THE CONTINUUM HISTORY
OF APOCALYPTICISM

THE
CONTINUUM
HISTORY OF
APOCALYPTICISM

Edited by
Bernard J. McGinn
John J. Collins
Stephen J. Stein

continuum
NEW YORK · LONDON

2003

The Continuum International Publishing Group Inc
15 East 26th Street, New York, NY 10010

The Continuum International Publishing Group Ltd
The Tower Building, 11 York Road, London SE1 7NX

This work derives from *The Encyclopedia of Apocalypticism,* Volume 1: *The Origins of Apocalypticism in Judaism and Christianity,* Volume 2: *Apocalypticism in Western History and Culture,* Volume 3: *Apocalypticism in the Modern Period and the Contemporary Age,* copyright © 1998 by The Continuum International Publishing Group.

Library of Congress Cataloging-in-Publication Data

The continuum history of apocalypticism / edited by Bernard J. McGinn,
    John J. Collins, and Stephen J. Stein.
      p. cm.
    Includes bibliographical references and indexes.
    ISBN 0-8264-1520-2 (hardcover : alk. paper)
    1. Apocalyptic literature—History and criticism. I. McGinn, Bernard,
1937- II. Collins, John J. (John James), 1946- III. Stein, Stephen J.,
1940- IV. Title.
BL501.C66 2003
291.2'3—dc21
                                                                 2003004123

Contents

v

INTRODUCTION

APOCALYPTICISM, BROADLY DESCRIBED as the belief that God has revealed the imminent end of the ongoing struggle between good and evil in history, has been a major element in the three Western monotheistic faiths of Judaism, Christianity, and Islam. While comparable beliefs about final reward and retribution are found in religions all over the world, there are genetic and historical links in the apocalyptic traditions of these three faiths that argue for a comprehensive and collective treatment. This volume attempts to provide such a treatment.

Apocalypticism (a recent word) is derived from "apocalypse," the Greek word for revelation and the name of the last book of the Bible. Apocalypticism refers to the complex of ideas associated with the New Testament Apocalypse, especially the imminent end of history and the catastrophic events that it entails. Apocalypticism is an analogous term, and it admits of different emphases. Some material is recognized as apocalyptic because it relates to the end of history. Other material is apocalyptic insofar as it describes supernatural revelation and the activities of angelic and demonic powers. In this volume we have not attempted to impose a strict definition, but rather to include a broad range of materials that may be regarded as apocalyptic in various senses. The reader should be aware that different contributors may use the terminology in slightly different ways. We believe, however, that there will be little confusion, and that it is amply compensated for by the wealth of material brought to the discussion.

In modern scholarship apocalypticism has also been related to other terms, especially "eschatology" (teaching about the last things), "millennialism" or "chiliasm" (belief in a coming better age on earth, such as that described in the thousand-year reign of Christ at the end of the book of Revelation), and "messianism" (hope for a heaven-sent savior who will usher in the better age). Messianism is a distinct phenomenon, insofar as it focuses on specific savior figures. "Eschatology" can be used for all sorts of human goals (e.g., national liberation) that do not necessarily qualify as apocalyptic, and millennialism is properly speaking a narrower concept that concentrates on earthly utopias. Nonetheless, all these terms overlap and are often used interchangeably. The precise nuance given to them by a given author must be inferred from the context.

This volume is a condensation of *The Encyclopedia of Apocalypticism,* which was originally published in three volumes in 1998. We have retained the main historical surveys that provide the spine of the *Encyclopedia,* while omitting essays of a thematic nature, and a few whose subject matter is not central to the historical development. The *History* is divided into three parts, corresponding to the three volumes of the *Encyclopedia.*

PART ONE: THE ORIGINS OF APOCALYPTICISM IN THE ANCIENT WORLD

The main flowering of apocalyptic writing and thinking in the Western world took place in Judaism in the Hellenistic period, and was carried on, intermittently, in Christianity, down through the Middle Ages. The roots of the phenomenon, however, lie further back. The proximate roots of Jewish and Christian apocalypticism can be found in the Hebrew prophets, especially in the oracles of judgment and predictions of the day of the Lord. But the imagery of the apocalypses of the Hellenistic age is much more full and vivid than that of the prophets. To a great extent it harks back to the ancient mythologies of the Near East, known to us now through the rediscovered Akkadian and Ugaritic literatures. The Hebrew Bible stands in a cultural continuum with these ancient Semitic mythologies, and much mythological lore that is not reflected in the Bible lived on in oral traditions down into the common era. It is possible to trace a direct line of development from the myths of the second millennium B.C.E. to the apocalypses of the Hellenistic and Roman periods. There was also, however, an independent apocalyptic tradition in ancient Persia, which may itself date back to the second millennium. This tradition exercised some influence on Judaism and Christianity, and some scholars would argue that it is the primary fountainhead of apocalypticism in the Western world. We should be wary, however, of attempts to trace all of Western apocalypticism to a single source.

Our survey of the ancient roots of apocalypticism begins with two essays on pagan antiquity, by Richard Clifford and Anders Hultgård. Clifford traces the roots of apocalypticism in ancient Near Eastern myth, primarily in the great combat myths represented by the Akkadian *Enuma elish* and the Ugaritic Baal Cycle. In these myths we find the theme of the battle with the chaos monster, which figures prominently in such apocalyptic writings as the books of Daniel and Revelation. This is not to suggest that apocalypticism can be reduced to the combat myth. Clifford also notes the relevance of a neo-Assyrian vision of the netherworld to the theme of otherworldly journeys and the relevance of Akkadian prophecies to the apocalyptic motif of prophecy after the fact (*ex eventu*). But the combat myth undeniably provides one major motif of apocalyptic writings and is the aspect of Near Eastern myth that exercised the greatest influence on apocalyptic tradition. Hultgård provides a magisterial exposition of Persian apocalypticism. Discussions of Persian literature are bedeviled by problems of dating. The Pahlevi literature that contains the most extensive Persian apocalyptic writings is admittedly late—much later than the Jewish and early Christian apocalypses. Some scholars accordingly dismiss Persian religion as a source of apocalypticism in the West. Hultgård, however, sides with those who argue for the antiquity of Persian apocalypticism and makes a strong case that the main features of the tradition were already in place in the Achaemenid period.

Three essays are devoted to the development of apocalypticism in ancient Judaism. John Collins discusses three major phases in this development. The first is located after the Babylonian Exile, in the sixth century. In the later prophetic writings we find a tendency to picture the future in cosmic terms, with less specific reference to the concrete particularities of the prophet's own situation than was the case in the earlier period. The major development, however, takes place in the Hellenistic period, when the belief in the judgment of the dead begins to find acceptance in Judaism. The hope for a blessed hereafter is one of the major factors that distinguish the eschatology of the apocalyptic writers from that of the prophets. A third phase of the development, found in apocalypses from the Roman period (about 100 C.E.) is distinguished by the attempt to synthesize different traditions and provide a more systematic exposition of future hope. New light has been shed on Jewish apocalypticism by the Dead Sea Scrolls. The evidence is presented by Florentino García Martínez. The Scrolls provide extensive reflections on the origin of evil, the periods of history, the final battle, and most distinctively, on human participation in the heavenly world. It remains a puzzle why the authors of the Scrolls make so little use of the genre apocalypse, which was well known in this period, but they undeniably give expression to an apocalyptic worldview, expressed in different genres. James VanderKam discusses the relation between apocalypticism and messianism. The earliest Jewish apocalypses do not look for messianic savior figures. The hope for the restoration of the Jewish kingship was nourished by circles different from those who wrote the first apocalypses. Later, however, the two traditions are synthesized in the Dead Sea Scrolls and in the apocalypses of the Roman period.

The first part of the volume is rounded out by three essays dealing with early Christianity. A century ago, Albert Schweitzer revolutionized New Testament scholarship with his thesis that the teaching of Jesus was characterized by thoroughgoing eschatology. This thesis is often challenged in modern times, but is defended vigorously here by Dale Allison. Allison has little difficulty in showing the pervasiveness of apocalyptic motifs in the Jesus tradition, as preserved in the Synoptic Gospels. It is difficult to avoid the conclusion that modern resistance to the eschatological Jesus arises from the fact that such a Jesus is too strange and uncomfortable for modern tastes. Martinus de Boer deals with the writings of Paul. The thought of Paul is complex, and many factors play a part in it. De Boer shows that one major factor is the apocalyptic belief that the day of judgment and resurrection is close at hand. Adela Yarbro Collins expounds the most influential of all apocalyptic texts, the book of Revelation. Her essay deals not only with the original setting and purpose but also with major themes in the history of interpretation. A distinctive feature of this essay is a discussion of the role of female symbolism in Revelation.

☞ PART TWO: APOCALYPTIC TRADITIONS
FROM LATE ANTIQUITY TO CA. 1800 C.E. _____

The survey of the historical development of apocalypticism continues with Brian E. Daley's essay, "Apocalypticism in Early Christian Theology," which studies the use of apocalyptic ideas in major Christian thinkers from the second through the sixth centuries C.E. David Olster's essay, "Byzantine Apocalypses," begins in the patristic period with a consideration of how the fourth-century conversion of the Roman Empire to Christianity provided the basis for a new form of apocalyptic understanding of the relation between Christianity and "Romanity" (*romanitas*), a political theology that was decisive throughout Byzantine history and that was also imported to the European West. Olster concentrates on the formative period of the Byzantine troubles from the seventh through the tenth centuries C.E., during which this political theology was challenged by the rise of Islam and was forced to respond with adaptations of its apocalyptic outlook. He does not treat later Byzantine apocalypticism, which depends in large part on this earlier patrimony.

Bernard McGinn's essay, "Apocalypticism and Church Reform: 1100–1500," after some introductory remarks on early medieval apocalypticism in Western Europe, concentrates on the high and late Middle Ages. This essay emphasizes "mainline" uses of apocalypticism as providing a resource for, and in some cases even creating, reform models for repristination of the essential institutions of medieval Christianity. The following essay, "Radical Apocalyptic Movements in the Late Middle Ages," by Gian Luca Potestà, covers some of the same period but takes a different perspective. Potestà seeks to reconstruct the intellectual and (where possible) social background of those apocalyptic thinkers and movements of the late Middle Ages who were conceived of as "radically" apocalyptic in the sense that they sought to undermine ecclesiastical structures. (They were often condemned as heretics, sometimes imprisoned, even executed.) Although the line between reform and revolution was sometimes a fine one, essential differences remained.

The period studied by Robin Barnes in his contribution, "Images of Hope and Despair: Western Apocalypticism ca. 1500–1800," is more limited than those surveyed in the preceding essays. Nevertheless, the proliferation of apocalyptic movements as Western Christianity fragmented in the sixteenth century and the sheer mass of evidence concerning the three centuries he reviews make any synoptic view difficult. Barnes, however, manages to provide a readable and remarkably complete picture of both the advances and the declines in European apocalypticism as it confronted the Reformation and early modernity. As a complement to Barnes's essay, Jean-Robert Armogathe's offering, "Interpretations of the Revelation of John: 1500–1800," studies one particular but central aspect of the changes in apocalypticism during the transition to modernity, namely, the ways in which diverse interpretations of the Revelation of John open a window on disputes and transformations in apocalyptic mentalities.

The last two essays in part 2 turn to the apocalyptic traditions of Judaism and Islam. Although apocalypticism played a less important role in Judaism after the formation of rabbinic Judaism than it had in earlier periods, it was still by no means negligible, as Moshe Idel shows in his essay "Jewish Apocalypticism: 670–1670." Idel presents both an original perspective on the phenomenology of apocalypticism and also an argument that the contribution of Jewish mysticism, especially Kabbalah, to Jewish apocalypticism has been undervalued in the past. Finally, Saïd Amir Arjomand, "Islamic Apocalypticism in the Classic Period," sets out a revisionist agenda in arguing that the apocalyptic origins of Islam have been ironed out of Islamic historiography and often ignored in modern scholarship. In presenting his case, Arjomand must be necessarily selective, surveying only the classic period from the seventh century through the Mongol invasions of the thirteenth century, and concentrating primarily on the first two centuries of the formation of Islam.

☞ PART THREE: APOCALYPTICISM
IN THE MODERN AGE

Part 3 opens with two essays dealing with the transplantation of European traditions of apocalypticism to the New World and their adaptation to new circumstances. Alain Milhou's essay, "Apocalypticism in Central and South American Colonialism," spans the period beginning with the voyages of discovery by Christopher Columbus and extending until the struggle for independence from Spain led by Simon Bolivar in the opening decades of the nineteenth century. Milhou documents how apocalyptic traditions of messianism and millennialism operative during the Middle Ages and early modern period in the Mediterranean world, especially in the Iberian peninsula, motivated Spanish and Portuguese explorers and conquerors in the New World as well as Franciscans, Dominicans, and Jesuits in their spiritual campaigns. The application of biblical symbols and apocalyptic imagery as well as Joachite notions to the complex societies discovered, created, destroyed, and sometimes recreated in Central and South America proved a powerful influence on both the social and the political imaginations and on the religious worlds constructed by natives, Creoles, and Europeans.

The companion to Milhou's piece is Reiner Smolinski's essay, "Apocalypticism in Colonial North America," an examination of the preoccupation with apocalyptic among clerical and lay leaders in Puritan New England. His essay also documents continuities between Europe and America, in his case between influential Protestant exegetes in Old England as well as in other parts of Europe and commentators on the Apocalypse in New England. Smolinski scrutinizes the debate surrounding the role of millennialism in the founding and settlement of the New England colonies and the subsequent controversy regarding its contribution to the formation of a distinctive sense of American identity both before and after the American Revolution. Together, Milhou and Smolinski make the case for the importance of the transatlantic context for the study of early American apocalypticism.

The next two essays form a natural pair because they examine apocalypticism in the United States in contrasting religious and cultural locations, namely, inside and outside the religious mainstream. James H. Moorhead's "Apocalypticism in Mainstream Protestantism, 1800 to the Present" charts the changing fortunes of postmillennialism among representatives of the dominant Protestant denominations in this nation. He measures dramatic changes between the antebellum period in the nineteenth century, when the rational progressivist vision combined with apocalyptic modes of thought to fuel the reform movements of that day, and the decades after the turn of the twentieth century, when all apocalypticism became an embarrassment to theological liberals, who set out to manage scientifically and professionally the affairs of a "this-worldly" kingdom of God. Moorhead documents the end of a sense of the end for those who were once describable as advocates of post millennialism. Stephen Stein's essay, "Apocalypticism Outside the Mainstream in the United States," explores the very different fate of apocalyptic among religious groups located on the margins of America's religious and cultural worlds. Apocalyptic speculation has been a growth industry among outsiders in the United States, providing them resources for constructing their own unique religious and social identities. This essay catalogues the variety of outsider religious communities in the United States that have experimented with apocalyptic notions from the earliest years of the new republic until the recent past. Among such groups there is no waning of interest in apocalypticism.

Paul Boyer's "The Growth of Fundamentalist Apocalyptic in the United States" complements both of the preceding essays. The same years that witnessed the decline of postmillennial interests among theological liberals saw the rise to prominence of a system of dispensational premillennialism, the product of ideas imported from England and nurtured in the United States. Boyer describes the convergence of factors giving birth to an explicit fundamentalist apocalyptic perspective based on a literalistic reading of the prophetic portions of the Bible. He documents the ways in which this powerful and malleable tradition has gained growing religious and political influence in America throughout the twentieth century. Boyer also identifies several significant outsider religious groups, including a number discussed in the preceding essay, that hold variant versions of this fundamentalist apocalypticism.

The story of apocalypticism begun by Alain Milhou is continued by Robert M. Levine in "Apocalyptic Movements in Latin America in the Nineteenth and Twentieth Centuries." His essay examines Latin American millenarian movements, many of which exploited the sharp contrast between the traditional religious views of the underclass and the modernizing outlook of elites. But Levine challenges overly facile interpretations of apocalypticism that deal only with socioeconomic tensions or the undue influence of charismatic individuals. He argues for greater complexity in the explanation of millenarian movements in Latin America during the past two centuries. He explores the tension between those advocating modernist views and those committed to an apocalyptic perspective—a theme articulated in several essays in this volume.

The next two essays in the collection treat aspects of apocalypticism in Judaism and in Islam, respectively, during the past two centuries. Both reach back to earlier times in order to contextualize recent developments. Aviezer Ravitzky's essay, "The Messianism of Success in Contemporary Judaism," examines twentieth-century examples of messianic revival within Judaism as part of his argument that such ferment may arise not only from calamity or catastrophe but also from success and triumph. He frames his case studies of contemporary messianism—Lubbavitcher Hasidism and religious Zionism—by discussing historical precedents from earlier periods in Judaism and by exposing the theological logic that informs these movements, namely, a notion of divine immanence. Abbas Amanat's essay, "The Resurgence of Apocalyptic in Modern Islam," provides a broad view of apocalyptic developments during the past two centuries, though he too reaches back to an earlier age—in his case, the early modern period—for perspective on the nature of messianism and millennialism within Islam. His essay features the links between religious developments and social and political circumstances. Amanat distinguishes the Sunni and Shiite appropriations of Islamic eschatological ideas and especially the ways in which the expectations of the leaders gave rise to new religious and political movements, including the Baha'i faith, the Ahmadiyya movement, and the contemporary Islamic Revolution. He demonstrates how both messianic impulses for salvation and utopian hopes derive from Islamic apocalyptic traditions.

The final essays in the volume deal principally with historical developments within Christian apocalypticism in Western and Eastern Europe, respectively, during the nineteenth and twentieth centuries. "Apocalypticism in Modern Western Europe," by Sandra L. and Paul F. Zimdars-Swartz, describes the ways cultural and political events—for instance, the French Revolution—triggered apocalyptic speculation and prophetic movements among both Protestants and Roman Catholics, as well as among secular thinkers. Their essay also underscores the rising apocalyptic significance accorded miracles, signs, and Marian apparitions by Roman Catholics in this period. "Apocalypticism in Eastern Europe," by J. Eugene Clay, focuses on eschatological traditions in Russia as an extended case study of the ways in which Orthodox Christianity has shaped and been shaped by apocalypticism. His examination of the Old Believers movement, for example, demonstrates how traditional apocalyptic ideas were adapted to the particular circumstances of Eastern Europe. Clay also discusses the secular apocalypticism of the Soviet Union as it developed out of the Bolshevik Revolution and under Communism and its impact on Orthodox Christianity. His essay concludes with a discussion of changes that have occurred since the fall of the Soviet Union.

To stress the significance of apocalypticism is not to deny its ambivalence. Apocalypticism has been the source of hope and courage for the oppressed, but has also given rise, on many occasions, to fanaticism and intolerance. The essays in this volume seek neither to apologize for the extravagances of apocalyptic thinkers nor to excuse the perverse actions of some of their followers. Rather, they strive to understand a powerful, perhaps even indispensable, element in the history of Western religions that has been the source of both good and evil, and still is today.

Our thanks are due to Frank Oveis for his initiative in conceiving the condensed volume.

JOHN J. COLLINS   BERNARD MCGINN   STEPHEN J. STEIN

PART 1

The Origins of Apocalypticism
in the Ancient World

1

The Roots of Apocalypticism in Near Eastern Myth

Richard J. Clifford, S.J.
Weston Jesuit School of Theology

A POCALYPTIC LITERATURE as such is not found in the period covered by this article (the third to mid-first millennia in the ancient Near East) but chiefly in the period from the third century B.C.E. to the second century C.E., and, in some Christian circles, down to the Middle Ages. The ancient roots of apocalyptic literature, however, can be traced to far earlier literature of the ancient Near East (back to the late third millennium). Its early history is not merely of antiquarian interest, but illuminates the purpose and rhetoric of mature apocalyptic works. These latter works fall within a venerable tradition of theological and philosophical reflection on divine and human governance, a kind of ancient "political theory." Read apart from their literary history, works such as the books of Daniel and Revelation, *1 Enoch*, 4 Ezra, and *2 Baruch* can appear to modern readers as bizarre in imagery and confusing in logic.

The first modern scholar to have seriously attempted to trace the roots of apocalyptic literature in ancient texts was Hermann Gunkel (1862–1932), whose *Schöpfung und Chaos in Urzeit und Endzeit: Eine religionsgeschichtliche Untersuchung über Gen 1 and Ap Joh 12* appeared in 1895. He belonged to the history-of-religions school, or *religionsgeschichtliche Schule*, which championed autonomous historical-critical scholarship and insisted that the Bible be seen against its environment. Gunkel argued that Genesis 1 and Revelation 12 consisted of "basically the same material, which [in Revelation] surfaces a second time, but in a different form. In the ancient instance it is the myth of *Urzeit*, which travels from Babylon to the Bible, in the new a prediction concerning the *Endzeit*" (p. 398).

His book demonstrated that Genesis 1 and Revelation 12 were not free compositions of their authors but adaptations of traditions from outside, ultimately from Babylon. He concluded that the combat myth entered Israelite literature in the monarchic period, rather than in the patriarchal era or the Babylonian Exile, the periods of borrowing suggested by earlier

3

scholars. It is a mark of Gunkel's genius that with the little material available to him he did not simply list motifs and themes but concentrated his attention on the one *Gattung* (the combat myth) that included so much else: the *Urzeit* ("primal time") *Endzeit* ("end-time") equation, creation and new creation, the monster symbolizing evil, and divine kingship. Gunkel's pioneering work retains its usefulness despite its obvious deficiencies: he had access to only a fraction of the Akkadian texts now available and knew nothing of the combat myth in the Canaanite texts from Ugarit (first discovered in 1929); he had a romanticist tendency to overstress origins as explanation and undervalue reception and particular usage.

Later scholars have been able to make use of the Ugaritic texts, which are closely related to early Biblical Hebrew and are composed in the same poetic tradition, as well as the enormous amount of Sumerian and Akkadian literature unearthed and published since Gunkel. It is now possible to chart the history of relevant genres, motifs, and themes in a variety of works over many centuries. In particular, scholars can describe the interaction of Canaanite and early Israelite traditions and sketch the inner-biblical development that led to fully developed apocalyptic works such as Daniel and Revelation. A number of points are still under discussion. These include the way in which traditions from Mesopotamia came into Canaan as well as the date and extent of their influence and the inner-biblical sources of apocalyptic literature.

This article is selective, examining in the early literature only those genres, motifs or recurrent elements, and ideas that were important in the later mature apocalyptic works. Among the genres, the most important by far is the combat myth, for it provided not only imagery but also a conceptual framework for explaining divine rule over the world. Other genres are the *vaticinia ex eventu* ("prophecies after the fact") found in some Akkadian texts, and the dream vision (though the relevance of the specifically Akkadian form of this last genre is disputed). Among the recurrent elements are the divine assembly under the high god responding to a major threat, cosmic enemies portrayed as monsters, various heavenly beings, divine decrees or secret knowledge, and a sage-mediator of heavenly knowledge. Among the topics are explorations of the nature of evil and new creation or restoration of the original order.

☞ MESOPOTAMIA

History and Religion

The course of Mesopotamian history shows two impulses, one toward local rule exemplified in the city-states, and the other, more sporadic, toward large and complex political systems aimed at dominating large areas. The first period for which there is a record is the Early Dynastic (2900–2350 B.C.E.), a period when families ruled various cities. The Akkadian and Ur III dynasties at the end of the third millennium represent a shift from city-state to nation-state. The Akkadian system, in contrast to the earlier Sumerian system, featured a centralized state around king and court. Though Sumerian and Akkadian languages and populations were distinct, the culture itself was a common Mesopotamian one.

In the second millennium, Mesopotamia became divided into two geopolitical regions, Babylonia and Assyria. From the eighteenth century B.C.E. to the end of the millennium, Babylon and Assyria were the two great nation-states. Babylon and Assyria were international in ambition and contacts, and their fortunes unfolded in an international context. Northern Syria came into the picture as its coastal cities—Ugarit, Byblos, Tyre—rose to prominence. Northwest Mesopotamia became a meeting point of Mesopotamian and Levantine culture. The essentially cooperative international atmosphere was ended, however, by population movements in the last two centuries of the second millennium. The dominant empires of the first millennium were the Neo-Assyrian empire (935–612 B.C.E.) and its successor, the Persian empire (539–333 B.C.E.), both complex and vast in extent.

The chief gods in the pantheon were Anu (Sumerian An), "sky," the god of heaven and head of the older generation of gods, whose consort was Antu; Ellil (Sumerian Enlil), son of Anu, father of Ninurta, "king of all populated land," head of the younger generation of Sumerian and Akkadian gods whose consort was Ninlil or Ninhursag and whose cult center was Nippur; and Ea (Sumerian Enki), god of water, wisdom, and incantations, whose consort was Ninmah or Damkina and whose cult center was Eridu. With the rise of the Amorites and of the city-state Babylon, the warrior-god Marduk became important, taking over titles of other gods. In Old Assyrian religion Asshur was the national god, to whom the king regularly reported his activities, especially war. After the middle of the fourteenth century B.C.E., the Assyrian pantheon became babylonized. In the Assyrian version of *Enuma elish,* Asshur took the place of Marduk.

The assembly of the gods was an important part of the organization of the divine world and the major decision-making body; all the gods were subject to its decrees. The members were of two groups, the fifty "great gods" and "the seven gods of the fates (*šīmātu*)." The divine triad of Anu, Enlil, and Ea was preeminent, with Anu presiding over the assembly. In a democratic give-and-take, the member gods made decrees affecting matters in heaven and earth and responded to various crises. Indeed, the divine assembly can be viewed as a reflection of "democratic" practices that once prevailed in Sumerian city-states. The Akkadian term is *puḫru ilāni,* "assembly of the gods." The institution is also attested in Canaan: Ugaritic *pḫr [bn] ʾlm,* Phoenician *mpḫrt ʾl,* and biblical *ʿēdâ* (Ps 82:1) and *sôd* (Jer. 23:18, 22; Job 15:8; Ps. 89:8). In Mesopotamia, the members are specifically identified and act as individuals, but in Canaan the assembly as a whole or its head, El, acts rather than individual members (Mullen 1980).

The major office of divine governance was kingship. Kingship over the gods could be won by a particular god resolving a crisis or defeating a threat to cosmic order. Human kingship is age-old in Mesopotamia and was the dominant form of government everywhere from the early second millennium forward. The Sumerian King List seeks to demonstrate that the country was always united under one king, ruling successively in different cites: "When kingship was lowered from heaven, kingship was (first) in Eridu," and so on; it existed in heaven independently of any earthly king. When kings are mentioned in creation myths, they organize the human race so it can carry out its basic task of providing for the gods. Kings were not ordinarily considered divine but had to be appointed by the gods. A supernatural aura surrounded the king, for he was the regent of the gods, represented divine order on earth, and conversely, represented the people before the gods.

A common way of resolving threats to cosmic order was force of arms. The gods were involved in the wars that kings waged on earth; war was both political and religious. The new order resulting from the war could be said to represent the will of the god or gods. War was thus a way for the gods to exercise their rule and oversee the rise and fall of kingdoms.

Literature and Themes Relevant to Apocalyptic Literature

Genres

THE COMBAT MYTH. One of the most long-lived genres in ancient literature was the so-called combat myth. It lasted as a live genre into the period of full-blown apocalyptic works and had an enormous influence on them. In fact, the genre provided ancient poets with a conceptual framework for reflecting on divine power and human kingship, and on the rise and fall of nations. Instances of the myth in Mesopotamia are *Lugal-e, Anzu,* and *Enuma elish.* In Canaan it is represented by the Baal Cycle. In early biblical poetry it is found in Yahweh's victory over Pharaoh at the sea (Exodus 15) or over the sea itself (several psalms). No ideal form of the combat myth exists, of course, but a consistent plot line can be abstracted: a force (often depicted as a monster) threatens cosmic and political order, instilling fear and confusion in the assembly of the gods; the assembly or its president, unable to find a commander among the older gods, turns to a young god to battle the hostile force; he successfully defeats the monster, creating the world (including human beings) or simply restoring the pre-threat order, builds a palace, and receives acclamation of kingship from the other gods.

There are three combat myths sufficiently preserved to be analyzed: the Sumerian *Lugal-e* of the late third millennium; the Akkadian *Anzu,* extant in an Old Babylonian and a Standard (early-first-millennium) version; and *Enuma elish,* dated variously to the eighteenth, fourteenth, or, more commonly, the twelfth century. Each influenced its successor.

The best way of analyzing the myths is by attending to their plot rather than to their ideas, a method somewhat contrary to modern analytical habits. For us stories are usually regarded as entertainment or as illustration of a "point" derived from discursive reasoning, but for ancient Near Easterners narrative was the medium for expressing serious thought. The plots of the three combat myths will be briefly told with attention to "discourse time," the time taken in the telling.

Lugal-e tells how the young warrior-king Ninurta (god of thunderstorms and floods) defeated the mountain-dwelling monster Azag, restored the flow of the river Tigris, after which he judged the stones that had taken part in the battle, assigning them their various functions. The story begins with Sharur, Ninurta's weapon, reporting to his master that in the mountains the plants and stones have made Azag king and that the monster is planning to take over his domain. Ninurta's first foray against them, made against the advice of Sharur, is defeated by the dust storm Azag raises. Sharur now brings to Ninurta strategic advice from Enlil, Ninurta's father: send a rainstorm to put down the dust. The strategy works; Ninurta defeats Azag. Ninurta then collects the waters that had been trapped in the mountain ice and routes them to the Tigris. Ninlil, his mother, lonesome for her absent son, pays him a visit. Ninurta sends her home before exercising judgment over the stones. Each is judged according to its degree of participation in the battle against him. Ninurta returns to Nippur to receive the acclamation of his father and the other gods.

Five features of *Lugal-e* are relevant for other combat myths, including those found in apocalyptic literature. (1) The relationship of the older god (Ninurta's father, Enlil) and the younger god (Ninurta)—a common relationship in combat myth—is perennial in ancient Near Eastern palace life, as Thorkild Jacobsen points out: "Under the early political forms, which are here reflected, the king (*lugal*) was usually a young man whose task it was to lead the army in war. The supreme ruler was an older experienced administrator, here Ninurta's father, Enlil. Thus his military exploits serve to impose and maintain Enlil's authority" (Jacobsen 1987, 236 n. 4). The same relationship holds for Anu and Marduk in *Enuma elish*, El and Baal in the Ugaritic texts, the Ancient of Days and the Son of Man in Daniel 7, and the one seated on the throne and the Lamb in Revelation 4–5. (2) The "evil," or threat to order, in this story is that the water necessary to fertilize the fields of Mesopotamia is trapped in mountain ice. The victory over or defeat of the evil consists in making that water once again available to the inhabitants, thus restoring the fertility intended by the gods. The nature of the victory casts light on the meaning of divine kingship in the myth. Kingship (including its permanence) is proportional to the threat that has been put down. The more profound the threat, the more profound the victory undoing it. Yet, as Neil Forsyth recognizes, not every warrior-god's victory is a cosmogony (1987, 44–45). Marduk's victory over Tiamat in *Enuma elish* surely is cosmogonic, but Ninurta's victory in *Anzu* is not so wide-ranging, nor is Baal's victory over Mot in the Ugaritic tablets. (3) The evil is portrayed as a "natural" force (water trapped in mountain ice), but here, as in other references to nature, there is an implied historical reference, for the northern and eastern mountains were the homelands of historical invaders of the plains. A dichotomous distinction between myth and history cannot be drawn; the two domains are related. (4) Judgment of enemies (and allies as well) follows the victory, an action that occurs also in *Enuma elish* (VI 11–32) and in the apocalypses in Daniel 7 and 8–12 and Revelation 17–19. (5) The victorious god reestablishes the original order; *Urzeit* becomes *Endzeit*. Rev 21:1 is a succinct expression of the victory: "Then I saw a new heaven and a new earth; for the first heaven and the first earth had passed away, and sea was no more."

The observations just made also apply to the second of our three Mesopotamian examples of the genre of combat myth, *Anzu*. It is partially preserved in an Old Babylonian version (first half of the second millennium) and much more completely in an early-first-millennium Standard Babylonian version, originally consisting of about 720 lines on three four-column tablets. It was canonical, in "the stream of tradition," that is, copied by scribes in their training and widely distributed. It influenced *Enuma elish*.

The prologue sings of Ninurta, "the Mighty One," a title that recurs throughout the myth. The world is in a crisis: the beds of the Tigris and Euphrates have been laid out, but no water flows in them to fertilize the land of Mesopotamia. At a certain point, the fresh waters of the Apsu are released to supply the two rivers, a happy turn of the plot somehow caused by the birth of Anzu (the text is not clear). Anzu is a birdlike creature with a monstrous head, conceived by earth and born in a mountain fastness. Such a creature would make an ideal gatekeeper for the gods, thinks Anu, the head of the older generation of gods, and recommends him to Enlil, head of the younger generation of gods. Anu's judgment proves disastrous, however, for Anzu uses his post to steal from Enlil the Tablet-of-Decrees, which determines the destiny of things, the "software program of the world." To meet the crisis, the assembly of the gods meets. Anu promises to any god who can capture back the tablet a great name and recognition as mighty. Anu turns first to Adad, then Gerra, and finally Shara, but all refuse to lead the army. They know that Anzu and not Enlil possesses the Tablet that makes its possessor's commands all-powerful.

Then Belet-ili, the mother goddess, asks Ninurta, the son of Enlil, to go out against Anzu. Family honor is at stake, she explains, for Anzu rejected his father. In contrast to the verbose refusals of the three gods, Ninurta's answer is a quick yes. He loses the first battle when Anzu's authoritative word turns his arrows back. Wise Ea's advice enables him to succeed: shake feathers loose from the birdlike Anzu and in the moment when he calls his loose feathers back to his body, release your feathered arrow so that it will be caught up in the irresistible stream toward Anzu's body. Caught up in the flow, Ninurta's arrow pierces and kills Anzu. Then Ninurta drenches the mountain open stretches with water. Wind-borne feathers from Anzu's dead body signal the gods that Ninurta is victorious. The gods summon Ninurta home and, declaring that he has avenged his father Enlil, acclaim him with a series of new names.

Analysis of *Anzu* in discourse time shows what events the poet chooses to delay on:

Prologue	Water crisis and solution	Assembly: three gods refuse to go	Appointment of Ninurta	Battle and victory	Celebration grant of names
I.1–14	1.15–83	1.84–155	I.156–II.27	I.28–III.22	
14 lines	69 lines	71 lines	79 lines	ca. 144 lines	ca. 48 lines

The initial crisis (Anzu's theft of the Tablet-of-Decrees) is quickly told (69 lines). The poem dwells on the deliberations of the assembly (Anu's attempts to persuade the three gods to recapture the tablet [71 lines] and the commission of Ninurta [79 lines, the two scenes totaling 150 lines]), Ninurta's battle and victory (ca. 144 lines), and the gods granting him new names (ca. 48 lines).

Four features of the combat myth *Anzu* should be noted as relevant to later apocalyptic works. (1) The threat from the lack of water in the opening lines is resolved somehow by Anzu's birth, but this resolution leads to the much more dangerous threat from the loss of the Tablet-of-Decrees. This turn breaks up the simple plot and foreshadows the complex two-part structure of *Enuma elish*. (2) The evil here is the dissolution of political as well as cosmic order. The assembly is rendered ineffectual as a *political* body, for it is unable from its senior members to muster an army to get back the tablet. It is *family* rather than political considerations that send Ninurta into the field. His victory restores the political office of king; with Anzu out of the way, the assembly is again effective and can acclaim him king: "They assigned to you full shepherdship of the people. As king they gave (you) your name 'Guardian of the throne'" (III.129–30). (3) The fundamental issue is kingship. Ninurta takes the kingship of the other gods; Anu, the head of the older generation, proved inadequate, as did Enlil and the three gods who refused to fight. They must yield to Ninurta, who has won the title Mighty One and restored the civic and political order destroyed by the loss of the Tablet. Ninurta's restoration of political order does not seem to be cosmogonic, though one should keep in mind that political order was part of what the ancients meant by creation. (4) Relevant to later apocalyptic literature are several recurrent elements: the monster Anzu as a composite animal (lion-headed eagle, or perhaps bat-headed, as befits one born in a cave), the active role of the assembly of the gods, and the god's personified weapon. In Daniel and Revelation, evil can be symbolized by composite animals, and the heavenly assembly plays a similar role though it is much less prominent.

The third Mesopotamian example is *Enuma elish* (named after its opening line), seven tablets in length, much copied and commented on in antiquity, and recited on the fourth day of the New Year festival.

The dramatic structure of *Enuma elish* is more complex than its predecessors, being in five acts.

1. I.1–20. The first twenty lines are a theogony, in which a series of gods are born when the primordial waters Apsu and Tiamat were an undifferentiated mass and there was no land. The emergence of the gods is also the emergence of two rival dynasties: Apsu-Tiamat versus Anshar-Anu-Ea-Marduk (Goldfless 1980, 127–30). The monster Tiamat thus represents both a natural force (cosmic waters) and a political reality. "Myth" and "history" are intertwined. Another indication of the historical interest in the entire myth is the large amount of discourse time devoted to political debate in the divine assembly.

2. I.21–79. In the initial confrontation of the rival dynasties, Ea defeats Apsu and builds his palace to celebrate the victory.

3. I.79–VI.121. Foreshadowed by the first confrontation, the major conflict between the son of Ea, Marduk, and the widow of Apsu, Tiamat, is the theme of the bulk of the work. Tiamat, still angry over the death of her husband Apsu at the hands of Ea, plots an assault against the rival dynasty. When they learn of her plans, the assembly is frightened and seeks to appoint a military commander. After two gods refuse to go, Marduk agrees on the condition that the assembly make his decree supreme. He slays Tiamat in single combat and from her body builds the universe and his shrine Esagil.

4. VI.122–VII.144. The gods, grateful for Marduk's victory and obliged by their oath, give him "Anu-ship." He in turn promises them that Babylon will be their new residence and that man, a new creature, will be their servant. From the blood of the slain Kingu (Tiamat's general), Marduk forms man. The gods build Marduk a city and a temple and give him fifty names of honor.

Many of the remarks already made about *Lugal-e* and *Anzu* also apply to *Enuma elish*. As in these other myths, one god is exalted over gods and humans. In contrast to the other myths, however, in *Enuma elish* Marduk does not *reestablish* a threatened or disturbed order but forms a world that never existed before. He creates. The genre of combat myth has been expanded not only in length and complexity but conceptually as well.

What does it mean to create in the ancient Near East? The concept of creation in the ancient Near East differs from the modern Western view, shaped as the latter is by evolutionary and scientific concerns (Clifford 1994, chap. 1). Ancient accounts usually imagined creation on the model of human activity (molding clay, building a house, fighting a battle) or natural processes (life forms left by the ebbing Nile flood). What emerged from the process for the ancients was a *populated* universe, human society organized for the service of the gods with a king and culture, and not, as with modern accounts, the physical world (often only the planet earth in its solar and stellar system). Ancient accounts were often portrayed as dramas, which is not surprising in that the process was imagined as personal wills in conflict. This is far from the impersonal interaction of modern scientific accounts. Lastly, the criterion for truth in ancient accounts is dramatic plausibility in contrast to our need for one complete explanation.

In *Enuma elish*, creation of the world is possible because a hostile rival dynasty has come to an end with the death of Tiamat. A new stage has been reached with the exaltation of Marduk. As part of this settlement, Marduk builds a palace or palace-city where he can be acknowledged by the other gods as supreme. He forms the human race to work and provide for the gods. Creation is thus intimately linked to his victory. Later biblical texts link divine victory exaltation to creation and envision creation as the building of a temple or temple-city, for example, Isaiah 65–66 and Revelation 19–22.

VATICINIA EX EVENTU. Five texts from Mesopotamia, some of them formerly designated "prophecies" from their alleged resemblance to biblical literature, are now widely judged to be relevant to apocalyptic literature. They are best described as prophecies after the fact (*vaticinia ex eventu*). Sections typically begin with "a prince shall arise." No kings are named, presumably so that the vagueness will give the impression that future events are being predicted. Kings and kingdoms, however, can be identified from the historical details. Reigns are judged sweepingly as either good or bad. The surveys are very much like the historical surveys in later works such as Daniel 7, 8, and 11 and the Apocalypse of Weeks and the Animal Apocalypse in *1 Enoch*.

Whether all five texts represent a single genre is not certain, but there are two clear sub-categories: prophecies in the third person (Text A, the Dynastic Prophecy, and the Uruk Prophecy), and prophecies in the first person (the Shulgi and Marduk Prophecies).

Text A, from seventh-century Asshur, is organized by the refrain "and a prince shall arise" (repeated eight times in a fragmentary tablet). The number of years in each reign is given as well as a characterization of the major events in that reign, historical, meteorological, and agricultural. The events in Text A took place in the twelfth century, five centuries before its composition, so they all are *ex eventu* by definition.

The *Uruk Prophecy,* possibly composed in the reign of Amel-Marduk (biblical Evil-Mero-dach, 561–560), preserved mainly on the reverse side of the tablet, narrates the rise of six kings. The fifth king is Nebuchadnezzar II (604–562). The genuine prediction comes in lines 16–19: "After him (Nebuchadnezzar II) his son will arise as king in Uruk and become master of the world. He will exercise rule and kingship in Uruk and his dynasty will be established forever. The kings of Uruk will exercise rulership like the gods." The past "predictions" are intended to lend credibility to the last statement. The course of history has been determined by the gods: Nebuchadnezzar's son is meant to rule forever.

The *Dynastic Prophecy,* a Late Babylonian text, speaks successively of the fall of Assyria, the rise and fall of Babylonia and Persia, and the rise of the Hellenistic monarchies. The victory of Alexander the Great over Darius at Issus in 333 B.C.E. is described. After this comes the genuine prophecy, a prediction of another battle, in which Darius is victorious over Alexander: "Enlil, Shamash, and [Marduk] will be at the side of his army [and] the overthrow of the army of the Nanaean (= Thracian, i.e., Alexander) he will [bring about]. He will carry off his extensive booty and [*bring (it)*] into his palace. The people who *had* [*experienced*] misfortune [*will enjoy*] well-being. The mood of the land [will be a happy one]." By its detail, length, and climactic placement of the final prediction, the text gives the impression that the gods have determined the victory of Darius over Alexander. The predicted victory, however, never took place; Darius never defeated Alexander.

In the second subcategory—prediction in the first person (by a god or king)—are two texts that were paired in scribal editions, the Shulgi Prophecy of the late second or early first millennium and the Marduk Prophecy, perhaps from the reign of Nebuchadnezzar I (1125–1104).

In the *Shulgi Prophecy,* unfortunately heavily damaged, Shulgi, a Sumerian king of the Third Dynasty of Ur (2112–2004), who was considered a god and the founder of the city of

Nippur, speaks of the kings who will come after him. His successor will submit to Assyria, and Nippur will be cast down. The reign of the Babylonian king, however, will be cut short by the command of Enlil. Another king will arise, restore the shrines, and rebuild Nippur.

In the *Marduk Prophecy*, Marduk describes his (i.e., his statue's) peregrinations, which can be dated to the first millennium: the statue's journey to Hatti and back to Babylon, to Assyria and back to Babylon, and finally to Elam and back to Babylon. The god brought prosperity wherever he went, but his stay in Elam spelled disaster for Babylon. After Marduk returned from Elam to Babylon, however, "a king of Babylon will arise" (probably Nebuchadnezzar I, 1124–1103) who will make the city prosperous and punish Elam. The last part is the genuine prophecy, made credible by the post-factum "prophecies" preceding it. The text is a propaganda piece for Nebuchadnezzar.

The many similarities between the genre of "post-factum prophecy" and the historical surveys in apocalyptic literature suggest possible influence of the older literature on the younger. The most important similarity is that past events are "predicted" to lend credibility to the last-mentioned event, as in the Uruk Prophecy, the Dynastic Prophecy, and the Marduk Prophecy. Textual damage prevents us from knowing if the same is true in the other tablets. Daniel 7, 8, 9, and 11; *1 Enoch* 83–90, 91; and the *Sibylline Oracles,* likewise "predict" some events that are already past and some that are still future, the accuracy of the "predictions" making the genuine prediction at the end more believable. Further, history is seen as a sequence of kingdoms rather than, say, the dominance of a particular city, shrine, or deity. Even in the Marduk Prophecy, the emphasis falls on the king of Babylon. Persons are not named, as they are not named in apocalyptic literature. History is painted with a broad brush; details are few and conventional; reigns are either good or evil. The apocalyptic predictions in apocalyptic literature come to the speaker through revelation. The predictions in the Shulgi and Marduk prophecies come from a deity; perhaps this is true of the other tablets, but their beginnings are too poorly preserved to tell. Lastly, the language of omen texts has stamped the language of the "prophecies," a fact that should warn us against distinguishing too sharply between mantic wisdom (the science of divination) and prophecy/apocalypticism.

There are also important differences between the prophecies and apocalyptic literature. The most important is that the apocalypticists incorporated predictions of kingdoms into a new scenario. That scenario was cosmic threat, combat, and rule of the victorious god; it envisioned the end of the present world and divine judgment upon it. One text, however, already has a certain affinity to the scenario: the Uruk Prophecy predicts that after Nebuchadnezzar II, "his son will arise as king in Uruk and become master of the world. He will exercise rule and kingship in Uruk and his dynasty will be established forever. The kings of Uruk will exercise rulership like the gods [= forever]." In summary, the prophecies show that the apocalypticists were anthologists, borrowing genres such as the post-factum prediction to demonstrate that the course of history was under God's control and that in their day history as they knew it had come to an end and a new age was about to dawn.

DREAM VISION. A late-seventh-century B.C.E. Akkadian text, "The Vision of the Nether World," has been proposed as a source of the dream vision of Daniel 7 (Kvanvig 1988, 389–555; *ANET* 1969, 109–10). In the relevant thirty-four lines on the obverse side, a visionary, Kummāya, sees in the night a vision of the netherworld: fifteen gods in hybrid form (human or animal heads, hands, and feet) standing before him, and "one man, his body was black like pitch. His face was similar to that of an Anzu bird. He was wearing a red robe. In his left hand he was holding up a bow. In his right hand he was holding a sword." The seer then sees the warrior Nergal on a throne, who, enraged, intends to put him to death because he has dishonored Ereshkigal, Nergal's wife. Ishum, Nergal's counselor, dissuades his master. A description of an ideal king follows, though the context is unclear: "This [spirit] which you saw in the netherworld, is that of the exalted shepherd: to whom my father [   ], the king of the gods, gives full responsibility. . . ." Next comes a prediction and an admonition, and the section concludes with brief reports in the first person and in the third person.

Though the text bears a general resemblance to Daniel 7, with the night dream of gods in hybrid form and the warrior-god on a throne pronouncing judgment, there are major differences. Judgment is given against the visionary himself, whereas in Daniel it is against the beasts from the sea; the ideal ruler in the *Vision* is extremely shadowy, whereas in Daniel he receives an eschatological kingdom. The *pattern of relationships* in the two texts is quite different. Finally, the texts have little in common with regard to aim. In the *Vision,* the aim is to encourage piety to the god of the netherworld; in Daniel, it is to encourage Jews to resist the hellenizing policies of the Seleucid kings (J. J. Collins 1993, 283–86). The "Vision of the Netherworld" is of interest, however, as a precedent for the tours of heaven and hell that are popular in later, especially Christian, apocalypses.

Recurrent Elements

One of the important and persistent recurrent elements in the genre of combat myth is the divine assembly, thrown into confusion yet charged with the responsibility of resisting the monster's threats. A considerable amount of discourse time is devoted to its discussions in *Anzu* and *Enuma elish.* Dramatically, the magnitude of the threat is expressed through the terror and consternation of the gods as they meet. The decrees of the assembly are powerful and binding in heaven and on earth; they are prominent in all the combat myths. Nonetheless, its decrees are not automatically effective against every cosmic threat, for they can be rendered ineffective by a monster. A warrior-god must do away with the evil before the decrees are effective. At the end of *Lugal-e* (lines 679 forward), Ninurta receives the homage of the Anunnaki gods and his father Enlil grants him new status. In *Anzu,* the victorious Ninurta receives names of honor and authority from the gods, a harbinger of the fifty names that Marduk in *Enuma elish* receives from the gods. In *Enuma elish* the assembly's decree plays an extraordinarily important role. Before he sets out, his destiny is declared supreme: "Your destiny (*šīmtu*) is unequalled, your word (has the power of)! . . . From this day forwards your command shall not be altered. Yours is the power to exalt and abase. . . . We hereby give you sovereignty over all of the whole universe" (IV.4–14). In the final tablets (end of IV to VII) Marduk constructs the universe and the assembly's earlier decree takes effect as they acclaim his fifty names.

The decree of the assembly that exalts one deity because of his victory over cosmic enemies is a theme found in a transposed form in apocalyptic literature. Though heavenly decrees in the combat myth are primarily concerned with kingship, they can also be concerned with broader questions of the divine will and human activity. In the Bible, a vestige of the decision-making assembly is found in Gen 1:26 ("Let *us* make man in our image") and 11:7 ("Let *us* go down and confuse their language"), in the designation of heavenly beings as the host or army (the literal meaning of Y<small>HWH</small> ṣĕbāʾôt), and in affirmations that Yahweh is incomparable to other heavenly beings (e.g., Exod. 15:11; Deut. 3:24; 1 Kgs. 8:23; Pss. 86:8; 95:3). Apocalyptic literature in particular exploits the heavenly assembly. God is often in the assembly, surrounded by heavenly beings, messengers or angels, and there is constant reference to "destinies," and decrees (Brown 1958a; 1958v; 1959).

Related to the decree of the assembly is the Tablet-of-Decrees (ṭuppi šīmāti), which in Akkadian narratives occurs only in *Anzu* (where it plays a central role), *Enuma elish* (I.57; IV.121; V.69, presumably derived from *Anzu*), and *Erra* (IV.44). The tablet was worn around the neck of the god in charge, and it could be put on and taken off like a garment—for Enlil removed it to take a bath in *Anzu*. Neither English "destiny" nor "fate" is a satisfactory translation of šīmtu, for these English words imply inevitability, whereas the Akkadian word connotes something *decreed* but not necessarily unalterable. "Destinies" were subject to change through magic; they were usually transmitted from a higher power, from god to king, king to subject, father to child. In mythology and literature, the highest gods, usually Anu, Enlil, and Ea, decreed the destinies establishing the nature and pattern of things in heaven and on earth. Šīmāti were regarded as introduced at creation, for *Enuma elish* (I.8) describes pre-creation as a period when "no destines had been decreed." Other words for similar determination of things and events are Sumerian *me* or *giš.ḫur* (= Akkadian *parṣu, uṣurtu*). In later apocalypses, the seer is frequently shown heavenly visions of meteorological and natural phenomena and of future events. Such visions should be understood against the ancient Near Eastern background of "destinies"—things and events that have been determined by the divine.

Another relevant recurrent element of the genre of combat myth is the enemy as monster. Azag is a monster. Anzu's strange appearance was proverbial; his face, possibly that of a bat, inspired terror. Though Tiamat, personified Sea, is not described clearly in *Enuma elish*, scholars assume that the dragon depicted fighting a god on many seals is Tiamat; the seven-headed Hydra of some seals may have been later identified with Tiamat. The monsters are often interpreted as natural forces: for example, the storm-god's attack on the monster in the mountains reflects thundershowers sweeping into the mountain ranges. Though such a natural reference cannot be denied, there are as well historical and political dimensions to the monsters. Azag and Anzu reside in the northeastern mountains, the homeland of the enemies of the Mesopotamian plain dwellers. *Enuma elish* views Apsu, Tiamat, and Kingu as usurpers of the legitimate throne that belongs by right to Anu and Marduk. H. H. Schmid notes:

> In Mesopotamia, Ugarit, and Israel, *Chaoskampf* appears not only in cosmological contexts but just as frequently—and this was fundamentally true right from the first—in political contexts. The repulsion and the destruction of the enemy, and thereby the maintenance of political order, always constitutes one of the major dimensions of the battle against chaos. The enemies are not other than a manifestation of chaos which must be driven back. (1984, 104)

An important motif is the seer-hero who is brought into or ascends to the world of the gods to receive wisdom and knowledge about the future. It is his task to communicate this wisdom to the human race. The preeminent seer in apocalyptic literature is Enoch, the hero of the several booklets that make up *1 Enoch*. He is also the hero in other writings and is mentioned in

Sirach, Wisdom of Solomon, and the New Testament. As one raised up to heaven and given special knowledge, he served as the model for Daniel, John, and Ezra. Enoch has antecedents in Mesopotamian tradition.

A key biblical text that mediated Mesopotamian lore to Levantine literature and applied it to Enoch was Gen 5:21–24. There Enoch is seventh in a ten-member genealogy of pre-flood patriarchs. The Priestly writer makes comments about Enoch that are not made about the other nine patriarchs: instead of describing his death, the Priestly writer has "he walked with 'God' (*hā'ĕlōhîm*); then he was no more because God (*'ĕlōhîm*) took him." The Hebrew spellings noted above are significant. The prefaced definite article *hā-* in the first occurrence suggests that the correct translation is not "God" but "divine beings," the heavenly beings who lived with God. The Genesis text thus says that even while on earth Enoch associated with heavenly beings, unlike the other patriarchs. Further, the end of his stay on earth did not mean the end of his communion with heavenly beings; he was taken up into the heavens to be with God.

The Sumerian King List, a schematic history of pre-flood kings, which exists in copies ranging from ca. 1500 b.c.e. to 165 b.c.e., has long been recognized as a source of Genesis 5. The kings in the lists, like the ancestors of Genesis, are extraordinarily long-lived; in some versions of the list, there are ten kings, the last of whom is the flood hero. Some versions have in seventh place a figure like Enoch, named Enmeduranki or Enmenduranna, who ruled in Sippar, a city sacred to the sun-god. Enoch's age of 365 years, which differs so dramatically from the other pre-flood heroes in Genesis, is most naturally explained as a reflection of the solar calendar, another link to Enmeduranki of Sippar. Most important, two texts show Enmeduranki in the presence of the gods Shamash (the sun-god) and Adad. In one he is brought in to the assembly and given special wisdom.

> Shamash in Ebabbarra [appointed] Enmeduranki [king of Sippar], the beloved of Anu, Enlil [and Ea]. Shamash and Adad [brought him in] to their assembly, Shamash and Adad [honoured him], Shamash and Adad [set him] on a large throne of god, they showed him how to observe oil on water, a mystery of Anu [Enlil and Ea], they gave him the tablet of the gods, the liver, a secret of heaven and [underworld], they put in his hand the cedar-(rod), beloved of the great gods." (VanderKam 1984, 39–40; cf. Kvanvig 1988, 185–86)

Enmeduranki is brought into heaven and there is taught divination, how to read the future. He is the prototype of the biblical Enoch, who in Genesis is taken up to heaven to walk with the heavenly beings.

Further refinement to the Enmeduranki tradition has been provided by recently published texts that have made it possible to reappraise the so-called *bīt mēseri* ritual series.[1] The texts list the *apkallu*, legendary pre-flood creatures of great wisdom; seven in number, they taught the human race wisdom and craft.

Kings	Sages
1. Alulim	U-An
2. Alagar	U-An-dugga
3. Ammeluanna	Enmedugga
4. Ammegalanna	Enmegalamma
5. Enmešugalanna	Enmebulugga
6. Dumuzi	An-Enlilda
7. Enmeduranki	Utuabzu

They are followed after the flood by four more sages. The text gives each *apkallu* a short notice. Utuabzu, the sage of Enmeduranki, has an especially interesting notice: "Utuabzu, who was taken up into heaven, the pure *purādu* fishes, the *purādu* fishes of the sea, the seven of them, the seven Wise, who arose in the flood, who direct the plans of heaven and earth." Riekele Borger, the editor, believes that the text strengthens the possibility that Enmeduranki as predictor of the future and the seventh ruler in primordial time was the prototype of Enoch. He notes, however, that the myth of Enoch's journey to heaven comes ultimately from Enmeduranki's sage, the seventh pre-flood sage, Utuabzu.

Genesis 5:21–24 is the oldest surviving example of the Enoch tradition in the Bible. From this modest source text a mighty stream was destined to flow.

Themes

The two themes most relevant for later apocalyptic works are cosmic threat and new creation. Though the threat is undeniably prominent in the combat myth, the most important thing is the god's defeat of it and consequent exaltation to the top rank. In *Lugal-e* the evil is that the water destined to irrigate the Mesopotamian plains is trapped in the ice of the northern and eastern mountains. This is not simply a natural malfunction but the conscious strategy of the mountain-dwelling monster Azag, who has been made king by the mountain plants and stones. Azag thwarts the gods' intent that Mesopotamian fields be fertile and support human workers to care for and feed them. Azag's act is against gods and human beings. Azag and his constituency of plants and stones are not purely mythical, for the northern and eastern mountains were the homeland of the plains dwellers' historical enemies. The evil in *Lugal-e* is therefore (in modern terms) both "natural" and "historical," affecting both gods and human beings. By defeating Azag, Ninurta truly restores the cosmos as a coherent system.

In the first part of the two-part *Anzu* the evil is the same as in *Lugal-e*, that is, the failure of the mountain waters to reach the plains. How that problem was solved (at the beginning of the epic) cannot be determined from the fragmentary text. The major evil, however, is Anzu's theft of the Tablet-of-Decrees from its rightful custodian, Enlil. The divine decision regarding all reality encoded in the tablet is in the power of a monster hostile to the divine assembly. The evil is that things will not work right because the tablet is in the wrong hands. By getting the tablet back, Ninurta ensures the survival of the world the gods have created.

Enuma elish is more complex, and so is the evil in its two sections. In the first section (I.1–79), the evil is the rival dynasty represented by Apsu, who is killed by Ea. In the second part, the evil is the rival dynasty represented by Tiamat. She is violent and irrational; the world would never have been created if she were to rule. Marduk's victory establishes the legitimate dynasty and eventuates in creation.

The three combat myths see the universe as threatened once upon a time by a monster with sufficient power to destroy it or change it for the worse. The divine assembly—that is, the gods as deciding and acting—cannot by itself resolve the problem. The evil is not simply a cosmic malfunction but is willed by a particular being. The evil plays itself out on the natural and historical planes.

Closely related to the evil is the god's victory over it. Is the victory merely a restoration of the pre-threat order, or is it new creation? At the very least, *Endzeit* becomes *Urzeit*, for the original order is renewed. This is surely true for *Lugal-e* and *Anzu. Enuma elish,* however, is a differ-ent case. It is true creation. Marduk makes the world as we know it. The world did not exist prior to Tiamat, for it is from her body that the cosmos is constructed.

☞ CANAAN

History and Religion

By the third millennium Syria-Palestine was populated by West Semitic peoples speaking an Old Canaanite language. After 1200 B.C.E., the Old Canaanite area was divided into three areas: Palestine (the area south of Mount Hermon, later conquered by the tribes of Israel), the areas of the Aramaean city-states, and Phoenicia, the long narrow strip of land along the Mediterranean from Arvad to Mount Carmel in the south. In a Ugaritic text, "Canaanite" refers to an area dis-tinct from the city of Ugarit, but in modern usage "Canaanite" is customary for the whole lit-toral.

A common literary tradition is attested for the Old Canaanite (Phoenician) culture. Reli-gious and mythological poetic texts excavated at the Late Bronze (mostly fourteenth century B.C.E.) city of Ugarit display vocabulary, especially word pairs, recurrent elements, and tech-niques found also in Phoenician inscriptions and in early biblical poetry. The Ugaritic texts provide a northern sampling of literary and religious traditions shared by Canaan and Israel.

Canaanite scribes in the employ of royal courts in the major cities knew Mesopotamian lit-erature. Canonical texts have been found at Boghasköy (ancient Hattuša) in the Hittite empire, at Ugarit, at Meskene (ancient Emar, a crossroads of east and west), and even at Megiddo in Palestine (a fragment of *Gilgamesh*). These texts were understood by Levantine scribes, for Akkadian was a diplomatic language in the late second and early first millennia. One can assume that some scribes employed in Canaanite and Israelite temples and palaces were trained in the traditional manner—by copying canonical texts. It is thus not surprising to find Mesopotamian influence on Canaanite and biblical literature. A good example of a western borrowing of an eastern literary genre is the creation-flood story. Attested in the *Sumerian Flood Story, Atrahasis, Gilgamesh XI, Berossus,* and some versions of the Sumerian King List, it is echoed in the flood story found at Ugarit, and has strongly influenced the Bible in Genesis 2–11 (Clifford 1994, 144–46).

The god lists of Ugarit, like those of Mesopotamia, list many more deities than the few who play prominent roles in myths, but we are here chiefly concerned with the executive deities. The most important mythological texts found at Ugarit (in excavations from 1929 forward) are the story of King Keret, the story of Aqhat, and the cycle concerning Baal's combat. They are writ-ten in a cuneiform adaptation of the Canaanite alphabet.

The head of the pantheon is the patriarch El, creator of heaven and earth. His consort is Asherah. There is no sacred triad in Ugarit; Mesopotamian Enlil and Ea have no real analogues. El presides over the assembly of the gods, whose members in Ugaritic texts (unlike Mesopotamia) are not precisely identified nor shown engaged in lively debate. El or the assem-bly *tout ensemble* speak and act. El is portrayed as old and wise, though there are hints that in olden days he was a feared warrior-god. His decree, approved by the assembly, is of extraordinary importance. Both Anat and Asherah confess: "Thou art wise, O El, and thy decree is long life." The young god Hadad (Baal) is a warrior. The assembly decrees, "Our king is Aliyan Baal, our judge above whom there is no other." His weapons are those of the storm—lightning, thunder, wind, and rains that bring fertility—and his bellicose consort is Anat. Two divine beings play significant roles as Baal's enemies: Mot (Death) and Yamm (Sea). One of the major interpretative problems of the Baal Cycle is El's relation to Baal and to Baal's enemies Yamm and Mot. Mot is called "son of El," and Yamm in *KTU* 1.1 is given a name and palace by El. Elsewhere El favors Baal and grants him permission to build his palace.

Literature and Themes Relevant to Apocalyptic Literature

Genre of Combat Myth (Baal Cycle)

The six tablets of the Baal Cycle (*KTU* 1.1–6 = *ANET* 129–42[2]) belong to the genre of combat myth, which we have singled out as having extraordinary influence on apocalyptic literature. The similarities of the Baal Cycle to the Mesopotamian combat myths are striking: (1) the enemy is Sea in *KTU* 1.1–3 = *ANET* 129–31, 135–38, recalling Tiamat in *Enuma elish;* (2) the divine assembly under its president An or El is threatened and commissions a young warrior-god to battle the foe, though in the Baal Cycle the commission must be inferred from the goddesses' quote of the decree that their king is Baal; (3) events are decided by a battle that is cosmic in scope; (4) the warrior-god's victory is symbolized by a palace and dedication feast for all the gods. Some scholars have proposed that this combat myth originated among West Semites on the grounds that the sea phenomenologically is important only in Syria-Palestine. The theory is unlikely, however, because the word "sea" in Mesopotamian myths can refer not only to the ocean but to the waters in the northern mountains, as it does in *Anzu.* It is now clear that the literary antecedent of the Marduk–Tiamat conflict in *Enuma elish* is not the West Semitic Baal–Yamm story but the native *Anzu* (Lambert 1986).

The Ugaritic combat myth is in the same poetic tradition as early biblical poetry and thus is much more pertinent to later apocalyptic literature than the Akkadian works analyzed above. Unfortunately, four of the six tablets of the Baal Cycle cannot be put in their proper sequence because of broken beginnings or ends. Hence we cannot be certain of the plots. Here the Akkadian works are useful, for they can supply the sequence and plot only dimly discernible in the Ugaritic texts. In the Baal Cycle only tablets V (*ANET* 138–39) and VI (*ANET* 139–41) preserve the ending and the beginning that demonstrate their sequence. (Normally the last line of a tablet is repeated as the first line of the succeeding tablet.) Tablets I–III (*ANET* 129–31, 135–38) tell of the Baal–Yamm conflict and tablets IV–V (*ANET* 131–35, 138–41) of the Baal–Mot conflict. The majority of scholars assume a single cycle, which first depicts Baal's war with Yamm and then describes his war with Mot. It is more probable, however, that the two conflicts are not two acts in a single drama but variants of the same myth. There are good indications that the two stories are variants: tablets III (*ANET* 135–38) and IV (*ANET* 131–35) show an identical sequence of actions (Baal has no palace like the other gods, an embassy is sent to the goddess to ask her to intercede with El for Baal's palace, the goddess prepares for her journey and departs for El's abode, the goddess praises El's decree, El grants permission, the craftsman god is summoned to build it. Positing two versions of a single myth avoids a dramatically implausible never-ending seesaw battle between Baal and his enemies.

Baal–Yamm. Tablets I–III (*ANET* 129–31, 135–38) are about the Baal–Yamm conflict. We do not know the original sequence of the tablets, and so any summary of the plot must be regarded as tentative. At a certain point Yamm (Sea) is given authority ("a name") by El, who charges him to drive Baal "from his royal throne, the resting place, the throne of his domination." El commands the craftsman-god Koshar wa-Hasis to build a palace for Yamm. (Throughout the cycle, the palace plays an extremely significant role as the concretization of kingship.) So commissioned, Baal sends ambassadors to the assembly presided over by El, ordering them to surrender Baal. The assembly is terrified at the approach of Yamm's messengers, and El immediately hands Baal over, "Baal is your servant, O Yamm" ("your subject" in political language). Baal tries to fight but is restrained by Anat and Ashtart, presumably because they regard the assembly's action as legally binding. After some major gaps in the tablets, Baal eventually has the opportunity to attack his enemy with Koshar wa-Hasis at his side. Koshar fashions two magic weapons against Yamm, the second of which succeeds in knocking Yamm to the ground, where Baal finishes him off. Baal is acclaimed king: "Yamm is dead! Baal reigns!"

The Baal–Yamm story is more fragmentary than the Baal–Mot story; the plot is uncertain and important matters are left unexplained. Why does El commission Yamm and give him a palace? Why does the assembly hand Baal over to Yamm, and why is Baal later able to best him in combat? A major problem in Ugaritic mythology—the unclear relationship of El to Baal, Yamm, and Mot—keeps us from fully comprehending the essential point of this myth.

Baal–Mot. The Baal–Death combat myth is told in tablets IV–VI of the Baal Cycle (*ANET* 138–42); the extant material is greater and in surer sequence than is the case with the Baal–Yamm story. Most scholars believe that tablets IV-V-VI are the proper sequence. Tablet VI (*ANET* 139–141) immediately continues tablet V (*ANET* 138–39), since its first line repeats the last line of tablet V, but the proper placement of tablet IV (*ANET* 131–35) is far from certain. The story begins with Baal complaining that he has no palace like the other gods and must live in the home of El. Anat intercedes with Asherah, El's wife, to bring the plea to El, reminding him, "Thy decree is wise. . . . Thy decree is: Our king is Puissant Baal, our sovereign second to none; all of us must bear his gift, all of us must bear his purse." Although Baal has been given authority by the assembly, El's permission is still needed for his palace, the full sign of his kingship. El gives his permission. Baal gathers the material and Koshar wa-Hasis builds it. At its completion, Baal declares: "My house I have built of silver, my palace of gold" (*KTU* 1.4.vi = *ANET* 134–35) and invites all the gods to a dedicatory banquet. He marches triumphantly through numerous towns in the vicinity of his Mount Zaphon and from his palace proclaims his kingship in thunder as his enemies flee. In this moment of triumph, Baal instructs his messengers to proclaim his kingship to the underworld and invites Mot.

If *KTU* 1.5 (*ANET* 138–39) directly continues, as most scholars assume (though there are difficulties), then Baal's triumph is suddenly turned upside down as Mot invites, or rather commands, Baal to come to *his* underworld domain. Baal must descend with his whole entourage, and he says to Mot, "Your servant am I, and that for ever (= no set time)." Eventually messengers report back to El that "we came upon Baal fallen to the earth. Dead is Aliyan Baal, departed is Prince, Lord of the earth!" (*KTU* 1.5.vi.8–10 = *ANET* 139). El and Anat engage in mourning rites. Anat finds the body and brings it for burial to Mount Zaphon (*KTU* 1.6.i = *ANET* 139). El is unable to find among his and Asherah's children a suitable replacement for Baal, which makes dramatically clear that Baal is irreplaceable (*KTU* 1.6.i.132–67). Afterward the bereaved

Anat encounters Mot, who callously tells her he consumed Baal "like a lamb in his mouth." Later, she seizes him in rage, cuts him up and sows him far and wide (*KTU* 1.6.ii.30–37). After a break of forty lines, El declares that "Aliyan Baal lives, existent is Prince, Lord of the earth," for he sees in a dream the signs of Baal's return to life: the heavens raining oil and the wadis running with honey. El's dream shows that Baal is alive; Shapshu, the sun-goddess, is asked to search for him. After a break, Baal appears, defeats rebellious sons of Asherah and takes the throne. In the seventh year of his reign, Mot comes to exact vengeance for the humiliation inflicted upon him by Anat: "Because of you, Baal, I experienced winnowing in the sea. Give me one of your brothers that I may eat." After about sixty lines of uncertain text, Mot comes to Baal on Mount Zaphon and accuses him of giving him his own brothers to eat (*KTU* 1.6.vi.14–16). Baal and Mot then fight like animals until both fall in exhaustion. At this point Shapshu intervenes and rebukes Mot: "How dare you fight with Aliyan Baal. . . . [Bull El your father] will uproot the base of your dwelling. Surely he will overturn your royal throne. Surely he will shatter your scepter of judgment" (1.6.vi.24–29). Mot stops out of fear. Baal remounts his throne and the cycle ends with a banquet of the gods. Shapshu is lauded as judge, probably for her role in settling the conflict of kingship.

The overall interpretation of the Baal Cycle is made difficult by the uncertain sequence of tablets I–IV (and columns within tablet II), many broken passages, and our ignorance of its social location. Was the cycle recited in the temple? Was it used to support the authority of the king? Several interpretations have been proposed: ritual and seasonal, cosmogonic, and rhetorical and political. Each has some validity yet no single theory does justice to all the data. Few would deny any reference to the change of seasons. Mot represents the dry summer season or dry areas, and Baal represents the fertilizing rains of the Levantine winter. An exclusively seasonal explanation, however, neglects the obvious political features of the myth. Mot and Baal act more like generals and politicians than natural forces, and Baal's kingship has to have some reference to the Ugaritic king, who, like Baal, needed military power in order to reign. Others see in the cycle a cosmogony or creation account, in which Baal creates a cosmos after defeating some form of chaos. This interpretation accounts for the life–death struggle, and the prominence of cosmic order and the palace, but in the Ugaritic texts only El and Asherah are given the title creator; the most that Baal accomplishes by his victory over sea and death is to reconstitute cosmic and political harmony. Historical interpretations see the myth as reflecting the rise and fall of the gods of different peoples; for example, the rise of Baal allegedly at the expense of El reflects the god of a new dynasty in the history of Ugarit. This interpretation is unsatisfactory, however. Baal does not replace El but is commissioned by him, and the commission of a young god by a senior god in the face of a cosmic threat is a characteristic feature of ancient palace life and of the genre of combat myth.

The best approach is to view the cycle according to its genre, the combat myth, and to reconstruct its plot by analogy with the better-known combat myths of Mesopotamia. In the typical plot, a monster threatens the cosmic order; the assembly of the gods meets amid considerable trepidation; finding no willing warrior among the senior deities, it turns to a young outsider, who successfully defeats the monster and returns to the assembly to be acclaimed king. This abstract plotline does not completely resolve several puzzles in the Baal Cycle (e.g., the relation of El to Baal, Mot, and Yamm), but it allows us to arrange the tablets in order with some confidence. It also explains the prominent role of Baal's palace, the need for El's permission, the fact that Yamm and Mot, despite their names, are portrayed not as primordial forces but as seekers of political power. Baal's royalty explains the relation of these mythic texts to the people of Ugarit, for human kingship is a reflection of divine kingship. These myths must support the authority of the Ugaritic king, whose proper rule ensures fertility, upholds family and civic order, and sees to the proper honoring of the gods.

Recurrent Elements

The assembly of the gods plays a significant role in the Baal–Yamm story.

> The gods sat to eat, / the holy ones to dine. / Baal stood before El. / When the gods saw them [the hostile messengers of Yamm], / . . . . . / the gods lowered their heads / upon their knees, / and upon their princely thrones. / Baal rebuked them. / "Why have you lowered, O Gods, / your heads upon your knees / and on your princely thrones? / I see, O gods, you are terrified / from fear of the messengers of Yamm, / the emissaries of Judge River. / Lift up your heads, O gods, / from upon your knees, / from upon your princely thrones!" (*KTU* 1.2.I.20–28)

Despite Baal's protests, the assembly surrenders him to Yamm's messengers, and their decision, even though made in fear, is binding.

In biblical passages such as 1 Kgs. 22:19–23; Isaiah 6; and 40:1–8; Psalm 82; and Job 1–2, the assembly plays a major role, and in apocalyptic literature it sometimes forms the context in which God acts, e.g., Daniel 7 and Revelation 4–5. The biblical emphasis on the unicity and absolute power of Yahweh reduces the members of the assembly to spectators, choristers, or messengers, but the assembly persists as part of the heavenly scene.

Sea is apparently a monster. In *KTU* 1.3.III.39–IV.3, Anat recalls the allies of Yamm, the enemies of Baal: El's river Rabbim, the dragon, the crooked serpent, Shilyat with seven heads. In *KTU* 1.5.I., Lotan is the ally of Mot. Lotan appears in the Bible under the name Leviathan in Ps. 74:13–14; Job 3:8; 26:12–13; 41:1–34; Isa. 27:1; Rev. 12:3; 17:1–14; 19:20; 21:1; 2 Esdras 6:49–52. Mot is not described but may also be a monster. To judge by their names, Yamm and Mot represent forces hostile to the human race and terrify the divine assembly. Unfortunately the precise nature of their threat is unclear.

The decree is ascribed to El. The assembly is not recorded as issuing decrees on its own. When the goddesses Anat and Asherah ask El to permit Baal to build a palace after his victory over Mot and Yamm, they praise his decree: "Your decree, O El, is wise. Your wisdom is eternal. A life of good fortune is your decree. Our king is Aliyan Baal, our judge without a peer" (*KTU* 1.3.V.30–33; 1.4.IV.41–44). The kingship of Baal needs the decree of El in order for it to be realized in a palace. In the Bible, Yahweh is acclaimed king by the denizens of heaven. Psalm 29 is the most explicit: "Give to Yahweh, O sons of El, give to Yahweh glory and might. . . . Yahweh is enthroned on Flood-dragon, Yahweh reigns as king forever!"

A recurrent element in apocalyptic literature—the use of animal names for human beings—has precedents in Ugaritic and in early biblical poetry, suggesting that it was part of the Canaanite literary repertoire. Animal names convey fleetness, ferocity, or strength. King Keret's dinner guests include "his bulls" and "his gazelles" (*KTU* 1.15.IV.6–8, 17–19), which are to be interpreted as "peers" and "barons." Baal's allies include "eight boars" (*ḥnzr* = Hebrew *ḥzr*), parallel to "seven lads" (*KTU* 1.5.V.8–9). The Bible has even more examples: *ʾabbîr* ("bull," "stallion") *ʿayil* ("ram") *kĕpîr* ("young lion") *ʿattûdîm* ("he-goats") among others (Miller

1971). Daniel 7 and 8 as well as the Animal Apocalypse in *1 Enoch* 85–90 describe human heroes under the figure of animals.

Themes

The best clue to the nature of the cosmic threats in the Ugaritic texts is their names, Death (Mot) and Sea (Yamm). Death seems to represent death and sterility, and Sea, the Mediterranean Sea bordering on and perhaps threatening to overrun the coast. In the Bible the monsters have an implicit historical and political reference, but the Ugaritic texts are silent on such references. One can probably assume that the conquests of Baal have some reflex in royal ideology: for example, the king of Ugarit has been commissioned by El and his rule continues the work of Baal.

Because the nature of the cosmic evil is unspecified, the nature of Baal's victory over it must also be uncertain. Does Baal reestablish an order or does he create? He does not seem to attain the uncontested rank among the gods that Marduk attains in *Enuma elish* or to create the world. Only El and his consort Asherah are ever called creator. In comparison with the Mesopotamian accounts, Baal's royalty seems limited. At one point in the story, his enemies are actually supported by the assembly of the gods and El, and at another point he himself declares he is Mot's servant. Baal cannot defeat Mot in *KTU* 1.6.VI until Shapshu warns that El will hear and retaliate against Mot. Baal's characteristic thunderstorm is a phenomenon of winter, a hint perhaps that it is not effective in the summer season. The evidence suggests that Baal—and probably the Ugaritic king, his regent on earth—enjoy limited kingship. The limit differs strikingly from the triumph of Ninurta in *Anzu*, Marduk (or Asshur) in *Enuma elish*, and Yahweh's victory in the Bible.

The above survey of Mesopotamian and Canaanite material prompts four observations.

1. One must be careful methodologically about describing the elements of the genre of combat myth in the ancient Near East. There is no ideal form of the myth but only diverse realizations. What is essential? Joseph Fontenrose's initial classification in *Python: A Study in Delphic Myth* (1959) was useful but relied too much on the personal qualities of the actors and too little on their function. Neil Forsyth's *The Old Enemy: Satan and the Combat Myths* adapts Vladimir Propp's description in *Morphology of the Folk Tale* to provide the following scheme (Forsyth 1987, 448–51).

1. Lack/ villainy.	2. Hero emerges/ prepares to act.	3. Donor/ Consultation.	4. Journey	5. Battle	6. Defeat	7. Enemy ascendant.

7. Hero recovers/ new hero.	8. Battle rejoined.	9. Victory.	10. Enemy punished.	11. Triumph.

2. Kingship and cosmic order are inextricably bound up with each other in that the god's restoration of pre-threat order (*Lugal-e, Anzu*; Baal–Mot, Baal–Yamm?) or creation of order (*Enuma elish*) is *the* great act and sign of his kingship. The kingship of the victor god is in a sense

"monotheistic"; that is, *one* god is singled out at the expense of the other gods' sovereignty, usurping their supremacy in the pantheon and over the universe.

3. What modern thought distinguishes as "nature" and "history" is not clearly distinguished in ancient thought. Natural forces are described as historical enemies. Monsters engage in political activities (stealing the Tablet-of-Decrees), lead armies, and conduct campaigns.

4. Do the texts look forward to a permanent final state? Norman Cohn concludes that Mesopotamian, Canaanite, and early biblical faith views were essentially "static yet anxious" (Cohn 1993, 227) and that Zoroastrianism introduced hope for a permanent phase of absolute peace. One can argue, however, that the combat myth, even outside the Bible, already contains a hope for a permanent kingdom, or, better stated, the unimpeded rule of a single deity. One god became supreme over all the other gods and over a particular cosmic evil. People presumably hoped for the abiding order, though perhaps they were not surprised when fresh cosmic threats arose. But endless repetition, eternal return, is not the *message* in the combat myths considered above.

⮞ THE BIBLE ───

History and Religion

By ca. 1200 B.C.E., a group of tribes occupied part of Palestine and formed a league of tribes known as Israel, which shared a common story. Yahweh their God had rescued them from Egypt, made a covenant, and brought them into Canaan. Some poetry from this period survives.

To judge by this early poetry, Israel made use of the poetic repertory and concepts of Canaanite religious literature. The fixed pairs of words, vocabulary, and poetic syntax found in the largely fourteenth-century Ugaritic texts also occur in Hebrew poetry such as Exodus 15, Judges 5, Deuteronomy 33, and Psalm 114. The well-known animosity of the Bible to "Canaanite" religious practices should not mislead us into thinking the Israelites were a hermetically sealed enclave in Canaan. The very vehemence of the Bible shows the affinity between Canaanite and Israelite culture.

Israelite poets described Yahweh in the language used of the gods El and Baal in Canaan. The exploits of Yahweh were sometimes depicted in the genre of the combat myth. Yahweh is a storm-god using weapons of wind, rain, and lightning to defeat his foes (e.g., Pss. 18:8–20; 29; 77:12–21). Though sharing much with their neighbors, Israelite poets were distinctive in their explicit *historical* interest and reference. The poets celebrated Yahweh's victories not over other gods or monsters but over the army of Pharaoh in Egypt. Yahweh fought *Israel's* battles. These historical acts were nonetheless celebrated with mythic language and concepts, which deepened their significance and gave them a cosmic scope. The combined historical and mythic reference enabled Israel, relatively insignificant in comparison with other peoples, to reckon itself as extraordinary, the special people of the Most High God.

In the course of Israel's history, the prominence given to either the mythic or the historical dimension in religious writings varied. Early poetry generally maintained a balance between mythic and historical elements: for example, Yahweh fights on the heavenly plane for Israel (e.g., Judg. 5:4–5, 20–21), but the poem is mainly about a historical battle between Israel and a coalition of northern kings. In some works borrowed from neighboring courts and temples, Israelite scribes left mythological elements "untranslated," that is, not referred to historical events. Though some postexilic writings such as Isaiah 24–27, 65, and Zechariah 9–14 do not immediately refer mythological description to historical events, one must be cautious about making the myth–history correlation a criterion for charting the development of apocalyptic literature. Myth and history are not dichotomous concepts. Historical reference can be implicit in nonbiblical mythology, which may well have in view a historical people and dynasty (Roberts 1976). The prominence of myth or history in a literary work may depend on the genre rather than on a "worldview."

It has been argued that historical and sociological changes in the postexilic period, particularly the end of native kingship and the related "office" of prophecy, encouraged the development of apocalyptic writing. In sixth-century literature such as Isaiah 34–35, 40–55, and the later oracles of the book of Ezekiel, a change in the character of prophecy is already discernible. New traits or patterns have emerged. One is the democratizing and eschatologizing of classical prophetic themes and forms. A second is the doctrine of two ages, an era of "old things" and an era of "new things," the beginning of a typological treatment of historical events. The significance of history was increasingly discovered in future fulfillment. A third element is the resurgent influence of myths of creation used to frame history and to lend history transcendent significance (Cross 1973, 343–46).

Literature and Themes Relevant to Apocalyptic Literature

Genre of Combat Myth

We can distinguish four stages in the use of the combat myth by Israel: (1) early poetry such as Exodus 15, (2) liturgical poetry (psalms) of the monarchic period, (3) Second Temple literature such as Isaiah 40–66 and Zechariah 9–14, and (4) fully developed apocalyptic literature such as Daniel 7 and Revelation 12. In the first stage, the old hymns celebrate a past event, Yahweh's victory, which has brought Israel into existence. Yahweh defeated threats (Pharaoh, the Red Sea) to Israel's existence enabling the people to live safely in their land. In the second stage, hymns such as Psalms 93, 96, and 114 praise the ancient past victory that brought Israel into being. In communal laments such as Psalms 74, 77, and 89, Israel is threatened by enemies. The psalmist narrates before God in liturgy ("remembers") the original combat whereby God defeated its enemies. The purpose is to persuade God to repeat the primordial victory and defeat the present threat. In the third stage, the postexilic period, Israel has been destroyed in that it has lost its land and Temple. The validity of Yahweh's past victory has been annulled. Hence the psalmist beseeches God to fight and win a victory over Israel's enemies *in the future*. In the fourth stage, exemplified in Daniel 7 and Revelation 12, a seer is told that the victory *has already taken place* in heaven; the seer is to bring the news of victory to the beleaguered faithful on earth.

The criterion for distinguishing the stages above is how the combat myth is viewed by each. In the first stage the combat-victory is a past and still valid event (the victory over Pharaoh at the Red Sea), and it is the reason for Israel's present existence. In the second stage, liturgical hymns praise the past victory as still potent. Communal laments, however, view the community as profoundly threatened to the point that the old saving event has lost its efficacy and must be renewed. In the third stage, the combat victory has been annulled, for Israel lies in ruins. Hence the community prays God to act again on the model of the ancient deed. In the fourth stage, the period of Daniel and Revelation, the combat has taken place and the victory has been won in the real or heavenly world, but only the seer (and his readers) knows it. We now turn to a representative work from each of the four stages.

1. Exodus 15 is the best known adaptation of the combat myth of the early poetry. Its early date is strongly suggested by archaic linguistic features (Cross 1973; Sáenz Badillos 1993). The first part of the poem celebrates Yahweh's defeat of Pharaoh *on* the sea (sea itself is not the enemy), and in the second part, Yahweh's leading the people to his shrine, where his kingship is acclaimed. Its genre—hymn—differs of course from the narrative realizations of the combat myth we have so far seen. The structure is not identical to Forsyth's ideal outline of the plot, which is drawn from purely narrative realizations. The first scene, "lack or villainy," occurs in v. 9, "I will purse, I will overtake, I will overtake, my desire shall have its fill of them." The assembly of gods is only vestigially preserved because of the demands of Israel's monotheistic faith. The battle is described in v. 8. Yahweh is exalted to kingship over the other gods (v. 11): "Who is like you, Yahweh, among the gods, / Who is like you, majestic in holiness, / Awesome in splendor, working wonders! You stretched out your right hand, the earth swallowed them"; (v. 18): Yahweh will reign for ever and ever!" A special emphasis is the procession of the people through Canaan to Yahweh's shrine, where his kingship will be celebrated. The narrative plot has been broken up for the sake of liturgy.

The hymn celebrates a specific historical event in the myth—Yahweh's victory over Pharaoh at the Red Sea. "Historical" here means only that the Israelites believed the exodus took place at a particular time and place. Though the extant extrabiblical combat myths did not have an explicitly historical reference, they depicted creation or reestablishment of a particular cosmic order and must have therefore had in mind a specific king and people. The Bible is, nonetheless, much more explicit about historical events and gives them much more emphasis than nonbiblical texts.

2. In liturgical poetry of the monarchic period the combat myth is discernible in some hymns, for example, Psalms 93, 96, and 114, in which it functions as in the early hymns. The combat myth functions differently, however, in communal laments such as Psalms 74, 77, and 89. In this genre Israel, threatened by enemies, recites before God ("remembers") the old combat victory at the beginning. The purpose is to persuade God to repeat the primordial victory and defeat the present threat. This use differs from the previous stage and points forward to stage 3: the victory is a past historical event but its present potency is now in doubt. People have to pray that the original deed be renewed.

Psalm 89 is a good example of how the combat myth functions in communal laments. Recent commentators rightly regard it as a literary unity (Clifford 1980). It "remembers" before Yahweh his ancient world-creating victory (in this psalm it includes the installation of the Davidic king) in order to appeal to God's *noblesse oblige:* Will you allow the king who represents your combat victory to be defeated in battle? Verses 6–19 describe that cosmic victory as a single event that includes a procession and consecration of a king.

¹⁰You rule the raging Sea;
    you still its swelling waves.
¹¹You crushed Rahab with a mortal blow;
    your strong arm scattered your foes.
¹²Yours are the heavens, yours the earth;
    you founded the world and everything in it.
[Verses 16–19 describe a triumphant procession to Yahweh's shrine, after which
the Davidic king is consecrated.]
²⁰Then you spoke in a vision to your consecrated one and you said,
    I have set (my) servant above the mighty men,
    I have raised up a man of (my) choice from the army.
   . . . .
²⁸Yes, I make him my firstborn,
    the highest of the kings of the earth.

3. After the capture of Jerusalem, the destruction of the Temple, and the end of the monarchy, it was understandable that Israelites concluded that God's work had come to an end. Texts such as Isa. 51:9–11 view the combat victory as no longer in effect and ask God for a new deed similar to the ancient one.

⁹Awake, awake, clothe yourself with power,
    arm of Yahweh!
Awake as in days of old,
    generations long ago.
surely it was you that hacked Rahab [sea monster] in pieces,
    that pierced the Dragon.
¹⁰It was you that dried up Sea
    the waters of the Great Deep,
that made the abysses of Sea
    a road for the redeemed to walk on.
¹¹So let the ransomed of Yahweh return,
    let them come with shouting to Zion.

Second Isaiah imagined the ancient deed that gave birth to Israel as the exodus conquest and a cosmogonic victory (43:16–17). God is about to do something new modeled on the old (43:18–21). In the prayer of 51:9–11, the prophet asks God to do again the ancient combat victory over Sea, which will result in the return of the exiles to Zion. The ancient deed is a thing of the past; it is now projected into the future. May God bring it about!

4. In Daniel 7, written in the 160s B.C.E., vestiges of the combat myth appear. In the plot of the Mesopotamian and Canaanite examples examined earlier in this essay, the young warrior, after vanquishing the sea monster and restoring order, receives kingship from the chief god and the assembly. Though no one would argue that fourteenth-century Canaanite texts directly shaped Daniel 7, there can be little doubt that the combat myth has influenced the scene: the Son of Man coming with the clouds of heaven (v. 13) recalls the epithet of Canaanite Baal, "rider of the clouds"; the Ancient of Days (v. 9) evokes the epithet of Canaanite El, ʾb šnm, "Father of Years." The pattern of relationships is further proof of influence: the interaction of two god-like figures is unprecedented in the Bible but common in the Ugaritic texts; there is opposition between the sea and the cloud rider. There are, of course, major differences such as the introduction of the motif of the four kingdoms, and the beast is slain not in combat but by

judicial decree (J. J. Collins 1993, 286–94). Knowledge of the Canaanite background can high-light important points in Daniel 7: the earthly kingdoms symbolized by the four beasts are agents of a more primordial evil, Sea; no battle needs to be fought, the victory is already won; Israelite monotheism has made the old warrior-god into an angelic representative of Israel.

The book of Revelation has also drawn on the combat myth. One could perhaps argue that chaps. 4–5 are a vestigial reflection of the divine assembly thrown into consternation by its inability to find within its ranks a defender of divine rule; the Lion turned Lamb would be the heavenly hero. Revelation 12 is more certain. The enemy is a seven-headed dragon, for which there is no biblical parallel but a clear one in the Ugaritic Baal cycle, "Lotan (Leviathan) the twisting serpent. . . . Shalyat with seven heads" (*KTU* 1.5.i.1–3 = *ANET* 138). The dragon's ten horns show an attempt to relate it to the fourth beast in Daniel 7. As in Daniel 7, Revelation 12 uses the combat myth (however vestigial) to show that the victory has been won (A. Y. Collins 1976). It has happened in the heavens, the real world, but is not yet displayed on earth. An event of *Urzeit* is now an event in *Endzeit*. When the beasts and the dragon will be destroyed on earth (Rev. 17:1–20:15), the new heavens will appear.

The above survey shows the various ways in which the genre of the combat myth appears in biblical literature. In many old poems and psalms the combat is past and undergirds the present order. With the exile, the present order has collapsed, and so the combat is moved to the future, with a view to restoration.

☞ CONCLUSIONS

What can we learn about apocalyptic literature by studying its early antecedents? First of all they teach us that the imagery and themes of apocalyptic literature are not bizarre and obscurantist, as is sometimes claimed. For example, the combat myth was a customary ancient way of thinking about the world. Ancient Near Eastern "philosophical" thinking was normally done through narrative. Retelling one basic narrative in slightly different versions enabled ancients to reflect about the governance of the world and explain the course of history, especially the history of their own nation. Their era took for granted the existence and power of the gods and factored them into their reflection, as our era takes for granted and reckons with a different (and less ultimate) range of forces, for example, the power of ideas, of free trade, of energy resources. To do philosophy, theology, and political theory, modern thinkers employ the genre of the discursive essay rather than the narrative of the combat myth. Despite the differences, one should not forget that ancients and moderns share an interest in ultimate causes and both are intent on explaining the cosmos, the nature of evil, and the validity and the functions of basic institutions. Apocalyptic literature at bottom is not bizarre and opaque, but is rather a narrative way of reflecting about theology, philosophy, and history, and of inculcating a way of life.

Some of the exotic elements of apocalyptic literature, however, are intended by their authors. For example, the *post-factum* prophecies are deliberately vague, without place or personal names, to make them appear as prophecies of a future only dimly discerned. Heavenly visions are deliberately portrayed as wondrous and radically different from everyday life. Their exotic details are a narrative way of conveying the numinous quality of the heavenly world.

This article has focused on the combat myth as an important key to understanding some of the underlying issues of apocalyptic works. The genre always deals with the supremacy (kingship) of *one* god in the pantheon or heaven. Despite the mythic language, there is a "historical" perspective in all the instances of the genre because they refer to the personal and political realities of the human beings who tell them. In the Bible the historical reference is explicit, and the use of mythic language to interpret historical happenings is clear.

☞ NOTES

1. The most important text was published by R. Borger, "Die Beschwörungsserie *bīt mēseri* und die Himmelfahrt Henochs," *JNES* 33 (1974): 183–96. Discussions are in Kvanvig 1988, 191–213; and J. C. Greenfield, "Apkallu," in *Dictionary of Deities and Demons in the Bible,* ed. K. van der Toorn and P. W. van der Horst, 134–38 (Leiden: E. J. Brill, 1995).

2. There have been several systems of reference to the Ugaritic texts, but *KTU* is now the standard text. A widely used English translation is that of H. L. Ginsberg in *ANET.* The equivalences of tablets of the Baal Cycle in *KTU* and *ANET* is as follows: *KTU* 1.1 = *ANET* VI AB iv; *KTU* 1.2 = *ANET* III AB, C, B, A; *KTU* 1.3= *ANET* V AB; *KTU* 1.4 = *ANET* II AB; *KTU* 1.5 = *ANET* I AB; *KTU* 1.6 =*ANET* I AB.

☞ BIBLIOGRAPHY

Abbreviations
ANET   Pritchard, James B., ed. *Ancient Near Eastern Texts Relating to the Old Testament.* 3rd ed. Princeton, N.J.: Princeton University Press, 1969.
KTU   Dieterich, M., O. Loretz, and J. Sanmartín. *The Cuneiform Alphabetic Texts,* 1–28. Münster: Ugarit Verlag, 1995. The standard edition of the alphabetic cuneiform (still abbreviated *KTU* after the earlier German title).

Primary Texts
Mesopotamia
Lugal-e:
Jacobsen, Thorkild. 1987. *The Harps that Once . . . : Sumerian Poetry in Translation,* 233–72. New Haven: Yale University Press. A free translation with brief introduction and notes.
van Dijk, Jan. 1983. *LUGAL UD ME-LÁM-bi NIR-ĜÁL: Le récit épique et didactique des Travaux de Ninurta, du Déluge et de la nouvelle Création.* Leiden: E. J. Brill. A magisterial edition and commentary.

Anzu:
Dalley, Stephanie. 1991. *Myths from Mesopotamia,* 203–27. Oxford: Oxford University Press. An up-to-date translation with brief introduction and notes.
Moran, William L. "Notes on Anzu." *Archiv für Orientforschung* 35 (1988): 24–29. Authoritative discussion of new manuscripts.

Enuma elish:
Dalley 1991, 228–77. Translation and notes.
Speiser, E. A. "The Creation Epic." In *ANET,* 60–72, 501–3.

Akkadian Prophecies, Text A:
ANET, 451–52.

Akkadian Prophecies, Uruk Prophecy:
Hunger, H., and S. A. Kaufman. 1975. "A New Akkadian Prophecy Text." *Journal of the American Oriental Society* 95:371–75.

Akkadian Prophecies, Dynastic Prophecy:
Grayson, A. K. 1975. *Babylonian Historical-Literary Texts,* 24–37. Toronto: University of Toronto Press.

Akkadian Prophecies, Shulgi Prophecy, and Marduk Prophecy:
Borger, Riekele. 1971. "Gott Marduk und Gott-König Šulgi als Propheten: Zwei prophetischen Texte." *Bibliotheca Orientalis* 28:3–24.
Foster, Benjamin R. 1993. *Before the Muses: An Anthology of Akkadian Literature,* 270–72, 304–7. Bethesda, Md.: CDL.

Canaan
Baal Cycle:
del Olmo Lete, G. 1981. *Mitos y Leyendas de Canaan,* 81–233. Madrid: Ediciones Cristiandad. Richly annotated Spanish translation.
Dieterich, M., O. Loretz, and J. Sanmartín. 1995. *The Cuneiform Alphabetic Texts,* 1–28. Münster: Ugarit Verlag. The standard edition of the alphabetic cuneiform (still abbreviated *KTU* after the earlier German title).
Gibson, J. C. L. 1978. *Canaanite Myths and Legends,* 38–81. 2nd ed. Edinburgh: Clark. English translation.
Ginsberg, H. L. "Ugaritic Myths, Epics, and Legends." In *ANET,* 129–42. English translation.
Smith, M. S. 1994. *The Ugaritic Baal Cycle.* Vol. 1. Leiden: E. J. Brill. *KTU* 1.1–1.2 only, with lengthy discussion.

Secondary Studies
Batto, Bernard. 1992. *Slaying the Dragon: Mythmaking in the Biblical Tradition.* Louisville: Westminster/John Knox. A good survey of the combat myth in Mesopotamia, Ugarit, and the Bible.
Brown, R. E. 1958a. "The Pre-Christian Semitic Concept of 'Mystery.'" *Catholic Biblical Quarterly* 20:417–43.
———. 1958b. "The Semitic Background of the New Testament *Mystērion.*" *Biblica* 39:426–28; 40 (1959): 70–87.
Clifford, Richard J., S.J. 1980. "Psalm 89: A Lament over the Davidic Ruler's Continued Failure." *Harvard Theological Review* 73:35–47.
———. 1994. *Creation Accounts in the Ancient Near East and in the Bible.* CBQMS 26. Washington, D.C.: Catholic Biblical Association. A study of all the cosmogonies, some of which are combat myths, with up-to-date bibliography.
Cohn, Norman. 1993. *Cosmos, Chaos, and the World to Come: The Ancient Roots of Apocalyptic Faith.* New Haven: Yale University Press. A survey of the roots of apocalyptic thinking among the Egyptians, Mesopotamians, Vedic Indians, Zoroastrians, with attention to how belief in the end of history arose.
Collins, Adela Yarbro. 1976. *The Combat Myth in the Book of Revelation.* Harvard Dissertations in Religion 9. Missoula, Mont.: Scholars Press. Draws on the combat myth in ancient Near Eastern literature to clarify Revelation 12 and the structure of the entire book of Revelation.
Collins, John J. 1993. *Daniel: A Commentary on the Book of Daniel.* Hermeneia. Minneapolis: Fortress Press. Contains a thorough discussion of ancient Near Eastern antecedents to Daniel.
Cross, Frank Moore. 1973. *Canaanite Myth and Hebrew Epic.* Cambridge, Mass.: Harvard University Press. Contains a penetrating discussion of the Israelite borrowing of Canaanite myth with a sketch of "proto-apocalyptic" material.

Day, John. 1985. *God's Conflict with the Dragon and the Sea: Echoes of a Canaanite Myth in the Old Testament.* Cambridge: Cambridge University Press. A competent and detailed discussion of Ugaritic and biblical texts.

Fontenrose, Joseph. 1959. *Python: A Study in Delphic Myth.* Berkeley: University of California Press.

Forsyth, Neil. 1987. *The Old Enemy: Satan and the Combat Myth.* Princeton: Princeton University Press. An authoritative history of Satan from third-millennium Sumer through the Old and New Testaments, Gnosticism, up to Augustine.

Goldfless, Sanford K. 1980. "Babylonian Theogonies: Divine Origins in Ancient Mesopotamian Religion and Literature." Dissertation, Harvard University.

Kvanvig, Helge S. 1988. *Roots of Apocalyptic: The Mesopotamian Background of the Enoch Figure and of the Son of Man.* WMANT 61. Neukirchen-Vluyn: Neukirchener Verlag. A detailed study of Mesopotamian antediluvian traditions and of Akkadian dream visions and their reuse in apocalyptic literature.

Lambert, W. G. 1986. "Ninurta Mythology in the Babylonian Epic of Creation." In *Keilschriftliche Literaturen: Ausgewählte Vorträge der XXXII Rencontre assyriologique internationale,* edited by K. Hecker and W. Sommerfeld. Berliner Beiträge zum vorderen Orient 6. Berlin: Reimer.

Miller, P. D. 1971. "Animal Names as Designations in Ugaritic and Hebrew." *Ugarit-Forschungen* 2:177–86.

Mullen, E. T., Jr. 1980. *The Assembly of the Gods in Canaanite and Early Hebrew Literature.* Harvard Semitic Monograph 24. Chico, Calif.: Scholars Press.

Propp, Vladimir. *Morphology of the Folk Tale.* Austin: University of Texas Press.

Roberts, J. J. M. 1976. "Myth *versus* History." *Catholic Biblical Quarterly* 38:1–13. A nuanced statement of the relation between myth and history in the Bible.

Rochberg-Halton, F. 1982. "Fate and Divination in Mesopotamia." *Archiv für Orientforschung* Beiheft 19:36–71.

Sáenz Badillos, A. 1993. *A History of the Hebrew Language.* Cambridge: Cambridge University Press.

Schmid, H. H. 1984. "Creation, Righteousness and Salvation: 'Creation Theology' as the Broad Horizon of Biblical Theology." In *Creation in the Old Testament,* edited by B. W. Anderson. Philadelphia: Fortress Press.

VanderKam, James C. 1984. *Enoch and the Growth of an Apocalyptic Tradition.* CBQMS 16. Washington, D.C.: Catholic Biblical Association. Thorough and reliable discussion of the sources and usage of the figure of Enoch in apocalyptic literature.

2

Persian Apocalypticism

Anders Hultgård
Uppsala University

PERSIAN OR IRANIAN APOCALYPTICISM presents a unique interest because of its striking similarities with the Judeo-Christian tradition, making at the same time a somewhat alien and unfamiliar impression that is due to a different cultural background. For almost two centuries the problem of Iranian influence on Jewish and Christian eschatology has attracted Western scholarship and also stirred up an ardent debate. Could it be that the entire worldview of Western apocalypticism up to the present time ultimately derives from ancient Iran? The end and renewal of the world, the apocalyptic time reckoning, the signs and tribulations of the end, the struggle of God and his Messiah against evil, personified in the figure of Satan and his demons, would thus be ideas having a foreign origin. The fact is that all these ideas are found in Iran and, what is more, they are essential and well integrated in the Zoroastrian religious worldview. Or—as the opposite party contends—does Jewish and Christian apocalypticism represent a natural and continuous development out of biblical prophecy?

The discussion is further complicated by the nature of the sources. The origins of Persian apocalypticism are not apparent, since the older texts, the Avesta, contain only isolated eschatological assertions or allusions to ideas that may be interpreted in an apocalyptic framework. In fact, no coherent apocalyptic tradition can be restored from the Avesta that has come down to us. It is not until medieval times—that is, the early Islamic period—that we meet with full descriptions of cosmogony and eschatology that enable us to delineate a coherent apocalyptic tradition.

The purpose of this essay will be to describe and interpret the primary texts of Persian apocalypticism, to consider the historical and social context, and to address the questions of origins and influence on the Judeo-Christian tradition. By apocalypticism I here understand primarily ideas of the end and renewal of the world set in a framework of cosmic history, often transmitted in a revelatory context and particularly actualized in crisis situations. Seen in isolation from their cosmic and revelatory context, these ideas may equally well be classified as eschatological and messianic. The genre of texts describing visionary journeys to paradise and hell, like the Ardāy Wirāz Nāmag is also treated in this essay, although they are largely concerned with individual eschatology.

☞ THE APOCALYPTIC TRADITION
OF THE PAHLAVI BOOKS: AN INTERPRETIVE DESCRIPTION_____

The Primary Sources

For the reasons stated above it seems convenient to begin with a description and analysis of the Pahlavi texts. This is the common designation for the religious literature of the Zoroastrians compiled or written down in the late Sassanian and early Islamic periods (sixth to eleventh centuries C.E.) in the Middle Iranian literary language called Pahlavi. Being a predominantly priestly literature, it has generally a conservative character in the sense that it is largely based on authoritative tradition which was either passed on orally for generations or recorded in written form during the late Sassanian period (fifth to sixth centuries C.E.). This authoritative tradition, oral or written, is usually referred to in the texts with specific terms such as *dēn* ("the religion"), *āgāhīh* ("the knowledge"), *zand* ("the commentary of sacred texts"), and *abestāg* ("the Avesta"). The formulas introducing cosmogonical and eschatological sections normally contain such a reference combined with verbal expressions denoting the authoritative or revelatory character, for example, *pad dēn paydāg kū* ("it is revealed in the religion that . . .") or *andar dēn ōgōn nimūd ēstēd kū* ("it has been shown in the religion that . . .") (see Widengren 1983, 101–3; Hultgård 1983, 391–92 for further examples). The dating of most Pahlavi texts to the early Islamic period does thus not a priori preclude their use as sources for the history of religious ideas in centuries long before. On the other hand, some of the materials are clearly contemporary with the compilers and authors or reflect beliefs and institutions in the Sassanian era (third to sixth centuries C.E.). The argument of the present essay, however, is that the bulk of cosmogonic and apocalyptic-eschatological traditions preserved by the Pahlavi compilers originated in earlier periods.

The fact that apocalyptic-eschatological ideas are well integrated in the general worldview of Zoroastrianism has not favored the composition of independent literary apocalypses as we find them in Judaism and Christianity. The only text that might claim the status of independant apocalyptic writing is the *Bahman Yašt* (see below). By contrast, apocalyptic-eschatological sections are a significant component in most Pahlavi writings and occur generally toward the end of the composition.

By way of introduction, the main Pahlavi books will be described in a few words and their apocalyptic-eschatological chapters briefly characterized. The huge compilation known as the *Dēnkard* (literally, "acts of the religion") was put together in the tenth century on the basis of a partly lost work from the ninth century and can be characterized as an encyclopedia of Mazdean theology and wisdom. Originally the *Dēnkard* included nine books, of which the first two are no longer extant. Besides apocalyptic allusions and fragments dispersed throughout the work, a systematic description of the apocalyptic events from the fall of the Sassanian empire up to the restoration of the world (Av. *frašōkərəti*) is found in chapters 7–11 of book 7, which for the rest consists of a "Life of Zoroaster" (chapters 1–5) and of a report on "miracles" in the reign of Vištaspa (chapter 6).

The *Bundahišn* (literally, "the primal creation") is essentially a compilation on cosmogony and cosmology with important sections on general eschatology. The beginning of the work states that it conveys *zand-āgāhīh*, that is, "knowledge (derived) from the *zand*." The basic materials may have been compiled from *zand* sources already in late Sassanian times, but the final redaction of *Bundahišn* took place in the early Islamic period, since there are clear allusions to the Arab-Muslim conquest of Iran. In Western scholarship, *Bundahišn* is usually treated as consisting of two different "recensions" or "compilations," referred to by two different names—the *Indian Bundahišn* and *Greater Bundahišn* respectively—the former, which is shorter, denotes the Indian manuscript tradition, and the latter the more complete Iranian one. This is misleading terminology since in fact we have to do with a common original subsequently split into two manuscript branches. In chapter 33 an apocalyptic survey of the history of *ērān-šahr* ("the land of the Iranians") is given, as indicated by the heading *abar wizend hazārag hazārag ō ērān šahr madan* ("on the calamities to hit the land of the Iranians millennium after millennium"). Beginning with the irruption of the Evil Spirit in the creation of Ahura Mazdā, the description proceeds through the millennia of cosmic history up to the appearance of the last savior, the Saoshyant. This account is supplemented in chapter 34 with a more detailed description of the resurrection of the dead and the renewed existence: *abar ristāxēz ud tan ī pasēn* ("on the resurrection and the final body"; heading of the chapter).

A work closely akin to the *Bundahišn* is the *Wizīdagīhā ī Zādspram* (literally, "the selections of Zādspram"), which from the literary point of view is more coherent. Unlike *Bundahišn*, the *Wizīdagīhā ī Zādspram* also has an important section on the "life of Zoraster" (chapters 4–24). Its author, Zādspram, lived in the late ninth century and compiled his work from traditional sources to which he explicitly refers in some passages. Dāmdād, one of the nasks (sections) in the collection of sacred texts (cf. Dk. IX,5), is thus mentioned in 3:43 and 57 and the Spand nask in 35:18. The two last chapters of the *Wizīdagīhā ī Zādspram* (chapters 34 and 35) contain descriptions of the eschatological events presenting much original and valuable information.

The *Dādestān ī Dēnīg* was composed in the ninth century by Manuščihr, high priest of the Zoroastrians in Iran and also a brother of the above mentioned Zādspram. The composition has the form of questions and answers. No fewer than ninety-two questions (*pursišn*) are directed to Manuščihr covering a wide variety of issues. Questions 34 to 36 deal with eschatological matters, especially the resurrection of the dead and the nature of the world immediately before and after the Renovation (Phl. *frašgird*). Also cast in the form of questions and answers is the late Sassanian composition known as *Dādestān ī Mēnōg ī Xrad* (literally, "Judgments of the Spirit of Wisdom"), in which a fictive figure called Dānāg (literally, "wise, knowing") addresses questions to the Spirit of Wisdom. Scattered references to apocalyptic world history and to the events of the end-time occur throughout the book (e.g., chapters 2:93–95; 8:11–16; 27:27–31; 57: 6–7, 30–31).

The *Pahlavi Rivāyat*, a compilation of traditional materials from the early Islamic period, presents an important section on apocalypticism and eschatology (chapter 48). It deals with the two last millennia of world history, as well as the end-time and the restoration of the universe.

A short text with interesting apocalyptic materials is the one that goes under the name of

Jāmāsp Nāmag (literally, "Book of Jāmāsp"). The text consists more precisely of some Pahlavi fragments of a more extensive writing that probably is reflected in the *Ayādgār ī Jāmaspīg* (literally, "Memoirs of Jāmasp"), a compilation of Pahlavi materials transcribed into Arabic-Persian script (= *pārsi*).

The *Bahman Yašt,* or *Zand ī Wahuman Yasn,* is not an original apocalypse, but it would more accurately be described as "a secondary compilation of apocalyptic materials of a diverse origin" (see Hultgård 1983, 388). The redaction of the materials included is minimal, and this reduces the literary quality but, on the other hand, enables the historian to get a clearer idea of the sources used. It can be divided into five different parts of unequal length:[1] (1) the vision of the four ages (I,1–5); (2) the appearance of Mazdāk and the prescription of king Xosrov Anōšurvān concerning liturgical texts (*yasna*) and their *zand* (I,6–8); (3) the vision of the seven ages and of the rich man in hell and the poor man in paradise (II,1–22); (4) the signs announcing the end of the millennium of Zoroaster (II,23–63); (5) the ultimate onslaught of enemies and demons on the lands of Iran, the liberation and the restoration of Mazdāism through Kay Wahrām and Pišyōtan, and other events of the end-time (III,1–62).

Finally there is the important text known as *Ardā Wirāz Nāmag* ("The Book of the righteous Wirāz"), which belongs to the genre of revelatory texts that purport to describe a tour of heaven and hell. In its present redaction the book must be ascribed to the ninth or tenth century but it is based on a late Sassanian version. The book presents a striking similarity with Dante's *Divina Comedia,* which it antedates by several centuries. Scholars have supposed an Oriental influence on Dante but the precise nature of this influence remains to be shown.

Forms of the Apocalyptic-Eschatological Traditions

The ideas of cosmic history and of the end and renewal of the world are embedded in a variety of forms and genres. For the evaluation of the Pahlavi texts as sources for Iranian apocalyptic beliefs in periods before the early Islamic time it is important to notice the form-historical setting of relevant passages and texts (for an attempt at form-historical analysis, see Hultgård 1983, 399–400). In many cases the determination of the forms and genres underlying the post-Sassanian compilations is difficult because citations from earlier texts are usually too short or have been reworked beyond identification.

For the tradition-historical analysis the most important genres are the *zand*-type and the *hampursagīh* form. The *zand* is an Avestan tradition that has been summarized or paraphrased into Pahlavi and enlarged with glosses and other interpolations. *Zand* texts are found especially in parts of the *Bahman Yašt* and in much of the *Dēnkard* book 7. The *hampursagīh* form ("consultation" with Ahura Mazdā) is characterized by its setting as an oracular encounter between Ahura Mazdā and Zoroaster. Extensive passages of the *Dēnkard* book 7, the *Bahman Yašt,* the *Bundahišn,* and the *Wizīdagīhā ī Zādspram* are cast in the *hampursagīh* form. Some texts seem to be a mixture of *zand* and the *hampursagīh* form. The *zand* texts were composed during the Sassanian period, but the underlying traditions may well go back farther in time. The *hampursagīh* form is a genuine Avestan genre perpetuating much traditional material in the Pahlavi books.

The otherworldly journey that may serve as a frame for some of the *hampursagīh* texts constitutes a particular apocalyptic genre that is concerned with visions of heaven and hell and is well known from Jewish and Christian traditions. The ecstatic otherworldly journey seems to have been in ancient Iran an important way of receiving direct transcendent knowledge.

Cosmogony and World History: The Mythic Basis of Iranian Apocalyptic Traditions

One cannot understand Persian apocalypticism without taking into consideration its context within cosmic history. There is an inner coherence between the beginning and the end that is unique to the Iranian worldview. The creation myth gives meaning to world history at the same time that it divides its course in great periods of world ages and millennia.

In ancient Iran there seem to have been competing cosmogonies. One myth probably saw creation as a vivification of the primordial elements through a primeval sacrifice performed by the supreme deity, be it Ahura Mazdā or Mithra. This myth is alluded to in the *Fravardin yašt* of the Avesta (Yt. 13:2–3, 9–10). The oldest Avestan text, the *Gāthās,* pay homage to Ahura Mazdā as father and "creator" of the universe (Y. 44:3–5; the word *dātar* meaning here "one who sets [chaos] in order"). A myth imagining the "creation"of the world as setting up a cosmic tent may lie behind the references to Ahura Mazdā as "creator" in the *Gāthās.* The cosmogony that became prominent in Zoroastrianism certainly has roots far back in time and might have evolved out of the older myths. This cosmogonic myth with its strongly dualistic character has survived only in the Pahlavi texts, but it is attested already by Plutarch in *De Iside et Osiride* chaps. 46–47. Plutarch most probably drew on Theopompos, who wrote in the early fourth century B.C.E. It is thus possible to follow the dualistic creation myth at least back to late Achaemenian times, when it probably had replaced other myths as the standard version of Zoroastrian cosmogony.

The most complete versions of the basic cosmogony are found in *Bundahišn* (1:1–59; 1A:1–21; 4:1–28 and 6A–J) and in the *Wizīdagīhā ī Zādspram* (1:1–27; 2:1–22; 3:1–86), which both refer to earlier normative sources for their account: "In the good religion it is thus revealed that . . ." (Bd. 1:1) and "Now it is thus revealed in the religion that . . ." (WZ 1:1). There are some differences between the two accounts, but they clearly reflect the structure and contents of the same basic myth. To elucidate the intimate connection between cosmogony and eschatology we have to turn to the first part of the myth (Bd. 1:1–59; WZ 1:1–27), where the course of world history is determined. In summary it runs as follows:

In the very beginning there existed two opposed cosmic entities. One was Ohrmazd (Av. Ahura Mazdā), the supreme god who dwelt on high in omniscience and goodness. For endless time he was ever in the light. The other was Ahreman (Av. Angra Mainyu), the Evil Spirit, who had his abode down in the darkness. He was slow in knowledge but full of lust to destroy. Both powers were limitless, and there was no connection between them, since a void separated them. But they were limited at the border of the void. Ohrmazd knew in his omniscience that the Evil Spirit existed and that he would attack the realm of light, but he also knew that through creation he would be able to bring about the final defeat of Evil. Ahreman, unaware of Ohrmazd, moved around in the darkness but happened to catch a glimpse of the realm of light. Eager to destroy it, he rose up from the depths to the border and rushed forward. Ohrmazd went against him for battle, but the Evil Spirit fled back to the darkness. Now Ohrmazd created in spiritual form (*mēnōg*) the main elements of the world to come, and they remained with him in the *mēnōg* state for three thousand years. Ahreman on his side brought forward a terrible counter-creation in that he fashioned a multitude of destructive demons and evil spirits, and toward the end of the first period of three thousand years he reappeared with his host of demons at the border and threatened to destroy the creation of light. Ohrmazd foresaw that it was necessary to fix a time for battle against Ahreman, otherwise the Evil Spirit would never desist from aggression. He therefore offered him peace and proposed a treaty, knowing that thereby he would make the Evil Spirit powerless in the end. To that purpose Ohrmazd created out of eternal boundless Time historical time, which was to be limited in extension (also called "time of long dominion"). The decisive battle would be postponed for nine thousand years, and during that limited time the sovereignty would be shared between Ohrmazd and Ahreman in the way stated in *Bundahišn* 1:28:

> This too Ohrmazd knew in his omniscience that within these nine thousand years, three thousand years would pass entirely according to the will of Ohrmazd, three thousand years in the period of mixture according to the will of both Ohrmazd and Ahreman and that in the last battle it would be possible to make the Evil Spirit powerless and that he (Ohrmazd) would (thus) prevent aggression against the created world.

The Evil Spirit agreed to the terms of the treaty, being unable to foresee the end. Ohrmazd then chanted the *Ahunawar* (a text in the *Gāthās* that became the most sacred prayer of the Zoroastrians), thereby revealing to the Evil Spirit his ultimate defeat. When Ahreman became aware of this he fell stupefied back into the darkness, where he remained in torpidity for three thousand years. During this period Ohrmazd gave material form (*gētīg*) to his first creation, which had been in the *mēnōg* state. Now the sky, the water, the earth, the primordial plant, the beneficent animal, the primordial man (*Gayōmard*) and the fire took visible shape. The world was in a state of perfection and purity. The three thousand years completed, Ahreman rose from his torpidity, took his host of demons, and made an assault on the creation of Ohrmazd. He succeeded in penetrating into the world which was ravaged and defiled by the evil powers, and it became thus the mixture of good and evil (*gumēzišn*) that it still is. After his initial success Ahreman met resistance from the primordial elements trying to counteract him each in its own way. The Sky hardened itself and closed the passage through which Ahreman and his demons had entered to keep him captured within the world. With the help of the star Tištar and the Wind, clouds and raindrops emerged out of the Water; the rains while drowning many of Ahreman's noxious creatures gave rise to oceans, lakes, and rivers. The Earth shook upon the attack of the Evil Spirit and from that shaking mountains, hills, and valleys were produced where water could stream and plants grow. The primordial Plant withered and died from Ahreman's poisonous breath but its seeds, which contained thousands of species, were saved by Amurdād, divine guardian of plants, and spread with the rain all over the earth to be used by mankind for cure of the diseases sent by Ahreman. The beneficent Animal and the primordial Man were both struck with deadly diseases by Ahreman. The light in the semen of the beneficent Animal was saved by divine intervention and purified by the Moon, and from it came the species of animals. When the primordial Man died, he emitted his semen on the ground and after forty years the first humans, man and woman, grew up from the soil in plant form and then evolved to human shape. From them all humankind is descended.

The significance of this great cosmogonic myth is twofold. First, creation is a long process, which begins with the fashioning of spiritual prototypes by the supreme god and ends with the assault of Evil on the material primordial creation. The good creation counteracts the irruption of Evil through differentiation of the physical universe and through multiplication of the vegetative, animal, and human prototypes, and by this final stage the creation process is completed. The purpose of creation is also to entrap evil and finally to eliminate it. The basic tenets of the Zoroastrian worldview are thus determined by the cosmogonic myth.

Second, the cosmogonic myth sets the course of world history at nine thousand years and divides it in three large periods of three thousand years, which may be termed world ages, each having its own characteristics. History thus begins with the prototypical material creation, which remains in light and purity for three thousand years, and continues with a period of three thousand years in the mixed state, the beginning of which also signifies the fulfillment of the last stage in creation. At the completion of the last period of three thousand years, history ends when evil is eliminated, the dead are resurrected, and the world is restored to its original purity and perfection.

It has been argued that in Zoroastrianism world history comprises twelve thousand years divided into four world ages. This number is arrived at by including the first three thousand years, when creation was in the *mēnōg* state. Yet the Pahlavi tradition is quite clear on the point that history begins with the creation of the world in its material form, the *gētīg* state. If the twelve-thousand-year scheme was the original one, it is difficult to explain why the Pahlavi texts insist on nine thousand years as a determined traditional number (see further Hultgård 1995, 85–101). In fact, the number twelve thousand for the world's history occurs only in Arabic and Neo-Persian sources from the Islamic period (see Zaehner 1972, 97).

The cosmogonic myth provided a world history in outline which could be elaborated in further detail. It is difficult to say with certainty whether the more detailed apocalyptic schemes of the Pahlavi books constitute developments during the Sassanian period or whether they reflect yet more ancient traditions transmitted orally in Hellenistic and Parthian times. These problems will be dealt with in the second section of this essay.

The most important elaboration in the Pahlavi texts is the division of the last period of three thousand years into three millennia with similar characteristics. This period begins with the appearance of Zoroaster, and the first millennium is consequently named after him. As to the two remaining millennia, each one starts with the manifestation of a savior figure: the first is called in Pahlavi Ušēdar and the second Ušēdarmāh. Together with the last savior, Sōšāns, they are considered Zoroaster's descendants (see for this mythical complex, see Hultgård 1995, 130–49). When the third millennium of the last world age comes to an end, the final messianic figure appears, the Sōšāns (Av. *saošyant*). He is really a world savior because he ushers in the restoration (*frašgird*) and the state of eternal bliss, which lies outside history.

The Expectation of the End

As pointed out above, the last period of three thousand years is subdivided into three different millennia, and the end of each millennium is characterized by tribulations and disasters presaging the coming of the new savior. The coming of the first messianic figure initiates a gradual amelioration of human conditions, of moral standards, and of nature itself, which continues through the last millennium, that of Ušēdarmāh. This idea may be seen as an anticipation of some elements belonging to the ultimate world restoration (Phl. *frašgird).* The post-Sassanian

Pahlavi books all presuppose this traditional scheme, which has the appearance, however, of being a later development of an earlier and simpler scheme (see below). Without deviating from the main scheme of cosmic history, more detailed divisions of particular periods are sometimes found in the sources. The *Bundahišn* presents in chapter 33 a world history of six millennia over which mythical and historical events are distributed, from the irruption of Ahreman in the first millennium of the mixed period to the coming of Sōšāns at the end of the sixth millennium. *Bahman Yašt* divides the millennium of Zoroaster according to a quite different scheme, which sees history as a gradual deterioration. This scheme, which occurs in two variants—one with four ages and one with seven—begins with the appearance of Zoroaster (the golden age) and ends with the calamities that will affect the Iranian lands at the close of the millennium (the age of mixed iron). The ages are characterized by different metals and are represented symbolically as branches of a tree. This scheme, where history during different periods declines from a golden age to a last evil one, is paralleled in the Greek myth of the five succeeding races (*genos*) of humans (Hesiod, *Works and Days* 109–201) and in the Indian doctrine of the four world ages (e.g., *Mahābhārata* III,186–89).

THE APOCALYPTIC SIGNS AND TRIBULATIONS. The apocalyptic woes are described in most detail for the end of Zoroaster's millennium, which was the first eschatological time to come. Analysis of the Pahlavi texts shows that there is a wide variety of signs and tribulations announcing the end-time. There are nevertheless so many correspondences in motifs and details that we have to assume a basic tradition which the authors and compilers had at their disposal, elaborating it differently according to the particular purposes they set themselves. At the same time fresh details were added to make the allusions to contemporary events clearer. In presenting the signs of the end, their character and function, the traditional scheme of a subdivision of the last three-thousand-year period into three millennia is here followed, although it is not always clear from the texts to which particular millennium the signs described originally belonged.

The most extensive descriptions are found in the *Bahman Yašt*, the *Dēnkard* book 7, and the *Jāmāsp Nāmag* and refer to the millennium of Zoroaster. In the analysis of the apocalyptic sign tradition these descriptions will serve as the basic source material. The tribulations and disorders to come are termed "signs," and they are explicitly seen as phenomena that inevitably announce the coming of an evil time and the end of the millennium. The signs do not happen by chance, but they are part of world history, which is determined by divine will. When Zoroaster asks what sign will announce the end of his millennium, Ahura Mazdā answers: "The sign of the end of thy millennium and of the coming of the lowest [i.e. 'worst'] time is that . . ." (BYt. II,24). The *Dēnkard* introduces the account of the tribulations preceding the destruction of the reign and religion of the Iranians in the following way: "On the signs of the coming of those who shall destroy . . ." (Dk. VII,7: 29).

The motifs that make up the textual body of the signs of the end may be grouped in different categories. There are signs pertaining (a) to family, society, country, religion, and culture, (b) to subsistence and property, (c) to cosmos and nature, and (d) to biological aspects of human life. A prominent mark of the evil time to come is the inversion of values and social order. Paradoxical statements and the use of rhetorical figures are characteristic features of the style. The catalogues of apocalyptic tribulations may also be interpreted as a mirror of the traditional values and ideas that shape the worldview of a given society and religion.

THE MILLENNIUM OF ZOROASTER. The drawing near of the end begins to be seen in the dissolution of society and religion. Lawlessness, deceit, and falsehood will spread. As it is said in *Jāmāsp Nāmag:* "By night one with another they will eat bread and drink wine, and walk in friendship, and next day they will plot one against the life of the other and plan evil" (JN 13, trans. H. W. Bailey). Families will split in hatred, the son will strike the father, and brother will fight against brother. Traditional ideals and values will be abandoned and foreign customs adopted. The social order will be dissolved and also reversed. Men from the lower classes will marry the daughters of the nobles and the priests (BYt. II,38). Slaves will walk in the path of nobles; the horseman will become a man on foot; and the man on foot a horseman (JN 35–36). Religious duties will be neglected; apostasy will abound; the rituals will hardly be performed; and the sacred fires will no longer be upheld. In hyperbolic statements this is described in *Bahman Yašt* II,37: "Of hundred, of thousand, of ten thousand, only one will believe in this religion, and even this one believer will not do what is a religious duty. And the Wahrām-fire will be destroyed and disgrace will be brought on it, a thousand fires will be reduced to one only and this one fire will not be properly cared for."

There will also be physical changes in the cosmos and in nature that will announce the coming end. The sun will become smaller and will be less visible; months, weeks, and days will become shorter (BYt. II,31). Clouds will darken the whole sky; hot and cold winds will blow at the same time and carry off all fruits and grains of corn (BYt. II,42; JN 26–27). The rain will not fall at its due time, and when it falls, it will rain more noxious creatures than water (BYt. II,42). The earth will contract; crops will not yield seed; and plants, bushes, and trees will be small. This general corruption of the cosmos, which manifests itself as a diminution and deterioration of both astral and earthly phenomena will also affect humans and animals. The consequences are described in the *Bahman Yašt* as follows: "Horses, cattle and sheep will be born smaller and have bad ability, they take little burden, their hair will be shorter, their skin thinner. Their milk will not increase and they will have little fat" (BYt. II,43). A similar degeneration affects humans. They will be born smaller and have less strength (BYt. II,32) and the young will look like the old (Dk. VII,8:12).

The disasters to follow are indicated by presages. The sun darkens; in the moon different colors become visible; various portents can be seen in the sky; dark clouds spread over the earth; and storms and earthquakes ravage the world. Then men will know that the end is imminent. A heavy onslaught of enemies and demonic forces will come upon the lands of the Iranian peoples. The invasion occurs in waves that carry each time new demonic figures and hosts of enemies. In the words of *Bahman Yašt* II,24–25:

> Hundreds, thousands and ten thousands of kinds of demons (*dēw*) with parted hair, descendants of Fury (*hēšm*), the basest race, will appear from the direction of the East and rush into the land of the Iranians (*ērān šahr*). They have raised banners and carry black weapons, their hair is parted falling down on the back. They are small, the basest of servants, but powerful and most skilled in smiting.

In similar wording, the *Bundahišn* mentions hostile invasions: "Thereafter Chionites and Turks in large numbers and with many banners will rush into the land of the Iranians; they will devastate this prosperous sweet-smelling land of the Iranians" (Bd. 33:26).

The *Jāmāsp Nāmag* speaks of attacks by the *Tāzigs*, who will "daily grow stronger and seize district after district" and correlates these attacks with the disintegration of social and moral order in the Iranian lands. The Tāzigs may here denote the pre-Islamic Arabs, as in early Armenian tradition, but this usage is not exclusive. The confusion of demonic hosts and human armies is characteristic of the whole Zoroastrian tradition. The political enemies of the Iranians will take joint action with the demons of Ahreman in destroying the world.

When the woes are at their height, apocalyptic expectation sees salvation to be near. Two messianic figures will appear who are thought of as both forerunners and co-helpers of the first future savior, Usēdar. The appearance of these two messianic figures marks the turning point of history. One of them is Kay Wahrām, whose epithet indicates that he is thought of as a reappearance of one of the early mythic rulers of Iran (Av. *kavi*, MIr *kay*). It is told that "on the night when the Kay is born, a token will come to the world: a star will fall from the sky" (BYt. III,15). Kay Wahrām will gather a multitude of victorious men, and from the East they will storm forward with uplifted white banners to the Iranian lands. They will slay enemies and demons in large numbers and liberate land and people from their oppressors. As Ohrmazd tells Zoroaster in the form of a simile: "When the end-time comes, Spitaman Zardušt, these enemies will be destroyed like a tree upon which the night of a cold winter comes and throws off the leaves" (BYt. III,23). The legend of Kay Wahrām is told only in the *Bundahišn* (33:27) and in the *Bahman Yašt* (III,14–23). The other messianic figure, called Pišyōtan, is mentioned in several Pahlavi texts which devote to his coming rather elaborate descriptions (BYt. III,25–42; Bd. 33:28; JN 99–103; Dk. VII,8:45–48). Together with his retinue of 150 holy warriors, the immortal Pišyōtan will leave Kangdiz, the stronghold of the Kayanians, the early mythic rulers of the Iranian lands, and restore the worship of Ohrmazd and purify the holy places that have been desecrated (on Kangdiz, see further Boyce, 1984). Pišyōtan clearly appears as the hidden hero who in a secluded place awaits the end-time when he will go forth with his followers and defeat the enemies. The very end of Zoroaster's millennium is thus already colored by the shift from an evil time to a new happier era. This expectation is condensed in a saying that concludes the descriptions of the millennium in both *Bahman Yašt* and the *Jāmāsp Nāmag*: "The time of the wolves will pass away, and the time of the sheep will arrive" (BYt III,40, JN 105).

THE MILLENNIA OF USĒDAR AND USĒDARMĀH AND THE COMING OF SŌŠĀNS. The manifestation of Usēdar, the first of Zoroaster's three mythical sons, is then the confirmation of the beginning of a new era that has in fact been ushered in by his immediate forerunners. The legend of Usēdar's conception, which takes place in the same miraculous way as that of the other coming saviors, is briefly told in *Dēnkard* VIII,55–57 and in *Bundahišn* 33:36–38 and 35:60 in slightly different versions. When only thirty winters remain of the millennium, a virgin of noble descent goes down to a lake. She walks out in the water, drinks some, and becomes pregnant from the semen of Zoroaster that has been preserved there in the form of his shining glory (Phl. *xwarrah*) protected by the goddess Anāhīd (Av. Anāhita). The *Bundahišn* adds that one can see at night the glory of Zoroaster as three lights shimmering deep down in the water. When time is ripe, each light in turn will rise to the surface and join with a young woman.

In a sense Kay Wahrām and Pišyōtan have already anticipated the task of the first savior. Usēdar is not primarily described as the one who saves the Iranian lands from enemies and demons but rather as the spiritual figure under whose authority the world begins slowly to be transformed toward its final perfection in the *frašgird* state. The religion of the Mazdā worshipers will be revealed to him, just as it once was to Zoroaster. Nature is being recovered and the conditions of humankind are ameliorating. The Pahlavi texts speak of this progress in much similar terms: Water will fill rivers and lakes. Plants and trees will be green for three years. Famine, distress, and misery will disappear. Peace and nonviolence will increase all over the world, as also generosity. The compiler of *Dēnkard* book 7 cites a saying of Ohrmazd taken from sacred tradition (the *dēn*): "In this way, O Zardušt, when the one who receives is less distinguished than the one who gives, then generosity and giving will remain among the living beings" (Dk.VII,9:6). The demonic powers will lose strength, but an outbreak of evil will come with the appearance of the demon Malkūs, who will let loose terrible winters with heavy rains and snowfall during several years (Dk. VII,9:3; PR 48:10–17; Bd. 33:30; AJ 17:4). According to some texts this will happen in the fifth century of the millennium (so Dk. VII,9:3; PR 48:10), but the *Bundahišn* (33:30) places the calamity toward the end of the millennium, which seems more in accordance with the original apocalyptic scheme. Malkūs will be vanquished, however, and the subterranean *war* (literally, "enclosure," Av. *vara*) of Yima, where people and cattle had taken refuge, will be opened and the earth will flourish again and be repopulated. The tradition of the demon Malkūs and of the opening of the *war* draws clearly on the Avestan myth of Yima (Vd. chapter 2), the chief figure in Persian primordial history. This myth tells of how Yima is warned by Ahura Mazdā that bad winters will come. Therefore he is instructed to build a large subterranean refuge for humans and animals where they will be able to survive the winters. The narrative, which belongs to the same category of such myths as the flood stories of the ancient Near East (e.g., Genesis 6), is set in a mythic past but has been transferred to an eschatological context in the Pahlavi texts. An eschatological motif that may seem strange from a Western Judeo-Christian viewpoint is the appearance of wild animals from mountains and plains after the winters of Malkūs have come to an end (Dk. VII,9:8–12; PR 48:19–21). They seek refuge with the Mazdeans, thinking that "they will treat us like their own children." Then Ašawahišt, one of the lesser divinities, cries out from heaven: "Do not kill these beneficent animals any more as you used to do!" The Mazdeans will kill and eat an animal only upon its own request before it dwindles away: "Oh Mazdeans, eat me while I am still in vigour before reptiles and serpents shall devour me" (Dk. VII,9:9 in a citation from sacred tradition). The text then goes on to say that the Mazdeans will be satisfied to slaughter and to eat, and the animals to be slaughtered and eaten. In the afterlife—presumably at the resurrection—Mazdeans and animals will come together in friendship as it is said in the *Dēnkard:* "When they take on spiritual form those who slaughtered will meet those who were slaughtered, those who cut those who were cut, those who ate those who were eaten" (Dk, VII,9:12). This eschatological motif should be understood in the light of the sacrificial ideology of Zoroastrianism. In sacrifice the soul of the victim is sent to Ahura Mazdā and to the Spirit of the animals (Phl. *Gōšurwan*). The souls of both humans and beneficent animals will enjoy divine protection beyond death. This testifies to the care for animals taken by Zoroastrians.

The shift to the last millennium, that of Ušēdarmāh, is not marked by apocalyptic tribulations if we do not follow the *Bundahišn* in placing the appearance of Malkūs and the bad winters at the end of that millennium. The birth of Ušēdarmāh is believed to have happened in the same miraculous way as that of Ušēdar. His reign is characterized by further progress toward the final transfiguration of the world. The savior will make one cow give milk to a thousand persons (Dk. VII,10:2). Hunger and thirst will be less strong (Dk. VII,10:2; Bd. 34:2). Plants will now be green for six years (Bd. 33:32; PR 48:24). Humankind will not eat meat any more; first they will feed on milk and plants, toward the end only on water and plants (Dk. VII,10:8–9). They will not die except when their allotted time is come or when they happen to be killed by the sword (Dk. VII,10:7; BYt. III,53). Part of the demons and noxious creatures will be vanquished and made powerless (PR 48:26–29; Bd. 33:32; BYt. III,52). Joy, peace, and generosity will increase in the world (Dk. VII,10:3). When the millennium is near its end, there will happen a disastrous event. The dragon Azdahāg (Av. *Aži Dahāka*), who up to this time has been fettered in the mountain Dumawand will come loose and together with the demons he will devour one third of humankind and one third of the animals. Upon the complaint of water, fire, and plants that have suffered hard from his violent dominion, Ohrmazd and the Amahraspand "the Bounteous Immortals" (Av. Aməša Spənta) will appear on earth and wake up the hero Karsāsp (Av. Kərəsāspa) who will slay the dragon (Bd. 33:33; BYt. III,55–59; PR 48:30–36; Dk. VII,10:10; AJ 17:5–7).

Now the final savior Sōšāns (Av. Saošyant) will appear. The description of his birth, the miracles accompanying his reaching thirty years of age, and his coming into consultation with Ahura Mazdā follow the same basic pattern as found in the legends of the two preceding saviors. The preeminence of the last savior in this legend is indicated by the fact that the sun will stand still for thirty days. At the appearance of Ušēdarmāh this miracle lasted twenty days and for Ušēdar ten days. The fifty-seven years assigned to his activity of restoring the world are mentioned in several texts (Dk VII,11:1, 4 and 7; PR 48:49; WZ 34:46) and have a symbolic meaning because they correspond to the fifty-seven years during which the religion of the Mazdā worshipers once was propagated all over the seven continents of Zoroastrian mythical geography (WZ 34:47–48).

THE ULTIMATE CONFRONTATION OF GOOD AND EVIL. The final apocalyptic events will then follow closely upon one another. The texts present roughly the same events and motifs, but have arranged them somewhat differently. The evil powers will be ultimately vanquished in a great eschatological battle (WZ 34:53) fought by Ohrmazd, the Amahraspand, Sōšāns and his fellow heroes. Some texts talk about the elimination of evil in more vague terms, but it seems nevertheless clear that the tradition of the great battle in one way or another lies in the background. The final struggle takes place in different stages. First, Sōšāns will muster an army and make a holy war against the demon of perverted truth. They will defeat the demon primarily by ritual means, since their chief weapon will be the performance of a *yasna* ceremony (PR 48:73–85). Other demons will also be vanquished by the aid of divine ritual (PR 48:89). The decisive moment is the combat between the chief deities and their demon enemies. Ohrmazd and the other divinities will appear on earth, and they will choose each his own adversary. The *Bundahišn* and the *Wizīdagīhā ī Zātspram* present this idea in the form of a systematic opposition between Ohrmazd and the Amahraspand on one side, and Ahreman and his principal demons on the other:

> Thereafter Ohrmazd will take the Evil Spirit, Wahuman will take Akōman, Ašwahišt will take Indar, Šahrewar will take Sāwal, Spandarmad will take Tarōmad, that is Nanghayt, Hordād and Amurdād will take Tayriz and Zayriz, Truthful Speech will take False Speech, the righteous Srōš will take Hēšm with the bloody club. (Bd 34:27; so also with slight variations WZ 35:37)

Other texts give a less detailed scheme of paired opponents but concentrate on the chief adversaries: "Ohrmazd and Ahriman, Srōš and Az, will appear on earth. Ohrmazd will smite Ahriman" (WZ 34:44; see also PR 48:94–95; MX 8:10). There is also a tradition that emphasizes the role played by the god Mihr (Av. Mithra) in the end-time struggle. According to the *Bah-*

man Yašt, Mihr discloses to the Evil Spirit that the nine thousand years have already passed and that the demonic powers have held sway for a thousand years more than stipulated by the treaty concluded in the beginning of world history. When the Evil Spirit hears this, he will become stupefied just as he was in the primordial time when Ohrmazd revealed his own future victory at the end of time. Mihr then smites the demon Hēšm (Av. Aēšma), who becomes powerless (BYt. III,33–35). The same tradition is reflected in *Jāmāsp Nāmag* 77, which states that Mihr and Hēšm will fight against each other in an eschatological encounter. Both *Bahman Yašt* and *Jāmāsp Nāmag* place this mythologoumenon vaguely within the context of the shift from Zoroaster's millennium to that of Ušēdar, but this is most probably a secondary development.

The eschatological confrontation is clearly considered a duel between divine beings and figures of evil on the model of the first hostile encounter between Ohrmazd and Ahreman described in the cosmogony. Here it is told that the decisive confrontation was postponed for nine thousand years but when these had elapsed Ohrmazd and the Evil Spirit would meet in a final battle. According to the myth, this was agreed upon by both parties, and the narrator of the myth adds the simile: "in the same way as two men who shall fight a duel fix a time saying: let us do battle on the so-and-so day until night" (Bd. 1:13).

All traditions are unanimous in emphasizing the belief that Ahreman and evil will be eliminated from the world to come. The way commonly used to express that fact is the statement that the Evil Spirit will be made powerless and incapable of doing any more harm. This is the significance of the Pahlavi term *agār,* which frequently occurs in the texts dealing with this motif (e.g., MX 8:10; PR 48:96). In the cosmogonic myth the end of evil after the completion of the nine thousand years was already foreseen: "He [Ohrmazd] knew that by fixing a time the Evil Spirit would be made powerless" (*agār;* Bd. 1:26–28). The details concerning the elimination of evil vary but a distinctive idea is that Ohrmazd and the other divinities will chase Ahreman and the surviving evil powers out of the world and push them back to the depths of darkness whence they came (Bd. 34:30–32; PR 48:94–96).

The disappearance of evil is hastened, according to some texts, by internal dissolution and enmity within the realm of Ahreman. In this "civil war" the female arch-demon Az (Concupiscence, Greed) figures prominently. The cosmogonic myth, in one version, tells that if Ahreman during the allotted time of nine thousand years did not succeed in converting humankind to hate Ohrmazd and to love himself, the demon Az would start to devour the other evil beings, because she would no longer be able to find food from the creatures of Ohrmazd. This prediction comes true in the very end-time. Az begins to starve and turns her greed toward the demons and even toward the Evil Spirit himself, whom she deserts and even threatens to devour. In the eschatological battle she will be overcome first and then the Evil Spirit will be weakened and easier to defeat (WZ 34:34–45; PR 48:90–93).

THE RESTORATION OF THE WORLD, THE FRAŠGIRD. After the coming of Sōšāns, all people living at that time will not die. Those who are dead will be raised to life in a great act of general resurrection called *ristāxēz* in Pahlavi ("raising of the dead"). This is usually thought of as taking place after the elimination of evil. In some traditions the resurrection is thought to be performed by Sōšāns with the help of other eschatological figures (Bd. 34:3, 7–8; PR 48:54), in others it is Ahura Mazdā himself who recreates the body of the dead (Bd. 34:5–6; WZ 34:19–20). In three texts the resurrection is described in more detail, and these accounts, taken from sacred tradition, reflect the concern of explaining an idea that might have encountered questions and doubts (Bd. 34:4–9; WZ 34:1–20; 35:18–30; PR 48:53–65). These questions are put in the mouth of Zoroaster and addressed to Ohrmazd. How is it possible that those who are long dead can receive a new body? The answer is through a reference to creation:

> When I [Ohrmazd] set the sun, the moon and the stars in motion to be shining bodies in the sky [literally, "the atmosphere"], when I created seed to be thrown on the ground, to come up and grow and to bear fruit in abundance, when I gave color to the plants according to the diversity of their species, when I gave fire to plants and other things so as not to be consumed by it, when I formed a child [literally, "son"] in its mother's womb, preserved it and fashioned forth separately hair, skin, nails, blood, fat, eyes and ears. . . . then all these things were more difficult for me to create than the raising of the dead. Because at resurrection I am helped by things that once were in existence but at that time [i.e., the creation] did not exist. (Bd. 34:5; cf. WZ 34:20)

This assertion is based on the idea that in death the different parts of the human person are received by the elements of nature, whence, on divine command, they are carried back and recreated at the time of resurrection. Flesh and bones from the earth, blood from the waters, hair from the plants, the spirit of life from the wind (Bd. 34:5; WZ 34:7; PR 48:55).

The resurrection of the dead includes both righteous and wicked, Iranians and non-Iranians. It is conceived of as a ritual process enacted by Sōšāns and his helpers. Through the celebration of successive *yasna* ceremonies, all humankind will be raised in five stages, the primordial man Gayōmard and the first couple of humans, Māšē and Māšēnē, having been resurrected first (Bd. 34:6; WZ 34:18–19; 35:19–30; PR 48:56).

The question of the wicked and their destiny seems to have preoccupied the Zoroastrians in a particular way. While the belief in the separation of the souls after death, the righteous coming to paradise (Phl. *garōdmān*) and the wicked to hell (Phl. *dušox*) is uncontroversial and firmly rooted in ancient Iran, the fate of the wicked in resurrection did pose a problem, and diverging solutions are reflected in the Pahlavi books (see, e.g., PR 48:66–68). The general idea of an elimination of evil and a purification of the world and of humankind did, however, favor the belief that even the wicked could not be punished by eternal damnation but had to be purified and included in the new community of the restored world. The idea of a temporary punishment of the wicked after their souls and bodies had been reunited at resurrection imposed itself as the most satisfying solution.

The restoration of humankind to the new state of perfection is resumed in the idea of the "future body" and is believed to take place in successive moments in which also the purification of the wicked is included. Although the themes and the moments are the same in the underlying tradition, their precise order of realization does not emerge clearly from the texts, and the confusion that one senses may be due both to redactional incongruences and to different opinions recorded in the basic Sassanian sources or expressed at the time of compilation in the early Islamic period. The moments of the restoration are here described in the order in which they are presented in the *Bundahišn*.

After the raising of the dead, all people will come together in a great assembly which recalls the judgment scenes of Jewish, Christian, and Islamic eschatologies. In the Pahlavi books it is called "the assembly of Isadvāstar" so named after the eldest son of Zoroaster. In that gathering every person will recognize those whom he or she knew during life: "this is my father, this is my mother, this is my brother, this my wife and this is someone in my family" (Bd. 34:9; cf. also PR 48:57). The wicked are already by outward appearance distinguished from the righteous like "black horses from white horses" (WZ 35:32), and the *Bundahišn* explains this by saying that the deeds of everyone will be made manifest: "at that assembly every person will behold the good deeds and the evil deeds that he or she did; the righteous shall be visible among the wicked like white sheep among black sheep" (Bd. 34:11).

Punishment and reward will be distributed. The wicked will be thrown back again to hell for three days and three nights, where they suffer much pain in body and soul, whereas the righteous are taken to paradise (Bd. 34:13–14; WZ 35:40–45). The separation is vividly depicted: "they will cause every person to pass before his own deeds, a righteous person will weep over a wicked, a wicked will weep over himself, there will be a time when a father is righteous and a son is wicked . . ." (Bd. 34:15), or "at that moment all humankind will lament together and shed tears on the ground, because the father shall see his son be thrown into hell, the son his father, the wife her husband, the husband his wife, the friend his friend" (WZ 35:41).

After punishment has been inflicted on the wicked for the three days, they are brought back to the earth and finally cleansed from their evil in streams of fire. This cleansing process is part of the universal renovation (Phl. *frašgird*) which may be seen as a purification of the world which once had been contaminated through the irruption of Ahreman and the evil powers. The metal of all the mountains will be caused to melt and to flow over the earth and burn away the stench and impurity that still are left from the evil (Bd. 34:31). All humankind must pass through these streams of molten metal. For the righteous it will be like walking through warm milk, but for the wicked it will be the real pain of passing through molten metal (Bd. 34:18–19; PR 48:70–72). The tradition behind the *Wizīdagīhā ī Zādspram* does not speak about the molten metal but of a universal conflagration that is clearly conceived of as a means of eliminating evil but also serves the purpose of separating the righteous from the wicked. The great fire is likened to a huge human figure holding in his hand a tree with the branches above and the roots below. The branches will take the righteous and bring them to paradise; the roots will seize the wicked and drop them in hell (WZ 35:40, 44). The world conflagration is seen in this tradition as part of the great eschatological battle and is compared to the primordial battle when creation offered resistance to the attack of Ahreman and the rains drowned the noxious creatures: "But as the great battle in the beginning was with the raining of water and the wind driving it, so in the end it will be with the heat of burning fire and the hard wind that makes the fire to blaze" (WZ 34:53).

The renovation of the world also implies that it is made eternal and humankind immortal. As it is said in the *Dēnkard*, translating a lost Avestan passage: "Then I who am Ohrmazd shall restore the world according to my will (to exist as) eternal, for ever prospering and powerful" (Dk. VII,11:11). For humankind the *frašgird* means immortalization and an everlasting experience of bliss and divine goodness. The ritual impact on the eschatological ideas appears also in the description of the last moments of the renovation. According to the *Bundahišn* and some other texts, Sōšāns and his followers will perform a sacrifice by slaughtering the bull Hadayōš in order to prepare the elixir of life: "From the fat of that bull and the white sacred juice (Phl. *hōm ī spēd*) they will prepare the beverage of immortality and give all humankind to drink. All humans will be immortal for ever and ever" (Bd. 34:23; cf. WZ 35:60).

The Pahlavi *Rivāyat* tells that in the *frašgird* the earth will rise toward the sky through successive acts of worship so that there will be one and the same place for the divine beings and humankind (PR 48:98–99). Despite statements on the limited nature of human knowledge of the world to come (e.g., PR 48:102) the traditions on the renovation sometimes convey rather detailed views on what life in the renewed world will look like. Besides the assertion that humankind shall behold and praise Ohrmazd and the other divinities—just as in Jewish and Christian descriptions of paradise the righteous are said to behold and praise God—other ideas are presented that reflect the Zoroastrian attachment to what is good in life. Adults will be restored to the age of forty and youth and children to the age of fifteen. Those who in life had no woman will be given one. Men and women will continue to have desire for each other, and they will be joined in love without there being any births from them (Bd. 34:24; PR 48:101, 107; cf. WZ 35:52). Plants and beneficent animals will be restored, and they will not diminish any more (PR 48:103, 107). The earth will be extended without steep mountains and hills, and it will flourish like a garden (PR 48:61; Bd. 34:33).

The significance of the renovation is strongly emphasized in the Pahlavi tradition although its details are described only in a limited number of passages. One may best sense the impact of the idea of the *frašgird* on the minds of the Zoroastrians from the short similes about its appearance that were circulated among the Persians down to the compilation of the Pahlavi books. The *Wizīdagīhā ī Zādspram* have preserved some of them: "And again the Renovation is like unto a dark night when the night draws towards its end and the sun rises over the three boundaries of the world and completes its course having returned to its proper place. Then it comes to shine anew and smites darkness and gloom" (WZ 34:25), or "The resurrection of the dead is like unto dry trees and shrubs from which new leaves shoot forth and buds open" (WZ 34:28).

THE OTHERWORDLY JOURNEY AND ESCHATOLOGY. The main Pahlavi text describing an other-worldly journey is the *Ardā Wirāz Nāmag*. The immediate reason for the otherworldly journey of Wirāz is that the Mazdeans were in doubt about the utility of their prayers and religious ceremonies, and to get divine guidance they decided to send a pious man to the heavenly world. Wirāz was chosen, and he was taken to a fire temple where he prepared his ecstatic journey by drinking wine mixed with henbane. When he fell asleep, his soul left the body and passed by the Činwad bridge into paradise. On the seventh day the soul of Wirāz returned and he rose up "as from a pleasant sleep, happy and with dreamful thoughts" (AWN 3:3). After having taken food and drink and performed a religious ceremonial, Wirāz ordered that a learned scribe be brought to him and the scribe "sat in front <of him> and everything that Wirāz said, he wrote down correctly, clearly and in detail" (3:24). On his journey to the other world Wirāz was accompanied by two heavenly figures—Srōš, the guardian angel of the Zoroastrian community, and Adur, the divinity of fire—and they function as guides and "interpreting angels." Srōš and Adur declare that they will show him the splendor and bliss of paradise, the reward of the righteous, and the darkness and torments of hell, the abode of the sinners (AWN 5). Wirāz is led along the same path on which the souls of the righteous travel after death. First Wirāz comes to a place where he sees "the souls of a number of people standing together (at an equal height)" and he asks his divine guides: "Who are they? Why are they standing here? The righteous Srōš and the god Adur said: this place is called *hammistagān* and these souls are standing in this place until the day of bodily resurrection and they are the souls of those persons whose good deeds and sins were equal" (AWN 6:3–7).

Here one of the characteristic teachings of Persian individual eschatology is presented. The *hammistagān* literally means "raised together (to an equal height)" but generally denotes the place for those souls whose merits and sins weighed on the balance of the divinity Rašn turned out to be equal. The *hammistagān* is a place similar to the purgatory of Dante, but it does not seem to have any purifying function.

Wirāz is then led by his divine guides into the first of the three heavens, to "the station of the stars," where those righteous dwell who did not observe the religious practices and had no leading position; yet they were righteous through their other good deeds. In the second heaven Wirāz comes to the station of the moon, which curiously holds the same kind of righteous people as in the "station of the stars" except that no mention of their social position is made. The text seems here incomplete or clumsily redacted and there are other passages that show the same lack of coherence (see also Gignoux 1984, 16). Having entered the third heaven Wirāz sees in the "station of the sun" the righteous sitting on golden thrones and carpets. These are those who in life exercised "good sovereignty, rulership, and authority." The Pahlavi terms indicate a stratified leadership with "sovereignty" coming at the top. Finally Wirāz arrives in paradise itself (*garōdmān*), where he is introduced by the god Wahuman (Av. Vohu Manah) to the supreme deity and the beneficent immortals (*amahraspandān*):

> This is Ohrmazd, Wahuman said. I wished to prostrate myself in front of Him but He said: "be welcome, truthful Wirāz, you have come safely from the world of troubles to this pure and radiant place." And he ordered righteous Srōš and god Adur saying: "take pious Wirāz and show him the places and the rewards of the righteous and also the punishments of the wicked." (AWN 11:3–6)

Up to this moment Wirāz has followed the path of the souls of the righteous dead, and he has been greeted by Ohrmazd with the same words with which the souls of the dead are greeted after having achieved their heavenly journey. After having visited the other places where different groups of righteous souls dwell (chapters 12–15), Wirāz is brought back to the Činwad bridge. From here he is led by his guides along the path that the wicked souls take leading them through three stations down to hell. In accordance with the strict dualistic thinking of Zoroastrianism the road to hell is described as the inversion of that to heaven. Wirāz then tours the many different places in hell and sees the punishments inflicted on the souls of the wicked. Finally he gets a short view of the Evil Spirit himself who is constantly pouring scorn on the damned in hell. The touring of hell occupies the main part of the book (chapters 18–100); in this respect Zoroastrianism does not differ from other religions—for example, Christianity, Islam, and Buddhism, in which the descriptions of the punishments in hell are far more extensive and detailed than those of the heavenly pleasures. After the tour of hell Wirāz returns to paradise, where once more he is addressed by Ohrmazd and charged with the task of telling the Mazdeans what he saw and enjoining on them to follow "the one way of righteousness, the way of the primal teachings, because the other ways are no ways" (AWN 101:7). Ohrmazd then bids him farewell saying that all purifications and ablutions performed by the Mazdeans in concord and in mind of the divinities have verily come to his knowledge.

The purpose of Wirāz's otherwordly journey has thus been fulfilled; the community is reassured of the effectiveness of their rituals; and confidence in the normative tradition of "the primal teachings"of Mazdāism is restored.

By comparing the way in which Wirāz prepares his ecstatic journey and the details of the path he follows to enter the other world with descriptions in Middle Iranian texts of similar visionary journeys, a pattern emerges that suggests a well-established tradition in ancient Iran of mystical and visionary experience. This experience is associated with prominent figures of ancient Zoroastrian legend such as Zoroaster, Vištāspa, Jāmāspa, and historical persons from the early Sassanian period, the high priest Kirdīr being the most well-known example. The *Bahman Yašt* has recorded two dream visions of Zoroaster (I,1–6 and II,4–22) that are but two variants of the same legend. It is told that Zoroaster prayed Ohrmazd to make him immortal. Ohrmazd refused for reasons not immediately disclosed but which he intended to show by conferring on Zoroaster the quality of divine omniscience (see for this theme Hultgård 1995, 139–49):

> Ohrmazd . . . put the wisdom of omniscience in the form of water in the hands of Zardušt and said: "Drink." Zardušt drank from it, and he [Ohrmazd] mingled his wisdom of omniscience with Zardušt. For seven days and nights Zardušt remained in the wisdom of Ohrmazd. (BYt. II,5–6)

On the seventh day Ohrmazd takes away the omniscience from Zoroaster, who awakes from the vision as from a pleasant sleep. Ohrmazd asks him what he saw in his sleep, and Zoroaster relates how he saw a rich man in hell and a poor man in paradise and a huge tree with seven ("four" in the first variant) branches each representing a different metal. Ohrmazd explains the vision of the tree to Zoroaster: "The tree that you saw is the world created by me Ohrmazd. The seven branches that you saw are the seven ages to come" (BYt II,15). These are then described and characterized in the following passage (II,16–22). In all probability the vision and its explanation by the deity are thought to take place during an otherworldly journey. After having consumed the "wisdom of omniscience," Zoroaster sees the seven world continents and he is able to distinguish the finest details of humans, cattle, and plants. This is best explained on the assumption of a movement in space. In fact, we find a reference to an otherworldly journey undertaken by Zoroaster in a short citation from sacred tradition preserved in the *Dēnkard*. Ohrmazd and the beneficent immortals address Zoroaster with the following words: "You have come to paradise (*garōdmān*); now you know the actions that are done in the corporeal world and those that will be done, even in secret" (Dk IX,28:2).

An otherworldly journey was, according to the *Dēnkard*, the chief instigation for Vištāsp to embrace the religion preached by Zoroaster (Dk. VII,4:84–86). In a citation from a *zand* text we learn that Ohrmazd sent a messenger to the beneficent immortal Ardvahišt telling him to give to Vištāsp a beverage consisting of the sacred juice (*hōm*) and henbane (*mang*). Vištāsp drank it and afterwards he lay as "a dead corpse." Having regained consciousness he immediately called upon Zoroaster that he might teach him "the religion of Ohrmazd and Zardušt." The introduction to this *zand* quotation summarizes the rewards promised to Vištāsp if he accepted the religion: victory over the enemies, lasting power, richness, and divine glory (*xwarrah*). The *Dēnkard* text does not explicitly mention an otherworldly journey, but the parallel passage in *Pahlavi Rivāyat* 47:15–19 shows that this was the case: "when he [Vištāspa] had consumed the drink he fell unconscious on the spot and they led his soul to paradise (*garōdmān*)."

The Pahlavi texts show that the trance preparing the mystical experience is induced by a specific technique performed in a ritual context. The drinking of a cup with sacred juice and henbane seems to have been the usual means of achieving the trance state. The expression "in the form of water" in the *Bahman Yašt* to denote the drink Zoroaster consumed before his vision does not mean that it was water but only that it was a liquid.

Toward the end of the third century C.E. Kirdīr, the chief Magus of three succeeding Sassanian kings, had four inscriptions set up to commemorate his achievements. In two of them there is mention of an otherworldly journey that the Magus undertook to assure himself and his compatriots of the veracity of his religious mission. Although the text of the inscriptions has some lacunae, the main content is clear and its eschatological bearing is likewise apparent. Kirdīr wants to know whether he belongs to the righteous and shares in their afterlife in paradise or to the damned, who will end up in hell. Having induced a trance—the text runs "I made myself like dead"—Kirdīr, represented by his spiritual person (denoted in the text as "the one having the same form as Kirdīr"), proceeds along the same path as the souls of the dead. He is met by a beautiful woman, the *daēna*, who takes the hand of Kirdīr; they walk together along a path "radiant of light." Before arriving at the Činwad bridge they get a glimpse of suffering souls in hell. Crossing the bridge and still walking in the direction of the East, they come to a heavenly palace of incomparable beauty and brilliance into which they enter. Unfortunately the text becomes fragmentary at this point, but there is clearly mention of a golden throne, of bread, flesh, and wine that are being distributed. A divine figure then smiles on Kirdīr. Here a short lacuna follows after which the vision has come to an end. The concluding part of the inscriptions emphasizes the importance of Kirdīr's vision, that the Mazdean beliefs in the afterlife, in heaven and hell, are true, and that Kirdīr by the journey into the other world has received divine confirmation of his own mission.

The significance of Kirdīr's inscriptions is that they attest the tradition of ecstatic otherworldly journeys for a date of more than five hundred years before the compilation of the Pahlavi books. The descriptions of the otherworldly journeys in the *Dēnkard* and the *Bahman Yašt* are based on *zand* texts which in turn go back to Avestan texts. It is important to notice that the "Oracles of Hystaspes" were said to derive from "a wonderful dream vision" (*admirabile somnium*) which Hystaspes (= Vištāspa) received and which was interpreted by a prophesying child.

The tradition of visionary otherworldly journeys performed in a state of trance is characteristic of Iranian culture and is intimately bound up with eschatological and apocalyptic teachings.

☞ QUESTIONS OF ORIGIN, HISTORICAL DEVELOPMENTS, AND INFLUENCE _____

The Avestan Background of the Pahlavi Apocalyptic Traditions

The Pahlavi books of the early Islamic period usually refer their apocalyptic ideas to an earlier authoritative tradition which we have every reason to place in the fifth and sixth centuries of the Sassanian era. By that time the Avestan script had been invented in order to record the sacred texts—in the first place those that were recited in the Zoroastrian liturgies. Only a few written copies of the complete Avesta could have been in circulation, and oral transmission had still to be relied on, be it Avestan texts or religious traditions in Middle-Iranian language. The process of translating Avestan texts into Middle-Iranian language is likely to have begun in the same period. There is evidence pointing to an authoritative collection of Avestan traditions with Pahlavi translations in the late Sassanian period to which also mythic and legendary traditions were added. There emerged then a body of texts in Pahlavi which constituted basically a translation of Avestan traditions but was to a large extent also a reinterpretation. These texts, which were transmitted both in oral and written form, came to be the main source for the compilers of the Pahlavi books with respect to eschatological and apocalyptic beliefs.

How far back in time can we follow the apocalyptic eschatology of the late Sassanian period? If we assume that the main ideas of that eschatology were based on Avestan texts composed when Avestan was still a living language—that is, before the early third century B.C.E.— we would have a useful criterion for dating these traditions. The problem is, however, that we do not know to what extent the Zoroastrian priests composed new texts in Avestan during the Parthian and Sassanian periods. Being an Old Iranian language, Avestan as a living spoken language would have been replaced by Middle-Iranian long before the Sassanian era, but it lived on as a ritual language of Zoroastrianism as it still does today. Some texts in the heterogeneous Younger Avesta present an epigonic character with a defective use of Old Iranian, which shows that the authors no longer mastered Avestan. Texts may have been composed in an imperfect Avestan all along the Sassanian period; however, for one category—namely, the Avestan traditions on which the Pahlavi *zand* texts were based—we have to assume that they were genuine and had a pre-Sassanian origin (see also Shaked 1994, 29–30). It would otherwise be hard to imagine that Sassanian priests first composed texts in Avestan which they then commented on in Pahlavi (see further Hultgård 1995, 80; Widengren 1983, 153–54). The linguistic argument is, however, intricate and not always applicable. In the first place we will, therefore, turn to other evidence for the continuity of apocalyptic-eschatological traditions in ancient Iran up to the ninth- and tenth-century Pahlavi books. This evidence can adequately be grouped in two categories: (1) native Iranian traditions contained in the Avesta, and (2) information preserved by Greco-Roman authors.

THE AVESTA AND ITS TRANSMISSION. The term *Avesta* (from Middle Iranian *abēstag*) refers to a collection of primarily ritual texts that came to be considered sacred scriptures of Zoroastrianism in the late Sassanian and early Islamic periods. The impact of the "book religions" of the ancient Middle East (Judaism, Christianity, Manicheism, and Islam) inspired the formation of a Zoroastrian canon, which had the invention of the Avestan script as its prerequisite. According to the summary in *Dēnkard* book 7, the normative traditions of Mazdāism in the late Sassanian period were divided into twenty-one minor collections called *nasks* (literally, "bundles, branches"). Comparing the present Avesta with the summary found in the *Dēnkard,* scholars have concluded that approximately three-fourths of the Sassanian Avesta were lost in the turmoils following the Arab-Islamic conquest. There is, however, uncertainty concerning the extent of a *written* Avesta in the Sassanian period, and the summary in the *Dēnkard* may partly refer to oral texts. What survived of written Avestan traditions were texts used in post-Sassanian rituals, and in these only scattered references to apocalyptic teachings occur.

The Avesta is a heterogeneous body of texts in which the *Gāthās* together with the short text called the "Yasna of Seven Chapters" stand out as having been composed in a slightly different and presumably older dialect termed Old Avestan. Linguistic evidence suggests a date around 1000 B.C.E. for the Old Avestan texts. The other parts form what is called the Younger Avesta, which contains texts of different age and origin.

THE GĀTHĀS AND ESCHATOLOGY. The *Gāthās,* which are composed in a complicated poetic style, are allusive in character and to modern interpreters still obscure in much of their contents. The worldview and rituals presupposed by the *Gāthās* are unknown to us. Using the Younger Avesta and the Pahlavi books as keys of interpretation we may in many passages discover ideas that are typical of classical Mazdāism. We cannot be sure, however, that these passages originally conveyed precisely the meaning they had for later Mazdāism. In some cases concepts and beliefs undoubtedly changed and acquired a different and sometimes more fixed and narrow content, as, for example, with the term *saošyant* (see Hinze 1995). One thing is evident, however. Later Avestan texts, as well as the Pahlavi books, associated the apocalyptic-eschatological beliefs with words and expressions found in the *Gāthās*, although their original meaning might have been different.

The *Gāthās* are pervaded by dual oppositions on several levels. There is a cosmic dualism between the good ordering of the universe, the Truth, and a bad ordering, the Deceit or Lie, coupled with the opposition day and light against night and darkness. Correspondingly, there are on the human level two opposing groups: "the truthful" and the "deceitful." In the divine world good deities (*ahuras*) confront bad deities (*daēuuas*). On the ritual level, there are good sacrifices and bad sacrifices. A fundamental opposition exists also between two "spirits" (*mainiiu-*), be they conceived of as mental attitudes within the human person or supernatural spiritual entities. The more developed dualism on cosmic and human levels characteristic of the Younger Avesta and the Pahlavi books is certainly in line with the Old Avestan ideas.

A "final turning point" is alluded to in some passages (Y. 43:5 and 51:6), and here the context suggests an eschatological interpretation, since at that "turning point" recompense for the individual's actions will be given, "evil to the evil one, (but) a good reward to the good one" (trans. Humbach 1991). A key passage is Yasna 44:14–15, which may allude to the ultimate confrontation between Truth and Lie. In stanza 14 the antagonism of Truth and Lie is proclaimed and the reciter prays Ahura Mazdā to "bring his impetuous weapon (down) upon the deceitful (and) bring ill and harm over them" (trans. Humbach 1991). In the following stanza there is mention of two opposing armies that will confront each other, and the reciter asks Mazdā rhetorically: "to which side of the two (sides), to whom wilt Thou assign victory?" (trans. Humbach 1991). To Zoroastrian tradition this was—probably rightly so—a clear allusion to the great eschatological battle between Good and Evil.

An important notion in the *Gāthās* is *ahu-* ("existence"), which seems to have several connotations. Qualified by *astuuant-* ("of bone") it means the corporeal existence of humans and animals; and, linked with *mainiiu-*, it denotes their spiritual existence. It may also refer to different forms of existence, ritual as well as human in general. The term *ahu-* may further denote individual existence, "life," and universal existence, "world."

The belief in the afterlife of the human person represented by the "soul" (Av. *uruuan*) is a prominent element in the *Gāthās*, the presence of which seems undisputed among modern interpreters. One may see in this eschatologization of the sacrifice one of the main innovations of the *Gāthās* (Kellens and Pirart 1988, 35). The final destiny of the truthful will be with Ahura Mazdā in the "house of Good Thought" (Y. 32:15), whereas the deceitful will in the end come to "the house of Lie" (Y. 51:14) or "the house of Worst Thought"(Y. 32:13). To arrive in paradise the truthful cross a bridge called *cinuuatō pərətuš* (Y. 46:10), meaning "the account-keeper's bridge" (Humbach, 1991), "the bridge of the Judge," or "the bridge of the mason" (Kellens and Pirart 1988). The souls of the deceitful will recoil from them, when they reach the bridge, and they will "be guests for ever in the house of Lie" (Y. 46:11; see also Y. 51:13).

Eschatological reward and punishment, which both seem to be realized through an ordeal of divine fire, are promised in *Yasna* 43:4 and 47:6 (possibly also in Y. 31:3). In *Yasna* 43, stanza 5 sets the distribution of reward and punishment to "the final turning point of creation." In *Yasna* 51:9 this eschatological recompense through fire is linked to (or specified as) an ordeal of molten metal (see aslo Y. 32:7). Several other passages seem also to include allusions to the different postmortem existence of the individuals although they may at the same time refer to divine rewards and punishments to be distributed during their earthly life (Y. 30:4; 34:13; 43:12; 44:19; 47:5).

The idea of a perfection of the world may underlie the references to making or creating the existence "brilliant," "blissful," or "abundant" in *Yasna* 30:9 and 34:15. The mention in 30:9, which is set in the context of a defeat and punishment of Deceit, expresses the wish of the Gāthic community to be among those who help to bring about this perfection. The other mention is a prayer to Ahura Mazdā to make the existence "brilliant." The claim for a continuity of beliefs between the *Gāthās* and the Pahlavi texts is also supported by the fact that *Yašt* 19 predicts the renovation of the world through the final savior in close similarity with the contents of the Gāthic stanzas (Yt. 19:89).

The otherworldly journey as a means of acquiring divine knowledge, which is characteristic of Iranian visionary experience as attested in the Pahlavi apocalypses *Ardā Wirāz Nāmag* and *Bahman Yašt,* may well have its origin far back in time. The *Gāthās* include some passages that can be interpreted as reflecting such visionary journeys. In *Yasna* 33:5 there is mention of "the straight paths on which Mazdā Ahura dwells" (or, according to Kellens and Pirart, "at the end of which, O Mazdā, the [or: an] Ahura dwells") and which are attained by the reciter. Similarly in *Yasna* 43:3 we find the wish that a particular man should teach the community "the straight paths of benefit" which can be compared to the prayer in *Yasna* 34:12 addressed to Ahura Mazdā: "Show us with Truth the paths of Good Thought, easy to travel." *Yasna* 34:13 prays Ahura Mazdā to teach the path on which "the *daēnas* of the *saošyants*" walk toward the recompense. The above passages mentioning the divine paths may refer to the good ritual behavior which bestows on the sacrificer an eschatological reward, but they may also contain allusions to the paths of divine vision. Two other passages allude to a journey undertaken by the soul (*uruuan*) or by a named person. In *Yasna* 44:8 the reciter asks along which road his soul may proceed to attain the things to come and in *Yasna* 51:16 Vištāspa is said to proceed along the paths of Good Thought to the insight (*cisti-*) conceived by Ahura Mazdā. The journey mentioned in these two passages seems to refer in the first place to the ascent of the soul after death to paradise, but may also allude to otherworldly journeys to acquire divine insight (note the word *cisti*). As we have seen, the path on which the soul after death will reach paradise in classical Zoroastrian tradition is the same along which the visionary proceeds, and the goal is also the same—namely, the encounter with the supreme deity. The description of the ecstatic vision of Vištāspa in the *Dēnkard* (Dk. VII,4:84–86) is explicitly described as a journey to paradise in the parallel account in the *Pahlavi Rivāyat* (47:30). Here the connection with *Yasna* 51:16 is obvious and implies an early interpretation of that stanza as an otherworldly journey made by Vištāspa in his lifetime.

THE RESTORATION OF THE WORLD ACCORDING TO THE YOUNGER AVESTA. The most important text in the Younger Avesta dealing with the final battle between Good and Evil and the renovation of the world is *Yašt* 19, composed most probably in the sixth century B.C.E. In stanzas 88–94 a unique eschatological prediction has been preserved which presents the basic themes of the apocalyptic eschatology as it is found in the Pahlavi books. *Yašt* 19 is dedicated to the divine glory and enumerates the heroes and figures whom the "glory" has accompanied in the past to help them fulfill their renowned actions. For the last figure the scene is set in the future and depicts the appearance and mission of Astvat.ərəta, who is characterized as a *saošiiant;* the *Yašt* thus takes up a concept from the *Gāthās* and applies it to an individual eschatological savior (see for this development Hinze 1995). The myth of the Saošyant's birth is alluded to when stanza 92 tells us that he will appear from the waters of Kansaoya and that his mother is named Vīspa.taurvairī. He is the final and most victorious among the group of *saošyants* in which the *Gāthās* also included the truthful believers who through their good thoughts, words, and actions have a part in the perfection of the existence (Y. 34:13; 46:3; and 48:12). The final battle between Good and Evil is clearly announced. Astvat.ərəta will carry the victorious weapon which the divine hero Thraētona had when he slew the dragon Aži Dahāka. He will overcome the great enemy, "the evil Lie of evil roots and born of darkness" (stanza 95). Lie will be expelled from the world of Truth. The followers of Astvat.ərəta described as a retinue of truthful, religious, and morally outstanding men, will drive away the destructive Aēšma (the demon Hēšm of the Pahlavi books). Some of the divine beings and entities surrounding Ahura Mazdā will choose each his own adversary: Vohu Manah ("Good Thought") will defeat Aka Manah ("Evil Thought"), the Truly Spoken Word will overcome the Falsely Spoken Word, "Immortality" and "Integrity" will overcome Hunger and Thirst, and Angra Mainyu ("the Evil Spirit") will flee bereft of his power (stanza 96). The theme of eschatological duels between divinities and demons found in the Pahlavi texts is thus already present in the Zoroastrianism of the early Achaemenian period. It seems to be an Indo-European motif, as it is characteristic of Old Scandinavian eschatology (the *Ragnarok* tradition) and ancient Indian epic mythology (the great battle in Mahābhārata).

The belief in the resurrection of the dead and in the renovation of the world is clearly set out in *Yašt* 19. Astavt.ərəta will make the world "perfect" a belief that we have seen is in line with Old Avestan ideas (Y. 30:9; 34:15). The world will be "non-aging, immortal, non-fading, non-decaying, forever living, forever prospering" (Yt. 19:89). The dead will rise when the Saošyant "who restores life" appears and the living beings who exist at that time will not die (stanzas 89–90). The renovation is conceived of as a gazing with spiritual power, and through the eyes of the Saošyant the whole material world will be made undying (stanza 94).

Scattered allusions to this coherent picture of the end-time are found in other passages of the Younger Avesta. The final Saošyant is mentioned in several passages and is there always associated with the epithet "victorious" (Yt. 13:129 and 145; Vd. 19:5; Y. 26:10; and 59:28). In Yt. 13:129 his two names are explained: Saošyant insofar as he will make the entire corporeal existence prosper, and Astvat.ərəta "insofar as being corporeal (and) living he will provide corporeal freedom from danger" (trans. Hinze 1995, 92). The course of world history is summarized in the expression "from the primordial man (*gaya marətan,* Phl. *gayōmard*) to the victorious Saošyant" (Yt. 13:145; Y. 26:10). The myth of his birth is alluded to in *Vidēvdād* 19:5: "until the victorious Saošyant will be born out of Lake Kansaoya." The renovation as a desired goal is prayed for in Yt. 13:58 (see also Y. 62:3; Vd. 18:51). The hope for the resurrection of the dead is expressed in Yt. 19:11: "when the dead will rise, the one who restores life, the Undying (i.e., the Saošyant) will come" and in Y. 54: "The dead will rise in their lifeless bodies."

Greek Authors on Persian Apocalypticism

The Avestan evidence is, with the exception of *Yašt* 19:88–96, both scarce and allusive in character and contrasts sharply with the rich picture of the end-time that the Pahlavi books depict. Were it not for the testimony of Greek authors, the argument for a continuity of Iranian apocalypticism from the Avesta down to the Pahlavi books of the early Islamic period would be less convincing.

Among these testimonies the one given by Plutarch, writing in the decades around 100 C.E., stands out as the most decisive. In his treatise *De Iside et Osiride* chaps. 46–47 he gives a short but rather detailed picture of Zoroastrian cosmogony and eschatology. In this part of the treatise Plutarch intends to illustrate a general opinion "held by most people and the wisest men" concerning the two incompatible principles of good and evil both having, however, their source and origin in Nature itself. To this purpose the Persian doctrine of two opposing cosmic powers presented itself as a very appropriate example. From the literary point of view his account is not uniform, and Plutarch seems to draw on different sources and informants. He thus gives two variants of the primordial state of the cosmos in which the content is the same but the terminology different (see Hultgård 1995, 96–98).

In the first place, Plutarch clearly attests the basic cosmogonic myth that we otherwise only know from the Pahlavi texts. Several points show a surprising correspondence in details, which emphasizes the reliability of the oral transmission of that myth through centuries.

The initial state of the cosmos, with Good and Evil as two opposing entities from the beginning, is described with almost identical wording to what we find in the opening of the first chapter of the *Bundahišn* and the *Wizīdagīha ī Zādspram*. The good deity, says Plutarch, is called Oromazes and the evil one is called Areimanios; the former is of all things perceptible to the senses to be compared with light, the latter by contrast with darkness and ignorance (first variant in chapter 46). The wording of the second variant (chapter 47) is slightly different in that Oromazes is said to be born out of the purest light and Areimanios out of darkness. In the first variant there is also a mention of the intermediary space that separates the two cosmic powers: "midway between the two is Mithras." This should be compared with the opening of the myth in *Bundahišn* 1:1–3: "Ohrmazd was on high in omniscience and goodness, for endless time he was ever in the light. . . . Ahreman was deep down in the darkness, ignorant and full of lust to smite. Midway between them was the void" (similarly also WZ 1:1–2).

In *Bundahišn* 1:3 a variant tradition is recorded in which the "void" appears as *way* ("wind, atmosphere") at the same time considered as a deity (Av. Vayu) of the same dignity as Mithra. Plutarch adds that Oromazes and Areimanios "are at war with one another," and he then goes on to describe briefly the work of creation, how the former fashions forth six divinities who clearly correspond to the group of the Aməša Spəntas, the "Beneficent Immortals" (Bd. 1:53). Areimanios responds by creating six opposing entities, just as Ahreman brings forth the archdemons as an anti-creation according to the Pahlavi myth (Bd. 1:47–49, 55). Oromazes adorned the sky with luminaries, and "one star he set before all others as a guardian and watchman, the Sirius" (*De Isid. et Osir.* 47). The first assertion recalls the wording of *Bundahišn* 2:1: "Ohrmazd fashioned forth the luminaries between the sky and the earth." The line on Sirius appears to be virtually a citation in Greek of a passage from the Avestan *yašt* dedicated to the stargod Tištriya, who is the equivalent of Sirius: "The bright and glorious star Tištriya we worship whom Ahura Mazdā set as lord and watchman over all the stars" (Yt. 8:44).

Twenty-four other divinities are created by Oromazes and placed within the cosmic egg. A countercreation by Areimanios follows again, and he produces twenty-four demons. Areimanios and his demons then pierce the cosmic egg, and in this way, says Plutarch, was the mixture between good and evil brought about. Here the allusion to the irruption of Ahreman into the creation of Ohrmazd and as a result the emergence of the present world as a "mixed state" of good and evil is obvious.

Plutarch then passes directly to the eschatological era: "A destined time will come when as decreed Areimanios having brought on pestilence and famine will be entirely destroyed by these and made to disappear." Plutarch's emphasis on what has been decreed tallies well with the idea that the ultimate defeat of Ahreman was determined by Ohrmazd already at creation. The tribulations of the end-time are also alluded to by the words "pestilence and famine," and the idea that they are produced by Ahreman but also will cause his destruction is in accordance with the Pahlavi tradition on the deadly internal strife within the camp of the demons. When the end draws near, a heightened activity of evil is expected, as stated in the *Bahman Yašt*: "when the moment of his destruction is close, the deceitful Evil Spirit will be more oppressive and his regime worse" (BYt. II,54).

The bliss of the renovation is also touched upon by Plutarch: "the earth will become a level plain, and there shall be one manner of life and one form of government for a blessed humankind who all speak the same tongue." These ideas can be shown to have their background in the Pahlavi texts' description of the renovation. For the first statement a clear parallel is found in *Bundahišn* in a citation from sacred tradition: "This earth will become a plain, level without slopes, and there will be no hollows, hills, and peaks, no up and down" (Bd. 34:33). The other assertions can likewise be understood in the light of the *frašgird* tradition. Scholars have pointed to *Bundahišn* 34:21, where it is said that when the soul is reunited with the body "humankind will altogether be of the same voice and loudly bring praise to Ohrmazd and the Beneficent Immortals" (Bidez-Cumont 1938, 2:77; Widengren 1983, 132). It is, however, not clear if this is the meaning that should be attributed to the statement of Plutarch. The eschatological unity in manner of life and form of government alluded to in the Greek text and to which good parallels so far have not been adduced (see Widengren 1983, 132), can in fact be interpreted in the light of some Pahlavi passages concerning the renovation. In the *Dēnkard* it is said: "All humankind will gather around the religion of Ohrmazd in one community" (Dk. VII,11:6). The unity in thinking, speech, and action that exists among the Aməša Spəntas will also characterize humankind after the renovation, as is expressed in the following statement proclaimed by the Beneficent Immortals: "being of the same thought, the same speech and the same action you will be without aging, without sickness and without corruption as we the Amahraspand are" (WZ 35:2).

In the last part of his account Plutarch mentions explicitly an earlier source from which he gives a brief citation—the historian Theopompos of Chios, writing in the fourth century B.C.E., whose work unfortunately survives only in fragments. It is of great importance that the Persian periodization of world history here appears as it is told in the basic cosmogonic myth of the Pahlavi texts, although with a somewhat different distribution of the sovereignty between Ohrmazd and Ahreman. In referring explicitly to the Magi, Theopompos says that each deity in turn will rule for three thousand years and that during another period of three thousand years they will fight and make war and undo the work of the other. World history consists of nine thousand years and is subdivided into three periods of three thousand years each with its own characteristics. The final destruction of evil and the bliss of the renewed world is also briefly touched on. Areimanios (here called Hades) will perish and all humankind will be blessed and happy "without having need of food and without casting any shadow." These strange details are in accordance with Persian eschatological tradition. The *Bundahišn* and the *Dēnkard* predict that humankind will gradually feel less need of food when the end-time approaches. First one meal will be sufficient for three days. Then people will desist from eating meat and will nourish themselves with milk and vegetables and: "Thereupon they desist from drinking the milk, then they renounce the vegetables and drink only water. Ten years before the coming of Sōšans they will be entirely without food and drink and they shall not die" (Bd. 34:3; Dk. VII,10:8–9; WZ 34:38–41).

This process is the inverse of that which the first human couple underwent who began by drinking water, then added vegetables, milk, and finally also meat (Bd. 34:1). For the idea of the blessed casting no shadow, similar beliefs were propagated also by the Pythagoreans, who said that "the souls of the dead do not cast a shadow" (Plutarch *Quaest. Graecae* 39). The Iranian background may be found in the Avesta as suggested by Bidez-Cumont (1938, 2:78), and it has been plausibly argued that the idea is also related to the renouncing of food (Widengren 1983, 132). The citation from Theopompos concludes with the curious statement that the god (Oromazes) who had brought about the final bliss for humankind now "will have quiet and repose for a time." This may be explained from the idea that Ohrmazd having achieved the renovation, does not have to perform any action (PR 48:101; see also Bd. 34:22).

The detailed concordances between the account of Plutarch and the Pahlavi texts show that Plutarch and his source Theopompos were well informed on Iranian ideas of cosmogony and eschatology and suggest in addition that this knowledge derived directly from Persian informants. Through the testimony of Theopompos we further know that the basic cosmogonic myth, with its apocalyptic-eschatological implications, was in circulation in the late Achaemenian period and probably also in the fifth century B.C.E.

The belief in the resurrection of the dead is not explicitly mentioned in the account of Plutarch but is certainly implicit in what he says of the blissful state of humankind after the disappearance of evil. Other Greek writers refer to Theopompos as their chief source in attributing the resurrection of the dead to teachings of the Magi and Zoroaster. So does Diogenes Laertius in his Proemium: "who [Theopompos] says that according to the Magi humankind will become alive again and be immortal. That is also told by Eudemos of Rhodes." Eudemos is another fourth-century B.C.E. author who apparently knew about Persian beliefs but whose works have not survived. Aenas of Gaza (sixth century C.E., excerpt in Bidez-Cumont 1939, 2:70) also refers to Theopompos for the idea of resurrection: "Zoroaster predicts that there shall be a time when a resurrection of all the dead will come. Theopompos knows what I say and he teaches also the other (writers)."

The "Oracles of Hystaspes"

The diffusion of Iranian apocalyptic beliefs in antiquity is not only echoed among Greco-Roman writers but can also be seen in the emergence of apocalyptic compilations with a more or less strong Iranian influence. These texts related to the Sibylline tradition were usually attributed to Hystaspes, being the Greek form of the Iranian Vištāspa, and propagated in different versions and by different groups during the Hellenistic period and the first centuries of our era (see Colpe 1991). The "Oracles of Hystaspes" owed their origin to a milieu where Iranian apocalyptic ideas were used to maintain spiritual and political resistance against Macedonian and Seleucid rule in western Asia. The Oracles were reused among various groups during subsequent centuries now with an anti-Roman tendency. The opposition against Roman imperial rule rallied Iranians with Syrians, Jews, and other Oriental peoples and the "Oracles of Hystaspes" enjoyed a wide popularity as an apocalyptic pamphlet. No original version of a Hystaspes text has survived; we know their content only through incomplete paraphrases and summaries given by Lactantius mainly in his *Divine Institutions,* written in the beginning of the fourth century C.E. Although Lactantius was a Christian, his knowledge of the Bible seems to have been limited. On the other hand, he was well versed in Greek and Latin literature and the source for his paraphrasing extracts was most probably an intermediate Hystaspes text compiled from a Greco-Persian prophecy. It has been suggested that this intermediate text was a compilation in Greek produced by Jews in Asia Minor before the destruction of the temple in Jerusalem (so Flusser 1982). The Iranian substratum of that version of the Oracles, as condensed and reworked by Lactantius, is not easily distinguished from the Hellenistic Jewish layer. The problem is that we do not find many characteristic details that can be unambiguously associated solely with Zoroastrian apocalyptic ideas, as is the case, for example, with the account of Plutarch. As scholars have long noticed, the description of the apocalyptic signs in the Lactantius paraphrase recalls strikingly those found in the Pahlavi texts, in particular the *Bahman Yašt.* On the other hand, the similarities with Jewish and early Christian apocalypses are equally apparent, a fact that may be explained by the universal content of these signs and by cross-cultural influences. This makes the separation of genuine Iranian ideas from Jewish and Christian traditions an intricate matter. The changes in cosmos and nature announcing the end-time predicted in Lactantius, *Inst. Div.* 7.16.6–11 present unmistakable affinities with *Bahman Yašt* II,31–32 as also with the prophecy of the Astronomical Book 80:2–8 in the Jewish Enoch collection (*1 Enoch*) and the predictions in 4 Ezra 5:1–12 and 6:20–25. There is a closer correspondence in formulation, however, between the *Divine Institutions* and the *Bahman Yašt.* Lactantius says, for example, that "the year will be shortened and the month diminished and the day contracted into a short space" (16:10). The parallel predictions of *1 Enoch* 80:2: "And in the days of the sinners the years shall be shortened and the crops delayed in their land and fields"; and the one in 4 Ezra, "The sun will suddenly begin to shine in the middle of the night, and the moon in the day-time" (5:4) certainly attest the dissolution of cosmic order. However, only *Bahman Yašt* gives the precise equivalent: "The sun will be less visible and smaller, year and month and day shorter" (BYt. II,31). Rhetorical statements of the type: "from the place where a thousand had gone forth, scarcely a hundred will go forth" (*Div. Inst.* 7.16.14) are characteristic of the Iranian apocalyptic tradition but rarely occur in Jewish and Christian apocalypses. The eschatological fire described by Lactantius (*Div. Inst.* 7.21.3–7) corresponds by its function clearly to the Iranian concept and not to the Judeo-Christian one. The "Oracles" emphasize that the divine fire will burn both the righteous and the wicked, and that the wicked will be tried by the divine fire but it will not hurt the righteous: "but they whom full justice and maturity of virtue have imbued will not perceive that fire" whereas it will affect the wicked "with a sense of pain" but not destroy them. The fire "will both burn the wicked and will form them again, and will replace as much as it shall consume of their bodies." This is precisely the character of the eschatological fire that is described in the Iranian apocalyptic texts.

The scenario of the end-time in the "Oracles" resembles much the one found in Jewish and Christian "historical" apocalypses, but there are details and formulations that reveal the original Persian background. When the eschatological tribulations are at their height, the righteous will separate themselves from the wicked and flee to a mountain. The evil king who dominates the world is filled with wrath on hearing this, and he will encircle the mountain with a great army. The faithful shall implore God for help; they will be heard and God will send them a savior from heaven who with his followers shall rescue the righteous and destroy the wicked. The expectation of the coming savior in the "Oracles of Hystaspes" originally meant a Persian savior figure be it Mithra (e.g., Bidez-Cumont 1938; Widengren 1983), the final Saošyant (so Hinnells) or Darius *redivivus* (so Colpe 1991). The savior is called the "great king" (*rex magnus*), an obvious allusion to Iranian kingship terminology, and in another passage Lactantius mentions "the leader of the holy retinue" (*dux sanctae militiae*), which clearly alludes to the followers of the Saošyant, and perhaps their "leader" is none other than Pišyōtan. The scenery with the mountain is best explained from Persian customs of worshiping on the top of hills as described by Herodotus (*Hist.* 1.131–32). The righteous are called "followers of the truth" (*sectatores veritatis*), which recalls the Zoroastrian emphasis on Truth and the believers as the truthful. In an explicit reference to the prophecy of Hystaspes (*Div. Inst.* 7.18) Lactantius reproduces more directly the wording of the Oracles in saying that the faithful besieged on the mountain will implore Jupiter for help and "Jupiter will look to the earth and hear the voices of the humans and he will exterminate the wicked" (cf. the wording in the summary above from *Div. Inst.* 7.17). Jupiter here stands for Zeus, which was the established Greek name for Ahura Mazdā. It is improbable that Christians or Jews would have used Zeus in their own writings instead of the general Greek term *theos*. Lactantius is aware of this in his comment following the citation: "All this is true except one thing, namely, that he [Hystaspes] said that Jupiter shall fulfill what God shall do" (*Div. Inst.* 7.18.2).

The Iranian background of Lactantius's paraphrase of the "Oracles of Hystaspes" is thus ascertained (cf. also Shaked 1994, 31), and it seems, therefore, reasonable to conclude that the passages in the "Oracles" that show similarities of equal pertinence both with the Iranian tradition and the Jewish-Christian apocalypses should in the first place be interpreted as Persian elements. The "Oracles of Hystaspes" is undeniably an important testimony to the impact of Persian apocalyptic ideas on the western Greco-Roman world.

Historical Developments, Social and Political Settings

Eschatology, both individual and universal, is from the very beginning strongly integrated in the Iranian worldview. The *Gāthās* and the Younger Avesta show these beliefs to be deeply rooted in the sacrificial cult. As in ancient India sacrifice nourished cosmic speculation, so the Old Iranian sacrificial worship also inspired meditation on the creation and history of the world. These reflections were given concrete expression in sacral poetry, memorized and transmitted by the priests who administered the cult. They became the chief tradents of apocalyptic and eschatological ideas, but these were not kept as esoteric teachings and we may assume that beliefs in the afterlife and the ultimate victory of Good over Evil were known to wider circles of the Iranian society, the aristocracy as well as the common people.

There is a basic continuity in the Persian expectation of the end from the time of the

Gāthās (ca. 1000 B.C.E.) down to the early Islamic period (seventh to tenth centuries C.E.). In the course of time, however, new versions of the apocalyptic eschatology evolved as a result of changing cultural and historical situations but keeping the fundamental ideas intact. The most striking innovation appears to be the triplication of the end-time and its eschatological events. This innovation seems to be the result of "deliberate scholastic developments" (Boyce 1984, 68–69). The last period of world history was subdivided into three millennia, each having its own key figure. The first millennium, that of Zoroaster, has already begun and draws to its end, but before the final restoration of the world two further savior figures are expected whose appearance ushers in each a new millennium. At the shift of the millennia broadly similar events occur characterized first by deterioration and then by improvement. The original apocalyptic tradition appearing in *Yašt* 19 and still current in early Hellenistic times as appears from Theopompos and the "Oracles of Hystaspes" was reinterpreted and its themes distributed over three "end-times." Traces of the rearrangement of traditions can still be found in the incongruences and blurrings found in some apocalyptic passages of the Pahlavi books. We may take as an example Pišyōtan and the tradition linked to him. Originally one of the comrades of the final savior Astvatarta, Pišyōtan and the tradition linked to him were later transferred to the end of Zoroaster's millennium, where he and his followers appear as forerunners of Ušēdar, the first savior to come. In the *Bahman Yašt* it is said that Ahura Mazdā and the Beneficent Immortals will manifest themselves on earth and summon Pišyōtan to restore the Mazdean religion (BYt. III,25–31). According to the *Dēnkard,* Pišyōtan will smite the Evil Spirit and the demons (Dk. 7.8.47). Both the *Bahman Yašt* and the *Dēnkard* place these events at the turn of Zoroaster's and Ušēdar's millennia. However, the appearance of the supreme deity and his "archangels" on earth and the defeat of Ahreman clearly are expected at the end of world history and these ideas were originally connected with the *frašgird* tradition.

Since eschatological beliefs were at the center of ancient Mazdāism, they could easily be actualized in times of crisis and take on new formulations. It seems that in the wake of Alexander's conquest of the Achaemenian empire apocalypticism received a fresh stimulus. New prophecies resembling the genre of Sibylline predictions were promulgated among the Iranians to encourage resistance and to give hope for a future salvation. The Iranian prophecies served the interests of a more widespread anti-Macedonian and subsequently anti-Roman movement in the eastern provinces. The late Avestan traditions underlying the present *Bahman Yašt,* the *Jāmāsp Nāmag* and the "Oracles of Hystaspes" most probably took shape in the early Hellenistic period. These traditions were faithfully preserved and presumably reused down to the Sassanian period, during which further reinterpretations were added.

The downfall of the Sassanian kingdom and the Arab-Muslim conquest of Iran profoundly affected the Zoroastrian communities. From the position as the most favored religion, Mazdāism became in a couple of centuries an oppressed minority religion. These dramatic changes gave new impetus to apocalyptic expectations, which have left their traces on the eschatological strands of the Pahlavi books. New prophecies were added, and the Sassanian apocalyptic tradition was subjected to a general reinterpretation. *Bundahišn* chapter 33 outlines the history of "the Iranian lands" according to a millennial scheme which is retrospective down to the early Islamic period mentioning the defeat of the Iranians by the Tāzīgs, the death of Yazdagird and the flight of his son into Xorasan to raise an army. Then it turns into eschatology, giving predictions of coming events leading up to the advent of Pišyōtan and the beginning of Ušēdar's millennium. The Tāzīgs have here become the Muslim Arabs, and their wicked rule is briefly described. The impact of this national disaster on the Zoroastrians is clearly stated: "From the primal creation until the present day no evil greater than this has come" (Bd. 33:22).

Movements of resistance and insurgence against the rule of the Caliphate emerged in various parts of the Iranian territories. They were led by persons who legitimated their activity by associating themselves with traditional Zoroastrian salvation hopes. In the *Jāmāsp Nāmag* a number of oracles have been preserved that partly are events after the fact and testify to the apocalyptic effervescence of the first troubled centuries of Islamic expansion (see Kippenberg 1978).

In conclusion it must be emphasized that apocalyptic eschatology is one of the prominent elements of Zoroastrianism and all along its history the expectation of the end has been transmitted as a living doctrine. Zoroastrians were thus spiritually prepared to deal with major crisis situations that came upon the "religion of the Mazdā worshipers," the Macedonian conquest of Iran through Alexander and the Arab-Muslim destruction of the Sassanian kingdom nearly a thousand years later being the most spectacular.

The Problem of Iranian Influence on Jewish and Christian Apocalypticism

The degree and extension of Iranian influence on early Judaism and indirectly on Christianity have long been a controversial issue. The adherents of the *religionsgeschichtliche Schule* in the first three decades of the twentieth century (e.g., Wilhelm Bousset, Richard Reitzenstein, and Eduard Meyer) suggested a thoroughgoing influence from Iranian traditions especially on Jewish and Christian apocalypticism, messianism, and eschatology. The criticism leveled by Carsten Colpe (1950) against the results of the *religionsgeschichtliche Schule* did not have the general impact it aimed at. The discovery of the Qumran texts gave fresh impetus to the discussion of the Iranian impact on early Jewish religion, especially the dualistic ideas professed by the Qumran community. In modern scholarship the controversy goes on, but it seems that the tendency to admit Iranian influence prevails to varying degrees. Recent advocates for a decisive influence are Mary Boyce from the Iranist side and Norman Cohn from the side of cultural historians (Boyce 1991; Cohn 1993). Conversely, critical voices are heard that emphasize the difficulty in proving Iranian influences usually with a reference to the late date of the Pahlavi writings. Arguments for inner-Jewish developments as a sufficient explanation for the emergence of new eschatological beliefs have frequently been presented. In addition, there is a growing tendency to argue that Hellenistic, Jewish, and Gnostic ideas have influenced anthropological, cosmological, and apocalyptic ideas of the Pahlavi books. The description of the world ages symbolized by different metals in the *Bahman Yašt* is thus, according to some scholars, dependent on the book of Daniel (Duchesne-Guillemin 1982; Gignoux 1984). The microcosmos–macrocosmos speculations in some Pahlavi texts have been adduced as another example influence from late antiquity on Iranian thinking.

The issue of religious influence with respect to ideas and doctrines is delicate to handle since the evidence is seldom clear-cut and also open to different interpretations. Before an influence from one religion on another can be assessed properly two basic preconditions must be fulfilled. First, the priority in time for a particular idea in one of the religions subject to comparison; second, the possibility of religious and cultural contacts between the religions involved. Both these preconditions are present in the case of Persian influence on Judaism and Christianity.

As pointed out above an apocalyptic eschatology is firmly attested in Zoroastrianism already in the sixth century B.C.E. and is in addition well integrated in the general Iranian worldview. Jews and Persians were in close geographical contact from the Achaemenian period down to the fall of the Sassanian empire. Palestine was under Achaemenian rule for two hundred years, from 538 B.C.E. to the Macedonian conquest. The large Jewish population in Mesopotamia remained under Iranian sovereignty also in the Parthian and Sassanian periods. Iran proper included important Jewish communities within its territory from the Hellenistic period onwards; subsequently Christians too became numerous. In Asia Minor, Iranians and Jews had likewise good opportunities for cultural and personal contacts since both groups were represented by important local communities, for the Iranians already from the Achaemenian period. From the liberation of the exiled Jews by Cyrus—hailed as a Messiah in Deutero-Isaiah—down through the centuries there were strong bonds of political sympathy between Jews and Persians. As shown by Greek and Roman writers Iranian beliefs were well known in antiquity and could not have gone unnoticed in the Hellenistic Jewish milieu as indicated by Philo of Alexandria. One may also point to religious and social affinities between the priestly classes of Jews and Persians in the Hellenistic period. The Zadokites among the Jews fulfilled the same religious functions and occupied the same position in society as the Magi among the Persians. These common interests would have facilitated contacts on both personal and official levels, and it is in fact possible to distinguish a particular strand of Iranian influenced ideas in the pre-Essene Zadokite writings (see Hultgård 1988).

The core of the question must briefly be addressed: How much does the Judeo-Christian tradition owe to Persian apocalypticism? There was no direct and general borrowing of the Iranian apocalyptic eschatology as such by Judaism and Christianity. Instead, the influence exerted itself in an indirect way but was of no less importance. The encounter with Iranian religion produced the necessary stimulus for the full development of ideas that were slowly under way within Judaism. The personification of evil in the form of figures like Satan, Belial, or the Devil, the increasing importance of the dual opposition between Good and Evil as well as their eschatological confrontation are ideas that are unlikely to have emerged without external influence. The doctrine of the two Spirits as professed by the Qumran community provides a striking example of Persian religious impact that had wider and long-lasting effects on Jewish and Christian traditions (see Philonenko 1995). This is also the case with the belief in the resurrection of the dead, which can be shown to have some Israelite antecedents in the exilic period but was not fully developed until Hellenistic-Roman times, and in addition was not accepted by all Jews. The Persian impact is also shown by many details in Jewish and Christian eschatology, both universal and individual, that appear to be Iranian borrowings (see further Hultgård 1978; Boyce 1991).

As a conclusion one may say that the emergence of an apocalyptic eschatology among Jews and Christians in the Hellenistic and Roman periods was propelled by the fruitful encounter with a religion deeply concerned with the struggle of good and evil and firmly assured of the ultimate restoration of the world.

⮑ NOTES _____

1. The *Bahman Yašt* is here cited according to the division of chapters and paragraphs found in the translation of E. W. West in *The Sacred Books of the East, Pahlavi Texts Part I* (Oxford, 1880).

⮑ BIBLIOGRAPHY _____

Abbreviations

AWN	*Ardāy Wīrāz Nāmag*	MIr	Middle Iranian
AJ	*Ayādgār ī Jāmāspīg*	MX	*Mēnōg ī Xrad*
Av.	Avestan	Phl.	Pahlavi
Bd.	*Bundahišn*	PR	*Pahlavi Rivāyat* accompanying the *Dādestān ī Dēnīg*
BYt.	*Bahman Yašt*	WZ	*Wizīdagīhā ī Zādspram*
DD	*Dādestān ī Dēnīg*	Vd.	*Vidēvdāt (Vendidād)*
Dk.	*Dēnkard*	Y.	*Yasna*
JN	*Jāmāsp Nāmag*	Yt.	*Yašt*

Primary Texts

Anklesaria, B. T. 1956. *Zand-Akāsīh: Iranian or Greater Bundahišn.* Bombay: Bode.

Cereti, C. G. 1995. *The Zand ī Wahman Yasn: A Zoroastrian Apocalypse.* Rome Oriental Series 75. Rome: Istituto italiano per il medio ed estremo oriente.

Gignoux, P. 1984. *Le Livre d'Ardā Vīrāz: Translittération, transcription et traduction du texte pehlevi.* Paris: Editions Recherche sur les Civilisations.

Gignoux, P., and A. Tafazzoli. 1993. *The Wizīdagīhā ī Zādspram: Anthologie de Zādspram.* Studia Iranica—Cahier 13. Paris: Association pour l'avancement des études iraniennes.

Humbach H., J. Elfenbein, and P. O. Skjærvø. 1991. *The Gāthās of Zarathushtra and the Other Old Avestan Texts.* Part I, *Introduction—Text and Translation.* Part II, *Commentary.* Heidelberg: Carl Winter. The most important English translation of the *Gāthās* and the *Yasna Haptanghaiti.*

Kellens, J., and E. Pirart. 1988, 1990, 1991. *Les textes vieil-avestiques.* Vol. I, *Introduction, texte et traduction.* Vol. II, *Répertoires grammaticaux et lexique.* Vol. III, *Commentaire.* Wiesbaden: Ludwig Reichert. A comprehensive study with a new interpretation of the *Gāthās.*

Molé, M. 1967. *La légende de Zoroastre selon les textes pehlevis.* Travaux de l'Institut d'Etudes Iraniennes de l'Université de Paris 3. Paris: C. Klincksieck.

Wahman, F. 1986. *Ardā Wirāz Nāmag: The Iranian 'Divina Commedia.'* Copenhagen: Curzon Press.

Williams, A. V. 1990. *The Pahlavi Rivāyat Accompanying the Dādestān ī Dēnīg.* 2 vols. The Royal Danish Academy of Sciences and Letters, Hist.-filosof. Meddelelser 60:2. Copenhagen: Munksgard.

Secondary Studies

Bidez, J., and F. Cumont. 1938. *Les mages hellénisés. I–II.* Paris: Société d'éditions "Les Belles lettres." A collection of Greek, Latin, and Syriac texts on Persian religion with useful comments and interpretations.

Boyce, M. 1984. "On the antiquity of Zoroastrian apocalyptic." *Bulletin of the School of Oriental and African Studies* 47:57–75. A short but penetrating survey of the development of Persian apocalypticism.

Boyce, M., and F. Grenet. 1991. *A History of Zoroastrianism. III, Zoroastrianism under Macedonian and Roman Rule.* Leiden: E. J. Brill. Deals with Zoroastrianism outside Iran proper during the Hellenistic period; includes important considerations of the question of Iranian influence on Judaism and Christianity as well as on Greco-Roman religions.

Cohn, N. 1993. *Cosmos, Chaos and the World to Come: The Ancient Roots of Apocalyptic Faith.* New Haven/London: Yale University Press. A broad account of the ancient Near Eastern roots of apocalyptic ideas, including Zoroastrianism.

Colpe, C. 1994. "Hystaspes." In *Reallexikon für Antike und Christentum,* 16:1057–82. Stuttgart: Hiersemann. Analyses in a lucid manner the intricate tradition-historical development of the Hystaspes texts.

de Jong, A. 1997. *Traditions of the Magi: Zoroastrianism in Greek and Latin Literature.* New York: E. J. Brill. Deals with the same topic as Bidez and Cumont but is more comprehensive with respect to Iranian traditions.

Duchesne-Guillemin, J. 1982. "Apocalypse juive et apocalypse iranienne." In *La Soteriologia dei Culti Orientali nell' Impero Romano,* edited by U. Bianchi and M. Vermaseren, 753–59. Leiden: E. J. Brill. Argues that the *Bahman Yašt* depends on the book of Daniel.

Flusser, D. 1982. "Hystaspes and John of Patmos." In *Irano-Judaica: Studies Relating to Jewish Contacts with Persian Culture throughout the Ages,* edited by Shaul Shaked, 12–75. Jerusalem: The Ben-Zvi Institute. A penetrating study of the "Oracles of Hystaspes" and its influence on the book of Revelation.

Hinnells, J. 1973. "The Zoroastrian Doctrine of Salvation in the Roman World: A Study of the Oracles of Hystaspes." In *Man and His Salvation,* edited by E. Sharpe and J. R. Hinnells, 125–48. Manchester: Manchester University Press. Argues that the savior figure of the Oracles is the Zoroastrian *saošyant.*

Hinze, A. 1995. "The Rise of the Saviour in the Avesta." In *Iran und Turfan: Beiträge Berliner Wissenschaftler, Werner Sundermann zum 60. Geburtstag gewidmet,* edited by Ch. Reck and P. Zieme, 77–98. Wiesbaden: Harrassowitz. Traces the development of the *saošyant* concept from the *Gāthās* to the Younger Avesta.

Hultgård, A. 1979. "Das Judentum in der hellenistisch-römischen Zeit und die iranische Religion—ein religionsgeschichtliches Problem." In *Aufstieg und Niedergang der römischen Welt* 19,1, edited by W. Haase, 512–90. Berlin/New York: de Gruyter. A detailed study of the question of Iranian influence on Judaism.

———. 1983. "Forms and Origins of Iranian Apocalypticism." In *Apocalypticism in the Mediterranean World and the Near East,* edited by D. Hellholm, 387–411. Tübingen: Mohr-Siebeck. Analyzes the forms in which Iranian apocalyptic materials are transmitted.

———. 1988. "Prêtres juifs et mages zoroastriens—influences religieuses à l'époque hellénistique." *Revue d'historie et de philosophie religieuses* 68:415–28. Points out the similarities between Jewish priesthood and the Magi, and traces Iranian influence in Jewish Zadokite writings.

———. 1995. "Mythe et histoire dans l'Iran ancien: Étude de quelques thèmes dans le Bahman Yašt." In *Apocalyptique iranienne et dualisme qoumrânien,* edited by G. Widengren, A. Hultgård, and M. Philonenko, 63–162. Paris: Maisonneuve. The study deals with apocalyptic and mythic themes in Zoroastrian tradition with an emphasis on the *Bahman Yašt.*

Kippenberg, H. G. 1978. "Die Geschichte der mittelpersischen apokalyptischen Traditionen." *Studia Iranica* 7:49–80. A useful survey with emphasis on the interaction of apocalypticism and sociopolitical history in the late Sassanian and early Islamic periods.

Philonenko, M. 1995. "La doctrine qoumrânienne des deux Esprits: Ses origines iranniennes et ses prolongements dans le judaïsme essénien et le christianisme antique." In *Apocalyptique iranienne et dualisme qoumrânien,* edited by G. Widengren, A. Hultgård, and M. Philonenko, 163–212. Paris: Maisonneuve. A comprehensive study of the influence of Persian dualism on Jewish and Christian traditions.

Shaked, S. 1994. *Dualism in Transformation: Varieties of Religion in Sasanian Iran.* London: School of Oriental and African Studies. Includes an important chapter of Zoroastrian eschatology in the Sassanian period.

Widengren, G. 1983. "Leitende Ideen und Quellen der iranischen Apokalyptik." In *Apocalypticism in the*

Mediterranean World and the Near East, edited by D. Hellholm, 77–162. Tübingen: Mohr-Siebeck. A detailed account of Persian apocalyptic ideas that emphasizes their historical continuity.

Zaehner, R. C. 1972. *Zurvan: A Zoroastrian Dilemma, with a New Introduction by the Author.* New York: Biblo and Tannen. A comprehensive discussion of Zurvanism with edition and translation of important passages in the Pahlavi books.

From Prophecy to Apocalypticism: The Expectation of the End

John J. Collins
University of Chicago

I N POPULAR CONSCIOUSNESS, no idea is more characteristic of apocalyptic eschatology than the expectation of the end of the world. Eschatology, after all, means "talk about the end," even though, as we shall see, it can never be reduced to just the end of anything. While some scholars have traced this idea to the teaching of Zoroaster in ancient Iran (Cohn 1993), a clearer line of transmission can be traced to the Hebrew prophets. The ultimate roots of the concept lie in the combat myths that can be found in various cultures of the ancient Near East. In Israel, this mythology was adapted to celebrate the triumph of God over the forces of chaos, in the Psalms (e.g., Psalms 96, 98). The prophets, however, projected the conflict into the future and used the mythology to evoke the judgment of God, both on the Gentile nations and on Israel itself.

It was the prophet Amos in the eighth century B.C.E. who first proclaimed that "the end" (Amos 8:2; Hebrew *haqqēṣ*) was at hand. By this Amos meant that the kingdom of northern Israel was doomed. There was no concept as yet of an end of this world. Amos also spoke of this event as "the day of the Lord," which would be darkness and not light (Amos 5:18–20). In the centuries that followed, other prophets used poetic hyperbole to expand this notion into a day of cosmic judgment. An oracle preserved in the book of Isaiah predicts the fall of Babylon in cosmic terms: "the day of the Lord comes, cruel, with wrath and fierce anger, to make the earth a desolation and to destroy its sinners from it. For the stars of heaven and their constellations will not give their light; the sun will be dark at its rising and the moon will not shed its light. . . . Therefore I will make the heavens tremble and the earth will be shaken out of its place at the wrath of the Lord of hosts, in the day of his fierce anger" (Isa. 13:9–13). Here the prophet is still concerned with the destruction of a specific city, Babylon, but his language evokes a catastrophe of cosmic proportions. Thus, the notion of the end of this world has its origin in the cosmic imagery of Hebrew prophets in their oracles of destruction against specific places, including Jerusalem.

This imagery, however, underwent significant development in the period between the Babylonian Exile (586–539 B.C.E.) and the rise of Christianity. We will consider three phases in the development. The first is located in the latter part of the sixth and early fifth centuries B.C.E., at the time of the Jewish restoration in Jerusalem under the Persians, and is often called "proto-apocalyptic." The second occurs in the Hellenistic period and reached its climax in the time of persecution under Antiochus IV Epiphanes (168–164 B.C.E.) and the Maccabean revolt. The third is contemporaneous with the rise of Christianity and arises in the context of Jewish reflection on the second destruction of Jerusalem, by the Romans in 70 C.E.

☞ POSTEXILIC PROPHECY

In the period that followed the Babylonian Exile we often find heightened cosmic imagery in oracles that are difficult to pin down as to their specific historical referents. Some of the most colorful examples are found in Isaiah 24–27, a passage of uncertain historical provenance that may be related to the sack of Babylon by Xerxes in 485 B.C.E.. (These chapters are sometimes called "the apocalypse of Isaiah," but in form they are simply prophetic oracles.) "Now the Lord is about to lay waste the earth and make it desolate, and he will twist its surface and scatter its inhabitants" (24:1); "for the windows of heaven are opened, and the foundations of the earth tremble. The earth is utterly broken, the earth is torn asunder, the earth is violently shaken" (24:19). These oracles also draw motifs from ancient Canaanite myths, by promising that God "will swallow Death (*Môt*) forever" (25:7) and that he will punish Leviathan and slay the dragon that is in the sea (27:1). Significantly, we also find here the language of resurrection: "Your dead shall live, their corpses shall rise. O dwellers in the dust, awake and sing for joy" (26:19). Most probably, the reference here is to the restoration of the Israelite nation, in contrast to their erstwhile rulers, of whom it is said that their dead will not live (26:14). Resurrection of the dead was already used as a metaphor for the restoration of Israel in Ezekiel's vision of the valley full of dry bones in Ezekiel 37, which dates from the time of the exile. In any case, the resurrection language here reminds us that these oracles are not only predictions of destruction. They are also looking for a new beginning beyond the disaster.

We can only guess at the historical and social matrix that inspired the prophet of Isaiah 24–27. There is clearly resentment against "the fortified city, the palace of aliens" (25:2; Babylon is perhaps the most plausible candidate). There is also a great desire for the restoration of Israel, likened to a resurrection of the dead. In the prophet's vision, the physical world symbolizes the political order; the world as constituted must be broken apart to allow a new order to emerge. The prophet evidently identifies with the poor and disenfranchised, but the poor may be the Jewish people in relation to the Gentiles, or some smaller group within Israel. The lack of historical specificity is characteristic of many eschatological oracles from the postexilic period. Another example is found in Ezekiel 38–39, where the prophet conjures up the fantastic figure of Gog from the land of Magog. (The name may be suggested by Gyges of Lydia, but Gyges had no contact with Israel.) Gog becomes a generic representative of Gentile power, which is to be brought low by God on the mountains of Israel. Yet another example is found in Joel 3:9–16, where God judges the nations in the valley of Jehoshaphat. Again, we can only guess at the historical context of this oracle. (Joel 3:6 rebukes Tyre, Sidon, and Philistia for selling Jews as slaves to the Greeks, but the slave trade flourished throughout the Persian and Hellenistic periods.)

All of these passages were probably composed with specific crises in mind. Since we no longer know the historical circumstances, however, the oracles take on the character of general eschatological predictions that evoke an expectation of the end of history, which may or may not be imminent. Since these oracles were embedded in scripture, later generations could interpret them in various ways and could see their fulfillment in various historical circumstances.

Only in the period immediately after the exile can the emerging eschatological expectations of the later biblical period be set in historical and social context. In the year 518 B.C.E. the prophets Haggai and Zechariah were instrumental in motivating the returned exiles to complete the rebuilding of the Temple. Haggai told the people that their lack of material prosperity was due to the fact that they had given higher priority to their own houses. When the building of the Temple was finally undertaken, he told them to take courage:

> For thus says the Lord of hosts: Once again, in a little while, I will shake the heavens and the earth and the sea and the dry land; and I will shake all the nations, so that the treasure of all nations shall come, and I will fill this house with splendor, says the Lord of hosts. (Hag. 2:7)

In the brief text of Haggai's oracles, there are signs that the promised transformation was delayed. Haggai is insistent: "From this day on I will bless you" (2:19). It is apparent, however, that the Jewish community did not experience a transformation of fortune such as Haggai had promised.

Haggai expected the rebuilding of the Temple to be the catalyst for a new age. Not all his contemporaries shared his views. The final section of the book of Isaiah (chapters 56–66) preserves a skeptical view of the Temple project:

> Thus says the Lord: Heaven is my throne and the earth is my footstool; what is the house that you would build for me, and what is my resting-place? All these things my hand has made, and so all these things are mine, says the Lord. But this is the one to whom I will look, to the humble and contrite in spirit, who trembles at my word. (Isa. 66:1–2)

The tremblers (ḥārēdîm) have given their name to apocalyptically oriented ultraorthodox Jews in modern Israel. They probably constituted a distinct group also in the Persian period (Blenkinsopp 1990). They were no less eschatological in their outlook than the proponents of the rebuilding: "For I am about to create new heavens and a new earth" (Isa. 65:17) and "as the new heavens and the new earth, which I will make, shall remain before me, says the Lord; so shall your descendants and your name remain . . ." (65:22).

In a seminal study published in 1975 Paul Hanson argued that Isaiah 56–66 represented *The Dawn of Apocalyptic.* He posited a sharp division in the postexilic community between the hierocratic party, represented by Haggai, Zechariah 1–8, and Ezekiel 40–48, whose piety focused the preservation of the sacred, and a visionary party, represented by Isaiah 56–66, that gave a higher priority to social and humanitarian concerns. In the categories of the sociologist Karl Mannheim, the hierocrats were ideological, while the visionaries were utopian. While both sides used eschatological symbols, the use made of them was different: one side used them to underpin the existing power structures of the Temple and priesthood, while the other side used them to undermine these structures. Hanson used a complex system of prosodic typology (that is, the changing poetic style of the prophets), to reconstruct the history of the visionary party, from the initial enthusiasm shown in Isaiah 60–62 to eventual disillusionment with history and the desperate hope for a new creation.

This ingenious reconstruction has been criticized on several grounds. The twofold division of postexilic society is almost certainly too simple, and the unsympathetic portrayal of the hierocratic movement requires modification. The hierocrats must be credited with genuine religious motives and not merely the desire to maintain the current power structures. Moreover, the "hierocratic" books of Zechariah and Ezekiel 40–48 are no less visionary than Isaiah 56–66 and may equally well be considered forerunners of apocalypticism (Cook 1995; Tigchelaar 1996). The reliability of prosodic typology as an instrument for tracing historical development is also open to question. Nonetheless, Hanson must be credited with an imaginative reconstruction of a situation where the hope for a new heaven and earth made sense: it arises from profound alienation and a sense of hopelessness in the present world. While it is certainly possible to find "millennial groups in power" (Cook 1995, 55), we must remember that even those who wielded power in postexilic Judah experienced relative deprivation in the broader context of the Persian empire. Haggai and Zechariah may have been close to the center of power in Jerusalem, but they were very marginal figures in the broader Persian context. The significance of Hanson's work, however, lies in the light it shed on the role of inner-community conflict in the rise of apocalypticism. Eschatological hope in the early postexilic period was not only prompted by the powerlessness of the Jewish people in the international context. It also arose from division and alienation within the Jewish community. Both factors, the international situation and internal division, continue to play a part in generating eschatological expectations throughout Jewish history.

The hope for a new heaven and a new earth (Isa. 65:17) is certainly relevant to the history of apocalypticism, but it should not be labeled "apocalyptic" without serious qualification. Formally, the last chapters of Isaiah are prophetic oracles, just like the oracles of the preexilic prophets. The content of the oracles also has much in common with older prophecy. The conditions of the new creation that are spelled out in Isaiah 65 are closer to the expectations of the prophets of old than to those of the later apocalyptic visionaries:

> No more shall there be in it an infant that lives but a few days or an old person who does not live out a lifetime; for one who dies at a hundred years will be considered a youth, and one who falls short of a hundred will be considered accursed. They shall build houses and inhabit them; they shall plant vineyards and eat their fruit . . . for like the days of a tree shall the days of my people be. (Isa. 65:17–25)

The passage concludes by evoking Isaiah 11: "The wolf and the lamb shall feed together." What is envisaged here is an earthly life such as we know, but longer and free of pain and care. This is a utopian hope, which can properly be called eschatological. It is very different, however, from the hope that we will find in the apocalyptic literature of the Hellenistic age.

We may summarize the developments of the early postexilic period as follows. There is increased use of cosmic imagery to express the hope of a radical transformation of human affairs. In many cases, the expected judgment takes on a general character that cannot be tied specifically to any known historical events. The ancient myth of God's combat with the dragon is projected into the future as a paradigm for a new creation. We find eschatological hopes in various theological traditions, some oriented toward the Temple cult, some critical of it. Eschatological hopes arise both to compensate for the powerlessness of Israel among the nations and to console groups that were alienated from the power structures within Jewish society. The hopes that we find in these late prophetic texts, however, are still oriented toward a restored earthly society in a way that has more in common with earlier prophets than with later visionaries.

It must be conceded, however, that we know extremely little about the groups that transmitted eschatological expectations in Judaism in the Persian period. When apocalypticism emerges full-blown in the books of Enoch and Daniel in the Hellenistic period, it is a far more developed and complex phenomenon than is the case in any of the fragmentary prophetic texts hitherto discussed. It is not possible to show any social continuity between the visionaries of the Persian period and their Hellenistic successors. The prophetic oracles were taken up into the canon of scripture, and so became part of the source material of the apocalyptists, who picked up motifs like the creation of a new heaven and a new earth. The apocalypticism of the Hellenistic period, however, is a new phenomenon in many crucial respects.

☞ THE HELLENISTIC PERIOD _____

The Books of Enoch

The oldest Jewish apocalypses are found in the *Book of Enoch,* a composite work that is fully preserved only in Ethiopic. Greek fragments of the work have long been known, and Aramaic fragments have been found among the Dead Sea Scrolls (Milik 1976). The book includes at least five distinct works: the Book of the Watchers (chapters 1–36), the Similitudes (chapters 37–71), the Astronomical Book (chapters 72–82), the Book of Dreams (chapters 83–90), and the Epistle (chapters 91–105). Within these books, the Animal Apocalypse (chapters 85–90) and the Apocalypse of Weeks (93:1–10 + 91:11–18) stand out as distinct compositions, while the concluding chapters of the book, 106–8, contain further material. (Chapters 106–7 deal with the birth of Noah; 108 is "another book" Enoch wrote for his son Methuselah.) The Similitudes are not attested in the Dead Sea Scrolls and can be dated no earlier than the first century C.E. The other books, however, must be dated to the third or early second centuries B.C.E. on the basis of the paleography of the Dead Sea fragments and also on internal evidence. (The Apocalypse of Weeks and the Animal Apocalypse allude to historical events and also presuppose the story of the Book of the Watchers.)

While the prophets of old had spoken in their own names, and oracles such as Isaiah 24–27 probably circulated anonymously, the books of Enoch are pseudonymous, since they are ascribed to an antediluvian patriarch who cannot possibly have been their actual author. Pseudonymity henceforth is a trademark of Jewish apocalypses. Other pseudonymous authors include Daniel, Moses, Ezra, Baruch, and Abraham. There was a precedent for pseudonymity in Jewish tradition: the book of Deuteronomy was ascribed to Moses, although it was promulgated by King Josiah in 621 B.C.E. and probably took its present form during the Babylonian Exile. In the Hellenistic period the device was widespread. New oracles were uttered in the name of the sibyl in the Greek world, and in the names of Zoroaster and Hystaspes in the Persian world. But pseudonymity was not peculiar to oracles and apocalypses. In Hellenistic Judaism we find new psalms of David and Solomon and a new wisdom book also in the name of

Solomon. New writings circulated in the Greek and Roman world in the names of Plato and Heraclitus. Pseudonymity, then, was something of a literary fashion and could serve different purposes in different contexts. In all cases, it presumably enhanced the authority of a work by giving it an aura of antiquity. While the authors of such works must have been aware of the fiction involved, their effectiveness depended on the credulity of the masses. This is not to say that the authors sought to deceive; they may have had a sophisticated understanding of their literary device. In general, the pseudonyms are appropriate to their material. Enoch is the authority on heavenly mysteries, since he had been taken up to heaven before the flood (Gen. 5:24). Solomon is the authority for wisdom teaching, and Moses for matters pertaining to the law.

In the context of apocalyptic writing, pseudonymity offered some other advantages. It permitted the author to create an extended "prophecy" of history, most of which could be verified, because it was written after the fact. The actual prophecy of future events was thereby rendered more credible. Such prophecies conveyed a sense that the course of history was predetermined, since events could be predicted so far in advance. They also allowed the readers to identify their own place in the unfolding drama and to see the events of their time in a cosmic perspective.

The oldest parts of the Enoch tradition are found in the Astronomical Book and the Book of the Watchers. The Astronomical Book is largely taken up with the movements of the stars. These were important for establishing the true calendar, which was a major cause of sectarian division in ancient Judaism. Much of this material is scientific, or pseudo-scientific, in character, and it suggests that the tradents of the Enoch literature were learned scribes, even if their learning was crude and outdated by Greek or Babylonian standards. Enoch views the stars as animated beings and speaks of their leaders, who are responsible for their movements. Moreover, he warns that at a future time "many heads of the stars in command will go astray, and these will change their courses and their activities, and will not appear at the times which have been prescribed for them" (1 Enoch 70:6). We are also told that the regulations in this book are valid "until the new creation shall be made which will last forever" (72:1). Apart from these hints, however, there is little eschatology in the Astronomical Book of Enoch. The book is primarily a treatise on the movements of the stars (VanderKam 1984, 76–109).

The Book of the Watchers also contains much material that might be regarded as speculative and that suggests that the authors were learned scribes rather than prophets. In this case, however, eschatology also has an important role. There are two major themes in the Book of the Watchers, the story of the Watchers, or fallen angels, in 1 Enoch 6–11 and the story of Enoch's ascent to heaven and his journeys to the ends of the earth (chapters 12–36; the two themes overlap in chapters 12–16). The story of the Watchers has its point of departure in Genesis 6, where the "sons of God" become enamored of the daughters of men and come down and beget giants. In 1 Enoch, this story is developed into an explanation of the spread of sin on earth. (Enoch also knows the story of Adam and Eve, but he does not use it to explain the prevalence of sin in later generations.) On this explanation, sin results from the influence of supernatural, demonic forces on human behavior. The fallen angels impart to humanity forbidden knowledge: "and they taught them charms and spells and showed to them the cutting of roots and trees" (7:2).

> And Azazel taught men to make swords and daggers and shields and breastplates, and he showed them the things after these, and the art of making them: bracelets, and ornaments and the art of making up the eyes and of beautifying the eyelids and the most precious and choice stones and all kinds of colored dyes. And the world was changed. And there was great impiety and much fornication, and they went astray, and all their ways became corrupt." (8:1–2)

Later we are told that evil spirits come out of the flesh of the giants, to cause evil and sorrow on earth (15:8–16:1). This myth is developed in the book of *Jubilees,* where Mastema, the chief of the spirits, gets permission from God for one-tenth of the spirits to remain on earth so that humanity can be corrupted and led astray (*Jub.* 10:7–11).

Paolo Sacchi has argued that the story of the Watchers is the kernel in which the essence of apocalypticism is contained and from which the whole tradition grows (Sacchi 1996). The underlying problem that all apocalyptic literature addresses is the problem of evil. The characteristic apocalyptic explanation lies in the appeal to supernatural, demonic forces. There is no doubt that Sacchi has highlighted a very fundamental element in the Enoch tradition, but its importance must be seen in perspective. Even the story of the Watchers is not concerned only with the origin of evil; it also entails judgment and punishment. Moreover, we find various explanations of the origin of evil in apocalyptic tradition. The Qumran *Community Rule* says that God created two spirits, one of light and one of darkness, an explanation that is patently indebted to Zoroastrian dualism. Later apocalypses (4 Ezra, *2 Baruch*) make extensive use of the story of Adam and Eve and ignore the Watchers. But nonetheless, Sacchi has performed an important service in highlighting the role that the origin of evil plays in several apocalyptic texts. It should also be noted that the story of the Watchers very probably has an allegorical quality. The passage cited above from *1 Enoch* 8 complains that "the world was changed." It is difficult not to read this passage as a loose allegory for the cultural crisis brought on by the advent of Hellenism, which entailed the spread of information and new ideas of morality that were often scandalous to traditional Jews. The story of the Watchers, then, is not only an etiology of the spread of wickedness before the flood. It is also paradigmatic of the way the world was changed in the author's own time in the Hellenistic age.

The author evidently perceived the way the world was changed as negative, but his composition does not end in despair. Rather, he offers two resolutions of the crisis. First, the story of the Watchers ends with their imprisonment by the archangels; second, Enoch's tour reveals that the apparatus of judgment and retribution is already in place.

In *1 Enoch* 11, the punishment of the Watchers is described. The angel Raphael is bidden: "Bind Azazel by his hands and his feet, and throw him into the darkness. And split open the desert which is in Dudael, and throw him there . . . and cover his face that he may not see light and that on the great day of judgment he may be hurled into the fire. And restore the earth, which the angels have ruined" (10:4–7). Again, the angel Michael is told to bind Shemiḥaza, the other leader of the rebel angels, "for seventy generations under the hills of the earth until the day of their judgment and of their consummation, until the judgment which is for all eternity is accomplished" (10:12). The passage goes on to describe how the earth will be transformed and cleansed from corruption. The prospect of a final judgment provides the ultimate solution to the crisis of the Watchers. We do not, however, get the impression that this judgment is imminent. In the narrative context of the book, it is deferred for seventy generations, until the end of history.

The eschatology of the Book of the Watchers is filled out in the account of Enoch's journeys. Enoch is introduced in chapter 12 as a "scribe of righteousness," whom the Watchers ask to intercede for them. There follows an intriguing scene in which Enoch sits down "by the waters of Dan" and reads out the petition of the Watchers until he falls asleep. Then in his vision clouds call him and the winds lift him up to heaven. We have no way of knowing whether the author was reporting his own visionary experience here, but the recitation and the proximity of water are often associated with visions in many cultures. Enoch then describes his entry into the heavenly palace and the presence of God enthroned (chapter 14). He is told to tell the Watchers that they should intercede for humans, not the reverse, and that they should have remained spiritual and holy, living an eternal life, and not have lain with women and begotten children. We see here that the fundamental antithesis in the Book of the Watchers is between heaven and earth, spirit and flesh (although the latter distinction should not be confused with the Greek distinction between body and soul). The ideal life is the holy, spiritual, eternal life in heaven, which the Watchers have forsaken. Enoch, in contrast, is a human being admitted to the heavenly court, whose elevation betokens a new possibility for human existence. The negative attitude toward sex and procreation should also be noted. A similar tendency toward asceticism is found in the Dead Sea Scrolls and in the Greek accounts of the Essene sect, some of whose members are said to have been celibate.

Enoch's actual tour begins in chapter 17 and takes him to the ends of the earth, accompanied by angelic guides. He sees the storehouses of the winds and the elements and the cornerstone of the earth and other such cosmological marvels. A major part of his revelations, however, concerns places of judgment. In chapters 18 and 19 he sees the prison of the stars and the host of heaven, where the Watchers also are kept until the great judgment day, and another form of this vision is repeated in chapter 21. In chapter 22 he sees chambers inside a mountain, where "the spirits of the souls of the dead" are kept to await judgment. While there is some confusion in the text as to whether there are three chambers or four, it is clear that distinctions are made between the righteous and the wicked, while they await the judgment day. *This is earliest attestation of the judgment of the dead in Jewish tradition.* The following chapters go on to describe the place where God's throne will be set when he comes down to visit the earth for good (chapter 25), the tree of life whose fruit will be given to the chosen after the judgment (chapter 26), and the valley of judgment (chapter 27). In a later chapter (32) Enoch sees the tree of knowledge, from which Adam and Eve ate.

The world that Enoch tours in chapters 17–36 is normally hidden from human sight and is accessible here only by supernatural revelation. It is antithetical to the world defiled by the Watchers. The message of the book is that all is not as it seems on earth. In the hidden regions, all is in order. The places of judgment are prepared to ensure the triumph of justice and provision has been made for retribution on an individual basis. Moreover, the holiness of the divine throne and its surroundings provide the greatest contrast to life on earth. The expectation of a future day of judgment is of basic importance in this book, but it is not the only, or even the primary, focus of the author's attention. Rather, the emphasis is on the present reality of everything that Enoch sees. While most human beings can only hope for access to the angelic world after death, the revelation of Enoch assures them that it is already there, waiting for them.

The hope for fellowship with the angels in the heavenly world is more explicitly stated in the Epistle of Enoch (chapters 91–105), which probably dates from the early second century B.C.E. Much of this document is taken up with woes against the rich, who trust in their wealth and do not remember the Most High, and exhortation to the righteous. The hope of the righteous is expressed in chapter 104: "you will shine like the lights of heaven and will be seen, and the gate of heaven will be opened to you . . . you will not have to hide on the day of the great judgment . . . for you shall be associates of the host of heaven." Even though the author of the Epistle cares deeply about injustice on earth, his ultimate hope is not just for a reversal of earthly fortune but for an angelic life in heaven.

While both the Book of the Watchers and the Epistle of Enoch anticipate a day of judgment, their focus is on the contrast between the heavenly and the earthly, the hidden and the visible. Concern for chronology appears more clearly in two Enochic apocalypses from the Maccabean era, the Apocalypse of Weeks and the Animal Apocalypse. The Apocalypse of Weeks divides history into ten "weeks" (presumably weeks of years), which will be followed after a new creation by "many weeks without number forever." The turning point of history comes in the seventh week, when there is an apostate generation, but at the end of the week "the chosen righteous from the eternal plant of righteousness will be chosen, to whom will be given sevenfold teaching concerning his whole creation" (93:10). The eighth week will be that of the righteous and "a sword will be given to it that the righteous judgment may be executed on those who do wrong" (93:12). If the apocalypse was written in the eighth generation, the sword would presumably be a reference to the Maccabean revolt. It is more likely, however, that it was written in the seventh week, at the time of the emergence of the chosen righteous. It is clear, however, that this apocalypse envisages a militant role for the righteous in the last generations. In the ninth generation, the world will be written down for destruction, and in the tenth there will be an eternal judgment on the Watchers. Then the first heaven will vanish and pass away, and a new heaven will appear. The Apocalypse of Weeks is probably the first Jewish document to envisage the end of the world in a literal sense.

This apocalypse is also noteworthy for literary reasons. The revelation takes the form of an extended prophecy, most of which is after the fact. The time of the author can be identified as the point of transition in the apocalypse, from the woeful present to the glorious future. The idea that history can be divided into a set number of periods is a very common idea in Jewish, and later Christian, apocalyptic literature. The division into ten periods most probably derives from Persian eschatology, which expected a great transition at the end of a millennium (e.g., in the *Bahman Yašt,* chapter 1). We find here a distinctively historically oriented apocalypse that is formally quite different from the otherworldly journeys of Enoch in the Book of the Watchers. It is closer to much of what we will find in the book of Daniel. It conveys a sense that history is predetermined and serves to legitimate the group called "the chosen righteous" (to which the author surely belonged) as playing a providential role in history.

The Animal Apocalypse is another extended prophecy after the fact, although the division into periods is less clearly defined. The apocalypse gets its name from its dominant literary device—the representation of human beings as animals. Adam is a white bull; the fallen angels are stars who have members like the members of horses and whose offspring are elephants and camels and asses, and so forth. In the postexilic period, Israel is subjected to the rule of seventy shepherds. The turning point of history comes when small lambs are born and horns grow upon them, and a big horn grows on one of them. The lamb with the big horn is clearly Judas Maccabee, and the context is the Maccabean revolt. The outcome of the revolt, however, is not described simply in historical terms. The Lord of the sheep comes down in anger, and a judgment scene unfolds. A big sword is given to the sheep (Israel) to kill the wild animals (Gentiles). The judgment extends not only to the seventy shepherds (the patron angels of the nations) but also to the Watchers of old. Here again the device of prophecy after the fact serves to locate the author and his group at the turning point of history. Like the Apocalypse of Weeks, this apocalypse is unabashed in its endorsement of violence as a means of executing justice. As in all of these Enochic writings, however, the final judgment is executed by God, and it affects all generations simultaneously. The sheep that had been destroyed are assembled at the judgment (90:33), which is a figurative way of giving expression to the resurrection of the dead.

In the writings attributed to Enoch, then, we can trace a progression, from those that are more speculative in content to those that are more concerned with history. The pseudonym of Enoch was chosen presumably because Enoch was preeminently qualified to disclose the mysteries of the heavenly world. Already in the Book of the Watchers, which shows no awareness of the Maccabean crisis, these mysteries include the judgment of the individual dead. There are indications in several of these apocalypses that the authors belonged to a group that considered itself to be chosen by God. In the heat of the Maccabean crisis, the interest shifts from the mysteries of the cosmos to those of history, and the sense of imminent expectation becomes greater. At least the Animal Apocalypse, and possibly the Apocalypse of Weeks, expresses outright support for the militant policies of the Maccabees.

The Book of Daniel

The book of Daniel is also a composite book. Chapters 1–6 contain a collection of traditional tales, often legendary in character, about Daniel and his companions in the Babylonian Exile. These tales were written down sometime in the third or early second century B.C.E. Chapters 7–12 report the visions of Daniel, interpreted by an angel. Already in antiquity the Neoplatonist Porphyry showed that these visions did not come from the time of the Babylonian Exile. They give an accurate report of history down to the time of Antiochus Epiphanes (to about 167 B.C.E.) but not beyond that point. Although Porphyry did not realize it, the account of the death of the king "between the sea and the holy mountain" (11:45) was inaccurate, and so we know that this prophecy was completed before the news of his death reached Jerusalem. (He died in Persia, late in 164 B.C.E.) The visions of Daniel are pseudonymous, just like those of Enoch. Even though Daniel is supposed to have lived during the Babylonian Exile, it is likely that his name was derived from ancient myth. Ezekiel, who certainly lived during the exile, associated Daniel with Noah and Job (Ezek. 14:14) and regarded the wisdom of Daniel as legendary (28:3). A hero named Daniel is found in the Ugaritic myths from the late second millennium, but it is uncertain whether the name of the biblical figure was suggested by the mythic tradition.

The stories in Daniel 1–6 represent the tradition lying behind the apocalyptic visions in chapters 7–12. In the stories, Daniel is preeminently an interpreter of dreams and mysterious signs. Most notable for our purpose is the interpretation of Nebuchadnezzar's dream in chapter 2. The king refuses to tell his dream, so Daniel can only know it by divine revelation. The dream concerns a large statue composed of different metals: the head of gold, the chest and arms of silver, the middle and thighs of bronze, and the feet of iron mixed with clay. Daniel interprets the statue in terms of four kingdoms, in declining succession, beginning with Nebuchadnezzar as the head of gold. The use of metals to symbolize a declining sequence has a famous parallel in Hesiod's *Works and Days,* where the ages of humankind are represented as gold, silver, bronze, and iron. A closer parallel to Nebuchadnezzar's vision is found in the Persian *Bahman Yašt,* where Zoroaster sees "the trunk of a tree, on which there were four branches: one of gold, one of silver, one of steel, and one of mixed iron." While the Persian text in its present form is several centuries later than Daniel, it is likely to derive from a common source. There is no reason to think that it was influenced by the biblical book. In the context of the book of Daniel, the four kingdoms must be identified as Babylon, Media, Persia, and Greece. (Daniel introduces the fictitious figure of Darius the Mede to represent the Median empire.) This sequence also points to Persian influence, since the Medes never ruled over Judea.

The sequence of four kingdoms followed by a fifth of a different character was well known throughout the Near East in the Hellenistic and Roman periods. Another Jewish example is found in the fourth *Sibylline Oracle*. Assyria, rather than Babylon, is usually the first kingdom. In Daniel 2, the end of the sequence is represented by a stone cut from a mountain that destroys the statue. The stone represents the kingdom of God, which will last forever. In Daniel 2, however, there is no sense of imminent expectation. The coming of the kingdom of God is in the distant future from the viewpoint of Daniel and Nebuchadnezzar. The point is rather that the God of Israel is in control of history and that this control will eventually be made manifest.

The theme of four kingdoms is picked up again in Daniel's vision in chapter 7, but this time the imagery is very different. Daniel sees four beasts coming up out of the sea, one more fearsome than the other, and the fourth, which has ten horns plus an additional upstart one, is the most fearsome of all. Then he sees thrones set, and the deity, in the form of an ancient one, takes his seat and passes judgment on the beasts. Then "one like a son of man" appears with an entourage of clouds and is presented before the ancient one. He is given "dominion and glory and kingship" that shall never be destroyed. An angel subsequently explains to Daniel that the four beasts are four kings, or kingdoms, and that "the holy ones of the Most High will receive the kingdom." Finally the angel explains further that the little horn will attempt to change the times (i.e., the cultic calendar) and the law, and that "the people of the Holy Ones of the Most High" will receive the kingdom.

Daniel 7 is arguably the most influential passage in Jewish apocalyptic literature, and it had a profound influence on the Synoptic Gospels, where Jesus is identified as the Son of Man. It is also a powerful vision in its own right. Like some of the passages we have cited from Isaiah 24–27, it draws on the imagery of the Canaanite combat myth, where Baal, rider of the clouds, triumphs over Yamm, the turbulent sea. It is clear that the little horn represents Antiochus Epiphanes, and that the vision predicts his overthrow. But as Daniel sees it, the struggle is not just between Greeks and Jews. It is a reenactment of the primordial struggle where the beasts of chaos rise from the sea in rebellion against the rightful God. The most striking aspect of the imagery is that there seem, prima facie, to be two divine figures. Elsewhere in the Hebrew Bible it is always YHWH, the God of Israel, who rides on the clouds; here he must be identified with the Ancient of Days. This anomaly reflects the Canaanite background of the imagery. In the ancient myth, El is the ancient one while Baal is the rider of the clouds. In the Jewish context, the "one like a son of man" has often been taken as a symbol for Israel. He does indeed represent Israel in some sense, but such an interpretation misses the significance of the imagery. Elsewhere in Daniel, human figures in visions often represent angels (e.g., 10:5, 18; 12:5–6). "Holy Ones" nearly always represent angels both in Daniel and in the contemporary Jewish literature. In the context of Daniel, the one like a son of man is most satisfactorily identified as the archangel Michael, who is introduced as the "prince" of Israel in 10:21 and 12:1. The Holy Ones of the Most High are the angelic host and Israel is the people of the Holy Ones. The vision predicts the exaltation of Israel, but the real conflict is between the angelic hosts and the infernal beasts. (See further Collins 1993, 274–324.)

This reading of Daniel 7 is confirmed by the dialogue between Daniel and the angel Gabriel in chapter 10. There the angel explains that he is engaged in conflict with "the prince of

Persia," and that shortly "the prince of Greece" will come, but he is aided in his struggle by "Michael, your prince." Conflicts between peoples on earth are understood as reflections of struggles between their patron angels. Chapter 11 continues with an extended "prophecy" of the history of the Hellenistic age. At the end Michael arises in victory (12:1) and the resurrection and judgment follow.

Much of the "prophecy" of Hellenistic history is focused on the persecution of the Jews by Antiochus Epiphanes in the Maccabean era. Unlike the Enochic apocalypses, however, Daniel evinces no support for the Maccabees. Instead, the heroes of the drama are the "wise" (maśkîlîm), who instruct the common people and some of whom are killed. Their instruction presumably corresponds to the understanding of events found in the book of Daniel itself. They are not said to fight. At the resurrection, however, these wise teachers are said to shine like the brightness of the firmament and be like the stars forever and ever. Like the righteous in the Epistle of Enoch, they become companions to the host of heaven. They can afford to lose their lives in this world, because they are promised a greater glory in the next. They cooperate with the angelic hosts in defeating the enemy, not by fighting but by keeping themselves pure. A very similar viewpoint is found in the *Testament of Moses* 9–10, where a man called Taxo reacts to persecution by taking his sons into a cave and telling them to die rather than transgress the commandments of the Lord, "for if we do this and die, our blood will be avenged before the Lord and then shall his kingdom appear throughout all his creation . . . and God will exalt you and set you in heaven above the stars." The innocent righteous are, in effect, martyrs. By sacrificing their lives they ensure their eternal reward and also hasten the coming of the kingdom of God.

Two other motifs in the book of Daniel are especially important for the development of apocalypticism. In chapter 9, Daniel ponders Jeremiah's prophecy that Jerusalem would be desolate for seventy years (Jer. 25:11–12; 29:10). The angel Gabriel appears to him and explains that the seventy years are really seventy weeks of years, or 490 years. This passage is important for several reasons. First, it shows the importance of biblical prophecy in apocalyptic thought. But the prophecies are not understood in their historical context. Rather, they are reinterpreted in light of the circumstances of the apocalyptic author. The logic behind this move is expressed very clearly in the commentary on Habakkuk from the Dead Sea Scrolls (col. 7): "God told Habakkuk to write what was going to happen to the last generation, but he did not let him know the end of the age." Biblical prophecy is treated like the writing on the wall or Nebuchadnezzar's dream. It is a coded message, to be deciphered by the inspired interpreter. Second, Daniel 9 offers a calculation of the duration of the period from the end of the exile to the end of the persecution. The seventy weeks of years would be reinterpreted over and over again in early Christianity in an attempt to calculate the end of the world (see Collins 1993, 116–17).

The final motif in Daniel that influenced later apocalypticism is related to this. In chapter 12 we are told the exact number of days until the coming of "the end." This is in fact the only instance in an ancient Jewish apocalypse of an attempt to calculate the exact number of days. According to Dan. 8:14 the Temple cult would be disrupted for 2,300 evenings and mornings, or 1,150 days. At the end of the book, however, we are given two further calculations: "From the time that the regular burnt offering is taken away and the abomination that makes desolate is set up, there shall be 1,290 days. Happy are those who persevere and attain the 1,335 days" (Dan. 12:11–12). Two things about this latter passage are remarkable. First, we are given two different numbers side by side. Both may be regarded as approximations of three and a half years, but the fact that two different figures are given strongly suggests that the second calculation was added after the first number of days had passed. The phenomenon of re-calculation is well known in later apocalyptic movements such as the Millerite movement in nineteenth-century America (Festinger et al. 1956, 12–23). Second, Daniel is not specific as to what will happen when the number of days has passed. Since the days are calculated from the time that the Temple cult was disrupted, we might expect that the expected "end" is simply the restoration of that cult, and this would seem to be the implication in Dan. 8:14. But, according to 1 Macc. 1:54; 4:52–54, Judas purified the Temple three years to the day after it had been polluted, so both numbers in chapter 12 point to a date after that restoration. At least the last date must have been added after the purification had taken place. Presumably, the author of Daniel did not think that the restoration under Judas was satisfactory. But there is probably more at stake here. The numbers in Daniel 12 follow the prophecy of the victory of Michael and the resurrection of the dead. In Dan. 12:13 Daniel is told that he will rise from his rest at the end of the days. The end, then, is the time when the archangel Michael intervenes and the resurrection takes place, roughly what later tradition would call the end of the world.

A New Kind of Literature

One of the major modern debates about Jewish apocalypticism has concerned the origin of the phenomenon. The most influential schools of thought have seen it either as a child of prophecy (e.g., recently Hanson) or as a product of wisdom circles (von Rad). There is manifest influence of biblical prophecy in both Enoch and Daniel, especially in the crucial expectation of a day of judgment. It is also true that both Enoch and Daniel are depicted as wise men rather than as prophets (von Rad 1965). But this whole debate about the origins of apocalypticism is misplaced. In the books of Enoch and Daniel we are dealing with a new phenomenon in the history of Judaism, which was very much a product of the way in which "the world was changed" by the impact of Hellenism on the Near East. The apocalyptic visionaries drew on materials from many sources: ancient myths, biblical prophecies, Greek and Persian traditions. But what they produced was a new kind of literature that had its own coherence and should not be seen as a child or adaptation of something else. The vision form as we find it in Daniel has prophetic precedents (e.g., Zechariah) but is also indebted to Babylonian dream interpretation. Neither prophetic oracles nor wisdom instructions can be said to play a major role in these books.

There has also been debate as to whether these books, and the later Jewish and Christian apocalypses, can be said to constitute a literary genre. Von Rad argued that they were a "*corpus permixtum*," embracing various *Gattungen* (von Rad 1965, 330). In this he was thinking of the constituent forms that make up the apocalypses: visions, heavenly journeys, *ex eventu* (after-the-fact) prophecies, dialogues, etc. But on a higher level of abstraction, these books also have significant commonalities in form and content. The common elements of apocalypses are summed up in the following definition (Collins 1979, 9):

> [A]n apocalypse is a genre of revelatory literature with a narrative framework, in which a revelation is mediated by an otherworldly being to a human recipient, disclosing a transcendent reality which is both temporal, insofar as it envisages eschatological salvation, and spatial insofar as it involves another, supernatural world.

Every individual apocalypse has some distinctive features, but this common core identifies a new macro-genre in the history of Jewish religious literature.

The definition of an apocalypse given above should be qualified in a few respects. As Paolo Sacchi especially has argued, this literature has a history and evolved over time. In the early books of Enoch and Daniel, the genre is in an experimental stage. No subsequent otherworldly journey is quite like that of Enoch in the Book of the Watchers. Both the early Enoch books and Daniel incorporate material that would not be considered apocalyptic if taken on its own (e.g., the stories in Daniel 1–6). Further, it is important to recognize at least two distinct types of apocalypses—the otherworldly journey, typified by the Book of the Watchers, and the histori-cally oriented apocalypses, such as the Apocalypse of Weeks or Daniel 7–12. The popular stereotypes of apocalypticism are dominated by the historical type, but the otherworldly jour-neys also have an illustrious history in mysticism and even in literature (culminating in Dante's *Inferno*). Finally, while the functions of apocalypses may vary from one situation to another, one may say, on a fairly high level of abstraction, that they serve to exhort and console their addressees. The books of Enoch and Daniel arise out of a cultural crisis precipitated by Hel-lenism and aggravated by the persecution of Antiochus Epiphanes. Regardless of their status within the Jewish community, the authors of these books surely felt relatively deprived, because of the impact of foreign culture and religious persecution. The nature of the crises may vary, however, in other apocalyptic situations.

The definition given above concerns a literary genre. Implicit in that genre, however, is a worldview that can also find expression in other ways (Collins in Collins and Charlesworth 1991, 11–32). The crucial elements of this worldview are (1) the prominence of supernatural beings, angels and demons, and their influence on human affairs and (2) the expectation of a final judgment not only of nations but of individual human beings. Both of these elements can be paralleled elsewhere in the Hellenistic world, but in Jewish tradition they constituted a new and distinctive worldview, as can be seen if we contrast the book of *Enoch* with the Deutero-nomic tradition or with the roughly contemporary writings of Ben Sira or 1 Maccabees. Espe-cially important was the belief in the judgment of the dead and the hope for a blessed immortality. Ancient Israel was exceptional in the ancient world in its reluctance to embrace such notions. In most of the Hebrew Bible, the hope of the individual was for long life, prosper-ity, and offspring, in the context of a prosperous nation. In the apocalyptic literature we still find hope for a glorious kingdom, but the hope of the individual is for eternal glory with the angels. Consequently, the Enoch literature could look on sexual relations with women as defil-ing activity, unworthy of spiritual beings, and the wise men of Daniel could let themselves be killed rather than compromise their convictions. The expectation of judgment after death brought with it a profound change of values and laid the foundation for one of the more signif-icant shifts in spirituality in the Jewish tradition.

☞ THE ROMAN ERA _____

The Spread of Apocalyptic Ideas

The first major cluster of Jewish apocalyptic writings originated in the period shortly before and during the Maccabean revolt. For another comparable cluster of writings we must wait until the next great crisis in Jewish history, the revolt against Rome in 66–70 C.E., which led to the destruction of the Jerusalem Temple. In the intervening period of more than two centuries we do not find many apocalypses, but we find considerable evidence of the spread of apocalyptic ideas in several areas of Jewish life. The following are some examples:

The Dead Sea Scrolls are the subject of a separate essay in this volume. While they do not yield many apocalypses in the literary sense (there are a few fragmentary works of uncertain genre), they provide plenty of evidence for apocalyptic eschatology, most strikingly in the *Scroll of the War of the Sons of Light against the Sons of Darkness.* The sect that produced the major scrolls evidently adapted the apocalyptic tradition for its purposes. We find very little resurrection language, but several texts speak of present fellowship with the angels. It would seem that the sectarians claimed to enjoy in the present the exalted life that was promised to the faithful after death in Daniel and Enoch. The Scrolls are remarkable also for their strongly exegetical character, and the foundational role given to the Torah of Moses. This exegetical focus, coupled with the charismatic authority of the Teacher of Righteousness, may explain why the sectarians did not compose apocalypses in the names of ancient heroes or base their revelations on visionary experience.

The Dead Sea sect is most probably to be identified with the Essenes, whom Josephus describes as one of the three main Jewish groups around the turn of the era. The Sadducees, according to Josephus, rejected belief in angels and in life after death, and so can have had little sympathy for apocalyptic ideas. The Pharisees are said to "attribute everything to Fate and to God; they hold that to act rightly or otherwise rests, indeed, for the most part with men, but that in each action Fate co-operates" (*Jewish War* 2.163). They are also said to believe in some form of resurrection ("the soul of the good passes into another body"). Whether Josephus's account of the Pharisees is accurate is open to question, but presumably it has some basis. By analogy with this account, the *Psalms of Solomon,* which were composed some time after the Roman general Pompey entered Jerusalem in 63 B.C.E., are sometimes ascribed to the Pharisees. These Psalms clearly affirm resurrection and also express the hope that God will raise up an heir to the Davidic line—in effect, a kingly Messiah. Whether the *Psalms* are Pharisaic or not, they show that other groups besides the Essenes were interested in messianism and eschatology.

The *Testament of Moses* is a further witness to eschatological ideas around the turn of the era. We have already referred to this text in our discussion of Daniel. There are indications that the text was originally composed in the Maccabean era and updated later, after the death of Herod the Great in 4 B.C.E. The *Testament* purports to be the parting speech of Moses and is heavily influenced by Deuteronomic theology, with its tendency to see historical crises as punishment for sin. Most important for the present context is the fact that Moses concludes his prediction with the coming of the kingdom of God and the exaltation of Israel to the stars. The *Testaments of the Twelve Patriarchs* are also permeated with an eschatologically oriented view of history, but the *Testaments* are Christian in their present form, and it is difficult to reconstruct a Jewish stratum with any confidence.

One apocalypse that should be dated before 70 C.E. and probably originated in the land of Israel is the Similitudes of Enoch (*1 Enoch* 37–71). The Similitudes are presented as heavenly visions of Enoch, but their content is most notably indebted to the book of Daniel. In *1 Enoch* 46:1, Enoch sees "one who had a head of days and his head was white like wool; and with him there was another, whose face had the appearance of a man, and his face was full of grace, like one of the holy angels." The latter figure is subsequently referred to as "that Son of Man." It is said that his name was named before creation, and later he is seated on a throne of glory, just like the Most High (chapter 62). The wicked are confounded when he is revealed, but the righteous share his life in heaven forever. In chapter 71, Enoch is told "you are the Son of Man who is born to righteousness." There are literary indications that this chapter is a secondary addition to the Similitudes, added perhaps to contradict the Christian claim that Jesus was the Son of Man. In later Jewish tradition, however, Enoch is identified with Metatron, a heavenly viceroy who has much in common with Enoch's Son of Man. The Similitudes are not found among the Dead Sea Scrolls and presumably were the work of a different sect. They are typically apocalyptic in their focus on the coming judgment and the hope for a heavenly afterlife for the righteous.

The *Sibylline Oracles* constitute a distinct genre that flourished in the Jewish Diaspora. Books 3 and 5 of the standard collection were composed in Egypt between the middle of the second century B.C.E. and the early second century C.E. These were in the form of oracles or inspired speech; they include no vision reports or interpretations. They were modeled to some degree on pagan sibylline oracles, but they also show significant similarities to apocalypses of the historical type, insofar as they claim to predict the course of history, which is often divided into periods, and culminate in eschatological change. Surprisingly, neither book 3 nor book 5 of the *Sibylline Oracles* envisages resurrection or the judgment of the dead. Book 5 is considerably more pessimistic and hostile to the Gentiles than book 3, and it probably reflects the atmosphere of the great Diaspora revolt of 115–117 C.E. The fourth book of *Sibylline Oracles* reflects a different tradition (possibly originating in Syria). Here history is divided into four kingdoms and ten generations, and the oracle concludes with a prediction of cosmic conflagration and resurrection. In its present form, book 4 dates from the period after the destruction of the Temple in 70 C.E. There is evidence that an older, Hellenistic oracle has been updated. The fourth kingdom and tenth generation is that of Macedonia; Rome is introduced after the end of the numerical sequence. It is impossible to be sure, however, whether the older oracle included the predictions of conflagration and resurrection, or whether these were part of the update in the Roman era. A somewhat similar oracle is found in books 1 and 2 of the *Sibyllines,* which also divide history into ten generations and end with conflagration, resurrection, and judgment. In this case, however, a Jewish oracle has been updated by a Christian, and the provenance of the Jewish original is uncertain, although there are some grounds for locating it in Asia Minor, around the turn of the era.

One particular motif that appears in the fourth and fifth books enjoyed a prolonged afterlife in sibylline and apocalyptic prophecy. This is the motif of *Nero redivivus* (*Sib. Or.* 4.138; 5.28–34, 138–53, 215–24, 363–70). At the time of Nero's death there was a popular belief that he had escaped and fled to the Parthians. Several pretenders appeared subsequently claiming to be Nero. In the *Sibylline Oracles,* however, the expectation is no longer for the historical Nero but for a figure of mythic proportions: "A man who is a matricide will come from the ends of the earth. . . . He will destroy every land and conquer all. . . . he will destroy many men and great rulers, and he will set fire to all men as no one else ever did" (5.363–69). The figure of *Nero redivivus* also appears in the book of Revelation (Rev. 17:11) and was assimilated to the Antichrist in later tradition.

Finally, mention should be made of the proliferation of eschatological prophets and messianic pretenders in Judea in the first century C.E. John the Baptist and Jesus were most probably eschatological prophets, and several other figures are described by Josephus. When Fadus was governor of Judea (about 45 C.E.) a man named Theudas "persuaded most of the common people to take their possessions and follow him to the Jordan River. He said he was a prophet, and that at his command the river would be divided and allow them an easy crossing" (*Antiquities* 20.97–98). Theudas apparently presented himself as a new Joshua, but his actions might also bring to mind Moses and the exodus. A decade later, a similar movement was instigated by an Egyptian, who "made himself credible as a prophet and rallied about thirty thousand dupes and took them around through the wilderness to the Mount of Olives. From there he intended to force an entry into Jerusalem, overpower the Roman garrison and become ruler of the citizen body" (*Jewish War* 2.261–62). But in another account (*Antiquities* 20.169–71) Josephus says that "he said that from there he wanted to show them that at his command the walls of Jerusalem would fall down and they could then make an entry into the city," clearly evoking the capture of Jericho. Josephus distinguishes prophets of this kind from armed rebels:

> Besides these (the "dagger-men") there arose another body of villains, with purer hands but more impious intentions, who no less than the assassins ruined the peace of the city. Deceivers and impostors, under the pretense of divine inspiration fostering revolutionary changes, they persuaded the multitude to act like madmen, and led them out into the desert under the belief that God would there give them tokens of deliverance. (*Jewish War* 2.258–60)

Unfortunately, these prophets left no writings, but the authors of the books of *Enoch* and Daniel, in their day, could equally well have been said to be fostering revolutionary changes under the pretense of divine inspiration. We have no apocalyptic books that can be dated either to the period leading up to the revolt or to the revolt itself. Yet it seems likely that eschatological prophecies of the kind reported by Josephus played a part in fomenting the rebellion, just as the apocalypses of Daniel and Enoch had played a part in the turmoil of the Maccabean revolution. Josephus claims that "what more than all else incited them to the war was an ambiguous oracle, likewise found in their sacred scriptures, to the effect that at that time one from their country would become ruler of the world" (*Jewish War* 6.312). It is not clear what scriptural passage is in question. (Daniel 7 is often considered a possibility.) Evidently the passage in question was popularly understood as a messianic oracle, but Josephus argues that it actually predicted the rise of Vespasian, who was proclaimed emperor on Jewish soil.

Apocalypse as a Medium of Reflection:
4 Ezra, 2 Baruch, 3 Baruch

The second major cluster of Jewish apocalypses dates from the end of the first century C.E., in the aftermath of the Jewish revolt. 4 Ezra, *2 Baruch,* and *3 Baruch* are all reflections on the catastrophe that had come to pass. While they continue to console and exhort, they represent a rather different use of the genre from that of the early Enoch writings and Daniel. Unlike the "ambiguous oracle" of Josephus, they could scarcely have incited anyone to revolt. Instead they are attempts to understand and come to terms with failure and destruction.

4 Ezra, which is preserved in Latin and several other secondary translations, stands out among the Jewish apocalypses as the most acute formulation of a theological problem. Ezra, located anachronistically in Babylon thirty years after the destruction of Jerusalem, acknowledges the familiar Deuteronomic theory that the destruction was punishment for sin, but then raises an all-too-obvious question: "Are the deeds of Babylon better than those of Zion? Or has

another nation known thee besides Israel? Or what tribes have believed thy covenants as these tribes of Jacob?" (3:31–32). The angel with whom he speaks does not respond to this question directly but tells Ezra: "Your understanding has utterly failed regarding this world, and do you think you can comprehend the way of the Most High?" (4:2). He assures him, however, that "the age is hastening swiftly to its end" (4:26) and proceeds to tell him the signs that will precede the eschaton. Ezra, however, is not easily deterred. He renews his questions about the justice of God, only to be again diverted with an eschatological prediction (6:17–28). Yet a third time Ezra probes more deeply: "O sovereign Lord, behold, thou has ordained in thy law that the righteous shall inherit these things, but that the ungodly shall perish" (7:17). But in that case most of humankind is doomed to perish: "For all who have been born are involved in iniquities, and are full of sins and burdened with transgressions" (7:68). The angel's reply is harsh: "You are not a better judge than God, or wiser than the Most High! Let many perish who are not living, rather than that the law of God which is set before them be disregarded!" (7:19–20). The angel urges Ezra to think about what is to come rather than about what now is (7:16) and discourses on the messianic age and the judgment after death. The Most High, we are told, made not one world but two (7:50), this world for the sake of the many but the world to come for the sake of the few (8:1). Ezra is not consoled:

> It would have been better if the earth had not produced Adam, or else, when it had produced him, had restrained him from sinning. For what good is it to all that they live in sorrow now and expect punishment after death? O Adam, what have you done? For though it was you who sinned, the fall was not yours alone, but ours also who are your descendants. (7:116–18)

Even though he gradually resigns himself to the will of God, he still comments ruefully on the paucity of those who will be saved (9:15).

After the third dialogue, Ezra is told to go into the field and eat the flowers (9:24, 26). After this he has a vision of a woman in mourning. At first Ezra scolds her, for being concerned with her personal grief while "Zion, the mother of us all" is in affliction. Then he tells her not to dwell on her grief but to "let yourself be persuaded because of the troubles of Zion, and be consoled because of the sorrow of Jerusalem" (10:20). While he is speaking, she is transformed into a city with massive foundations. Then the angel Uriel appears and explains to Ezra that the woman was Zion and that God had shown him the future glory of Jerusalem because of his wholehearted grief over her ruin. From this point on, Ezra raises no further complaints. In chapters 11–12 he sees a vision of an eagle rising from the sea that is confronted by a lion. The eagle stands for Rome, and the lion for the Davidic Messiah. In chapter 13 a man rises on clouds from the heart of the sea. He takes his stand on a mountain and repulses the Gentiles, and then gathers in the lost tribes of Israel. In the final chapter, Ezra is inspired to reproduce the Torah that has been burnt, but also seventy secret books that are to be given to "the wise among your people, for in them is the spring of understanding, the fountain of wisdom and the river of knowledge" (14:46–47).

4 Ezra is remarkable for the fact that the pseudonymous author, Ezra, adheres to a theology that is rejected by the angel. Some scholars have argued that Ezra is the voice of heresy, which the author meant to refute, but it is surely implausible that heresy would be given such an authoritative voice. Rather, the dialogue between Ezra and the angel must be taken to reflect the conflict of theologies in the author's heart and mind (Stone 1990, 21–36). In this respect, it is reminiscent of the book of Job, which also articulates a deeply felt problem before submitting

to a divinely imposed solution. Ezra articulates the traditional Deuteronomic theology but finds it wanting. The angel does nothing to rehabilitate this theology, but tells Ezra in effect that God's ways are inscrutable in this world, and that he must be content to wait for the revelation of justice in the world to come. In the end, the eschatological visions carry the day. The high value placed on the seventy secret books in the final chapter is highly significant. While the Torah remains important, it does not contain "the spring of understanding and the fountain of wisdom." That wisdom requires higher revelation, such as Ezra receives in this apocalypse.

The actual eschatology of 4 Ezra, however, is based on the Hebrew Scriptures, although the themes are developed in original ways. There is no influence here from the Enoch tradition. The origin of sin is discussed with reference to Adam. There is no mention of the Watchers. The picture of the future combines various strands of traditional eschatology. In chapter 7 the Messiah (called "my son") is said to reign for four hundred years and then die. After this, there will be seven days of primeval silence, followed by the resurrection and judgment. In this way, the apocalypse accommodates both the expectation of national restoration under a messianic king and the more typically apocalyptic hope for a new creation. We find a similar two-stage eschatology in the roughly contemporary book of Revelation, where Christ reigns on earth for a thousand years before the resurrection and new creation (Revelation 20). In chapters 11–13, 4 Ezra draws heavily on the book of Daniel. The Roman eagle rises from the sea like the beasts in Daniel 7 and is identified as "the fourth kingdom which appeared in a vision to your brother Daniel. But it was not explained to him as I now explain or have explained it to you" (11:11–12). The lion, who has no place in Daniel's vision but is derived from Gen. 49:9, is "the messiah whom the Most High has kept until the end of days, who will arise from the posterity of David." In chapter 13, the man who rises from the sea on clouds is clearly a reinterpretation of the "one like a son of man" in Daniel. He is identified, however, as the Davidic Messiah ("my son"), and the description of his stand on the mountain (Zion) is reminiscent of Psalm 2. The messianic age serves to restore Israel and thereby partially answer one of Ezra's complaints. Ultimately, however, this apocalypse insists that the Most High made not one world but two, and full retribution can only be expected after the resurrection, in the world to come. It should be noted that 4 Ezra has virtually no interest in the heavenly world, despite the role of the revealing angel. There is no sense that the other world is already present, as it is in the Dead Sea Scrolls. Nonetheless, like all apocalypses, it requires the belief that this world is not all there is; hope is based on belief in an alternative universe.

2 Baruch is in many ways a companion piece to 4 Ezra. It is similar in structure and contains both dialogues and visions. Baruch also raises questions about the justice of God, but he does not probe them the way Ezra does. He is more easily satisfied that justice is served by a judgment based on the law (54:14: "justly do they perish who have not loved thy law"). Like Ezra, Baruch asks, "O Adam what have you done to all those who are born from you" (48:42), but a little later he answers his own question: "Adam is therefore not the cause, save only of his own soul, but each of us has been the Adam of his own soul" (54:19). In the end, Baruch warns the tribes that "we have nothing now save the Mighty One and His law" (85:4). The message of the book is that the Jewish people should keep the law and trust in the justice of God. The teaching accords well with that of mainstream rabbinic Judaism.

This message is framed, however, by an eschatological teaching very similar to that of 4 Ezra. "The youth of the world is past, and the strength of the creation already exhausted and the advent of the times is very short" (85:10). There is an elaborate division of history into twelve periods in a vision of a cloud that rains alternately black and white waters (chapters 53–74). The twelfth period, however, is not the last but the restoration after the exile. This in turn is followed by a dark period, which presumably includes the time of the real author. Finally comes the messianic age, symbolized by lightning. In chapters 27–32 the time of tribulation is divided into twelve woes. Then the Messiah is revealed, but after a time "he will return in glory." This presumably corresponds to the death of the Messiah in 4 Ezra, although it is expressed in more positive terms. The resurrection and judgment follow. In chapters 35:1–47:2 there is an allegorical vision, in which a vine rebukes a cedar. The vine, representing the Messiah, rebukes the cedar, just as the lion rebuked the eagle in 4 Ezra. Although there is no allusion to Daniel in the vision, the interpretation identifies a sequence of four kingdoms (chapter 39). Like 4 Ezra, 2 Baruch shows no awareness of the Enoch tradition, but integrates the eschatology of Daniel and of traditional messianism into a Deuteronomic theology.

4 Ezra and 2 Baruch can be seen as two voices in the discussion of theodicy in the wake of the destruction of Jerusalem. Both have much in common with emerging rabbinic Judaism and place a high value on the law, although neither deals with specific halakic issues. The common eschatological presuppositions of these works show that such ideas were widely shared in Palestinian Judaism at the end of the first century. Whatever role apocalyptic ideas may have played in stirring up revolutionary fervor at the outbreak of the war, they are not used for that purpose in these books. Here eschatology becomes an element in theological reflection. Although both books assure us that the time is short, neither conveys a great sense of urgency. What is important is that there will be an eventual judgment that will establish that God is in control. Hope is sustained but deferred. There is a clear attempt here to integrate different strands of Jewish eschatology, providing both for national restoration on earth and for the resurrection of the dead in a new creation.

A quite different reaction to the destruction of Jerusalem can be found in the Greek apocalypse of 3 Baruch, which was most probably composed in the Egypt (Harlow 1996). This text opens with Baruch grieving over the destruction of Jerusalem. An angel appears to him and tells him: "Do not be so distressed about the condition of Jerusalem . . . argue with God no more, and I will show you other mysteries greater than these. . . . Come and I will show you the mysteries of God." The angel then escorts Baruch on an upward tour of five heavens. (There has been much speculation as to whether there were originally seven, the usual number in apocalypses of this period, but there is no good reason to believe that anything has been lost. Rather, Baruch's revelation is limited insofar as he is not taken up to the highest heaven.) In the course of this ascent he sees various cosmological mysteries and also the places where the dead are rewarded and punished. In the fifth heaven he sees the archangel Michael, who takes the merits of the righteous up to the presence of the Lord. It appears that people are judged strictly on their individual merits regardless of their membership in a covenant people. The final chapter of the apocalypse indicates that Israel has suffered the curses of the covenant:

> Inasmuch as they angered me by what they did, go and make them jealous and angry and embittered against a people that is no people, against a people that has no understanding. And more—afflict them with caterpillar and maggot and rust and locust and hail with flashes of lightning and wrath and smite them with sword and with death, and their children with

demons. For they did not heed my voice, neither did they observe my commandments nor do them. (16:2–3)

The reference to "a people that is no people" alludes to Deut. 32:21, while the remainder of the passage recalls the curses of the covenant (Lev. 26:16; Deut. 32:24). A Jew might take some comfort in the thought that the Romans are "a people that is no people," but there is little consolation for Israel here. Whereas 4 Ezra and 2 Baruch had held that individuals who broke the law deserved to perish, 3 Baruch seems to hold that Jerusalem deserved its fate on the same grounds. All that is left in this apocalypse is the merit of individuals and the consolation of pondering the heavenly mysteries.

3 Baruch does not express the only reaction to the destruction of Jerusalem in the Hellenistic Diaspora. The fifth Sibylline Oracle, written around the time of the Diaspora revolt of 115–117 C.E., rages against Rome for its insolence in destroying the Temple. In the tradition of the Third Sibyl, however, this oracle lacks the typically apocalyptic motifs of resurrection and judgment of the dead. While it contains some prophecies of hope for a restored Jerusalem, it ends on an extraordinarily pessimistic note by describing a battle of the stars, at the end of which all the stars are destroyed and heaven is left starless. While the anger against Rome that we find in these oracles may have been a factor in the events that led to revolt in the Diaspora, the sibyl ultimately ends on a note of bitter resignation.

The Decline of Historical Apocalypses

After the failure of a series of revolts against Rome in the late first and early second centuries C.E., the rabbis who undertook the codification of Jewish tradition seem to have turned away from apocalypticism. Mythological and eschatological motifs can still be traced in the Talmud and midrashim, but the primary emphasis in rabbinic Judaism was placed on the Torah and its interpretation. Claims of higher inspiration were viewed with skepticism and suspicion. With the exception of the book of Daniel, the apocalypses of the Hellenistic and Roman periods were not preserved by the rabbis. Those books have come down to us through Christian hands, in various translations—Greek, Latin, Syriac, Ethiopic, Old Church Slavonic. Only in the last half-century have we recovered fragments of apocalyptic literature in Aramaic and Hebrew in the Dead Sea Scrolls.

In general, the "historical" type of apocalypse fades from view in the second century C.E., both in Judaism and in Christianity, although it would reemerge in the Byzantine period and in the Middle Ages. The heavenly journey becomes the standard medium of apocalyptic revelation. The ascent through a numbered sequence of heavens had its origin in Judaism, as can be seen in 3 Baruch and 2 (Slavonic) Enoch, although the provenance of the latter work is far from clear. This strand of apocalypticism finds its continuation in Judaism in the mystical Hekalot literature, notably in the work known as 3 Enoch or Sefer Hekalot, which represents the culmination of the Enoch tradition. Apocalypses of this type also proliferate in Christianity after the first century C.E. They reflect a world with little anticipation of revolutionary change but with a strong orientation toward another, heavenly world beyond this one.

CONCLUSION

The Apocalyptic Worldview

Our rapid sketch of developments over a period of six hundred years allows us to draw some conclusions about the origins of apocalypticism in ancient Judaism. Apocalypticism is a worldview that is indebted to ancient Near Eastern myths and to Hebrew prophecy, but which arose in response to the new challenges of the Hellenistic and Roman periods. The essential ingredients of this worldview were a reliance on supernatural revelation, over and above received tradition and human reasoning; a sense that human affairs are determined to a great degree by supernatural agents; and the belief that human life is subject to divine judgment, culminating in reward or punishment after death. In the context of Israelite and Jewish tradition, this worldview was novel in the Hellenistic period, especially in its expectation of a final judgment, which had far-reaching implications for ethical values and attitudes in this life. The dominant form of Jewish apocalypticism, which we have traced in this essay, also anticipated a denouement of history, culminating in divine intervention and a judgment of all nations on a cosmic scale. This judgment, however, would typically be followed by a resurrection of the dead, which allowed for retribution on an individual as well as a national scale. This worldview found its typical medium of expression in the rather loose macro-genre "apocalypse," which was a report of supernatural revelation, with an eschatological dimension. But the worldview could also come to expression in other genres, that were not directly reports of visions or otherworldly journeys.

The worldview that we have sketched here is fairly broad and could be embodied in different sociological formations and theological schools. The Enoch literature says little, at least explicitly, about the law of Moses. In contrast, the Torah is fundamental to the priestly apocalypticism of the Dead Sea Scrolls. The "proto-apocalyptic" prophecies of Isaiah 65–66 seem to question the importance of Temple and sacrifice. Even though the Dead Sea sect was evidently alienated from the Jerusalem Temple, it evidently still attached great importance to cultic worship. The origin of evil might be variously understood in terms of the myth of the Watchers, with an emphasis on the role of fallen angels, or in terms of the sin of Adam, underlining human responsibility. Finally, we should not think that apocalyptic ideas were confined to sectarians living apart from the rest of Judaism, on the model of the Qumran community. The book of Daniel was accepted as canonical scripture by all Jews and Christians. 4 Ezra and especially *2 Baruch* have much in common with rabbinic theology and give no indication that they were produced in sectarian communities. Apocalypticism, then, was not the exclusive property of any one sect or movement, although it was characteristic of various movements from time to time.

The Functions of Apocalyptic Literature and Ideas

Most scholars would probably agree with the view of David Hellholm that apocalypses are "intended for a group in crisis with the purpose of exhortation and/or consolation, by divine authority" (1986, 27). A few qualifications are in order, however. All the texts we have considered in this essay can be said to have been written for a group in crisis, if only because the entire Jewish people can be said to have been in crisis for most of the period in question. The crises were of various kinds. For the authors of the Book of the Watchers, it was a cultural crisis, when the world was changed by Hellenism; for the author of 4 Ezra it was a crisis of theodicy, the apparent failure of divine justice in light of the destruction of Jerusalem. Since the "group in crisis" can be either the whole Jewish people or a specific group with a specific problem, like the Qumran sect, the designation is only of limited help. The same may be said of the sociological theory of relative deprivation: almost everyone can feel deprived relative to someone or something. Nonetheless, it is true that all the apocalypses we have considered here are born out of a sense that the world is out of joint. The visionaries look to another world, either in the heavens or in the eschatological future, because this world is unsatisfactory. This sense of dissatisfaction is not necessarily an invariable aspect of apocalyptic expectations. In principle, it is possible to conceive of an apocalypticism of the powerful. Divine revelation can be used to buttress established authority and one might look for its ultimate confirmation in the eschatological judgment. (Virgil's *Aeneid* might arguably be taken to exemplify this kind of apocalypticism.) But in practice none of the Jewish apocalyptic writings of the Second Temple period reflects the viewpoint of established power. Typically, the appeal for divine intervention is necessitated because the world is believed to be in the grip of hostile powers.

Apocalypses surely were written to exhort and console. We should note, however, that exhortation and consolation are not the same thing, and that the nature of the exhortation is in no way implied in the apocalyptic form. Some of the apocalypses we have reviewed here were militant: the Apocalypse of Weeks and the Animal Apocalypse may be understood to exhort their readers to support the Maccabean revolt. The "ambiguous oracle" reported by Josephus was also evidently understood as a call to arms. Other apocalypses are quietistic. Daniel shows little enthusiasm for the Maccabees. 4 Ezra and *2 Baruch* are primarily reflections on a catastrophe that has befallen. The exhortation of *2 Baruch* is quite explicitly directed to Torah observance. In some of these texts, the expectation of an "end" seems to neutralize any urge toward militant action: God will act in the proper time; the pious person should wait patiently.

The consolation of apocalyptic hope may have been considerable in the short term, but it was highly prone to disillusionment. It is in the nature of apocalyptic eschatology that it cannot be fully realized in this life. Even when the hopes could be realized in principle, they most often failed to materialize. The Jewish visionaries rarely ventured specific dates for their predictions, and so avoided the pitfalls that beset such groups as the Millerites in modern times. Nonetheless, the eventual rejection of the apocalypses by the rabbis bespeaks a sense of disillusionment that is readily understandable. The pathos of apocalyptic hope is nicely captured in the alleged exchange between Rabbi Akiba and R. Yoḥanan b. Torta at the time of the Bar Kokhba revolt. When Akiba hailed Bar Kokhba as "the king, the Messiah," Yoḥanan allegedly replied: "Akiba, grass will grow between your cheekbones and he [the Messiah] will not have come." Apocalyptic hope is invariably hope deferred. Nonetheless, it has persisted as a recurring feature of Western religion for over two thousand years. While it can never deliver on its promises, it continues to speak eloquently to the hearts of those who would otherwise have no hope at all.

⮞ BIBLIOGRAPHY

Blenkinsopp, J. 1990. "A Jewish Sect of the Persian Period." *Catholic Biblical Quarterly* 52:5–20.

Charlesworth, J. H., ed. 1983. *The Old Testament Pseudepigrapha,* Volume 1. New York: Doubleday. Translations and annotations of most of the relevant noncanonical literature.

Cohn, N. 1993. *Cosmos, Chaos, and the World to Come.* New Haven: Yale University Press. Review of mythological backgrounds, arguing for the primacy of Zoroastrianism.

Collins, J. J. 1984. *The Apocalyptic Imagination.* New York: Crossroad. Reprint, Grand Rapids: Eerdmans, 1998. Introduction to the Jewish apocalypses in historical context.

———. 1993. *Daniel.* Hermeneia. Minneapolis: Fortress Press. Comprehensive introduction to the book of Daniel.

Collins, J. J., ed. 1979. *Apocalypse: The Morphology of a Genre.* Semeia 14. Chico, Calif.: Scholars Press. Analytical outline of the genre in the ancient world.

Collins, J. J., and J. H. Charlesworth. 1991. *Mysteries and Revelations.* Apocalyptic Studies since the Uppsala Colloquium. Sheffield: Sheffield Academic Press. Eight studies on developments in the study of apocalypticism in the 1980s.

Cook, S. L. 1995. *Prophecy and Apocalypticism: The Postexilic Social Setting.* Minneapolis: Fortress Press. Study of late prophecy with extensive anthropological parallels.

Festinger, L., H. W. Riecken, and S. Schachter. 1956. *When Prophecy Fails: A Social and Psychological Study of a Modern Group That Predicted the Destruction of the World.* New York: Harper.

Hanson, P. D. 1975. *The Dawn of Apocalyptic.* Philadelphia: Fortress Press. Ground-breaking sociological study of postexilic prophecy.

Harlow, D. C. 1996. *The Greek Apocalypse of Baruch (3 Baruch) in Hellenistic Judaism and Early Christianity.* Leiden: E. J. Brill. Study of *3 Baruch* in both its Jewish and its Christian redactions.

Hellholm, D. 1986. "The Problem of Apocalyptic Genre." *Semeia* 36:13–64.

Hellholm, D., ed. 1983. *Apocalypticism in the Ancient Mediterranean World and the Near East.* Tübingen: Mohr. Proceedings of International Colloquium at Uppsala in 1979, with comprehensive coverage of ancient sources and rich diversity of viewpoints.

Himmelfarb, M. 1983. *Tours of Hell: An Apocalyptic Form in Jewish and Christian Literature.* Philadelphia: University of Pennsylvania Press.

———. 1993. *Ascent to Heaven in Jewish and Christian Apocalypses.* New York: Oxford University Press.

Milik, J. T. 1976. *The Books of Enoch.* Oxford: Clarendon Press. First publication of the Enoch fragments from Qumran.

Murphy, F. J. 1985. *The Structure and Meaning of Second Baruch.* Atlanta: Scholars Press. Excellent recent study of *2 Baruch.*

Nickelsburg, G. W. E. *1 Enoch.* Hermeneia. Minneapolis: Fortress Press, 2001. Comprehensive commentary on *1 Enoch.*

Rowland, C. 1982. *The Open Heaven.* New York: Crossroad. Synthetic treatment of apocalyptic literature emphasizing its mystical aspects.

Sacchi, P. 1996. *Jewish Apocalyptic and its History.* Sheffield: Sheffield Academic Press. Collected essays on Jewish apocalypticism, originally published in Italian.

Stone, M. E. 1984. "Apocalyptic Literature." In *Jewish Writings of the Second Temple Period,* edited by M. E. Stone, 383–441. Philadelphia: Fortress Press. Excellent short survey of apocalyptic literature.

———. 1990. *Fourth Ezra.* Hermeneia. Philadelphia: Fortress Press. Comprehensive commentary on *4 Ezra.*

Tigchelaar, E. C. 1996. *The Prophets of Old and the Day of the Lord.* Leiden: E. J. Brill. Study of Zechariah and the Book of the Watchers.

Tiller, P. A. 1993. *A Commentary on the Animal Apocalypse of 1 Enoch*. Atlanta: Scholars Press. Detailed commentary on the Animal Apocalypse.

VanderKam, J. C. 1984. *Enoch and the Growth of an Apocalyptic Tradition*. Washington: Catholic Biblical Association. Study of the early Enoch tradition against its Mesopotamian background.

von Rad, G. 1965. *Theologie des Alten Testaments*. 4th ed. Munich: Kaiser. Argument that apocalyptic literature is rooted in ancient wisdom.

4

Apocalypticism in the Dead Sea Scrolls

Florentino García Martínez
University of Groningen

IF "APOCALYPTICISM" IS BROADLY DEFINED (as it is in this Encyclopedia) as "the belief that God has revealed the imminent conclusion of the ongoing struggle between good and evil throughout history," there can be no doubt that the Qumran community was an "apocalyptic" community. The writings that most probably can be considered a product of the Qumran community and which better represent its thought show clear indications that the authors believe that their own lives and the life of the community were part of the ongoing struggle between good and evil, that God had revealed to them the approaching end of the struggle, that they were preparing themselves for an active participation in the final climax, and even that they were already living somehow in the final phase.

Since some of the elements that show the apocalypticism of the Scrolls, such as the participation in the final struggle of several messianic figures have been dealt with in other articles in this volume (see especially chapter 6 below) I will present a summary of the other most relevant topics: the origin of evil; the periods of history and expectation of the end; the communion with the heavenly world; and the eschatological war.

At the outset, it seems necessary to offer a short *status quaestionis* with reference to the literature on the topic listed at the end of this article.

The hard questions posed by Klaus Koch (1972) definitively ended the optimism of the previous decade of research, which saw in the Dead Sea Scrolls the solution to all the problems that had vexed scholarship in the field of apocalypticism. The announcement that the most characteristic apocalypses, such as Enoch or Daniel, were abundantly represented in the new finds, the discovery that other compositions previously unknown had characteristics similar to these apocalypses and could therefore be legitimately considered new apocalypses, the awareness that the most typical sectarian writings had a remarkable eschatological dimension and showed a very radical dualistic thinking, and above all the fact that the group from which the manuscripts were supposed to have come was a secluded community, providing for the first time a model for the sociological background of the apocalypses all helped to create a *pan-Qumranism* in the investigation of apocalypticism. But after many years of intensive research, this optimism proved to be ill grounded, and the contribution of Hartmut Stegemann to the Uppsala Colloquium in 1979 concluded that the expected master key to unlock the secrets of apocalypticism had not been found in the Dead Sea Scrolls. The Qumran manuscripts had not provided the solutions hoped for; the apocalyptic elements to be found within the Scrolls were scanty, and they could be foreign bodies, to which it is impossible to assign any central position in the life or organization of the Qumran group (Stegemann 1983). At the same time, there was a growing awareness of the inadequacy of the traditional way of defining apocalypticism by a mélange of literary and thematic elements, or by a mixing of form and content. On the one hand, a large number of elements used to characterize apocalyptic were to be found in many compositions that no one would dream of defining as apocalypses, and, on the other hand, many compositions recognized as apocalypses were lacking elements that were thought to be characteristic of apocalypticism. The intensive efforts of the Society of Biblical Literature group on the genre apocalypse, which culminated with the publication of *Semeia* 14, brought the necessary refinement of the terminology used to chart the problem and provided a definition of apocalypse commonly accepted today (Collins 1979). The definition of *Semeia* 14 and its distinction of two basic types of apocalypses—the *historical* and the *heavenly ascent* types—proved very fruitful and paved the way for the developments of the next decade. In these years we saw the development of the *syntagmatic* or *text-linguistic* analysis of several apocalypses as well as the *sociological approach* to apocalypticism (in which the insights gained by the study of millenarian movements through history [medieval millenarianism, Puritan groups in England in the sixteenth century, etc.], or by means of anthropological study of contemporary sectarian apocalyptic movements or groups [fringe groups in the United States, for example] were applied to the study of apocalypticism, but also the detailed study of single apocalypses [such as VanderKam 1984; Stone 1990]) and a systematic mapping of the developments of apocalypticism in a historical perspective, both in a synchronic (Collins 1984) and in a diachronic way (Sacchi 1996 [English 1997]). As a result, we can observe a decline in the importance of the Dead Sea Scrolls for understanding the phenomenon of apocalypticism, and a more differentiated way of understanding the individual apocalypses and the phenomenon of apocalypticism. Nonetheless, the contribution of the Scrolls to this field of study remains considerable.

As I formulated the issue in the introduction to my book *Qumran and Apocalyptic*:

> The study of the Qumran manuscripts has completely transformed the way in which we nowadays understand the most ancient apocalypses, those composed within the Enochic tradition, has had a profound effect on the study of the origins and the development of the apocalypse of Daniel and has indicated a number of new factors demonstrating the variety and the ideological richness of the apocalypses written within, or transmitted by, the Qumran community itself. (García Martínez 1992, xi)

I think this is still a fair, and rather nonpolemical, representation of the situation. Everybody agrees now on the characteristics of the literary genre apocalypse and its basic division of "cosmic" and "historical" apocalypses. Everybody agrees also that in the definition of the literary genre apocalypse the function of the genre (absent in the definition of *Semeia* 14) should be included in one way or another. And most tend to agree that this function could be defined as was done in *Semeia* 36: an apocalypse is "intended to interpret present earthly circumstances in the light of the supernatural world and of the future, and to influence both the understanding and the behavior of the audience by means of divine authority." This has resulted in a better understanding of the best representatives of both basic types: the books of Enoch and the book of Daniel. This would also, in my opinion, allow some of the compositions from Qumran lately published to be categorized as apocalypses despite their fragmentary condition.

Everybody also agrees that apocalypticism cannot be reduced to the literary genre apocalypse. The number, certainly limited, of apocalypses found at Qumran (or the even smaller number of apocalypses that can be attributed to the activity of the group) (Dimant 1994) do not need to limit us in the study of the apocalypticism of the Scrolls. The major sectarian scrolls, which are certainly not apocalypses, provide us in spite of their generic differences with a worldview similar to the worldview we find in the apocalypses, a worldview that can be considered representative of the group's way of thinking. Since this worldview has been clearly influenced by ideas characteristic of well-known apocalypses, mainly Enoch and Daniel, it can be described as "apocalyptic." In the words of John J. Collins:

> A movement or community might also be apocalyptic if it were shaped to a significant degree by a specific apocalyptic tradition, or if its worldview could be shown to be similar to that of the apocalypses in a distinctive way. The Essene movement and Qumran Community would seem to qualify on both counts. (Collins 1997b, 37)

Everybody also agrees that the worldview we find in the Scrolls presents also obvious differences from the ideas of these apocalypses. But there are several ways to interpret these differences, and so scholars are divided.

The basic question seems to be: Are the different solutions given to the same problem in Qumran and in some apocalyptic writings disagreements within a common framework in the interpretation of the same original myth (as seems to be the case between the Book of Watchers and the Epistle of Enoch, for example, or between 4 Ezra and *2 Baruch*), or are they due to the use of different premises, referring to different myths? Should we see the relationship as one of continuity within a certain tradition or rather of discontinuity and derivation from different traditions?

For Paolo Sacchi, the differences remain within the same basic framework and we can speak thus of a continuity within the tradition (Sacchi 1996). For Collins, they indicate derivation from a different tradition. In the words of Collins: "I agree with Sacchi, against Carmignac and Stegemann, that apocalypticism can not be reduced to a literary genre. . . . I do not agree, however, that apocalypticism can be reduced to a single stream of tradition, or to a single socially continuous movement" (Collins 1997b, 298).

It is usually assumed that the circles responsible for the different Enochic compositions formed a single movement or belonged to a single tradition in spite of the differences, implying something more than a common worldview. After all, we usually speak of a "prophetic tradition" and of "a wisdom tradition," and we imply by this something more than a common worldview, in spite of our ignorance of the concrete sociological basis for these "prophetic" and "sapiential" traditions. In this way it does indeed seem appropriate to speak of an "Enochic tradition" even if the sociological basis remains rather vague. And because the Enoch books are apocalypses, it seems also appropriate to speak of an "(Enochic) apocalyptic tradition" (VanderKam 1984). By the same token it would be equally legitimate to speak of a "(Qumranic) apocalyptic tradition," and it would be equally legitimate to investigate the relationships (genetic or other) between the several apocalyptic traditions.

In my opinion, the *status quaestionis* boils down to the following: Is apocalypticism simply a worldview (an umbrella term for different apocalyptic traditions), or it is something more? Can the cluster of ideas we find in the Qumran writings be attributed to an apocalyptic tradition? As we shall see in the following summaries, the cluster of ideas appearing in the sectarian scrolls is something more than an umbrella term; it represents a genuine apocalyptic tradition, connected with, but different from, other apocalyptic traditions.

THE ORIGIN OF EVIL AND THE DUALISTIC THOUGHT OF THE SECT

The core of the oldest part (the Book of the Watchers) of the oldest apocalypse (*1 Enoch*) is dedicated to giving an explanation of the origin of evil in the world. And the explanation given to this topic, using the old myth of the "rebellion in heaven," is that evil was not introduced into the world by men, but is the result of the sin of the Watchers, the fallen angels lead by Asael and Shemiḥaza, who consorted with women and taught them heavenly secrets. The fallen angels introduce a disruption in the harmonic order of nature: "The whole earth has been devastated by the works of the teaching of Asael; record against him all sins" (*1 Enoch* 10:7). Sin originates in heaven not in earth, and it is introduced on earth by the action of angelic beings. Within the Enoch tradition itself, we will find a direct refutation of the conclusion of the Book of the Watchers about the heavenly origin of evil. In the last composition incorporated into the Enochic collection, the Epistle of Enoch, we can read (in Ethiopic, the Greek version is somewhat different): "I swear to you, sinners, that as a mountain has not, and will not, become a slave, nor a hill a woman's maid, so sin was not sent to the earth, but man of himself created it" (98:4). It is impossible not to conclude that the author of the Epistle is completely turning around the conclusion of the Book of the Watchers in order to arrive at the opposite conclusion. In spite of this direct rebuttal, both compositions, the Book of the Watchers and the Epistle of Enoch, seem to have originated within the same ideological tradition (which some people call the Enoch school, much in the same way others talk about a Johannine school); they were in any case considered compatible enough not only to fraternize in the same shelves of a library but to be included as part of the same book, our *1 Enoch*.

I thus conclude that it was perfectly possible within one and the same tradition to hold divergent (and even opposite) views on some central theological problem; and that we cannot expect dependence to be expressed only as agreement.

We do not know precise antecedents for the idea put forth by the author of the Book of the Watchers. In the short form in which we find the myth in Genesis 6 it is not put to use to explain the origin of evil. Nor is it used in this way by the book of *Jubilees*, which is dependent on the Book of the Watchers in many respects, but does not accept the idea that evil comes into the earth through angelic mediation and gives a different explanation of the origin of evil. For *Jubilees*, sin begins in the earth with the fall of Adam, long before the fall of the angels. *Jubilees*, on the other hand, presents the fallen angels as an army, led by Mastema, who is described as a prince, and who obtains from God that a tenth of the fallen spirits will not be directly destroyed but will be left under his command in order to harass, mislead, and destroy humanity. The idea that evil originates in heaven is also dismissed in the wisdom tradition as represented by Sir. 15:11: "Do not say, 'It was the Lord's doing that I fell away.'" But Sirach does not attribute evil either to the sin of Adam, which he never mentions (some manuscripts even change the famous reference to the sin of Eve in Sir. 25:24, attributing it to the "enemy"). Sirach introduces the idea of the "inclination" (the *yēṣer*): "God created man in the beginning and placed him in the hand of his inclination" (15:14). But he also insists that everything is in the hands of God: "In the fullness of his knowledge the Lord distinguished them and appointed their different ways. Some he blessed and exalted, and some he made holy and brought near to himself; but some he cursed and brought low, and turned out of their places" (33:11–12). Most of the interpreters rightly insist that the *yēṣer* in Sirach is very different from the *yēṣer* as it will be understood in 4 Ezra (the *cor malignum*) and especially in the rabbinic tradition, where it is even identified with Satan. Sirach does not exploit the potentiality of the *yēṣer*, and at the end, he is unable to resolve the tension created by his adherence to the traditional biblical conception, which preserves free will and the equally biblical conception that underlines God's omnipotence. As Collins says: "Sirach's over-all position remains ambiguous" (Collins 1997b, 370), and he limited himself to observing the duality of evil and good: "As evil contrasts with good, and death with life, so are sinners in contrast with the just" (33:14).

It is my contention that all these strands of thought are interwoven in the thought on the origin of evil that we find in the Dead Sea Scrolls, and that all of them contribute in some way to shape the new solution they gave to the problem. It is clear that the Scrolls know the myth as it is presented in the Book of the Watchers. Not only have several copies of the composition appeared in Cave 4, but the story itself is used in some other Qumran compositions such as 4Q180, a *pesher* on the periods, in which Asael plays a leading roll. Even more significantly, the *Damascus Document* (CD) uses the story of the Watchers as the first example in a review of human unfaithfulness to the will of God (CD 2:15–16). Similarly, *Jubilees* has had a deep influence in the thought of the community, which sees the angelic forces as organized armies under an angelic leader, and which even knows Mastema as one of the names used for this leader. Copies of *Jubilees*, of course, are among the compositions best represented in their library, as are (to a lesser extent) copies of Ben Sira. No wonder then that the *yēṣer* of the wisdom tradition has also left its traces within the Dead Sea Scrolls. As expected, its presence is more notorious in the wisdom texts, such as *4QSapiential A*, where we find expressions such as: "Do not be deluded with the thought of an evil inclination" (4Q417 2 ii 12), but it is also used in more clearly sectarian compositions such as CD 2:15–16: "so that you can walk perfectly on all his paths and not follow after the thoughts of a guilty inclination."

However, the most characteristic explanation of the origin of evil, the one we find in the Treatise of the Two Spirits, does not limit itself to incorporating and blending together these influences but offers us an original solution to the problem. This treatise, embodied in the *Community Rule* (1QS 3:13–4:26; all translations from the Dead Sea Scrolls are taken from García Martínez 1996), is at the same time the most systematic exposition of the dualistic thinking of the community.

The treatise begins with a solemn introduction (3:13–15), followed by the basic principle: "From the God of knowledge stems all there is and all there shall be. Before they existed he made all their plans, and when they come into being they will execute all their works in compli-

ance with his instructions, according to his glorious design without altering anything"
(3:15–16).

From this deterministic formulation the author deduces the basic dualistic structure of
humankind, expressed with the traditional symbols of light and darkness: "He created man to
rule the world and placed within him two spirits so that he would walk with them until the
moment of his visitation: they are the spirits of truth and of deceit" (3:17–19). The author
develops in detail his dualistic conception, applying it not only to each individual but to all
humanity, which he describes as divided into two camps (two dominions), led respectively by
the Prince of Light and the Angel of Darkness: "And in the hand of the Prince of Light is dominion over all the sons of justice; they walk in the paths of light. And in the hand of the Angel of
Darkness is total dominion over the sons of deceit; they walk in the path of darkness"
(3:20–21). He even extends this dualistic division explicitly to the angelic world, which is
divided, as are humanity and each individual, in two camps: "He created the spirits of light and
of darkness and on them established all his deeds, and on their paths all his labors. God loved
one of them for all eternal ages and in all his deeds he takes pleasure for ever; of the other one he
detests his advice and hates all his paths forever" (3:25–4:1). The treatise goes further, describing the characteristic deeds that result from the dominion of each one of the two angelic hosts,
the conflicting human conduct that results from the influence of the opposing spirits, and the
contrasting retribution of each person according to their share of light and darkness.

Not only the origin of sin is explained by the treatise in this way. The sin of each individual
also finds an explanation in this dualistic context. Human life is seen as a battle between the
forces of light and darkness, a violent conflict in which there is little left to human initiative:

> Until now the spirits of truth and of injustice feud in the heart of man and they walk in wisdom
> or in folly. In agreement with man's birthright in justice and in truth, so he abhors injustice;
> and according to his share in the lot of injustice he acts irreverently in it and so abhors the
> truth. For God has sorted them into equal parts until the appointed end and the new creation.
> (4:24–25)

A person can, of course, sin; even the righteous do. But these sins are explained as caused by the
influence of spirits of darkness:

> Due to the Angel of Darkness all the sons of justice stray, and all their sins, their iniquities, their
> failings and their mutinous deeds are under his dominion in compliance with the mysteries of
> God, until his moment, and all their punishments and their period of grief are caused by the
> dominion of his enmity; and all the spirits of their lot cause the sons of light to fall. (3:21–24)

At the end, at the time of God's visitation, however, sin will disappear and justice will triumph:

> God, in the mysteries of his knowledge and in the wisdom of his glory, has determined an end
> to the existence of deceit and on the occasion of his visitation he will obliterate it for ever. Then
> truth shall rise up forever in the world which has been defiled in paths of wickedness during the
> dominion of deceit until the time appointed for judgment. Then God will refine, with his
> truth, all man's deeds, and will purify for himself the configuration of man, ripping out all
> spirit of deceit from the innermost part of his flesh, and cleansing him with the spirit of holi-
> ness from every irreverent deed. He will sprinkle over him the spirit of truth like lustral water
> (in order to cleanse him) from all the abhorrences of deceit and from the defilement of the
> unclean spirit. In this way the upright will understand knowledge of the Most High, and the

wisdom of the sons of heaven will teach those of perfect behavior. For these are those selected by God for an everlasting covenant and to them shall belong the glory of Adam. (4:18–23)

This eschatological perspective is an essential part of the treatise and puts in perspective the solution to the problem of evil given by its author.

For him, as for the Book of the Watchers, evil clearly has its origins not on earth but in heaven. But the author the Treatise of the Two Spirits is apparently not satisfied with the solution given in the Book of the Watchers; after all, if the Watchers are the origin of evil on earth, their own capability of doing evil also needs to be explained. The solution given to the problem by the author of the Treatise is much more radical than the one given in the Book of the Watchers. For him there is no rebellion in heaven. The Watchers are part and stock of the evil spirits, the army of the Prince of Darkness; they are created as evil spirits directly by God. Evil comes thus from heaven, and directly from God. The author also has used the conception of the angelical army as represented in *Jubilees*, and has fully developed the deterministic and dualistic implications of the *yēṣer* of the wisdom tradition. But its thought has a radicality that cannot be explained only by these influences. It was recognized almost as soon as the scroll was published that the thought of the Treatise of the Two Spirits is most akin to the myth of Persian dualism with its twin spirits, the twin sons of the supreme God, one identified as good and the other as evil from the beginning, and one associated with light and the other with darkness. This myth is already present in the oldest part of the Avesta, the *Gāthās*, generally considered to be the work of Zoroaster. The dualism of the Treatise of the Two Spirits does not imply the initial option of humans for one or the other spirit in the manner of the Persian myth, and, even more importantly, the Treatise emphatically views the two spirits as created by God and completely subordinate to him. It is thus far removed from the later Persian thought that considers evil to be primordial. Yet it seems clear that the thought of the author of the Qumran text is deeply indebted to some form of Zoroastrian thought and has used it in order to radicalize the ideas he has received from the apocalyptic and sapiential traditions.

It is true that the Avesta is known to us in a collection from the Sassanian period, but the centrality of dualism in Zoroastrian thought is already attested by Plutarch (*On Isis and Osiris*), and, although we do not know the exact channels of transmission, the possibility of its influence in a Jewish context poses no special problem during the Hellenistic period.

Although the explanation of the origin of evil and the expression of dualistic thought in the Treatise of the Two Spirits is perhaps not the most widespread idea in the Dead Sea Scrolls, we find it attested in enough different writings that we may consider it one of the trademarks of the thought of the Qumran community. I have already quoted a sentence of the *Damascus Document* in which the human *yēṣer* is qualified as "guilty." One of the parenetic sections of the same document, CD 2:2–13, shows not only a very close verbal parallel to the Treatise of the Two Spirits, but the same emphatic deterministic outlook. Another section, CD 4:11–18, describes Israel under the dominion of Belial and the people falling in his three nets, and CD 5:18–19 offers a perfect example of dualistic thinking presenting Moses and Aaron raised up by the Prince of Light and Jannes and his brother Jambres by the hand of Belial. The end of the original composition (as shown by 4QD[b] 18 v) contains a ceremony of expulsion from the assembly which exactly parallels the ceremony of entry into the covenant of 1QS 1–2 and has the same general dualistic overtone.

Another composition closely related to the worldview of the Treatise is 4QAmram, an

Aramaic composition recovered in five copies, all very poorly preserved. In it, Amram tells his sons about a vision he has had in which two angelic figures who "control all the sons of Adam" quarrel over him. One of them "rules over darkness"; the other "rules over all what is bright." Each figure has apparently three names, although the only name preserved is Melchireša'. The assumed counterpart, Melchizedek, is the central figure of another composition from Cave 11, where he is the agent of the eschatological judgment and saves "the men of his lot," freeing them from the hand of Belial and the spirits of his lot. Although visions and revelations are involved, the literary genre of the composition is more that of testament than apocalypse. The Qumranic origins of 4QAmram have been disputed because it is in Aramaic, but the fact that the same cluster of ideas and expressions is to be found in a series of liturgical texts (4Q280–4Q287) which explicitly mention the Council of the *yaḥad* and abound in curses against Melchireša', Belial, and other angelic figures seems to me to place the composition within the corpus of sectarian writings.

The deterministic view of the Treatise appears also in a good part of the *Hodayot*, especially in the so-called Hymns of the Teacher, to the point that some people have speculated that both compositions were penned by the same author, the Teacher of Righteousness. The dualistic understanding of the world is equally obvious in the *War Scroll*. There it is not related to a description of human nature but concerns the development of human history and its final denouement in the eschatological war.

Summarizing the evidence on this point, I think we can conclude that the Dead Sea sect inherited from the Enochic tradition a view of the origin of evil that it further developed using elements coming from other traditions (like the Sapiential tradition and Zoroastrianism) so as to arrive at a full dualistic and deterministic view of the world.

☞ THE PERIODS OF HISTORY AND THE EXPECTATION OF THE END

One of the most characteristic features of the "historical" apocalypses is the division of history into periods and the expectation that God will intervene in the last of these periods in order to bring an end to evil in the world. Introducing these periods into history allows the apocalypses the possibility to integrate the past and the present reality with the future that the author intends to "reveal" and with the expected intervention of God, which will bring the end of history. The systems used to divide history into periods, bringing in this way some order into the chaos, are based on the numbers 4, 7, 10, 49 (7 x 7), 70, and even 490 (70 x 7 or 10 x 49). We find different ways of indicating this division of history into periods in different apocalypses, or even within the same composition. Daniel, for example, uses the schema of four successive kingdoms but also, and most characteristically, the schema of seventy weeks (of years), transforming the seventy years of Jeremiah into 490 years, which equals ten jubilees and can be correlated with the use of the number 10 in other apocalyptic compositions.

Within the different components of *1 Enoch*, we find different ways to express the division of history into periods. In the Book of the Watchers there is an allusion to a division of seventy periods before the end: "Bind them (the Watchers) for seventy generations under the hills of the earth until the day of their judgment and of their consummation, until the judgment which is for all eternity is accomplished" (10:12). The so-called Animal Apocalypse, which presents the protagonists in the history of Israel as various animals, also introduces periods into history; seventy shepherds pasture the sheep, each at his own time (89:59), and these seventy shepherds are divided into four unequal groups which pasture the sheep during four periods of different length (corresponding to the four kingdoms of Daniel). At the end of these periods the judgment takes place, the Messiah comes, and all the sheep become white bulls. But the most interesting view of the division of history is the one found in the so-called Apocalypse of Weeks, embedded in the Epistle of Enoch and now restored to its original order (disturbed in the Ethiopic translation) with the help of the Aramaic fragments from Qumran. As in Daniel, history is here divided into "weeks," presumably weeks of years, but the schema is based on the number 10, or, better said, on a combination of 7 and 10. The author compresses history from the birth of Enoch to his own days in seven weeks, and places himself obviously at the end of the seventh week, a week in which an apostate generation has arisen and at the end of which "the chosen righteous from the eternal plant of righteousness will be chosen [or "rewarded" according to other Ethiopic manuscripts], to whom will be given sevenfold teaching concerning his whole creation" (93:10). He obviously belonged to the chosen group to which he addresses his composition. Similarly, the author of Daniel belonged to the *maśkîlîm*, and the author of the Animal Apocalypse to the *ḥāśîdîm*. The great originality of the Apocalypse of Weeks lies in the fact that history does not end with this week. The Apocalypse goes on to reveal what will happen in the following weeks, introducing the organizing principle also in the future, and unfolding the progressive development of meta-history: in the eighth week a sword will be given to the righteous, who execute judgment on the sinners, and at its end "a house will be built for the great king in glory forever" (91:12–13); in the ninth week "the judgment of the righteous will be revealed to the whole world, all the deeds from the impious will vanish from the whole earth, and the world will be written down for destruction" (91:14); in the tenth week (in its seventh part) there will be apparently the judgment of the Watchers (the Ethiopic text is rather confused) and "the first heaven will vanish and pass away, and a new heaven will appear" (91:15–16) Then: "And after this there will be many weeks without number forever in goodness and in righteousness, and from then on sin will never again be mentioned" (91:17). The author of the Apocalypse of Weeks periodizes not only history but meta-history; the "end" is for him not one event, but rather the unfolding of a process in which several moments can be discerned.

In the Dead Sea Scrolls we find attested almost all the models used in the apocalyptic writings to periodize history, and also a conception of the "end" of history as an unfolding process in which several moments can be discerned.

A composition in Aramaic, preserved in two copies, 4Q552 and 4Q553, contained apparently a division of history following the model of the four kingdoms of Daniel; but the text is so badly preserved that we can say almost nothing. There is at least one vision and there is question of an interpretation. There is a king and there are trees that are able to talk and answer questions; one of the trees gives his own name as Babel, and of him it is said that he rules over Persia. This is almost all that can be gathered from the surviving fragments, but because it is also said that these trees are four, we can assume the author was following the well-known model of the four kingdoms.

Another very fragmentary text contained a commentary expressly dedicated to the division of history into periods that comprise the diverse phases of human history, which have been preordained by God and engraved in the heavenly tablets (4Q180–181). It begins: "Interpretation concerning the ages which God has made." This composition, certainly authored within the Qumran community and marked by the strongly deterministic outlook of the Treatise of the Two Spirits, could have provided us with a complete view of the problem within the community, but unfortunately it has also been badly preserved. Even combining the material of the two manuscripts (which are not necessarily part of the same composition) only part of the assertions concerning the first period (the ten generations from Noah to Abraham) can be recovered: the first is characterized by the sin of the fallen angels; the last by the sin of Sodom and Gomorrah. It is not clear how many periods were reckoned, but one of the fragments used the expression "in the seventieth week," apparently implying that a system of subdivisions was worked out inside the main divisions.

Another composition (4Q390) uses a system of jubilees to offer a review of the history of Israel, similar to the historical reviews of the apocalypses and of the beginning of the *Damascus Document*, but put into the mouth of God: "And when this generation passes, in the seventh jubilee of the devastation of the land, they will forget the law, the festival, the sabbath and the covenant, and they will disobey everything and do what is evil in my eyes" (4Q390 1:6–9). The author also uses other units to mark the divisions: a week of years ("and there will come the dominion of Belial upon them to deliver them up to the sword for a week of years" (4Q390 2:3–4), and a period of seventy years: "and they will begin to argue with one another for seventy years, from the day on which they break this vow and the covenant. And I shall deliver them to the hands of the angels of destruction and they will rule over them" (4Q390 2:6–7). Curiously enough, all the periods preserved in this document are characterized by a negative connotation: infidelity to the covenant and all sorts of transgressions, and especially the dominion of Belial and the "angels of destruction," a clear allusion to the Mastema of the book of *Jubilees*.

More clear, although also fragmentary, is the system we find in 11QMelchizedek, a thematic *pesher* that interprets Leviticus 25 (the jubilee year), Deuteronomy 15 (the year of release), and Isaiah 52 and 61 (which proclaim the liberation of the prisoners), applying these (and other biblical texts) to the eschatological period, the "last days." In this text, which knows Daniel and refers explicitly to it, history is divided into ten jubilees. The preserved part of the composition concentrates on the last of these ten jubilees: "This will happen in the first week of the jubilee which follows the nine jubilees. And the day of atonement is the end of the tenth jubilee in which atonement will be made for all the sons of God and for the men of the lot of Melchizedek" (11Q13 2:6–8). The protagonist of the text is Melchizedek, who is presented as a heavenly figure. The remission of debts of the biblical text is interpreted as referring to the final liberation, which will occur during the Day of the Expiation. Melchizedek, the agent of this liberation, is presented as the eschatological judge mentioned in Ps. 7:8–9 and Ps. 82:1–2. He is also presented as the chief of the heavenly armies, the leader of the "sons of God," who will destroy the armies of Belial, identifying his figure in terms of practical functions with the "Prince of Light" (a figure we find in 1QS 3:20, CD 5:8, and 1QM 13:10) and with the angel Michael (a figure appearing in 1QM 17:6–7). The victory of Melchizedek against Belial and the spirits of his lot, will usher in an era of salvation, which is described in the words of Isaiah.

In this text we have encountered the most usual expression within the Dead Sea Scrolls to indicate the period of the end, the phrase *ʾaḥărît hayyāmîm*. The expression is well attested (in Hebrew and once in Aramaic) within the Hebrew Bible. The phrase occurs more than thirty times in the nonbiblical scrolls and is especially frequent in exegetical compositions. The phrase originally meant "in the course of time, in future days," and this (noneschatological) meaning seems to be best suited to many of the biblical occurrences of the expression, although its use in Isaiah 2, Micah 4, Ezekiel 38, and Daniel 2 and 10 may have a more specifically eschatological meaning.

In Qumran this is certainly the case, as the expression seems to be used to designate the final period of history. Nowhere are the precise limits of this period defined, but it is the last of the divinely preordained periods and the period in which the community exists. According to the latest study published on *'aḥărît hayyāmîm* in the Scrolls (Steudel 1993), the phrase may refer, depending of the context, to the past, to the present, or to the future from the point of view of the writer. The last days are thus a period already started but not yet completed, somehow coextensive with the present of the community. As CD 4:4 put it: "the sons of Zadok are the chosen of Israel, 'those called by name' who stood up at the end of days."

The text most often quoted as asserting that the last days have already begun is 4QMMT, where the complete expression occurs twice in the hortatory section. But in the first occurrence (C 13–15) the expression may have a meaning more akin to the biblical usage, and the second—"And this is the end of days" (C 21)—can be linked both to the preceding sentence in the past tense ("We know that some of the blessings and the curses as written in the book of Moses have come, and this is the end of days," and to the following sentence in the future tense: "And this is the end of days, when in Israel they will return to the Law." In neither case will the phrase have the fully developed eschatological connotation characteristic of other Qumran usages; it will rather represent a first stage in the development of Qumranic thought.

The most characteristic usage is the one we find in the exegetical compositions, where the meaning of the biblical text, "for the last days," is directly applied to the life of the community, which is seen as fulfillment of the prophetic text. The phrase has two different aspects in the Scrolls. The last days are a period of testing and refining, a period of trial, but the expression also designates the time beyond the trial, the period in which salvation will start.

The first element is explicit in 4Q174, which interprets Ps. 2:1 as referring to the elect of Israel in the last days and continues: "That is the time of refining which comes . . . ." The participle used can be translated with a past or with a future meaning, but there is no doubt that the time involved is a time of trial: Belial is mentioned, and also a remnant, and the text explicitly refers to Dan. 12:10, where the just "shall be whitened and refined." Other texts use the same expression, "time of refining," referring to the persecution of the Teacher of Righteousness or of the men of the community (4QpPs^a 2:17–19) or to locate during the last days the hostile actions of the "violators of the covenant," as well as the suffering and tribulations of its members and its leaders (1QpHab, 4QpNah, etc.).

The second element is equally explicit. The last days comprise the beginning of the messianic age. The same 4Q174 locates in the last days the rising up of the "shoot of David" and the construction of the new temple. A *pesher* on Isaiah (4Q161), commenting on Isa. 11:1–5, presents the same "shoot of David" (also called the Prince of the Congregation in the same document, and the Messiah of Israel in other writings) waging the eschatological war against the Kittim in the last days, destroying its enemies and judging and ruling over all the peoples. CD 6:11 extends the duration of age of wickedness "until there arises he who teaches justice at the end of days." 11QMelchizedek announces the ushering in of the age of salvation in the last days. The *Rule of the Congregation of Israel in the Last Days* (1QSa), which legislates for the eschatological community, assumes as a matter of fact that the Messiahs are present in these last days and take an active part in the life of the community. One of the most famous and disputed passages of the Scrolls announces God's begetting the Messiah "with them." For the rest, as L. Schiffman (1989) put it: the document describes the eschatological future as a mirror of the present. 1QSa reflects the everyday life of the community as we know it from the *Community Rule*—its purity concerns, its hierarchical structure, and its meals—but addresses at the same time particular concerns of the communities of the *Damascus Document*, as if indicating that in the last days the *yaḥad* community and the communities of the camps will be reunited in a single eschatological congregation.

The precise limits of the end of days are nowhere clearly stated, but it is said that this period of time will be closed by God's "visitation." In the Treatise of the Two Spirits we read: "God, in the mysteries of his knowledge and in the wisdom of his glory, has determined an end to the existence of deceit and on the occasion of his visitation he will obliterate it forever" (1QS 4:18–19). It is thus a period of time of limited duration, and it would be surprising if the members of the community had not attempted to calculate exactly the moment when the evil would be obliterated forever. Indeed, in some texts indirect traces of these calculations can be found. I do not think (as Steudel does) that the Day of Atonement of the tenth jubilee of 11QMelchizedek could gives us this date, nor that it can be provided by the 390 years of the beginning of the *Damascus Document* (the year 72 B.C.E.). But I do think that other texts, the *pesher* Habakkuk and the *Damascus Document* preserve traces of these calculations.

This last text tells us that the traitors to the covenant "shall not be counted in the assembly of the people and shall not be inscribed in their list, from the day of the gathering in of the unique Teacher until there arises the Messiah of Aaron and Israel" (19:35–20:1). A little further on it adds: "And from the day of the gathering in of the unique teacher, until the destruction of the men of war who turned back with the man of lies, there shall be about forty years" (20:13–15). If we identify the "men of war who turned back with the man of lies" with the traitors "who turned and betrayed and departed from the well of living waters," and if we understand both the coming of the Messiahs and the destruction of the men of war as an indication of the beginning of the divine visitation, we can see here a trace of these calculations: the end will come *about* forty years after the death of the Teacher. I do not think we can calculate an exact date on the basis of this "about forty years," but its presence in the *Damascus Document* is a sure indication that such calculations were made.

The other text, 1QpHab 7:1–14 does not offer any more precision, but it is a precious witness to the way the community coped when the calculations proved to be wrong and the expected end did not materialize. The text concerns Hab. 2:1–3, which is quoted, section by section, and interpreted:

> And God told Habakkuk to write what was going to happen to the last generation, but he did not let him know the end of the age. And as for what he says: "So that the one who reads it may run": Its interpretation concerns the Teacher of Righteousness, to whom God has disclosed all the mysteries of the words of his servants, the prophets. "For the vision has an appointed time, it will have an end and will not fail." Its interpretation: the final age will be extended and go beyond all that the prophets say, because the mysteries of God are wonderful. "Though it might delay, wait for it; it definitely has to come and will not delay." Its interpretation concerns the men of truth, those who observe the Law, whose hands will not desert the service of truth when the final age is extended beyond them, because all the ages of God will come at the right time, as he established for them in the mysteries of his prudence.

In its extreme conciseness, this text teaches us many things: that the true meaning of the word of the prophet concerns the last period of history, the last days in which the community lives, although this meaning is not known by the prophet; that this deep meaning is known to the community thanks to the revelation the Teacher of Righteousness has received; that the core of this revelation is that the community lives in the last days, but this revelation does not include the exact time of arrival of the final salvation; that this arrival is part of the divine mystery, which includes prolongation as part of the divine plan; that the moment of salvation will come anyway, at the precise moment God has decreed; and that what really matters for the members of the community is not to abandon the service of truth during this prolongation.

The text clearly implies that the community has calculated the arrival of the end but that their prediction has not been fulfilled at the moment of the writing of the *pesher:* "the final age has extended beyond them." The text also shows that the community has already found a way to explain this delay without losing either the certainty of living already in the last days or the hope of the approaching final salvation.

This calculation of the end is nothing new. Daniel had already attempted to make even more specific calculations of the same end, and the biblical text shows traces of new calculations when the end did not come (Daniel 12).

Summary

The historical apocalypses were characterized by the division of history into periods and the expectation that God would intervene in order to bring an end to the evil in the world. These ideas are abundantly represented in compositions we can attribute to the Qumran community that are of very different literary genres. They also seem to have profoundly shaped the worldview of the sect, which considered itself to be living in the last period of history.

COMMUNION WITH THE HEAVENLY WORLD

One of the elements that distinguishes apocalyptic literature from the traditional biblical worldview is an increased interest in the heavenly world. This is shown by the number, and the concrete names, of the heavenly beings, be they angels or demons, that we encounter in this literature (Mach 1992). These heavenly beings appear named for the first time in such books as *1 Enoch* and Daniel, where their numbers "cannot be counted," but they are no fewer than "a thousand thousands and ten thousand times ten thousand." The angelology of *1 Enoch* is particularly developed, where a multitude of angelic beings exercise multiple functions. They are servants of the deity who stand before the throne of glory or outside the heavenly residence; they are intercessors before God, ministers of the heavenly liturgy but also executioners of the divine will. They are intimately related to the seer; they interpret dreams for him and disclose to him heavenly secrets. They guide the visionary in his heavenly tours and communicate to him divine decisions. They are also deeply involved in the affairs of this world. They rule over the stars, the winds, the rains, the seasons, and over all celestial elements which form part of their own names. They record the deeds of human beings and execute the punishment of the Watchers and of the sinners, but also they help the righteous and watch over Israel.

Already in the classical description of the Essenes it is said that they cherished "the knowledge of the names of the angels." So it comes as no surprise that the angelology of the scrolls is rather developed, more in line with the angelology of *1 Enoch* than with the sober angelology of the biblical texts. We have already mentioned the dualistic division of the angelic world with the Prince of Light and the Angel of Darkness at the head of two angelic hosts, and we have also alluded to Belial, the most common name for the demonic leader in the Scrolls, to the "angels of destruction" (a designation that echoes the proper name of Mastema, their angelic leader in the book of *Jubilees*), and to Michael, the opponent of Belial in the eschatological war. But in the Scrolls we find also explicitly stated that another of the names of this angelic prince is Melkireša^c; (4Q544), in parallel to Melchizedek (11Q13), who in the Scrolls is apparently identified with Michael and with the Prince of Light.

In the Scrolls we find also a strongly hierarchical structure of the heavenly world, similar to the one that appears in the apocalypses, with different roles and different degrees of proximity to the deity. The Scrolls also attribute to angels many of the functions assigned to angelic beings in *1 Enoch* and other apocalyptic writings: angels interpret dreams and visions to the seer (such as to Amram); they guide the visionary on a tour to the future city and the future temple (as in the New Jerusalem), or read for him from a heavenly book or inscription in the temple (as in 11Q18, 19 5–6). A fragmentary Aramaic composition (4Q529) even records "The Words of the book which Michael spoke to the angels of God."

But the most characteristic view of the heavenly world we find in the sectarian scrolls is the idea, expressed several times, that the angels are present in middle of the community, and consequently that its members somehow share already the life of the angels. This communion with the heavenly world and fellowship with the angels is explicitly stated as the reason for the high degree of purity required of those who take part in the eschatological battle: "And every man who has not cleansed himself of his 'spring' on the day of battle will not go down with them, for the holy angels are together with their armies" (1QM 7:5–6). But it is also invoked as an absolute reason to refuse entry into the eschatological community to anyone with an imperfection:

> No man defiled by any of the impurities of a man shall enter the assembly of these; and everyone who is defiled by them should not be established in his office amongst the congregation. And everyone who is defiled in his flesh, paralyzed in his feet or in his hands, lame, blind, deaf, dumb or defiled in his flesh with a blemish visible to the eyes, or the tottering old man who cannot keep upright in the midst of the assembly, these shall not enter to take their place among the congregation of famous men, for the angels of holiness are among their congre[gation.] (1QSa 2:3–9)

That this fellowship with the angels is not something reserved for the eschatological time, for the "last days" to which these two documents are addressed, is proved by one of the copies of the *Damascus Document* from Cave 4, which legislates who can become members of the present community:

> And no-one stupid or deranged should enter; and anyone feeble-minded and insane, those with sightless eyes, and the lame or one who stumbles, or a deaf person, or an under-age boy,

none of these shall enter the congregation, for the holy angels are in its midst. (4Q267 17 i 6–9)

It is also shown by the repeated use of this idea both in *Rule of the Community* and in the *Hymns*, perhaps the most characteristic documents of the Qumran community, as indicated by the following two samples:

To those whom God has selected he has given them as everlasting possession; until they inherit them in the lot of the holy ones. He unites their assembly to the sons of the heavens in order (to form) the council of the Community and a foundation of the building of holiness to be an everlasting plantation throughout all future ages. (1QS 11:7–9)

And I know that there is hope for someone you fashioned out of clay to be an everlasting community. The corrupt spirit you have purified from the great sin so that he can take his place with the host of the holy ones, and can enter into communion with the congregation of the sons of heaven. (1QH 11:20–22)

The idea of communion with the heavenly world gives us the key to understanding the document in which the angelology of the Qumran group is most explicitly stated: the *Songs for the Sabbath Sacrifice*. This composition, the title of which has been taken from the sentence that begins each one of its thirteen songs, has been found in ten fragmentary copies: eight from Cave 4, one from Cave 1, and another one found in the excavations of Masada. All of them were made between the second half of the first century B.C.E. and the first half of the first century C.E. (Newsom 1985, 19). The peculiarities of the language, dominated by nominal and participial sentences with elaborate construct chains, the omnipresence of constructions with the preposition *l-*, many lexical novelties, and peculiar syntax, indicate that the original composition should not be dated very much earlier than the oldest copy.

The composition comprises thirteen songs intended for consecutive sabbaths, apparently designed to be repeated in each quarter of the year. Each song starts with a fixed formula but has no fixed end, and each one consists of a call to different sorts of angelic beings to praise the deity. Although the angels are insistently exhorted to praise, nowhere in the composition is their praise recorded, except as "the serene sound of silence" (4Q405 19 7), or "the voice of a divine silence" (4Q405 20–22 7) of the blessing.

The first four songs deal with the establishment of the angelic priesthood, its responsibilities and functions in the heavenly sanctuary ("[Because he has established] the holy of holies among the eternal holy ones, so that for him they can be priests [who approach the temple of his kingship,] the servants of the Presence in the sanctuary of his glory" [4Q400 1 i 3–4]), as well as with the relationship of the angelic priesthood to the human priesthood: "And how will our priesthood (be regarded) in their residences? What is the offering of our tongue of dust (compared) with the knowledge of the divinities?" (4Q400 2 6–7). The fifth song deals with the eschatological battle: "the war of the gods in the per[iod . . .] for to the God of the divinities belong the weapons of war [. . .] the gods run to their positions, and a powerful noise [. . .] the gods in the war of the heavens" (4Q402 4 7–10), placing this eschatological battle in the same deterministic perspective we have seen in the Treatise of the Two Spirits: "Because from the God of knowledge comes all that existed for ever. And through his knowledge and through his decision all that is predestined exists for ever. He does the first things in their ages and the final (things) in their appointed periods" (4Q402 4, completed with the copy from Masada). The sixth and eighth songs detail respectively the seven praises uttered by the seven sovereign angelic princes who are the seven high priests of the seven heavenly sanctuaries, and the praises by their seven deputies, "those second among the priests who approach him, the second council in the wonderful dwelling among the seven . . . among all those having knowledge of eternal things." The seventh song, the center of the whole cycle, contains a very elaborate exhortation to praise, followed by the praise uttered by the different elements of the heavenly temple: "the foundations of the holy of holies, the supporting columns of the highest vault, and all the corners of his building," but also "all its beams and walls, all its shape, the work of his construction." This praise is continued in more detail in songs 9–11, which proceed with the description of the praise of the elements of the heavenly temple, described as animate beings, from the outside in the ninth song ("the lobbies of their entrances, spirits who approach the holy of holies"), to the inside in the tenth song, as far as the veil of the sanctuary with all that is engraved there, to reach finally in the eleventh song the inside of the *děbîr*, which describes the praise uttered by all its elements "living gods are all their works and holy angels the images of their forms." The twelfth song describes the appearance of the chariot-throne, the movement of the heavenly beings which surround it and the praises they utter:

> They bless the image of the throne-chariot (which is) above the vault of the cherubim, and they sing the splendor of the shining vault (which is) beneath the seat of his glory. And when the *ofanim* move forward, the holy angels go back; they emerge among the glorious wheels with the likeness of fire, the spirits of the holy of holies. Around them, the likeness of a stream of fire like electrum, and a luminous substance with glorious colors, wonderfully intermingled, brightly combined. The spirits of the living gods move constantly with the glory of the wonderful chariots. And (there is) a silent voice of blessing in the uproar of their motion, and they praise the holy one on returning to their paths. (4Q405 20–22 8–13)

The climax of the whole composition is reached in the thirteenth song, in which the sacrifices that appear on the heading of each song are finally mentioned: "agreeable offerings," "the sacrifices of the holy ones," "the odor of their offerings," "the odor of their libations." The angels are described as officiating priests wearing the ephod and the breastplate, and the praise of the whole heavenly temple is summarized (11Q17 cols. 10–11).

Although the *Songs* do not preserve personal names of the angels (except perhaps the name of Melchizedek in two broken instances) and it is difficult, not to say impossible, from the generic names used (gods, holy ones, glorious ones, spirits, angels, princes, priests, deputies, angels of the face, angels who approach, angels who serve, and so on) to extract the assigned or intended functions of the different classes of angels, there is no doubt that the number of beings and the differentiation of the heavenly world in the *Songs* is as great and variegated as it is in other apocalypses. In the *Songs* even all the material elements of the heavenly abode—the structures of the heavenly temple and the components of the chariot-throne—are presented as animated heavenly beings of angelic nature who utter praise and participate in the heavenly liturgy. And, though the hierarchical structure of the angelic realm is somewhat blurred in the *Songs,* at least there is explicit mention of the seven princes and their seven deputies in the sixth and eighth songs. These are clearly two categories of angelic beings superior to the others, the first corresponding perhaps to the seven archangels of the Greek text of *1 Enoch* or to the four archangels of the Ethiopic text, who are also named in other Qumran scrolls.

In spite of the nonpolemical and neutral character of the *Songs* and of the absence of clearly sectarian terminology in the composition, the abundant parallels with other clearly sectarian scrolls, such as the 1QH or 1QS, suggest that the *Songs* are a product of the Qumran community. Other considerations supporting this view include the use of *lĕmaśkîl* in the headings (which is common to many sectarian compositions); the close parallels between the description of the angelic praise and the heavenly temple in the *Songs* and in compositions such as 4QBerakot (4Q286–290) and the *Songs of the Maskil* (4Q510–511), whose sectarian character cannot be doubted; the great number of copies found; the late date of all of them and the equally late date assumed for the original. The idea of communion with the angels, which we find to be characteristic of the Qumran community, provides the most illuminating setting for the composition.

The function of the *Songs* within the community has been diversely explained. For those who value most the detailed descriptions of the components of the heavenly temple, the text would function as revelation of the heavenly realities. For those who underline the numinous character of the language used and the importance of the description of the chariot-throne, the *Songs* would function as an instrument of mystical meditation or even mystical ascent to the divine throne, similar to the mystics of the *Merkavah*. For those who emphasize the priestly character of the *Songs,* its function would be to validate and justify the priestly character of a community that has no control over the earthly temple by its association with the heavenly cult. In my view the most likely function of the *Songs* within the Qumran community was to substitute for the participation in the sacrifices of the earthly Temple the association with the heavenly liturgy and the sabbath offerings. We know that the community, in the expectation of the new situation "at the end of the days" had developed an interim theology of the community as spiritual temple, in which praise substituted for the sacrifices (see 1QS 8:4–10; 9:3–6). We have also seen (in the texts from 1QSa and 1QM quoted above) that the community had developed the idea of fellowship with the angels, and other texts show that the priests of the community considered themselves to be associated with the angelic priesthood. The blessing over the priests, the sons of Zadok, says: "May the Lord bless you from his holy residence. May he set you as a glorious ornament in the midst of the holy ones. For you may he renew the covenant of eternal priesthood. May he grant you a place in the holy residence" (1QSb 3:25–26), and even more clearly in the next column: "You shall be around, serving in the temple of the kingdom, sharing the lot with the angels of the face and the council of the community . . . for eternal time and for all the perpetual periods" (1QSb 4:25–26). The recitation of the *Songs of the Sabbath Sacrifice* on the successive sabbaths of the four quarters of the year gave the members of the community the possibility of participating in the sabbath sacrifice of the heavenly temple, compensating for their absence from the sabbath sacrifice of the Jerusalem Temple and giving a concrete expression to the life shared with the angels already in the present.

Summary

The complexity and structured organization of the heavenly world that we find in the apocalypses are represented also in the Scrolls, which add a most notable element: the idea that the angels are already living among the members of the community. This fellowship with the angels is not restricted to the future but is a reality also of the present and allows participation in the liturgy of the heavenly temple.

☞ THE ESCHATOLOGICAL WAR

One of the basic themes of the prophets is the announcement of the final triumph of God and of the people of Israel against the evil forces and against the enemies who oppress the people in the present. Very often this triumph takes the form of a future military victory in which the Israelites will destroy the hostile powers who actually oppress them. This expectation is rooted in the realities of the political history of the people of Israel with its repeated experience of invasions and defeats by foreign powers and in the confidence that the God of Israel, who has overpowered the forces of chaos, will deliver his people from oppression. Although in some cases this liberation takes the form of a victory against a very concrete enemy (such as in the various oracles of Jeremiah against different nations), very often it is generalized in the form of a victory against all the nations (Psalm 2) or against a mythical enemy, such as Gog, king of Magog, who represents all the hostile powers (Ezekiel 38–39); a famous oracle of the prophet Joel links this victory with the day of the Lord, when the nations will be judged (Joel 3:9–16)

The apocalypses develop further this idea of the victory over all the nations, placing it in a clear eschatological perspective (as in the Animal Apocalypse, which ends with the destruction of all the hostile nations [1 Enoch 90]), and introduce in this eschatological war, as participants or as protagonists, the angelic forces with a celestial leader (as in Daniel, where Michael is the leader who overpowers the angels of the nations).

In the Scrolls the biblical elements of the final victory against all the nations are clearly present, and they are placed in an eschatological perspective. 4QFlorilegium (4Q174) interprets Psalm 2 in the context of the "end of days" and "the time of the trial"; 4QpIsaᵃ (4Q161) refers to Magog and "the war of the Kittim" together with the Branch of David, the Davidic Messiah who participates in the eschatological victory; the same figure, called there "the Prince of the Congregation," appears in the Damascus Document as "the scepter" of the oracle of Balaam "who will smite the children of Sheth" (CD 7:20–21). The angelic participation in the final battle is also well attested in the Scrolls, which refer to "the war of the heavenly warriors" (1QH 11:35), and which (as we have already seen) anticipate the final victory of the forces of light against the forces of darkness "at the time of his visitation" in the Treatise of the Two Spirits (1QS 3–4).

But in the Scrolls the eschatological battle does not simply coincide with the biblical and apocalyptic vision of the final victory against the foreign nations, because it comprises the victory against all evil forces. The dividing line is not between Israel and the foreign nations but between the Sons of Light (which are the elected ones of Israel) and the Sons of Darkness (a term that covers not only pagans but also unfaithful Israelites). In the thought of the Qumran community, the eschatological battle will not be restricted to a battle against the foreign nations; it will also be a battle against all the evildoers, including the part of Israel that has not joined the community.

The document in which the thought of the group on the eschatological battle and final victory is best reflected is the Rule of the War of the Sons of Light against the Sons of Darkness (1QM), which has been best preserved in a copy from Cave 1, but which is also attested in several fragmentary copies from Cave 4 (4Q492, 4Q494–496). Other manuscripts, such as 4Q491 and 4Q493, have preserved materials related to this composition or even different recensions of the same composition, while two other manuscripts (4Q285 and 11Q11) that also deal with the eschatological war may represent part of the lost end of 1QM or may come from another composition dealing with the same topic (Duhaime 1995).

The contents of 1QM may be summarized as follows:

Column 1 and part of column 2 contain a summary of the development of the war, which ends with the victory of the Sons of Light and the restoration of the cult in Jerusalem.

Columns 2–9 record the organization and the military tactics that should be employed in this war: rules of the trumpets to conduct each one of the phases of the war (2:15–3:11); rules of the banners with their inscriptions (3:13–5:2); rules of the formation of the battle arrays, the weapons, and the tactical movements (5:3–7:7); and the rules to conduct the war with the different trumpets (7:9 until the end of column 9).

Columns 10–14 contain the prayers that are to be said during the different phases of the war: in the camps (cols. 10–12), during the battle (col. 13), and after the victory (col. 14).

Column 15 to the end of the manuscript preserves another version of the war against the Kittim, with the exhortation of the high priest before the battle, the first engagement, the use of the reserve troops when the Belial army seems to have the upper hand, the final battle and the celebration after the victory.

The unity and coherence of the document in its present form have led some scholars to defend the unity of composition of 1QM. But, because of certain repetitions, inconsistencies, and especially because there are two basically different conceptions of the eschatological war, most scholars recognize that 1QM is the result of the fusion of at least two documents.

One of them, inspired by Daniel 11–12 and Ezekiel 38–39, developed the idea of an eschatological conflagration on seven lots in which each one of the sides has the upper part during three lots and which ends with the victory of God. As stated in col. 1: "In the war, the sons of light will be the strongest during three lots, in order to strike down wickedness; and in three (others), the army of Belial will gird themselves in order to force the lot of [. . .] to retreat. . . . And in the seventh lot, God's great hand will subdue [Belial, and a]ll the angels of his dominion and all the men of [his lot]" (1QM 1:13–15). The same idea is found in cols. 14–19, in which, in spite of the bad state of preservation, we can discern that these seven lots alternate, a victory following a defeat, until the final victory of the Sons of Light in the seventh lot, when "the Kittim shall be crushed without a [remnant . . .] when the hand of the God of Israel is raised against the whole horde of Belial" (1QM 18:2–3). This war is envisaged in two levels, the human and the angelic: "On this (day), the assembly of the gods and the congregation of men shall confront each other for great destruction" (1QM 1:10), but the angelic hosts appear to have no leader apart from God himself, who at the end decides the victory. These two ideas characterize cols. 1 and 14–19.

These two elements allow us to distinguish this original document from the second one, reflected in cols. 2–13, in which the war of seven lots is transformed in a progressive battle of forty years against each one of the nations enumerated in Genesis 10, and in which the angelic army is guided by an angelic leader, the Prince of Light: "From of old you appointed the Prince of Light to assist us, and in [. . .] and all the spirits of truth are under his dominion" (1QM 13:10). This progressive battle, which evidently is based on the forty-year schema of Exodus, does not know any interruption other than the obliged rest of the sabbatical years, five in a forty-year period. This leaves thirty-five years for the conduct of the war. For the author of this document (or for the redactor who has united it with the previous one), the war of seven lots of the first document seems to be understood as the first seven of the forty years, of which the seventh year is not the final victory but the first sabbatical year, and the other six either a general preparation for the war or a general battle of the whole congregation against the main enemies, according to the interpretation one gives to the problematic expression of 2:9. The remaining twenty-nine years are dedicated to eradicating all the enemies of Israel: nine years of war against the sons of Shem, ten years against the sons of Ham, and the last ten years against the sons of Japheth:

> During the remaining thirty-three years of the war, the famous men called to the assembly, and all the chiefs of the fathers of the congregation shall choose for themselves men of war for all the countries of the nations; from all the tribes of Israel they shall equip for them intrepid men, in order to go out on campaign according to the directives of war, year after year. However, during the years of release they shall not equip themselves in order to go out on campaign, for it is a sabbath of rest for Israel. During the thirty-five years of service, the war will be prepared (or waged) during six years; and all the congregation together will prepare it (or wage it). And the war of the divisions (will take place) during the remaining twenty-nine years. (1QM 2:6–10)

If the idea of the forty-year war is clearly based on the biblical tradition and reminds us of the wandering in the wilderness, it is difficult to find a biblical precedent for the idea of the war of seven alternate lots, although there is an obvious similarity between the seven lots and the sabbatical structures that inform so much of Jewish thought. The closest parallel to this idea is provided by a passage in Plutarch that attributes a similar idea to the Persians: "Theopompus says that, according to the Magians, for three thousand years alternately the one god will dominate the other and be dominated, and that for another three thousand years they will fight and make war, until one smashes up the domain of the other. In the end Hades shall perish and men shall be happy "(*On Isis and Osiris* 47; see chapter 2 above).

Although there are many uncertainties in this text, it provides some basic elements, like two supernatural forces that battle each other and alternately hold sway until the victory of the supreme God, which may have helped to give shape to the thought of the author of the *War Scroll*. This possible Persian influence comes at no surprise since we have already noted the most plausible Persian influence on the Treatise of the Two Spirits, and the first document of the *War Scroll* shares the characteristic dualistic framework of this tractate.

The redactor who has combined both documents to form the *War Scroll* that we have in 1QM has also used other elements. Most prominent is a collection of prayers for the time of the war, which could have had an autonomous existence. This is suggested by the text itself:

> The High Priest will take up position, and his brothers the priests and the levites and all the men of the rule shall be with him. And he will say in their hearing the prayer for the time of war, [as it is written in the "Bo]ok of the Rule for this time," with all the words of thanksgiving. (1QM 15:4–5)

This clearly echoes the biblical order: "before you engage in battle, the priest shall come forward and speak to the troops" (Deut. 20:2), but the specific reference to a "book" seems to indicate that these prayers were already at the disposal of the redactor of the composition, an assumption that is corroborated by the use of the same prayers in other closely related but different compositions on the same topic such as 4Q491. These prayers are mostly grouped in cols. 9–14, but we can find them also in other places of the scroll. The prayers are very closely based on biblical material; many of them recall incidents from biblical history that show examples of divine intervention in favor of Israel, and their language is mostly a mosaic of biblical expressions. They are put in the mouths of levites, of priests, or of the high priest (who are also the ones who exhort the people by means of speeches and enforce the purity regulations), and they help to accentuate the priestly preeminence in guiding the people and the ritualistic character of the whole war.

The redactor has also sought inspiration from Greco-Roman tactical military manuals to specify the regulations for warfare that he applies to the development of the war in cols. 2–9. These regulations for warfare show some general similarity to Maccabean battles, but they are more akin to the Roman military tactics (such as the use of the "gates of war," the Roman *intervalla* [see Yadin 1962]). The knowledge of these tactics and the descriptions of the weaponry (such as the square shield, the Roman *scutum*) indicate a certain familiarity with the Roman army but do not imply that the redaction of 1QM is posterior to the intervention of Pompey, because this knowledge could be obtained well before the Roman conquest of Palestine. The author has been influenced by the biblical tradition more than by Greco-Roman military manuals or Maccabean warfare. The organization of the army in thousands, hundreds, fifties, and tens is patterned after the Israelite army as described in Exodus 18; the overall use of the banners to distinguish each unit and their elaborate inscriptions are dependent on Numbers 2 and 17; and the use of the trumpets has its basis in Numbers 10, although in the *War Scroll* the use of trumpets is much more complex and elaborate than in the biblical tradition, and its function in conducting each phase of the war goes far beyond the biblical text. This use of trumpets and horns accentuates the ritualistic character of the whole composition and recalls the ritual character of the conquest of Jericho in Joshua 7.

Because we do not have the end of the 1QM manuscript, we do not know in detail what expectations its author had for the time after the eschatological war or how he imagined the life of the community after the final divine intervention. But if he accepted, as it seems, the summary of the first document of the war of seven lots, one of the first results of the final victory (col. 2) would be the reconstruction of the temple service according to the proper order and the right calendar of 364 days. This implies return to Jerusalem after the necessary purification of the earth from the corpses of those slain in battle, and the reorganization of the whole of life according to the regulations of the community, which would be no more in exile but would control the whole country. Because all the Sons of Darkness, the "army of Belial," would be completely destroyed, the Sons of Light would no longer be a remnant but would be the whole of Israel. Hence, the *War Scroll* shares the perspective of other sectarian documents, such as the *Rule of the Congregation* (1QSa), in which membership of the community seems to be coextensive with the Israel "of the last days." Characteristically, the same people who are excluded from the community "of the end days" are also excluded from participating in the final battle (compare 1QM 7:4–5 with the already quoted text of 1QSa 2:5–8).

The function of the *War Scroll* has been defined in very different terms by various scholars: as the apocalyptic revelation of the several phases, enemies, and general development of the eschatological war; as a composition designed to instruct the perfect soldier, a manual to be used on the battlefield to oppose the enemy; as a propaganda pamphlet to oppose the way rival Jewish leaders were conducting the war indicating the right way to proceed; as a composition written more for liturgical than for practical purposes, more to celebrate the future victory than to prepare for or to conduct the war. But in fact these readings of the function of the text do not need to be mutually exclusive, and perhaps the best way to understand this complex document is by combining these apparently contradictory functions. The *War Scroll*, by representing the dramatic final conflict of the forces of good and evil as a liturgy in which the trumpets are as effective as the weapons, the priestly prayers as necessary as the movements of the troops, and the purity regulations as essential as the presence of the heavenly warriors, stimulates the hope for the future intervention of God, helps to organize the present as a preparation for this intervention, justifies the present opposition to other forces, and conveys the certitude that the actual dreams and hopes will be fulfilled in the final victory.

Summary

The apocalypses developed the traditional idea of a final victory against the enemies of Israel and placed it in an eschatological context, with participation of angelic forces. In the Dead Sea Scrolls this idea is further developed and transformed into an eschatological war of seven lots or of forty years which will end with the final victory against all forces of evil.

⌒ CONCLUSION _____

In the four topics examined we have seen that characteristic ideas of the apocalyptic tradition have not only contributed to the thought of the Qumran community but have undergone there equally characteristic developments. The idea of the origin of evil has been developed to a fully dualistic and deterministic view of the world; the apocalyptic division of history into periods and the expectation that God will intervene to bring an end to the evil in the world have profoundly marked the worldview of the community, which considers itself living in the last of these periods; the Scrolls add to the complexity and structured organization of the heavenly world of the apocalypses the idea that the angels are already living among the community, allowing its members to participate in the liturgy of the heavenly temple; the Scrolls also develop the apocalyptic idea of an eschatological war in which the heavenly forces help Israel to defeat the nations in a final war in which all evil will be destroyed.

We can thus conclude that the apocalypticism indicated by this cluster of ideas in the sectarian scrolls is something more than an umbrella term. It represents genuine continuity with the worldview of Daniel and *1 Enoch* even while it adapted the tradition inherited from these earlier apocalypses in its own distinctive ways.

⌒ BIBLIOGRAPHY _____

Collins, J. J. 1984. *The Apocalyptic Imagination.* New York: Crossroad. Second edition, Grand Rapids: Eerdmans, 1998. Broad introduction to the Jewish apocalypses in their historical context.

———. 1997a. *Apocalypticism in the Dead Sea Scrolls.* London: Routledge. The most comprehensive and detailed analysis of apocalypticism in the Scrolls.

———. 1997b. *Seers, Sibyls and Sages in Hellenistic-Roman Judaism.* Leiden: E. J. Brill. Important essays on apocalypticism and the Scrolls.

———, ed. 1979. *Apocalypse: The Morphology of a Genre. Semeia* 14. Chico, Calif.: Scholars Press. Definition of the literary genre Apocalypse, description of the paradigm and classification of the two main subtypes.

Dimant, D. 1994. "Apocalyptic Texts at Qumran." In *The Community of the Renewed Covenant,* edited by E. Ulrich and J. C. VanderKam, 175–91. Notre Dame, Ind.: University of Notre Dame Press. Classification of the Qumran texts that can be labeled apocalyptic.

Duhaime, J. 1995. "War Scroll (1QM; 1Q33; 4Q491–496; 4Q497)." In *The Dead Sea Scrolls: Hebrew, Aramaic, and Greek Texts with English Translation,* edited by J. H. Charlesworth, 2:80–203. Tübingen: Mohr; Louisville: Westminster/John Knox Press. Critical edition of all the fragments of the *War Sroll* and some related documents.

García Martínez, F. 1992. *Qumran and Apocalyptic.* Leiden: E. J. Brill. Collection of articles on Aramaic texts relevant to apocalypticism from Qumran.

———. 1996. *The Dead Sea Scrolls Translated. Second Edition.* Leiden: E. J. Brill; Grand Rapids: Eerdmans. Translations of most of the nonbiblical Dead Sea Scrolls.

Hellholm, D., ed. 1983. *Apocalypticism in the Ancient Mediterranean World and in the Near East.* Tübingen: Mohr. Proceedings of the Uppsala Colloquium on Apocalypticism and the most complete collection of articles on the phenomenon of apocalypticism, the literary genre of apocalypses, the sociology of apocalypticism, and the function of apocalypticism.

Koch, K. 1972. *The Rediscovery of Apocalyptic.* Naperville, Ill.: Allenson. German original, *Ratlos vor Apokalyptik.* Critical analysis of the problems posed by the indiscriminate use of the term "apocalyptic."

Mach, M. 1992. *Entwicklungsstadien des jüdischen Engelglaubens in vorrabbinischer Zeit.* Tübingen: Mohr. Comprehensive and detailed study of the developments of Jewish angelology.

Newsom, C. 1985. *Songs of the Sabbath Sacrifice: A Critical Edition.* Atlanta: Scholars Press. Critical edition of all the preserved copies of the composition and analysis of its contents.

Sacchi, P. 1996. *Jewish Apocalyptic and its History.* Sheffield: Sheffield Academic Press. Italian original, *L'Apocalittica Giudaica e la sua Storia* (Brescia: Paideia, 1990). Collection of articles on the development of apocalypticism, focusing mainly on *1 Enoch.*

Schiffman, L. H. 1989. *The Eschatological Community of the Dead Sea Scrolls.* Atlanta: Scholars Press. Comprehensive and detailed analysis of 1QSa

Stegemann, H. "Die Bedeutung der Qumranfunde für die Erforschung der Apokalyptik." In Hellholm 1983, 495–530. Critical view of the importance of the Scrolls for the study of apocalypticism.

Steudel, A. 1993. "ʾaḥărît hayyāmîm in the Texts from Qumran." *Revue de Qumrân* 16:225–46.

Stone, M. E. 1990. *Fourth Ezra.* Hermeneia. Minneapolis: Fortress Press.

VanderKam, J. C. 1984. *Enoch and the Growth of an Apocalyptic Tradition.* Washington: Catholic Biblical Association. Monograph on the early Enoch tradition and its Mesopotamian background.

Yadin, Y. 1962. *The Scroll of the War of the Sons of Light against the Sons of Darkness.* Oxford: Oxford University Press. Comprehensive and detailed commentary on 1QM.

5

Messianism and Apocalypticism

James C. VanderKam
University of Notre Dame

I N ONE FORM OR ANOTHER Jewish beliefs about a messiah surface in a number of texts dating from the Greco-Roman period. The presence of the term *messiah* in a series of Jewish texts and especially the large role the title plays in the New Testament works have ensured the popularity of the topic to the present day. The purpose of this essay is to explore and document the varied messianic ideas present in the Jewish texts and to study their connections (or lack of them) with apocalypticism. The introductory section will be devoted to clarifying terms and to the biblical roots of messianism and apocalypticism. The next section will present the evidence for messianic expectations in early Jewish texts, and the final part will summarize the results for the variety of messianic expectations and their relations with apocalyptic concerns.

INTRODUCTION

Messiah and Messianism

The first term to be defined is *messiah*, a word reflecting the Greek transcription of the Hebrew *māšîaḥ*, which refers to a person who has been anointed with oil. The Hebrew term appears moderately often in the Bible in connection with several types of officials or characters. It is used for the following: (1) Kings of Israel who have oil applied to their head as a way of marking divine designation of them for the role (e.g., 1 Sam. 12:3, 5; 16:6; 24:7, 11). A distinction should be drawn between those historical passages that refer to Saul or David or the like as anointed monarchs and a passage such as Ps. 2:2, in which the king, in a more mythical or ideal context in which he is identified as the son of God, is mentioned together with the deity himself as the object of assault by the rulers of the earth (see also Ps. 18:51 = 2 Sam. 22:51; Ps. 89:39, 52; 132:10, 17). (2) High priests of Israel, whom the Priestly writer calls "the anointed priest" (Lev. 4:3, 5, 16; 6:15; Ps. 84:10). (3) Cyrus of Persia, who was set apart for the purpose of carrying out the Lord's will (Isa. 45:1). (4) A future prince (Dan. 9:25, 26). (5) The patriarchs (Ps. 105:15 = 1 Chr. 16:22). While the third usage (for Cyrus) is consistent with the general concept that an anointed one is a high-ranking person who has been set aside to a lofty position or chosen by God for a noble purpose, numbers (1) and (2) are the most important for the present purposes. In the Bible both the king and the high priest can be designated the anointed ones of the Lord, and at times the term is put to a specialized use for a leader of the future (as also in the fourth usage).

From the normally mundane biblical employment of the term, the belief that there would be a divinely marked ruler in the future developed over time. Dan. 9:25–26 predicts: "from the time that the word went out to restore and rebuild Jerusalem until the time of the anointed prince, there shall be seven weeks; and for sixty-two weeks it shall be built again with streets and moat, but in a troubled time. After the sixty-two weeks, an anointed one shall be cut off and shall have nothing. . . ." The "anointed prince" in v. 25 may be the first postexilic high priest, Joshua, and the "anointed one" in v. 26 is often understood to be the high priest Onias III, who was forcibly removed from office in 175 b.c.e. and eventually executed (Collins 1993, 355–56). Passages such as Ps. 2:1–2 document the belief that an anointed Davidic ruler would also be a world ruler: "Why do the nations conspire, and the peoples plot in vain? The kings of the earth set themselves, and the rulers take counsel together, against the Lord and his anointed. . . ." This anointed king is later identified in the psalm as God's king (v. 6) and as the divine son (v. 7) who will conquer the nations and possess the ends of the earth (v. 8).

If one were to confine the survey only to the term "anointed one," the results from the Hebrew Bible would not be overly impressive. There are some thirty-eight occurrences of the word, and in all cases it is used for a leader. However, there has been a debate about the proper use of the terms *messiah* and *messianism*: Should these words be restricted to those places in which an anointed one is mentioned and those eschatological contexts in which a person explicitly designated Messiah appears? Or is it permissible to use the words more broadly to refer to any leader of the end-time and the thought patterns that include such characters?

If we go by the usage of ancient texts, there can be little doubt that the broader under-standing is an acceptable one. A variety of prophetic texts in the Hebrew Bible make reference to a royal leader of the future but do not call him Messiah. For example, Isaiah prophesies: "A shoot shall come out from the stump of Jesse, and a branch shall grow out of his roots" (11:1). He will be given extraordinary qualities; his reign will be ideal; and in his time the dispersed will be gathered and their enemies defeated (11:2–16). Or Jeremiah, in one of his pictures of the future, quotes the Lord as saying:

> The days are surely coming, says the Lord, when I will raise up for David a righteous Branch (*ṣemaḥ*), and he shall reign as king and deal wisely, and shall execute justice and righteousness in the land. In his days Judah will be saved and Israel will live in safety. And this is the name by which he will be called: "The Lord is our righteousness." (23:5–6)

Neither Isaiah nor Jeremiah resorted to the term *anointed* in these contexts, but they do make clear that the present earthly "anointed" ones, that is, the Davidic kings, will have successors in the future of God's reduced people (see also Isa. 7:14; 9:1–6; Jer. 33:14–16; Ezek. 17:22–24; 34:23–24; 37:24–25; Mic. 5:1–3; Hag. 2:20–23; Zechariah 4 and 6). That point also emerges from the promise to David:

> When your days are fulfilled and you lie down with your ancestors, I will raise up your off-spring after you, who shall come forth from your body, and I will establish his kingdom. He shall build a house for my name, and I will establish the throne of his kingdom forever. I will be a father to him, and he shall be a son to me. . . . Your house and your kingdom shall be made sure forever before me; your throne shall be established forever. (2 Sam. 7:12–14a, 16)

In later texts, *anointed* and other titles for end-time leaders are used side by side or interchanged for the same individual (see, e.g., the Similitudes of Enoch). Hence, despite the absence of the title Messiah from such contexts, it is possible to speak of at least an incipient messianism in the Hebrew Bible in that the prophetic pictures of the future at times include a new leader from the line of David, whether he is called a king or a prince or given some other title. As John Collins writes, "a messiah is an eschatological figure who sometimes, but not necessarily always, is desig-nated as a משיח in the ancient sources" (Collins 1995, 12). Messianism, then, would be a mode of thought centering about such a leader or in which he plays a significant role. Postbiblical Jewish literature evidences a richer flowering from these rather limited biblical roots.

Apocalypse and Apocalypticism

There has been an extensive discussion in modern times concerning the proper usage of *apoca-lypse, apocalypticism,* and related terms. Since the definitions of these words have been dis-cussed in the introduction to this volume, it suffices simply to note that here *apocalypse* is being used in the sense of Collins's expanded definition (see Collins 1991, 19 for the added section about the function of apocalypses). The tendency among scholars has been to focus on the eschatological side of teachings in the apocalypses and less on the other kinds of material found in them, but the future was not the only concern of the seers. They contain revelations about cosmological or heavenly phenomena as well as about eschatological mysteries. Yet it is accu-rate to say that disclosures about noneschatological subjects (e.g., about the heavens) are often if not always connected in some way with eschatological matters and are intended to reassure the reader that God ultimately reigns over the universe and is thus able to rectify what is now wrong with the world. It should be noted, too, that apocalyptic ways of thinking are not con-fined to works formally defined as apocalypses; they are also to be found in other genres such as testaments and oracles.

Collins and the other authors in the *Semeia* volume distinguished two major types of apocalypses: some apocalypses have and others lack an otherworldly journey by the individual who receives the revelation. Both those with and without otherworldly journeys can be further subdivided:

> (a) the "historical" type which includes a review of history, eschatological crisis and cosmic and/or political eschatology; (b) apocalypses which have no historical review but envisage cos-mic and/or political eschatology . . . ; and (c) apocalypses which have neither historical review nor cosmic transformation but only personal eschatology. (Collins 1979, 13)

As with Messiah/messianism, the Hebrew Bible supplies the foundations for later Jewish apocalyptic writing and thinking. The only unmistakable apocalypses in the Hebrew Bible are the several visions disclosed to Daniel in chaps. 7–12, but a number of scholars have regarded earlier, especially prophetic texts as being *proto-apocalypses*. If one adopts Collins's definition of *apocalypse*, none was written by a Jewish author before the Hellenistic period began. This implies that those who consider passages such as Isaiah 24–27 or Zechariah 1–8 to be apocalypses or at least proto-apocalypses are operating with different definitions. F. M. Cross, who argues that "the origins of apocalyptic must be searched for as early as the sixth century B.C." (1973, 343), has pointed to "reformulations of the prophetic tradition and of the royal ideology" in some later prophetic texts in the Hebrew Bible; these manifest "rudimentary traits and motives of apocalypticism." He lists three: "democratizing and eschatologizing of classical prophetic themes and forms"; the doctrine of two ages; and "the resurgent influence of myths of creation used to frame history and to lend history transcendent significance, significance not apparent in the ordinary events of biblical history" (1973, 346). O. Plöger and P. Hanson have also located the first literary examples of apocalyptic phenomena at the beginning of postexilic history and have tried to describe the nonhierocratic, eschatologically minded groups who were responsible for the birth of apocalyptic thinking (Plöger 1968; Hanson 1975). Although it is obvious that the authors of the apocalypses drew upon earlier scriptural material and to a certain extent imitated biblical forms, no Jewish writer composed an apocalypse in Collins's sense of the term until the third century B.C.E. The evidence now suggests strongly that the most ancient Jewish apocalypses were texts that centered on the antediluvian seer Enoch.

Important models and sources for the apocalypses were supplied by the biblical prophetic literature. One prophetic model was the throne vision report in which the prophet was given access to the divine presence and the discussion of earthly matters that transpired between God and his angelic advisors (1 Kings 22; Isaiah 6; see *1 Enoch* 14). Another model came from passages such as Ezekiel 40–48, in which an angel gives the prophet a tour of the renewed Jerusalem, Temple, and country. Mention should also be made of symbolic visions that are disclosed to a prophet and explained by God or an angel (e.g., Amos 7–9; Zechariah 1–8) or of other cryptic messages that were clarified for a prophet (Daniel 9). In general the sequence in prophetic eschatology of decisive judgment followed by extraordinary renewal for a purged remnant is reflected in even stronger form in the apocalypses. However, there is also evidence that divinatory procedures and assumptions (as in dream interpretations) have left their mark on apocalyptic works. For example, in the apocalypses cryptic, symbolic dreams are disclosed to the seer who also receives a celestial explanation of the encoded message. The explanations reveal information about the future which will arise out of the circumstances of the past and present (see Daniel 7 for an example; VanderKam 1984, 52–75).

☞ MESSIANISM IN EARLY JUDAISM

The purpose of this section is to survey the references to messiahs in early Jewish texts and to gather information about who the Messiah(s) was (were) thought to be and what he (they) was (were) expected to do. The survey falls into two parts. First, those texts that belong to the genre *apocalypse* as defined above will be examined; second, texts that are not apocalypses but in which a Messiah appears will be studied. It should be remembered that it is not only instances of the title Messiah that will be under consideration; others that are applied to the future ruler(s) and the nature of the qualities and roles assigned to these leaders will also be studied.

Messianic Leaders in the Early Jewish Apocalypses

Collins has identified a series of early Jewish texts that qualify under his definition as apocalypses. These should be studied in chronological order (insofar as that is possible) to determine which apocalypses assign a role or roles to messianic leaders, understood in a broad sense, and which do not. The survey will show that it is not until the first century C.E. that messianic leaders begin to appear consistently in the texts; even then, however, not all apocalypses envision such a leader in their eschatological tableaux.

THE ASTRONOMICAL BOOK OF ENOCH (1 ENOCH 72–82). Ever since J. T. Milik published some of the Qumran Aramaic fragments of the Astronomical Book, it has become customary to date it to the third century B.C.E. (Milik 1976, 7–11). It is at times considered an apocalypse because it claims to be the record of Uriel's revelations to Enoch (who is on a tour of the universe) about astronomical and geographical matters; however, the work does not consist of such instructions alone. According to 72:1 the disclosures are "for each year of the world and for ever, until the new creation."[1] In this early, perhaps apocalyptic work there is no hint of a messianic leader at the end-times.

THE BOOK OF THE WATCHERS (1 ENOCH 1–36). A third-century date has also been advocated for this collection of what appear to have been a series of originally separate works (Milik 1976, 22–23). Parts of the booklet have apocalyptic traits (see chapters 1, 10–11, 14–15, and 17–36). While these chapters contain many eschatological topics, not a word is said about a Messiah or any human leader. That is, the earliest Enochic apocalypses (if they may be called apocalypses) do not include a Messiah in their vivid pictures of the end. God and his angels act without messianic assistance.

THE APOCALYPSE OF WEEKS (1 ENOCH 93:1–10; 91:11–17). This short historical apocalypse, which appears in the correct order in the Aramaic fragments from Qumran but has been split and the parts reversed in the Ethiopic, presents Enoch as speaking from extraordinarily authoritative sources (books, heavenly vision, words of holy angels, tablets of heaven [93:1–3]). From them he reveals to his children the course of history and the judgment divided into ten schematic segments called *weeks*. Weeks 8–10 detail the different stages of the judgment. In week 8 the righteous receive a sword to punish the sinners; in week 9 righteous judgment is revealed to the entire world and the deeds of the impious vanish, with the world recorded for destruction; and in week 10 there is an eternal judgment on the watchers and the creation of a new heaven. These stages will be followed by innumerable weeks forever in which sin has been entirely eliminated. The text of the Apocalypse of Weeks is exceptionally brief and allusive, but no character in it can be construed as a messianic leader.

THE ANIMAL APOCALYPSE (1 ENOCH 85–90). The Animal Apocalypse, which follows an apocalyptic-sounding vision in chapters 83–84, also surveys biblical history and moves beyond it, as the Apocalypse of Weeks does. The experience behind the text is termed a dream and dream vision (85:1–2). The apocalypse uses animals as symbols for people, while people represent angels or the like. The numerous details of the symbolic biblical history are not pertinent in this context, but as the overview reaches the author's time (in the 160s B.C.E.) it refers to defeat after defeat for the sheep (= Israel), "until a big horn grew *on* one of those sheep" (90:9). The enemies "wished to make away with its horn, but they did not prevail against it" (v. 12). This sheep or ram (both terms are used) becomes the object of a unified assault by Israel's enemies. However, "it fought with them and cried out that its help might come to it" (v. 13). A recording angel assures the ram that divine assistance for it was coming (v. 14). A final assault by the combined foes leads to decisive divine intervention and victory for the sheep (vv. 16–19). It is possible to understand the sheep/ram with the large horn as a Messiah, but the conclusion seems unlikely, and commentators often identify it as a representation of Judas Maccabeus (yet note the reference to "that ram" in v. 31 [Tiller 1993, 62–63, 355]). One argument against seeing the sheep/ram with the large horn as the Messiah is the fact that he appears before another figure who seems to be a Messiah.

A more likely candidate for a Messiah is the individual called "a white bull" in 90:37. One learns that it was born at the end, and "its horns (were) big, and all the wild animals and all the birds of heaven were afraid of it and entreated it continually. And I [= Enoch] looked until all their species were transformed, and they all became white bulls; and the first one among them was a wild-ox, and that wild-ox was a large animal and had big black horns on its head. And the Lord of the sheep rejoiced over them and over all the bulls" (vv. 37–38). The image of the white bull reverts to the symbol used for the patriarchs from Adam through Isaac (85:3–89:12). Yet the bull hardly stands out as unusual in the end-time, since "all their species" became white bulls. "The function of this end-time figure seems to be unique in the literature of the period. Like the 'one like a son of man' in Daniel 7, he comes at the end of world history and is granted universal dominion. Contrary to Daniel's figure, he is a human individual, as is shown by the fact that he is symbolized by an animal" (Tiller 1993, 384). The fact that the white bull is soon joined by others entails that his mission is "apparently only to be a sort of catalyst for the transformation of all humanity" (Tiller 1993, 385). Consequently, the Animal Apocalypse appears to be the earliest Jewish apocalypse that mentions a messianic leader of the end-time. He is a special individual who exercises power over the nations, although he is not a different kind of being from his contemporaries.

DANIEL. Several sections in the second half of Daniel, the only fully apocalyptic unit in the Hebrew Bible, qualify as apocalypses.

1. Daniel 7. Daniel's famous vision of the four beasts who emerge from the sea climaxes in a scene of judgment in which "an Ancient One" (that is, God) serves as the enthroned judge before whom the horned fourth beast was executed and the other beasts were deprived of their dominion. "As I [= Daniel] watched in the night visions, I saw one like a human being [traditionally and more literally: one like a son of man] coming with the clouds of heaven. And he came to the Ancient One and was presented before him. To him was given dominion and glory and kingship, that all peoples, nations, and languages should serve him. His dominion is an everlasting dominion that shall not pass away, and his kingship is one that shall never be destroyed" (7:13–14). This figure appears to have clear messianic qualities and has traditionally

been so identified, but there is a good chance that the "one like a son of man" is a symbol either for the people of God (see v. 27, where the dominion is given to the "people of the holy ones of the Most High") or for the angel Michael (Collins 1993, 304–10). In either case, the "one like a son of man" would not be a messianic individual who belonged at least in part to the human realm.

2. Daniel 8. After his vision of the four beasts, Daniel sees another in which a ram with two horns (specifically explained as the kings of Media and Persia), a goat (interpreted as the king of Greece; see 8:20–21), and four kingdoms into which the great horn of the goat was split play the central parts. The vision pertains, as the text says, to "the appointed time of the end" (v. 19). The judgment that will be meted out to the last foe is that "he shall be broken, and not by human hands" (v. 25). No Messiah or other human representative of the good appears in this vision about the end of time.

3. Daniel 9. As Daniel ponders Jeremiah's prophecy that Jerusalem would lie desolate for seventy years (Jer. 25:11–12; 29:10), he prays for national forgiveness and for the Lord to remember his ravaged sanctuary and city. The scene is an example of how the mantic tradition has influenced apocalyptic writers, since Daniel is attempting to derive a message from an encoded text that requires expert handling. The message lies hidden beneath the surface appearance of the medium. The angel Gabriel then came to explain the meaning of the puzzling prophetic words to him. Gabriel points out that the seventy years actually mean seventy weeks of years and further notes that there is to be a seven-year period from the command to restore Jerusalem "until the time of an anointed prince" (9:25). "After the sixty-two weeks, an anointed one shall be cut off and shall have nothing, and the troops of the prince who is to come shall destroy the city and the sanctuary" (v. 26). As noted above, this anointed one is thought to be the high priest Onias III, who was ousted from his position in 175 B.C.E. and eventually murdered. There is no indication in the text that he functioned as a messianic leader in any other than the most literal sense that he, like the high priests of old, had been anointed with oil upon taking the position. He does nothing specifically "messianic"; his appearance and death serve only to mark the turning point from a troubled time to one of catastrophe.

4. Daniel 10–12. In the longest of the visions (see 10:1, 7, 8) Daniel encounters a "man clothed in linen" (10:5–6) who had a frightening appearance and who came "to help you [= Daniel] understand what is to happen to your people at the end of days. For there is a further vision for those days" (10:14). The man was sent "to tell you what is inscribed in the book of truth" (10:21). The apocalyptic vision contains a historical survey covering individuals who are identified as the kings of Persia (11:2) and of Greece and successor kingdoms (11:3–45), but it provides particularly detailed information about the kings of the south (the Ptolemies) and of the north (the Seleucids). Antiochus IV (175–164), "a contemptible person on whom royal majesty had not been conferred" (11:21), receives the largest amount of attention (11:21–45). The only leaders of eschatological times who are portrayed in a positive way appear to be "the wise among the people" (11:33), who give understanding to others, suffer violence and execution, and receive "a little help" (v. 34) from others whom commentators regularly identify as the Maccabees. After Antiochus meets his lonely end (11:45), "Michael, the great prince, the protector of your people, shall arise" (12:1). A time of anguish will occur, but Daniel's people, "everyone who is found written in the book" (12:11), will be delivered and many of the dead

will rise, some to everlasting life, others to everlasting contempt (12:2). Throughout the relatively detailed scenario sketched by the author, not a word is said about a Messiah or any other eschatological leader, apart from the angel Michael.

Thus, the viewpoint expressed in all the apocalyptic visions in the second half of the book of Daniel is that there is no messianic king or the like at the last times. The only leader of God's people in those tumultuous and fateful days is an angel through whom God himself works.

THE BOOK OF JUBILEES. Various sets of internal and external data point to approximately the mid-second century B.C.E. as the time when the book was written. Although the book itself, which is presented as a revelation to Moses, is not formally an apocalypse, it does contain two passages that could be classified as apocalypses. One is the first chapter, which is set on Mount Sinai, where God is speaking directly to Moses. Much of the Lord's address deals with Israel's future apostasy from the covenant despite remarkable divine faithfulness and patience. The pattern that the Lord predicts to Moses is that Israel will sin and God will send witnesses (= prophets) to warn them but their missions will fail to accomplish a return to the covenant. God will then hide his face from his people and hand them over to the nations. When they are separated from their land, they will continue sinning but will later repent in their places of dispersion. As a result the Lord will gather them and transform them into a righteous plant in their own land, build his temple among them, and reestablish proper covenantal relations with them. Nothing that is said in the first chapter, however, even affords a hint that the author anticipates the rise of a Messiah. One learns there only about God's relations with the entire people and the mediating role that Moses plays in those relations.

The same may be said about parts of chapter 23, which are more clearly apocalyptic in character. The Lord will eventually arouse the nations against an especially wicked generation, and only later will a new generation of people who study the law be born. They will obey by returning to the right path, and the ages of God's people will again become as lengthy as and even longer than they were before the flood. There are several participants in the eschatological drama—the Lord, the nations, and the new generation who are called "children"—but there is no Messiah.

Before leaving *Jubilees* a note should be added about a theme in the book that caused messianic repercussions in later literature. The author highlights Levi and Judah as the most important among Jacob's twelve sons; their grandfather, Isaac, predicts that Levi and his descendants will serve as the Lord's priests and that Judah's line will provide the kings of Jacob's offspring (31:11–17, 18–20; cf. 30:18). *Jubilees* depicts neither Levi nor Judah as a leader in eschatological days, nor does it anticipate that one or two will arise from their children; nevertheless, its emphasis on priestly and kingly leadership seems to be an earlier stage in the development of the dual messianism found at Qumran (see below).

SIBYLLINE ORACLES 3. Much of the third *Sibylline Oracle* was written around the mid-second century B.C.E. It has been claimed that *Sib. Or.* 3.652–795, although a king is mentioned only at the beginning of the section, is "almost exclusively messianic in content" (Schürer 1979, 501), but Collins thinks that the king who comes from the sun is a "benevolent Ptolemy," not a Jewish Messiah. "The Sibyl, then, resembles Deutero-Isaiah in endorsing a Gentile king as the agent of deliverance. The hopes of most Jews in the period 550–150 B.C.E. were for a benevolent over-

lord who would protect and promote the Jewish people, rather than for national independence" (Collins 1995, 39).

TESTAMENT OF LEVI 2–5. It is not at all certain that the *Testament of Levi* belongs at this point
in the chronological survey. In its present form the testament is Christian (see the reference to
Jesus Christ in 4:4), but there is reason to believe that an older Jewish work underlies the extant
text. The Aramaic Levi text from Qumran appears to be one of the sources (whether direct or
indirect) from which the author drew in composing the testament, and the Aramaic Levi may
be a third-century B.C.E. work.

In the *Testament of Levi* 2–5 Levi recounts a dream vision that he experienced while feeding the family flocks in Abelmaul. His dream vision belongs to the tour-of-heaven class of apocalypses: an angel shows him three heavens, and he learns about four others. He is told that the
Lord will save the whole human race through him and through Judah (2:11). The angel
explains to Levi the nature of the seven heavens, speaks of the baffling character of human sin,
and predicts that various natural disasters will occur when the Lord judges humanity (chapter
3). Levi prays that he may be separated from unrighteousness and serve in the divine presence;
his request is accepted. In chapter 5, during a throne vision in which he sees God in his heavenly
temple, Levi is appointed as God's priest (5:1–2). This appointment, however, is presented as
an event of the past and as affecting an ancient character. The vision does not describe Levi's
investiture as eschatological priest. Only Jesus Christ, whose arrival is predicted in the passage,
is accorded a messianic title; he is called God's son.

The situation is different in chap. 18, where the writer predicts that, at the end of history,
"the Lord will raise up a new priest" (v. 2), whose accomplishments will be extraordinary:
among other feats, he will execute judgment, remove darkness through the light he will dis-
pense, receive the spirit of understanding and sanctification, enlighten the Gentiles, and
remove sin. There is ample reason for thinking, however, that this chapter belongs to the Christian redaction of the testament and relates to Jesus Christ, not to a priestly Messiah who will be
descended from Levi (Hollander and de Jonge 1985, 179–82).

The *Testament of Levi* and the *Testament of Judah,* along with several other statements elsewhere in the *Testaments of the Twelve Patriarchs,* present a teaching about Levi and Judah parallel to what we find in *Jubilees,* but they usually do not present their descendants as Messiahs.
Testament of Reuben 6:12, in which the patriarch is speaking about Judah's posterity, predicts
that he (or his descendants) will die in visible and invisible wars and be an eternal king. Such
sentiments are probably Christian (Hollander and de Jonge 1985, 108). *Testament of Dan*
5:4–15, a pericope dealing with the last days, predicts unsuccessful opposition to Levi and
Judah (v. 4) and that the Lord's salvation will come from Judah and Levi (v. 10). Once again,
however, the passage has Christian motifs. An especially clear case is found in *Testament of
Joseph* 19:11, where one reads about the lamb of God who takes away the sin of the world and
saves all the nations; this lamb is to arise from the seed of Levi and Judah (see also *T. Sim.* 7:1–2;
T. Naph. 8:2–3; *T. Gad* 8:1; and also *T. Levi* 2:11; 8:14–15).

It is particularly two, somewhat parallel texts that have been understood messianically—
Testament of Levi 18 and *Testament of Judah* 24. The former was considered above; it refers to
Jesus as the new priest who will not be from Levi's line. The latter (which like *Testament of Levi*
18 directly follows a sin–exile–return passage) forecasts:

And after these things a star will arise to you from Jacob in peace and a man will arise from my seed like the sun of righteousness, walking with the sons of men in meekness and righteousness, and no sin whatever will be found in him. And the heavens will be opened to him to pour out the blessing of the spirit of the holy Father, and he will pour out the spirit of grace upon you; and you will be sons to him in truth and you will walk in his commandments from first to last. This (is) the branch of God Most High and this (is) the fountain unto life for all flesh. Then the sceptre of my kingdom will shine, and from your root a stem will arise; and in it a rod of righteousness will arise to the nations to judge and to save all who call upon the Lord.

Commentators such as Hollander and de Jonge have noted the author's heavy reliance on a variety of passages from the Hebrew Bible but have also determined that several parts of the chapter clearly betray a Christian hand (e.g., the reference to Jesus' baptism). Hence, it is safest to say that, at least in its present form, *T. Judah* 24 is Christian and not a witness to a type of specifically Jewish messianism. After surveying all the relevant passages in the *Testaments of the Twelve Patriarchs,* Hollander and de Jonge conclude: "In any case, there is no 'double messianism' in the *Testaments.* Whenever a saviour figure occurs in L.J. passages [i.e., passages dealing with Levi and Judah], there is only one, and clearly Jesus Christ is referred to" (1985, 61).

The Similitudes or Parables of Enoch (*1 Enoch* 37–71). The lengthy section of *1 Enoch* that contains three parables uttered by the antediluvian patriarch is the earliest Jewish apocalypse to provide an extended and complicated treatment of a messianic individual. There has been a long scholarly debate about when the booklet was written, and that debate has taken on a new character after it was learned that no fragments of this part of *1 Enoch,* unlike the case with the other four sections, had been identified in Qumran Cave 4. Milik, the editor of the Qumran Aramaic copies of *1 Enoch,* argued that the Similitudes is a Christian work, written in the late third century C.E.; it was only later incorporated into *1 Enoch* when the Book of Giants was removed from the collection (Milik 1976, 89–98). Other scholars have continued to debate whether it dates from the first century B.C.E. or the first–second century C.E. There appears to be no decisive evidence for dating it any later that the end of the first century B.C.E.

There are four titles given to a messianic leader who is identified in 71:14 as Enoch himself. Two of the four occur only rarely, while the other two are more frequent. The first of these, *the righteous one,* seems to be used collectively in 47:1, 4, but it is used for an eschatological individual in 53:6: "And after this the Righteous and Chosen One will cause the house of his congregation to appear." The term "righteous one" is a descriptive word applied here to the character designated often in the book as the chosen one (see below). In 53:6 he seems to have a congregation associated with him. This same individual is explicitly termed Messiah in two places in the Similitudes. The first is in *1 Enoch* 48:10: "And on the day of their [= the kings' and the mighty ones'] trouble there will be rest on the earth, and they will fall down before him and will not rise; and there will be no one who will take them with his hands and raise them, for they denied the Lord of Spirits and his Messiah." Here, echoing the words of Ps. 2:2 about the Lord and the Davidic king, the writer pictures evil groups as finding no help at the end because they have denied both God himself and his anointed one. In 52:4, the only other use of "Messiah" for this leader, an angel explains to Enoch that some natural phenomena which he sees will serve the dominion of his anointed one. Thus, the messianic individual is to exercise some sort of rule.

While "righteous one" and "anointed one" appear infrequently in the Similitudes, the titles *chosen one* and *son of man* figure much more often. "Chosen one" is used in fifteen or six-

teen passages, and "son of man" in sixteen. The chosen one is associated with a group appropriately designated the "chosen ones" (e.g., 39:6; 40:5; 45:3–4; etc.); on the day of judgment he will
sit on a glorious throne (45:3; 51:3; 55:4; 61:8) and judge the different classes of evildoers (55:4).
He is a source of comfort and strength for the chosen; his glory is eternal (see 49:2); and "all the
secrets of wisdom will flow out of the counsel of his mouth" (51:3). Mountains will melt like
wax before him (52:6), and various metals will be destroyed when he appears (52:9). It should
be recalled that in 53:6 this figure is also called the "righteous one."

The sixteen cases in which "son of man" is employed for an eschatological figure also disclose important information about the functions he is expected to perform. For reasons that are
not evident in every case, the Ethiopic text uses three different formulations for "son of man."
One (*walda sab'*) appears only in 46:2, 3, 4; 48:2, where the vision of Daniel 7, with its "one like
a son of man," exercises a noticeable influence. A second (*walda be'si*) is employed in 62:5;
69:29 (two times), and 71:14, that is, at later points in the Similitudes. The son of man sits on
his glorious throne, evil passes from his presence, and his word is strong. The most interesting
use of *walda be'si* comes in 71:14, where Enoch himself is identified as the son of man who was
born for righteousness. Despite efforts to emend the text, the reading is secure. The third way of
formulating the title (*walda 'egwāla 'emma-ḥeyāw* = son of the offspring of the mother of the
living) occurs eight times and is thus the most frequent one. It, like the second form, figures in
the latter parts of the Similitudes. *1 Enoch* 62:7 says that the son of man is hidden but is revealed
to the chosen. The kings and mighty ones fall before him (62:14; 63:11), while the righteous and
chosen ones will live with him eternally. According to 69:25–27 the ones to whom the son of
man was revealed will be happy but the sinners are destroyed by his judgment; and 70:1 and
71:17 say that Enoch, the son of man, after his removal from earth, is to enjoy a long life in the
heavens.

Scholars have debated whether chapters 70–71 belong to the original form of the Similitudes and thus whether the teaching that Enoch was the son of man is the conclusion intended
by the author of the three parables (that is, of chapters 37–69). It can be argued that all of chapters 37–69 are set within Enoch's 365-year life and that the three stages of exaltation pictured in
chapters 70–71 are a natural conclusion to that life as they describe his final removal (the one
mentioned in Gen. 5:24). It has also been claimed that the Similitudes speak of the son of man
as preexistent—a condition incompatible with identifying him as Enoch the son of Jared and
seventh from Adam. It is reasonable to infer, however, that in passages such as *1 Enoch* 62:7 the
son of man is not preexistent but was elected before the world began. Or possibly the verse
means only that from an early time Enoch was hidden (see *1 Enoch* 12:1), that is, removed from
human society (see VanderKam 1992, 176–82).

All four terms for the eschatological leader refer to the same individual, as equivalences
and interchanged titles in the text demonstrate (VanderKam 1992, 185–86). It appears that in
much of the material that describes the eschatological leader, the author of the Similitudes is
dependent on the servant passages in Deutero-Isaiah; these he interprets as referring to a messianic individual. His messianic individual does not, however, suffer as the servant does in Isaiah. Some passages (especially *1 Enoch* 46–48) show heavy indebtedness to Daniel 7, whose
"one like a son of man" the author has also read in an individualistic sense. The complicated
messianic leader in the Similitudes is an exalted individual who will judge the wicked at the end
and vindicate the suffering chosen ones, thus bringing about the great reversal from the present
miserable conditions of oppression.

2 BARUCH. One of the literary responses by a Jewish author to the defeat and destruction to which the Romans subjected the Jews in 70 C.E. is *2 Baruch,* which has been preserved only in Syriac. It may date from near the end of the first century C.E. The book contains a lengthy dialogue between Baruch and God about the disaster that has occurred and the reasons for it. Statements about God's long-term purpose in what he has done lend themselves naturally to predictions about the end-time. In those predictions the author has lodged several references to a Messiah.

An apocalypse begins in chapter 26 with Baruch's question: "That tribulation which will be, will it last a long time; and that distress, will it embrace many years?"[2] The divine reply indicates that the calamitous time in question will be divided into twelve parts, which will overlap with one another to some extent. Baruch learns that what is being said to him applies to the entire world, although God will protect only those found in the holy land. "And it will happen that when all that which should come to pass in these parts has been accomplished, the Anointed One will begin to be revealed" (29:3). The end of time (29:8) will be marked by the act of consuming the two monsters Behemoth and Leviathan, by extraordinarily abundant crops, and by the reopening of the treasury of manna. The reader soon learns that the epiphany of the Messiah does not go unnoticed: "And it will happen after these things when the time of the appearance of the Anointed One has been fulfilled and he returns with glory, that then all who sleep in hope of him will arise" (30:1). The souls of the righteous rejoice, while the souls of the wicked waste away, knowing that the time of their torment has arrived (30:5).

Later, during an apocalypse that uses the images of a forest, vine, fountain, and cedar (chapters 35–40), the Messiah reappears. In a night vision (36:1) Baruch sees the vine with a fountain running under it submerge and uproot the forest and overthrow the mountains that surround it. Eventually the fountain grows so powerful that just one cedar is left. The vine condemns the cedar for making evil endure and consigns it to present pain and future judgment. Eventually the cedar was burned, the vine grew, and the valley around it became full of unfading flowers. Baruch requests an explanation for the night vision (chapter 38) and receives it from God. The forest is a fourth power, as in Daniel's vision of the four beasts. "And it will happen when the time of its fulfillment is approaching in which it will fall, that at that time the dominion of my Anointed One which is like the fountain and the vine, will be revealed. And when it has revealed itself, it will uproot the multitude of its host" (39:7). It turns out that the cedar is the last ruler who, after his army is killed, is brought to Mount Zion:

> . . . my Anointed one will convict him of all his wicked deeds and will assemble and set before him all the works of his hosts. And after these things he will kill him and protect the rest of my people who will be found in the place that I have chosen. And his dominion will last forever until the world of corruption has ended and until the times which have been mentioned before have been fulfilled. (40:1–3)

2 Baruch includes the Messiah one more time in a picture of the future. In chapter 53 the reader encounters an apocalypse that centers on clouds. There is a long explanation of alternating periods of darkness and light, represented by clouds of the corresponding color. At the very end of the explanation the Messiah appears: ". . . all will be delivered into the hands of my Servant, the Anointed One. For the whole earth will devour its inhabitants" (70:9–10). Chapters 72–73 detail what will happen at the time of bright waters following black ones. "After the signs have come of which I have spoken to you before, when the nations are moved and the time of my Anointed One comes, he will call all nations, and some of them he will spare, and others he will kill" (72:2). Once all of this has been completed, "after he has brought down everything which is in the world, and has sat down in eternal peace on the throne of the kingdom, then joy will be revealed and rest will appear" (73:1). Idyllic conditions ensue.

2 Baruch's Messiah is a conquering king whose glorious appearance marks a change after the eschatological calamities have occurred. He defeats the last, hideous foe and rules until the world of corruption ends. He judges all peoples, and when he sits on his throne in everlasting peace there is great joy. Those who have hoped in him, even if they have died, share in the benefits of his splendid reign.

2 ESDRAS (= 4 EZRA). Another response to the Roman destruction of Jerusalem, the Temple, and the nation was written under the pseudonym of Ezra, a leader during reconstruction more than a century after the first Temple was burned to the ground. The book has survived only in Latin but has the traits of a Jewish work composed in Hebrew, perhaps around the same time that 2 Baruch was written. Like 2 Baruch, 4 Ezra consists of dialogues in which the Jewish seer questions how God could justify the calamity that his people had experienced. In this case the dialogue takes place between Ezra and the angel Uriel, whom God had dispatched to converse with Ezra (see 4:1). As it has survived, the Jewish portion of the work is found in chapters 3–14, while chaps. 1–2 (= 5 Ezra) and 15–16 (= 6 Ezra) are Christian booklets that testify to the fact that Christians preserved and transmitted the Jewish work. 5 Ezra contains teachings about a savior who is pictured as a young man of great stature, but, as one expects in a Christian work, this savior is Jesus Christ.

The Jewish composition (chapters 3–14) offers its own distinctive picture of a Messiah. In the third vision (6:35–9:25) the angel makes the first disclosure to Ezra concerning the Anointed One:

> For behold, the time will come, when the signs which I have foretold to you will come to pass. . . . And everyone who has been delivered from the evils that I have foretold shall see my wonders. For my son the Messiah shall be revealed with those who are with him, and those who remain shall rejoice four hundred years. And after these years my son the Messiah shall die, and all who draw human breath. And the world shall be turned back to primeval silence for seven days, as it was at the first beginnings; so that no one shall be left. And after seven days the world, which is not yet awake, shall be roused, and that which is corruptible shall perish. (7:26–31)[3]

After the resurrection the Most High exercises judgment for about one week of years (7:32–44).

The Messiah, then, is God's son, who will have a temporary messianic reign of four hundred years, after which he will die. Nothing is said about whether he will rise to take part in the judgment.

The next reference to a Messiah occurs in the fifth, or eagle, vision (chapters 11–12). The eagle, which "had twelve feathered wings and three heads" (11:1), came from the sea and exercised rule over the entire earth (v. 5). The sundry parts of this amazing creature and their functions are set forth in chapter 11. Eventually a lion emerges to excoriate the eagle for its misrule and to announce its annihilation (11:36–46). The eagle, which is identified as the fourth beast of Daniel's vision (11:39; 12:11), is finally destroyed (12:1–3). Ezra requested an explanation of the strange vision and received one from the angel. The wings and heads of the creature are clarified, and the eagle is again presented as the fourth beast in Daniel 7.

> And as for the lion that you saw rousing up out of the forest and roaring and speaking to the eagle and reproving him for his unrighteousness, and as for all his words that you have heard, this is the Messiah whom the Most High has kept until the end of days, who will arise from the posterity of David, and will come and speak to them; he will denounce them for their ungodliness and for their wickedness, and will cast up before them their contemptuous dealings. For first he will set them living before his judgment seat, and when he has reproved them, then he will destroy them. But he will deliver in mercy the remnant of my people, those who have been saved throughout my borders, and he will make them joyful until the end comes, the day of judgment, of which I spoke to you at the beginning. (12:31–34)

Here, unlike in chapter 7, the Messiah carries out the function of judging, but the object of his sentence is the eagle, although it is addressed in the plural. Also, the final judgment is not under consideration here; it is mentioned at the end of v. 34 as coming after the blissful rule of the Messiah. In that sense, the picture in chapter 12 is consistent with the temporary messianic reign in chapter 7. The Davidic Messiah is also the agent through whom God's people are delivered or saved.

Ezra's sixth vision provides the final scene in which the Messiah is mentioned, although he is not called an "anointed one." In a dream Ezra sees a wind stirring the sea and making "something like the figure of a man come up out of the heart of the sea. And I looked, and behold, that man flew with the clouds of heaven; and wherever he turned his face to look, eveything under his gaze trembled, and whenever his voice issued from his mouth, all who heard his voice melted as wax melts when it feels the fire" (13:3–4). When an enormous multitude of people from all directions gathered to attack the one resembling a man, "he carved out for himself a great mountain, and flew upon it" (13:6). The attack took place nevertheless. The manlike being did not use normal weapons to fight but "sent forth from his mouth as it were a stream of fire, and from his lips a flaming breath, and from his tongue he shot forth a storm of sparks" (13:10). These combined long-range weapons consumed the attackers. "After this I saw the same man come down from the mountain and call to him another multitude which was peaceable. Then many people came to him, some of whom were joyful and some sorrowful; some of them were bound, and some were bringing others as offerings" (13:12–13).

As was his practice, Ezra requested an interpretation. He learns that the man coming from the sea "is he whom the Most High has been keeping for many ages, who will himself deliver his creation; and he will direct those who are left" (13:26). The attack that Ezra had observed meant that in a time of universal war and confusion

> when these things come to pass and the signs occur which I showed you before, then my son will be revealed, whom you saw as a man coming up from the sea. And when all the nations hear his voice, every man shall leave his own land and the warfare that they have against one another; and an innumerable multitude shall be gathered together . . . desiring to come and conquer him. But he will stand on top of Mount Zion. And Zion will come and be made manifest to all people, prepared and built, as you saw the mountain carved out without hands. And he, my Son, will reprove the assembled nations for their ungodliness . . . and he will destroy them without effort by the law. . . . And as for your seeing him gather to himself another multitude that was peaceable, these are the ten tribes. . . . (13:32–40)

Ezra is later told that the man's rising from the sea signified that "no one on earth can see my Son or those with him, except in the time of his day" (13:52).

In 2 Esdras (= 4 Ezra), then, the messianic leader, termed God's son, is hidden until the end, when he as conqueror destroys the wicked and reunites God's people on Mount Zion. He is from David's line, and his joyful, four-hundred-year reign ends with his death and the deaths of all others just before the last assize.

THE *APOCALYPSE OF ABRAHAM.* Another Jewish apocalypse written after the disastrous result of the war against Rome is the *Apocalypse of Abraham,* which is preserved now only in Old Slavonic, transmitted by Christians. It is likely, however, that it was written in Hebrew and that it dates from some point at the end of the first or beginning of the second century c.e.[4] The first part of the work (chapters 1–8) deals with the youthful Abraham's rejection of his father's idolatry, while the second (chapters 9–32) is an apocalypse that is introduced into the scene of Abra(ha)m's sacrifice in Genesis 15. God tells him on that occasion: "in this sacrifice I will place the ages. I will announce to you guarded things and you will see great things which you have not seen" (9:5–6; cf. vv. 9–10). God sends the angel Iaoel to make the revelations to him (10:3).

In the course of many disclosures, Abraham is told about the messianic leader at the end of time. Not all of the details are crystal clear, but in chapter 29 some twelve periods of impiety leading up to the end are under discussion. Abraham looks down at a picture that is being shown to him and says: "I looked and saw a man going out from the left, the heathen side. From the side of the heathen went out men and women and children, a great crowd, and they worshiped him. And while I was still looking, those on the right side came out, and some insulted this man, and some struck him and others worshiped him. And I saw that as they worshiped him Azazel ran and worshiped and, kissing his face, he turned and stood behind him" (29:4–6). Abraham asks who the man is and is told:

> [H]e is the liberation from the heathen for the people who will be (born) from you. In the last days, in this twelfth hour of impiety, in the twelfth period of the age of my fulfillment, I will set up this man from your tribe, the one whom you have seen from my people. All will imitate him, . . . (you) consider him as one called by me . . . (they) are changed in their counsels. And those you saw coming out from the left side of the picture and worshiping him, this (means that) many of the heathen will trust in him. And those of your seed you saw on the right side, some insulting him, some beating him, and others worshiping him, many of them shall be offended because of him. It is he who will test those of your seed who have worshiped him in the fulfillment of the twelfth hour, in the curtailing of the age of impiety. (29:8–12)

The text goes on to speak about ten plagues that will be sent on creation. Once they are past, "I will sound the trumpet out of the air, and I will send my chosen one, having in him one measure of all my power, and he will summon my people, humiliated by the heathen" (31:1). The judgment follows this scene.

Thus, in the *Apocalypse of Abraham* the messianic figure is called a man who is worshiped by some but insulted by others. He liberates Abraham's descendants from the control of the heathen, but some of the nations and some of Abraham's descendants will worship him. He will summon God's people after they have been humiliated by the nations. Textual problems in chap. 29 prevent one from understanding more fully what is said there, but it is difficult to avoid the impression that this passage is a Christian interpolation.

OTHER APOCALYPSES. A few other apocalypses that are of uncertain date and origin should be mentioned briefly here. The *Apocalypse of Zephaniah* may be attested as early as Clement of Alexandria's *Stromata*, and arguments have been offered that it is a first century B.C.E. to first century C.E. work.[5] Much of the fragmentarily preserved text tells of the prophet's experiences and encounters in the fifth heaven, of Hades and the abyss, the heavenly city, and so on. Though the last days seem to be envisioned, no messianic figure plays a role.

The same is the case for the lengthy *2 Enoch*. It is set in Enoch's final earthly days and involves revelations given to him before he bids farewell to his children. The topic that receives an extended treatment is the creation. Throughout the apocalypse, while the end is in view, there is no Messiah. Enoch himself also does not seem to play any such role. Instead, he receives spectacular revelations, conveys the key information to his children, and is finally removed.

The *Testament of Abraham* (first to second century C.E.) is, of course, placed near the time when Abraham is to die. He resists God's various messengers (Michael, Death) who are to take him and is shown what sorts of judgments the different kinds of souls undergo after leaving their bodies. While the judgment does play a major part in the story, nothing is said about an end-time leader.

Finally, *3 Baruch* may also belong here. It was written in the early centuries of the Christian era and contains a tour by Baruch through the five heavens. Among the mysteries disclosed to Baruch are the results of obedience and disobedience to God's commandments. The final judgment is not an important theme in the book, and it never mentions a Messiah.

Messianic Leaders outside the Apocalypses

Another way in which to approach the question of the relation between messianism and apocalypticism is to survey those texts that are not apocalypses in a formal sense but in which a messianic figure appears. The earliest such occurrences of "anointed one" for a leader of the last times are in the Dead Sea Scrolls and the *Psalms of Solomon*. The Scrolls present the unusual picture of two messianic figures, while *Psalms of Solomon* 17–18 speaks of a single Messiah from the line of David. The Qumran Scrolls are associated in some way with what may be termed an apocalyptic community, but a community that seems to have produced no apocalypses of its own. That is, it inherited apocalypses, such as the ones in the Enochic tradition, but there is no evidence that any author at Qumran wrote an apocalypse (see below for two possible exceptions).

MESSIAHS IN THE SCROLLS. A series of passages documents the fact that in the Qumran texts both a priestly and a Davidic/secular Messiah were expected to come. Each of the two Messiahs is designated by three different titles. The Davidic/secular Messiah is also called Branch of David and Prince of the Congregation. Besides Messiah, the priestly leader is named Interpreter of the Law and (High) Priest. In the following paragraphs those passages in which both are or may be referred to as Messiah in the same expression will be examined. Once those passages have been considered, other messianic ones will be studied to isolate the functions they attribute to these eschatological individuals and also to check whether the Scrolls preserve evidence of other messianic expectations.

1. The Two Messiahs Together. The Scrolls speak of a Messiah from Israel and a Messiah from Aaron, that is, of a Davidic and a priestly Messiah. What appears to be the earliest such reference is also the best known one. The *Rule of the Community* includes the following statement: "They should not depart from any counsel of the law in order to walk in complete stubbornness of their heart, but instead shall be ruled by the first directives which the men of the Community began to be taught until the prophet comes, and the Messiahs of Aaron and Israel" (1QS 9:9–11).[6] While the number of Messiahs is not specified here, the fact that the words "of Aaron and Israel" complete the construct phrase favors the conclusion that there are two. The plural Messiahs is an unmistakable reading in the manuscript, but the genuineness of the passage has been disputed because one of the Cave 4 copies of the *Rule of the Community,* which on paleographical grounds is considered by some scholars to be the oldest copy, lacks these and surrounding lines. Although ten copies of the work have been identified among the myriad fragments from Cave 4, only the fourth and fifth are relevant because they alone preserve the general part of the text found in the vicinity of the ninth column in the Cave 1 copy (where the messianic reference occurs). The fourth copy (4Q258) is broken in the context (although it contains the equivalent of 9:10 at the end of frag. 2 col. ii and has the equivalent of 9:15 at the beginning of frag. 2 col. iii), but the text preserved in 4Q259 moves from the equivalent of 8:15 in the Cave 1 copy to the equivalent of 9:12 in the Cave 1 copy. That is, it (apparently uniquely) lacks all the material between 8:15 and 9:12, including the reference to the Messiahs. The correct explanation for this state of affairs is not clear. Absence of the material could be explained as omission of a full column (similar expressions precede and follow the missing text), in which case the material would be original and the shorter text defective; or the extra material in the Cave 1 copy could be an addition (see VanderKam 1994, 212–13). Since 4Q259 may be the oldest copy of the *Rule of the Community,* some scholars have concluded that the work did not refer to the Messiahs in its original form. While there is clear evidence of conceptual development in the different copies of the work (the role of the sons of Zadok is a case in point), it remains debatable whether 4Q259 retains a more ancient form of the text than the Cave 1 copy in this place. The important point is, nevertheless, that a text dating from ca. 100 B.C.E. (1QS) contains a reference to a priestly and to a secular Messiah. In the text the appearance of the prophet and Messiahs serves to mark the end of an era: the members of the community are to follow the original directives of the group until they arrive. That is, their advent ushers in the end of this evil age. Nothing more is said about the Messiahs' activities in the *Rule of the Community.*

The evidence from the *Damascus Document* should probably be understood in the same sense. This work, which stems from the larger movement of which the Qumran community was a small part, resorts to similar but not identical language in speaking about messianic matters. The key distinction between the formulation in the *Rule of the Community* and that in the *Damascus Document* is that while the former uses the plural "Messiahs" the latter has the singular "Messiah." There are four passages in the *Damascus Document* that remind one of the messianic statement in 1QS. In CD 12:23–13:1 we read: "Those who walk in them, in the time of wickedness until there arises the messiah of Aaron and Israel. . . ." CD 14:18–19 is similar: "And this is the exact interpretation of the regulations by which [they shall be ruled until there arises the messiah] of Aaron and Israel. He shall atone for their sins]." CD 19:10–11 speaks of a military situation, as it explains Zech. 13:7: "These shall escape in the age of the visitation; but those that remain shall be delivered up to the sword when there comes the messiah of Aaron and Israel." Finally, 19:33–20:1 uses the messianic arrival to define the end of the present era: "And thus, all the men who entered the new covenant in the land of Damascus and turned and betrayed and departed from the well of living waters, shall not be counted in the assembly of the people and shall not be inscribed in their [lis]ts, from the day of the session {of him who te<aches>/ of the teacher} of the unique Teacher until there arises the messiah of Aaron and Israel." Although in all four instances the term *messiah* is singular and in the only case where a finite verb is used with the title it, too, is singular, the Messiah has both Aaronic and Israelite qualities. In fact, each of the two terms *Aaron* and *Israel* in CD 20:1 is supplied with a preposition (literally: from Aaron and from Israel). The fragmentary Cave 4 copies offer little help since they usually do not preserve the relevant parts of the text, but in the only instance in which one of the messianic passages is extant—4QD[a] 10 i 12–13 for 14:18–19 (cf. 4QD[d] 11 i 2)—it verifies the reading of the Geniza copy quoted above.

2. Messiah and Priest. There are no other occurrences of the expressions "the Messiahs of Aaron and Israel" or "the Messiah of Aaron and Israel" in the Scrolls, but there are several passages in which the Davidic Messiah appears together with a priest. These may reflect the same dual messianism even though they do not give the title Messiah to the priest. 1QSa (the *Rule of the Congregation*), which was copied on the same scroll as 1QS (the *Rule of the Community*), describes an eschatological meal in which the Messiah and a priest play roles. The text opens by saying, "this is the rule of the congregation of Israel in the final days, when they gather" (col. 1, line 1). The section dealing specifically with the messianic meal contains several lines that are important for the present purposes. According to García Martínez's rendering, 2:11–12a reads: "This is the assembly of famous men, [those summoned to] the gathering of the community council, when [God] begets the Messiah with them." However, the term "God" has to be imported into the text, and "begets" is an emendation. E. Puech has now shown that the verb, owing to a supralinear correction, is to be read "reveals," not "begets" (1994, 351–65). In other words, the text is speaking about an assembly at which God reveals the Messiah together with the members of the community. At that time, the text continues:

> the chief [priest] of all the congregation of Israel shall enter, and all [his brothers, the sons] of Aaron, the priests [summoned] to the assembly, the famous men, and they shall sit befo[re him, each one] according to his dignity. After, [the Me]ssiah of Israel shall ent[er] and before him shall sit the chiefs [of the clans of Israel, each] one according to his dignity, according to their [positions] in their camps and in their marches. (2:12–15)

Then, when the meal is ready,

> [no-one should stretch out] his hand to the first-fruit of the bread and of the [new wine] before the priest, for [he is the one who bl]esses the first-fruit of bread and of the new wine [and stretches out] his hand towards the bread before them. Afterwards, the Messiah of Israel shall stretch out his hand towards the bread. [And after, he shall] bless all the congregation of the community, each [one according to] his dignity. And in accordance with this regulation they shall act at each me[al, when] at least ten m[en are gat]hered. (2:18–22)

The last line suggests that this messianic meal is a recurring event, while the beginning of the text declares that the rules found in it are for the last days. The nonpriestly leader alone is given the title Messiah in the extant portions of the text. The priest may also be considered a Messiah, but the title is never specifically attached to him.

This pattern found in the *Rule of the Congregation*, according to which the two eschatological leaders appear together though the title Messiah is not assigned to both, is repeated in a number of other texts from the Qumran caves. 4Q174 (*Florilegium*) is a prime example. In a section of the text that deals with the promise of an eternal dynasty to David, the writer says: "This (refers to the) 'branch of David,' who will arise with the Interpreter of the law who [will rise up] in Zi[on in] the last days" (1–3 i 11–12). There is no doubt that Branch of David is a title for the Davidic Messiah, and Interpreter of the Law is one of the epithets used for the priestly Messiah. The text is explicit about the expectation that the two will appear together in the last days. It seems that 4Q252 (*Commentary on Genesisa*) fits in the same mold. In his interpretation of the blessing on Judah in Gen. 49:10 the expositor writes:

> A sovereign shall [not] be removed from the tribe of Judah. While Israel has dominion there will [not] lack someone who sits on the throne of David. For "the staff" is the covenant of royalty, [the thou]sands of Israel are "the feet." Until the messiah of justice comes, the branch of David. For to him and to his descendants has been given the covenant of royalty over his people for all everlasting generations, which he has observed [. . .] the Law with the men of the Community. (5:1–5)

It is likely that in the gap in the last line quoted (the space indicated as [. . .] before "the Law") the term "Interpreter of" should be restored; if so, then the Interpreter of the Law is present with the leader, who is called both Messiah and Branch of David (thus showing that the two royal titles refer to the same individual).

The *Damascus Document* contains a similar passage, one that supports the idea that in the recurring expression "Messiah of Aaron and Israel" (see above) two Messiahs are envisaged. The passage in question is CD 7:14–21, where the writer is clarifying the meaning of Amos 5:26–27 by using the complementary information found in Amos 9:11 and in Num. 24:17. About the star in Amos 5:26 ("Kaiwan your star-God") he writes: "the star is the Interpreter of the Law, who will come to Damascus, as it is written: 'A star moves out of Jacob, and a sceptre arises out of Israel' [= Num. 24:17]. The sceptre is the prince of the whole congregation and when he arises he will destroy all the sons of Seth" (7:18–21). The expositor finds that Num. 24:17 refers to two future leaders, and these two are the two Messiahs of the *Rule of the Community* and the *Damascus Document*.

4Q161 (4QpIsaᵃ) seems to belong in this category as indicated by 7–10 iii 22–29, where the writer is commenting on Isaiah 11. The long citation of Isa. 11:1–5 occupies lines 15–20, and an empty line separates the biblical lemma from the commentary. The Isaian text furnishes an obvious peg on which to hang statements about a Davidic Messiah. The name *David* appears immediately after a gap in line 22; it is followed by a reference to the end of days in the same line and by "throne" and "crown" in line 24 and the verbs "rule" and "judge" in line 25. Line 27 then gives a recitation of Isa. 11:3. The interpretation of the verse is broken, but lines 28–29 say: "28. [. . .] as they teach him, so will he judge, and according to their command 29. [. . .] with him. One of the priests of repute will go out. . . ."[7] The reputable priest is not identified as a Messiah, but at least he seems to be with the Davidic Messiah described in the preceding lines, and a group of priests appear to be the ones who provide instruction for the Messiah in matters of justice.

4Q285 (the so-called *War Rule*) frags. 4–5 also associate a Davidic leader with a priest. Here again the biblical base is from Isaiah, specifically Isa. 10:34–11:1. Frag. 4 refers to the Prince of the Congregation twice (lines 2 and 6) and apparently describes a war that he conducts against the Kittim. Frag. 5 opens with a quotation from Isa. 10:34–11:1 and continues with: "3 [. . .] the bud [= branch] of David will go into battle with [. . .] 4 [. . .] and the Prince of the Congregation will kill him, the bu[d of David . . .] 5 [. . .] and with wounds. And a priest will command [. . .] 6 [. . .] the destruction of the Kittim [. . .]." The Davidic Messiah, under two of his Qumran titles, figures prominently, but a priest, not further identified, also plays a commanding part in the battle.

3. Other Messianic References in Qumran Texts. Another group of texts mentions a single Messiah, whether Davidic or priestly, but fails to employ the title Messiah. The *War Rule* includes one reference to the Prince of the Congregation (1QM 5:1), on whose shield names representative of all groups in Israel are inscribed. 1QM 15:4 introduces the high priest as offering a prayer before the final struggle with the Kittim; he strengthens the troops with his words during the battle (16:13); during the last assault he and his fellow priests bless God (18:5; see also 2:1). 1QSb (the *Rule of the Blessings*) 5:20–29 contains a benediction for the prince of the congregation. The blessings heaped upon him are based on those given to the davidic shoot in Isaiah 11. He is to defeat the nations, establish the covenant, and rule with justice. The same text should contain a blessing for the high priest, but no rubric marks where it might have occurred.

Two Qumran texts that have been labeled apocalypses also preserve passages that should be treated in this context. It is debatable whether, under the definition offered above, either of these works should be assigned to the genre *apocalypse*. Perhaps if more of the texts had survived the point would be clear, but in their present, fragmentary form they lack some of the ingredients of apocalypses. 4Q521 (*Messianic Apocalypse*), at the top of what is called col. 2 in frag. 2, reads: "1 [for the heav]ens and the earth will listen to his Messiah 2 [and all] that is in them will not turn away from the holy precepts." The text goes on to speak of mighty deeds and miracles that will take place, but they are apparently performed by the Lord. The second text under this rubric, 4Q246 (*Aramaic Apocalypse*), predicts the rise of a remarkable ruler:

> 1 7 [. . .] and he will be great over the earth 8 [. . .] they will do, and all will serve 9 [. . .] great will he be called and he will be designated by his name. 2 1 He will be called son of God, and they will call him son of the Most High. Like the sparks 2 of a vision, so will their kingdom be; they will rule several years over 3 the earth and crush everything; a people will crush another people, and a city another city. 4 *Blank* Until the people of God arises and makes everyone rest from the sword.

Some scholars maintain that a messianic figure is here being called "son of God" and "son of the Most High" (as Jesus is in Luke 1:32, 35); but the pattern of the text seems to be that of Daniel 7, in which the quintessentially evil fourth kingdom is replaced by the rule of the saints. If so, the sequence would entail that the titles are ascribed falsely to a ruler in this last, wicked kingdom and hence are not being attributed to a Messiah.

THE *PSALMS OF SOLOMON*. The set of poems that were transmitted under the name of Solomon was written in the latter part of the first century B.C.E. Psalms 17 and 18, the last two in the collection, express a vivid, detailed hope for a Messiah from the line of David. The author takes pains to locate his beliefs about a Messiah within the context of a repeated confession that God is the eternal king (17:1, 26; cf. v. 34, where the Lord is the Messiah's king) who is the savior and whose kingdom is also forever (17:3). He refers to the promise of an eternal dynasty for David but also notes that national sin has led to the rise of evil, non-Davidic rulers (apparently the Hasmoneans, "[t]hose to whom you did not [make the] promise" [v. 5]) who established themselves as kings. The Lord judged and overthrew them through an alien, who seems to be Pompey (vv. 6–9). Terrible times ensued because of the arrogance and violence of the foreign conquerors. In this context of all that had gone wrong during the periods of rule by the Hasmoneans and Romans, the author enunciates his yearning for a new Anointed One from David's line (17:21–44). The passage is too lengthy to quote, but its teachings and those of the shorter section in chap. 18:5–9 can be summarized under four headings.

1. The Nature of the Messiah. He is a king (17:21, 32) who is a descendant of David (17:21); he is called Lord Messiah,[8] is said to be free from sin (17:36), and whatever he does is characterized by righteousness.

2. The Messiah's Relation with God. God, the eternal king, is always the superior one who acts and is in control. God will raise the Anointed One in his own time (17:21) and will support him with the ability to drive out the Gentiles (17:22). The people led by the Judge-Messiah are the ones whom God sanctified (17:26; cf. v. 27). The Messiah will glorify God in an exalted place (Jerusalem, v. 30) where the nations see the Lord's glory (v. 31). As a righteous king he will be taught by God (17:32). The Lord is the Messiah's king, the one on whom he relies (17:32–34, 37). "God made him powerful in the holy spirit and wise in the counsel of understanding, with strength and righteousness" (v. 37). God's blessing remains with him (17:38), and his hope lies in the Lord (17:39), as he is "strong in the fear of God" (17:40). He will shepherd the Lord's flock (17:40). God is the one who will cause Israel's good fortune at the time of the Messiah (17:44), and he is the one who will cleanse Israel in preparation for that blessed time (18:5). The fear of the Lord will be the mark of the Messiah's reign (18:7–9).

3. The Messiah's Relation with Israel. The Messiah is to reign over God's servant Israel (17:21, 35; 18:5). He will gather and lead them in righteousness (17:26), will judge them (17:26, 43), and will be their righteous king (17:32). He purges Jerusalem of Gentiles (17:30–31). He blesses the Lord's people with wisdom and happiness (17:35); he shepherds them and leads them in holiness and discipline (17:40-42; see 18:7). He also directs them in righteous acts in the fear of the Lord (18:8-9).

4. The Messiah's Relation with the Nations. The Messiah is to purge Jerusalem of Gentiles (17:32), and he will destroy "the unlawful nations with the word of his mouth" (17:24). The nations will flee from him when he warns them (17:25). As one might expect, he judges "peoples and nations in the wisdom of his righteousness" (17:29). The nations will serve him (17:30) and will stream to Jerusalem to observe his and the Lord's glory (17:31). He will be compassionate to the peoples who revere him (17:34).

     In the *Psalms of Solomon* the Messiah is an extraordinary individual to whom God will grant great gifts such as wisdom, righteousness, holiness, and the fear of the Lord, but he remains a human monarch who is subservient to God, the eternal king.

PHILO AND JOSEPHUS. Philo has left no clear indication about any messianic beliefs he may have entertained, although he may be hinting in this direction in *On Rewards and Punishments* 95. There, in his explanation of the Greek version of Num. 24:17 ("there shall come forth a man"), he writes that the man, aided by God, will subdue many nations. He does not stipulate whether the text intends an eschatological or a historical ruler. Josephus does resort to the term *messiah* in a few instances and uses other terms for future leaders. However, he does not tell the reader what his views about a Messiah might have been. One passage that has messianic overtones is the familiar "ambiguous oracle" that he reports in the *Jewish War* in a section in which he is reflecting on portents the Jews had received before the war against Rome.

> But what more than all else incited them to the war was an ambiguous oracle, likewise found in their sacred scriptures, to the effect that at that time one from their country would become ruler of the world. This they understood to mean someone of their own race, and many of their wise men went astray in their interpretation of it. The oracle, however, in reality signified the sovereignty of Vespasian, who was proclaimed emperor on Jewish soil. (6.312–13)[9]

Josephus does make two references to Jesus and includes the term *messiah* in both. In *Ant.* 18.63 the text has "[h]e was the Messiah," while in *Ant.* 20.200 he is said to be "Jesus who was called the Christ."[10] The first of these passages has, of course, been widely regarded as the product of at least some Christian editorial interference, while the second is simply a noncommittal report by Josephus.

Josephus also adduces several instances in which men whom he regarded as impostors tried to gather a crowd of followers by evoking historical themes such as the exodus, the trek in the wilderness, and the crossing of the Jordan. He alludes to a Samaritan who, during the procuratorship of Pontius Pilate (26–36 C.E.) assembled an armed crowd which he led to the sacred Mount Gerizim to show them the holy vessels still buried where, curiously, Moses was supposed to have placed them. Pilate's troops brought a premature halt to the movement (*Ant.* 18.85–87). At the time of Fadus (ca. 45 C.E.) a man named Theudas, claiming to be a prophet, attracted a fairly large number of followers who were to accompany him to the Jordan River. It was to part at his command, just as it had for Joshua. Roman troops again intervened and Theudas was beheaded (*Ant.* 20.97–99). Rabbi Gamaliel refers to the same incident in Acts 5:36, where he puts the number of Theudas's followers at "about four hundred." While Felix ruled in Judea (ca. 52–59 C.E.), another claimant to the prophetic mantle, a man called only "the Egyptian," lured some thirty thousand people to the wilderness and then to the Mount of Olives with the promise that the walls of Jerusalem would collapse at their approach. The predictable military response of the Roman regime ended this scheme as well (*Ant.* 20.169–72). In *War* 2.262–63 Josephus writes that the Egyptian intended to rule as a tyrant. The Egyptian appears to be the man for whom the apostle Paul was mistaken by the tribune in Acts 21:38. Josephus never refers to any of these individuals as Messiahs or even so-called Messiahs.

MESSIAHS AND REVOLTS. The Jewish revolts against Rome in 66–70 and 132–35 and the Diaspora uprising in 115–17 could be considered prime occasions for potential Messiahs to appear. There is really no evidence for any such claim during the first revolt. Menahem, the son of Judas the Galilean (see *War* 2.433–48), and Simon bar Giora (see *War* 7.26–36) had royal pretensions, but Josephus reports nothing regarding messianic assertions by or about them.

The Diaspora revolt in the time of Trajan may have involved a messianic leader or leaders. Eusebius calls the chief in Cyrene *Lucuas* (*Ecclesiastical History* 4.2) and attributes to him the titles Leader and King; Dio Cassius gives his name as *Andreas* (*Roman History* 68.32). The latter also mentions a certain rebel leader on Cyprus named Artemion. While some scholars view the uprising as messianic in nature, the evidence for the character of the revolt is really very sparse.

The second Jewish revolt against Rome (132–35) was certainly messianic in the sense that the Jewish military leader, Simon bar Kosiba, was identified as King Messiah by Rabbi Akiba according to rabbinic sources (e.g., *y. Taʿan.* 4.8 [68d]). Akiba is supposed to have related to him the prediction of Num. 24:17 that a star (*kôkāb*) would come forth from Jacob. This brought about the wordplay on Simon bar Kosiba's name so that it became *bar Kokhba*, or son of the star (see also Eusebius, *Ecclesiastical History* 4.6, 2). The same talmudic passage (*y. Taʿan.* 4.8 [68d]) also indicates that Rabbi Akiba's opinion was not shared by all. The letters and coins associated with Simon's rule use neither the title King nor Messiah for him; rather, they designate him Prince of Israel. When the revolt failed, Simon's memory was condemned by dubbing him Simon ben Koziba, or son of the lie (Horsley and Hanson 1985, 127–29).

☞ CONCLUSIONS _____

The survey of the evidence for messianic teachings within Jewish apocalypses and outside them has yielded important if diverse results. These may be summarized briefly.

Chronology

No Jewish text written before the second century B.C.E. mentions a messianic leader. Some of the later works in the Hebrew Bible offer suggestive words and images that point in this direction (e.g., Isa. 9:1–6; Hag. 2:20–23), and others were later interpreted as referring to a Messiah (e.g., the suffering servant in Deutero-Isaiah, the one like a son of man in Daniel 7), but no pre-200 work describes a person who could be called a Messiah in the eschatological sense of the term. Texts failing to mention a Messiah in eschatological contexts continued to be composed throughout the period covered by the preceding survey. Nonmessianic portraits of the end-times were a frequent phenomenon in early Judaism.

Apocalypses and Messianism

None of the earliest Jewish apocalypses (the Astronomical Book, the Book of the Watchers, the Apocalypse of Weeks, parts of *Jubilees*, Daniel 7–12) contains references to messianic leaders. The earliest one to make such an allusion—the Animal Apocalypse—dates from the late 160s B.C.E. After that time a number of apocalypses include messianic teachings (the Similitudes of Enoch, *2 Baruch*, *4 Ezra*, *Apocalypse of Abraham*), but others do not (the *Apocalypse of Zephaniah*, *2 Enoch*, the *Testament of Abraham*, and *3 Baruch*). If one divides the apocalypses into the categories defined in *Semeia* 14, four types are represented in the early Jewish apocalypses. Type Ia ("Historical" Apocalypses with No Otherworldly Journey) includes some with a messianic figure (the Animal Apocalypse, *2 Baruch*, *4 Ezra*) and some without (Daniel 7-12, the Apocalypse of Weeks, *Jubilees* 1 and 23). The same is the case for IIb (Otherworldly Journeys with Cosmic and/or Political Eschatology) in which the Astronomical Book, the Book of the Watchers, *2 Enoch,* and *Testament of Levi* 2–5 lack a Messiah, while the Similitudes of Enoch has one. Type IIa ("Historical" Apocalypses with an Otherworldly Journey) includes only the *Apocalypse of Abraham* among the works considered here, and it has a messianic leader. Type IIc (Otherworldly Journeys with only Personal Eschatology) contains the *Apocalypse of Zephaniah,* the *Testament of Abraham,* and *3 Baruch,* none of which mentions a Messiah (Collins 1979, 14–15). No author explains why a Messiah is not mentioned, but those texts which lack such a figure are able to emphasize the actions of God, perhaps executed through angels, to a greater extent than are those which include a Messiah.

Messiahs and Writings That Are Not Apocalypses

Some works that are not formally apocalypses but offer apocalyptic or eschatological teachings contain references to or entire sections on messianic figures, but few of them do so. That is, the vast majority of Second Temple Jewish texts have no reference to a messianic leader of the end-time. A number of works, such as historical reports, would not be expected to include one, but it is still obvious that messianic thinking was not a dominant approach among Jewish writers whose works have survived from that period.

Images of the Messiah(s):

The texts that speak about messianic beliefs present not a unitary but a varied picture of who the Messiah(s) was (were) thought to be and what he (they) would do.

1. The texts show that some writers anticipated the arrival of one and others awaited two Messiahs. Expectation of one Messiah is much more frequently represented; a dual messianism is attested only in the Dead Sea Scrolls.

2. Early Jewish authors used several titles for the Messiah(s):

Messiah	Similitudes of Enoch, *2 Baruch,* 4 Ezra, the *Rule of the Community,* the *Damascus Document,* the *Rule of the Congregation,* the *Commentary on Genesisa,* 4Q521 (*Messianic Apocalypse*), *Psalms of Solomon* (where he is called Lord Messiah), Josephus, *Antiquities,* Talmud Yerushalmi
Righteous One	Similitudes of Enoch
Chosen One	Similitudes of Enoch, *Apocalypse of Abraham*
Son of Man	Similitudes of Enoch; 4 Ezra refers to one having the figure of a man, and the *Apocalypse of Abraham* calls him a man.
Son (of God)	4 Ezra
(God's) Servant	*2 Baruch*
Prince of the Congregation	*Damascus Document,* 4Q285 (*War Rule*), *War Scroll,* the *Rule of the Blessings*
Branch of David	4Q174 (*Florilegium*), *Commentary on Genesisa,* 4Q285 (*War Rule*), 4Q161?

Interpreter of the	
Law	*Damascus Document*, 4Q174 (*Florilegium*), 4Q252
	(*Commentary on Genesisa*)
(High) Priest	*Rule of the Congregation*, 4Q161?, 4Q285 (*War Rule*), *War Scroll*

Other symbolic references are attested: a white bull (the Animal Apocalypse), a vine/fountain (*2 Baruch*), and a lion (4 Ezra).

3. The most common belief was that the Messiah would be from the lineage of David, that he would engage in warfare to defeat the nations, and that he would judge the wicked. In these senses he would be involved in delivering God's people and would appear at the turning point of history. His rule would be marked by justice. 4 Ezra alone expresses the belief that the messianic reign would be temporary and that the Messiah would die.

4. Only texts in the tradition prepared for by *Jubilees* (and perhaps Aramaic Levi; cf. the *Testaments of the Twelve Patriarchs*) and embodied in the Dead Sea Scrolls articulate the belief that there would be two Messiahs, one Davidic and one priestly. Their appearance with a prophet will mark the end of this evil age and usher in a new era. The Davidic Messiah is associated with ruling and judging, while the priest instructs and blesses. In one place it is said that the Messiah(s) will atone for the sins of the chosen.

5. Other than in the *Jubilees*-Qumran tradition, there is no clear evidence in early Jewish texts about the messianic beliefs or lack of them among the Jewish parties such as the Pharisees or Sadducees.

Concluding Speculations

The evidence does not permit sure conclusions about the reason(s) why messianism arose when it did and appeared where it is attested, but some tentative suggestions may be offered. The lack of messianic expectation in the Second Temple and the fact that the most ancient apocalypses do not envisage a Messiah may in part be related to Jewish attitudes toward non-Jewish rule over them. The Jewish nation had centuries of experience with such a governmental arrangement, and there is evidence that Gentile rule was at times viewed neutrally or even somewhat positively, as long as the regime permitted exercise of Judaism. The first authors to include Messiahs in the scenarios for the future were hostile to the reigning power. The Animal Apocalypse includes the periods of rule by all the foreign powers in exilic and postexilic history within the time of despotic rule by the seventy shepherds; it does, however, show a positive attitude toward native rule (Judas Maccabeus). Parts of Daniel show, nevertheless, that attitudes to Gentile rule were not the sole cause for the rise of messianism, since in its apocalyptic sections, unlike some of the court narratives, the foreign powers are pictured most negatively and the Maccabees are presented somewhat positively.

    In the Qumran texts, the *Psalms of Solomon,* and the Similitudes of Enoch both foreign and native rulers are castigated and hopes are placed on a Messiah (or Messiahs) who will end the present evil age of injustice. Much later, in the aftermath of the first Jewish revolt against Rome (66–70 c.e.) the gross failure of both Gentile and Jewish leadership led to the despair found in works such as *2 Baruch* and 4 Ezra and the yearning for the arrival of a Davidic Messiah. If attitudes toward the Gentile power were a strong factor in arousing messianic hopes, it is quite understandable that neither Philo nor Josephus would have a place for a Messiah in their writings.

The factors that determined the status assigned by the different authors to their Messiahs are not clear. It may be that the choice of which biblical passages to use in developing the picture of the Messiahs played a role, but that would leave unexplained why those passages were selected in the first place. Of all the texts surveyed, the Similitudes of Enoch presents the most exalted portrait of a Messiah; other apocalypses such as *2 Baruch* and *4 Ezra* also view him as a highly impressive individual but not one of the same heavenly status as the Messiah of the Similitudes. It is difficult to define the status of the Messiahs in the Qumran texts, but they appear to be human leaders; the same is true for the great and righteous descendant of David in the *Psalms of Solomon.* Moreover, there is no reason for thinking that Simon bar Kosiba was envisaged as superhuman. Consequently, while it may be the case that the apocalypses anticipate a somewhat more exalted messiah than the leaders one finds in the nonapocalyptic texts, the contrast is not a strong one in most cases.

NOTES

1. Quotations from *1 Enoch* are taken from M. Knibb, *The Ethiopic Book of Enoch,* 2 vols. (Oxford: Clarendon Press, 1978), vol. 2.

2. The translations of *2 Baruch* are from A. F. J. Klijn in *Old Testament Pseudepigrapha,* ed. J. H. Charlesworth, 2 vols. (= *OTP*) (Garden City, N.Y.: Doubleday, 1983, 1985), vol. 1.

3. The translation used for *2 Esdras/4 Ezra* is that of B. M. Metzger in *OTP,* vol. 1.

4. See R. Rubinkiewicz in *OTP,* 1:682–83. The translations of the *Apocalypse of Abraham* are those of Rubinkiewicz.

5. See O. Wintermute in *OTP,* 1:499–501.

6. Translations of the Dead Sea Scrolls come from F. García Martínez, *The Dead Sea Scrolls Translated* (Leiden: E. J. Brill, 1994).

7. The translation of this passage is from M. Horgan, *Pesharim* (CBQMS 8; Washington: Catholic Biblical Association, 1979), 76.

8. For the textual situation here, see R. B. Wright in *OTP,* 2:669–70, n. z. Quotations are from Wright's translation.

9. The translation is that of H. St. J. Thackeray, *Josephus* III: *The Jewish War, Books IV–VII,* Loeb Classical Library (Cambridge, Mass.: Harvard University Press; London: Heinemann, 1979).

10. These renderings are from L. H. Feldman, *Josephus* IX: *Jewish Antiquities, Books XVIII–XIX,* Loeb Classical Library (Cambridge, Mass.: Harvard University Press; London: Heinemann, 1981); and idem, *Josephus* X: *Jewish Antiquities, Book XX,* Loeb Classical Library (Cambridge, Mass.: Harvard University Press; London: Heinemann, 1981).

BIBLIOGRAPHY

Charlesworth, J. H., ed. 1992. *The Messiah: Developments in Earliest Judaism and Christianity.* Minneapolis: Fortress Press.

Collins, John J. 1991. "Genre, Ideology and Social Movements." In *Mysteries and Revelations: Apocalyptic Studies since the Uppsala Colloquium,* edited by J. J. Collins and J. H. Charlesworth, 11–32. Journal for the Study of the Pseudepigrapha Supplements 9. Sheffield: Sheffield Academic Press.

————. 1993. *Daniel.* Hermeneia. Minneapolis: Fortress Press.

————. 1995. *The Scepter and the Star.* Anchor Bible Reference Library. New York: Doubleday.

Collins, John J., ed. 1979. *Apocalypse: The Morphology of a Genre. Semeia* 14. Chico, Calif.: Scholars Press.

Cross, F. M. 1973. *Canaanite Myth and Hebrew Epic.* Cambridge, Mass.: Harvard University Press.

García Martínez, F. 1994. *The Dead Sea Scrolls Translated.* Leiden: E. J. Brill.

Hanson, Paul. 1975. *The Dawn of Apocalyptic.* Philadelphia: Fortress Press.

Hollander, H. W., and M. de Jonge. 1985. *The Testaments of the Twelve Patriarchs.* Studia in Veteris Testamenti Pseudepigrapha 8. Leiden: E. J. Brill.

Horsley, R. A., and J. S. Hanson. 1985. *Bandits, Prophets, and Messiahs: Popular Religious Movements at the Time of Jesus.* Minneapolis: Winston.

Milik, J. T. 1976. *The Books of Enoch.* Oxford: Clarendon Press.

Neusner, J., W. S. Green, and E. Frerichs, eds. 1987. *Judaisms and Their Messiahs.* Cambridge: Cambridge University Press.

Oegema, G. 1994. *Der Gesalbte und sein Volk.* Göttingen: Vandenhoeck & Ruprecht.

Plöger, O. 1968. *Theocracy and Eschatology.* Richmond: John Knox. An English translation of the second German edition, which appeared in 1962.

Puech, E. 1994. "Préséance sacerdotale et messie-roi dans la Règle de la Congrégation (*1QSa* ii 11–22)." *Revue de Qumran* 16/63:351–65.

Rowland, C. 1982. *The Open Heaven.* New York: Crossroad.

Schürer, E. 1979. "Messianism." In *The History of the Jewish People in the Age of Jesus Christ,* Volume 2, revised and edited by G. Vermes, F. Millar, and M. Black, 2:488–554. Edinburgh: T. & T. Clark.

Stone, M. 1968. "The Concept of the Messiah in IV Ezra." In *Religions in Antiquity: Essays in Memory of E. R. Goodenough,* edited by J. Neusner, 295–312. Leiden: E. J. Brill.

Tiller, P. 1993. *A Commentary on the Animal Apocalypse of I Enoch.* Society of Biblical Literature Early Judaism and Its Literature 4. Atlanta: Scholars Press.

VanderKam, J. 1977. *Textual and Historical Studies in the Book of Jubilees.* Harvard Semitic Monographs 14. Missoula, Mont.: Scholars Press.

————. 1984. *Enoch and the Growth of an Apocalyptic Tradition.* CBQMS 16. Washington: Catholic Biblical Association.

————. 1989. *The Book of Jubilees.* 2 vols. Corpus Scriptorum Christianorum Orientalium 510–11, Scriptores Aethiopici 87–88. Louvain: Peeters. Translations of *Jubilees* are taken from this volume.

————. 1992. "Righteous One, Messiah, Chosen One, and Son of Man in 1 Enoch 37-71." In *The Messiah,* edited by J. H. Charlesworth, 169–91. Minneapolis: Fortress Press.

————. 1994. "Messianism in the Scrolls." In *The Community of the Renewed Covenant,* edited by E. Ulrich and J. VanderKam, 211–34. Christianity and Judaism in Antiquity 10. Notre Dame, Ind.: University of Notre Dame Press.

6

The Eschatology of Jesus

Dale C. Allison, Jr.
Pittsburgh Theological Seminary

W HAT JESUS BELIEVED about the last things is a controversial topic. Throughout most of
church history Christian readers of the New Testament have related Jesus' prophecies
primarily to three things—to Pentecost and the life of the church, to the destruction of
Jerusalem in 70 C.E. and God's supposed abandonment of the Jewish people, and to the resurrection of the dead and final judgment at the distant end of the world. Many modern scholars,
however, now believe that Jesus had little if anything to say about the church, that he anticipated not God's abandonment of Israel but Israel's eschatological restoration, and that he
spoke of the end not as distant but as near to hand. Indeed, many are convinced that much of
Jesus' message can be fairly characterized as apocalyptic eschatology. This chapter will clarify
just why this is the case and why other interpretations of the evidence are unlikely to be correct.

THE OLD CONSENSUS

The modern discussion of Jesus and eschatology began with the first edition of Johannes
Weiss's *Die Predigt Jesu vom Reiche Gottes,* which appeared in 1892. In this Weiss argued that
Jesus' proclamation of the kingdom, rightly understood, was consistent with neither traditional
Christian piety nor the nineteenth century's liberal lives of Jesus. When Jesus spoke of the kingdom, he was not referring to the church, that is, the body of dead and living saints, nor was he
speaking of God's rule in the human heart. He was, rather, announcing the imminent advent of
an eschatological reality that would transform the physical world. That reality would be ushered in by the final judgment, which would mean punishment or annihilation for the condemned and reward in paradise for the righteous. According to Weiss, although Jesus originally

139

thought the end to be very near, later, after his call for repentance went widely unheeded, he came to believe that the kingdom would not come before he had died as a ransom for the people.

In 1906 Albert Schweitzer, when surveying the nineteenth century's quest for Jesus, wrote that Weiss's little book "seems to break a spell. It closes one epoch and begins another" (1961, 239). Schweitzer had independently come to the same conclusion as Weiss: Jesus was an apocalyptic preacher. Schweitzer, however, believed that Weiss "showed a certain timidity" (1961, 351 n. 1), for he failed to see that Jesus' conduct in its entirety was ruled by an eschatological scenario. This was the significance of Schweitzer's famous term "thoroughgoing eschatology" (*konsequente Eschatologie*). More so than Weiss, Schweitzer explained every aspect of what Jesus said and did by reference to eschatology. Schweitzer indeed went on to contend that we must choose between two alternatives, between thoroughgoing eschatology and thoroughgoing skepticism. By this he meant that either Jesus lived in the same imaginative world as those responsible for the old Jewish apocalypses, or the Gospels are so unreliable that we know next to nothing about him.

Since Schweitzer, many have accepted his dichotomy and embraced the eschatological option. Even when disagreeing with Schweitzer about this or that, they have believed that Jesus expected God to put an end to the normal course of things by raising the dead, judging the world, undoing evil, and transforming the earth into a perfect reflection of the will of God. They have also thought that for Jesus this eschatological metamorphosis was near to hand. The generalization includes Rudolf Bultmann, who affirmed that "Jesus' message is connected with the hope . . . primarily documented by the *apocalyptic* literature, a hope which awaits salvation not from a miraculous change in historical (i.e. political and social) conditions, but from a cosmic catastrophe which will do away with all conditions of the present world as it is" (1951, 4). The generalization also includes the more conservative Joachim Jeremias, who attributed a whole series of very concrete eschatological expectations to Jesus—that eschatological suffering would soon fall upon the saints, that Satan would soon be defeated, that angels would soon separate the living righteous from the wicked, that the dead would soon be raised, that Gentiles would soon stream in from east and west to the mountain of God (1971, 122–41, 241–49). More recently, E. P. Sanders has argued that Jesus was an eschatological prophet who prophesied the eschatological destruction and rebuilding of the temple and looked forward to the restoration of the twelve tribes of Israel.

☞ REJECTION OF THE CONSENSUS

Schweitzer's interpretation of Jesus as an apocalyptic preacher has always had its opponents. One suspects that in this matter theological sentiment has unduly interfered with intellectual history. However that may be, perhaps the foremost among Schweitzer's opponents in the first half of the twentieth century was the British scholar C. H. Dodd. In *The Parables of Jesus*, first published in 1935, he sought to counter the seemingly humiliating discovery that Jesus was, in effect, a false prophet. (In the 1960 Preface he states candidly that "my work began by being orientated to the problem as Schweitzer had stated it.") Dodd urged that "Jesus conceived His ministry as moving rapidly to a crisis, which would bring about His own death, the acute persecution of His disciples, and a general upheaval in which the power of Rome would make an end of the Jewish nation, its city and temple" (1935, 50–51). But all this trouble was not to be followed by a supernatural age of bliss. For the sayings that can be so understood (e.g., Matt. 19:28; Mark 14:58) point rather to "the transcendent order beyond history" (1935, 53). Dodd believed that on the historical or mundane plane the kingdom had already arrived, or was already, so to speak, accessible. Jesus proclaimed the kingdom as "a present fact" (1935, 29). As Matt. 12:28 has it, "the kingdom of God has come upon you."[1] What the prophets foretold was for Jesus a matter of present experience.

Although most have judged Dodd to be unpersuasive in much of his exegesis and appraised his work a failed attempt to find the eschatology of John's Gospel in the sayings of the historical Jesus, his rejection of a Jesus who expected the natural course of things to be interrupted by God's supernatural intervention is shared by many. Perhaps the most prominent exponent of a noneschatological Jesus today is John Dominic Crossan. As early as 1973 he wrote that the scholarly consensus that Jesus' message was "apocalyptic eschatology" had become "extremely problematic." For Jesus "was not announcing that God was about to end the world (i.e., for us, the planet), but he was proclaiming God as the One who shatters the world repeatedly and always. If, for instance, he forbade calculations of the signs of the end, it was not calculations nor signs he was opposed to, but end" (Crossan 1973, 109).

Crossan has continued to forward this view in recent books. While Jesus, as a follower of John the Baptist, began as an apocalyptic believer, he did not, for Crossan, so continue. Jesus broke with the Baptist and developed his own program.

Crossan's method of developing a Jesus dissimilar from Schweitzer's is different from that of Dodd. Although Dodd believed the eschatological discourse in Mark 13 to be "a secondary composition," so that it cannot stand as evidence of Jesus' "own forecast of the future" (1935, 36–37), Dodd took the Synoptics to be very reliable. So his dismissal of Schweitzer was based primarily on a reinterpretation of pertinent passages. Crossan, unlike Dodd, freely confesses that a great many sayings in the Jesus tradition state and presuppose eschatological expectations that contradict his reconstruction; he simply regards these as not authentic. In this Crossan carries forward the project of Norman Perrin, who, although he did not go as far as Crossan in eliminating eschatological elements from the tradition, ousted so-called apocalyptic items as secondary, that is, argued that they were not from Jesus himself.

It has recently been claimed that the position staked out by Crossan has become the new consensus. While this is debatable, many do now reject Schweitzer's old dichotomy. Although denying that Jesus thought something like a millennial kingdom or the rabbinic world-to-come to be just around the corner, they do this without giving up the quest for the historical Jesus. They contend rather that earlier scholars made at least two big mistakes. First, they attributed to Jesus eschatological texts that should instead be attributed to the early church. Second, they misinterpreted other texts that Jesus did compose.

As illustration of the first error, many now doubt that Jesus uttered any of the sayings that feature "the Son of Man" and the last judgment. Mark 8:38 ("Those who are ashamed of me and of my words in this adulterous and sinful generation, of them the Son of man will also be ashamed when he comes in the glory of his Father with the holy angels") and related texts are thought to have been created by Christians. There is said to be no convincing evidence that "the Son of Man" was a recognizable title for a messianic figure among Jesus' Jewish contemporaries, so Jesus could not have used it. The appellation was rather created by Jesus' followers and applied to him on the basis of a Christian interpretation of Dan 7:13–14. On this view of things, if Jesus ever used "son of man" (as most think he did on at least a few occasions) he was only using a common Aramaic idiom for speaking about oneself in a roundabout fashion.[2] The expression had nothing to do with the last things (see Vermes 1973).

As illustration of the second supposed error, some now say that Jesus' sayings about the kingdom or rule of God have been roundly misunderstood, because it has been assumed that the kingdom—the central theme of Jesus' proclamation—was imminent and eschatological. The common conviction may seem an obvious inference from Mark 14:25 ("I shall not drink again of the fruit of the vine until that day when I drink it new in the kingdom of God"). But the authenticity of these words is now disputed, and there are other texts that clearly indicate that Jesus spoke of the kingdom as present. Matt 12:28 = Luke 11:20, for instance, declares that "the kingdom has [already] come to you," and Luke 17:20–21 says that "the kingdom of God is not coming with things that can be observed; nor will they say, 'Look, here it is!' or 'There it is!' For, in fact, the kingdom of God is among you." Crossan and others have urged that Jesus proclaimed a "sapiential" kingdom, one having to do with living under God's power and rule in the here and now.

Two catalysts in particular have disturbed the old consensus regarding Jesus and eschatology and have encouraged the new position. The first was the discovery of the *Gospel of Thomas*, part of the Nag Hammadi library, a corpus of Gnostic texts discovered in 1945 in Egypt. This extracanonical collection of sayings of Jesus, which seems in part independent of the canonical Gospels, was, according to many, composed sometime between the middle of the first century C.E. and the middle of the second century C.E. So it is relatively early. It moreover contains not a word about the eschatological Son of Man. Nor is there any sense that the world is about to undergo an eschatological transformation. Several scholars have proposed that *Thomas* reflects a very early stage of the Jesus tradition, one that had not yet been touched by the apocalyptic expectation of the Son of Man. For them, *Thomas* is reason to suppose that the sayings in the Jesus tradition which promote an apocalyptic eschatology are secondary.

A second catalyst toward the new picture of Jesus has been discussion of the compositional history of Q, the hypothetical document supposedly used by both Matthew and Luke. Several recent scholars have decided that the earliest, or at least an early, version of Q contained no future Son of Man sayings, and that the eschatological pathos present in Q as it was known to Matthew and Luke was a secondary development (so Kloppenborg 1987). If accepted, this result would be consistent with the theory that the Christian tradition, without help from Jesus, was responsible for the eschatological character of so much in the Gospels.

☞ DEFENSE OF THE OLD CONSENSUS _____

But there are problems. Some would hesitate to put much confidence in the hypothetical compositional history of the hypothetical document Q. Others would offer alternative histories of Q that do not eliminate a strong eschatological element from the earliest stratum.

For the sake of argument, however, what follows if one grants that the first level of Q was indeed empty of eschatological feeling? Probably very little. One can readily imagine that the initial compiler of Q had interests different from the compiler of some later, expanded edition.

But why those first interests, as opposed to later interests, would alone favor the preservation of authentic sayings is unclear to many of us. If we were envisaging a documentary history that spanned generations, then an earlier contributor would certainly be in a privileged position. Q, however, was opened and closed within, at most, a thirty- or forty-year period. One might accordingly even suppose that the enlarged Q, by virtue of additional, authentic material, resulted in a fuller and less distorted impression of the historical Jesus. Is arguing that the first stratum of Q alone gives us an accurate picture of what Jesus did or did not say about eschatological matters really any more persuasive than urging that the first biography written about, let us say, John F. Kennedy, must be more reliable than all of those that have come later? Should we, because we learn of Jesus' crucifixion not from Q but from other sources, perhaps entertain the notion that Jesus was not crucified? Obviously Q leaves much out of account, even much of importance, which it must have known.

As for the *Gospel of Thomas,* whatever its compositional history may be, there is every reason to believe that its final redactor had no fondness for sayings promoting an apocalyptic eschatology. The truth is that *Thomas* both knows and disparages an eschatological understanding of Jesus. This being so, *Thomas* shows only that competing interpretations existed at an early period. It does not tell us which of those interpretations was congruent with Jesus himself.

There is, however, yet another reason for questioning the old consensus. Contemporary work on the Jesus tradition has plausibly urged that Jesus was a teacher of subversive wisdom, an aphorist, a creator of sapiential sayings. This matters for us because wisdom is about coping with the present whereas apocalypticism seemingly rejects the present in the hope of a better future. We appear to have here two different ways of looking at the world. If so, and if Jesus saw things through the wisdom tradition, is it not natural to intuit that he did not also see them through the apocalyptic tradition? Many have discerned a tension between sayings that assume the continuing flow of the natural order and others that prophesy the end of that order.

Although one sees the point, surely Jesus the eschatological prophet could have uttered provocative one-liners and lived partly out of the wisdom tradition. As historians of Second Temple Judaism are well aware, significant connections run between wisdom literature and the apocalypses. Further, an imminent expectation or strong eschatological interest is combined with wisdom materials in Daniel, the *Testaments of the Twelve Patriarchs,* the Synoptics, and Paul. So why not also with Jesus? One needs only a little knowledge of contemporary American fundamentalism to realize that fervent attention to practical social questions can go hand in hand with authentic belief in a near end. In any case both the subversive and often unconventional wisdom of the Jesus tradition and its expectation of a quick end to things as they now are function similarly, namely, to undo the status quo.

Those who reconstruct a noneschatological Jesus sometimes defend their position with the claim that Jesus' message was misunderstood or misinterpreted within a generation. As Robert Funk has affirmed,

> We can understand the intrusion of the standard apocalyptic hope back into his [Jesus'] gospel at the hands of his disciples, some of whom had formerly been followers of the Baptist: they had not understood the subtleties of Jesus' position, they had not captured the intensity of his vision, and so reverted to the standard, orthodox scenario once Jesus had departed from the scene. (Funk 1996, 164)

This strategy is not new. C. H. Dodd, in trying to save Jesus from Schweitzer's brand of eschatology, wrote that Jesus' reporters, "understandably anxious to find his words relevant to their own urgent preoccupations, have given them a twist away from their original intention" (1970, 123).

This sort of apology against eschatological error indeed has a very long and ancient pedigree. For it already appears in the New Testament itself. Luke tells us that as Jesus went up to Jerusalem he told his disciples a parable, "because they supposed that the kingdom of God was to appear immediately" (Luke 19:11). Luke, like Dodd, is telling us that while the disciples got it wrong, Jesus got it right. He made no mistake. He was just misunderstood.

Now, of course, great figures who stand above their times can be misunderstood. But this is too easy a way out. Rabbinic texts tendentiously explain sectarianism by positing that the disciples of Antigonus of Socho and Shammai and Hillel inadequately understood their masters' teaching. Is not Luke 19:11 equally tendentious? If the early Christians really failed to comprehend Jesus' pronouncements about the kingdom, then is it realistic to think that we, who have access to him only through their erroneous memory, can ever understand him aright? Would it not be more realistic just to give up the quest for Jesus?

More worthy of our attention is the proposition that the presence of the kingdom in certain sayings is incompatible with a Jesus who believed in a yet-to-come eschatological kingdom. One way around this—more plausible than is often imagined—is simply to assert that the sayings so often taken to mean that the kingdom was in some sense present mean no such thing. But even if one thinks this a desperate strategy, one still would not have sufficient reason for attributing one idea to Jesus, another to his followers. Rudolf Otto, observing that although Muhammad announced the day of Allah to be near, the prophet nonetheless gave himself to long-term political and military projects, stressed what he called the "essential irrationality" of eschatological thinking (63). He had a point; and when we remember how often people have found tensions and outright contradictions within the authentic letters of Paul, we should perhaps hesitate to apply with any confidence criteria that demand consistency from Jesus.

In this particular, however, there seems to be a natural resolution. First, Jesus' Bible itself exhibits a similar tension. Dan. 2:44 announces that "in the days of those kings the God of heaven will set up a kingdom that shall never be destroyed." Here the kingdom is eschatological and yet to come. But in 4:34 we read that God's "kingdom endures from generation to generation." Here the kingdom is somehow already present.

Second, Judaism was familiar with the notion that the eschatological transition would be a protracted process, a series of events taking place over a period of time; and this notion appears in texts for which the process has already begun, for which eschatological blessings have entered the present.

The author of *Jubilees,* for example, writing around the middle of the second century B.C.E., believed that the eschatological era had already begun. This is evident above all in chapter 23, which first describes the Maccabean revolt and then apparently moves on to allude to the author's present as a time when "people will begin to study the law and the commandments anew and to return to righteousness" (v. 26; trans. Wintermute, in Charlesworth 1983). The text, then, draws no sharp line between the happy present and the days of eschatological redemption when people will live to be a thousand years old and "there will be no Satan or evil creature" (v. 29). The one time will gradually become the other: "And the days will begin to increase and grow longer" (v. 27). Evidently the eschatological tribulation is past. The kingdom of God has begun to arrive.

The so-called Apocalypse of Weeks (= *1 Enoch* 93 + 91:12–17) offers a similar eschatology. Here history is divided into ten weeks. The first six weeks run from Adam to the destruction of the Temple. The seventh week then introduces eschatological time. There is first a period of great wickedness, after which the elect become manifest and receive knowledge. There follow three weeks of eschatological judgment. The author clearly belongs to the end of the seventh week, when eschatological tribulation ceases and eschatological knowledge enters the world. So although God's kingdom has not yet come in its fullness, God is already bestowing the blessings of the new age.

One can take Jesus' statements about the presence of the kingdom to imply that he thought himself to be in the middle of the unfolding of the eschatological scenario. The term "inaugurated eschatology" has often been used to refer to this sort of idea.

A point regularly missed by those who give us a noneschatological Jesus is that, among sayings thought to declare the kingdom present, we find the language of advent, not reference to a changeless reality. Luke 10:9 says that the kingdom has come or has come near. Similar is Luke 11:20: "upon you has come the kingdom of God." Whatever else these statements mean, they give a temporal character to the kingdom. Presumably there was a time when the kingdom of God had not come upon people. Does this make sense if Jesus had in view an "always available divine dominion"? (Crossan 1991, 292). Does not the use of temporal verbs with the kingdom reflect Jesus' belief that something new and unprecedented had happened? Are we not impelled to think in terms of an eschatological scenario?

Given the inconclusive nature of the arguments so far considered, it is no surprise that the old consensus still has its vigorous supporters. Declarations of its demise or of its replacement by a new consensus are premature. In addition to Sanders, John P. Meier has recently written a major work in which Jesus looks much more like Schweitzer's Jesus than the nonapocalyptic, Cynic-like sage of Crossan. Many in fact remain confident that the eschatological Jesus must be the historical Jesus. Among their reasons are the following.

1. The apocalyptic writings put us in touch with a type of eschatology that was well known in the Judaism that nurtured Jesus. Not only did the sacred collection itself contain apocalyptic materials—Isaiah 24–27, Daniel, Zechariah 9–14—but portions of *1 Enoch*, some of the Jewish *Sibylline Oracles,* and the *Testament of Moses* were in circulation in Jesus' day; and the decades after Jesus saw the appearance of *4 Ezra, 2 Baruch,* and the *Apocalypse of Abraham*. His time was also when the Dead Sea Scrolls, so many of which are charged with eschatological expectation, were presumably being composed or copied and studied. The point, reinforced by Josephus's remarks on the general popularity of Daniel (*Antiquities* 10.268), is simply that the sort of eschatology Schweitzer attributed to Jesus was indeed flourishing in Jesus' day. The sense of an imminent transformation appears to have been shared by many. So to propose that Jesus thought likewise is just to say that he believed what many others in his time and place believed.

2. The apocalyptic view of things was not just held by many Jews in general; it was also held by many of the first Christians in particular. Passages from a wide variety of sources leave little doubt that many early followers of Jesus thought that the eschatological climax was

approaching. Examples include Acts 3:19–20; Rom. 13:11; 1 Cor. 16:22; 1 Thess. 5:1–11; Heb. 10:37; Jas. 5:8; 1 Pet. 4:17; 1 John 2:8; Rev. 22:20; and *Didache* 16.

If in the post-Easter period there were Jesus people who believed that "the ends of the ages have come" (1 Cor. 10:11), in the pre-Easter period Jesus was associated with John the Baptist, whose public speech, if the Synoptics are any guide at all, featured frequent allusion to the eschatological judgment, conceived of as imminent.[3] According to Q (as preserved in Matthew 3 and Luke 3), John warned people "to flee from the wrath to come," asserted that "even now the axe is laid to the root of the trees," prophesied a baptism "with fire," affirmed that the winnowing fan of judgment was about to clear the threshing floor, and spoke of him "who is coming after me."

The direction of all this is unambiguous. For Jesus himself was baptized by John. Further, we should not doubt that Jesus had positive things to say about his baptizer (see, e.g., Mark 11:30; Luke 7:24–28 [Q], 31–35 [Q]). Obviously then there must have been significant ideological continuity between the two men. So, as many have observed over and over again, to reconstruct a Jesus who did not have a strong eschatological orientation entails unexpected discontinuity not only between him and people who took themselves to be furthering his cause but also between him and the Baptist, that is, discontinuity with the movement out of which he came as well as with the movement that came out of him. Presumption is against this. Certainly the Synoptic evangelists seem to have been unaware of major discrepancy between John and Jesus, for they tended to assimilate the two figures.

Crossan resists the inference from Jesus' relationship to John by citing *Gos. Thom.* 46 ("whoever among you becomes a child will know the kingdom and shall become higher than John"; trans. Guillaumont et al.) and its parallel in Luke 7:28 (Q) ("the least in the kingdom of God is greater than he"). This tradition supposedly shows that if—as Crossan admits—Jesus once shared and "even defended" John's "apocalyptic" vision, he must later have "changed his mind" (1991, 237). But Crossan's interpretation of *Gos. Thom.* 46 and Luke 7:28, which sets Jesus at odds with John, is far from obvious. So one can hardly be chided for preferring the plain and unqualified endorsement of John's message ascribed to Jesus in Luke 7:26 (Q): "What did you go out to see? A prophet? Yes, I tell you, and more than a prophet." One also wants to ask Crossan why, if Jesus abandoned John's apocalyptic vision, the contributors to Q thought it fit to preface their collection of Jesus' sayings with John's sayings about eschatology. Did they not understood that Jesus had "changed his mind" and gone far beyond John? Did they fail to see what Crossan sees?

Marcus Borg for his part resists the natural implication of the expectation of the early churches by crediting that expectation "to a deduction based upon the Easter event itself. . . . To some within the church, the fact that a resurrection had occurred was an indicator that the general resurrection must be near; Christ was the 'first fruits' of those to be raised from the dead" (1986, 95–96). This seemingly sensible suggestion, however, leaves the big question unanswered: Why did anyone proclaim a resurrection in the first place? "The fact that a resurrection had occurred" is an infelicitous formulation. How can one here speak of a "fact"? The declaration of Jesus' resurrection was not the recording of a clear observation but an act of interpretation. So what made that particular interpretation the favored one among certain people?

Borg himself observes that "'resurrection' (as distinct from resuscitation) in Judaism was an event expected at the end of time" (1986, 96). Given this and the observations already made, does not the post-Easter, eschatological interpretation of Jesus' vindication—God has already raised Jesus from the dead—imply a closely related pre-Easter eschatological expectation?

3. The Synoptics contain statements that almost certainly regard the eschatological kingdom of God as temporally near:

> Truly, I tell you, there are some standing here who will not taste death until they see the kingdom of God has come with power. (Mark 9:1)

> Truly, I tell you, this generation will not pass away until all these things have taken place. (Mark 13:30)

> When they persecute you in one town, flee to the next; for truly, I tell you, you will not have gone through all the towns of Israel before the Son of Man comes. (Matt. 10:23)

The Synoptics also contain parables admonishing people to watch for the coming of the Lord or of the Son of Man (e.g., Luke 12:39–40 [Q]; Luke 12:35–38 [Q?]; Matt. 25:1–13), pronouncements of eschatological woes on contemporaries (e.g., Mark 13:17; Luke 6:24–26; 10:12–15 [Q]), and miscellaneous traditions that either announce or presuppose that the final fulfillment of God's saving work is nigh (e.g., Mark 1:15; 13:28–29, 33, 37; Luke 18:1–8; 21:34–36).

If Jesus uttered just one of these sayings, then Schweitzer was probably close to the truth. But even in the unlikely event that they were all created by the early church, that is still no sound reason to deny an apocalyptic outlook to Jesus. That some Christians believed one thing is no strong reason to hold that Jesus believed something else. It is theoretically possible that the Jesus tradition was so amorphous or devoid of character that it could not resist the wholesale importation of foreign ideas into it. But it is more likely that people felt free to compose eschatological sayings and add them to the tradition because they thought them in accord with Jesus' message.

4. In ancient Jewish literature "kingdom (of God)" is associated with both imminence and eschatology proper. Consider the following texts:

> Then his [God's] kingdom will appear throughout his whole creation. Then the devil will have an end. Yea, sorrow will be led away with him. (*Testament of Moses* 10:1; Priest, in Charlesworth 1983)[4]

> But when Rome will also rule over Egypt . . . then indeed the most great kingdom of the immortal king will become manifest. (*Sibylline Oracles* 3.46–48; Collins, in Charlesworth)

> And then, indeed, he will raise up a kingdom for all ages. (*Sib. Or.* 3.767–68; Collins in Charlesworth)

> Their kingdom will be an everlasting kingdom and all their path will be truth. They will jud[ge] the earth in truth and all will make peace. The sword will cease from the earth, and all provinces will pay homage to them. (4Q246)[5]

> He will glorify the pious on the throne of the eternal kingdom. . . . (4Q521 frag. 2, col. 2)

> May you attend upon the service in the Temple of the kingdom and decree destiny in company with the Angels of the Presence. . . . (1QSb 4:25–26)

> May he establish his kingdom in your lifetime and in your days, and in the lifetime of the whole house of Israel, speedily and at a near time. (Kaddish prayer)

No one would dispute that many first-century Jews were indeed "looking forward to the consolation of Israel" (Luke 2:25), nor that this consolation was often conceived of as an eschatological transformation of the world, nor that this transformation was sometimes spoken of as "the kingdom (of God)." So when we find that the Jesus tradition links "the kingdom (of God)" with eschatological imagery in sayings that are not obvious creations of the community, it is natural to suppose that for Jesus himself the kingdom had strong eschatological associations. One thinks, for example, of the following sayings, which make the kingdom something to be experienced in the future:

> How hard it will be for those who have wealth to enter the kingdom of God. (Mark 10:23)

> I will never again drink of the fruit of the vine until that day when I drink it new in the kingdom of God. (Mark 14:25)

> Then people will come from east and west, and north and south and will eat in the kingdom of God. (Luke 13:29 [Q])

> Your kingdom come. (Luke 11:2 [Q])

5. A common Jewish conviction about the latter days was that God would finally defeat Satan and the forces of evil. As it says in *Jub.* 23:29, then, "there will be no Satan and no evil (one) who will destroy" (Wintermute, in Charlesworth 1983; compare *1 Enoch* 10:4–6; 54:4–6; *Testament of Zebulon* 9:8; Rev. 20:1–15). This matters because the Jesus tradition contains sayings which refer to Satan's downfall:

> I watched Satan fall from heaven like a flash of lightning. (Luke 10:18)

> But if it is by the finger of God that I cast out the demons, then the kingdom of God has come to you. (Luke 11:20 [Q])

> No one can enter a strong man's house and plunder his property without first tying up the strong man; then indeed the house can be plundered. (Mark 3:27)

Three things may be said about these sayings. First, at least the last two are widely thought to come from Jesus himself. Second, the tradition associates these same two sayings with Jesus' ministry of exorcism. Third, the three sayings naturally reflect the conviction that Satan has already begun to be defeated. The devil has fallen from heaven. He has been cast out. He has been tied up and plundered. These are very strong statements. It is not just that the devil is meeting opposition but rather that he is being routed—as people expected him to be in the latter days. So are we not invited to believe that Jesus was a successful exorcist who, given his eschatological convictions, associated the defeat of Satan in his ministry with Satan's expected defeat before the eschatological coming of the kingdom?

6. Despite its moral focus, the Jesus tradition fails to supply guidance for changing political or social realities. This very strongly implies that if Jesus hoped for better circumstances he must have assumed that they would be brought about by God himself. In other words, Jesus' imperatives are not akin to the *Analects* of Confucius: they do not offer human solutions to concrete problems but rather look forward to God himself, through a miracle, setting all things right.

7. Many early Christian texts associate the death and resurrection of Jesus with what appear to be eschatological events. According to Matt. 27:51–53, when Jesus died there was strange darkness (cf. Amos 8:9–10), a strong earthquake (cf. Zech. 14:5), and a resurrection of the dead (cf. Ezekiel 37; Zech. 14:4–5). According to John's Gospel, Jesus' death was "the judgment of the world" (12:31) and brought down the reign of Satan (16:11). And according to Paul, Jesus is "the first fruits of those who have died" (1 Cor. 15:20)—a metaphor which assumes that the eschatological harvest (see below) is under way, that the resurrection of Jesus is only the beginning of the general resurrection of the dead.

Given its attestation in Paul, the Synoptics, and John, the habit of associating the end of Jesus with eschatological motifs must go back to very early times. What explains it? The most natural answer is that, while Jesus was yet with them, his followers—as Luke 19:11 plainly tells us—"supposed that the kingdom of God was to appear immediately." That is to say, they foresaw eschatological suffering followed by eschatological vindication, tribulation followed by resurrection. So when Jesus was, in the event, crucified and seen alive again, his followers, instead of abandoning their eschatological hopes, did what one would expect them to do: they sought to correlate expectations with circumstances. This is why they believed that in Jesus' end the eschaton had begun to unfold.

JESUS' EXPECTATIONS

It seems more likely than not, despite recent arguments to the contrary, that Jesus and those around him held strong eschatological hopes, which they thought would soon be realized. But beyond that, what details can we offer?

The Eschatological Judgment

To begin with what we can know with assurance: the theme of eschatological reversal runs throughout the sayings of Jesus, and this theme presupposes that the eschatological judgment is just around the corner. Consider the following:

> Blessed are you who are hungry now,
>   for you will be filled. (Luke 6:21 [Q])

> For all who exalt themselves
>   will be humbled,
> and those who humble themselves
>   will be exalted. (Luke 14:11 [Q])

> Those who try to make their life secure
>   will lose it,
> but those who lose their life
>   will keep it. (Luke 17:33 [Q])

> Many who are first
>   will be last
> and the last
>   will be first. (Mark 10:31)

Regarding authenticity, perhaps no words in the tradition are more often reckoned authentic than the beatitudes in Luke 6:20–21; and Rudolf Bultmann spoke for many when he included Luke 14:11; 17:33 (cf. Mark 8:35); and Mark 10:31 among those sayings of which he said, "here if anywhere we can find what is characteristic of the preaching of Jesus" (1963, 105).

As for interpretation, these pithy sayings are neither secular proverbs begotten of experience, akin to "pride goes before destruction" (Prov. 16:18), nor expressions of hope for a world reformed by better people. The first half of each declaration picks out a circumstance in the mundane present, while the second half declares its reversal in the surprising future. What conviction underlies the certainty with which it is announced that unhappy present circumstances will be undone? One supposes that it was only his firm belief in God's near judgment that allowed Jesus to prophesy the reversal of present circumstances. One recalls the story in the Talmud, in which Rabbi Joseph ben Joshua ben Levi catches a glimpse of the next world, which is "topsy–turvy," because "those who are on top here are at the bottom there, and those who are at the bottom here are on the top there" (Babylonian Talmud *Pesaḥ* 50a). This is not secular wisdom but an affirmation, based upon revelation, about what God will do. One may compare Isa. 60:22:

> The least of them
>   shall become a clan,
> and the smallest one
>   a mighty nation;
> I am the Lord;
>   in its time I will accomplish it quickly.

Also closely related are the promises of reversal in *Testament of Judah* 25:4:

> And those who died in sorrow
>   will be raised in joy;
> and those who died in poverty for the Lord's sake
>   shall be made rich;
> those who died on account of the Lord
>   shall be awakened to life.

If the Synoptic sayings quoted above presuppose, as do Isa. 60:22 and *T. Jud.* 25:4, a coming judgment that will overthrow the current state of things, other sayings often ascribed to Jesus plainly refer to God's judgment. Consider the following three sayings, all from Q:

Do not judge, and you will not be judged. (Luke 6:37)

I tell you, on that day it will be more tolerable for Sodom than for that town. (Luke 10:12)

The queen of the South will rise at the last judgment with the people of this generation and condemn them. . . . The people of Nineveh will rise at the judgment with this generation and condemn it. (Luke 11:31–32)

Sayings about the judgment appear throughout the Synoptic tradition. While this in itself does not guarantee that Jesus himself spoke of the judgment, surely the sayings offer some reason for supposing that he did.

The interesting question is not whether Jesus believed in or spoke of eschatological judgment but whether he gave that belief definite shape, whether he offered a picture of it. Was Norman Perrin right to affirm that Jesus expressed confidence in divine vindication but said "nothing about its form" and that, when this result is compared with the ancient sources, Jewish and Christian, the difference is "spectacular" (1967, 203)?

The Synoptics contain only one detailed picture of the last judgment. In Matt. 25:31–46 the Son of Man, accompanied by angels, comes in glory, sits on a throne, and, like a shepherd who separates sheep from goats, divides humanity into two groups, one for the kingdom, one for exclusion from the kingdom. This scene, however, appears only in Matthew, and it seems to owe as much to the evangelist and to the Similitudes of *1 Enoch,* where the Son of Man also sits on his glorious throne in judgment, as it owes to Jesus.

We have no good evidence then that Jesus ever painted a picture of the last judgment, but the implications of this are not large. We have here only a difference in emphasis or style from the apocalypses, not a difference in conviction. If Jesus did not depict the last judgment in detail, the explanation is not that he thought such depiction inappropriate but that he could take such detail for granted. That is, his tradition already supplied his audience with pictures of the last judgment, so Jesus could simply assume them. Certainly there is no evidence that he rejected traditional images or sought to correct them. To go by the extant evidence, Jesus' focus was not on depicting the judgment but on drawing out its ramifications for behavior in the present. When he warned that one would be taken, another left (Luke 17:34–35 [Q]), he did not elaborate on how that would happen. The point was instead to get people to change their behavior. Christianity began as a sectarian movement precisely because Jesus, following John the Baptist, denied that membership in Israel—that is, physical descent from Abraham—would place one well in the afterlife. Jesus, like his first followers, believed that the verdicts of heaven and hell corresponded to acceptance and rejection of Jesus and his cause.

The Resurrection of the Dead

Soon after his crucifixion, several of Jesus' pre-Easter followers declared, "God raised Jesus from the dead." Upon this fact the canonical Gospels, traditions in Acts, and the letters of Paul all concur.

To proclaim a man's vindication by "the resurrection of the dead" (Acts 4:2) was to proclaim the occurrence of an eschatological event. There is no evidence that Christians ever understood Jesus' resurrection to be (like Lazarus's experience) a return to earthly life. It was, rather, always conceived of as an entrance into heavenly glory. But to say this, to say that God had raised somebody from the dead, was to claim that God had already begun to do what he had formerly been expected to do only at history's culmination.

Why do we have texts that associate Jesus' postmortem vindication with the language of resurrection? Why not texts announcing the heavenly vindication of Jesus' spirit, or declaring his *future* resurrection from the dead, or interpreting Jesus as an angel who only appeared to die before he returned to heaven, or using terms linked with the assumptions to heaven of earlier Jewish heroes such as Enoch and Elijah?

The best answer is that several influential individuals came to their Easter experiences—whatever they were—with certain categories and expectations already fixed, that they already envisaged the general resurrection to be imminent. This would explain why Jesus' vindication was interpreted not as an isolated event but as the onset of the consummation. As anyone familiar with the sociology of messianic movements knows, every effort is usually made to clothe the unfolding of events with material already to hand. In the year 1666, the so-called Old Believers in Russia declared that the end would come shortly. When it did not, they did not throw away their expectation but rather decided that the Antichrist ruled in the Russian Orthodox Church.

That Jesus expected the general resurrection is not just an inference. Mark 12:18–27 has Jesus, in debate with Sadducees, arguing that God can raise the dead. The unit has often been reckoned to rest on a pre-Easter encounter. The early church, as far as we know, did not engage Sadducees in debate,[6] and to judge from the New Testament, the early church argued for the resurrection and speculated on its nature by reference to Jesus' resurrection, not scripture. But Jesus' resurrection is not part of Mark 12:18–27. We seemingly have here an inner-Jewish debate, which makes sense on the level of the historical Jesus.

There is also a pertinent Q saying, Luke 11:31–32 par. According to this, "the queen of the south will be raised at the judgment with this generation and will condemn it," and "the people of Nineveh will be raised at the judgment with this generation and will condemn it." Although these words do not offer details, the universal judgment is presupposed, and it is natural, in view of the future tenses, to give "will be raised" its literal sense.[7]

The general resurrection is further presupposed in Mark 9:43–47, where Jesus says it is better to enter life maimed or lame or with one eye than to be thrown into hell whole. The language, like that of some rabbinic texts, implies that the body is raised exactly as it was buried. If a limb has been cut off, then it is missing at the resurrection. The language may, to be sure, be hyperbolic and so intended to startle. Still, Mark 9:43–47 presupposes that speaker and audience expect the dead to come forth from their graves.

Belief in the resurrection of dead appears not only in Mark 9:43–47; 12:18–27; and Luke 11:31–32 but also in the explicit passion predictions (Mark 8:31; 9:31; 10:33–34). These are often dismissed, perhaps rightly, as obviously composed after the event. But Jesus probably did anticipate an untimely death, and it would hardly be surprising to learn that he hoped that God would, notwithstanding all opposition, vindicate his cause. So it is at least possible that, in accord with his eschatological outlook, Jesus foretold tribulation and death for the saints, including himself, and their and his subsequent vindication at the general resurrection. The passion predictions as they now stand would then supply an example of what is so common in the history of broken eschatological expectations, namely, the reinterpretation of a prediction in order to align it with its fulfillment.

Whatever one makes of the passion predictions, there is reason enough to believe that Jesus looked forward to a general resurrection. The implications of this are considerable. Jesus' eschatological future was not mundane but was rather some sort of new, supernaturally wrought state. Whether he thought of something like a millennial kingdom, or a transformed world in which the boundaries between heaven and earth would begin to disappear, or something like the supramundane rabbinic "world to come," he expected its inauguration to be marked by extraordinary events, including the resurrection of the dead. We are not here in the world of preexilic prophecy but in that of Daniel and the apocalypses.

The Restoration of Israel

Turning now to things that are less certain but still probable, it seems likely enough that Jesus, despite his focus on individuals, expected the eschatological restoration of Israel. The hope was common. It appears in the First Testament as well as intertestamental literature.[8]

The widespread expectation is found in the earliest Jesus tradition. In Luke 22:28–30 (Q) Jesus promises his disciples that they will sit on thrones "judging the twelve tribes of Israel." "Judging" here almost certainly means not "condemning" but "ruling," and the saying presupposes the belief that the gathering of the lost and scattered twelve tribes belongs to the eschatological events.

But can we attribute this conviction to Jesus himself? Whether Luke 22:28–30 goes back to Jesus is unfortunately an open question that cannot be definitively answered. But surely it is suggestive that Jesus associated himself with a special group of twelve disciples. Did he not thereby indicate his belief in the eschatological restoration of the twelve tribes?

There is another Q saying, one whose authenticity is usually accepted, in which Jesus speaks of many coming from east and west and reclining with Abraham, Isaac, and Jacob in the kingdom of God (Luke 13:28–29; cf. Matt. 8:11–12). Most exegetes have assumed that the "many" should be identified with Gentiles. But a minority of interpreters have entertained the possibility that Jesus had in mind the eschatological ingathering of Israel (e.g., Sanders 1985, 119–20). The minority is probably right. For the Q context (see Luke 13:24–30) says nothing about Gentiles, and the phrase "east and west" occurs in Jewish texts in connection with the return of Jews to the land promised to Abraham.[9] On the other hand, there does not appear to be a single text in which "east and west" refers to an eschatological ingathering of Gentiles. Further, there is otherwise little or no evidence that Jesus spoke of the eschatological coming of the Gentiles. So Luke 13:28–29 appears to tell us that Jesus drew a stark contrast not between unbelieving Jews and believing Gentiles but between saved and unsaved Jews. In this case he made a prophetic threat that while Jews scattered abroad who had not had the benefit of encountering him or his message would find eschatological salvation, those in the land who had heard him would not. The meaning would then be close to Jer. 24:1–10, where the good figs are identified with the exiles from Judah, whom God will return to the land and make his own, while the bad figs are identified with Zedekiah, his princes, the remnant of Jerusalem in the land and those in Egypt, who will be condemned. One may also compare Ezekiel 11, which promises return to Palestine for those in exile but foretells terrible punishment for those who have remained in the land.

One final point about Luke 13:28–29 is that it assumes that the land of Israel will be the geographical center of the eschatological scenario. This accords with traditional expectations. At the same time, the saying seemingly negates any advantages that might accrue from dwelling in Palestine. We have here the rejection of the sort of thinking found in *2 Bar.* 29:2; 71:1; 4 Ezra 9:7–8; and Babylonian Talmud *Ketub.* 111a. In these and other texts it is prophesied that the land will protect its own from the dangers of the latter days. In Jesus' proclamation, however, inhabitants of the land will be cast out. Their living in Palestine will not bring them merit. Quite the contrary. It is precisely those inside the borders of Israel, those who have been blessed with the presence of God's eschatological herald, who will face the more dire consequences. Of those to whom much is given, will much be required.

Eschatological Tribulation

Jewish apocalypticism is by nature catastrophic; that is, it stresses the difficulties that lie between the painful present and the ideal future; and ancient Jewish sources regularly depict the birth of a better world as accompanied by terrible labor pains (Allison 1985, 5–25). The rabbis spoke of the "birth throes of the Messiah," and the sorts of disasters catalogued in Mark 13 can be found in many documents, Jewish and Christian. As Dan. 12:1 says, "there shall be a time of anguish, such as has never occurred since the nations first came into existence."

Some have, with good reason, supposed that when Jesus looked into the future he saw what so many others did—not just a new world coming but its attendant birth pangs—and further, that he, like other ancient Jews (Allison 1985, 6–22), interpreted his own work in terms of those pangs. Schweitzer suggested that Jesus originally anticipated, in a generalized fashion, suffering for himself and his followers before the coming of the kingdom; but later, as this expectation went unfulfilled, he conceived the notion that he would die in Jerusalem and take unto himself alone the tribulation of the latter days. According to Joachim Jeremias, Jesus believed instead that his death would be "the prelude to the time of the sword," that the eschatological time of distress would commence with his passion and cover the period of his subsequent absence (1971, 241–44).

What is the evidence that Jesus took up and used to his own ends the traditional motif of the messianic woes? Jesus saw difficulties all around him. He used the image of lambs in the midst of wolves (Luke 10:3 [Q]). He said he had no place to lay his head (Luke 9:58 [Q]). He spoke to people who were poor and hungry and in mourning (Luke 6:20–21 [Q]). He said that those who were not against him and his cause were for him (Mark 9:40)—implying that some were against him (Luke 11:23 [Q]). He told a story in which the invitations to a banquet were roundly rejected—a fictional circumstance surely mirroring his own experience (Luke 14:15–24 [Q]). He spoke of disciples hating their parents (Luke 14:26 [Q]). He may also have enjoined people to take up a cross (Mark 8:34), and he may have composed a parable in which the workers of a vineyard shamefully treat the owner's messengers, a parable that perhaps climaxed with a murder (Mark 12:1–9).

To all this one may add that Jesus' self-conception and experience together pointed to difficulties ahead. For (a) Jesus considered himself a prophet (see below), and Jewish tradition had many tales about the persecution of prophets;[10] (b) Jesus came out of the Baptist movement, and the Baptist was arrested and killed; and (c) Jesus was a controversial figure, and his activities put him into conflict with some Jewish authorities. Certainly someone put him to death, and we may doubt that he was blind to the fact that his provocations might lead to trouble. Now because the Jewish prophetic and apocalyptic traditions foresaw a time of tribulation for the saints before God's final victory, and because Jesus spoke of that victory as near, one wonders whether he might not have spoken of his own present and expected suffering as belonging to that time.

It is possible that the Lord's Prayer alludes to the eschatological woes. In Luke 11:4 (Q) the disciples are to pray that they not be brought to the time of trial. Whether or not the rest of the Our Father is given an eschatological interpretation, its concluding line probably envisions not the trials or temptations of everyday life but the final time of trouble which precedes the renewal. Here, as in Rev 3:10, the Greek word *peirasmos* can stand for the messianic woes, from which one prays to be delivered (Jeremias 1971, 202).

Whatever one makes of the Lord's Prayer, that Jesus interpreted his own difficult time as the eschatological trouble appears from the Q text behind Luke 12:51–53 and Matt. 10:34–36. It included something close to the following: "Do you think that I came to give peace on the earth? I did not come to give peace but a sword. For I came to divide a man against father and daughter against mother and a daughter-in-law against mother-in-law." This passage depends on Mic. 7:6: "For the son treats the father with contempt, the daughter rises up against her mother, the daughter-in-law against her mother-in-law; your enemies are members of your own household." In *Mishnah Soṭa* 9:15 this biblical text is drawn upon to characterize the discord of the time right before the Messiah's coming: "Children shall shame the elders, and the elders shall rise up before the children, for the son dishonors the father, the daughter rises up against her mother, the daughter-in-law against her mother-in-law; a man's enemies are the men of his own house." Similar statements appear in other texts.[11] The conviction that the eschatological trial would turn those of the same household against each other was common. That Q's adaptation of Mic. 7:6 should be given an eschatological sense is confirmed by the statement about the sword. For talk of the sword within prophecies of eschatological affliction and judgment was also widespread.[12] For Jesus, then, the eschatological time of affliction had come or was near.

Possible confirmation appears in Luke 16:16, which is usually assigned to the historical Jesus and which in Q was close to the following: "The Law and the prophets were until John; from then the kingdom of God has suffered violence and violent men take it by force." Norman Perrin strongly argued that here "the use of the kingdom of Heaven . . . evokes the myth of the eschatological war between God and the powers of evil and interprets the fate of John the Baptist, and the potential fate of Jesus and his disciples, as a manifestation of that conflict" (1976, 46). In other words, Jesus linked opposition to the Baptist's cause with opposition to his own cause and saw both as part and parcel of the eschatological tribulation. This may very well be the correct interpretation.

Luke 12:49–50, which may have stood in Q even though it has no Matthean parallel, makes Perrin's reading all the more plausible. Here Jesus declares, "I came to cast fire upon the earth; and would that it were already kindled! I have a baptism to be baptized with; and how I am constrained until it is accomplished!" Throughout the Jesus tradition fire is associated with eschatological judgment. Moreover, Jewish tradition commonly uses water and flood as symbols of calamity (e.g., Ps. 18:16; Isa. 43:2; Amos 5:8). Jewish tradition also links fire and water together as symbols of judgment, as in Isa. 43:2: "When you pass through the waters I will be with you; and through the rivers, they shall not overwhelm you; when you walk through fire you shall not be burned, and the flame shall not consume you" (compare Ps. 66:10–12; Isa. 30:27–28; *Sib. Or.* 3.689–91). Jewish tradition, presumably under the influence of Iranian eschatology, where a flood of molten metal burns up sinners but refines saints at the end of time, also combines fire and water into one eschatological symbol. In Dan. 7:10 there is a stream of fire; in Rev. 19:20 a lake of fire (compare *1 Enoch* 14:19; *Sib. Or.* 3:54; 4 Ezra 13:10–11). In view of all this, one can make a very good case that in Luke 12:49–50 Jesus is relating his own fate to the end of the eschatological trial, when flood and fire will come upon all. As Mark 9:49 says, "every one will be salted with fire." In Luke 12:49–50, however, Jesus shrinks from this prospect; he is torn between conflicting attitudes toward the fearful expectation. One is reminded of the words attributed to both Ulla and Rab in Babylonian Talmud *Sanhedrin* 98b concerning the terror of the latter days: "Let him [the Messiah] come, but let me not see him!"

One final point should be made about the messianic woes. Schweitzer observed that certain traditions seem to join Jesus' fate with the fate of his disciples, yet others focus entirely on Jesus and his solitary passion. Schweitzer eliminated the tension between these two traditions by positing a change within Jesus' thought. At an early time Jesus expected the tribulation to encompass all; later he anticipated taking it up in himself alone. If, however, one takes account of the post-Easter reinterpretation of the Jesus tradition, there is no need to postulate development in Jesus' thinking here. Jesus expected to suffer in the final drama. This accounts for the traditions that link his fate with the fate of his followers (see, e.g., Mark 10:35–45). The church then interpreted and modified his words in the light of what actually happened. This accounts for the texts that focus on Jesus' fate alone. On this view it becomes possible that even the so-called passion predictions are, as already suggested, reinterpretations and specifications of more general prophecies. Any prediction of death and resurrection would originally have meant this: suffering lies ahead for the saints, but afterwards God will vindicate us. Such a pre-Easter forecast, if Jesus gave one, would naturally have been revised, after the fact, to correspond to his isolated suffering and belief in his isolated resurrection.

JESUS' SELF-CONCEPTION

Anointed Prophet

According to Mark 6:15 and 8:27–28, some of Jesus' contemporaries thought him a prophet (see also Matt. 21:11, 46; Luke 7:39; 24:19). There is no reason to reject this testimony, and every reason to suppose that Jesus himself shared this evaluation. In Mark 6:4 he says that a prophet is without honor except in his own hometown. The implication is that Jesus understood his own ministry in prophetic terms. Again, in Luke 13:33 (whose authenticity is less assured) Jesus says that he must be on his way today and tomorrow and the day following, for it cannot be that a prophet should perish away from Jerusalem.

Given that Jesus apparently considered himself a prophet, and given that he thought himself to belong to the latter days, did he associate his ministry with any particular eschatological prophecies? Q's beatitudes, now found in Luke 6:20–23, suggest that he did. The beatitudes draw upon Isaiah 61, which opens thus:

> The spirit of the Lord God is upon me,
>   because the Lord has anointed me;
> he has sent me to bring good news to the poor,
>   to bind up the broken-hearted,
> to proclaim liberty to the captives,
>   and release to the prisoners;
> to proclaim the year of the Lord's favor,
>   and the day of vengeance of our God;
> to comfort all who mourn.

Q's "Blessed are those who mourn, for you will be comforted" borrows from Isa. 61:2.[13] "Blessed are the poor, for yours is the kingdom of God" alludes to Isa. 61:1. One may also observe that "Rejoice and be glad" recalls Isa. 61:10. What follows?

The Dead Sea Scrolls (11QMelchezedek and the fragmentary 4Q521) use Isa. 61:1–3 to portray the eschatological liberation of Israel's captives, and an eschatological interpretation of these verses also appears in the targum on Isaiah. Moreover, another Q text, Luke 7:22, takes up Isaiah 61 to demonstrate that Jesus is to be identified with the eschatological figure of John's proclamation. When John the Baptist asks whether Jesus is the Coming One, Jesus says, among other things, that the poor have good news preached to them—a clear reference to Isa. 61:1.

Unfortunately, the authenticity of Luke 7:22 is controverted; there is no consensus that it goes back to Jesus. But the beatitudes by themselves tell us that Jesus linked his work with Isaiah 61. And, given that we have other reasons for believing that he took himself to be a prophet, the inference that Jesus identified himself with the eschatological prophet of Isaiah commends itself.

Jesus' interpretation of his own ministry in terms of Isaiah 61 may also help explain why early Christians came to confess him as Messiah. The indications that Jesus associated himself with Davidic hopes are, as scholars have long recognized, few and far between. The two scenes that must bear the burden of proof—Peter's confession at Caesarea Philippi (Mark 8:27–30) and Jesus' confession before the Sanhedrin (Mark 14:61–62)—are often dismissed, rightly or not, as post-Easter products. At the same time, no persuasive explanation for the post-Easter confession of Jesus as the Messiah has been forthcoming. But if Jesus was already, in his own lifetime, thought to be an eschatological figure "anointed" by God (Isa. 61:1), then the step to confession of him as "the Messiah," that is, "the Anointed One," would perhaps not have been such a large one. Particularly suggestive in this connection is 4Q521 (4QMessianic Apocalypse). This says that "[the hea]vens and the earth will listen to His Messiah," then goes on to list miraculous healings reminiscent of Luke 7:22 (see below), and finally cites Isa. 61:1 ("He will heal the wounded, and revive the dead, and bring good news to the poor"). The case has been made that "His Messiah" not only preaches good news to the poor but performs the miracles listed (Collins 1994). We seem to have here an example in Judaism of how one who was thought to fulfill the oracle in Isaiah 61 could be identified as "Messiah."

Son of Man

Several Synoptic sayings refer to the eschatological coming of "the Son of Man" (e.g., Matt. 10:23; Mark 13:26; 14:62; Luke 12:40; 18:8). But many now suppose that the church created all these sayings. Jesus may have used the Aramaic idiom "the son of man" to speak about himself in a roundabout fashion, but he could not, it is said, have used this circumlocution to prophesy his own coming on the clouds of heaven. The church, with its belief in the *parousia,* or second coming of Jesus Christ, used Daniel 7, where one like a son of man comes on the clouds of heaven, to depict Jesus as the judge of the last day.

This solution to the puzzle of the Son of Man sayings has become popular of late (Vermes 1973), and it could be correct. But some remain troubled by the fact that outside the Gospels "the Son of Man" rarely appears. The point has all the more force because we know that although Lord and Christ were all-important titles in the early church, they have left scarcely a trace in the sayings of Jesus. One may doubt that the church freely introduced christological titles into the Jesus tradition.

Another approach to the Son of Man sayings holds that Jesus did in fact refer to the coming of the Son of Man, but he was not speaking about himself. This position was held by Bult-mann and was once very popular; its adherents are fewer today. The parables of *1 Enoch* as well as 4 Ezra show us that even if "the Son of Man" was not a recognizable title in Jesus' day, there was at least an exegetical tradition that identified Daniel's humanlike figure with a preexistent Messiah. This makes it reasonable, for those who recognize Jesus' kinship with Jewish apoca-lypticism, to suppose that he looked forward to the heavenly appearance of the Son of Man. On this view of things, the formal distinction between Jesus and the Son of Man in Luke 12:8–9 makes sense: those who confess Jesus will be confessed by the Son of Man; those who deny Jesus will be denied by the Son of Man.

One objection to this viewpoint is that outside the Son of Man sayings there is no evidence that Jesus looked for or spoke of eschatological figures other than the Baptist and himself. It has been replied, however, that the church would hardly have been anxious to preserve references to such a figure, and also that, after the resurrection, Jesus' followers would have identified him with the figure of Dan 7:13. Still, why could they not have been content to proclaim Jesus' res-urrection and simultaneously look forward to the coming of another figure, the Son of Man?

Another objection to the proposal that Jesus did not think of himself as the Son of Man is that he may well have believed himself to be Israel's messianic king. That he was crucified as a messianic pretender, that his first followers confessed him to be the Messiah, and that he associ-ated his own work with that of the anointed herald of Isaiah 61 may tell us, when taken together, that he took himself to be not just an important prophet but Israel's eschatological king. This conclusion is consistent with the fact that he apparently placed himself outside of the symbolic group of twelve that he assembled: he stood above them as their leader and so, per-haps, implicitly made himself out to be the leader of regathered Israel.

All this matters because those who believe that Jesus took himself to be Israel's king might also believe that he spoke of himself as the Son of Man coming on the clouds. Both the Simili-tudes of Enoch and 4 Ezra, which are literarily independent, identify Daniel's "one like a son of man" as the Messiah; so if Jesus took himself to be the latter, he could have made himself out to be the former. It can be retorted that the identification of Jesus with Daniel's "one like a son of man" would not have made sense before the crucifixion, when Jesus was on earth. But this protest is not decisive if Jesus interpreted his own time in terms of the eschatological tribula-tion, for he then could have thought of vindication on the far side of suffering and death. Cer-tainly Judaism was familiar with the notion that God's chief agent in the final judgment might be a character from the past who was now waiting in heaven.[14]

Given the current lack of scholarly consensus about the Son of Man problem, this is not the place to put forward my own conclusions on this matter. But two final observations may be offered. First, even if Jesus took himself to be the messianic king in Jerusalem, he might still have expected the coming Son of Man to be someone else. Jewish messianism was quite varie-gated, and if some of the Dead Sea Scrolls speak of two Messiahs, or two Anointed Ones, Jesus could have done something similar. If he believed in two eschatological prophets—the Baptist and himself—he could, at least in theory, have also believed in two Messiahs or messianic deliv-erers.

Second, it has occasionally been asserted that without the authenticity of the coming Son of Man sayings, there is little reason to suppose that Jesus' teaching about the kingdom had anything to do with an imminent end. This is untrue. Neither Johannes Weiss's nor Albert Schweitzer's account of things rested solely or even mainly on the Son of Man sayings; nor did

Rudolf Bultmann's, nor E. P. Sanders's. The truth is that even if Jesus never said anything about "the Son of Man," one could still construct a solid case for an apocalyptic Jesus. The popularity of apocalyptic eschatology in Jesus' day, Jesus' close relationship to John the Baptist (attested in Q, Mark, and John's tradition), the selection of a symbolic body of twelve men, the eschatological expectations of so many in the early church, the primitive proclamation of Jesus' resurrection, and Jesus' execution as "king of the Jews," a would-be deliverer, all cohere with the view that Jesus' words were from the beginning linked with a strong eschatological expectation.

☞ THEMES AND MOTIFS RELATED TO ESCHATOLOGY

When Schweitzer spoke of "thoroughgoing eschatology" he was urging not just that Jesus promoted a certain sort of eschatology but that Jesus' entire ministry, including just about everything he said, could be directly related to it. In what follows it will be argued that, in accord with Schweitzer's contention, many different themes in the authentic Jesus tradition, over and above those already introduced, can and indeed should be closely linked with Jesus' imminent apocalyptic eschatology.

Revelation

Consider the following sayings:

> I thank you, Father, Lord of heaven and earth, because you have hidden these things from the wise and the intelligent and have revealed them to infants; yes, Father, for such was your gracious will. (Luke 10:21 [Q])

> Blessed are the eyes that see what you see. For I tell you that many prophets and kings desired to see what you see but did not see it, and to hear what you hear, but did not hear it. (Luke 10:23 [Q])

> To you has been given the secret of the kingdom of God, but for those outside, everything is in parables. (Mark 4:11)

These three sayings, which depict the present as a time of unprecedented divine disclosure, are easily associated with the conviction that the eschatological consummation will bring special knowledge to the elect. Already Jer. 31:34 says, "No longer shall they teach one another, or say to each other, 'Know the Lord,' for they shall all know me, from the least of them to the greatest, says the Lord." Hab. 2:14 puts it this way: "The earth will be filled with the knowledge of the glory of the Lord, as the waters cover the sea." The commentary on Habakkuk from the Dead Sea Scrolls, when commenting on this line, similarly declares that "afterwards knowledge will be revealed" in "abundance" (1QpHab 11:1). The author of this commentary probably connected his own ability to fathom Habakkuk's prophecies with this sort of eschatological expectation. Certainly this conviction lies behind the composition of the apocalypses, in which eschatological revelations are made known. In Daniel the seer explicitly announces that his book will be sealed until "the time of the end," when "the wise will understand" (compare *1 Enoch* 104:12–13; *Testament of Judah* 18:3, 5).

Particularly interesting in this regard is the Apocalypse of Weeks (= *1 Enoch* 93 + 91:12–17). As already observed, in this work the present is already eschatological time, and it is characterized by the entrance of eschatological knowledge into the world: in the latter days the righteous will be given "sevenfold instruction." Do we not have something similar in the Jesus tradition? And do we not have it precisely because Jesus himself interpreted his own teaching not just as revelation but precisely as eschatological revelation? Is this not how we should account for Luke 10:21, 24 and Mark 4:11? One remembers that, in the Dead Sea Scrolls, God has "made known all the mysteries of the words of his servants the prophets" to the so-called Teacher of Righteousness, who belongs to "the last generation" (1QpHab 7:1–5). One also recalls that *1 Enoch* 51:3 prophesies that God's Elect One will sit on the divine throne and pour forth all the secrets of wisdom, and that in the Animal Apocalypse in *1 Enoch* the final events commence with snow-white sheep beginning to open their eyes and see (90:6)—an allegorical way of saying that near the end special revelation will be given to the righteous (compare also CD 3:13–14).

Harvest

The tradition assigns three parables of harvest to Jesus: the parable of the sower (Mark 4:2–9), the parable of the scattered seed (Mark 4:26–29), and the parable of the tares (Matt. 13:24–30). It also has Jesus say that "the harvest is plentiful" (Luke 10:2 [Q]; compare John 4:35–38). Crossan (1991) accepts the authenticity of this saying and the three parables, but he does not seem to recognize that they speak against his nonapocalyptic Jesus. For the Jewish Bible uses the images of threshing, winnowing, and harvesting in prophecies of judgment,[15] and in apocalyptic literature the same images are associated with the eschatological consummation. In Rev. 14:14–16 the judgment comes when a man seated on a cloud puts forth his sickle and reaps the fruit of the eschatological harvest. In 4 Ezra the end can be called without explanation "the time of threshing" (4:30, 39). In *2 Bar.* 70:2 we read that the last days will come when "the time of the world has ripened and the harvest of the seed of the evil ones and the good ones has come." We evidently have here a common way of speaking into which Jesus' talk of harvesting, if given an eschatological sense, fits nicely. One may cite as a parallel a saying that Q assigns to the Baptist: "His winnowing fork is in his hand, to clear his threshing floor and to gather the wheat into his granary; but the chaff he will burn with unquenchable fire" (Luke 3:17). This, whether or not it goes back to John, shows us how those steeped in Jewish tradition naturally construed language about harvesting.

That Jesus' use of such language should turn our thoughts to eschatology is strongly suggested by the yields in the parable of the sower: the good soil offers yields of thirty- and sixty- and a hundredfold. Recent study has seemingly demonstrated that these yields would be truly miraculous in Jesus' time and place. This matters so much because the theme of supernatural fertility or yield was strongly associated with God's eschatological restoration of the land.[16] Once again, then, the Jesus tradition moves one to think of eschatology.

Periodization of History

The Jesus tradition reflects the conviction that the present is a time of unprecedented significance:

> When you see a cloud rising in the west, you immediately say, "It is going to rain"; and so it happens. And when you see the south wind blowing, you say, "There will be scorching heat"; and it happens. You hypocrites! You know how to interpret the appearance of earth and sky, but why do you not know how to interpret the present time? (Luke 12:54–56 [Q])

These words are readily given eschatological sense: even though the consummation is near, people fail to recognize the fact and to take it into account. That this is the correct interpretation appears from another Q saying, that behind Matt. 11:12 (compare Luke 16:16):

> The law and the prophets were until John. From then the kingdom of God has suffered violence and the violent take it by force.

We have already looked at these enigmatic words in connection with the subject of eschatological tribulation. Here it may be remarked that John the Baptist marks a division within history. After him, or with his appearance, the kingdom of God suffers violence. Now it is a characteristic of several Jewish apocalypses that they divide history into segments. Daniel 7 offers a vision of four beasts, which are four consecutive kingdoms. Daniel 9 tells us about the seventy weeks of years. The *Testament of Moses* divides the time between Moses and God's eschatological advent into 250 units. The Apocalypse of Weeks teaches that seven weeks of world history are past and three weeks are yet ahead. Compared to these detailed schemes Matt. 11:12 is relatively rudimentary. Nonetheless, the division of times it offers reminds one of nothing so much as the systematization of history one finds in apocalypses.

Dualism

Jesus was undoubtedly known as an exorcist, and it is perhaps this above all else which, in his lifetime, made him so popular with so many. It has already been observed that Jesus probably associated the defeat of Satan in his exorcisms with Satan's defeat before the eschatological coming of the kingdom. That is, Jesus seems to have interpreted his own work within the context of the great battle between good and evil.

This cosmic dualism has its natural correlate in the tendency of the Jesus tradition to see things in black and white, to divide people into two groups or types. There are those who build their houses on the sand and those who build their houses on the rock (Luke 6:47–49 [Q]). There is Lazarus and there is the rich man (Luke 16:19–31). There are the two sons, one who speaks well but does wrong, one who speaks wrongly but does rightly (Matt. 21:28–32). There are those who use the money entrusted to them to gain wealth for their master, and there is one who fails to do so (Luke 19:11–27 [Q]). There are the wise and intelligent from whom things are hidden, and there are the infants who possess revelation (Luke 10:21 [Q]). There are those who are for Jesus and those who are against him, and seemingly no one in between (Luke 11:23 [Q]; but note Mark 9:40).

These traditions, some of which surely go back to Jesus, reflect more than the excessive clarity of the moral visionary. For in some of these units those who do the wrong thing are punished. Floods sweep away the house without a foundation. The rich man who does not feed Lazarus is tormented in Hades. The man who buries the talent has everything taken away from him. Throughout church history these images have most often been taken to stand for the final judgment of God, for the sentence of judgment that is to be passed upon the wicked. Here, it seems, the church has got it right. Jesus' division of his hearers into two groups carries forward the old biblical prophecies of salvation for the righteous and disaster for the wicked, and it pre-supposes that at the eschatological judgment only two sentences will be passed.

Ethics

Jesus' ethical teaching—his demand to love enemies, to hate father and mother, to lose one's life, to forgive seventy times seven—has often been thought to be at odds with a fervent escha-tological orientation. C. H. Dodd urged that the ethical teaching of Jesus "appears to contem-plate the indefinite continuance of life under historical conditions" (1935, 79). But the objection is misguided. For one thing, Jesus' prohibition of divorce, according to which the monogamy of creation overrides Moses' permission (Mark 10:2–9), may well presuppose that the end will match the beginning (a common belief): the coming of the kingdom will bring the restoration of paradise, when Adam and Eve were united as man and wife (Sanders 1985, 256–60). For another thing, the Dead Sea Scrolls show us that people expecting a near end could also draw up detailed institutional rules, while *2 Baruch* combines the conviction that "the youth of the world has passed away" (85:10, trans. Klijn, in Charlesworth 1983) with con-ventional exhortations to keep the Torah (32:1; 46:3; etc.). The situation is similar in the *Testa-ments of the Twelve Patriarchs:* the ethics and the eschatology are not logically linked, but they nonetheless appear side by side. So it would be unwise to set eschatology over against impera-tives that seem to us to envisage "the indefinite continuance of life under historical conditions." When Mark summarizes Jesus' proclamation by combining the nearness of the end with a call to repent (1:15), the evangelist probably catches the spirit of Jesus' exhortations. It is just com-mon sense, confirmed by the experience of those who are told that they have little time to live, that the present takes on added seriousness if the end is near. Even if most of Jesus' imperatives have parallels in noneschatological texts, that is no reason to deny that, on his lips, imminence lent them an added earnestness.

Healing

The tradition has Jesus healing the blind, curing the lame, and raising the dead. It also has him interpreting these remarkable events as eschatological signs: "Go and tell John what you have seen and heard: the blind receive their sight, the lame walk, the lepers are cleansed, the deaf hear, the dead are raised, the poor have good news brought to them" (Luke 7:22 [Q]). This list is offered as evidence that Jesus is an eschatological figure, John's "coming one." Whether or not Bultmann was right to suppose that the words just cited go back to Jesus, they do plainly connect healing miracles with eschatology. This connection is now illuminated by a fragmen-tary Dead Sea Scroll, 4Q521, which includes the following:

> [the hea]vens and the earth will listen to his Messiah, and none therein will stray from the commandments of the holy ones. . . . The Lord will consider the pious and call the righteous by name. Over the poor his Spirit will hover and will renew the faithful with his power. And he will glorify the pious on the throne of the eternal kingdom, he who liberates the captives, restores sight to the blind, straightens the b[ent]. . . . He will heal the wounded, and revive the dead and bring good news to the poor. . . .

Whether or not the miracles which the Lord performs in this text are done through his Messiah, we have here evidence that at least some pre-Christian Jews expected miracles of the sort Jesus worked to belong to the eschatological scenario. The point is that even Jesus' healing ministry can, if one is so inclined, be associated with eschatological expectation.

To conclude this section: if the nonapocalyptic Jesus were the historical Jesus, it is peculiar that so much in the tradition, even so much that is regarded as authentic by those who offer us such a Jesus, can be so easily related to apocalyptic eschatology.

☞ FINAL REMARKS _____

In most respects the eschatology of Jesus must be regarded as conventional. The nearness of the consummation, the coming of judgment, and belief in the general resurrection were all things handed to him by his tradition. What was new was the connection he made with his own time and place. He probably interpreted John the Baptist as an eschatological prophet who suffered during the messianic woes. He interpreted his own ministry as a fulfillment of the prophecies of Isaiah 61. He foresaw judgment upon those who rejected his proclamation, and he associated his own teaching with the special revelation expected to be made known to the righteous in the latter days. In other words, Jesus, like the sectarians of Qumran, construed what he saw around him in terms of certain eschatological expectations.

Focus on matters eschatological and hope for a near end often arise out of suffering or dissatisfaction with the present. It was almost surely the same with Jesus. Not only was Judea under the Roman thumb, but his words, as observed above, have much to say about difficult times. Moreover, the many polemical barbs against scribes and Pharisees and the stories of conflict with them tell us that Jesus was disillusioned with and alienated from many religious authorities. Beyond this, however, it may be impossible to go. There may have been some particular political or social crisis that fostered his eschatological enthusiasm and gave him a receptive audience, but, if so, the details sadly appear to be lost to history.

☞ NOTES _____

1. Biblical quotations are from the NRSV, although the author has occasionally made minor revisions.

2. E.g., Mark 2:28 ("the Son of man is lord even of the sabbath") has been taken to mean that human beings in general (including therefore Jesus in particular) stand above the sabbath.

3. It might be argued that one should follow not the Gospels but Josephus, whose John is not an apocalyptic prophet but a social reformer (*Ant.* 18:116–19). Josephus, however, sought to underplay the eschatological fervor of Judaism. It is telling that his portrait of the Essenes includes nothing about the restoration of Israel, cosmic dualism, or messianic hope. Only from the Dead Sea Scrolls—presumably written by Essenes—do we learn these things.

4. The context encourages the reader to hope that this kingdom will come soon.

5. All translations of the Dead Sea Scrolls are from Vermes 1995.

6. There is no evidence of real Christian debate with Sadducees in Q or any of the four Gospels (with

the possible but unlikely exception of Matthew), and Sadducees are missing entirely from the New Testament epistles. They are only marginal in Acts (4:1–2; 5:17–18; 23:6–10).

7. Jewish sources vary as to who will be raised. Most refer only to the righteous being resurrected; see, e.g., *Psalms of Solomon* 3; *1 Enoch* 83–90; and Josephus, *Jewish War* 2.163 (compare Ps. 1:5 LXX?). Luke 11:32–33 par. seems to indicate that Jesus on the contrary believed that all the dead would be raised. His belief in this matter may explain why a universal resurrection appears in some early Christian sources (e.g., John 5:28–29). But a universal resurrection also appears in *Sib. Or.* 4.179–90; *Testament of Benjamin* 10:8; and perhaps Dan. 12:1–3, which says that "many" (= "all"?) will be raised, some to life, some to shame.

8. E.g., Isa. 27:12–13; 43:5–6; Hos. 11:11; 2 Macc. 1:27; 2:18; Bar. 4:37; 5:5; *Psalms of Solomon* 8:28; 11:2–3; *1 Enoch* 57:1; 11QTemple 57:5–6; 4 Ezra 13:32–50; *2 Bar.* 78:1–7; *Sib. Or.* 2.170–73; *Testament of Joseph* 19:3–8 (Armenian); *Mishnah Sanhedrin* 10:3.

9. E.g., Deut. 30:4 LXX; Zech. 8:7–8; Bar. 4:4; 5:5; *Pss. Sol.* 11:2; *1 Enoch* 57:1. While Matt. 8:11–12 uses "east and west," Luke 13:28–29 uses the longer expression "from east and west and north and south." This phrase too was traditionally associated with Israel's return: Ps. 107:2–3; Isa. 43:5–6; Zech. 2:6 LXX; *Pss. Sol.* 11:2–3.

10. See, e.g., 1 Kgs. 18:4, 13; 19:10; Neh. 9:26; Jer. 2:30; 26:20–24; *Jub.* 1:12; Josephus, *Ant.* 10.38; *Ascension of Isaiah* 5:1–16; Letter of Jeremiah 9:21–32.

11. E.g., *Jub.* 23:16, 19; *1 Enoch* 56:7; 99:5; 100:1–2; 4 Ezra 5:9; 6:24; *2 Bar.* 70:3.

12. E.g., Isa. 66:16; *Jub.* 9:15; *1 Enoch* 63:11; 90:19; 91:11–12; *Pss. Sol.* 15:7; *Sib. Or.* 3.796–99; 4.174; Rev. 6:4; *2 Bar.* 27:6.

13. Matthew's form is here original.

14. See, e.g., 11QMelchizedek; *1 Enoch* 71 (if v. 14 identifies Enoch with the earlier "one like a son of man"); and *Testament of Abraham* A 12–13. Also relevant are 1 Cor. 6:2 and Rev. 20:4. One might protest that Daniel's "one like a son of man" is an angel, maybe Michael, but in any case not a man (a plausible interpretation). But Jewish eschatology (including the teaching of Jesus) could erase the line between humans and angels. The Dead Sea Scrolls turn Melchizedek into an angelic figure (11QMelchizedek) and perhaps even identify him with the archangel Michael (see 4Q401 frag. 11).

15. E.g., Isa. 41:14–16; Jer. 15:7; 51:33; Hos. 6:11; Joel 3:13; Mic. 4:12–13.

16. Cf. Isa. 51:3; Ezek. 36:35; 47:7–12; Rev. 22:2; *1 Enoch* 10:19; *2 Bar.* 29:4–8; Papias in Irenaeus *Against Heresies* 5.33.3–4; Babylonian Talmud *Ketubot* 111b–112a; *Šabbat* 30b.

⌒ BIBLIOGRAPHY _____

Allison, Dale C., Jr. 1985. *The End of the Ages Has Come: An Early Interpretation of the Passion and Resurrection of Jesus.* Philadelphia: Fortress Press. This study argues that many early Christian passion traditions are best explained as attempts to reconcile Jesus' fate with his eschatological prophecies.

Beasley-Murray, G. R. 1986. *Jesus and the Kingdom of God.* Grand Rapids: Eerdmans. A detailed exegesis of every Synoptic saying about the kingdom of God. It consistently reviews the history of the discussion.

Borg, Marcus. 1986. "A Temperate Case for a Non-Eschatological Jesus." *Forum* 2 (September): 81–102. A clear presentation of what the title indicates.

Bultmann, Rudolf. 1951. *Theology of the New Testament.* Vol. 1. New York: Charles Scribner's Sons. Contains a very influential portrait of Jesus as an eschatological prophet.

————. 1963. *History of the Synoptic Tradition.* Oxford: Basil Blackwell.

Charlesworth, James H., ed. 1983. *The Old Testament Pseudepigrapha.* 2 vols. Garden City, N.Y.: Doubleday.

Collins, John J. 1994. "The Works of the Messiah." *Dead Sea Discoveries* 1:1–15.

Crossan, John Dominic. 1973. "The Servant Parables of Jesus." In *Society of Biblical Literature 1973 Seminar Papers,* edited by G. W. MacRae, 2:94–118. Cambridge, Mass.: Society of Biblical Literature.

———. 1991. *The Historical Jesus: The Life of a Mediterranean Jewish Peasant.* San Francisco: Harper. According to Crossan, Jesus was a Cynic-like sage who began as a follower of the apocalyptic Baptist but later adopted another view of things. The work is characterized by the use of extracanonical sources.

Dodd, C. H. 1935. *The Parables of Jesus.* London: James Nisbet. The classic presentation of "realized eschatology," according to which Jesus proclaimed not an apocalyptic message but the presence of the kingdom.

———. 1970. *The Founder of Christianity.* New York: Macmillan.

Funk, Robert W. 1996. *Honest to Jesus: Jesus for a New Millennium.* New York: Macmillan.

Guillaumont, A., et al., eds. 1959. *The Gospel according to Thomas.* Leiden: E. J. Brill.

Jeremias, Joachim. 1971. *New Testament Theology.* New York: Charles Scribner's Sons. This summation of Jeremias's conclusions after a lifetime of study interprets the entire message of Jesus in terms of the expectation of a near end.

Kloppenborg, John S. 1987. *The Formation of Q.* Philadelphia: Fortress Press.

Meier, John P. 1994. *A Marginal Jew: Rethinking the Historical Jesus.* Vol. 2, *Mentor, Message, and Miracles.* New York: Doubleday. This contains a long and thorough discussion of the meaning of Jesus' proclamation of the kingdom. Meier concludes that Jesus believed both in the presence of the kingdom and in a near end.

Otto, Rudolf. 1943. *The Kingdom of God and the Son of Man: A Study in the History of Religion.* London: Lutterworth.

Perrin, Norman. 1976. *Jesus and the Language of the Kingdom.* Philadelphia: Fortress Press. Here Perrin argues that Jesus used "kingdom" as a "tensive symbol," that is, as something whose meaning cannot be exhausted or adequately expressed by any one referent.

———. 1967. *Rediscovering the Teaching of Jesus.* New York: Harper & Row. This influential book argues that Jesus expressed confidence in God's future but did not give his expectation any definite form. He did not, for example, refer to Daniel's "one like a son of man."

Sanders, E. P. 1985. *Jesus and Judaism.* Philadelphia: Fortress Press. According to Sanders, Jesus was an eschatological prophet who looked forward to the restoration of Israel.

Schlosser, Jacques. 1980. *Le Règne de Dieu dans les dits de Jésus.* Etudes bibliques. 2 vols. Paris: J. Gabalda. A systematic examination of Synoptic sayings about the kingdom which Schlosser judges to be from Jesus.

Schweitzer, Albert. 1961. *The Quest of the Historical Jesus.* New York: Macmillan. This is the standard review of nineteenth-century research on Jesus. It concludes with Schweitzer's memorable portrait of a Jesus consumed by eschatological expectation.

Vermes, Geza. 1973. *Jesus the Jew.* London: Collins, 1973.

———. 1995. *The Dead Sea Scrolls in English.* Revised 4th ed. London: Penguin.

Weiss, Johannes. 1971. *Jesus' Proclamation of the Kingdom of God.* Philadelphia: Fortress Press. This book opened the modern discussion of Jesus and eschatology and remains interesting reading.

7

Paul and Apocalyptic Eschatology

M. C. de Boer
Vrije Universiteit, Amsterdam

THIS CHAPTER DISCUSSES eschatology or, more precisely, *apocalyptic* eschatology, in the writings of Paul the Apostle (d. ca. 65 C.E.). The New Testament contains thirteen letters under Paul's name. According to many scholars, Paul may actually be the author of only seven of these (Romans, 1 and 2 Corinthians, Galatians, Philippians, 1 Thessalonians, Philemon). The authorship of the other six (Ephesians, Colossians, 2 Thessalonians, 1 and 2 Timothy, and Titus) remains disputed. In this article, therefore, references to Paul are in the first instance references to the Paul of the seven undisputed letters.

To the minds of many readers, Paul's apocalyptic eschatology is most readily, or even exclusively, discernible in those passages which present a scenario of events anticipated to occur at Christ's *parousia* ("presence," "coming," "advent"), an event that Paul can refer to as "the revelation [Greek *apocalypsis*, 'apocalypse'] of our Lord Jesus Christ" (1 Cor. 1:7; cf. 2 Thess. 1:7). 1 Thess. 4:13–18 and 1 Cor. 15:20–28, 50–56 are the classic examples from the undisputed letters. Both concern the resurrection of the dead. In the first, Paul claims:

> We [believers] who are alive, who are left until the coming [*parousia*] of the Lord, will by no means precede those who have died. For the Lord himself, with a cry of command, with the archangel's call and the sound of God's trumpet, will descend from heaven and the dead in Christ will rise first. Then we who are alive, who are left, will be caught up in the clouds together with them to meet the Lord in the air; and so we will be with the Lord forever.[1]

In the second, Paul writes:

> All will be made alive in Christ. But each in his own order: Christ the first fruits, then at his coming [*parousia*] those who belong to Christ. Then is[2] the end, when he hands over the king-dom[3] to God the Father, after he has destroyed every ruler and every authority and power. . . .

The last enemy to be destroyed is Death. . . . We will not all die, but we will all be changed, in a moment, in the twinkling of an eye, at the last trumpet. For the trumpet will sound, and the dead will be raised imperishable, and we will be changed. . . . (15:23–24, 26, 51–52)

A notable (and challenging) example from the disputed Pauline letters occurs in 2 Thess. 2:1–12, which reads in part:

As to the coming [*parousia*] of our Lord Jesus Christ and our being gathered together to him, . . . Let no one deceive you in any way; for that day will not come unless the rebellion comes first and the man of lawlessness is revealed, the son of destruction . . . whom the Lord Jesus will destroy with the breath of his mouth, annihilating him by the manifestation of his coming [*parousia*]. . . .

This study will indicate, however, that apocalyptic eschatology in the letters and thought of Paul cannot, and therefore must not, be confined to these scenarios of the *parousia*, nor then to the expectation of such a *parousia*.[4] Jesus' *parousia*, along with the events that will accompany it, is the culmination of a series of apocalyptic-eschatological events. This series began at least as early as God's raising Jesus from the dead, an event that has already taken place. As Paul writes in 1 Thessalonians, Christians eagerly await God's "Son from heaven, *whom he raised from the dead*—Jesus, who rescues us from the wrath to come" (1 Thess. 1:10). Here two references to the *parousia* (awaiting the Son from heaven, rescue from the wrath to come) sandwich a reference to Jesus' own resurrection. In 1 Corinthians 15, Paul claims that "Christ has been raised from the dead"; it is for this reason that he is "the first fruits of those who have died" (1 Cor. 15:20), the first installment of the full harvest of resurrection to come. God's raising of Christ here constitutes the first act in the apocalyptic-eschatological drama of which the *parousia* is but one element:

each in his own order: [1] Christ the first fruits, [2] then at his coming [*parousia*] those who belong to Christ. [3] Then is the end . . . . (1 Cor 15:23–24)

Paul's understanding of Christ and his saving work is permeated from beginning to end (from Christ's resurrection to his *parousia*) by the categories and the perspectives of apocalyptic eschatology. Indeed, Paul goes further, since he also applies these categories and perspectives not only to Jesus' resurrection but also to his death by crucifixion, and even, in some contexts, to God's sending of Jesus into the world (see, e.g., Gal. 4:4).

☞ PAUL AND JEWISH APOCALYPTIC ESCHATOLOGY

The understanding of Paul as an apocalyptic thinker owes most to Albert Schweitzer, who wrote two studies on Paul and his eschatology early in the twentieth century: *Paul and His Interpreters: A Critical History* (1912; German 1911) and *The Mysticism of Paul the Apostle* (1931; German 1930). The latter was actually drafted in 1906 and was intended as a sequel to the former. Schweitzer momentously claimed that Paul lived "in the conceptions of the dramatic world-view" of Jewish apocalyptic eschatology, which Schweitzer referred to, somewhat unfortunately, as "the late Jewish Eschatology" (1931, 11). Schweitzer thus interpreted Paul's eschatology with primary reference not to the eschatology of Jesus nor to that of other early

Christians but to the eschatology to be found among Jews of Paul's time. The writings attesting the Jewish eschatological view were for Schweitzer "mainly the Book of Enoch [*1 Enoch*], the Psalms of Solomon, and the Apocalypses of Baruch [*2 Baruch*] and Ezra [*4 Ezra*]." As additional sources, Schweitzer listed the book of *Jubilees,* the *Testaments of the Twelve Patriarchs,* and the "Ascension" (*Assumption*) of Moses, with a passing nod also to "the earlier and later Prophets" (1931, 54–55). (Schweitzer did not of course know the Dead Sea Scrolls.)

Ever since Schweitzer, students of Paul who have tended to label Paul's eschatology (and even his whole theology) as "apocalyptic" have done so largely because, following Schweitzer's lead, they have discerned conceptual affinities between Paul's eschatological ideas and first-century Jewish eschatological expectations, which are also understood to be "apocalyptic" in some sense (e.g., the resurrection of the dead). It is thus difficult, nay impossible, to discuss Paul's apocalyptic eschatology apart from Jewish apocalyptic eschatology and what scholars have said about the latter since the time of Schweitzer.

In recent years, many scholars of Jewish apocalyptic, though not all, have found it appropriate and useful (see especially Hanson 1976; 1979; 1992) to distinguish between apocalypses (a literary type or genre), apocalyptic eschatology (a religious perspective not confined to apocalypses), and apocalypticism (a socioreligious movement or community that has recourse to apocalyptic eschatology as a way of dealing with social or political alienation). Only the second of these (apocalyptic eschatology) can apply to Paul. He wrote no apocalypses and his apocalyptic-eschatological understanding of Christ did not emerge from social or political or any other kind of alienation. Indeed, according to his own testimony, exactly the *reverse* is true in his case, as in that of the communities he founded: social and political alienation (often leading to persecution) was a *consequence* of faith in Christ (the Christ whose *parousia* was eagerly awaited), *not* its cause (see, e.g., Phil. 3:5–9; 1 Thess 2:14). Hence, this chapter will discuss Paul's particular apocalyptic eschatology as it comes to expression in his letters.

According to Paul Hanson, "Apocalyptic eschatology is neither a genre, nor a socioreligious movement, nor a system of thought, but rather a religious perspective, a way of viewing divine plans in relation to mundane reality . . . it is a perspective which individuals or groups can embrace in varying degrees at different times" (1976, 29), and give a home in different genres of literature. In an important and influential article first published in 1964, Philipp Vielhauer maintained that "the essential characteristic" of the apocalyptic-eschatological perspective is what he called "the eschatological dualism" of two world ages, "this age" and "the age to come" (1992, 549; see *1 Enoch* 71:15; *4 Ezra* 7:50, 112, 119; *2 Baruch* 44:8–15; 83:4–9; *Mishnah* ʾ*Abot* 4:1; *Mishnah Sanhedrin* 10:1; *Mishnah Berakot* 9:5; cf. Mark 10:30; Matt. 12:32; Luke 18:30; Eph. 1:21; 2:7; Heb. 6:5). This claim was echoed by Hanson: as "a religious perspective," the "essential characteristics" of Jewish apocalyptic eschatology are two ages separated by "a great judgment" (1979, 432, 440). Similarly, D. S. Russell wrote that the "dualistic view of the world, which is characteristic of apocalyptic eschatology, finds expression in a doctrine of two ages" (1964, 269).

The dualism of the two ages is "eschatological" (and thus also temporal) because it entails the final, definitive replacement of "this age," which is completely evil or bad, by "the age to come." The latter puts an end to the former. There is and can be "no continuity" between the two ages (Vielhauer 1992, 550), since "this age" is the epoch and the realm (or sphere) of sin, evil, and death, whereas "the age to come" is the epoch and the realm (or sphere) of God and thus of righteousness, well-being, and life. As realms (or spheres) of activity, the categories "this age" and "the age to come" have spatial as well as temporal aspects. The locus of "this age" is the earth, whereas the locus of "the age to come" is heaven, from which the benefits of the new age will descend at the end of time or history. The dualism of the two ages characteristic of apocalyptic eschatology is thus *at once temporal and spatial*.

Furthermore, although Jewish apocalyptic eschatology naturally finds its focus in God's covenantal relationship to Israel, the scope of the two ages is cosmic: they both involve all people and all times. As Schweitzer pointed out, redemption in apocalyptic eschatology is "not a mere transaction" between an individual and God, but "a world-event in which he [or she] has a share" (1931, 54).

That Paul was familiar with some form of this eschatological dualism is minimally suggested by his use of the expression "this age" (*ho aiōn houtos,* Rom. 12:2; 1 Cor. 1:20; 2:6, 8; 3:18; 2 Cor. 4:4; cf. Eph. 1:21). In Gal. 1:4, he refers to "the present evil age." The phrase "this world" (*ho kosmos houtos*) is a synonym (1 Cor. 3:19; 5:10; 7:31; cf. Eph. 2:2; 4 Ezra 4:2; 8:1), as is shown by the parallelism in 1 Cor. 3:18–19:

> If you think that you are wise in *this age,* you should become fools so that you may become wise. For the wisdom of *this world* is foolishness with God.

The corresponding expression "the age (or world) to come" occurs only in Ephesians among the Pauline letters (1:21; cf. 2:7), though there may be an allusion to it in the reference to "the ends of the ages" (i.e., the end of the old age and the beginning of the new) in 1 Cor. 10:11. But the idea of a coming age is implied when the present world-age is characterized as *this* world-age (Keck 1984, 234). Moreover, such expressions as "the kingdom [kingly rule] of God" (Rom. 14:17; 1 Cor. 4:20; 6:9, 10; 15:24, 50; Gal. 5:21; 1 Thess. 2:12; see also Eph. 5:5; Col. 4:11; 2 Thess. 1:5; cf. *Testament of Moses* 10:1), "eternal life" (Rom. 2:7; 5:21; 6:22, 23; Gal. 6:8; see also 1 Tim. 1:16; 6:12; Titus 1:2; 3:7; cf. Dan. 12:2), and "new creation" (2 Cor. 5:17; Gal. 6:15; cf. *1 Enoch* 72:1; 4 Ezra 7:75; *2 Bar.* 32:6) are surely other ways of speaking about the age or world to come. These are eschatological realities, that is, the realities of the new age of God.

☞ APOCALYPTIC ESCHATOLOGY AND REVELATION

While a two-ages dualism characteristic of Jewish apocalyptic eschatology underlies Paul's thought, the apostle does not, of course, write about "apocalyptic eschatology." He does not use this technical phrase, nor do other ancient writers of his time. The phrase is an invention, and also a convention, of biblical scholars (see Sturm 1989). It provides a convenient, shorthand way of labeling and discussing a distinctive form of eschatology (teaching concerning "last things") that scholars have discerned not only in Paul's letters but also in other ancient Jewish and Christian literature. Christian versions of apocalyptic eschatology, including that of Paul, are deeply indebted to, or are modifications of, Jewish apocalyptic eschatology, which already existed in the time of Jesus and the early church. Jewish apocalyptic eschatology, in short, was the matrix within which Christian apocalyptic eschatology, including that of Paul, arose and developed (see Collins 1984).

Eschatology has traditionally (within the history of Christian thought) referred to the theological doctrines of heaven, hell, judgment, and life after death (see the *Oxford English*

Dictionary [1897]), often treated separately and with an eye on the destiny of the individual believer. *Apocalyptic* eschatology, however, concerns visible, objective, and public events that are cosmic in scope and implication, for example, the general resurrection of the dead and the last judgment.[5] Apocalyptic eschatology is fundamentally concerned with God's active and visible rectification (putting right) of the created world (the "cosmos"), which has somehow gone astray and become alienated from God.

This form of eschatology is in turn often differentiated from the eschatology of the Hebrew prophets (e.g., Amos, Isaiah, Jeremiah), which has a more limited frame of reference. This "prophetic" eschatology is often seen as the precursor of the apocalyptic variety (see Rowley 1963, 13–53; Russell 1964, 73–103), though this is a much-debated question (Collins 1984, 19–28). Prophetic eschatology—the eschatology of the Hebrew prophets—has in view a future divine intervention in the ongoing history of Israel. This divine intervention is a corrective measure in the continuing story of God's people. Furthermore, God's intervention is not publicly visible but is hidden in the historical process of national disaster or restoration. Postexilic or "late" prophecy (e.g., Ezekiel, Zechariah, Trito-Isaiah) tends to portray God's intervention in the affairs and history of Israel against a backdrop of cosmic upheaval and discontinuity, which gives this "late" prophecy a proto-apocalyptic flavor (see Hanson 1979). According to Collins (1992, 283), a "novelty" of apocalyptic eschatology (relative to prophetic eschatology) is a judgment of the dead as well as of the living (see already Isa. 25:8; 26:19, part of the so-called Isaiah Apocalypse; Dan. 12:1–3). A distinctive element of apocalyptic eschatology, at least in such works as *1 Enoch, 2 Baruch,* and *4 Ezra,* is its cosmic scope and interest: all times and places and thus all human beings are involved and at stake in the eschatological drama about to unfold, so that God's eschatological action of rectifying the creation reaches back to the beginning of human history even as it brings it to an end.

But why call this form of eschatology "apocalyptic"? The adjective is derived from the noun "apocalypse," a near transliteration of the Greek *apokalypsis,* literally meaning "unveiling" (which is also the meaning of the Latin *revelatio,* from which the English term "revelation" comes). The use of this term to characterize "apocalyptic" eschatology was inspired primarily by the New Testament book of Revelation (the Apocalypse of John). The opening verse, from which the traditional title derives, reads: "The revelation [*apocalypsis,* apocalypse] of Jesus Christ, which God gave him to show his servants what must soon take place" (Rev. 1:1). Apocalyptic eschatology refers, then, to the kind of eschatology found in the book of Revelation, and this eschatology is a matter of divine revelation: apocalyptic eschatology is *revealed* eschatology. It needs also to be recognized, however, that the book of Revelation is in many ways distinctive and cannot be taken as the measure of all expressions of an apocalyptic-eschatological worldview. The sheer quantity and richness of Revelation's symbolism and imagery are really without parallel in contemporary sources, whether Jewish or Christian (see Bauckham 1994, 9–12). Apocalyptic eschatology can be given expression in much less vivid, certainly less lurid, imagery and language, and Jewish apocalyptic eschatology, of course, would not have the Christian elements found in Revelation. Nevertheless, what is called "apocalyptic eschatology," whether in Jewish or Christian sources, is normally assumed to bear at least a "family resemblance" to the eschatology found in the book of Revelation; the family resemblance is discernible in the dualism of the two world ages, which is a matter of divine revelation.

For understandable reasons, apocalyptic eschatology has been closely associated with books that are seemingly of the same genre as the New Testament book of Revelation and thus sharing its distinctive generic features at least to some extent. The Jewish apocalypses Daniel, *1 Enoch*, *4 Ezra*, and *2 Baruch* are the commonly cited examples (though unlike these works Revelation is not pseudonymous). In recent years, in fact, some scholars have begun to insist that the term "apocalyptic" should be used exclusively in connection with works of this genre or with the themes attested in them. These scholars also maintain that the term "apocalyptic" cannot then be limited to eschatology (understood narrowly as expectations about future events) since eschatology is not always the sole or even the major concern or topic of an apocalypse. Christopher Rowland, the major champion of this approach, has argued that the term "apocalyptic" ought to be used only in connection with what, in his view, is distinctive about apocalypses, namely, their interest in the revelation of "divine mysteries" (1982, 1–3, 29–37, 70–72). "Apocalyptic," he claims, "seems essentially to be the revelation of the divine mysteries through visions or some other form of immediate disclosure of heavenly truths" (1982, 70). According to Rowland, such divine mysteries can include not only the future but also "the movement of the stars, the heavenly dwelling of God, angelology, the course of human history, and the mystery of the human plight." All of these "fall within the category of the mysteries which can only be solved by higher wisdom through revelation" (1990, 34). He concludes: "To speak of apocalyptic, therefore, is to concentrate on the theme of direct communication of the heavenly mysteries in all their diversity" (1982, 14). B. Matlock, in his extensive survey and critique of scholarship on Paul as an apocalyptic thinker, has followed Rowland's lead (Matlock 1996, 258–62, 282–87).

Rowland does make a significant contribution in his insistence that apocalyptic is not only concerned with future events:

> Apocalyptic is as much involved in the attempt to understand things as they are now as to predict future events. The mysteries of heaven and earth and the real significance of contemporary persons and events in history are also the dominant interests of the apocalypticists. There is thus a concern with the world above and its mysteries as a means of explaining human existence in the present. (1982, 2)

Thus, if the essential characteristic of apocalyptic eschatology is the dualism of two ages, cosmically conceived, the notion of revelation in "apocalyptic" eschatology encompasses *both* ages, not just the one to come, since it is only through the disclosure of the coming age that the present can be perceived as "*this* (evil) age," as one destined to be brought to an end by God. Along similar lines, J. L. Martyn has written that apocalyptic involves "the conviction that God has now given to the elect true perception both of present developments (the real world) and of a wondrous transformation in the near future." A central concern of apocalyptic is "the birth of a new way of knowing both present and future" (Martyn 1985, 424 n. 28; cf. 1967). The knowledge granted of the future, of the last judgment, and of the new age beyond the judgment thus bears a close and reciprocal relationship to the knowledge granted of "this age"—which is to say that the solution (the age to come) must address the problem (this age). In apocalyptic eschatology, then, the notion of revelation applies not only to the last judgment and the coming age but also to "this age," its true nature, and its destiny.

In other respects, however, Rowland's proposal contains considerable difficulties. First, in his account apocalyptic is reduced to something mystical and individualistic. The consequences for studying Paul as an apocalyptic thinker are considerable. As Matlock points out, Rowland's view that apocalypses are more concerned "with secret knowledge and with revelatory experience" than with eschatology means that when "applied to Paul, attention shifts from the 'apocalyptic eschatology' of 1 Corinthians 15 to the rapture to paradise in 2 Corinthians 12" (Matlock 1996, 286–87, pointing to Rowland 1982, 374–86; similarly Segal 1990, 34–71). This peculiar restriction of apocalyptic in Paul's thought and experience to his personal journey to the heavenly realm in 2 Cor. 12:1–10 (an ecstatic experience Paul recounts only in order to devalue its importance) is in stark contrast to what is normally understood by apocalyptic, in Paul or elsewhere, and cannot even be substantiated by Paul's own use of the language of revelation in a number of other passages (see below). For Rowland, apocalyptic becomes curiously focused on the human experience of the divine world, rather than on God's own revelatory action of rectifying a world gone awry.[6]

Second, John J. Collins has pointed out against Rowland that "the essential role" eschatology plays in the Jewish apocalypses must not be underestimated (1984, 8). In Rowland's account, the mysteries disclosed about contemporary persons or events, about the human plight, about angels, and much else are implicitly divorced from the expected future events, from eschatology, when such mysteries should probably be understood only (or at least primarily) in relation to this eschatology. The divine mysteries disclosed are arguably of no interest apart from the expectation of God's cosmic act of rectification.

Third, as I pointed out above, the definition of apocalyptic eschatology is partly a matter of scholarly tradition and convenience even though it is based, as it ought to be, upon the data of the available sources, namely, such books as Revelation, Daniel, *1 Enoch, 2 Baruch,* and *4 Ezra.* It really makes no difference to this definition that there are apocalypses that may contain no eschatology or an entirely different one. Nor does the fact that the language of revelation is used outside of the framework of apocalyptic eschatology affect the soundness of the basic definition.

Fourth, as also pointed out previously, apocalyptic eschatology (the revealed dualism of the two world ages) is not confined to apocalypses (see Collins 1984, 2; Hanson 1976, 29) even if it finds its most vivid and memorable expression in some works that seem to fit that genre. An apocalypse itself "is not constituted by one or more distinctive themes but by a distinctive combination of elements, all of which are found elsewhere" (Collins 1984, 8–9). There are some notable works, such as *Jubilees,* the *Testaments of the Twelve Patriarchs,* and the *Community Rule* (1QS) and the *War Rule* (1QM) from Qumran, which assume a clearly apocalyptic-eschatological perspective (the dualism of the two world ages) but are not apocalypses at all.[7]

Fifth, the book of Revelation itself, which is often regarded as the paradigmatic example of the genre apocalypse, has the formal framework of a letter reminiscent of Paul's own letters. Compare:

> John to the seven churches that are in Asia: Grace to you and peace from him who is and who was and who is to come. . . . (Rev. 1:4)

> Paul an apostle . . . to the churches of Galatia: Grace to you and peace from God our Father and the Lord Jesus Christ. (Gal. 1:1–3)

> The grace of the Lord Jesus be with all the saints. Amen. (Rev. 22:21)

> The grace of the Lord Jesus be with you. Amen. (1 Thess. 5:28)

The opening line of the book, "The revelation of Jesus Christ," may in fact describe not the genre of the book at all but its contents,[8] or the one to whom the contents point (Jesus Christ himself). It is even possible, given the Pauline flavor of its epistolary framework, that the opening line was derived from Paul (see Gal. 1:12 and below).

Sixth, the revelation that is an integral element of apocalyptic eschatology does not refer, as in Rowland's proposal, to the mere disclosure of information about the past, present, and/or the future to a seer who is to pass it on (in an apocalyptic writing, for example), but primarily to *God's expected eschatological activity itself*. That is, the final events themselves, when they occur, will constitute God's eschatological revelation (*apokalypsis*) of himself, of his justice or righteousness, and of his sovereign claim on the whole created world. The word "apocalyptic" properly evokes this idea of God's own eschatological and sovereign *action* of putting an end to this world-age and replacing it with the new world-age (the kingdom of God). To speak of apocalyptic, therefore, is to concentrate not on the theme of direct communication of heavenly mysteries to a human being (even if such can be involved) but on the theme of God's own visible eschatological *activity,* activity that will constitute the actual revelation, what we may call the apocalypse of God.

THE REVELATION (APOCALYPSE) OF JESUS CHRIST

The opening line of Revelation, with its claim that the revelation is "of Jesus Christ," points to a crucial modification of Jewish apocalyptic eschatology, one shared by Paul. In Revelation, the eschatological events of the imminent future take their point of departure from an eschatological event of the recent past, the resurrection (and thus ascension) of Jesus Christ to God's heavenly throne (cf. 1:9–20; 5:1–14). This event, in Paul as in Revelation, constitutes a crucial Christian modification of Jewish apocalyptic eschatology. For Paul (as for John of Revelation), the hour of the eschaton was not, as in Jewish apocalyptic eschatology, about to strike; it had already struck in God's raising of Jesus from the dead, an apocalyptic-eschatological event, as Schweitzer clearly perceived:

> While other believers held that the finger of the world-clock was touching on the beginning of the coming hour and were waiting for the stroke that would announce this, Paul told them that it had already passed beyond the point, and that they had failed to hear the striking of the hour, which in fact struck at the Resurrection of Jesus. (Schweitzer 1931, 99)

Paul's apocalyptic eschatology, like that of Revelation, is thus as much a matter of a *past* eschatological event (the resurrection of Jesus, the Messiah) as of an event still to occur (the *parousia*). Christians such as Paul and John of Revelation were convinced that God's Messiah had already made an appearance on the human scene and, just as important, that this appearance of the Messiah provided the essential and inescapable clue to a "right" understanding of this world and its events, of the human condition or plight, as well as of what was expected to happen in the near future. "For the man [person] of insight who dares to see things as they really are," Schweitzer wrote, "faith ceases to be simply a faith of expectation. It takes up present certainties into itself"; someone "who has true knowledge [a Christian] can be conscious of himself [or herself] as at one and the same time" living in both ages, in what Schweitzer here refers to as "the transient world and the eternal world" (1931, 99).

Paul also uses the term "revelation" (*apokalypsis*) in several passages. Indeed, as already noted, he can, like John in Rev. 1:1, speak of "the revelation of Jesus Christ" (Gal. 1:12; cf. 1 Cor. 1:7; 2 Thess. 1:7). Needless to say, the term is not a genre designation for Paul. However, it also cannot be assumed that the term as used by Paul is a technical one for his apocalyptic-eschatological understanding of Christ, as it is for modern scholars. Paul's use of the term and that of scholars may well diverge. It is clear that there are numerous instances where Paul uses this noun and its cognate verb (*apokalyptein,* "to reveal") in connection with the communication of heavenly or divine mysteries, particularly as mediated or induced by the Spirit. For example, he writes: "When you come together, each one has a hymn, a lesson, a *revelation,* a tongue, or an interpretation" (1 Cor. 14:26; cf. 1 Cor. 2:10; 14:6, 30; 2 Cor. 12:1, 7; Phil. 3:15; Gal. 2:2; Eph. 1:17). In 2 Cor. 12:1, he writes about "visions and revelations of the Lord." Paul's usage here approximates Rowland's linking of the term with the visionary disclosure of heavenly secrets or information to an individual (who mediates what he or she has seen and heard to others).

However, Paul also uses the term in connection with Jesus' *parousia:* the Corinthians, he writes, "are waiting for the *revelation* (*apokalypsis*) of our Lord Jesus Christ" (1 Cor. 1:7; cf. Rom. 2:5; 8:18–19; 1 Cor. 3:13). Paul continues: God "will strengthen" the Corinthians "to the End" (cf. 1 Cor. 15:24) so that they "may be blameless on the day [= *parousia*] of our Lord Jesus Christ" (1 Cor. 1:8). In this passage, then, the term *apokalypsis* does approach the technical usage of modern scholars when they talk about apocalyptic or apocalyptic eschatology: the "revelation" of Jesus concerns his visible eschatological appearance at his *parousia,* and this is clearly an apocalyptic *event,* as commonly understood. The Corinthians are "waiting" not for the direct communication of heavenly mysteries, of divine information, in a dream, mystical trance, or a moment of spiritual ecstasy, but for the visible reappearance on the world scene of Jesus himself. 2 Thess. 1:7 speaks similarly and more clearly of "the *revelation* (*apokalypsis*) of the Lord Jesus from heaven with his angels of power" (in 2 Thess. 2:3, 6, 8, it is Jesus' adversary who will "be revealed" at his *parousia*). The "revelation" here referred to is no mere disclosure of previously hidden heavenly secrets, is not simply information about future events, but is actual eschatological activity and movement, an invasion of the world below from heaven above, which is also in a sense an invasion of the present by the future.

Moreover, Paul does not confine this use of the language of revelation, of apocalypse, to the *parousia.* In Rom. 1:16–18, "the gospel" itself is decribed as "the power of God for salvation," and in this gospel "the righteousness (= rectifying act) of God is [now being powerfully] revealed through faith for faith." Indeed, "the [eschatological] wrath of God is [now also being] revealed from heaven upon all ungodliness and wickedness of those who by their wickedness suppress the truth." In Gal. 1:12, Paul claims that "the gospel that was proclaimed by me is not of human origin; for I did not receive it from a human source, nor was I taught it, but [it came or happened][9] through a *revelation* (*apokalypsis*) of Jesus Christ," an unmistakable allusion to the cataclysmic appearance of the risen Christ to Paul near Damascus (cf. 1 Cor. 9:1; 15:8–10; Phil. 3:7–9). A few verses later, he writes that "God . . . was pleased to *reveal* his Son to me (*en emoi,* in me, that is, in my life), so that I might proclaim him among the Gentiles" (Gal. 1:15–16). Paul did not travel up to heaven in a dream or a trance; rather, God came down (as it were) into Paul's Pharisaic life and shattered it: "I have been crucified with Christ; . . . it is no longer I who live, but it is Christ who lives in me" (Gal. 2:19–20); "the world has been crucified to me and I to the world" (Gal. 6:14). According to Paul's own understanding, God disclosed to him his Son, the Christ who faithfully died for sins "so as to deliver us from the present evil age" (Gal. 1:3–4). This Son, his saving death and resurrection, is the content of the gospel Paul proclaims (cf. 1 Cor. 15:1–5), a gospel that is not his gospel but God's (Rom. 1:1). Paul can even talk of faith itself as something "revealed" (Gal. 3:23), and this means that faith "came [on the scene]" as Christ himself did (3:24). Christ entered a world in subjection to inimical enslaving powers, here the law (Gal. 3:25).

> Now before faith came [on the scene], we were imprisoned and guarded under the law until faith should be revealed [*apokalyphthēnai*]. Therefore the law was our confining custodian until Christ came [on the scene], so that we might be justified by faith. But now that faith has come [on the scene], we are no longer subject to a confining custodian. (Cf. Martyn 1997)

Paul uses the language of revelation to characterize the whole of God's eschatological saving *activity* in Christ, from beginning to end. This activity includes the revelatory work of the Spirit in the churches (cf. 1 Cor. 14:26, etc. above), since the Spirit is the apocalyptic-eschatological presence of God and Christ on earth, in human history. And Paul's proclamation is itself part of the apocalyptic-eschatological drama inaugurated by the death-resurrection of Christ (cf. Rom. 16:25; Eph. 3:5), a drama that is to culminate in his *parousia*. The proclamation of the gospel elicits faith and creates eschatological communities that are the visible manifestations of God on the human scene, at least for those whose eyes have been opened by faith. The church is the community that lives at the juncture of the ages (cf. 1 Cor. 10:11), the point at which the forces of "this age" are being crushed (cf. 1 Cor. 1:18), to be replaced by a new world, the world of God disclosed in the person and the work of Jesus Christ.

PAUL AND THE TWO PATTERNS OF JEWISH APOCALYPTIC ESCHATOLOGY

According to Schweitzer, the Jewish eschatology that provides the interpretive background for Paul's own entails a dualistic contrast between the "natural" world or age and the "supernatural" world or age. The "natural" world-age is "characterized not only by its transience, but also by the fact that demons and angels exercise power in it . . . ," while the "supernatural" world-age "will put an end to this condition" (Schweitzer 1931, 55). Salvation is "thus cosmologically conceived" (Schweitzer 1931, 54), as the expurgation of evil demonic or angelic powers from the cosmos. The presence of angels and demons in such Jewish apocalyptic literature as *Jubilees, 1 Enoch,* or the *War Rule* (1QM) goes considerably beyond what is found in the canonical Old Testament, apart from Daniel. As Russell writes: "Details of their numbers, their names, their functions, their natures are given which, though in many cases having their beginnings in the canonical scriptures, far outstrip anything to be found there" (Russell 1964, 240). Furthermore, in contrast to the Hebrew Old Testament (apart from Daniel), the world of the angels "is divided into two. On the one side are the angels who remain true to God . . . on the other side are the fallen angels and demons who obey the chief of the demons and commit all kinds of wickedness upon the earth" (1964, 238; cf. *1 Enoch* 6–16; 54–56; 69; *Jubilees* 10, 15; 1QS 3–4; 1QM; Daniel 10).

It is noteworthy, however, that of the four Jewish works named by Schweitzer as his main witnesses to Jewish apocalyptic eschatology—*1 Enoch, Psalms of Solomon,* and the apocalypses of Baruch and Ezra—the latter three do not mention evil angelic or demonic forces, nor then a conflict between angelic forces at the eschaton. Schweitzer himself acknowledged this fact: "In the Psalms of Solomon the Angels have no role assigned to them at all. The Apocalypses of Ezra and Baruch mention angels only as obedient servants of God and never as adversaries and oppressors of men [people]." The *Apocalypse of Baruch* mentions an angel of death (21:23), but "he too is thought of as standing in the service of God," not as a cosmic opponent. But this then means that the angelology of such works as *1 Enoch, Jubilees, Testaments of the Twelve Patriarchs,* the *Community Rule* (1QS) or the *War Rule* (1QM) is not an essential component of the dualism of the two ages which fundamentally characterizes apocalyptic eschatology.

The dualism of the two ages, in fact, exhibits two distinct patterns (or "tracks") in the available Jewish literature, one cosmological, the other "forensic" (legal, juridical) in which cosmic, angelic forces play no part (see de Boer 1989).

1. According to one pattern, the created world has come under the dominion of evil, angelic powers in some primeval time, namely, in the time of Noah (for the idea of an angelic "fall," cf. Gen. 6:1–6; *1 Enoch* 6–19; 64:1–2; 69:4–5; 86:1–6; 106:13–17; *Jub.* 4:15, 22; 5:1–8; 10:4–5; *Testament of Reuben* 5:6–7; *Testament of Naphtali* 3:5; CD 2:17–3:1; *2 Bar.* 56:12–15; *Liber Antiquitatum Biblicarum* 34:1–5; Wis. 2:23–24; Jude 6; 2 Pet. 2:4). God's sovereign rights have been usurped and the world, including God's own people, has been led astray into forms of idolatry. But there is a righteous remnant, chosen by God, who by acknowledgment of and submission to the Creator, the God of Israel, bears witness to the fact that these evil cosmological powers are doomed to pass away. This remnant, the elect of God, await God's deliverance. God will invade the world under the dominion of the evil powers and defeat them in a cosmic war. Only God has the power to defeat and to overthrow the demonic and diabolical powers that have subjugated and perverted the earth. God will establish his sovereignty very soon, delivering the righteous and bringing about a new age in which he will reign unopposed.

This "cosmological" apocalyptic eschatology is to be found in perhaps its purest form in *1 Enoch* 1–36 but can best be illustrated here by *Testament of Moses* 10:

> And then his [God's] kingdom shall appear throughout all his creation,
> And then Satan shall be no more,
> And sorrow shall depart with him.
> . . .
> For the Heavenly One will arise from his royal throne,
> And he will go forth from his holy habitation
> With indignation and wrath on account of his sons.
> And the earth shall tremble. . . .

This form of Jewish apocalyptic eschatology, in short, appears to involve "a cosmic drama in which divine and cosmic forces are at work" (Russell 1964, 269). This drama in turn suggests that the two ages are not only temporal epochs but also two spheres or zones in which certain powers hold sway or in which certain kinds of activity take place. The final judgment entails God's defeat and destruction of evil cosmic forces.

2. The other pattern is a modified form of the first. In this pattern, the notion of evil, cosmological forces is absent, recedes into the background, or is even explicitly rejected (cf. *1 Enoch* 98:4–5; *Psalms of Solomon* 9:4–5). Instead, the emphasis falls on free will and individual human decision. Sin is the willful rejection of the Creator God (the breaking of the first commandment), and death is punishment for this fundamental sin. God, however, has provided the law as a remedy for this situation, and a person's posture toward this law determines his or

her ultimate destiny. At the last judgment, conceptualized not as a cosmic war but as a court-room in which all humanity appears before the bar of the judge, God will reward with eternal life those who have acknowledged his claim and chosen the law and observed its command-ments (the righteous), while he will punish with eternal death those who have not (the wicked).

This "forensic" form of apocalyptic eschatology is to be found in both 4 Ezra and *2 Baruch,* both of which emphasize the fall and the responsibility of Adam, the first and paradigmatic human transgressor (4 Ezra 3:5–7, 20–21; 4:30–31; 7:118–19; *2 Bar.* 17:2–3; 23:4; 48:42–43; 54:14, 19; 56:6; cf. *1 Enoch* 69:6; *Jub.* 3:17–25; 4:29–30; *LAB* 13:8–9; Sir. 25:24; Wis. 10:1). Evil angelic powers are absent from both works, as noted above. According to *2 Baruch,* for exam-ple, "Adam sinned first and . . . brought death upon all . . . each of us has become his [or her] own Adam" (54:14, 19; trans. Klijn, in Charlesworth 1983). The destiny of each person is in his or her own hands: "each of them who has been born from him [Adam] has prepared for himself [or herself] the coming torment . . . each of them has chosen for himself [or herself] the coming glory" (54:15; cf. 51:16; 85:7). To choose the law is thus to choose the coming glory (cf. 17:4; 38:1–2; 48:22; 54:5). The present age is the time of *decision.* This form of apocalyptic eschatol-ogy, whose marks can still be traced in rabbinic literature, is characterized by a legal piety in which personal responsibility and accountability are dominant.

Some works exhibit a blend of the two patterns, notably the Dead Sea Scrolls, where one finds both subjection to evil cosmological forces and human control of personal destiny, both predestination and exhortation to observe the law, both God's eschatological war against Belial and his cohorts and God's judgment of human beings on the basis of their deeds or works (see 1QS 1–4; 1QM; CD). According to the Scrolls, the community as a whole as well as the individ-ual members are under constant threat from evil cosmological powers (Belial, the Angel of Darkness, the Spirit of Falsehood or Deceit). To choose the law is thus to choose to stand in the protected sphere of God's own power (as represented by Michael, the Angel of Light, the Spirit of Truth). The law is God's powerful weapon whereby he enables the righteous believer to with-stand the superhuman power of the demonic forces (cf. CD 16:1–3). Present existence is thus marked by a struggle between two contending groups of cosmological powers or spirits that seek to lay their claim on human beings. This struggle manifests itself not only in the sociologi-cal separation of the righteous (the covenantal community) from the wicked (the world out-side) but also in the choice that the individual, especially the member of the community must make each day for God and his law. The struggle penetrates the heart of the individual (see especially 1QS 3–4). (See Sanders 1977, 237–321, especially 295.) Much the same could be said for the book of *Jubilees* and the *Testaments of the Twelve Patriarchs* (see Collins 1984, 111).

Paul's letters also exhibit the characteristic concerns and ideas, or at least the language, of these two different patterns or "tracks" of Jewish apocalyptic eschatology. His use of the story of Adam in 1 Cor. 15:21–22, 45–49 and Rom. 5:12–21 (cf. 2 Cor. 11:3; 1 Tim. 2:13–14) betrays the influence of the tradition of interpretation of Adam and his disobedience found in 4 Ezra and *2 Baruch,* while his not infrequent references to Satan, always as the power hostile to God and the gospel of Christ (Rom. 16:20; 1 Cor. 5:5; 7:5; 2 Cor. 2:11; 11:14; 12:7; 1 Thess. 2:18; cf. 2 Cor. 6:14; 1 Thess. 3:5), suggest his deep indebtedness to the worldview of "cosmological" Jewish apocalyptic eschatology (cf. "the god of this age" in 2 Cor. 4:4; "Beliar" in 2 Cor. 6:15). The angelology of "cosmological" Jewish apocalyptic eschatology probably also lies behind the ref-erences to "the rulers of this age" in 1 Cor. 2:6–8, the principalities and powers mentioned in

Rom. 8:38 and 1 Cor. 15:24, and Paul's personification of Sin and Death as oppressive cosmic powers that rule over human beings (cf. Rom. 5:12, 21; 1 Cor. 15:26, 56).

The two patterns of Jewish apocalyptic eschatology as just outlined have been reflected in the study of Paul, and particularly in the debate between Rudolf Bultmann and Ernst Käsemann. Bultmann acknowledged the importance of Schweitzer's insights but also argued that Paul had begun a process of existentially reinterpreting ("demythologizing") received apocalyptic tradition with its talk of cosmological powers and future cosmic transformation, a process that Bultmann sought to bring to fruition in his own existentialist interpretation of Paul (see Bultmann 1984; 1951, 185–352). Käsemann sought to refute Bultmann's approach in a series of essays published in the early 1960s (see especially 1969b). Bultmann's so-called anthropological approach maintained that Paul's primary concern was with the *individual* human being as he or she is addressed by the gospel message in the *present* and confronted with the *decision* of faith. Käsemann's "cosmological" interpretation maintained that Paul's primary concern was with God's destruction in the *future* of the inimical *cosmic powers* that now enslave the creation, a condition from which the individual human being cannot be abstracted. As Käsemann wrote:

> Man [the human being] for Paul is never just on his [or her] own. He [she] is always a specific piece of world and therefore becomes what in the last resort he [she] is by determination from outside, i.e., by the power which takes possession of him [her] and the lordship to which he [she] surrenders him[her]self. His [her] life is from the beginning a stake in the confrontation between God and the principalities of this world. In other words, it mirrors the cosmic contention for the lordship of the world and is its concretion. As such man's [a human being's] life can only be understood apocalyptically. (1969b, 136)

Both Bultmann and Käsemann sought in their respective interpretations of Paul to come to grips with the tension of "already" and "not yet" in Paul's thought. Nevertheless, Käsemann's interpretation was regarded as properly apocalyptic, whereas Bultmann's was regarded as a nonapocalyptic reading of Paul.

Both interpretations of Paul, however, assume the basic dualism characteristic of apocalyptic eschatology and for this reason both acknowledge in their own way the influence of Jewish apocalyptic traditions within Paul's thought, christologically adapted and modified of course. This can be seen most illuminatingly in their respective interpretations of Paul's theology of justification by faith, regarded by both as lying at the center of Paul's thought.

Bultmann argued that there was "complete agreement" between Paul and first-century Jews "as to the formal meaning of *dikaiosynē* ['justification,' 'righteousness,' 'rectification']: It is a forensic-eschatological term" (Bultmann 1951, 273; Bultmann appeals to Rom. 2:13; 4:3, 5, 6; Gal. 3:6). For Bultmann "righteousness" as a forensic term implies the imagery of the law-court and thus means the "favorable standing" one has in such a court; it does not mean "the ethical quality of a person," but "his [or her] relation to God" (1951, 272, 279). The event of Christ's death and resurrection, however, caused Paul to make two key modifications in the Jewish view:

1. *Present not future.* "What for the Jews," Bultmann wrote, appealing to Rom. 5:1, "is a *matter of hope* is for Paul a *present reality*—or, better, is also a present reality" (1951, 279 [emphasis original]). Thus, through the Christ-event, "God already pronounces His eschato-

logical verdict (over the man [person] of faith) in the present; the eschatological event is a present reality, or, rather, is beginning in the present" (p. 276). Christ's death and resurrection was "the eschatological event by which God ended the old course of the world and introduced a new aeon" (p. 278). Through that event "God's acquitting decision" (p. 279) has been declared, a verdict that becomes a reality for the individual "hearer of the gospel" (p. 275).

2. *Faith not works.* Whereas "the pious Jew endeavors . . . to fulfill the conditions which are the presupposition" of God's eschatological justifying (acquitting) verdict (to be given at the last judgment), namely, "keeping the commandments of the Law and doing good works" (p. 273), the Christian does not seek justification by works of the law but receives it by faith: "Righteousness, then," Bultmann wrote, "cannot be won by human effort, nor does any human accomplishment establish a claim to it; it is sheer gift" (pp. 280–81). The "righteousness of God" (*dikaiosynē theou*) is thus "God-given, God adjudicated righteousness" (p. 285).

It is evident from this brief summary of Bultmann's views that Paul's "anthropological" understanding of justification or of God's righteousness was, apart from the two modifications mentioned, the same as that found in the forensic Jewish apocalyptic eschatology outlined previously. According to Bultmann himself, "In the apocalyptic view the individual is responsible for himself [herself] only . . . and the individual's future will be decided according to his [her] works. And this is a judgment over the whole world" (1975, 31). In another work (1956, 80–86), Bultmann relies primarily on 4 Ezra for his account of Jewish apocalyptic eschatology, while in his famous *Theology of the New Testament* (1951, 230), he attributes talk of cosmological powers in Paul to the influence of "the cosmological mythology of Gnosticism," rather than to Jewish apocalyptic traditions.

In reaction to Bultmann, Käsemann (1969a) argued that the expression "the righteousness of God" (*dikaiosynē theou,* Rom. 1:17; 3:5, 21; 10:3; 2 Cor. 5:21) referred in the first instance to God's own righteous eschatological saving action and power. This unified expression was not coined by Paul; it occurs as a technical term in Deut. 33:21, in *Testament of Dan* 6:10, and in 1QS 11:12: "If I stagger because of the sin of flesh, my justification shall be by the righteousness of God which endures for ever" (trans. Vermes). Paul, Käsemann argued, retained this meaning in his appropriation of the term. For Käsemann, then, the undoubted character of righteousness as a forensic-eschatological gift (acquittal to eternal life) cannot be separated from its character as God's saving presence and power: "God's saving activity . . . is present in his gift; the righteousness of God "partakes of the character of power, insofar as God himself enters the arena with it" (1969a, 174). God's righteousness is a gift only insofar as it also signifies submissive obedience to God's saving power (p. 182), without which all claims to righteousness are merely illusion. In the process of establishing this thesis, Käsemann also attacked the two modifications Bultmann attributed to Paul:

1. *Present but also still future.* According to Käsemann, what made Paul's use of the expression "the righteousness of God" unique over against the Jewish apocalyptic use of it was not, as Bultmann claimed, the present reality of righteousness. The *Thanksgiving Hymns* from Qumran show that its present reality was also stressed in one stream of apocalyptic Judaism (p. 178). But Käsemann's basic point was not that Bultmann had misunderstood apocalyptic Judaism but that he had misunderstood *Paul.* Though Käsemann conceded that "Paul lays the strongest stress on the present nature of salvation" (p. 178), he emphasized that Paul's "present

eschatology cannot be taken out of its context of future eschatology. . . . Paul remained an apocalyptist" (p. 181). Käsemann here unfortunately, probably because he was reacting to Bultmann, equates apocalyptic eschatology in Paul with a future hope, with the "not yet"; elsewhere he can be more nuanced.

2. *God's cosmic act of salvation.* Similarly, in attacking Bultmann's second modification, Käsemann asserted that "the righteousness of God does not, *in Paul's understanding,* refer primarily to the individual and is not to be understood exclusively in the context of a doctrine of man [the human being]" (1969, 180 [emphasis added]). The Bultmann anthropological/individual constriction occurs when exclusive emphasis is laid on the gift character of righteousness and when the latter is interpreted in terms of the contrast between faith and works (pp. 172–73, 176). *Paul's* theology of God's righteousness is not "essentially concerned with anthropology" (p. 181), that is, with human activity and decision, but with God's own redemptive action in and for the world. It is here that the uniqueness of Paul's appropriation of the term "the righteousness of God" lies, according to Käsemann. Over against apocalyptic Judaism as well as pre-Pauline Jewish Christianity, the disclosure of God's righteousness in Christ can no longer signify only his covenant faithfulness but also, and primarily, his faithfulness toward the whole creation. It is "God's sovereignty over the world revealing itself eschatologically in Jesus" (p. 180), through whom, contrary to the Jewish view, God justifies not the godly but the ungodly (p. 178). The ungodly (Rom 4:5; 5:6) are not those who do bad things, nor those who willfully transgress the law, but those who *cannot* do the right thing, because they have become subjected to the enslaving powers of Sin and Death. God's righteousness is saving gift because it delivers human beings from these two cosmic powers, powers against which the law is weak and ineffectual.

It is evident from this summary that Käsemann's interpretation of God's righteousness in Paul's thought reflects the categories and perspectives of the "cosmological" Jewish apocalyptic eschatology previously outlined. The debate between Bultmann and Käsemann (and their respective followers) is a sufficient indication that the traditions of both patterns or "tracks" of Jewish apocalyptic eschatology, the forensic and the cosmological, are present in Paul's thought.

Schweitzer, however, had concluded that Paul, like Jesus, "stood *closer* to the world of thought represented by the Book of Enoch" than to that of "the Apocalypses of Baruch and Ezra" (1931, 57 [emphasis added]). This was of course also the view of Käsemann, in polemical opposition to Bultmann. That this is a correct interpretation of Paul would seem to be supported by Paul's argument in Romans 1–8. In the first five and a half chapters (Rom. 1:1–5:11), the language and perspectives of forensic apocalyptic eschatology are clearly prominent (not surprisingly, Bultmann found these chapters crucial to his own interpretation). In Romans 6–8, however, the language and perspectives of cosmological apocalyptic eschatology predominate (e.g., sin and death, righteousness, flesh, and the Spirit are conceptualized as cosmic powers in conflict). In Rom. 5:12–21, however, where Paul utilizes the figure of Adam, whose primeval disobedience and its result (death) play crucial roles in forensic Jewish apocalyptic eschatology (4 Ezra, 2 Baruch), forensic and cosmological ideas completely interpenetrate, and the passage marks the shift from predominantly forensic to predominantly cosmological categories in Paul's argument in Romans. That shift finds its anticipation in 1:16–17 and 3:9, two texts that occur at crucial junctures in Paul's argument in the first three chapters. Thus, while such passages as 8:1 and 8:33–34 indicate that forensic categories have hardly been given up or left behind, the structure and progression of Paul's argument in Romans 1–8 suggest that motifs proper to cosmological apocalyptic eschatology circumscribe and, to a large extent, overtake forensic motifs.

If this assessment of Romans 1–8 is correct, the question is: Why are forensic motifs present at all? Or why are they so prominent in the opening chapters? The answer may have something to do with Paul's assumed or imagined conversation partners, perhaps especially those in Rome. If one of these partners was Judaism (as interpreters of Romans have often claimed), then it was also probably a Judaism embracing the categories and the perspectives of forensic Jewish apocalyptic eschatology. In Rom. 2:5–8 (cf. 2:13), Paul reproduces a nearly pure specimen of Jewish forensic apocalyptic eschatology, with its adaptation of the Two Ways: "by your hard and impenitent heart you are storing up wrath for yourself on the day of wrath and the revelation of the righteous judgment of God, who will repay to each person according to his [or her] works. . . ." Since Paul is writing to Christians in Rome, it is also quite possible, perhaps probable, that these imagined conversation partners, whether of Jewish or of Gentile birth, had appropriated the categories and the perspectives of forensic Jewish apocalyptic eschatology. For such Christians, presumably, Christ's death would have been understood as a sacrifice atoning for past sins (Rom. 3:25–26; 4:25; cf. 1 Cor. 15:3; Gal. 1:4). This sacrificial death did not put an end to law observance but quite to the contrary obligated those so forgiven to obey it all the more (cf. Matt. 5:17–20).

Throughout Rom. 1:18–3:19, Paul embraces the presuppositions of forensic Jewish apocalyptic eschatology (and/or its Jewish-Christian adaptation), most notably its understanding of the role and function of the law, only to claim that by the standard of the law, through which "the whole world may be held accountable to God" (3:19; cf. 2:12–16), the human situation is in fact hopeless (cf. 3:10–20; 4:15; 8:1). It is hopeless because, for Paul, every one is "under the power of Sin" (3:9), a claim that presumes what is made abundantly clear later in Romans, namely, the inability of the law to provide deliverance from Sin's lethal clutches (cf. 7:7–8:8). Reliance on "works (observance) of the law" (3:20, 28) is quite literally a dead end (4:15a) and, in any event, is ruled out by the justifying death of Christ (3:21–30; cf. 5:1–11), good news indeed. Faith is the appropriate human posture to this event, replacing (as Bultmann rightly claimed) "works of the law." But Paul's cosmological understanding of God's righteousness (1:16–17) and of Sin (3:9) indicate that faith is not, as Bultmann seemed at times to think, analogous to what it replaces; that is, it is precisely not a matter of human choice or "decision" (cf. 10:17). It is in fact a matter of being grateful beneficiaries of God's gracious, liberating power revealed (made effectively present in the world) in the death and resurrection of Christ (cf. 5:11). Thus, while Paul speaks of faith (or of rectification by faith) primarily when he is combatting the claim (among both Jews and Christians of his time) that "works (observance) of the law" provide the righteousness that will lead to eschatological justification (acquittal) and thus to life in the new age, the meaning of faith is actually determined by the cosmological-apocalyptic disclosure of God's righteousness and of sin in the crucifixion of Christ. Christ's death cannot be understood in exclusively forensic terms, since it marks God's triumphant invasion of the world "under sin" (Rom. 3:9) to liberate human beings (the ungodly) from sin's deadly power.

☞ SOME SPECIAL PROBLEMS

What was the source of Paul's apocalyptic ideas?

In Phil 3:5, Paul declares himself a Pharisee (cf. Acts 26:5), and according to some interpreters Pharisaism was an essentially *non*apocalyptic form of first-century Judaism (see the overview of the debate in Russell 1964, 20–28, 73–103). Pharisaism was the immediate precursor of the rabbinic Judaism that developed after 70 C.E. (the year the Roman armies destroyed the Temple in Jerusalem), and the rabbis explicitly repudiated Jewish apocalyptic works such as *1 Enoch* (Daniel was the only apocalyptic work accepted into their canon of scripture.). It must be noted, however, that the rabbis shared and retained the two-ages dualism characteristic of apocalyptic eschatology, as indeed did the Pharisees before them (cf. Acts 23:6–8). But the apocalyptic eschatology of the rabbis was largely of the *forensic* variety attested in such works as the *Psalms of Solomon*, 4 Ezra, and *2 Baruch*. The Pharisaic rabbis thus repudiated only the "*cosmological*" manifestations of Jewish apocalyptic eschatology. As a former Pharisee, Paul's deep familiarity with the perspectives and assumptions of forensic Jewish apocalyptic eschatology is thus readily explicable.

But what then about his familiarity with, and even his preference for, the perspectives and categories of *cosmological* Jewish apocalyptic eschatology? Here it must be said that the precise character of Pharisaism *prior* to 70 C.E. is not easily ascertainable, since all the relevant sources (primarily Josephus, the Gospels, and Acts) date from after 70 C.E. There is one exception: Paul's own letters. In fact, Paul is the only known Pharisee who has left any writings behind at all. It cannot be excluded, therefore, that Pharisaism prior to 70 was characterized by, or could accommodate, the perspectives and categories of cosmological Jewish apocalyptic eschatology (cf. Acts 23:8, which mentions the Pharisaic beliefs in angels and spirits; Hengel 1991, 40–55, especially 51). By the same token, then, it cannot be excluded that Paul the Christian derived some of his cosmological-apocalyptic concepts from his earlier life as a devout Pharisee (cf. Gal. 1:13–14; Phil. 3:5–9).[10]

Does Paul simply fit his understanding of Christ into an apocalyptic-eschatological framework taken over from his pre-Christian past?

It could be argued in light of the foregoing discussion that while Paul the Christian repudiated the Pharisaic understanding of a righteousness predicated on observance of the law (Phil. 3:5–9; cf. Gal. 2:19–20; 6:14), he did not repudiate the apocalyptic-eschatological two-ages dualism of his previous Pharisaism. With respect to this dualistic understanding of time and history, there was no discontinuity between Paul's Pharisaic past and his career as an apostle of Christ. The conclusion is then at hand that Paul effectively fit his understanding of the gospel of Christ into the perspectives and assumptions of Jewish apocalyptic eschatology (whether that be forensic or cosmological). As Dodd wrote, "When Paul became a Christian, his new beliefs were fitted into this framework" (Dodd 1953, 109). According to J. C. Beker, despite the christological modifications, the coherent core of Paul's gospel remained "the imminent cosmic triumph of God" (Beker 1980, 19), which was the central hope of Jewish apocalyptic eschatology.

Paul imposes and insists on "a particularist Jewish apocalyptic ideology to communicate the truth of the gospel" (ibid., 170).

It is clear from the discussion of Bultmann and Käsemann above, however, that the reverse must be true: the crucified Christ whom God raised from the dead is Paul's criterion for the appropriation of Jewish apocalyptic-eschatological categories; the latter serve the former, not vice versa. Jewish apocalyptic ideas or categories have no validity whatsoever apart from the validation they receive from God's action in raising from the dead the crucified Christ. (The same is true of Paul's use of, for example, Stoic or Epicurean ideas). Paul does not preach apocalyptic eschatology, not even Christian apocalyptic eschatology; he preaches the crucified Christ whom God raised from the dead, nothing else (cf. 1 Cor. 1:23; 2:2).

Is there apocalyptic eschatology in Paul's letter to the Galatians?

This question arises from the fact that there are no explicit or even certain references to the *parousia* or a future consummation in Galatians. Gal. 5:5 is the clearest possibility: "we eagerly wait for the hope of rectification" (cf. 2:16). As a result, Beker claimed that in Galatians Paul's dominant apocalyptic-eschatological perspective was effectively suppressed for reasons having to do with the specific problems he was seeking to address in the churches of Galatia (Beker 1980, 37–58). Once Paul's apocalyptic eschatology is not limited to his expectation of the *parousia*, however, this appraisal of Galatians falls away (see Martyn 1985, 1997). The two-ages dualism of apocalyptic eschatology permeates this letter (see especially the conflict between flesh and spirit in 5:16–26), though it has of course been brought into the service of proclaiming the gospel: Christ's self-sacrificial atoning death "for our sins" delivers human beings from "the present evil age" (1:4).

Did Paul's views concerning the parousia and concerning the resurrection of the dead change or develop?

In 1 Thess. 4:13–18, Paul assumes that Christians (including himself) can expect to live to the *parousia;* the death of Christians in Thessalonica (4:13) before that event was an unexpected development, causing considerable consternation. In 1 Cor. 15:50–58, however, the death of Christians before the *parousia* is no longer regarded as unusual or unexpected: "We will not *all* die," Paul declares. Those who remain alive until the *parousia* now seem to be in the minority.

Furthermore, the way Paul conceives of the resurrection seems to change as well. The issue in 1 Thess. 4:13–18 is whether those who have died before the *parousia* are lost or at a disadvantage. Paul solemnly declares to the Thessalonians that such is not the case, that "we who are alive, who are left until the coming of the Lord, will by no means precede those who have died." In fact, at the final trumpet, "the dead in Christ will rise first." Then "we who are alive, who are left, will be caught up in the clouds together with them to meet the Lord in the air." Thus, the dead in Christ as well as the living shall "be with the Lord for ever." In 1 Cor. 15:50–58, Paul's conception of what will happen at the *parousia* is much more elaborate: "we will all be changed. . . . For the trumpet will sound, and the dead will be raised imperishable, and we [the living along with the dead] will be changed"; the perishable body shall "put on imperishability," and the mortal body shall "put on immortality." Death will then have been "swallowed up in victory." There is nothing here about being caught up in the clouds to meet the Lord in the air. The emphasis falls on transformation into a new bodily form of existence and God's triumph over the power of death (cf. 15:26).

2 Cor. 5:1–10 seems to go further. Paul here echoes the language used in 1 Cor. 15:50–58 ("we wish not to be unclothed but to be further clothed, so that what is mortal may be swallowed up by life") but the *parousia* is not mentioned, nor is a last trumpet signaling a final resurrection. Rather, Paul now seems to be concerned with what happens immediately after physical, bodily demise: "we know that if the earthly tent [the physical body] is destroyed [dies], we have a building from God, a house not made with hands, eternal in the heavens." Paul seems not only to contemplate his own death but even to prefer it: "we know that while we are at home in the body we are away from the Lord . . . we would rather be away from the body and at home with the Lord." Paul's focus seems thus to have shifted from the *parousia* and the (future) resurrection of the dead to the prospect of life with Christ immediately after death; he no longer talks about a corporate meeting of Christ in the air at the *parousia* (as in 1 Thess. 4:13–18), nor about eschatological bodily "change" for all who are raised at the last trumpet (as in 1 Cor. 15:50–58), but about personal release from the earthly body at death. Has Paul given up the apocalyptic-eschatological expectation of a *parousia*? Has the *parousia* receded in imminence and thus in importance? Some scholars have argued as much, especially Dodd (1953, 108–28).

Dodd saw "the turning point" in Paul's developing thought "to lie somewhat about the time of II Corinthians." The letter to the Ephesians was for Dodd "the climax of that development" (1953, 117–18). In Ephesians, as in Colossians, Christians are said to "have been raised with Christ" and to "have been made alive together" with him (Eph. 2:4–6; Col. 2:12–14); the future expectation, though not given up (Eph. 6:13; Col. 3:4), has receded in vitality and in importance (a conclusion that could also apply to the Pastoral Epistles; cf. 1 Tim. 6:14; 2 Tim. 4:1; Titus 2:3). Paul, Dodd argued, "outgrew" the dualistic mentality of Jewish apocalypticism and he also "revised" his eschatological timetable (1953, 126–27). Dodd's views are easier to maintain if Colossians and Ephesians (and the Pastoral Epistles) are deemed to be authentic letters of Paul, which most scholars today doubt with respect to Ephesians and the Pastorals (they are evenly divided over Colossians). But if we disregard these disputed letters, the claim that Paul's eschatology changed is doubtful.

In Galatians, as we saw above, there is no mention of the *parousia* and a future expectation plays a minor role in Paul's argument. If, as some scholars believe, Galatians (instead of 1 Thessalonians) was Paul's earliest letter, the thesis of a development in Paul's eschatological expectation (from vibrant to moribund) clearly falls to the ground. Galatians has much in common with Romans, a letter undoubtedly written toward the end of Paul's active missionary career. In Romans, the emphasis certainly falls, as in Galatians, upon the present benefits of Christ's death and resurrection (cf. Romans 5–6), but the expectation of a future cosmic transformation is neither absent nor peripheral to the theology (see especially Rom. 8:18–25; 13:11). In any event, Romans was written after Galatians and the future expectation is more vibrant in Romans than in Galatians. In Romans, furthermore, Paul still holds out hope for a bodily redemption (cf. 8:11). In Philippians, also probably written toward the end of Paul's active missionary career, the apostle combines the hope of being with Christ immediately after death with the expectation of a future consummation. His personal "desire is to depart [die] and be with Christ for that is far better [than remaining alive]"; indeed "dying is gain" (1:21–23). But Christians also await from heaven "a Savior, the Lord Jesus Christ" who "will transform" the lowly earthly body into a glorious one (3:20–21). The language here echoes 1 Thess. 1:9–10; 4:13–18; 1 Cor. 15:20–28, 50–58.

It is important to remember that Paul's undisputed letters are occasional works, addressing specific problems in specific places; they are not dogmatic nor systematic treatises on specified topics such as the *parousia,* the resurrection of the dead, or life after death. The differences from one letter to the next may not reflect changes in Paul's fundamental theological convictions (that Jesus will come again and that there will be a resurrection of the dead), but changes in the issues being addressed. Furthermore, the actual language Paul uses to describe the *parousia* and the resurrection of the dead is not only figurative and plastic (the last "trumpet," "put on" immortality as clothing, "change," "transform," etc.), but also contextually determined, that is, determined by the needs of the audiences being addressed (see Lindemann 1994). Paul's eschatology, then, may not have changed or developed but may have found constantly new forms of verbal and conceptual expression. His fundamental conviction, one that arguably unifies his thought, is expressed in Rom. 8:38–39:

> For I am convinced that neither death, nor life, nor angels, nor rulers, nor things present, nor things to come, nor powers, nor height, nor depth, nor anything else in all creation, will be able to separate us [both now and in the future] from the love of God in Christ Jesus our Lord.

Does Paul believe all human beings will be saved at the end?

The question arises from seemingly irreconcilable statements (see Boring 1986), even in the same work. For example, in 1 Cor. 1:18, Paul writes that "the message about the cross is foolishness to those who are perishing, but to us [i.e., us Christians] who are being saved it is the power of God." This statement seems to imply a limited salvation, as do others (cf., e.g., 1 Thess. 1:10; 4:13–18). In 1 Cor. 15:22, however, Paul claims that "as all die in Adam, so all will be made alive [saved] in Christ." Here salvation appears to be universal, as it is elsewhere (see especially Rom. 5:12–21). Scholars have sought to come to grips with these seemingly contradictory claims in various ways, for example, by arguing that Paul's thought developed from limited salvation to universal salvation (Dodd), that while Paul may have regarded salvation as universal in intent (salvation is "offered" to all) it would be only limited in actual result (Bultmann and many others), or that Paul's statements cannot finally be reconciled: he maintains both points of view (Boring). The issue comes down to two sets of passages: (1) those that envisage Christians appearing before the judgment seat of God or Christ (see 1 Cor. 3:17; 2 Cor. 5:10; Rom. 14:10; cf. Rom. 2:1–16; 1 Cor. 9:24–10:13), and (2) those that envisage ultimate salvation for nonbelievers as well as believers (especially 1 Cor. 15:21–22; Rom. 5:12–21; cf. Rom. 11:25–36; 2 Cor. 5:14–15, 19). The issue is thus whether Christians can lose or be denied salvation at the *parousia,* on the one side, and whether nonbelievers can or will ultimately be saved on the other.

The first group of texts bears the hallmarks of "forensic" apocalyptic eschatology because of their emphasis on individual responsibility and accountability for one's actions: for example, "For all of us [Christians] must appear before the judgment seat of Christ, so that each may receive recompense for what has been done in the body, whether good or evil" (2 Cor. 5:10); "we [Christians] will all stand before the judgment seat of God. . . . So, then, each of us will be accountable to God" (Rom. 14:10, 12). Does Paul, therefore, believe that the sinful actions of

Christians can and will put their ultimate salvation at risk? Will some of them be damned instead of saved? It is certainly true that Paul regards salvation in the *present* as under constant threat, and he cautions against the presumption of claiming to be already living beyond the *parousia,* especially in 1 Corinthians (see 1 Cor. 4:8; 9:24–10:13): "So if you think you are standing, watch out that you do not fall!" (1 Cor. 10:12; cf. Rom. 11:18–22). Christians are in danger and their faith is in jeopardy, but he goes on to assure his Corinthian readers that God is faithful and will enable those who put their trust in him to withstand such testing (1 Cor. 10:12–13; cf. 1:8). Thus, while Paul regards salvation as under constant threat in the short term (prior to the *parousia*), it is doubtful that he so regards it in the long term (Phil. 1.6). Christians will be held accountable for what they do, but their works have no effect on their salvation in the long term (for Paul, salvation is not a human achievement, or "work," in any sense of the word). When, in 1 Cor. 5:1–10, Paul counsels the Corinthian church to "drive out" an errant member (for gross sexual immorality) and no longer to associate with him, it is "so that his spirit may be saved in the day of the Lord," that is, at the *parousia.* The loss of even this person, whom Paul regards as a lapsed Christian, to the realm of Satan (where his behavior shows he belongs) is entirely temporary and provisional.

In 1 Cor. 15:21–22 and Rom. 5:12–21, both of which contrast the work of Christ with that of Adam, salvation seems to be universal. Scholars attempt to get around the difficulty of Paul's statement in 1 Cor. 15:22 ("all will be made alive in Christ") in three ways. First, they claim that Paul's *true* view is to be found in the following verse, which mentions only "those who belong to Christ" as being raised at his *parousia* (as in 1 Thess. 4:13–18). But this interpretation does not solve the problem presented by the wording of 15:22, while the reference to the raising of Christians in 15:23 may not in any case be meant exclusively. Indeed, some scholars argue that the phrase "Then is the end [*telos*]" could also mean "Then come the rest," that is, the remainder of the dead (see NRSV note). This would mean three groups: Christ, Christians, and the rest of humanity. Others would reject this interpretation of *telos,* probably rightly (cf. 1:8), but still discern a general resurrection, to occur at the end, given the parallelism of 15:21–22:

> through a human being, death,
> through a human being, *resurrection of the dead.*
>
> in Adam, all die,
> in Christ, *all* shall be made alive.

The parallelism demands that the "resurrection of the dead" encompass "all" people.

Second, some scholars attempt to get around this parallelism by claiming that the general resurrection in view is not a resurrection of all to salvation but of all to final judgment whereby those raised will be consigned *either* to salvation *or* to damnation (so Schweitzer 1931, 68, 93; cf. Luke 14:14; John 5:29). That this interpretation is improbable is once again shown by the parallelism in 15:21–22, where "resurrection of the dead" is parallel with "all shall be *made alive.*" Elsewhere Paul uses the verb "to make alive" (one word in the Greek) as a synonym for "to save" (Gal. 3:21; Rom. 4:17; 1 Cor. 15:45; cf. 15:36) and it seems likely that he does so here as well.

Third, some scholars claim that what Paul really means in 15:22 is that "all who are in Christ," that is, only believers, shall be saved. But this interpretation is not supported by the grammar or syntax, nor by the parallelism with "in Adam, all die." It also raises another problem: How can Christ's work be less effective, *less cosmic,* than Adam's transgression? The whole point of the comparison between Adam and Christ is that the effects of Christ's saving work (*all shall be made alive*) match the cosmic effects of Adam's primal transgression (*all die*). How could it be otherwise if God is to be "all in all" (1 Cor. 15:28)? Furthermore, Paul repeats the point in Rom. 5:12–21, where he reuses the Adam–Christ typology: "just as one man's trespass led to condemnation *for all,* so one man's act of righteousness leads to justification and life *for all*" (Rom. 5:18). The two italicized phrases are in parallel and must have the same reference and thus the same scope. There can be no doubt here that Paul's words signify universal salvation, even if here too there have been repeated attempts to suggest that that is not what Paul *really* means: Paul has merely been forced into this understanding of Christ's saving work, so the argument runs, only by the force of the analogy with Adam; he does not *really* mean to say this. However, the universality given expression in these passages is arguably consistent with Paul's fundamental theology. The universality of salvation corresponds to, and addresses, the universal hegemony of sin and death (1 Cor. 15:26, 54–56; Rom. 3:9; 5:12, 21). Unless salvation is universal, sin and death will not have been completely defeated, and God's saving action and thus his sovereignty will remain an extremely limited affair.

Furthermore, the claim of universal salvation has a significant rhetorical function in both 1 Corinthians 15 and Romans 5 (see de Boer 1988): it effectively destroys any notion that salvation is either a natural right (1 Corinthians) or a merited achievement (Romans). Salvation is thus no longer a matter of competition or triumphalist claims ("I am saved; are you?"). Paul's claim of a universal salvation is an expression of his "theology of the cross" (see 1 Cor. 1:18–2:4; cf. 2 Cor. 5:14–15). The upshot of this theology is that God justifies and thus saves not the righteous but the ungodly. In Paul's view, God saves only the ungodly, those who cannot save themselves, a category that includes all human beings from Adam onward ("for there is no distinction, since all have sinned and fall short of the glory of God" [Rom 3:23]). Adamic human beings cannot save themselves from the inimical cosmic powers of sin and death, and for this reason the gospel is not the "offer" of salvation (as is the law in forensic Jewish apocalyptic eschatology) whose saving effects depend on human acceptance or "decision" (Bultmann). Salvation is a gift granted by God and takes effect solely at God's initiative. The salvation God will bestow on all is thus no different in kind from the salvation to be bestowed on believers and in which they have already been graciously allowed to participate, having received the Spirit as "a first installment" (2 Cor. 1:22; cf. Rom. 8:23). The dualism between those perishing and those now being saved (1 Cor. 1:18), between unbelievers and believers, is thus entirely temporary and provisional.

Some would argue, as Boring does, that "Paul has statements in which salvation is . . . conditional on faith in Christ" (Boring 1986, 290; cf. Rom. 10:9) and thus limited, but faith for Paul involves the trustful acknowledgment that salvation is (has and will be) *un*conditionally given by God to the ungodly; that is, it is God who effects and thus freely grants salvation (cf. Rom. 5:9–11, 15–17). Faith for Paul is not a work that can lay claim to salvation as a just reward. Faith is the gracious result of God's prior saving act (the death and resurrection of Jesus), not the condition for it.

It is perhaps no surprise that Paul's assertion of a universal salvation just as much as his theology of the cross has proven to be a great stumbling block for Christians and non-Christians alike.

What is the destiny of unbelieving Israel in Paul's eschatology?

This question is closely related to the preceding, for in Rom. 11:25–32, Paul places the thorny issue of Israel's unbelief (more precisely, the unbelief of a *part* of Israel, probably the majority in Paul's time) within the context of the universality of salvation: "For God has imprisoned *all* in disobedience so that he may be merciful to *all*" (Rom. 11:32; cf. Gal. 3:22). God's universal mercy, extended to the ungodly Gentiles, is now paradigmatic for God's dealing with unbelieving, that is, ungodly, Israel (see Martyn 1988, 8–11). God's mercy is greater and more powerful than human disobedience, including the disobedience of his own people (cf. 11:1). Thus, this disobedience is temporary and provisional; it is also part of the divine purpose:

> I want you to understand this mystery: a hardening has come upon part of Israel [see 9:18], *until* the full number of Gentiles has come in. And so all Israel will be saved [by God]; as it is written, "Out of Zion will come the Deliverer; he will banish ungodliness from Jacob. And this is my covenant with them, when I take away their sins" . . . they have now been disobedient in order that, by the mercy shown to you [Gentile Christians], they may now receive mercy.

The unbelief of a part of Israel, whereby they have become God's enemies (11:28), does not nullify God's call and God's promises (9:4–5; 11:18, 28–29). Exactly how God will accomplish the salvation of all Israel is left rather vague, perhaps intentionally so. Does this salvation necessarily involve conversion, the recognition of Jesus as Messiah and Lord? Is "the Deliverer" in 11:26 Christ or God? Does "out of Zion" mean "out of heaven"? Does Paul have the *parousia* in view or some other event? What does "the full number of Gentiles" mean? What is the meaning of the verb "to come in"? It may be idle to speculate about such matters given Paul's words about God's inscrutable ways in 11:33–34 (though cf. 10:9–13; 11:14–15, 23). What is interesting here is that Paul's ambiguous scenario of events presupposes that the salvation of Gentiles precedes rather than follows the salvation of God's own people (the unbelieving part thereof), which is in effect a modification (tantamount to a reversal) of the Jewish tradition of an eschatological conversion and pilgrimage of the Gentile nations to Zion following upon God's deliverance of Israel (cf., e.g., Isa. 2:2–3; 25:6–9; 56:6–8). The key point, however, is that the salvation of all Israel (which is brought about *by God* in his own way and time, and not by human beings, not even by Christians) is part of the gospel itself and of its eschatological vision of cosmic redemption (see further Davies 1978).[11]

What about 2 Thessalonians?

2 Thessalonians is one of the disputed letters of Paul, one reason being its distinctive eschatology (see Menken 1994). This letter is very similar in structure and wording to 1 Thessalonians, and a comparison of the eschatology of the two letters is therefore instructive. The key passages are 1 Thess. 4:13–18 (with 1:9–10; 5:1–5) and 2 Thess. 2:1–12. Both passage speak explicitly about the *parousia,* as we saw at the beginning of this article. But in other respects the scenarios are strikingly different.

1. In 1 Thessalonians, the *parousia* is understood to be *imminent,* but in 2 Thessalonians it is understood to be *delayed.* The readers are instructed not to believe that "the day of the Lord is

already here [i.e., imminent, around the corner]" through some word or letter supposedly from Paul (a possible allusion to 1 Thessalonians, where that is precisely the assumption!).

2. In 1 Thessalonians, the *parousia* will come *suddenly,* without any warning, "like a thief in the night" (5:2); in 2 Thessalonians, however, the *parousia* will *not* come suddenly but will be preceded by a series of public events: "that day will not come unless the rebellion [Greek *apostasia,* 'apostasy'] comes first and the man of lawlessness is revealed, the son of destruction." The man of lawlessness "takes his seat in the Temple, declaring himself to be God." The passage continues: "And you know what is now restraining him, so that he may be revealed when his time comes. For the mystery of lawlessness is already at work, but only until the one who now restrains it is removed." It is extremely difficult to determine exactly what the author is here referring to (What is the rebellion? Who is the "man of lawlessness"? What and who does the "restraining"?), but that a series of discernible events is involved seems clear enough. The conception of the *parousia* here is really not compatible with that found in 1 Thessalonians (and indeed elsewhere in the undisputed letters of Paul).

3. In 1 Thessalonians, the tone is *warm* and the emphasis falls upon the *salvation* of (both dead and living) Christians and their eternal fellowship with the Lord. In 2 Thessalonians, however, the tone is *cold* and the emphasis falls upon the *eternal* destruction of unbelievers:

> For it is indeed just of God to repay with affliction those who afflict you . . . when the Lord Jesus is revealed from heaven with his mighty angels in flaming fire, inflicting vengeance on those who do not know God and on those who do not obey the gospel of our Lord Jesus. These will suffer the punishment of eternal destruction, separated from the presence of the Lord and from the glory of his might. (1:6–9; cf. 2:10)

These three features, taken together, set the eschatology of 2 Thessalonians apart from that of 1 Thessalonians, causing doubt about its genuineness as a letter of Paul (cf. 2:2, 15; 3:14, 17). Though the genuineness of 2 Thessalonians still has strong supporters, the theology of 2 Thessalonians is difficult, probably impossible, to reconcile with the theology of the undisputed letters in which God's love, mercy, and grace finally outweigh his justified wrath against human sinfulness (cf. Rom. 5:9; 1 Thess. 1:10; 5:9). Indeed, God's eschatological destructive action, his wrath, is finally directed not toward human beings at all, but toward the inimical spiritual forces (sin, death, flesh, Satan) that subjugate human beings and alienate them from God and life (1 Cor. 15:20–28; Rom. 5:12–21).

Does Paul contemplate a messianic interregnum between the parousia *and the end?*

The question arises from 1 Cor. 15:20–28, which refers to Christ's reign or rule:

> Christ has been raised from the dead, the first fruits of those who have died. . . . But each in his own order: [1] Christ the first fruits, [2] then at his *parousia* those who belong to Christ; [3] then is the End, when he hands over the kingdom to God the Father, after he has destroyed every ruler and every authority and power. For he must reign [rule as king] until he has put all his enemies under his feet. The last enemy to be destroyed is Death . . . so that God may be all in all.

Does this passage, then, envisage an extended period of time between the *parousia* (2) and the end (3)? And is this the time of Christ's reign, a reign that shall conclude with the destruction of the inimical powers, the last of these being Death? Some interpreters, most notably Schweitzer (1931), have drawn this conclusion, finding support in the thousand-year reign of Christ after his *parousia* in Rev. 20:4–6 (which has as its background the idea of a messianic interregnum in Jewish expectations, e.g., 4 Ezra 7:26–31 [four hundred years]; *2 Bar.* 29:1–30:5: 40:3 [no specified duration]). This interpretation then assumes the following scenario:

1. The resurrection of Christ
2. Then the *parousia* and the resurrection of Christians ("those who belong to Christ")

   Christ's reign (the messianic kingdom)

3. Then the end, when he hands over the kingdom to God the Father, after he has destroyed every ruler and every authority and power, Death being the last. The general resurrection of the dead occurs and God becomes "all in all" (15:28).

This interpretation of 1 Cor. 15:20–28 actually has little to commend it (see Davies 1967, 285–98). There is no real indication that there is a significant lapse of time between the *parousia* and the end, or that this interval was of any importance to Paul here. The "end" more probably immediately follows the *parousia* itself,[12] and signifies what the *parousia* will bring about. Christ's reign, during which he takes on and destroys the powers, thus takes place between his own resurrection and the *parousia* (cf. Col. 1:12–13). The following scenario results:

1. Christ's resurrection from the dead
   Christ's reign (the messianic kingdom)
2. Then the *parousia*: the resurrection of Christians;
3. Then the end, when he hands over the kingdom to God the Father, after he has destroyed every ruler and every authority and power, Death being the last. The general resurrection of the dead occurs and God becomes "all in all."

Christ's reign actually extends from his resurrection to the end, and the end is signaled by the *parousia*. Christians now live in the midst of Christ's reign, where he carries on spiritual warfare with the powers of this evil age, as we have seen previously.

Paul's scenario of a messianic interregnum finds its most important background in the *War Scroll* (1QM), where the Messiah (here called "the Prince of all the Congregation," 5:1) is a warrior king who destroys the enemies of Israel ("the Kittim," Romans) in an eschatological war lasting forty years (2:5f.). The earthly war reflects and corresponds to a cosmological battle between the spiritual forces of Belial and the angels of God. In short, the messianic era of forty years is a time of war (not peace, as in 4 Ezra or Revelation) and marks the transition (as in *2 Baruch*) from the old age to the new, when God will reign supreme and unopposed. For Paul, however, the enemies of the Messiah (Jesus) and of Christians are not other human beings but solely the malevolent spiritual powers who enslave them (see de Boer 1988, 132–36). In 1 Corinthians 15, death itself is the supreme and "last" enemy (cf. Isa. 25:8), the partner and outcome of sin (1 Cor. 15:56; Rom. 5:12–21); when Christ has destroyed death, his mission will have been accomplished and all human beings will have been saved from death's hegemony.

CONCLUSION

It was a key insight of Schweitzer that Paul's eschatology was not, as so often thought, "a kind of annexe to the main edifice of Pauline doctrine" (Schweitzer 1911, 53). As Davies has summarized the point:

> Schweitzer has criticized . . . those writers who in their treatment of Pauline theology have assigned their discussion of Paul's eschatology to the last section of their work, as if eschatology were an aspect of the Apostle's thought which could be neatly isolated and treated as a kind of addendum, whereas in fact it is his eschatology that conditions Paul's theology throughout. (Davies 1967, 285)

Schweitzer's insight has force to the extent that Paul's apocalyptic eschatology is not reduced to his understanding of the *parousia* and the end but also encompasses his understanding of Christ's advent, death, and resurrection. A full account of Paul's apocalyptic eschatology would thus have to be a full account of Paul's theology, an exercise clearly beyond the scope of this chapter.

NOTES

1. Translations follow NRSV, with occasional changes.
2. There is no verb in the Greek.
3. The sense here is kingly rule, not realm.
4. Scholars such as A. Schweitzer, E. Käsemann, and J. C. Beker, who have made significant contributions to an understanding of Paul as an apocalyptic-eschatological thinker, have also tended to identify the expectation of an imminent *parousia* as the central or defining element of Paul's apocalyptic eschatology (Schweitzer 1931, 52; Käsemann 1969b, 109 n. 1; Beker 1980, 18).
5. These events signal and effect the end of the world as previously known and experienced by human beings (i.e., the world characterized by sin, evil, death, and forces of lawlessness and rebellion, as in the scenarios of the *parousia* quoted above), as well as the transition to a new world marked by righteousness, peace, and life.
6. Schweitzer ran the same risk when he introduced the term "mysticism" in connection with Paul's eschatology and highlighted it in the title his seminal book *The Mysticism of Paul the Apostle* (1931). According to Schweitzer, however, Paul's mysticism was an "eschatological mysticism" whereby the individual believer participates in and benefits from God's *cosmic* act of eschatological salvation as effected in and through Christ (1931, 3). This distinctive eschatological mysticism was thus also a "Christ mysticism" (not a God mysticism), since the believer is "in Christ" or "in the Spirit," while Christ or the Spirit "lives" or "dwells" in the believer (Gal. 2:19–20; Rom. 8:9–11; cf. Gal. 3:26–28; 4:6; 5:24–25; 6:14; 2 Cor. 5:17; Rom. 6:10–11; 7:4; 8:1–2; 12:4–5; Phil. 3:1–11). Paul's "mysticism" does not, then, blur the boundaries between earth and heaven, or between the human and the divine, but between the present (existence in the flesh) and the future (the kingdom of God, now already effective in the activity of the Spirit). Furthermore, this mysticism encompasses all aspects of Christian existence (especially love, the primary fruit of the Spirit), not just (or even primarily) "out-of-body" experiences of the sort recounted in 2 Corinthians 12.
7. Collins also points out that in fact an apocalypse is "a generic framework" (1984, 3) within which passages of different literary genres can find a home.

8. The term "apocalypse" only clearly becomes a self-conscious genre designation in the course of the second century C.E. (Collins 1984, 3).

9. There is no verb in the Greek.

10. Various details of Paul's apocalyptic eschatology could well have been commonplace, even in the non-Jewish world. For example, Paul's claim that the creation is "in decay" (Rom. 8:21) may reflect the "widespread common acceptance of the idea of the world's senescence" (Downing 1995, 206), which also found a place in Jewish apocalyptic texts (4 Ezra 5:51; *2 Bar.* 85:10). This idea, "Epicurean in origin," was "in Paul's day widespread" (ibid.).

11. 1 Thess. 2:14–16, a disputed passage that some scholars do not believe to have been written by Paul, cannot speak against this view. Here certain Jews are charged with killing Jesus and the prophets, persecuting Paul, displeasing God, and hindering Paul from speaking to the Gentiles. "Thus," he concludes, "they have constantly been filling up the measure of their sins; but God's wrath has overtaken them at last" (NRSV). An alternate translation of the last phrase (*eis telos*) is "completely" or "forever" (so NRSV footnote), but this would be incompatible with Romans 11. If the passage stems from Paul he has moderated his views by the end of his apostolic career.

12. Again, there is no verb in the Greek. NRSV supplies "comes," which implies an event subsequent to the *parousia.*

⪜ BIBLIOGRAPHY

Bauckham, R. 1994. *The Theology of the Book of Revelation.* Cambridge: Cambridge University Press.

Beker, J. C. 1980 [1984]. *Paul the Apostle: The Triumph of God in Life and Thought.* Philadelphia: Fortress Press. A major study of Paul's theology which argues that apocalyptic, defined as the imminent cosmic triumph of God, is the unifying center of Paul's thought as a whole.

Boring, M. E. 1986. "The Language of Universal Salvation in Paul." *Journal of Biblical Literature* 105:269–92.

Bultmann, Rudolf. 1951. *Theology of the New Testament.* Volume 1. New York: Charles Scribner's Sons.

———. 1956 [1949]. *Primitive Christianity in its Contemporary Setting.* New York: Meridian.

———. 1975. *The Presence of Eternity: History and Eschatology.* Westport, Conn.: Greenwood.

———. 1984 [1941]. "New Testament and Mythology." In *New Testament & Mythology and Other Basic Writings,* edited by S. Ogden, 1–43. Philadelphia: Fortress Press. Bultmann's classic essay explores the problem of making sense of Paul's apocalyptic ideas in the modern world from an existentialist perspective.

Charlesworth, J. H. 1983. *The Old Testament Pseudepigrapha.* Vol. 1, *Apocalyptic Literature and Testaments.* Garden City, N.Y.: Doubleday.

Collins, John J. 1984. *The Apocalyptic Imagination: An Introduction to the Jewish Matrix of Christianity.* New York: Crossroad.

———. 1992. "Apocalypses and Apocalypticism (Early Jewish Apocalypticism)." In *Anchor Bible Dictionary,* edited by David Noel Freedman, 1:282–88. New York: Doubleday.

Davies, W. D. 1967 [1948]. *Paul and Rabbinic Judaism: Some Rabbinic Elements in Pauline Theology.* New York: Harper Torchbooks.

———. 1978. "Paul and Israel." *New Testament Studies* 24:4–39.

de Boer, M. C. 1988. *The Defeat of Death: Apocalyptic Eschatology in 1 Corinthians 15 and Romans 5.* Journal for the Study of the New Testament Supplement 22. Sheffield: JSOT Press. A detailed examination of two key passages in Paul's letters and an exploration of how Paul has adapted the two-ages dualism of Jewish apocalyptic eschatology especially in connection with his understanding of death.

———. 1989. "Paul and Jewish Apocalyptic Eschatology." In *Apocalyptic and the New Testament: Essays in Honor of J. Louis Martyn,* edited by Joel Marcus and Marion L. Soards, 169–90. Journal for the Study of the New Testament Supplement 24. Sheffield: JSOT Press. Argues that ancient Jewish apocalyptic eschatology exhibits two distinct patterns or "tracks" and that both provide important background for understanding Paul's own views.

Dodd, C. H. 1953 [1935]. "The Mind of Paul: II." In *New Testament Studies,* 108–28. Manchester: Manchester University Press. A classic exposition of the view that Paul's thought about the *parousia* and the resurrection of the dead developed and changed over time.

Downing, F. Gerald. 1995. "Common Strands in Pagan, Jewish and Christian Eschatologies in the First Century." *Theologische Zeitschrift* 51:196–211.

Hanson, Paul D. 1976. "Apocalypse, Genre" and "Apocalypticism." In *Interpreter's Dictionary of the Bible: Supplementary Volume,* 27–34. Nashville: Abingdon.

———. 1979. *Dawn of Apocalyptic: The Historical and Sociological Roots of Jewish Apocalyptic Eschatology.* 2nd ed. Philadelphia: Fortress Press.

———. 1992. "Apocalypses and Apocalypticism (Genre, Introductory Overview)." In *Anchor Bible Dictionary,* edited by David Noel Freedman, 1:279–82. New York: Doubleday.

Hengel, M. 1991. *The Pre-Christian Paul.* London: SCM; Philadelphia: Trinity Press International.

Käsemann, Ernst. 1969a [1961]. "'The Righteousness of God' in Paul." In *New Testament Questions of Today,* 168–82. Philadelphia: Fortress Press. A classic essay which argues that God's righteousness in Paul refers to God's eschatological saving action in Christ against the evil spiritual powers of this present evil age.

———. 1969b [1962]. "On the Subject of Primitive Christian Apocalyptic." In *New Testament Questions of Today,* 108–37. Philadelphia: Fortress Press. An important essay on early Christian apocalyptic, especially that of Paul.

Keck, Leander E. 1984. "Paul and Apocalyptic Theology." *Interpretation* 38:229–41. A plea for the idea that Paul's apocalyptic is not merely a matter of eschatology but of theology.

Lindemann, Andreas. 1994. "Paulus und die korinthische Eschatologie: Zur These von einer 'Entwicklung' im paulinischen Denken." *New Testament Studies* 37:373–99.

Martyn, J. Louis. 1967. "Epistemology at the Turn of the Ages: 2 Corinthians 5.16." In *Christian History and Interpretation: Studies Presented to John Knox,* edited by W. R. Farmer, C. F. D. Moule, R. R. Niebuhr, 269–87. Cambridge: Cambridge University Press. Also in *Theological Issues in the Letters of Paul,* 89–110. Edinburgh: T & T Clark, 1997. Introduced epistemological considerations into the discussion about Paul's apocalypticism.

———. 1985. "Apocalyptic Antinomies in the Letter to the Galatians." *New Testament Studies* 31:307–24. Also in *Theological Issues in the Letters of Paul,* 111–23. Edinburgh: T & T Clark, 1997. An argument for apocalypticism in Galatians.

———. 1988. "Paul and His Jewish-Christian Interpreters." *Union Seminary Quarterly Review* 42:1–15. Also in *Theological Issues in the Letters of Paul,* 37–45. Edinburgh: T & T Clark, 1997.

———. 1997. *Galatians: A New Translation with Introduction and Commentary.* Anchor Bible 33A. New York: Doubleday.

Matlock, R. Barry. 1996. *Unveiling the Apocalyptic Paul: Paul's Interpreters and the Rhetoric of Criticism.* Journal for the Study of the New Testament Supplement 127. Sheffield: Sheffield Academic Press. A searching appraisal of scholarship and the problems of talking about apocalyptic in Paul.

Menken, M. J. J. 1994. *2 Thessalonians.* New Testament Readings. London/New York: Routledge. An interpretation of 2 Thessalonians which pays particular attention to its eschatology.

Rowland, Christopher. 1982. *The Open Heaven: A Study of Apocalyptic in Judaism and Early Christianity.* New York: Crossroad.

———. 1990. "Apocalyptic." In *A Dictionary of Biblical Interpretation,* edited by R. J. Coggins and J. L. Houlden. London: SCM.

Rowley, H. H. 1963 [1944]. *The Relevance of Apocalyptic.* London: Athlone.

Russell, D. S. 1964. *The Method and the Message of Jewish Apocalyptic: 200 BC–AD 100.* Old Testament Library. Philadelphia: Westminster.

Sanders, E. P. 1977. *Paul and Palestinian Judaism.* Philadelphia: Fortress Press.

Schweitzer, Albert. 1912 [1911]. *Paul and His Interpreters: A Critical History.* London: Adam and Charles

Black. A survey of scholarship on Paul, originally intended as the introductory chapter of the following work. Schweitzer faults his predecessors for not seeing the importance of eschatology for understanding Paul's thought as a whole.

———. 1931 [1930]. *The Mysticism of Paul the Apostle.* London: Adam & Charles Black. A classic exposition of Paul's thought as thoroughgoing eschatology.

Segal, Alan F. 1990. *Paul the Convert: The Apostolate and Apostasy of Saul the Pharisee.* New Haven, Conn.: Yale University Press.

Shires, H. M. 1966. *The Eschatology of Paul in Light of Modern Scholarship.* Philadelphia: Westminster. A readable discussion of various aspects of Paul's eschatology.

Sturm, R. E. 1989. "Defining the Word 'Apocalyptic': A Problem of Biblical Criticism." In *Apocalyptic and the New Testament: Essays in Honor of J. Louis Martyn,* edited by Joel Marcus and Marion L. Soards, 17–48. Journal for the Study of the New Testament Supplement 24. Sheffield: JSOT Press. A helpful survey of scholarship and of the problems of definition.

Vielhauer, Philipp. 1992 [German 1989]. "Introduction" to "Apocalypses and Related Subjects." In *New Testament Apocrypha:* Vol. 2, *Writings Related to the Apostles; Apocalypses and Related Subjects.* Cambridge: James Clarke; Louisville: Westminster/John Knox. First published 1964.

Whiteley, D. E. H. 1964. "Eschatology." In *The Theology of St. Paul,* 232–73. Oxford: Blackwell. A brief, technical discussion of numerous special problems in Paul's eschatology.

8

The Book of Revelation

Adela Yarbro Collins
University of Chicago

No OTHER SINGLE WORK has had as great an influence on the apocalyptic tradition as the book of Revelation. Its opening word, "apocalypse" or "revelation," which serves as a kind of self-designation, has become the name of a kind of writing and the ideas and themes associated with it. Although its key images have precedents in Jewish literature and parallels in other early Christian writings, it is from the book of Revelation that the popular images of "Armageddon," the "tribulation," the "millennium," and the "New Jerusalem" come. The purpose of this essay is to place the book in its social-historical context and to consider its relationships with Jewish apocalypticism and the Jesus tradition.

☞ THE AUTHOR

The author of the book of Revelation refers to himself as "John" (Rev. 1:1, 4, 9; 22:8). Since the name was not uncommon among Jews and followers of Jesus at the time, we may not simply assume that this John is John the son of Zebedee, one of the Twelve, to whom the Gospel of John has also been attributed by Christian tradition. The author of Revelation never refers to himself as an apostle or a disciple of the Lord. Justin, surnamed Martyr, writing around 135 C.E., refers to the book and says that its author was John, one of the apostles of Christ (*Dialogue with Trypho* 81). Irenaeus refers to the author of Revelation as "John, the Lord's disciple" (*Against Heresies* 4.20.11; 5.35.2). The reliability of this tradition is called into question by a combination of two other factors. One is the likelihood that the book of Revelation was written in the mid-nineties C.E. (see below). The other is the tradition that John, the son of Zebedee, was killed for his allegiance to Christ, apparently before 70 C.E. (see Charles 1920, 1:xlv–xlix).

195

The attribution of the book of Revelation to John, the son of Zebedee, therefore, occurred either by mistake or as a way of increasing the authority of the book.

Since ancient times, some have argued that the book of Revelation is pseudonymous, that is, that it was written by someone who wanted those who received the work to think that it had been written by John, the son of Zebedee. The Alogi, a group active in the second century who strongly opposed the New Prophecy (Montanists), argued that neither the Gospel of John nor the book of Revelation was composed by John. Rather, they were written by Cerinthus, a teacher criticized for various reasons, including his ideas about a future kingdom of God on earth. The reason for this strange accusation seems to be that the Gospel of John and the book of Revelation supported certain ideas of the New Prophecy (see Swete 1917, cxi–cxiv). In modern times, some scholars have argued that the book of Revelation was written pseudonymously, because pseudonymity is a typical feature of ancient Jewish apocalypses. This argument is not compelling because there was a revival of prophecy among the followers of Jesus, which led, for a short time at least, to the willingness to prophesy and to write books of prophecy in one's own name. The apocalyptic work from the second century called *The Shepherd of Hermas*, for example, was written by a Christian in Rome, Hermas, in his own name. Another reason that this argument is unpersuasive is that the author would probably have taken care to specify more clearly that he was an apostle or a disciple of the Lord, if he had intended to be so recognized.

The most reasonable conclusion about the authorship of Revelation is that it was written by a man named John who is otherwise unknown to us (see Yarbro Collins 1984, 25–53). Although John never claims to be a prophet, he describes his work as a "prophecy" (1:3; 22:7, 10, 18, 19). Further, he comes very close to designating himself as a prophet when he attributes the following words to the revealing angel in 22:9, "I am a fellow servant with you and your brethren the prophets" (RSV). Thus, the author presented himself indirectly as a prophet, that is, as one whose task it was to mediate an intelligible message to his fellow Christians, a message that he claimed derived ultimately from God (1:1). His intimate knowledge of Jewish scriptures and evidence that he knew Hebrew and Aramaic indicate that he was probably a Jew by birth and a native of Judea. The fact that he addressed several different communities suggests that he was an itinerant prophet. His presence in Asia Minor and his attitude toward Rome may be explained with the hypothesis that he was a refugee from the first Jewish war with Rome, which erupted in 66 and climaxed with the destruction of the Temple in Jerusalem in 70 C.E.

☞ THE DATE

The earliest statement about the date of the book of Revelation is the remark of Irenaeus that the revelation was seen at the end of the reign of the Roman emperor Domitian (*Against Heresies* 5.30.3). There is no good reason to doubt this dating. Domitian ruled from 81 to 96 C.E. (see Yarbro Collins 1984, 54–83).

The most important internal evidence for the date consists of references to a city called "Babylon" and prophecies of its destruction (14:8; 16:19; 17:5; 18:2, 10, 21). It is unlikely that the author was referring to the city in Mesopotamia or the one in the delta of the Nile in Egypt, both of which bore that name. The name is not literal but symbolic, as the statement in Rev. 17:5 shows, "and on her forehead was written a name of mystery: 'Babylon the great, mother of harlots and of earth's abominations.'" The explanation of the "mystery" in 17:7–9 makes clear that the woman represents the city of Rome. She sits on a beast with seven heads; the heads represent seven hills on which the woman is seated. Writers of antiquity frequently referred to Rome as the city of seven hills. Furthermore, the woman is interpreted as "the great city which has dominion over the kings of the earth" (17:18). In the first century such a city could only be Rome.

It is likely that John took over this symbolic name from Jewish tradition current in his time. In ancient Jewish sources, "Egypt," "Kittim," "Edom," and "Babylon" are all used as symbolic or code names for Rome. "Kittim" is the most common name for Rome in the Dead Sea Scrolls, and "Edom" is the most common in rabbinic literature. Most of the occurrences of "Babylon" occur in apocalyptic works. In each occurrence, the reason for this choice of symbolic name is made clear in the context. It is the fact that Rome's forces, like those of Babylon at an earlier time, destroyed the city of Jerusalem and the Temple (4 Ezra = 2 Esdras 3:1–2, 28–31; *2 Baruch* 10:1–3; 11:1; 67:7; *Sibylline Oracles* 5.143, 159). The use of the name in Jewish tradition suggests that John used it not only to allude to the great power, wealth, arrogance and decadence of Rome but also and most especially to call to mind the events of 70 C.E. This interpretation implies that the book of Revelation was written after 70 C.E., but not necessarily immediately afterward. The two great Jewish apocalypses that react to those events, 4 Ezra and *2 Baruch,* were not written immediately after the destruction of Jerusalem, but around 100 C.E.

☞ SUMMARY OF THE CONTENTS

The book of Revelation opens with a preface in the third person; that is, in it John does not speak but is spoken about (1:1–3). It is difficult to determine whether the preface was added later by someone else or whether John used the third person here as a literary device. In any case, the style and content of the preface are very similar to those of the rest of the work.

The preface refers to the work as an "apocalypse" or "revelation" that was given by God to Jesus Christ to show his servants what must soon take place (1:1). This emphasis on the imminence of significant events is repeated at the end of the preface, "for the time is near" (1:3). The revelation was mediated in a series of steps: from God to Jesus Christ to an angel to John to the servants of God (1:1–2). The work is also called "words of prophecy" and a blessing is pronounced on the one who reads it aloud (in a communal setting) and on those who keep or observe the things written in it (1:3).

Apart from the preface, the book has the framework of an ancient letter (1:4–22:21). In this part of the work, John speaks in the first person and also quotes other speakers. This part of the work begins with the typical opening elements of an ancient letter: the salutation, that is, the naming of the sender and the addressees (1:4a); the greeting, in this case the wish that God and Christ grant grace and peace to the addressees (1:4b–5); and a doxology (1:5b–6). The latter corresponds to the thanksgiving that typically occurs near the beginning of the letters of Paul. The work closes with a concluding blessing, typical of early Christian letters (22:21).

Attached to the epistolary prescript are two prophetic sayings (1:7, 8), which hint that this work is not a typical letter. Similarly, a series of prophetic sayings precedes the epistolary conclusion (22:6–20). These sayings enclose what may be called the body of the work, 1:9–22:5.

This main part is a description of the revelation received by John and an account of how and from whom he received it. This report falls into two main parts: an account of an appearance of the risen Christ to John (1:9–3:22) and a description of visions and auditions of heavenly origin (4:1–22:5). The second part begins with a vision of the heavenly court (4:1–5:14), which introduces a series of symbolic visions (6:1–22:5).

☞ THE STRUCTURE OF THE BOOK

It is clear that an organizing principle in the book of Revelation is the number seven: seven messages, seven seals, seven trumpets, and seven bowls are presented. The symbolic significance of this number is cosmic. According to late Pythagorean tradition and to the Jewish exegete and philosopher Philo, all reality is ordered and that order expresses itself in patterns of seven (see Yarbro Collins 1996, 90–99, 122–27). Jewish writers argued that the observance of the sabbath is thus in accordance with the cosmic order, but John does not make this point, at least not explicitly.

It is not so clear, however, how each of the series of seven relates to the others. They manifest parallels among themselves and some repetition. The similarities between the trumpets and the bowls are so close that the latter seem in large part to repeat the former. Some scholars think that the repetition results from the use of written sources. Others think that it is part of the author's literary design. Within the latter group, some think that the literary design involves a linear sequence of events, whereas others argue that the same events are described repeatedly from different points of view.

The theory that the book of Revelation describes the same events from different points of view was adopted by the author of the oldest surviving commentary on the work, written ca. 300 C.E. by Victorinus of Pettau. He stated that both the trumpets and the bowls predict the eschatological punishment of unbelievers (Haussleiter 1916, 84, line 14–p. 86, line 7). Victorinus's principle of recapitulation was taken up by Tyconius as an independent rule in his exegetical work *Three Books of Rules,* written around 382 C.E. (Steinhauser 1987, 32, 250). Tyconius then applied this rule in his influential commentary on the book of Revelation, written about 385 C.E. This commentary has unfortunately been lost, but it survives in fragments and something of its nature can be known by its influence on others. The approach to Revelation pioneered by Victorinus has been called the recapitulation theory.

The source-critical approach was first applied to the book of Revelation by Daniel Völter in 1882. An extreme source-critical analysis was proposed by Friedrich Spitta in 1889, who argued that the seals, trumpets, and bowls each reflect a source based on a sevenfold series (see Bousset 1906, 109, 113–14). In the twentieth century, the source-critical approach has been adopted by M. E. Boismard, J. Massyngberde Ford, and Ulrich B. Müller. Boismard used the repetitions in the book to distinguish two sources, one written under Nero and the other somewhat later (Boismard 1949). Müller used differences in messianic ideas to distinguish sources in Revelation from the minimal editorial work of the author (Müller 1972). Ford suggested that chaps. 4–11 constitute a source containing the prophecies of John the Baptist and that chaps. 12–22 represent another, later source, originating from among the disciples of John the Baptist (Ford 1975). It is now generally accepted that the author of the book of Revelation used sources, but not as many or as extensive ones as some source critics have argued. The argument for an extensive use of sources has been undercut by the demonstration of the unity of style in the work as a whole (Bousset 1906, 159–77; Charles 1920, 1:lxxxviii–lxxxix).

Charles argued that the literary design of Revelation describes a linear sequence of events. Most of the events are given in strict chronological order, but there are significant exceptions. Chapter 12 is a flashback intended to provide the background for chapter 13. Three "proleptic" or anticipatory visions interrupt the orderly unfolding of events in order to encourage the audience by flashing forward to some more distant point of the future; these are 7:9–17; 10:1–11:13; and chapter 14. The adequacy of this theory was called into question both by these significant exceptions and by the hypothesis that the text had been thrown into disarray by an incompetent disciple of the author after his death (Charles 1920, 1:xxii–xxiii, l–lv, lix).

The failure of the attempt to interpret the plan of the book as a linear sequence of events led to the revival of the recapitulation theory. Scholars had been reluctant to admit the validity of this approach, because it had been used by those who argued that Revelation prophesied history from the time of its composition to the time of the interpreter (see below). But Günther Bornkamm was able to show that this theory was compatible with a historical-critical approach to the book, that is, with an interpretation that understands the prophecies to refer to the past and present of the author and otherwise to the eschatological future. Bornkamm pointed out the close parallel structure between 8:2–14:20 and 15:1–19:21. He suggested that the former passage describes the same series of events as the latter, but in a mysterious, fragmentary, and proleptic manner (Bornkamm 1937). Another way of retrieving the recapitulation theory is the argument that the book of Revelation is composed of two great cycles of visions, 1:9–11:19 and 12:1–22:5. Each of these cycles is made up of three series of seven: (1) seven messages, seven seals, and seven trumpets; (2) seven unnumbered visions, seven bowls, and another series of seven unnumbered visions. Beginning with the seven seals, each series expresses the message of the whole book in its own particular way. The constant elements of the message are (a) persecution, (b) punishment of the persecutors, and (c) salvation of the persecuted. These themes are introduced in the first cycle in a way that seems deliberately veiled and fragmentary. The second cycle maintains the symbolic and mythic language of the first, but presents the message of the book in a fuller and more coherent manner. In particular, the second cycle is more explicit about the historical contexts of the visions. The first cycle makes clear that persecution is of major importance, but it is only in the second cycle that the identity of the persecutors is made explicit, namely, the Roman authorities (see Yarbro Collins 1976, 32–44).

Structural, thematic, and text-linguistic approaches have also been offered. Elisabeth Schüssler Fiorenza discerned a pattern of inclusion or symmetry in the book of Revelation. The first (1:1–8) and the last (22:10–21) units are related to one another as promise and fulfillment. The second (1:9–3:22) and sixth (19:11–22:9) units correspond because they each have an "inaugural" vision of Christ (1:12–20 and 19:11–16). The third (4:1–9:21) and fifth (15:1, 5–19:10) units are related to each other because both evolve out of the scroll with the seven seals. The fourth unit is then the center and climax of the book (Schüssler Fiorenza 1985, 170–75). Charles Homer Giblin, building on the work of Ugo Vanni, argued that the themes of divine judgment and divine disclosure are articulated and correlated in chaps. 16–22. The narrative of the seventh bowl, wrath against "Babylon" (16:17–21), describes the negative aspect of divine judgment. The narrative of the elimination of all eschatological adversaries (19:11–21:8) is the fulfilled aspect of divine judgment that entails a new creation. The disclosure of the significance of "Babylon"

(17:1–19:10) is correlated with the disclosure of the New Jerusalem (21:9–22:6) (Giblin 1974). In his text-linguistic study of Revelation, David Hellholm concluded that the level of communication most profoundly embedded in the work is the speech of God in 21:5–8. This speech also occurs on the highest grade of the hierarchy of text sequences. This hierarchic embedment of divine speech enhances the authority of the message (Hellholm 1986, 45).

⌒ SOCIAL SETTING AND PURPOSE

The messages to the seven congregations in the seven cities reveal conflict among the followers of Jesus in this region and rivalry among their leaders. Each message is addressed to "the angel" of the congregation in that particular city. Since angels were equivalent to stars in Jewish tradition and the angels of the congregations are identified with stars in 1:20, it is clear that John refers to angelic beings in 2:1 and in the other messages, not to human messengers. This motif is a democratization of the Israelite and Jewish idea that each people or nation has an angel ruling over it, as representative and patron. At the same time, however, the address to the angel is a literary device through which the author can address each community as a whole, speaking in the name of Christ. It may be that the author employed this device in order to circumvent the institutional leaders of these communities (bishops, elders etc.) and to relativize their authority. The charismatic authority of the prophet may bypass the institutional authority of the local leaders.

The Christians in Ephesus are commended because they "cannot bear evil men but have tested those who call themselves apostles but are not, and found them to be false" (2:2). They are also praised for hating the works of the Nicolaitans, which Christ also hates (2:6). In the message to the followers of Jesus in Pergamum, the teaching of the Nicolaitans is equated with that of Balaam (2:14–15). According to Numbers 22–24, Balaam was a foreign priest and a diviner or seer, whom Balak, the king of Moab, paid to curse Israel. Moved by the power of the Lord, however, Balaam blessed Israel instead. But the book of Revelation seems to allude not to these mostly positive accounts but to Num. 31:16, which says that Balaam counseled the women of Midian to cause the people of Israel to act treacherously against the Lord in the matter of Peor. This text in turn alludes to the story in Num. 25:1–18, according to which some of the men of Israel married women of Moab and Midian, who then persuaded them to worship their god, Baal of Peor. The teaching attributed to Balaam which some in Pergamum are accused of holding involves eating food sacrificed to idols and practicing immorality (Rev. 2:14). It is not entirely clear whether either or both of these activities are meant literally or metaphorically. The eating of food, probably meat, sacrificed to idols is an issue addressed by Paul in 1 Corinthians 8–10. It could very well be meant literally here. Practicing (sexual) immorality could also be meant literally, but in some restricted sense regarding distinctions between permitted and forbidden types of marriage. If the terms are taken literally, the controversy here may be related to the so-called apostolic decree reported in Acts 15:29. Another possibility is that both terms are meant to symbolize laxness in monotheistic devotion to the one true god. "Harlotry" is a term used frequently in the prophetic books of the Jewish scriptures for honor paid to other gods. In either case, the point at issue seems to be how to live as a servant of God and a follower of Jesus in a pluralistic society. In antiquity there was no concept of a secular state; religious, social, economic, and political aspects of life were closely intertwined. John evidently disagreed with some traveling and local teachers in Ephesus and Pergamum on this question.

The issue is even more explosive in the message to Thyatira. The Christians in that place are criticized for tolerating the woman "Jezebel" (2:20). As "Babylon" is a symbolic name for the city of Rome, so "Jezebel" is a code name for a female prophet active in Thyatira. According to 1 Kgs. 16:31–33, Jezebel was the daughter of the king of Sidon and a worshiper of Baal. Ahab, the king of Israel, married her, presumably to form an alliance with Sidon. Ahab then built a temple for Baal in Samaria. A struggle then followed between the devotees of Baal and those of Yahweh. In the end, Jezebel was thrown from a window and her body was eaten by dogs (2 Kgs. 9:30–37). John's endowment of the otherwise anonymous prophet with the name "Jezebel" is already in itself a harsh condemnation of her teaching. Her teaching is described in the same way as that of Balaam: practicing immorality and eating food sacrificed to idols (2:20). The words attributed to Christ hint that her teaching also involved "the deep things of Satan" (2:24). This phrase could be understood to mean that her teaching was similar to Gnostic speculation or that she was involved in the practice of magic. It could, however, simply mean that she taught "mysteries," that is, apocalyptic or heavenly secrets, perhaps through the interpretation of texts, about Satan and the evil angels associated with him. Such teaching is intelligible entirely within the context of Jewish and Christian apocalypticism. But we do not have sufficient information to be sure about what this teaching was.

The messages also reflect a social setting in which followers of Jesus are in conflict with their Jewish neighbors. Although the movement that originated with the historical Jesus could still be defined as a type of Judaism in the nineties C.E., it is likely that considerable social differentiation had taken place. The use of the term *ekklēsia* ("congregation" or "church") in the book of Revelation (1:4, 20; 2:1 etc.) indicates that the followers of Jesus in each city had their own association, separate from the *synagōgē* ("synagogue"), the assembly of the local Jewish community. In the message to Smyrna, the speaker refers to "the slander of those who say that they are Jews and are not, but are a synagogue of Satan" (2:9). "Those who say that they are Jews and are not" could be Jewish or judaizing Christians condemned for some reason by John. For example, they could be Gentiles by birth who argue that those who would be saved in Christ must be circumcised and observe all or some commandments of the Torah. This line of interpretation seems unlikely, however, since John shows no interest in the theological principles dear to Paul, such as salvation by faith rather than works of the law. Furthermore, the rhetorical force of the saying implies that "Jews" is a positive designation. The implication is that the *ekklēsia*, the Christian congregation, is the synagogue of God, and that the local Jewish community, which does not recognize Jesus as the Messiah, is a synagogue of Satan. The polemic is analogous to that of the community of the Dead Sea Scrolls against other Jews who have not joined in their new covenant with the Lord. For example, the *Community Rule* states: "They shall separate from the congregation of the men of falsehood and shall unite, with respect to the Law and possessions, under the authority of the sons of Zadok, the Priests who keep the covenant, and of the multitude of the men of the Community who hold fast to the Covenant" (1QS 5:1–3; trans. Vermes). The men of falsehood are equivalent to the men of the lot of Satan (Belial) (cf. 1QS 4:9–14 and especially 1:4–10). In the *Thanksgiving Hymns*, the (probably Jewish) opponents of the Qumran community are designated "a council of deceit and a congregation of Belial" (1QH 2:22 Vermes = 10:22 García Martínez; my translation).

Immediately following the reference to "the synagogue of Satan" is encouragement in the face of expected persecution. John uses the word "tribulation" to speak of the sporadic persecutions that have already happened and continue to occur (1:9; 2:9) and for the persecutions that he expects to happen in the future (2:10; 7:14). He uses the term once for the punishment that may fall upon a false prophet (2:22). In the message to Smyrna, the speaker says, "Do not fear what you are about to suffer. Behold, the devil is about to throw some of you into prison, that you may be tested, and for ten days you will have tribulation. Be faithful unto death and I will give you the crown of life" (2:10). These words imply expectation of official arrest and imprisonment, presumably to await trial. Now at this time, the Roman officials did not seek out Christians to arrest and interrogate them. They took action only when a citizen or resident with civil rights brought an official accusation or charge against Christians, in accordance with the normal legal process. The juxtaposition of the two remarks suggests that in Smyrna, conflict between Christians and Jews had led, or was about to lead, to the formal accusation of Christians by Jews before the Roman authorities. The charge could have been disturbing the peace or introducing a new (unlawful or subversive) cult. The message to the congregation in Philadelphia also mentions a "synagogue of Satan" and "those who say that they are Jews and are not, but lie" (3:9). The promise that those who claim to be Jews will come and bow down before the feet of the congregation and know that Christ has loved them expresses the hope for a reversal of the present situation in which the Christian congregation has little or no status and power.

The need to endure and the need to avoid denying the name of Christ are prominent themes in the messages. These themes reflect a social situation in which it is difficult to maintain the identity of the group in light of the dominant symbolic system and lifestyle and in which there is active opposition to the Christian communities. The messages reveal tensions between Christians and non-Christian Jews. It is likely that there were tensions between Christians and non-Christian Gentiles as well. As already noted in the discussion of the date of the work, the book of Revelation manifests great antipathy to Rome because of the destruction of Jerusalem and the Temple. Another point of potential conflict was the imperial cult. This issue begins to emerge in chap. 12.

The revelatory report in chap. 12 consists of a vision with three scenes (vv. 1–6, 7–9, and 13–17) and an audition (vv. 10–12) that interprets the second scene of the vision. The first and third scenes constitute a birth narrative in which a suprahuman female figure gives birth to a son with a heroic or divine destiny. Mother and son are threatened by a great monster, but the mother receives divine aid and the child is saved. This narrative has similarities with several ancient texts, but it is most like stories about Leto giving birth to Apollo, in spite of the pursuit of Python, a monster who rightly fears that Apollo will take his place as ruler of Delphi and its oracle. During the period of the Roman Empire, Roman rule was likened to the golden age of Apollo, and various emperors were identified as Apollo manifest or incarnate. John co-opts this imperial propaganda to claim that the true golden age will come with the messianic reign of Christ (see Yarbro Collins 1976, 57–155).

The vision of the beast rising out of the sea (13:1–10) is a rewriting and adaptation of the vision of the four beasts rising out of the sea in Daniel 7. At the end of the previous vision, the dragon or serpent that threatened the woman is shown standing on the sand of the sea (12:17). The dragon thus watches as the beast arises from the sea in 13:1. The implication is that the beast is the agent of the dragon. This impression is confirmed by the statement in 13:2b, "And to it the dragon gave his power and his throne and great authority," and by 13:4, "Men worshiped the dragon, for he had given his authority to the beast, and they worshiped the beast, saying 'Who is like the beast, and who can fight against it?'" Since the dragon is identified with Satan (12:9), the beast is presented as an ally or agent of Satan. In the original context of Daniel, the four beasts represented the Babylonian empire, the Medes, the Persians, and the Greeks. Josephus provides evidence that the fourth beast was understood to be Rome in the first century C.E. That the beast of Rev. 13:1–10 represents Rome is clear from the statement in 13:7b, "And authority was given it over every tribe and people and tongue and nation." Rather than describe four beasts, each more terrible than the last, John has combined the attributes of all four to create one overwhelmingly monstrous creature. The result is a reduction of attention to history and a focus on the terrors of the recent past and the present.

The vision of the beast from the sea makes clear what the dominant concerns of John are. Like the beasts of Daniel 7, this beast, that is, Rome, is portrayed as rebelling against God, as an adversary of God. This theme is evoked by the very images of the sea and the sea monster (cf. Ps. 74:12–17; 89:10; Job 26:12–13; Isa. 27:1; 51:9). It is made explicit by the motif of the blasphemous name upon its heads and the mouth uttering haughty and blasphemous words (Rev. 13:1, 5). This theme reaches its climax in the statement that "it opened its mouth to utter blasphemies against God, blaspheming his name and his dwelling, that is, those who dwell in heaven" (13:6). So far, the language of conflict is symbolic or mythic. In 13:7a it becomes clear that this mythic conflict has a historical dimension: "Also it was allowed to make war on the saints and to conquer them." This statement may be understood in two ways. It reflects the incidents of persecution that have already occurred (cf. 2:13) and those that John expects to occur in the future (13:9–10; cf. 1:10). It also probably reflects the first Jewish war with Rome, which began during the reign of Nero. The Roman forces were at first under the command of the military leader Vespasian, until he was proclaimed emperor. His son, Titus, then took over the command. It was he who led the siege of the Temple mount and under whose command the Temple was burned and the city leveled. Later, he succeeded his father as emperor. Thus, the Romans made war on the saints (that is, the people of God; in Daniel, the "saints" or "holy ones" are angels and the people are "the people of the saints of the Most High"; cf. Dan. 7:27) and conquered them.

The blasphemous name and haughty and blasphemous words evoke not only rebellion and war but also the imperial cult. Worship of the living emperor was not a typically Roman phenomenon, but it was popular in the East. In the cultures of Mesopotamia and Egypt, it was traditional to view the king or pharaoh as a deity manifest or incarnate. The Greeks had a tradition of honoring the special dead with hero cults and of honoring living benefactors with religious rituals. When Alexander the Great conquered the Near East, he accepted and apparently even encouraged the peoples he ruled to give him divine honors. His successors did the same. Various ruler cults appeared among the Greeks during the Hellenistic period. When Roman hegemony was established in the eastern Mediterranean area, various cities established cults in which divine honors were given to Roma and Augustus and then to various other emperors, often while they were still alive. It is clear that these cults had important social and political functions. They expressed gratitude to Rome for creating social and political stability, and were part of a system of benefaction and patronage. The philosophical and religious dimensions of the phenomenon are debated. S. R. F. Price has argued that the imperial cult in the Hellenistic cities resulted from the attempt by Greek subjects of the Roman Empire to relate their ruler to their own dominant symbolic system (1984, 241).

The imperial cult was a ubiquitous and impressive phenomenon in the regions in which the seven cities of the book of Revelation were located. No resident could overlook it. There were eighty imperial temples in sixty cities in Asia Minor (Price 1984, 134). The cult was celebrated not only in temples but also in the major civic centers, the meeting place of the council, the theater, the stadium, and the gymnasium (ibid., 109). The emperor was regularly associated with the gods and sometimes presented as a god himself. For example, gold was normally used only in statues of the gods, but it was also often used in those of the emperors. Images of the emperor were often carried in processions (ibid., 186–89). Finally, many of the coins in use carried the portrait of the emperor, often depicted as Zeus, Apollo, or Hercules.

John's awareness of the imperial cult is evident in the remark, "and they worshiped the beast, saying, 'Who is like the beast, and who can fight against it?'" (13:4b). His disapproval of it is displayed in the statement that "all who dwell on earth will worship it, every one whose name has not been written before the foundation of the world in the book of life of the Lamb that was slain" (13:8). In the account of the last judgment, it is said, "and if anyone's name was not found written in the book of life, he was thrown into the lake of fire" (20:15). This lake of fire is the second death (20:14b). The remark in 13:8, then, is a heavy condemnation of those who worship the beast and a strong threat addressed to those who may be contemplating doing so. The threat in 14:9–11 is even more direct and terrifying.

By associating the emperor with the beast and the beast with Satan, John argued that honoring the emperor was betrayal of God. This position was not taken by all Christians. Paul instructed the Christians in Rome to be subject to the ruling authorities. He implied that the emperor is God's servant and minister and that he was worthy of respect and honor (Rom. 13:1–7). The author of 1 Peter similarly advised his audience to be subject to the emperor and to honor him (1 Pet. 2:13–17). Until the outbreak of the war with Rome, the Jewish people offered a daily sacrifice in the Temple in Jerusalem in behalf of the emperor. So early Christians may have debated with one another whether to honor the emperor and, if so, how to do so. Some, like John, chose to condemn, rather than honor the emperor. Others may have advocated praying for the emperor, as a kind of spiritual sacrifice. Yet others may have seen nothing wrong in pouring a libation to the emperor or in burning incense before his image. For John, however, doing so was idolatry, the worst offense imaginable.

Following the vision of the beast from the sea is a vision of a beast that arises out of the earth. On the mythic level, these two beasts recall Leviathan and Behemoth, primordial creatures that must be conquered by divine power (cf. Job 40:15–41:34). On the historical level, the beast from the sea represents the Roman Empire and its heads Roman emperors. The beast from the land is described as follows: "It exercises all the authority of the first beast in its presence and makes the earth and its inhabitants worship the first beast, whose mortal wound was healed" (13:12). Earlier it was said that one of the heads of the beast "seemed to have a mortal wound, but its mortal wound was healed, and the whole world followed the beast with wonder" (13:3). By adapting legends about Nero, John has created a picture of an Antichrist figure, even though he does not use the term (see Yarbro Collins 1976, 176–90). Both Jesus and the beast as Nero are kings who die and rise again. The vision of the beast from the land may refer to the future from John's point of view, but it reflects his present, a situation in which the local elite, wealthy, powerful families in Asia Minor, occupy positions of power with the blessing of Rome for mutual advantage. In order to maintain good relations with Rome and enhance their own prestige, local leaders in various cities of Asia Minor tried to outdo one another in building temples, statues, and other monuments honoring the emperor.

John says that the second beast had the power to cause those who refused to worship the first beast to be slain (13:15). This should not be taken to mean that the Roman governor or local leaders attempted systematically to force people to participate in the imperial cult. The pressure was cultural rather than legal. Since the imperial cult was a significant part of civic life in Asia Minor, it would have been difficult to resist joining in. The pressure to celebrate Christmas in American society today is formally analogous. The authorities did apply force, however, in one set of circumstances. They would not seek out Christians, but if anyone was accused of being a Christian, the governor would ask him or her to offer wine and incense before images of the gods and the emperor. If this act was refused, the individual would be executed (see Pliny *Letters* 10.96; Yarbro Collins 1984, 72–73).

John also says that "no one can buy or sell unless he has the mark, that is, the name of the beast or the number of its name" (13:17). As noted earlier, many of the coins in circulation in Asia Minor bore the image of the emperor with divine attributes and his name. This aspect of the vision expresses the offense caused by the virtual necessity of using such coins for strict monotheists and strict interpreters of the commandment against images (see Yarbro Collins 1996, 212–14). In the following verse, the allusion to "the number of its name" is explained as follows, "Here is wisdom: let him who has understanding calculate the number of the beast, for it is the number of a human being, and his number is six hundred sixty-six" (13:18). These remarks are based on the fact that Hebrew and Greek letters served sequentially as numerals. For example, the first letter of the alphabet is used as the numeral "one," the tenth as "ten," the eleventh as "twenty," and so forth. Thus, the letters of any name may be added up, and the sum may be used cryptically to refer to the name or the person bearing the name. The "wisdom" involved is not only the knowledge of what numerals the letters represent. To calculate the sum related to a name is easy; there is only one correct sum. But to determine what name is represented by a particular sum is difficult, since the same sum may represent the total of many different series of numerals. Two types of evidence support the theory that "Nero Caesar" is the name alluded to in Rev. 13:18. One is the fact that the references to the beast from the sea allude to the legend about Nero's death and return. The other is the fact that a number of manuscripts read "six hundred sixteen" rather than "six hundred sixty-six." Nero's name was sometimes spelled "Neron" and sometimes without the final *n*. If one uses Hebrew letters (another aspect of the "wisdom" needed to solve the riddle), the name "Neron Caesar" adds up to 666; without the final *n*, it adds up to 616.

John's thinking was dualistic in the sense that he perceived the situation in which he lived as characterized by a cosmic struggle between two diametrically opposed powers and their allies. God and Satan, along with their agents and spokespeople, were engaged in a struggle for the allegiance of the inhabitants of the earth. Jesus Christ, the primary agent of God, had been slain but would return to establish the rule of God on earth. At his return, he would be opposed by the primary agent of Satan. As the historical Jesus was transformed by his resurrection into a powerful, transhistorical figure, so Nero is presented as transformed by his descent into the underworld into an opposing, transhistorical figure. This symbolic or mythic construct expresses the insight, or makes the argument, that the primary conflict in John's time was the cultural tension between the views and lifestyles of a strictly monotheistic and exclusive type of Christianity, on the one hand, and the Roman imperial ideology on the other. A major purpose of the book of Revelation is to discourage its audience from accepting the ideology of the provincial elite, which involved a pyramid of power and patronage with the emperor at the pinnacle, and from participating in any form of the imperial cult, which was the religious aspect of that system. This purpose was accomplished by the imagery of the beast, which provided a highly negative redefinition of the imperial symbolic system, by threats, for example, the angelic proclamation of 14:9–11, and by promises, for example, the reward predicted for those who do not worship the beast (20:4).

The work's critical attitude toward Rome is also clearly expressed in the vision of the prostitute in chapter 17. As noted above, the depiction of the woman as sitting on a beast with seven heads and the explanation of the heads as seven hills show clearly that the woman is a symbolic representation of the city of Rome. The Hebrew prophets often personified cities. Isaiah exclaimed that the faithful city, Jerusalem, had become a prostitute, thereby condemning the corruption and injustice that occurred there (1:21). Ezekiel personified Jerusalem as a prostitute and associated this image with the worship of gods other than Yahweh (chapter 16). He also personified both Jerusalem and Samaria as prostitutes and defined their tributary alliances with other nations as prostitution (chapter 23). Given the lack of differentiation of politics and religion, such alliances would almost inevitably involve some recognition of the foreign religious symbolic system and thus of their deities. The prophet Nahum depicted Nineveh as a prostitute because of its deceitful and treacherous dealings with other cities (3:4). Isaiah described the commercial dealings of Tyre as prostitution (18:15–18). Analogously, and perhaps inspired by these texts, the author of the book of Revelation depicted the alliances and commercial activities of the city of Rome as prostitution (cf. 17:2 with 18:3 and 18:9–10 with 18:11, 15, 19, and 23). The association of prostitution with the worship of other gods is implied by the motifs of the blasphemous names and the abominations and impurities (17:3–4). The motif of injustice appears in the allusions to the persecution of the followers of Jesus in 17:6 and 18:24. Violence against non-Christians is also condemned in 18:24 and a critical attitude toward the slave trade is implied in 18:13.

Besides biblical precedent, the portrayal of the city of Rome as a prostitute may have another set of associations. Beginning with the second century B.C.E., cults of the goddess Roma appeared in cities of Asia Minor, the region to which the book of Revelation is addressed (Price 1984, 24, 40–43, 187–88, 250, 252, 254). Such a cult is attested for the city of Erythrae, which was situated on the mainland opposite the island of Chios, not far from Smyrna, one of the seven cities of the Apocalypse. Around the same time, the city of Chios voted to hold a procession, sacrifice, and games for Roma. When Octavian became emperor and the cities of Asia Minor wished to give him divine honors, he allowed himself to be worshiped only in conjunction with the goddess Roma. Temples dedicated to them are attested for the island of Samos and for the cities of Pergamum and Ephesus. If, as suggested above, the author of the Apocalypse was a native of Palestine, he may have seen the temple that Herod built in Caesarea Maritima in which stood a colossal cult statue of Augustus, modeled on the statute of Zeus at Olympia, and another of Roma, of the same size as that of Hera at Argos. The cult of Roma is a good example of the inseparability of the religious and the political in antiquity. She was a goddess and also a personification of the power of Rome. The cults of Roma probably arose in western areas under Greek cultural influence during the Roman republic, but soon spread to

Greece and Asia Minor and continued into the imperial period, so that John was probably familiar with them. From this perspective, the portrayal of the city of Rome as a prostitute in Revelation 17 has a polemical edge. Instead of depicting her as a goddess like Hera (as she was presented in the temple at Caesarea mentioned above) or Athena (as she appeared on coins [Price 1984, 44]), John portrays her as an ostentatious, luxury-loving woman of loose morals, displaying her wealth in the finest clothing and jewelry and drinking to excess, even drinking blood. By painting such a picture, John expressed the outrage already felt by many Jews and Christians because of the destruction of Jerusalem; the portrait also had the effect of challenging any members of the audience who accepted the dominance of Rome and the symbolic and social system connected with it to reconsider their perceptions and their loyalties.

As we have seen, the book of Revelation reflects conflict among Christians, conflict between Christians and Jews, and conflict between Christians and the representatives of Rome. The work attempts to interpret these conflicts and to resolve them in accordance with its own perspective. These interpretations and proposed resolutions are intended to win or reinforce the commitment of members of the audience to that perspective, and they are reinforced by admonitions and threats. They are also reinforced by promises of future rewards and glory. Each of the seven messages in chapters 2–3 contains a promise to "the one who conquers." The Greek phrase could also be translated "the one who overcomes" or "the one who is victorious." The notion of Christian victory in the book of Revelation is complex and paradoxical. It is a metaphor that has its deepest root in the experience and language of victory in battle. According to Hesiod, the goddess of Victory was honored by Zeus for assisting the gods against the Titans (*Theog.* 383–403). The poets depicted her as ruling over athletic and all other competitions, as well as military contests. She appeared in Roman allegorical art as a symbol of victory over death. The paradox of the image is expressed most vividly in Revelation 5. The statement that "the lion of the tribe of Judah, the root of David, has conquered, so that he can open the scroll and its seven seals" (5:5) evokes for the audience with its messianic language the idea of a military victory. The vision that follows the statement, however, focuses on the slain Lamb. According to the announcement of the heavenly voice in chapter 12, "the brothers" have conquered the Accuser (Satan) by the blood of the Lamb and by the word of their own testimony, and they are acclaimed as those who "did not love their lives unto death" (12:10–11). These two passages imply that it is by dying that Christ and his followers become victorious over Satan and all their enemies. But later in the book, military imagery is used; for example, according to the vision of Rome as prostitute in chapter 17, "[the beast and the ten kings] will do battle with the Lamb, and the Lamb will conquer them, because he is Lord of Lords and King of Kings, and those with him are called and chosen and trustworthy" (17:14). The battle alluded to here is announced already in chapter 16. After the sixth bowl is poured out, the beast will assemble the kings of the earth for battle on the great day of God the Almighty. The scene of this great battle is to be a place called "Armageddon" in Hebrew (16:12–16). "Armageddon" is a reference to Megiddo, an ancient city on a plain in northern Israel that was the scene of several decisive battles in the history of Israel (Judg. 5:19; 2 Kgs. 9:27; 2 Chr. 35:22). Christ is also pictured as a victorious warrior in 19:11–21. The vivid depiction of the past metaphorical victory of Jesus and the future military victory of the risen Christ encourages the audience to stand firm in their loyalty to him. The main way in which they conquer the beast is to refuse to participate in the activities that involved giving the emperor divine honors, even if such resistance resulted in death (cf. 15:2 with 20:4 and 7:14).

In the message to Ephesus, those who are willing to make such a commitment, those "who conquer," are promised that they will eat of the tree of life that is in paradise or the garden of God (2:7). This is a clear example of the way in which visions of definitive salvation in the final age are similar to myths of origin. The one who conquers will be allowed to enter the garden from which Adam and Eve were driven and to eat from the tree of life, to which they were denied access (Gen. 3:22–24). The implication is clear: in the new age, death will be no more. The promise to Smyrna is similar: "The one who conquers will not be harmed by the second death" (2:11). Some in Smyrna may be killed (2:10), but this first death, the death of the earthly body, is of little consequence. A death faced in commitment and loyalty is like a triumph in a contest, and it will be rewarded by "the crown of life" (2:10). The victor in athletic and other contests received a crown of laurels, but those who suffer this noble death will be spared the second death, the death of the soul or eternal torment (cf. 20:14–15 with 14:10–11), and will enjoy eternal life. Such beliefs provided powerful motivation for resistance.

The promise to Pergamum involves the gift of manna and a new name (2:17). Like the promise of the tree of life, the promise of manna compares the future, definitive salvation to a former time. In this case it is the time of the wandering in the wilderness, when God nourished the people in an extraordinary, if not miraculous, way. The intimacy between God and the people enjoyed in the time of the exodus will be restored in the new age. The motif of the new name implies a new beginning; the former name, the lack of status, the suffering—all will be removed and a new, secret name of power will be granted.

The promise to Thyatira, that the one who conquers will rule the nations with a rod of iron, evokes the military aspect of victory once again (2:26–27). The victors will share in Christ's messianic rule and power (cf. 5:10; 22:5). Christ also promises to give the victor the morning star (2:28). In ancient Near Eastern and Greek myths, the morning star was a deity. According to the book of Revelation, Christ is the morning star (22:16). This promise seems to be a figurative way of promising that the victor will share in Christ's glory and divinity. The promise to Sardis, that the victor will be clothed in white garments (3:5), is similar. The white garments signify a glorious, exalted state like that of the angels and other immortals.

The promise to Philadelphia, that Christ will make the victor a pillar in the temple of God, is odd, because John explicitly states in the description of the New Jerusalem that he saw no temple there (21:22). Yet he also says that the temple of the city is the Lord God Almighty and the Lamb. This implies that, in effect, the whole city takes the place of the temple in which God or his name traditionally dwelled. The promise to Philadelphia, therefore, may be read as a figurative way of saying that the victor will participate in an important way in the life of the city, the focal point of the new age. This interpretation is supported by the association of the gates of the cities with the twelve tribes of Israel and the foundations with the apostles of the Lamb (21:12, 14).

The promise to Laodicea, like the one to Thyatira, indicates that the one who conquers will share in the victory of Christ. Not only will the victor have power over the nations (2:26–27); he will even share the throne of Christ, which is also the throne of God (3:21). Such language suggests the identification of the follower of Christ with Christ himself, a kind of mystical union that involves the deification of the one who conquers. At the very least, the image signifies that the victorious follower of Jesus enjoys a fulsome delegation of authority and will act as an agent of God and Christ in the new age. The image is similar to the dream of Moses narrated by

Ezekiel the tragedian in the Greek drama *The Exodus* (Holladay 1989, 362–63). A figure, probably representing God, rises from a throne on Mount Sinai and commands Moses to sit on it.

A very important reward for those who resist the beast, especially those who lose their lives because of such resistance, is a share in the first resurrection. Those who have been beheaded for their testimony to Jesus and the word of God and who did not worship the beast are to come to life and to reign with Christ for a thousand years while Satan is bound. The rest of the dead are not to rise until after the thousand years are ended (20:4–6). This is the vision from which the apocalyptic theme of "the millennium" derives, "millennium" coming from the Latin word for a thousand.

The theme of the rewards of the victor is concluded with the words attributed to God in Rev. 21:7, "the one who conquers will inherit these things." "These things" include the new heaven and new earth (21:5) and the enjoyment of the intimate presence of God with God's peoples (21:6–7), symbolized by the water of life (cf. 22:1–2).

☞ WOMEN AND FEMININE SYMBOLISM

Actual, historical women are invisible in the book of Revelation with two exceptions. The first is the message to Thyatira with its attack on "the woman Jezebel" (2:20). Some readers take the criticism of this early Christian female prophet at face value, perhaps because they accept the claim that these words were spoken by the risen Christ or acknowledge the authority of the author, whom they assume to be John the son of Zebedee, one of the twelve apostles, or simply because of the canonical authority of the book of Revelation itself. A more critical reading starts from the assumption that here the author is claiming the authority of the risen Christ for his own point of view in a struggle within the early Christian movement (see above). "Jezebel" is criticized for encouraging followers of Jesus to eat "food sacrificed to idols." Like some of the Christians in Corinth (see 1 Corinthians 8–10), this female prophet may have argued that it was permissible to eat such food because the gods worshiped by the Greek, Roman, and other residents of Asia did not exist. She may have called upon the criticism of idols in the book of Isaiah for support. She may have argued that, since there is one God, the Creator, all food is clean and may be eaten after giving thanks. In 1 Cor. 8:6, Paul agreed with this point of view in principle. If she communicated revelations concerning Satan and the spirits associated with him (Rev. 2:24), she may have argued that this revelation endowed her followers with power over these intermediary beings, who were identified with the Greek and Roman gods. Such power would allow her followers the freedom to eat dedicated food unharmed and without sin.

For "the strong" in Corinth and the followers of "Jezebel," the issue of dedicated food was not an abstract theological debate, but a practical matter. A tolerant position on this matter would allow Christians to mingle socially with non-Christian Gentiles. Such social contact would have been important for Christians who wanted to maintain contact with non-Christian relatives or who wished to join or maintain membership in one of the numerous local associations. Meals taken in common virtually always had a religious dimension. The associations normally had a patron god or goddess who was honored at meetings. The club's common meals often took place on the grounds of a temple. Christians may have wished to join local burial associations or associations of artisans who shared the same craft. Inscriptions provide evidence that there were many such trade associations in Thyatira (Hemer 1986, 108, 246 n. 10). John's teaching advocated a form of Christianity that would remove Christians from the social fabric of their surrounding communities.

Besides allowing the consumption of dedicated food, "Jezebel" is accused of advocating the practice of prostitution (2:20). In the text to which allusion is made (Num. 25:1–2), the "prostitution" of the Israelites was twofold: intermarriage with non-Israelites and idolatry. It is not clear whether the "prostitution" mentioned in Rev. 2:20 is purely metaphorical and thus refers to idolatry only, or whether some actual sexual practice was involved. In vv. 22–23, the sexual metaphor is extended. Those who accept "Jezebel's" teaching (or her partners in leadership) are described as those who commit adultery with her. The reference to her "children" is probably a way of describing her followers. This figurative language suggests that "prostitution" means idolatry only, although tolerance of mixed marriages may also have been a factor. In ancient Jewish tradition, such marriages were often associated with idolatry, because of the assumption that the non-Jewish spouse would lead the Jewish spouse away from Jewish tradition and into polytheistic practices.

It is unlikely that an early Christian leader advocated polytheism in a theological sense. What was at stake was the question whether the Christian faith and way of life were compatible with Greek and Roman cultures. This was a difficult issue, since no ancient culture even attempted to be religiously neutral. John implies that they are not compatible and that Christians must avoid Greek and Roman cultural institutions and practices. The position of "Jezebel" was, therefore, not as extreme as it appears when the text is taken at face value. Persons who took a position similar to hers were accepted as members of the Christian congregation in Corinth. Paul attempted to modify their views and especially their practices, but he did not vilify them as John does his rivals. John says that the female prophet "calls herself a prophet" (2:20), implying that she was not a genuine prophet. But evidently, she not only claimed to be a prophet but was recognized as such by a considerable number of Christians in the vicinity. If she had not been well received, at least in Thyatira, John would not have been so concerned about her influence. Prophecy was a gift often received by early Christian women. Paul acknowledged the activity of female prophets in 1 Cor. 11:2–16. According to the book of Acts, the female daughters of Philip prophesied in Caesarea Maritima, a city in the land of Israel and the Roman capital of the province of Judea. John's mention of "Jezebel" is evidence that a woman, whose actual name has not been preserved, exercised the gift of prophecy in Asia Minor toward the end of the first century. It is unlikely that she was the only woman to prophesy in her time and region. John's name-calling has obscured the fact that we have here an important indication of the leadership of women in the early church of this region.

The other text that bears on the lives of actual Christian women of this period is 14:1–5. This vision belongs to the second great cycle of visions that extends from 12:1 to 22:5. The 144,000 who are seen with the Lamb are making in this passage their second appearance in the book. They were introduced first in 7:1–8, where they are portrayed as an assembly consisting of 12,000 persons from each of the twelve tribes of Israel. Since John can dispute the Jewishness of members of the local synagogues, it is likely that he included Gentile Christians among the 144,000. The number clearly has symbolic significance as a multiple of twelve, but the use of a specific number (as opposed to the innumerable multitude of 7:9–17) suggests that a particular group within the whole body of the faithful is intended. In 14:4 it is said that they "follow the Lamb wherever he goes." According to chapter 5, the most distinctive characteristic of the

Lamb is the fact that he was slain. The 144,000, therefore, seem to be those who are called to suffer death for the sake of their faith in Jesus. This hypothesis is supported by the citation of this passage in the *Letter of the Churches of Lyons and Vienne*. One of the martyrs, Vettius Epagathus is called "a true disciple of Christ, 'following the Lamb wherever he goes,'" because he laid down his life in defense of his fellow Christians (1.10). The description of the 144,000 is best understood as a rhetorical presentation of ideal discipleship. The description of the group includes the following statement, "These are the ones who have not defiled themselves with women, for they are virgins" (14:4). The language implies that any kind of heterosexual relation is defiling. The root idea, found both in Israelite and Jewish religion, on the one hand, and Greek and Roman religion, on the other, is that sexual relations make the parties unfit to enter the holy space of a sanctuary dedicated to a deity. But this was a temporary defilement, the removal of which was governed by certain regulations (see Lev. 15:18). But Rev. 14:4 goes beyond the idea of a temporary, removable defilement by speaking of the 144,000 as virgins. The passage thus expresses a point of view in which the defiling potential of sexual relations with women is to be avoided absolutely by avoiding such relations altogether. The question arises as to the occasion and rationale for this intensification of the quest for ritual purity and for the androcentric way in which the achievement of purity is expressed.

One possibility is that the occasion for the intensification of the value of purity was the adaptation of holy war tradition in the book of Revelation. The ancient Israelite notion of holy war involved the understanding that Yahweh and his angels fought alongside the men of Israel and were present in the military camp. Because of this heavenly presence, the camp had to be kept holy. Various regulations were developed to that end, among which were restrictions on sexual relations, which were forbidden for a time preceding the gathering of the military force and within the camp. The ancient holy war traditions had not been forgotten in John's time. The Maccabees had revived them in the second century B.C.E. (Yarbro Collins 1996, 199–200). The community of the Dead Sea Scrolls adapted the notion of holy war to articulate their understanding of the last days. Revelation also makes use of this tradition, especially in the account of the last battle in 19:11–21 (ibid., 205–7). The expectation that the faithful were to have an active role in the eschatological battle (Rev. 17:14) could be the occasion for the high value placed on sexual continence and for the androcentric point of view (warriors were normally men).

The ascetic tendencies in the Dead Sea Scrolls can also be understood as an intensification of the priestly purity regulations and their extension to the whole community. The notion of the priesthood of the whole Christian community is an important theme in the book of Revelation (1:6; 5:10; 20:6). As in the Dead Sea Scrolls, the notion that purity was necessary for holy war and the idea and practice of priestly purity may have reinforced one another in the milieu of the book of Revelation. The androcentric point of view would thus in part reflect the traditional Israelite-Jewish state of affairs in which only men were priests.

The priest had to be holy because of his special closeness to God. Similarly, around the turn of the era, in some contexts the prophet was seen as one especially close to God. Philo treated the priestly and the prophetic roles of Moses as virtually identical. Near the beginning of his treatment of the third aspect of the life of Moses, his priesthood, Philo states that Moses had to be clean in order to exercise his priesthood, which is the service of God. He had to purify himself from all the calls of mortal nature, food and drink and intercourse with women. Philo says that he disdained the latter almost from the time when, possessed by the spirit, he entered on his work as a prophet, since he had held it fitting to hold himself always in readiness to receive the oracular messages (*On the Life of Moses* 2.68–69). Philo's rationale for the sexual continence of Moses is clearly a metaphysical dualism in which material, earthly things are devalued in comparison with the heavenly. Nevertheless, one may ask whether the book of Revelation, as an apocalyptic work, did not link the prophet in a similar way to the heavenly world and thus to sexual continence.

Besides understanding themselves as priests and as potential holy warriors, the community of the Dead Sea Scrolls understood themselves to be living with and like the angels. This notion appears to be a characteristically apocalyptic one. The aim of apocalyptic revelation and piety is to share in the life of the heavenly world and to overcome the evils, dislocations, and limitations of finite, earthly life. This aim is often expressed by the expectation of human transformation into a heavenly or angelic existence (e.g., Dan. 12:3). In the present, special individuals may attain that angelic existence, at least temporarily (see the Book of the Watchers, i.e., *1 Enoch* 1–36, and the *Ascension of Isaiah*). The Book of the Watchers is especially interesting in relation to Rev. 14:1–5. This early apocalypse contains a narrative about the fallen angels that is similar to but much more elaborate than Gen. 6:1–4. It is said that some angels came down from heaven and took human wives for themselves. These angels taught the women heavenly secrets, including charms and spells, the arts of war, and so on. This illegitimate revelation (and the illegitimate children that they produced, the giants) was the cause of all the evils upon the earth (*1 Enoch* 6–9). The good angels comment that the fallen angels "lay with those women and became unclean" (9:8). Later in the text, the Lord, while decreeing the punishment of the wayward angels, remarks that they "have associated with the women to corrupt themselves with them in all their uncleanness" (10:11). Enoch, who had been "hidden" (cf. Gen. 5:24) and was dwelling with the angels, or Watchers, was sent to the fallen Watchers to inform them of the divine decree. They ask Enoch to intercede with the Lord in their behalf, so that they might be forgiven. Instead of forgiving the Watchers, the Lord instructs Enoch to go and say to them that they ought to petition in behalf of men and not men in behalf of them; they have left the high, holy, and eternal heaven and lain with the women and become unclean with the daughters of men; they were spiritual, holy, living an eternal life, but became unclean upon the women or through the blood of the women, begat children through the blood of the flesh, lusted after the blood of men, and produced flesh and blood as they do who die and are destroyed (15:2–4).

A clue for interpretation is the remark "You ought to petition in behalf of men, not men in behalf of you" (15:2). Enoch and some of the angels have exchanged places. The heavenly and spiritual existence of some angels has been transformed into an earthly existence, involving flesh and blood, procreation and death. Enoch's earthly and fleshly existence has been transformed into a heavenly and spiritual one. Sexual intercourse with women stands for earthly existence, as a part for the whole. The exchange by the angels of a spiritual existence for an earthly one is symbolized by their having sexual relations with women. Although it is not explicit in the narrative, the corollary is that a man's exchange of an earthly existence for a spiritual, heavenly one may be symbolized by abstaining from sexual relations with women. The underlying logic of Rev. 14:1–5 seems to be the same. The 144,000 exemplify the ideal of a Christian apocalyptic piety, in which the goal is a transformed human existence. Through a faithful death, Christians may participate in eternal, heavenly life (14:13; 12:10–11; 7:14–17). In the present, that existence may be anticipated by a life of sexual continence (14:4; cf. Luke 20:34–36).

Feminine symbols are prominent in the second half of the book of Revelation, which extends from 12:1 to 22:5. The three major feminine symbols are the woman clothed with the sun in chapter 12, the prostitute of chapter 17, and the bride of the Lamb in chapters 19 and 21. The roots and purpose of the image of the prostitute in chapter 17 were discussed above. A traditional interpretation of the woman clothed with the sun is that she is Mary, the mother of Jesus, since the child she brings forth is described as the Messiah. Other inner-biblical interpretations are that she is personified Israel, Jerusalem, or the people of God. Such personifications are common in the prophetic traditions of Israel. An approach based on the history of religions leads to the conclusion that the woman is presented as a high goddess with astral attributes: the sun is her garment, the moon her footstool, stars her crown. These attributes suggest that she is the queen of the universe who has power over the movements of the heavenly bodies and thus over human destiny. Only a few goddesses in Hellenistic and early Roman times were so depicted: the mother-goddess worshiped at Ephesus, who was identified with the Greek Artemis and the Roman Diana; the Syrian goddess Atargatis; and Isis, the Egyptian goddess who was worshiped in new forms all over the Mediterranean world in the Hellenistic and Roman periods. The plot of Revelation 12 involves an attack of a monster on a pregnant woman in order to destroy her and her child. As noted above, this narrative has similarities with several ancient texts, especially the pursuit of Isis by Seth-Typhon and of Leto by Python (Yarbro Collins 1993, 21–24). The author of Revelation has adopted motifs and stories about goddesses in order to create a glorious picture of the heavenly Israel. Her story serves as a model for the audience of the book. Like her, they have a heavenly identity: they are God's kingdom in the world, God's priests (1:6). But they are also vulnerable: some have been arrested, some killed; their legal status in the Roman Empire is precarious. The rescue of the woman and her being nourished in the wilderness suggest to the audience that God will deliver them as God delivered the people of Israel from Egypt.

The motif of the bride of the Lamb in chapters 19 and 21 is analogous to the sacred marriage of Zeus and Leto. Traditional interpretations have identified the bride with the church or with the soul of the individual Christian that is united with Christ after death. An approach based on the history of religions sees the influence of the mythic notion of a sacred marriage in the formation of this symbol. Such a marriage celebrates the establishment of cosmic, political, and social order, both on the narrative level and in the social world of the text. The vision of the bride has also been influenced by Isaiah 54, in which Jerusalem is portrayed as God's wife. The construction of the New Jerusalem out of precious stones may have been suggested by Isa. 54:11–12, "I will set your stones in antimony, and lay your foundations with sapphires. I will make your pinnacles agate, your gates of carbuncles, and all your wall of precious stones." In the Dead Sea Scrolls this text was interpreted as an allegorical description of the "Congregation of His Elect," the sectarian community that used the scrolls. The bride, the New Jerusalem, in Revelation symbolizes the community of the faithful at the time of their uniting with God and the Lamb in the new age. In this work, the fulfillment of God's creation and God's ultimate intimacy with humanity are not described in abstract terms or in metaphors that are only masculine. Both the masculine and the feminine are drawn upon to express the richness, complexity, and vitality of the created world and its fulfillment. This vision of the new creation as a wedding is a counterbalance to Rev. 14:1–5. Because of the present crisis, which John implied was about to intensify, the ideal was to renounce sexual relations and to prepare for the end. At the same time, as one of the fundamental characteristics of God's good creation, sexual union is a symbol of the new creation, of wholeness, of the time of salvation.

☞ THE HISTORY OF INTERPRETATION _____

At least since the time of the early Christian scholar and theologian Origen, the crucial issue in the interpretation of the book of Revelation has been whether to take it literally or spiritually. One focus of the controversy in the early church was the prophecy expressed in Rev. 20:1–6. Some early Christian writers, for example, Papias, Justin Martyr, Irenaeus, and Tertullian, believed that this passage predicted an earthly kingdom of Christ that would follow his second coming and last for a thousand years. This interpretation, especially in the case of Irenaeus, may have arisen in opposition to the purely spiritual notion of salvation held by the Gnostics. Origen, however, taught that hope for an earthly kingdom was an indulgence of unworthy desires. He rejected literal interpretations of prophecies of the new age and argued that they ought to be interpreted figuratively (*De Principiis* 2.11.2–5). This approach flowered in the work of the late-fourth-century Donatist Tyconius (see above and McGinn 1987, 531). He interpreted the book of Revelation exclusively in terms of the struggle between good and evil throughout the history of the church and excluded any hope for a coming earthly kingdom.

The tension between those who looked forward to an earthly reign of Christ for a thousand years (the chiliasts or millenarians, from the Greek and Latin words for a thousand respectively) and those who did not (the allegorists) was mediated by Augustine's synthesis of teaching about the last things (eschatology). He interpreted Rev. 20:1–6 figuratively as a reference to the ministry of Jesus, because during that time Satan was bound (with reference to Luke 10:18). Thus, the reign of a thousand years was understood as the age of the church, which was to be followed by the second coming of Christ. Augustine's interpretation of the beasts of chapter 13, as this wicked world and hypocrisy respectively, undercut the tendency to identify these beasts with the Roman Empire and its agents or with other specific political or social institutions. Even though Augustine understood the thousand years and the events of the end literally, his spiritual interpretation of the present and his location of the end in the distant future significantly reduced speculations about the end and expectation of its imminent advent.

Augustine's view of eschatology became dominant. Eventually, the thousand years of the age of the church came to be understood symbolically rather than literally. From about 400 to about 1100 C.E., the book of Revelation was interpreted primarily in terms of the moral struggle between vice and virtue. The notion of an earthly reign of Christ or new age remained dormant until it was revived by Joachim of Fiore. Although he maintained the moral perspective of the Augustinian approach and affirmed the literary structure of recapitulation in his *Exposition on Revelation,* Joachim provided a historical reading that correlated the symbols of the book of Revelation with the major events of the history of the church. This interpretation also divided all of history into three great epochs related to the three persons of the Trinity. According to Joachim, the third age of history, which is to begin after the defeat of the Antichrist, is one in which the Holy Spirit will bring about a reformed and purified monastic church. He did not teach that this new age would last a literal thousand years, but he did reintroduce millenarianism by predicting a coming perfect age of indefinite duration.

The book of Revelation was frequently read and intensely debated in England during the period of the Reformation. Truly millenarian readings revived in radical Puritan circles in the seventeenth century and often included the idea of England as an elect nation. In the nineteenth century, American and British heirs of the apocalyptic Puritan tradition continued to produce

treatises and commentaries giving apocalyptic interpretations of the American and French Revolutions and the activities of Napoleon I and Napoleon III.

In modern times, the issues have been analogous to those debated in the early church. In
the twentieth century the old debate between the chiliasts and the allegorists has gone on in
controversies between fundamentalists and modernists or between premillennialists and amillennialists. Those who expect a literal reign of Christ on earth for a thousand years believe that
they hold the historic faith of the church. As a movement, they have more proximate roots in
the teaching of John Nelson Darby, who founded the Plymouth Brethren in England, and in
various movements in nineteenth-century America, such as the Millerites. Today such believers
call themselves "premillennialists" because they believe that Christ will return before the thousand year reign on earth. They oppose the official eschatological teaching of the major denominations, which is rooted in Augustine, and describe it as "amillennial" because it does not
include an earthly reign of Christ between the second coming and the final state.

In the United States in the twentieth century, several points of view on the question of the
end may be distinguished. The position that has attracted the most attention and caused the
most concern is that which combines premillennial faith with imminent expectation. This
point of view sometimes includes calculations of various periods in history and a more or less
specific prediction of the date of the second coming. One of its fundamental principles is the literal interpretation of scripture. Its adherents accuse "amillennialists" of being inconsistent,
because they interpret other parts of scripture literally, but have a special hermeneutic for
prophecy. The books of Daniel and Revelation are important resources for this point of view.

The modern premillennial position may be seen as a contemporary analogue to ancient
chiliasm. A contemporary version of the spiritual or allegorical point of view is characterized by
commitment to the scientific method and thus by considerable skepticism and agnosticism
with regard to the actual events of the beginning and end of our universe. From this point of
view, Daniel and Revelation suggest the inner meaning of our universe or of the human experience of its processes. The biblical apocalypses are viewed not as forecasts of what is to be but as
interpretations of how things were, are, and ought to be. Their purposes are to inform and
influence human life by means of the values and insights expressed in symbolic and narrative
form.

⌒ CONCLUSION _____

For the historically minded critical reader, the book of Revelation is not a cryptic summary of
the history of the church or the world. It is not primarily a prediction of the timing of the end of
the world. Rather, it is a work of religious poetry, inspired by the prophets of Israel and by the
cosmic and political myths of the author's time. The author, an early Christian prophet by the
name of John, believed himself authorized by God and his Messiah to interpret the times for his
contemporaries. His message was harsh and demanding, both for insiders and outsiders. Insiders were to avoid compromise with the corrupt and idolatrous culture of the hellenized and
romanized cities of Asia Minor, no matter what the cost. Some chance for the repentance and
conversion of outsiders was envisaged (Rev. 11:13). But, for the most part, outsiders were
expected to continue doing evil and to be condemned to eternal torment in the lake of fire

(20:15; 22:11). The book of Revelation is also a work of religious rhetoric, intended to shape the beliefs and lifestyle of its audience. Its impact is far different from that of the teaching of Jesus as expressed in the Sermon on the Mount (Matthew 5–7), which calls for love of enemies and turning the other cheek. Historically speaking, however, the book of Revelation may have contributed to the survival of a Christian perspective that could not simply take its place as one ancient cult among many. Theologically and ethically speaking, it is a work that expresses the anguish of those who live on the margins. It expresses a vision of hope for the marginalized themselves and makes vivid and intelligible for the comfortable how the world of power relations looks from a perspective on the margins.

⌒ BIBLIOGRAPHY

Aune, David E. 1981. "The Social Matrix of the Apocalypse of John." *Biblical Research* 26:16–32. An illuminating study of the social context of Revelation.

———. 1987. "The Apocalypse of John and Graeco-Roman Revelatory Magic." *New Testament Studies* 33:481–501. A suggestive study regarding the similarities between Revelation and the magical papyri.

———. 1997. *Revelation 1–5*. World Biblical Commentary 52A. Dallas: Word. Major commentary that appeared after this article was written.

Barr, David. 1984. "The Apocalypse as a Symbolic Transformation of the World." *Interpretation* 38:39–50. A study of the way in which the book of Revelation affects its audience.

Boismard, M. E. 1949. "'L'Apocalypse' ou 'les apocalypses' de S. Jean." *Revue biblique* 56:507–27. A classic example of a source-critical study of the book of Revelation.

Boring, M. Eugene. 1989. *Revelation*. Interpretation: A Bible Commentary for Teaching and Preaching. Louisville: John Knox. An interpretation that argues that the message of the book of Revelation is compatible with the teaching of nonviolence attributed to Jesus.

Bornkamm, Günther. 1937. "Die Komposition der apokalyptischen Visionen in der Offenbarung Johannis." *Zeitschrift für die neutestamentliche Wissenschaft* 36:132–49. Also in *Studien zu Antike und Christentum: Gesammelte Aufsätze, Band II*, 204–22. Beiträge zur evangelischen Theologie 28. Munich: C. Kaiser, 1959. The article that revived the recapitulation theory in modern scholarship on Revelation.

Bousset, Wilhelm. 1906. *Die Offenbarung Johannis*. Rev. ed. Göttingen: Vandenhoeck & Ruprecht. Reprinted, 1966. A classic commentary from the point of view of the history of religions.

Charles, R. H. 1920. *A Critical and Exegetical Commentary on the Revelation of St. John*. 2 vols. International Critical Commentary. New York: Charles Scribner's Sons. A classic commentary, still valuable for its comparisons with Jewish apocryphal and pseudepigraphical texts.

Ford, J. Massyngberde. 1975. *Revelation: Introduction, Translation and Commentary*. Anchor Bible 38. Garden City, N.Y.: Doubleday. The source-critical theories of this commentary have not been accepted, but it is valuable for comparisons with the Dead Sea Scrolls.

García Martínez, Florentino. 1994. *The Dead Sea Scrolls Translated: The Qumran Texts in English*. Leiden/New York/Cologne: E. J. Brill. A comprehensive translation of all the significant fragments.

Giblin, Charles Homer. 1974. "Structure and Thematic Correlations in the Theology of Revelation 16–22." *Biblica* 55:487–504. An important literary study.

Haussleiter, I., ed. 1916. *Victorini Episcopi Petavionensis Opera*. Corpus scriptorum ecclesiasticorum latinorum 49. Leipzig: Freytag. The oldest surviving commentary on the book of Revelation.

Hellholm, David. 1986. "The Problem of Apocalyptic Genre and the Apocalypse of John." *Semeia* 36:13–64. A sophisticated study of the language of the book of Revelation and the implications for its structure and genre.

Hemer, Colin J. 1986. *The Letters to the Seven Churches of Asia in Their Local Setting.* Journal for the Study of the New Testament Supplement. Sheffield, JSOT Press. A comprehensive collection and discussion of geographical and social data related to the seven cities of Revelation.

Holladay, Carl R., ed. 1989. *Fragments from Hellenistic Jewish Authors:* Vol. 2, *Poets: The Epic Poets Theodotus and Philo and Ezekiel the Tragedian.* Society of Biblical Literature Texts and Translations 30, Pseudepigrapha Series 12. Atlanta: Scholars Press. Text, translation, and notes on the fragments of Ezekiel the Tragedian, a Jewish work that casts light on some aspects of Revelation.

McGinn, Bernard. 1987. "Revelation." In *The Literary Guide to the Bible,* edited by Robert Alter and Frank Kermode. Cambridge, Mass.: The Belknap Press of Harvard University Press. A magisterial history of the interpretation of Revelation.

Müller, Ulrich B. 1972. *Messias und Menschensohn in jüdischen Apokalypsen und in der Offenbarung des Johannes.* Studien zum Neuen Testament 6. Gütersloh: Mohn. An important study of the presentation of Jesus Christ in Revelation and other works from the same period.

Pippin, Tina. 1992. *Death and Desire: The Rhetoric of Gender in the Apocalypse of John.* Louisville: Westminster/John Knox. A reading of Revelation from a twentieth-century feminist perspective.

Price, S. R. F. 1984. *Rituals and Power: The Roman Imperial Cult in Asia Minor.* Cambridge: Cambridge University Press. A very insightful history and analysis of the practice of the worship of the Roman emperor in Asia Minor.

Schüssler Fiorenza, Elisabeth. 1985. *The Book of Revelation: Justice and Judgment.* Philadelphia: Fortress Press. A brief but important commentary from the perspective of liberation theology.

Steinhauser, Kenneth B. 1987. *The Apocalypse Commentary of Tyconius: A History of its Reception and Influence.* European University Studies, Series 23, vol. 301. Frankfurt am Main/Bern/New York: Peter Lang. An important study of the surviving evidence for the lost commentary of Tyconius.

Swete, Henry Barclay. 1917. *The Apocalypse of St. John: The Greek Text with Introduction Notes and Indices.* 3rd ed. London: Macmillan. A classic commentary on the Greek text.

Thompson, Leonard L. 1990. *The Book of Revelation: Apocalypse and Empire.* New York/Oxford: Oxford University Press. A learned, but ultimately unconvincing reading of Revelation as a nondualistic response to a nonthreatening social situation.

Vanni, Ugo. 1971. *La struttura letteraria dell' Apocalisse.* Aloisiana 8. Rome: Herder. An important analysis of the literary structure of Revelation.

Vermes, Geza. 1995. *The Dead Sea Scrolls in English.* Revised 4th ed. London/New York: Penguin. A highly readable translation of most of the significant texts.

Yarbro Collins, Adela. 1976. *The Combat Myth in the Book of Revelation.* Harvard Dissertations in Religion 9. Missoula, Mont.: Scholars Press. A study of the literary structure of Revelation, the major symbols of chapters 12, 13, and 17, and the mythic character of the whole work.

———. 1984. *Crisis and Catharsis: The Power of the Apocalypse.* Philadelphia: Westminster. An analysis of the book of Revelation in its social context.

———. 1993. "Feminine Symbolism in the Book of Revelation." *Biblical Interpretation* 1:20–33. A study of the feminine symbols in which two approaches are explored: the history of religions and Jungian interpretation.

———. 1996. *Cosmology and Eschatology in Jewish and Christian Apocalypticism.* Supplements to the Journal for the Study of Judaism 50. Leiden: E. J. Brill. Essays on the book of Revelation and related texts.

PART 2

Apocalyptic Traditions from
Late Antiquity to ca. 1800 C.E.

9

Apocalypticism in Early Christian Theology

Brian E. Daley, S.J.
University of Notre Dame

T HE APOCALYPTIC STYLE OF THOUGHT, throughout Christian history, has not been confined to works one might formally call "apocalypses." If one understands "apocalyptic" thinking as the use of dramatic, traditional religious symbols and literary devices to express the vivid expectation of a violent end to human history and the present world—an end preceded by conflict and the persecution of God's faithful ones, centered on the resurrection of the dead and the divine judgment, and culminating in the punishment of the wicked and the transformation of the cosmos into a glorious new home for the just—one can find this pattern, in all sorts of mutations and variations, throughout much of the religious literature of early Christianity.

Other chapters in this *Encyclopedia* deal with the origins and development of the apocalyptic genre itself in Judaism and other religions of the ancient Near East and in the early Christian period. Although much about the development of this powerful literary form, and even about its definition, remains the subject of debate, I will assume here that apocalypses are normally pseudepigraphic written texts, claiming the authority of a revered ancient religious figure for what purports to be the revelation of divine secrets; that they are usually narrated in the form of a dream or vision and often involve a marvelous journey through a vast yet ordered cosmos, in the course of which the seer is granted dramatic glimpses of the larger forces underlying the troubled surface of human history; and that the "message" of these works is normally both a sharp critique of the political and religious structures the author regards as oppressive and evil and a call to the audience to seek deeper religious commitment and stricter moral observance, as they await a resolution to the riddles of present history known only to them (see Collins 1979; Schüssler Fiorenza 1989). I will also assume that ancient apocalypses were normally "sectarian" productions: written for a community of faith that saw itself beleaguered or marginalized by the dominant religious and political systems of the society to which it belonged, even though it considered itself to be uniquely representative of humanity's best religious traditions (see Nickelsburg 1989; Meeks 1989). Apocalyptic rhetoric is, to a large extent, a rhetoric of defining religious and moral boundaries. The strong prophetic element of social and moral critique in most ancient Christian apocalyptic works, their frequent anti-Jewish animus, their exhortation to fidelity and endurance in the face of persecution present and future, and their claim to privileged access to God's secret plans for history all point to an origin among believers convinced that the religious resources generally accepted by their fellow Christians were insufficient to ground and preserve their own spiritual identity.

What we will study in this chapter, however, is not primarily early Christian apocalypses themselves (which are discussed in other parts of this *Encyclopedia*) but the use of apocalyptic themes and the presence of an apocalyptic style of thought in the theological, spiritual, and poetic writings of what might be broadly termed "mainstream" Christianity, during the time of its first intellectual maturing—the first six centuries of the present era. This is not to suggest that apocalypses in the more formal sense lack theological purpose or spiritual content, or to overlook works like the *Shepherd* of Hermas, which present the official pastoral program of a major church community (Rome) in a literary guise that shows many apocalyptic features. Our concern here, however, is to see what Christian poets, thinkers, and leaders, most of them writing in their own names and from recognized positions within the ecclesial structure of their day, managed to make of the elements of the apocalyptic tradition that remained alive in their own churches, precisely in the period in which orthodox Christianity took on its classical shape. The only works in the actual apocalyptic form that we will discuss in this chapter are isolated survivors of an earlier genre, documents of the fourth and fifth centuries that fall outside the chronological scope of the other chapters of this *Encyclopedia* and can best be understood against the background of the other, less strictly apocalyptic contemporary works to which we will devote most of our attention.

Before we consider the details of this use of apocalyptic themes in early Christian theology, it might be helpful to make a few broader generalizations:

1. Apocalypse as a living form of Christian literary composition became rarer toward the end of the second century c.e. This development seems to have accompanied the growing "establishment" of Christian religious communities as a loosely organized yet unified presence within Mediterranean society: their gradual recognition, in practice if not yet under the law, as a religious body distinct from Judaism; their deveopment of stable structures of authority, communion, and doctrinal continuity; and the general acceptance within these communities, in practice at least, of the beginnings of a canon of normative Christian texts or "scriptures." Apocalyptic writing, it seems, is usually not at home in large and stable religious bodies.

2. General agreement on the exact boundaries of the Christian canon was not reached until the fourth or even fifth century (McDonald 1995, 191–227), and the most disputed New Testament work in the Greek-speaking churches remained the book of Revelation, or Apocalypse of John (Eusebius, *Historia ecclesiastica* 3.24f.; 7.25). Even after the canonicity of that work was accepted, Greek theologians in our period remained noticeably hesitant to use it in theological argument or to comment on it as scripture; the first known Greek commentaries on the book come from the sixth century and are learned works that downplay its specifically "apocalyptic" features. In general, apocalyptic—like other literary and doctrinal features of early Judaic Christianity—remained more readily accepted in the Latin West than in the Greek East, and interest in the book of Revelation was more a Latin than a Greek phenomenon.

3. Nevertheless, the presence of apocalyptic themes and images in early Christian theol-

ogy after 200 seems mainly to have been due to their canonical status by virtue of their being included in the books of the New Testament. Most of the apocalyptic features of the theological works we will discuss here are drawn from a handful of biblical passages: in the Hebrew Bible, Dan. 9:24–27; 12:1–13; Mal. 3:23f.; occasionally Isa. 65:17–25; and in the New Testament, Matthew 24–25 (especially 24:15–44) and par.; 1 Cor. 15:20–28; 1 Thess. 4:13–18; 2 Thess. 2:1–12; and Revelation 13; 17:3–18; and 20:1–21:5. From their attempts to explain these passages within the context of a growing doctrinal consensus and a growing sense of the long-term stability of the church, early Christian writers developed a classical scenario for the end of history which drew the powerful, prophetic images of challenge and warning in these texts into their own unified understanding of history in its present form. Some theologians, particularly those inspired by Origen and his intellectual heirs, preferred to spiritualize these images by applying them to the individual's experience of death, or to institutionalize them by seeing them as metaphors for the present life of the church. The result was a "taming" of apocalyptic in order to integrate it into a larger picture of a Christian world order, a "history of salvation" culminating in the redeemed life of the disciples of the risen Christ.

4. At certain points within the period we are considering, however—times characterized by a sense within the Christian community of social instability or renewed marginalization—a more genuinely apocalyptic spirit reemerged within "mainstream" Christian literature, in which this biblical scenario was taken to be referring to the immediate future, and to be presaged by recognizable personalities and events in the contemporary world. These moments of apocalyptic revival within the main Christian body included periods of severe and widespread political persecution in the third and early fourth centuries—the persecutions under Decius (249–251) and Valerian (257–258), and the "Great Persecution" under Diocletian (303–311)—as well as longer periods of social malaise and anxiety during the Gothic incursions into western Europe in the first half of the fifth century, and the Lombard invasions of Italy at the end of the sixth. In addition, a strong sense of coming judgment and an occasional interest in the revival of the apocalyptic literary form are evidenced in writings cherished by fourth- and fifth-century monastic groups, from Gaul to Spain to Egypt to Asia Minor. In the circles of these "athletes of God," who had withdrawn from public society and the life of the larger church to do battle with the demons that ruled this cosmos and to wait for Christ's coming, the prophetic and sectarian features of earlier apocalyptic communities were realized anew.

☞ THE SECOND CENTURY _____

Besides the actual apocalypses produced by Christians, presumably of Jewish background, during the second century of our era, a number of works in other religious genres from the period show an interest in the expectations and images of apocalyptic literature. Since Adolph von Harnack, in fact, scholars have tended to assume that the normal pattern of ultimate Christian hope in the second century was colored not only by a vivid sense of the imminent return of Christ in judgment but also by chiliastic or millenarian expectations: by the hope that when Christ comes again, the just alone will first be raised from the dead to enjoy a thousand years of peace and fabulous plenty under his rule on a transformed earth, and that only after that period of first reward will the final conflict between the forces of good and evil come to its brief and bloody climax and the resurrection and judgment of all who have lived occur. Charles Hill, however, has recently shown, by careful analysis of the relevant texts, that millenarian expectations were in fact the exception rather than the rule among Christian writers of the second and third centuries; their more normal pattern of hope was to imagine the preparatory period for Christ's final judgment in terms of an immediate, personal judgment and recompense by God for individuals—presumably as bodiless shades or souls—at the time of their death, and to expect a second judgment of all after the common resurrection, at the end of history (Hill 1992).

Nevertheless, millenarian hopes did play an important part in the future expectations of a number of important Christian thinkers in the second and third centuries, not only in Asia Minor, as is often suggested, but also in Rome, North Africa, and Egypt. Eusebius of Caesarea (*Hist. eccl.* 3.28) quotes the third-century bishop Dionysius of Alexandria as attributing to Cerinthus (an early-second-century Gnostic teacher about whom little is known, but who may have been of Egyptian origin) the hope that the faithful will enjoy, under Christ's rule, a thousand-year "wedding feast" of material pleasures in Jerusalem after their resurrection. This, according to Dionysius, was the reason some went so far as to attribute the Apocalypse of John to Cerinthus, presumably because of the description there of such a millennial kingdom (Rev. 20:1–6). Irenaeus of Lyons, who strongly defended the millenarian tradition in the 180s, attributes his own understanding of it to the writings of Papias of Hierapolis, a Phrygian bishop of the early second century who had reportedly listened to the apostle John and who collected the teachings of earlier Asiatic "elders" in a work of five books (*Adversus haereses* 5.33f.; cf. Eusebius, *Hist. eccl.* 3.39.11), of which only a few fragments now survive.

The apologist *Justin* (d. ca. 165) is the first major Christian writer we know of who developed the tradition of Christian apocalyptic and millenarian hope into a more or less consistent picture. In his reported dialogue with the rabbi Trypho, Justin insisted that the fulfillment of Israel's messianic prophecies had been realized in the glorification of Jesus, and that the one who Daniel foretold would speak blasphemies against the Most High was "already at the door" (*Dialogue with Trypho* 32; cf. 110). In response to Trypho's questioning about the prophecy that Elijah would precede the Messiah on "the great and terrible day of the Lord" (Mal. 4:5, which Justin here wrongly attributes to Zechariah), Justin argues that scripture predicts "that two comings (*parousiai*) of the Messiah would occur," one in humility and suffering and the second in glory, and that just as John the Baptist, full of the Holy Spirit, was the herald of the first coming, Elijah—the bearer of the same Spirit—would inaugurate the second (*Dial.* 49; see 40, 110). Drawing on Daniel 7, Justin describes this second coming of Christ, which he expects soon, as a scene of great majesty (*Dial.* 31, 121); it will take place in Jerusalem (*Dial.* 40, 85) and will be a time of judgment and righteous recompense for all people (*Dial.* 28, 31f., 121). In his *Second Apology*, Justin says Christians believe that the world is to be judged and destroyed by an inundation of fire, which will purify the just and consume the wicked (*2 Apol.* 7; cf. *1 Apol.* 20, where he admits the similarity of this expectation to Platonic and Stoic traditions). The reason this ordeal is delayed, he argues in one passage, is the preserving presence of "the seed of the Christians" (*2 Apol.* 7); in other places, he suggests that God is offering humanity a period of grace, to allow more people to be converted to faith in Jesus (*1 Apol.* 28) or to complete the predestined number of the just (*1 Apol.* 45).

At the time of final judgment and revelation, in Justin's view, the just will rise to share in a life of ease and abundance in a restored Jerusalem for a thousand years, after which there will be an "eternal and general resurrection and judgment of all" and a radiant new world in which the just will be, in Jesus' words, "equal to the angels" (*Dial.* 81, alluding to Rev. 20:4f.; Isa. 65:17–25; and Luke 20:35f.). Justin concedes, in this passage, that although he is not alone in his millenarian hope, there are also "many, even Christians of pure and reverent faith," who imagine the end of history otherwise (*Dial.* 80). To deny the resurrection altogether, however, and to conceive of salvation simply as meaning that the souls of the just are taken to heaven at death—apparently, in Justin's eyes, the extreme alternative to his Christian millenarianism—would be blasphemy both for pious Jews and pious Christians (ibid.). For Justin, the prospect of a coming millennium of earthly peace for the just seems to be indispensable to a realistic understanding of a bodily resurrection. Elsewhere, however, Justin hints that the prophets' expectation of this time of peace and plenty is in some sense already realized in the peaceable community of the church (*Dial.* 110). Strong as it was, his millenarian hope seems to have been capable of various interpretations.

The other main representative of millenarian hope in the late second century was *Irenaeus of Lyons* (d. after 198). Like Justin, Irenaeus also insists that Christian faith includes the expectation of a real resurrection of the body and a real transformation of the present cosmos, at least as the penultimate chapter in the story of salvation; a primary interest in his theology, of course, is to counteract the dismissal of both body and cosmos by contemporary Gnostic teachers as irrelevant to human welfare. Second-century Gnosticism showed little interest in the future of the world or the body and little sense of an impending crisis of judgment (MacRae 1989, 319f.). Apart from speculating about a final cosmic conflagration that would consume all matter (see Irenaeus, *Adv. haer.* 1.7.1), Valentinian writers seem to have been mainly interested in a future for the enlightened few that lay totally apart from the world and its history, and to have interpreted Christian resurrection hope in entirely spiritual terms (see *Treatise on Resurrection*, Nag Hammadi I, 4). Those texts in the Nag Hammadi collection with strong apocalyptic features are probably of later origin, perhaps as late as the fourth century (see "The Revival of the Apocalyptic Genre" below).

As bishop of a small, sharply divided and cruelly persecuted community on the northern frontier during widespread social unrest and anxiety over foreign invasions in the later years of the emperor Marcus Aurelius (161–180), Irenaeus seems to have sensed the need both to affirm the public continuity of Christian teaching, as the belief of a worldwide community with a recognizable history, and to resist the attractions of more inward, individualistic forms of Christianity. Irenaeus has an unprecedented sense of the importance of time. His conception of human fulfillment and perfection—being created in the image of "the uncreated God," "seeing God," and participating, through that vision, in God's indestructible life—inevitably includes growth; because they are not uncreated, humans must advance toward fulfillment in God by a slow, at times frustrating process of learning and becoming, just as each human individual must begin life as an infant and grow slowly to the fullness of his or her powers (*Adv. haer.* 4.38). Christ's appearance, Irenaeus assumes, was "in these last times," since he is himself the fulfillment and summation of human history (ibid.).

Following a widely held tradition of Jewish and early Christian thought (Luneau 1964), Irenaeus seems to have taken it for granted that human history would be limited to a "week" of six thousand years (*Adv. haer.* 5.28.3), although he nowhere indulges in more precise calculations about just when the end is due. His conception of the scenario of history's end closely follows Christian scriptural sources. As suggested by 2 Thessalonians and Daniel, the end-time will be inaugurated, Irenaeus believes, by the appearance of the Antichrist, an unjust judge and ruler "who concentrates in himself every satanic error" and who will attempt to be worshiped as a god (*Adv. haer.* 5.25.1, 5; 28.2; 29.2). Irenaeus suggests possible ways of deciphering 666, "the number of the beast" in Rev. 13:18, as a cipher for the Antichrist's name; although he himself thinks *Teitan* the most probable rendering, he points out that *Evanthas* and *Lateinos* are also possible and urges against too much speculation on such things: "It is more certain and less hazardous to await the fulfillment of the prophecy than to be making surmises . . ." (*Adv. haer.* 5.30.3) Irenaeus vividly expects that Christ will come in fire and majesty to judge the world (4.4.3; 33.1; 36.3; 5.30.4), purifying the just by the same campaign in which he will annihilate his enemies (5.28.4; 29.1). He is particularly insistent that the picture of the thousand-year reign of the risen just with the triumphant Christ in Rev. 20:1–6 not be taken allegorically any more than one may take the promise of bodily resurrection as an allegory (5.35). Citing the teaching of Papias and other, unnamed "elders" of the past, Irenaeus sees a coming time of earthly peace and plenty as clearly prophesied by the Hebrew Bible, especially by various passages in Isaiah, and argues that such a "commencement of incorruption" for God's faithful ones is a necessary step to prepare them to "lay hold of God" in inconceivable but far closer intimacy, after the millennium has come to an end (5.35.2; 36.1, 3). For Irenaeus, both the millennial kingdom and the reality of a fleshly resurrection—for which he argues at length in *Adv. haer.* 5.1–15—are part of a larger understanding of human salvation which his anti-Gnostic elaboration of Christian faith implies: if the same God is at once creator, lawgiver, and savior, this whole order of creation, as described in the Hebrew and Christian scriptures, must be the recipient of God's saving activity and ultimately must come to share in God's incorruptible being.

> For as it is truly God who raises up the human person, so also does the human person truly rise from the dead, and not allegorically, as I have shown repeatedly. And as we rise in actuality, so also shall we be actually trained beforehand for incorruption, and shall go forward and flourish in the times of the [millennial] kingdom, in order that we might be capable of receiving the glory of the Father. Then, when all things are made new, we shall truly dwell in the city of God. (*Adv. haer.* 5.35.2)

☞ THE FINAL CENTURY OF PERSECUTIONS

As a religious group not officially sanctioned by the Roman state and as objects of widespread prejudice and ignorance, Christians were occasionally subject to arrest and persecution, on a variety of grounds, in the first two centuries of their history; it was only in the third century, however, that persecution became, in several brief but bloody episodes, systematic and universal. During the generally peaceful and prosperous reign of Septimius Severus (193–211), for instance, persecution broke out in Egypt (202–203) and in the province of Africa (197, 211–213), probably due in large measure to public anxiety about the growing influence and wealth of Christians in the larger cities there (Frend 1965, 303–46). Later, as the empire slipped into a half century of economic distress, social unrest, and a succession of unusually incompetent and repressive emperors (Jones 1964, 1:23–36), from the military coup of Maximinus Thrax in 235 until the accession of the reformer Diocletian in 284, Christians throughout the empire frequently became the scapegoats for society's ills, and attempts to force them into religious conformity led to several further waves of persecution. In such periods of common danger, apocalyptic expectations became a powerful vehicle for Christians to use in interpreting their situation and confirming their hope.

Eusebius of Caesarea, for instance, reports that in 202–203 an author named Judah—perhaps an Alexandrian, probably a Christian of Jewish origin—wrote an interpretation of Daniel's apocalyptic visions in which he predicted the imminent arrival of the Antichrist: "so completely," adds Eusebius, "had the upheaval of the persecution of our people at that time unsettled the popular mind" (*Hist. eccl.* 6.7). Hippolytus of Rome, in his *Commentary on Daniel* (ca. 204), reports that a number of bishops in Syria and Pontus had recently expressed the expectation that the world would soon end (3.18f.). Firmilian, bishop of Caesarea in Cappadocia, wrote to Cyprian of Carthage in the 250s that during the persecution of Maximinus in 236 a prophetess in central Asia Minor had urged Christians there to make their way to Jerusalem for the coming of Christ (Cyprian, *Epistles* 75.10.1–3); and Bishop Dionysius of Alexandria, also in the middle of the century, tells of having persuaded a millenarian sect in the Fayyum, led by a certain Korakion, to rethink their hope for a coming material kingdom (see Eusebius, *Hist. eccl.* 7.24.4).

The most articulate exponent of Christian apocalyptic hope in the Severan period was *Tertullian of Carthage* (ca. 160–after 220), the brilliant, often enigmatic polemicist who created a Latin theological vocabulary virtually single-handedly, in order to express stinging critiques of his Gnostic, pagan, and even Christian contemporaries. In his *On Spectacles* (*De spectaculis*), probably an early work, Tertullian contrasts the vanity of the theatrical and athletic shows so prized in Roman society with "the spectacle that is fast approaching," the coming of Christ in majesty. Then all people will be forced to see the resurrection of the just, he assures his readers, and their entry into the New Jerusalem.

> Other spectacles remain, as well: that last, unending day of judgment; that day unlooked for by the nations, regarded by them with derision, when the world, hoary with age, and all that it has produced, shall be consumed in one great flame! How vast a spectacle then will burst upon the eye! (*De spect.* 30)

In this coming "show," Tertullian gloats, his own delight will be to watch the public reversal of the present order of power: Rome's deified emperors being thrust "into the lowest darkness," pagan philosophers and poets being surprised by the reality of judgment and retribution, "governors of provinces, too, who persecuted the Christian name, in fires fiercer than those with which, in the days of their pride, they raged against the followers of Christ" (*De spect.* 30). In his *Apologetic Work* (*Apologeticum*), on the other hand (ca. 197), addressed to the Roman provincial governor, Tertullian insists that Christians do pray for the emperor and the state, precisely because they know that "the great disaster threatening the whole world, the very end of the age with its promise of dreadful sufferings, is held off by the continuing existence of the Roman Empire" (*Apol.* 32; see also *De carnis resurrectione* 24 [210–212]). Tertullian is convinced that a violent end of history, as promised in the apocalyptic tradition, is near: the Antichrist is "now close by, gasping for the blood of Christians" (*De fuga in persecutione* 12 [ca. 212]). The scenario for the drama he expects is that of the book of Revelation: plagues and wars, the temporary confinement of the devil and "the blessed prerogative of a first resurrection" for the just, then a "final and universal resurrection" (*De carn. res.* 25). In this context, Tertullian clearly

affirms, against Gnostic spiritualizing of Christian hopes, both the bodily character of this resurrection and the expectation of a millennium of peace and plenty on earth for the just, "for it is
both just and worthy of God that his servants should also have joy in that place where they have
suffered affliction in his name" (*Adversus Marcionem* 3.24).[1] He even cites reports from pagan
soldiers in Judea of visions of a distant city in the dawn sky as intimations of the coming of the
New Jerusalem of Revelation 21 (ibid.). Yet although the scriptures reveal these things, and
"concentrate the harvest of the Christian hope in the very end of the world," Tertullian is also
willing to recognize the truth of "spiritual" interpretations of the resurrection and the millennium (*De carn. res.* 25), and criticizes the Jews for interpreting these promises exclusively in
national and material terms (ibid., 26). Although he takes the Christian apocalyptic tradition
seriously, Tertullian is too sophisticated for a simple biblical literalism.[2]

A contemporary of Tertullian who largely shared his apocalyptic expectation was *Hippoly-*
tus, traditionally understood to be a Greek speaker of unknown origin who became a presbyter
and later a schismatic bishop in Rome, and who died in the persecution of Maximinus in 235.[3]
Hippolytus's treatise *On Christ and Antichrist* (*De Christo et Antichristo*) (ca. 200) is a carefully
arranged and sparingly annotated anthology of passages from the Hebrew Bible and the New
Testament that depict the end of history, especially the conflicts surrounding the figure of the
Antichrist. By linking the picture of the beast in Revelation 13 with a variety of earlier prophetic
texts, Hippolytus constructs a vivid portrait of this last rebel against the royal rule of Christ,
which anticipates the standard interpretation of succeeding centuries. A Jewish leader from the
tribe of Dan (15), the Antichrist will assume for himself the symbolic attributes of the Messiah
promised in scripture and "seek to liken himself in all things to the Son of God" (6). He will
rebuild the Temple in Jerusalem (6) and begin to build up a power base in the eastern Mediterranean, defeating Egypt and Libya and conquering Tyre and Berytus (52), apparently by overturning Roman rule (28–37). After gathering supporters—probably mainly Jews—from
throughout the world (56; cf. 54), he will begin a new persecution of the Christian church (56,
59–63) and will be defeated only when Christ, heralded by Elijah and John the Baptist, comes
again in glory, raises the dead, and holds final judgment (44f., 64–66). Notable here is not only
Hippolytus's effort to harmonize and schematize biblical apocalyptic imagery into a coherent
narrative but also his apparent unwillingness to speculate on details not in scripture. Following
Irenaeus, for instance, he offers the same conjectures for the name of the Antichrist signified by
the number 666, but he is even less willing than Irenaeus is to commit himself to one interpretation (50).

In his *Commentary on Daniel,* probably written also during the persecution of Septimius
Severus (ca. 204), Hippolytus takes a similarly sober approach to the apocalyptic intimations of
that prophetic book. Written in four discourses, this work—the oldest extant Christian scriptural commentary—expressly assumes the same scenario for the end of history that is sketched
out in *On Christ and Antichrist* (4.7) and echoes that work's caution about specifying its details
any further. On the date of the end, for instance, Hippolytus argues that it has been deliberately
concealed by Christ so that we do not slacken in keeping the commandments (4.16); but he
seems to feel that the end is not imminent (4.17) and even suggests that it will only come five
hundred years after the birth of Christ (4.23f.). This notion, later commonplace in both Eastern
and Western writers, was apparently based on the scheme of history as a cosmic "week" of six
thousand years, followed by a one-thousand-year "sabbath" of rest; the coming of the Messiah
was usually located halfway through history's millennial sixth "day." But Hippolytus does not

clearly espouse a millenarian interpretation of the future "sabbath" of the saints in the sense that Irenaeus does; Hippolytus says nothing about a "first" resurrection or a period of earthly rest before the final struggle, but simply identifies the final sabbath with "the coming kingdom of the saints, when they will reign with Christ" (4.23), leaving its relationship to the general resurrection and the final reward of the just somewhat vague (see 4.10, 39, 56). In his restraint and his deliberate focus on scriptural texts, Hippolytus stands closer to Augustine than to either Irenaeus or Tertullian.

Cyprian of Carthage (d. 258), bishop of that metropolitan city during the brief but violent persecutions of Decius (249–251) and Valerian (257–258), was mainly concerned, in his eloquent, closely reasoned letters and treatises, with questions of leadership and ecclesial legitimacy—questions that closely touched his own attempts to unify the sharply factionalized African church. Although eschatology is not a central theme in Cyprian's work, he frequently expresses the conviction that the present troubles of empire and church are signs of the world's final crisis. In his apologetic address to the proconsul Demetrianus (252), who had accused the Christians of causing the wars and disasters of the mid-third century by neglecting the traditional gods, Cyprian develops the Stoic theme of "the world's old age" (*senectus mundi*).[4] If natural resources seem now to be diminished all over the world, if human skills seem on the decline and famine and plagues increasing,

> You must in the first place know this, that the world has now grown old and does not remain in that strength in which it formerly stood; nor does it enjoy that vigor and force by which it once flourished. . . . Whatever is tending downwards to decay and its final struggle, with its end nearly approaching, must necessarily be weakened. (*Ad Demetrianum* 3)

In Cyprian's view, this general decline is due not simply to a natural depletion of human and cosmic powers but to the judgment of God:

> If wars continue frequently to prevail, if death and famine increase our anxiety, if health is shattered by raging diseases, if the human race is wasted by the desolation of pestilence—know that this was foretold: that evils should be multiplied in the last times, and that misfortunes should be varied; and that as the day of judgment is now drawing near, the censure of an indignant God should be more and more aroused for the scourging of the human race. (*Ad Demetrianum* 5)

Christ's own sacrifice, Cyprian suggests (*Ep.* 63.16), was a sign of "sunset and the evening of the world"; this nearness of the end is all the clearer in the dramatic conflicts of his own day, when persecutions unmistakably warn that "in the ending and consummation of the world the hateful time of the Antichrist is already beginning to draw near" (*Ad Fortunatum*, praef.; cf. *Ep.* 67.7). All of these trials, Cyprian tells his community during a local epidemic in 252, are but the fulfillment of scriptural prophecy and signs that better things cannot be far away.

> The Kingdom of God, dear brothers and sisters, has begun to be very near: the reward of life, the joy of eternal salvation, everlasting joy, the possession of the Paradise we once lost, are now approaching, even as the world declines; heavenly things now take the place of earthly ones, great things of small, eternal things of what passes away. What room is there now for anxiety or worry? (*De mortalitate* 2)

Like the proclamations of John the Baptist, Cyprian's letters to Bishop Lucius of Rome in 252 say that the sufferings of church leaders all over the empire simply make it clear that Christ is coming soon to confirm his faithful ones in joy (*Ep.* 61.4). All these passages reveal how, in Cyprian's hands, the imagery of the apocalyptic tradition—taken very much at face value—has become a powerful means of pastoral encouragement as well as a key to finding deeper meaning in the troubles of his time.

Unquestionably the writer of this dark period with the most long-lasting influence on later Christian thought was *Origen of Alexandria* (ca. 185–253/254). Origen's use of the apocalyptic tradition, like most of his thought on Christian doctrine and scripture, was complex and carefully nuanced. He was aware of the apocalyptic tradition, accepted its main features as referring to events in both past and future history, and was willing to employ some of its themes in his own preaching. Yet he was also aware of its potential abuse and preferred a less theatrical view of human salvation. Origen affirms clearly, in the last book of his apology *Against Celsus* (ca. 250), that his first goal as a Christian evangelist is to convince the pagan world that there will be judgment and retribution for all people based on their deeds (*Contr. Cels.* 8.52). So too, in two of his extant homilies on the Psalms, Origen calls on his hearers to do penance in this present life rather than undergo "the punishments of eternal fire" (*Homily 2 on Ps. 37* 1, 5; *Homily 5 on Ps. 36* 4). Despite his frequent speculation on the prospect of universal salvation (*apokatastasis;* see Daley 1991, 58f.), Origen clearly stressed individual moral responsibility and saw the punishment of sinners, at least for a time, as necessary for their cleansing and instruction—even if the traditional imagery of fire and "outer darkness" is to be taken metaphorically (*De principiis* 2.10.4–8).

History, in Origen's scheme, is far less mysterious than it seemed to writers in the classical apocalyptic tradition: not a dark decline toward impending dissolution, but a process of the fall and the gradual healing of free, created minds, securely guided by a triumphantly provident God—a process whose lines can be discerned by the spiritually aware (see esp. *De prin.* 1.5–6; 2.3; 3.1, 5–6). So when Origen sets out to explain the Bible's apocalyptic passages—something he only seems to do when the context of his exegesis makes it unavoidable—he tends to take them either as referring to past events or in what he understands as their deeper, "spiritual" meaning, rather than to see in them indications of unprecedented future disasters. His treatment of the Matthaean apocalypse (Matthew 24), in his *Series of Commentaries on Matthew* 32–60, generally identifies the sufferings predicted there for the faithful as referring to the sufferings of the Jewish people in 70 C.E., and takes Daniel's "seventy weeks of years" (Dan. 11:26) as referring to the time between the prophet and the fall of Jerusalem (*Comm. ser.* 40–42). Even the cosmic signs predicted for the end of the world are natural indications of the waning vitality of creation, not of some extraordinary cataclysm interrupting the normal plan of history (*Comm. ser.* 36f., 48); those who suffer in the future, like the Jews under Titus and Hadrian, will suffer only as a purgation for their sins and a means of salvation (see Monaci 1978; Daley 1991, 48f.). Alongside this historical interpretation of the apocalyptic tradition, Origen also suggests—for the more "advanced" of his readers (*Comm. ser.* 49f.)—a second, more allegorical, and (for him) "truer" way of reading Matthew 24, in terms of personal spiritual growth and the encounter with Christ as Wisdom in the scriptures: "the coming of Christ in perfected men and women" (*Comm. ser.* 32; cf. 38, 40–42, 50–52). Similarly, Origen's reading of John's Revelation usually focuses on passages of christological interest, on angelology, on martyrdom, or on the image of the heavenly Jerusalem; in his extant works, he never comments on chapters 13, 15, or 18, and only rarely on chapters 4, 8, 9, 11, 16, 17, or 22.[5] In *Against Celsus* 6.45f., Origen does defend the plausibility of a historical Antichrist figure, as representing utter evil in contrast to Christ, the embodiment of goodness, although he prefers elsewhere to see him simply as a symbol for "every word which is alien to truth, and claims to be the Word of God" (*Comm. ser.* 33; cf. 42). Alluding probably to the millenarian traditions Irenaeus had so eagerly accepted, Origen is also contemptuous toward those "disciples of the mere letter" who interpret scripture's promises of future beatitude in terms of material plenty in an earthly Jerusalem (*De prin.* 2.11.2; cf. 4.2.2–3). For Origen, the life-giving heart of all scripture, even of its apocalyptic passages, is its ability to reveal Christ as savior to the contemplative reader. In his view, that revelation is to be sought less in dramatic future events than in the long growth of personal knowledge.

Through the next four centuries, the theological and exegetical legacy of Origen—especially his stand on eschatological issues—was to become, at various points, the focus of bitter controversy in both the Greek- and Latin-speaking churches. We have already mentioned the dispute between *Dionysius of Alexandria,* one of his early disciples, and a group of schismatics in the Fayyum who used the writings of the Egyptian bishop Nepos, a contemporary and presumably a critic of Origen, to support their rejection of "spiritual" exegesis and their strong expectation of a millennial kingdom on earth. Although he criticized the group's "materialistic" understanding of the reward of the just, Dionysius himself was not ready to reject the authenticity of the Revelation of John, as some of his own party had done, simply on the grounds of the millenarian implications of chapter 20; but he did argue that its author was not the same John who was thought to be the author of the Fourth Gospel (Eusebius, *Hist. eccl.* 7.24f.).

Probably just before the end of the third century, the Asian writer *Methodius* began to use aspects of the apocalyptic and millenarian tradition in his own characteristically allegorical form. A follower of Origen, who became also his critic on a number of key issues (notably in affirming the material reality of the risen body [see Patterson 1997]), Methodius was a promoter of the ascetical life and wrote his longest extant work, the *Symposium,* for the edification of a women's ascetical community. In book 8 of that work, Methodius interprets the vision of the woman crowned with stars in Revelation 12 as a symbol of the church in the conflicts of this present history (8.5–8, 11), guarded by God from the constant assaults of the devil (8.10); the image is especially appropriate, he argues, because the church is strongly sustained in the struggle by the presence of its consecrated virgins (8.12f.). In book 9, Methodius weaves the imagery of Revelation 20 into a discourse on the eschatological meaning of the Jewish feast of Tabernacles. On the "first day" of the resurrection, he suggests, the just will celebrate a thousand-year feast, in which "the Lord will rejoice in us" (9.1); our participation will be proportionate to how we have "borne fruit" in this life, and a privileged share will be given to those who have lived in chastity (9.3). At the end of this millennial "sabbath," the faithful will undergo another transformation and will pass on to a new, inconceivable form of existence "in the house of God" (9.5). Here aspects of the apocalyptic tradition, particularly the millenarian vision of Irenaeus, are beginning to be employed in a new context, which, in the fifth century, will become increasingly its home: the world not of martyrdom but of monasticism.[6]

Official repression and martyrdom remained very real threats for the Christian churches into the second decade of the fourth century, especially during the "Great Persecution" begun by the emperor Diocletian in 303 and intermittently continued by his successors until the edict of universal religious toleration issued by Constantine and Licinius in 313 (Eusebius, *Hist. eccl.*

10.5; see Frend 1965, 477–535). Predictably, perhaps, this last outburst of anti-Christian fury seems to have aroused among Christians a renewed interest in the details of the Bible's apocalyptic hope, of which two very different witnesses remain.

The first was *Victorinus,* bishop of Poetovio in Noricum (Ptuj or Pettau in modern Slovenia), the first known Latin-speaking exegete, who commented on many books of the Bible and who died as a victim of persecution in 304. Jerome, who revised Victorinus's *Commentary on the Book of Revelation*—somewhat hastily—in 398 (see Dulaey 1991, esp. 203–7), makes the surprising assertions that Victorinus was both a follower of Origen, thoroughly dependent on the master for his own exegesis (so in Jerome, *Epp.* 61.2; 84.7; *Apologia adversus libros Rufini* 3.14; *Commentarius in Ecclesiasten* 4.13), and a millenarian with the same understanding of the thousand-year reign of the saints as Papias and Nepos (prologue to Victorinus's commentary: CSEL 49.14.8–10). Victorinus's commentary, as it presently exists in Jerome's edition, tends, in Origenistic fashion, to take the dramatic events and images of John's Revelation—the trumpets and phials of chapter 8, for instance—as referring to disasters within human history; one should not take their sequence in the text as indicative of chronological order or clues to their date, he argues, but "should rather examine their meaning (*intellectus*)—for this is a pseudo-prophecy" (CSEL 49.86.6–8). The Antichrist, in Victorinus's view, should be understood as a historical ruler yet to come, who will reestablish Jewish worship and law, have his image placed in the Temple in Jerusalem, and insist on being called "Christ" (ibid. 120.18–21; 128.5–130.8). Both in the commentary and in his brief treatise on the creation of the world (*De fabrica mundi*), Victorinus asserts that the seventh day of creation will find its typological fulfillment in a millennium of rest for the saints that will bring history to a close (*Comm.* 6.14f.; 140.12–144.12), but he offers few other details and gives no hint of the "materialistic" expectations so criticized by Origen. His interest in Revelation, in fact, seems more focused on its Christology than its narrative of the end, and he depends largely on the Synoptic apocalypses for his interpretation of its eschatology. Victorinus's work is clearly apocalyptic exegesis of a very subdued kind.

A far more exuberant and assertive reading of the New Testament scenario appears in the seventh book of the *Divine Institutes* of the learned rhetorician and Christian convert, *Lactantius.* Forced into retirement from his publicly supported position as professor of rhetoric in Diocletian's eastern capital, Nicomedia, because of his new faith, Lactantius spent his exile, the years 304–313, composing this long and erudite apology for Christian theology and practice. Its seventh and final book offers an elaborate scheme for the events of history's last days (7.14–27), as a serious form of Christian prophecy (7.26). Lactantius's sources here are not only the prophetic and apocalyptic sections of the Christian Bible but a wide range of ancient philosophical and literary speculations about the fate of the cosmos, as well as Hermetic and even Zoroastrian texts (Daley 1991, 68; for literature on Lactantius's sources, see also 239 nn. 8–9). Lactantius begins his prophetic narrative with the observation, familiar from Tertullian and Cyprian as well as from the Stoic tradition, that the world has grown old and is crumbling to ruin (7.14); it is now in the sixth and final millennium of its history, although that millennium will probably not be completed for another two hundred years (= 500 C.E.; see 7.25). During this final age, Roman rule will come to an end, after a period of continuing injustice and instability (7.15), and will be succeeded by the rule of ten tyrants. These will be overthrown by "a mighty enemy from the north," during whose time the cosmos will suffer devastation (7.16); then a Syrian king, a "son of the Devil," will appear to destroy the human race (7.17)—the

Antichrist, who will perform deceptive miracles and demand worship (7.19). After three and a half years of his misrule, Christ himself will come and defeat him (7.17–19); the living faithful will join Christ in destroying all vestiges of pagan religion, and the faithful dead will be raised to join them in victory (7.19–20). All the living will then be made to pass through a fire of judgment, and those whose evil deeds outweigh their good ones will be forced to remain in that fire forever (7.21); those who pass through the fire unscathed, as well as the just who have been raised from the dead, will reign with Christ on earth for a thousand years.

In a picture drawn as much from Virgil's *Fourth Eclogue* and the *Oracula Sibyllina* as from biblical sources, Lactantius describes the marvelous prosperity and peace of this millennial kingdom, in which the just will continue to propagate offspring to share their happiness (7.24). At the end of this age, the Prince of Demons will again be released from his restraint to lead a final assault on God's people; God will defeat him and devastate the world, and after seven more years of peace the saints will experience a total transformation of the natural order and will become like angels, while sinners will be raised from the dead to face eternal punishment (7.27). Lactantius's style of prophecy has been called apocalyptic for a learned elite rather than an expression of popular Christianity (Prete 1966, 102). Whatever its audience or its immediate effect, its influence on later Latin Christian apocalyptic writing was enormous, doubtless because of its literary resonances and the author's elegant style, and also because of the unsurpassed power with which it portrays the passing of a tired world.

☞ APOCALYPTIC IN A CHRISTIAN EMPIRE: THE FOURTH AND FIFTH CENTURIES _____

With the end of persecution, as the Christian community rapidly moved from being a large but legally marginal minority to being the empire's dominant religious entity, the apocalyptic tradition momentarily lost much of its appeal. Eusebius of Caesarea, the chief exponent of Constantinian optimism, showed open contempt for the millenarian hopes of past Christians (*Hist. eccl.* 3.39.13; 7.24.1) and saw in the life of his own age, as the church luxuriated in acceptance and civil peace, "the firstfruits of future rewards" (*Vita Constantini* 1.33; *Laus Constantini* 3.5). Some of the leading Christian writers of the mid-fourth century did draw on the apocalyptic tradition, especially in homiletic contexts, for their speculations on the future of humanity, but they tended to adopt the moderate, spiritualizing approach of Origen rather than the dramatic, challengingly prophetic stance of Lactantius.

Hilary of Poitiers (ca. 315–367), for instance, the great Gallic theologian of the mid-fourth century, follows Origen in accepting as a genuine prediction about future history the main features of the New Testament's apocalyptic program: the persecution of the Antichrist, the triumphant second coming of Christ, the resurrection of all the dead, the final judgment (e.g., *Commentarius in Evangelium Matthaei* 21.2; 25.3, 8; 26.2; 33.2 [before 356]; *Tractatus super Psalmum 118* 3.5, 12; 11.5 [ca. 365]). His interpretation of most of the other details in the apocalyptic discourse in Matthew (*In Matt.* 25.3–28), however, is relentlessly allegorical: the saying "Let those who are on the housetops not come down," for instance, urges those who have ascended to the "height" of human perfection through baptismal regeneration not to "descend" again to their old ways (*In Matt.* 25.5); so too, those who are "in the field" of Christian labor, keeping the commandments, must not return to reclaim their old "clothes" of sin (ibid.). Although Christ's appearance will imply judgment for all people, only those "midway between the faithful and the unfaithful," whose actual moral state is unclear, will need to be examined (*In Ps. 57* 7); the rest will simply be revealed for what they are in the light of the face of Christ, and the experience of his "turning his face" on the human race will be at once punishment for the sinner and reassuring mercy for the faithful (*In Ps. 118* 17.12). Although he occasionally uses the traditional scheme of six thousand years as the "week" of history (*In Matt.* 17.1; 20.6), Hilary insists that the time of the end always remains unknown, to afford humans both time for repentance and wholesome fear (*In Matt.* 26.4). He is hardly a millenarian, yet a trace of the Irenaean millenarian tradition may be present in his understanding of the gradual transformation of the church, as the collective Body of Christ, into the glorious kingdom of God. Connecting this transformation with 1 Cor. 15:27f. (on the "subjection" of all things to the Son and of the Son to the Father, "that God may be all in all"), Hilary argues that this "dispensation of the Mystery" is "an event within time" (*De trinitate* 11.30–33), even though its full realization is something yet to be achieved (ibid. 36, 39–40, 43). In some passages, he even seems to suggest that a process of gradual change will intervene between the final coming of Christ's kingdom among men and women and his "handing it over," in full submission, to his Father (*In Ps. 9* 4; *In Ps. 148* 8).

Hilary's younger contemporary and fellow bishop, *Ambrose of Milan* (ca. 334–397), was also steeped in the Origenist tradition of spiritual exegesis, which he enthusiastically propagated in the Latin church. In contemporary crises, like the death of the emperor Valens at the battle of Adrianople in 378, as well as in the conversion of the Goths and Armenians to Christianity, Ambrose perceived signs that the end was near (*Expositio Evangelii secundum Lucam* 10.9f., 14), and he used as his own the traditional theme of "the world's old age" (*De bono mortis* 10.46). Nevertheless, like Hilary, Ambrose is not a consistent herald of the approaching end and prefers to interpret the apocalyptic details of scripture in more personal, interior terms; he is more interested in the death and judgment of the individual than in the end of history (Daley 1991, 98–101). Approximating Hilary's theory that Christ's final act of judgment will essentially consist in his full knowledge of each person and will only involve an actual examination of the "sinful believers," whose final state remains somehow in doubt (*Exp. in Lucam* 10.46; *In Ps. 51* 56), Ambrose takes the "first" and "second" resurrections of Revelation 20 as referring to the distinction between those saints who will rise without need for judgment and will have immediate access to beatitude with God, and those who will need to be sifted and purified before attaining final salvation (*In Ps. 118* 3.14–17; 20.12–15). In making use of the apocalyptic tradition, Ambrose generally remains the learned pastor and rhetor rather than a prophet of approaching doom.

The last three decades of the fourth century, however, as well as the first half of the fifth, witnessed a gradual but steady revival in apocalyptic expectations of a more intense and literal kind. The reasons for this widespread sharpening of a sense of cosmic crisis are not easy to identify. Christians were now not only accorded full legal status and religious recognition but became, by the reign of Theodosius, the empire's favored and dominant religious body. The emperors and their political establishment had been Christian since the death of Constantine, with the exception of Julian's brief attempt to reestablish traditional religious practices (361–363). Christians participated fully in the relative abundance and cultural brilliance of the decades after Julian, often referred to as the "Theodosian renaissance." Nevertheless, many in the churches seemed suddenly to experience a loss of confidence in the prospects of human resources and institutions, and a new sense of vulnerability and impending doom, in sharp contrast to the boundless optimism of Eusebius and his imitators. One reason for this gradual change in mood may have been Julian's decision to ban practicing Christians from teaching in publicly supported schools, a brief but painful episode that seems to have reminded Christian intellectuals that their faith was never to be entirely compatible with the assumptions and values of Hellenistic culture. A new and widespread malaise was also introduced into Roman society by the movements of several waves of invading peoples from the East—Goths, Huns, Alans, and later Vandals—whose occasional clashes with, and eventual incorporation into, the imperial armies caused fear and a new sense of institutional impermanence among the empire's established citizenry (Jones 1964, 1:152–69). Christians were often blamed for this growing social instability, on the grounds of having led the empire to abandon the religious traditions that preserved its ancient character and institutions; as a result, many Christians in the late fourth century seem again to have developed a dark sense of alienation from society and the present world, an alienation that accorded well both with old apocalyptic traditions and with the new, widespread phenomenon of monastic withdrawal and the pursuit of ascetic heroism as a way to real salvation.

A first trace of this revived apocalyptic mood among Christian writers may be discernible in the statement by a number of his contemporaries that *Apollinarius of Laodicea* (ca. 310–ca. 390)—usually remembered for his distinctive view of the person of Christ—held "Jewish" expectations of a coming millennium, in which the Temple in Jerusalem would be restored and Israel's cult and ritual practices revived.[7] Strong apocalyptic expectations in this period, however—as throughout the patristic era—were rare in the Greek world, and more common in the provincial regions of the Latin West. The *Priscillianist* movement, for instance, which attracted followers in Spain in the last three decades of the fourth century, seems to have combined an interest in apocalyptic cosmology and eschatology (Augustine, *De haeresibus* 70) with a dualistic form of severe asceticism. Members of the sect were criticized for their use of apocryphal scriptures (Augustine, *Epistle* 237), perhaps of apocalyptic content, and they seem to have produced some documents with apocalyptic themes themselves.[8] The Spanish bishop *Pacian of Barcelona* (d. between 379 and 393), in his exhortation to penitents, urges sinners to undertake public confession and canonical penance by proclaiming that "the last time is quickly approaching; Tartarus and Gehenna are opening their bosoms wide for the wicked" (*Sermo de paenitentibus* 11.5; cf. 11.4 and 12.5). The African bishop *Quintus Julius Hilarianus* composed a brief chronological treatise, *On the Course of Times* (*De cursu temporum*), around 397, which concludes with a narrative of the coming end-times drawn from Revelation and which estimates that the date of Christ's second coming will be March 25, 500 (16–19).

More striking, perhaps, is the strong sense of apocalyptic anxiety and hope running through the elegant writings of *Sulpicius Severus* (d. ca. 420), the disciple and biographer of Martin of Tours who also composed a history of the world, dialogues, and letters. When he comes to treat of contemporary history in his *Chronicle* (completed ca. 402), Sulpicius speaks of "the times of our age" as "difficult and dangerous, since the churches are polluted by unprecedented evil and all things are in confusion" (*Chron.* 2.46.1).[9] For Sulpicius, as for his master, Martin, these conflicts were evidence that "the day of judgment is near" (*Vita Martini* 22.5) and that the need for repentance and conversion was now more urgent than ever before. Nine of the ten persecutions prophesied as preludes to the end of time were already over (*Chron.* 2.33.4);

false prophets were active: a young man in Spain was claiming to be Elijah, another in the East to be John the Baptist, the two expected heralds of the returning Christ (*Vita* 24.1–3). Sulpicius even remarks: "Since false prophets of this kind have appeared, we may infer from this that the coming of Antichrist is at hand, for he is already practicing in these persons the mystery of iniquity." Martin himself had encountered Satan in person, disguised as the triumphant Christ, and although the saint had easily seen through the deceit, many of his contemporaries, Sulpicius seems to suggest, might have been more easily fooled (*Vita* 24.4–8).

In the second of his *Dialogues* (2.14.1–4), Sulpicius recounts hearing Martin's version of the coming scenario for the end of time. First, Nero and the Antichrist must come to power. Nero—whose death had never been certified and who was suspected to have been miraculously kept alive in a secret place, awaiting the end-time (*Chron.* 1.29.5)—would rule in the West, the Antichrist in the East; the latter would rebuild the Temple in Jerusalem, impose circumcision, and claim to be the Messiah. Eventually the Antichrist would defeat Nero and rule all nations, until he is himself overthrown by the coming of Christ. Martin was convinced, Severus reports, that the Antichrist, "conceived by an evil spirit," was already alive as a young boy, and that "he would assume power as soon as he reached the proper age." "Now, this is the eighth year since we heard these words from his lips," Sulpicius adds, writing the *Dialogue* about 405; "you may guess, then, how soon those things which we fear in the future are about to happen" (*Dial.* 2.14.4).

As the fifth century neared the end of its first decade, this sense of impending worldwide disaster came to be more and more widely shared among Christian writers and preachers. At the death of the emperor Theodosius I, the Vandal general Stilicho, who had married Theodosius's daughter Serena, was appointed commander of the imperial armies (*magister militum*) throughout the empire. The armies themselves were already composed to a large degree of the federated immigrant peoples who had settled within its borders (Jones 1964, 1:182–87; Williams and Friell 1994, 91–102, 143–58). Tensions among these peoples led to protracted military power struggles, against which civilian institutions were virtually powerless. The sack of Rome by Visigothic warriors under Alaric—mainly Arian Christians—in 410 was simply the climax of almost a decade of their marauding in northern Italy, but it had a symbolic importance without precedent throughout the empire: the city where the law and unifying culture of the Mediterranean world had their deepest roots was now defenseless before the brutality of strangers, undisciplined thugs whom traditional pagans might see as the products of Christian decadence, while a biblically nourished imagination might identify them as the prophesied heralds of the "day of the Lord."

An apologetic fictive dialogue between a Christian and an unbeliever from this period— the *Consultations of Zacchaeus and Apollonius,* written perhaps by the North African bishop Evodius of Uzala about 412 (see Courcelle 1964)—reflects the new relevance of the traditional Christian apocalyptic scenario for believers during these anxious years (see especially 1.21–26, 3.7–9). Zacchaeus, the Christian speaker, is convinced by the violence of the time that the end of history is near. Christ came only shortly before that end, he argues, precisely so that his followers would not be corrupted by a long wait (1.21). The exact time of his return is known only to God, but the events predicted as signs of his coming seem already fulfilled in the violence of the contemporary world, and the universal preaching of the gospel (3.8). Zacchaeus's description of the events awaited in the end-time follows a familiar pattern: first Elijah will come (3.8);

then the Antichrist (who will be the devil himself in human form) will appear, will try to reestablish Jewish law, and will be regarded by many pagans as divine (ibid.). After three and one-half years of turmoil, Christ will come in triumph as judge, the dead will be raised and will receive their due reward or punishment, and a new heaven and a new earth will appear, where the just will live in glory, enjoying the vision of God. Zacchaeus is made to describe this new world in terms reminiscent of the Irenaean millenarian tradition (1.25–26; 3.9),[10] although the work does not explicitly espouse the idea of an earthly millennium of happiness for the just.

A number of Italian episcopal preachers from the first decades of the fifth century reflect this same sense of the impending end and occasionally make a similar use of apocalyptic themes and images, even when the theme of their preaching, like Pacian's at the end of the previous century, is more moral and disciplinary than eschatological. *Gaudentius of Brescia* (fl. after 406), for instance, observes in his Paschal homilies on the book of Exodus that Christ died "at the evening of the world," and that the transformation of the human body and the whole cosmos is coming soon (*Tractatus* 3.1f., 12). Gaudentius also alludes to a millennium of "sabbath rest" for the saints, which lies ahead (*Tr.* 10.14–16, 22), but it is not clear whether he understands this as a distinct final period of history or uses it simply as an image of eternal beatitude. *Maximus of Turin* (d. between 408 and 423), another bishop of the period whose sermons have survived, sees in the perils of the time a call for renewed moral seriousness in the light of the coming judgment (*Sermon* 32.2; 85.2; 91.2); yet he also finds comfort for his listeners in the thought that Christ and his reign are obviously so near (*Serm.* 85.1). Their influential younger contemporary, *Peter Chrysologus* (d. ca. 450), bishop of Ravenna, also occasionally echoes the old Latin theme that the world has grown weak with age (*Serm.* 167.3) and that his own era was "the end of time" (*Serm.* 36.3). Peter's outlook on his age, however, is considerably more optimistic than that of most Latin Christian writers at the turn of the fifth century. Like Maximus, he finds in the prospect of history's end hope and consolation for believers (*Serm.* 47.5).

The reign of Theodosius and the decades that followed were also the time of the first flowering of an expressly Christian Latin poetry: the product of highly educated Christian writers seeking, perhaps in response to Julian's exclusion of Christians from the cultural mainstream, to find themes from the Christian Bible in which the language and forms of classical poetry and rhetoric could achieve a new and edifying evangelical content, free of the moral dangers of the old mythology. As their contemporaries struggled with the turn-of-the-century anxieties we have been describing, some of these Christian poets made powerful use of apocalyptic themes in their own work. The earliest and probably the most gifted of these writers, the Spanish-born *Prudentius* (348–after 405), frequently works apocalyptic touches into his *Peristephanon,* celebrating Christianity's past heroes, the martyrs, and into his cycle of splendid poetic prayers for the Christian year, the *Cathemerinon.* The martyr Romanus, for instance, is made to warn Prudentius's readers that

> One day the heavens will be rolled up as a book,
> the sun's revolving orb will fall upon the earth,
> the sphere that regulates the months will crash in ruin. (*Peristeph.* 10.536ff.)

Other scenes portray the coming of the Lamb of God in majesty to defeat the Antichrist and banish the beast of Revelation 13 (*Cath.* 5.81–112), or his judgment of all men and women, living and dead, immediately after his victory (*Cath.* 9.106–14; 11.101–12). In that coming final spectacle, the intercession of the church's martyrs for their devotees and their native cities will be crucially effective in winning mercy from the divine judge (*Peristeph.* 4.9–60; 6.157–62; 10.1131–40).

Prudentius's contemporary, *Paulinus of Nola* (353–431), seems to have had an even more dramatic sense of the nearness of history's end. A native of Bordeaux, of distinguished family and education, Paulinus rose quickly in the imperial civil service, then underwent a conversion to a more deeply committed Christian life, along with his wife Therasia, in the early 390s. After this, the couple established a quasi-monastic community at Nola in Campania, where they spent the rest of their days. Writing to his former teacher Ausonius, Paulinus attributes his conversion to a suddenly deepened awareness of the brevity of life and a fear of the judgment to come (*Carm.* 10.304–10). To Paulinus, signs of the consummation of history seemed evident everywhere:

> All creation now waits in suspense for his [Christ's] coming,
> all faith and hope search intently for him, their king!
> The world, which is to be renewed, already gives birth
> to that end which approaches in the final days.
> True oracles in the holy books warn all people
> to believe in the prophecies and to prepare themselves for God. (*Carm.* 31.401–6)

Like Hilary, Ambrose, Jerome, and others, Paulinus imagined that only sinners whose deeds were not wholly depraved—not the just, but also not the *impii*—would actually have to pass through the fires of judgment and purification (*Carm.* 7.24–36); nevertheless, the prospect of that judgment seems to have been as awful to him as it was to his countrymen Martin and Sulpicius Severus, and to have drawn him, like them, to a life of retirement, prayer, and ministry to the poor, as well as to energetic literary activity as poet and correspondent. Living at the end of the ages gave powerful nourishment to the late Latin rhetorical imagination.

A third poet from Roman Gaul in the same period was *Orientius,* probably the bishop of Auch near Toulouse in the 430s, author of a long moralizing poem in two books, the *Song of Warning* (*Commonitorium*), in which a sense of social decay and the prospect of general destruction are still more dominant themes (see Daley 1991, 160–62 and literature cited there, as well as chapter 11 below). The dangers of contemporary society have convinced the poet that he is witnessing "the funeral rites of a collapsing world" (2.185; cf. 2.210) and have reminded him of the immediacy of death for all: "even now, while we are speaking, we anticipate death (*praemorimur*)" (2.196; see 195–262). In book 1 of the *Commonitorium*, Orientius depicts the coming resurrection of the dead in graphically literal terms and insists that the purpose of resurrection is that divine justice may be fulfilled: the guilty must be punished, the virtuous rewarded, in the bodies in which they have earned their fate (1.273–76). Book 2 draws a grand and vivid picture of Christ's triumphant return and judgment, in terms drawn from Matthew 24 but embellished with new and dramatic detail: earthquakes and lightning, angelic music, a throne of terrible majesty encircled with flame (2.347–92). This elaborate and extended use of Christian apocalyptic imagery would find few parallels in Latin poetry until the thirteenth-century *Dies irae.*

Latin theology and biblical scholarship at the turn of the fifth century, however, were clearly dominated by two figures, each with a somewhat ambivalent attitude toward the apocalyptic tradition, and each destined to leave an ineradicable mark on the future of Western

Christian thought: Jerome and Augustine. Of the two, *Jerome* (331–420) is the more enigmatic in intellectual and personal terms. A tireless scholar and insatiably curious student of the Bible, an enthusiastic promoter of the ascetic and monastic life, a man of letters—at times a reluctant one—who became a passionate defender of tradition and popular Christianity, an energetic correspondent and spiritual advisor, an ardent friend and an equally ardent enemy, Jerome had little interest in philosophical or theological speculation and was not deeply troubled by inconsistency, either in relationships or in his own ideas. His approach to interpreting the scriptures always drew its method and much of its content from the work of Origen, even after he had been persuaded by Epiphanius of Salamis, in 393, to regard Origen and all his admirers as heretical (Kelly 1975, 195–209). Like Origen, Jerome tended to assume that the main features of the traditional scenario for the end of history, drawn from the New Testament, referred to actual future persons and events, but that they were also capable of allegorical or spiritual interpretations, in terms of asceticism and the life of the church, that are often more important for the Christian reader.

In interpreting Daniel, for example, Jerome remained critical of the pagan Porphyry's approach, which took the book's symbolism simply to be referring to contemporary events. The figure of Antiochus IV Epiphanes, depicted as the "beast" in Daniel 8 and portrayed more prosaically in Daniel 11, must also be seen, Jerome insisted, as a type of the Antichrist to come (*Commentary on Daniel* [399] 7.7f., 11; 11.21), who would be not a demon but a human being, a Jew who would eventually overthrow the empire and rule the world (ibid. 7.8; *Epistle* 60.16 [396]; 123.16 [409]). On the other hand, Jerome was also willing to take predictions of a coming judgment in scripture to refer not only to the eschatological coming of Christ but also to an individual's encounter with Christ in death (*In Sophoniam* 1.14 [late 390s]), or even to one's anticipation of death in ascetical practice (*In Isaiam* 6.14.1 [408–410]). Although he is generally critical of millenarian hopes as "judaizing" materialism, he speaks with respect, in some texts, of earlier advocates of this position—writers such as Tertullian, Lactantius, and Victorinus among the Latins, and Irenaeus and Apollinarius among the Greeks (e.g., *Commentary on Ezekiel* 11.36 [411]).[11] Jerome's own preferred interpretation of Revelation 20:1–6 is *juxta ecclesiasticam intelligentiam* ("according to an ecclesiastical understanding"), as an image of the peace and growth of the church after the time of persecution (ibid.). In his edited version of Victorinus's commentary (398), on the other hand, Jerome argues that the thousand-year kingdom is a symbol of the life of virginity, in which the ascetic "reigns" with Christ while the devil remains "bound" through renunciation. So in his *Commentary on Matthew,* written also in the spring of 398, Jerome suggests that the grand apocalyptic scene depicted in Matthew 24 can legitimately be taken *juxta litteram,* as referring to historical events—both to the destruction of Jerusalem in 70 C.E. and to the coming end—but can be interpreted still more meaningfully (*magis*) in terms of the present life of the church: the "abomination of desolation" (Dan. 9:27; Matt. 24:15), for instance, can be taken as referring to an idol already erected in the Holy of Holies, to the coming role of the Antichrist as desecrator of the faithful community, or to "all kinds of heretical teaching (*omne dogma perversum*)," from which the careful believer must "flee to the eternal mountains" of true doctrine (*Comm. on Matt.* 24.15).

After the turn of the fifth century, however, and particularly after the shock of Rome's fall to the Visigoths in 410, Jerome shared the tendency of his contemporaries to see in the apocalyptic tradition more immediate and more sobering references to the present. In the preface to his *Commentary on Ezekiel* (411), for instance, he gives poignant expression to his shock at the sack of the city, compounded by news of the recent deaths of his friends Pammachius and Marcella;

> For days and nights I could think of nothing else but the safety of all the people; when my dear
> ones were captured, I felt myself a captive, too, sharing in the captivity of the saints. . . . After
> the brightest light of all the world had been extinguished, indeed the head of the Roman
> Empire had been cut off, and—to speak more truly—after the whole world died in one city,
> then "I became silent and lay on the ground, and spoke no good words" (Ps. 38:4). (PL 45:16)

In this work, and in the *Commentary on Isaiah* completed in the previous year, Jerome is more willing to acknowledge that the tensions and heresies that troubled the church of his day were realizations of what had been prophesied for the end-time (*In Isa.* 6.14.1; *In Ezek.* 11.38). As the philosophers had recognized long before, the world was indeed growing old (*In Isa.* 14.51.6). Yet even in his darker moods, Jerome always remained enough of the Irenaean to insist that the end of this world would only mean its transformation to a more glorious form of its present state (ibid.; also 18.65.17f.), and also enough of the Origenist to see the most profound significance of apocalyptic images in their spiritual typology.

An important influence on Augustine's interpretation of the apocalyptic tradition was his compatriot, the Donatist exegete *Tyconius,* who seems to have died in the 380s (see Daley 1991, 127–31). Following the principles for "unlocking" mysterious passages of scripture that he had outlined in his *Three Books of Rules* (*Libri regularum tres*), Tyconius produced a commentary on Revelation that is still partly recoverable from fragments and from the eighth-century commentary of Beatus of Liébana. There his usual method for interpreting biblical apocalyptic imagery is to apply it to the situation of the contemporary church—his own Donatist church, which saw itself as the isolated but faithful remnant of the apostolic community. As Augustine would do throughout his mature writings, Tyconius sees all humanity divided into two opposed "cities" or societies, represented in Revelation by the Great Harlot, dominating "the kings of the earth" (Revelation 17) and the Bride of the Lamb (Rev. 21:2, 9). These "are each one church, one body," he writes. "So then there are two cities, one of God and one of the devil" (Beatus 9.3.12), two "bodies" representing the opposed wills of their heads (*Lib. reg.* 1, 7; Beatus 6.4.75f.).

The last days of the faithful Body of Christ will be characterized by persecution, in Tyconius's view, such as the Donatist faithful had been undergoing for almost a century. The Antichrist was already active, he argued, although held in check by the faith of believers (Beatus 2.6.82f.); the end of history will mean an unmasking of his activity, currently being carried out in the guise of religion (Beatus 6.3.39), but it will also reveal the current activity of Christ in his church. As part of this interpretation, Tyconius understood the millennium of "rest for the saints" in Revelation 20 to refer to the time of the church, "from the passion of the Lord until his second coming" (Beatus 11.5.9). The "first resurrection" (Rev. 20:5) is the Christian's rebirth, through baptism, from the death of sin (Beatus 11.5.3; *Lib. reg.* 4)—an idea whose roots can be found in Origen (*Commentary on John* 10.243–45; *Commentary on Luke,* fr. 83; see n. 5 below) and which reappears in Ambrose (*In Ps. 1* 53) and Jerome (*Commentary on Luke* 18, 65.20), as well as in Augustine. So, for Tyconius, the blessings of the thousand-year reign with Christ are already available in a spiritual form for his faithful. When the church's allotted time of growth is over—a conclusion that Tyconius may possibly have thought was coming in his own lifetime[12]—Satan will be released from the "abyss" of the human heart, where he now lies chained, and people will sin openly, totally obscuring the church's teaching (Beatus 5.6.6ff.) and allowing Christians no further witness except the shedding of blood (Beatus, praef. 4.12; 4.3.11ff.). This final trial will be a time of purification for the faithful community, but it will simply bring to clearer and more public focus the triumphant state of union with Christ they already enjoy in a hidden way (Beatus 4.6.75–78). Tyconius offers here a kind of "realized apocalypticism" that his younger contemporary Augustine will approach without ever being able to share it completely, and which appropriates, in typically Donatist terms, the Western Origenist tradition of spiritual and ecclesial exegesis.

The use of apocalyptic themes by *Augustine of Hippo* (354–430) himself is at once more varied and more complex. As with most subjects, his thoughts on the world's final crisis and on Christian attitudes toward its coming were largely developed in response to questions from correspondents or the pastoral needs of his congregations, and these thoughts show the same lines of development that one finds with many issues in his work—from a more literary and philosophical approach in his early writings to a simple emphasis on biblical teaching in his later years. Throughout his writings, however, Augustine tends to take a moderately agnostic position on the actual details of eschatological hope, accepting the value of biblical apocalyptic prophecy as revealing future events, but stressing its spiritual interpretation as at least equally important and insisting always that it is not for the human mind to make exact calculations of the time of the end (Daley 1991, 131–50).

In some of his writings from the late 380s and early 390s, for example, Augustine makes use of the old Roman topos of dividing human history into a "week" of ages, the final stage of which will be a golden age of cosmic renewal (*De Genesi contra Manichaeos* 1.35–41 [388/389]; *De diversis quaestionibus LXXXIII* 58.2 [391/395]). He often connects this theme with the biblical scheme of the six "days" of creation, followed by a sabbath rest, which he identifies, in some early works, with the millennium of Rev. 20:1–6 (*Serm.* 259.2 [ca. 393]; *Serm. Mai* 94.4f. [393/395]; *Contra Adimantinum* 2.2 [394]). The reason for his interest in the millennial tradition at this early stage of his career is unclear; perhaps he may already have come into contact with Irenaeus's *Against Heresies,* the Latin version of which may have newly appeared in North Africa in those years. His own version of the millennial hope, however, always deemphasized its earthly delights and presented it mainly as an intra-historical period of peace for the church, before its final trials.

Augustine soon grew more tentative, however, about identifying the six days of creation with "ages" of a thousand years (see, e.g., *Enarrationes in Psalmos* 6.1f. [392 or 394]; *De trinitate* 4.4.7 [401–407]), and tended more and more to identify eternal beatitude not with an "eighth day" of new creation, as some earlier Christian writers had done, but with the symbol of the sabbath itself (e.g., *Confessions* 13.35.50 [401]; *De Genesi ad litteram* 4.18.31f. [401/414]). In the *City of God* 20.7 [425/426], Augustine explains that a spiritually understood millennium of rest for the saints, at the end of history, is a tenable Christian notion, and that "I myself once held this opinion." Now, however—having read not only Tyconius's fifth *Rule* but probably his *Commentary on Revelation* as well (see Dulaey 1986)—Augustine clearly identifies the rule of the saints with Christ in Revelation 20 as "his present kingdom, the church" (*De civitate Dei* 20.9), and sees the "binding" of the devil there as his providential restraint within the "abyss" of the hearts of the wicked (ibid. 7). As he explains with reference to Rev. 20:4f.,

So there are also two resurrections: the one the first and spiritual resurrection, which takes place in this life, and preserves us from coming into the second death; the other the second, which does not occur now, but at the end of the world, and which is of the body, not of the soul, and which by the last judgment shall dismiss some into the second death, others into that life which has no death. (*De civ. Dei* 20.6)

Because of his unwillingness to speculate about the exact time of the end of history, Augustine was always reluctant to see in the catastrophes of his age the same apocalyptic meaning that many of his contemporaries saw. In his "Sermon on the Fall of the City (Rome)," delivered in 410, Augustine compares the reported sufferings of Roman citizens with various biblical examples, to reinforce the point that God allows such disasters not to bring about our destruction but to lead us to conversion; thus, they are signs of his mercy and not of his wrath (7). He tells the story of similar eschatological panic that occurred in Constantinople a few years earlier and points out that although the end did not come then either, many people took the occasion to reform their lives (6).

Near the end of the same decade, a new mood of crisis gripped many people throughout the Mediterranean region, a result now not simply of continuing Germanic raids but also of alarming natural signs: drought, earthquakes in Palestine and North Africa, an eclipse of the sun on July 19, 418 (so *Serm.* 19.6 [December, 419]; *Serm.* 38.10f. [419?]). Sometime in late 418 or 419, Hesychius of Salonae, a well-known Dalmatian bishop, wrote to Augustine to ask if he too saw in these dire events fulfillment of the biblical prophecies of the approaching end (see Bouhot 1986). Augustine replied briefly but politely (*Ep.* 197), enclosing some excerpts from Jerome's *Commentary on Daniel* to support his insistence that there is no way we can calculate the time of Jesus' second coming. Since Augustine had asked for Hesychius's opinion on the matter, the bishop replied (*Ep.* 198) that he and many of his clergy and faithful were convinced that the end was indeed near. Even if Jesus told the Twelve (Acts 1:7f.), "It is not for you to know the times or seasons which the Father has fixed" for the coming kingdom, still those who wait eagerly for the Lord's return can hardly avoid seeing signs of his nearness in "what we suffer and the evils we are undergoing." Furthermore, the Gospel was now being preached everywhere in the known world and persecution had come to an end; all that remained for the church to look forward to was its final fulfillment. In his lengthy reply (*Ep.* 199)—a tract entitled "On the End of the World" in the manuscripts—Augustine begins by agreeing that "one must love and long for the coming of the Lord," and must wait vigilantly for his arrival (1–3). Nevertheless, he insists, the prophetic passages of the Bible are only meant to call the reader to vigilance, not to enable us to calculate the date of the end (6–13). "Loving the coming of the Lord" does not mean thinking it is distant or near, but waiting for it with sincere faith, firm hope, and ardent love (14f.). Turning to the apocalyptic sections of the New Testament, Augustine argues in some detail (like Jerome in his *Commentary on Matthew*) that some refer to the destruction of Jerusalem in 70 C.E., others to the "coming" of Christ in the life of the church, and still others to the end of time (25-45). The present disasters are not really worse than those suffered by God's people in the past; further, the gospel is clearly *not* yet being preached in all parts of the world, particularly those outside the frontiers of the empire (46–51). Augustine concludes his letter with the observation that three attitudes toward the coming end are possible for a Christian: one can expect it soon, but in the process risk damaging one's own or one's neighbor's faith if it does not happen; one can suppose it will be long delayed, and so both train oneself in patience and be happily surprised if it occurs sooner than expected; or one can simply be agnostic, as Augustine is: "The one who admits that he or she does not know which of these expectations is true hopes for the one, is resigned to the other, and is wrong in neither of them" (54).

Hesitant as Augustine always remained to calculate the time of the end, however, his later writings show no hesitation in spelling out the details of what Christians look forward to, on the basis of the apocalyptic sections of the Bible. The last three books of the *City of God* (425/426) especially spell out the traditional scenario in vivid detail, while remaining strictly within the limits of the biblical texts. A passage near the end of book 20 summarizes that narrative of the future modestly, but with stunning concision:

> In connection with the judgment, the following events shall come to pass, as we have learned: Elijah the Tishbite shall come; the Jews shall believe; Antichrist shall persecute; Christ shall judge; the dead shall rise; the good and the wicked shall be separated; the world shall be burned and renewed. All these things, we believe, shall come to pass; but how, or in what order, human understanding cannot perfectly teach us, but only the experience of the events themselves. My opinion, however, is that they will happen in the order in which I have related them. (*De civ. Dei* 20.30)

The clarity of Augustine's conflation of these apocalyptic texts into a single narrative, as well as the power of his prose and the authority of his person, ensured that these final books of his monumental Christian reading of history would become the classic source for further theological reflection on the apocalyptic tradition in the Latin West.

As the fifth century reached its midpoint, Augustine's synthesis had already begun to show this canonical character. The *Book of the Promises* (*Liber de promissionibus*), probably written by Augustine's disciple Quodvultdeus of Carthage in 445–449, catalogues 153 saving "promises" of God and "predictions" of sinful human and diabolical acts that appear in the Christian Bible and briefly discusses their mode of fulfillment on the basis of later scripture and history. The final thirty-three concern the end-time and form a florilegium of apocalyptic passages from scripture, each with a terse commentary, that the author sees as providing us with summary details about the end of the world. In their selection and arrangement, and to a large degree in their content, these chapters follow the narrative scheme outlined in the last three books of the *City of God*. Nevertheless, Quodvultdeus is occasionally willing to interpret contemporary events in more explicitly apocalyptic terms than Augustine had been: in citing the opinion of "some," for instance, who saw the Goths and Moors then ravaging North Africa as the fulfillment of the biblical Gog and Magog (*Liber de prom.* 14.23 [SC 102.634]; cf. Ezek. 38:2; Rev. 20:8).[13] This tendency for Christian pastors to see in the insecurities of their time signs of the imminent end is even more clearly evinced in two treatises written in the 440s by the presbyter *Salvian of Marseilles* (d. after 470), *To the Church* (*Ad ecclesiam*) (also known as *Adversus avaritiam*) and *The Governance of God* (*De gubernatione Dei*) (see Daley 1991, 154f.). These works of moral exhortation see both in the contemporary decay of Roman institutions and in the experience of rapid social change a divine judgment on society's sins and a sign that the final reckoning is near (*Ad eccl.* 1.7.35f.; *De gub.* 4.6.30). The prospect of judgment, Salvian urges, should work both as consolation for those already striving to live by the gospel, and as a call to renewed concern for the poor and to intensified generosity with one's worldly possessions (*Ad eccl.* 2.10.49; 3.3.13; 3.14.61).

A third Latin writer who may well also have been active in these middle years of the fifth century is the mysterious poet *Commodian,* whose two lengthy and powerful works, the anti-

Jewish *Song of the Two Peoples* (*Carmen de duobus populis*) and the *Instructions* (in two books of shorter poetic units), revive the tradition of Christian apocalyptic speculation with a vigor unknown since the time of Lactantius. Commodian's dates and homeland are uncertain; a number of scholars have argued for placing him in Italy or Africa in the time of Cyprian, the mid-third century, but the content of his works, as well as the few scraps of external evidence we possess, make it more likely that he was writing in southern Gaul or Africa shortly after 450 (see Daley 1991, 162–64 and notes). It has even been suggested, on the basis of the poems' moral rigorism, their emphasis on the persecution of the elect, and their critique of the social and ecclesiastical establishment, that the author may have been a late Donatist (Brisson 1958, 390–94).

Commodian's two works imitate the forms of apocalyptic narrative in their esoteric style as well as their urgently moralistic tone: acrostics and riddles, symbolic events within a visionary framework, and a call to conversion in the face of history's imminent and violent end recall the literary world of Jewish and Judeo-Christian apocalypses of three centuries earlier. Yet the scenario they spell out in detail is essentially a mixture of elements from Matthew 24, 1 Thessalonians 4, and Revelation, seasoned by echoes of Lactantius, Sulpicius Severus, Jerome, and Salvian. At the end of six thousand years of history, according to Commodian, a great struggle will break out between God's people and the forces led by Antichrist (*Carm.* 791; *Instr.* 2.35.8); after the usual cosmic disaster signals—the sound of a trumpet, earthquakes, fire, and darkness (*Carm.* 901–4; *Instr.* 1.43.1–3)—the final persecution of God's people will begin (*Carm.* 808, 942; *Instr.* 1.42.1f.). The Goths, who will then invade the Roman Empire, will treat the Christians as brothers and sisters (*Carm.* 809–22), but Nero will return from hell as Antichrist and make war on the church (*Instr.* 1.41).[14] Elijah will also return, prophesying against Nero (*Carm.* 825–36; *Instr.* 1.41.5–20). After much bloodshed (*Carm.* 880–90; *Instr.* 1.42.39–48), God will rain on earth a fire of judgment (*Instr.* 1.43.1–19; 2.35.10f.). Commodian then depicts a "first resurrection" of God's faithful poor, who will live for a millennium of prosperity and peace in "the heavenly Jerusalem" (*Instr.* 1.44.1–5). There they will beget children like themselves (*Carm.* 947–78; *Instr.* 1.44.9–15), while the nobles of the present age serve them (*Carm.* 987f.; *Instr.* 2.35.12–16) and God's enemies burn in the fire of judgment. At the end of this millennium, there will be new cosmic disasters: fire will rain from heaven; earth and sky will be shaken (*Carm.* 993–1012; *Instr.* 2.35.17–19); those on earth who have some good in them will be purged by these events; but the wicked will be completely consumed (*Carm.* 1018; *Instr.* 2.35.10). Finally, the humble Christ will appear (*Carm.* 1042), all the dead will rise, and the just will meet him in the air in a final reunion, as sinners are plunged into hell forever (*Carm.* 1045–55; *Instr.* 2.35.21f.). These two poems, unlike the works of devout literati such as Prudentius or Paulinus at the turn of the century, are less essays in biblically based craftsmanship than vehicles of sharp social protest and moral exhortation; the traditional Christian narrative of history's final conflicts has here been fully revived once again as a warning of imminent disaster.

☞ THE REVIVAL OF THE APOCALYPTIC GENRE

During the late fourth and early fifth centuries, a number of new works seem to have been composed in the Christian apocalyptic genre—works that make no attempt to follow the narrative scheme of the New Testament, but which claim to reveal new knowledge of the secrets of time through the familiar strategies of pseudepigraphy, revelatory speeches, and cosmic journeys. The most likely home for these works—for their preservation, at least, if not for their composition—is the monastic world, where a sense of the transitoriness of society and its material surroundings, along with a strong emphasis on personal reform, undoubtedly roused interest in apocalyptic speculations which might have been considered extreme in the more public and traditional context of the cities and their churches.

It was probably members of a Pachomian monastic community, for instance, which preserved and concealed the collection of Coptic Gnostic writings discovered at Nag Hammadi in 1947. Among these documents are two Christian works containing substantial sections in a recognizably apocalyptic style, both probably composed in Egypt during the fourth century: *On the Origin of the World* (II, 5 and XIII, 2), and *The Concept of Our Great Power* (VI, 4). The first of these documents draws on Jewish, pagan, Manichean, and Greek philosophical sources as well as the Christian tradition to offer a composite view of the origin and end of the world, and may represent an attempt to popularize Gnostic cosmology for a wider audience (NHLE, 161). In describing the end of the present world, it paints a scene of violence and cosmic disaster that will end in the fiery collapse of the heavens and the "abyss," the destruction of the inner-cosmic realm of the "prime parents," and the complete triumph of light over darkness (125.34–127.17).

The Concept of Our Great Power, which seems to date from the second half of the fourth century, also ends in a vivid description of the end of the present world (43.26–47.32), which will begin in the anger of the "archons" who rule it at the life of the enlightened faithful. The archons will first attack the East, introducing violence and widespread desolation. As "wickedness becomes dominant," the "archon of the Western regions"—a kind of Antichrist figure—will arise, perform miracles, and teach a spurious wisdom in order to confuse the faithful. He will introduce Jewish observances such as circumcision and rule with divine claims. Then "the cleansing of the souls will come" in cosmic disasters: the sea will dry up, the sky will give no rain, and the sun will cease to give light. Christ will then withdraw, with all his followers, into "the immeasurable light," where they will be clothed with holy, protective garments. Afterwards, Christ will return and destroy the archons and their subjects with fire, "and the sons of matter will perish." Then holy souls will appear in "the aeon of beauty of the aeon of judgment, will gaze on the Incomprehensible One and find rest in him," and even those souls who had "acted according to our birth of the flesh" and were being punished will "come to be in the unchangeable archon." Neither of these works gives a hint of bodily resurrection or of the eventual transformation of the material order, but *The Concept of Our Great Power* hints at the hope for a kind of universal salvation. Whatever religious community gave them birth, both of them show strong traces of apocalyptic style and themes, fitted into the doctrine and vocabulary of Gnostic religion, which in its earlier forms had shown little or no interest in such dramatic speculations. If anything, they indicate the continuing hybridization of Egyptian religious thought.

A more orthodox Christian composition incorporating many of the formal features of Jewish and early Christian apocalypses, the *Apocalypse of Paul* was probably composed in Greek—perhaps by charismatic Christian monks—during the first two decades of the fifth century (Piovanelli 1993).[15] In content, this work is not an apocalypse in the sense in which we have been using the term, because its main subject is not the mystery and crisis of humanity's future but the fate of individuals at death. Guided by an angel, the apostle Paul is given a tour of the regions beyond the present world where souls are rewarded or punished; he is allowed to see the role played by good and evil angels at the death of each individual (11–14), the divine judgment that follows (16f.), the joys of blessed souls in paradise before the general judgment (21–22), and the various punishments that the damned receive after death, suited to their particular histories of sin (31–42). The work seems to have been widely read in the fifth and sixth centuries, particularly in monastic circles in the West. It is apparently quoted by Caesarius of Arles, as well as in the *Rule of the Master* and the *Rule of St. Benedict* (Carozzi 1994, 12). It exercised an influence on a variety of later Western writers, probably including Dante. While its subject matter puts it outside the apocalyptic tradition, strictly speaking, it reflects both the preoccupation with mortality and judgment that characterized the early fifth century and a renewed interest in the form of a pseudepigraphical visionary narrative as a way of speculating on the unknown.

Less well known, but more genuinely apocalyptic, is the *Apocalypse of Thomas,* which exists in two Latin versions (the shorter of these seems to be the older and may depend on a Greek original from the fourth century). Echoes of Manichean ideas and parallels to some apocalyptic fragments identified as Priscillianist writings (see n. 8 below) suggest that this shorter version may have taken shape under gnosticizing influence. References to the emperors Arcadius (d. 408) and Honorius (d. 423) in the longer version place its composition around 420. In form, this brief work is a revelatory speech of the risen Christ to the apostle Thomas; in content, it relies heavily on the book of Revelation, although it divides that book's dramatic narrative into a scheme of seven days. On the sixth day, the heavens will be torn open, Christ will come in glory, and the fire surrounding paradise will become a conflagration devouring the whole cosmos. Then the souls of the saints, presently reposing in paradise, will come forth to receive their bodies again and will be changed with them into a new angelic form, putting on "the garment of eternal life." They will then be led off into the realm of light, where the Father lives, while angels destroy the wicked and annihilate material creation. In the longer version, this scenario is preceded by a period of conflict and tribulations, with a number of "prophecies" referring to events in the early fifth century. Chronological details here suggest that the redactor expected the end of the world about the year 500.

Another essay in the apocalyptic genre from the spiritual world of late-fourth- or early-fifth-century monasticism is the Coptic *Apocalypse of Schenute,* of which only a few fragments remain. The great Egyptian monastic leader Schenute (ca. 348–466), abbot of the Pachomian "White Monastery" in the early fifth century, often dwells vividly on details of the coming judgment in his moral instructions to his monks (e.g., *Opus* 42, *De iudicio Dei* [CSCO 42.189; trans. 96.110f.]; *Opus* 43, *De ira Dei* [CSCO 42.199; trans. 96.117]). The fragments of the apocalypse attributed to him (*Opus* 82: CSCO 73.199–202; trans. 108.121f.) narrate the meeting of St. Paul with a "gathering of saints" (perhaps a group of desert monks), in which the apostle depicts the scene of judgment in lurid terms. Terrifying angels will appear to carry out God's sentence; then Christ will appear to separate the sheep and the goats, and will give special attention to the judgment of monks and clerics, punishing with ultimate severity priests guilty of sins of the flesh. In the third fragment, Schenute also describes a vision of a procession of saints entering heaven, but his main emphasis is on the terrifying aspects of the final drama, which he describes with stark economy of detail. At one point, for instance, Schenute depicts an angel pouring water and hot steam on the earth and saying simply, "This is destruction and death" (Roquet 1993). Although the fragmentary state of this Coptic text makes it impossible to draw strong conclusions from it about the development of the apocalyptic mind in fifth-century Egypt, it does serve as proof of the continuing interest in such themes in the Nile Valley, precisely in the milieu of a large monastic community. Like many of their contemporaries in the West, alienated from traditional culture and unnerved by political and social instability, these monks seem to have found in their own withdrawal an invitation to confront the threat and the promise of their future on the grandly imagined stage of God's judgment and redemption.

As the fifth century drew to a close, speculation that the world's history would end with the year 500 was probably rife in many parts of the Mediterranean world. The last decades of the century were the time in which the Byzantine tradition of "political apocalypses" had their origin (see chapter 10 below). The *Seventh Vision of Daniel*, now only preserved in Armenian, and the *Oracle of Baalbek*, describing the "birth-pangs of the world" that were to begin shortly after the turn of the new century, may well both be based on Greek originals composed shortly before 500 (see Daley 1991, 178f. and n. 41). The *Theosophia*, a collection of pagan oracles and Christian imitations made during the reign of the emperor Anastasius I (491–518) and purporting to bring together all the wisdom of previous history, concludes with a brief summary of that history that predicts its end five hundred years after the birth of Christ. In the Syrian church, the great preacher *Narsai of Edessa* (399–503)—unlike earlier Syriac poet-theologians such as Ephrem or Jacob of Serug—strongly emphasized traditional apocalyptic themes in his eighty-one surviving metrical homilies. His scheme of the end, largely derived from Matthew 24, begins with a period of wars and natural catastrophes (*Homily* 18), followed by the appearance of the Antichrist, a human being totally controlled by Satan, and the coming of Elijah, who will confront the Antichrist and defeat him in single combat (*Homs.* 34, 51). After their struggle, Christ will appear in power, bathed in light and surrounded by a procession of saints (*Hom.* 34); he will crown Elijah and destroy the Antichrist so completely that even his soul will be annihilated (*Homs.* 18, 34, 44). Christ will then raise the dead by a simple gesture, clothe the living with immortality, and separate the good from the evil by "melting them down" in the fiery "furnace" of judgment (*Hom.* 18). The same anxieties that troubled Christians in other parts of the Roman Empire just before the half millennium seem to have made these images important also to their Syriac-speaking fellows across the Persian frontier.

⌒ THE SIXTH CENTURY: A RESPITE AND AN END _____

The first seven decades of the sixth century apparently offered a kind of respite to anxious spirits in the Mediterranean world. The violent effects of the immigration of warlike Germanic people were gradually mitigated as the fifth century drew to a close by their cultural and economic assimilation into the empire. Although the Goths and Vandals were Arian Christians, the Franks rapidly became Catholics after the baptism of Clovis in 497, and the institutional structures of the Catholic Church, both in Rome and throughout Gaul and Spain, grew markedly stronger and more unified in the early decades of the sixth century (Frend 1984, 791f.). In the Greek-speaking world, the successive reigns of Justin I (518–527) and his nephew Justinian I (527–565) offered almost a half century of stable, well-organized political life that gradually spread westward, until the whole Mediterranean basin, for a final brief period under Justinian, was unified under a single system of military and civil administration. The cultural life of the empire, in East and West, flourished once more: architecture and the visual arts, poetry and history, philosophy and theology reached by mid-century a level of quality and of international homogeneity that they would not approach again until the ninth and tenth centuries.

Predictably, perhaps, the use of apocalyptic themes in Christian preaching and theological literature declined markedly during this period. *Ceasarius of Arles* (ca. 470–543), for instance, often refers in his sermons to the certainty of judgment that awaits us at the time of the resurrection, and emphasizes with special relish the call to care for "the least of one's brethren" in the judgment scene of Matt. 25:31–46. Yet Caesarius is uninterested in the rest of the apocalyptic scenario and seems to assume that resurrection and judgment lie in a distant and indefinite future (*Serm.* 154.5; 157.1). The *Rule of St. Benedict,* too, in an early section taken wholly from the earlier and more severe *Rule of the Master* (2.5–10, 37–40), urges the abbot in the monastic community to see his responsibility in the context of the coming judgment of God, but there is practically none of the preoccupation with death and retribution here that one finds in monastic writings—Latin or Coptic—a century earlier.

Curiously, this very period witnessed the composition of four new commentaries on Revelation, two in Greek and two in Latin; yet all of them are scholarly works, balanced in tone and careful to avoid any sensational applications of the biblical apocalyptic text to the contemporary world. The first of these, the oldest extant commentary on the Johannine Apocalypse in Greek, is that of *Oecumenius,* probably the high military official (*comes*) who exchanged letters with Severus of Antioch. The commentary seems to date from the first decade of the sixth century (see Daley 1991, 179–83). Oecumenius takes a moderately spiritual approach to the text, in the spirit of Origen, and emphasizes the christological and practical meaning of Revelation rather than its value as a prediction of future events. He rejects a millenarian interpretation of Rev. 20:1–6, for instance, and takes the passage—as Tyconius and Augustine had done—to refer to Christ's present reign among the faithful on earth (Hoskier edition 213.16–19; 215.2–19). For Oecumenius, the struggles depicted by John point to actual events and persons of the future: barbarian tribes will harass the church; the Antichrist will be a human being dominated by Satan, who will kill Enoch and Elijah in the last days (Hoskier 225.14–20; 128–30; 131.3–13; 155.12–14); all the dead will rise in their physical bodies (Hoskier 221.1–3; 229.1–4) and undergo, with the material cosmos, transformation into a new, incorruptible, and spiritual mode of being (Hoskier 232.3–9). Oecumenius's understanding of the lot of sinners after the resurrection stresses their spiritual suffering (Hoskier 164.14–19; 231.114–17), and he guardedly recognizes the possibility of a progressive mitigation of their suffering and of universal final salvation (Hoskier 112.11–21; 113.1–10; 122.13–18). He also interprets the book's images of future beatitude in a predominantly spiritual way (Hoskier 62.4–15). In general, his commentary is anything but an expression of strong apocalyptic expectation, representing instead the calm attempt to integrate the Christian apocalyptic tradition into the intellectual mainstream of Greek biblical scholarship.

Andrew of Caesarea, metropolitan of Cappadocia sometime between 563 and 614, also commented on the whole book of Revelation in Greek, in a series of twenty-four homilies that apparently draw on Oecumenius's work (without mentioning him) but also seem to distance themselves deliberately from Oecumenius's rather tentative Origenism (Daley 1991, 198–200). Andrew's approach to the text is generally moralistic, and although he also stresses the spiritual character of the rewards of the blessed, he takes the eternal punishment of sinners more literally than his predecessor does. The Antichrist, in his view, will be a Jew from the tribe of Dan, a native of Bashan, who will pose as a Roman emperor but will also make claims of divinity (Schmid edition 35.7; 79.3f.; 102.6–8). Andrew, too, identifies the millennial kingdom with the present church (Schmid 216.13–18), and insists that the actual time of the end of history is known only to God (Schmid 221.15–222.6). Likewise, his hope is that the present material universe will share in the human transformation of the resurrection (Schmid 227.19–21; 229.11–13; 232.6f.). Along with Oecumenius, Andrew of Caesarea took a moderate approach to apocalypse interpretation that laid the groundwork for most later Byzantine exegesis of the work and won final theological acceptance for a book that had previously been regarded with suspicion in the Greek Christian world.

Two new Latin commentaries on Revelation also appeared near the middle of the sixth century. *Primasius of Hadrumetum* (d. after 553) produced a complete commentary sometime before 543, largely drawn from Tyconius's interpretation, as well as from the last three books of Augustine's *City of God*. It is a literal, rather cautious work that lacks all sense of an imminent end to history. *Apringius,* bishop of Beja in modern Portugal, wrote a briefer commentary shortly after 553, sizable fragments of which remain in the commentary of Beatus of Liébana. Like Oecumenius and earlier writers in the Origenist tradition, Apringius is more interested in the christological significance of the work than in connecting it with coming historical events. He gives no indication that he thinks the end is near.

In the 560s, however, the mood of quiet optimism that had characterized the sixth century until then seems once again to have changed and darkened. The end of Justinian's long and highly centralized reign left a leadership vacuum throughout the empire; its hard-won political and military unity gradually began to dissolve, and as city population continued to decline and land ownership became more and more unequal, the standard of living fell in both East and West (Frend 1984, 870–73). The bubonic plague appeared in the Mediterranean region for the first time: in Egypt, Palestine, and Syria in 542, and spreading to Asia Minor and the West by 570, everywhere bringing terrible distress and anxiety (Jones 1964, 1:287f.). Once again Germanic military depredation became a serious threat, this time at the hands of the half-pagan Lombards, who invaded Italy under Alboin in 568 and subjugated the northern part of the peninsula with unprecedented savagery (Ewig 1980, 574–79). A sense of social dissolution suddenly reemerged and found its most poignant and eloquent expression in the works of *Pope Gregory the Great* (ca. 540–604).

This highly cultivated Roman, who abandoned a bureaucratic career to become a monk (575), then deacon and papal representative in Constantinople (579–585), succeeded Pelagius II as bishop of Rome in 590. Pope Gregory's official correspondence, like his exegetical and hagiographical works, repeatedly confirms the portrait of John the Deacon, his ninth-century biographer: "In all his words and acts, Gregory considered that the final day and the coming judgment were imminent; the closer he felt the end of the world was coming, with its numerous disasters, the more carefully he pondered all human affairs" (*Vita* 4.65). Humanity, Gregory was convinced, had entered its final agony (*Homiliae XL in Evangelia* 1.1.5; *Homiliae in Hiezechielem* 2.6.22–24), and the signs of the end foretold in scripture were now visible in Italy, "like the pages of our books" (*Ep.* 3.29 [593]; cf. *Dialogi* 3.38.2f.; *Ep.* 3.61 [593]; *Hom. in Evang.* 1.1.1). The Antichrist—who, in Gregory's view, would be Satan incarnate rather than simply a human person—already was showing his influence in political and clerical arrogance, such as that displayed by Patriarch John of Constantinople (*Ep.* 5.39 [595]; 7.30 [597]). The Lombard threat, like the political corruption everywhere present within the empire, offered the church, in Gregory's view, both a warning of coming judgment and an urgent call to purification (Straw 1988, 81–89, 197–213). The end of the world was near, yet not so near that repentance and the conversion of unbelievers were no longer possible. In fact, Gregory saw in the troubles of his time an unusual opportunity for his contemporaries to turn to God and to learn not to love the "passing world" (*Hom. in Evang.* 1.1.1; 1.4.2; *Moralia in Iob* 13.14.28). The church, he recognized, was still internally at peace and still growing; this itself was a sign that history was not yet in its final struggles (*Mor. in Iob* 35.15.35). So he could assure King Ethelbert of Kent that not all the predicted signs of the end would happen in their day and that there was still time for the reform and christianization of society (*Ep.* 11.37).

In Pope Gregory's nuanced but impassioned apocalyptic consciousness, one senses traces of a more common awareness that an age was indeed coming to a close (Markus 1990, 213–28). The Christian Roman culture of the West was entering a period of retrenchment, of material poverty, of bureaucratic decentralization and weakened institutions that would isolate its citizens more and more from each other and from their past for the better part of two centuries. In the Greek and Semitic East, scholarship and artistic production would continue at a somewhat higher level than in the West until the mid-eighth century. Yet there too culture entered something of a holding pattern, and Christian thought in the seventh and eighth centuries—apart from bursts of genuine synthetic creativity in the work of a Maximus Confessor or a John of Damascus—gradually lost both scholarly precision and spiritual energy. A world had indeed grown old, and its transformation had not yet appeared. The apocalyptic expectation of early Christian thought, on the cultural and religious levels, at least, had begun to see its fulfillment.

☞ NOTES

1. Tertullian mentions here that he has treated Christian eschatological expectations more fully in a tract, now lost, entitled *De spe fidelium.* There, he says, he discussed the possibility of taking the restoration of the land of Israel also in a spiritual or allegorical sense, as "applicable to Christ and the church." According to Jerome (*Comm. in Ezek.* 11.36), this work also developed the millenarian hope in its more literal sense.

2. Tertullian's millenarianism is often seen as part of the legacy of the "New Prophecy" or Montanism, a charismatic and prophetic movement that he embraced about 207. However, although the Montanists seem to have shared his expectation of the imminent end, there is no clear ancient evidence that they were themselves millenarians. For a discussion of Montanist eschatology, see Trevett 1996, 95–100.

3. For references to recent discussion of the unity of authorship of the works attributed to Hippolytus, see Daley 1991, 233 n. 9.

4. For this theme in Cyprian's works, see also *Ep.* 58.2 and *De mortalitate* 25. For sources and parallels in classical literature, see Daley 1991, 234 n. 12.

5. The authorship of the fragments of commentary on Revelation attributed to Origen in the catenae and published by C. Diobouniotis and A. von Harnack (*Die Scholien-kommentar des Origenes zur Apokalypse Johannis,* Texte und Untersuchungen 38 [Leipzig, 1911]), is still disputed; see Daley 1991, 235 n. 10; Dulaey 1991, 209 n. 55. If they are not the work of Origen, they are at least in the Origenist tradition and show the same tendency to take the images of Revelation as referring primarily to intra-historical events. For a discussion of Origen's "spiritual" interpretation of Rev. 20:1–6, in which the "first resurrection" is taken as referring to conversion to a knowledge of Christ and to the forgiveness of sins in baptism,

see Henri Crouzel, "La 'première' et la 'seconde' résurrection des hommes d'après Origène," *Didaskalia* (Lisbon) 3 (1973): 3–20.

6. For a discussion of these and other passages in the *Symposium* that seem to represent a modified interpretation of Irenaeus's millenarian scheme, see Lloyd G. Patterson, "Methodius' Millenarianism," *Studia Patristica* 24 (1993): 306–15.

7. See, e.g., Basil of Caesarea, *Ep.* 263.4; 265.2; Gregory of Nazianzus, *Ep.* 101.63; 102.14; Jerome, *Comm. on Daniel* 3 (on Dan. 9:24), translating a passage from Apollinarius's treatise *Against Porphyry,* predicting the coming of Antichrist about 490; also Jerome, *Comm. on Isaiah* 18, praef.; *Comm. on Ezekiel* 11 (on Ezek. 36:1–15); *De viris illustribus* 18. Martine Dulaey sees Apollinarius also as the unnamed opponent whom Jerome criticizes in the preface to his *Commentary on Malachi* for thinking that Elijah, when he comes as herald of Christ's return, will restore the covenant with Israel: see Dulaey 1988, 93f. Epiphanius of Salamis, however, denied that Apollinarius was a millenarian (*Panarion* 77.36.5).

8. The last eight of Priscillian of Avila's ninety Pauline canons dealt with the coming of Antichrist, the judgment, and resurrection (see Chadwick 1976, 61f.). For further fragments that may be of Priscillianist origin, which show strong interest in apocalyptic themes, see D. De Bruyne, "Fragments retrouvés d'apocryphes priscillianistes," *Revue Bénédictine* 24 (1907): 323f., 326f., 328–30.

9. Sulpicius probably is thinking above all of the atmosphere of fear and mutual recriminations caused in the Spanish churches by the execution of Priscillian in 386 and the persecution of his followers. The mood of apocalyptic expectation shared by the Priscillianists seems to have spread quickly through the mainstream churches of Spain and Gaul, verified by the very conflicts it aroused. See Sulpicius, *Chron.* 2.51.7–10; *Dialogue* 3.11 (on Martin's opposition to the persecution of the Priscillianists).

10. This parallel would be all the more striking if the Latin translation of Irenaeus's *Adversus haereses* was actually made, as has been argued, in North Africa during the 390s. For arguments for and against this view, and further bibliography, see Dominic J. Unger and John J. Dillon, introduction to *St. Irenaeus of Lyons: Against the Heresies* 1 (Ancient Christian Writers 55; Paulist: New York 1992), 14–15 and 121–123, nn. 74–75.

11. See Dulaey 1988 for a careful analysis of all the passages where Jerome deals with the millenarian tradition. Dulaey argues that the main targets of Jerome's hostility on this subject are Lactantius and Apollinarius.

12. Although no direct citations from Tyconius exist in which he made such calculations, passages in later commentaries that seem to be drawing on his, notably in that of Beatus, suggest that Tyconius took the three and one-half days in which the Gentiles will gaze triumphantly at the dead bodies of God's two witnesses (Rev. 11:9–11) to signify three and one-half centuries of steady persecution from the time of the death of Christ until the end (Beatus 5.6.6; 6.3.38: ed. E. Romero-Pose [Rome: Typis Officinae Polygraphicae, 1985] 2.67f., 82). This would put the time of the world's final crisis at about 380, roughly the time of his own writing. See, however, Paula Fredriksen Landes, who argues from the lack of clear references to apocalyptic chronology in Tyconius's *Libri regularum,* as well as from his generally deeschatologizing approach to apocalyptic prophecy, that he did not make such clear predictions of the end of history ("Tyconius and the End of the World," *Revue des études augustiniennes* 18 [1982]: 59–75).

13. For a discussion of the differences between Quodvultdeus's conception of history and that of Augustine, see Herve Inglebert, "Un exemple historiographique au Ve siècle: La conception de l'histoire chez Quodvultdeus de Carthage et ses relations avec la Cité de Dieu," *Revue des études augustiniennes* 37 (1991): 307–19, especially 313–18.

14. Here a discrepancy arises in the narrative structure of the two works. In the *Carmen de duobus populis,* a second Antichrist will come in the East and will perform miracles in Judea (837–41, 891–926); in the *Instructions,* Nero will be the only Antichrist, but he will go to Jerusalem and be accepted there as the Messiah, once he has conquered the West (1.41.13–20).

15. In an elaborate study of the *Apocalypse of Paul* and its parallels, C. Carozzi has argued that the work as we now have it is based on a Greek original, composed in Egypt in the last three decades of the second century and cited by Origen. The present text is a Latin translation, in Carozzi's view, of an expanded Greek version of that work, made in monastic surroundings and related to the Pseudo-Macarian corpus;

it may have been composed in the neighborhood of Constantinople (Carozzi 1994, 165–72). Piovanelli seems right, however, in being more skeptical about the relationship of the extant text with the *Apocalypse* referred to by Origen (Piovanelli 1993, 37–59). In any case, the story told by the historian Sozomen (*Historia Ecclesiastica* 7.19) of the discovery of such an apocalypse by monks, in the foundation of Paul's house in Tarsus ca. 420, suggests that it began to be circulated in monastic groups about that time.

BIBLIOGRAPHY

Abbreviations

CSCO   *Corpus scriptorum Christianorum orientalium.* Paris, Louvain, Washington: 1903–.
CSEL   *Corpus scriptorum ecclesiasticorum Latinorum.* Vienna: 1866–.
NHLE   James M. Robinson, ed. *The Nag Hammadi Library in English.* San Francisco: Harper & Row, 1977.
PL   Jacques-Paul Migne, ed. *Patrologia Latina.* Paris, 1841–64.
SC   *Sources chrétiennes.* Paris, 1941–.

Studies

Bouhot, Jean-Paul. 1986. "Hesychius de Salone et Augustin (lettres 197–198–199)." In *Saint Augustin et la Bible: Bible de tous les temps,* edited by Anne-Marie la Bonnardière, 3:229–50. Paris: Beauchesne.

Brisson, Jean-Paul. 1958. *Autonomisme et christianisme dans l'afrique romaine de Septime Sévère à l'invasion vandale.* Paris: Boccard. On Commodian, see pp. 378–410, esp. 390–94.

Carozzi, Claude. 1994. *Eschatologie et au-delà: Recherches sur l'Apocalypse de Paul.* Aix-en-Provence: Publications de l'Université de Provence. The fullest recent survey of the background and parallels of the Apocalypse of Paul; includes a corrected Latin text.

Chadwick, Henry. 1976. *Priscillian of Avila.* Oxford: Clarendon Press.

Collins, John J., ed. 1979. *Apocalypse: The Morphology of a Genre. Semeia* 14. Missoula, Mont.: Scholars Press. The fullest recent discussion of the apocalyptic genre.

Courcelle, Pierre. 1964. "Date, source et génèse des consultationes Zacchaei et Apolonii." *Revue de l'histoire des religions* 146:174–93 (= *Histoire littéraire des grandes invasions germaniques* [Paris: Études Augustiniennes, 1964], 261–75).

Daley, Brian E. 1991. *The Hope of the Early Church: A Handbook of Patristic Eschatology.* Cambridge: Cambridge University Press. The most complete survey of early Christian eschatology, with extensive bibliography.

Dulaey, Martine. 1986. "L'Apocalypse: Augustin et Tyconius." In *Saint Augustin et la Bible: Bible de tous les temps,* edited by Anne Marie la Bonnardière, 3:369–86. Paris: Beauchesne.

———. 1988. "Jérôme, Victorin de Poetovio et le millénarisme." In *Jérôme entre l'Occident et l'Orient,* edited by Yves-Marie Duval, 83–98. Paris: Études Augustiniennes.

———. 1991. "Jérôme 'éditeur' du *Commentaire sur l'Apocalypse* de Victorin de Poetovio." *Revue des Études Augustiniennes* 37:199–236.

Ewig, Eugen. 1980. "The Missionary Work of the Latin Church." In *History of the Church,* edited by Hubert Jedin and John Dolan, 2:517–601. New York: Seabury Press. These chapters in Jedin's handbook of church history survey the situation in the Latin church during the period of great missionary activity from the fifth to the eighth centuries. The author discusses Italy during the Lombard invasions on pp. 574–584.

Fredriksen, Paula. 1991. "Apocalypse and Redemption in Early Christianity: From John of Patmos to Augustine of Hippo." *Vigiliae Christianae* 45:151–83.

Frend, W. H. C. 1965. *Martyrdom and Persecution in the Early Church: A Study of Conflict from the Maccabees to Donatus.* Oxford: Basil Blackwell, 1965. The fullest and most balanced account of the persecution of early Christians.

———. 1984. *The Rise of Christianity.* Philadelphia: Fortress Press. A full, lively, often unconventional survey of early Christian history.

Gry, Léon. 1914. *Le millénarisme dans ses origines et son développement*. Paris: Picard.

Heid, Stefan. 1993. *Chiliasmus und Antichrist-Mythos: Eine frühchristliche Kontroverse um das Heilige Land*. Bonn: Borengässer.

Hellemo, Geir. 1989. *Adventus Domini: Eschatological Thought in Fourth-Century Apses and Catecheses*. Leiden: E. J. Brill.

Hill, Charles E. 1992. *Regnum Caelorum: Patterns of Future Hope in Early Christianity*. Oxford: Clarendon Press. A thoughtful reexamination of second-century millenarianism.

Jones, A. H. M. 1964. *The Later Roman Empire, 284–602*, 3 vols. plus maps. Oxford: Basil Blackwell. The most comprehensive survey of the economic and social history of the late Roman Empire.

Kelly, J. N. D. 1975. *Jerome: His Life, Writings and Controversies*. London: Duckworth.

Lauras, Antoine. 1966. "Le commentaire patristique de Lc 21.25–33." *Studia patristica* 7:505–12. Includes a discussion of Origen's treatment of the Lucan apocalypse.

Luneau, Auguste. 1964. *L'Histoire du salut chez les pères de l'église: La Doctrine des âges du monde*. Paris: Beauchesne.

MacRae, George W. 1989. "Apocalyptic Eschatology in Gnosticism." In *Apocalypticism in the Mediterranean World and the Near East*, edited by David Hellholm, 317–25. Tübingen: Mohr-Siebeck.

Markus, Robert A. 1990. *The End of Ancient Christianity*. Cambridge: Cambridge University Press. A masterly interpretation of the changes in Western Christian culture and thought after the end of persecution, from the fourth to the sixth centuries.

McDonald, Lee M. 1995. *The Formation of the Christian Biblical Canon*. Revised ed. Peabody, MA: Hendrickson. A full, careful account of the formation of the Christian canon.

Meeks, Wayne A. 1989. "Social Functions of Apocalyptic Language in Pauline Christianity." In *Apocalypticism in the Mediterranean World and the Near East*, edited by David Hellholm, 687–705. Tübingen: Mohr-Siebeck.

Monaci, Adele. 1978. "Apocalisse ed escatologia nell'opera di Origene." *Augustinianum* 18:139–51.

Nickelsburg, George W. E. 1989. "Social Aspects of Palestinian Jewish Apocalypticism." In *Apocalypticism in the Mediterranean World and the Near East*, edited by David Hellholm, 641–54. Tübingen: Mohr-Siebeck.

Patterson, Lloyd G. 1997. *Methodius of Olympus: Divine Sovereignty, Human Freedom and Life in Christ*. Washington: Catholic University of America Press, 1997. The first comprehensive study of Methodius's theology since 1903, with special emphasis on his complex relationship to Origen's thought.

Piovanelli, Pierluigi. 1993. "Les origines de l'*Apocalypse de Paul* reconsidérées." *Apocrypha* 4:25–64.

Prete, Serafino. 1966. *La Escatologia e parenesi negli scrittori cristiani Latini*. Bologna: Zanichelli. A thoughtful study of early Latin eschatology.

Rauh, Horst Dieter. 1973. *Das Bild des Antichrist im Mittelalter: Von Tyconius zum deutschen Symbolismus*. Münster: Aschendorff.

Roquet, Gérard. 1993. "L'Ange des eaux et le dieu de la crue selon Chenoute: Sur un fragment copte des visions de l'*Apocalypsis Sinuthii*." *Apocrypha* 4:83–99.

Schüssler Fiorenza, Elisabeth. 1989. "The Phenomenon of Early Christian Apocalyptic: Some Reflections on Method." In *Apocalypticism in the Mediterranean World and the Near East*, edited by David Hellholm, 295–316. Tübingen: Mohr-Siebeck.

Straw, Carole. 1988. *Gregory the Great: Perfection in Imperfection*. Berkeley: University of California Press. An excellent synthetic account of Gregory's theology and spirituality.

Timmermann, Johannes. 1968. *Nachapostolisches Parusiedenken*. Munich: Hueber.

Trevett, Christine. 1996. *Montanism: Gender, Authority and the New Prophecy*. Cambridge: Cambridge University Press. The fullest recent account of the Montanist movement.

Williams, Stephen, and Gerard Friell. 1994. *Theodosius: The Empire at Bay*. New Haven: Yale University Press. A revealing new account of cultural and social changes in the Roman Empire at the end of the fourth century.

10

Byzantine Apocalypses

David Olster
University of Kentucky

WITHOUT DOUBT, one of the most overlooked genres of Byzantine literature is eschatology. Hans-Georg Beck's encyclopedic handbook *Kirche und theologische Literatur im byzantinischen Reich* briefly mentions Byzantine apocalyptic themes that appear in genres such as homilies, but offers the reader no general survey of Byzantine apocalypses themselves. Indeed, with the exception of the posthumous (and incomplete) survey of Byzantine apocalyptic by Paul J. Alexander, no modern monographic survey of Byzantine apocalypses and apocalyptic literature exists. Such oversight characterizes the study of Byzantine apocalypses, which hardly compares either in detail or in depth with the study of Western medieval apocalypses. And although many of the most prominent scholars in Byzantine studies have made important contributions to the study of Byzantine apocalypses, Byzantine apocalyptic has remained for the most part understudied and underexploited. Ironically, Byzantinists have been for the most part less interested in the cultural impact of their own apocalyptic traditions and texts than those in other, chronologically related fields. Western medievalists have long recognized the close ties that link several Eastern and Western apocalyptic traditions; Slavicists readily acknowledge the influence of Byzantine apocalyptic on the development of Slavic literature; and translations of Byzantine apocalypses appear as far away as Armenia and Ethiopia. But on the whole, Byzantinists have not pursued such research avenues.

Why Byzantine scholars have overlooked this prominent and influential literary genre is not easily explained, but the most obvious reason is that there is no "great" Byzantine apocalyptic author or apocalypse. Certainly, there is no figure in the corpus of Byzantine apocalypses to compare with a Joachim of Fiore, nor does Byzantine apocalyptic possess the cultural diversity, broad spectrum of themes, and variety of visions that early Christian apocalyptic enjoys. But these characteristics of Byzantine apocalyptic hardly explain scholarship's general lack of interest.

Perhaps more influential in determining the historiographic disinterest in Byzantine apocalyptic is the sharp distinction that Byzantinists often make between "high" and "low" literature, contrasting a classical, "high" literary tradition against a perceived Christian, "low" literary tradition, much to the detriment of the latter. In fact, Byzantine authors who wrote in classical genres like history may have themselves contributed to the marginalization of apocalyptic as an expression of "low" culture. The sixth-century author Agathias wrote contemptuously of the popular reaction to an earthquake:

> Fantastic stories and amazing predictions that the apocalypse was near began to circulate among the people. Charlatans and self-appointed prophets roamed the streets prophesying whatever came into their heads and terrifying the majority of the people. . . . Society never fails to throw up a bewildering variety of such people in times of misfortune. (*Historiarum libri quinque* 4.5.1–3)

Such striking passages may well reflect, or even have influenced, scholarship's view of Byzantine apocalyptic as a "popular" genre, suitable as evidence for eschatological theology, or the christianization of society (and for many this implies a sort of cultural decline), but not for the study of Byzantine literature or history itself (see Alexander 1968). On the contrary, Byzantine apocalypses can be vital historical evidence for poorly documented periods of Byzantine history, especially the Byzantine "dark age" of the seventh through ninth centuries.[1] Not surprisingly, this is also the period that saw the development and maturation of the Byzantine apocalypse as a genre.

In fact, Byzantine apocalypses can show a surprising degree of literary sophistication. They often incorporated elements drawn from genres and texts entirely distinct from apocalyptic: *Pseudo-Methodius,* for example, incorporated elements of the *Alexander Romance,* and the *Homily* of Leo of Constantinople incorporated extensive hagiographic material.[2] On the other hand, apocalypses could be written into other genres, such as hagiography (e.g., the *Apocalypse of Andrew the Fool*) or even anti-Jewish works such as the *Doctrine of Jacob the Newly Baptized.* The Byzantines' general reliance on the prophecies of Daniel led to several "Visions" of Daniel, who is perhaps the most common pseudonymous author of apocalypses, but other apocalypses were attributed to church fathers such as Methodius, Ephrem, John Chrysostom, and even to the emperor Leo VI the Wise. Byzantine apocalypses tended to borrow heavily from one another and often conform to the Byzantine literary practice of *mimesis* or literary imitation. Indeed, the *mimetic* tradition of the genre and the evident borrowings from one text to another illustrate at least one sort of literary circle of Byzantine readership and authorship within the imperial cultural sphere. Despite regional distinctions that appear in different texts, Byzantine apocalyptic is a further demonstration of cultural homogeneity within the empire. This fact might also give the reader pause before simply dismissing these texts as "low" literature, for such borrowings show a literate, if not elite, audience. Indeed, at times the literary affectation of some apocalypses has led scholars to pronounce them romances or a peculiar sort of antiquarian literature (Alexander 1985, 124–25).

A possible second reason why Byzantine apocalypses have not received the study they deserve is that, notwithstanding its necessity as a category, Byzantine apocalyptic is actually a misnomer: it would be far more accurate to call it *very* late Roman apocalyptic. Those we call Byzantines used that name only as an archaism for the inhabitants of Constantinople (formerly Byzantium), their capital. Despite the fact that they spoke Greek, that for most of the period of our survey they had little if any political control or influence in Rome, and that they themselves generally conceded that the Roman Empire was not what it once was, they defied modern historical logic and called themselves Romans, a title that was generally conceded also by their Latin contemporaries, even those competing for the imperial title with them. And, if we were to construct Roman history solely from their frame of reference, we would find a seamless Roman imperial continuity from Augustus to the fall of Constantinople to the Turks in 1453. Their apocalypses participated in this cultural conceit; indeed, many were written to uphold it, and their apocalyptic writings powerfully reflected this uneasy synthesis of their historically anomalous position. Perhaps that is why the Byzantines' apocalyptic traditions had more influence on, and were more interesting to, a medieval world fascinated by the restoration or preservation of the God-guarded Roman Empire than to our own.

Nonetheless, although the Byzantines insisted that they were Romans, institutionally and geopolitically the transition from the "later" Christian Roman Empire to the "very late Roman" Byzantine Empire followed in the wake of three crucial events: the conversion of Constantine and consequent imperialization of Greek Christian political thought; the foundation of Constantinople and eventual identification of that city as legitimate capital of the Roman Empire and the Christian *oikoumenē*; and the barbarian invasions, above all the seventh-century Slav and Arab invasions that shattered the Greco-Roman cultural unity of the Mediterranean and challenged the ideals and principles that had guided post-Constantinian, Christian Roman political thought. These three events generally define modern periodization; and the third, the Slav and Arab invasions of the seventh century, initiated not only the geopolitical and institutional crises that shaped Byzantine history, but it also inspired an ideological crisis that led to the creation of a "Byzantine," as opposed to late antique or late Roman, apocalyptic perspective.

Above all, the diminution of the empire in the seventh century inspired in Byzantine apocalyptic the theme of imperial restoration that most clearly distinguishes Byzantine from late Roman apocalyptic. For although the Byzantines did not like to admit it, the geopolitical dissonance between the "classical" Roman Empire and the "medieval" Roman Empire was so great that they built an entire historical and apologetic apparatus in order to bring historical time and events within the sphere of their imagined time. Apocalyptic was a primary literary vehicle to achieve this end.

The biblical sources of Byzantine apocalyptic both contributed to and reinforced the Byzantine interest in imperial continuity. On the whole, Byzantine apocalyptic drew inspiration from the prophecies of Daniel (especially the "weeks" of Daniel 9 and the prophecy of "four kingdoms" in Daniel 2) and Ezekiel (Gog and Magog of Ezekiel 38–39), rather than those of John's Revelation.[3] (It is noteworthy that the *Apocalypse of Pseudo-Ephraim* is the only Byzantine apocalypse specifically to name Revelation.) This is not to say that the Byzantines altogether ignored Revelation: there are four extant commentaries on the book, including a tenth-century comment by the important literary figure, Arethas of Caesarea. Of course, the Byzantines maintained a lively interest in the millennium and the Antichrist. Nonetheless, the Byzantines were often more attracted to the successions of kingdoms (generally considering their own to be the last) and the invasions of Gog and Magog (which they incorporated into a scenario exalting Christ as the successor to the last Byzantine emperor) than to the end of the world and the final judgment (though the latter plays a role in Byzantine art). Typically, although *Pseudo-Methodius,* perhaps the most influential Byzantine apocalypse, concludes with the final judgment, it gives merely a sentence or two announcing that Christ will reward the righteous and punish the unrighteous. Furthermore, the last judgment passage cites 2 Thessalonians and Philippians, but not Revelation. Similarly, several ninth-century Daniel "visions" end with the overthrow of the Antichrist and a brief reference to the final judgment, but their primary interest is the succession of Byzantine rulers leading up to the manifestation of the Final Enemy and an account of his career. These texts constructed a historical and apocalyptic process of imperial past and future in order to create a future framework in which to set the restoration and eventual victory of the Roman Empire. Although, as we shall see, not all Byzantine apocalypses followed this pattern, nevertheless, the theme of imperial restoration and Christ's relationship with the empire remained a central theme in the apocalyptic genre, just as in other genres of Byzantine literature.

Byzantium, however, did not develop its apocalypticism in a cultural vacuum. Local cultures and apocalyptic traditions crowded the Near East, and Byzantium dynamically interacted with its neighbors, both influencing and being influenced. *Pseudo-Methodius* was originally a Syriac (and likely Monophysite) product, but its Greek translation and succeeding redactions were the most influential Byzantine apocalypse both within and without Byzantium.[4] Armenian and Ethiopian apocalyptic text collections include translations of Greek originals, and the Byzantines also may have been in contact with Coptic apocalyptic thought, although the ties between these two powerful cultural traditions in the middle Byzantine period have not been extensively studied.

In addition to Byzantine relations with other Christian apocalyptic traditions, the Byzantines also interacted with Jewish traditions and texts: in particular, the Sibylline apocalyptic tradition, which, although christianized in late antiquity, retained something of the Jewish reticence toward the Roman Empire. However, Judeo-Byzantine apocalyptic relations seem to have at times been more direct in the period of our survey. The Jewish *Dream and Prophecy of Zerubbabel* places Armilus, the Antichrist or "little horn" of Daniel, among the ten royal "horns" of the prophecy and refers to Armilus as "the destroyer of peoples," explaining that the name comes from the Greek, which would be *Hermolaos*.[5] Whether the name actually came from Greek or not, it is clear that Christian and Jewish authors drew on a tradition that transcended religious lines.[6] In fact, an *Armaleus* turns up in *Pseudo-Methodius,* not as the Antichrist but as an alternative name for Romulus, the king of Rome who receives the promise of Rome's eternal rule.[7] Thus, although Christian and Jewish apocalypses shared the name of a Roman ruler, they employed him very differently. Hermolaos also appears as the Antichrist in *The Doctrine of Jacob the Newly Baptized,* an anti-Jewish dialogue that contains an extensive apocalyptic apparatus and was translated into both Slavic and Ethiopic. "For when the ten horns arise, and Hermolaos the evil one comes, there will be great confusion among the peoples."[8] Not only does the *Doctrine* share this name for the Antichrist with the Jewish apocalypses; it also incorporates the same apocalyptic schedule in which God kills Armilus/Hermolaos himself.[9] Regardless of how these intermingled apocalyptic schemes are sorted out, and the degree and nature of Judeo-Byzantine cultural interaction, they evidence the powerful appeal of apocalyptic traditions across religious lines in the medieval Near East.

Before turning to Byzantine apocalyptic itself, let us investigate the themes and ideas that Byzantium inherited from its late Roman predecessors, for the imperial model that the Byzantine apocalypses sought to recover was one that was initiated at the beginning of the Christian empire. The victory of Constantine inaugurated a new age that for Eusebius was the fulfillment of a divine plan for Rome. Following Origen's lead, Eusebius asserted that the coincidence of Augustus and Christ was no temporal accident: on the contrary, it was part of a divine plan to join Christianity to the Roman Empire and to achieve the conversion of the *oikoumenē* ruled by the universal empire of Rome. This idea never left Byzantine political rhetoric and thought. Even as late as the fifteenth century, when the empire's days were numbered, churchmen still claimed that there was no church without empire and emperor. The successors of Eusebius treated Constantine's conversion as the final seal of God's divine choice of the Romans as the Christian nation or race chosen by God.[10]

Indeed, the successors of Eusebius described the Romans as God's chosen people even before their conversion. By the middle of the fifth century, Christians assumed an organic union of Christianity and imperialism that aimed at the attainment of two complementary ends under the aegis of Christ: to spread the Christian faith and to achieve universal peace. The Christian universal mission blended with the *pax romana* so that, according to Eusebius, "As the knowledge of one God was imparted to all men, a single sovereign arose for the entire Roman Empire, and a deep peace took hold of all" (*Tricennial Oration* 16.4–5).[11] The empire's victorious march was the undeniable proof of Christianity's efficacy and Christ's power, so that the Roman Empire was "further destined to obtain all those not yet united [with the empire] right up to the limits of the inhabited world" (ibid. 16.6).[12] The universal missions of Christianity and the empire drew all races together "in order to merge every race into one unity and concord" (ibid.).[13] Civilization, empire, and religion had long been inseparable in classical Roman political thought, but the pagan Romans had not possessed the Christian apocalyptic framework that redefined the historical ends of religion and empire. By the seventh century, the association of Christian and Roman universalism led Byzantine authors to refer to themselves as the "new Israel." This use of the title of God's chosen people was not simply an echo of the new Israel rhetoric justifying Gentile appropriation of Jewish prophetic and especially messianic promises, but was a claim that the prophecies that pertained to the kingdom of Israel now properly belonged to the Christian empire of the Romans. In particular, the Byzantines applied the Daniel prophecy of the four empires to themselves so that they became the last empire, the empire that prepared the way for Christ's return.

As the Christians adopted and adapted the rhetoric of classical imperial universalism, they slowly assumed the entire panoply of Roman triumphal discourse. In the wake of Constantine's victory, Eusebius employed the classical topoi that identified victory and God's favor to create historical legitimacy for a Christian empire and religious legitimacy for Christianity. Thus, Christianity and "Romanity" (*romanitas*) came to depend on each other in a sort of religio-historical tautology: imperial victory demonstrated Christianity's power, efficacy, and legitimacy; Christ's demonstrated power through victory proved his love for his chosen empire and its emperor. At the end of the sixth century, the church historian Evagrius had demonstrated God's blessings on the empire by pointing to the stability of the imperial succession: no emperor had been overthrown between Constantine and the end of the sixth century.[14] Imperial wars became a further demonstration of Christ's power and love for his empire, so that the fifth-century church historian Theodoret concluded, "These wars [against Christians] and the victory of the church have been predicted by the Lord, and the event teaches us that war brings us more blessing than peace" (*Ecclesiastical History* 5.38).[15] On the one hand, the "wars" against Christians referred to the persecutions of Christians of which even Roman emperors were guilty. But the wars of the Romans against barbarians were equally part of Christian history, and even Theodoret asserted that military victory was the seal of Christ's favor.[16] Theodoret's contemporary, the church historian Sozomen, explained how a plague sent by God struck the barbarians with fear, "not so much because they had dared to take up arms against a nation of such valor as the Romans possessed, as that they perceived them to be assisted by a mighty God" (*Eccl. Hist.* 7.43).[17]

Roman wars thus became increasingly imbued with religious significance. By the fifth century, the church historian Socrates could claim that the Romans had gone to war "for the sake of the Christian religion" (*Eccl. Hist.* 7.18),[18] and that through the imperial armies Christ had taken vengeance on the Persians through the Romans "because they shed the blood of so many of his pious worshippers" (ibid. 7.20).[19] From the seventh century, this identification of war and persecution, of a struggle between Christians and heathens rather than Romans and barbarians intensified, and war became ever more closely associated with the exercise of Christian as well as Roman power. Both the emperors Heraclius (610–641) and Nicephorus II Phocas (963–969) unsuccessfully attempted to have battlefield death declared a form of martyrdom. As one Byzantine military treatise explained, "It is right that [the soldiers'] homes be preserved free of every outrage, according to the laws of the ancient Romans, and that they should be honored as defenders of the Christians."[20]

The Byzantines also inherited the Hellenistic assumption that God's favor was especially dependent on the emperor. Sozomen explained that "we have continually included the emperors in these historical narratives, because from the time they began to profess the Christian religion, the affairs of the church have depended on them" (*Hist. Eccl.,* introduction). Piety, the virtue that assured divine favor, thus ranked high on the imperial list. When Theodosius I charged his sons to remain steadfast in the orthodox faith, his admonition was traditional: "For in this way, peace is maintained, war ended, foes defeated, trophies raised, and victory proclaimed" (Theodoret, *Eccl. Hist.* 5.25).[21] Theodosius II, if hard-pressed, could call upon divine aid, "If at any time war was raised, he, like David, placed his trust in God because he knew he was the judge of battles" (Socrates, *Ecclesiastical History* 7.22). When the emperor marched in the field, Christ accompanied him; as the twelfth-century emperor Alexius I Comnenus explained, "My majesty makes itself ready to march with God against the enemies of the Roman Empire."[22] Byzantine apocalyptic retained an abiding interest in the role of the emperor in eschatological history, as well as the means by which the heavenly emperor Christ would aid the emperor, or assume the imperial throne himself. Characteristically, the Byzantines thought of Christ as *symbasileus,* coemperor, with the earthly emperor. Ultimately, for the Byzantines, Christ was as Roman as themselves.

For all the claims of divine aid in warfare, before the seventh century Christ and the Virgin almost never personally intervened in battle.[23] In the wake of seventh-century defeats, however, human means came to appear increasingly inadequate, and the Virgin in particular participated in the successful defense of Constantinople against the Avars in 626, walking along the walls according to one report. At the same time, icons of Christ and the Virgin assumed an increasingly prominent role on the battlefield and in sieges. The icons that protected Constantinople during the Avar siege were not simply apotropaic, but represented the presence of Christ and the Virgin in the battle itself. As Theodore Syncellus, whose homily celebrates the victory over the "Gog and Magog" of the Avars explained, "For the Lord will go to war on our behalf, and the Virgin, the Mother of God, will be the defender of the city if indeed we might run to them with full hearts and willing souls."[24]

The siege of Constantinople also illustrates a second theme that further identified Romanity with Christianity: the Byzantine construction of Constantinople as not only the center of the Roman world but the center of the entire Christian world. By the middle of the fifth century, Constantinople had truly assumed the mantle of Rome as the imperial capital. And by the beginning of the sixth century, Constantinople had also begun to take the title New Jerusalem, a fitting name for the capital of the new Israel.

The sixth century also saw the identification of Constantinople as a city protected by and devoted to the Virgin. By the seventh century, the Virgin intervened to preserve Constantinople from the attacks of the Avars; and in the fifteenth century, only a few years before the city's fall, Byzantine writers still called on the Virgin to preserve her city from assault once more. Equally important, not only did Constantinople acquire the relics and protection of the Virgin, but its churches became a veritable storehouse of holy relics. When Robert of Clari sacked the city with the Fourth Crusade in 1204, he listed with reverent glee the holy loot that his companions acquired. With the loss of Jerusalem as a pilgrimage city and central locus of Christian worship, Constantinople assumed that role. As the seventh-century churchman Theodore Syncellus wrote:

> And what other place could be named the "navel of the world" except the city where God has set the imperial residence of the Christians, and that he has created, by its central position, even that it might itself serve as the intermediary between East and West. It is against this city that the kings of the tribes and the peoples assemble. And it is their power that the Lord makes vain, who said to Zion, "Be without fear, Zion! Do not throw up your hands! Behold, your God is in your midst and it is he that will save you." (*On the Attack of the Avars,* 307)

Theodore wrote these lines after the Avar siege of 626, and it is noteworthy that he had also interpreted the Gog and Magog prophecies to refer to Constantinople instead of Jerusalem. Constantinople's geographic centrality was complemented by its ideological centrality as the crossing point of both Christian and Roman universal apocalyptic expectations, and one that allowed the redefinition and appropriation of apocalyptic prophecies of the restoration and glorification of Jerusalem.[25]

The Christian Romans' firm belief that their empire was, by definition, victorious did not of course prevent defeat, and defeat brought with it a challenge to the assumptions of Christian triumphalism: that the love and favor of God guaranteed victory. That military defeat was evidence of God's condemnation and the weakness of the loser's deity was a classical idea with a long history.[26] It was one that the Christians, well before Eusebius and Constantine, had heartily embraced. Christianity was God's true faith, and the Christian Romans' victories proved they were God's chosen people. The Jews' defeat and loss of their kingdom were an important foil for this historical apologetic;[27] it followed that Christians would never suffer such a loss because God would not allow his chosen people to be overthrown.

For this reason, even before the seventh century, Christian Romans were faced with the historical and religious dilemma of defeat when warring against Persians, Goths, and Huns. Military disasters puzzled the Byzantines, and even Procopius was forced to concede that he was unable to explain the fall of Antioch to the Persians in 540 "for no cause that appears to us" (*Wars* 2.10.4–5).[28] The extent of these defeats, however, was far less than in the seventh century:

defeats in the West were distant, the Balkans expendable, and the Persian successes in the East remained raids. Christian triumphalism bent but did not break, and by and large both ecclesiastical and secular writers followed a triumphalist historical perspective, even if occasionally they did so uneasily.[29] Rather than challenge the triumphal model, Byzantine writers explained defeat as momentary diversions caused by an individual ruler's, rather than the citizens', sins—a distinction that preserved the claims for Christ's power, and the sanctity of the Christian imperial office.

Nonetheless, during the first Christian imperial centuries, a different explanation of defeat also emerged, although it was far less popular than that of the emperor's vice.[30] Trying to explain the events that led to Constantine's and the church's victory, Eusebius proposed an explanation of the Great Persecution that held the Christian community's own sins responsible for its calamities:

> God himself has at all times been the guide of our affairs, at the right time punishing and correcting his people through misfortunes, and again thereafter, following sufficient punishment, showing mercy and goodwill to those holding their hopes in him. (*Hist. eccl.* 9.8.15)

The battle of the Milvian bridge brought the arrival of an imperial protector and demonstrated Christianity's truth: it also was the ultimate proof of God's forgiveness. The Christians' new power to confront persecutors with their own weapons transformed the way in which Christ's people saw the favor of their God. Once the empire became Christian and Christ was put to the martial test, it was unthinkable that defeat, the failure of Christ to protect his own, could stem from Christ's weakness. The shock of Rome's fall was so strong in the West that, through Augustine, it unhinged the triumphalist formula of victory and divine favor (see chapter 9 above). In the East, the effect was not as severe, yet it was strong enough that Sozomen could assert that "all persons of good sense were aware that the calamities which this siege entailed upon the Romans were indications of divine wrath sent to chastise them" (*Eccl. Hist.* 9.6). Significantly, the argument that the citizens' sins were responsible for military disasters was limited at this time to the West. Procopius had Gaiseric claim that he chose to attack Rome because its inhabitants were those "against whom God is angered" (*Wars* 3.5.25).

The sixth-century Byzantines endured few disasters that severely tested their patience and optimism. The seventh century, however, was something else altogether. The disasters of this age—Jerusalem captured twice by heathens; the loss of the Balkans, the Levant, and Egypt; and three sieges of Constantinople within one hundred years—were constant, geographically close, and quite unprecedented. They shattered the post-Constantinian, triumphalist identification of Christian truth and Roman victory. Throughout the seventh century, Byzantine authors lamented how their enemies taunted them with their God's evident weakness. For as long as the Heraclian dynasty held the throne (610–711), which was during the worst of the invasions, Christian defeat could not be officially explained by an emperor's personal vice. Religious dissidents like Dyotheletes and the Monophysites might accuse the emperor of heresy, but they hardly represented an official or—even within the empire—a majority view. New political conditions required a new model of Christian imperialism and a different explanation of seventh-century Christian disaster.

It was above all the psychological effects of defeat that demanded a response. The archbishop John of Thessalonica, who wrote the *Miracles of Saint Demetrius* around 615–620, recorded the saint's paternal care of his city's hard-pressed congregation; and, not surprisingly, the majority of the miracles narrate the city's often narrow escapes from the attacks of the Slavs and Bulgars. But a generation earlier the Romans had stood on the Danube, and John conceded that the reversal of fortune had shaken the faith of his congregation:

> For the soul, weakened and suffering with various and assorted ills of the body, [at first] made ardent with the memory of God, becomes finally increasingly weaker in the faith, and falls, from a feeling of frustration into anger, even uttering and murmuring abominations against God.[31]

As bad as conditions in Thessalonica became, it had at least held off barbarian attacks. In Jerusalem, God's chastisements had climaxed in the Persian capture of the city in 614, and then, after its eventual recovery by the Byzantines in 628–630, its fall into Arab hands. Antiochus Monachus, whose *Fall of Jerusalem to the Persians in 614* recorded the siege, fall, and sack of the city, explained that the greatest threat to the souls of the inhabitants was not the Persians but the temptation by the devil to despair:

> For the devil stands and tempts your hearts . . . and says to you, "Oh Christians, how you err and fool yourselves. For Christ has washed his hands of you and ignored you. . . . For you are hated by him and are his enemies, not his friends; for did he not aid your enemies and strengthen them more than you, and strip you of his armor and take away from you his protection?"[32]

The temptation to doubt Christ's power was real enough, and even Antiochus was forced to admit that "a few weak-minded" Christians actually renounced Christ (*Fall of Jerusalem* 18.6). The anti-Jewish dialogue *Papiscus and Philo* evidences Christian conversion to Islam in the wake of its victories. When the Christian considers the effect that heathen victories have had on Christians and Jews, he defends his religion only by contrast, "If some Christians have apostasized, they are not as many as you [Jews] have had apostasize, even though you are not being murdered for being Christian."[33]

The sense that the last times had arrived inspired the Byzantines to adopt extraordinary measures to reaffirm Christianity and its imperial institutions. Perhaps one of the most radical of these was the forced baptism of Jews. Yet even here contemporaries judged events with an apocalyptic eye. Maximus the Confessor objected strongly to such measures, not out of any concern for the Jews but out of anxiety over the apocalyptic implications of their baptism:

> I have reservations about their expected apostasy according to the holy apostle [2 Thess. 2:3], lest, initially, there take place their assimilation with the faithful people, through which they would be able, without raising suspicion among the more naive, to harvest a crop of scandals against our holy faith, and that clear and unambiguous sign be discovered of the disturbances of the final consummation.[34]

Times were such that while Maximus as a Christian objected to the baptism of Jews on apocalyptic grounds, it was commonly recognized that the Antichrist would arise from the Jews. On the other hand, at least some of the baptized Jews accepted their baptism because the destruction of the Roman Empire meant the end of the world (*Doctrine of Jacob* 63) and consequently argued:

> Therefore, let none of us disdain the faith in Christ, lest, when we have fallen into such an indescribably great chaos of destruction, we not be saved; rather, let us believe in Christ the king of

glory, offering thanks to God and to the men through whom God commanded us to be baptised violently. (*Doctrine of Jacob* 79)

The seventh-century imperial crisis led contemporaries to seek explanations and redress for the "indescribably great chaos of destruction," and led Christians, and perhaps some Jews as well, to undertake actions that would have been unthinkable in the fifth or sixth century. The challenge to the Christian's faith in Christ's power that was raised by defeat required a reaffirmation of Christ's love for the Roman Empire and a historical framework that could supply Christians with a pattern that would restore order to a world turned upside down. This search for order created Byzantine apocalypticsm: a literary genre designed to fill the jagged gap between reality and ideal.

The rupture of imperial history and the consequent religio-political crisis led to the creation of apocalyptic historical schemes of imperial restoration. This eschatological dynamic remained strong until the end of Byzantium. The historical perspective that drove Byzantine apocalypticism was a tripartite historical cycle that required God's punishment of the Christians' collective sins, divine forgiveness, and the eventual restoration of the empire. Two further elements were vital to this eschatological cycle: the critical role of the imperial office and emperor; and the centrality of Constantinople, the New Jerusalem in the divine plan.

The seventh century, the period of the Arab and Slav invasions and the final shattering of the imperial hegemony, stands as the formative period of Byzantine apocalypticism. It produced the founding works that established the general, and in many cases, the specific, parameters of Byzantine apocalyptic traditions. This period of crises and historical redefinition lasted until the ninth or tenth century, when Byzantium's recovery no longer seemed to require an apocalyptic scenario. By the tenth century, a Byzantine emperor was once more campaigning in the Holy Land, and the restoration of the empire that might in the early ninth century have seemed possible only in a distant future was very much present. The period extending from the seventh into the ninth century constitutes the golden age of Byzantine apocalypses, when the formative texts and models were created. As Paul Magdalino explained, after the eleventh century, "the discreet silence of intellectuals on eschatological matters probably does reflect growing scepticism or indifference" (Magdalino 1993, 32).

The most important text for the later development of Byzantine apocalypticism ironically was written not within the political boundaries of Byzantium at all but in Syria (in Syriac) shortly after the Muslim conquest: the *Apocalypse of Pseudo-Methodius*. The author of *Pseudo-Methodius* appropriated the name of the third-century bishop of Patara, although different manuscripts name Methodius as the bishop of Olympus, or even Rome. A firm supporter of the imperial order, the author seems to have been a Monophysite, although doubt remains about this identification. Originally written around 690, shortly after the fall of Syria to the Arabs, *Pseudo-Methodius* was translated into Greek very quickly after its composition.[35] It shares with other contemporary texts a preoccupation with the effects of the invasion on Christian morale. It excoriated apostates, "All those who are weak in the faith will be made manifest and they will voluntarily separate themselves from the holy churches" (*Pseudo-Methodius* 12.6; ed. Lolos, 114). Characteristically, the author transformed apostasy from a sign of Christian weakness to a part of God's plan for the greater glory of the faithful. "And why does God allow the faithful to undergo these trials? Why, so that the faithful will appear and the unfaithful will be made manifest, the wheat separated from the chaff; for this time is a fire of trial" (13.4, ed. Lolos, 118).

Pseudo-Methodius can be divided into two sections: a "historical" section, which narrates the history of Rome and Byzantium; and an "apocalyptic" section, which narrates the Arab invasion (as still in the future), the invasion of the "unclean races" and Gog and Magog, and the final defeat of the Antichrist. A comparison of the Greek and Syriac versions of *Pseudo-Methodius* reveals how authors of apocalypses modified their historical narrative according to the varying fortunes of the empire in the seventh century in order to ensure that the Christians would be rewarded and their empire preserved. Both versions highlight the defeat of Rome's historical enemies, the Arabs, followed by her mythic enemies, Gog and Magog. But the later Greek version also incorporates the Arab siege of Constantinople in the 670s into the apocalyptic scheme of imperial restoration. Indeed, the Greek author wove this victory at the gates of the city into the repentance and restoration cycle as the moment of God's decision to relent:

> Woe to you, Byzas, that Ishmael possesses you; every horse of Ishmael will tread over you; and their leader will set his tent before your face, Byzas, and begin to make war. And he will break the Xylocercus gate, and march up to the Bous [in Constantinople]. Then the Bous will bellow, and the Xylocercus will scream as it is struck by the Ishmaelites. Then a voice will come out of heaven, saying, "This punishment is sufficient for me." (13.9–10; ed. Lolos, 120–22)

Pseudo-Methodius presented a siege of Constantinople as the final trial of the Byzantines. The Syriac version had no contemporary victory on which to hang its narrative; the Greek version simply fitted the victory at Constantinople into a historical framework plastic enough to assimilate it. Such an apocalyptic "moment" at Constantinople was used in several other apocalypses. In the *Apocalypse of Pseudo-Chrysostom* the Arabs advance to the center of Constantinople before God relents and eventually leads the Byzantines to victory over the invaders.

The centrality of Constantinople, its imperial tradition, and the conflict with the Arabs begins, however, in the "historical" section. There the author wove elements of the Genesis narrative and the *Alexander Romance* together to produce an unusual demonstration of the power of Rome and the destructiveness of the Arabs and an equally unusual reconstruction of the origin of Constantinople. Already at the time of Ishmael himself, the Arabs had raided as far as Rome, and only at the time of Gideon was Israel delivered from the "sons of Ishmael." Yet even as they were driven back to the desert, *Pseudo-Methodius* predicted that "they will lay waste the land and conquer all the world. . . . And there will be no people or empire under heaven strong enough to fight them" (5.8–9; ed. Lolos, 68–70). *Pseudo-Methodius,* however, predicted that ultimately the Arabs would be defeated by the Romans, "for that empire will be exalted over all the kingdoms of the peoples, and it will certainly not be overcome by any of them until the end of time for it has a shield by which all will be defeated by it" (ibid., 70). Thus, the historical section set up the confrontation between Ishmaelites and Romans that is the highlight of the "apocalyptic" section, foreshadowed the divine aid that Rome would receive, and confirmed the marriage of Romanity and Christianity that underlay the imperial ideal.

To establish further the imperial credentials of Constantinople, *Pseudo-Methodius* links Byzantium to the imperial tradition of Alexander the Great. According to *Pseudo-Methodius,* Alexander was the son of Philip and Chouseth, the daughter of the king of Ethiopia. After the death of Alexander, Chouseth was given in marriage to Byzas, founder of Byzantium. Their daughter was Byzantia, who was given in marriage to Romulus, who, greatly in love with her, gave her Rome as his wedding gift. Thus, *Pseudo-Methodius* reverses as it were the donation of Constantine, so that it is Constantinople that receives the rule of Rome. And once again,

Pseudo-Methodius links Christianity and empire. Citing Psalm 67:32, that the princes of Ethiopia will hold out their hands to God, the author affirms that the offspring of Chouseth will rule for all time, only transferring the rule to Christ himself at the time of the Antichrist. Until that time, the author affirms a second time that "there is no people or kingdom under the sky able to conquer the empire of the Christians" (9.8–9; ed. Lolos, 88).

The "apocalyptic" section of *Pseudo-Methodius* is in some respects more historical than the "historical" section, for it contains the narrative of the Arab invasion in an apocalyptic setting. As we saw above, the Arabs would carry their victories up to Constantinople itself. But the victory at Constantinople is only the climax of an actual historical narrative of Arab victories that includes Arab raids against Cyprus, Cappadocia, and Rhodes. This section begins with a further reaffirmation of Rome as the final empire, meant to endure until Christ receives its rule from the hand of its emperor. It goes on to explain the cause of Arab victories: the apologetic end of the apocalypse. The author clearly outlines a cycle of sin, repentance, and restoration to explain Christian Roman defeat. Arab victories were not due to God's love for them, but rather as a punishment of the sinful Romans:

> The Lord says to Israel through Moses, "Not because the Lord God loves you does he lead you into the promised land to settle it, but on account of the sins of those who dwell there." Likewise for the sons of Ishmael, the Lord God does not give them the power to rule the lands of the Christians because he loves them, but on account of the sinfulness abounding among the Christians. (11.5, ed. Lolos, 98)

Pseudo-Methodius put Jews and Arabs on the same level as instruments of God's chastisement. In both cases, God permitted a rejected race to conquer because of the inhabitants' sins, not the victors' virtues. Nor was the comparison of Jews and Arabs accidental; the Jews were the model for the Arabs. "Did not the Hebrews rule for one thousand years?" But they ruled no longer. In a ninth-century Daniel "vision" (the Slavonic Daniel) the author makes the same point without employing the Jews as a foil:

> And Daniel said to the angel, "Tell me, Lord, why do these afflictions befall the entire world?" And the angel said to me, "Because the Lord does not love Ishmael will he give him strength to encompass the land of Rome? [No], but because of the sins of those residing in it."[36]

Both texts were careful to affirm that the victories of the Arabs had no relationship to God's favor but were merely a means of drawing the Romans to repentance. In fact, *Pseudo-Methodius* went on to affirm that the Christian Romans possessed an eternal *imperium*, "For every realm and every power of this world will be destroyed except this: for it will war and not be subdued" (10.3; ed. Lolos, 92).

The defeat of the Arabs inaugurates an era of peace that is broken by the appearance of the "unclean races," led by Gog and Magog, who were locked up by Alexander the Great behind a great bronze gate between two mountains. They are initially victorious, but are destroyed by an angel sent by God "in one moment." After this, the Roman emperor will move to Jerusalem, where, when the Antichrist is revealed:

> The emperor of the Romans will go up to Golgotha, there at the place the wood of the cross is set up. . . . And the emperor of the Romans will take his crown, and set it upon the cross and stretch his hands to heaven, and hand over his empire to God the Father. (14.3; ed. Lolos, 132)

The cross and crown rise and are accepted into heaven, whereupon the last earthly emperor dies and the Antichrist comes into his own, eventually sitting enthroned in the renewed Temple in Jerusalem. Christ then appears, destroys the Antichrist, and brings the world and the apocalypse to an end.

This narrative of the last emperor, which was one of the most compelling apocalyptic passages of the Middle Ages and which had a profound influence in various guises beyond the borders of Byzantium, served a more limited role in the context of *Pseudo-Methodius* itself. There it primarily maintains the link between Christ and the empire beyond the end of the world. The placement of the crown on the cross is the symbolic climax of the union of the Roman imperialism and religion. The Antichrist does not rule as a Roman emperor; on the contrary, after the death of the last emperor, "every realm and rule will cease," including the earthly Roman Empire. Ultimately, even at the end of the world, the emperor remains the connection between heaven and earth and the means by which Christ's aid is enlisted.

Pseudo-Methodius illustrates well the three basic themes of (1) divine forgiveness and imperial restoration, (2) Constantinople as an apocalyptic catalyst, and (3) the imperial office as a divinely ordained institution ultimately to be assumed (or assimilated) by Christ himself. Other apocalypses emphasize different aspects of these themes. Several also introduce lists of historical emperors in the apocalyptic future by means of *vaticinia ex eventu* (i.e., history disguised as prophecy). An example can be found in the twelfth-century *Oracles of Leo* attributed to the emperor Leo VI the Wise (late ninth century), which is more interested in imperial succession than in the end of the world.

Pseudo-Methodius represents the dominant stream of Byzantine apocalyptic that emphasized imperial restoration, but a second, less imperialized stream was also part of the Byzantine apocalyptic tradition. It is represented by a series of Daniel "Visions" and related texts. In contrast to *Pseudo-Methodius's* affirmation of imperial restoration and especially the importance of Constantinople in that process, the *Apocalypse of Daniel* shows little concern for imperial restoration and even submits Constantinople itself to destruction.[37] This apocalypse, like *Pseudo-Methodius,* can be divided into two parts: a historical one and an apocalyptic one. Unlike *Pseudo-Methodius,* however, the historical section of the *Apocalypse of Daniel* is in fact based on recent Byzantine history. This apocalypse reflects, if not historical Byzantine reverses, then the psychological effect of earlier reverses. Nonetheless, it was written in the early ninth century after the worst of the Arab invasions, and although other ninth-century apocalypses take note of Arab successes, like the conquest of Sicily in the 820s, the *Apocalypse of Daniel* shows less direct concern for the Arabs or worry that they are an immediate threat to the empire. Instead, a different threat begins to take shape from the West, not the East.

The text begins with the rise of Islam and the victories of "the sons of Hagar," who, in their pride, exclaim, "Where is the God of the Romans? There is no one who aids them, for truly they are defeated" (3.5; ed. Berger, 12). Once again, an attack on Constantinople is the moment at which God intervenes. The Arab leader strikes the "seven-hilled" city and the inhabitants despair: "And then the lords of the Romans blaspheme, saying, 'Woe is me, woe is me! We have no emperor either on earth or in heaven.' And after this cry, the Lord pours his mercy upon the Romans" (5.2; ed. Berger, 13). At this point, there will be a "roar" from heaven, a "cry of angels," and God will raise up an emperor who defeats the Arabs. The parallels with *Pseudo-Methodius* are obvious, but the *Apocalypse of Daniel* adds the detail in chapter 3 that the first letter of the emperor's name is *kappa.* Although the close literary ties between the *Apocalypse of*

Daniel and *Pseudo-Methodius* create a generic image of the emperor, and qualify any positive identification, it is possible to propose that the victorious emperor is Constantine IV (668–685), who defeated the Arabs in the siege that inspired the Byzantine version of *Pseudo-Methodius*. Thus, unlike *Pseudo-Methodius*, whose "history" is largely mythological and whose apocalyptic immediacy made the Arab siege the first sign of the end, the *Apocalypse of Daniel* set the Arab siege within a historical framework that included divine intervention but went on with a highly elliptical survey of eighth-century Byzantine emperors, beginning with Leo III (717–740), continuing through his successors,[38] and ending with an evil empress (chaps. 5–6). The descriptions of these rulers employ many generic clichés, and it is difficult to identify any-one but Leo III, a ruler with a "name like a beast," although the empress might be Irene (797–802).[39]

Generally, we view the eighth century in the light of iconoclasm, but the author makes no direct mention of this. What interests him is the destruction of Byzantium by a flood, as well as the transfer of imperial power from Byzantium to Rome in the reign of the evil empress. It is this event that climaxes the historical section of the apocalypse and brings it to an end:

> Woe to you miserable Babylon, mother of cities, because God pours his anger, full of fire, upon you and your high walls will fall. And nothing will remain of you except one column of the great scepter of Byzantium, Constantine the Great, so that those sailing on the sea there will mourn you. (*Apoc. Dan.* 9.3–5; ed. Berger, 15)

The destruction of Constantinople, the "seven-hilled Babylon," uses passages on the end of Tyre and Babylon found in Ezekiel 26–27 and Revelation 18. The apocalypse in the *Life of Andrew the Fool* gives further information about the destruction of Constantinople. A disciple of Andrew claims that "some say" that Hagia Sophia will survive the flood by floating over the waters, a notion of which he is swiftly disabused. Andrew explains, however, that the column will survive because it contains the holy nails with which Christ was fastened to the cross.[40]

The destruction of Constantinople does not end the Roman Empire. "The empire will depart from you. . . . For at that moment, the rule will be taken from Byzantium and given to Rome" (9.6–9; ed. Berger, 15). The combination of an evil empress and the transfer of imperial power from Byzantium to Rome may possibly reflect one Byzantine reaction to the coronation of Charlemagne in 800. Whether or not the author had Charlemagne in mind, the *Apocalypse of Daniel*'s vision has discovered the West in a way that is very different from the first redaction of *Pseudo-Methodius,* whose primary concern is the Arabs.[41]

The "apocalyptic" section of the *Apocalypse of Daniel* details the rise and career of the Antichrist. Characteristically, the Antichrist is a Jew from the tribe of Dan. The thematic use of the Antichrist is quite unlike that found in *Pseudo-Methodius*, whose main interest is explaining how the Roman Empire will eventually be restored and therefore employs Old Testament prophecies of Israel's restoration to that end. On the contrary, the *Apocalypse of Daniel* and related texts seek to explain away such prophecies not by applying them to the restored empire but by referring them to the Jewish kingdom of the Antichrist. As the related *Apocalypse of Andrew the Fool* explains: "For Paul said that they will be saved not from eternal punishment, but from so many years wandering around in foreign lands, and from the abuse of the gentiles and their extraordinary shame" (ed. Rydén, 210). Far from restoring the Roman Empire, the Jews, led by the Antichrist, "will oppress the nation of the Christians throughout all the earth, and they will torment the Romans unto death," as the *Apocalypse of Daniel* makes clear (10.6–7;

ed. Berger, 15). Eventually, plagues and famine will cover the earth, and three men will come forth, "two from heaven, one from the earth," to denounce the Antichrist and be martyred by him. This inaugurates a final persecution of Christians and the appearance of Christ, who defeats the Antichrist and casts him with his demons into hell.

One can only guess the cause of the *Apocalypse of Daniel*'s failure to argue for imperial restoration. If its editor, Klaus Berger, is correct and it was written in the wake of the coronation of Charlemagne, the text's pessimism can perhaps be understood as a reflection of the sudden appearance of an imperial competitor. Whatever the cause, this and other ninth-century texts introduce new nations into Byzantine apocalyptic (see Pertusi 1988). It is in this period that the "blond race" makes its appearance to replace the receding threat of the Arabs: "There is a prophecy that the race of the Hagarenes will enter the city and kill many by the sword. But I say that the blond race will also enter here, whose name begins with the seventeenth letter."[42] The seventeenth letter is *rho*, and the "blond race" is the Rus, who raided the outskirts of Constantinople in 860. But the Rus are not the only "blond race." The *Slavonic Daniel* narrates the victory of the Roman emperor in the West, and the reunion of the eastern and western Roman lands against the Arabs. "And [the emperor] will send his forces into the inner Roman lands, and they will tame the Blond Beards. Both will drive away Ishmael."[43] In the twelfth century and especially following the Fourth Crusade, when the Latins conquered and held Constantinople, apocalyptic authors found it increasingly easy to assimilate the "blond race" into their apocalyptic schemes (Pertusi 1988, 50–62).

The victories over barbarians and over Gog and Magog are generally accomplished either by a Roman emperor or during the historical period of the empire. The last act of the apocalyptic drama, the account of the Antichrist's career, is almost always introduced by the end of the Roman Empire—most often by the surrender of the last emperor's crown, rule, and life in Jerusalem. The Antichrist himself, then, is not associated with the empire at all. On the contrary, he is often said to arise from the Jews, specifically following Gen. 49:17, from the tribe of Dan. Often, in accordance with Matt. 11:21 and Luke 10:13, he is said to be conceived at Chorazin, born at Bethsaida, and ruling at Capernaum. Eventually, he will return to Jerusalem, where he will be denounced by Enoch and Elijah (and occasionally a third prophetic figure as well), all of whom he will martyr. He will then begin the last and worst persecution of Christians. The Byzantine apocalypses' Antichrist is certainly their most scripturally based apocalyptic element; it is also among the consistent elements from text to text.

The Antichrist not only arises from the Jews but is generally accepted by them and becomes their leader. In some apocalypses, he gathers the Jews again to Jerusalem in order to initiate his persecution of Christians. Thus, the transition from the Roman Empire to the Jewish "empire" is an important consequence of the last emperor motif in Byzantine apocalypses, and effectively juxtaposes not only the Christ, who has received the crown and rule of the Romans from the last emperor, with the "Jewish" Antichrist, but also the Christian Romans and their empire with the Jews and their restoration claims. This contrast is a motif developed by the Byzantines in the seventh century as well, a further apologetic method of imperial renewal that juxtaposed the Jews, who were hated by God and whose kingdom was never to be restored, with the Christians, who were loved by God, and whose empire would be restored after their punishment and repentance.[44] As the *Apocalypse of Andrew the Fool* shows, the Byzantines remained uneasy about entirely dismissing the Old Testament claims of Jewish restoration. The Antichrist legend allowed the Byzantines to establish their own claims to Old Testament restoration prophecies; maintain their apologetic juxtaposition between Jewish and Christian claims to restoration and forgiveness; and, finally, explain Jewish restoration in a manner that complemented their exegetical goals.

Byzantine apocalyptic reveals itself to be remarkably single-minded in its defense of Romanity, although at times somewhat limited in its imagination. The apocalypses' use of traditional motives argues for a homogeneous literary culture whose authors were aware of these literary traditions and at least some other works of the genre: a literary ethos that characterizes other Byzantine genres, both ecclesiastical and secular. Nonetheless, it would be misleading to see Byzantine apocalypses as artificial literary creations. Nor would it be fair to dismiss these works as merely "apologetic." Apologetic they were, but the problem that they addressed ran throughout Byzantine society and transcended any narrow political definition. On the contrary, the empire's geopolitical crisis in the seventh century went to the heart of the Byzantine religious sensibility by disrupting the accepted divine imperial order. The evidence of the seventh century demonstrates that Christ's power was challenged, and at least some despaired. The Byzantine apocalypses did not resolve that psychological tension, for the Roman Empire was never restored. For this reason, the themes that dominate Byzantine apocalypses at the beginning of the genre remained dominant to the end. But these works also show how the medieval mind confronted the transition from antiquity and the end of the classical, Mediterranean order. The Byzantine need for *taxis*—the appropriate order of things—found emotional expression in their apocalypses and reveals with a clarity found in almost no other genre how Byzantium's historical dilemma was at the same time political, social, and religious, as well as how close together the Byzantines set the heavenly and the earthly realms.

NOTES

1. See, for example, the use of apocalyptic sources in Walter E. Kaegi, "Initial Byzantine Reactions to the Arab Conquest," *Church History* 38 (1969): especially 145–48.

2. Its historical perspective is decidedly iconodule, as shown by R. Maisano, *L'Apocalisse Apocrifa di Leone di Constantinopoli* (Naples: Morano, 1975).

3. The Byzantines entertained some suspicions about the authorship of Revelation; see Podskalsky 1972, 77ff.; Alexander 1980, 62; and Magdalino 1993, 4ff.

4. There is no full critical edition of the Syriac form of *Pseudo-Methodius* at present. For a discussion, as well as an English translation from the text of one manuscript, see Alexander 1985, chap. 1. There are four redactions of the Greek text edited by Anastasios Lolos in two volumes: *Die Apokalypse des Ps.-Methodios* (Meisenheim am Glan: Hain, 1976), containing the first two redactions; *Die dritte und vierte Redaktion des Ps.-Methodios* (Meisenheim am Glan: Hain, 1978). (The first redaction will be cited throughout this essay.) The longer form of the Latin translation was edited by Ernst Sackur, *Sibyllinische Texte und Forschungen* (Halle: Niemeyer, 1898), 59-96, of which there is a partial English translation in Bernard McGinn, *Visions of the End: Apocalyptic Traditions in the Middle Ages* (New York: Columbia University Press, 1979), 77–78.

5. See I. Levi, "*L'Apocalypse de Zerubabel,*" *Revue des Études Juives* 68 (1914): 149–50 and 153 n. 1. On the etymology of the name, see p. 152, especially n. 6. In fact, the etymology of *Hermolaos/Armilus* is

confused. Lolos (*Die Apokalypse des Ps.-Methodios*) suggests that it is a Syrian or Hebrew transliteration of Romulus, while Levi agrees with the explanation given by *Zerubbabel*. (See chapter 14 below.)

6. On Byzantine, as well as later Jewish views of the Antichrist, including the Armilus figure, see Bernard McGinn, *Antichrist: Two Thousand Years of the Human Fascination with Evil* (San Francisco: HarperSanFrancisco, 1994), chap. 4 (also see chapter 14 below).

7. *Pseudo-Methodius* 9.5 (ed. Lolos, 86). See Alexander 1985, 57–59.

8. *Doctrina Jacobi nuper baptizati*, ed. N. Bonwetsch, Abhandlungen der königlichen Gesellschaft der Wissenschaften zu Göttingen, phil-hist. Klasse, n.s. 13 (Berlin: Weidmann, 1910), 74; see also pp. 59, 70–71, 76.

9. See *Doctrine* 75; cf. *Apocalypse of Zerubbabel* (ed. Levi, 155).

10. On the views of salvation history and the role of the empire in Eusebius and the other church historians considered here, see Glenn F. Chesnut, *The First Christian Historians: Eusebius, Socrates, Sozomen, Theodoret and Evagrius* (Paris: Beauchesne, 1977).

11. Ed. I. A. Henkel (Leipzig, 1902).

12. The victory of Constantine at the Milvian bridge was only one example of the triumphal nature of Christian political thought; see Eusebius, *Life of Constantine*, ed. I. A. Henkel (Leipzig, 1904), 1.28–38.

13. The identification of imperialism and religion had been asserted in the second century by Plutarch, who had described how Alexander had brought not only his arms but also "[t]he power of religion: O wondrous power of philosophic teaching, that brought the Indians to worship Greek gods" (Plutarch, *The Fortune of Alexander* [Loeb edition], 4:393). Before Plutarch, Strabo had made the same point, namely, that barbarians were brought into the circuit of civilized races not only through Roman secular culture but through the gods that gave their conquerers the power of victory.

14. Evagrius Scholasticus, *Ecclesiastical History*, ed. J. Bidez and L. Parmentier (London, 1898) 3.41.

15. Ed. L. Parmentier and F. Schweidweiler, 2nd ed. (Berlin, 1954).

16. Theodoret, *Ecclesiastical History* 5.24, for the victory of Theodosius. See Sabine MacCormack, "Christ and Emperor, Time and Ceremonial in Sixth Century Byzantium and Beyond," *Byzantion* 52 (1982): 303–4, on victory as proof of Christian and imperial universalism.

17. Ed. J. Bidez and G. Hansen (Berlin, 1960); see also 7.23, where God opens a miraculous path for Theodosius II's army.

18. Ed. W. Bright (Oxford, 1878).

19. Procopius, whose *Wars* had a very different literary ethos from that of the church historians, explained that the Persian king Chosroes's fourth invasion of the empire had been undertaken "not against Justinian, the emperor of the Romans, nor indeed against any other man, but only against the God whom the Christians worship" (*Wars* 2.26.2).

20. *Three Byzantine Military Treatises*, ed. George Dennis (Washington: Dumbarton Oaks, 1985), 320.

21. See also the guarantees of victory that Theodosius receives for his faith in Socrates (*Ecclesiastical History* 7.18 and 20); cf. Sozomen, *Ecclesiastical History* 9.16.

22. See Herbert Hunger, *Prooimion: Elemente der byzantinischen Kaiseridee in den Arengen der Urkunden* (Vienna, 1964), 74.

23. On one occasion angels appear to announce victory to some travelers; see Socrates, *Ecclesiastical History* 7.18.

24. Theodore Syncellus, *On the Attack of the Avars*, ed. L. Sternbach, Analecta Avarica (Cracow, 1900), 303. See also the discussion of the apocalyptic role of icons in Magdalino 1993, 15–18.

25. See David Olster, *Roman Defeat, Christian Response, and the Literary Construction of the Jew* (Philadelphia: University of Pennsylvania Press, 1994), 72–79.

26. See L. Bonniec, "Aspects réligieux de la guerre à Rome," in *Problèmes de la guerre à Rome* (Paris, 1969), 101–15, especially 111–15; A. Michel, "Les lois de la guerre et les problèmes romains dans la philosophie de Cicéron," ibid., 171–77; and R. M. Grant, "War—Just, Holy, Unjust—in Hellenistic and Early Christian Thought," *Augustinianum* 20 (1980): 174–78.

27. For Eusebius on the fall of the Jewish kingdom and its proof of the Christian religion, see *Tricennial Oration* 16.5. On this, consult R. M. Grant, *Eusebius as Church Historian* (Oxford: Clarendon Press, 1980), 97–113; idem, "Eusebius, Josephus and the Fate of the Jews," in *Society of Biblical Literature 1979 Seminar Papers,* ed. P. J. Achtemeier (Missoula, Mont.: Scholars Press, 1979), 2:69–86.

28. See also Chosroes's speech on the fall of Antioch proclaiming that sorrows must necessarily accompany good fortune. Antioch's fall also puzzled Menander Protector, but he found a rather different explanation than Procopius: "This is God's way of punishing the excessive good fortune of the Romans, lest they think that they differ greatly from others" (*Fragmenta Historicorum Graecorum,* vol. 4; fr. 6.1). Menander thus ascribed Persian victory to God's will as well, but hardly to the chastisement of sin.

29. See Walter Kaegi, *Byzantium and the Decline of Rome* (Princeton: Princeton University Press, 1968), 176–223; and Chesnut, *First Christian Historians,* 223–42.

30. Perhaps the reason for this is that this idea was appropriated by pagans to explain Roman decline. Ironically, one of the last pagan historians of Rome, Zosimus, first insisted that the Roman Empire had fallen on account of its citizens' sins. His claim left a powerful impression on succeeding generations of Christian authors. Evagrius, writing nearly a hundred years later, felt constrained to refute Zosimus in his *Ecclesiastical History* and insisted on the empire's health just on the eve of the Arab invasions.

31. P. Lemerle, *Les plus anciens recueils des Miracles de Saint Démétrius* (Paris: CNRS, 1979), 1:76.20–24; see also 149.11–12, for a description of God as teacher.

32. *Antiochus Monachus: La prise de Jérusalem par les Perses,* ed. G. Garitte, CSCO 203 (Louvain: Peeters, 1952), 13.65.

33. *Dialogue between a Christian and a Jew Entitled Antibolê Papiskou kai Philônos pros monaxon tina,* ed. A. C. McGiffert (New York, 1889), 75.

34. From R. Devresse, "La fin inédite d'une lettre de saint Maxime: un baptême forcé de Juifs à Carthage en 632," *Revue des sciences religieuses* 17 (1935): 35.

35. The dating of *Pseudo-Methodius* has been a source of disagreement. Although some would date the Syriac original close to the middle of the seventh century, a strong case has been made for the later dating, especially by G. J. Reinink, "Pseudo-Methodius und die Legende vom römischen Endkaiser," in *The Use and Abuse of Eschatology in the Middle Ages,* ed. Werner Verbeke, Daniel Verhelst, and Andries Welkenhuysen (Leuven: Leuven University Press, 1988), 82–111.

36. Adapted from the translation in Alexander 1985, 69.

37. The *Apocalypse of Daniel* has been edited in *Die griechische Daniel-Diegese: Eine altkirchlichen Apokalypse,* ed. Klaus Berger (Leiden: E. J. Brill, 1976). There is an English translation of a somewhat different version by G. T. Zervos in *The Old Testament Pseudepigrapha: Apocalyptic Literature and Testaments,* ed. James H. Charlesworth (Garden City, N.Y.: Doubleday, 1983), 763–70.

38. Perhaps the civil war that is mentioned is a reference to the war between Leo III's son, Constantine V, and his general Artavasdos.

39. Lennart Rydén argues that the evil empress in this apocalypse (clearly related to the *Apocalypse of Daniel*) cannot be associated with Irene ("The Andreas Salos Apocalypse: Greek Text, Translation, and Commentary," *Dumbarton Oaks Papers* 28 [1974]: 249–51); he supplies a variety of biblical citations to demonstrate the generic character of the evil empress theme. Rydén's argument represents the difficulty of measuring topos and authorial intent. Nevertheless, Berger (*Daniel-Diegese,* 6), who is equally aware of apocalyptic topoi of the evil empress, does not hesitate to read the figure in that apocalypse as Irene.

40. See *Apocalypse of Andrew the Fool* (ed. Rydén, 211).

41. The related *Apocalypse of Andrew the Fool* also describes imperial rule passing from submerged Constantinople to Rome, Thessalonica, and "Sylaion" (ed. Rydén, 211).

42. This is taken from one of the manuscripts of the *Apocalypse of Andrew the Fool;* see the edition of Rydén, 201, and the translation on p. 215 n. 8.

43. As translated in Alexander 1985, 70.

44. See Olster, *Roman Defeat,* 116–37.

⌐ BIBLIOGRAPHY _____

Agathias. 1967. *Historiarum libri quinqui.* Edited by R. Keydell. Berlin: de Gruyter.

Alexander, Paul J. 1968. "Medieval Apocalypses as Historical Sources." *American Historical Review* 73:997–1018. One of the seminal works of Byzantine apocalyptic scholarship, which demonstrates the importance of Byzantine apocalypses for understanding the broad scheme of medieval thought, as well as their significance as records of historical events.

———. 1980. "The Diffusion of Byzantine Apocalypses in the Medieval West." In *Prophecy and Millenarianism: Essays in Honour of Marjorie Reeves,* edited by Ann Williams, 53–106. Suffolk: Longmann.

———. 1985. *The Byzantine Apocalyptic Tradition.* Berkeley and Los Angeles: University of California Press. The best introductory text for Byzantine apocalypses.

Berger, Klaus. 1976. *Die griechische Daniel-Diegese: Eine altkirchliche Apokalypse.* Leiden: E. J. Brill. One of the most detailed and encyclopedic commentaries of a Byzantine apocalypse, incorporating material from a wide variety of apocalyptic traditions.

Magdalino, Paul. 1993. "The History of the Future and Its Uses: Prophecy, Policy and Propaganda." In *The Making of Byzantine History: Studies Dedicated to Donald M. Nicol,* edited by Roderick Beaton and Charlotte Roueché, 3–34. Centre for Hellenic Studies, King's College London Publications II. London. One of the most recent and successful efforts to follow the course of Byzantine apocalyptic from late antiquity to the fall of Byzantium in order to show how tied apocalyptic was to the Byzantine worldview.

Patlagean, Evelyne. 1981. "Byzance et son autre monde: Observations sur quelques récits." In *Faire Croire: Modalités de la diffusion et de la réception des messages religieux du XIIe au XVe siècle,* 201–22. Collection de l'École Française de Rome 51. Rome. Treats four later medieval apocalypses and otherwordly journey narratives.

Pertusi, Agostino. 1988. *Fine di Bisanzio e fine del mondo: Significato e ruolo storico delle profezie sulla cadulta di Constantinopoli in Oriente ed Occidente.* Rome: Istituto Storico per il Medio Evo. A comprehensive analysis of not only Byzantine but neighboring apocalyptic traditions about New Rome, its enemies and its competitors during the last half century of Byzantium.

Podskalsky, Gerhard. 1972. *Die Byzantinische Reichseschatologie: Die Periodizierung der Weltgeschichte in den 4. Grossreichen (Daniel 2 und 7) und dem tausendjährigen Friedensreiche (Apok. 20).* Munich: Fink. The best and most comprehensive survey of the political "theology" of Byzantine apocalypticism.

11

Apocalypticism and Church Reform: 1100–1500

Bernard McGinn
University of Chicago

> When I was a young man I heard a sermon about the end of the world preached before the people in the cathedral of Paris. According to this, as soon as the number of a thousand years was completed, the Antichrist would come and the last judgment would follow in a brief time. I opposed this sermon with what force I could from passages in the Gospels, Revelation, and the book of Daniel. (Abbo of Fleury, in McGinn 1979a, 89–90)

THIS PASSAGE FROM A FRENCH MONK has often been cited as evidence for the "terrors of the year 1000"—the notion that as the first Christian millennium drew to a close paralyzing fear of the end of the world was widespread. There are, to be sure, a number of texts from the late tenth and the early eleventh centuries that witness to the continued strength of apocalyptic traditions at the time, but it is by no means clear that fears of the end were more general ca. 1000 than at other periods in the Middle Ages, let alone that they focused on January 1, 1001 (the real beginning of the millennium now approaching its end).[1] Exaggerated emphasis on the turn of the millennium, or indeed any specific date in the list of the many at some time identified with the end during the five centuries between 1000 and 1500, tends to minimize the pervasiveness of apocalypticism throughout these centuries. Medieval folk lived in a more or less constant state of apocalyptic expectation difficult to understand for most of us today. Their sense of the imminent final events involved both fear and hope, as the apocalyptic scenario of the end-time had always portended from the time of its Jewish origins.

During the period from ca. 500 to 1000 C.E. Western views of history and its end supported an uneasy tension between the thought of Augustine of Hippo, who rejected predictive apocalypticism, and various forms of more direct expectation of the last days, especially the imperial apocalypticism created in Eastern Christianity but also influential in the West.[2] Augustine had denied the validity of attempts to make correlations between current historical events and biblical prophecies about the end (*City of God* 18.52–54; *Letter* 199). His theology of history rejected the sacralizing of the Roman Empire and its ruler that was crucial to Byzantine and later Western imperial apocalypticism (*City of God* 5.24–25). Although Augustine accepted the interpretation that identified the church with the thousand-year reign of Christ and the saints predicted in the twentieth chapter of Revelation (*City of God* 20.7–9), he did not view this in an optimistic or triumphalist manner. The church was God's instrument of salvation, but it would remain an imperfect mixture of good and evil down to judgment day.

Despite the pervasive influence of Augustine, early medieval views of the end-time maintained the interaction between pessimism and optimism characteristic of apocalyptic traditions.[3] The pessimistic pole centered on the coming persecution of the Antichrist and the fear of the last judgment. Although Augustinianism worked against precise predictions concerning these events, early medieval Christians were fascinated with the Antichrist's coming and Doomsday.[4] The optimistic aspect of early Christian apocalypticism, centering on hope for an earthly thousand-year reign of Christ and the saints (Rev. 20:1–6), had been effectively rebutted by Augustine, Jerome, and others; but a new form of nonliteral "millennial" optimism was created in imperial apocalypticism by means of the legend of the Last Roman Emperor.[5] In reaction to threats to Rome (now the "good" final empire), especially the unprecedented rise of Islam in the seventh century, supporters of the Eastern Roman emperors reworked ancient imperial legends to create the picture of a coming Last Emperor who would defeat all opponents of Christianity, reconquer Jerusalem, and initiate a time of peace and plenty until the day when he voluntarily surrendered the imperial regalia, thus ending Rome's domination and allowing for the public manifestation of Antichrist (see chapter 10 above).[6] This legend, as well as the widespread expectation that there would be a brief period allowed for repentance between the destruction of the Antichrist and judgment day, showed that not all views of the end-time were pessimistic in the early medieval era.[7]

This inherited amalgam was decisively recast in the eleventh and twelfth centuries as apocalypticism took on a new role in the debates over the nature of the church and the necessity for ecclesiastical "reform in head and members." Early medieval apocalypticism was not rejected, but such elements in the scenario of the end-time as the Last Emperor legends and the picture of Antichrist came to be seen in a different way.

The notion of reform-renewal (*reformatio/renovatio*) has been an essential element in Christian history from the beginning.[8] Paul exhorted the Romans, "Be not conformed to this world, but be transformed in the renewal (*in renovatione*) of your mind" (Rom. 12:2; cf. 2 Cor. 3:18; 4:16; Eph. 4:23; Col. 3:10). In the patristic period, especially before the conversion of the Roman Empire, reform was essentially personal, the moral effort to restore the damage done to the image of God in the soul through sin. While the individual aspect always remained significant, in the early medieval period the gradual emergence of the question, How is Christendom (*christianitas*) to be rightly ordered and governed? meant that the administrative, ecclesiological, and broadly sociopolitical aspects of reform received increasing attention. This development reached a culmination in the mid-eleventh century when a papally directed movement to restore moral purity to the clergy and right order to church governance challenged the traditional imperial understandings of the nature of Christendom. This Great Reform, as it has been called, is primarily associated with the name of Hildebrand, or Pope Gregory VII (1073–1085), who on several occasions explained his efforts by invoking the traditional understanding that the struggle between good efforts for reform and evil resistance would grow greater the nearer the approach of the end:

> From the moment when by divine inspiration Mother Church raised me, unworthy and God knows unwilling, to the apostolic throne, I have labored with all my power that Holy Church . . . might come again into her own splendor and might remain free, pure, and catholic. But because this was not pleasing to our ancient enemy, he stirred up his members against us to bring it to nought. . . . And no wonder! For the nearer the day of Antichrist approaches, the harder he fights to crush out the Christian faith. (*Collected Letters* 9.46)

Gregory VII's psychological sense of the imminence of the end is reminiscent of that of his predecessor Gregory I (590–604). Though Gregory I was a good Augustinian in refusing to make any predictions about the time of the end, his writings display a profound conviction that he was living in the last days, as well as a fascination with the Antichrist's activity, especially as present in his growing body composed of heretics and religious hypocrites. What sets Gregory VII apart from Gregory I is not his sense of the psychological imminence of the end but his joining that sense to an explicit program of institutional reform. Hildebrand and the circle of reformers around him began as monastic reformers, and there was a strong monastic flavor to their attempts to realize the true "order" (*ordo*) of Christian freedom in the world.

The imminence of the end was certainly not the only motive for the actions of Gregory VII and his friends, and it is not easy to determine how far his use of Antichrist language implies a real apocalyptic view of history. However we evaluate it, one thing is clear—Gregory's model of a totally purified church in which "the priests of Christ" would be the true "fathers and masters of kings and princes and of all believers" (*Collected Letters* 8.21) was not finally realized. Rather, a compromise was worked out in the early decades of the twelfth century between the respective claims of kingship and clergy (*regnum* and *sacerdotium*) which tried to allow each its proper sphere of action.

The consequences of the failure of the Great Reform movement to realize Gregory's goals were far-reaching, not least for the history of apocalypticism. These decisive events in the history of the medieval West marked the beginning of an ongoing debate about reform that was to continue into the sixteenth century and beyond. Such quarrels involved not only questions of church government and the proper life-style for the clergy but also the relationship between the church and Christian kings and emperors. Different modes of understanding *reformatio* were bound to have a powerful effect on conceptions of the end, since in the Christian teleological view of history the final events are what validate all efforts to attain moral good and proper order. Just as the last judgment vindicates or "justifies" individual struggle between good and evil, so too major historical changes in the history of Christianity were justified and given a transcendental significance by being accorded a place in the scenario of the end-time. The conversion of the Roman Empire to Christianity made possible (one might say even demanded) the apocalyptic validation of Christian Rome through the creation of the legend of the Last Roman Emperor. Similarly, the rise of the papacy to the position of effective moral and administrative leadership of the Western church through the Great Reform (especially the way in which the popes claimed for themselves the position of arbiters of religious reform) required the papacy to be given a special role in the last days. The apocalyptic view of the papacy, which had its own positive and negative aspects (the *pastor angelicus* versus the papal Antichrist), was among the major creations of later medieval speculation on the end-time (Reeves 1993, part 4).

The relationship between expectations of the end and conceptions of reform enables us to discern important aspects of the social and political significance of medieval apocalypticism, at the same time that it undercuts interpretations, like that of Norman Cohn, that overemphasize the deviant or sectarian character of apocalyptic ideas and movements (Cohn 1957).[9] To be sure, apocalyptic ideology often did fuel the protests of dissidents who sought radical change in the structure of Christendom, sometimes even by force of arms—though most often these groups began under the same umbrella of "return to apostolic purity" used by mainstream proponents of reform (see chapter 12 below). Most medieval apocalyptic beliefs, however, were employed as ecclesio-political rhetoric in the service of dominant institutions and officeholders (popes and other ecclesiastical leaders; emperors, kings, and their propagandists). As a part of what we would call foreign policy, apocalypticism was called upon to encourage the defense of Christendom and its institutions from external foes, especially Islam. As a part of domestic policy, its primary role was to advance programs of reform viewed as necessary for a Christian society that continued "to live in the shadow of the Second Coming."[10]

FOUR MODELS OF APOCALYPTIC REFORM

The ways of linking reform programs and beliefs about the imminent end during the Middle Ages were many.[11] This article will attempt to provide a picture of the evolution of these linkages between 1100 and 1500 C.E. Though the variations are many, they can be seen as falling into four broad types or models, which were often combined in particular thinkers. It will be helpful to lay out their essential features before undertaking a chronological overview.

The first model can be called "Gregorian," since it follows the path laid down by Gregory VII and his twelfth-century successors, who strove to reform the lives of both clergy and laity and to repair the diseased state of the church in light of the imminence of the end, usually conceived of in a nonpredictive way. Gregorian reform was influenced by the monastic sense of corporate *reformatio,* though it sought to expand this to the whole of Christian society and not just an enclosed community. Paradoxically, it looks both ahead and behind in the sense that if its main reforming motive was the necessity for purification before the end, the model for the reformed *ecclesia* was the apostolic age, howsoever conceived. This mode of reform was generally nonmillennial, emphasizing the effort for reform in head and members more than the possibility of ever attaining the goal—the harder the good struggle, the more fiercely the Antichrist and his emissaries will work to block reform and persecute its adherents until the last judgment vindicates the just and condemns the wicked.

The second type of apocalyptic reform was that initiated by Joachim of Fiore at the end of the twelfth century (see Grundmann 1927; Mottu 1977; McGinn 1985). The Joachite view was connected with the standard Gregorian model in its desire to expand traditional monastic imperatives to the whole of *christianitas,* but it broke with Gregorianism (as well as with the older imperial models to be treated below) in a decisive way. Like Augustine, Joachim gave no positive role to the Christian empire; indeed, he emphasized that Christian emperors often were persecutors of the church and thus served among the heads of Antichrist as symbolized in the great dragon of Revelation 12. Unlike Augustine, though, Joachim was convinced that the "spiritual understanding" (*intellectus spiritualis*) of the Bible allowed the inspired exegete to discern the parallel patterns of events, or "concords" as he called them, between the Old Testament, the *status,* or era, of the Father, and the unfolding of the history of the church in the New

Testament era, the time of the Son. Thus, real predictions about imminent events could be made, if only with caution. Joachim went beyond this piecemeal level of prophecy, however, in his most original insight. As a created image or icon of the Trinity, history must reveal the work of all three Persons, so the abbot announced an imminent third *status* of the Holy Spirit, an era that would fulfill the predictions of Revelation 20 about the millennium, though not in any materialistic or numerical way (see Mottu 1977; Crocco 1986).

Joachim's revival of millennial hopes differed from that found in the usual forms of the Last Emperor legend both chronologically and substantively. His third *status* comes after, not before, the time of Antichrist. (It would be more correct to say that it comes *between* Antichrists, since Joachim believed that there would also be an Antichrist at the end of the third *status* revealed in the figure of Gog in Rev. 20:8.) More importantly, Joachim's hope for the future centered on a new form of *ecclesia* of a totally monasticized character, rather than on the reform of the present religio-political entity of *christianitas*. The abbot's imminent, perfect earthly church placed the magnet of reform in the future and not in a return to the idealized past of the apostolic age. Though he lived in an era that he viewed as one of growing moral evil and persecution that was soon to culminate in the arrival of the final Antichrist of the second *status,* Joachim was essentially optimistic in his belief in a divinely inspired progress built into history.

The Calabrian abbot's notion of church reform differed from the Gregorian model not only by locating the archetype or ideal model of the church in the future rather than in the past, but also by how it related it to extra-monastic institutions. Joachim was not interested in such things as reviving canon law, correcting ecclesiastical finances, reforming church administration, and the like—major concerns of the Gregorians. None of this counted for much in the midst of the looming terror of Antichrist (Joachim and his followers also had a more predictive sense of the imminent end than the Gregorian reformers).

Joachim's third *status* would be the time of the *ecclesia spiritualis* in which all three orders of the church (laity, clergy, and monks in the full sense) would live according to a monastic rule of life emphasizing the sharing of goods, contemplative prayer, and the study of scripture in the era of the full flowering of the *intellectus spiritualis*. As set forth in his utopian diagram or *figura* entitled "The Arrangement of the New People of God Pertaining to the Third *Status* after the Model of the Heavenly Jerusalem," Joachim's conception of the triumph of reform was different from anything that had gone before.[12]

The abbot of Fiore also made a major contribution to the evolution of the role of the papacy in the scenario of the last events. Although the development of clearly delineated apocalyptic roles for popes, both positive and negative ones, was a process that stretched over several centuries, Joachim's predictions concerning the activities of a coming pope who would withstand Antichrist at the end of the second *status,* as well as his announcement of "a new leader who will ascend from Babylon, namely a new universal pontiff of the New Jerusalem, that is, of Holy Mother the Church,"[13] were significant milestones in the creation of the figure of the holy pope of the last days. The abbot also seems to have feared that Antichrist or one of his henchmen would take over the papal office itself to fulfill the apostle Paul's prediction in 2 Thess. 2:4 that the "Man of Perdition" would sit enthroned in the Temple of God (i.e., the church) and demand to be worshiped (McGinn 1994b, 135–42).

The third model of reform was the imperial one, originating in Eastern Christianity in the seventh century and gradually westernized from the tenth century on. In its original appearances in *Pseudo-Methodius* and the *Tiburtine Sibyl* little attention was paid to the church and none to the necessity for institutional reform as such. Rather, ecclesiastical officials and their functions were viewed as parts of the Christian world empire, whose power was tottering because of the moral failure of its subjects. The rise of Islam, as the predecessor of Antichrist, was seen as divine chastisement for these sins. After this necessary cleansing, however, God would raise up a Last Roman Emperor, whose "sanctity" would be essentially political in nature—defeat of the enemies of Christianity and the establishment of a pre-Antichrist millennial period modeled on the golden age ascribed to the great emperors of the past (see chapter 10 above). In later forms of the imperial legend (i.e., post-1100) the reformation of church and clergy often emerged as an explicit part of the Last Emperor's agenda (Reeves 1993, and the treatment below).

In the thirteenth century expectations concerning the role of good and evil popes in the last days produced a fourth type of apocalyptic reform, which can be called "angelic reform" since it centers on the figure of the Angelic Pope (*pastor angelicus*). This type is usually found in hybrid modes, allied with aspects of imperial and Joachite motifs. As the thirteenth-century papacy became increasingly mired in the territorial struggles and financial exactions needed to support its political agenda, hopes for a radical change that would elevate holy pastors to the most eminent position in the church took on increasing apocalyptic dimensions. Only divine intervention to come at the end was seen as capable of correcting the present massive deformations of the church. As early as the 1270s, Roger Bacon had expressed the view that "it was necessary that the church be cleansed through the best of popes and the best of princes as if joining together the material sword and the spiritual sword" (Bacon, *Compendium of the Study of Philosophy*). Individual popes, such as Gregory X (1271–1276) and especially Celestine V (1294), were hailed as possible agents for such ultimate reform. Shortly after 1300, in texts like the famous *Prophecies of the Supreme Pontiffs* and *The Book of Fiore,* the legend of the holy reforming pope of the time immediately before Antichrist emerged in clear fashion.

NEW FORMS OF APOCALYPTICISM IN THE TWELFTH CENTURY

The twelfth century was fascinated with the problem of history—sacred and profane, particular and universal.[14] The dramatic changes Western Europe was undergoing at this time helped foster a concern for the meaning of events in the light of God's providential plan and encouraged new forms of apocalyptic thinking that focused on understanding the present state of the *ecclesia* in relation to the approaching end. Most of the twelfth-century apocalyptic thinkers were "Gregorians" in the sense that they saw their efforts to reform contemporary evils in the church as an integral part of the approach of the end. Where they went beyond Gregory was in their willingness to make literal connections between biblical descriptions of the last days and their own times, and also in the hopes that at least some of them expressed for a possible better age of the church before the end.

A good example of the first generation of apocalyptically minded Gregorians can be found in Rupert of Deutz (ca. 1070–1129). This reforming monk does not appear to have harbored any millennial hopes, but his poem "The Calamities of the Church of Liège" applies images of

John's Revelation to the events of the struggle between his hero, Gregory VII, and the emperor, Henry IV. Rupert also composed an important commentary on Revelation, one that broke, if only in tentative fashion, with the seven-hundred-year Latin tradition of essentially moral exegesis of the text by suggesting that the Apocalypse might contain prophecies that could also illuminate present and imminent events.[15]

Like Gregory I and Gregory VII, Rupert does not appear to have expected the immediate end of the world, but other religious reformers of the early twelfth century did. Bernard of Clairvaux tells us that he once had a conversation with Norbert of Xanten (d. 1134), the founder of the Premonstratensian order, in which this reforming canon insisted that the Antichrist had already been born (Bernard, *Letter* 56). Similar beliefs remained strong among his followers and their confidants. In 1147 the priest Gerard of Poehlde wrote to the Premonstratensian Evermord of Magdeburg claiming that the evils of the day indicated that the thousand years of Satan's binding (Rev. 20:2) were ending ahead of schedule.[16] Another contemporary Premonstratensian, Eberwin of Steinfeld, interpreted the six waterpots of the marriage feast of Cana (John 2) as signifying six ages of the church's history, identifying the fifth pot with the current rise of heresy and seeing the sixth pot (Antichrist's coming) as proximate.

The clearest example of an apocalyptic Gregorian reformer in the twelfth century is to be found in the figure of the Bavarian canon Gerhoh of Reichersberg (1093–1169).[17] Gerhoh wrote his major apocalyptic works, *The Investigation of Antichrist* and *The Fourth Watch of the Night* during the 1160s, the time of the conflict between Alexander III and Emperor Frederick Barbarossa, the second round in the ongoing struggle between popes and emperors over the leadership of Western Christendom. Gerhoh read Matthew's account of the four watches of the night during which the apostles rowed upon the stormy waters of the Sea of Galilee (Matt. 14:22–33) as a type of the history of the church over the course of four trials inflicted by Antichrist. The first watch is the age of the "bloody Antichrist" of Roman persecution; the second that of the "fraudulent Antichrist" of heresy. For Gerhoh the career of Gregory VII saw the culmination of the third age of the church, the time of the struggle against the "impure Antichrist," that is, the church's inner corruption through clerical simony and unchastity. Gregory's conflict with the German emperors marked the loosing of Satan's thousand-year captivity and the beginning of the time of the "avaricious Antichrist," the swelling avarice not only of simoniacs but now even to be found in the papacy itself. The canon viewed the venality of the Roman curia as a sign that Peter was sinking beneath the waves, but he believed that Christ would stretch forth his hand to save the sinking papacy (Matt. 14:30–32). "Before the final coming," he noted, "the church which is the true and living house of the living God, is to be reformed to its ancient practice of apostolic perfection in those who are called and ought to be spiritual men" (*Investigation of Antichrist* 1.44). During this time, as he had predicted in a work he personally delivered to Pope Eugene III in 1152, "the high priest presiding over the Apostolic See [would be] crowned and exalted over all kingdoms" (*Commentary on Psalm 64*). Gerhoh, therefore, put the reformed papacy devoted to poverty at the center of his hopes for a coming better age of the church. In this sense he represents an optimistic, even a moderately millennial, perspective that would have been anathema to Augustine and his followers, and even to Gregory VII.

Less of a Gregorian-style reformer but no less original a thinker, the German abbess Hildegard of Bingen (1098–1179) also confronted the ecclesiastical disputes of the day from the perspective of an apocalyptic theology of history (Töpfer 1964, 33–44; Rauh 1973, chap. 7; Kerby-Fulton 1990, chap. 2). Hildegard was primarily concerned with the necessity for the moral reform of the clergy in the era begun with Henry IV's attack on the church, the age that she described as the *tempus muliebre,* "the womanish time" of weakness and decline.[18] Essentially conservative and pessimistic, by the last decades of her life Hildegard held out little hope for either the empire or the papacy as true agents of reform. She vigorously attacked the immorality of the clergy, both financial and sexual, in her writings and in the unprecedented (for a woman) public preaching campaigns she conducted between 1159 and 1170 (see, e.g., *Letters* 8, 15, 17, 26, 149, 223). Her reformist prophetic stance was to find subsequent echoes in the careers of Mechthild of Magdeburg and Birgitta of Sweden.

The abbess's theology of history is based on a gender symbolism emphasizing how the evil male figure of Satan attacks humanity, the female bride of Christ, progressively figured in Eve, the synagogue, Mary, and the church. Hildegard made no chronological predictions, but she clearly saw the contemporary ecclesiastical situation in the light of her visions about the approach of the end. In a famous showing recounted in her *Scivias* she described an apocalyptic scenario in which the present "womanish time" figured as the first of five periods before the coming of the end.[19] Hildegard's vision of what lay ahead combined both purging of sinful clerics through forced confiscation of their wealth and the conviction that a more perfect clergy was not far off. Nevertheless, her perspective was still fundamentally pessimistic—Antichrist, pictured as the final and worst sexual criminal of Satan's line, was in the process of being born from the body of the church in a violent expulsion that is like a reverse rape. The abbess was the first to combine the traditional idea that Antichrist would stage a pretended death and resurrection with the notion that he would be destroyed by divine power when he would attempt to mock Christ by ascending to heaven from the Mount of Olives. Nevertheless, the persecutor's death does not mark the end. Building on the notion of the forty-five-day respite after Antichrist's death, Hildegard also proclaimed a final period of triumph for the church. Such oscillation between positive and negative moments in the ongoing task of apocalyptic reformation of the church before the end was to be typical of many late medieval thinkers.

In opposition to these rich new veins of apocalyptic of a more or less Gregorian nature, the twelfth-century examples of imperial apocalypticism stressed that the only reform needed was a strong Roman emperor and a clergy who would not hypocritically try to restructure the divinely established order of *christianitas.* A good illustration of this view of how to act in light of the approaching end can be found in the "Play of Antichrist," which is contemporary with Gerhoh but adopts a diametrically opposed position on the issue of the role that church leaders should take in the time of the Antichrist.[20] In response to the attacks on the imperial office both of popes and rising national monarchs, this liturgical drama, which may have been written for Emperor Frederick Barbarossa, insists that the fate of the church in the last days ultimately rests with Christ alone.

The drama opens with seven royal thrones arranged in a circle. *Ecclesia* enters accompanied by the pope on the right and the emperor on the left. (The pope, significantly, has no speaking role; he is merely the court chaplain of the emperor.) The kings of the earth then assemble to dispute world leadership. The emperor rapidly subdues the arrogant king of France, accepts the fealty of the kings of the Greeks and of Jerusalem, and defeats the pagan king of Babylon. There is no millennial period at this point, because the emperor immediately surrenders the imperial regalia in Jerusalem and returns to his ancestral position as king of Germany. The end of the empire is the signal for the advent of Antichrist, who is preceded by a crowd of hypocrites, bowing low in feigned humility to win over the laity, and accompanied by the personifications of hypocrisy and heresy. The hypocrites hail Antichrist as a reformer who attacks the wealth and worldliness of the clergy with this song:

> Holy religion has already long faltered,
> Vanity has seized Mother Church.
> Why this waste through these adorned ones? [i.e., clergy]
> God does not love worldly priests.
> Climb to the height of kingly power!
> Through you the remnants of what is old will be changed!

Antichrist as hypocritical church reformer next wins over the rulers of the world by force, bribery, and deception. The king of the Germans resists and confutes the hypocrites (as the German emperors had done with Gregory VII and his followers), but he too is won over when Antichrist performs three miracles.

The remainder of the "Play of Antichrist" adheres to the traditional view of the final enemy's career. The two witnesses predicted in Revelation 11, Enoch and Elijah, come from heaven to convert the Jews and confront Antichrist. He slays them, but is himself then struck down from heaven. There is no last judgment, but the final lines may hint at some form of post-Antichrist millennial period: "*Then, as everyone returns to the faith, Ecclesia, welcoming them, begins:* Praise our God. . . ."[21] The message of "The Play of Antichrist" is that contemporary efforts at ecclesiastical reform are really hypocritical deceptions of Antichrist.

The role that the apocalyptic city of Jerusalem plays in the "Play of Antichrist" and throughout much Christian apocalyptic literature raises the question of the relationship between the crusades and the apocalyptic currents of the late eleventh and twelfth centuries. Guibert of Nogent's version of Urban II's speech at Clermont in 1095, the event that sparked the First Crusade, includes a strong apocalyptic element, but this is a later creation that probably tells us more about Guibert's mind than about Urban's intentions (McGinn 1979a, 91–92). Still, it would be difficult to deny that fascination with the earthly Jerusalem as the place of the last events, including the descent of the heavenly Jerusalem (Rev. 21:2), played some role in popular excitement for the sacred and bellicose pilgrimage that resulted in the recapture of the apocalyptic city *par excellence*.[22] What is clear is that the fate of Jerusalem, especially after the city had been retaken by Islamic forces in 1187, was increasingly important in late medieval apocalyptic expectations.

While much of the evidence concerning medieval apocalypticism comes from commentaries, treatises, and letters produced by the learned elite, we need to be attentive to the wider social dimensions of apocalyptic thought, difficult as these are to reconstruct. The careers and self-understanding of apocalyptic propagandists themselves provide us with some access to the broader aspects of the significance of apocalypticism. Rather than representing a semi-educated and alienated fringe of society, most of the major apocalyptic thinkers of the twelfth century were figures situated in high echelons of intellectual and political power. They sought to make their views effective both on a popular level through preaching and also with the leadership of *christianitas,* especially with the popes of the era. A good illustration can be found in the greatest medieval apocalypticist, Joachim of Fiore (ca. 1135–1202), whose unique new theology of apocalyptic reform was briefly described above.

Joachim was born into an influential bourgeois family and was educated to become an official in the Norman court of the kingdom of Sicily. After a conversion experience, he lived the life of a wandering holy man for some years before entering the monastic life. Visions that he experienced in 1183–1184 launched him on his career as an apocalyptic writer and propagandist, as well as the founder of a new monastic order in the isolated Sila plateau of his native Calabria. Joachim, however, was no lonely prophet on a mountaintop. Rather, he sought to convey his message of impending crisis and coming millennial peace both to the whole body of believers (see his "Letter to All the Faithful" in McGinn 1979b, 113–17), and especially to the leadership of society—popes, emperors, and kings. In effect, he served as a kind of "apocalyptic advisor" to a number of popes in the troubled last two decades of the twelfth century. His reputation was international. Richard Lionheart of England, on his way to the Holy Land to try to recapture Jerusalem, sought an interview with the famous seer in the winter of 1191 and heard from him the troubling announcement that the Antichrist, whose persecution would end the second *status* of history, had already been born. Not all the apocalyptic thinkers of the later Middle Ages were as involved as Joachim was with advising and at times castigating the elite of the time, but most demonstrate the Calabrian abbot's concern to disseminate as broadly and effectively as possible the critical message that the last times had come.

☞ CONFLICTING APOCALYPTIC PERSPECTIVES ON REFORM (1200–1350)

This century and a half saw the full evolution of the various models of apocalyptic reform described above. It is worth remembering that the Gregorian impetus for reform of the church in head and members (especially the clergy) remained an underlying motif of much late medieval apocalypticism. After 1200, however, it rarely is found in a pure form, but is usually part of views of the last events that include elements taken from the thought of Joachim, and often from the imperial and/or angelic models. An illustration of this process can be seen in the writings of the English Franciscan Roger Bacon (ca. 1215–ca. 1292).

Bacon is noted for his concern with the necessity of reforming the education of the clergy found in the monumental *Greater Work* (*Opus maius*) that he sent to Pope Clement IV in 1267. But, as the quotation cited above reminds us, the irascible friar viewed educational reform of the clergy within a broad perspective of the need for total reform of the church, which he declared must be the work of both pope and emperor. Bacon searched a wide range of prophetic authorities (he names the Sibyls, Merlin, Joachim, Methodius, and others unknown today) in order to determine whether the Mongol attack on Islam in 1258 meant the end of "the law of Muhammad" and the proximity of Antichrist (see chapter 14 below, for Jewish reactions to this crisis). Bacon called for increased apocalyptic education: "I know that if the church wished to study the sacred text and the holy prophecies, . . . and also histories and the books of the philosophers, along with the paths of astronomy, she would find a sufficient conception and greater certitude about the time of Antichrist" (McGinn 1979a, 156). The Franciscan was also open to apocalyptic optimism, as is shown in his citation of the prophecy of an Armenian seer named Akaton, who predicted the defeat of the Mongols, the conversion of all nations to Christ, and a coming period of universal peace.

Women seers continued to play a role in the call for reform of the church in the light of the approach of the terrible events of the last days. The German mystic and visionary Mechthild of Magdeburg (ca. 1208–ca. 1282), in her vernacular *The Flowing Light of the Godhead,* advanced a unique apocalyptic theology in which she attempted to recapitulate the whole of salvation history in her visionary and intercessory role as an instrument of God's call for repentance. In one place she asks Divine Love: "When I consider that my body shall so fade away at death that I shall no longer suffer or praise my beloved Jesus, then I feel such pain that I desire, if that were possible, to live till the last day." To which the Lord responds: "I declare that your being (*wesen*) shall remain until the end of humanity" (*Flowing Light* 6.15; cf. 4.27; 6.21; 6.26). Mechthild appears to have had some contact with Joachite thought, as reflected in her detailed picture of a coming order of "spiritual men" (*viri spirituales*) who will sustain the church at the time of Antichrist's attack, but the seer's distinctive visions of the events of Antichrist's life and her willingness to take on the suffering of the martyrs of the last days at the time of the second pouring out of Christ's blood (a form of apocalyptic crucifixion of Christ's body, the church; see *Flowing Light* 5.34) are essentially pessimistic.

Concern for the role of Islam in contemporary events and especially in the coming crisis of history was another important feature of most late medieval apocalyptic scenarios. Islam had a clear place in the imperial legends, especially in the popular *Pseudo-Methodius,* as the predecessor of Gog and Magog and of Antichrist. Dramatic events in the East, from the conquest of Jerusalem through the ongoing crusades, the Mongol onslaught, and the loss of the last Western presence in Palestine with the fall of Acre in 1291, fueled the production of prophetic texts, sometimes connected with Jewish and Islamic sources. These both helped "explain" the events through the device of history disguised as prophecy (*vaticinium ex eventu*) and also encouraged the faithful by predicting coming victory over the forces of evil. Many of these oracles were couched in a prophetic obscurity that allowed them to be revised and updated to interpret new crises for many centuries. For example, the "Cedar of Lebanon" prophecy was originally composed to "predict" the Mongol invasion of Eastern Europe, but was subsequently revised and reinterpreted in relation to ongoing Islamic threats down to the seventeenth century (Lerner 1983).

Perhaps the best illustration of how the rich stew of late medieval apocalyptic expectations could be served up for very different, indeed opposing, political agendas can be found in the history of the struggle between a succession of medieval popes and the emperor Frederick II that stretched from 1227 to the emperor's death in 1250, and beyond.[23] The involvement of the medieval papal court with apocalyptic ideas was more widespread than hitherto imagined. Innocent III (1198–1216), though traditionally held responsible for the condemnation of Joachim's views on the Trinity at the Fourth Lateran Council, may actually have maneuvered to obtain the relatively mild language in which the objection was expressed.[24] Some of Innocent's curial circle were influenced by Joachite speculation, including Cardinal Rainer of Viterbo (d. 1250), who was the most important papal propagandist in the struggle against Frederick.

The emperor was first excommunicated by Gregory IX in 1227 for his failure to undertake the crusade he had pledged, but it was not until his second excommunication in 1239 that the struggle of the popes against Frederick and his descendants reached it most savage, polemical, and also apocalyptic stage. Gregory IX's letter of June 21, 1239 (drafted by Rainer), beginning "The Beast Ascends from the Sea" (referring to Rev. 13:1–2), identified the emperor with one of the traditional images of Antichrist's associates. Frederick responded in kind with a letter claiming that the pope was the monstrous red horse (cf. Rev. 6:4) who takes away peace from the earth. Yet more, the letter went on to say: "Construing his words in the true sense, he is that great dragon who leads the world astray (Rev. 12:9), Antichrist, whose forerunner he says we are. . . ." As open warfare between the emperor and the pope and his allies heated up, apocalyptic rhetoric continued to be used on both sides. In 1243, Gregory IX was succeeded by Innocent IV, who fled to southern France and deposed Frederick at the Council of Lyons in 1245. At this juncture Cardinal Rainer composed another series of apocalyptic broadsides now clearly identifying Frederick with Antichrist: "Since Frederick has in his forehead the horn of power and a mouth bringing forth monstrous things, he thinks himself able to transform the times and the laws and to lay truth in the dust" (Letter "According to Isaiah's Prophecy"). Frederick's followers responded with pamphlets showing that *Innocencius papa* numerically equaled 666, the number of Antichrist (Rev. 13:18), and by calling for imperial reform of the corrupt papal church within an apocalyptic context.

In the second and third stages of this fascinating example of the use of apocalyptic rhetoric in politics (respectively 1245–1250 and 1250–1268) most of the ammunition was anti-imperial and was created by Franciscan followers of Joachim of Fiore to show that Frederick and his successors had been predicted by the Calabrian abbot as the final enemy of the church, who (even when dead) was ready to attack the righteous, especially the faithful followers of the poverty of Francis.[25] In order to understand this new moment in the history of medieval apocalypticism it is helpful to reflect on how Francis and his practice of poverty came to be given a transhistorical and apocalyptic significance through ideas originating with Joachim, the Calabrian seer.

In his account of the crisis of the second age of history, Joachim predicted that the forces resisting Antichrist would be led by two groups he referred to as "spiritual men" (*viri spirituales*), conceived of as new religious orders who would resist the Antichrist not by force of arms but by prayer and preaching.[26] This turned out to be one of those rare apocalyptic prophecies whose apparent fulfillment encouraged acceptance of the entire system of its creator. Only a few years after Joachim's death, the Franciscan and Dominican orders of mendicants burst upon the scene and decisively changed the history of the medieval church. Francis of Assisi (1182–1226) saw his own preaching of poverty and desire for worldwide missionization in the light of the Christian eschatological view of history, but there is no evidence that he had any interest in apocalyptic expectations.[27] Dominic appears to have been even less apocalyptically minded. The channels by which Joachim's prophecies came to be adopted with enthusiasm by many Franciscans and at least a few Dominicans are not totally clear, but the story had important consequences for the late Middle Ages.

Joachim's early fame, based on his preaching and popular reputation, saw him primarily as a prophet of the advent of Antichrist. It was only in the 1240s, when some Franciscan defenders of the radical poverty of Francis came upon the Calabrian's predictions of the role of the *viri spirituales* in the imminent crisis of history, that the other implications of Joachim's new apocalyptic theology of history became evident.[28]

Franciscan Joachitism was not the only form of ongoing adaptation of the seminal thought of the Calabrian, but it was the most potent. This apocalyptic theology involved elements drawn from Joachim's own thought, as well as important additions that form a new chapter in the story of our second model of reform. The exact origins and the major creators of Franciscan Joachitism are still subject to dispute, but its major components are clear. The first was the identification of the Franciscans and Dominicans as Joachim's two hoped-for orders of *viri spirituales,* something already found in the *Commentary on Jeremiah,* a text pseudonymously ascribed to the abbot, but (at least in its present form) a product of the early 1240s.[29] This identification was given official approbation by both orders in the joint encyclical letter issued by the Minister General of the Franciscans, John of Parma, and the Dominican Master, Humbert of Romans, in 1255. The second element was singling out absolute poverty of life as the characteristic sign of the spiritual men of the end of the present era (Joachim had emphasized contemplation over poverty). Finally, Franciscan Joachitism gave Francis a unique historical role by identifying him with the Angel of the Sixth Seal, "bearing the sign of the living God" (Rev. 7:2), that is, the stigmata which proclaimed his position as the perfect model of Jesus Christ and harbinger of the final age.[30]

Where did Frederick II and his conflict with the papacy fit into this new form of apocalypticism stressing the centrality of poverty of life for reforming the church in the light of the approaching end? Like Rainer of Viterbo and his circle, the Franciscan Joachites saw Frederick as the Antichrist, but they went beyond the curial polemicists in locating Frederick's persecution within a new understanding of the last times, one which (in partial dependence on Joachim) predicted that the end of the second *status* would take place in the year 1260. They also looked forward to a millennial third *status* of the purified church when all would live according to the Franciscan model of true poverty.

According to the Franciscan chronicler Fra Salimbene, in 1247 an abbot of Joachim's Florensian order, fleeing from the armies of Frederick, deposited Joachim's works in the Franciscan convent at Pisa in the conviction that "at that time all the mysteries were to reach fulfillment in Frederick since he was in conflict with the church" (*Chronicle;* in Verbeke 1988, 362). Contacts like this encouraged the Franciscans and their followers to a burst of prophetic activity in the period ca. 1245–1250 aimed at showing that Frederick was the Antichrist who was to persecute the church down to the dawn of the new era in 1260.[31] This apocalyptic scenario, however, was shattered by Frederick's unexpected death in 1250. But once again (as has so often been the case in the history of apocalyptic expectations) discomfiture proved to be the seedbed of ingenuity. Just as the death of the persecutor Nero in the first century produced the picture of the emperor as the head of the beast wounded unto death but then revived (Rev. 13:3; see chapter 8 above), so too rumors began to circulate that Frederick had not really died. As a widespread prophetic verse found in some chronicles and incorporated into a number of apocalyptic treatises put it:

> His death will be hidden and unknown.
> Among the people will resound: "He lives," and "He does not live!"
> (McGinn 1979a, 171)

The idea of a return from the dead, however, put a strain on the credulity of many, so a more satisfactory answer was created in the legend of the "Third Frederick," that is, the belief that the dread emperor would return in the person of one of his descendants to complete the work of Antichrist's final persecution. The *Commentary on Jeremiah* had predicted that Frederick, typologically identified with the basilisk of Isaiah 14:29, would "afflict the church throughout the whole breadth of the empire," and would "swallow the bird [i.e., the church] . . . either in his own person or in his seed" (*Commentary,* Venice ed., 1525, f. 46r). The explicit figure of a persecuting *Fredericus tertius* already occurs in the *Book of the Burdens of the Prophets,* ascribed to Joachim of Fiore but written by an Italian Franciscan about 1255. It was to have a considerable history in the later Middle Ages. As the popes of the 1250s and 1260s pursued their vendetta against the descendants of Frederick, this Franciscan Joachite apocalypticism proved useful, even if it was not directly cited in papal propaganda.

Frederick II's own understanding of his role in the clash of apocalyptic propaganda remains ambiguous. He may well have been quite comfortable inspiring fear as a great persecutor; but, as Ernst Kantorowicz noted, "The whole life of Frederick could be interpreted either in the Messianic or in the Anti-Christian spirit."[32] Like many late medieval rulers, Frederick was not averse to making personal use of messianic legends about the Last World Emperor as the restorer of Christianity and reformer of the church when it suited him (McGinn 1979a, 172–73), though it is doubtful that this was a major aspect of his ideology.

The imperial model of apocalyptic reform was initially applied to the German emperors as heirs to the glory and name of Rome, but in the late Middle Ages national monarchs also sought to lay claim to apocalyptic status. A Sibylline oracle circulating in France at the time of the Second Crusade promised the French king Louis VII conquest in the East and a messianic role. About 1220 a Francophile reworking of the *Tiburtine Sibyl* glorified the French monarchy and identified Philip Augustus (1180–1223) as the Last Emperor. When the papacy called in Charles of Anjou, the younger brother of Louis IX, to exterminate the heirs of Frederick II, curial propaganda also hailed him as the Last Emperor. Strangely enough, even the originally anti-imperial legends concerning the return of Frederick, either in himself or in his progeny, later took on a positive valence (what appears as persecution from one perspective can be seen as legitimate chastisement from another). Hence, among those opposed to clerical and papal corruption, especially in Germany, we find evidence of a good "Third Frederick," who is seen as a divinely sent rod to chastise a hopelessly deformed church, clergy, and social order. The Franciscan chronicler John of Winterthur, under the year 1348, noted widespread belief in Germany concerning Frederick's return, "even if he had been cut up into a thousand pieces and burned to ashes." According to this account, the revived emperor would effect a social transformation, marrying poor girls to rich men, allowing nuns and monks to wed, and giving full justice to all. This is a truly radical picture of imperial reform:

> He will persecute the clergy so harshly that they will spread cow dung over their crowns and tonsures . . . so that they do not seem to be tonsured. He will drive the religious, especially the Franciscans, from the land. . . . After he has governed the empire that he has resumed more justly and gloriously than before, he will cross the sea with a great army and on the Mount of Olives or at the dry tree will resign the empire. . . . (McGinn 1979a, 251)

Franciscan Joachite apocalypticism was created not primarily as a polemical tool to counter Frederick but as a way for the minorites to understand the role of Francis and his order in the crisis of the last days. Its development is integral to comprehending the interaction of the various models of apocalyptic reform in the century between 1250 and 1350. During the first half of this period the evolution comprised three dramatic chapters: (1) the crisis of the "Eternal Gospel"; (2) Bonaventure's modified Joachite theology of history; and (3) the apocalypticism of the Spiritual Franciscans.

Gerardo of Borgo San Donnino, a young Italian friar and protégé of the Joachite Minister

General John of Parma, had been sent to Paris about 1250. In 1254 he produced a work entitled the *Introduction to the Eternal Gospel*, a summary and interpretation of Joachim's writings which announced that the present age of the church would end in 1260 to be succeeded by a franciscanized church in which the abbot's works would replace the Old and New Testaments. The enemies of the mendicants, especially the Paris secular priests who taught at the university, used Gerardo's ill-advised work as an excuse to attack the new orders, even to the extent of claiming that their novelty and heresy were a sign of the advent of Antichrist (Szittya 1986). Although these charges were rebutted by the rising intellectual stars of both orders (Thomas Aquinas for the Dominicans and Bonaventure for the Franciscans), Franciscan Joachitism was seriously compromised. Gerardo was condemned and imprisoned for life while John of Parma was compelled to step down as Minister General in 1257 to be succeeded by Bonaventure.

Later propaganda of the Franciscan Spirituals painted Bonaventure as an enemy of the strict interpretation of Franciscan poverty and an opponent of Joachim and apocalyptic speculation. Modern scholarship, however, has shown that the great scholastic and mystic actually created an original apocalyptic theology of history in which he made considerable use of the abbot of Fiore's methods of exegesis and a modified version of Franciscan Joachite theology (Ratzinger 1971; McGinn 1985, chap. 7). Increasingly, Bonaventure appears as one of the greatest Christian apocalyptic thinkers.

In the spring of 1273, Bonaventure delivered an unfinished series of lectures to the Franciscans at Paris, the *Collations on the Hexaemeron*. Making use of Joachim's historicizing concordances, which demonstrated exact parallels between events of the Old and events of the New Testaments, in *Collations* 15–16 he warned the friars that they were witnessing the crisis of the sixth age of the church immediately before the coming of the seventh "day" of rest and peace before the end of the world (i.e., another form of post-Antichrist millennialism). Among the negative signs of the ending of the age, ongoing persecution plays a role, but Bonaventure (ever the good scholastic) identified the major evil sign of the times as the influence of the pernicious philosophy of Aristotle on sound doctrine. But the present time of crisis mingles optimism with pessimism, for the great sign of the dawning of an era of contemplative theology and perfect poverty was the coming of St. Francis, the Angel of the Sixth Seal (*Coll.* 16.16, 29; *Coll.* 22.22–23). Bonaventure avoided referring to a new *status* of the Holy Spirit, but he believed that in the imminent seventh era announced by the figure of Francis "the church militant will be conformed to the church triumphant as far as is possible in this life" (*Coll.* 16.30).

Bonaventure attempted to mediate between rigorist Franciscan views of the necessity for true poverty of life and the relaxed attitude of the majority, who claimed that they were following Christ and the apostles in *owning* nothing but merely *using* the goods the popes possessed and allowed the order access to. The issue of the correct practice of apostolic poverty, however, soon became intertwined with the Franciscan Joachite theology of history created by John of Parma and his friends and modified by Bonaventure. During the years 1280–1330 the great conflict between the rigorist, or Spiritual, understanding of the Franciscan way of life and the Conventual, or majority, position tore the order apart, troubled the church, and produced an apocalyptic movement that wound up condemning the popes opposed to the Spiritual view as Antichrists.

The Spiritual party developed in several areas in Italy, especially Umbria and the Marches, as well as in Provence. Its intellectual leader was the Provençal friar, Peter John Olivi (ca.

1248–1298), a former student of Bonaventure's who wrote an important *Lecture on Revelation* in 1297 (the best study is Burr 1993). Olivi shared much of Bonaventure's revised Joachite apocalypticism, but he went beyond his master in several important ways. First of all, Olivi was more directly critical of the contemporary carnal church than Bonaventure had been, an invective that was to serve his followers well when they decided that the papacy was the incarnation of such carnality. Even more important was the fact that Olivi's complicated view of Antichrist, involving both a "Mystical Antichrist" and a "Great Antichrist," predicted that the former would be a false pope who would attack the evangelical poverty of the Franciscan life. As he put it in his *Lecture*, the prophetic authorities "think that Frederick with his seed is like the slain head [Rev. 13:3] in this age, and that he will revive in the time of the Mystical Antichrist. . . . He will set up as pseudopope a certain false religious who will contrive something against the Evangelical [i.e., Franciscan] Rule" (McGinn 1979a, 211). Finally, Olivi also was more detailed than the cautious Bonaventure had been about the Franciscan character of the coming millennial period after this persecution and was also willing to identify it with Joachim's *tertius status,* by now suspect to many.

Olivi's *Lecture* was written after the 1294 resignation of Pope Celestine V, the briefly reigning supporter of the Spirituals. The new pontiff, Boniface VIII (1294–1303), began a persecution of the Spirituals, many of whom had refused to accept his election. Olivi did not take this path, but it comes as little surprise that some of his Italian followers, such as Ubertino of Casale in his *Tree of the Crucified Life of Jesus Christ* (1305), used Olivi's corporate view of Antichrist to identify Pope Boniface and even his successor Benedict XI with the two aspects of the Mystical Antichrist—savage persecution and hypocritical deception. The real crisis (though not quite the end of the world) came under Pope John XXII (1316–1334). Pope John reopened the whole question of Franciscan claims to be following Christ (and Francis) in renouncing all personal possession (*dominium*). He first moved against the Spirituals, whose failure to observe obedience to their superiors had been an irritant for decades, condemning Olivi's view of Franciscan poverty, as well as the apocalyptic expectations of his followers, the Provençal beguins and later the Italian *Fraticelli,* or "Little Brothers." (In 1326, after a lengthy investigation, Olivi's *Lecture* was also condemned.) But the drama was not over. Pope John had become convinced that the whole Franciscan ideology about the absolute poverty of Christ and the apostles (which implied that the Franciscans alone adhered to this central mark of apostolic perfection) was a sham. On the advice of a theological commission he summoned, in 1323 John renounced papal ownership of the things "used" by the Franciscans and declared that it was heretical to claim (as Bonaventure and many other friars had done) that Christ and the apostles owned nothing. Olivi's prophecy was fulfilled. A pope had attacked the evangelical rule of poverty, thus proving himself "pseudo-pope" and Antichrist. Both the remnants of the Spiritual Franciscans and members of the Conventual party denounced John XXII and his sucessors as Antichrists and moved off into the shadowy world of heretics in the later fourteenth century.[33]

The apocalyptic drama that began with the confrontation between Frederick II and the papacy and that progressed over the next eight decades, especially within the Franciscan order, played an important role in the maturation of the fourth model of apocalyptic reform outlined above (i.e., "angelic reform"), which placed hopes for a future better age primarily in the figure of a new kind of pope, whether conceived of as reigning before or after Antichrist. (Given the proliferation of kinds of Antichrist we have already seen, pre- and post-Antichrist millennial periods begin to lose much practical specificity.) As pointed out above, the apocalyptic legend of the "Angelic Pastor" had a long germination rooted in the new position of the papacy achieved by the Great Reform movement, and, like so many apocalyptic symbolizations, it developed in dialectical fashion with its evil counterpart, the papal Antichrist, who seemed the natural fulfillment of Paul's predictions about the "Son of Perdition" who would seat himself in God's Temple (2 Thess. 2:3–4). The involvement of individual popes with the quarrels within the Franciscan order ca. 1280–1330, while not the only factor, was a major catalyst in the full-blown scenario of this final model of reform, which reached its classic form about 1300.[34]

Angelic reform, as we have termed it, was most often a hybrid type, involving roles for both a good Last World Emperor and a Holy Pope, and often expressed within the contours of a more or less Joachite theology of history. The marked contrast (at least in the eyes of Spiritual Franciscans) between the holy hermit Celestine V and the persecuting Boniface VIII is reflected in the Pseudo-Joachim *Angelic Oracle of Cyril* and its accompanying *Commentary* probably written in the 1290s, which identifies the former as the "correct pope" (*orthopontifex*) while condemning the latter as "false pope" (*pseudopontifex*) without going so far as to call him Antichrist. The most popular source for the angelic model of reform, however, was the *Prophecies of the Supreme Pontiffs* (*Vaticinia de summis pontificibus*).[35] These obscure oracles, like so much late medieval apocalyptic literature, were ascribed to Joachim of Fiore, but they actually show no trace of the distinctive marks of his apocalypticism, especially belief in the third *status*. Based on the Byzantine *Leo Oracles* of the twelfth century, their precise origin, dating, and development are still under dispute, but the work was certainly circulating in its finished form soon after 1300.[36] After a succession of pictures and brief vatic texts describing occupants of the papal throne from Nicholas III to Boniface VIII, the *Prophecies* conclude with a series of five captioned scenes representing a pre-Antichrist millennialism in which a Holy Pope replaces the traditional Last World Emperor as the one who will bring peace and prosperity to *christianitas*.[37] The *Prophecies* are a purely papal view of apocalyptic reform, but a contemporary work (the first in which the term *pastor angelicus* is actually found) testifies to the combination of the imperial and papal models hinted at by Roger Bacon. The *Book of Fiore* was written shortly after 1304.[38] Like the *Prophecies,* the *Book of Fiore* (again ascribed to Joachim) lists a series of good and evil popes that can be historically identified through *vaticinia ex eventu* (in this case the line extends from Gregory IX to Boniface VIII). In passing from history disguised as prophecy to real apocalyptic prediction, the *Book of Fiore* breaks new ground, however, in predicting a succession of four such holy pontiffs, a continuity which allows for a fairly significant millennial period before the arrival of the Final Enemy. The first of these popes, who is described as both *pastor angelicus* and the *rectificator* of Christianity, will make an alliance with "a noble king of Pippin's posterity" (i.e., a king of France) and will anoint him emperor of East and West. In tandem, the Angelic Pope and Last Emperor will miraculously accomplish the political and religious reform of Christendom, reuniting the Eastern and Western churches, recapturing Jerusalem, pacifying Italy, purifying the church and restoring it to a life of true poverty, and, finally, destroying all weapons of war. The three successors of this *pastor angelicus* are described as accomplishing equally impressive miracles of reform subsequent to the death of the Last Emperor, who is clearly a secondary player. This fusion of the figures of holy pope and pious emperor of the last days was to find many imitators in the next two centuries.

CONTINUITY AND CHANGE IN REFORM
   APOCALYPTICISM (1350–1500)

The seeds sown in the twelfth century and developed in such a rich fashion between 1200 and 1350 continued to bear fruit in the next century and one-half (see Rusconi 1979; *L'attesa* 1962; and Potestà 1991). The major new creation in Western apocalypticism during this time, that is, the identification of the office of the papacy itself (not merely individual bad popes) with Antichrist was the work of movements whose story will be told in the following essay. Here it remains to describe how the four heuristic models proposed at the outset of this essay allow us to grasp something of the ongoing power of apocalypticism in the late Middle Ages.

The mid-fourteenth century provides a transitional point not only because the essential modes of relating expectations of the end and the reform of Christendom were all fully formed by that time but also because of the way in which the horror of the Black Death (whose major onslaught took place in 1347–1349) created a caesura in medieval history. A simplified view of apocalypticism that sees the heightening of fears of the end only as a reaction to contemporary trials and crises would lead one to expect that this unrivaled disaster would have had a major effect on late medieval apocalypticism. There were, to be sure, some popular prophecies of the end that circulated at the time of the plague, and it is also noted as one of the signs of coming judgment in contemporary apocalyptic treatises, such as the Franciscan John of Rupescissa's *Book of Secret Events*.[39] Nevertheless, the Black Death did not effect a major shift in Western apocalypticism, largely because the models for understanding the end were already set and particular crises, small or large, were more easily incorporated into existing structures than productive of new scenarios, at least in the fourteenth and fifteenth centuries.

A number of more or less apocalyptic preachers of the time were proponents of the Gregorian model; that is, they announced reformation of the church in head and members in the light of the impending second coming, usually without millennial hopes. This is arguably also the view that inspired William Langland's great poem "Piers Plowman" (three versions composed between 1365 and 1385).[40] It is clearly the approach found in prophecies of Birgitta of Sweden (ca. 1303–1373), who was commanded to go to Rome by Christ in order to offer "revelations for the reformation of the church" to both the pope and the emperor. The Swedish seer's pronouncements were usually threats of divine retribution directed to individuals, but they include generalized apocalyptic messages as well (McGinn 1979a, 244–45). A number of apocalyptic prophecies were later pseudonymously ascribed to Birgitta. More directly apocalyptic are two reform preachers of the early fifteenth century, the Dominican Vincent Ferrer (ca. 1350–1419) and the Observantine Franciscan Bernardino of Siena (1380–1444).

These two figures, arguably the most important preachers of their era, provide ample evidence for the ongoing significance of a broadly Gregorian reformist stance in the late medieval church, especially during the time of the Great Western Schism (1378–1417) when popes installed at Avignon vied with those at Rome for ecclesiastical leadership. Vincent and Bernardino are also interesting in representing different reactions to the ultimate usefulness of apocalyptic preaching.

Vincent Ferrer managed to be officially canonized by the eventually triumphant Roman line of popes despite his lifelong adherence to their Avignon opponents. The sad events of the papal schism had convinced him that Antichrist had already been born, that terrible persecution was imminent, and that moral reform of both clergy and laity was the only hope of salvation for those who were witnessing these last events. In his widespread preaching missions in France and Spain, Vincent used both biblical texts and contemporary visions to proclaim the message that Antichrist was alive and the last times were already under way. His more optimistic hopes for what would soon unfold did not exceed the traditional forty-five-day period of repentance allowed for those who gave way to Antichrist, though he was pessimistic about how many might be willing to convert:

> Only with difficulty will those who followed the Antichrist return to repentance. The reason is that those who received great treasures will not want to return them. The religious who received many beautiful diabolical wives and bore many children to increase their guilt will have become accustomed to their solace. . . . And the same in the case of nuns or laity of any state of life. After these days, there will immediately come a fire from East to West. . . . The whole earth and anything that is in it will burn so that it will be like ashes in a furnace. (McGinn 1979a, 258)

If the Dominican preacher is a good example of a rigorist reformer with no doubts that the end was not just near but really at hand, Bernardino of Siena represents the case of someone who began preaching a message of imminent chastisement before the end but who then modified his message in the light of what seemed like more promising times for a newly reformed church. In his early preaching at the time of the crisis of the conciliar attempts to solve the schism (1413–1417), Bernardino's message was essentially pessimistic, centering on the necessity for repentance as Antichrist's persecution dawns; but, after the end of the schism through the Council of Constance in 1417 and the election of Martin V, the Franciscan gradually altered his message, first to one emphasizing the necessity of opposition to the spirit of Antichrist present in immorality (like the widespread practice of usury), and subsequently to a form of moralizing homiletics in which the evils of the day were condemned along with attacks on preachers who were announcing Antichrist's imminence.[41] Many mendicant preachers and publicists of the fifteenth century followed in the wake of Vincent and Bernardino. In the 1490s the Dominican Savonarola, for example, began from a reformist position close to those of Vincent and the early Bernardino, though (as chapter 4 shows) the situation of late Quattrocento Florence moved him in directions neither of his predecessors would have condoned.

In the late medieval period the reputation of the abbot Joachim continued to grow, especially through the pseudonymous works ascribed to him. If Joachim's name was widespread, it must nevertheless be said that there were relatively few late medieval apocalyptic texts that were direct representatives of the Joachite model of reform, in the sense that they were based on a three-age view of history which saw in contemporary events the signs of the ending of the second era and the dawning of the third. Among the most interesting of these was a treatise written in Spain about 1350 entitled *The Summary of the Concordance of the New and the Old Testaments,* one of the few texts in the late Middle Ages that took the abbot's original model of biblical exegesis seriously not only by attempting to work out "concords" between the ages of the Old and the New Testaments, but also by being more specific about how such parallels reveal information about the dawning third *status* (Lee 1989). Nevertheless, the distance from the real Joachim, and even from his most faithful disciple Olivi, is evident in the loss of the trinitarian foundation of the three-age model. Much of the late medieval apocalyptic literature ascribed to the Calabrian abbot, or influenced in one way or another by his thought, abandoned his distinctive theology of history in favor of a concentration on political prophecy.

Political prophecy in the later Middle Ages, to be sure, was not restricted to the Joachite camp. There were, for example, non-Joachite updatings of the Last Emperor traditions. "The Second Charlemagne Prophecy," which Marjorie Reeves has described as having "the widest vogue of any political prophecy in the fifteenth and sixteenth centuries" (Reeves 1993, 330), was originally composed for the French king Charles VI on his accession in 1380, hailing him as the descendant of Charlemagne who would be crowned emperor by the Angelic Pastor, conquer Europe, subdue all the enemies of Christendom, and eventually surrender his crown on the Mount of Olives. Francophile versions of the Last Emperor were countered by new oracles insisting on the German identity of the final world ruler, not only the "Third Frederick" texts noted above, but new creations like the "Prophecy of Gamaleon." According to this prophecy of the early fifteenth century, the new Charlemagne's attempt to take power away from Germany would induce the Germans to elect an emperor from the Rhineland who would attack and slay the second Charles, transfer the papacy to Mainz, strip the church of its worldly possessions, and kill all priests! (McGinn 1979a, 251–52).

Some of the most interesting prophecies of the late Middle Ages, however, while not using an explicit three-age pattern of history, combined political expectations (both imperial and papal) with hopes originally stemming from Joachim for a coming era of a renewed Christianity after the destruction of the Antichrist of the present era. The prime example is a treatise known as *The Great Tribulations and the State of the Church,* which announces itself as a vision that came to "humble brother Telesphorus of Cosenza, a poor priest and hermit," in 1386 (Telesphorus is probably a pseudonym). Since 1300 at least, prophecies had been announcing a coming schism that would pit an Angelic Pastor against a Papal Antichrist. Thus, the outbreak of the Great Schism in 1378 was another fortuitous example of prediction fulfilled that confirmed the authority of the entire prophetic scenario. The Telesphoran text, which Roberto Rusconi has described as "the ultimate development of the Joachimite prophetic tradition" (Rusconi 1979, 182), appears to be a conflation of two texts relating to the schism, the first written ca. 1360 predicting an "imminent schism," and an updated version from the 1380s, which includes *vaticinia ex eventu* about the "present schism." Its complicated apocalyptic scenario unfolds in three acts. First, the Mystical Antichrist (a German), born about 1365, is crowned as Frederick III by a false German pope. A terrible struggle then breaks out, pitting the evil pope and emperor against the Second Charlemagne, who is crowned legitimate world ruler by the *pastor angelicus* (fig. 1). In the second act, the triumphant forces of good have to face the Great Antichrist (*antichristus magnus*), who arises in 1378 and leads the church into schism. Telesphorus predicts that the good pope and emperor will finally defeat him in 1393 and usher in a succession of holy popes who will reign down to 1433. The third act begins with the Second Charlemagne laying down his crown in Jerusalem so that Gog, the Final Antichrist, can be revealed to begin his persecution of the church. Telesphorus predicts that he too will be defeated and that there will be a second messianic period of peace before the end. Confusing as it is, the Telesphoran treatise remained popular in the fifteenth and sixteenth centuries, often being produced in richly illustrated versions (Guerrini 1997).

The fifteenth century witnessed a rich proliferation of popular preachers of the end, whose ideas were widely disseminated toward the close of the century through the new medium of the printed page. The ability of apocalypticism to combine deep fear about savage persecution and final destruction with fervent hope for a perfect age of peace in a fully purified church took on special flavors in the cultural atmosphere of the Renaissance. The more optimistic side of medieval apocalypticism also played a role in the discovery of the New World, or at least in the effort to understand the meaning of this epochal event. Christopher Columbus had dabbled in prophetic texts since about 1480. His was scarcely a pessimistic view, since he believed the end was some 150 years off. Following a line of Iberian imperial prophecies which stressed the role of Spanish rulers in leading crusades against the Muslims and recapturing Jerusalem, Columbus believed that his discoveries were proof of a dawning millennial age. In 1501, during the break between his third and fourth voyages, with the help of the Carthusian Gaspar Garritio, he put together a compilation of texts from the Bible, the church fathers, and various medieval authors that he called *The Book of Prophecies*. Its intention was to show how his three earlier voyages were connected with the project he now proposed to his patrons Ferdinand and Isabella—the recovery of the Holy Land from the Muslims, the rebuilding of the Jerusalem Temple with gold from the Indies, and the beginning of a millennial age of Spanish rule and worldwide conversion. The same hope is expressed in the account he wrote of his fourth and final voyage (1502–4), which reads in part:

> Jerusalem and Mount Zion are to be rebuilt by the hand of a Christian; who this is to be God declares by the mouth of his prophet in the fourteenth psalm [Ps. 14:7–8]. Abbot Joachim said that he was to come from Spain. . . . The emperor of Cathy some time since sent for wise men to instruct him in the faith of Christ. Who will offer himself for this work? If our Lord brings me back to Spain, I pledge myself, in the name of God, to bring him there in safety.[42]

Apocalyptic hopes—and fears—were soon to migrate to the New World itself (see chapter 16 below).

These four models of relating apocalyptic expectations and the imperative for reform are designed to provide an overview of what can be described as the central core of apocalypticism between 1100 and 1500. Obviously, there were many other applications and implications of the fears and hopes of medieval people for the events that they believed would come, sooner or later, to close off history. The complex story of various popular prophecies, recorded and unrecorded, and what these have to tell us about the social dynamics of apocalyptic prophecy are certainly a major part of this broader story, but it is not clear that such beliefs form a different model of apocalyptic thinking from those analyzed above.

Apocalypticism can be thought of as constituting a broad stream of religio-political beliefs and practices that can be used by many different groups in a society (both high and low), as well as for a variety of purposes, both those that try to "reform," and therefore generally support and strengthen societal order, and those that threaten or subvert it. This essay has concentrated on movements that stress how apocalypticism was employed to consolidate the medieval sense of the correct order of *christianitas* through calls for reform in the light of the second coming. The following essay will show how apocalyptic reform often contained within it the seeds of more radical, even revolutionary, potential. In the long run it is impossible to separate these two aspects of the dynamics of apocalypticism.

☞ NOTES _____

1. The "Legend of the Year 1000" goes back to the church historian Cesare Baronio (1538–1607) and was given wide dissemination by Jules Michelet (1798–1874). Without attempting to revive older forms of the legend of the terrors, some recent studies have sought to show that there was an increase in apocalyptic expectations, both positive and negative, in the tenth and eleventh centuries; see Johannes Fried, "Endzeiterwartung um die Jahrtausendwende," *Deutsches Archiv* 45 (1989): 381–473; Richard Landes, *Relics, Apocalypse and the Deceits of History: Ademar of Chabannes, 989–1034* (Cambridge, Mass.: Harvard University Press, 1995), 285–327; idem, "Rodolfus Glaber and the Dawn of the New Millennium: Eschatology, Historiography, and the Year 1000," *Revue Mabillon* n.s. 7 (1996): 57–77.

2. For Augustine's attitude toward apocalypticism, see chapter 9 above, while Byzantine apocalyptic expectations are treated in chapter 10.

3. For early medieval apocalyptic views in Western Europe, see Bernard McGinn, "The End of the World and the Beginning of Christendom," in *Apocalypse Theory and the End of the World,* ed. Malcolm Bull (Oxford: Blackwell, 1995), 58–89; and Fried, "Endzeiterwartung um die Jahrtausendwende."

4. On the Antichrist, see Emmerson 1981, and McGinn 1994b.

5. In this essay the term "millennial" implies any belief in a final age of peace on earth before the end, whether of a literal thousand years or not.

6. Three texts disseminated this legend in the early Middle Ages. The Pseudo-Methodian *Revelationes,* written in Syriac ca. 690, were soon translated into Greek and Latin and were widely read. Adso's *Epistola de Antichristo* contained a westernized version of the legend. The surviving Latin forms of the Greek *Sibylla Tiburtina,* which began to proliferate from ca. 1000, also have a Last Emperor figure.

7. See Robert E. Lerner, "Refreshment of the Saints: The Time After Antichrist as a Station for Earthly Progress in Medieval Thought," *Traditio* 32 (1976): 97–144. This period after Antichrist (usually forty-five days) is based on the discrepancy in Dan. 12:11–12 between two numerations of the reign of the Abomination (= Antichrist). Hippolytus and after him Jerome were the sources of the tradition.

8. For a classic analysis of the early development, see Gerhart B. Ladner, *The Idea of Reform: Its Impact on Christian Thought and Action in the Age of the Fathers* (Cambridge, Mass.: Harvard University Press, 1959). A summary of later views and literature can be found in Gerald Strauss, "Ideas of *Reformatio* and *Renovatio* from the Middle Ages to the Reformation," in *Handbook of European History 1400–1600,* ed. Thomas A. Brady, Jr., Heiko A. Oberman, James D. Tracy (Grand Rapids: Eerdmans, 1995), 2:1–30. Strauss defines reform as "healing reversion to a prior norm" (p. 4).

9. For an early critique, see Herbert Grundmann's review in *Historische Zeitschrift* 196 (1963): 661–65.

10. The phrase is taken from Timothy P. Weber, *Living in the Shadow of the Second Coming: American Premillennialism 1875–1982,* 2nd ed. (Chicago: University of Chicago Press, 1987).

11. The connection between apocalypticism and reform has been investigated by Kerby-Fulton (1990, especially 1–9), who identifies "reformist apocalypticism" primarily with the cleansing of abuses in the clerical life. The term is taken in a wider sense in this essay. See also the forthcoming work of E. Randolph Daniel, *History of Reformist Apocalypticism.*

12. On this *figura,* see McGinn 1979b, 142–48; the most detailed study is in Reeves 1972, 232–48.

13. See Joachim's *Liber de Concordie* 4.1.45 (ed. E. R. Daniel, 402; Venice ed. f. 56rb). This latter figure, whose type is the "angel ascending from the rising of the sun having the sign of the living God" (Rev. 7:2), seems identical with the *pater spiritualis* who presides over the monastic utopia of the third *status.*

14. See M.-D. Chenu, *Nature, Man and History in the Twelfth Century* (Chicago: University of Chicago Press, 1968), chaps. 4–5; and Richard W. Southern, "Aspects of the European Tradition of Historical Writing," *Royal Historical Association, Transactions,* 5th series, 20 (1970): 173–96; 21 (1971): 159–79; 22 (1972): 159–80.

15. On early medieval exegesis of Revelation, see Paula Fredriksen and E. Ann Matter in Emmerson

and McGinn 1992, 20–50. On Rupert of Deutz, the standard work is John H. Van Engen, *Rupert of Deutz* (Berkeley: University of California Press, 1983).

16. For a translation, see McGinn 1979a, 113–14. Seeing contemporary troubles as marking the freeing of Satan after his one-thousand-year captivity was not completely new, since the eleventh-century monk Raoul Glaber had already done so in the second book of his *Quinque libri historiarum.*

17. See Karl F. Morrison, "The Exercise of Thoughtful Minds: The Apocalypse in some German Historical Writings," in Emmerson and McGinn 1992, 352–73.

18. For Hildegard's views of the necessity of clerical reform, see also Kathryn Kerby-Fulton, "A Return to the 'First Dawn of Justice': Hildegard's Visions of Clerical Reform and the Eremitical Life," *American Benedictine Review* 40 (1989): 383–407; and the same author's forthcoming paper on Hildegard as "Prophet and Reformer" in *Voice of the Living Light: Hildegard of Bingen and Her World,* ed. Barbara Newman (Berkeley: University of California Press, 1998).

19. See Hildegard *Scivias* 3.11 (a work completed in 1151). In her *Liber divinorum operum* 3.10–11 (finished in 1174) she expands on the *Scivias* showing. These five periods are symbolized by animal figures, as found in much early and medieval apocalyptic literature.

20. There is an English translation by John Wright, *The Play of Antichrist* (Toronto: PIMS, 1967).

21. Wright (*The Play of Antichrist,* 46–47) plausibly suggests that the abrupt ending in the manuscript, *Laus Deo nostro,* reflecting Rev. 19:5, is merely the introduction to a longer hymn based on the heavenly victory song that in Revelation comes after the fall of Babylon and *before* the final events.

22. Control over Jerusalem, however, was traditionally associated with imperial apocalyptic legends, so the success of the papally sponsored crusade undercut imperial claims and is another example of the clash of apocalyptic models.

23. For a survey of the quarrel and translations of key texts, see McGinn 1979a, 168-79; and chapters 9 and 10 below. Also consult Töpfer 1964, 155–82; and Hans-Martin Schaller, "Endzeit-Erwartung und Antichrist-Vorstellung in der Politik des 13. Jahrhunderts," in *Festschrift für Hermann Heimpel* (Göttingen: Vandenhoeck & Ruprecht, 1972), 2:924–47.

24. For this suggestion and proof of Innocent's use of Joachim's ideas, see Fiona Robb, "Did Innocent III Personally Condemn Joachim of Fiore?," *Florensia* 7 (1993): 135–42.

25. Robert E. Lerner, "Frederick II, Alive, Aloft, and Allayed, in Franciscan-Joachite Eschatology," in Verbeke 1988, 359–84.

26. On the *viri spirituales* and their history in the Middle Ages and beyond, see Reeves 1993, part 3; and McGinn, "Apocalyptic Traditions and Spiritual Identity in Thirteenth-Century Religious Life," in McGinn 1994a, chapter 7.

27. See E. Randolph Daniel, *The Franciscan Concept of Mission in the High Middle Ages* (Lexington: University Press of Kentucky, 1975).

28. In later centuries this apocalyptic theme was to be widespread among a number of religious orders, especially Augustinians and Jesuits.

29. The *Super Hieremiam* was one of the most widely read of the works that circulated under Joachim's name. While the text may contain a core that goes back to the abbot himself, in its surviving forms it appears to be the work of Franciscans anxious to find support for the historical significance of their order under the name of the famous prophet. There is no modern edition; for a study, see Robert Moynihan, "The Development of the 'Pseudo-Joachim' Commentary 'Super Hieremiam': New Manuscript Evidence," *Mélanges de l'école français de Rome: Moyen age-temps modernes* 98 (1986): 109–42.

30. We are not sure where this identification, which is not in Joachim, began, though it seems quite possible that it was with John of Parma himself. See Stanislao da Campagnola, *L'Angelo del sesto sigillo e l'"alter Christus"* (Rome: Laurentianum, 1971).

31. During this time the other major Sibylline text of the Middle Ages, the *Sibylla Erythraea,* an imperial oracle translated from Greek to Latin in the late twelfth century, was reworked by Joachite Franciscans to include *vaticinia ex eventu* of the evil Frederick and his family.

32. Ernst Kantorowicz, *Frederick the Second, 1194–1250* (London: Constable, 1931), 608.

33. This account partly overlaps with that given in the following chapter, largely because the Spiritual Franciscans, beguins, and their *Fraticelli* successors represent a good example of how difficult it is distinguish when reformist apocalypticism passes over into radical uses of apocalyptic ideology.

34. There were, of course, contributions to the hopes for a coming final holy pope which appear to be largely untouched by Joachite speculation, as in the case of Roger Bacon and also the Dominican visionary Robert d'Uzès (d. 1296). It is still controversial how far some of the major texts relating to the *pastor angelicus* can be proven to have been composed by Franciscans.

35. The *Vaticinia* were among the most popular of medieval apocalyptic texts. Over sixty manuscripts are known, many richly illustrated; there were twenty-four printings between 1505 and 1670.

36. For important recent contributions to the history of the *Vaticinia*, see Andreas Rehberg, who shows that the prophecies were first applied to cardinals rather than popes ("Der 'Kardinalsorakel'-Kommentar in der 'Colonna'-Handschrift Vat. lat. 3819 und die Enstehungsumstände der Papstvatizinien," *Florensia* 5 [1991]: 45–112); and Robert E. Lerner, "Recent Work on the Origins of the 'Genus Nequam' Prophecies," *Florensia* 7 (1993): 141–57.

37. The popularity of this first series of *Vaticinia* led to the creation of a second set by Provençal beguins ca. 1330 (see chapter 12 below).

38. There is no modern edition of the work, which appears to survive in only five manuscripts. For an account, see McGinn 1994a, chapter 6.

39. For more on John, whose basic apocalyptic scenario combined Franciscan Joachitism, Francophile imperialism and hopes for the coming *pastor angelicus,* consult chapter 12 below. For the role of the Black Death in apocalypticism, see Robert E. Lerner, "The Black Death and Western European Eschatological Mentalities," *American Historical Review* 86 (1980): 533–52.

40. There has been considerable debate as to whether "Piers Plowman" shows evidence of an optimistic current of hopes for the church, perhaps even of Joachite persuasion, or is primarily pessimistic.

41. Among these were the Dominican Manfred of Vercelli, whose popular preaching of Antichrist's imminence had inspired a penitential movement which believed that flight to Jerusalem was the only way to escape destruction.

42. From the so-called *Lettera Rarissima* (McGinn 1979a, 285). The exact identity of text of Joachim to which Columbus refers has been disputed, but it is most likely the pseudo-Joachite prophecy *Ve mundo in centum annis* written in Catalonia ca. 1300.

⌒ BIBLIOGRAPHY ────────────────────────────────────

Given the extensive literature dealing with medieval apocalypticism, this list contains only monographs and collections of essays, not individual articles.

L'attesa dell'età nuova nella spiritualità della fine del medioevo. Todi: L'Accademia Tudertina, 1962. A collection of fifteen essays, mostly Italian, dealing with apocalypticism in the fourteenth and fifteenth centuries.

Burr, David. 1993. *Olivi's Peaceable Kingdom: A Reading of the Apocalypse Commentary.* Philadelphia: University of Pennsylvania Press. The best study of Olivi's apocalypticism.

Capitani, Ovidio, and Jürgen Miethke, eds. 1990. *L'attesa della fine dei tempi nel Medioevo.* Bologna: il Mulino. Eight essays in Italian on aspects of medieval apocalypticism.

Cohn, Norman. 1957, with later editions. *The Pursuit of the Millennium: Revolutionary messianism in Medieval and Reformation Europe and its bearing on modern totalitarian movements.* New York: Essential Books. A provocative and seminal work, though its conclusions about the radical nature of apocalyptic movements have been modified by subsequent research.

Crocco, Antonio, ed. 1986. *L'età dello Spirito e la fine dei tempi in Gioacchino da Fiore e nel gioachimismo medievale: Atti del II Congresso Internazionale di Studi Gioachimiti, 1984.* S. Giovanni in Fiore: Centro Internazionale di Studi Gioachimiti. Twenty papers in various languages dealing with Joachim's third *status* and reactions to it.

Emmerson, Richard Kenneth. 1981. *Antichrist in the Middle Ages: A Study of Medieval Apocalypticism, Art, and Literature.* Seattle: University of Washington. A fine survey of medieval uses of Antichrist across a broad range of materials.

Emmerson, Richard Kenneth, and Bernard McGinn, eds. 1992. *The Apocalypse in the Middle Ages.* Ithaca: Cornell University Press. Seventeen essays dealing with the use of Revelation in medieval thought, art, and literature.

Grundmann, Herbert. 1927. *Studien über Joachim von Fiore.* Leipzig: Teubner. The first major study devoted to Joachim; still valuable. The recent Italian version, *Studi su Gioacchino da Fiore* (Genoa: Marietti, 1989), contains a helpful introduction.

Guerrini, Paola. 1997. *Propaganda politica e profezie figurate nel tardo medioevo.* Naples: Liguori. Studies late medieval illustrated apocalyptic texts.

Kerby-Fulton, Kathryn. 1990. *Reformist Apocalypticism and 'Piers Plowman'.* Cambridge: Cambridge University Press. An analysis of how clerical reformist apocalypticism influenced the later Middle Ages and shaped Langland's "Piers Plowman."

Lee, Harold, with Majorie Reeves and Giulio Silano. 1989. *Western Mediterranean Prophecy: The School of Joachim of Fiore and the Fourteenth-Century 'Breviloquium.'* Toronto: PIMS. Edition of an important Joachite text from Catalonia with a lenthy introduction on fourteenth-century Joachitism.

Lerner, Robert E. 1983. *The Powers of Prophecy: The Cedars of Lebanon Vision from the Mongol Onslaught to the Dawn of the Enlightenment.* Berkeley: University of California Press. A study of the transformations of one later medieval prophetic text.

———. 1995. *Refrigerio dei santi: Gioacchino da Fiore e l'escatologia medievale.* Rome: Viella. Collects and translates from English eight of the author's most important studies of medieval apocalypticism.

McGinn, Bernard. 1979a. *Visions of the End: Apocalyptic Traditions in the Middle Ages.* New York: Columbia University Press. An anthology and commentary on medieval apocalyptic texts from 400 to 1500. 2nd ed. 1998.

———. 1979b. *Apocalyptic Spirituality: Treatises and Letters of Lactantius, Adso of Montier-en-Der, Joachim of Fiore, the Spiritual Franciscans, Savonarola.* New York: Paulist Press.

———. 1985. *The Calabrian Abbot: Joachim of Fiore in the History of Western Thought.* New York: Macmillan. Sets forth the main lines of Joachim's life and thought, as well the reaction to Joachim by Thomas Aquinas and Bonaventure.

———. 1994a. *Apocalypticism in the Western Tradition.* Hampshire: Variorum. Reprints twelve essays dealing with medieval apocalypticism.

———. 1994b. *Antichrist: Two Thousand Years of the Human Fascination with Evil.* San Francisco: HarperSanFrancisco. A general history of the Antichrist from biblical roots to the twentieth century.

Mottu, Henry. 1977. *La manifestation de l'Esprit selon Joachim de Fiore.* Neuchâtel/Paris: Delachaux & Niestlé. An original hermeneutical approach demonstrating the radical implications of Joachim's view of the third *status*.

Potestà, Gian Luca, ed. 1991. *Il profetismo gioachimita tra Quattrocento e Cinquecento: Atti del III Congresso Internazionale di Studi Gioachmiti, 1989.* Genoa: Marietti. A rich collection of twenty-nine essays in varying languages dealing with the heritage of Joachim of Fiore.

Potestà, Gian Luca, and Roberto Rusconi, eds. 1996. *Lo statuto della profezia nel Medioevo (Cristianesimo nell Storia 17/2 [Giugno, 1996]).* Seven essays in English and Italian dealing with medieval understandings of the role of prophecy.

Ratzinger, Joseph. 1971. *The Theology of History of St. Bonaventure.* Chicago: Franciscan Herald Press. Translation of ground-breaking study of Bonaventure's apocalypticism, originally published in German in 1959.

Rauh, Horst Dieter. 1973. *Das Bild des Antichrist im Mittelalter: Vom Tyconius zum Deutschen Symbolismus.* Münster: Aschendorff. Detailed study of German apocalyptic thinkers of the twelfth century.

Reeves, Marjorie. 1993. *The Influence of Prophecy in the Later Middle Ages: A Study of Joachimism.* Notre Dame: University of Notre Dame Press. Second, slightly revised, edition of Reeves's most important work on late medieval apocalypticism. A rich mine of information.

————, and Beatrice Hirsch-Reich. 1972. *The Figurae of Joachim of Fiore.* Oxford: Clarendon Press. Most detailed study of Joachim's noted *figurae,* or diagrams, illustrating his apocalyptic view of history.

Rusconi, Roberto. 1979. *L'attesa della fine: Crisi della società, profezia ed Apocalisse in Italia al tempo del grande scisma d'Occidente (1378–1417).* Rome: Istituto Storico Italiano per il Medio Evo. Important contribution to the understanding of apocalypticism in late medieval Italy.

Szittya, Penn R. 1986. *The Antifraternal Tradition in Medieval Literature.* Princeton: Princeton University Press. Shows how the crisis of the "Eternal Gospel" of the mid-thirteenth century established an important apocalyptic topos in late medieval literature.

Töpfer, Bernhard. 1964. *Das kommende Reich des Friedens: Zur Entwicklung chiliastischer Zukunftshoffnungen im Hochmittelalter.* Berlin: Akademie Verlag. What appears to be a rigidly Marxist view of medieval apocalypticism actually turns out as one of the most insightful accounts ever given of the period ca. 1100–1300.

Verbeke, Werner, Daniel Verhelst, and Andries Welkenhuysen, eds. 1988. *The Use and Abuse of Eschatology in the Middle Ages.* Leuven: Leuven University Press. Perhaps the most important recent collection of papers on medieval apocalypticism (twenty essays in various languages).

Williams, Ann, ed. 1980. *Prophecy and Millenarianism: Essays in Honour of Marjorie Reeves.* Essex: Longman. Sixteen essays dealing with medieval and early modern apocalyptic themes.

12

Radical Apocalyptic Movements in the Late Middle Ages

Gian Luca Potestà
Catholic University, Milan

The field of eschatological movements and thinkers in the late Middle Ages is extremely vast. This essay will be limited to analyzing their apocalyptic aspects, thus paying no attention to professional exegetes, ecclesiastical preachers on Revelation, and collectors of prophetic and apocalyptic texts. I will focus exclusively on those movements and thinkers who behaved according to the belief that the final events were at hand and would bring about dramatic changes. These thinkers held that some texts, such as commentaries on the book of Revelation as well as prophecies and other predictions, supported their convictions. I will examine these texts in order to understand how these apocalyptic thinkers prepared for the end (almost always for "their" end).

In the past, historians focused on the social structure of the apocalyptic movements in the late Middle Ages. Scholars wished to discern if and to what extent these groups could be seen as precursors of the revolutionary movements in the modern era. This essay results from a more recent concept of historiography and aims to reconstruct the conceptual background of the radical apocalyptic movements. In particular, it will investigate how their patrimony of creeds, doctrines, and behaviors originated, was transmitted, and was modified. As a consequence, the highly debated issue concerning the mental condition of the apocalypticists loses its interest.[1] Although we admit that in some cases these thinkers may have been insane, we must recognize that their insanity had historical relevance. In most cases they were persecuted by the ecclesiastical authorities not because of their folly but because they expressed creeds and behaviors that were radically apocalyptic.

An apocalyptic interpretation of reality, however, does not necessarily entail a revolutionary attitude. Joachim of Fiore succeeded in combining an apocalyptic sensitivity with a substantial respect for contemporary ecclesiastical authority. In the thirteenth century, the Franciscans easily interpreted Joachim's message according to their propaganda, thus showing that an apocalyptic lexicon could be used for religious self-promotion. In the last part of the century, however, sects and secondary movements of Franciscan origin reappropriated Joachim's perspectives, highlighting aspects of his message that had subversive undertones. At the beginning of the fourteenth century the revival of apocalyptic thought acquired a heretical connotation.

We will examine briefly the social classes, the milieus, the cultural levels, and the ecclesiastical and political groups that were involved in each new apocalyptic movement. Indeed, it is impossible to fit these complex and multifaceted experiences into one all-encompassing interpretation. Nevertheless, we may say that one common tendency is recognizable: although they maintained their original religious elements, the new apocalyptic movements of the late Middle Ages acquired a much stronger social and political connotation. Their discourse tended to move from a criticism against the worldly church and hope for its reformation toward a longing for deep changes in society in all its political aspects.

THE APOSTOLICS AND DOLCINO

In the last decades of the thirteenth century the so-called movement of the Apostolics, founded in Parma by the layman Gerardo Segarelli, became very popular. Originating in the vast undercurrent that gave rise to the mendicant orders, this movement became a particularly dangerous rival for the Friars Minor. Their similar origin explains the polemic and ironic statements made about them by the Franciscan chronicler Salimbene of Parma. According to him, the Apostolics should resume their original activities—as cowherds, herdsmen of pigs, and peasants.[2] If we believe his testimony, the Apostolics came from the countryside. Although their social positions were modest, they were neither poor nor marginalized. When he initiated his religious movement, Gerardo had sold his "little house." Similarly, when they joined the new fraternity, his disciples sold "their little houses, their gardens, their fields and vineyards."[3] Women represented a comparatively large section of the movement (Orioli 1988, 187–213).

When Segarelli was burned at the stake as a heretic (July 1300), Fra Dolcino replaced him as the leader of the Apostolics. A layman with some knowledge of theology, Dolcino gave his message a clearly apocalyptic tone. The author of the treatise *The Sect of Those Who Say They Belong to the Order of the Apostles* (1316) mentions that Dolcino sent three letters to his followers, and transcribes passages from two of them (the original texts have been lost).[4] In the first letter (August 1300), introducing himself as the new leader of the Apostolics, Dolcino divides history into four major *status*, or states: (1) the state under the law of the Old Testament, which allowed marriage; (2) the state under the church from its origins until Constantine and Pope Sylvester (in this era chastity and poverty were steps of perfection superior to married life and worldly goods); (3) the state of the church after Constantine (this era began with the conversion of the pagan peoples and had the clergy and the monks and friars as its main figures); and (4) the state of the imminent *reformatio* of the church and its return to its pristine life-style. A specific category of saints characterizes each of the four states: first, the patriarchs and prophets of the Old Testament; then Christ and the apostles; later, Benedict, Francis, and Dominic; finally, Gerardo Segarelli, described as the martyr and the defender of the return to the apostles' life-style. According to this letter, the church undergoes four crucial transformations. It is good, chaste, and persecuted during the period between Christ and Sylvester; in the following period the church is wealthy, praised, and devoted to goodness and chastity; then, in the era after Francis and Dominic, it becomes bad, rich, and proud. Finally, it will be poor, pure, and suffering in the era inaugurated by Gerardo Segarelli.[5]

In this case Franciscan-Joachite elements have molded an original vision of history. Joachim's scheme of the three states (which was appropriated by significant Franciscan groups in the thirteenth century) has been modified through the division of the state of the church into two different periods, before and after Constantine. This partition results from the belief that the contemporary church does not follow the original church any longer.

In the final part of the letter, whose content is simply summarized, Dolcino addresses the church's contemporary condition and expresses himself on what, according to his personal "revelations," would occur in the future. He criticizes the entire ecclesiastical institution, every religious order and in particular Boniface VIII, the ruling pope. According to Dolcino, this church will be soon destroyed by Frederick of Aragon, king of Trinacria. Frederick will be elected emperor and will select nine kings (in this way the apocalyptic number of ten horns or kings from Rev. 17:12–14 would be reached). Then he will take Boniface prisoner and will kill him along with those who deserve to die. Finally, a Holy Pope (*pastor angelicus*) will lead the church. This pope will be the Angel of Philadelphia, who had been preceded by six historical figures (St. Benedict, Pope Sylvester, St. Francis, St. Dominic, Segarelli, and Dolcino himself), each corresponding to one of the six angels mentioned in Revelation 2–3. Frederick's empire and the pontificate of the Holy Pope will last until the arrival of the Antichrist.[6] These eschatological expectations interpret themes that were quite common in the contemporary prophetic literature and propaganda. In particular, when he states that Frederick of Trinacria will free and renew the corrupt church, Dolcino refers to the hope, born in some Ghibelline groups, that a "third" Frederick would come and complete Frederick II's attack against the Roman Church (see chapter 11).

In 1303 Dolcino, his wife Margherita, and some friends had already been active north of the Lake Garda, where he was probably preaching in the attempt to make new proselytes. His second letter was written during this period (December 1303). In his first letter, Dolcino had already presented himself as the Angel of the Church of Thyatira, so his epistles are in fact apocalyptic messages, like the letters sent to the Angels of the Seven Churches of the Apocalypse. In the second letter, Dolcino explains his expectation of the "Holy Pope" in more detail. He presents a series of popes, in which the first is good (Celestine V, who had stepped down in 1294), the next two bad (Boniface VIII and his successor), and the final one the "Holy Pope," whose arrival is considered to be at hand.[7] Dolcino may have borrowed from the prophetic literature on the popes that had become popular at the time. He probably had a vague and indirect knowledge of this kind of writing, especially the *Prophecies concerning the Supreme Pontiffs* (*Vaticinia de summis pontificibus*).

In his second letter, Dolcino still believed that Frederick would be able to purify the corrupt church. His insistence on the king's historical role sprang from his expectations for the Italian Ghibelline party. In 1304 Dolcino moved to Piedmont with his family and disciples, first settling in the Sesia valley, then on the mountain of the "Parete Calva," and finally (1306) on the Monte Rubello. At least at the beginning, he chose high and inaccessible places not for military reasons but because he was convinced that, according to the prophetic texts of the Old Testament (Ezekiel and Obadiah), only the mountains could save the elect from the dread final events. In Piedmont his followers became more numerous, at least initially, perhaps about a thousand. Most of them were peasants from the Campertogno area.[8]

Dolcino did not think that he would carry out the church's forceful liberation himself. However, given that he had to support a large number of men and women, he was compelled to some acts of violent expropriation which brought about armed conflicts with the troops of Novara and Vercelli. Dolcino's forces were able to hold out on the Monte Rubello for almost a year, thanks to an initial series of positive sallies. Only in 1307 did the militias succeed in overcoming the stronghold of the famished Apostolics. More than four hundred people died. Dolcino was arrested, prosecuted, tortured, and finally burned at the same stake (June 1, 1307) where Margherita had just died.

Dolcino's story constitutes a significant moment in the history of medieval apocalyptic movements. Although the main themes of his prophetic discourse were familiar, such as the church's reformation according to poverty and purity, the "Holy Pope," the emperor who would purify the church, and so on, for the first time, thanks to Dolcino, these themes reached some sections of lay society that had no theological background. A small "congregation," as Dolcino's followers defined themselves, initially inspired by purely religious motivation, became involved in a broad social and political debate. Although Dolcino's message focused on the church's purification and reformation according to the gospel's teachings with no specific sociopolitical program, nonetheless, he became the head of a heretical group that acted autonomously in a particular territorial and social context (Orioli 1988, 224–32). Thanks to Dolcino, apocalyptic expectations finally moved outside of a restricted theological milieu and revealed revolutionary potential with ecclesiastical, social, and political implications.

THE FRANCISCAN SPIRITUALS

Inside the order of the Friars Minor, the Spirituals strongly criticized the evolution of the order itself, believing that it had abandoned Francis's original path. The first traces of the Spiritual movement can be found immediately after the Second Council of Lyon (1274), when a revolt was rapidly repressed.[9] Between the end of the thirteenth and the beginning of the fourteenth century, the Spirituals were active both in Italy and in southern France. When Pope Celestine V welcomed a delegation of Italian dissidents and allowed them to break away from the order (1294), the Spirituals believed that they were about to accomplish their objective of a Franciscan life outside the Friars Minor. But when Celestine resigned immediately after, his decisions could not be validated and legalized (for this story, see Potestà 1990, 27–35). Disappointed and upset because of the sudden political change, the Italian Spirituals came to believe that Celestine V's resignation and the election of Boniface VIII were illegal. Their opinion, shared by other ecclesiastical groups, was fostered by the cardinals Giacomo and Pietro Colonna.

This rigid political stand caused a substantial break between the Spirituals in southern France and those in central Italy, a crisis confirmed by the severe letter sent by Peter John Olivi to Conrad of Offida in 1295. Stressing the differences between the real "Spirituals" and the "erroneous and heretical extremists," the Provençal theologian regrets the Spirituals' decision of "fleeing the carnal society and its errors, wishing to fulfill Revelation's command: 'Come out, my people, away from Babylon, so that you do not share in her crimes' (Rev. 18:4)."[10] Indeed, during those months a group of Spirituals from the Marche region in Italy was heading east, while other groups stayed in Italy, composing prophetic and apocalyptic texts against Boniface VIII and fostering belief in an imminent resurrection of Francis of Assisi.[11] These Italian Spirituals produced works such as *Oracle of Cyril* (*Oraculum angelicum Cyrilli*) (ca. 1298) and the *Book of Fiore* (*Liber de Flore*).[12]

In the meantime Olivi had written a commentary on Revelation that would become the most influential book of Franciscan dissidence in the first decades of the fourteenth century.[13] In this *Lecture on Revelation* (*Lectura super Apocalipsim*) (1296–1297) Olivi offers a Franciscan reading of Joachim of Fiore. His apocalyptic perspective is unquestionably more controlled and cautious than that expressed by the contemporary circles of the Italian Spirituals. Olivi accepts Joachim's vision of the three *status*, but he modifies it by combining it with the doctrine of the three advents of Christ.[14] Between the first coming in the flesh and the last in the glory of judgment day, Olivi inserts an intermediate advent in the Spirit, one that will bring the church back to its original purity. He thinks that this second advent was embodied in Francis of Assisi, who thus represented the beginning of the third state of the world. The plan of the three advents entails a revision of Joachim's perspective, because it posits the Spirit's era within a Christocentric field and celebrates Francis of Assisi as a Christ-like figure corresponding to a specific apocalyptic character, that is, the Angel with the Seal of the Living God (Rev. 7:2; see Burr 1993, 118–21).

Olivi holds that, notwithstanding Francis's advent, the contemporary church is almost identical to the apocalyptic Babylon and that only a few elect are outside the "carnal church" (Burr 1993, 93–95). According to Olivi, these people will be attacked both by the mystic Antichrist and the open Antichrist. The first's coming is imminent; he might be a king, a pseudo-pope, or maybe the two of them together. Those few who will still be faithful to the gospel will be forced to run away. Within the church, Olivi says, they will be heeded more by the laity than by clerics and they will receive unexpected support from a pagan army that will destroy Babylon, that is, overthrow Rome and the carnal church. After the defeat of the mystic Antichrist, for a short while the elect will be given repose and a contemplative order will preach the gospel. This period will be interrupted by the arrival of the open Antichrist. After his rout, the third, or sabbatical, state will start, free of every form of temptation and adversity because it marks the time for the preparation of Jesus' final coming. Whereas Joachim was convinced that the sabbatical era would be very short, Olivi seems to believe that it will last almost seven-hundred years (Burr 1993, 163–78).

To explain how these apocalyptic expectations, created by some radical religious groups with a Franciscan background, spread throughout southern France, the Pyrenees, and Catalonia in the first half of the fourteenth century (the fundamental work remains Pou y Martí 1930; 1991), it is crucial to bear in mind the role played by Arnold of Villanova, the prime supporter of apocalyptic beliefs in those areas during the first decade of the century. Arnold was a layman, a physician with many spiritual and religious interests. A great bibliographer, he made use of Sibylline texts, oracles, and other predictions to interpret biblical apocalyptic passages announcing the imminent final events. In the beginning, Arnold thought that he could establish the exact date of the Antichrist's arrival. To support his conclusions, he wrote a *Treatise on the Time of Antichrist's Coming*, which he presented to the Parisian teachers in 1300. Because of their censure, he was indicted for heresy. Although in the following years the Dominicans repeatedly accused him of being *relapsus*, that is, an unrepentant heretic, Arnold was able to continue his exegetical work thanks to the protection of his patient, Boniface VIII. In the *Treatise* Arnold's calculation is based on a reckless exegesis of Daniel 12:7ff., a text he believed revealed the date of the Antichrist's coming, predicted for about 1368.[15]

In 1304 Arnold went to Benedict XI's court at Perugia in order to defend himself against the Dominicans, who accused him of heresy, as well as to support the cause of the Spirituals, with whom he had become aligned. At the time of the next conclave (1304–1305), Arnold modified his eschatological theories, referring to a series of "particular revelations," that is, some prophetic and apocalyptic texts (e.g., the *Book of Fiore*) that he had just encountered thanks to his contacts with the Spirituals of central Italy. In his unpublished *Exposition on the 24th Chapter of Matthew,* composed at that time, he interpreted this apocalyptic chapter of the Gospel in a way that allowed him to determine the following series of final events: (1) an ongoing tribulation, lasting no more than thirty years and starting from the reign of Nicholas III (1277–1280); (2) reformation of the church and advent of the Angelic Pope; (3) Antichrist's advent and the battle between the devil and the elect; (4) a short period of peace granted to the elect so that they can repent; and (5) the final coming of Jesus as judge (see Potestà 1994). In comparison with the earlier *Treatise,* in this text Arnold introduced an intermediate period characterized by the advent of a pope who would cherish the perfection of early Christianity and honor those who practice it. Rather than stressing Antichrist's advent (one Antichrist, since he rejected Olivi's theory of a double figure), Arnold highlighted the role of the Angelic Pope, whose coming precedes the Final Enemy. Through this theoretical shift, Arnold aimed to comfort the dissident groups with the idea that their beliefs would soon prevail and their sufferings be rewarded.

Arnold confirmed this scheme of final events in his *Exposition on the Book of Revelation* (1306).[16] Here he wished to reinforce the expectation for a coming spiritual pontiff who would succeed the reigning Clement V.[17] Arnold identified this spiritual pontiff with a series of figures from Revelation—the Angel that John hears speaking behind him (Rev. 1:10–12), the Angel of Philadelphia (Rev. 3:7), the Strong Angel of Rev. 5:2, the Angel with the Seal of the Living God (Rev. 7:2), and the other Strong Angel of Rev. 10:1.[18] After him, the time of the church's reformation will last for not more than five pontificates. Then the Antichrist will manifest himself, whose coming Arnold now calculated for 1332.[19]

In the meantime, Ubertino of Casale, one of the most visible of the Italian Spirituals, had written the *Tree of the Crucified Life of Jesus* (*Arbor vitae crucifixae Iesu*) on Monte Alverna in 1305. His first four books contain a life of Jesus; the fifth one offers a history of the church in apocalyptic terms. Its structure is based on Olivi's commentary on Revelation, from which Ubertino copied long sections. Ubertino modified Olivi's text, however, in order to express the more radical sensitivity of the Italian Spirituals. He identified the carnal church with the Roman curia, the prostitute of Revelation 17. For Ubertino, Boniface VIII was the angel of the abyss (Rev. 9:11) and the beast from the sea (Rev. 13:1ff.). Benedict XI was the beast from the earth (Rev. 13:11ff.). While Olivi did not describe the traits of the mystical Antichrist, Ubertino believed that he was identified with the past two popes.[20] Ubertino postponed expectation of the Angelic Pope, although he still believed that the "clarification of the sixth state" (or *renovatio prima*) was at hand.[21]

A strong presence primarily in southern France, the Spirituals hoped in vain that Pope Clement V would recognize them as an autonomous order. The new pope, John XXII (1316–1334), summoned them to obey the Franciscan authorities and resumed a vehement repression of the Spirituals. Those who did not abide by the pope's order were arrested and prosecuted. Four were burned at the stake in Marseille in 1318.

THE BEGUINS

A few years after Olivi's death, some of his proselytes began to consider him to be the long-expected Angel of Philadelphia.[22] His followers stressed the fact that he had fathomed the history of the church and foreseen the final events. In the meantime, the Franciscan Spiritual vision of Christianity based on rigorous humility and poverty, devotional practices, and a firm confidence in an imminent relief from their difficulties had spread over large areas of lay people, commonly called *beghini,* or beguins. The beguins, both men and women, wished to live a religious life either in a community or by themselves. In one of these groups we encounter someone who, like Dolcino, considered himself to be one of the angels of Revelation.

Guiard of Cressonessart was arrested toward the end of 1308, accused of having secretly helped and defended the heretic Marguerite Porete.[23] When the Inquisitor questioned him about his personal beliefs, Guiard stated that, thanks to a special revelation, he knew that he was the Angel of Philadelphia, directly sent by Christ. For Guiard, the church had gone through some distinct periods in its history that were mysteriously marked by the Seven Churches of Revelation 2–3. In particular, the members of the church of Philadelphia are those "runners" who "give up everything, wishing to preserve the discipline of the pristine church." They are "the followers of the Lord." His task was to lead and defend them, as he had done for several people, among them Marguerite Porete. For these "followers of the Lord" he had exposed himself to the attack of Dominicans and Franciscans, particularly in Reims and Paris. Guiard distinguishes among members of the church in the broad sense, those "followers of the Lord" who could either "wear a cloak" or "secular clothes," and the members of his *societas* in a strict sense, who wore a long tunic and, as a fundamental mark, a leather belt. The cloak and the tunic instantly remind us of the ecclesiastically dubious clothes of the beguins. According to the judicial records, during the first trial the canonists treated Guiard as a *beguinus;* during the second they called him a *pseudoreligiosus,* which is probably the equivalent (Lerner 1976, 350). As far as the leather belt is concerned, it indicated that the *beguinus* embraced the life-style of John the Baptist.

The ecclesiastic authorities could not accept Guiard's conviction that Christ himself had asked him to defend those who followed poverty. The fact that Guiard identified himself with the Angel of Philadelphia had threatening implications. In particular, it suggested that he granted himself a charismatic role, one that claimed to have a divine origin and thus was an alternative to that of the hierarchy. Whereas Marguerite Porete did not withdraw her statements and was burned at the stake as a relapsed heretic in 1310, Guiard finally abjured and thus was condemned to life imprisonment. (Arnold of Villanova had urged Guiard to retract his statements, because he feared that Guiard's stubbornness might convince Clement V to deny the Spirituals a favorable solution.)[24]

A central aspect of beguin culture was the oral transmission of their religious message. In southern France and in southern Italy several works by Olivi and Arnold were translated into the vernacular. Olivi's *Lecture,* for example, was translated into Provençal, although it had been placed under examination from 1317 and was finally condemned by John XXII in 1326 (see Burr 1993, 198–239). This translation and others must have enhanced the informal circulation and memorization of Olivi's and Arnold's theories. It is significant, however, that while some manuscripts containing translations of Olivi's ascetical works have been preserved, no text of the translation of the *Lecture* remains. (It is actually impossible to determine whether this was a complete translation or a synopsis.)[25] However, the fact that such a complex and ponderous text, corresponding to more than a thousand printed pages, was translated means that groups of lay people found Olivi's apocalyptic message extremely fascinating.

The story of the beguin Na Prous Boneta shows how intense the debate on Olivi's apocalyptic message had become in those years. Na Prous, accused of heresy along with her sister and a friend, was arrested and prosecuted. When she related the content of her visions and beliefs and refused to recant, she was sentenced to death in 1325 (see May 1955). Na Prous was convinced that John XXII's condemnation of Olivi meant the destruction of the gospel. Since the pope's condemnation, divine grace had stopped flowing through the church's body. Na Prous compares Pope John with Caiaphas, and the *beghini* with the innocent children slaughtered by Herod. She even likened the pope's sinful attack on Olivi's books to Adam's fall. According to her, Christ had placed Elijah and Enoch—that is, Francis of Assisi and Peter John Olivi—in his new Eden, that is, the church. Although Francis and Olivi had received Christ's message, they were killed by the Antichrist, who is none other than John XXII. Na Prous also mentioned a spiritual hierarchy opposed to the antichristian one of Pope John. According to her, the first pope ordained by the Holy Spirit was the Franciscan Guillaume Guiraud (see May 1955, 19–20), one of the twenty-five Spirituals who were arrested and questioned in 1317 because they had refused to obey John XXII.[26] Na Prous identified the Angel with the Seal of the Living God (Rev. 7:2) with Francis of Assisi, the Angel with the Face like the Sun (Rev. 10:1) with Olivi, and the Angel with the Keys of the Abyss (Rev. 9:11) with the Holy Spirit, which she had received from God. The abyss will close for those who believe in her words, and it will open for those who will not believe in them (see May 1955, 29–30).

THE FRATICELLI

Several circles of Franciscan dissidents accused John XXII of being a heretic and, more or less openly, identified him as the Antichrist. This view was advocated by many dissident groups, both in southern France and in Italy, in particular by the Spirituals. At the beginning of the fourteenth century these Spirituals were generally called *fraticelli* (literally, "little brothers"). Some sources distinguish between the *fraticelli de paupere vita,* direct descendants of the Spirituals, and the *fraticelli de opinione,* who supported the view on poverty expressed in 1322 by the General Chapter of the Friars Minor in opposition to Pope John.

The most visible representative of the fraticelli was Angelo of Clareno from the Marche region (d. ca. 1337). After having spent most of his youth in prison because of his support of the first revolts after 1274, Clareno was part of the group of dissidents Celestine V had allowed to break away from the order. This group had formed a family of *pauperes eremitae.* After having fled to the East for a decade, he went back to Italy. In 1311 he was at the curia of Avignon, where, together with Ubertino, he tried his best to help the dissidents obtain official authorization to break away from the Franciscans. Between 1312 and 1318 Clareno's letters were cautious and reserved, devoid of any apocalyptic connotations. Only after the failure of his efforts and his return to Italy did this follower of Olivi fill his writings with more and more prophetic and apocalyptic references.

In the *Chronicle or History of the Seven Tribulations* (1323–1326), his most famous work, Clareno interpreted the history of the Franciscan order in an apocalyptic way in which Francis's few legitimate children experience a series of adversities with brief periods of peacefulness, whereas the order of Friars Minor increases in size and slowly abandons its original intentions. Clareno investigated the contemporary tribulation, the seventh and the last. According to him, this final trial has just started. At its end, a new era will dawn on the world.[27]

In some letters of the same period, Clareno states that the current trial is the "great tribulation" that Jesus had predicted (Matthew 24), and that the Gospel's allusion to the "Abomination of Desolation" in the "holy place" refers to John XXII, who became a heretic when he condemned evangelical poverty. Given the situation, Clareno suggests that his companions behave in a cautious, alert, and sensible way. Clareno constantly invites his followers not to believe in any immediate change in the church. The apocalyptic vision in his letters is accompanied by a constant emphasis on patience and silent resistance, in order to avoid any form of yielding to delusion and abandonment (Potestà 1990, 215–95).

These letters and the depositions of some fraticelli prosecuted in 1334 help us understand who Clareno's followers were and how they lived. They gathered in small groups, in places (*loci*) in central and southern Italy close to small towns or villages (see Potestà 1990, 284). Some of Clareno's addressees were also Augustinian friars, others laity. An important factor in their choice of location was the protection offered them by the Colonna cardinals and the Angevin dynasty. (For instance, the abbey of Subiaco, where Clareno took shelter from 1318 to 1334, was in Colonna territory.) In Naples, Philip of Maiorca, brother-in-law of King Robert and faithful disciple of Clareno, sided with the fraticelli. During the last years of Clareno's life, the fraticelli acquired the status of an actual religious order, one that considered him its leader.

After Clareno's death, the fraticelli movement decomposed in central-southern Italy. Those groups dedicated to voluntary poverty survived with fewer difficulties under some bishops' protection or at least tolerance. Such groups supported new attempts to reform the Franciscan order in the second half of the fourteenth century, the movements that led toward the "Observance" form of Franciscanism. On the contrary, the segments with strong apocalyptic expectations and revolutionary inclinations (fostered by the posthumous controversy against John XXII as a heretic) became clandestine.[28]

The above tendencies had difficulty in emerging because of the Inquisition's pressure against them. When this pressure became less intense, as in Florence between 1348 and 1382, the fraticelli revived and preached their apocalyptic and radical message. However, as soon as the Florentine Signoria and the Inquisition reached an agreement, their opposition to the fraticelli resumed, culminating in the prosecution and execution of Michael of Calci (1389). One of his supporters' narration gives the impression that the people supported the fraticelli martyr, who remained firm in his principles, openly referring to the words directed to the Church of Philadelphia in Rev. 3:11.[29] The fraticelli certainly brought instability to the social order. The Florentine oligarchy disliked them because it thought that they amplified popular unrest and discontent. However, in contradiction to traditional historiography, we need not believe in a direct relationship among the fraticelli, the common people, and the urban proletariat. The

fraticelli always kept a sectarian and fundamentally elitist character; their radical antihierarchical propaganda failed to address larger issues of social change (Rusconi 1979, 79–84). Nor can
we believe that they directly supported any plan for social and political reform. Indeed, the
encounter of the Roman tribune Cola of Rienzo with their groups did not have a deep influence
on his ideas.

A new series of papal prophecies, which, unlike the previous one, circulated almost exclusively among their groups, clarified how the fraticelli perceived the current ecclesiastical situation. In this text, composed ca. 1328–1330 and updated in the fourteenth century several times
in order to make it useful in new controversies, the fraticelli clearly state that their major concern is to face the "great tribulation."[30] Whereas the first series of *Prophecies of the Supreme Pontiffs* (*Genus nequam*) concluded with a series of portraits of the Angelic Pope, the second series
(*Ascende calve*) ends with the description of a pope with bestial features. In opposition to the
corrupt church, the fraticelli proclaim that they belong to a distinctly apocalyptic community.
In 1419, in the Marche region we still find a group of fraticelli who were led by a certain Friar
Gabriele. His followers had elected him bishop, shepherd of the Church of Philadelphia, and
Minister General of the "true" Friars Minor (Rusconi 1979, 77).

LOLLARDS

Between the fourteenth and fifteenth centuries the Inquisition succeeded in repressing apocalyptic movements both in France and in Italy. The situation was different in countries where
the Inquisition's measures were less timely or were not totally supported by the civil authorities.
Indeed, in these areas, starting from the last years of the fourteenth century, popular radical
movements were able to proclaim their message and to make a number of proselytes in lay
circles. Their attacks against the church's oppression was increasingly accompanied by a criticism of the contemporary forms of power and social relationships.

In the second half of the fourteenth century in England, John Wyclif, a master at Oxford,
expressed a severe criticism of the hierarchical church. Wyclif set the visible church, whose
hierarchy and canon law were corrupt, against the invisible church of the elect, based on the
scriptures. The former church is the see of the Antichrist. Although his writings and sermons
frequently make use of the notion of the Antichrist, Wyclif's interpretation is less apocalyptic
than political. In most cases, the term "Antichrist" refers to the Roman curia and the pope,
often considered to be God's main enemy and thus the "Greatest Antichrist" (*maximus
antichristus*) and the "Open Anti-christ" (*patulus antichristus*).[31] For Wyclif, the Antichrist and
the pope—the latter seen not as a specific figure but rather as the highest expression of an institution—are synonyms. The English reformer clearly rejects any apocalyptic and millenarian
allusion,[32] but this kind of extreme terminology gave his discourse a tone of radical gravity that
lent itself to an interpretation that did not coincide with its author's.

In the initial and chaotic phase of the Great Schism (1378) Wyclif distanced himself from
those reformers who had looked at him as a possible ally. It was at that point that the ecclesiastical hierarchy reacted against him and his followers, calling them "Lollards." The hostility of
the social and political power structures was triggered by the suspicion that the Lollards'
preaching was somehow responsible for the "Peasants' Revolt" of 1381. In fact, Wyclif's mes-

sage was accepted by academics, lower clergy, and lay people, especially manual workers, craftsmen, knights. At the beginning some intellectuals played a major role in spreading and simplifying the message, so that it could reach uneducated people as well.

One learned adherent, who had certainly studied at Oxford, composed the *Lofty Work* (*Opus arduum*) between Christmas 1389 and Easter 1390. This Latin commentary on Revelation was primarily a treatise aimed at sustaining the Lollards, who had been persecuted as supporters and participants in the Peasants' Revolt. The author interprets Revelation in reference to the pope's persecution of the "evangelical people." The writer composed his text in jail but did not reveal his identity. Following Wyclif, the *Opus arduum* identifies contemporary popes—or, better yet, the whole papacy—with the Antichrist. Unlike Wyclif, however, the author interprets the Antichrist's historical embodiments in light of the apocalyptic narration of Revelation. Sometimes using a cryptic and obscure language, the author of the *Opus arduum* reads the most recent events, such as Wyclif's condemnation and the persecution of the Lollards, as chapters of God's mysterious plan. He also encourages the "Preachers of the Gospel" not to give in, but to continue their teaching, preaching, and study of the gospel.[33]

Apocalyptic believers and adherents gave close attention to those evangelical texts which either had a clearly apocalyptic character or alluded to the Antichrist. In particular, a vernacular commentary on Matthew 24 became popular among English Lollards (seventeen manuscripts of this text survive). In some manuscripts this work is called *Of Mynistris in the Chirche*. Following Wyclif's cautious perspective, the author avoids any specific calculation regarding Doomsday. Matthew's chapter enables him to identify the pope as Antichrist, his members with the cardinals and new orders, and the false prophets with the friars. This work is a forceful polemic, especially against the papacy and the mendicant orders.[34]

The events that took place in 1413 and 1414, in particular the arrest of Sir John Oldcastle and the subsequent revolt in which the Lollards were directly involved, marked the ultimate break between the English government and the Lollard movement. Thereafter, the Lollards were forced to become clandestine. They survived until the Reformation, thanks to the episcopacy's inconsistent repression and the Lollards' withdrawal into small communities and families. The strength of their intellectual endeavors and theological awareness slowly weakened, but a sporadic apocalypticism resurfaced as one of their strongest sources of inspiration. The most relevant example is a group found in Newbury in 1490–1491, some of whom hoped that in the course of ten years Christians would become one flock led by one shepherd and every heretic and Lollard would be able to preach freely. Others believed that only the Lollard faith would save the world from total destruction. Others feared that before the end there would be a disastrous conflict between the Lollards and the clergy.[35]

☞ THE SPREAD OF APOCALYPTIC LITERATURE ON THE CONTINENT _____

During the first decades of the fifteenth century, Wyclif's doctrines, directly imported from England, acquired a remarkable importance in Bohemia, especially because of the increasing suspicion there of the Roman Church. The growth of apocalyptic and millenarian tendencies within Bohemia derived from a gradual absorption of texts coming from different western

European countries. An analysis of the manuscript distribution may explain how apocalyptic doctrines circulated, though originally their transmission must have been primarily oral.

All the surviving manuscripts of the *Opus arduum* were produced on the continent. The oldest (Brno, University Library, Mk 28) dates from 1415. Starting from this text it has been possible to reconstruct the ways through which the Lollard commentary reached Bohemia from England. The *Opus arduum* mentions Joachim of Fiore, Olivi, and the fourteenth-century apocalypticist John of Rupescissa. However, the unknown author distances himself from Joachim and holds that Olivi's *Lecture* and some of Rupescissa's writings had been withdrawn from Oxford and Salisbury as a result of the persecution against the Lollards. In fact, it is difficult to determine to what extent the works of these three authors were known in England between ca. 1350 and 1500. Nor is it clear how familiar the author of the *Opus arduum* was with their doctrines.

In order to get a sense of the role of radical apocalyptic movements on the continent, it will be helpful to consider John of Rupescissa (Jean de Roquetaillade). This French friar spent most of his life in houses of detention, where he composed several works with visionary and prophetic content. His *Handbook in Tribulation* (*Vademecum in tribulatione*) (1356) was a compendium of his apocalyptic views. In this text John describes imminent tribulations and exhorted his readers to prepare for the Antichrist's arrival. He believed that in a few years the clergy would undergo unparalleled plagues. As a result, the religious would be forced to resume the life-style of Christ and the apostles:

> The world will be filled with indignation against the ostentation of wealth, against the temporal glory of the clerics' worldly pride. The lay and oppressed peoples will rebel in an unexpected and sudden way, and will take the temporal goods away from the clergy.

At that time the "people's justice" will devour noblemen and tyrants, and many powerful princes will lose their dignity and wealth.[36] Later, the double Antichrist will arrive (an Eastern and a Western one). This tribulation will last for the traditional three and one-half years. The Antichrist will be followed by a pontiff, sent by Christ, as *reparator orbis*. He will be the mystical Elijah. In his activity of restoration this pontiff will be supported by a French king who will become emperor. These two monarchs will inaugurate the sabbatical millennium, whose opening will witness the resurrection of the martyrs and the conversion of the Jews.[37] Finally, the last Antichrist (*ultimus antichristus*) will arrive with Elijah himself. Doomsday will be the final act.

The Eastern Antichrist was expected by 1365, whereas the Western one (a heretic emperor) was supposed to arrive before 1370. These dates came from the calculations of Arnold of Villanova, whose interpretation of Daniel 12 was faithfully reproduced by John.[38] However, contradicting a well-known prophetic tradition of Franciscan-Joachite nature, John held that a revolt of the laity, and not the violent action of a sovereign, would bring about the imminent purification of the church (see Töpfer 1964, chap. 4). For the first time the subversion of the church was linked to belief in a social upheaval and in a *justitia popularis* opposing nobles and the rich.

In its original Latin version, the *Handbook* had a rather large diffusion on the continent. Abridged versions were published in Latin, French, German, Czech, Catalan, and Castilian. Rupescissa's other works were less successful. Nevertheless, the *Pamphlet* (*Libellus*), written by an anonymous author known only through the pseudonym Telesphorus of Cosenza, spread

Rupescissa's apocalyptic ideology. The *Libellus* saw Rupescissa's apocalyptic expectations as one aspect of the more general request for a reformation of the church (see chapter 11 above).

We can conclude that the circulation of Rupescissa's visionary teaching was connected with the increasing desire for a reform of the church. Particularly in Bohemia, where expectations and programs of renewal became prominent, that message helped shape apocalyptic and millenarian theories.[39]

☞ REFORMERS, APOCALYPTICS, AND MILLENARIANISTS IN BOHEMIA

The Bohemian reform movement arises from the activity of preachers who, starting from the fourteenth century, focused their message on the imminent advent of the Antichrist (e.g., Jan Milič of Kroměřiž), as well as on the behavior necessary to defend oneself against his attacks (e.g., Matthew of Janov). Thanks to the involvement of some masters at the University of Prague, as well as the diffusion of Wyclif's works and Jan Hus's preaching, the first decade of the fifteenth century saw the birth of a new movement which criticized the Roman Church on the basis of strong nationalistic elements (Czechs against Germans). Issues involving the meaning and mode of distributing the Eucharist were among the most significant themes debated by the reformers, both as internal polemics and as forms of propaganda against the Roman Church. These debates show how important lay people had become within the church. In their campaigns against imperial armies the Hussites insisted that the laity should be allowed to receive the Eucharist under both forms, that is, by drinking from the chalice and eating the consecrated bread (a view called Utraquism).

In this situation apocalyptic expectations were a rather limited phenomenon, at least at the outset. However, they help us understand how the Hussites perceived their historical situation. All in all, apocalyptic expectations played a secondary role in the works and preaching of the most famous reformers (Nicholas of Dresden, Jacobellus of Stříbro, Jan Hus). Their frequent allusions to the Antichrist have in fact no real eschatological connotations. When they speak of Antichrist, they interpret him according to Wyclif's notion, that is, as an expression of their polemic against Rome.[40]

When the Council of Constance (1415) sentenced Hus to death, the reformers' movement left the academic and ecclesiastical circles and involved larger sectors of the population. This was the beginning of the Hussite revolution, which in the following years involved Bohemia and Moravia, subverting political institutions, ecclesiastical structures, and social relationships. When large sections of the lower classes joined the movement, a cultural and social polarization took place within Hussitism. The precarious and intricate balance among its diverse components fell apart in 1419.

At the beginning of that year, Wenceslaus IV tried to reinstate Catholicism, but the lower classes strongly opposed his effort. In southern Bohemia Hussite priests created congregations of believers that were independent of the local parishes. Trying to reproduce an evangelical and apostolic life-style, these congregations were the embryo of a new social organization. Their most famous center was on a hill close to the Castle of Bechyně which was named Tabor (from Matt. 28:16–20). Those who attended that center were called Taborites. In the meantime, another radical wing of Hussitism was born in Prague. Its most visible representative was Jan Zelivský, the first preacher to make use of the *Opus arduum* in one of his sermons.[41] In the Czech capital, the radicals opposed a composite formation, including Catholic and royalist forces, Bohemian noblemen, and moderate Hussites. The balance broke down when the city councilors still faithful to the king were thrown out of the window of the town hall (the "Defenestration" of Prague). King Wenceslaus died immediately after (August 1419).

The different phases of the harsh conflict among Hussitism's different "souls" are detectable in the evolution of the radicals' and Taborites' apocalyptic doctrines. According to some contemporary chronicles, in the beginning the most common trend was what modern historians have described as "Fatalistic Chiliasm,"[42] or, more exactly, "Adventism."[43] As a response to the emperor Sigismund's attacks on the "Wyclifites," that is, against Hussitism's extreme wing, the Taborite priests exhorted believers to leave their homes and to take shelter in one of the five cities they controlled. In opposition to the university masters and the nobles of the capital, in November of 1419 the Taborites identified Prague with the Babylon they wished to abandon. They invited their followers to move to the mountains in order to flee the corrupt establishment, as Lot once fled from Sodom (see Kaminsky 1967, 310–29).

As a consequence of this action, the characters of the different congregations changed. If in the beginning they were virtual communities which gathered only for periodic eucharistic celebrations and sermons, later they turned into actual communities whose schedules and life-style depended on their expectation of imminent tribulations and the eschatological conflict with the Christian forces ranged against them. In this context the rebels rejected their original pacifism and justified the use of violence as a form of self-defense.

After leaving Plzen ("the city of the sun") in March 1420, the "Wyclifites" settled in Písek, in southern Bohemia. Here they founded a regime based on the communal administration of goods, on their distribution according to each person's needs, and also on the confiscation of private property. In the meantime, the Taborites had appropriated the abandoned fortress of Hradiště, where they had started to build the new city of Tabor. The foundation of the fortified city stirred the hopes of the Wyclifites, who rushed to the new Tabor from every part of the country to find safe shelter.

In this climate a significant change occurred in these groups in terms of apocalyptic views. Many became convinced that Christ's millennial kingdom would be established on earth soon and would take revenge on every sinner (see Kaminsky 1967, 336–60). The combination of these two elements marks a significant shift in medieval apocalyptic theories. On the one hand, the idea of the imminent millennial kingdom transcends the circles of visionaries, prophets, and readers of manuscripts to become the motto of a popular movement that believes in the imminent realization of a perfect satisfaction and joy and in the return of the sinless earthly paradise without any form of domination and private property. On the other hand, the concept of "the time of revenge," in particular theorized by the Taborite priest John Čapek, justified the use of aggression and violence and thus the realization of a revolutionary ideal.

Tabor was organized as a sort of city-state. In the beginning, the priests probably distributed the goods. Their resources derived both from productive and commercial activities and from heavy taxes levied upon the surrounding territories (Kaminsky 1967, 384–97). The peasants were under considerable fiscal pressure. Primarily during the first phase, the Taborite clerics played a central role from a sociopolitical standpoint. The two most notable were Martin

Húska and Nicholas of Pelhřimov (also known as Nicholas Biskupec). Húska soon became the most noted proclaimer of the imminent kingdom of the saints in which every suffering would be erased.

When the Taborites returned to Prague (May 1420) and their priests reacted against the university masters who had condemned them, the movement's unity broke down. Our sources, which stress Hussitism's different views on the Eucharist, do not clarify the origins and reasons for this crisis completely. Probably these theological debates expressed deeper strategic differences, primarily on how to pursue the revolutionary process and how to relate to the moderate Hussites in Prague. Húska, attacked by both the Utraquists and the Taborites, remained isolated with a small group of followers. Imprisoned in January 1421 under the charge of being a heretic "Picard" (i.e., a follower of the "Free Spirit"), he was tortured and burned in August of 1421. In the meantime, some hundreds of "Picards" were expelled from Tabor. This was the first step toward their total annihilation, achieved in the fall of the same year. In Prague, after the murder of Zelivský (March 1422), the moderate forces regained control of the situation.

For decades Tabor continued to exist as an independent entity, with a remarkable military potential and an extraordinary defensive structure. Only in 1452 George of Poděbrady, the governor of Bohemia, succeeded in overcoming what had become nothing but the shadow of that pristine institution. Among the few Taborites who were imprisoned was the old Nicholas of Pelhřimov. After being ordained "senior" (bishop) in 1420 by some priests including Húska, Nicholas had broken with Húska during the tense and confused phase that concluded with the annihilation of the "Picards." From that moment on he became the major theoretician of the Taborites and the author of their historical memory.

Nicholas's unpublished *Postil on Revelation* (ca. 1430) reveals a perspective that is very different from the "Adventist" and millenarian expectations formulated at the time of the foundation of the city. This work is a series of Latin sermons with key passages translated into Czech. Speaking to the Taborite clergy, Nicholas follows the medieval exegetical tradition. Among contemporary sources Nicholas refers to the *Commentary on the Book of Revelation* by Jacobellus (Jakoubek) of Stříbro (written in Czech in 1421), which he interprets in a Taborite manner, as well as to the *Opus arduum,* which he quotes directly.[44] Reproducing the traditional vision of history divided into seven phases, Nicholas is convinced that he is living during the fifth. At the beginning of the sixth age, the world will witness the arrival of the Antichrist, and, slightly afterward, Doomsday; and the seventh period will see the Lord's triumph beyond history. Explicitly attacking millenarian visions, which he considers "fables" nobody believes in anymore,[45] Nicholas limits himself to foreseeing a "brief and modest peace" between the advent of the Antichrist and judgment day, thus following a rather inoffensive exegetical theme.[46]

According to Nicholas, the conflict against evil has two levels. On the one hand, it corresponds to an interior battle in which the soul attempts to overcome its negative drives. On the other, it is also a historical, social struggle in which the saints are asked to oppose the attacks of Antichrist, whose mystical body is the Roman Church. At this second level, Nicholas's vision presents some uncertain and apparently ambiguous elements. On the one hand, he sees the attacks and persecutions suffered by the Taborites as apocalyptic manifestations. By so doing, he consecrates the myth of the city as the bulwark of the Hussite legacy, when in Prague many were starting to advocate a new relationship with the empire and a reunification with Rome. However, he does not hide his disappointment vis-à-vis the contemporary historical situation. The exciting experience of the original Tabor is over. The new rituals, especially the reception of the Eucharist in its two forms, hide old vices, among others a widespread drunkenness. People pay much less attention to sermons and communion; many criticize and deride those who believed it would be possible to reproduce the life-style of the first Christian community and still speak about a possible reform of the church. Nicholas believed that the meaning of Tabor lay in its attempt to revivify the pre-Constantinian church, and not in its millenarian expectations. The way he described the contemporary situation and future events reflected the fact that the most sensible groups were aware of the failure of the movement.

APOCALYPTIC MOVEMENTS IN GERMANY

We can explain the magnitude and strength of the radical apocalyptic movement in Bohemia and Moravia if we consider that in the fifteenth century those territories were free from the Inquisition's and the German empire's power. In the areas where those institutions were able to exert their control, radical apocalyptic tendencies were promptly stifled.

Nevertheless, in German territories we can still find traces of several examples of apocalyptic movements limited to single individuals or small groups.[47] The modest extent of these phenomena certainly depends on the fact that the ecclesiastical powers promptly and vigorously attacked these tendencies, which they viewed as clearly heretical. Since the church usually destroyed the writings of these individuals, we obtain information about them only with difficulty from various chronicles, annals, and trial records that were produced by their adversaries and by external observers. Thus, it is difficult to tell if these heretics were actually aware of their connections or relationships to earlier apocalyptic movements, or, better yet, if these connections were corroborated by their own writings. These relationships may have been created by the theologians and inquisitors according to their own theological background and knowledge of heretical doctrines.

The main apocalyptic tendencies in Germany often echo themes coming from the Franciscan apocalyptic theorists (e.g., Olivi, John of Rupescissa and Telesphorus of Cosenza). The principal figure of the first significant occurrence is Frederick of Braunschweig, a Franciscan who advocated a form of literal millenarianism which spread in southern Saxony and the Rhineland between 1389 and 1392.[48] In 1389 a treatise written by his fellow Franciscan Dietrich of Arnevelde accused Frederick of following the "fables of the Jews" and the "ravings of Brother John of Rupescissa."[49] In 1392 he was sentenced to life imprisonment because he had upheld the following errors: the advent of Antichrist within four and one-half years; the imminent restoration of the Jews' temporal power, including the reconstruction of Jerusalem; the coming of a "humble person," a friar minor, who would be a *reparator* and would kill the Antichrist; and, finally, the beginning of Christ's millennial kingdom on earth, which would be ruled by the *reparator* (at once pope and emperor) under the law of the Holy Spirit. This kingdom would last until the final advent of Christ and the general resurrection. Frederick believed that he would play the role of John the Baptist; that is, he would be the precursor of the *reparator,* proclaiming his coming to both clergy and laity. He thought that only in the time of the *reparator* would the world have real priests, because contemporary priests were not really "anointed."[50]

As the Council of Constance had been marked by the execution of Hus, the Council of Basel also ended with the execution of a heretic. In this second case, however, no one protested the burning at the stake of Nicholas of Buldesdorf in 1446. According to the sentence, Nicholas was a layman, author of theological and exegetical texts, among them a book with the title *Testimonies of the Holy Spirit in Prophecies,* as well as commentaries on the Our Father, on the Psalms, and on Revelation. During his process, Nicholas claimed that his texts were well known in Germany, France, and Spain, but no copies have survived, probably because the council condemned them to the flames. Seeing himself as a divine messenger, Nicholas had rashly gone to Basel, had been immediately arrested, and had eventually been condemned by a committee formed in 1443 to examine his doctrines.[51]

The articles condemned and reproduced in his death sentence offer a detailed explanation of his teaching. Nicholas announced that the seventh era of the world and the third gospel of the Holy Spirit were imminent. According his view, the final age would be characterized by the advent of a *pastor angelicus* who would combine the pope's and the emperor's powers. This *pastor* and his followers would be omnipotent; he would have David's key to open the scriptures (see Rev. 3:7). He would be a man, but his body would live forever.

Among the articles condemned, one is an almost literal quotation from Olivi's *Lecture on Revelation.*[52] John of Segovia, a cardinal who participated in the investigating committee, recognized that Nicholas had been influenced by Telesphorus's doctrines. Another element of Nicholas's theories probably derives from John of Rupescissa or Telesphorus, namely, his stress on the future role of the Jews. Nicholas's position was so radical that it is possible to theorize a direct influence of Jewish apocalyptic views. He thought, for example that the Angelic Pope was the same as the Messiah expected by the Jews and that he would free them from their captivity and make them rule over the world. The candelabrum of the church (Rev. 4:5) will be returned to the synagogue. To be saved, the Jews will not need to convert to Christianity; they need only be faithful to the Mosaic law and to their fathers' traditions.

Between 1465 and 1466 in the city of Eger a new group was born, the "sect of the Wirsberger."[53] Wirsberg in Franconia is the place where the family came from. As far as we know, the sole members of this "sect" were the brothers Livin and Janko. In recent years two texts by the Wirsberger brothers have been found in the library of the University of Augsburg,[54] a discovery that gives us direct contact with their theories, which previously were known only through some indirect sources in the archives of Eger and a scholastic *quaestio* of the Augustinian theologian John of Dorsten. From these documents we can hypothesize that they believed in a third *status* on earth before judgment day, one marked by the arrival of a messianic figure. They describe this person as the "Anointed of the Savior," a sort of new Christ of the Holy Spirit's era. Born from the Virgin in a spiritual way, he will unveil the mysteries of revelation and will lead the 144,000 elect of the final times to their salvation (see Rev. 7:1–8). Like Christ, he would be preceded by a John the Baptist. (It seems that Janko attributed the role of precursor to himself.) In the claims of the Wirsbergers we can detect themes and perspectives also present in the preaching of Frederick of Braunschweig and Nicholas of Buldesdorf. The Wirsbergers also must have been familiar with the doctrines of the radical apocalyptic movements of Franciscan origin. (Janko used to visit the Observant Franciscan convent in Eger.) Livin was sentenced to life imprisonment in 1468 but died shortly thereafter. We have no clue of what happened to Janko after 1466.

In comparison with the former two figures, the case of the Wirsberger brothers has a clearly political connotation. We can interpret their story in light of the specific geopolitical situation of Eger, a German city that had an old connection with the Bohemian kingdom, a kind of Catholic island in Hussite territory. In reality, the case of the Wirsbergers reflects the more general evolution of Eger. In this context, it becomes apparent why Janko was accused of being a "Hussite." However, their doctrines themselves had evident political undertones that came from the fact that the Wirsbergers belonged to a lower nobility. It seems that they predicted that the military, rebelling because they had not received their pay, would soon rise up to slaughter both princes and clerics. The Wirsbergers also believed that in the coming third *status* social classes would be eliminated, in particular high nobility.

In conclusion, in Germany apocalyptic insurrections were rather limited, although manifestos and projects involving social and political revolutions were composed and discussed.[55] These texts testify to a permanent dissatisfaction with the church and society, a discontent that would come to the surface during the first decades of the sixteenth century in the Protestant Reformation.

☞ APOCALYPTIC TENSIONS IN ITALY
(CA. 1480–1520)

In fifteenth-century Italy, preachers often used apocalyptic themes and proclaimed that the Antichrist was at hand. The most famous preachers were the Dominicans Vincent Ferrer and Manfred of Vercelli and the Franciscan Bernardino of Siena (see chapter 11 above). Warning their listeners about the imminent end in their sermons, they advocated moral reform, penance, and conversion of life. Expectations of a new age also soon became popular in humanistic circles. In the last part of the century, proclamations of imminent catastrophes were linked to hopes for a general renewal and reformation of the church. Several documents describe the itinerant preachers and circles of learned ecclesiastics who at once worried about the imminent Antichrist and trusting in the advent of an Angelic Pope.

Only in Florence did these expectations become a significant aspect of the city's social and political life, primarily because of the Dominican preacher Girolamo Savonarola, who played a crucial role in the period of Piero de Medici's expulsion from the city and the invasion of the French king Charles VIII (1494). For some time the debate on Savonarola has been dominated by polemical or apologetic positions (see Weinstein 1991). Only in recent years have scholars understood how Savonarola's teaching evolved. The different stages of his doctrine must be read in light of Florence's civil life and of the destiny of his "party": the *Piagnoni* or *Frateschi*. If we consider the evolution of Savonarola's beliefs from this standpoint, we can perceive both their fascination and their ambiguity. Interpreting his dramatic death as the symbol of his entire life, many scholars have extolled him as a martyr of prophecy.

During his first stay in Florence (1482–1487) the young Savonarola demonstrated a firm background in Thomistic theology, to which he remained faithful until the end.[56] When he returned to Florence in 1490, he gave a series of *Lessons on Revelation,* which advocated penance and self-abnegation and constantly referred to the imminent end.[57] Until 1494 his preaching did not deal with themes directly connected with Florence's political life and with its historical destiny, nor did he oppose the Medici.

After the fall of the Medici and their flight from Florence, different political figures alternated as heads of the local government. In the midst of these changes in the governing powers, the Piagnoni imposed themselves as a decisive element of the new political and social situation, one that was particularly complicated, given the impending threat of Charles VIII's invasion of Italy. In this difficult climate Savonarola suddenly became a crucial reference for social groups that previously had not been particularly sensitive to his preaching. The Dominican friar was considered the architect of the peace established between Florence and Charles VIII and thus acquired a much more powerful role within Florentine civic institutions.

At this point, Savonarola radically changed the tone of his preaching, proposing his message as the unifying expression of the conscience of the city. Making much use of a well-known arsenal of apocalyptic rhetorical figures, the Dominican prophesied that Florence would be elected by God as the "New Jerusalem," becoming the model of a renewed Christian purity.[58] More and more directly, he identified Pope Alexander VI with the Antichrist and foresaw the imminent overthrow of the Roman "Babylon."[59] Savonarola's increasingly more radical attack against the pope finally led to Alexander VI's reaction. The pope threatened Florence with an interdiction unless it distanced itself from the friar. The pope's position was supported both by the factions opposing the Piagnoni and those preachers, in particular Franciscans, who did not accept Savonarola and his circle as the representatives of the entire Florentine people. Savonarola's fall was quick. In the spring of 1498 he was arrested, questioned, tortured, and finally burned at the stake.

Even during the most inflamed phase of Florence's civil life, Savonarola's apocalyptic vision was only one facet of his more general project, which aimed to christianize and moralize Florentine society. In order to achieve his plan, Savonarola tried to build a larger consensus within the city by using words and images evoking the myth of the elect city destined to obtain vast political and economic power. Nevertheless, the apocalyptic dimension was not a secondary aspect of his preaching. His attacks against the sins of Babylon and the announcement of the church's imminent reform thanks to a coming holy pope were the major characteristics of the last period of his preaching and the main reason for Alexander's decisive reaction against him.

Just as Savonarola's doctrinal system was rather nuanced, his followers were also socially and ideologically heterogeneous. Although he aimed at a gradual involvement of the masses, Savonarola's message was successful primarily among intellectuals, the middle class, and craftsmen, as well as among the higher classes. After his death, the Piagnoni continued to be a significant presence of Florence's social life for decades. As far as Savonarola's call for a moral and religious reform was concerned, it survived in different forms: some tried to realize it in their inner life; others attempted to renew the religious life within the ecclesiastic structures; others stressed the radical and revolutionary aspects of his message (see Polizzotto 1994).

Among the last group, the craftsman Pietro Bernardino was one the most important. While Savonarola was still alive, Bernardino had been rather successful, first as a lay preacher in fraternities of young boys, then as the leader of a small group of activists.[60] Believing that he had received a special call from God in 1497, Bernardino was convinced that the education of the young Florentines was his particular mission. Led by their innocence and intuitive knowledge of grace, these Florentine children had great potential for future plans of reformation in Bernardino's view.

Although many scholars see Bernardino's teaching as mystical, aspects of his message and the very structure of his small congregation, which became clandestine after Savonarola's death, share similarities with apocalyptic sects. He held that the clergy were hostile toward scripture and Christ's example; he stated that God had unveiled his plans only to the poor, the weak, and the persecuted. He also anointed his followers with oil and held that they were the "Anointed" of the Holy Spirit, as they were later called. Forced to flee Florence, he interpreted his flight as God's gift to the "Anointed" to separate from the wicked (Polizzotto 1994, 134). Eventually, Bernardino and some of his followers were imprisoned, tortured, and finally burned at the stake in 1502.

The last major representative of radical Savonarolism was a would-be Camaldolite monk named Theodore, arrested in Florence in 1515. Before the ecclesiastical court he stated that Savonarola had appeared to him and had announced the imminent renovation of the church. This reform would result from the united attack of all the princes of the world against the priests, the friars, the pope, and all the Christians who would not recognize the Angelic Pope, who would support a church deprived of all temporal goods.[61] Theodore claimed that he was sustained by the archangel Michael, and he also identified himself with the Angelic Pope. He was condemned to prison for ten years, but escaped in 1519 and resumed his previous preaching. Finally, he was arrested a second time and condemned to life imprisonment (see Polizzotto 1994, 276–79, 310).

The balance sheet from this investigation of the more radical aspects of apocalyptic traditions in late medieval Europe is a mixed one. These movements did not begin as revolutionary ideologies in the modern sense. Nevertheless, more than a few represent the voice of deprived groups and usually silent sectors of medieval society. These supposedly marginalized adherents to positions that were often condemned as heretical found in the language of Christian apocalypticism a way to express their hopes.

Translated by Armando Maggi

⌒ NOTES

1. For an analysis of medieval apocalyptic movements as forms of fanaticism, see Norman Cohn, *The Pursuit of the Millennium: Revolutionary messianism in Medieval and Reformation Europe and its bearing on modern totalitarian movements* (New York: Essential Books, 1957).

2. *Cronica fratris Salimbene de Adam ordinis Minorum,* ed. O. Holder-Egger (Hannover: Monumenta Germaniae Historica, 1905–13), 273, 257, 259.

3. Ibid., 271.

4. The *De secta illorum qui se dicunt esse de ordine apostolorum* was edited by A. Segarizzi in volume 9/5 of *Rerum Italicarum Scriptores* (Città di Castello: Lapi, 1907), 17–36. Its attribution to the Dominican inquisitor Bernardo Gui is questionable.

5. Ibid., 20–21.

6. Ibid., 21–22.

7. Ibid., 22–23.

8. For an accurate description of Dolcino's life in Piedmont, see *Historia fratris Dulcini heresiarche,* an anonymous text that extolls the bishop of Vercelli. It was edited by A. Segarizzi in volume 9/5 of *Rerum Italicarum Scriptores,* 3–14.

9. Antonino Franchi, "Il Concilio di Lione II (1274) e la contestazione dei francescani delle Marche," *Picenum Seraphicum* 11 (1974): 53–75.

10. Livarius Oliger, "Petri Iohannis Olivi De renuntiatione Papae Coelestini V: Quaestio et Epistola," *Archivum Franciscanum Historicum* 11 (1918): 372. For a meticulous presentation of the letter and its themes, see Burr 1989, 112–24.

11. This belief was spread by Conrad of Offida, as Ubertino of Casale clearly states in a description

contained in the *Arbor vitae crucifixae Iesu* (Venetiis: Andrea de Bonettis, 1485; anastatic reprint, Turin: Bottega d'Erasmo, 1961), book V, chap. 4, 442b–443a.

12. See chapter 11 above, as well as Töpfer 1964, chap. 5. More detail on the *Liber de Flore* can be found in Herbert Grundmann, "*Liber de Flore:* Eine Schrift der Franziskaner-Spiritualen aus dem Anfang des 14. Jahrhunderts," in *Ausgewählte Aufsätze* (Stuttgart: Hiersemann, 1977), vol. 2, esp. 108–9 (for its date) and 148–50 (for its authorship); and Bernard McGinn, "*Pastor angelicus:* Apocalyptic Myth and Political Hope in the Fourteenth Century," in *Santi e santità nel secolo XIV: Atti del XV Convegno Internazionale della Società internazionale di studi francescani* (Assisi: Università di Perugia, Centro di studi francescani, 1989), 219–51.

13. A critical edition has not yet been published. Available are copies of the typed critical edition by Warren Lewis, *Peter John Olivi, O.F.M.: Prophet of the Year 2000* (diss., Tübingen, 1972). A fundamental study is Burr 1993.

14. For previous texts on the same theme, see Burr 1993, 116.

15. Josep Perarnau i Espelt, "El text primitiu del *De mysterio cymbalorum Ecclesiae* d'Arnau de Vilanova: En apèndix, el seu *Tractatus de tempore adventus Antichristi,*" *Arxiu de Textos Catalans Antics* 7/8 (1988–89): 148–49. The number results from the addition of the following digits: 33 (the years of Christ's life) + 42 (the years between Jesus' death and the destruction of the Temple of Jerusalem) + 3.5 (three years and a half in which the Jews kept offering sacrifices even though the Temple had been destroyed) + 1290 (the days, considered as years, which according to Daniel would correspond to the advent of the Antichrist. They were calculated starting from the "tempus in quo ablatum fuit iuge sacrificium," Dan. 12:11).

16. Arnaldi de Villanova, *Expositio super Apocalypsi,* ed. I. Carreras i Artau, O. Marinelli Mercacci, and I. M. Morató i Thomàs, Arnaldi de Villanova Scripta spiritualia I (Barcelona: Institut d'Estudis Catalans, 1971), 135.

17. Ibid., 227.

18. Ibid., 22, 59, 81, 111, 141.

19. Ibid., 153, 177 (the number is the double of the beast [666] in Rev. 13:18).

20. Ubertinus de Casali, *Arbor vitae,* book V, chap. 8, 459a–467a. See also Potestà 1980, 146–54.

21. Ubertinus, *Arbor vitae,* book V, chap. 8, 467b and chap. 9, 470b–471b.

22. See the act of accusation that the leaders of the Franciscans composed against the Spirituals on March 1, 1311: "Communitatis accusatio," in Franz Ehrle, "Zur Vorgeschichte des Concils von Vienne," *Archiv für Literatur und Kirchengeschichte* 2 (1886): 371.

23. Robert E. Lerner has reevaluated this important historical figure and has also published the acts of his condemnation and the canonists' judgments on him. See Lerner 1976, 343–64, 529–40.

24. On this, see Oriana Cartaregia and Josep Perarnau, "El text sencer de l' *Epistola ad gerentes zonam pelliceam* d'Arnau de Vilanova," *Arxiu de Textos Catalans Antics* 12 (1993): 7–42.

25. Robert E. Lerner, "Writing and Resistance among Beguins of Languedoc and Catalonia," in *Heresy and Literacy, 1000–1530,* ed. Peter Biller and Anne Hudson (Cambridge: Cambridge University Press, 1994), 198–99.

26. Conradus Eubel, ed., *Bullarium Franciscanum,* tomus V (Romae: Typis Vaticanis, 1898), n. 293, p.133a. The four men condemned to death in Marseille the following year were part of this group.

27. This text is available in a noncritical edition by Alberto Ghinato (Rome: Antonianum, 1959). On its apocalyptic aspects, see Potestà 1990, 195–213.

28. The following text is significant: Fraticelli cuiusdam "Decalogus evangelicae paupertatis an. 1340–1342 conscriptus," ed M. Bihl, *Archivum Franciscanum Historicum* 32 (1939): 411. In this text a disciple of Clareno describes John XXII as the "king of locusts who destroys Christ's life." A similar perspective is found in a letter (1353–1354) of the fraticelli to the municipality of Narni in Livarius Oliger, "Documenta inedita ad historia fraticellorum spectantia," *Archivum Franciscanum Historicum* 6 (1913): 518.

29. For an account of the episode, see Rusconi 1979, 73–79.

30. See Robert E. Lerner, "Illuminated Propaganda: The Origins of the Ascende Calve Pope Prophecies," *Journal of Medieval History* 20 (1994): 157–91.

31. Alexander Patschovsky, "'Antichrist' bei Wyclif," in Patschovsky and Šmahel 1996, 83–98, especially 88 nn. 62 and 63.

32. Michael Wilks offers a different interpretation, arguing that Wyclif's message has traces of prophetic and apocalyptic traditions of Franciscan Joachimite origin; see Wilks, "Wyclif and the Great Persecution," in *Prophecy and Eschatology,* ed. Michael Wilks (Oxford: Blackwell, 1994), 29–63.

33. Anne Hudson, "Lollardy and Eschatology," in Patschovsky and Šmahel 1996, 99–113, esp. 106–7.

34. Ibid., 109–10.

35. Ibid., 99.

36. Johannis de Rupescissa, "Vademecum in tribulatione," in *Appendix ad Fasciculum Rerum Expetendarum et Fugiendarum,* ed. Edward Brown (London: Chiswell, 1690), 496–508, esp. 499.

37. Ibid., 500–501, 506.

38. Ibid., 507.

39. For this aspect, see Robert E. Lerner, "'Popular Justice': Rupescissa in Hussite Bohemia," in Patschovsky and Šmahel 1996, 39–52.

40. For the first two preachers, see Kaminsky 1967, 40–51, 75–85. For the third preacher, see Alexander Patschovsky, "Ekklesiologie bei Johannes Hus," in *Lebenslehren und Weltentwürfe im Uebergang vom Mittelalter zur Neuzeit,* ed. Hartmut Boockmann, Bernd Moeller, and Karl Stackmann, Abhandlungen der Akademie der Wissenschaften in Göttingen, Phil.-Hist. Klasse, Dritte Folge, Nr. 179 (Göttingen: Vandenhoeck & Ruprecht, 1989), 370–99, esp. 396–99.

41. Hudson, "Lollardy and Eschatology," 112.

42. Robert Kalivoda, *Revolution und Ideologie: Der Hussitismus* (Cologne/Vienna: Böhlau, 1976), 131–42.

43. Howard Kaminsky, "Chiliasm and the Hussite Revolution," *Church History* 26 (1957): in particular 47ff.

44. Nicholas's *Postilla* is present only in one manuscript (Vienna, NationalBibliothek 4520) As far as its content is concerned, see Howard Kaminsky, "Nicholas of Pehlrimov's Tabor: An Adventure into the Eschaton," in Patschovsky and Šmahel 1996, 139–67 (for the problem concerning its sources, see p. 143 n. 12).

45. Whether Nicholas himself had believed in these during the dramatic phase of the revolutionary process (1419–1420) is still moot. See Kaminsky, "Nicholas of Pehlřimov's Tabor," 158 n. 75.

46. Ibid., 145 n. 18. On the exegetical tradition concerning the brief period of *refrigerium* that the saints would have before the end, see Robert E. Lerner, "Refreshment of the Saints: The Time after Antichrist as a Station for the Earthly Progress in Medieval Thought," *Traditio* 32 (1976): 97–144.

47. Apart from the three cases examined here, see a list of other minor episodes in Alexander Patschovsky, "Die Wirsberger: Zeugen der Geisteswelt Joachims von Fiore in Deutschland während des 15. Jahrhunderts?" in *Il profetismo goachimita tra Quattrocento e Cinquecento: Atti del III Congresso Internazionale di Studi Gioachimiti,* ed. Gian Luca Potestà (Genoa: Marietti, 1991), 253–54 n. 72.

48. Alexander Patschovsky, "Chiliasmus und Reformation im ausgehenden Mittelalter," in *Ideologie und Herrschaft im Mittelalter,* ed. M. Kerner (Darmstadt: Wissenschaftliche Buchgesellschaft, 1982), 475–96; also Patschovsky 1990.

49. For the sources concerning the first phase of Frederick's career as a supporter of a literal millennium in southern Saxony and for the accusation expressed in Dietrich's *Silencium contra prophecias prophetarum Saxoniae,* see Robert E. Lerner, "The Medieval Return to the Thousand-Year Sabbath," in *The Apocalypse in the Middle Ages* (Ithaca/London: Cornell University Press, 1992), 70 n. 71.

50. A fragment of Frederick's trial has been published in *Die Rektorbücher der Universität Heidelberg, Band I. 1386–1410, Heft I,* ed. Jürgen Miethke (Heidelberg: Carl Winter, 1986), 29–30.

51. Alexander Patschovsky, "Nicolaus von Buldesdorf: Zu einer Ketzerverbrennung auf dem Basler Konzil im Jahre 1446," in *Studien zum 15. Jahrhundert: Festschrift für Erich Meuthen,* ed. Johannes Helm-

rath, and Heribert Müller (Munich: R. Oldenbourg, 1994), 269–90 (the council's condemnation is on pp. 281–90).

52. Ibid., 286 and n. 89.

53. On this sect, see Patschovsky, "Die Wirsberger," 225–57.

54. This writing is a letter to a "John of the East" and a long circular letter to the city of Nuremberg; see Patschovsky, "Die Wirsberger," 245.

55. On two of the most important texts of the fifteenth century, see Heinrich Koller, *Reformation Kaiser Siegmunds* (Stuttgart: Monumenta Germaniae Historica, 1964); and K. H. Lauterbach, *Geschichtsverständnis: Zeitdidaxe und Reformgedanke an der Wende zum 16. Jh. Das oberrheinische 'Buchli der hundert capiteln' im Kontext des spätmittelalterlichen Reformbiblizismus* (Munich, 1985). In particular, for an analysis of the text's millennialism, see pp.198ff.

56. For this phase, see Giulio Cattin, *Il primo Savonarola: Poesie e prediche autografe dal Codice Borromeo* (Florence, 1973).

57. Armando F. Verde, "Le lezioni o i sermoni sull'Apocalisse di Girolamo Savonarola (1490): 'Nova dicere et novo modo,'" in *Immagine e parola retorica, filologico-retorica, predicatoria (Valle e Savonarola), Memorie Domenicane* 19 (Pistoia 1988), 5–109.

58. Particularly significant are Savonarola's sermons on Haggai (Advent 1494). See Girolamo Savonarola, *Prediche sopra Aggeo e Trattato circa il reggimento e governo della città di Firenze,* ed Luigi Firpo (Rome: Belardetti, 1965), esp. 144–45, 151, 340–41. Weinstein (1970, chaps. 4–5) has brought this important aspect to the fore. However, I am not sure that Savonarola's vision can be considered millenarian.

59. Girolamo Savonarola, *Prediche sopra i Salmi,* I, ed P. G. Ricci (Rome: Belardetti, 1955), 135–45, 165–75, 200–203, 291–93; and *Prediche sopra l'Esodo,* I, ed. P. G. Ricci (Rome: Belardetti, 1955), 119–21. These two series were composed in 1495 and 1498.

60. On Bernardino and his sect, see Cesare Vasoli, "Une secte hérétique florentine à la fin du 15e siècle: les 'oints,'" in *Hérésies et sociétés dans l'Europe pré-industrielle: 11e–18e siècles,* ed. Jacques Le Goff (Paris/The Hague: Mouton, 1968), 259–71. Also Polizzotto 1994, 119–38, esp. 122, where Bernardino is described as the organizer of a "small activist élite [. . .] like a task force."

61. Adriano Prosperi, "Il monaco Teodoro: Note su un processo fiorentino del 1515," *Critica storica* 12 (1975): 71–101 (the text of the process is in the appendix).

⸙ BIBLIOGRAPHY

Burr, David. 1989. *Olivi and Franciscan Poverty: The Origins of the 'Usus Pauper' Controversy.* Philadelphia: University of Pennsylvania Press.

———. 1993. *Olivi's Peaceable Kingdom: A Reading of the Apocalypse Commentary.* Philadelphia: University of Pennsylvania Press. The most important study of Olivi's apocalypticism.

Kaminsky, Howard. 1967. *A History of the Hussite Revolution.* Berkeley/Los Angeles: University of California Press. The best study of Hussitism in English. Also examines the Taborites and other millenarian groups.

Lambert, Malcolm. 1992. *Medieval Heresy: Popular Movements from the Gregorian Reform to the Reformation.* 2nd ed. Oxford: Blackwell. A survey of medieval heresy with up-to-date bibliography.

Lerner, Robert E. 1976. "An 'Angel of Philadelphia' in the Reign of Philip the Fair: The Case of Guiard de Cressonessart." In *Order and Innovation in the Middle Ages,* edited by W. C. Jordan et al., 343–64. Princeton: Princeton University Press.

Manselli, Raoul. 1959. *Spirituali e beghini in Provenza.* Rome: Istituto Storico Italiano per il Medio Evo. A general account of both the Spirituals and their beguin followers.

May, W. H. 1955. "The Confession of Prous Boneta Heretic and Heresiarch." In *Essays in Medieval Life and Thought presented in Honor of Austin P. Evans,* edited by J. Mundy, R. Emery, and B. Nelson, 3–30. New York: Columbia University Press.

Molnar, Amedeo. 1986. *I Taboriti: Avanguardia della rivoluzione hussita (sec. XV): Gli scritti essenziali.* Turin: Claudiana. A Brief history of Tabor, including an anthology of texts translated into Italian and a bibliography.

Orioli, Raniero. 1988. *Venit perfidus heresiarcha: Il movimento apostolico-dolciniano dal 1260 al 1307.* Rome: Istituto Storico italiano per il Medio Evo. The most complete work.

Patschovsky, Alexander. 1990. "Eresie escatologiche tardomedievali nel regno teutonico." In *L'attesa della fine dei tempi nel Medioevo,* edited by Ovidio Capitani and Jürgen Miethke, 221–44, Annali dell'istituto storico italo-germanico, Quaderno 28. Bologna: Il Mulino. The most synthetic of Patschovsky's important contributions to this area of study.

Patschovsky, Alexander, and František Šmahel, eds. 1996. *Eschatologie und Hussitismus: Internationales Kolloquium Prag 1.–4. September 1993.* Prague: Historisches Institut. See especially the essays of Anne Hudson, Robert E. Lerner, and Howard Kaminsky.

Polizzotto, Lorenzo. 1994. *The Elect Nation: The Savonarolan Movement in Florence 1494–1545.* Oxford: Clarendon Press. Detailed account of the evolution of the Savonarolan movement.

Potestà, Gian Luca. 1980. *Storia ed escatologia in Ubertino da Casale.* Milan: Vita e Pensiero.

———. 1990. *Angelo Clareno: Dai poveri eremiti ai fraticelli.* Rome: Istituto Storico Italiano per il Medio Evo.

———. 1994. "Dall'annuncio dell'anticristo all'attesa del pastore angelico: Gli scritti di Arnaldo di Villanova nel codice dell'Archivio generale dei Carmelitani." *Arxiu de Textos Catalans Antics* 13:287–344.

Pou y Martí, José Maria. 1930. *Visionarios, Beguinos y Fraticelos Catalanes (siglos XIII–XV).* Vich: Editorial Serafica. Still the most complete account. It has been recently republished with an introduction by Ana Mary Arcelus Ulibarrena (Madrid: Colegio Cardenal Cisneros, 1991).

Reeves, Marjorie E. 1993. *The Influence of Prophecy in the Later Middle Ages: A Study in Joachimism.* 2nd ed. Notre Dame/London: University of Notre Dame Press. This book offers a detailed description of late medieval and early modern apocalyptic movements. The author is primarily interested in reconstructing a map of the diffusion of Joachim's doctrines.

Rusconi, Roberto. 1979. *L'attesa della fine: Crisi della società, profezia ed Apocalisse in Italia al tempo del grande scisma d'Occidente (1378–1417).* Rome: Istituto Storico Italiano per il Medio Evo. A work that treats the later Fraticelli and that is important also for its analysis of apocalyptic preaching and the diffusion of prophetic and eschatological texts.

Šmahel, František. 1993. *Husitska Revoluce.* 4 volumes. Prague, 1993. This monumental study of the Hussite revolution is available only in Czech; the third volume deals with the revolutionary conflict.

Töpfer, Bernhard. 1964. *Das kommende Reich des Friedens: Zur Entwicklung chiliastischer Zukunftshoffnungen im Hochmittelalter.* Berlin: Akademie Verlag. An important general survey of radical movements. In the introduction to the recent Italian translation, the author includes an important *retractatio: Il regno futuro della libertà: Lo sviluppo delle speranze millenaristiche nel medioevo centrale* (Genoa: Marietti, 1992).

Weinstein, Donald. 1970. *Savonarola and Florence: Prophecy and Patriotism in the Renaissance.* Princeton: Princeton University Press. The best study of Savonarola's relation to Florence.

———. 1991. "Hagiography, Demonology, Biography: Savonarola Studies Today." *Journal of Modern History* 36:483–503. Summarizes the most recent research.

13

Images of Hope and Despair: Western Apocalypticism ca. 1500–1800

Robin Barnes
Davidson College

T HE GREAT WESTERN TRANSITION from medieval to modern civilization involved basic shifts in prevailing conceptions of space and time, the human and the divine, shifts that we cannot begin to fathom apart from the developing traditions of Judeo-Christian apocalypticism. While older models of "secularization" held that the central tendency of the early modern period was the general dissolution of inherited Christian and pagan myths about nature and history, recent studies force upon us a much more complex picture. The broad outlines of this picture suggest that the changes commonly associated with emerging "modernity," including the religious reformations, the rise of experimental science, and even the development of political liberalism, were themselves intimately related to the continuing evolution of Western prophetic and apocalyptic visions. What follows is an attempt to survey the dominant lines of European apocalyptic thought, both learned and popular, from the age of the Reformation to the era of the French Revolution. We seek to explore the ways in which ancient and medieval images of crisis and a coming end, transformed in the ferment of latter-day experience, created a fundamental matrix for the emergence of "modern" attitudes and ideas.

The historian Marjorie Reeves explained that "from its birth Christian thought held within it both a pessimistic and an optimistic expectation concerning history; its end could be conceived either as a mounting crescendo of evil or as the Millennium, a Messianic Age of Gold" (Reeves 1993, 295). This paradoxical potential was realized in ever starker forms toward the end of the Middle Ages, when extreme foreboding and burning hope both appear dramatically in the same people. By around 1500, this bipolar aspect of Western expectancy was becoming more pronounced and pervasive than ever. In giving form to this radical psychological vacillation and tension, early modern apocalypticism both shaped and revealed the efforts of Europeans to wrestle with basic spiritual and social issues. This discussion will try to show that the experience of historical disillusionment and despair was at least as formative as the rise of forward-looking hope in the evolution of characteristically modern attitudes. In the broadest sense, our inquiry has to do with new forms of self-consciousness, new concepts of identity, as Europeans struggled to reconcile highly paradoxical perceptions into some universal scheme of meaning.

It is possible to view the early modern age as both bringing to a climax and gradually overcoming late-medieval spiritual and psychological anxieties. Outwardly, the Renaissance-Reformation age witnessed a considerably higher level of apocalyptic expectancy than did the subsequent era of the Enlightenment. Studies of the European "crisis" of the seventeenth century often emphasize the waning of earlier religious, intellectual, and social tensions after about 1660. This presentation, however, will maintain that powerful underlying strains of mixed fear and hope remained very much alive in the late seventeenth century and throughout the eighteenth. Although traditional forms of apocalypticism were to some extent challenged by the insistent claims of Enlightenment rationalism and skepticism, inherited assumptions and images did not fade as fully as is commonly assumed. Indeed, they maintained a great deal of potency, often just beneath the surface of public discourse. And these currents once again came to the fore, transformed but marked with clear signs of their ancestry, at the end of our period, in the era of the French Revolution.

☞ THE PERCEPTION OF TIME IN RENAISSANCE CULTURE

Among the main features of Renaissance culture, none was more significant than the intensified perception of time. By the decades around 1500, as Renaissance learning blossomed on a European scale, a newly pronounced and pervasive awareness of time's passage—both in the experience of the individual and in history—was everywhere in evidence. It is difficult to explore the meaning of this waxing awareness apart from the thesis that in the later Middle Ages European civilization witnessed a unique swelling of apprehension and guilt; for, as one distinguished historian has put it, "anxiety is a function of man's attitude to time," and especially of prevailing visions of the future.[1] With the growing complexity of Western urban culture, involving new forms of bureaucratic control, novel technologies (including clocks and printed calendars), and ever more ambiguous social relationships, Europeans developed a heightened sense of future possibility, and hence a rising general level of anxiety.

We need not look far, of course, to find striking disclosures of darkest dread toward the end of the Middle Ages. We might consider, for example, the prevalence of morbid themes in art and literature, or countless desperate acts of repentance, or the frequent outbreaks of anti-Semitic violence in many parts of Europe. At the close of the fifteenth century and in the years leading up to the great religious explosion of the 1520s, these and other manifestations of social anguish were becoming more widespread than ever. So too were apocalyptic prophecies of doom. Predictions of the advent of the Antichrist competed with forecasts of a Christian bloodbath at the hands of the Turks. In the 1490s, at the very seat of Renaissance culture, Savonarola's terrifying preaching on the wrath to come ignited a fireball of religious panic that heated even the city's most urbane minds (see chapter 12 above). For virtually every part of western and central Europe we have evidence that the same sort of message was very common, and that the fear of an angry God was likely affecting more people than it had in earlier generations.

But while Savonarola's message included terrifying warnings, it also held out the promise of a great spiritual and moral renewal of the whole world, in which Florence would enjoy the role of the New Jerusalem. Indeed, the high Renaissance era also brought dramatic bursts of positive hope for the earthly future. Inherited prophetic traditions that awaited a future time of deliverance could and did blend easily with the humanistic vision of a returning golden age. The joys of classical learning, the growing sense of the power of language, the desire to find dignity in creative human pursuits were all able to build on medieval dreams of a *renovatio mundi*, the sorts of prophetic hopes conveyed by Joachimism and related medieval currents. Advances in trade and technology likewise helped to convince some that Christendom was on the verge of a great flowering. Perhaps the most important development came with printing, regarded especially among the learned as a wonderful gift of God. Among the most expansive of all Renaissance enterprises were the famous voyages of discovery, and here recent studies have demonstrated a clear role for hopeful strains of apocalyptic thought. Christopher Columbus, for instance, was inspired in large measure by the belief that by sailing to the Indies he was helping to fulfill the divine plan, according to which all lands and peoples would be converted to Christ before the end (see chapter 11 above).

In many cases, however, hopeful schemes were patently direct reactions to a fearful sense of breakdown. While traditional predictions of a quasi-messianic savior-emperor continued and even intensified, as did dreams of an Angelic Pope who would reform the whole world, these projections were obvious mental reversals of the perceived chaos in both political and religious life. Indeed, it is hard to avoid the impression that especially outside the confines of humanist circles, the general tendency of this era was toward the anticipation of terrible disasters and suffering for the world; the dominant outlook was one of dread. In northern Europe particularly, a sense of breakdown and the feared day of judgment were pervasive. Events were spinning completely out of human control; the forces of evil seemed to be running rampant in a decaying world; rumors of the birth or imminent disclosure of Antichrist were common. The German preacher Gailer von Kaisersberg echoed the sentiments of many when he declared bleakly that "there is no hope that things will go better for Christendom."[2]

The Renaissance revival of ancient forms of prophecy and divination was by this time exercising a powerful influence, which began to extend beyond the bounds of a learned elite. Ancient methods and traditions provided a massive new arsenal of tools by which inherited hopes and fears could be articulated and reinforced. Humanistic learning made prophetic inquiry more systematic in its methods and more ambitious in its goals. Far and away the most important of the revived ancient divinatory methods was astrology, which had grown ever more pervasive since the twelfth century, when the translation of Arabic texts into Latin had begun (for the role of astrology in Jewish apocalypticism, see chapter 14 below). In the last decades of the fifteenth century, a host of classical and Arabic sources appeared in print, contributing to broader knowledge and sophistication in both astronomy and its practical sister-science. The analysis of celestial motion had a long and close association with apocalyptic thought, and the link was very much in evidence as astrology became more pervasive. Thus, for example, the Arabic doctrine of "great conjunctions," by which universal history was divided into precisely measurable epochs, helped inspire new precise efforts at prophetic speculation.

The star-obsession of elites in the high Renaissance era is well known; less commonly appreciated is the popular spread of astrological imagery around this time. Already before 1500 relatively cheap annual booklets and broadsheets were extremely common in Italy and Germany. Vernacular editions became especially numerous in the German cities, where by the early years of the new century lay culture was positively saturated with the revived star lore of the ancients. These publications directed attention to the dangers anticipated for the coming months, threats to the vital equilibrium both within the individual and in nature at large. They came to reflect a preoccupation with the universal destructiveness of time, a notion frequently conveyed in the image of Saturn devouring his children. Thus, they helped evoke fears of lunar imbalance, Saturnine chaos, and universal disorder. Almost all astrologers insisted that "the stars incline; they do not force," and nearly all emphasized that theirs was a Christian art that honored the power and glory of God. But the tendency to apply classical divination in a Christian context served to focus the religious imagination on the apocalyptic elements of Christian prophecy.

In this atmosphere of prophetic ferment the motley predictions of stargazers such as the famous Johann Lichtenberger (d. 1503) stirred widespread unrest and awe. Lichtenberger's *Prognostication* (*Pronosticatio*), first published at Heidelberg in 1488 and many times thereafter, was a potent brew of astrology with biblical and medieval prophetic traditions, including Joachimism and Last Emperor myths. His forecasts included the nightmare of invasion by the Turks along with many other hair-raising predictions, but also held out hopes for imperial, even universal, reformation. The *Prognostication* marks a key stage in the move to publication of prophetic materials in the vernacular, a trend that was particularly strong in the German-speaking lands. More generally, Lichtenberger's work exemplifies the way in which the varied strains of medieval apocalypticism entered a new phase of intensification and dissemination around the midpoint of the second millennium C.E. It is also a monument to the highly blurred boundaries between learned and popular expectations at that time; at both levels of culture we see predictions of general disaster and woe as well as dreams of glory. Equally important, religious and political themes were thoroughly mixed.

As had been true throughout the late Middle Ages, apocalyptic and millenarian schemes could function either to support or to undermine established political structures. Thus, while Lichtenberger's predictions, for example, were basically conservative and defensive of traditional institutions, the same era saw the appearance of revolutionary tracts such as the *Book of a Hundred Chapters* by the so-called "Upper Rhenish Revolutionary" (ca. 1500), which foresaw the overthrow of a thoroughly corrupt social order and the onset of a new age. Whether or not any particular apocalyptic vision was viewed as socially threatening depended on which groups or forces understood and accepted the divine plan for history, and which ones opposed that plan. If the activist forms of apocalypticism were most often expressed in movements calling for social transformation, there were also more defensive forms that were generally linked with an attitude of passive watchfulness, with the effort to cling to whatever bulwarks of meaning and order remained in a crumbling world.

The most dramatic example of the swelling prophetic excitement of this era lay in a complex of imagery that was inherently neither conservative nor revolutionary, but evoked a deep sense of existential apprehension. By the second decade of the sixteenth century, a wave of flood fears swept over much of the continent, especially central Europe. We have considerable evidence showing widespread reaction to astrologically inspired predictions of a second universal deluge that might well bring the end of the world. These fears became focused on February of 1524, when there were to be no fewer than sixteen planetary conjunctions in the "watery" sign of Pisces. While many writers sought to restore calm in the rising atmosphere of panic, it seems clear that the flood imagery served to articulate a wide range of psychological and spiritual fears that were coming to a head by the early 1520s. The sense of impending chaos or annihilation made one crucial question profoundly immediate and pressing: What did the Lord require of the faithful?

☞ RADICAL OUTPOURINGS

A range of responses to a widespread sense of crisis marked the religious and social explosion of the early Reformation. In the push to throw off Roman authority, in the forceful reform of local ecclesiastical structures and practices, and in militant action for the final cleansing of a corrupt world, we have movements in which an activist apocalyptic message played a central role. On the other hand, a more defensive, passive aspect is evident in the evangelical emphasis on the nearness of deliverance, in the prevailing acknowledgment of secular authority, and in strident preaching for personal repentance in the face of the universal judgment. Here again, apocalypticism was by no means the preserve of social revolutionaries; a pervasive atmosphere of expectancy marked the age. An essentially passive attitude of watching and waiting could and often did evoke a high level of psychological tension, as intense as any experienced by those who believed they were called to help bring on the kingdom themselves.

We should also be on guard against the notion that those groups and individuals commonly associated with "radical" reform shared the expectation of an earthly millennium. "Chiliasm" in the strict sense—namely, belief in a coming thousand-year reign of Christ on earth (Revelation 20)—did appear among a few early Reformation radicals, such as the Anabaptist Augustin Bader. But hopes for the consummation of the kingdom within historical time remained exceptional among "radical" as well as mainline reformers. Thomas Müntzer, for example, who began as an ally of Luther but soon broke away entirely and became a revolutionary preacher in the German Peasants' War of 1525, does not seem to have anticipated a literal earthly millennium. Rather, his vision was of a final destruction of the godless by the elect, who would reestablish the apostolic church and thus prepare the world for the second advent and the eternal kingdom. Müntzer was heavily influenced by medieval mystical as well as activist apocalyptic traditions. He preached the advent of the kingdom in the hearts of the elect, but stressed that it was the responsibility of the faithful to see that the divine will should be done on earth, as it was in heaven.

A similar view was shared by the early Anabaptist leader Hans Hut, who calculated that the final purification of the world, and the end of time, would come in the summer of 1528. The fiery figure Melchior Hoffman, another early evangelical turned Anabaptist, came to preach a final outpouring of the spirit and worldwide cleansing by the people of God. In 1530 he conceived of himself as Elijah, one of the "two witnesses" predicted in Rev. 11:3. The city of Strasbourg was to be the spiritual New Jerusalem, the beacon for the final triumph of the Word before the return of Christ, which he predicted for 1533. The precise shapes of Hoffman's apocalyptic visions were fluid; the same was true for many apocalyptic spiritualists of that era. Along with many other "radical" preachers of this era he seems to have been influenced to some extent by medieval Joachimism. But in fact it is often difficult to determine whether a particular thinker looked to the spiritual or physical advent of Christ, whether the destruction of the forces of evil would precede the last judgment in such a way that one could speak of an earthly realization of the kingdom, or whether the second advent would actually bring the end of time or not. Religious or psychological importance lay less in the precise apocalyptic scenario than in the general belief that a final outpouring of the spirit was under way.

Among the early evangelical reformers, the idea of a final victory for the faithful within history was not unknown. It was put forward, for example, in the first Protestant commentary on the book of Revelation, issued in 1528 by Francis Lambert, a key figure in the organization of the reform in Hesse. Another notable early-Reformation "millenarian" was Martin Borrhaus (Cellarius), who was likewise no Anabaptist radical or social revolutionary. Borrhaus was an early student and associate of Martin Luther and Philipp Melanchthon at Wittenberg, who, despite later flirtations with spiritualism became a respected professor at Basle. In a 1527 work titled *The Works of God* (*De Operibus Dei*), which may have influenced Melchior Hoffman among others, Borrhaus put forward an interpretation of scriptural prophecies in which a coming period of general calamity and suffering would be followed by a universal renovation and fulfillment. When in 1530 the Augsburg Confession denounced "certain Jewish opinions which are even now making their appearance and which teach that, before the resurrection of the dead, saints and godly men will possess a worldly kingdom and annihilate all the godless" (Article XVII), the intended targets most likely included Borrhaus.

In short, then, it was neither apocalyptic expectancy in general nor the teaching of a coming millennial kingdom in particular that actually set radicals and revolutionaries apart from the mainstream in the early Reformation. Rather, what seems to have most threatened established structures were the notions of immediate spiritual inspiration and the believer's responsibility for social cleansing. It was above all this sort of spiritualist perfectionism, the belief that the faithful could have direct knowledge of God's will in the here and now and that they had an active role to play in the drama of the last days, that had the potential to threaten social order. Those who received the gift of the spirit shared responsibility for the purification of the church and the world, a rooting out of evil in preparation for the end itself.

Melchior Hoffman himself never became a preacher of social revolution; this point illustrates again that the apocalyptic sense of contingency regarding all human structures had no fixed social implications. But radical followers in the Netherlands and in northwest Germany used his thinking to take a more active stance, and the disastrous result was the famous Anabaptist rising at Münster in 1534–1535. Here, in perhaps the most notorious early modern outbreak of revolutionary apocalypticism, the idea of a final Davidic kingdom to precede the second advent inspired a takeover of the city led by Jan Matthijs, Bernhard Rothmann, Bernard Knipperdolling, and finally by Jan van Leiden. All citizens who resisted the movement of the godly were expelled; communism of goods and a severe moral code were enforced. Ultimately Jan van Leiden procaimed himself king of the New Jerusalem and established what became essentially a reign of terror, during which he instituted a form of polygamy, citing the model of the Old Testament patriarchs. After an increasingly desperate resistance against a siege raised by neighboring princes, the city was finally overrun in June of 1535. Most of the inhabitants of the Münsterite kingdom were slaughtered outright, while Jan van Leiden and his associates were tortured at length. Their bodies were placed on public display, where they remained long afterward as a grim memento.

The debacle at Münster was basically an aberration within the early Reformation movement known as Anabaptism. Most "Brethren," as they called themselves, waited quietly, peace-fully, and fervently for the return of the Lord, though they commonly sought to remove them-selves from the corruption they saw throughout the old creation. Among Mennonites and other Anabaptists, who managed to maintain their communities through the severe persecu-tions of the sixteenth century, trust in the divine promise of deliverance from and judgment upon history continued to be central. But this belief in itself did little or nothing to distinguish Anabaptists or other "radicals" from large numbers of mainline evangelical Protestants.

☞ HOPES AND FEARS IN THE REFORMATION

Of greater long-term importance than the sporadic outbursts of revolutionary apocalypticism were the common hopes and fears that emerged with the broader spread of the Reformation. In general, Protestant piety directed the focus of religious attention away from traditional rituals, turning it toward prophecy and prayer. This shift concentrated the outlook of believers on the promise of future salvation, the threat of the coming last judgment, and the avenues by which these things were revealed. The piety of the Middle Ages had offered a wide range of intermedi-aries between humanity and the divine, through which the faithful could in some measure ease their spiritual anxiety. In one sense the new evangelical preaching brought liberation from the burdens of this spiritual regiment. On the other hand, it also did away with the sense of security that the traditional channels had allowed. It would therefore be a serious mistake to assume that the Reformation overcame the widespread prophetic anxiety of the late Middle Ages. Quite the contrary, the sixteenth-century reform movements witnessed a major reshaping and refocus-ing, as well as a massive new social dissemination, of apocalyptic visions.

Of all the major reformers, Martin Luther revealed the most consistently pronounced apocalyptic outlook. Luther's expectancy was clearly influenced by common, late-medieval prophetic ideas and assumptions. His conception of world history, for example, owed much to inherited notions of universal decline and degeneracy. Yet Luther was without question a highly original apocalyptic interpreter; indeed, his readings of scripture and his re-visioning of prophetic truth became the key source of inspiration for a long tradition of Protestant apoca-lypticism both in Germany and elsewhere. Luther's revival of the New Testament hope included a heavy emphasis on the literal imminence of universal judgment and deliverance. His religious outlook was founded on the sense of an all-encompassing struggle between God and the devil. Luther saw his own movement to revive the gospel as the last act in this great conflict. God was allowing the light of truth to flash over the world with a final burst of clarity even as true believers were subject to unprecedented threats and persecutions.

Essential to Luther's prophetic understanding was his discovery of the biblical Antichrist in the Roman papacy. Departing from the long medieval tradition in which individual popes were reviled as Antichrist, Luther identified the institution of the papacy itself as the incarna-tion of a corrupted gospel. In accordance with Antichrist prophecies such as that found in 2 Thessalonians 2, this discovery indicated that the last days had arrived. The struggle was now out in the open; nothing more was to be awaited before the end. Luther did believe that secular authorities had the responsibility to guard peace and protect lives in whatever ways they could, but individual believers were simply to bear the multiplying horrors on earth as they joyfully awaited the day of redemption. This attitude of essentially defensive apocalyptic expectancy became pervasive among Luther's evangelical followers. Although most of the Western world was affected to some extent by the heightened expectancy of the age, the authority of the Wittenberg reformer helped to sanction among his German heirs the most consistently pronounced apocalyptic atmosphere in sixteenth-century Europe.

Luther rejected most of the eschatological visions that had bubbled up in the rising prophetic ferment of earlier centuries: Last-Emperor myths, prophecies of an Angelic Pope, Joachimite dreams of a third historical dispensation, forecasts of a final flowering of the church after the rise and fall of Antichrist. To be sure, he was not averse to using medieval prophetic traditions when he believed they could help the cause of the gospel, but he never left room for doubt that the chaos of history would continue until the last judgment itself, which would bring time to an end. While the basic shape of Luther's prophetic outlook did not change after his break from Rome, in his later years his tone became more markedly and consistently apocalyptic as his interest in the historical dimension grew, and also as he perceived this world's plight becoming more desperate. Thus, while at first he found the book of Revelation obscure and confusing, as time went on and the swirl of events became ever more distressing he found it to be a rich and necessary source of prophetic insight. The increasingly bleak utterances of his later years left a heavy imprint on the preaching of his heirs, reinforcing the powerful emphasis on worldly disillusionment, on the utter hopelessness of the temporal world.

Circumstances continued to nourish the common perception that the crucial hour was at hand. The nightmare of an invasion by the Turks, which would come as a final punishment on a sinful world, had never seemed closer to realization than it did by the late 1520s. Such a feeling spurred Luther to complete his vernacular translation of the Bible so that the word might spread as widely as possible in whatever brief time remained. While Luther and most of his colleagues generally worked to discourage too-precise calculations and predictions, the desire to gain insight into the order and timing of critical events was ever-present. Among fervent evangelicals the excitement sometimes reached a fever pitch, as it did in a village near Wittenberg when Luther's friend Michael Stifel predicted from his pulpit that the world would end at 8:00 A.M. on October 19, 1533.

Luther's sermons, polemical writings, and prophetic utterances gave weight to the assumption that the last times were at hand; in 1541 he even issued a major world chronology, the *Supputatio annorum mundi*, in which he reckoned the age of the world and made clear his conviction that time was running out. His calculations generally complemented those of the highly popular *Chronica* of Johann Carion, a universal history edited by Philipp Melanchthon that first appeared at Wittenberg in 1532. Although the notorious affair at Münster, as well as the scandal raised closer to home by Michael Stifel, helped to dampen public predictions for a time, the quest for prophetic insight went on. The Nuremberg reformer Andreas Osiander gave a major push to Protestant reckoning both in Germany and elsewhere with his *Conjectures on the Last Days and the End of the World* (1544). Osiander proposed that while the precise day and hour of the end could not be known, God in fact commanded the faithful to pursue research into the order and timing of events as the judgment approached.

Despite the centrality of Luther's biblical discoveries, evangelical propaganda continued to draw on the large stock of medieval apocalyptic lore and imagery. Thus, for instance, popular expectations of a final great prophet, a last Elijah who would come to prepare the way for the Lord's return, were frequently understood as referring to Luther himself. The so-called Cedar of Lebanon vision, a powerful formulation of the Last World Emperor myth, was adapted to support the Protestant convictions that Luther's movement was divinely ordained, that the godless would soon be punished, and that deliverance was imminent for the faithful (for Jewish use of this prophecy, see chapter 14 below). The heritage of Joachimism was not left unused. In 1527, for example, Andreas Osiander updated and published an old Joachimist prophecy and a prediction of Hildegard of Bingen, both of which looked to a recovery of the true church before the last judgment and the end of the world.

Again, as in earlier generations, monstrous births and other natural wonders were almost universally viewed as divine signs and warnings. Luther and Melanchthon sanctioned such interpretations with publications about the prophetic significance of grotesque appearances in nature. These included the famous "Monk-Calf" and "Papal Ass," hideous creatures revealing the abominations of the Roman Church and the nearness of the judgment. Although 1524 passed without a flood, the signs in the heavens continued to draw intense interest. The appearance of a great comet in 1531 (later named Halley's) drew the rapt attention of many observers as an almost certain warning of divine punishment to come. While Luther himself turned a mostly cold shoulder to systematic astrological predictions of human fate, it was difficult to keep biblical prophecies and sidereal forecasts fully separate. Recognizing the power of Lichtenberger's *Pronosticatio*, Luther issued his own edition of the work, emphasizing its anti-Roman elements. More important, the full embrace of astrology by the highly influential Melanchthon, "the teacher of Germany," guaranteed a major role for the art in later Lutheran apocalypticism.

While neither Ulrich Zwingli nor John Calvin shared the sort of apocalyptic expectancy that prevailed among the German evangelicals, the sense of the present as a decisive moment in universal history was in evidence almost everywhere the Reformation spread. Such feelings could easily crystallize into explicit apocalyptic convictions. Anti-Romanism in almost every form seized avidly upon passages such as Revelation 11, which spoke in gripping terms of the two witnesses who would appear before the last judgment to oppose the beast from the bottomless pit. We will see that as the sixteenth century progressed, Protestantism in particular witnessed a growing tendency to articulate apocalyptic attitudes in precise analyses of past, present, and anticipated events. This development had highly complex causes, but among them were surely the general spread of humanistic learning, the continuing rise in lay literacy, and the increasingly pressing needs of emerging confessional, social, and political groups to achieve or maintain a clear sense of identity and purpose in a world riddled with conflict.

GERMAN LUTHERAN APOCALYPTICISM

In the decades after Luther's death (1546), German Lutherans propounded an increasingly explicit, eclectic, and strident apocalypticism. With the rise of severe factional strife among Luther's heirs, the emergence of Calvinism and other competing confessions, and with the inevitable waning of early-Reformation exuberance, evangelical preachers and writers expressed a growing sense that the plight of this world was hopeless. Typical of this trend was

Andreas Musculus (d. 1581) of Frankfurt an der Oder, who tirelessly pounded on the sobering theme of universal breakdown. Everywhere there was evidence of the drying up of true faith and love, of unparalleled religious and moral decay. The devil appeared to be more active than ever before. The only hope lay in the promise of deliverance at the last day; trust in its closeness was absolutely central to Christian faith.

After Luther's death, ever-larger collections of his prophecies also appeared, mostly those he made in the period after 1530. On virtually every page of these collections—which were huge publishing successes—one finds a blood-curdling picture of whatever short time remained to this world. In the troubled period around mid-century and later, as German evangelicals split into feuding factions and their movement appeared to falter and stall before a host of hostile forces, these dramatically negative predictions seemed to confirm Luther's status as a true prophet—indeed, as the third or last Elijah, sent to announce the final advent. Equally significant was the spate of eschatological tracts issued in the third quarter of the century by evangelical clergymen. Perhaps the most widespread of all was a treatise by Basilius Faber, *Necessary and Useful Christian Instructions about the Last Events of the World*, first published at Eisleben in 1565. This work laid out abundant evidence for the approach of the last day and also explained essential teachings on the resurrection, the judgment, heaven, and hell. Like many others, Faber made prominent reference to the grim forecasts of Luther to help confirm the closeness of the end. These predictions he took to be inspired explications of biblical prophecy.

Further expressions of apocalyptic appeared in the wonder books, another popular genre that expanded massively after mid-century. Sensational as they often appear, these volumes breathed heatedly the expectation of a great, imminent outpouring of divine wrath upon the godless world, and of the last judgment itself. The wonders were a form of preaching, and the authors of the broadsheets and books illustrating them were like Old Testament prophets. Among the most widely read writers of such popular collections was the pastor Job Fincel, whose book *Marvellous Signs* (*Wunderzeichen*) (1st ed. Nuremberg, 1556) emphasized the multiplication of natural wonders since Luther had revived the true gospel. Again the message was one of spiritual urgency, for the wonders screamed of worldly disorder; the old creation was patently crumbling.

Inspired by the humanist inquiries into nature and history led by Melanchthon, students of prophecy eagerly applied the tools of chronology, mathematics, and astrology to this field of inquiry. The traditional historical scheme of the four world monarchies from the book of Daniel was now frequently complemented by the so-called Prophecy of Elias. This was an adaptation of the Augustinian scheme of six world ages: the world was allotted two thousand years before the law, two thousand years under the law, and two thousand years after the coming of the Messiah. A well-worn passage from Matthew (24:22) made it clear that the last age would be cut short, for "except those days should be shortened, there should no flesh be saved." Over fifteen hundred years of that era had already passed. If one now included the evidence supplied by countless astrologers regarding the celestial signs, including unusual conjunctions of the planets and the frightening new star of 1572, one could hardly refute the conclusion that the end was very close. After mid-century we see the full-scale adoption of astrology among many German Lutherans as a prophetic tool, a means of reading the book of nature, the truths of which necessarily complemented scripture.

There was a major buildup of expectations that 1588 would bring some sort of universal upheaval, if not the end itself. But that year was only one of numerous foci for expectation in the apocalyptically charged late-Reformation era. Most learned calculations avoided open date-setting, in keeping with the continuing Protestant emphasis on passages such as Matt. 24:36: "But of that day and hour knoweth no man, no, not the angels of heaven, but my Father only." Nevertheless, historical reckoning became rife in German burgher culture. Typical of the trend was a work by Nicholas Raimarus entitled *Chronological, Certain, and Irrefutable Proof, from the Holy Scripture and Fathers, That the World Will Perish and the Last Day Will come within 77 Years* (Nuremberg, 1606; reckoned from 1596). This tract inspired a long debate among both learned and popular writers, many of whom argued that Raimarus had estimated too loosely and that the judgment would certainly come upon the present generation within a decade, or sooner still. As late as the 1620s, we find Lutheran clergymen as well as layfolk fixing their prophetic attention on dates in the not-too-distant future, an enterprise in which they commonly used both scriptural and astronomical/astrological evidence. In its most baroque forms this sort of chronological reckoning merged with complex kabbalistic calculations with biblical letters and numbers (see chapter 14 below).

The decades around 1600 witnessed a flurry of earnest and excited but confused efforts to unravel the crucial secrets of the last times. A pervasive sense of dualism between the fallen present and the redeemed future, along with the belief that hidden truths would be revealed to the faithful in the last times, propelled countless magical efforts to discover the deepest secrets of creation. The intense pursuit of prophetic assurance commonly amounted to a quest for gnosis, or universal saving knowledge. As scholars have shown, it is no accident that the origins of the Faust legend lay in Lutheran Germany. It was above all here, and in the tense setting of the empire and central Europe as a whole, that apocalyptic astrology, alchemy, number mysticism, and related arts buoyed desperate dreams of a new and truly universal Reformation. The great wave of excitement over the appearance of the first "Rosicrucian" tracts (1614–1615) is best understood in this context.

By 1620 a reaction was building among Lutheran theologians against what they regarded as the prophetic mania that surrounded them. Yet not until the era of the Thirty Years' War (1618–1648), with its widespread destruction and sordid realities, was there any significant dissipation of this pervasive atmosphere of apocalyptic tensions and gnostic striving. The bloodshed and suffering that overcame central Europe in the 1620s and 1630s did evoke a swelling of popular millenarian visions such as those of the Silesian Christoph Kotter. These dreams of a messianic ruler and final world conversion followed a familiar late-medieval pattern (see chapter 11). But the dominant note was one of disillusionment. By the middle decades of the seventeenth century we can see among German Protestants a general turn toward the more purely subjective piety that would give rise to Pietism.

☞ THE OUTLOOK OF REFORMED PROTESTANTS

The historical and prophetic outlook of Reformed Protestants tended to be less pessimistic and less radically apocalyptic than that of Luther's heirs. Yet a major tradition of Reformed prophecy nonetheless developed after the mid-sixteenth century, which in several settings took genuinely apocalyptic forms. In Zurich, for example, the leaders of Swiss-German Protestantism developed prophetic teachings that were far more historical and literal than Zwingli's had been. Heinrich Bullinger helped set this new tone in his *In Apocalypsim Iesu Christi . . . Conciones centum* (*One Hundred Sermons on the Apocalypse*), first published in 1557. In the subsequent era, Reformed prophecy showed a growing tendency to be hopeful about the progress of God's kingdom within history. Calvinism would prove especially fertile ground for the emergence of a forward-looking millenarianism that often bordered on historical meliorism.

Although John Calvin himself was perhaps less inclined to apocalyptic thought than any other early Protestant leader, and though early Calvinist interpreters tended to avoid the explicit analysis of current events in prophetic terms, in the late sixteenth and early seventeenth centuries Calvin's heirs showed growing interest in understanding how the current struggle against the Roman Antichrist and his allies fit into a divine scheme. Already in the 1580s, in the midst of the turmoil of the French religious wars, the Italian convert Jacopo Brocardo (d. ca. 1600) adopted the trinitarian scheme of Joachim of Fiore for defense of the Huguenot cause. Brocardo's vision of a new historical dispensation was hardly welcomed among most Calvinists, but his perception that he was living in a time of culminating crisis, and his desire to correlate contemporary events with the prophecies of Revelation, were in line with broader trends in Reformed Protestantism.

More typical of continental Calvinism was the Heidelberg professor David Pareus (d. 1622), whose massive commentary on Revelation saw the book as a historical drama with clearly identifiable acts. Pareus looked to the future destruction of Rome and Roman power; he also helped keep alive old predictions for a "Second Charlemagne," a messianic emperor figure. The worldly confidence of Calvinist thinkers shaped readings that included increasingly explicit visions of future victory. Among the continental scholars who contributed notably to this development was Johann Heinrich Alsted of Herborn (d. 1638). Alsted engaged in apocalyptic computations that included astronomical evidence, reflecting a move toward "scientific" prophecy among Calvinists just at a time when Lutheran orthodoxy was trying to distance itself from such efforts. His most important work was the 1627 *Diatribe de Mille Annis Apocalypticis* (*Discourse concerning the Thousand Years of the Apocalypse*), a commentary on Revelation 20, which engaged in complex mathematical reckoning to predict the full and final fulfillment of saintly rule in 1694.

Equally if not more influential was Alsted's student Jan Amos Comenius (d. 1656), who promoted the ideal of a universal reform of education serving advancement toward the millennial fullness of knowledge. His ideas amounted to a sort of progressive pansophism that built upon the spreading millenarian confidence among Calvinists. Even among more strictly theological thinkers, including relatively staid Dutch Calvinists, positive historical hopes became common. While Dutch Reformed thought retained a good deal of Calvin's own disinclination toward apocalyptic research, particularly into Revelation, the rising sense of prophetic assurance demanded formulation. Daniel van Laren, for instance, developed a carefully studied millenarian vision; like many others he looked to the conversion of the Jews as central to the final transformation. More broadly influential was the important covenant theologian Johannes Cocceius (d. 1669), who pointed to the worldly promise inherent in the covenant of grace. To label this sort of hope "apocalyptic," however, would be to stretch the term beyond useful limits.

☞ CATHOLIC APOCALYPTIC THOUGHT_____

Apocalyptic thinking certainly did not die out in Catholic Europe during the age of the Reformation. But here the continuing traditional integration of the sacred and the social, along with mounting efforts to suppress most forms of prophetic speculation, made for an atmosphere in which historically focused hopes and fears were generally less prominent. In the early sixteenth century there was an active and tense culture of prophecy in war-torn Italy, common to elite and popular culture, and often markedly apocalyptic. The sack of Rome by imperial troops in 1527 was commonly regarded in eschatological terms among both enemies and defenders of the papacy. After around 1530, this atmosphere of popular prophetic discourse was increasingly opposed by a deeply defensive clerical establishment. Yet the growing constraints on preachers and printers could not, of course, eliminate inherited prophetic attitudes and images.

Not surprisingly, Catholic prophecy in Italy, Spain, and elsewhere sometimes identified Luther or other Protestant leaders as the Antichrist; the rapid spread of heresy could easily be seen as a sign of the nearing end. Messianic emperor prophecies continued to circulate; in the 1540s, for example, the Viennese physician and historian Wolfgang Lazius brought together many strands of traditional millenarian hope, focusing them mainly on the emperor Charles V. A competing tradition in France looked to Francis I. Indeed, the theme of a universal Catholic monarchy would remain very much alive well into the seventeenth century, as would medieval dreams of an Angelic Pope. Through much of the Counter-Reformation era Venice in particular saw the continuation of Joachimist and related currents. Venetian prophetic thinkers showed especially lively interest in the idea of a great reforming pope, a tendency with obvious links to the Venetian resistance to papal power.

Apocalyptic ideas had a weighty role among various religious orders. Many Jesuits, for instance, adopted Joachimite assumptions about their order as a prophetic elite with a divinely ordained role to play in the final acts of the historical drama. Various, more or less domesticated forms of Joachimite prophecy continued to support the hopes of numerous Catholic thinkers. Hence, for instance, the overseas missions of groups such as the Franciscans were broadly inspired by beliefs about the final worldwide flowering of Christ's church and the establishment of the millennial kingdom (see chapter 16). Hopes for a coming golden age were often buried in learned biblical commentaries, where they could serve to console scholars but remained largely out of public view.

The general Catholic muting of public prophecy was perhaps least evident in France. While scholars are divided over the level of eschatological fear and anguish among French Catholics in the period before ca. 1560, it is clear that a number of influential preachers and writers, such as Pierre Turrel and Richard Roussat, expressed the view that the last times had arrived, not hesitating to find countless correlations between current events and biblical prophecy and basing their insights in part on Arabic astrological conjunction theory. French preaching on the last judgment most often took the form of grim warning; the message was that salvation was difficult, the saved would be very few. Often these warnings were directed essentially to the individual penitent without reference to the framework of historical or natural events. In this sense the atmosphere among French Catholics would remain less openly apocalyptic, if often no less intensely eschatological, than that which prevailed among many Protestants, especially in Germany.

Popular astrological prediction spread less quickly and pervasively in France than in Germany, but by the 1550s, when Nostradamus began to gain fame, vernacular almanacs had become an established genre and helped to impress a sense of impending catastrophe. Nostradamus himself, for all the attention he drew as a predicter of future events, was not especially concerned with apocalyptic warning or consolation, though he was among those who suggested that a major planetary conjunction in 1565 might herald the second coming. Much of the violence of the French Wars of Religion (ca. 1562–1595) was impelled by popular Catholic prophecies about the forces of God and Satan. It has been argued that the formation of the Catholic League in 1588–89 was essentially a collective response to a sense of eschatological crisis.

Serious public airings of apocalyptic schemes increasingly became linked with heresy in Catholic lands. In the 1540s, Guillaume Postel's breathtaking visions of universal restitution, heavily influenced by Joachimism, became too much for the Jesuit order, from which he was expelled. Later he was declared insane and was imprisoned. Toward the end of the century, millenarian projections made an even more spectacular appearance in the thinking of figures such as Tommaso Campanella and Giordano Bruno, both of whom projected images of a unified and peaceful world. But these thinkers faced their famous troubles with the Inquisition mainly on account of dangerous metaphysical and natural scientific ideas, rather than for their prophetic notions.

Under the Counter-Reformation Habsburg monarchy, Catholic officials waged an ongoing war against all forms of prophecy and divination, which were increasingly viewed in association with popular magic and doctrinal deviance. Apocalyptic ideas surfaced mainly in the form of millenarian hopes in support of Protestant resistance. Protestant chiliasm served this function already after the 1620 Habsburg victory in Bohemia and continued until at least the last decades of the century. Here, and elsewhere in Catholic Europe, by the seventeenth century a popular culture that offered numerous forms of contact with the heavenly world showed only a limited tendency to expect divinely effected transformation of the world at large.

Catholic preaching leaned toward a thoroughly individual eschatology stressing salvation through the unchanging mediating institutions of the church. On the whole, Catholic eschatology remained more individualized and spiritualized, less concerned with the history and future of the world, than the outlook of Protestants. Nevertheless, there can be little doubt that fears of divine wrath and the last judgment remained a pervasive undercurrent throughout Catholic Europe. As late as the mid-seventeenth century a figure such as the Jesuit Fulvio Fontana could still deliver powerful sermons on the theme in his tours of Italy, Switzerland, and Austria. In addition, Catholic prophecy continued to include some medieval traditions, such as the "Fifteen Signs before Doomsday," that were largely abandoned by Protestants because they were judged unscriptural.

REFORMATION APOCALYPTICISM IN ENGLAND _____

The tradition of Reformation apocalypticism in England followed a unique trajectory, which paralleled in several ways the rise of Puritanism. By the middle decades of the sixteenth century,

English writers were beginning to translate and adapt German apocalyptic ideas showing the crucial significance of the struggle against the Roman Antichrist and of the current preaching of the purified gospel. The experience of the Protestant exiles during the reign of Mary Tudor (1553–1558) would help shape the English Puritan vision, in which the struggle against the Antichrist defined both the true church and the people of God.

Early English Protestants showed much of the sort of worldly pessimism that prevailed in Lutheran Germany, yet already in such writers as John Bale (d. 1563) and John Foxe (d. 1587) we can see some different emphases. Their works gave special attention to the English Reformation and its place within the context of providential history. In his famous *Actes and Monuments* (English ed. 1563), Foxe gave England an explicit and central role in the advance of Christ's kingdom. These thinkers were not openly millenarian in outlook, but they helped prepare the way for a confident, militant apocalyptic hope, at the heart of which stood England and English Protestantism. This apocalyptic outlook was already in evidence by the time of the failed Spanish Armada (1588).

In England as elsewhere, powerful strains of non-millenarian apocalypticism certainly continued. Judgment-day sermons were a staple of Elizabethan culture. In 1583 the bishop of London, Edwin Sandys, expressed a traditional and pessimistic belief in the coming end of the world: everywhere there was breakdown; Satan was active as never before. In part, this worldly pessimism reflected the continuing dependence on continental readings of biblical prophecy. Growing confidence and independence, however, are manifest among British writers toward the end of the century. *A Plaine Discovery of the Whole Revelation* (1593) of the Scottish mathematician John Napier was widely read among both British and continental writers. This work offered a highly detailed chronology from the birth of Christ and a systematic analysis of the imagery of Revelation. While Napier avoided definite date setting, he presented numerous detailed speculations, showing the likelihood of the Roman Antichrist's fall in 1639 and the coming of the last judgment by 1700. This notion that the main enemies of Christ might be destroyed before the end itself was in effect a way to legitimize hopes for a final time of peace and justice within history without adopting more explicit and controversial forms of millenarianism. It was proffered with less learned calculation, but more anti-Roman militancy, in Arthur Dent's highly popular *The Ruine of Rome* (1603).

With the apocalyptic researches of Thomas Brightman (d. 1607), we enter into a phase of great flowering in English millenarian thought, most clearly manifest among the Puritans. The Presbyterian Brightman was among the highly influential writers of the day. He saw the millennial age as already in progress; the future would bring ongoing triumph for the true church, until the final defeat of the Antichrist and the full flowering of the kingdom on earth. Of equal if not still greater weight, particularly among Puritans, were the writings of Joseph Mede, above all his 1627 *Clavis Apocalyptica* (*Apocalyptic Key*). Mede's scheme, based like many others on years of intensive study, was less gradualist than Brightman's; it saw all fulfillment as still in the future. Both these writers, however, encouraged a confident, militant Protestantism that deeply affected English society and culture. In the decades prior to the outbreak of the Civil War (1642), the translated works of Alsted and other continental authorities added to the current. On a more popular level, the common astrological almanacs were a main channel for the articulation of expectancy.

How theologically and socially respectable millenarian expectation had become by the 1630s is still a debated question. But it was accepted broadly enough to be a mental framework that served many varied needs, from revolutionary commitment to spiritual comfort. Here again, we find the paradox that fearful belief in the imminence of Doomsday coexisted or alternated rapidly with hopes for the coming of an earthly paradise. As in other settings, a wide variety of apocalyptic scenarios circulated, and even among convinced millenarians there was no simple correlation between prophetic expectations and political positions. To many committed Protestants, however, it appeared that the Antichrist was regaining a hold over both the English church and the state. The surging millennial hopes for a godly society were thus expressed partly in the Puritan migration to the New World, where the elect might yet properly prepare the way of the Lord.

During the upheavals of the Civil War and Interregnum (ca. 1642–1660), the sense of a world-historical turning point came to a climax: "These are days of shaking . . . ," cried one preacher in 1643, "and this shaking is universal."[3] Popular millenarianism became an integral element of propaganda for a cause that linked strident Protestantism with parliamentary or republican government and the establishment of a "godly kingdom." In the absence of all censorship, zealous opponents of the Stuart monarchy openly declared the conflict to be the showdown between the forces of Christ and Antichrist, and even particular battles were correlated with prophetic passages of the Bible. For some radical Independents, even the strictures of Presbyterianism were signs of the beast of Revelation 13, threats to the conscience of the true believer. Here apocalyptic activism verged on Christian anarchism.

With the defeat of Charles I and the uncertainties of the years after 1648 there was a still greater explosion of prophetic hopes. The programs of radical groups such as the Levellers, the Diggers, and the Ranters were heavily laced with revolutionary millenarianism. The most famous case of radical expectancy in this period was that of the Fifth Monarchy Men, who saw it as the responsibility of believers to help bring on the final and most perfect historical age through militant action. The Fifth Monarchists became rapidly disillusioned by the early 1650s: "Lord, wilt thou have Oliver Cromwell or Jesus Christ to reign over us?" asked a Fifth Monarchist in 1653.[4] The apparent answer was deeply frustrating. This highly confused and tense atmosphere witnessed the rise of other, quite different radical religious groups, including those of the Muggletonians, the Philadelphians, and the Quakers, all of which shared a general anticipation of universal spiritual breakthrough. Although George Foxe and most of his early fellow Quakers stressed the advent of the Kingdom as a spiritual transformation in the hearts of believers, the origins of the movement cannot be understood apart from the apocalyptic agitation of that era.

The broader disillusionment with reformist zeal that brought about the Restoration of 1660 would also manifest itself in attitudes toward apocalyptic prophecy. The reaction echoed what had taken place among German Lutherans more than a generation earlier. A 1658 commentary on Revelation by the Scottish Calvinist James Durham already reflected a turning away from too-precise interpretations, maintaining a more or less spiritualized view of the millennium, and emphasizing the book's value for the prophetic goals of admonition and consolation. After the Restoration there was a general retreat from openly politicized prophetic visions, although predictably there were those who greeted Charles II as a messianic savior-king. More pervasive was attention to the year 1666, long a focus of fears and hopes because of its inclusion of the number of the beast (Rev. 13:18). The disasters of plague and fire preceding that year contributed to the desire to search the future for promises of order and security rather than for dreams of heavenly anarchy.

THE SEVENTEENTH CENTURY _____

Science and Skepticism

In the early and mid-seventeenth century, a period of pandemic war, revolution, witch-hunting panics, and intellectual confusion, the apocalyptic tension between fear and hope was perhaps more powerful and pervasive than it had ever been in Europe. Both Renaissance "fortune" and Reformation "providence" had emphasized human helplessness in the face of the last things, and now even the most immediate realities often appeared as deeply threatening. Especially with reference to Protestant regions, it may not be going too far to speak of a dominant culture of melancholy in this era, a climate of extremes in which fear, intolerance, and near-paralysis competed with idealistic hope and action. Thus, violent persecution of witches and heretics, for example, was accompanied by the continuance of medieval hopes for the conversion of the Jews. Even as intolerance was at its height among the Christian confessions, the seventeenth century saw a significant movement of millenarian philo-Semitism, both on the continent and in England.

Despite the political and social quieting that was beginning by 1660, dramatic bursts of idealistic expectancy continued. We might point to the all-but-forgotten figure of Petrus Serrarius, a Netherlander who refused to identify himself with any confession, styling himself "a servant of the universal church." In his *Awakening to the Wofull World* (1662), he combined astrology (in particular an expected conjunction of all the planets) with biblical interpretation to predict the collapse of all existing secular power, the conversion of the Jews, and the return of Christ. Related notions played a role in the strange career of the wandering prophet Quirinus Kuhlmann. In Rotterdam and London during the late 1670s, Kuhlmann announced the imminence of worldwide crisis and issued calls for a great pan-Protestant confederation and a universal Reformation. If these were more or less fringe thinkers, we need not look far for more widespread excitement. Thus, for instance, the 1660s brought the greatest wave of messianic fervor in the history of medieval and modern Jewry. Throughout Europe Jews came to accept the figure of Sabbatai Sevi as the Messiah himself. Tremendous shock and disappointment followed when the Sabbatai underwent forced conversion to Islam in 1666. The whole affair helped to turn educated opinion against millenarian or messianic "enthusiasm" of any sort.

The great tide of expectancy and speculation that peaked in the seventeenth century appears from one perspective as mainly a late and extreme articulation of medieval ideas and images, a cacophony of final, desperate attempts to achieve a coherent world picture incorporating all genuine revelations, all true wisdom, both ancient and latter-day. On such a view, the rise of modern rationalism and science required a fundamental reshaping of attitudes toward human knowledge, a reshaping that ultimately rejected the Judeo-Christian concept of revelation, and hence all traditional apocalyptic visions of reality. We may accept the general validity of this view, but we should not allow it to obscure the ways in which apocalyptically inspired explorations of nature and history helped to establish characteristically "modern" patterns of thought. Attempts to achieve a proper understanding of the universal forces at work in a time of crisis were the creative basis from which many new questions emerged in the seventeenth century.

The rise of the new natural and mathematical philosophy is in fact impossible to separate clearly from the late-Renaissance blossoming of prophetic science, the search for insight into the ultimate plan of the universe. The increasingly systematic and "scientific" apocalypticism of the late sixteenth and early seventeenth centuries involved sophisticated efforts to grasp the universal patterns of both history and nature. Thus, the science of historical chronology emerged in close association with apocalyptic reckoning of the age of the world and the periods of universal history. The Irish archbishop James Ussher (d. 1656) rejected several inherited errors as he worked carefully to establish the date of creation. He found it in 4004 B.C.E., believing he now had a *terminus a quo* for prophetic calculation. Similarly, advances in mathematics frequently issued from efforts to gain insight into biblical prophecy. Michael Stifel, who calculated a precise date and time for the end during the early German Reformation, was a respected academic mathematician, as was John Napier in Scotland, the inventor of logarithms. So too was Isaac Newton, who invested great effort delving into the mysteries of biblical prophecy.

Our concern, however, is less with particular inventions or discoveries than with the relationship between apocalyptic thinking and characteristically "modern" attitudes. Scholars have often seen connections between the forward-looking hope of seventeenth-century millenarians and the modern idea of historical progress. In this view, the modern faith in history is a secularized version of one pole within the Christian apocalyptic tradition: the aspect of worldly hope. Indirectly through Joachimism, with its vision of a new historical age, and more immediately through Protestant millenarianism, the early modern age brought the gradual triumph of progressive hope over the inherited medieval view that the world was in decay and decline. Those who adopt this interpretation emphasize that the Enlightenment vision of progress "retained a smuggled Providence" (Tuveson 1949, 201). The directing spirit had simply become immanent, indeed had become one with history itself.

Much recent work in the history of science is basically complementary to this view. There is strong evidence, for example, to show that millenarian thinking, particularly in its English Puritan forms, was intimately related to the emergence of new attitudes toward the investigation of nature. In the intense atmosphere of expectant hope that came to a head in the period of the Civil War and Interregnum (ca. 1642–1660), millenarian schemes "promoted a confident, active, and exploratory approach to nature" (Webster 1975, 8). In short, natural science was the God-given instrument that allowed humanity a role in establishing the kingdom. Interpreters regularly cited the words of Dan. 12:4, giving them a thoroughly positive spin: "But thou, O Daniel, shut up the words, and seal the book, even to the time of the end: many shall run to and fro, and knowledge shall be increased." Francis Bacon's program of a "Great Instauration," a profound intellectual reform and return to an Edenic dominion over nature, gained momentum largely as a blueprint for movement toward the millennial goal. The foundation of the Royal Society (1661) and the institutionalization of science need to be understood at least in part against this background.

There is, however, a very different perspective to be taken into account. Among some Protestants, such as the radical Dutch Collegiants (descendants of early Reformation Anabaptism and spiritualism), it was precisely the belief in the ongoing decay of the world and despair at the possibility of establishing the true church before the advent of the millennial kingdom that was central to the formation of a "modern" outlook in the period ca. 1660–1680. In figures such as Galenus Abrahamsz, a Collegiant leader in Amsterdam, disillusionment resulting from the failure to gain reliable prophetic insight, along with frustration over the follies and embarrassments to which millennial speculation had led, resulted in a new reliance on practical reason as a provisional guide in human affairs. Many Collegiants did not abandon belief in the coming millennium itself; in this sense they did not cease to think in apocalyptic terms. Rather they came to doubt human capacity to know anything about, much less contribute to, the means by which God would carry out his plan. This newly powerful skepticism implied a retreat from ideals of world reform; the new emphasis was on tolerance and on the life of practical virtue. Thus, too, it meant a strengthening of reason in its own limited sphere and extreme caution about all claims to a larger gnosis.

We need to notice not only relatively sudden disillusionments such as that of the Dutch Collegiants but also the persistent Protestant tendency, perhaps most clearly evident in Germany and the Netherlands, to combine historical pessimism with an awareness of paradox often bordering on fideism. Where apocalyptic terror remained the dominant pole, all imaginative structures were potentially suspect. If history was essentially a story of degeneration, and this world a vale of tears from which one sought deliverance, and if in addition one's speculations about the end of the story were finally reminders of human weakness and ignorance, the serious believer was never without reason to conclude that the most faithful life was also the most practical and sensible one, a life that dealt with one problem at a time, without any more system than was immediately necessary.

To the extent that it manifested itself in Protestant culture this sort of restraint was not the fruit of good-natured skepticism in the mode of Michel de Montaigne (d. 1592). It was more closely allied with feelings of sin and disgust at human pretensions. Such an attitude had been implicit in Reformation apocalypticism—especially in its Lutheran forms—from the beginning. To be sure, caution about the dangers of a too-lively curiosity in divine matters was frequently forgotten in the tense late-Reformation era. Yet throughout the period a central theme of evangelical preaching was to warn against any form of false consolation in the face of worldly fears. Indeed, preachers and writers often played on those very fears, making the most of them; they reveled in the cultivation of worldly anxiety. The believer was forced to encounter a world neither reformable nor redeemable by human efforts. The only hope lay in Christ, whose advent would bring a change utterly beyond the grasp of the human mind. This sort of apocalyptic worldly pessimism tended to reassert itself even among confident and militant believers at those moments when their millennial confidence was shaken.

The connections between apocalyptic pessimism and modern skeptical reason may be less obvious than those between millenarianism and the secular vision of progress, but it appears difficult to deny that there was a continuity here. It was no doubt easier for the enlightened progressivist to retain the outward forms of a biblical faith than it was for the despairing skeptic. But just as in the sixteenth century apocalyptic affirmation and alienation had stood together in constant tension, so in the eighteenth century the idea of human progress and the attitude of critical skepticism evolved in a most uneasy alliance.

Natural Law and Providence

It is hardly possible to deny that the second half of the seventeenth century saw some waning of Reformation-era expectancy, especially among the elites within European society. The reasons for this development were as manifold and complex as the whole historical problem of the transition from Renaissance to Enlightenment. We have noted several manifestations of the general turn toward more individualistic and subjective piety, and it would be an easy matter to multiply examples. Historians of the age of Louis XIV, for instance, have often pointed out a trend toward various forms of mysticism and religious quietism in France. In Germany, the mid- and late seventeenth century saw a cooling of the Reformation passion for world history and the discovery of its prophetic shape. It is not going too far to say that the age saw a broad shift from interest in the universal dimensions of time to greater concern with the unchanging universal laws of nature.

There is broad evidence for the rise of a religious and intellectual outlook that looked essentially to nature, not to history, for its evidences, to a truth grasped through uniform laws rather than through a providential historical process. Already in the early part of the century, deistic conceptions of natural law were circulating far more openly than they had earlier in the Reformation era. Natural religion was hostile to prophetic revelation in general and to apocalyptic expectations in particular. The rational religion proposed by Lord Herbert of Cherbury in his 1624 *De Veritate* (*On Truth*), for example, clearly involved an abandonment not only of apocalyptic teachings as such but also of the whole effort to discover a universal meaning in history. It was not until later in the century, however, that significant numbers of western European thinkers began to explore the implications of a "natural" religion. The spread of mechanistic conceptions of nature, closely associated with the growing acceptance of the new heliocentric cosmology, bespoke new commitment to the search for an order that was not historically grounded, revealed, or shaped in any way, the quest for a purely objective natural law.

By 1700 the conception of the world as a machine that operated according to invariable laws had made significant inroads among the learned classes of western Europe and was beginning to extend to a broader reading public. Works such as the famous *Historical and Critical Dictionary* (1697) of Pierre Bayle had little but ridicule for all claims to historically unique revelation. Bayle, a great propagandist for the intellectual avant garde, attacked virtually all the beliefs that had accompanied the apocalyptic worldview: portents, visions, attempts to correlate historical events with biblical prophecy, all claims to prophetic authority. This sort of skepticism gained ever greater currency among self-consciously enlightened thinkers in the eighteenth century. It carried the potential to arouse a new form of terror: the specter of history as an endless and meaningless series of cycles.

Growing hesitancy to trust claims about the future was also manifest in far more mundane ways. The development of the insurance industry, for example, already well advanced by 1700, reflected the new option of regarding the future in terms of statistical probabilities. One could not take out insurance against the last judgment, of course, but the principle of probability did help to reduce anxiety in daily life and hence eased the psychological need for an image of universal resolution. Under such circumstances, many Christian theologians in the eighteenth century showed a tendency to discard the traditional forms of Christian apocalypticism as the baggage of outmoded superstitions and to reduce all eschatology to the doctrine of personal immortality. Despite the dangers of practical skepticism to all religious meaning, it appears that the anxiety and anticipations of the Renaissance and Reformation had been at least partly calmed by the smiling face of the goddess Reason.

We must not, however, overestimate the speed or the scope of this calming. In much of Europe, apocalyptic thinking may have become less popularly visible, but it was still clearly in evidence even among the elites. There is strong evidence, for example, that among the urbane latitudinarian bishops of late-seventeenth- and early-eighteenth-century England, visions of the dawning millennium retained powerful currency. Despite the work of humanistic scholars going back as far as Jean Bodin (d. 1596) to show the inadequacy of the traditional schemes of biblical chronology, serious thinkers continued efforts to establish a historical scheme consistent with scripture and to conjecture—most often in a hopeful mode—about the completion of the universal pattern. Indeed, throughout the Enlightenment era we encounter ongoing labors to develop a "scientific" treatment of prophecy.

The Cambridge Platonist Henry More (d. 1687), for example, a key figure in the early growth of natural-scientific interests at the English universities in the mid-seventeenth century, was a millenarian who adopted much of his interpretation from Joseph Mede and who continued the tradition of detailed correlation between biblical prophecies and historical events. In his *Revelation of Revelation* (*Apocalypsis Apocalypseos*, 1680), he looked explicitly to the destruction of the papacy, the defeat of Islam, and the conversion of the Jews as signs of the millennium. To be sure, More was concerned to distance himself from the radical political prophecies of the Civil War era. He insisted that it was not possible to calculate precisely when the millennium itself would come. This was less a matter of objective prophetic research than a question for individual believers. The more genuine the personal spiritual progress of true Christians, the more hopeful they could be of the final downfall of the Antichrist and the coming of the millennial kingdom. Yet despite the contemplative and personally practical tone of his thinking, More was unquestionably a fervent millenarian.

Numerous studies attest to the broad continuation of such interests. Among the many academicians and pastors who published their prophetic researches was Nathaniel Homes (d. 1678), who calculated that a millennial age of spiritual union would begin before 1710. But there is no more striking instance than that of Isaac Newton (d. 1721), who devoted great energy and learning to the investigation of world chronology and biblical prophecy. In his *Observations of the Prophecies of Daniel and the Apocalypse of St. John* (not published until 1733), Newton calculated the fall of the apocalyptic beast for 1867, the coming of the millennium for the year 2000. As advances in astronomy contributed to ever greater sophistication in the dating of historical events, thinkers well into the Enlightenment continued a tradition inherited from the encyclopedic scholars of the late Renaissance era. For this long line of eighteenth-century thinkers the scriptures remained the ultimate framework of all world chronology. Futhermore, the continuing Protestant association of the Roman Church with the forces of Antichrist helped ensure that most such calculations projected a view of the present and the future that was implicitly apocalyptic.

Newton's own preoccupation with prophetic studies could not, however, overcome some potential and highly troubling implications of the new philosophy he had so dramatically advanced: Why should it be assumed that the divinely constructed mechanism of nature would ever cease to exist? Could not matter and motion continue *ad infinitum*? The most widely cited answer in defense of traditional views was that of Bishop Thomas Burnet (d. 1715), whose *Sacred Theory of the Earth* was first published in Latin in 1681 and appeared in English three years later. In 1689–1690 he issued a reinforcement entitled *On the Conflagration of the World and the Future State of Things*. These works put forward an old argument in updated form: the universe could not be a perpetual motion machine, for the creation by its very nature was contingent rather than eternal. Like any clock, nature would finally wind down, and when this happened God would carry out his promised destruction and renewal.

Burnet's work provoked numerous and lengthy quarrels among scientists, philosophers, and divines. Probably the most popular contribution to the debate was the *New Theory of the*

Earth (1696) by William Whiston (d. 1752), a highly earnest and energetic Newtonian and churchman. Whiston believed that biblical prophecy taught not the destruction of the world but rather its renewal; a good God would perfect his creation. Intensely devoted to showing the necessity of the literal fulfillment of all biblical prophecy, he lectured on meteors, eclipses, and other celestial phenomena and their connection to the divine plan. For over a half-century he preached on these convictions; in 1746 he even announced that the millennium would begin in twenty years. Another figure in the same English tradition was the philosopher and theologian David Hartley (d. 1757), who foresaw in 1749 that the millennium would be heralded by a series of enormous upheavals in both the natural and political realms. He expected the imminent dissolution of all human structures of government, the conversion of the Jews and their restoration to the Holy Land, and the spread of the true faith to all peoples.

The writings of men like Burnet, Whiston, and Hartley sought to combine all the latest scientific and historical as well as scriptural research. Their debates provoked ridicule from skeptics and deists but were taken seriously by a large proportion of those who were exposed to them. These English figures were part of a larger Protestant tradition that continued to draw scholars into detailed apocalyptic reckonings of both millenarian and nonmillenarian varieties.

☞ THE ENLIGHTENMENT AND MILLENNIALISM

Some scholars argue that the distinction between what have come to be called the "pre-millennial" and "post-millennial" teachings became increasingly important in the Enlightenment period. *Premillennialism* refers to the idea that Christ's second advent will inaugurate his kingdom on earth. This view often conceived of the period immediately preceding that return as bringing a culmination of earthly disasters. The transition to the millennial kingdom will thus involve a sudden and decisive conflict between Christ and his enemies, and the ensuing rule of the saints will begin at once. *Postmillennialism,* by contrast, conceives of the personal return of Christ and the last judgment as coming after the triumph and rule of the true church. The transition to the millennium can in this case be viewed in terms of historical progress, a series of victories by which the world finally enters into a stage of spiritual fulfillment. It is often suggested that only this latter form, because of its compatibility with humanistic visions of progress, became intellectually respectable. The more literal pre-millennial view was more commonly associated with vulgar myth.

While this interpretation has much to recommend it, we need to be careful not to oversimplify what necessarily remains a highly complex and varied picture. There are so many exceptions to the thesis just outlined that its usefulness is limited. It does appear that in regard to apocalyptic prophecy, as in other aspects of culture, a divide between elite and popular attitudes became increasingly pronounced by the eighteenth century. Especially among intellectual elites there was a new emphasis on religious toleration and social stability. Hence, while scholars and churchmen continued heated debates over religious prophecy and basic questions of worldview, they began to view the public preaching of most apocalyptic ideas as a form of "enthusiasm," a danger to society and the state. But rising concerns about the implications of prophetic teachings for public order did not imply any uniform view of what constituted "vulgar" prophecy.

Moreover, apocalypticism continued to retain its full range of political uses. During the Enlightenment era the defining issue was once again not so much the level of expectancy as the sources and nature of spiritual understanding. Even as basically conservative and latitudinarian scholars reasoned out the details of prophetic chronology, there arose groups such as the Philadelphians, inspired by the visions and illuminations of the widow Jane Lead, whose aim was to form a spiritual association of the truly reborn and to spread the message of love around the world in its last days. "Philadelphian" societies sprang up throughout northern Europe in the years around 1700, largely among educated town-dwellers who found little satisfaction in institutional churches that seemed merely props to a problem-ridden social order. Throughout the eighteenth century, popular political dissent retained links with religious movements that sanctioned special revelations, spiritual illuminations, and visions. Again, it was far less apocalyptic excitement than the form and nature of the revelations that determined the social implications of expectancy.

In France, Louis XIV's revocation of the Edict of Nantes in 1685 spurred a major wave of millenarian prophecies among Huguenots, continuing for several decades. Most widely heeded were the so-called child prophets, who issued announcements of the final fulfillment of biblical prophecies, the return of Christ, and the triumphant spread of the gospel over the whole earth. The Huguenot prophets preached an urgent message of repentance and promised deliverance for the faithful. According to one popular belief, the final downfall of the Catholic Church in France was to come in 1690. This prophetically inspired resistance movement became rapidly more violent after 1700. In the Cévennes mountains of central France, Huguenot prophetic preachers led the Camisard rebels in a guerrilla war against the military forces of Louis XIV. The revolt peaked around 1702–1704 and was finally put down by 1710; but even afterward the millenarian visions it had inspired continued to echo among Protestants throughout the European world.

A less violent but no less earnest prophetic movement arose among French Catholics a generation later in the wake of Louis XV's decision to enforce the papal bull *Unigenitus* (1731), which condemned the theology of Jansenism. For nearly a century the Jansenists had defended a heavily Augustinian teaching that included criticisms of the worldliness and moral laxity of the French church as a whole. There had in fact been expressions of apocalyptic expectancy among them well before the 1730s. Now driven into open prophetic opposition, the Jansenist "Convulsionaries" believed they were witness to the final outpouring of the Spirit prophesied in the book of Joel. They predicted doom for the persecutors of the Christian truth. The Abbé Etémare foresaw the imminent conversion of the Jews, the coming of Elijah, and the renewal of the universal church following the final defeat of the beast.

In some of its forms Jansenist millenarianism evolved into a continuing protest against the worldly society of eighteenth-century France. Various offshoots persisted through the century among proponents engaged in zealous evangelizing, but most often such teachings were pushed underground by official opposition. Ironically, many similar apocalyptic themes were taken up later by the Jansenists' traditional foes, the Jesuits. The suppression of their order in 1773 led to a renewal of long-standing prophecies in which the Jesuits held a central role. As in earlier eras, these scenarios often included Joachimite ideas of worldwide tribulation preceding a final spiritual breakthrough and triumph.

If millenarianism often took shape through movements of political and social opposition in France, we can see a different tendency in late-seventeenth- and eighteenth-century Germany, particularly in those regions where Lutheran Pietism took strong hold. Early Pietism shared with Calvinist Puritanism the tendency toward a forward-looking millenarian hope, which in some of its forms might be described better as historical meliorism than as apocalypticism. Yet because of its intensely biblical, eschatological character and its general sense of urgency, Pietist millenarianism deserves attention as a significant form of early-modern expectancy. A key seventeenth-century figure was the famous Philipp Jakob Spener (d. 1705), leader of the Lutheran clergy at Frankfurt am Main, later active in Saxony and Brandenburg. Spener held to the strong conviction that the last times would bring the conversion of the Jews and the fall of the papacy; biblical prophecy proved that "God promised his church here on earth a better state than this" before the last judgment.[5] Pietist preaching in this vein encouraged proposals for sweeping social reform throughout Lutheran Germany both before and after 1700. But Pietist millenarianism was by no means politically revolutionary; on the contrary, most Pietists accepted the state as part of the divinely instituted order of the world.

Later Pietist leaders did not uniformly share Spener's brand of explicit millenarian hope. August Hermann Francke (d. 1727), for example, the central figure in the educational, spiritual, and social reform impulses emanating from Halle after 1700, represented a far more subjective and individualistic form of piety that played down hopes for the fulfillment of an objective divine plan. But the prophetic element again emerged strongly in the Württemberg Pietist leader Johann Albrecht Bengel (d. 1752), who in the 1730s and 1740s issued numerous influential writings on biblical chronology and Revelation. Bengel saw the history of the world as the story of the divine education of the human race, a course of inevitable progress. He engaged in detailed prophetic calculations and correlations, estimating that the millennium was likely to begin around 1836. Pietism's deeply earnest mixture of apocalyptic conviction and spiritualist fervor helped extend the influence of the movement throughout northern Europe and across the Atlantic. Pietist hopes were everywhere felt during the great popular religious revival of the eighteenth century.

Among those who felt the spiritual energy emanating from Germany was John Wesley, the founding spirit of Methodism. In his earlier years Wesley's preaching often suggested that Christ's return was near. If later he tended to play down this element, his movement saw continuing expressions of apocalyptic excitement. Perhaps the most notable came early in 1763, when the zealous preacher George Bell predicted the return of Christ for 28 February. Wesley himself opposed the prediction and tried to calm the great wave of popular agitation, preaching through the final night to huge London crowds and struggling to combat the disillusionment that followed. Yet the excitement that boiled over into such notorious affairs was a continuing current, not only among Wesley's followers but in the broader popular evangelical culture of the eighteenth century. A wide range of groups agreed that they were working to help complete the divine plan by which true Christian faith would triumph everywhere, certainly and soon. It was in just this atmosphere of excitement over the fulfillment of prophecy and the coming of Christ that the popular ecstatic movement of Shakerism began in Lancashire during the 1740s. In this case the advent of Christ was understood to be at least partially fulfilled in the person of Mother Ann Lee.

THE PROGRESSIVE HOPE OF
THE ENLIGHTENMENT

The first half of the eighteenth century seems to have witnessed the crest of learned skepticism toward efforts to discern the larger meaning and direction of human history. After about 1760, such agnostic resistance faded in the glow of a waxing eschatology of human progress. Across the social spectra history was more and more viewed as an inevitable forward movement toward some sort of social utopia. If in earlier decades prophetic disillusionment and critical skepticism had gained momentum, the pendulum now swung toward an explosion of Enlightenment progressive hope. But while the new revolutionary era brought the radical social expression of "rational" millennial myths, it also manifested the continuing power of inherited apocalyptic imagery.

There are in fact good reasons to believe that by the late eighteenth century, Enlightenment optimism and Christian millenarian hopes entered into a new stage of mutual reinforcement and ferment: the great and liberal mansion of Christian (largely Protestant) universalism had room for all these forward-looking ideals. Traditional prophetic hopes such as that of a final conversion of the Jews merged with the Enlightenment vision of a rational and universal faith producing harmony among all humanity. The Reformed pastor Johann Caspar Lavater spoke for growing numbers of educated middle-class Europeans when in 1769 he openly challenged the Jewish leader Moses Mendelssohn to embrace liberal Christianity, hoping in this way to help further the divine plan and thus bring on the consummation of world history.

The liberal vision of progress pushed the meliorism implicit in much post-millennial thinking to its logical extreme by all but eliminating apocalyptic dualities, regarding the ascent to the final age of perfection as entirely peaceful. In his classic *On the Education of the Human Race* (1780), Gotthold Ephraim Lessing saw in universal history a series of three revelations: the Jewish, the Christian, and the dawning universal revelation. The pattern harked strongly back to Joachim of Fiore, but in this Enlightenment conception the apocalyptic birth pangs of the new age were reduced to insignificance. Historic Christianity was one of several major stages in the education of humanity, which had begun with human life itself and would culminate in the supreme and final understanding. This image of world history as a process of education was broadly revealed in a more benign conception of God's paternal role. By the eighteenth century we see God far less as the traditional stern and majestic judge and much more as a benevolent figure who disciplines his children and guides them to their ultimate goal.

Many Enlightenment theorists of history in effect simply reversed the traditional Danielic vision of world-historical descent through four monarchies; the new model was one of ascent to a golden age of reason. Again, this approach had important roots in Joachimism and especially in Calvinist meliorism. In its most zealous devotees, however, historical progress was divorced from all transcendent guidance. The ultimate statement of progress made immanent in humanity came in a document that has often been regarded as a virtual manifesto of Enlightenment thought: the *Sketch for a Historical Picture of the Progress of the Human Mind* (1795) by the Marquis de Condorcet. Here the progressive emancipation of the human mind became itself a law of nature. Condorcet's faith was fully in history. His hope did not lie in the future; it was the future itself.

The most widespread forms of future hope, however, retained more explicitly religious elements. Outside the established Christian traditions, perhaps the most important avenue for the propagation of visions mixing secular and spiritual progressivism lay in international Freemasonry. The eighteenth century had seen the appearance of various Masonic organizations throughout Europe, most of which offered broad scope for mystical and even occultist visions of the coming spiritual regeneration of the world. By the 1770s and 1780s, Freemasons were caught up in a broad revival of Renaissance magical traditions based on the supposed wisdom of the ancient East, the recovery of which was crucial to the anticipated blossoming of universal truth. Masonic millenarianism was quite eclectic; in its many forms it included astrological, alchemical, and numerological speculation, the mystical teachings of Emanuel Swedenborg (d. 1792), and even a revival of biblical apocalypticism.

Adding to the atmosphere of excitement in the pre-revolutionary years was the surging popularity of the new science of Mesmerism. The theories of the Viennese physician Franz Anton Mesmer (d. 1815) about "animal magnetism" appeared in many minds to promise a solution to all the secrets of the natural world. At the same time, they were commonly invested with a heavy religious significance, for they seemed to offer clear proof of the workings of divine providence in the world. The universal magnetic force was nothing less, for some Mesmerists, than "the demonstrated presence of God" (see Garrett 1975, 20). Here again, especially as Mesmerism spread to a broad middle-class audience, there developed a potent brew of scientific theory and religious hope, adding to the general ferment of expectancy.

It is not surprising that this atmosphere included intense fears as well as hopes. The observation of sunspots in 1777 and numerous outbreaks of severe weather in the 1780s sparked rumors that the world was coming to an end. Several novels on the theme of the end of the world appeared during the prerevolutionary years. Both on the continent and in England there was a marked renewal of a tendency toward coexisting feelings of hope and terror. When the momentous events of the French Revolution began in 1789, they did not so much create apocalyptic expectations as give new focus and new urgency to preexisting patterns of thought.

Political liberals everywhere commonly regarded the early revolution as a turning point of world-historical, indeed of cosmic, significance. Reason and liberty were emerging triumphant at the heart of European civilization; it seemed certain that the victory would very soon be universal. But the revolution also brought forth a torrent of publications of ancient, medieval, and more recent prophecies, all showing that these world-changing events were in some way fulfilling a divine plan. Especially appealing were the many predictions attributed to Nostradamus, now reissued to show that gifted forecasters had long regarded 1789 and subsequent years as a time that would bring earth-shaking upheaval. In the realm of popular political prophecy, the writings of this famous figure had long since taken on a nearly canonical status. The prophet had in fact suggested that profound changes could be expected around 1790, and now, according to some popular interpreters, he had predicted the Revolution in precise detail. While the Nostradamic predictions were not essentially apocalyptic, their deeply portentous tone and delphic quality guaranteed their use by a wide variety of interests, from those who saw the current upheavals as a millennial dawn to those who saw in it nothing but diabolical disaster.

The Revolution drew into the limelight not only old prophetic authorities but numerous new prophets as well. Suzette Labrousse was one of many who saw the Revolution as the great movement that would usher in the millennium, which she expected to dawn fully in 1800. In 1792 this prophetess made a pilgrimage to Rome, hoping to share with the pope her revelation that the Revolution was the beginning of a divinely decreed worldwide spiritual regeneration. Around the same time, a *Journal Prophétique* began publication, dedicated to showing that the Revolution was bringing on the millennium. Not surprisingly, many French Catholic clergy were drawn to end-time speculations that depicted the acts of the revolutionary leaders—above all the Civil Constitution of the Clergy (1790)—as the final great raging of Satan. In England, on the other hand, efforts to understand the revolutionary developments in terms of the long tradition of hopeful biblical millenarianism were legion.

The revolutionaries' own conviction that they were witnessing the event of a new age was hardly apocalyptic or millenarian in any Christian sense. Revolutionary eschatology could be nothing less than antibiblical, anti-Christian. Here was the rational parallel to Protestant anti-Romanism: as Rome had been to European evangelicals, so all Christian teaching became for the new faith.

Nothing could have made clearer the advent of the post-Christian dispensation than official announcement of the new decimal calendar, in which the week became ten days, and each month was three weeks. More important, the *Anno Domini* system was officially abolished, along with all other vestiges of the Christian year. The founding of the Republic in the fall of 1792 became the beginning of the Year 1, marking a clean sweep in the history of the world. Even more radical was Robespierre's Cult of Reason, later softened to acknowledge a Supreme Being. In these respects, the revolutionaries were going beyond secularized forms of expectancy; they were preaching what amounted to a rationalized gospel. For them the messianic age had begun.

In England the debate over the meaning of the Revolution became nearly all-consuming: What was the place of this tremendous upheaval in the divine plan? Here traditional apocalyptic ideas remained more widespread and respectable than in contemporary France. Many continued in the belief that current events revealed a countdown to the second coming. The London Baptist minister James Bicheno issued a regular journal, *The Signs of the Times*, keeping readers on both sides of the Atlantic informed about the evident unfolding of prophetic events. In other cases, however, we find the old prophetic categories reordered in basic ways. The philosophers and political radicals Richard Price (d. 1791) and Joseph Priestley (d. 1804), for example, held a fundamentally millenarian conception of a universal providence that was leading the world ineluctably toward a state of perfection.

The dawning new age looked to a general outpouring of reason and thus at first required no individual savior figure. But as the gospel of the Revolution appeared increasingly threatened in the 1790s, the eyes of the faithful searched the horizon for the one who could ensure their redemption. Into the savior-emperor role stepped Napoleon, with perhaps greater effect than any other ruler of the three centuries we have surveyed. It is not surprising that many throughout Europe saw in the emperor no world hero but rather the Antichrist. For some this image had itself become secularized: Napoleon was the incarnation of political evil. Others did not hesitate to apply the biblical prophecies of the Antichrist in a fully literal sense, thus pointing to the continuing power of the traditional images into the modern age.

⌒ CONCLUSION _____

While the role of apocalyptic ideas in the broad movements of nationalism and romanticism remain outside the scope of this essay, we may point ahead by noting that in 1800 a variety of powerful reactions against Enlightenment universalism and skepticism were drawing on the stock of Western images of crisis and coming resolution. In one sense, new critical attitudes had turned history and nature themselves into the main texts into which Western thinkers peered for self-understanding. Yet biblical apocalypticism and the various structures of expectation that had grown up around it were still very much alive. And even while the traditional imagery had lost much of its immediate resonance among educated Europeans, it continued to carry enormous weight in what we may call the collective unconscious.

A main goal of this discussion has been to show that the heritage of Judeo-Christian apocalypticism was central to the major transformations in Western self-consciousness that took place over the course of the early modern era. Throughout the centuries we have surveyed, European thinkers were deeply influenced by the assumption that they were living in a time of world-historical crisis or transformation. This assumption drove continual efforts to reconceive the place of present experience within a universal scheme of meaning. Both apocalyptic hope and despair had a role in the continuing drive to reimagine the world: in millenarian hope lay the seeds of the modern idea of progress, while apocalyptic disillusionment moved in the direction of practical skepticism and agnosticism. It appears that the characteristic apocalyptic vacillation between terror and hope receded to some extent, at least among European elites, with the spread of a new sense of universal order in the late seventeenth and early eighteenth centuries. But by the close of our era, we see the return of widespread expectancy, the forms of which were still shaped in fundamental ways by ancient, medieval, and early modern traditions.

The "corrosive" and "creative" aspects of apocalyptic visions are difficult to disentangle from each other. The evidence we have surveyed, however, suggests that early modern apocalyptic visions had a basic role both in undermining inherited myths and in creating new ones. As the main reflection of continuing Western efforts to reimagine the world in time, apocalyptic conceptions reveal the radical spiritual and psychological tensions that drove Europeans to a modern world in perpetual revolution.

⌒ NOTES _____

1. William J. Bouwsma, "Anxiety and the Formation of Early Modern Culture," in *After the Reformation: Essays in honor of J.H. Hexter*, ed. Barbara C. Malament (Philadelphia: University of Pennsylvania Press, 1980), 218.

2. Quoted in Preuss 1906, 6.

3. Quoted in Hugh Trevor-Roper, "The General Crisis of the Seventeenth Century," in Hugh Trevor-Roper, *The Crisis of the Seventeenth Century: Religion, the Reformation, and Social Change* (New York/Evanston: Harper & Row, 1968), 46.

4. Quoted in Bernard Capp, "The political dimension of apocalyptic thought," in Patrides and Wittreich 1984, 116.

5. Quoted in Richard L. Gawthrop, *Pietism and the Making of Eighteenth-Century Prussia* (Cambridge: Cambridge University Press, 1993), 108.

☞ BIBLIOGRAPHY

Ball, Bryan W. 1975. *A Great Expectation: Eschatological Thought in English Protestantism to 1660.* Leiden: Brill.

Barnes, Robin Bruce. 1988. *Prophecy and Gnosis: Apocalypticism in the Wake of the Lutheran Reformation.* Stanford: Stanford University Press. An interpretation of the nature and the cultural implications of Lutheran apocalypticism in the sixteenth and early seventeenth centuries.

Bauckham, Richard, ed. 1978. *Tudor Apocalypse: Sixteenth-Century Apocalypticism, Millenarianism and the English Reformation.* Appleford: Courtenay.

Becker, Carl. 1932. *The Heavenly City of the Eighteenth-Century Philosophers.* New Haven: Yale University Press. A valuable older study of Enlightenment perfectionism.

Bloch, Ernst. 1986. *The Principle of Hope.* 3 volumes. Cambridge, Mass.: MIT Press. A challenging theoretical and historical discussion that includes early modern eschatology.

Capp, Bernard. 1972. *The Fifth Monarchy Men: A Study in Seventeenth-Century English Millenarianism.* Totowa, N.J.: Rowman & Littlefield. The definitive study of this famous group.

———. 1979. *Astrology and the Popular Press: English Almanacs 1500–1800.* Ithaca: Cornell University Press. Considers the influence of popular astrology on apocalyptic thinking among other realms of society and culture.

Christianson, Paul. 1978. *Reformers and Babylon: English Apocalyptic Visions from the Reformation to the Eve of the Civil War.* Toronto: University of Toronto Press.

Clouse, Robert. 1987. "The Millennium that Survived the Fifth Monarchy Men," in *Regnum, Religio, et Ratio: Essays Presented to Robert M. Kingdon,* edited by Jerome Friedman, 19–29. Kirksville, Mo.: Sixteenth Century Journal Publishers.

Cohn, Norman. 1961. *The Pursuit of the Millennium: Revolutionary Messianism in Medieval and Reformation Europe.* 2nd ed. New York: Harper. A classic study; its overall theoretical framework is no longer accepted by most students of the subject.

Crouzet, Denis. 1990. *Les Guerriers de Dieu: La Violence au Temps des Troubles de Religion (vers 1525–vers 1610).* 2 volumes. Seyssel: Champ Vallon. Views religious violence as the logical result of apocalyptic anguish.

Delumeau, Jean. 1978. *La Peur en Occident (XIVe–XVIIIe siècles).* Paris: Fayard.

———. 1990. *Sin and Fear: The Emergence of a Western Guilt Culture, 13th–18th centuries.* New York: St. Martin's Press. An extensive treatment of the psychology of guilt in the late medieval and early modern periods.

Deppermann, Klaus. 1987. *Melchior Hoffman: Social Unrest and Apocalyptic Visions in the Age of the Reformation.* Edinburgh: T. & T. Clark. An excellent treatment of a major radical apocalyptic thinker.

Firth, Katharine. 1979. *The Apocalyptic Tradition in Reformation Britain 1530-1645.* Oxford/New York: Oxford University Press. The best among many works on apocalypticism in sixteenth- and seventeenth-century Britain.

Fix, Andrew. 1991. *Prophecy and Reason: The Dutch Collegiants in the Early Enlightenment.* Princeton: Princeton University Press. A path-breaking argument regarding the connections between apocalyptic disillusionment and the rise of rationalism.

Froom, Leroy Edwin. 1946–54. *The Prophetic Faith of Our Fathers: The Historical Development of Prophetic Interpretation.* 4 volumes. Washington, D.C.: Review & Herald. A truly remarkable survey of Christian eschatology by a scholarly Seventh-Day Adventist. Volume 2 surveys the pre-Reformation and early modern eras.

Fruchtman, Jack, Jr. 1983. *The Apocalyptic Politics of Richard Price and Joseph Priestley: A Study in Late Eighteenth-Century English Republican Millennialism.* Transactions of the American Philosophical Society, Vol. 73, Part 4. Philadelphia: American Philosophical Society.

Garrett, Clarke. 1975. *Respectable Folly: Millenarians and the French Revolution in France and England.*

Baltimore/London: Johns Hopkins University Press. Focuses mainly on traditional millenarian thinking rather than the secularized visions of the revolutionaries.

Gow, Andrew C. 1995. *The Red Jews: Antisemitism in an Apocalyptic Age, 1200–1600.* Leiden/New York: Brill. A valuable contribution on a little-studied aspect of apocalypticism.

Haase, Roland. 1933. *Das Problem des Chiliasmus und der dreissigjährige Krieg.* Leipzig: G. Gerhardt. Surveys numerous popular figures, mostly German, from the Thirty Years' War era (1618–1648).

Haller, William. 1963. *Foxe's Book of Martyrs and the Elect Nation.* London: J. Cape. Shows Foxe's role in establishing a prophetic nationalism in England.

Headley, John. 1963. *Luther's View of Church History.* New Haven: Yale University Press. Places Luther's eschatology in the context of his approach to history.

Hill, Christopher. 1971. *Antichrist in Seventeenth-Century England.* London/New York: Oxford University Press, 1971.

Hofmann, Hans-Ulrich. 1982. *Luther und die Johannes-Apokalypse.* Tübingen: J. C. B. Mohr (Paul Siebeck). Detailed and useful analysis of the reformer's waxing engagement with the images of Revelation.

Jacob, Margaret C. 1976. *The Newtonians and the English Revolution 1689–1720.* Ithaca: Cornell University Press. A convincing argument about the compatibility of millenarian views with the new science.

Klempt, Adalbert. 1960. *Die Säkularisierung der universalhistorischen Auffassung: Zum Wandel des Geschichtsdenkens im 16. und 17. Jahrhundert.* Göttingen: Musterschmidt. Analysis of the growing challenges to universal prophetic history in the post-Reformation era.

Kurze, Dietrich. 1960. *Johannes Lichtenberger (†1503): Eine Studie zur Geschichte der Prophetie und Astrologie.* Lübeck/Hamburg: Matthiesen Verlag. The authoritative study of Lichtenberger.

Lamont, William. 1969. *Godly Rule: Politics and Religion, 1603–60.* New York: St. Martin's Press. Argues that millenarianism was widespread, respectable, and politically potent in seventeenth-century England.

———. 1979. *Richard Baxter and the Millennium: Protestant Imperialism and the English Revolution.* Totowa, N.J.: Rowman & Littlefield.

Lerner, Robert. 1983. *The Powers of Prophecy: The Cedar of Lebanon Vision from the Mongol Onslaught to the Dawn of the Enlightenment.* Berkeley: University of California Press. Traces a single apocalyptic tradition.

List, Günther. 1973. *Chiliastische Utopie und Radikale Reformation.* Munich: Fink. A somewhat forced argument, linking chiliasm to the disappointment of expectations for social change.

Löwith, Karl. 1949. *Meaning in History: The Theological Implications of the Philosophy of History.* Chicago: University of Chicago Press.

Niccoli, Ottavia. 1990. *Prophecy and People in Renaissance Italy.* Princeton: Princeton University Press. Breaks much new ground in an analysis of interactions between popular and learned attitudes in early-sixteenth-century Italy.

Oberman, Heiko A. 1989. *Luther: Man Between God and the Devil.* New Haven/London: Yale University Press. Far and away the best study of Luther's apocalyptic worldview.

Patrides, C. A., and Joseph Wittreich, eds. 1984. *The Apocalypse in English Renaissance thought and literature: Patterns, antecedents, and repercussions.* Ithaca: Cornell University Press. Includes an extremely valuable bibliography.

Petersen, Rodney L. 1993. *Preaching in the Last Days: The Theme of 'Two Witnesses' in the Sixteenth and Seventeenth Centuries.* New York/Oxford: Oxford University Press. Offers a useful handle on the issue of Protestant prophetic self-awareness.

Peuckert, Will-Erich. 1976. *Die Grosse Wende: Das apokalyptische Saeculum und Luther.* 2 volumes. Darmstadt: Wissenschaftliche Buchgesellschaft. A highly colorful picture of late-fifteenth- and early-sixteenth-century expectancy.

Phelan, John Leddy. 1970. *The Millennial Kingdom of the Franciscans in the New World.* Berkeley: University of California Press.

Popkin, Richard H., ed. 1988. *Millenarianism and Messianism in English Literature and Thought 1650–1800*. Leiden: Brill.

Preuss, Hans. 1906. *Die Vorstellungen vom Antichrist im späteren Mittelalter, bei Luther und in der konfessionellen Polemik*. Leipzig: J. C. Hinrichs. Still valuable despite a very dated interpretative framework.

———. 1933. *Martin Luther, der Prophet*. Gütersloh: C. Bertelsmann.

Reeves, Marjorie. 1993. *The Influence of Prophecy in the Later Middle Ages: A Study in Joachimism*. 2nd ed. Oxford: Clarendon Press. The classic study of Joachimism; extends into the sixteenth century.

———. 1977. *Joachim of Fiore and the Prophetic Future*. New York: Harper & Row. Includes a highly informative treatment of the ways in which various Protestants adopted Joachimite ideas.

Rusconi, Roberto, ed. 1996. *Storia e figure dell'Apocalisse fra '500 e '600: Atti del 4° Congresso Internazionale di studi gioachimiti*. Rome: Viella. A valuable collection on apocalypticism ca. 1500–1700; includes articles in English as well as Italian.

Scholem, Gershom. 1973. *Sabbatai Zevi: The Mystical Messiah, 1626–1676*. Princeton: Princeton University Press. The essential study of a fascinating episode in Jewish messianism.

Schwartz, Hillel. 1980. *The French Prophets: The History of a Millenarian Group in Eighteenth-Century England*. Berkeley: University of California Press.

———. 1990. *Century's End: An orientation manual toward the year 2000*. New York: Doubleday. A popular work offering some valuable insights on the way Westerners have regarded the final years of each century since ca. 1000 C.E.

Scribner, Robert. 1981. *For the Sake of Simple Folk: Popular Propaganda for the German Reformation*. Cambridge/New York: Cambridge University Press. Pioneering work on the uses of imagery by sixteenth-century publicists.

Seifert, Arno. 1986. "Reformation und Chiliasmus: Die Rolle des Martin Cellarius-Borrhaus." *Archiv für Reformationsgeschichte* 77:226–64.

———. *Der Rückzug der biblischen Prophetie von der neueren Geschichte: Studien zur Geschichte der Reichstheologie des frühneuzeitlichen deutsche Protestantismus*. Cologne/Vienna: Böhlau.

Staehelin, Ernst. 1957. *Die Verkündigung des Reich Gottes in der Kirche Jesu Christi: Zeugnisse aus allen Jahrhunderten und allen Konfessionen*. 4 volumes. Basel: F. Reinhardt.

Talkenberger, Heike. 1990. *Sintflut: Prophetie und Zeitgeschehen in Texten und Holzschnitten astrologischer Flugschriften, 1488–1528*. Tübingen: Max Niemeyer. A comprehensive survey of texts and images related to the great flood panic of the early 1520s in Germany.

Thomas, Keith. 1971. *Religion and the Decline of Magic*. New York: Charles Scribner's Sons. A classic study of popular belief, focusing on England.

Tonkin, John. 1971. *The Church and the Secular Order in Reformation Thought*. New York: Columbia University Press.

Toon, Peter, ed. 1970. *Puritans, the Millennium, and the Future of Israel: Puritan Eschatology 1600–1660*. Cambridge: James Clarke.

Tuveson, Ernest Lee. 1949. *Millennium and Utopia: A Study in the Background of the Idea of Progress*. Berkeley: University of California Press. The main statement of the thesis that the modern idea of progress is essentially a secularized form of Christian millenarianism.

Warburg, Aby. 1920. *Heidnisch-antike Weissagungen in Wort und Bild zu Luthers Zeiten*. Heidelberg. Reprinted in *Gesammelte Schriften* (Leipzig: Teubner, 1932), 2: 487–558. A study of the paradoxical flowering of pagan divination at the time of the evangelical Reformation.

Webster, Charles. 1975. *The Great Instauration: Science, Medicine, and Reform 1626–1660*. New York: Holmes & Meier. A powerful argument for millenarianism as crucial to the emergence of the new science in the mid-seventeenth century.

Weinstein, Donald. 1970. *Savonarola and Florence: Prophecy and Patriotism in the Renaissance*. Princeton: Princeton University Press.

Wilks, Michael, ed. 1994. *Prophecy and Eschatology*. Oxford/Cambridge: Blackwell.

Zambelli, Paola, ed. 1986. *"Astrologi hallucinati" Stars and the End of the World in Luther's Time*. Berlin/New York: Walter de Gruyter.

14

Jewish Apocalypticism, 670–1670

Moshe Idel
Hebrew University

⟿ PROBLEMS OF DEFINITION: APOCALYPTICISM AS THE "TIME OF THE END"

THE MEANING OF APOCALYPTICISM is disputed among scholars. In the following, I shall not address the issue of the literary genre commonly designated as apocalypse, but I shall concentrate on the concept expressed by the phrase ʿēt qēṣ, "time of the end," which recurs in the book of Daniel (e.g., Dan. 11:35). I assume that this phrase implies not only the calculation of the date of a fateful event for humanity and/or the world but also the end of a given order, consonant with Jacques Ellul's understanding of apocalypticism as the unveiling of a collapsing reality, and a "metastatic faith," to use Eric Voegelin's term. These treatments may or may not be part of a messianic scenario, but for the sake of our discussions here, the messianic elements will be addressed only peripherally.

Since the end of time is the main topic, we can distinguish between various types of time, each having a different sort of end. The private time, which starts with birth and ends in death, in religious systems involves a personal eschatology dealing with postmortem retribution and punishment and will not concern us here. The category I propose to designate as *microchronos*, which includes the ritualistic life recurrent cyclically in small units of time (days, weeks, or years) was little concerned with an end, because ritual was conceived of as a perfect mode of existence. However, the *mesochronos*—a term I prefer to use for the time of an extended group, a tribe or a nation—measures time by hundreds of years and commonly is involved in dealing with the end of one form of order and the entrance of another. This form of time is generally pertinent for most of the discussions of what we can call imminent apocalypticism. Last but not least, the *macrochronos* refers to cosmic time, measured in units of time that exceed hundreds of years. It concerns the life of the universe rather than the fate of a nation or even of humanity. Unlike the processes concerning the *mesochronos,* the end of the *macrochronos,* or "great time," is commonly predetermined by factors that far transcend human activity. They constitute the widest form of historical processes, while the apocalyptic *mesochronoi* are part of traditional messianic scenarios. In the following, we shall be concerned with transpersonal events that allegedly affect larger human communities or the entire universe. However, the above categorizations of times and their ends sometimes intersect, in the writings of one school, one author, or even in one passage, as we shall see below.

The concept of messianism was promoted from a secondary status in biblical literature to one of much greater importance in subsequent Jewish literature, even sometimes reaching the status of an essential article of faith (see chapter 5). This was never the case with apocalypticism. Calculations of the end were often attacked explicitly in rabbinic literature, and attempts to determine the date of the coming of the Messiah by invoking angels or demons have been discounted by medieval authors. Hence, we may distinguish some forms of messianism from apocalyptic speculations, though the two modes of thought are often closely related. The relation is one-sided, a fact that should be emphasized, though it is possible to imagine forms of nonapocalyptic messianism, as is the case in Maimonides' theory of messianism. Nevertheless, we can hardly imagine an explicit or imminent apocalypticism (unlike the implicit form) that is detached from the messianic scenario. In fact, apocalyptic material was often conjugated into a larger scheme that culminated in a messianic *renovatio mundi.* Thus, in the explicit forms of apocalypticism the "collapsing" vision of reality is never detached from its more positive sequel dealing with the dramatic improvement that follows the collapse of the older order.

Most messianic dramas of the advent of the Messiah, or Messiahs, consist of a sequence of events, some having distinct apocalyptic features, such as natural upheavals, religious conversions, bloody wars ushering in mass murder, the death of messianic figures, etc. These upheavals were conceived of as being so painful that rabbinic figures confessed that they would prefer not to live to see them. Here, the apocalyptic nature of the eschaton is so strong that it deters people from wishing to witness the advent of the messianic age.

⌒ MEDIEVAL APOCALYPTICISM
IN MODERN RESEARCH _____

One of the great merits of Gershom Scholem's scholarship was to put in relief the importance of apocalyptic thought—previously marginalized in scholarship—for the better understanding of Jewish thought and history. The historical approach he initiated emphasized the apocalyptic aspect of Jewish messianism, as well as its translation into mass movements, to such an extent that a cluster of different concepts generally referred to as messianism has come to be implicitly identified with apocalypticism in its entirety. Though manifesting ways of thought and types of experience at odds with genuine apocalyptic trends, the more radical among the Jewish spiritualists would nonetheless very rarely reject the apocalyptic mythologies in an explicit manner. Rather, they attempted to interpret them spiritually, or to offer an additional eschatological discourse on top of the apocalyptic one. Thus, a continuity between the various phases of Jewish literature on messianism could be demonstrated by restricting the scholarly analysis mostly to explicitly apocalyptic elements. Consequently, the dominant scholarly surveys discerned a rather monolithic strand of apocalypticism running over millennia.

The precise forms of the transmission of apocalyptic elements throughout the centuries, either written or oral, still demand detailed inquiry. In such a framework, however, one of the medieval forms of Jewish mysticism, Kabbalah, was accorded by Scholem a significant role for only two centuries (from the middle of the sixteenth century to the mid-eighteenth). Only in this period were apocalyptic elements combined with Kabbalistic ones in his view. In other words, though apocalypticism was continuously influential, Kabbalah was a conduit for this approach only for a short period. Scholem did not address the issue of the channels of the lasting influence of apocalyptic messianism, but there is no problem in accepting the view that in popular sources messianic ideas, in a variety of apocalyptic variations, were propagated either in a more active form or in a dormant one through widespread types of texts.

I wish to propose an alternative to Scholem's reductive approach to the role of Kabbalah in the overall economy of Jewish apocalypticism and messianism. This proposal attributes to the various Kabbalistic schools a greater concern with apocalyptic themes, beliefs, and experiences, without restricting them to apocalyptic messianism alone. This perspective will give new insight into neglected aspects of the history of Jewish apocalypticism. For example, Abraham Abulafia's treatment of apocalypticism demonstrates that his form of Kabbalah was deeply involved in formulating his own spiritual interpretation of the coming end. Moreover, his efforts to preach this eschatological vision to Christians, and even more to Jews, demonstrate a strong propagandistic tendency not matched by earlier or later messianic figures. Another example can be found in the apocalyptic themes found in the book of the *Zohar*, themes that suffice to elicit a more continuous relationship between the Kabbalah, in all its major forms, and apocalypticism.

☞ SOURCES OF MEDIEVAL JEWISH
APOCALYPTICISM _____

Apocalypticism is a religious phenomenon whose impact on the Western monotheistic religions stems from its creation in the intertestamental period. Possibly of Iranian origin (see chapter 2), apocalypticism was appropriated in Judaism within specific political and religious circumstances, especially those of prolonged expectations for the return of the Israelite king, and the events connected to his—oftentimes miraculous—advent. The details of these eschatological events were in most cases related as a revelation given from above, something inherent in the very etymology of the term "apocalypticism." Though rooted in earlier forms of literature, apocalypticism's impact in the general economy of biblical literature is small, though it is paramount in the book of Daniel. Nevertheless, with the passage of time the topic gradually grew, though it never attained a status similar to other main aspects of Judaism, such as the law (*halakah*).

If European philosophy can be described as a series of footnotes to Plato, as Alfred North Whitehead put it, Jewish apocalypticism, and substantially also Western apocalypticism, may be conceived of as footnotes to the apocalyptic visions of Daniel and the drama of redemption described in Exodus. The content of the enigmatic prophecies of Daniel, perhaps the most puzzling writing in the whole biblical corpus, has tantalized generations of Jewish and Christian authors who attempted to explore the "messages" alluded to by the prophet. To a great extent, Jewish apocalyptic writings were indebted to the various hints related to the future history of the Jews and of the Gentile nations spread throughout the obscure verses of this book. The mysterious figures, beasts, and kingdoms in Daniel invited allegorical interpretations that attempted to discern the precise dates and protagonists of the end. Daniel combines several aspects of apocalypticism that sometimes appear separately, though they are part of the apocalyptic complex: the nature of the apocalyptic events; the protagonists of the apocalyptic drama; and the precise date or dates of that drama and its place or places. Given the relatively minor role of Daniel in the rabbinic tradition, however, apocalypticism did not become a main topic in later rabbinic literature. The other major source for many of the medieval discussions of the drama of the end of time is the exodus from Egypt, envisioned as the prototype for the events of redemption. While the role of Moses was played by the Messiah, Pharaoh was allegorically conceived of as representing the powers of evil. Thus, the exodus from Egypt was understood as adumbrating the return of the Jews to their homeland.

Apocalyptic literature flourished in the intertestamental period, but it is important to note that messianic figures played a relatively restricted role in the original apocalypses. The further developments of apocalypticism in Judaism represent the combination of a gradually growing role of a redeemer figure and a more complex evolution of messianism, which includes many apocalyptic components. Jewish apocalypticism, as found in the talmudic and midrashic literature, is always related to a more comprehensive topic—messianism. Since the advent of the messianic age is the main focus of discussion in these texts, we should perhaps view apocalypticism as one of the possible components of messianism, though not tantamount to this broader phenomenon. It is hard to imagine nonmessianic forms of apocalypticism in Jewish sources. It is easier, though rare, to discover messianic scenarios that are totally devoid of apocalyptic motifs. However, the focus of messianic scenarios in talmudic and midrashic texts is not to describe apocalyptic sequences in themselves but to serve as preludes for the description of the advent of the Messiah and the messianic age. Rabbinic literature did not devote special space to theological and historical issues, and this is also the case insofar as messianism is concerned. Only sporadic discussions are extant in the vast rabbinic literature.

In the early medieval period, however, a series of short treatises dealing with the messianic drama were composed. Most of them were pseudepigraphical, attributed, for example, to the biblical figure of Zerubbabel, or to the early rabbinic author Rabbi Shimeon bar Yohai. The most famous and widely influential on a whole range of medieval messianism is the *Sefer Zeruvabel*. These writings were collected and edited with critical apparatus in Yehuda Even Shmuel's fundamental anthology *Midreshei Ge'ullah*, the *Midrashim of Redemption*. They elaborate on the signs preceding the coming of the Messiah, the wars and death of the Messiah ben Joseph, as well as the arrival and final victory of the Messiah ben David. Though written during a period of several hundred years (between the seventh and the twelfth centuries), this literature is relatively unified from the conceptual point of view. It is mythical in its approach to reality: God and the Messiah are conceived of as powerful enough to disrupt the course of nature and of history. This messianism is strongly oriented toward a redemption that will take place in both time and space, and, unlike the more mystically oriented individualistic forms of redemption, it has an obvious restorative nature, one that includes the rebuilding of the Temple, the descent of Jerusalem from above, and the victory of Judaism as a universal religion. It should be emphasized that the main target of the whole process is the redemption of the chosen among the people of Israel. Individual spiritual redemption does not play any role in this popular form of Jewish literature. The apocalyptic material collected by Even Shmuel, modest in quantity, nevertheless exercised considerable influence on the popular understanding of messianism. In some cases, the very criteria of the truth of someone's messianic claim were based on this literature. This was the case with disputations regarding the seventeenth-century Messiah Sabbatai Sevi.

Besides the biblical, rabbinic, and apocalyptic literature that nourished most medieval Jewish apocalyptic discussions, there are additional sources that played significant roles in its development. First and foremost is the astrological worldview, which made substantial inroads among Jewish thinkers, especially after the middle of the twelfth century. This produced a variety of macrochronic views. Sometimes astrology was combined with Christian theology, as, for example, in a Kabbalistic corpus of writings composed in Spain around 1470:

> The mystery of "a virgin, neither has any man known her" . . . there is an actual virgin, made of fire, and she is sexually receptive [namely, has a receptive vessel] and this likeness was created for Israel, as a wife and as a virgin. . . . At the end of the redemption the mystery of the Messiah will come forth for Israel. Until that time, she will remain a virgin and then the supernal spirit will enter her mouth and a spirit of consuming fire will come forth at her opening and will emerge from that sanctuary, for there it will reside, shut away. At that same time, when the spirit emerges, it will take the form of fire. This is the mystery of the constellation of Virgo. Therefore, it is the constellation of Israel, and this is the esoteric meaning of the verse: "Rise, virgin of Israel!" . . . that is the secret interpretation of the verse "a virgin, neither has any man known her" until the Lord's anointed will come. (*Sefer ha-Meshiv*, MS Jerusalem-Mussayoff 24, fol. 34b; MS Jerusalem-Mussayoff 5, fol. 120)

The "end of redemption" points to the event that will usher in the birth of the Messiah from a supernal virgin, a conspicuously Christian view that is projected into the future but also has a cosmic-astral quality. She is the zodiacal sign of Virgo. Her description is close to that of the Kabbalistic last *sefirah,* also designated as *Shekhinah,* but its fiery nature is reminiscent of conflagrations related to apocalyptic events, especially the *ekpyrōsis* of the Stoics.

As pointed out by David Ruderman, there was a certain osmotic relationship between the Jewish and Christian apocalyptic views, at least after the late fifteenth century. It was apparently in this period that one of the most important apocalypses in the Christian Middle Ages, the "Tripoli Prophecy," composed in the mid-thirteenth century, was translated into Hebrew. Another factor that contributed to the growth of medieval Jewish apocalypticism was the course of history itself. Historical upheavals, such as the invasion of Eastern Europe and the Middle East by the Mongols, created apocalyptic expectations among the Jews, as they did among the Christians, as the "Tripoli Prophecy" demonstrates.

In the following pages, the modest corpus of medieval Jewish apocalyptic literature will be examined according to some major parameters. It should be emphasized that though they subscribed to the view that the redemptive acts were still ahead, Jewish writers produced only a few apocalyptic documents during this era. (Christianity, which assumed that the main redemptive act had already taken place in the past, produced much more apocalyptic literature.) In comparison to other Jewish bodies of literature, such as the *halakic,* Kabbalistic, philosophical, or poetic, the apocalyptic corpus is quantitatively small.

APOCALYPTICISM AS THE TIME OF THE END

Mesochronoi

In the following, I shall deal mainly with forms of *mesochronoi,* namely, calculations of imminent occurrences that were conceived of as radical turns in a linear sort of history, and only secondarily with the cyclical *macrochronoi.* While the latter were also a matter of calculation, this was done on nonscriptural bases (basically astrological ones), while the mesochronoi were much more dependent on the biblical text.

How do the Jewish calculators of the time of the end claim that they get the dates of the apocalyptic redemption? The major source of apocalyptic information is the interpretation of the apocalyptic parts of the Bible, especially the book of Daniel. Also important was the eschatological interpretation of passages describing the defeat of the nations and the triumph of the Israelite king, such as some verses from Psalms. These eschatological interpretations attempt to decipher the biblical text by means of allegorical codes, or by numerological calculations, the best known being *gematria* (i.e., the process of interchanging words whose letters have the same numerical value). Apocalypticism, characterized by the assumption that redemption is either imminent or both imminent and immanent, was concerned with scriptural validation of dates for the end-time, either rough or precise. Hence, the importance of complex allegories and calculations based on biblical passages.

BIBLICAL VERSES. One of the most recurrent verses in eschatological calculations is Gen. 49:10, where the phrase "Until Shiloh will come" is found. The noun *Shiloh,* whose meaning is not clear, was understood in rabbinic literature as pointing to the Messiah. Later on it was taken as a gematria pointing to the year of the return of the scepter to Judah. Its numerical value is 335, which in the Jewish calendar amounts to this year in any millennium. In the sixteenth century, the year corresponds to 1575, and many authors were preoccupied with the messianic significance of that year.

Another example comes from Daniel. In the manuscript *Commentary on Sefer ha-ʿEdut,* one of the most important prophetic writings of Abraham Abulafia, we learn that the famous passage in the Bible where generations of Jewish thinkers strove to find the clue for the date of the redemption (namely, Dan. 12:7—"a time, two times, and a half time") points to the year 1280. This computation is based on the numerical value of the word *ʾĕmet* ("truth") counted in a way that amounts to 1440. The initial letter *aleph* stands for thousand and Abulafia proposes to count this figure three times, because of the terms *môʿēd* ("time") and *môʿădîm* ("times," understood as pointing to two times), so that with the addition of the numerical value of the other letters, the whole amounts to 4320. To this figure he adds the half of *ʾĕmet* counted as 1440 (i.e., 720). He calculates this because the Danielic verse says *wāḥēṣî* ("and a half"). The total thus comes to 5040, the Jewish year corresponding to 1280 C.E.

ASTROLOGICAL CALCULATIONS. Calculations dealing with the dates of the conjunctions of two major planets (e.g., Saturn and Jupiter in the house of Pisces) were common in Arabic and Jewish astrology. The belief was that major religious changes take place under this sign, described as *coniunctio maior*. Jewish authors believed that the conjunction signified the emergence of the Messiah. Such calculations started with the Muslim astrologer Abu Mashar, but were cultivated by Jewish authors from the twelfth century on and remained in use until the seventeenth century. The assumption that change is immanent in the very nature of mundane reality presided over by celestial bodies and their revolutions rendered this astrological view sometimes apocalyptic, especially because of its deterministic nature.

REVELATION. In other cases, the date of the end is revealed by a direct message coming from above. So, for example, Abraham Abulafia confesses:

> When I arrived at [the knowledge of] the Names, by my loosening of the bonds of the seals, "the Lord of All" appeared to me and revealed to me his secret and informed me about the time of the end of the exile [*ʿēt qēṣ haggālût*] and about the time of the beginning of redemption. He compelled me to prophesy. (*Ve-Zot Li-Yhuda*, pp. 18–19, corrected according to MS New York, JTS 1887)

According to this messianic Kabbalist, redemption will occur in 1290, which in the Jewish calendar corresponds to the year 5050, a date deemed to be hinted at by the word *hakkôl*, which is part of the expression, "the Lord of All" (*ʾādôn hakkôl*). Therefore, the Lord of All revealed to this Kabbalist the time of redemption. Written approximately a year before the expected date, this is a fine example of messianic expectations.

COMBINATIONS. Obviously, the different sources were sometimes combined, as we learn from another discussion of Abulafia where the special significance of the figure 5040 is emphasized. According to Abulafia, 180 solar revolutions multiplied by 28 amounts to 5040. The figure 28 (Hebrew *kôaḥ*) means "power," but in the medieval understanding of the word it points to potentiality. Thus, the revolution of the sun is explained as a preparation for something to emerge out of its potentiality. The actualization of this potentiality is conceived to be the time of the end. This will be attained ten years later, when to the number 180 a decade will be added, and 190 will emerge. (The number 190, when translated into Hebrew letters, is *qēṣ*, "end.") In other words, the very term for end contains a hint at the date of the end.

Cyclical Macrochronoi

While the mesochronoi deal with an imminent expectation of the collapse of the old order, and thus with an acute and explicit apocalypticism, the cyclical macrochronoi imply a more hidden apocalyptic worldview. Originating in astrological perspectives, some ideas about cyclical time were adopted in the Kabbalistic schools, which envisioned the end of the universe at a determined and recurrent date. In Hebrew this complex of ideas was designated as the theory of *Shemittot* and *Yovelim*. This is a cosmic interpretation of the biblical commandments to cease from working the earth each seventh and fiftieth years and to liberate slaves. According to some thirteenth-century Kabbalists, each year in the Bible stands for a millennium, thus creating a frame of reference corresponding to astrological rhythms. In some views, the seventh millennium is the time of the cessation of all living creatures, vegetable, animal, and human, while the fiftieth millennium marks a cessation of the whole material universe. According to these views, each unit of seven millennia (designated as *shemittah*) is presided over by one of the lower seven *sefirot*, which determines its nature. During the *Yovel*, or the cosmic Jubilee, the seven lower *sefirot* will return to their source to be absorbed within the third *sefirah*, *Binah*. According to some Kabbalists, the present *shemittah* is presided over by the *sefirah* of *Din* ("Stern Judgment"), which entails harsh religious precepts and the laws of transmigration. This strict determinism of astral extraction was often coupled with a negative vision of reality.

Apocalyptic Complexities

Apocalyptic significance resides not only in the nature of events whose concatenation is conceived of as constituting "history" but also in the attitude toward time that is embedded in these events and factually bestows on them a certain surplus. The same event will be understood differently when interpreted in a cyclic approach to time rather than in a linear one. Moreover, the same event can be understood in different ways if it can be located, concomitantly, within different frames of time. We can adduce a general example from a Kabbalist who expressed all the varieties of religious times mentioned above in his various writings. The mid-thirteenth century rabbi, Moses ben Nahman (Nahmanides), one of the most famous Jewish thinkers of the Middle Ages, composed an apocalyptic book named *Sefer ha-Ge'ullah* (*Book of Redemption*), which calculated the precise time of the arrival of the Messiah as 1358, thus subscribing to a linear view of time. On the other hand, Nahmanides also held to a theory of cyclical macrochronoi (*Shemittot* and *Yovelim*) regarding them as pulses of the divine organism similar to the rhythm of inspiration and expiration. Furthermore, he subscribed to the microchronic cycle related to Jewish ritual. These varying views of time did not create tensions within his system.

Beyond this general example, a more concrete discussion combining two different conceptions of time will illustrate the complexity of chronology in Jewish apocalypticism. In a sixteenth-century book, we read the following about the date for the advent of the Messiah:

> The great purpose of the advent of the king Messiah and of the World to Come, [was not disclosed as it is said] "The heart did not disclose to the mouth," neither to the crowd nor to all of the elite, but to the few ones who merit this [i.e., the knowledge of the secret]. It is forbidden to the recipient of this secret to disclose it even to the elite, except to a friend exceptionally close to him. And in the year of the Messiah, namely in the year whose secret is 358 of the sixth millennium, which is the year *Shannah*, then the Messiah will arrive. [However,] in an occult manner he has already arrived during the several cycles of the worlds which have already passed before the present one in which we are, since at the time when he has already arrived, then he will come again also in this time. And what was said, that "and then he will come," means that the Messiah will come in the future at the time he comes in our time, namely our world. (*Sefer Ginnat Beitan*, chap. 52, MS Oxford 1578, fol. 63b)

The assumption here is that in each and every cosmic cycle the Messiah will always come in the year pointed out by the gematria of the term *māšîaḥ*. Thus, while the overt subject of the passage is redemption according to linear time, redemption takes place, according to the esoteric teaching of this master, time and again in the future cosmic cycles.

☞ SPACE AND APOCALYPTICISM

As suggested above, time is a central factor in discussion of apocalypticism. Its end is the main concern of the calculators. However, time manifests itself in place, sometimes in different places. Two cities loom larger than any others in the apocalyptic scenarios in Jewish texts: Jerusalem and Rome.

The former is the place where the apocalyptic process will find its final fulfillment, as is evident from innumerable texts. The descent of the celestial city upon the mundane one, the rebuilding of the Temple and the return of the Jews and of the divine presence are leitmotifs permeating all the popular forms of Jewish apocalypses. They are also present in some of the more elitist ones. So, for example, we read in the sixteenth-century author Shlomo Molkho's messianic poem:

> Israel shall rejoice—Nations shall expire;
> Then repaid—Manifold
> Heavenly Mercy may be—Upon the city of Jerusalem.

From this perspective, Jewish apocalypticism, more than its messianism, is topocentrically oriented. It involves dislocation, returning, immigrations of masses, battles over sacred space.

Some of the events that precede the final scenario of the end of time address matters related to Rome. It is there that some Jewish apocalyptic writers placed the birth of Armilus, the Jewish counterpart of Antichrist. This horrible creature will be born, according to some texts, out of a marble stone in that city. According to several medieval texts, the Messiah has to first come to Rome, to live with the paupers of the city, and then to approach the pope, before he can be recognized as the Redeemer. This is a typological reading of the exodus events where the redemption of the Jews began with Moses going to Pharaoh. The eschatological journey to Jerusalem starts at Rome.

One of the most influential texts dealing with the end of time is a passage in the writings of Nahmanides. In his polemical text relating his debate with Paulus Christianus in Barcelona, he claims that the Messiah has not yet come,

> [But] only that he was born on the day of the destruction [of the Temple]: for was it on the day that Moses was born that he immediately went to redeem Israel? He arrived only a number of days later, under the command of the Holy One, Blessed be He, and [then] said to Pharaoh: "Let my people go that they may serve Me!" So, too, when the end of time will have arrived, the Messiah will go to the Pope under the command of God and say, "Let my people go that they may serve Me," and until that time we will not say regarding him that he arrived, for he is not [yet] the Messiah. (Eisenstein 1928, 88)

Under the impact of this and similar traditions, Abraham Abulafia described his stay in Rome in 1280 as part of his expected instauration as Messiah:

> He said that he was in Rome at that time and they told him what was to be done and what was to be said in his name, and that he told everyone that "God is King, and shall stir up the nations," and the retribution of those who rule instead of Him. And he informed him that he was king and he changed [himself] from day to day, and his degree was above that of all degrees, for in truth he was deserving such. But he returned and again made him take an oath

when he was staying in Rome on the river Tiber. . . . And the meaning of his saying, "Rise and lift up the head of my anointed one," refers to the life of souls. "And on the New Year" and "in the Temple"—it is the power of the souls. And he says: "Anoint him as a king"—rejoice in him like a king with the power of all the names. "For I have anointed him as a king over Israel"—over the communities of Israel, that is, the commandments. And his saying: "And his name I have called *Shadday,* like My Name"—whose secret is *Shadday,* like My Name, and understand all the intention. Likewise his saying, "He is I and I am He," and it cannot be revealed more explicitly than this. But the secret of the "corporeal name" is the "Messiah of God." Also "Moses will rejoice," which he has made known to us, and which is the five urges; and I called the corporeal name as well. . . . Now Raziel started to contemplate the essence of the Messiah and he found it and recognized it and its power and designated it as David, the son of David. (MS Rome-Angelica 38, fols. 14b–15a; MS Munich 285, fol. 39b)

An apocalyptic passage from the book of the *Zohar* combines descriptions concerning both Jerusalem and Rome:

Some of these things were fulfilled at that time, while some others were fulfilled later on, and others are left for the time of the King-Messiah. . . . We have learned that the Holy One, Blessed be He, will rebuild Jerusalem and will reveal one fixed star that shoots as sparks seventy mobile stars, and seventy sparks that are illumined from this star [are found] at the center of the firmament, and from it another seventy stars will draw [their light] and will illumine and shine brightly for seventy days. And on the sixth day [and] on the twenty-fifth day of the sixth month the star will appear, and will be gathered to the seventh day. And after seventy days, it will be covered up and will be seen no more. On the first day it will be visible in the city of Rome and on that day three high walls of the city of Rome will fall, and the great palace there will collapse and the ruler of that city will die. In that time the star will expand and become visible over the world and then mighty wars will arise in all the four quarters of the world and faith is going to be absent among them. (*Zohar,* vol. 3, fol. 212b)

Rome was also the site of the activities of two other figures closely associated with messianism. In the late twenties of the sixteenth century, Shlomo Molkho, a former *converso,* arrived at the city and became well acquainted with, in fact a protégé of, the pope. According to a legendary testimony, he accomplished a magical circumambulation, presumably in Rome, that was intended to destroy idolatry. A similar performance, historically reliable, is mentioned in connection with Nathan of Gaza, the Sabbatean prophet, in 1668. In a Sabbatean apocalypse extant in a Yemenite version the Messiah is still portrayed as born in Rome, though he will be translated to Jerusalem.

APOCALYPTIC DRAMATIS PERSONAE

Apocalyptic literature presents a variety of protagonists involved in the scenario of the end-time. The main actor in ancient forms of Jewish apocalypticism was God, while in later texts the Messiah, or Messiahs, preceded by Elijah as a forerunner, gradually come to the fore as miraculous figures able to change the natural and political course of events. A relatively new figure, emerging in the early Middle Ages, is Armilus, whose role is reminiscent of the Christian Antichrist (see chapter 10). Indeed, his name (in an elliptic spelling) is related, by means of gematria, to one of the most common names of the Messiah, the son of David, namely,

Menahem ben ʿAmiel. (Both have the same numerical value: 341.) Some angels, like Michael, Yahoel, and Metatron recur in the apocalyptic literature, either as sources for eschatological revelation or as playing an active role in the apocalyptic battles. These conflicts were sometimes portrayed as taking place both below and on high, between angels representing the nations and the angel appointed for the Jewish nation.

In the more speculatively oriented forms of medieval Jewish thought, where the concept of nature became more evident, the possibility of change in history was attributed to immanentistic factors rather than to heterogeneous ones. The most important examples are the astrological visions of the end. The main thrust of apocalyptic descriptions has to do with the events in history and nature, rather than with the deeds of the Messiah and his psychology. Worldviews based on complex and systematic forms of order tended to exclude from apocalyptic events the unpredictable interventions that characterize popular messianism.

Another important issue concerns the historical authors who created, elaborated, reiterated, and propagated apocalyptic worldviews. Visions of history centering on crisis may reflect personalities who interpreted historical events from a special angle. Like the personalities portrayed in the literary exposition of the apocalyptic drama, the authors of these texts often seem to be in search of a role in history.

☞ APOCALYPTICISM AND REVELATION _____

The term "apocalypticism" is etymologically related to revelation from above. Indeed, one of the sources of apocalyptic information is often such a revelation. But the revelation of the time of the end is only one of the contents of such revelations. The imminence of redemption produces deep changes in the pattern of available religious knowledge; the restructuring of reality is accompanied by the disclosure of hidden forms of knowledge. The messianic times are often described in Kabbalistic literature as the moment of the disclosure of the secrets of the Torah, as well as their broad dissemination. So, for example, we learn from a late-thirteenth-century Kabbalistic treatise belonging to ecstatic Kabbalah:

> During the time of the Exile, the activity of the names has been obliterated and prophecy has been canceled from Israel because of the hindrance of the attribute of Judgment [*Din*]. This state will go on until the coming of the one whom God has chosen, and his power will be great because of what has been transmitted to him related to their power, and God will reveal the name to him and transmit to him the supernal keys. Then he will stand against the attribute of Judgment . . . and the attribute of Mercy will guide him. The supernal [entity] will become lower, and the lower will become supernal, and the Tetragrammaton, which has been concealed will be revealed, and ʾ*Adonai,* which was revealed will be concealed. Then it will happen to us what has been written [Jer. 31:33]: "For they shall all know me from the least of them to the greatest of them." Then the natural, philosophical sciences will be canceled and concealed, because their supernal power was canceled, but the science of names and letters, which are for now unknown to us, will be revealed, because their [supernal] power is gradually enhancing. Then [Esther 8:16] "The Jews will have light and gladness," and sadness and worry will be [the part of] the deniers, and "Many of the people of the land become Jews" [Esther 8:17] and "Your sons and daughters will prophesy" [Joel 3:1]. (Porush 1989, 17)

Here the messianic figure chosen by God is taught the secrets and power of the divine names, and, using this knowledge, he is able to start his messianic activity. Redemption is a consequence of the Messiah's use of the divine names, just as the instauration of the Messiah was attained by means of the power of these names.

Revelation of the divine name and messianism are conspicuous in ecstatic Kabbalah. Indeed, this issue is not just one of the many topics of this brand of Kabbalah, but is the core of the whole system. Revealing the divine names is tantamount to revealing Kabbalah itself, and this is essential for knowing the secret of the advent of the messianic era. It is quite important to dwell on the sequence of the events related by Abulafia in the text cited above. His spiritual life, described here as knowing the names and loosing the bonds, brought him to a subsequent revelation of the eschatological secrets. Spiritualization is here a condition of redemption, not vice versa. However, the revelation of the divine name is only one aspect of the relationship between name and redemption.

Another messianic figure, Rabbi Shlomo Molkho, also mentions the revelation of secrets as part of the apocalyptic upheaval:

> With words concealed—I shall reveal to men
> Choice words—Like spices.
> From Mount Carmel—You were sent by God
> [To be] the man [who] brings tidings—[And takes] revenge
>   upon the nations
> Nations shall war—Warriors will be crushed
> Foreigners shall be vanquished—And to us peace.
> He arose from the North—To seek daughter and son
> Esau who is Edom—The young Shlomo
> Will consecrate—His polished sword
> In aid of his nation—To redeem from nights.
> Nations shall fear—And gifts bestow
> Full with indignities—Due to Salvation.
> Israel will rejoice—Nations will expire.
> Then repaid—Manifold
> Heavenly Mercy may be—Upon the city of Jerusalem.
> The scales are set—For Judgment in Yemen. (Kaufmann,
>   1897, 121–25)

Sometimes, the revelation of the secrets is necessary because of deterioration due to the moral corruption that at times is described as preceding the messianic advent. Rabbi Hayyim Vital, who had messianic aspirations, claims:

> The disclosure of this lore nowadays, in these bad generations, is to safeguard us by its means, . . . because in those [earlier] generations, the majority was [constituted by] men of deeds and piety, and even scanty [parts of Kabbalah] were able to save them from all the opponents [meqatregim]. But now, as we are far remote from the supernal source, just as yeast at the bottom of a barrel, who will safeguard us, if not our reading this wondrous and profound lore? Especially as our Rabbi Isaac [Luria] said: "The secrets have become exoteric [knowledge], because in this generation prostitution and delation and slander and hate in the heart rule and the shell [qelippah] has become widespread to such an extent that persons are ashamed to behave in a pious manner; God shall safeguard us and forgive our sins." (Rabbi Hayyim Vital's preface to ʿEtz Hayyim, fol. 5c)

Some of Rabbi Hayyim Vital's dreams also exhibit an element of apocalyptic messianism. In his diary there are descriptions of eschatological battles, reminiscent of much earlier Jewish messianic literature, but they are integrated into passages characterized exclusively by an individual-messianic aspect. These passages differ from more theoretical perceptions, where the apocalyptic aspect does not play a major role. In any case, these testimonies revealing Vital's messianic consciousness remained sealed in his manuscript diaries, hardly known outside his family. According to his account, Vital's success in convincing the people of his city to repent was scant. Nevertheless, the importance of dreams as carriers of messianic, and even apocalyptic, messages is evident not only from Vital's collection of dreams but also from several instances among the Sabbateans.

In other cases, we learn about attempts to appease the fears of imminent apocalyptic wars by instituting vigils to safeguard those involved in them from the pangs of the Messiah. This can be seen in the case of the sixteenth-century Kabbalist Rabbi Abraham ben Eliezer ha-Levi in Jerusalem.

☞ APOCALYPTICISM AND HISTORICAL EVENTS

Apocalypticism describes events that are imagined to occur in future history. Thus, the boundary situation of apocalypticism served as the arena for imagining present problems and/or solving them through religious imagination. Apocalyptic eschatology is dramatic, much more than spiritual salvation, or individual eschatology, which deals with psychological processes. The middle of the thirteenth century witnessed clashes between groups of people moving into the same areas from different directions. These involved Christians, driven by their religious goal to liberate the holy places and maintain their strongholds in the land of Israel; Mongols, pushing into Eastern Europe in the late 1220s and on to Syria and the land of Israel in the late 1250s; and, finally, the Mameluks, inhabitants of the areas surrounding the Holy Land, who succeeded in restoring the hegemony of Islam in this region after bloody encounters with both Christians and Mongols. The specter of conflagrations and real bloodshed built up sharp tensions in Europe. Beginning with the Hungarian kingdom, which faced the imminent danger of Mongolian invasion, rumors about the savage behavior of these godless warriors speedily spread all over Europe. Some indigenous European apocalyptic prophecies, mostly from the circle of Joachim of Fiore and apparently unrelated to the panic awakened by the Mongols, contributed scholarly speculations to the patrimony of popular eschatological expectations, enriching them in numerous ways. In Joachimite circles, the belief in the arrival of the Angelic Pope (see chapter 11), as well as various eschatological computations, added an important tone to the apocalyptic symphony of the time. The Jews, a small and oppressed minority both in Europe and in the land of Israel, could not actively participate in a meaningful way in those fateful events. However, the news spreading in Europe, and perhaps also written apocalypses produced there, excited their hopes and stirred their imagination. Mongols were metamorphosed into "the hidden" (*haggĕnûzîm*), to be identified with the Ten Lost Tribes who were to return on the eve of the eschaton and to play an important role in the apocalyptic events. In some cases, expectations arose among the Jews that these tribes would avenge the sufferings inflicted on them and their ancestors by their Christian neighbors. It seems that this understanding of historical events was shared by a major Christian apocalypse, the well-known "Tripoli Prophecy," or the "Prophecy of the Cedars of Lebanon":

> The sons of Israel will be liberated from captivity. A certain people called "without a head" or reputed to be wanderers, will come. Woe to the clergy! A new order thrives: if it should fall, woe to the church! There will be many battles in the world. There will be mutations of faith, of laws, and of kingdoms. The land of the Saracens will be destroyed. (Lerner 1983, 16)

This vision implies the identity between the Mongols and the sons of Israel. This point, highly significant in the documents to be discussed below, is combined with the assumption that the clerical establishment, the church and the existing orders, will be the object of punishment. We may assume that the anonymous author, as part of an opposition faction in Christianity, exploited the historical event of the Mongol onslaught in order to express his hope in an imminent change. A Hebrew document written in Spain and Christian descriptions of the Jews testify to a deep belief that finally the account with the oppressors will be settled. In some of these documents, the repercussions of these expectations on Christians are documented. We learn of anti-Jewish riots motivated by the hopes expressed by the Jews that the Mongols, namely, the lost tribes, would conquer Europe.

The Hebrew documents mentioned can be dated shortly after the middle of the thirteenth century. At least in one case the author of the document was a Kabbalist, the Catalan poet Rabbi Meshullam da Pierra. It seems, however, that the overt reaction to these historical events was not a single expression of Jewish longing for, and hope in, an immediate redemption. A comparison of the concerns of the Provençal Kabbalists and their followers in Catalonia in the first third of the thirteenth century with those of the Kabbalists after the middle of the century, demonstrates a certain ascent in messianic expectations. Rabbi Isaac the Blind of Lunel refers to the eschatological confrontation with Amalek, the ancestral enemy of Israel. His student, Rabbi Ezra of Gerona, mentions messianic issues in his *Commentary on the Song of Songs;* however, these references seem to betray the classical concern with eschatology which never ceased in Jewish sources in general. As Gershom Scholem has aptly remarked, the early Kabbalists were rather indifferent to actual messianism. It is a matter of debate whether the explanation he proposed—namely, that those early Kabbalists were immersed in the contemplation of the processes of the beginning, that is, the theosophical interpretations of the talmudic account of creation—is valid, or whether such indifference was due to Neoplatonic influence, which was not much interested in history.

In the writings of Rabbi Yehuda ben Nissim ibn Malka in Morocco, Rabbi Isaac ben Jacob ha-Cohen, and in the book of the *Zohar* in Castile, as well as in the writings of Abraham Abulafia, messianism plays a far more important role than in the texts of their predecessors. One may explain this change as the result of the greater literary production that characterizes Kabbalah in the second half of the thirteenth century rather than as evidence of a greater emphasis on messianic issues. This production of voluminous books may allot a larger share to messianism than had been the case. Though this argument seems sound, it cannot explain the emergence of elaborate messianic discussions motivated by a deep conviction in the messianic mission that characterizes Abulafia's writings. Further, the messianic speculations differ from each other in substantial ways. It is highly unlikely to assume that these authors depend on each other as far as the details of their speculations are concerned.

Abulafia's messianism combines a spiritualistic understanding of eschatology with his

consciousness that he is the Messiah. He firmly believed that he had a definite role in the historical scene, as his attempt to meet the pope demonstrates. Isaac ha-Cohen emphasizes the eschatological fight between the powers of good and evil that received cosmic dimensions in his
vision of the end. The importance of the confrontation between the two camps is absent from
the Kabbalah of Abulafia. According to Rabbi Yehuda ibn Malka, the advent of the end of days
is a matter we learn from astrology, a lore that is rather marginal in the speculation of Abulafia
and Isaac ha-Cohen. Last but not least, the Zoharic eschatology, following some early medieval
Jewish treatises dealing with eschatological events, adds an important dimension by its emphasis on the importance of the theurgical activity of the Kabbalist, namely, by his intentional and
mystical performance of the commandments.

It seems that the existence of a common background in the messianic expectations connected to the imminent arrival of the lost tribes has to be considered a major reason for the
renewed concern with messianism among the Kabbalists. The theory advanced by Joseph Dan
(Dan 1988), who regards the messianic discussions of Rabbi Isaac ha-Cohen as mere figments
of this Kabbalist's imagination without any historical background, fails to mention the repercussions of the Mongol invasion on the Jews at the time of Isaac ha-Cohen. Rabbi Isaac was well
acquainted with the impact of the advent of the Mongols on the Christians. His older contemporary, the poet Rabbi Meshullam da Pierra (whose verses will be discussed in detail below),
knew that "at the limit of Ashkenaz, cities are terrified, some of them being afraid of the sword."
Writing in Gerona, this Kabbalist was aware of the panic that prevailed among Christians in
Germany. In any case, it seems that in Castile rumors concerning the Mongols also reached the
Kabbalists. In the book of the *Zohar*, composed or at least edited in Spain in the late 1280s, we
read:

> The sons of Ishmael will cause fierce wars in the world and the sons of Edom will gather and
> wage battles against them, one on the dry earth, another on the sea, and one near Jerusalem.
> And each of them will rule over the other. And the land of Israel will not be given to the sons of
> Edom. At that same time, a nation [coming] from the end of the world will awake against the
> wicked Rome and will fight there for three months. And [other] nations will gather there and
> fall into its hands, until all the sons of Rome will gather together from all the corners of the
> world . . . and it will expel the sons of Ishmael from there.

Here the third nation, described as the victorious one that will arrive from the corner of
the world and fight both Christianity and Islam, seems to fit the Mongols. From the context of
this quotation, it is obvious that the author or the editor of the *Zohar* conceived of the Mongol
wars as part of the eschatological processes. This seems to have been the case throughout the
second part of the thirteenth century. European Jewry had the impression that the emergence
of an unexpected superpower of an obscure extraction, namely, the Mongols, and the change of
military status of the Christians in the Holy Land were portents with messianic overtones. More
than the suffering of the Jews, the defeats of their enemies, the Christians, nourished messianic
expectations. The belief that international conflagrations were signs of Gog and Magog foretold
in the Bible (Ezekiel 38–39) was the natural conclusion from a reading of the apocalyptic literature produced in the period between the sixth and the tenth centuries. A talmudic dictum to the
effect that when someone sees confrontations between kingdoms he may expect the advent of
the Messiah seems to summarize one major reason for the apocalyptic stirring that characterized medieval messianic expectations. The arrival of the Mongols that terrified so much of

Christian Europe must be considered the catalyst of renewed interest in a more active messianism among the Jews.

Let me exemplify the connection between the rumors regarding the Mongols and the
heightening of eschatological expectations as expressed in Meshullam da Pierra's poem:

> There is a witness to Redemption / and visions and legends widespread, And the kingdom will
> be renewed in our days / for the lost nation and the dispersed communities, And an offering
> will be brought to the son of David and Ishai / and to My secretaries and My officers donations,
> And My Temple will be built up and consolidated. . . . The tribes that were dispersed in the
> ancient days / Now they have left the country of their sojourn, And the sign that they sent by
> God is / that many princes are afraid. And their [the tribes'] time has come / to [perform] an
> act of great redemption, and they have [already] passed the passages . . . . See how Babylonia
> was seized, and Aleppo, / and Damascus, and the towns were devastated.

The fears of the princes apparently refer to the situation in the poet's vicinity in Christian Spain,
and possibly also to German towns mentioned in a verse quoted above. The devastated cities in
the Orient were an eloquent intimation of what was expected to be the fate of Europe; but what
really terrified the Christians, according to the poet, was the hope of the Jews. The poem explicitly indicates that the Temple will be rebuilt and the sacrifices renewed.

The same conviction about the imminent construction of the Temple is expressed later on
in the same poem. It seems no exaggeration to describe Rabbi Meshullam's tone in this poem as
one of acute messianism. The tribes are depicted as the messengers of God, who is the speaker
throughout these verses. Before turning to the revelatory tone of the poem, attention should be
drawn to the Hebrew term translated here as "passages" (*ma'bārôt*). According to Biblical
Hebrew, the main source of imagery in Spanish Jewish poetry, this word means "passages over
a river." Indeed, a river is mentioned shortly afterwards in the poem. It seems that the poet
hints at the Sambatyon River, which allegedly surrounds the ten lost tribes and does not allow
them to return to the civilized world. The tribes' arrival at the "passages over the river" is an
implicit hint of the imminent redemption. The use of the divine voice might be taken as a
poetic device, not to be taken too seriously, but this cautious approach is not a definitive interpretation of the text. As we know, Rabbi Meshullam had good relationships with the Kabbalists
Rabbi Ezra and Rabbi Azriel of Gerona, and apparently also with Nahmanides. These were Kabbalists who cannot be considered unsympathetic to revelations. At least in the case of the master
of Ezra of Gerona, that is, Rabbi Isaac the Blind, traditions extant at the end of the thirteenth
century describe him as the recipient of revelation from Elijah. Scholars assume that Meshul-
lah's poem was composed in the summer of 1260 in Catalonia. It is unequivocal evidence for
the messianic excitement provoked by the Mongol rumors among the Jews in northern Spain.

In the same year the young Abraham Abulafia left Tudela in the search of the river Sambatyon. Exactly at the same time that Meshullam was stirring messianic expectations in Catalonia, Abulafia undertook an enterprise that includes elements relevant to the expectations of his
contemporaries. The search for the mythical river, as scholars have correctly surmised, is to be
understood as part of a messianic scheme, because beyond this river the ten lost tribes were hidden. Abulafia's attempt to reach this river, taking the land of Israel as a starting point, may be
connected to the presence of Mongols in the area. However, his attempt could not be fulfilled
because of a battle that took place in the vicinity of Acre. He designated the protagonists of this
fight using biblical terms, a fact that complicates the precise identification of the belligerent

parties. "Ishmael" is a classical reference to the Muslims, in this case the Mameluks. In Christian sources, it may refer to the Mongols. On the other hand, "Esau" in Jewish medieval texts is the conventional allegory for Christianity, and it seems that no exception to this use was available. Therefore, the fight that prevented Abulafia from proceeding was apparently a battle between Muslims or Mongols and Christians. This battle apparently was waged late in 1260 or at the very beginning of 1261 in the environs of Acre. This dating is based on Abulafia's statement that he went to the land of Israel directly. It seems reasonable to assume that between his departure and his arrival no considerable span of time passed. The fact that Abulafia does not mention any town in the land of Israel besides Acre seems to support the assumption that he did not spend much time in the Holy Land but returned immediately to Europe. On these grounds, it seems reasonable to identify this battle as that between the Mameluks and the Mongols which took place in September 1260, at En Jalud, not far from Acre. This identification, however, is complicated by the fact that Christians did not participate in this battle. An inspection of the historical data concerning battles fought in late 1260 or early 1261 does not offer a better alternative. We are in a situation where we may assume either that Abulafia's description does not use the classical allegories when pointing to the belligerent parties or that, twenty-six years later, he misrepresented the armies involved in the war.

Abulafia presents his traveling as a response to the call of the divine spirit, which he mentions in connection with his journey to the land of Israel. The search for Sambatyon, however, is referred to as his own intention. If this peculiar formulation of Abulafia is intentional, then the divine revelation included no more than a command to visit the Holy Land. This reading is not strictly necessary, though, since grammatically we may consider his phrase "the Spirit of God awoke me and moved me" as dealing with a revelation that incited his travels without referring to a specific goal. In any case, the attempt to find the Sambatyon was not the result of a specific revelation or vision, but seems to have been a decision of his own. Twenty years later, Abulafia explicitly states that the beginning of his prophetic experience is to be dated to 1270, so that the earlier experiences would be considered, at least in retrospect, nonprophetic ones.

What could be the possible significance of the finding of the legendary river? We can only speculate that on the basis of the relationship between the lost tribes and the river Abulafia wished to see with his own eyes the exodus of the ten tribes. According to the verse of Rabbi Meshullam, the tribes arrived at the "passages," but the Latin "Prophecy of the Cedars of Lebanon" describes the "sons of Israel" who "will be liberated from captivity." Perhaps Abulafia only wanted to verify the rumors concerning the massive exodus of the tribes. Such an attempt would not necessarily involve any active role in the liberation of the tribes, namely, any messianic mission on the part of Abulafia, such as he will assume later on. Given the obscurity of the incident, no conclusion is definitive. According to an important apocalyptic document, the *Sefer Eliahu,* the ten tribes were supposed to leave the river of Sambatyon on the twenty-fifth of Tishrei, that is, less than a month after the New Year. Did Abulafia plan his arrival in the Holy Land on the eve of the New Year in order to witness such a fateful event?

As seen above, Rabbi Meshullam's poem of 1260 included sharp messianic overtones. According to a contemporary treatise dealing with the Hebrew letters and astrology, redemption was to begin in 1260, when the reign of Saturn, a sign favorable to the Jews, would start. The same year was envisioned by Joachite apocalypticists as the date when the powers of evil would be overcome and the third *status* would begin. This was the historical context for the first possibly messianic enterprise of Abulafia.

These considerations invite some broader reflections regarding the dynamics of Jewish messianism. The major question to be addressed is, What are the basic catalysts of the dormant apocalyptic elements in Judaism? Are they to be conceived of as a form of antidote for the tragic events connected to the fate of the people of Israel, a medicine that suffices to kindle messianic hopes and transforms them into a consuming fire? If so, the reaction of the Jews to the unprecedented massacres by the Crusaders in 1096 in France and Germany, or to the pogroms in Spain in 1391, was not a messianic response. Eschatologically speaking, the Jews were much more excited following the fall of Constantinople in 1453. They mentioned this year as fraught with messianic significance. After the expulsion from Spain, the messianic expectations of Rabbi Abraham ben Eliezer ha-Levi, a Kabbalist more interested in eschatology than any other Kabbalist of his generation, envisioned the defeats of the Christians in the Mediterranean as a messianic sign, whereas he ignored the date of the expulsion as a meaningful step in the apocalyptic scenario.

☞ SOCIOLOGICAL ASPECTS OF APOCALYPTICISM

Were the elitist groups of Kabbalists open at all to popular apocalyptic elements? Was their messianism of a radically different sort, one shaped by relatively more sophisticated types of thought according to the models I described at the beginning of this article? The tensions between popular apocalypticism and more elitist views is already well known in the rabbinic attitude toward the last times, and it is exemplified by the reactions of great Halakists like Maimonides, or Rabbi Shlomo ibn Adret. Leaders of mystical groups, like Rabbi Yehuda he-Hasid in Germany and Ibn Adret in Catalonia, were much more reticent about, if not openly hostile to, popular and sometimes even elite forms of messianism. As Vladimir Jankelevitch has audaciously formulated it: "The depersonalization of the Messiah who remains personal only in popular beliefs is an essential phenomenon to the philosophical history of Judaism." Thus, independent of their own visions of messianism (and I assume that all these figures professed one version or another of messianic traditions), it seems that the approach of the philosophical and *halakic* elite with respect to new forms of popular messianism was often both cautious and suspicious.

More open toward apocalyptic themes were two major Kabbalistic bodies of material—the book of the *Zohar* and the Kabbalists from the circle of *Sefer ha-Meshiv*. In these two cases we may assume that we are dealing with secondary elite figures and that the cloak of anonymity they assumed was protective of their real identity. In other words, messianic claims and ideas have been the prerogative of figures who belong to what I would describe as the secondary elite. These figures may be characterized as more eager to engage new ideas. They took a greater role in the reinterpretation of traditional ideas; they were also more mobile and more eager to disseminate their insights to the larger masses. Abraham Abulafia, Shlomo Molkho, Sabbatai Sevi, Abraham Michael Cardoso, Nathan of Gaza, Moshe Hayyim Luzzatto, and the Besht were all itinerant figures. Messianic ideas, as exposed by this secondary elite, should be understood as part of the cultivation of a broad range of topics characteristic of their creativity, including complex forms of hermeneutics, a propensity for exotericism, and an interest in magic. As one of their most characteristic constellations of ideas, messianism has been interpreted in a variety of ways, using many new imported concepts. This is one of the most convincing examples of the cosmopolitan nature of some important segments of the Kabbalistic elite. Like the Jewish philosophers, they were in significant dialogue with systems of thought formulated outside the pale of rabbinic Judaism. Kabbalah was sometimes a major factor in the processes of acculturation and also one of the significant influences of Jewish thought on general intellectual culture.

While apocalyptic elements were more congenial with popular segments of Jewish society, the more sophisticated amalgams of ancient Jewish eschatological material and speculative approaches were more consonant with the secondary elites. The primary elites attempted to preserve the canonical eschatology as a theological and teleological dogma, but they significantly moderated its catastrophic apocalyptic cargo. Only rarely did they feature strong spiritualistic interpretations of the rabbinic material concerning the Messiah. Each significant segment of Jewish society created its own sort of messianism, or was attuned to a certain wavelength from the past that fitted its expectations. Thus, notwithstanding the shared stock of eschatological themes, the various parts of Jewish society over the ages have cultivated specialized forms of messianic tendencies and their apocalyptic ingredients. The intensity of experiencing messianic themes presumably differed from one sector to another, as we have attempted to distinguish above with regard to the categories of Messiahs, the propagators of the ideas or self-consciousness of those Messiahs, and finally also with their followers. In lieu of speaking of messianism in general, a more nuanced concept of distribution of experiences, concepts, and beliefs will foster a better understanding of the way in which messianic themes and motives worked. We should differentiate between the reverberations of the various facets of what is vaguely called messianism and the much more stratified groups of the Jewish population involved in a messianic event. The apocalyptic messianism of the masses sometimes induced messianic figures to interpret less apocalyptic terms in a radical fashion. In fact, we may assume a pyramidic structure of messianic movements, with the top of the pyramid representing the messianic leader often involved in less apocalyptic speculations, even when discussing messianism. The apostles of these messianic figures, who had to translate the message to the base of the pyramid, had to resort to apocalyptic imagery, dominant in popular imagination.

The ongoing concerns with the preservation of the spiritual identity of the group, its national continuation and physical existence, have strengthened the apocalyptic elements in popular Jewish circles. However, the emergence of the axial spiritual attitudes, with their emphases on spiritual attainments more than on physical survival, or individual achievements rather than group well-being, produced a variety of syntheses between the primal and the axial values as hermeneutical moves that enabled the primal elements to survive while differentiating into new forms.

APOCALYPTICISM AND LITERARY GENRES

The feeling that the time of the end is imminent is obvious in some Jewish messianic figures who not only point out their confidence that they are living the last moments of the old order but also depict it as the time for a dramatic upheaval. To what extent the worldviews of the secondary elites in the Middle Ages subscribed to a literal interpretation of apocalyptic motifs is a matter that requires detailed analyses. There can be no doubt, however, that the most significant part of elitist medieval literature still resorts to apocalyptic rhetoric. The apocalyptic imagination, whether interpreted metaphorically or not, served as an important form of mediation between messianic elites and popular circles. This is evident in one of the most important apocalypses composed by a Jew in the Middle Ages, Abraham Abulafia's *Sefer ha-ʾOt* (*The Book of the Sign*). Even an extreme spiritualist like Abulafia claims:

> The coming day is the Day of Judgment,
> And it is called the day of remembrance.
> And the time of the trial has arrived,
> And the time of the end has been accomplished.
> The heaven will become earth,
> And earth will become celestial,
> Because the Lord of the trial is called by the name Yhwh
> And his judgment is one of truth,
> And his trial is upright. (*Sefer ha-ʾOt*, p. 69)

Subsequent passages repeat the message:

> Until the passage of the time of wrath and of the moment of fury
> When the new shepherd has slept,
> Then Yhwh, the Lord of Israel,
> Has aroused the heart of the shepherd;
> And he will wake from his sleep,
> And he will rouse the hearts of the sleepers of dust.
> And the dead will live. (*Sefer ha-ʾOt*, p. 78)

And again:

> He did not do this to every people and nation,
> As he did to Israel his servant and his nation
> For the sake of his Name.
> And the end of delivery and the day of redemption has arrived,
> But no one is paying attention to this issue today to know it.
> There is no redemption but by means of the name of Yhwh.
> And his redemption is not for those who do not request it
> In accordance to his Name.
> This is why I, Zekhariyahu,
> The destroyer of the building,
> And the builder of the destruction,
> Have written this small book
> By the name of Adonay, the small,
> In order to disclose in it the secret of Yhwh the great.
>   (*Sefer ha-ʾOt*, p. 76)

There is no doubt that the "new shepherd" is none other than Abulafia himself, or, as he calls himself in this book, "Zekhariyahu the Shepherd." Though one of the most propagandistic among the Kabbalists, as is evident from his attempt to speak with the pope and numerous efforts to disseminate his messianic Kabbalah to Christians, Abulafia's language in this apocalypse is strongly reminiscent of the anti-Christian attacks found in earlier apocalypses. For example:

> The end of abomination has arrived
> And behold, the destruction of the worshippers of the Cross
>   has come
> Because God has examined and tested by means of his Name
> The heart of his servants. (*Sefer ha-ʾOt,* p. 68)

The poetic and allegorical qualities of Abulafia's work have something to do with the solemnity of the message. Later apocalypses composed in Sabbatean circles, such as those by Nathan of Gaza and another by an anonymous Sabbatean believer, lack the poetic quality of Abulafia's *Sefer ha-ʾOt.*

⮞ ON THE PHENOMENOLOGY OF
JEWISH APOCALYPTICISM _____

The apocalypticism represented by most Jewish sources that deal with explicit expectations, unlike implicit apocalypticism, which is much less acute, reflects a binary structure obvious in the opposition Rome–Jerusalem, in the different fates of the two Messiahs (Ben Joseph, the suffering and dying one, and Ben David, the victorious one), and in the confrontation of the latter with Armilus. The Messiah's name in Hebrew is numerically equal to 358, the same as that of his great enemy, *Nahash,* the Serpent. This binary structure is conspicuous in mesochronic discussions, though not in the macrochronic ones. It is in the former that the crisis is conceived of as an interim moment between two opposite forms of order. This form of explicit apocalypticism does not preach forms of total destruction (*annihilatio mundi*) but rather moderate forms of renewal (*reformatio mundi*). Since the gist of Jewish apocalypticism is not a hope for or a description of the total obliteration of reality but its radical restructuring, the main movement of this form of religious thought is not a gradual one that attenuates the gap between the preapocalyptic and the post-apocalyptic. Rather, Jewish apocalypticism attempts to emphasize it by creating a liminal situation pointing to events taking place between diverging types of aeons, events that both separate and connect them. It depicts a strong transformation, not a process of evolution, as we learn from Abulafia:

> The end of the change of the times has arrived, and so is the end of the order of the stars, in accordance with the [divine] attributes. And the attributes and names will change, and the languages will be mixed, and the nations and the believers will be distorted, and the diadem of the Israelite [nation] will return to its former state, and the rank of Jews will be related to the name of the essence [of God], not to the name of [his] attribute. [Then] the revealed will become concealed, and the concealed will become revealed, and the ranks of the gentiles—men and women—will be lowered and they will be vanquished, and the rank of the Jews—men and women—will ascend and rise. (*ʾOtzar ʾEden Ganuz,* MS Oxford, Bodleiana 1580, fol. 41a)

The rupture described here concerns political status more than spiritual perfection.

Unlike nonapocalyptic forms of messianism, the apocalyptic discussions in Kabbalah, including some forms of Sabbateanism, capitalized on the binary opposition of the Messiah to the Serpent (both having the same numerical value in Hebrew) and depicted the final struggle between them as that between ultimate good and evil. Thus, popular apocalyptic mythology was not abandoned but was reinterpreted in metaphysical terms. So, for example, we learn from a manuscript fragment of Shlomo Molkho:

> Abel is Moses, who is Abel, because all the deliverances are done by him, because his soul will transmigrate into the Messiah. And this is why he [Moses] has been buried abroad. "What is the gain of man from all his labor that he labors under the sun," if the redemption does not come? And he [Solomon] answered: "One generation goeth another generation cometh," namely, it is a necessity that the Messiah will come, because he is the power of Satan [and] the Serpent and he removed the impurity of the Serpent from the world; and this is the reason that he goes, because in the very moment and time that Israel will repent, they will immediately be _____ every generation there was a person [stemming] from _____ prepared to become the Messiah, and to fulfill what _____ tion goeth and another generation cometh, and earth _____ not subsist without the Messiah, because of the impu- _____ eres and comes from the power of the seventh lower _____ oscow-Guensberg, 302)

_____ historically imminent, dependent on repentance, and _____ confrontation. This form of metaphysical myth had a _____ atean apocalypticism.

_____ xplicit apocalypticism believed in and sometimes even _____ ne commonly related to preaching the need to repent. _____ apocalyptic expectations implies a supernatural revo- _____ n that exploits potentialities inherent in ordinary _____ tween the recurrent emphasis that apocalyptic litera- _____ emergence of worldviews based on more stable, natu- _____ nption is evident. These latter occur in many of the _____ Ages.

_____ ontinuation, apocalyptic salvation involves drastic _____ nst an existing order of things. Apocalypticism strives _____ nmunity, whether a tribe or a nation. It starts not only _____ t also from quandaries related to the specific vicissi- _____ ome points of view, this is an escapist approach, espe- _____ divine power.

_____ t in the Middle Ages, either in the case of different philosophical strands, or in the diverse forms of Kabbalah, brought to the fore more articulated forms of spirituality, ultimately dependent on Greek sources and sometimes influenced by Sufi spirituality. These moved away from the old vision of salvation in terms of national, objective, temporal, and geographical changes: apocalypticism, and even some forms of messianism, have been understood in these new terms, which emphasize changes, but of a nature that prefers spiritual changes over material ones. This new approach did not obliterate beliefs in more general apocalyptic messianism, either in the masses or among some of the elite. Even extreme expressions of spiritual salvation were not automatically divorced from apocalyptic elements, either because of political reasons (i.e., because they had to address large audiences), or because their vision was more complex than a simple subscription to one form of religiosity. Interpretations of apocalypticism in spiritualistic terms should, therefore, be seen not as automatically obliterating the impact of more objective forms of apocalypticism but as one of the possible modes of its appropriation. There is no reason to create a stark contrast between an objective apocalyptic consciousness and its spiritualization, conceiving of them as completely incompatible.

From this perspective, the existence of apocalyptic discussions and treatises among some medieval mystics, as in the *Zohar* and Abraham Abulafia, should be seen as a case of addressing different issues on different levels. In describing Kabbalistic literature of the thirteenth century, we may assume a coexistence of different forms of discourse that deal with both spiritual and corporeal forms of salvation. Abraham Abulafia, a mystic who conceived of himself as a Messiah, composed at least one book that should be considered as belonging to the genre of the apocalypse. He also engaged issues related to spiritual redemption, both within this apocalyptic treatise and elsewhere in his writings. The detailed analysis of his vision of the end-time will help one understand not only the view of a mystical Messiah but also the complexities of eschatological issues found in bodies of literature belonging to later phases of Jewish mysticism. Thus, for example, we can discern that the coexistence of a variety of meanings of the term Messiah (explicitly identified with both the human person and the independent Agent Intellect) did not preclude a more popular usage involving the person who will bring redemption by his power. (See Abulafia's commentary on *Sefer ha-Melitz,* MS Rome-Angelica 38, fol. 9a.) The power of the human Messiah, however, is dependent on his spiritual attainment, namely, the union of his intellect with the Agent Intellect understood as a cosmic entity. By establishing a link with the spiritual world, the messianic figure is able to change the course of events in the mundane world.

From another perspective, apocalypticism was more concerned with the violent break occurring in history due to the intervention of supernatural powers, either those of God, or of the Messiah conceived of as a supernatural warrior. According to most of the Jewish apocalyptic visions, the Messiah would be a scion of David. Therefore, the break in history would be done by a person, extraordinary as he may be, who was somehow related to the glorious past. God, too, is conceived of as a savior; however, the extraordinary intervention of supernal figures will be obvious only because their redemptive action is not yet visible in the ordinary sequence of events. Though invisibly present throughout history, the apocalyptic Messiah and the apocalyptic God, both conceptualized as warrior figures, refrain from acting salvifically now, if only by creating a crisis of the present order. However, the transcendent, nonpersonalistic Messiahs of the ecstatic Kabbalah—namely, the angel Metatron and the Agent Intellect, or the *sefirah* of *Malkut* in the case of the theosophical-theurgical Kabbalah, are omnipresent salvific entities. No crisis makes manifest their miraculous intervention, but rather the perfection of the present order, that is, the human intellect in the ecstatic Kabbalah, and the Kabbalistic performance of the commandments in the case of the theosophical school.

To a certain extent, this is also the case with regard to the conception of the Messiah as combating the evil powers in the present, as we have seen in the passage of Shlomo Molkho cited above. The apocalyptic approach to crisis deals fundamentally with horizontal fields. That is to say, apocalypticism presupposes a dramatic change in the present order of reality but sees the next step in terms of a continuation with the present, despite the crisis in the world. On the other hand, some of the Kabbalistic systems discussed above may be better described as vertical, because the human Messiah does not descend into history, nor have his goal achieved within the normal experiences of this world, but achieves his destiny by adhering to another, spiritual world. It is this "vertical" move that allows the mystic to experience redemption now. The nature of the supernal Messiah and his constant presence ensure an experience that is immediately available to the elite, one unrelated to the advent of any historical redemptive figure.

The Kabbalistic treatments analyzed above moved in three different directions, each so powerful that it marginalized crisis-oriented apocalyptic and the political versions of messianism. First, there was an inward movement among some Kabbalists, one more powerful than even that of the Jewish philosophers. Second, among the theosophical-theurgical Kabbalists there was a movement above toward the heavenly world reminiscent of the apocalyptic authors of intertestamental Judaism. Finally, there was an activist political approach found among those Kabbalists who resorted to magical practices. An analysis of the various forms of messianism can detect two major developments related to these three approaches and also to Judaism in general. In addition to the more historical and nationally oriented forms of religion represented in the Bible and rabbinic literature, some forms of Kabbalah offered a more inward version, influenced by Greek philosophy, as well as a more cosmic version, influenced by astrological views. By detecting the ultimate flaw less in outward history and more in the various spiritual domains, such as the psychological or noetic processes or the divine or the demonic forces, Kabbalah made those realms the main subject of discussion. It should be emphasized, however, that when contemplated from a modern skeptical point of view, the three realms may be conceived of as more orderly and controllable than the political world, where the play of powers is hardly predictable. Even a flaw in the divine system is still understood as part of the possibilities inherent in a set system and can be therefore repaired. There is a rationale, a certain inner logic, in the theosophical-theurgical Kabbalah transcending the totally mythical discourse concerning the Messiah and his deeds in more popular apocalypses.

The soteriology of this brand of speculative Kabbalah is built on the double assumption that God's realm on high should be restored, and also on the assumption that this restoration can be achieved with tools taken from ordinary religious life, that is, the performance of the commandments. When God's absolute reign over historical processes was envisaged as weakened or flawed, humanity was conceived of as being called to help toward consolidating it through devotion to the perfect system of behavior, namely, *halakic* obligation. Thus, a certain "rationalizing" picture of the bond between God and humanity emerges. Humans are responsible for and in the case of the Kabbalists even able to know the reason for the flaw in the divine. Humans also have the tools to repair it. What should be stressed is the fact that most Kabbalists, unlike the more apocalyptically oriented Jewish thinkers, took as their point of departure no national and religious catastrophes, such as the destruction of the Temple (a historical event), but rather the sin of Adam, a prehistorical or metahistorical event that took place before the formation of a Jewish nation and kingdom.

During the Middle Ages regular and ordinary Jewish life had to a great extent acquired a new sense rooted in the awareness that the Jews, more especially the Kabbalists, may and should perfect basic processes shaping reality in general and human nature in particular. This is most evident in the ecstatic-mystical Kabbalah, where the study of philosophy and the practice of mystical techniques were available and recommended tools for generating "messianic" experiences of individuals. Apocalypticism had been projected into the spiritual realm of the individual.

⌒ BIBLIOGRAPHY _____

Aescoly, Aaron Zeev. 1987. *Jewish Messianic Movements* (in Hebrew). 2nd ed. Jerusalem: Mossad Bialik.

Baras, Zvi, ed. 1983. *Messianism and Eschatology: A Collection of Essays* (in Hebrew). Jerusalem: Zalman Shazar Center.

Berger, Abraham. 1959. "The Messianic Self-Consciousness of Abraham Abulafia—A Tentative Evaluation." In *Essays on Jewish Life and Thought Presented in Honor of Salo Wittmayer Baron,* 1:55–61. 3 vols. New York: Columbia University Press.

———. "Captive at the Gate of Rome: The Story of a Messianic Motif." *Proceedings of the American Academy for Jewish Research* 44:1–17.

Berger, David. 1980. "Three Typological themes in Early Jewish Messianism: Messiah Son of Joseph, Rabbinic Calculations, and the Figure of Armilus." *Association for Jewish Studies Review* 10:141–64.

Bloch, Joshua. 1952. *On the Apocalyptic in Judaism.* Philadelphia: Dropsie College.

Dan, Joseph. 1988. "The Emergence of Messianic Mythology in the 13th Century Kabbalah in Spain." In *Occident and Orient: A Tribute to the Memory of A. Schreiber,* 57–68. Leiden: E. J. Brill.

Eisenstein, J. D. 1928. *'Otzar ha-Wikkuhim.* New York: Y. Eisenstein.

Eliot, Rachel. 1986. "Messianic Expectations and Spiritualization of Religious Life in the Sixteenth Century." *Revue des Études Juives* 155:35–49.

Even Shemuel, Yehuda, ed. 1954. *Midreshei Geʾullah: Pirqei ha-ʿApocalypsah ha-Yehudit.* 2nd ed. Tel Aviv: Mossad Bialik.

Idel, Moshe. 1983. "Types of Redemptive Activities in the Middle Ages" (in Hebrew). In Baras 1983, 253–79.

———. 1990. "The Beginnings of the Kabbalah in North Africa? The Forgotten Document of R. Yehuda ben Nissim ibn Malka" (in Hebrew). *Peʾamim* 43:8–12.

Jankelevitch, Vladimir. 1965. "L'esperance et la fin des temps." In *La conscience juive, face à l'histoire: Le Pardon,* edited by Eliane Amado Levy-Valensi and Jean Halperin, 7–21. Paris: Presses Universitaires de France.

Jellinek, A. 1988. "'Sefer Ha-Ot': Apokalypse des Pseudo-Propheten und Pseudo-Messias Abraham Abulafia." In *Jubelschrift zum Siebzigsten Geburtstage des Prof. Dr. H. Graetz,* 65–85. Breslau: F. Schottlander.

Kaufmann, David. 1897. "Un poeme messianique de Salomon Molkho." *Revue des Études Juives* 34:121–25.

Lerner, Robert E. 1983. *The Powers of Prophecy.* Berkeley: University of California Press.

Levi, Israel. 1880. "Apocalypses dans le Talmud." *Revue des Études Juives* 1:108–14.

Liebes, Yehuda. 1986. "Jonas as Messiah ben Joseph" (in Hebrew). In *Studies in Jewish Mysticism, Philosophy, and Ethical Literature, Presented to Isaiah Tishby,* edited by J. Dan and J. Hacker, 269–311. Jerusalem: Magnes Press.

———. 1993a. *Studies in Jewish Myth and Jewish Messianism.* Translated by Batya Stein. Albany: SUNY Press.

———. 1993b. *Studies in the Zohar.* Translated by A. Schwartz, S. Nakache, and P. Peli. Albany: SUNY Press.

Mann, Jacob. 1925–26. "The Messianic Movements in the Period of the First Crusades" (in Hebrew). *Ha-Teqqufah* 23:243–61; 24:335–58.

Marx, Alexander. 1921. "Maʾamar ʿal Shenat ha-Ge-ullah" (in Hebrew). *Ha-Tzofeh le-Hokmat Yisrael* 5:194–202.

Patai, Raphael. 1979. *The Messiah Texts.* Detroit: Wayne State University Press.

Porush, J. E., ed. 1989. *Sefer Shaʿarei Tzedeq* (in Hebrew). Jerusalem: Makhon Shaʿarei Ziv.

Ruderman, David. 1991. "Hope Against Hope: Jewish and Christian Messianic Expectations in the Late Middle Ages." In *Exile and Diaspora: Studies in the History of the Jewish People Presented to Prof. Haim Beinart,* 185–202. Jerusalem: Makhon ben Tzvi.

Saperstein, Marc, ed. 1992. *Essential Papers on Messianic Movements and Personalities in Jewish History.* New York: New York University Press.

Scholem, Gershom. *Be-'Iqvot Mashiah* (in Hebrew). Jerusalem: Sifrei Tarshish.

———. 1972. *The Messianic Idea in Judaism.* New York: Schocken Books.

———. 1973. *Sabbatai Sevi: The Mystical Messiah, 1626–1676.* Translated by R. J. Z. Werblowsky. Princeton: Princeton University Press.

———. 1974. *Studies and Texts Concerning the History of Sabbateanism and its Metamorphoses* (in Hebrew). Jerusalem: Mossad Bialik.

———. 1991. *Studies in Sabbateanism* (in Hebrew). Edited by Yehuda Liebes. Tel Aviv: 'Am 'Oved.

Sharot, Stephen. 1982. *Messianism, Mysticism, and Magic: A Sociological Analysis of Jewish Religious Movements.* Chapel Hill: University of North Carolina Press.

Silver, Hillel. 1978. *A History of Messianic Speculation in Israel from the First through the Seventeenth Centuries.* Gloucester, Mass.: Peter Smith.

Tamar, David. 1984. "The Messianic Dreams and Visions of R. Hayyim Vital." *Shalem* 4:211–29.

Tishby, Isaiah. 1985. *Messianism in the Time of the Expulsion from Spain and Portugal.* Jerusalem: Merkaz Zalman Shazar.

———. 1990. *The Messianic Idea in Jewish Thought: A Study Conference in Honor of the Eightieth Birthday of Gershom Scholem* (in Hebrew). Jerusalem: Israeli Academy of Science.

Werblowsky, R. J. Zwi. 1973. "Mysticism and messianism, the case of Hasidism." In *Man and His Salvation: Essays in Memory of S. G. F. Brandon,* 305–14. Manchester: Manchester University Press.

15

Islamic Apocalypticism in the Classic Period

Saïd Amir Arjomand
State University of New York, Stony Brook

THE APOCALYPTIC ORIGINS of Islam were ironed out of Islamic historiography and have generally been ignored in modern scholarship.[1] The modern secondary literature on the subject has, furthermore, largely focused on the apocalyptic features of sectarian Shiʿite Islam while neglecting those of the mainstream Sunni Islam. To rectify these shortcomings, this essay will pay full attention to the place of apocalypticism in the origins of Islam and the *Qurʾān* itself (first section). The next two sections will examine the sociopolitical setting of the first two centuries of Islam as the formative period of the Islamic apocalyptic tradition. The reification of apocalyptic traditions through astrological determination, another topic that has not received adequate attention in the secondary literature, is treated in the fourth section. The next section covers the orthodox response to apocalypticism in the form of attempts to contain it. The chiliastic movements and instances of action motivated by apocalyptic beliefs are too numerous to be covered in one article. The sixth section is therefore inevitably selective and focuses on the most spectacular instances of the realization of apocalyptic in revolutionary action by the Ismaʿili Shiʿites in the tenth and twelfth centuries. The final section alludes to the plethora of popular chiliastic movements beyond the classic period, which comes to an end with the Mongol invasion in the thirteenth century.

☞ THE QURʾĀN AND THE ORIGINS OF ISLAMIC APOCALYPTICISM _____

There is ample evidence of apocalypticism in the early, Meccan verses of the *Qurʾān*, which speak of the coming of the Hour as the prelude to resurrection: "The Hour has drawn near and the moon is split" (Q. 54:1); "The Hour is coming, no doubt of it" (Q. 22:7; 40:59[61]); "Haply the Hour is near" (Q. 33:63; 42:17[16]); and "surely the earthquake of the Hour is a mighty thing" (Q. 22:1).[2] The apocalyptic Hour is the earthly prelude to eschatology. It is the hour of calamity that precedes resurrection. The *Qur'ān* uses a number of mostly obscure catastrophic terms for the occurrence at the Hour which the early commentators identify with the Day of Resurrection (*yawm al-qiyāma*). These include *āzifa* ("the imminent") (Q. 40:18; 53:58), *wāqi'a* ("terror") (Q. 56; 69:15; TZ 4:444–45), *rājifa* and *rādifa* ("quake" and "second quake") (Q. 79:6–7), *ṣākhkha* ("blast") (Q. 80:34–36), *ghāshiya* ("enveloper") (Q. 88), *zilzila* and *zalzāl* ("earthquake") (Q. 99:1), and *qāri'a* ("clatterer") (Q. 69:4, 101; 101:1–3). In addition, the appearance of the beast ("We will bring forth the Beast from the earth to speak upon them" [Q. 27:82]), as well as such cosmic cataclysms as the smoke (*dukhān*) (Q. 44:10), the rolling up (*takwīr*) (Q. 81) of the sun, the darkening of the stars and the movement of the mountains (Q. 81:2–4), the splitting (*infiṭār;* Q. 82) of the sky, the scattering of the stars and the inundation of the seas (Q. 82:2–4) are evidently the signs of the Day of Resurrection "when the tombs are overthrown" (Q. 82:5).

The vision of the sixth seal in the book of Revelation (Rev. 6:12–14) suggests itself as a likely source of inspiration for the cosmic disorder and destruction spoken of in these verses. The image of the apocalyptic earthquake (Q. 99:1–3), "When the earth is shaken with a mighty shaking, and earth brings forth her burdens, and Man says, 'What ails her?'" seems to echo 4 Ezra 4:42 ("For just as a woman in travail . . . do these places hasten to give back those things that were committed to them from the beginnings"). The apocalyptic figure of the beast (*dābba*) of the earth is probably the "second beast, like a bear (*dôb*)" of Dan. 7:5. In contrast to the Judeo-Christian apocalyptic beasts, however, the Koranic beast is relatively benign. Accord-ing to one influential tradition attributed to the Prophet, the beast comes out with the staff of Moses and the seal of Solomon. He brightens the faces of the believers with the staff and brands the infidels with the seal so that the two groups can be distinguished (*Fitan*, 403). The ancient myth of primal combat between the God of creation and the beasts of chaos that had given rise to the beasts of the Judeo-Christian apocalypses is now totally submerged under the Islamic monotheistic doctrine of salvation.[3]

The *Qur'ān* also speaks (14:49) of "the day the earth shall be transformed to other than the earth." The early commentators variously interpreted this verse to mean that the earth will become white like silver; it will become a white loaf from which the believers can eat; the earth will become silver and the sky gold; and similar transformations (TR 7:41–42). The Smoke that descends from the sky and envelops and suffocates the earth (TR 10:114–15; *Fitan*, 364–67) must be the smoke from the cosmic conflagration of the end (Cumont 1931). The transforma-tion of the mountains shows clear traces of Zoroastrian influence, presumably mediated through the Judeo-Christian apocalyptic lore (see chapter 2). The mountains will be pulverized into dust (Q. 56:4–6; TR 11:7), or become like plucked tufts of wool (Q. 70:9; 101:5; TR 11:262–63; 12:156; TZ 5:782–83; Gätje 1996, 176–77). Some mediated Zoroastrian influence can also be seen in the signs of social disorder that accompany cosmic cataclysms: "And when the Blast shall sound, upon the day when a man shall flee from his brother, his mother, his father, his consort, his sons" (Q. 80:33–36; TT 30:61–62; TR 11:398). The Muslim traditions elaborate on the distortion of order in time, nature, and social relations at the end of time (*Fitan*, 390).

At the Hour, "the Trumpet (ṣūr) shall be blown; that is the Day of the Threat. . . . And listen thou for the day when the caller shall call from a near place. On the day they hear the Cry (ṣayḥa) in truth, that is the day of coming forth" (Q. 50:19, 40–41). The Cry is not unprecedented; it is a portent of God's physical destruction of the nations which had disowned their prophets in sacred history (Q. 11:67, 94). But the final day has no precedent. It is indeed "the day when the earth is split asunder about them as they hasten forth" (Q. 50:43).

What follows when the trumpet is blown naturally captured the imagination of the Qurʾān commentators. According to Surah 39:

> For the Trumpet shall be blown, and whosoever is in the heavens and whosoever is in the earth shall swoon, save whom God wills. Then it shall be blown again, and lo, they shall stand, beholding. And the earth shall shine with the light of its Lord. . . . (Q. 39:69–70)

This final transfiguration of the earth is presumably "the new creation" (Q. 14:22).

According to the companion of the Prophet, Anas b. Mālik, Muhammad identified the exceptions to the universal death to come after the first blow as Gabriel, Michael, Isrāfīl (the blower of the trumpet), and the Angel of Death (ʿIzrāʾīl). The learned Jewish convert Kaʿb al-Aḥbār (d. 654), however, added eight angelic bearers of the divine throne (ʿarsh) mentioned in Q. 69:17,[4] raising the total number of exceptions to twelve (TR 9:420–21). As one would expect, the Shiʿite commentators expand on the details of the termination of life on earth and in the heavens and the ensuing resurrection. According to a tradition attributed to ʿAlī b. al-Ḥusayn, the fourth Imam, Isrāfīl blows the trumpet several times. The people of the earth die first. Then die the people of the heavens, the angels, and then the four archangels one by one until it is Isrāfīl's turn. Then God (al-jabbār) himself blows the trumpet, and there remains no other living being in the cosmos. God blows the trumpet again, and the angelic carriers of the throne are resurrected, followed by the people of the earth, with Gabriel descending to the Baqīʿ cemetery, where the Prophet and his family are buried, and leading Muhammad out of his grave first. The commentary on the following verse is attributed to the sixth Imam: "The Lord of the earth with whose light it shall shine is said to be the Imam of the earth" (TQ 2:252–53). Here we have the apocalyptic figure of the Imam of the end of time, which has no counterpart in Sunni Islam.

The references to the apocalyptic personalities of the Judeo-Christian tradition in the Qurʾān are few. Elijah (Ilyās) is mentioned as a monotheistic prophet (Q. 37:123, also 6:85; 37:130), but not as a figure of the end of time. The variant of Mesopotamian origin, Khir, who was to appear in the traditions and gain special popularity in later Islamic apocalyptic lore, is not mentioned at all. If we accept the common identification in Sunni legend, Enoch is mentioned twice as Idrīs among the prophets (Q. 19:57; 21:85) and thus functions as an apocalyptic figure: "He was a true man, a Prophet; we raised him to a high place" (Q. 19:57). There is also a rare tradition on Elijah and Enoch (khanūk) at the end of time (Fitan, 329) that follows a Christian tradition of identifying the two unnamed prophetic witnesses of the book of Revelation (11:1–13) as Elijah and Enoch (see Bousset 1896, chap. 14; VanderKam 1995, 181–82).[5]

The Paraclete is referred to in Q 61:6, where Jesus son of Mary gives the children of Israel "good tidings of a messenger who shall come after me and whose name shall be Ahmad (ismūhu aḥmadu)." W. Montgomery Watt has argued persuasively for an adjectival reading of the term aḥmad (Watt 1953, 110–17). Given one possible meaning of the term as "greater in praising," the Koranic statement is a reasonable paraphrase of the promise of the coming of the Paraclete in John 16:13–14: "When the Spirit of truth comes . . . he will not be speaking of his own accord but will only say what he has been told; and he will reveal to you the things to come. He will glorify me. . . ." Quite apart from the identity of the terms for "praising" and "glorifying" the Lord, this passage is substantively important because it corresponds exactly to the Koranic concept of revelation as the unaltered recitation, by the Prophet, of the divine words brought down by Gabriel (Q. 75:16–19; TZ 4:648–49; Gätje 1996, 48), who is indeed the [holy/trustworthy] Spirit (*rūḥ*) (Q. 5:110 [109]: 16:102[104]: 26:193). The *Qur'ān* (Recitation) is the latest revealed portion of the heavenly book, the "Preserved Tablet" (*lawḥ maḥfūẓ*) (Q. 85:22). The influence of the Gospel of John may have been reinforced through Manicheism (Widengren 1955, 58–62). Indeed, Bīrūnī's statement is a striking presentation of the great Babylonian prophet Mānī (d. 277) as the forerunner of Muhammad: "In his gospel . . . he says that he is the Paraclete announced by the Messiah, and that he is the seal of the prophets (i.e., the last of them)" (al-Bīrūnī 1879, 190). Be that as it may, the Muslim tradition came to consider Ahmad a variant of Muhammad and another name for the Prophet (TZ 4:513; Gätje 1996, 69–70), and identified him with the Paraclete (Ibn Rabbān 1922, 140–41). Ahmad and other variants of Muhammad were also identified with the Immanuel promised by Isaiah (Isa. 7:14) and the prophet whose coming was foretold by a host of other prophets. The idea of the Paraclete is thus de-apocalypticized to confirm the "realized messianism" of triumphal Islam (Ibn Rabbān 1922, 95–138; Lazarus-Yafeh 1992, chap. 4).

What remained inescapably apocalyptic, however, was the belief in the second coming of Christ. Jesus "is the sign of the Hour" (Q. 43:61). The Prophet's companion, ʿAbd Allāh b. ʿAbbās, associated the coming down of Jesus with the apocalyptic Smoke amidst which he herds people into the place of resurrection (TR 10:115). Jesus will return to Jerusalem and kill the Antichrist (*dajjāl*). This assured Jerusalem a central place in the topography of Islamic apocalyptic tradition. The Sea of Tiberias, on whose shores Jesus had revealed himself to the disciples after the crucifixion (John 21), also figured in the Islamic apocalyptic topography. In one interesting set of traditions, Gog and Magog first appear there and "drink its water dry" (*Fitan*, 356–60). Later commentators somewhat modify the picture to celebrate Islam. After slaying the Antichrist, Jesus kills the swine and breaks the crosses, destroys churches and synagogues, but confirms the Muslim prayer leader and prays behind him (Baiḍāwī, translated in Gätje 1996, 129). One curious tradition identifies the Muslim prayer leader of the end of time as the caliph of the [southern Arabian] migrants (Madelung 1986a, 167–68), but he is generally identified as the Mahdi (*Fitan*, 352).[6]

Ezra is mentioned once in the *Qur'ān* in the diminutive form of ʿUzayr. By the time of 4 Ezra and in the subsequent literature, Ezra the scribe had become Ezra the prophet (Stone 1982, 2). Ezra was identified with Enoch and appears as the key figure in the mystical speculations of the Jewish communities of Arabia (Newby 1988, 60–61). At the beginning of 4 Ezra, which circulated not only in Syriac but also in Arabic, Ezra is clearly presented as a Second Moses (4 Ezra 14:1–6) (Knibb 1982, 62),[7] and it is as the messianic "prophet like Moses" that he enters into Islam. The assertion in the *Qur'ān* (9:30) that "the Jews say ʿUzayr is the son of God as the Christians say the Messiah is the son of God" should be understood in this light (TR 9:178). It was thus natural that the unnamed person whom God caused to die on the outskirts of the ruined city but brought back to life a hundred years later to witness the resurrection of his donkey (Q. 2:261) should be commonly identified as Ezra (Lazarus-Yafeh 1992, 56–58), even though Jeremiah was sometimes preferred, just as the ruined city was taken to mean Jerusalem (TTkh 1:666).[8] This verse, as we shall see, formed the basis for the apocalyptic conception of the century in early Islam. Furthermore, the tradition that secrets had been written in a book and kept secret begins with 4 Ezra (Knibb 1982, 65). In the Muslim tradition, this was combined with the legend of the book thrown into the sea by Daniel (TTkh 1:2566–67).[9] It is interesting to note that the legend of Daniel is traceable to ʿAbd Allāh b. Salām (d. 663), the learned rabbi who accepted Muhammad as the prophet of the end of time, the gentile "brother of Moses" (*Life,* 240) (Grotzfeld 1969, 84).

The *Qurʾān* does not mention Daniel. This is surprising in view of the evident influence of the book of Daniel, which we must assume was mediated by Judeo-Christian apocalyptic lore, as well as the Gnostic-Mandean literature (Widengren 1950, 59–61). The reference to Abraham as the friend of God (Dan. 3:35) is carried over to the *Qurʾān* (4:124). Gabriel and Michael, the two archangels who are introduced to the Hebrew Bible in the book of Daniel, are both mentioned in the *Qurʾān*.[10] In fact, Gabriel's role in hierophany and audition (Dan. 10:4–11:1) becomes central in the *Qurʾān,* and the Islamic tradition sees Gabriel not only as the angel of revelation but also as Muhammad's frequent counselor (Pedersen 1954–, 2:363). Last but not least, the Danielic notion of setting the seal on prophecy (Dan. 9:24), as we shall see, crucially influenced Muhammad's idea of final prophecy.

The earliest reference to Daniel occurs in the account of the conquest of Susa (Shūsh) in 638, six years after Muhammad's death. After entering Susa in a suitably apocalyptic fashion to be described presently, the conquering Muslims were then shown the remains of Daniel and found a seal/signet ring depicting a man between two lions. The seal was first taken but was returned to the body by ʿUmar's order. The commander of the Muslim forces "had the body wrapped in shrouds and the Muslims buried it" (TTkh 1:2567; English trans. 13:147). According to a more interesting tradition, upon the conquest of Shūshtar (Tustar), where the presumed tomb of Daniel was located, the Muslims found a book in the treasury of the Persian commander, Hurmuzān, above the head of a corpse identified as Daniel. "They carried the book to ʿUmar, who was the first Arab to read it and sent it to Kaʿb, who copied it in Arabic. In it was what will occur of civil disorders (*fitan*)" (*Fitan,* 18–19).

With the civil wars of 656–661 and 680–692, the term *fitan* was soon to become synonymous with *malāḥim*—apocalyptic woes and tribulations on which a book is attributed to Daniel. I suspect that this tradition anachronistically renders *malāḥim* as *fitan,* but its referent is most probably the apocalyptic battles of the kings of the South and the North, and especially the battles of the end of time against earthly kings in which the archangels Gabriel and Michael will lead the army of angels against earthly kings (Dan. 10:13–12:1). The use of the term *malḥama* for the woes and tribulations of the end of time is striking. Its derivation from the Hebrew cognate, *milḥāmâ* ("war"), has not been explored; nor has the possible influence of the apocalyptic "War Rules" in the Dead Sea Scrolls (see chapter 4). But if my reading of this tradition on the content of the book of Daniel is correct, the original derivation of the *malāḥim* may be from the Danielic description of the battles of the end of time. Others doubtless thought that the book also contained the eternal wisdom that the father of humanity, Adam, had hidden in the Treasure-Cave mentioned in the Syriac texts soon to be translated into Arabic (al-Bīrūnī 1879, 300).

The idea of the dam or wall built by Alexander to keep out Gog and Magog, which represents the fifth-century C.E. fusion of the coming of these monstrous people with the legend of the building of the Caspian Gates by Alexander (Alexander 1985, 147), is elaborated in the *Qurʾān* in considerable detail (Q. 18:92–99). The account of the "Two-Horned" (*dhuʾl-qar-*

nayn) echoes the "two-horned ram" (i.e., the king of Persia) who opposes the "he-goat" (i.e., Alexander) in Dan. 8:6. But in Islamic tradition, the Two-Horned is commonly identified as Alexander, and his tale is prefaced by the story of the long sleep of the Companions of the Caves—the seven sleepers of Ephesus (Paret, 1954–, 1:691). The inhabitants of the region threatened by Gog and Magog, identified by the commentators as Bāb al-Abwāb (Gate of Gates; Darband), agreed to pay tribute to the Two-Horned for the construction of two ramparts in the mountainous passes, one of iron, the other of brass. Having completed the task, the Two-Horned told the people: "This is a mercy from my Lord. But when the promise of my Lord comes to pass, He will make it into powder; and my Lord's promise is ever true." This is immediately confirmed: "Upon that day We shall leave them surging on one another, and the Trumpet shall be blown" (Q: 18:97–99). This passage establishes the Two-Horned as an apocalyptic figure, and places the horror of the breaking of the dams holding back Gog and Magog firmly in the Islamic apocalyptic image of the end of time.[11] Last but not least, the one mention of the signs (*ashrāṭ*) of the Hour (Q. 47:20) opens the gate for the subsequent reception of the rich Judeo-Christian and Zoroastrian lore on the signs of the end. Predictably, it is Kaʿb al-Aḥbār, the expert on Judaism, who appears in the eighth-century papyri and other sources as an authority on the signs of the Hour (Khoury 1986, 249, 264–65).

The apocalyptic elements should be placed within the overall worldview of pristine Islam. According to Franz Rosenthal, "Muhammad's early preoccupation with the end of the world and his apparent belief in its imminent arrival . . . soon gave way to an attitude more congenial to him" (Rosenthal 1962, 37). This better-known attitude rested on the conviction that history was God's plan for the salvation of humanity and was "one of supreme confidence in presenting his people with a unique opportunity for salvation" as the final prophet. How much of this supreme confidence and anti-apocalyptic triumphalism reflects historical reality and how much of it is due to the flattened reconstruction of the life of the Prophet over a century after his death by Ibn Isḥāq and others must remain an open question. We know, for instance, that an anti-apocalyptic explanation of the splitting of the moon as an actual miracle performed by Muhammad is offered rather early (TT 27:84–88; TR 10:364). Rosenthal himself injects an element of doubt in his categorical statement with the following remark: "He is the final prophet (if finality is the main idea implied by the disputed expression 'seal of the prophets' in 33.40)" (1962, 37).

In fact, the grammatical dispute over its vocalization notwithstanding (TT 23:16), there can be little doubt that the notion of Seal (*khātam*) is apocalyptic. The Hebrew cognate *ḥôtām* is the messianic signet-ring of Haggai 2:23, where Yahweh declares to Zerubbabel: "I shall take you . . . and make you like a signet-ring; for I have chosen you." The apocalyptic connotation of the term is made explicit, and is, furthermore, applied to prophecy by Daniel, who speaks of the time for setting the seal on prophecy (Dan. 9:24) and is told by Gabriel to "keep the book sealed until the end of time" (Dan. 12:1). The basic tenet of primitive Islam (according to Casanova 1911, 8) was that "the time announced by Daniel and Jesus had come. Muhammad was the last prophet chosen by God to preside, at the end of time, . . . over the universal resurrection and last judgment." His argument for equating the expression "Seal of the Prophets" (*khātam al-nabiyyīn*) with "the prophet/messenger of the end of time" (*nabiy/rasūl ākhir al-zamān*) is persuasive (Casanova 1911, 18, 207–13, 228). According to one well-known tradition, used by Rāzī in his commentary on Q. 33:40, the finality of Muhammad's prophecy itself is apocalyptic: "I am Muhammad, and I am Ahmad and I am the resurrector (*ḥāshir*)—the people are resurrected upon my steps—and I am the final one—there is no prophet after me" (see TR 9:162; *Concordance* 1:470).[12] Even more decisive is the epithet "Prophet/Messenger of the *malḥama*" attested for Muhammad in several early traditions (Casanova 1911, 49–53; Ibn Saʿd 1904, 1:65; *Concordance* 6:107).

Muhammad, the Prophet of the end of time, did begin the conquest of Arabia as the Prophet of the *malḥama;* his apocalyptic battle was none other than the battle of Badr in 624, when God sent down three thousand angels to fight alongside his army (Q. 3:123–25). The Muslim tradition follows Daniel in having Gabriel and Michael each lead a thousand angelic troops to the right and the left of Muhammad (and archangel Isrāfīl is added at the head of another thousand to reach the number given in the *Qurʾān*).[13] Tradition also considers the battle of Badr as "the day of redemption/deliverance (*furqān*)" mentioned in Q. 8:41 as a parallel to Exodus 14:13 (Wagtendonk 1969, 261–62).

Other apocalyptic traditions are also worth noting. One tradition, suggestive of the idea of a preexistent Last Adam, attributes to Muhammad the statement: "I was the first of men to be created and the last of the prophets to be chosen" (Ibn Saʿd 1904, 1:96). Another reports Muhammad saying: "I was chosen prophet together with the Hour; it almost came ahead of me" (*Concordance* 3:29). In a third tradition, the seal of prophecy is associated with Elijah, the prophet like Moses. An old Jewish authority is reported to have told Kaʿb al-Aḥbār that he had read in the Torah that God would send "a prophet at the end of time . . . with a red spot in his eyes and the seal of prophecy between his shoulders. He will ride an Arabian ass and be an Arab from the descendants of Ishmael" (TQ 2:180). It should also be noted that the early traditions (*Concordance* 2:9) consider the seal of prophecy a physical mark of prophecy between Muhammad's shoulders, or alternatively on his chest, variously described as a dark mole or a lump the size of a pigeon's egg (*Life,* 80; see also Ibn Saʿd 1904, 1:106–7, 2:131–32).[14] The most curious of these traditions is reported in a tenth-century Persian translation of Tabari's *Commentary.* When the Prophet was approaching death, a certain ʿUkkāsha insisted on beating him on the chest with a stick in retaliation for having been beaten on his bare chest by the Prophet and injured years earlier. When the frail Prophet agreed to bare his chest, the Seal of Prophecy on it became visible. ʿUkkāsha dropped the stick and kissed the Prophet's chest, saying the purpose of the whole charade had been to do so because he had heard anyone whose face touched the Seal would not go to hell. The Prophet said, "O ʿUkkāsha, you are indeed spared the fire of hell."[15] What is interesting about this tradition is that it reports an event at the end of Muhammad's life and not early in his career when his apocalyptic preoccupations are acknowledged.

Nor are other indications of apocalyptic expectation centered on the Prophet at the end of his life lacking. ʿUmar, one of his closest companions and the second caliph, reportedly refused to give the Prophet on his deathbed ink to write his will, saying: "The Prophet will not die until we conquer the cities [of Rome], and even if he dies, we shall expect him as the children of Israel expected Moses" (Ibn Saʿd 1904, 4:38). When Muhammad did die, ʿUmar stood up in the mosque and said: "Do not let me hear anyone say Muhammad is dead. It is only that his soul is summoned for a gathering, as Moses son of ʿAmran was separated from his people for forty days." Others too denied the death of the Prophet, asserting: "He is not dead; his soul has been taken to the heavens as Moses' soul was taken" (Ibn Saʿd 1904, 4:53). Some of Muhammad's companions thus expected that he would return as "a prophet like Moses." It should be pointed out that all this is consistent with the common belief in late antiquity that

Moses had not died and would return as one of the two unnamed witnesses of Rev. 11:1–13 (VanderKam 1995, 181).

Much more apocalyptic material enters Islam after the death of the Prophet. Jewish messianic expectations at the time of the rise of Islam are well attested in Jewish, Greek, and Syriac sources (Lewis 1950).[16] A prophet like Moses "from among their brethren" was expected on the basis of Deut. 18:15 and 18 (see Ibn Saʿd 1904, 1:103; al-Bīrūnī 1879, 22–23). Not long before the Syriac-Byzantine apocalypse known as the *Pseudo-Methodius* indignantly reported the saying by the Muslim conquerors that there is no redeemer (*perūqā*) for the Christians (Alexander 1985, 154), the Jews of Damascus made the conquering ʿUmar the object of their apocalyptic expectations by acclaiming him the *Fārūq* (redeemer):

> They spoke thus: "Greeting to thee, O Fārūq! Thou art the lord of Aelia [Capitolina = Jerusalem]. We adjure thee by God, do not return until you conquer it." He asked them as to the Dajjāl, whereupon they answered: "He will be one of the tribe of Benjamin. By God, you, O nation of the Arabs, you will kill him at a distance of ten to twenty yards from the gate of Lydda." (al-Bīrūnī 1879, 196)

An earlier tradition is emphatic that it was not the Prophet but the "people of the Book" who called ʿUmar the Fārūq (TTkh 1:2729).[17]

The Dajjāl—an adjective of Syriac origin[18]—is also referred to as "the deceiving Messiah" (*masīḥ al-dajjāl*) and brands those he has deceived with his mark like cattle (Bousset 1896, 200). In due course, the Dajjāl assumed the identity of the Antichrist in the Islamic tradition. He is the one-eyed false prophet of the end of time (TR 9:457). He is also the first apocalyptic figure behind whom a real historical person can be found. It is intriguing that we find the Dajjāl mentioned in connection with the conquest of Susa in 638, as is Daniel. The monks and priests of Susa reportedly "looked down upon the Muslims, shouting,

> "Hey, you Arabs, do not bother, for no one will conquer this fortress but the Dajjāl, or the forces that have the Dajjāl in their midst." . . . Ṣāfī ibn Ṣayyād was with [the] cavalry. . . . Ṣāfī, furious as he was, strode to the gate of Susa, and, kicking it with his foot, shouted: "Open up!" and then it blew open! (TTkh 1:2565; English trans., 13:146)

Ibn Ṣayyād is given a different first name, ʿAbd Allāh, in other traditions. He is once reported to have asked Muhammad to acknowledge him as a messenger of God and engaged with him in a clipt and enigmatic exchange about the apocalyptic Smoke Verse (Q. 44:10; see *Fitan*, 334) (Morabia 1979). This Jewish practitioner of the Merkabah mysteries was the first historical person identified as the Dajjāl (see Halperin 1976, 223–26; Morabia 1979).

⌖ HISTORY AND THE APOCALYPTIC TRADITIONS _____

The conspicuous place of the near-synonymous terms *fitna* ("civil disorder") and *malḥama* ("tribulation/war") point to the unusual importance of history as the matrix of the Islamic apocalyptic traditions. The three civil wars (*fitan*) of classical Islam (656–61, 680–92, and 744–50 C.E.), the last of which ended with the ʿAbbasid revolution, are the easily recognizable context of a large number of apocalyptic traditions that usually take the form of *ex eventu* prophecies. As the events of these civil wars underwent apocalyptic transformation and elaboration, however, the term *fitna* itself acquired the sense of premessianic tribulation and was included among the signs of the Hour. The apocalyptic expectation with which ʿUmar had invested the projected conquest of Rome has already been mentioned. Rome (Byzantium) itself did not fall, and repeated wars against it remained a focus of apocalyptic speculation. In fact, the Muslim–Byzantine wars constituted the generative historical matrix of a considerable number of apocalyptic traditions on the tribulations of the end of time (Bashear 1991; see chapter 10 above). In addition, it is in the context of the civil wars that post-Koranic apocalypticism was born and the two foremost apocalyptic figures of the Islamic tradition, the Mahdi and the Qāʾim, arose. So did such relatively minor figures as the Sufyānī, the Qaḥṭānī, the Manṣūr and the Hādī.

The First Civil War (656–661) was considered a great disorder (*fitna*) and inspired horror in the surviving companions of the Prophet, who by then constituted the aristocracy of a vast empire of conquest. The non-Arab Muslims were few, and there is no evidence of any messianic movement to mobilize the conquered masses. The idea of *fitna* suggested disorder and drastic deterioration in the world, but the typical response was quietist rather than apocalyptic (Aguadé 1979, 72–82). This quietist response gave birth to the early neutralism (*iʿtizāl*) that is best expressed by the famous words of Abū Mūsā al-Ashʿarī that when the *fitna* befalls the Muslims, "He who sits in it is better than he who stands, he who stands better than he who walks, he who walks better than he who runs, and the silent better than the speaking and the sleeper better than the awake" (*Fitan,* 32). Nevertheless, when ʿAlī was assassinated in 661, one of his formerly Jewish Yemenite followers, ʿAbd Allāh b. Sabāʾ, who had at one time reportedly formulated the idea of the return (*rajʿa*) of Muhammad on the model of the second coming of Christ (TTkh 1:2942; Humphreys 1990, 146), claimed divinity for him, denied his death and said that Satan had been assassinated in his place. Ibn Sabāʾ may well have adopted the Danielic-Enochic image of the "one like the Son of Man" riding on the clouds,[19] as he reportedly claimed that ʿAlī was "the one who had gone on the clouds, and thunder was his voice and lightning his smile. He would indeed descend to the earth later and fill the earth with justice as it is filled with tyranny" (al-Sharastānī 1986, 1:174). The image, however, did not take root in the Islamic apocalyptic tradition, though the claim for the divinity of the Imam and denial of his death were taken over by extremist Shiʿite sects from time to time.

It is, however, the Second Civil War that marks the true birth of the apocalyptic figure of the Mahdi. As W. Madelung has shown, the dispersal in the desert in 683 of an army sent by the Umayyad caliph Yazīd against the anti-caliph ʿAbdallāh b. al-Zubayr upon hearing the news of the caliph's death generated what may be the first *ex eventu* prophecy about an unnamed restorer of faith who was later taken to be the Mahdi (Madelung 1981). Two notable historical features of the event—the pledge of allegiance by the people of Mecca between the Rukn and the Maqām, and the swallowing up (*khasf*) of an army in the desert (between Mecca and Medina)—were absorbed into apocalyptic literature. The term Mahdi, however, acquired its apocalyptic significance during that civil war, not in connection with Ibn al-Zubayr but through its application to his rival, ʿAlī's son, Muḥammad b. al-Ḥanafiyya.

The term *mahdī,* used for "the rightly-guided one," as the expected restorer of true religion and redresser of injustices, is a derivation of the root *h-d-y,* which denotes divine guidance—a Koranic notion as central to Islam as salvation is to Christianity. Unlike "savior," however, it is not an active but a passive participle. Indeed, its first attested usages are nonmessianic. However, when Mukhtār accepted the pledge of allegiance as the helper (*wazīr*) of Muḥammad b. al-Ḥanafiyya at the onset of his rebellion in Kufa in 683, the term clearly had messianic connotations:

> I have come to you from he who is in authority (*walī al-amr*), the source of virtue, the legatee (*waṣī*) of the Legatee, and the Imam the Mahdi, with an authority in which there is restoration of health, *removal of the covering.* . . . obey my command, and then rejoice and *spread the good news.* (TTkh 2:534)[20]

The apocalyptic connotations of the idea of the Mahdi were augmented under the influence of the two main groups among Mukhtār's followers. The first consisted of the southern Arabian tribes who reportedly held processions carrying ʿAlī's chair in imitation of the ark of the covenant (Madelung 1954b, 4:836). Thousands of Persian newly converted clients (*mawālī*) led by Kaysān Abū ʿAmrah, who was himself a client, constituted the second group. They were also familiar with apocalyptic beliefs, but these derived from Zoroastrian sources and included the idea of the awakening of the demon-slaying heroes from long sleep. It is quite possible that Kaysān survived Mukhtār, but in any event he organized both groups of his followers into a sect that became the major bearer of radical apocalypticism: the Kaysāniyya.

Despite the failure of Mukhtār's rebellion, the Kaysāniyya affirmed that they "hoped for a revolution (*dawla*) that would culminate in the Resurrection before the Hour" (cited in Arjomand 1996a, 492). When Muḥammad b. al-Ḥanafiyya died in the year 700, the Kaysāniyya maintained that he was in concealment or occultation in the Raḍwa mountains and would return as the Mahdi and the Qāʾim. The Kaysānī poet Kuthayyar (d. 723) said of him, "He is the Mahdi Kaʿb al-Aḥbār had told us about," and also affirmed that "he is vanished in the Raḍwa, not to be seen for a while, and with him is honey and water" (al-Masʿūdī 1970, 3:277). Another Kaysānī poet, the Sayyid al-Ḥimyarī (d. after 787), affirming that "he will not savor the taste of death" (al-Masʿūdī 1970, 3:278), testified:

> That [is] the one in authority (*walī al-amr*) and the Qāʾim . . .
> For him [is decreed] an occultation (*ghayba*); inevitably will he vanish.
> And may God bless him who enacts the occultation.
> He will pause a while, then manifest his cause
> And fill all the East and West with justice (cited in Arjomand 1996a, 493).

When Muḥammad b. al-Ḥanafiyya's son, Abū Hāshim, who had succeeded him, died childless in 717–718, some of his followers maintained that he was, like his father, the Mahdi and was alive in concealment in the Raḍwa mountains. The Kaysāniyya also spread the idea of *rajʿa*, return of the dead, especially the Imams, with the help of such Koranic precedents as the resuscitation of the Companions of the Cave. Furthermore, it is very probable in connection with the expectation of the return of this Mahdi from occultation that the term *al-qāʾim* (the Standing One, the Riser) became a major ingredient of the Shiʿite apocalyptic tradition. A valuable Syriac text, which predates Islam and is suggestive of the influence of Kaysānī Persian clients on the development of the notion, foretells that the Antichrist (*dajjāl*) will beguile the Magi by telling them that Pashūtan, one of the Zoroastrian immortals, has awakened from his sleep, "and he is the Standing One (*qāʾem*) before the Hurmizd, your God, who has appeared on earth."[21] In any event, the notion of occultation soon acquired chiliastic connotations through its association with the manifestation or *parousia* (*ẓuhūr*), of the apocalyptic Qāʾim.

The apocalyptic belief in the Qāʾim became a distinctive feature of the radical Shiʿite sects. Widengren derives the term *qāʾim* from the Aramaic Samaritan *qaʾêm* ("the living one," or "the one standing permanently") and the Syriac *qāʾem*, both of which are used to translate the Greek *ho hestōs* (the Standing One) in the Gnostic Samaritan literature (Widengren 1950, 44–49; 1955, 79). On etymological grounds, this derivation is supported by a Shiʿite tradition in which the sixth Imam allegedly explains the term *qāʾim*: "Because he rises after he has died" (al-Ṭūsī 1965/1385, 260). The substantive support for Widengren's proposition is even stronger. According to a tradition related by the chiliastic Jābir al-Juʿfī, it was ʿAlī himself who spoke of the Second Christ (*al-masīḥ al-thānī*) as "the one rising in truth" (*al-qāʾim biʾl-ḥaqq*) who is the king of this and the other world," while affirming "I am he and he is I" (Manṣūriʾl-Yaman 1952, 8).

The tenth-century Ismāʿīlī tract in which this tradition is reported also contains other early Shiʿite materials in its commentaries on the apocalyptic verses of the *Qurʾān* in which the expected redeemer rises as the redresser of the cause of God (*al-qāʾim bi amr Allāh*) and the riser by the sword (*al-qāʾim biʾl-sayf*) (Manṣūriʾl-Yaman 1952, 62, 72, 87–89; also *Biḥār* 51:50), wearing the armor of the Prophet and wielding his sword, the *dhuʾl-fiqār* (Manṣūriʾl-Yaman 1952, 34). This picture can be supplemented by the early Imami Shiʿite traditions which present the Qāʾim as the redresser of the house of Muhammad (*qāʾim āl Muḥammad*) (*Biḥār* 51:53–54), modeled clearly on the Messiah as the restorer of the house of David (al-Qummī 1983–84/1404, 259). He is at the same time the Lord of the Sword (*ṣāḥib al-sayf*) (Ṣaffār, *Baṣāʾir*, 151) and the avenger of the wrong done to the House of Muhammad by the usurpers of their rights: "The weapon [of the Prophet] with us is like the ark with the children of Israel" (several variants, Ṣaffār, 176–89). The Qāʾim will establish the empire of truth (*dawlat al-ḥaqq*) (*Biḥār* 51:62–63). One interesting Shiʿite tradition (transmitted through Qumm)[22] distinguishes the Qāʾim from the Mahdi, asserting that there are twelve Mahdis—identified as ʿAlī and his descendants, only the last of whom "is the Imam, the Qāʾim in truth (*al-qāʾim biʾl-ḥaqq*), through whom God will revive the earth after its death" (Ibn Bābūya 1975/1395, 317). Imam Jaʿfar al-Ṣādiq is reported as interpreting the Koranic verse here alluded to, "Know that God revives the earth after its death" (Q. 30:18), to mean "God Most High revives it after its death, meaning due to the infidelity of its inhabitants, as the infidel is a dead being" (Ibn Bābūya 1975/1395, 668).[23]

According to an early Twelver Shiʿite commentary, "'The Hour has drawn near' (Q. 54:1) means the rising of the Qāʾim" (*Biḥār* 51:49). The Ismāʿīlīs, the radical sect that surfaced during the last decades of the ninth century as a widespread revolutionary movement developed this apocalyptic connection into a new notion of the Qāʾim. They believed in the return from occultation of a descendant of ʿAlī, Muḥammad b. Ismāʿīl b. Jaʿfar, who would bring justice to the world as the Mahdi, and then preside over the end of the world and the last judgment as the *qāʾim al-qiyāma* (Riser of the Resurrection) (Manṣūriʾl-Yaman 1952, 11, 22, 28; Daftary 1990, 140). The origins of the idea is obscure; the parallel that comes to mind is Dan. 12:1–2, where "Michael will arise" at the time of the end, and his rising is immediately followed by the resurrection "of those who are sleeping in the Land of Dust."[24] It is interesting to note that the Qāʾim traditions are exclusively Shiʿite and do not enter the six canonical Sunni compendia.

The southern Arabian tribes who supported Mukhtār were a main source of the apocalyptic ideas spread through Kufa during the Second Civil War. Their important role in the formation of the Islamic apocalyptic tradition was, however, by no means confined to this instance.

Quite apart from the transmission of much of the Judeo-Christian apocalyptic lore through the learned southern Arabs,[25] Kaʿb al-Aḥbār and Wahb b. Munabbih (d. 728 or 732), the southern Arab tribes settled in Syria introduced a major nonbiblical tribal trend into classical Islamic apocalypticism. The leading role in this trend was played by Kaʿb's Ḥimyarite tribe whose apocalyptic imagination was kindled by the sense of dispossession resulting from the loss of the kingdom to the Quraysh (Madelung 1986a, 141–43): "This matter (= the reign) was among the Ḥimyar, then God took it away from them and placed it among the Quraysh. But it will return to them" (cited in Madelung 1986a, 151). The agent of this restoration will be the Qaḥṭānī (the descendant of the tribal ancestor of the southern Arabs). The Qaḥṭānī is the oldest nonbiblical figure in the Islamic apocalyptic tradition and was already recognizably so at the time the term Mahdi acquired its definitive messianic connotation. The southern Arabian tribes settled in Syria were split during the Second Civil War and fought on opposite sides in the decisive battle of Marj Rāhiṭ in 684. The apocalyptic output it occasioned introduced the figure of the Qaḥṭānī alongside details from the early Umayyad history (Madelung 1986a, 180–83).

The Qaḥṭānī was to rule after the final demise of the Quraysh until the end of time. His reign would witness the apocalyptic battles (*malāḥim*) that would culminate in the conquest of Constantinople: "Under the reign of this Yemenite Caliph who will conquer Constantinople and the Roman domain, the Dajjāl shall come forth, Jesus will descend in his time" (Madelung 1986a, 155). A tradition asserting that the Qaḥṭānī was a Yemenite Qurayshite "according to Kaʿb foreknowledge" is indicative of the appropriation, by the ruling Quraysh, of the southern Arabian Qaḥṭānī. This also required that the legendary hero be killed at the Greatest Tribulation (*al-malḥama al-ʿuzmā/al-kubrā*)[26] (*Fitan*, 251).

In addition, our apocalyptic traditionists introduced the southern Arabian deliverer, Manṣūr, whose name was frequently invoked on the battlefield with the cries of "*yā Manṣūr, yā Manṣūr!*" According to his great-great-grandson, Zayd b. ʿAlī (d. 740), Muhammad himself had adopted the slogan "*yā Manṣūr amit* (O Manṣūr, kill!)" in the apocalyptic battle of Badr (al-Wāqidī 1966, 1:72). In due course, the Manṣūr was also appropriated by the ruling Quraysh. The tradition "Manṣūr is the Manṣūr of the Ḥimyar" was accordingly modified to "the Manṣūr is the Manṣūr of Banū Hāshim [the clan of the Prophet]" (Madelung 1986a, 156–57; *Fitan*, 66, 247). Another apocalyptic figure contributed by the southern Arabs was the Saffāḥ, which means both the shedder of blood and the generous spender (of gold and silver). The southern Arabian traditionists claimed that the Saffāḥ's name was mentioned in the Old Testament: "The Saffāḥ will live for forty years; his name in the Torah is the flier of the sky (*ṭāʾir al-samāʾ*)" (*Fitan*, 66).

The southern Arabian input into the Islamic apocalyptic tradition was not restricted to the above cases recorded in the Sunni sources. The Ashʿarites and Ḥimyarites of Kufa settled in Qumm in central Iran after the suppression of the Mukhtār's rebellion (687), and in another wave after the failure of the rebellion of ʿAbd al-Raḥmān b. al-Ashʿath (d. 700) (Faqīhī n.d., 38–49). They acted as an important channel for the transmission of apocalyptic lore to Shiʿism.

The apocalyptic figure of the Sufyānī had been made possible once the Sufyanids had lost the caliphate after the battle of Marj Rāhiṭ. This makes Yazīd, who died at the beginning of the Second Civil War, a very likely first prototype. The probable provenance of the Sufyānī legend from Shiʿite circles tends to confirm the hypothesis that he was originally a "Yazīd *redivivus*" held responsible for the martyrdom of Imam Ḥusayn and elevated to the rank of the second evil personality of the Islamic apocalypse—second to the Dajjāl (Madelung 1986b, 9). In the Kufan

Shiʿite apocalyptic traditions, the Sufyānī, who is typically said to rule for the time of "the pregnancy of a woman," becomes the sender of the army that will be swallowed in the desert and is made to appear simultaneously with the Mahdi at the end of time. Furthermore, with this body of traditions, the destruction of Kufa becomes one of the signs of the end of time (Madelung 1986b, 11–19). Sunni traditions too are supportive of pre–ʿAbbasid-revolution evidence for the Sufyānī. One such tradition considers ʿUmar II one of three Mahdis, and places him *after* the Sufyānī (*Fitan*, 222). Thus, the leader of the first Syrian rebellion against the ʿAbbasids in 751, Abū Muḥammad al-Sufyānī, claimed to be this apocalyptic figure, "the Sufyānī who had been mentioned" (Ṭabarī's phrase cited in Madelung 1986b, 14). Nevertheless, the rebellion of this only real historical Sufyānī formed the basis of the later Sufyānī legend and supplied quite a few of its details which also echo many other contemporary events of the ʿAbbasid revolution (Madelung 1986b, 15–48).

In all these waves of political apocalypticism many historical details, *ex eventu*, entered apocalyptic traditions. Many of the main actors of early Islam were transformed into apocalyptic figures: Muʿāwiya became "the head of Kings" (*raʾs al-mulūk*); Marwān b. al-Ḥakam, "the son of the blue-eyed woman" (*ibn al-zarqāʾ*); and Marwān II, "the red [-haired]" (*aṣhab*) and the "Ass of the Jazīra." Others, such as the "Lord of the West" (*ṣāḥib al-maghrib*) were generated by forgotten historical figures such as ʿAbd al-Raḥmān al-Fahrī, who had led the great Berber rebellion of 740 in North Africa. The latter's apocalyptic disguise was especially complimentary: the commander of his vanguard is "a man whose name is the name of Satan" (*Fitan*, 156). Real cities are transformed into apocalyptic ones, as Baghdad was into the Round City (*madīnat al-zawrāʾ*) (Madelung 1986a, 147, 149, 176-77; 1986b, 13, 34).

Unlike Iran, Rome (Constantinople) did not fall to the Muslims, even though it lost Syria and Egypt. The intermittent wars against the Byzantines were persistently invested with messianic significance (see chapter 10 above). The Prophet was held to have said,

> Persia is (only a matter of) one or two thrusts and no Persia will ever be after that. But the Byzantines with horns are people of sea and rock; whenever a horn goes, another replaces it. Alas, they are your associates to the end of time.

Another tradition reports the Prophet as saying: "The Byzantines are the severest of all people on you, but their perishing will be with (the coming of) the Hour" (Bashear 1991, 191). The apocalyptic traditions generated by the intermittent wars with the Byzantines in the seventh and eighth centuries made a truce with and betrayal by the Byzantines one of the signs of the Hour, alongside a great civil disorder (*fitna*). Yet a third tradition (on papyrus) counts three separate calamities: "The calamities are three, Persia, Rome and the Hour," and affirms, "The perishing of Rome is with the Hour." The following belongs to the most notable series of traditions to emerge from the matrix of the Muslim-Byzantine wars: "An army of theirs [the Muslims] will go to the Roman domain, conquer it, taking the jewelry of the Holy House (Jerusalem) and the Ark of Immanence (*tābūt al-sakīna*), the table, the Staff (of Moses) and the garment of Adam. Then a youth from the people of Yemen is acclaimed" (Khoury 1986, 302–3). Other traditions explain that the Ark of Immanence, containing the original Torah and Gospel, will be retrieved from a cave in Antioch (Madelung 1986a, 149).

Truces and wars thus became the mark of premessianic events. Apocalyptic numbers— twelve kings, twelve banners with twelve thousand men under each—occur repeatedly. The notion of the birth pangs of the Messiah must incidentally be behind several references to "the length of a woman's pregnancy" which we find in several *malāḥim* traditions (Bashear 1991, 175–77) and those of the Sufyānī. The naval wars against Byzantium generated the suitably apocalyptic notion of the Day of the Depths (*aʿmāq*) as a premessianic event. The conquest of Constantinople, sometimes referred to as the City of Infidelity (*madīnat al-kufr*), thus becomes the prelude to the appearance of the Dajjāl. With the passage of time, the connection with the wars against Byzantium was lost and the term came to denote not the final wars but the general premessianic woes and tribulations.

An interesting feature of the *malāḥim* traditions is the praise for the role of the *mawālī*, the (non-Arab) Muslims who constituted the client estate. According to one tradition, "when the tribulations (*malāḥim*) occur, a contingent of the *mawālī* will come out of Damascus. They are among the Arabs best equipped with horses and weapons and with their God will support the religion." According to another, while a few Arab tribes will join the Roman army, the *mawālī* refuse to do so. A third tradition states that the non-Arabs (*ʿajam*) refuse to revert to infidelity while a third of the Muslims succumb to doubt and are swallowed up. According to a fourth: "the one who will defeat the Byzantines on the Day of the Depths is the Caliph of the *mawālī*" (Bashear 1991, 179, 187–89). Indeed, in these traditions the non-Arab Muslims assume a distinct apocalyptic identity as the Reds (*al-ḥamrāʾ*). According to yet a fifth tradition, the Romans would tell the Muslims: "Leave our land to us and return to us every *aḥmar* and half-breed (*hajīn*) among you, and the sons of (Byzantine) concubines (*abnā al-sarārī*)." The clients are to be given the option to choose the side they prefer by the Muslims. "The half-breeds (*banū hujn*), sons of the concubines, and the Reds will get angry and tie a banner for a man of the Reds (*ḥamrāʾ*). He will be the ruler (*sulṭān*) who is promised to Abraham and Isaac at the end of time. They will pledge allegiance to him, fight Rome alone, and will be given victory over her." The sympathy of the dispossessed southern Arabian Ḥimyarites was in part responsible for the place of honor: "Good tidings on the day of the Greatest Malḥima to Ḥimyar and the Ḥamrāʾ. By God, God will surely give them this world and the Hereafter, even if the people dislike it" (these traditions are cited in Madelung 1986a, 161–62).

The place of the Turks in the Islamic apocalyptic tradition is an interesting one. Fear of the Turks evidently predated their conversion to Islam and migration. The Khazars have been suggested as the referent of those tradition which speak of ramparts against their cattle,[27] and their breaking through "the gate of Armenia" (presumably the Caspian Gates; *Fitan*, 127 n.1). The risings of the Turks and the Romans are often coupled and connected to the rise of the Sufyānī and the Mahdi. Some traditions mention two risings of the Turks, one in Azerbaijan, the other in northern Mesopotamia, the Jazira—with "the *malḥima* of the Turk in the Jazira" being the truly apocalyptic one that ends in the extirpation of the Turks in "the greatest holocaust of God (*dhibḥ allāh al-aʿẓam*)" (*Fitan*, 128–29).

The apocalyptic idea of the Mahdi spread widely beyond the Kaysāniyya and other extremist Shiʿite groups. As it became dissociated from its historical archetype, Muḥammad b. al-Ḥanafiyya, other groups projected the image of the Prophet unto him. According to an influential tradition attributed to ʿAbd Allāh b. Masʿūd, Muhammad foretold the coming of a Mahdi coined in his own image: "His name will be my name, and his father's name my father's name" (*Fitan*, 227). Furthermore, widespread traditions assert that the number of the Mahdi's companions in battle is exactly the same (usually put at 313) as those of Muhammad in the apocalyptic battle of Badr (*Fitan*, 213; *Biḥār*, 51:44, 55, 58). One Sunni tradition goes even further and affirms that "on his shoulder is the mark of the Prophet" (*Fitan*, 226), while some

Shiʿite traditions have Gabriel to the right of the Mahdi on the battlefield and Michael to his left (*Biḥār*, 52:311). Political apocalypticism did have its opponents, however. The pious opposition to the revolutionary Mahdism of the followers of Muḥammad b. al-Ḥanafiyya found a resource in the belief in the second coming of Jesus. A tradition attributed to Ḥasan al-Baṣrī, who was a leading figure in this opposition, categorically states: "There will be no Mahdi other than Jesus son of Maryam" (Madelung 1954c, 5:1234). This tradition has survived the later traditions that affirm the return of both Jesus and the Mahdi.

The approach of the year 100/718–719 kindled centennial apocalyptic speculation on the events of the Year of the Ass (*sanat al-ḥimār*) so referred to after the resurrected Lord (*ṣāḥib*) of the Ass (see Q. 2:261). The apocalyptic conception of the century was reinforced by a set of traditions the most important of which is the statement attributed to the Prophet: "There shall not remain on the face of the earth after a hundred years a single individual but that he dies" (al-Masʿūdī 1970, 3:38). The Umayyad caliph Suleymān b. ʿAbd al-Malik (715–717) sought advantage from this trend by encouraging the belief that he was the Mahdi (al-Masʿūdī 1894, 335). He did not, however, live long enough, and it was his successor ʿUmar II b. ʿAbd al-ʿAzīz, who ruled in the year 100 and was recognized as the Mahdi by the pious traditionists of Arabia (Madelung 1954c, 5:1231).

We find apocalyptic elements already in the abortive attempt at revolution from above at the onset of the Third Civil War in 744 by Yazīd III, the first Umayyad Caliph with a non-Arab (Persian) mother. He rose against his cousin at the head of a revolutionary coalition of the newly humiliated southern Arabian tribes and the *mawālī* leaders of the Qadarite movement. A southern Arabian tradition attributed to Kaʿb al-Aḥbār had predicted the appearance of the Messiah, Jesus son of Mary, at the eastern gate of Damascus (Madelung 1986a, 167). Yazīd III rode to Damascus on a black ass surrounded by twelve men (TTkh 2:1789–90).[28] The apocalyptic significance of the act must have been evident to the Muslims who had not forgotten the Lord of the Ass, not to mention the Jews and the Christians for whom the reference to Zech. 9:9 must have seemed obvious. We also know that Yazīd was addressed as the rightly guided (*rāshid*) and the Mahdi (van Ess 1970, 279). We may assume that Yazīd III was the beneficiary of those southern Arabian Mahdi traditions attributed to Kaʿb al-Aḥbār which portray the Mahdi as a Syrian caliph of Yemenite descent who would defeat Rome and find the Ark of Immanence (Madelung 1986a, 148-49; *Fitan,* 220, 231).

✑ SECTARIAN PROTEST: THE ʿABBASID REVOLUTION AND THE DEVELOPMENT OF THE APOCALYPTIC TRADITION _____

The apocalyptic anticipation of the end of the first century was not confined to the Muslims, who were still a minority—probably one-fifth—of the population of the empire. A messianic Jewish leader known as the Shepherd (*al-Rāʿī*), who claimed to be "the forerunner (*muqaddama*) of the Mahdi," emerged during the reign of Suleymān.[29] He paved the way for the better known Obadiah, Abū ʿĪsā of Isfahan, who may well have identified the Shepherd as the Messiah,[30] claimed to be one of the five messengers of Jesus Christ, and gathered a large following during the Third Civil War (744–750). He was defeated by an army sent by the second

ʿAbbasid caliph, presumably in the following decade, and was in turn succeeded by a certain Yudghān (Shahrastānī 1:174–75; see Nemoy 1930, 328–29, 382–83). This syncretic Jewish messianic movement in central Iran, recorded in heresiography in its successive phases as the ʿĪsawiyya, the Yudghāniyya and the Mushkāniyya, demonstrates the spread of the Kaysānī idea of occultation (*ghayba*). According to our report, the Shepherd was believed to have disappeared/gone into occultation after Suleymān's agents put him in prison in Damascus (al-ʿAlawī 1964/1342, 57). ʿAbd Allāh b. Muʿāwiya had a large Kaysānī following and ruled central and southern Iran for some three years during the Third Civil War from 747 to 749. When he died in the prison of the rival revolutionary leader, Abū Muslim, his followers said he was alive and in occultation in the mountains of Isfahan.[31] Similarly, when the messianic Jewish leader Abū ʿĪsā Isfahānī was killed by the ʿAbbasid forces in Rayy, his followers claimed that he was in occultation in the mountains of Rayy. Thence, the notion of *ghayba* (occultation) made its way, via a Jewish messianic movement in eleventh-century France, to the original Arabic version of Maimonides' *Iggeret Têmān* (Friedlaender 1911–12, 488–92). Abū ʿĪsā's movement also generated an idea that found a conspicuous place in Muslim apocalyptics: the Dajjāl will rise in Isfahan at the head of seventy thousand Jews (*Fitan*, 335).

The Christians of Iran were not immune to the apocalyptic fever either, and a certain Syriac of Sistan (a province in eastern Iran) reportedly produced an *Apocalypse of Enoch* in 737.[32] The *Apocalypse of Enoch* is not extant, but its date of publication is close to the original source of a remarkable work that has survived in a Persian translation in a tenth- or eleventh-century book entitled the *Umm al-Kitāb* (*Mother of Books*). It is the only early Islamic work I know that is apocalyptic not only in substance but also in form (Halm 1982, 139–98). H. Halm has appropriately called it "the *Apocalypse of Jābir*." Jābir b. Jaʿfar al-Juʿfī, who died between 745 and 750, was a client of the clan of Juʿf from the southern Arabian tribe of Madhij and a follower of the fifth Shiʿite Imam, Muḥammad al-Bāqir (d. 733). He became the leader of the Mughīriyya, who have been aptly described as "gnostic revolutionaries" (Wasserstrom 1985, 27). In the *Apocalypse of Jābir*, Imam Muḥammad al-Bāqir, introduced in the later preface as a divinely inspired child of five who manifested "the divine glory of wisdom (*farr-e īzadī-ye ḥikmat*)" (*Umm*. 12), reveals the secrets of gnosis to his disciple, Jābir. The secrets include the development of the cosmos from the fall of the souls to their salvation, the fall of archangel ʿAzāzīʾil (Azazʾel of the book of Watchers in *1 Enoch* 1–36), the rise of the seven heavenly spheres (*Umm*. 120–53), the creation of the earth and the seven planet angels, as well as the metamorphosis of doubting angels into phantoms (*ashbāḥ*) and of the followers of Satan into shadows (*aẓilla*) who are placed in paradise and hell respectively (*Umm*. 204–10). The work offers a kabbalistic hermeneutics of letters and numbers, beginning with $19 = 7 + 12$ as the numerological equivalent of "In the Name of God, the Merciful, the Compassionate," and it includes speculations on the homology between the macrocosm (*ʿālam-e buzurg*) and microcosm (*ʿālam-e kuchak*) (*Umm*. 222–23). As for the feminine imagery, it is interesting to note that, on the one hand, Satan transformed the shadows he sends to the doubting angels and the humans into beautiful women. On the other hand, the numinous divine vision vouchsafed through Gabriel to the doubting angels is the face of Fāṭima on the highest heavenly sphere with her father Muhammad as her crown (*Umm*. 212–14).

Five lights emanate from the divine throne as holy spirits (*Umm*. 83). These five lights are continuous with the Speaking (*naṭiqa*) Spirit which is God, and which shines into the hearts of Muḥammad, ʿAlī, Fāṭima, Ḥasan, and Ḥusayn (*Umm*. 113). In the human world, the spiritual hierarchy consists of twelve trustees (*naqībs*) in twelve countries at the highest level, and twenty-eight nobles (*najībs*) in twenty-eight islands (*jazīras*) below them (*Umm.* 173–77). Twelve is the number of the trustees of the children of Israel (Ibn Bābūya 1975/1395, 272–73), as well as that of the disciples of Jesus. The twelve trustees of the *Apocalypse of Jābir* are the twelve spirits (*rūḥ*) created by Salmān's words (*Umm.* 133). The incidental terms "country" and "twenty-eight" were not to survive, but the gnostically significant notions of "island" and "twelve" were passed on to Ismaʿilism. According to one report, the organizer of the Ismāʿīlī mission selected twelve trustees (*naqīb*) and told them, "You are like the apostles of Jesus, son of Mary" (TTkh 3:2126).[33] Each trustee was put in charge of an "island" (*jazīra*). The Gnostic influence in this model is clear, stemming from the division of the world into twelve islands under twelve apostles in the apocryphal "Acts of Apostles" (Widengren 1955, 77).

In the *Apocalypse of Jābir*, Salmān, the Persian companion of the Prophet, occupies the special position of the demiurge, akin to that of Metatron in *4 Enoch*. God tells him:

> You are my gate (*bāb*), my book . . . and my right hand. . . . I am your God, and you are god of the believers. I have put the command of heaven and earth in your hand. I am your God and you are the god of all the heaven and earth. (*Umm.* 172)

Salmān is thus delegated God's creative power (*qudra*) and is in particular responsible for the punishment, in several stages, of ʿAzāziʾīl and his followers, who persist in their rebellious protest and are progressively darkened at millennial intervals into shadows and finally condemned to seven thousand years of carnal existence on earth (*Umm.* 141, 144, 154, 206). This introduction of the notion of millennium into the Islamic apocalyptic tradition has an echo of the Zurvanite myth of creation of Ahura Mazda and Ahriman and the division of the nine millennia before the final defeat of the latter (see chapter 2).

The apocalyptic form introduced by Jābir al-Juʿfī was developed by another Gnostic extremist Shiʿite, Muḥammad b. Sinān (d. 835), whose *Book of Shadows* (*Kitāb al-aẓilla*) is notable for its theory of the Seven Adams sent by God before our Adam who is the Qāʾim (Halm 1982, 112). The shadows seem to represent the Manichean mixture (*ikhtilāṭ al-mizāj*) of darkness and light and correspond to the mixing of believers and nonbelievers (Halm 1982, 260–61). The Gnostic-Mandean idea of the heavenly ascent of the souls saved by gnosis (Widengren 1950, 66–67) can be detected in the background. In the era of the last Adam the cycle of transmigrations of the souls will come to an end. When a believer dies, his soul will ascend to heaven. "He will take his light-body (*al-badan al-nūrī*) and abide under the angels of Paradise" (Halm 1982, 268).

The intense apocalyptic character of the ʿAbbasid revolution (744–763) remains largely unrecognized. The year 125 (743–744 C.E.) was before long seen as the year of the *fitna* and of the *malāḥim*: "Woe to the Arab after the year 125" (*Fitan*, 418–19). Nor are the traditions that tell of the turn in power of the House of ʿAbbās (e.g., *Fitan*, 116) in substance anachronistic. Traditions that show the ʿAbbasid leaders assumed the messianic titles of Saffāḥ, Manṣūr, and Mahdi abound (*Fitan*, 52, 66–67, 97, 247, 424). There is both literary and epigraphic evidence of the assumption of the title of the Mahdi by the first ʿAbbasid caliph, Abūʾl-ʿAbbās (al-Masʿūdī 1894, 338; al-Dūrī 1981, 136). There is also evidence that he claimed to be the Qāʾim, even though this evidence has been generally overlooked (al-Dūrī 1981, 128).[34] ʿAbd Allāh b. ʿAlī, the winner of the decisive battle of Zab and the destroyer of Marwān II and the Umayyads, was the original bearer of the title al-Saffāḥ,[35] which was later anachronistically assumed to be the regnal title of the first ʿAbbasid caliph.

In an imperial society that was torn asunder by strife among the ruling stratum and whose subjects were mostly non-Muslims and recent converts, it is not surprising to find the kindling of apocalyptic hope among the Jews and the Christians, as well as various Iranian movements (Browne 1956, chap. 9; Arjomand 1994, 10–12, 23). The most interesting movement among the latter was the syncretistic mission of the prophet Bih-Âfarīdh whose followers maintained "that the prophet had ascended into heaven on a common dark-brown horse, and that he will again descend unto them in the same way as he ascended, and will take vengeance on his enemies" (al-Bīrūnī 1879, 194; Browne 1956, 308–10). Nor is it surprising to find revolutionary parties appealing to non-Muslim and Muslim groups alike by adopting apocalyptic ideas for popular revolutionary mobilization. The revolution is in fact the outcome of the messianic movements that were converting the subject populations to Islam, beginning with the Murjiʾite rebellion in Transoxania (Madelung 1988, chap. 2; see also the next section), the Kaysānī followers of ʿAbd Allāh b. Muʿāwiya, and the ʿAbbasid movement itself.

The apocalyptic traditions supply some very valuable information about the Khurasanian partisans of the ʿAbbasid revolution who fought under the messianic black banners. "They have long hair, villages [and not tribes] are their genealogy, and their names are their honorific titles (kunā)" (Fitan, 118). And they spoke Persian, because according to some rare traditions: "Their slogan is 'bokosh, bokosh'!" ("Kill, kill!") (Fitan, 118–19). Their leader, Abū Muslim, "a man from the mawālī who rises in Marw" (Fitan, 420), is the subject of several pejorative traditions: "Scoundrel son of scoundrel (lakaʿ b. lakaʿ) will conquer the world." "The Hour will not rise until Scoundrel son of scoundrel is the happiest of the people" (Fitan, 115–16). These traditions place Khurasan firmly and conspicuously in the Islamic apocalyptic topography (Fitan, 188–93).

The twelve kings of the fifth vision of Ezra (4 Ezra 12:14), a remarkable text in political apocalypticism as the sequel to Daniel's vision of the fall of empires, was the likely source of inspiration for the particular tradition on the apocalyptic war (malḥima) against the twelve kings, the least of whom is the king of Rome (Fitan, 293; also 279). More generally, it also influenced the expectation that the Umayyad ruler after Yazīd III would be the last. This expectation finds expression in a large number of traditions concerning "the Twelve caliphs from the Quraysh," which were evidently first circulated by those who hoped there would be no more caliphs from the Quraysh. This political oracle in due course became an autonomous cultural form, serving as a source of speculation for many groups. It inspired the Twelver Shiʿites with the idea of ending the era of perplexity by fixing the number of their Imams at twelve (Ibn Bābūya 1975/1395, 338–39).

The culmination of the revolutionary apocalypticism of the period for the ʿAlids was the uprising, in 762, of the Ḥasanid Muḥammad b. ʿAbd Allāh, al-nasf al-zakiyya (the Pure Soul), whom the ʿAbbasids themselves had accepted as the Qāʾim and the Mahdi of the House of Muhammad before coming to power. ʿAbd Allāh, the father of the Mahdi, claimed to be in possession of the sword and the armor of the Prophet which would evidently be put at the disposal of his son as the Lord of the Sword. The Ḥusaynid Imam Jaʿfar al-Ṣādiq denied his Ḥasanid cousins' claim, asserting that he himself had inherited the sword and the armor of the Prophet from his grandfather and was holding them in his house in the jafr (Ṣaffār, 150–53, 184).

The long-delayed rebellion of the Mahdi of the House of Muhammad in Arabia in 762 was followed by that of his brother, Ibrahim, who assumed the title of Hādī in Iraq. Although Jaʿfar al-Ṣādiq dissociated himself from that uprising, he does not seem to have been able to prevent his sons from joining. His son, Mūsā b. Jaʿfar al-Kāẓim (d. 799), is reported among the participants in the uprising of the Pure Soul, and he in fact learned to harness its persistent chiliasm more subtly to long-term designs of his own. The rebellion of the Pure Soul contributed richly to the Shiʿite apocalyptic tradition. Indeed, "the killing of the Pure Soul" became one of the signs of the Hour: "There are only fifteen nights between the killing of the Pure Soul and the rising of the Qāʾim" (Ibn Bābūya 1975/1395, 649; al-Ṭūsī 1965/1385, 271). Further, "Five [are the signs] before the rising of the Qāʾim: the Yamānī [presumably the Qaḥṭānī], the Sufyānī, the caller who calls from the sky [sometimes identified as Gabriel], the swallowing in the desert, and the killing of the Pure Soul" (Ibn Bābūya 1975/1395, 649; variant in al-Ṭūsī 1965/1385, 267).

Mūsā al-Kāẓim, the first Shiʿite Imam, whose mother was a non-Arab slave, competed in clandestine political activism with the surviving Zaydis followers of his cousin, the Pure Soul. He followed the example of the latter in claiming to be the apocalyptic Qāʾim, although the Shiʿite tradition has systematically expunged the traces of this claim. Caliph Hārūn al-Rashīd imprisoned Mūsā in 793; he was released and then imprisoned for a second time. His two periods of imprisonment gave rise to the idea, circulated by his followers, that the Qāʾim would have two occultations, a short one followed by a longer one extending to his rising. Among several groups of Mūsā's followers who refused to accept that he had died, and/or maintained instead that he was the Qāʾim and the Mahdi and had gone into occultation, the Wāqifiyya (cessationists) were the most important channel for the direct transmission of chiliastic ideas to Imami (Twelver) Shiʿism. They considered Mūsā the Qāʾim and maintained that the Imamate had ceased with him. Books on the occultation by the Wāqifites were especially important for introducing apocalyptic notions into Imami doctrine, as the leading figures in the movement later rejoined the Imami fold under the eighth Imam, ʿAlī al-Riḍā (Arjomand 1996a, 493–94).

The formative era of Islamic political apocalypticism that had began in the Second Civil War (680–692) came to a close after the civil war between the sons of Hārūn al-Rashīd, Muḥammad al-Amīn and ʿAbd Allāh al-Maʾmūn (809–813). This devastating civil war, which triggered a series of ʿAlid Shiʿite uprisings, as well as the end of the second Islamic century in 815, spread the fire of apocalyptic imagination from sectarian groups to the Muslim society at large. The massive apocalyptic output of this civil war included one of the rare apocalyptic elaborations of social justice: "The caller will call from the sky: the earth is God's earth, and the servants God's servants. [Let] God's wealth be [divided] among his servants equally" (*Fitan*, 126).

The seventh ʿAbbasid caliph, ʿAbd Allāh al-Maʾmūn (813–833) undertook his bold initiative to unify the ʿAlid and ʿAbbasid houses—termed "the second calling" (*daʿwa thāniyya*) in comparison with the ʿAbbasid revolution as the first calling—amidst widespread expectation that he would be the last member of the ʿAbbasid dynasty to rule "before the lifting of the veil" and "the advent of the Qāʾim, the Mahdi." Apocalyptic centennialism was clearly the source of the expectation of the parousia of the Mahdi in the year 200 (815). According to one apocalyptic tradition later excised from Nuʿaym b. Ḥammād's *Kitāb al-fitan*, the last of the Banū ʿAbbās was called ʿAbd Allāh "and he is the last lord of the ʿayn among them . . . ; he will be the key to the tribulation and sword of perdition." As a letter of Maʾmun's brought to light by Madelung proves, the caliph himself shared this expectation as he had been told by his father "on the authority of his ancestors and what he found in the Book of Revolution (*Kitāb al-dawla*) and elsewhere that after the seventh of the descendants of al-ʿAbbās no pillar will remain standing for the Banā al-ʿAbbās" (Madelung 1981, 343, 345 [translation slightly modified]). There is some evidence to suggest that ʿAlī b. Mūsā, who was brought to Khurasan by the caliph, given the title of al-Riḍā (the one agreed upon [from the House of the Prophet]) and made his successor designate, shared al-Maʾmūn's apocalyptic expectations. In a valuable tradition, he is reported to have corrected a tradition in which his father is considered the Qāʾim in order to suggest that the latter's apocalyptic rising was imminent in the month of Rajab (*Biḥār* 52:182–83). However, Maʾmūn's grand reconciliation of the Houses of ʿAbbās and ʿAlī in 817 brought to a close an era of revolutionary chiliasm (Arjomand 1996a, 491–96).

We have already come across the exclamation "Woe to the Arab!" during the ʿAbbasid revolution (*Fitan*, 122). To some, it still would have meant "the perishing of the kings and the humiliation of the Arabs until the rise of the people of the West" (*Fitan*, 118). But as the massive conversion of the non-Arabs to Islam continued for the next century, the doom of the Arabs and the expectation of the shift of sovereignty to other nations became more definitive in the minds of the apocalyptic traditionists. The tenth-century *Book of Occultation* by Nuʿmānī contains several traditions in which the Mahdi will be hard on the Arabs, and his companions will be non-Arabs (ʿajam) (Nuʿmānī 1983, 154–55; Amir-Moezzi 1995, 294–96). The appearance of the regions of Daylam and Rayy in the apocalyptic topography of these traditions (Nuʿmānī 1983, 156, 201; also Ibn Bābūya 1975/1395, 311) is interesting, as these are also areas of Ismāʿīlī activity in central Iran. Even more interesting are the traditions concerning the rise of a false "Manichean" (*zandīq*) rising in Qazvin, who, to my knowledge, has not been identified (al-Ṭūsī 1965/1385, 269–70).

A question of great comparative import can only be posed and not answered here. Is the close connection between history and the apocalyptic we have described particular to Islam, or are the historical connections more visible because they are closer to us in time than those of other apocalyptic traditions? Whatever the answer, in this formative period it was largely history that was transformed into apocalyptic, not apocalyptic material that was historicized. It would be the other way around in the later periods. Historical details in the formative period, even one as recurrent and persistent as the clash with Rome, were ultimately submerged in the apocalyptic vision of the end. The six conditions of the Hour according to the great apocalyptic traditionist Wahb b. Munabbih are "first the banner of Rome, then the Dajjāl, third Gog and Magog, forth Jesus son of Mary, fifth the Smoke, and sixth the Beast" (*Fitan*, 402). In other traditions, historical events underwent even greater sublimation and became *fitan* and *malāḥim*, woes and tribulations of the end of time.

☞ REIFICATION OF APOCALYPTIC _____

Apocalyptic revelation of a new creation here and now transforms the present into a moment of revolutionary liminality, a time of great opening and freedom from tradition. Liminality means the removal of structural constraints upon human agency. We know that the liminality of political revolutions at the onset also engenders considerable fear of freedom that can account for the wide popularity of deterministic philosophies of history. Similarly, liminal anxiety generated by apocalypticism is a source of constant pressure for certainty and results in the reification of the apocalyptic future. The oldest techniques for the fabrication of predetermined futures are numerology and astrology (for parallel phenomena in medieval Judaism, see chapter 14 above).

Numerology is an ancient technique for the calculation of the predetermined future. Its reception in Islam as the science of *Jafr* was quite early, that science being attributed to Daniel and also to the sixth Shiʿite Imam, Jaʿfar b. Muḥammad, presumably on account of the red leather bag known as the *jafr*. The Shiʿites believed that it contained secret scrolls, as well as the weapons of the Prophet. It was said to be in possession of Jaʿfar, who had inherited it from his father and grandfather (Ṣaffār, 150–61).

The distinctive Muslim science for the prediction of the predetermined future, however, is what I call political astrology. This science for the astral determination of political upheavals was developed after the ʿAbbasid revolution. It adopted Sassanian astrological techniques for predictions of dynastic change on the basis of Ptolemaic astronomy, superimposed on Zoroastrian millennialism (de Goeje 1886, 116–19; Kennedy and Pingree 1971, vi–viii, 75). It was developed by MāshāʾAllāh, the Jewish astrologer who, together with the Zoroastrian astrologer Nawbakht, advised the second ʿAbbasid caliph, Manṣūr, on the time and location of the new City of Peace (*madīnat al-salām,* i.e., Baghdad) in 762.[36] A practitioner of this science who was a contemporary of MāshāʾAllāh's disciple, Abū Maʿshar, Ibn Abī Ṭāhir Ṭayfūr (d. 893), saw the heavenly revolution of stars replicated in a great revolution in *imperium,* or world domination. MāshāʾAllāh's calculations had shown the rise of Islam, and the Arabs' turn in power/domination (*dawla*) had been determined by the Shift of Triplicity on March 19, 571 (Kennedy and Pingree 1971, vi). Using this and other horoscopes, Ṭayfūr demonstrated that the next major event on earth occurred at the conjunction of Saturn and Jupiter at the vernal equinox in March 749. This had determined "the shift (*taḥwīl*) in the conjunction of the Arabian world domination to the Hāshimite Imams,"—that is, the ʿAbbasid revolution, which Ibn Abī Ṭāhir Ṭayfūr described as "the general revolution in religion and the state" (*al-inqilab alkulli fiʾl-din waʾl-mulk;* British Library, Oriental ms Add 7473, f. 60a). Apocalyptic numerological speculations continued through the centuries, producing endless calculations of the Hour and of lesser events.[37] However, it was political astrology that became the most respected science of prediction of the predetermined future revolutions in world domination. This stimulated numerous apocalyptic uprisings throughout Islamic history.

We only need to remember the widely cast horoscope of the Shift of Triplicity at the vernal equinox of the year 809 (Kennedy and Pingree 1971, vii) to realize that the maturation of the science of political astrology had much to do with the civil war of 809–813, which brought the era of Islamic political apocalypticism to a close. Al-Faḍl b. Abī Sahl b. Nawbakht, who made a major contribution to this science, was al-Maʾmūn's astrological advisor during and after the civil war (Ibn Bābūya 1970/1390, 2:145–47).

Political astrology played an important role in the history of the chiliastic Ismāʿīlī movement (to be considered more fully below under "Realization of Apocalypticism"). The conjunction of Saturn and Jupiter in the year 296 (908–909 C.E.) must have stimulated the Ismāʿīlī missionary, ʿAbū ʿAbd Allāh al-Shīʿī, who set up the Fatimid state for the Mahdi in North Africa in 909 (de Goeje 1886, 122). Our documentation for the consequences of the next conjunction twenty years later is much better. Bīrūnī mentions a prediction, based on erroneous astronomical calculations, of the appearance of the Qāʾim at the eighteenth conjunction after the birth of Muhammad, which is made to coincide with "the tenth millennium, which is presided over by Saturn and Sagittarius." At that time, the era of Islam and the rule of the Arabs will come to an end. The Qāʾim will rise and "will restore the rule of Magism" (al-Bīrūnī 1897, 196–97). In Rayy, a city in central Iran to the north of Isfahan, Abū Ḥatim al-Rāzī had been spreading the same astrological prediction of the coming of the Qāʾim (Madelung 1988, 96). We can further read in Bīrūnī that the Ismāʿīlīs who had established the Qarmatian state in Bahrain "promised each other the arrival of the Expected One (al-muntazar) in the seventh Conjunction of the Fiery Triplicity" (al-Bīrūnī 1879, 197 [translation slightly modified]; see de Goeje 1886, 122–23). When that conjunction occurred in 928, as we shall see below, a young man from Isfahan was ready to set out off for Bahrain to claim to be the expected Qāʾim.

The great tenth-century Ismāʿīlī encyclopedia, the Epistles of the Brethren of Purity (Rasāʾil ikhwān al-ṣafā), developed political astrology into an astrally determined cyclical theory of history. The revolution of the stars determines major changes in world history. Changes in the sovereignty of the dynastic houses (ahl bayt) and civil wars occur at the conjunctions of Saturn and Jupiter every twenty years, changes in world domination from one nation to another at the Shifts from one Triplicity to another every 240 years, and the greatest revolutions of all, changes in religion by the great prophet-lawgivers, occur every 960 (solar) years, or every (lunar) millennium at the great conjunction of Saturn and Jupiter at the Shift back to the initial Triplicity of the signs of fire (Marquet 1972, 53–56). The Brethren of Purity reconciled this duodecimal system of the zodiac with the heptads of the Judeo-Christian sacred history. The Prophet is made to say: "The life of this world is seven thousand years; I have been sent in the last of these millennia" (Marquet 1972, 51). Each millennium (= 960 solar years) is divided into two complete cycles, each consisting of four 120-year quarters of ascension, apogee, decline, and clandestinity. The term Qāʾim is given a new meaning in this astrological theory of history. Each 120-year quarter cycle is inaugurated by a Qāʾim, who is followed by six Imams. The seventh Imam, who completes the heptad, is the Qāʾim of the next quarter-cycle. The Qāʾim of the resurrection would be expected at the end of the millennium of Muhammad, which is the final millennium (Marquet 1972, 60–62).

Two and a half centuries later, Ḥasan II, the lord of the castle of Alamūt and the head of the Ismāʿīlī state established in a number of inaccessible mountain fortresses, evidently did not have the patience to wait until the end of the Islamic millennium, the time appointed by the Brethren of Purity. Using a different horoscope, on the 17th of Ramaḍān 559/558 (August 1164), at midday, under the ascendancy of Virgo and with the sun in Cancer, he came to the pulpit as deputy of the Imam and the Qāʾim of the resurrection and proclaimed the Great Resurrection on earth (Lewis 1985, 72; Jambet 1990, 35–43).

Needless to say, astrological speculations were by no means particular to heterodoxy. On the contrary, it was common to all Muslims, as can be seen in a short apocalypse from the period of the Crusades that was originally written in Egypt in the late twelfth century (Hartmann 1924, 90–91). The news of the Mongol invasion of northern Iran a few decades later inspired apocalyptic oracles on the destruction of Cairo at the tenth conjunction of the Earthly Triplicity in 1226. In a poem recorded by al-Maghrīzī, we can read, "Fear the Tenth Conjunction, my son, and flee with your family before the trumpet sounds" (de Goeje 1886, 127).

CONTAINMENT OF APOCALYPTICISM

The containment of apocalypticism is an indispensable step toward the institutionalization of authority in the Abrahamic religions. In Islam, this statement applies to both political and religious authority. That political authority is premised on the containment of apocalypticism would explain the appropriation of the messianic titles by Abū Ja'far, the second 'Abbasid caliph and the consolidator of the 'Abbasid revolution. His assumption of the messianic title of al-Manṣūr after suppressing the rebellion of the Pure Soul (al-Mas'ūdī 1894, 341) and the appropriation of the titles of al-Mahdī and al-Hādī for his son and grandson amounted to his effective long-term response to revolutionary chiliasm. This mode of containment of apocalypticism can be characterized as the routinization of apocalyptic charisma by the ruling temporal power.

The containment of apocalypticism seems, however, equally necessary for the institutionalization of religious authority. The constant crisis of authority and succession was the cost of apocalypticism in early Shi'ism, and as a rule the Imams themselves led the effort to contain it. The problem became acute after the death of the eleventh Imam and the onset of what would turn out to be the period of complete occultation to the end of time. Apocalyptic expectation persisted for decades after the death of the eleventh Imam, during what is termed the era of perplexity (ḥayra). Several traditions from the early decades of this era reported, with unmistakably apocalyptic tone, the clandestine existence of the Imam near Mecca. According to one of them, the hidden Imam told an old agent of his father who had visited him secretly to prepare the brethren for the uprising and to look for the "signs of parousia" (imārāt al-ẓuhūr). When asked about the time of the uprising, in one version, the Qā'im said it was the year of the appearance of beast (dābbat al-arḍ) who carries the staff of Moses and the seal of Solomon and herds the people into the place of resurrection (maḥshar). According to another version, he simply recited the Koranic verse (54:1), "The Hour has drawn near: the moon is split" (Arjomand 1997, 6).

In this period of perplexity, the hierocratic interests of the Twelver Shi'ite elite required that the idea of occultation, borrowed from the Wāqifites in a desperate crisis, be detached from its chiliastic matrix. Two important early theologians took the lead in the modification and rationalization of the idea of ghayba. Their knowledge of the Mu'tazilite rational theology suggested to these doctors that the idea could only be deapocalypticized with the help of a theology of occultation. The strategy chosen by them was, accordingly, to find a theological solution that would conjoin the rational discussion of occultation with the nature of the Imamate. The rationale of the theological argument had the advantage of establishing the necessity of the occultation or absence of the apocalyptic Mahdi. On the foundations thus laid at the beginning of the tenth century, the idea of occultation was definitively detached from its original chiliastic context and transformed into a fixed component of the Shi'ite theodicy and theology. In the second half of the fourth/tenth century, the Shaykh al-Ṣadūq, Ibn Bābūya, greatly developed the analogy between the occultation of the Imam and the absence of the prophets. The rationalist doctors of the eleventh century vigorously rebutted the charge that the occultation of the Imam meant the abeyance of the divine law. They recast the explanation of occultation within the framework of their Mu'tazilite-inspired nomocratic theology. The idea of occultation was no longer a cause for perplexity because, thanks to the divine law and grace (*lutf*), the believer knew what to do in the absence of the Imam. The rationalist eleventh-century doctors thus reconciled the idea of occultation with a stable system of hierocratic authority (Arjomand 1996).

The Shaykh al-Ṭūsī, however, the great theologian who put forward the systematic theology of occultation as the introduction to his *Book of Occultation,* also retained many of the apocalyptic traditions as the proof of the occultation. Needless to say, the expectation of the return of the hidden Imam remained a popular apocalyptic belief. By 1092, the subterranean passage to a water well (*sardāb*) in Sāmarrāʾ, where the hidden Imam was believed to have disappeared, had become a place of pilgrimage. At about the same time, the Shiʿites of the city of Kashan in central Iran are reported to have expected the return of the Mahdi and regularly paraded on horseback, fully armed, only to return without him. Similar outward demonstrations of Shiʿite apocalyptic expectancy are reported by Ibn Bābūya and Ibn Khaldūn in the fourteenth century (Friedlaender 1911–12, 496–97).

☞ REALIZATION OF APOCALYPTICISM

Apocalyptic ideas have motivated various instances and types of action in Islamic history, many of which we have already surveyed. Only a few additional examples can selectively be mentioned. Even though the southern Arabian apocalyptic figures play a minor role in Islamic apocalyptics, they have from time to time generated significant action. In 699, for instance, we have the serious albeit unsuccessful rebellion of ʿAbd al-Raḥmān b. al-Ashʿath, who called himself the Qaḥtānī (al-Masʿūdī 1894, 314; Madelung 1954c, 5:1231). An unpublished coin in the Tübingen collection (inventory no. 94-33-1) that dates from the great Murjiʾite rebellion of 734 in Transoxania has the legend "For the Manṣūr, and Justice," suggesting that its leader Ḥārith b. al-Suaryj, who unfurled the black messianic banner a decade earlier than the ʿAbbasid partisans, assumed the title of Manṣūr. The spread of revolutionary Ismaʿilism in the Yemen in the 880s, to give a last example, was the work of the missionary who appropriately assumed the title of the Manṣūr of the Yemen.

One of the more curious instances of action motivated by apocalyptic beliefs concerns the gate built by Alexander to keep Gog and Magog out. The caliph al-Wāthiq (842–847) dreamed that the Gate of the Two-Horned, which was holding back Gog and Magog, was broken, and he sent a special commissioner who knew thirty languages to Bāb al-Abwāb/Darband to inspect it. The commissioner, Sallām, gave a detailed account of his travels to the geographer Ibn Khurdādhbih. According to this account, it took him sixteen months to travel to Darband and to inspect the Caspian Gates/Gates of the Alān. Then, following the suggestion of a guide, he proceeded to Samarqand in search of Gog and Magog.[38] Twenty-two of his companions died in that trip. After another twelve months, he returned to Baghdad with fourteen survivors, carrying scraps of old metalloid rock from Alexander's gate and the reassurance that it was still intact.[39]

The claimants to Mahdihood and the Mahdist movements they have generated in Africa, the Middle East, and India are too numerous to survey. It does seem appropriate, however, to end this treatment of classical Islamic apocalypticism with its realization in the Qarmaṭī and the Nizārī branches of Ismāʿīlī Shiʿism in the tenth, and yet again in the twelfth century. The

Ismāʿīlīs, as was pointed out, considered Muḥammad b. Ismāʿīl as the Qāʾim,[40] and they expected his apocalyptic return. The Ismāʿīlī missionaries first appear in Iraq and the Yemen during the last quarter of the ninth century, engaged in propaganda on behalf of the expected Mahdi-Qāʾim, whom they considered the seventh and last Imam of the Islamic era. God was "preparing the paradise of Adam for Muḥammad b. Ismāʿīl."[41] He was soon to remove the veil of external reality by abolishing the law and revealing the true religion. Each missionary (dāʿī) was in charge of an "Island" (jazīra) where he established a communistically organized "abode of migration" (dār al-hijra), so designated after the model built by the Prophet after his migration to Medina. The missionaries were directed by the Proof (ḥujja) of the hidden Imam who moved to Salamya in Syria and established the headquarters of the clandestine revolutionary movement.

Around the year 885, the Ismāʿīlīs first took up arms in the Yemen (Halm 1996, chap.1). According to Halm's careful reconstruction of this obscure early phase of the movement, in the late 890s, the Proof in Salamiya decided to split the mythical seventh Imam-Mahdi-Qāʾim to its component parts, claiming the Imamate for himself and designating his nephew (he had no son) the Mahdi, and the latter's young son, the Qāʾim. The nephew, Saʿīd b. al-Ḥusayn, renamed himself ʿAbd Allāh al-Mahdī and his infant son, Muḥammad al-Qāʾim. Not only had the latter become Muḥammad b. ʿAbd Allāh, like the Prophet, but he was also given the latter's kunya, Abūʾl-Qāsim. This decision caused a split in the Ismāʿīlī movement.

Those who accepted the New Mahdi availed themselves of secondary apocalyptic titles. The chief of the mission in the Yemen, Ibn Ḥawshab, as we have seen, assumed the title of "the Manṣūr of the Yemen." The two sons of the missionary Zakaroye, who established an ephemeral state for the Mahdi in Syria in 903, also put forward apocalyptic claims of their own. The older one appeared with the name Yaḥyā b. Zakaroye, conveniently close to Yahya b. Zecharaia (= John the Baptist in Q. 21:89–90). He claimed to be a descendant of Muḥammad b. Ismāʿīl and maintained that his crippled arm was a miraculous sign. He was named the Shaykh by his followers, who called themselves the Fatimids (after the daughter of the Prophet, from whom the Imams, including Muḥammad b. ʿIsmāʿīl descended). He was also known as the Man of the She-Camel (ṣāḥib al-nāqa), as he claimed the camel mare he rode on the battlefield was divinely guided, evoking the She-Camel of God (nāqat Allāh, in Q. 11:64), whose killing by the nation of the prophet Ṣāliḥ brought about their destruction. When the Shaykh fell in battle, his brother, al-Ḥusayn, saw to the disappearance of his body and took over the leadership of the Fatimids. He claimed his birthmark was his sign, and accordingly he became known as the Man of the Birthmark (ṣāḥib al-shāma). His aide and cousin assumed the obscurely apocalyptic Koranic title of al-Mudaththir (Q. 74:1), "the one who covers himself" (TTkh 3:2218–20).[42]

In the fall of 903, while the Mahdi remained in hiding in Palestine, the Man of the Birthmark had the Friday sermon read in the name of "the Lord of the Age (ṣāḥib al-zamān), the Commander of the Faithful, the Mahdi" (Halm 1996, 82). The uprising for the Mahdi was suppressed by the forces of the caliph, and the Mahdi himself fled from Palestine to Egypt, and thence to Sijilmāsa in North Africa. Here he was robbed by bandits, who took his books of astrological oracles and secret writings. The books on political astrology, which were later recovered in Egypt by his son, al-Qāʾim, can safely be assumed to have contained the prediction of the passing of world domination from the Arabs at the conjunction of Saturn and Jupiter in the year 296 (908–909 C.E.) (see de Goeje 1886, 121–22). As was pointed out, in the year 909, the missionary who had been active on the Mahdi's behalf in North Africa in fact established the Fatimid state for ʿAbd Allāh al-Mahdī, who was in due course succeeded by his son, Muḥammad al-Qāʾim (Halm 1996). The Fatimids conquered Egypt in 969, and their empire, extended to Egypt and Syria, lasted two more centuries until it was overthrown by Saladin (Ṣalāḥ al-Dīn al-Ayyūbī) in 1171.

The Ismāʿīlīs who refused to accept the authority of the new Mahdi and remained faithful to the apocalyptic belief in the imminent return of Muḥammad b. Ismāʿīl as the Mahdi-Qāʾim after the schism became known as the Qarmaṭīs (Qarmatians) after their putative original leader, Ḥamdān Qarmaṭ. The Qarmatians predominated in the "islands" of Iraq and Bahrain (al-Baḥrayn). They succeeded in establishing a state in the latter region shortly after the schism. At the beginning of the tenth century, the Qarmatians proclaimed the sovereignty of the Qāʾim-Mahdi in their communally organized state. The tenth-century geographers Muqaddasī and Ibn Ḥawqal report respectively that in the Qarmatian state there was a "treasury (khazīna) of the Mahdi" and one-fifth of the revenues were kept for the Lord of the Time (ṣāḥib al-zamān) (Madelung 1996, 40). In the year of the seventh conjunction of the Fiery Triplicity (928) a young man from Isfahan who claimed to be the descendant of the Persian kings had joined the Qarmatians in Bahrain. A few years earlier, presumably in anticipation of the astrally determined turn in domination, a man claiming to be Muḥammad b. Ismāʿīl appeared in January 925 and gathered a large band of bedouin around him (Halm 1996, 64). Later that year, the caliphal police discovered a group of Qarmatians, called the Baqliyya, whose members carried clay seals stamped with the inscription, "Muḥammad b. Ismāʿīl, the Mahdi-Imam, the friend of God." What appears as spontaneous Mahdistic agitation among the Baqliyya was suppressed, and some of the survivors drifted to Bahrain and became known as the Ajamiyyūn, that is, the non-Arabs (Madelung 1996, 50).

In 930, the Qarmatians attacked Mecca, massacred the pilgrims and carried away the black stone to mark the end of the era of Islam. Meanwhile, the young man from Isfahan soon found his way to the inner circle of the Qarmatian elite and was told by one insider to approach the de facto ruler of Bahrain and the son of its founder:

> Go to Abū Ṭāhir and tell him that you are the man to whose allegiance his father and he himself had summoned the people. If he then asks your for signs and proofs, reveal these secrets to him. (de Goeje 1886, 132; and Madelung 1996, 46)

Abū Ṭāhir, whose poetry declaims that he would live until the coming of Jesus, son of Mary, recognized the signs and publicly surrendered the sovereignty to the Qāʾim from Isfahan in 931. According to the eyewitness account of the physician Ibn Ḥamdān, Abū Ṭāhir declared:

> Know then, community of men, that the [true] religion has henceforth appeared. It is the religion of our father Adam, and all the belief we had was false. All the things missionaries made you hear, their talk about Moses, Jesus and Muhammad, was falsehood and deceit. The [true] religion is in fact the religion of Adam, and those are all wily Dajjāls; so curse them." (Madelung 1996, 46–47 [translation slightly modified])

The Mahdi of Isfahan ruled for eighty days that ended in disaster. The apocalyptic Ismāʿīlīs of Iran had sought to put Islam in the perspective of the history of religions and identified Zoroaster with Abraham. At least one of their theorists, Nasafi, had presented the religion of Adam as the natural religion, religion without the law. The Isfahani Mahdi, who evidently

took the astral sign to indicate the end of the era of world domination by the Arabs and beginning of the domination of the Persians, ordered the worship of fire, established links with the
Zoroastrian clergy in Iran, and had the biblical prophets as well as the Imams, including ʿAlī,
cursed in public. All this was too much for Abū Ṭāhir, who had him seized and killed
(Madelung 1988, 99).

Far less disastrous and longer lasting was the proclamation of the Great Resurrection or
the Resurrection of the Resurrections by the Nizārī Ismāʿīlīs two centuries later. The Nizārīs
had broken off from the Fatimids in another schism in 1094, upholding the Imamate of Nizār,
the ousted older son of the Fatimid caliph al-Mustanṣir. Some Nizārīs believed that their Imam
was in occultation and would return as the Qāʾim-Mahdi. Their redoubtable leader, Ḥasan
Sabbāḥ (d. 1124), however, soon propounded "the new preaching" (daʿwat-e jadīd) and opted
for a hidden Imam with a visible Proof (ḥujja) as the head of the mission and the supreme
authority in the authoritative teaching (taʿlīm) of the adepts. The Nizārīs, who called each other
"comrade" (rafīq), held a number of impregnable fortresses in the mountains of Iran and Syria,
which they used for training zealous devotees (fidāʾi) and developing the technique of political
assassination in the revolutionary struggle against the Seljuq empire (Lewis 1985, 48–49).

As we have seen, on the astrologically determined date of August 8, 1164, the ruler of
Alamūt and other Nizārī Ismāʿīlī fortresses, Ḥasan II b. Muḥammad b. Bozorg-Omīd proclaimed the Resurrection as the Deputy (khalīfa) and Proof (ḥujja) of the Imam and the Riser of
the Resurrection (qāʾim al-qiyāma).[43] This meant that the era (dawr) of the law and external
reality had come to an end and the era of inner reality had begun. All believers could know God
and the cosmic mysteries through the Imam, and God would constantly be in their hearts. The
essence of their creed, in Juwaynī's words,

> [W]as that, following the Philosophers they spoke of the world as being uncreated and Time as
> unlimited and the Resurrection as spiritual. . . . It was laid down in the Law that men must
> worship God five times a day and be with Him. That charge was only formal but now in the
> Resurrection they must always be with God in their hearts and keep the faces of their souls con-
> stantly turned in the direction of the Divine Presence for such is true prayer.[44]

Ḥasan II was fatally stabbed in January 1166, but his son Muhammad II confirmed the
continuation of the resurrection, which lasted for a total of 46 years to 1210. The mission was
now "the call to [or perhaps 'the preaching of'] the resurrection (daʿwat-e qiyāmat)" (see
Juwaynī 3:240), and the Nizārīs considered themselves "the saved community of the Qāʾimites
(qāʾimiyān)."[45] As time went on, the doctrine of the Resurrection as developed by Muhammad
II, who claimed the Imamate for himself and his father as putative descendants of Nizār, made
the Imam the manifestation of the word and command of God through whose vision the
believers could find themselves in paradise. He added the Sufi level of truth (ḥaqīqa) to the
Ismāʿīlī levels of external and inner reality and identified it with the resurrection (Daftary 1990,
388–95).

Ḥasan II, "upon whose mention be peace," was now considered the Qāʾim as well as the
Imam, but the meaning of the term changed radically because of the declaration of resurrection. A treatise written some forty years into resurrection, reaffirmed the old Ismāʿīlī idea that
ʿAlī was the Qāʾim of the resurrection, but also asserted that "all the Imams are ʿAlī (bless him)
himself, and will be" (Haft Bāb 14.18).[46] It is true that the Qāʾim of the resurrection, "in this
period of ours, . . . in the clime of the sun, . . . in the land of Babylon among the lands of the

ʿAjam [non-Arabs], ... in the midst of the Jabal [mountainous region] ..., at the castle of Alamūt, he was Our Lord [Ḥasan II]" (*Haft Bāb*, 41; Hodgson 1955, 322). But the Qāʾim is no longer restricted to that particular incarnation. He is the eternal Imam and the primordial Adam who completes the cycle of revelation (*kashf*) (Jambet 1990, 62–66, 307, 311). With the resurrection, the Qāʾim as the New Adam is and will ever be in the heart of the people of truth, imparting to them the authoritative teaching (*taʿlīm*) that transcends the duality of external and inner reality and makes possible the full pantheistic plenitude of existence (Buckley 1984, 144; Jambet 1990, 96–99). By completing the cycle of revelation (*kashf*), the Great Resurrection is the apocalyptic appropriation of the world through the universal integration of saving knowledge into the daily lives of the people of truth. With this kenosis of apocalyptic into Sufi mystical pantheism, the ultimate potential of Gnostic Ismāʿīlī apocalypticism was realized as mystical life in posthistory.

☞ LATER DEVELOPMENTS

The fourteenth and fifteenth centuries were the era of realization of apocalyptic in history in a variety of Mahdistic popular movements. While the apocalyptic impulse of Ismaʿilism emptied itself into popular Sufism and the defeated Ismāʿīlī Imams became Sufi shaykhs, the opposite trend was far more typical in the fourteenth and fifteenth centuries. With the Mongol overthrow of the caliphate in 1258, the learned hierocracy lost the support of the state and the position of the *ulema* became shaky in the face of the challenge of popular Sufism. Containment of political apocalypticism by the doctors of law, be they Sunni or Shiʿite, fell apart. The chiliastic Qāʾim-Mahdi of the traditions burst through the rationalized integument of the theology of divine grace and pushed aside the nomocratic order for millennial activism under the leadership of several Mahdistic incarnations of divine charisma (Arjomand 1984, chap. 2).

In this era of Turko-Mongolian domination, which preceded the Ottoman championship of orthodox Islam, a variety of chiliastic popular movements arose among the Sufi orders which dominated the religious life of the masses without serious competition from the orthodox doctors of law. The Sufi shaykhs who led these movements claimed to be the Mahdi and/or his forerunners. Most notable among these movements were the Sarbidār movement in Khurasan, in the fourteenth century, the Ḥurūfiyya in Iran and Anatolia at the end of the fourteenth and beginning of the fifteenth century, the extensive rebellion of Shaykh Badr al-Din against the Ottomans, the Mahdist movements of Nurbakhsh (in Iran and Central Asia) and Mushaʿshaʿ (in Khuzistan), and last but not least the Safavid movement (in northwestern Iran and Anatolia) in the fifteenth century. The social setting for these Mahdist movements is complex, and the range of variation considerable.[47]

The Safavid revolution, set in motion by this last instance of Mahdism at the very end of the fifteenth century, however, swung the pendulum once more from political apocalypticism to law. The consolidation of nomocratic order in the Ottoman, Safavid, and Mughal empires in the sixteenth century put an end to the late medieval era of chiliastic popular movements. A new era was opened with the approach of the Islamic millennium toward the end of the sixteenth century, which continued to modern times.[48]

NOTES

1. P. Casanova's *Mohammed et la fin du monde* (Paris, 1911) has inspired little subsequent research and remains a rare exception.

2. For other verses, see H. E. Kassis, *A Concordance of the Qurʾān* (Berkeley/Los Angeles: University of California Press, 1983), 1111–12; and for a typical interpretation of the Hour, see Gätje 1996, 172–73.

3. Traces of the primeval combat between God and the beasts of chaos subsist in some of the apocalyptic traditions (*Fitan,* 356–62, 401–5). The only case of direct divine intervention I have noticed, however, is the end of Gog and Magog: "God lifts [the smoke] after three days; and Gog and Magog are indeed thrown into the sea" (*Fitan,* 362). See chapter 1.

4. An earlier verse (Q. 40:7) does not give a number for the throne-bearers. Some of the early commentators who must have known Ezekiel's vision of the throne with four angels (Ezek. 1:5–7, 26) attributed to the Prophet the explanation that four additional angels will help the regular throne-bearers on the Day of Resurrection (TR 11:251). A tradition that links the Prophet with the Jewish practitioner of *merkabah* mysticism, Ibn Ṣayyād, mentioned the arabicized form of the Hebrew *ḥayyôt* ("living creatures") for the throne-bearers, thereby suggesting the *merkabah* and its pseudepigraphic sources as the channel for the reception of the idea in the Qurʾān. See Halperin 1976, 217.

5. Presumably this was conveyed through such pseudepigrapha as the "Oracle of Baalbek"; see P. J. Alexander, *The Oracle of Baalbek* (Washington, D.C.: Dumbarton Oaks, 1967), 29; and the Syriac Ezra (see J.-B. Chabot, "L'Apocalypse d'Esdras," *Revue Sémitique* 2 [1894]: 340).

6. To suggest that most Jews and Christians would find the final call of the Mahdi irresistible, one tradition predicts that he will recover the ark of covenant from the Sea of Tiberias (*Fitan,* 223).

7. Still later he was to become the revealer of magico-astrological secrets (see Stone 1982, 16).

8. See the English translation of this text by M. Perlmann, *The Ancient Kingdoms* (Albany: State University of New York Press, 1987), 62.

9. See the English translation by G. H. A. Juynboll in *The Conquests of Iraq, Southern Persia and Egypt* (Albany: State University of New York Press, 1989), 147.

10. Michael is mentioned once (Q. 2:92). Gabriel is explicitly named only three times (Q: 2:91–92; 66:4), but there are also several references to the [holy/trustworthy] spirit (*rūḥ*) who brings down God's messages.

11. In one tradition, it is placed after the killing of the Antichrist by Jesus (*Fitan,* 362).

12. See Abūʾl-ʿAlī b. al-Ḥusayn al-Masʿūdī, in *Murūj al-Dhahab,* ed. C. Pellat (Beirut, 1970), 3:7.

13. Muḥammad b. ʿUmar al-Wāqidī, *Kitāb al-Maghāzī,* ed. J. Marsden Jones (London: Oxford University Press, 1966) 1:72–78; see also Ibn Saʿd 1904, 3:9.

14. Ibn Rabbān considers this sign foretold in Isa. 9:6[5] (1922, 95).

15. H. Yaghmāʾī, ed., *Tarjuma-ye Tafsīr-e Ṭabarī* (Tehran: Tūs, 1977/1356) 6:1704–6.

16. See also P. Crone and M. Cook, *Hagarism: The Making of the Islamic World* (Cambridge: Cambridge University Press, 1977), chap. 1.

17. See the English translation by G. R. Smith, *The Conquest of Iran* (Albany: State University of New York Press, 1994), 96. See also TTkh 1:2403, 2409; English translation by Y. Friedmann, *The Battle of Qādisiyya and the Conquest of Syria and Palestine* (Albany: State University of New York Press, 1992), 189, 196; as well as Bashear 1990.

18. *Daggālā,* meaning "deceiver," is found in Ephraem and other apocalyptic writers. See Abel 1954–, 2:76.

19. Some three decades later *Pseudo-Methodius* was to use this biblical image (see Bousset 1896, 227).

20. English trans. by G. R. Hawtig, *The Collapse of Sufyānid Authority and the Coming of the Marwānids* (Albany: State University of New York Press, 1989), 120 (emphasis added).

21. Bidez and Cumont 1938, 2:115; the significance of the term *qāʾem* is lost in the French translation on the following page.

22. Through the *Qurʾān* commentator ʿAlī b. Ibrāhīm.

23. The variant given in Muḥammad b. Ibrāhīm, Ibn Abī Zaynab al-Nuʿmānī, *Kitāb al-ghayba* (Beirut, 1983), 14, is as follows: "Indeed God revives it by the justice of the Qāʾim upon his manifestation (*ẓuhūr*) after its death due to the injustice of the Imams of error [i.e., illegitimate rulers]."

24. The verb ʿ*md* used in the verse is the postexilic synonym for *qwm,* to rise, whose active participle is *qāʾêm* (riser). See Collins 1993, 390.

25. The Judeo-Christian apocalyptic lore was known in the region since the Southern Jewish Kingdom of Dhū Nuwās in the early sixth century (see Newby 1988, chap. 4).

26. He is killed in arms before the appearance of a man from the House of Ahmad who will in turn be followed by the Dajjāl and Jesus.

27. Interestingly attributed to al-Walīd II b. Yazīd, whose murder started the Third Civil War in 744.

28. For an English translation of this text, see C. Hillenbrand, *The Waning of the Umayyad Caliphate* (Albany: State University of New York Press, 1989), 142–43.

29. Abū ʿĪsā al-Warrāq, cited in Muḥammad b. al-Ḥusayn al-ʿAlawī, *Bayān al-Adyān,* edited by H. Raḍī (Tehran: Farāhānī, 1964/1342), 56–57.

30. I take Shahrastānī's incomprehensible *al-dāʾī* on 1:175 to be a corruption of *al-rāʾī.*

31. A tradition that displaces the Raḍwa mountain to Fars in southern Iran (*Biḥār,* 52:153) may have originated around this time.

32. Or in the following decade, as he is supposed to have presented it to Marwān II. A. Abel, "L'Apocalypse de Bahîra et la notion islamique de Mahdî," *Annuaire de l'Institut de philologie et d'histoire orientales et slaves* (Bruxelles) 3 (1935): 5; idem, "Changements politiques et littérature eschatologique dans le monde musulman," *Studia Islamica* 2 (1954): 28.

33. English trans. by P. M. Fields, *The ʿAbbasid Recovery* (Albany: State University of New York Press, 1987), 171.

34. See also Ibrāhīm b. Muḥammad al-Farsī al-Isṭakhrī, *Masālik al-Mamālik,* ed. M. J. de Goeje, 2nd ed. (Leiden: E. J. Brill, 1927), 77 note e. The medieval Persian translation of the manuscript quoted in the note is now published (see I. Afshār, ed., *Masālik wa Mamālik* [Tehran, 1989/1368], 79).

35. ʿA.-ʿA. al-Dūrī and ʿA.-J. al-Muṭallabī, eds., *Akhbār al-Dawla al-ʿAbbāsiyya* (Beirut, 1971), 148.

36. Also important was his disciple Abū Maʿshar al-Balkhī (d. 886) on whom see Pingree 1968, 6–13.

37. It is interesting to note that Ibn Abī Ṭāhir's treatise in political astrology is followed, in the same manuscript, by the Book of Jafr, "extracted from the Books of Daniel and Solomon, son of David." (BL Oriental MS Add 7473, f. 63b.)

38. The wall he looked for in Samarqand was presumably the one built by another Sassanian king, Pīrūz, against the Heptalite Turks, who nevertheless killed him in 483 C.E. See Ḥamza b. al-Ḥasan al-Iṣfahānī, ed. M. E. Gottwaldt, as corrected by J. I. Tabrīzī (Berlin: Kaviani, 1921/1340), 38.

39. ʿAbd Allāh b. ʿAbd Allāh Ibn Khurdādhbih, *Kitāb al-Masālik waʾl Mamālik,* ed. M. J. de Goeje (Leiden, 1889), 139–45.

40. Ismāʿīl was the designated successor of the sixth Imam, Jaʿfar al-Ṣādiq, but he predeceased him.

41. Nawbakhti's *Firaq al Shiʿa,* as cited in H. Halm, *The Empire of the Mahdi: The Rise of the Fatimids,* trans. M. Bonner (Leiden: Brill, 1996), 21.

42. See F. Rosenthal, *The Return of the Caliphate to Baghdad* (Albany: State University of New York Press, 1985), 114–16; cf. Halm 1996, 70-81.

43. He later hinted that he himself was the Imam and the Qāʾim of the Resurrection.

44. ʿAlaʿud-Dīn ʿAṭa Malik-i Juwaynī, *The Taʾrīkh-i Jahān-gushā,* ed. M. Qazvīnī (Leiden, 1937) 3:236–37; see Lewis 1985, 73–74.

45. *Haft Bāb-i Bābā Sayyid-na,* ed. W. Ivanov, in *Two Early Ismaili Treatises* (Bombay, 1933), 5, 7.

46. English trans. in M. G. H. Hodgson, *The Order of Assassins* (The Hague: Mouton, 1955), 293, 296.

47. Rather than offering a perfunctory survey, I refer the interested reader to Babinger 1921. Unfortunately, there is no good study of this movement in English. See also Mazzaoui 1972; and Arjomand 1984, chap. 2.

48. The subsequent history of Islamic apocalypticism will be treated in chapter 23.

⮞ BIBLIOGRAPHY

Abbreviations

Biḥār   Muḥammad Bāqir al-Majlisī. *Biḥār al Anwār.* 110 volumes. Beirut: al-Wafāʾ, 1983.

Condordance   A. J. Wensinck. *Concordance et Indices de la Tradition Musulmane.* 2nd ed. 8 vols. Leiden: E. J. Brill, 1992.

EI   *The Encyclopaedia of Islam.* New edition. 8 volumes to date. Leiden: E. J. Brill, 1954–.

Fitan   Nuʿaym b. Ḥammad al-Marwazī. *Kitāb al-Fitan.* Edited by S. Zakkār. Mecca: n.d. [1991].

Life   A. Guillaume. *The Life of Muhammad: A translation of Ibn Isḥāq's Sīrat Rasūl Allāh.* Oxford: Oxford University Press, 1955.

Q.   The *Qurʾān.* Some of the short Meccan chapters, notably 79–82, 99–101, are entirely apocalyptic. In addition, apocalyptic verses are scattered throughout the *Qurʾān.* The most important of these are cited in the essay.

TQ   ʿAlī b. Ibrāhīm al-Qummī. *Tafsīr.* 2 volumes. Edited by T. al-Mūsawī al-Jazāʾirī. Qumm: Maṭbaʿat al-Najaf, 1965–66/1387.

TR   Abūʾl-Futūḥ al-Rāzī. *Tafsīr.* 13 volumes. Edited by ʿA.-A. Ghaffārī. Tehran: Islāmiyya, 1977–78/1398.

TT   Muḥammad b. Jarīr al-Ṭabarī. *Jāmiʿ al-Bayān fī Tafsīr al-Qurʾān.* 30 volumes. 1905–12.

TTkh   Muḥammad b. Jarīr al-Ṭabarī. *Taʾrīkh al-Rusul waʾl-Mulūk.* Edited by M. J. de Goeje et al. 3 series. Leiden: 1879–1901.

TZ   Maḥmūd b. ʿUmar b. Muḥammad al-Zamakhsharī. *al-Kashshāf.* 4 volumes. Edited by M. A. Shāhīn. Beirut: Dār al-Kutub al-ʿIlmiyya, 1995.

Umm.   "*Umm al-Kitāb,* edited by W. Ivanow." *Der Islam* 23 (1936): 1–132. [References are to paragraphs.] Includes a tenth- or eleventh-century Gnostic *Apocalypse of Jābir.*

Studies

Abel, A. 1954a. "Dadjdjāl." In *EI.*

———. 1954b. "Changements politiques et littérature eschatologique dans le monde musulman." *Studia Islamica* 2.

Aguadé, J. 1979. "Messianismus zur Zeit der frühen Abbasiden: Das Kitāb al-Fitan des Nuʿaim ibn Ḥammād." Ph.D. dissertation. Tübingen.

Alexander, P. J. 1985. *The Byzantine Apocalyptic Tradition.* Berkeley/Los Angeles: University of California Press.

al-ʿAlawī, Muḥammad b. al-Ḥusayn. 1964/1342. *Bayān al-Adyān.* Edited by H. Raḍī. Tehran: Farāhānī.

Amir-Moezzi, M. A. 1995. *Divine Guide in Early Shiʿism.* Albany: State University of New York Press.

Arjomand, S. A. 1984. *The Shadow of God and the Hidden Imam: Religion, Political Order and Societal Change in Shiʿite Iran from the Beginning to 1890.* Chicago: University of Chicago Press. Chapter 2 of this work offers a conspectus of the late medieval Mahdist movements.

———. 1994. "ʿAbd Allāh Ibn al-Muqaffaʿ and the ʿAbbasid Revolution." *Iranian Studies* 27.

———. 1996a. "Crisis of the Imamate and the Institution of Occultation in Twelver Shiʿism: A Sociohistorical Perspective." *International Journal of Middle East Studies* 28.

———. 1996b. "The Consolation of Theology: The Shiʿite Doctrine of Occultation and the Transition from Chiliasm to Law." *Journal of Religion* 76.

———. 1997. "Imam *Absconditus* and the Beginnings of a Theology of Occultation: Imami Shiʿism around 900 CE/280/90 AH." *Journal of the American Oriental Society* 117.

Babinger, F. 1921. "Schejch Bedr ed-Dīn, der Sohn des Richters von Simāw." *Der Islam* 9.

Bashear, S. 1990. "The Title 'Fārūq' and its Association with ʿUmar I." *Studia Islamica* 72.

———. 1991. "Apocalyptic and Other Materials on Early Muslim–Byzantine Wars: A Review of Arabic Sources." *Journal of the Royal Asiatic Society,* Series 3, 1.2

Bidez, J., and F. Cumont. 1938. *Les Mages hellénisés.* Paris.

al-Bīrūnī, Abū Rayḥān. 1879. *The Chronology of Ancient Nations.* Translated and edited by C. E. Sachau. London.

Bousset, Wilhelm. 1896. *The Antichrist Legend.* London: Hutchinson.

Browne, E. G. 1956. *A Literary History of Persia.* Cambridge: Cambridge University Press.

Buckley, J. J. 1984. "The Nizārī Ismāʿīlītes' Abolishment of the Sharīʿa during the 'Great Resurrection' of 1164 A.D./559A.H." *Studia Islamica* 60.

Casanova, P. 1911. *Mohammed et la fin du monde.* Paris: Geuthner.

Collins, J. J. 1993. *Daniel: A Commentary on the Book of Daniel.* Minneapolis: Fortress Press.

Cumont, Franz. 1931. "La Fin du monde selon les mages occidentaux." *Revue de l'histoire des religions* 104.

Daftary, F. 1990. *The Ismāʿīlis: Their History and Doctrines.* Cambridge: Cambridge University Press.

de Goeje, M. J. 1886. *Mémoire sur les Carmathes du Bahrain et les Fatimides.* Leiden: E. J. Brill. Although dated with respect to some details, this work remains valuable for its rare treatment of the role of astrological calculations in Islamic apocalyptic speculations.

al-Dūrī, ʿA.-ʿA. 1981. "al-Fikra al-mahdiyya bayn al-daʿwa al-ʿabbāsiyya waʾl-ʿaṣr al-ʿabbāsī al-awwal." In *Studia Islamica et Arabica: Festschrift for Iḥsān ʿAbbās.* Edited by Wadād al-Qāḍī. Beirut.

Faqīhī, ʿA.-A. n.d. *Tārīkh-e Madhhabī-ye Qumm.* Qumm: Hikmat.

Friedlaender, I. 1911–12. "Jewish-Arabic Studies." *Jewish Quarterly Review* n.s. 2:488–92.

Gätje, H. 1996. *The Qurʾān and Its Exegesis.* Translated by A. T. Welch. Oxford: Oneworld.

Grotzfeld, S. 1969. "Dāniyāl in der arabischen Legende." In *Festgabe für Hans Wehr,* edited by W. Fischer. Wiesbaden: Otto Harrassowitz.

Halm, H. 1982. *Die islamische Gnosis.* Zurich/Munich: Artemis. A selection of early Shiʿite apocalyptic texts in German translation with introductions and commentary.

———. 1996. *The Empire of the Mahdi: The Rise of the Fatimids.* Translated by M. Bonner. Leiden: E. J. Brill. A superbly clear account of the confusing beginnings of the Ismāʿīlī movement translated from the original German edition of 1991.

Halperin, D. J. 1976. "The Ibn Ṣayyād Traditions and the Legend of al-Dajjāl." *Journal of the American Oriental Society* 96.

Hartmann, R. 1924. *Eine islamische Apokalypse aus der Kreuzzugszeit.* Schriften der Königsberger Gelehrten Gesellschaft Geisteswissenschaftlische Klasse 1.3. Berlin.

Hodgson, M. G. S. 1955. *The Order of Assassins: The Struggle of the Early Nizārī Ismāʿīlīs against the Islamic World.* The Hague: Mouton.

———. 1968. "The Ismāʿīlī State." In *The Cambridge History of Iran.* Volume 5, *The Saljuq and Mongol Periods,* edited by A. J. Boyle. Cambridge: Cambridge University Press. An updated abridgment of Hodgson 1955.

Humphreys, R. S. 1990. *The Crisis of the Early Caliphate.* Albany: State University of New York Press.

Ibn Bābūya, Muḥammad b. ʿAli b. al-Ḥusayn. 1970/1390. *ʿUyūn Akhbār al-Riḍā.* Edited by M. M. al-Kharsān. Najaf.

———. 1975/1395. *Kamāl al-dīn wa tamām al-niʿma fī ithbāt al-ghayba wa kashf al-ḥayra.* Edited by ʿA.-A. Ghaffārī. Tehran: dār al-Kutub al-Islāmiyya. The most comprehensive source for the early Shiʿite traditions on the Mahdi and the Qaʾim.

[Ibn Rabbān]. ᶜAli [Ibn Rabbān] Tabari. 1922. *The Book of Religion and Empire*. Translated and edited by A. Mingana. Manchester: Manchester University Press.

Ibn Saᶜd, Muḥammad. 1904. *Kitāb al-Ṭabaqāt al-kabīr*. Edited by E. Sachau et al. Leiden.

Ivanow, W. 1933. *Two early Ismaili Treatises*. Bombay. The first of these, the *Haft Bāb*, written about 1200, expounds the Ismāᶜīlī theory of the resurrection on earth, and is translated into English with commentary as an appendix to Hodgson 1955.

Jambet, Charles. 1990. *La grande résurrection à Alamūt*. Paris: Verdier.

Kennedy, E. S., and David Pingree. 1971. *The Astrological History of Māshā ᵓAllah*. Cambridge, Mass.: Harvard University Press.

Khoury, R. F. 1986. *ᶜAbd Allāh ibn Lahīᶜa (97–174/715–790: Juge et grand maître de l'école égyptienne*. Wiesbaden: Otto Harrassowitz.

Knibb, M. A. "Apocalyptic and Wisdom in 4 Ezra." *Journal for the Study of Judaism* 13.

Lazarus-Yafeh, Hava. 1992. *Intertwined Worlds: Medieval Islam and Biblical Criticism*. Princeton: Princeton University Press.

Lewis, Bernard. 1950. "An Apocalyptic Vision of Islamic History." *Bulletin of the School of Oriental and African Studies* 13.

———. 1985. *The Assassins: A Radical Sect in Islam*. 2nd ed. London: Al Saqi Books.

Madelung, Wilfred. 1954a. "Ismāᶜīlīyya." In *EI*.

———. 1954b. "Kaysāniyya." In *EI*.

———. 1954c. "Mahdī." In *EI*.

———. 1981a. "ᶜAbd Allāh b. al-Zubayr and the Mahdi." *Journal of Near Eastern Studies* 40.

———. 1981b. "New Documents concerning al-Maᵓmūn, al-Faḍl b. Sahl and ᶜAlī al Riḍā." In *Studia Islamica et Arabica: Festschrift for Iḥsan ᶜAbbās*, edited by Wadad al-Qadi. Beirut.

———. 1986a. "Apocalyptic Prophecies in the Umayyad Age." *Journal of Semitic Studies* 31.

———. 1986b. "The Sufyānī between Tradition and History." *Studia Islamica* 63.

———. 1988. *Religious Trends in Early Islamic Iran*. Columbia Lectures in Iranian Studies 4. New York: Bibliotheca Persica.

———. 1996. "The Fatimids and the Qarmatis of Bahrayn." In *Medieval Ismaᶜili History and Thought*, edited by F. Daftary. Cambridge: Cambridge University Press.

al-Majlisī, Muḥammad Bāqir. 1983. *Biḥār al-Anwār*. 110 volumes. Beirut: al-Wafāᵓ. The encyclopedic compendium of Shiᶜite traditions on the Qāᵓim and the Mahdi from the beginning to the seventeenth century.

Manṣūriᵓl-Yaman, Jaᶜfar b. 1952. *Kitabu'l-Kashf*. Edited by R. Strothmann. London: Oxford University Press.

Marquet, Y. 1972. "Les Cycles de la souveraineté selon les Épîtres des Ihwān al-ṣafāᵓ." *Studia Islamica* 36.

al-Marwazī, Nuᶜaym b. Ḥammād. n.d. [1991]. *Kitāb al-Fitan*. Edited by S. Zakkār. The most important collection of Sunni apocalyptic traditions compiled after the end of the second Islamic century by Nuᶜaym b. Ḥammād (d. 844).

al-Masᶜūdī, Abūᵓl-ᶜAlī b. al-Ḥusayn al-Masᶜūdī. 1894. *al-Tanbīh waᵓl-Isrāf*. Edited by M. J. de Goeje. Leiden.

———. 1966–79. *Murūj al-Dhahab*. 7 vols. Edited by B. de Meynard and P. de Courteille, corrected by C. Pellat. Beirut.

Morabia, A. 1979. "L'Antéchrist (ad-Dajjāl) s'est-il manifesté de vivant de l'envoyé d'Allāh?" *Journal Asiatique* 267.

Nemoy, L. 1930. "al-Qirqisānī's Account of the Jewish Sects." *Hebrew Union College Annual* 7.

al-Nuᶜmāni, Muḥammad b. Ibrāhīm Ibn Abī Zaynab. 1983. *Kitāb al-ghayba*. Beirut.

Newby, G. D. 1988. *A History of the Jews of Arabia*. Columbia: University of South Carolina Press.

Paret, R. 1954. "Aṣḥāb al-Kahf." In *EI* 1.

Pedersen, J. 1954. "Djabrāᵓīl." In *EI* 2.

Pingree, David. 1968. *The Thousands of Abū Maᵓshar*. London: Warburg Institute.

al-Qummī, Muḥammad b. al-Ḥasan al-Ṣaffār. 1983–84/1404. *Baṣāʾir al-Darajāt.* Qumm: Makataba Āya-tullāh al-ʿUzma al-Marʿashī al-Najafī.

Rosenthal, Franz. 1962. "The Influence of the Biblical Tradition on Muslim Historiography." In *Histori-ans of the Middle East,* edited by F. Rosenthal, B. Lewis, and P. Holt. London: Oxford University Press.

al-Sharastānī, Muḥammad b. ʿAbd al-Karīm. *al-Milal waʾl-Nihal.* Edited by M. S. Kaylānī. Beirut.

Stone, M. E. 1982. "The Metamorphosis of Ezra: Jewish Apocalypse and Medieval Vision." *Journal of The-ological Studies* n.s. 33.

Tucker, W. F. 1975a. "Rebels and Gnostics: al-Muġīra ibn Saʿīd and the Muġīriyya." *Arabica* 22.1.

———. 1975b. "Bayān b. Samʿān and the Bayāniyya: Shiʿite Extremists of Umayyad Iraq." *The Muslim World* 65.4.

———. 1977. "Abū Manṣūr al-ʿIjlī and the Manṣūriyya: A Study in Medieval Terrorism." *Der Islam* 54.

al-Ṭūsī, Muḥammad b. al-Ḥasan. 1965/1385. *Kitāb al-Ghayba.* Edited by A. B. al-Ṭihrānī. Najaf. An eleventh-century treatise on the occultation of the Twelfth Imam that contains many earlier tradi-tions on the Mahdi and the Qāʾim.

VanderKam, J. C. 1995. *Enoch: A Man for All Generations.* Columbia: University of South Carolina Press.

van Ess, J. 1970. "Les Qadarites et la Gailānīya de Yazīd." *Studia Islamica* 31.

Wagtendonk, K. 1969. "Muhammad and the Qurʾān: Criteria for Muhammad's Prophecy." In *Liber Ami-corum: Studies in Honor of Professor Dr. C. J. Bleeker.* Leiden: E. J. Brill.

al-Wāqidī, Muḥammad b. ʿUmar. 1966. *Kitāb al-Maghāzī.* Edited by J. Marsden Jones London: Oxford University Press.

Wasserstrom, Steven. 1985. "'The Moving Finger Writes': Mughīra b. Saʿīd's Islamic Gnosis and the Myths of Its Rejection." *History of Religions* 25.

———. 1995. *Between Muslim and Jew: The Problem of Symbiosis under Early Islam.* Princeton: Princeton University Press. An informative but historically slippery treatment of the relation between Jewish and early Islamic, especially Shiʿite, millenarian themes.

Watt, W. Montgomery. 1953. "His Name is Aḥmad." *Muslim World* 43:110–17.

Widengren, Geo. 1950. *The Ascension of the Apostle and the Heavenly Book.* Uppsala: Uppsala Universitets Årsskrift.

———. 1955. *Muhammad, the Apostle of God, and His Ascension.* Uppsala: Uppsala Universitets Årsskrift.

PART 3

Apocalypticism in the Modern Age

16

Apocalypticism in Central and South American Colonialism

Alain Milhou
University of Rouen

T HE CRUSADERS HAD THEIR EYES set on the levant, toward the *umbilicus mundi,* where the celestial and earthly Jerusalems became superimposed. Joachite or millennial-inspired movements, all those in the Middle Ages who were concerned with eschatology or with the foreboding signs of the world's end and the final struggle against the Antichrist, who yearned on a more spiritual level for a *renovatio mundi,* looked toward the promised land.

But from the time of Christopher Columbus on, eyes would now be cast in a different direction. The discoverer himself was divided between his obsession with the Jerusalem crusade and his celebration of the "new skies and the new land." The New World, located to the west, associated with the world's end, now rose as a new promised land, a land of all things possible. This New Jerusalem was born in an apocalyptic clash: that produced by the struggle against the devil, master of the new continent, if things are seen from the point of view of Iberian providentialist history; or that produced by the devilish excesses of the conquerors, if Las Casas's indigenist viewpoint is adopted. This essay, therefore, will examine the lengthy path that leads from Columbus to the Independence generation early in the nineteenth century, who could well have conceived this remarkable sentence written by Chateaubriand in *Les Natchez:* "The Eternal Father revealed to his beloved Son his designs about America: he was preparing for all mankind a renovation of existence in that part of the world" (1986, 227). One may well recognize under such a romantic form of expression the *renovatio mundi* of medieval and Renaissance prophets.

America was truly a promised land for all Christians, but less so for Jews. For the indigenous peoples, the conquest was acknowledged as one of the cyclical catastrophes that were mentioned in their cosmologies. But those who managed to escape from the apocalyptic demographic plunge—or, at least, part of them—were also able to integrate their own values into Christian messianism, which sometimes produced surprising forms of syncretism.

☞ COLUMBUS AND HIS TIMES:
FROM THE CRUSADES TO THE MESSIANIC
CELEBRATION OF THE NEW WORLD_____

When Christopher Columbus (1451–1506) arrived in Spain in 1485 while the war of Reconquest of the peninsula's last Muslim kingdom was being waged, he was able to witness the development of those prophecies applied to the Catholic monarchs Ferdinand of Aragon and Isabella of Castile. A *romance,* set to music that same year by the royal chapel, expresses the wish to see the two sovereigns, after the fall of Grenada, stamp out the "sect of Muhammad" and reconquer the "Holy Mansion," or *Casa Santa.* (In medieval and sixteenth-century Spain, Christians, following the Jews in that respect, frequently used the expression the "Holy Mansion" when referring to the holy Temple and thus, by extension, to Jerusalem as a whole.) Columbus, the Genoese adventurer steeped in the environment of business concerns and messianism that characterized Portugal at the time of the major discoveries, could then appropriately witness the birth or renewed growth of his obsession concerning the crusade and the Holy City.

It was during the messianic atmosphere following the fall of Grenada (January 2, 1492) that Christopher Columbus finally obtained the royal agreement (April 17) to his mad project of reaching India by the western route. It was in fact such a propitious atmosphere that enabled him to present his glimmering project of a planetary struggle against Islam, thanks to the alliance with the Great Khan of Cathay as well as with the hidden Christendoms, such as the mythical kingdom of Priest John. The bringing together of all Spanish provinces (Castile, Aragon, and Grenada) and religious unification ensured by the inquisitorial persecutions against heretics and crypto-Jewish *conversos*[1] and by the expulsion of all Jews who refused to convert (decree of March 31)—were not these the foreboding signs of the heyday that would witness the fall of Islam, the reconquest of Jerusalem, and the gathering together of all humanity, Muslims, Jews, and pagans, within the bosom of the church: in other words, the formation "of a single flock" under the crook of a single shepherd (John 20:16)? Such a messianic vision frames the prologue of Columbus's first logbook, where he places, by personal conviction or by flattery, his own messianism within the official messianism inspired by the Catholic monarchs.

Indeed, Ferdinand of Aragon and later on his successors of the Hapsburg dynasty appeared as "Last Emperors," as "hidden kings" (*Encubert* in Catalan, *Encubierto* in Castilian Spanish) in numerous prophecies from the most diverse cycles. These included prophecies by the Pseudo-Methodius and the Pseudo-Joachim, introduced in the Catalan provinces as early as the thirteenth century, and by Franciscan visionaries linked to the House of Aragon, such as Arnold of Villanova (ca. 1240–1311) and Francesc Eiximenis (1340–1409); astrological predictions, sometimes of Muslim origin; Celtic traditional vaticinations attributed to Merlin; and, finally, lamentations on the destruction of Spain (in other words, the Muslim invasion, aided and abetted by the Jews) as well as visions of its final restoration in the Reconquest attributed to the emblematic figure of Castilian messianism, St. Isidore of Seville, the Hispano-Roman polygraphist who had celebrated the Visigothic monarchy at the beginning of the seventh century.

But is the discoverer a mere spokesman for the official messianism of the crowns of Castile and Aragon? Could not his taste for Old Testament prophecies—the fact that he compares himself to, and even identifies himself with, David, as well as his obsession concerning Jerusalem and the restoration of its Temple—be seen as clues of barely hidden Judaism? This is what the Spanish historian Juan Gil has recently claimed (1989, chap. 7). Therefore, could not the discovery of this New World be credited to Jewish messianism insofar as the eschatological concerns of the Hebrews, then persecuted within Spain, were definitely on the rise? Is it not significant that many Jews, more or less converted, actually did enlist as members of Columbus's first voyage crew? Some historians claimed that they wanted to flee from a land that expelled those Jews who retained the faith of their ancestors in order to find again the lost tribes of Israel, those tribes which had once left Assyrian captivity for an unknown destination.

It is true that on three occasions Christopher Columbus mentions a prophecy attributed to Joachim of Fiore (d. 1202) according to which "he who would rebuild the House on Mount Zion, was to leave from Spain." This, however, is a very ancient vaticination formulated around 1300 by the Valencian "spiritual" Arnold of Villanova. Once applied to a Spanish sovereign, it enjoyed an extraordinary application all the way up to the beginning of the seventeenth century. According to the Franciscans, heirs to the *spirituals,* it was the image of church reform. Did the admiral interpret the prophecy in this allegorical sense, as did observant Franciscans of more or less Joachite inspiration? It would be somewhat surprising, for the themes of church renovation and of the return of evangelical purity and simplicity are totally absent from his concerns. And as for the material reconstruction of the Temple, which Columbus did mention explicitly, could not such an idea be suspected of Judaism, or at least of a dangerously heterodox Judeo-Christian syncretism?

It seems more reasonable to think that for him, as for many others, the reconstruction of the Temple, evidently changed into a church, was rather the eschatological sign of the bringing together of all peoples converted to the Christian faith into God's house. Such an image had already been used in a similar fashion by Jean de Roquetaillade (b. 1346), a fourteenth-century Franciscan from the Auvergne, whose prophecies had considerable impact in the Iberian peninsula, first in Aragon, then in Castile, and later still, during the sixteenth century, in Portugal. It was also used later by two Jesuits who were closely linked to the history of the New World, Vieira and Lacunza. In the year of the discoverer's death, 1506, King Manuel of Portugal, in a letter to Cardinal Cisneros, then regent of Castile, mentioned this "Holy Mansion," where, once the crusade had ended, he would receive the body of Christ from the hands of the archbishop of Toledo, together with his father-in-law, King Ferdinand the Catholic.

But even if one day a document were to be discovered proving that Columbus was a converted Jew, or even a crypto-Jew, it still would not alter the main point, namely, that on the spiritual level Western expansion and, particularly, the discovery of the New World were carried by a Judeo-Christian messianism that reaches back beyond the Crusades, back to Isaiah and his evocation of faraway islands being converted, a fact that is recalled in the *Book of Prophecies,* the famous documentary compilation brought together by the discoverer himself.

An opposite thesis to that of a Jewish origin has also been proposed, namely, that Columbus would have considered himself the messianic herald of the era of the Holy Ghost, following the ternary structure (i.e., ages of the Father, the Son, and the Holy Spirit) inherited from Abbot Joachim.[2] In 1498 during his third trip, the admiral finally reached the shores of the new continent near the Paria peninsula in front of the island on which he significantly bestowed, with his acute sense of religious symbolism, the name of Trinidad. He had become aware of both the size and novelty of these southern lands, unknown to the ancients and different from the Asian continent, which he believed he had already discovered while cruising along the coasts of Cuba. He bestowed on it the most extraordinary epithets, "Holy Island" and "Isle of Grace," before assuming that this might be a new continent where the Garden of Eden could be located far inland in an inaccessible place. As one can read in the *Letter to the Wet Nurse of Prince Don Juan,* these were "the new skies and the new land mentioned by Our Lord through St. John's Apocalypse, after having been revealed by the words of Isaiah" (ed. Varela-Gil, p. 430). Columbus also proclaimed that God had chosen him as a "messenger" in order to announce the discovery of these lands, sanctified both by the memory of the original paradise and by the announcement of the Apocalypse. Was this not also the prophecy of the spiritual age or of the millennium? Was not Columbus tempted to think of himself as the new David? In the eyes of many Joachite-inspired visionaries, King David was but the prefiguration of the Christ-King, the new David, and of the messianic king-priest, the third David of the spiritual age. Other texts tend to suggest that Columbus may have been influenced, albeit in an indirect way, by Pseudo-Joachimism. But it would still be somewhat hazardous to declare that he considered himself the millennial Messiah. Even though he may have been tempted to do so, Columbus did not go any further, being too respectful of established order, both ecclesiastical and temporal.

If such caution must be emphasized, one may readily admit that with his messianic celebration of the southern continent, Columbus truly did open a capital line of thought in the history of humanity: America as a substitute for Jerusalem, as a promised land, as a New Jerusalem. Such a line of thought runs through the entire history of the New World. In this respect, Columbus, the merchant-crusader from the Middle Ages, inaugurated modernity.

☞ THE AMERICAN DREAM IN IBERIAN CONSCIOUSNESS DURING THE SIXTEENTH AND SEVENTEENTH CENTURIES _____

Because of his restless devotion and his sense of eschatology, Columbus represents the exception within the large crowd of discoverers, conquerors, and settlers. These latter overwhelmingly professed a simple form of religion, essentially defined by its external features; they quickly passed on to the native Indians their taste for statues of the Christ of the Passion and of the Virgin Mary. Insofar as their messianism was concerned, the long centuries of Reconquest fought against the Moors and the rise to power of Spain had given them an extraordinary sense of self-confidence; they considered themselves, in a way, representatives of a new chosen people, assured of their salvation in the struggle against the Other—not long ago the infidel, and now the pagan. Bearing no moral concerns with respect to the Indians until the time missionaries were able to make their voices heard and to introduce the demands of Christian ethics, they sought primarily to become wealthy, to lead an easy life, and to climb the social ladder.

The pursuit of quick wealth and of an easy life could acquire messianic features, though in a degraded form. As soon as the news about the discovery of the riches of Peru was known, the New World definitely became in popular imaginations an ideal country which partook both of the Garden of Eden and of the fabulous land of plenty (Milhou 1986, 7–20). This is, at any rate, what a peasant from the Toledo region expressed in May 1534, only one year after the affair of Atahualpa's ransom. (The Inca Atahualpa [1485–1533] then the prisoner of Francisco Pizarro [1480–1541], had his subjects assemble an incredible amount of precious metals in the hope, soon deceived, of buying his freedom.) "While I was at the village blacksmith's with some friends discussing the news of Peru and of all these amounts of gold and silver that were brought back from there, one of them said that this was the country where Our Lord Jesus Christ had lived, since the grass where he walked had changed into gold and silver and this was why there was so much of it to be found" (Archivo Historico Nacional de Madrid, Inquisición, legajo 47, expediente 14). Memories of apocryphal gospels as well as folk traditions must have intermingled in the heated mind of this Sancho Panza. Soon afterwards, for the Spaniards the land of plenty identified itself with the name of a Peruvian valley, "the land of Jauja." It was then that the legend of El Dorado developed. We shall consider other examples showing how the pagan theme of the paradise of all delights was able to contaminate that of the Garden of Eden.

The conquerors' and early settlers' concern for social ascent sometimes achieved an almost messianic dimension in the sense of a liberation from Old World constraints. From the early decades on, as one can read of it in a magnificent chapter of Las Casas's *History of the Indies* (book 3, chap. 105), the New World was, for peasants wishing to free themselves from lordly tutelage, a "free and royal" land, a "blessed country," where Spaniards, equal in dignity, would have no lord except the king. The tragedy, as Las Casas bitterly observes, was that the conquerors and settlers, nobles or laymen, all aspired to become *encomenderos*,[3] that is, lords of Indians. Only a small minority was successful in such an endeavor, hence the frustrations that generated new expeditions, unrest, or even revolts.

The Peru of postconquest times was, between 1537 and 1561, the setting of prolonged civil wars among the conquerors. The part played by those who were called in Peru the *soldados,* or soldiers, in other words the proletarians of the conquest, was particularly significant in Francisco Hernández Girón's rebellion (1553–1554). Hernández Girón (d. 1553) was a wealthy *encomendero* from Cuzco who raised the banner of revolt against the policies of the Lima authorities, who in turn wished to apply the royal ban on the use of indigenous forced labor. At the start, therefore, he was just a representative of the local oligarchy, even if he introduced himself as the "captain of the freedom of the realm" and, as such, as the defender of all the Spaniards of Peru, from the *encomenderos* all the way down to the *soldados.* But the former, duly instructed by the failure of Gonzalo Pizarro's major rebellion (1544–1548), preferred to stick to a benevolent neutrality, while taking due advantage of any concessions the royal authorities agreed upon in order to calm the situation. The defection of these elites thus left Hernández Girón at the head of a movement essentially made up of *soldados* and marginal elements. Hernández Girón was also surrounded by many sorcerers and soothsayers, particularly a Moorish woman who claimed to interpret dreams. In order to reinforce his army, he promised black slaves their freedom if they joined him. He also encouraged some of the millennial wishes of the poor *soldados.* He wore a medal engraved with the words *Edent pauperes et saturabuntur* ("The poor shall eat and be satisfied"), borrowed from a messianic psalm on the trials of the righteous and traditionally applied to the suffering Christ who satiates all the hungry (Ps. 22:26). He claimed to be the defender of the *pobrecitos,* a Franciscan-inspired word (*poverello*), and even declared that St. Francis of Assisi (1182–1226) himself, the favorite saint of Christian millennialism, had appeared before him to encourage him in his endeavor. Moreover, the rumor spread that he had set fire to the Potosí silver mines. Such a rumor was the sign of the bucolic dream of some of the *soldados* who finally burnt what they had hitherto worshiped, perhaps because of the frustration of an unsatisfied desire, perhaps also because of the influence of some cleric who had thundered against the "mouth of hell" of Potosí.

Let us now consider the more specifically religious forms of apocalypticism and messianism. It was from the years 1520/1530 on, after the conquest of central Mexico by Hernán Cortés (1485–1547) and the crossing by Magellan (ca. 1480–1521) of the straits to which he gave his name, that the New World finally revealed both the sheer size and the novelty of its geography and population. In his letter of January 20, 1531, to the Council of Indies, Bartolomé de Las Casas (1474–1564) considered that the New World was much larger and richer than the old one and contained "the major part, indeed almost all of mankind." Thus the moral responsibility of the Spanish crown, who had been unable to put an end to the cruelties and massacres—thus also its spiritual responsibility since so many Indians, yet to be baptized, would go to hell, where they would be joined by their exploiters in a state of mortal sin. Las Casas is probably the first to have emphasized so strongly America's importance in the history of humanity.

At that same time the Franciscans of "New Spain," the name Cortés had now given to Mexico, considered that the evangelization of large and apparently receptive native populations on a land that until then had been the privileged domain of devilish idolatry meant that eschatological times were near, thus fulfilling Christ's message as to the coincidence between the final evangelization and the end of all time (Matt. 24:14). For several Franciscans in New Spain, an association between the New World and the end of the world seemed obvious. Did not the Latin word *novissima* designate the latter day? Franciscans were certainly not the only ones to develop these eschatological variations; they can also be found, for instance, in an extraordinary 1550 Joachite text, written to the glory of the Jesuit Order.

One can witness the birth of the "good savage" myth in Columbus's first log book (1492/1493) as well as in his letter to Luis de Santángel (1493), in Pedro Váz de Caminha's letter to King Manuel of Portugal (1500) announcing the discovery of Brazil, in Amerigo Vespucci's *Mundus novus* accounts (1503?) and *Quatuor navigationes,* and in the *Decades de orbe novo,* written between 1493 and 1525 at the Spanish court by the Milanese humanist Pietro Martire d'Anghiera (1455–1516). The themes of the gentle Indian, naked and innocent, unaware of the difference between private and common property, which could be found in varying degrees in all these writings, would soon foster utopian or messianic theories. The West Indies thus appeared as a New World in which one could create with its innocent and pliant inhabitants a utopian Christian republic, an ideal Christendom worthy of the church's early times, or even a latter-day church.

The first accounts of the American discoveries provided Thomas More (1478–1535) with the starting point for his *Utopia* (1516), a communitarian model for the Old World perverted by its own selfishness, its unjust hierarchies and its rising capitalism. Inspired by the English chancellor's message, Vasco de Quiroga (1470–1556), a judge in the *Audiencia* that was then Mexico's governing body and the future bishop of Michoacán, imagined as early as 1532/1533 that a Christian society which would revive the golden age of the poets and philosophers of the Greco-Roman classical age as well as the early apostolic times might be created among the Indians of New Spain. An acknowledged disciple of Thomas More, Quiroga also had been indirectly influenced by Abbot Joachim through a text by St. Antonino of Florence that he interpreted in the following way. The church was bound to age and decay, but from its ruins a newborn church would rise, guided by reformed pastors called upon to rebuild it among these Indians, who were closer to the golden age than their European counterparts concerned exclusively with power, pomp, and riches.[4] Like him, the Franciscans in New Spain also dreamed of creating a church made up of poor and humble Indians separated from the reach of the greedy settlers. But, as it has been argued, was all this really a form of Joachite and millennial Christendom? We shall see how such an argument can be assessed. But, at any rate, it would be wrong to limit to the Franciscans alone the yearning to create a model form of Christendom in the New World. The Dominican Las Casas, basing his views on the testimony of Columbus's log book as well as on his own experience, was the most eloquent exponent of the native Indian's pre-Christian qualities. Moreover, he did not merely celebrate the Indian as such, but even thought about the ideal model of a *mestizo* Christian republic, something quite exceptional in colonial times.

The case of the Jesuit missions, the *reducciones,* particularly those of Paraguay (1609–1767), is more complex. They were unquestionably part of a Christian utopian vision, which the Jesuits adorned in their propaganda with the colors of the true primitive church, as opposed to the countermodel of the society made up of the Spaniards together with their creole and *mestizo* offspring. But the Jesuits did not conceive of their missions as a latter-day church based on the qualities of innocent savages. As rational and efficient instruments of the Counter-Reformation, the Jesuits were globally hostile to Joachite and millennial illusions despite several well-known exceptions like Andrés de Oviedo (1518–1580) and António Vieira (1606–1697). They also had given up the illusions of the good savage myth. But while they might have had a low estimation of the barbarous nature of the Moxo, Chiquito, Tupi, and Guarani Indians, they did try to make the best possible Christians out of them through fatherly and stern methods. In that respect, they were following the moderate thesis, far removed from any kind of messianism, of Father José de Acosta (1538–1599), the celebrated author of one of the most outstanding colonial missionary treatises, the *De procuranda Indorum salute* (1588).

Much could be said about the ambiguous nature of the good savage myth. The earlier visions of the Indian were quite ambivalent. The other face of the innocent native was that of the evil savage, both faithless and lawless, barbarous, man-eating, and sodomite. The countermodel of the peaceful Lucay and Taíno was the ferocious Carib, the cannibal. But even the Taíno Indians of Hispaniola, idealized by Columbus, became cowardly, slothful, and beastly creatures in the eyes of European settlers. The discovery of Aztec civilization convinced Cortés that this was a relatively civilized population, but the polytheism and human sacrifices of central Mexico's inhabitants reinforced the image of a barbarous continent ruled by the devil.

The almost hopeless barbarity and the devilish nature of indigenous religions were the dominant features of the vision reported by the official chronicler, Gonzalo Fernández de Oviedo, in his *General and Natural History of the Indies,* published in 1535. Oviedo's pessimism on the nature of the Amerindian provoked the strong enmity of Las Casas, the most optimistic of all the chroniclers with regard to the perfectibility of the Indian. Yet even without attaining Oviedo's degree of pessimism, similar considerations can also be found in the writings of many missionaries who were otherwise keen to defend the cause of the Indians and were utterly convinced of their ability to become good Christians. Vasco de Quiroga himself strenuously insists on the fact that evangelization and the teaching of "proper" human "polity" should draw the Aztecs and Tarascs away from their "barbarity" so as to "restore" among them the innocence of a golden age to which they were nonetheless closer than Europeans. As for Motolinía (d. 1568), the other Mexican Franciscans, or the Jesuit Andrés de Oviedo, they considered evangelization an apocalyptic struggle against the devil, the lord and master of the Indies. Thus their approval of armed conquest, despite critical comments about its excesses, since it was for them the first indispensable step toward the destruction of devilish idolatry. One can appreciate therefore the originality of Las Casas, for whom the devil was embodied not in the Indian but in the greedy and violent conqueror.

Paradoxically, such an emphasis on the theme of a devil's land could lead to the messianic exaltation of the New World. Following the model of pagan Rome, which became the center of Christendom, Mexico, the ancient capital city of Aztec idolatry, was hailed by eighteenth-century preachers as a new Rome or a New Jerusalem. The Virgin of the Apocalypse, venerated in the Guadalupe sanctuary, had defeated the dragon and the beast, the shapes of which could be detected in the drawings made of the lakes and rivers on the Mexican maps. Therefore there were those who did not hesitate to move even farther and predict that Mexico one day would become the new capital city of Christendom.

The messianic vision of the New World was strengthened also by the fear of an eventual renewal of "Spain's destruction," that is, by the return of the Muslim invasion of eight centuries. Throughout the sixteenth and even up to the beginning of the seventeenth century, numerous apocalyptic prophecies referred to such destruction, the instruments of which would now be the Turks and the inhabitants of Barbary, helped from within Spain by the *Moriscos,* those imperfectly converted descendants of the peninsula's former Muslim population. Strangely enough, such fears did not cease after the victory of Lepanto in 1571, but continued until the final expulsion of the *Moriscos* in 1609. To this traditional anxiety caused by the Moorish and Turkish perils now was added also the fear of Protestantism. The Inquisition was keen to play upon this new fear, particularly in 1559 with the arrest of Toledo's Archbishop Carranza, falsely accused of Lutheranism, and with the stamping out of "Protestant"—actually Evangelical—centers in Valladolid and Seville. According to the Holy Office's propaganda, the good Spaniard, faithful to his king, could be nothing but Catholic, while those Spaniards suspected of Protestant beliefs and practices were seen as foreign agents.

One cannot emphasize enough the fact that within the Spain of Philip II and Philip III, apparently so proud and sure of itself, prevailed an underlying sense of concern in the wake of both foreign and internal perils. Were not *Moriscos,* crypto-Protestants, or even crypto-Jews a fifth column within the heart of Catholicism's besieged fortress? Such fears were extended beyond 1640 through the phantasms conjured up by the possible collapse of Spain's overseas empire, which was then undergoing a severe crisis. In the wake of these Old World perils, the New World appeared to some as the ultimate refuge for the threatened Catholic faith. Such a theme is suggested in the later works of the Dominican Luis of Grenada. It clearly appears in the treatise *Light of the Soul,* published in 1554 by the Dominican Felipe de Meneses, as well as in the *History of the Indies* by his order brother Bartolomé de Las Casas, in a sermon by the Augustinian St. Thomas of Villanueva, and in the *History of the Indies of New Spain,* written between 1565 and 1581 by Diego Durán (d. 1588), a Dominican missionary in Mexico. All these authors even go so far as to consider the eventual transfer of the Catholic Church to the Indies following its destruction in Europe.

Portuguese messianism stemmed from a triple heritage: a political-religious messianism based on the epic plight of the African and Asian discoveries; the eschatological Iberian tradition; and Jewish messianism, the proportion of Marranos being, indeed, much higher in Portugal and Brazil than in the Hispanic world. One can ascertain the mixture of these three trends in the *Trovas* of Bandarra, a collection of rhymed prophecies that began its extraordinary notoriety as early as the 1530s. The poet, self-taught, announced the coming of a mysterious latter-day king, *o Encoberto* (the Portuguese equivalent of the Catalan *Encubert* and the Castilian *Encubierto*), who would restore justice and destroy Islam. After the disappearance of King Dom Sebastian in his foolish Moroccan crusade, Portugal was annexed by the Spanish crown from 1580 until 1640. Even though Portugal and its empire continued to enjoy a large degree of autonomy, the union of both crowns was, nonetheless, seen by a growing majority of the population on both sides of the Atlantic as an actual annexation. Many Jesuits, linked from the beginning of their order to the Portuguese monarchy, were keen (particularly in Brazil, where they were the dominant order) to encourage Sebastianism, that is, the belief in the missing king's return. He would either come back in person or through the providential member of a national dynasty. After revealing himself, this "hidden king" would accomplish Portugal's messianic vocation by first liberating the empire from the Spaniards in the Iberian peninsula and from the Dutch who had invaded and occupied northeastern Brazil, and then by establishing a universal millennial kingdom. We may observe that if it is true that Hispanic American messianism became more and more of a rival with regard to Spanish messianism, it is difficult to dissociate the American and Portuguese components of Luso-Brazilian messianism. The reason probably is that Brazil had become the Portuguese empire's cornerstone shortly before Spanish annexation, and would remain so until Independence, which was achieved without any kind of dramatic severance and, what is more, with the presence at its head of a legitimate descendant of the Portuguese dynasty.

For the Diaspora Jews, no New Jerusalem may ever be worthy of rivaling the unique and only one, even though some cities, like seventeenth-century Amsterdam, or some promised lands, like America, could eventually be used as substitutes. Many were the Jews—more or less converted—who did emigrate, despite official bans, to the Indies of Castile and Brazil. Quite soon America became part of the Jewish cosmology, not quite exactly as a promised land but as a peripheral space where Jews could enjoy a greater degree of peace despite the establishment of Inquisition courts in Lima (1570), Mexico (1571), and Cartagena de Indias (1610). As for Brazil, it witnessed only inquisitorial visits, but without the creation of a permanent court.

This peripheral American space, however, gradually became a cornerstone of Jewish messianism. According to beliefs based on the fourth book of Esdras, which developed from the middle of the sixteenth century among Christians as well as among the sons of Israel, America had been the host land to all or at least part of the ten tribes lost at the time of the Babylonian Exile. Such belief gave birth to two theories, namely, that the Indians were the descendants of those lost tribes, or that, according to another version, the Jews lived hidden among the Indians. These hidden Jews were those whom the Portuguese *marrano* Antonio de Montezinos claimed to have discovered in the forests of New Grenada, present-day Colombia. Soon after Montezinos's return to Amsterdam, Rabbi Manuel Dias Soeiro, who had assumed the name of Menasseh ben Israel (1604–1657), incorporated his compatriot's and coreligionist's narrative in a celebrated messianic text, *The Hope of Israel,* published in Spanish, Latin, and English in 1650, then later on in Dutch (1666), Yiddish (1691), and Hebrew (1698). Menasseh was the leader of a prosperous middle-class community, well established in a tolerant town that some did not hesitate to qualify as the "Jerusalem of the West" or "of the North." This did not prevent him from keeping his eyes fixed on Palestine's Jerusalem, since the discovery of these American Jews was for him the prophetic announcement of the return of all dispersed, or even hidden, Jews from all over the world, the dark parts of which were now gradually unveiled. The reading of such a work probably prepared the minds of Amsterdam's Judeo-Portuguese community for the enthusiastic welcoming in 1666 of the news that the Messiah, in the person of Sabbatai Sevi (1626–1676), had shown himself in Smyrna, thus announcing the return to Zion in Palestine.

MAJOR FIGURES OF APOCALYPTICISM AND IBERO-AMERICAN MESSIANISM

Las Casas, the famous Dominican friar, is well known for his actions in favor of the Indians. He is less well known for his eschatological and messianic tendencies. In fact, these two aspects of his enthralling personality are closely tied together. Indeed, Bartolomé de Las Casas established an apocalyptic relationship among the following: (a) the "destruction of Spain" when the country fell into the hands of Islam at the beginning of the eighth century; (b) the "destruction of the Indies" by way of an armed conquest, which he qualified as "Mahometan" and as "much worse than that which the Turk had carried out in order to destroy the church," and also through the colonial exploitation particularly embodied in the *encomienda* institution; and (c) the renewal of the "destruction of Spain," which God would surely allow as a punishment for the sins committed in the Indies if colonial injustices were not corrected. This certainty, expressed in 1542 in the *Eighth Remedy* against the *encomienda* and in the famous *Brief Account of the Destruction of the Indies,* haunted Las Casas until his death, as one can ascertain from his 1564 will.

There is probably a fourth element present in Las Casas's apocalyptic vision. Heresiarch Francisco de la Cruz invoked Brother Bartolomé's authority to justify his belief in the transfer of Christendom to the Indies after its destruction in Europe. This idea is expressed as a possibility in the *History of the Indies* (book 1, chap. 29). The new continent would constitute "apparently the major part of the universe, . . . where God must extend his Holy Church and, perhaps, transfer it altogether, while enabling his holy faith to shine among so many infinite nations who will know about it."

But whereas such an idea logically derives from the concern expressed by Las Casas about the possible destruction of European Christendom, it also follows on his approach celebrating the Indies and its inhabitants. His defense of the Indians and of their ability to accept the true faith is well known. And as for his descriptions of the American provinces, they abound with messianic connotative epithets such as "God's paradise" and "blessed lands." It seems as though Las Casas dreamed about setting up an ideal Christendom on the New World's paradisal lands, based on a union between Indians and Spanish farmers: "with both groups united through the bonds of marriage, these two republics could be turned into a single one, one of the best, one of the most Christian and one of the most peaceful in the world" (*History of the Indies,* book 3, chap. 102). This Brother Bartolomé wrote around 1560 when referring to his 1518 agrarian colonization projects. But even after the destruction of the Indies had also destroyed his utopia, yet he still retained his dreams that maybe one day Indians, friars, and good settlers would ensure the triumph of his prophetic ideas and welcome the remains of European Christendom.

The paradisal description of the Indies and the reference to the destruction of Spain and the transfer of Christendom to the New World may be considered revealing elements of Las Casas's belief in a first rough sketch of American millennialism. Other clues may also be found, among them the ban placed by Las Casas on the publication of his *History of the Indies* as long as the truth of his ideas did not prevail. But one should not project upon Las Casas the millennial thesis of Francisco de la Cruz, even if the latter acknowledges his debt to his Dominican brother. Las Casas's messianic or even millennial dreams are unquestionably less important than his apocalyptic denunciation of the "Indies hell" and his ceaseless fight in favor of the oppressed Indians.

In June 1524, solemnly greeted by Cortés, the *Twelve* made their entry into Mexico. Led by their superior Martín de Valencia (d. 1533), an ascetic who frequently had apocalyptic visions about the world's evangelization, these strict observance Franciscans set out to repeat the feat of the original twelve apostles. We have already stressed their conviction of actually living in the latter days of the world as well as the apocalyptic meaning they gave to their struggle against the demon of idolatry as the extension of an armed conquest of which they approved.

Would it not then be possible to build a Christendom worthy of the primitive church, purified from the pomp and vices of European Christendom, with the help of these Mexico Indians, looked upon as poor, humble, and obedient, as well as lacking the Spaniards' greed and pride? This "Franciscan" vision of the Indian can be found in Toribio de Benavente (d. 1569), who wanted in a way to reincarnate his master, St. Francis, the *Poverello*, by accepting for himself the name given to the deliberately miserable-looking group of the *Twelve*—*Motolinía*, "the poor one," in Náhuatl. This vision can be found also in his disciple Jerónimo de Mendieta, who, in his *Historia eclesiástica indiana* completed at the end of the sixteenth century, bemoaned the failure of the Franciscan dream. However, should one accept the arguments of Georges Baudot and John Leddy Phelan, the two leading specialists on Motolinía and Mendieta, when they analyze the Joachite-inspired "millennial kingdom" project of the Mexico Franciscans? In the light of recent studies, it seems that their interpretation must be questioned.

For Joachim of Fiore and his *spiritual* disciples such as Ubertino da Casale, the third *status* of the world, that of the Spirit, would witness the heyday of filial and unselfish love and of the *intelligentia spiritualis*, as opposed to servile obedience, fear, and public ceremony. In addition, there are those subversive millennialists who distorted Joachimism in an antihierarchical sense. Yet none of this can be found in Mexico's Franciscans, who never mentioned a millennial kingdom. Martín de Valencia, the leader of the *Twelve*, was deeply concerned with eschatology and was probably also influenced by Joachimism, like Motolinía or Mendieta; but he was not a millennialist, nor were his disciples. As his first biographer, Friar Francisco Jiménez, who was one of the initial *Twelve*, noted, Martín de Valencia "doubted that the New Church could be solidly grounded among these natives." Despairing of the Indians with whom coercion ultimately had to be used, he even prepared himself in 1532 to leave for China, where this ideal church could be built with populations "of greater capability," accessible to meditation and contemplation, all of which was impossible with the barbarians of New Spain, who could never become "spiritual men." It is also true that Motolinía had a much more positive vision of the humble Indians, but the ambiguity of this notion of "humbleness" must be emphasized. Neither Motolinía nor Mendieta questioned the power of the *encomenderos*, as did Las Casas. They did not question the Spanish domination of an indigenous society that would always need, according to them, the fatherly tutelage of missionaries. Indians would always be the last ones within the earthly world, even if they were to be granted the first place in the kingdom of God. In order to justify the refusal to ordain Indians, Mendieta unwaveringly declared, "they are not fit to command or lead, but to be commanded and led" (*Historia eclesiástica indiana,* book 4, chap. 23).

Even if they described New Spain as a promised land, neither Motolinía nor Mendieta considered that the salvation of humanity was to come from the Indies, contrary to what the visionaries Francisco de la Cruz and Gonzalo Tenorio claimed. Mendieta clearly stated that the messianic mission for the reform of Indian society, for the "universal destruction" of those "perverse sects" widespread all over the world, and for the "conversion and gathering together of all peoples in the bosom of the Church," rested with the king of Spain called upon to bear the burden of universal monarchy (*Historia eclesiástica indiana,* book 1, chap. 2). This was the most typical classical version of the Spanish crown's official messianism.

Likewise, the matters of the millennium and the New Jerusalem were raised by Gregorio López (1542–1596), the mysterious Madrilenian *hidalgo* who left the mother country in 1562 to lead the life of a hermit in New Spain until his death in 1596. His actions at first raised considerable suspicion, then curiosity, and finally veneration. But the eschatological concerns of his very orthodox *Treatise on the Apocalypse,* even if not millennial, do reveal a deep obsidional feeling: Roman Catholic countries are a fortress besieged by Turks and heretics. One may thus legitimately assume that this man, who left Spain without any explanation and settled in Mexico, without trying to evangelize the Indians, in order to devote himself to mortification, contemplation, and study, was infected by the idea that the New World was a Catholic sanctuary where one could meditate in due peace on the final ends of humanity.

Gregorio López was quite probably influenced by illuminism (or *alumbradismo*[5]), the typically Spanish heresy which frightened the Inquisition so much that it developed a systematic suspicion about any kind of mysticism in general. One may even consider *Venerable* Gregorio López, whose beatification trial was stopped abruptly, as the precursor of quietism. His orthodoxy, though, was never questioned despite close surveillance on the part of the Holy Office, which did arrest and condemn several of his creole disciples. These Mexican *alumbrados* present a number of typical features of millennialism. To be sure, the matter is not one of a messianic hailing of the New World, as with Las Casas, Francisco de la Cruz, or Gonzalo Tenorio, and even up to a certain point Motolinía or Mendieta. But a typically Hispanic American slant can be observed in the dreams of these disciples of Gregorio López; some believed in the permanence of sexual life and generation in millennial society. Like Francisco de la Cruz, they thus justified ideally the greater looseness of morals that existed in America when compared to Spain. In another region of the New World, Paraguay, where it seems that concubinage and even polygamy had reached a scandalous level in the eyes of censors, Asunción, the province's capital city, was characterized as being "Muhammad's paradise."

In 1550 an anonymous Jesuit, probably Andrés de Oviedo, sent to Francis Borgia, who had just joined the order, a messianic treatise to the glory of the recently founded *societas Iesu,* which had just started its work of Catholic reform in Europe together with its missionary activity in Portugal's Asian empire (1542), as well as in Brazil (1549). This particular text, which has remained in manuscript form, bears witness to the soon-to-be-repressed Joachite temptation present within the Jesuit Order at its beginnings (Milhou 1994–95, 193–239). Its author celebrates in its pages the coming of the third *status* in world history, that of the Spirit. Based on Joachim of Fiore's *Expositio in Apocalypsim* and *Psalterium decem chordarum,* as well as on Ubertino da Casale's *Arbor Vitae Cruxifixae Iesu,* he provides an exegesis of the Vulgate's Psalm 106, of the hymn in Habakkuk's third chapter, and of several passages from the book of Revelation (particularly Rev. 3:7–13). In these times of gradual decay and aging of the world's second *status,* the Company of Jesus, the spiritual order announced by Abbot Joachim, was to be the instrument of rebirth, of the *renovatio mundi.* To achieve such a renovation of European Christianity, religion was to become an internal process through general meditation as taught by the Jesuits according to their method of *Spiritual Exercises.* The coming of the third *status* would also bring about a universal evangelization, now taken over by the Jesuits, particularly in the New World. In the previous phase, corresponding to the second *status,* evangelization remained superficial; it had followed an armed conquest deemed terrible but indispensable in order to defeat the devil, the former absolute lord of the new continent. The conquerors were cruel and greedy, but they did play their part as *flagellum Dei.* As for the suffering inflicted on the Indians, particularly the demographic catastrophe the author seemed to be perfectly aware of, it was the embodiment of God's punishment for the monstrous sins they had committed— idolatry, cannibalism, human sacrifices, and sodomy. Adapting Joachimism to the new times of church reform and the geographic opening of the world, the anonymous author merely mentioned the age of the Spirit, but without any reference to a millennial kingdom, thus restating, beyond the Pseudo-Joachimism of medieval vaticinations, Joachim of Fiore's true spiritual message, which was far removed from any explicit millennial belief.

As for the Portuguese Jesuit António Vieira, he was openly a millennialist, but only a remote influence of Joachimism can be detected in his writings. While he was a missionary in Brazil, he became the apostle for restoration of the independence of the Portuguese crown. The sermon he preached in Salvador da Bahia in 1634 on the occasion of Saint Sebastian Day was the clearest of encouragements for all Sebastianists. When he returned to Portugal several months after the 1640 restoration, he was arriving in a country that was living a heyday of messianic euphoria. Henceforth, from Portugal, Holland, Rome, and Brazil, where he died in 1697, he never ceased to prophesy the coming of the fifth empire in Daniel's vision (Dan. 2:31–45) to the benefit of the new Sebastians, the successive kings of the new Braganza dynasty—Joao IV, Alfonso VI, and Pedro II. It would be a mistake, however, to reduce Vieira to mere celebration of the Portuguese empire. His message reveals a deep yearning for universal harmony through peaceful means, setting aside the inevitable crusade against the Turks. Particularly worth noting is his ecumenical feeling toward Jews: in the Temple once rebuilt could coexist both the old covenant sacrifices performed by Jews, though converted to Christianity, and the sacrifice of the new covenant, that is, the Catholic mass.[6] Perhaps himself a *converso,* Vieira had been exposed in Brazil, Portugal, and Holland to Jewish messianism. In Amsterdam in 1647 he even had a lengthy discussion with Menasseh ben Israel about problems concerning the coming of the Messiah and the alleged Jewish origin of Indians.

Whereas Father Vieira's importance must be emphasized in the history of Luso-Brazilian and, more generally, of Christian apocalypticism, it must be pointed out that his system is not specifically American, as are those of Francisco de la Cruz or Gonzalo Tenorio. But his views are, nonetheless, an expression of the strength of eschatological beliefs in Brazil as early as the colonial period.

The most complete work of Catholic millennialism—*The Return of Christ in Glory and Majesty* by the Chilean Jesuit Manuel Lacunza (1731–1801), published in 1812 after his death in Italian exile—is, in a similar fashion, not directed toward a messianic celebration of America. It is the Palestine Jerusalem that the former Jesuit mentions as the meeting place where Jews, Christians, and Gentiles could make their peace. Influenced by Vieira, but as far removed from him as from true Joachimism, he interpreted much more literally the contents of chap. 20 of the book of Revelation. Whereas the Portuguese Jesuit merely admitted the coming of Christ in spirit upon the establishment of his millennial reign, his Chilean brother firmly believed in the presence of Christ among men as priest-king.

There are, nonetheless, subtle links between America and Lacunza's millennialism. A victim of the expulsion of the Jesuit Order (1767) and thereby forced to leave his native Chile, Lacunza compensated for this double frustration by seeking refuge in the millennium. Whereas Columbus had the "new skyes" descend on America's southern lands, Lacunza transferred far-away America to the Jerusalem descended from the skies into Palestine. On the other hand, his work did raise a continuing interest within Latin America: it was in answer to a petition from the archbishop of Santiago that his book and, more generally, the belief in the visible reign of Christ on earth, were condemned by Rome in 1944.

☞ THE CREOLIZATION OF MESSIANISM

In America as in Spain, Portugal, or other countries of the Old World, messianism was a privileged instrument for national consciousnesses in the making. Grounding himself on various Lascasian arguments, which he then twisted so as to find a justification for colonial society, Francisco de la Cruz was the first to systematize the full scope of messianic tendencies in early creole society. Yet Brother Francisco was not a creole. Having joined the Dominican Order, he received a thorough theological training at San Gregorio de Valladolid, the famous university college where Las Casas had set up his headquarters between 1553 and 1560. De la Cruz steeped himself in the ideas of the *Defender of the Indians* concerning peaceful evangelization and agrarian colonization as well as in his prophecies on the destruction of Spain. These vaticinations, those of another Dominican, Felipe de Meneses (ca. 1572), as well as the tragic events of 1559— the arrest of Archbishop Carranza and the burnings at the stake of the Seville and Valladolid "protestants"—must also have deeply impressed him. All this might help explain his departure for Peru in 1561, a year before that of Gregorio López for Mexico, probably for the same reasons. One may assume he was running away from a European Christendom the destruction of which, he believed, was imminent, as well as from a Spain that was resolutely moving along the path of inquisitorial intolerance. Upon his arrival in Lima, he was soon acknowledged as a renowned preacher, but he was also rapidly won over to the creole mentality. He progressively renounced Lascasian rigorism, admitting the legitimacy of armed conquest and the *encomienda*. He was also seduced by the loose morals of Limenian society, secretly fathering a child from his relationship with a noble lady penitent. But a more serious matter was to come— his participation, together with other churchmen of great prestige, in a small *alumbrado* and millennial party. This is why he was arrested by the Holy Office in 1572 and sentenced to be burnt at the stake in 1578.

According to Francisco de la Cruz, the Turk would destroy the whole of European Christendom. Hence the transfer of the church to the Indies and of the papal see to Lima, the New Jerusalem where Solomon's Temple would be rebuilt, the new Rome where brother Francisco would reign, cumulating the offices of pope and king of the New World. A distant and heterodox disciple of Joachimism, he used the system of harmonization among the three ages to proclaim himself a "third David." In his megalomania, he held his illegitimate son to be the new Solomon of the Third Testament. Together with him, he would inaugurate the American millennium, ruling over the Spaniards, creoles, and *mestizos,* as well as over the Indians, whom he saw as the degenerate descendants of the lost tribes of Israel, opposed to the Europeans qualified as "genteel Christians." This latter belief enabled Francisco de la Cruz to justify the armed conquest since it allowed the return to the fold of the Indians, considered "heretical Jews" who had forgotten their covenant with the true God by sinking back into idolatry.

Francisco de la Cruz announced the coming of a millennial society that would prosper far from the attacks of Satan, who would remain in chains for a thousand years, following the classical reference. The millennium, according to him, would represent the ideal model of a colonial society ruled by a creole aristocracy, and not too rigorous as far as social and family morals were concerned. The *encomienda* system would continue indefinitely; all civil and church authorities would be confirmed in their posts; polygamy would become lawful as would the marriage of priests; the descendants of the Inca dynasty would be definitely dispossessed, the Indian masses paternally submissive, and black slavery confirmed. Francisco de la Cruz also incorporated in his dream of an ideal and hierarchical society the Lascasian theme of a peaceful colonization achieved by Spanish peasants who, by intermingling with the native Indian society, would pave the way toward generalized cross-breeding. As for the merchants and mine owners, they simply had no place in this Edenic and autarchic Peru, since all its inhabitants would now dedicate themselves exclusively to "farming, cattle-raising, and handicraft."

Brother Francisco's millennial system could be attractive to creole society inasmuch as it justified a major part of colonial interests, setting mines aside, and led to ultimate praise of the New World as a true chosen land. Peru's viceroy, Francisco de Toledo, took very seriously the potential political threat of this Americanist heresy and put due pressure on the Holy Office to secure a particularly harsh sentence. As a matter of fact, it was unthinkable for the creole aristocracy to follow Francisco de la Cruz along the path of his separatist ravings. But, on the other hand, there was in Peru a large number of impoverished adventurers seeking new fortunes, genuine conquest dropouts who had nothing to lose and might have been eager to follow any illuminated *caudillo* who would promise them paradise on earth, as had been the case with Francisco Hernández Girón's rebellion.

A similar type of creole triumphalist spirit, based on the theme of Christendom's transfer to the New World, can be found in the works of a seventeenth-century Peruvian creole, the Franciscan Gonzalo Tenorio. Unlike Francisco de la Cruz, he kept to orthodoxy and was not disturbed by the Inquisition. The sixteen manuscript volumes he produced before 1663 constitute a monument to the glory of the Immaculate Conception and of America, the land favored above all others by the Holy Virgin Mary. God had restored in the person of the Virgin, conceived without sin, all the primitive innocence of the Garden of Eden. Mary was thus a *Paradisus restitutus* and embodied the revealing image of what the future New World messianic Christendom should be.

In one of the multiple eschatological schemes he drew up, based on a sermon quoted by St. Thomas of Villanueva, Friar Gonzalo imagined that European Catholicism would soon be destroyed by Protestants and transferred to America. Probably adapting a Franciscan tradition previously developed by Jean de Roquetaillade and Francesc Eiximenis, Friar Gonzalo supposed that persecutions would force the pope to flee from Rome. He would then seek refuge in America, where he would continue to exercise his spiritual authority, together with a king destined to bear the crown of universal monarchy and who would be none other than a hidden descendant of the chosen Hapsburg dynasty. Here again one may find the messianic theme of the "hidden king" who will make himself known in the latter days. Tenorio restates the rumor that had circulated in Mexico concerning the mysterious Gregorio López, whom many considered to be a hidden (*encubierto*) son of Philip II. He also mentions the turmoil recently caused in Peru by the presence of an adventurer who was the living portrait of Philip IV and to whom some had predicted that he would one day come to rule. Tenorio did not merely conceive of the New World as a place of refuge. From America, where the New Jerusalem was soon to prosper, would come the final evangelizing wave that would extend itself over the whole world and ensure the ultimate triumph of Christ and Mary.

Genuine products of creole pride, Gonzalo Tenorio's theories were also an answer to contemporary woes, namely, the overall decadence that was affecting the Spanish empire since the 1640 crisis that had made it totter. Such a decline prompted in Friar Gonzalo an attitude of messianic compensation which he directed in favor of Spanish America. Both Francisco de la Cruz and Gonzalo Tenorio illustrate extreme, even pathological, cases of Hispanic American messianism. They are, nonetheless, representative of the creole consciousness which throughout the colonial centuries rested its claim upon the dignity of the New World as opposed to the Old and to the peninsular motherland, thus preparing the way for spiritual emancipation, if not for political independence.

The theme of Christendom's transfer to the Indies was, to them, a sort of sacred metaphor that expressed the dormant yearning for the time when Hispanic America would succeed both Spain and Europe. Such a theme was linked to that of the promised land, which could, in turn, take on several aspects. One was that of a Garden of Eden, following Christopher Columbus's initial lucubrations; even in the middle of the seventeenth century, the learned jurist Antonio de León Pinelo, a famous *converso* whose Portuguese family had sought refuge in Peru, devoted a long and erudite treatise to the matter of *Paradise in the New World*. We have also mentioned significant examples of the belief in a New Jerusalem or a new Rome to be located in America. But even without arriving at such messianic excesses, many creole authors described their continent as a land of Canaan, overflowing with wealth and beauty. Peruvians and Mexicans did not merely celebrate, from a biblical point of view, the bountiful fertility of tropical lands, but actually saw in the mining wealth of their respective countries the unequivocal sign of divine election. Such a "plutolatric" theme was often linked to its "mariolatric" counterpart as if in a strange form of spiritual alchemy.

These same images can be found in the celebratory rhetoric of Our Lady of Guadalupe, whom the civil and religious authorities of Mexico City proclaimed as Patron Virgin of Mexico "in the name of the Mexican nation" in 1737, while papal approval arrived only in 1754. According to this Guadalupean cult encouraged by both creole Franciscans and Jesuits, Mexico—the land of Mary and of mining wealth—by harboring the seat of the New Jerusalem as well as of the new Rome, was thus called upon to be the center of the world as well as the capital of Christendom. In 1749 the Jesuit Francisco Javier Carranza (b. 1703) published in Mexico a book that bore a significant title, *The Transmigration of the Church to Guadalupe*. In it he developed an exegesis of chapter 12 of the book of Revelation, identifying the Virgin pursued by the dragon as both the image of the Virgin of Guadalupe who had chosen to appear on Mount Tepeyac and the image of the church which, in order to escape from the persecutions of the Antichrist, would come to seek refuge in New Spain on the eve of the latter day.

☞ RELIGIOUS MESSIANISM AND POLITICAL
MESSIANISM AT THE TIME OF INDEPENDENCE _____

What would eventually remain at the time of Independence from this theme of a church transfer to the Indies? In his *Prophetic Letter* of 1815, Simon Bolivar (1783–1830) mentioned the transfer of European civilization to America, clearly a secularized version of the transfer of Christendom: "Then the sciences and the arts, once born in the Orient and having enlightened Europe, will take their flight towards free Colombia, who will grant them asylum." In the same letter he predicted that Panama would be the future "emporium of the Universe" and the "future capital of the Earth." In his 1819 *Angostura Speech* he presented the new fatherland over the birth of which he had presided, Gran Colombia, as the "center," the "heart of the Universe." In this famous speech delivered at a time when political reaction was triumphant in Europe, Bolivar conjured up the image of his motherland, a model for all nations, "seated on the throne of Liberty, holding in her hands the sceptre of Justice, crowned by Glory, showing to the ancient World the majesty of the new World." Such an allegorical vision of the motherland associated with liberty seemed to anticipate yet another allegory, the Statue of Liberty, which would be erected later on at the entrance of New York Harbor. This would be, in fact, the last stop in a long journey leading from the Judeo-Christian concept of a Jerusalem-navel of the world to the utopia of a *libertador* who dreamed that Gran Colombia's Panama could become the center of a secularized universe where Liberty would replace all forms of previous bondage.

Yet the image of Liberty's throne should not induce one to believe that secular thought had triumphed throughout the America of the *libertadores*. Another image, religious in this case, also imposed its presence, that of Guadalupe, bearing the features of the Virgin of the Apocalypse which the first two leaders of Mexico's Independence, the priests Hidalgo the creole and Morelos the *mestizo*, bestowed as a banner to their armies, largely made up of Indians. A religious image, moreover a maternal and apocalyptic one, could, in a much more effective way than an abstract symbol, achieve the union between the elite and the illiterate masses. The strength of this Marian cult came precisely from its Indian origins and its later revivification by creoles. According to the legend finally established by the middle of the seventeenth century, the Virgin Mary allegedly appeared in 1531 on Mount Tepeyac to a poor Indian under the features of the Virgin of the Apocalypse worshiped at the Guadalupe monastery in Spain. Yet on that same hill located on the outskirts of Mexico City, Tonantzin, the mother of the gods, had been venerated before the arrival of the Spaniards. But as the cult developed during the seventeenth and eighteenth centuries, Mary-Tonantzin became the mother of all Mexicans.

One might also mention the Sebastianist movement of Sierra do Rodeador, which also developed in the Pernambuco region between 1817 and 1820 shortly before Brazil's Independence. A former soldier, Silvestre José dos Santos, presented himself as the prophet of a new era that would be inaugurated by the return of King Dom Sebastian. The sermons he preached in what he called the "City of Earthly Paradise" invited all men and women to do penance, but not to revolt. Despite its pacifism, the group was exterminated by order of the governor. But even though this had not actually been an independence movement, its memory was later taken up by Pedro I, Brazil's first emperor. The millennialist sect of the Sierra do Rodeador was to be the first one in a long series of apocalyptic movements that developed throughout nineteenth- and early-twentieth-century Brazil, sometimes blended with elements borrowed from Indian and African mythologies.

☞ INDIAN APOCALYPTICISM AND CHRISTIAN MESSIANISM _____

Most Amerindian cultures had both cyclical and apocalyptic conceptions of history. Present-day humanity, like previous generations, was doomed to disappear in a cosmic disaster. But anguish could be compensated for by messianic hope in the new times to come. Chosen ones could escape from ultimate destruction either by revolt or by a spatial quest, but always by the sacred dance that accompanied either one of these salvation paths. The new humanity that these chosen few would have access to was announced by messianic shamans or by the return of the civilizing god-hero, a common feature of most indigenous mythologies. Rather than being entirely new, this after-doomsday earth shared the ancient and paradisal colors of what had once been the earth of divine ancestors.

Quite logically, therefore, the Spanish conquest was seen as an apocalyptic catastrophe duly integrated within the traditional perception of time. This is, at any rate, what may be read in the indigenous accounts of the conquest. According to their astrological calculations and their omens, the fifth sun of the Aztecs was about to disappear. Thus the increase of human sacrifices in order to preserve a threatened cosmic order. Had not Quetzalcóatl, the civilizing hero-god, returned under the features of Cortés? The latter understood Aztec doubts and anxieties and cleverly played upon them. He did not hesitate to smash the temple statues, a religious and political gesture that was to inspire a sacred awe. The Spaniards also had an unintentional weapon on their side that was also seen as part of a cosmic disaster—the epidemics. The gods were truly dead and left the Indians as orphans.

Ancient Peruvians also believed that they belonged to a fifth humanity. Less prone to anguish than their Mexican counterparts, the Inca lords and their subjects did suffer from a combination of fear and hope—anxiety concerning the upcoming prospect of a *pachacuti,* the Quechua word for an upheaval of world, time, and space; hope for the return of the civilizing god-hero Viracocha. The events that took place were indeed illustrative of the *pachacuti:* the capture and execution of Atahualpa, the Inca who ruled the northern half of the empire (1532/1533); the plundering of Cuzco, the holy city and center of the world (1533/1534); and the capture and execution of Túpac Amaru, the descendant of the Inca dynasty's rebel branch, which had kept up a dissident power center for thirty-five years in the remote regions of the Vilcabamba Andes. A Spanish eyewitness described the atmosphere of apocalypse that accompanied Túpac Amaru's execution in 1572 on Cuzco's main square in the presence of Viceroy Toledo. "The crowd of Indians uttered such a cry of grief that one may have thought Judgment day had arrived. . . . The [Inca's] head was stuck on the end of a pike near the scaffold. Each day that went by, it grew handsomer. . . . After nightfall, the Indians came to worship it. . . . A report was made to the Viceroy. He then had the head buried together with the body in one of the cathedral's chapels." After Atahualpa's tragic death, the Inca, in the person of Túpac Amaru, had now died a second time, but his head, handsomer after decapitation, announced a messianic resurrection. This was a variation on the legend that had begun to spread concerning Atahualpa's own head.

It is true that many of the recently subdued populations, both in central Mexico and in the Andean countries, had reasons to rejoice about their liberation from Aztec or Inca yokes. But even if many ethnic groups did collaborate with the Spaniards, the latter were not considered messianic liberators. Their assimilation to the civilizing god-hero did not last long. There were, on the other hand, among the revolts that stirred the indigenous world, a number of messianic movements led by prophets who, confronted by the first wave of colonization and evangelization now under way, preached the coming of new times or, in other words, the return to ancient times when there was no Spanish tribute and there were no missionaries or diseases. Some of these nativistic movements were violent, like the revolt in the Guadalajara region in 1541–1542, which involved several of western Mexico's sedentary and nomadic tribes. Mention should also be made of the Tepehuanes rebellion of 1616–1618, which, after twenty years of Jesuit evangelization, shook most of the Durango region in northwest New Spain. But it is probably in the peaceful *Taqui Oncoy*—that is, "the dance disease"—movement that the apocalyptic and messianic features of Indian nativism expressed themselves with greatest force. That movement developed in the central Andes between 1564 and 1572. The *Taqui Oncoy* prophets announced the upcoming destruction of the Spanish-ruled world, the end of all injustices, and the resurrection of the *huacas,* those sacred places and objects inhabited by the spirits of the ancestors. Such destruction/restoration would be accelerated by the trances of those who surrendered themselves frantically to the dance that would bring back the world as it was even before Inca domination.

Nativistic movements may be analyzed in terms of a rejection both of colonization and of evangelization, even though they abide by the internal logic, cyclical as well as apocalyptic, of time's indigenous vision. On the other hand, it is in the light of such logic that the quest for the *Land without Evil* of the Brazil Tupis and of their Paraguay and Brazil Guarani cousins must be understood (see Clastres 1975). In other words, the European presence may have heightened their anxieties, but it did not create them. These two major ethnic groups, similar in language and mythology, lived in apocalyptic dread of the world's destruction through fire and flood. But at regular intervals prophets would appear—the *karaï*—messengers of the civilizing god-hero who, after performing sacred dances, led their followers toward the *Land without Evil,* the ancestors' paradise where no one died, where the chosen ones would escape from universal destruction, where the earth itself produced everything, and where men would become gods, free from all social constraints. Portuguese chronicles recorded many such Tupi migrations between 1539 and 1609. The great achievement of the Jesuits in their Paraguay missions (1609–1767) was to christianize the Guaranis' yearning for immortality. Acknowledged by the latter as being *karaïs,* the Jesuits were able successfully to convince those ethnic groups they brought together in their *reducciones* that the *Land without Evil* was not of this world, but beyond it. Thus, the Paraguay missions were not a messianic land but merely the antechamber to paradise. The Guarani apocalypse did not develop into a Christian messianism. It died in the Catholic utopia of the *reducciones,* except for those tribes who remained untouched by evangelization and who undertook long-lasting migrations toward the *Land without Evil* in the nineteenth and the beginning of the twentieth century.

The example of the Guarani *reducciones* should not imply that Indian tradition and Christian messianism did not frequently intermingle. From a very large number of examples, we shall only mention three, located at different stages on the scale of syncretism. In the case of Yaguacaporo (1635–1637), the Indian apocalypse is the dominant feature. This Guarani chief claimed to be the reincarnation of the divinity who had created the world and announced the imminence of the final disaster. It would be the crowning achievement of the holy war he intended to wage against the Paraguay Jesuits. But he organized his followers by naming "bishops," "vicars," and "apostles" who left for the forest to preach the new religion. This was still an Indian apocalypse; it was no longer the *Land without Evil*, but it was not Christian messianism.

The Chiapas Tzeltales belonged to the Mayan cultural area, which had always been, since pre-Columbian times up to the present, a privileged territory for prophetism. In 1712 a young girl of the Cancuc community discovered a "talking statue" of the Virgin, who supposedly had ordered a general uprising of the Tzeltales and the restoration of ancient order. The whites were to be either submissive or massacred, and the town of Ciudad Real (present-day San Cristóbal de Las Casas) destroyed. Despite its appearances, this was not a nativistic movement yearning for a return to former "idolatry," nor did it claim to be the birth of a new religion. Evangelization had clearly been effective here. The Tzeltales essentially claimed to reappropriate Catholicism by forming, with the help of the European clergy's indigenous auxiliaries, an entirely Indian ecclesiastical hierarchy, from priests to pope. As for the whites, they were accused of being "Jews who did not believe in the Cancuc Virgin." More than a millennial society, the Tzeltales dreamed of an upside-down world where the last would effectively be the first and where Indians would give alms to whites.

The best example of a fusion between Indian and Christian messianisms is the myth of the *Inkarri,* the return of the Inca. Its origins, typically nativistic, were Inca legends surrounding the resurrection of Atahualpa and Túpac Amaru, and the millennial apocalypticism of the *Taqui Oncoy* relating to ancestral beliefs, previous or even hostile to Inca domination. But little by little throughout the seventeenth and eighteenth centuries, the myth of the return of the Inca was modified; it was the apparition of a Christian Inca, more than his actual return, that was now expected. This hope, the unexpected product of a fundamentally repressive evangelization, paradoxically served to unite the yearnings of the Andes Indians who had been far from willing before the Spanish conquest to accept the yoke of Inca rulers.

One of the major stages of this christianization of Andean expectations is represented by the Indian Felipe Guamán Poma de Ayala's illustrated chronicle, completed in 1615. Both deeply Indian and deeply Christian, Guamán Poma depicts colonization under the mixed light of Christian Apocalypse and Andean *pachacuti*. Particularly worth mentioning are his portraits of Atahualpa and Túpac Amaru, who die "in a very Christian-like way, like martyrs" and that of the Indian "poor in the image of Jesus Christ," surrounded by his exploiters represented in the shape of monsters directly inspired by medieval apocalyptic bestiaries.

In the eighteenth century, the *Inkarri* myth supported several major rebellions that went beyond the Indian world, which was a sign of the latter's Christianization and of its evolution toward a liberating messianism for all oppressed peoples. It was a *mestizo* and former pupil of the Jesuits, Juan Santos Atahualpa, named after the Inca emperor, who led a long, drawn-out revolt in Peru's Amazon fringes between 1742 and 1752. But the largest revolt of the entire colonial period was led, in central and southern Peru, by a *cacique* descendant of the Incas, José Gabriel Condorcanqui. Also a former pupil of the Jesuits, he was totally Christian but chose to take the name of his ancestor, Túpac Amaru. Like him, he was executed on Cuzco's main square, in 1781. This liberating messiah had successfully incorporated into his cause, apart from the Indians, *mestizos;* blacks, whose slavery he declared to be abolished; creole dropouts; and even priests. It is true that the war waged by his Indian troops quickly turned into a racial conflict from which non-Indians finally felt alienated. But despite such drift, his name, still used by various contemporary liberation movements, conjures up a messianism borrowed from both Indian and Christian sources.

Translated from the French by Nikita Harwich

☞ NOTES

1. The word *converso* was applied to converted Jews as well as to their descendants. Crypto-Jews, often called *marranos,* were *conversos* who returned to the beliefs and practices of Jewish religion; they could therefore be brought before the Inquisition courts.

2. For a good updating on this matter, see Roberto Rusconi, "Cristoforo Colombo e Gioacchino da Fiore," *Florensia: Bollettino del Centro Internazionale di Studi Gioachimiti* (Italy) 7 (1993): 95–108.

3. The *encomendero* had certain rights over the Indians who were granted to him by *encomienda* (collecting the tribute and/or labor services) in exchange of certain duties (protection and financing their evangelization).

4. Carlos Herrejón Peredo, "Fuentes patristicas, jurídicas y escolásticas del pensamiento quiroguiano," in *Humanitas Novohispanos de Michoacán* (Morelia [México], 1983), 9–23. See the classical work by Fintan B. Warren, O.F.M., *Vasco de Quiroga and his Pueblo-Hospitals of Santa Fe* (Washington: Academy of American Franciscan History, 1963).

5. The *alumbrados* (literally, the "illuminated ones") insisted on inner illumination as a result of contemplation and tended to dispute any ecclesiastical mediation. The first *alumbrados* were condemned by inquisitorial edict in 1525. This trend of thought lasted, under less radical, less theological and more sentimental forms, until about 1630.

6. See Cantel 1960, 138–42. Vieira's proposal is later taken up by Lacunza, who quotes him: *Tercera Parte de la Venida del Mesías . . . ,* chap. 9, pp. 276–81.

☞ BIBLIOGRAPHY

Primary Texts

Chateaubriand, François-René de. 1986. *Les Natchez.* 1826; *Oeuvres romanesques et voyages.* Paris: Gallimard, Collection La Pliade.

Colón, Cristóbal. 1992. *Textos y Documentos completos: Nuevas Cartas.* Edited by Consuelo Varela and Juan Gil. 2nd rev. ed. Madrid: Alianza Universidad. Must be complemented by *Libro de las Profecías,* edited by Juan Fernández Valverde (Madrid: Alianza Editorial, 1992; also available in English with a commentary: *The 'Libro de las Profecías' of Christopher Columbus,* edited by D. C. West and A. Kling [Gainesville: University of Florida Press, 1991]).

Guamán Poma de Ayala, Felipe. 1980. *El Primer Nueva Corónica y Buen Gobierno.* Edited by John V. Murra, Rolena Adorno, and Jorge L. Urioste. 3 vols. México City: Siglo XXI. This illustrated chronicle, completed in Peru in 1615, falls into the line of the various indigenous testimonies referring to the conquest (e.g., Miguel León Portilla, *El Reverso de la Conquista: Relaciones aztecas, mayas e incas* [México City: Joaquín Mortiz, 1964]). But Guamán Poma, deeply Indian and Christian at the same time, brings the traumatism of the vanquished within the framework of Christian eschatology.

Huerga, Alvaro. 1986. *Historia de los alumbrados.* III, *Los alumbrados de Hispanoamérica (1570–1605).*

Madrid: Fundación Universitaria Española, Madrid. Half of this work consists of the reproduction of inquisitorial trial documents concerning visionaries infected by millennialism: Peru-based Dominican friar Francisco de la Cruz (pp. 314–504) and the Mexican disciples of hermit Gregorio López (pp. 787–914). The publication of Francisco de la Cruz's complete trial records is currently being prepared by Vidal Abril Castelló (Madrid: C.S.I.C.).

Lacunza y Díaz, Manuel. 1978. *Tercera Parte de la Venida del Mesías en gloria y majestad.* Edited by Adolfo Nordenflicht. Madrid: Ed. Nacional. Written in Italy by a Chilean Jesuit after the 1767 expulsion, this book, first published in Cadix in 1812, offers the most complete systematic approach to a literal interpretation of Revelation 20–21.

Las Casas, Fray Bartolomé de, O.P. 1990–96. *Obras completas.* 14 vols. Madrid: Alianza Editorial. Those works, which best illustrate the apocalyptic and messianic spirit of the Defender of the Indians, are the *Historia de las Indias* (vols. 3–5), the *Brevísima relación de la destrucción de las Indias,* and the *Octavo Remedio* (vol. 10: *Tratados de 1552*).

León Pinelo, Antonio de. 1943. *El Paraíso en el Nuevo Mundo: Comentario apologético, Historia natural y peregrina de las Indias Occidentales, islas de Tierra Firme [sic] del Mar Océano.* Edited by R. Porras Barrenechea. 2 vols. Lima: Impr. Torres Aguirre. Written in the middle of the seventeenth century by a *converso* established in Peru, this book bears witness to the inclination of creoles toward a messianic celebration of the New World.

Menasseh ben Israël. 1979. *Esperança de Israël: Amsterdam,* "en la impresión de S. ben Israël Soeiro, 5410" (i.e., 1650). Edited with an introductory study and translated (*Espérance d'Israël*) by Henri Méchoulan and Gérard Nahon. Paris: Vrin. This book shows the place of the New World within the revival of Jewish eschatology at the time of Sabbatianism.

Mendieta, Fray Jerónimo de, O.F.M. 1971. *Historia eclesiástica indiana.* Edited by Joaquín García Icazbalceta. 2nd ed. fac-sim. México: Porrúa. This chronicle, written by a disciple of Motolinía and completed in 1596, expresses the Franciscan long-abandoned dream at the time to create, together with the Indians of Mexico, a church worthy of the early years of Christianity.

Molina, Cristóbal de, and Cristóbal de Albornoz. 1989. *Fábulas y mitos de los Incas.* Edited by Henrique Urbano and Pierre Duviols. Madrid: Historia 16, Crónicas de América 48. These two chronicles, written in the 1570s, are still an invaluable source on the *Taqui Onqoy* messianic movement which caused many Indians of Central Peru to rise against Christianity.

Motolinía, Fray Toribio de Benavente, O.F.M. 1985. *Historia de los indios de la Nueva España.* Edited by Georges Baudot. Madrid: Castalia. Fray Toribio, one of the first twelve evangelists to arrive in Mexico, draws up in this chronicle, completed in 1541, an ideal picture of Franciscan evangelization among the "poor" Indians.

Major Interpretations

Bataillon, Marcel. 1965. *Études sur Bartolomé de Las Casas.* Paris: Centre de Recherches de l'Institut d'Études Hispaniques. On the messianism of Las Casas and his heterodox disciple Francisco de la Cruz, the essays "Estas Indias (hipótesis lascasianas)" (pp. 249–58) and "La herejía de Fray Francisco de la Cruz y la reacción antilascasiana" (pp. 309–24) are of particular interest. On Francisco de la Cruz, the recent studies by Alvaro Huerga and Vidal Abril Castelló (see above) as well as the one by Jean Pierre Tardieu (*Le Nouveau David et la réforme du Pérou: L'affaire María Pizarro-Francisco de la Cruz: 1571–1596* [Bordeaux: Maison des Pays Ibériques, 1992]) may also be consulted.

Baudot, Georges. 1983. *Utopía e Historia en México: Los primeros cronistas de la civilización mexicana (1520–1569).* Madrid: Espasa Calpe. In this book (1st French ed., 1977) concerning the Franciscan chroniclers of Mexico, following John Phelan's line of investigation (see below) even more than Marcel Bataillon's ("Nouveau Monde et Fin du Monde," *L'Éducation Nationale* [December 11, 1952]: 3–6) upholds the thesis of Martín de Valencia and Motolinía's Joachite millennialism.

Bernand, Carmen, and Serge Gruzinski. 1991, 1993. *Histoire du Nouveau Monde.* I, *De la Découverte à la Conquête, une expérience européenne: 1492–1550.* II, *Les métissages: 1550–1640.* 2 vols. Paris: Fayard. Among Gruzinski's many works concerning what he has called "la colonisation de l'imaginaire," this summary treatise clearly stands out and enables one to understand better, from the inside, the sheer size of the upheaval brought about by the colonization of the New World.

Burga, Manuel. 1988. *Nacimiento de una utopía: Muerte y resurrección de los Incas.* Lima: Instituto de Apoyo Agrario. Through this work of historical anthropology, the author shows how, once the trauma caused by the conquest and the eradication had passed, Andean society created, as early as the seventeenth century, the myth of a pre-Hispanic golden age and of the messianic coming of a Christian Inca. On this topic, the essay by Alberto Flores Galindo (*Buscando un Inca: Identidad y utopía en los Andes* [Lima: Instituto de Apoyo Agrario, 1987]) should also be consulted.

Cantel, Raymond. 1960. *Prophétisme et messianisme dans l'oeuvre d'António Vieira.* Paris: Ediciones His-pano-Americanas.

Clastres, Hélène. 1975. *La Terre sans Mal: Le prophétisme tupi-guarani.* Paris: Seuil.

Eguiluz, Antonio, O.F.M. 1959. "Fr. Gonzalo Tenorio, O.F.M., y sus teorías escatológico-providencialistas sobre las Indias." *Missionalia Hispanica* 48:257–322. A study of the sixteen manuscript volumes written in the middle of the seventeenth century by a Peruvian creole, to the glory of the New World as being the land chosen by Mary.

Frost, Elsa Cecilia. 1990. "¿Milenarismo mitigado o milenarismo imaginado?" In *Memoria del simposio de historiografía mexicanista,* 73–85. México: UNAM, Comité mexicano de ciencias históricas. The author disputes the theses of Phelan and Baudot concerning Mexico's Franciscan missionaries' Joachimite millennialism to which she had previously adhered (see her "El milenarismo franciscano en México y el profeta Daniel," *Historia Mexicana* 26/101 [1976]: 3–28). Phelan's and Baudot's interpretations have also been revised by J. Saranyana (see below) and by Marco Cipolloni, *Tra Memoria apostolica e Racconto profetico: Il compromesso etnografico francescano e le cosas della Nuova Spagna: 1524–1621* (Rome: Bulzoni, 1994).

Gil, Juan. 1989. *Mitos y utopías del Descubrimiento,* I, *Colón y su tiempo.* Madrid: Alianza.

Lafaye, Jacques. 1976. *Quetzalcóatl and Guadalupe: The Formation of Mexican National Consciousness: 1531–1813.* Chicago: University of Chicago Press. A translation of the 1974 French edition of his book concerning the eschatological components of Mexican identity. The cult of the Virgin of Guadalupe, which originated among the native Indians, was recuperated by the creoles, who thus felt comforted in the idea that Mexico was, indeed, a chosen land.

Milhou, Alain. 1983. *Colón y su mentalidad mesiánica en el ambiente franciscanista español.* Cuadernos colombinos 11. Valladolid: Universidad de Valladolid-Casa Museo de Colón. The messianism of Columbus and of the times of the discovery and conquest is seen as a continuation of medieval mes-sianism.

———. 1986. "Du pillage au rêve édénique: Sur les aspirations millénaristes des *soldados pobres* du Pérou." *Caravelle: Cahiers du Monde Hispanique et Luso-Brésilien* [Toulouse] 46:7–20.

———. 1994–95. "La tentación joaquinita en los principios de la Compañía de Jesús: El caso de Francisco de Borja y Andrés de Oviedo." *Florensia: Bolletino del Centro Internazionale di Studi Gioachimiti* [Italy] 8–9:193–239.

Pease, Franklin. 1984. "Conciencia e identidad andinas: Las rebeliones indígenas del siglo XVIII." *Bolívar et son temps: Cahiers des Amériques Latines* 29–30: 41–60. A summary that continues Burga's treat-ment of the earlier period into the eighteenth century (see above), on the relationships between Andean revolts, particularly that of Túpac Amaru, and the messianic hope in the coming of a Chris-tian Inca.

Pereira de Queiroz, Maria Isaura. 1978. *Historia y Etnología de los movimientos mesiánicos: Reforma y revo-lución en las sociedades tradicionales.* México: Siglo XXI. Spanish translation of a book originally published in French (Paris: Anthropos, 1968). Comparative historical anthropology of syncretic and indigenous messianisms in Africa and America, with special emphasis on Brazil.

Phelan, John L. 1970. *The Millennial Kingdom of the Franciscans in the New World.* 2nd rev. ed. Berke-ley/Los Angeles: University of California Press. This classical work, dealing mainly with Mendieta, has been the first (1st ed., 1956) to outline the thesis of the Joachite millennialism of Mexico's evan-gelists.

Saint-Lu, André. 1981. "Significado histórico de la sublevación de los indios zendales (Chiapas, 1712)."
      Anales de la Academia de Geografía e Historia de Guatemala 54:93–98. The revolt of the *Zendales* or
      Tzeltales shows a deep syncretism: the Virgin who appears calls for the restoration of the ancient
      order.
Saranyana, Josep I., and Ana de Zaballa. 1995. *Joaquín de Fiore y América.* 2nd rev. ed. Pamplona: Eunate.
      Strongly critical regarding the theses of Phelan and Baudot, though more ambivalent with regard to
      those of Bataillon and Milhou, the authors tend to question the actual influence of Joachim of Fiore
      in America, particularly on the Franciscan friars of New Spain.
Wachtel, Nathan. 1977. *The Vision of the Vanquished: The Spanish Conquest of Peru through Indian Eyes:
      1530–1570.* Hassocks, England: Harvester Press. In this classical book of historical anthropology (1st
      French ed., 1971), Wachtel not only studies Peru's social and mental upheavals but also broadens
      the scope of his analysis through comparisons with Mexico, Guatemala, and Chile. Particularly wel-
      come and relevant are the pages concerning the "death of the indigenous gods," the "dance of the
      conquest," and the Indian millennial movements.

17

Apocalypticism in Colonial North America

Reiner Smolinski
Georgia State University

MUCH HAS BEEN WRITTEN about the origin and rise of the national mythology of the United States in the Puritan endeavor to set up their New Jerusalem in the New World. According to this familiar argument, American Puritans saw themselves as God's chosen people on an "Errand into the Wilderness," there to set up a city upon the hill as a shining beacon to the rest of the world. Come the millennium, New England and the American continent at large, would be transformed into the eschatological New Jerusalem, where Christ would set up his throne to govern the effete nations the world over. In short, the appropriation of the City of God to the American hemisphere, modern scholars have argued, instilled in the colonists a sense of purpose that came to fruition during the First Great Awakening, the American Revolution, and in the American missions to the Third World in the nineteenth century. Whether or not English Puritans justified their removal to the New World in eschatological terms is an issue that has divided the scholarly community since the 1980s. One school of thought (historians of religion and literary scholars) argues that the Puritan fathers' emphasis on purity of doctrine and church discipline, on conversion as a prerequisite to church membership, and on de facto separation from the lukewarm Church of England was informed by a fully articulated millenarian credo that sought to anticipate the City of God in America. These ideas were inscribed into the typology of their errand and invoked in the jeremiads of their descendants, who summoned the ghosts of their illustrious ancestors to revitalize their mission whenever a crisis threatened their survival. The creation of this mythic errand occurred in the decades after the Half-Way Covenant (1662) and proved so adaptable to the changing needs of the revolutionary pulpit a century later that it was constantly reinvented as the Puritans' own usable past, this time as a quest for a civil millennium in which God's American Israel was now called upon to defend its civil and religious liberties against the encroachments of the British Antichrist.

441

Modern historians tend to project this errand back into the motivation of the first settlers and thus read the literature of the transmigration in light of its later manifestation. Be that as it may, a second school of thought examines much more mundane factors of economic and political pressures that encouraged relocation. These historians stress specific "push" and "pull" factors that led English citizens to abandon their old home for opportunities in the New World. Promotional tracts of the period emphasized overcrowding, poverty, lack of opportunity, or simply political and religious oppression as reasons for leaving England. Conversely, economic improvement, free tracts of land, exploitation of natural resources, and religious freedom are listed as pull factors for those who could be lured away by new opportunities in America. More recently, a third school of intellectual historians has challenged the old paradigm that end-time visions invested the Puritan errand from the very start. Members of this group argue that *no* millenarian ideology informed the Puritan exodus during the first wave of emigration, because such issues did not become pronounced until a full decade *after* the first wave of settlers had arrived in New England. Still others have amplified this ongoing revisionism by demonstrating that Puritan New England did *not* proclaim Boston as the future site of Christ's millennial throne (as is commonly believed), but located the eschatological New Jerusalem in Judea and expanded the Christianography of salvation to include America. For better or worse, it is against this background that apocalypticism in colonial America must be examined.

MILLENNIALIST THEORIES IN THE CONTEXT OF THEIR DEVELOPMENT

The codification of apocalyptic hermeneutics was slow in coming—the plethora of diverging interpretations may strike modern readers as a veritable confusion of Babylonish tongues. Many seventeenth-century millennialists were dismayed to discover that there was no consensus about the state of the golden age: whether literal, spiritual, in heaven, or on earth; or indeed when the millennium was to occur, whether past, present, or future. To appreciate how American eschatologists fit into this debate, when and why they departed from their European colleagues, and how three basic patterns of millenarian interpretation became codified at the beginning of the eighteenth century, we briefly need to turn to the eschatological theories of the late sixteenth and seventeenth centuries in order to understand their development. Such English Reformation theologians as John Bale (1495–1563) and John Foxe (1517–1587) did their share in unlocking the prophetic mysteries. While Bale correlated the prophetic peregrination of the church in its fight against Satan with specific events in secular history, he dated the thousand-year reign of the "church invisible" (Rev. 20:4–5) from Christ's resurrection, in 33 C.E., and with St. Augustine asserted that Christ ruled in human hearts rather than in any visible organization. John Foxe inherited Bale's ideas and contributed his famous martyrology *Acts and Monuments* (1573). This work greatly influenced Elizabethan reformers in their efforts to portray the English nation as God's chosen people on the vanguard of the Protestant Reformation.

Whereas many reformers employed prophecy as a means to spur on the Protestant Reformation, the more radical-minded successors in the first half of the seventeenth century tried to turn England into a Puritan stronghold. Apocalypticism furnished them with ideological direction. Among the late-sixteenth-century Protestant heirs to Bale and Foxe was the Cambridge-trained theologian Thomas Brightman (1562–1607), whose *Apocalypsis Apocalypseos* (Frankfurt, 1609) is a fresh commentary on Revelation, greatly appealing to the congregationalist movement of the period. While both Bale and Brightman read John's Revelation as prophetic history of the periods before, during, and after the millennium, they parted company on the nature of Christ's kingdom. Brightman's fervent millennialism sought to establish a pure church polity this side of paradise, because particular visible churches and their largely Presbyterian polity could be identified with the invisible kingdom of God. Brightman did not correlate the millennium with Satan's concomitant binding, but rather saw them as two separate events following each other: Satan's binding began with Constantine the Great becoming the first Christian emperor of Rome (ca. 306) and ended in 1300, with the invasion of the Ottoman Turks; next, Christ's millennial reign began from the reformation of Wyclif (ca. 1300), ending in the day of judgment, a thousand years later (in 2300). For Brightman, then, Christ's spiritual reign was already in progress, and his saints of the "first resurrection" (Rev. 20:4–6), consisting of his martyrs and witnesses, were presently ruling through their spiritual successors in the church militant on earth.

If Thomas Brightman thus made the church militant part of the ongoing millennium and placed the church triumphant after the day of judgment, then his German colleague, Johann Heinrich Alsted (1588–1638), at Herborn University, significantly revised our understanding of prophetic periodization. In his tract *Diatribe de Mille Annis Apocalypticis* (Herborn, 1627), Alsted did not place the millennium of Antichrist's binding in the past (as did Bale), nor as Brightman in the present, but, with Francisco Ribeira (1537–1591) at his elbow, projected it into the future. This revision was a decisive break from traditional interpretations of these matters. Significant for later Puritan interpretations in England and America is Alsted's insistence on Christ's spiritual reign on earth and a *corporeal* first resurrection "in which the Bodies of the Martyrs [only] shall rise" (*The Beloved City, Or, The Saints Reign on Earth A Thousand Yeares*, 2nd ed. [London, 1643], 17). The remaining saints, less holy than the martyrs but far different from the wicked, would not rise until the "Universal Resurrection of all the dead" (p. 19). This hyperliteralism of the first resurrection marks a hermeneutic split between those who allegorized the first resurrection as a conversion of individuals by grace "common unto all good men and happeneth daily" (p. 18) and those for whom this event was a literal and corporeal resurrection of Christ's martyrs. The allegorists would eventually give rise to a so-called postmillennialism of which Daniel Whitby (1638–1726), Jonathan Edwards (1703–1758), Joseph Bellamy (1719–1790), and Samuel Hopkins (1721–1803) are eighteenth-century representatives, whereas the literalists would evolve into the so-called premillennialist camp as represented in Cotton Mather's mature eschatology. However, these handy (albeit too neat) distinctions remain problematic for most of the seventeenth century in that both groups spoke of an inchoate, progressively unfolding millennium of mortals who would not attain eternal life until judgment day, in the second resurrection (Rev. 20:11–15). Perfection and immortality would not be the lot of this mixed multitude of saved nations until they, too, had undergone death, corporeal resurrection, and life everlasting in the church triumphant. Not until the concept of the saints' Rapture at Christ's second coming (2 Thess. 4:15) was fully understood did the inevitable consequences of Alsted's hermeneutical break become the deciding factor in the split between pre- and postmillennialists.

Alsted's eschatology, then, stands at the crossroads between a premillennialism of the supernatural type advocated in Cotton Mather's "Triparadisus" (1724–1727) and a postmillennialism of the developmental type erroneously attributed to Daniel Whitby's *Treatise on the True Millennium* (1703) and proliferated in America by the disciples of Jonathan Edwards and the nineteenth-century apostles of progress. The much-touted postmillennialism (which has been attributed to Jonathan Edwards as its first American progenitor) seems therefore little more than a variation on a familiar theme outlined by Alsted more than a century earlier. The point of departure between the two systems, then, is determined not by whether Christ's visible return occurs at the beginning or end of the millennium, but by whether the first resurrection was to be understood as a literal and corporeal resurrection of the saints and martyrs or merely as a spiritual resurrection of the saints through conversion or of the church's reformation. Indeed, the nucleus of both systems was already present in Alsted. As I shall demonstrate below, the millennialist systems of American theologians, from the Puritan exodus to the Revolution, were little more than variants of Alsted's system—even if his eighteenth-century emulators employed the trappings of Enlightenment thought to clothe their received ideas in new garb.

The next step in the development of apocalypticism that affected how Americans viewed the millennium came through Joseph Mede (1586–1638), a nonconformist with Anglican sympathies, master of Christ College, Cambridge. His most significant work for our purposes is *Clavis Apocalyptica* (London, 1627), a commentary on Revelation that described St. John's visions as coterminous prophecies about the development of church and state. Mede's most important contribution is his analysis of the inner coherence of John's Apocalypse, which led Mede to identify (even coin the phrase) "the Synchronisme and order of the Prophecies of the Revelation." By this *Synchronisme* he meant "an *agreement in time or age*: because prophecies of things falling out in the same time, run on in time together, or Synchronize" (*Key of the Revelation*, 2nd ed. [London, 1650], pt. 1, p. 1). According to Mede's eschatology, Antichrist's reign of 1260 years was to be dated either from 456, the fall of Rome under Genseric the Vandal or twenty years later, in 476, when the last of the Roman emperors, Romulus Augustulus, was deposed by Odoacer the Hun. Antichrist's fall, Satan's binding, and Christ's second coming— all could therefore be expected either in 1716 or 1736. With this Archemedian fulcrum in place, Mede had at once solved the types of problems that had plagued the systems of John Bale and Thomas Brightman.

Like Alsted before him, Mede situated the millennium in the future upon the fall of Antichrist and made Satan's binding for a thousand years coterminous with the corporeal resurrection of the raised saints (first resurrection). Moreover, those alive at the beginning of the millennium would reign on earth: "Those who shall be Partakers of this Kingdome are described to be of two sorts: 1. The deceased Martyrs, who . . . shall resume their Bodies and Reigne in Heaven. 2. Such of the living as have not worshipped the Beast, nor his Image, neither received his marke, &c. These shall Reigne on Earth" (*Paraleipomena:. Remaines On some Passages in The REVELATION* [London, 1650], 24–25). It is significant that, unlike Alsted, Mede placed the corporeal saints of the first resurrection in the heavens as permanent occupants of Christ's celestial city. Yet like his predecessors, Mede also asserted an inchoate millennium. While more or less free from Satan's encroachment, the saved nations of "Virgin-Christians of the *Gentiles*" and "the Nation of the *Jewes*" now converted to Christianity (p. 25) would still retain the sting of mortality, their sinful dispensation, and ultimate disease and death not obviated until the second resurrection at the end of the millennium. By all accounts Alsted and

Mede are perhaps the most significant Protestant millennialists of the early seventeenth century. Their guidelines became the touchstone for all those who shared similar concerns.

Mede's colleague John Cotton (1584–1652), vicar of St. Botolph's in Lincolnshire, was guided by similar expectations after he had established himself in New England in 1633. Cotton's calculations about the coming millennium, however, centered on 1655 and were not formulated until roughly 1639, six years after his establishment in the First Church of Boston, in New England. By that time, he was preaching a series of sermons on the Apocalypse that linked the covenant, regeneration, and church membership with the visible church. In his *The Churches Resurrection, or the Opening of the Fift and Sixt verses of the 20th Chap. Of the Revelation* (London, 1642), his *Powring Ovt of the Seven Vials* (London, 1642), and *Exposition upon the Thirteenth Chapter of the Revelation* (London, 1655), Cotton adapted Thomas Brightman's Augustinian First Resurrection (Rev. 20:4–6) as a *spiritual rebirth* of individuals and of reformed churches that excluded the unregenerate by making conversion the litmus test for church membership. With Thomas Goodwin's *Exposition of the Book of Revelation* (London, 1650) at his elbow, Cotton charged the holy ministers with examining applicants' regeneration before admitting them to the communion table. Cotton's *Churches Resurrection* deserves detailed attention because it has been at the center of the recent critical debate. As mentioned above, many intellectual historians and literary critics point to John Cotton's emphasis on individual conversion prerequisite to church membership in New England as having been galvanized by his millennialist endeavor to set up the New Jerusalem in the American wilderness. What is often ignored, however, is that in his *Churches Resurrection* Cotton is as much preoccupied with positioning his own theories between those of Bale and Brightman on the one hand and Mede and Alsted on the other, as with the purity of New England's church ordinances, doctrine, and polity. To shed new light on the issue we need to understand exactly what Cotton's millennium looked like in order to determine if at any time before or after his migration to America he tried to establish the New Jerusalem church in New England. The millennial reign of the saints would begin with Antichrist's fall and Satan's binding in 1655. At that point, God would employ "powerfull Ministers" who would bind Satan with "the strong chaine of God's Ordinances Word and Sacraments and Censures" (*Churches Resurrection*, 5).

Satan's binding during an inchoate millennium signifies to Cotton the purity of church discipline, doctrine, and polity by admitting only regenerate members. As with Alsted, the rulers with Christ in heaven would be his martyrs: "those that were branded before as Hugunots, and Lollards, and Hereticks" would nearly be the only ones worthy to wear crowns of righteousness. Yet unlike Alsted, Cotton's martyrs "lived in their Successors," among the regenerate of saved nations during the millennium. And as in the case of Alsted and Mede, these saved nations were little more than a mixed multitude of regenerate and unregenerate (both still mortal and sinful), of church members and the wicked nations now bound "in chaines of . . . Admonition and Excommunication" (p. 6). The unregenerate among them "remaine dead in sinne" and would be excluded from the spiritual blessings bestowed upon the saved nations. The first resurrection then is twofold: a resurrection of particular persons dead in sin but renewed by regenerating grace (Eph. 2:1; 5:14; John 5:25, 28) and of particular churches recovered from their spiritual apostasy and dead estate in idolatry and superstition (Rom. 11:15; Ezek. 37:1–10). The martyrs and witnesses would invisibly govern through "Men of the same Spirit" (p. 6) the nations of the earth, "either keeping them out, and binding them, leaving them under Satan if they would not come in: Or if they be come in, binde them with this great chaine that they shall not trouble the Church any more, as carnall members use to doe" (p. 10). This context then establishes why Cotton emphasized church purity and admissions tests. Not, as some critics have argued, because Cotton and company wanted to set up their own New Jerusalem in Boston—for that belonged to the church triumphant following judgment day at the end of the golden age (in 2655)—but to make sure New England's churches would not be excluded from the millennial church, shut out as it were from God's ordinances, and thus share in the lot of the wicked nations as they rise with Gog and Magog against the camp of the saints. Individual regeneration and the resurrection of individual churches were therefore crucial to Cotton, if New England was to have a share in the millennium.

Mere church membership, however, was not enough: "If we do not now strike a fast Covenant with our God to be his people . . . then we and ours will be of this dead hearted frame for a thousand yeares; we are not like to see greater incouragements for a good while then now we see . . ." (p. 17). In short, Satan was being bound gradually through the ongoing reformation; the first resurrection of the churches, however, still lay in the future and would not begin until Antichrist's fall: "Therefore let it be a serious warning to every one not to rest in Reformation and formes of it, and to blesse yourselves in Church Membership, because to this day, this first Resurrection [of the churches] hath not taken its place, nor will not take his place till Antichrist be ruinated" (p. 20). Communicants had to experience true regeneration, or else their church membership would remain inefficacious. Likewise, true reformation of the church could be achieved only after Satan's binding, through a process of clerical preaching and censuring that would not achieve completion until the church triumphant. It is therefore absolutely imperative to Cotton's millennial system that New England's churches have tests of regeneration to *anticipate* the pure church, or else New England, like her unregenerate sister in Old England, would become part of Gog and Magog's final destruction by forfeiting her present opportunity to join in Christ's salvation. Notwithstanding the emphasis on high admission standards for new applicants to church membership, Cotton was fully aware that New England's churches could no more than anticipate the New Jerusalem state this side of the millennium. But he was quick to point at the vast gulf that separates anticipation from accomplishment, the church militant from the church triumphant. Not even during the millennium could complete purity be actualized.

Although Cotton's millennial fervor did not reach its full flower until about six years after his establishment in the First Church of Boston, his stringent requirements of regeneration of every communicant and exclusion of the unregenerate are clearly informed by his millenarian theories about the resurrection of the churches in an imminent millennium. Certainly, Cotton's position was not an isolated case but was shared by a number of his colleagues whose efforts to purify New England's churches through admissions tests were informed by the same millenarian concern for their survival into the millennium. These ideas were shared by his New Haven colleagues Peter Bulkeley (1583–1659) in *The Gospel-Covenant* (London, 1645), by William Hooke (1601–1678) in *A Short Discourse of the Nature and Extent of the Gospel-Day* (London, 1673), and by John Davenport (1597–1670) in "An Epistle to the Reader," published in Increase Mather's *Mystery of Israel's Salvation* (London, 1669).

Like Thomas Goodwin in England, John Davenport became an ardent congregationalist through Cotton's preaching in 1633. Davenport ultimately joined Cotton in New England in 1636, but settled in the New Haven Colony in 1648. There Davenport set out to make the visible as close to the invisible church as a means of anticipating the New Jerusalem condition on earth, by attaining "perfection of light, and holiness, and love, as is attainable on this side of heaven" ("Epistle," in Increase Mather's *Mystery* [1669], n.p.). His millennialist ideology differed from that of Goodwin, Alsted, and Cotton only in that Davenport's chiliasm led him to embrace the idea of Christ's physical and visible co-regency on the millennial earth with his corporeal and immortalized raised saints over the still mortal saved nations. More significantly, Davenport singles out for praise those who rescued millennialism from this stigma of infamy, including Thomas Goodwin in *The World To Come; Or, The Kingdom of Christ Asserted* (London, 1651) for having restored "the literal exposition of *the first Resurrection*" to the millennial system and for proving that "the *world to come*" (Heb. 2.5) carries a double signification: first, an inchoate millennium of the church militant, "a state between the state of the world as now it is"; and, second, the perfection of the church triumphant at the end, "the state of things after the day of judgment, when *God shall be all in all*" ("Epistle"). Davenport commends Mede's *Key to the Revelation* for making his synchronism of parallel events the key to unlocking the mystery of John's Apocalypse. Lastly, he celebrates Alsted's *Beloved City* for demonstrating that the millennium was not past but future. Perhaps that is why Davenport was so adamant about his chiliasm that he did not renounce it even after the collapse of Cromwell's Interregnum and the anathema of the Fifth-Monarchists. Davenport's millennialism expressed here is also informed by the momentous events of Sabbateanism in Europe, which prompted Increase Mather (1639–1723) to write his *Mystery of Israel's Salvation* in the first place. For Davenport, then, the return of European and Ottoman Jews to Jerusalem betokened the nearness of the second coming—all the more reason to press on with the reformation of the churches in New England.

This agreement between these notable New Englanders of the first generation should not lead one to assume that there was a consensus among the millenarians of the period. Far from it. In fact, their views on the millennium often differed as much as their views on church government and admissions tests. Thomas Parker (1595–1677), pastor of Newbury, Massachusetts, is a case in point. His Presbyterian leanings and standards of church admission had more in common with those later held by Jonathan Edwards's maternal grandfather Solomon Stoddard (1643–1729) of Northampton, than with John Cotton of the Boston church. If Cotton, Davenport, and Hooke tried to keep the visible church as close to the invisible by limiting church membership to the elect, Thomas Parker admitted virtually anyone with the faintest stirrings of grace. The church doors in his Newbury congregation were open as wide as any barn door in New England—or at least as wide as those of Stoddard in the Connecticut Valley fifty years later. In his *Visions and Prophecies of Daniel Expounded* (London, 1646), Parker argued for a chronological scheme of the millennium that had more in common with the preterist systems of Augustine, Bale, and Brightman than with the futurist systems of Cotton, Alsted, or Mede. According to Parker's system, the millennial reign was already in progress in his lifetime, intermitted only by the destruction of Gog and Magog, in the last forty-five years before the last judgment. The ministers of "particular Churches," who admit the yet unconverted elect "into the community of the whole Church of New Jerusalem[,] shall hereby be instruments of bringing them into the heavenly perfection, and shall therein be glorified with their converts" (pp. 148–49). Parker's views on the millennium, then, shaped his position on church membership as well: even the weakest must be admitted to safeguard their membership in the church triumphant.

Thomas Shepard (1605–1649), minister at Cambridge, had a view of church admission similar to those espoused by Davenport and Cotton, but Shepard was far less willing to let the unpredictable nature of millennialist exegesis determine his views on such crucial issues. The most interesting of his sermons on the topic is his *Parable of the Ten Virgins* (London, 1660). Here Shepard speculated about two comings of Christ—the one, a spiritual appearance to call Jews and Gentiles in their final ingathering before the destruction of Antichrist; the other, a literal, corporeal appearance of Christ to judge the world at the end of the one-thousand-year reign (*Works*, 3 vols. [1971 ed.], 2:24–26, 507–10). Either way, the Bride of Christ had to be holy and clean to receive the groom—even though there would remain enough foolish virgins left unprepared at his coming. But lest New England deem itself wise beyond safety, Shepard made sure that no carnal hypocrites might delude themselves with false security. He shared John Cotton's emphasis on an inchoate millennium or "Middle Advent," even as both deferred Christ's literal return in the clouds of fire to the day of judgment. Since both preparationists like Shepard and anti-preparationists like Cotton described the sequence of events leading up to and during the millennium in essentially the same terms, the issue of premillennialist gloom or postmillennialist optimism, as critics are wont to argue, seems altogether moot. Even if Shepard (unlike Cotton) still expected the slaughter of the martyrs and witnesses to occur before the golden age, it was the preparation of the heart in terms of personal conversion (Cotton's spiritual first resurrection) that safeguarded an individual's entrance into the millennium. Even on this issue, then, both clergymen saw eye to eye.

Matters of church government and the purity of its members were also much on the mind of John Eliot (1604–1690) of Roxbury, New England's Apostle to the Indians. He began his missionary work among the Indians in 1646, translated the Bible into their Algonquian language, and published several Indian grammars, to speed their conversion. Cultural differences notwithstanding, Eliot's admission requirements for his communities of praying Indians were as stringent as for any English settler and required years of preparation. Guided by his belief in the Indians as the remnants of the Lost Tribes of Israel in America, he tried to do his best to convert them to the gospel of Christ and thus to bring home Indian Jews. As could be expected, Eliot's millennialism grew more fervent with the rise of Cromwell's Interregnum, and in the wake of the execution of Charles I, Eliot wrote a tract on the form and nature of Christ's millennial government. It does not come as a surprise that when Eliot's *Christian Commonwealth* belatedly appeared in London, in 1659, on the eve of the Restoration, he caused his fellow New Englanders great embarrassment. To appease English critics, the Massachusetts General Court forced Eliot to recant and had his tract publicly burned in 1661. The bone of contention was his insistence on Christ as "the only right Heir to the Crown of England"—a rather impolitic if not seditious argument that could do anything but please the more mundane interests of Charles II ("Preface," Bv).

Eliot's millennialism has much in common with that of Thomas Goodwin and John Cotton. Like his colleagues, Eliot allegorized Christ's millennial reign on earth as the leadership of holy ministers who were preeminently guided by the Bible. For Eliot, then, Oliver Cromwell's Interregnum had "*cast down not only the miry Religion, and Government of Antichrist, but also the former form of civil Government, which did stick so fast unto it, until by an unavoidable necessity, it fell with it*" ("Preface," Bv), and the millennial reign was imminent. What then did Eliot's government look like? It was a covenanted community of visible saints in which civil and ecclesiastical society would be modeled after the patterns established by Moses and evident in the division of angels in myriads: in the order of tens, hundreds, thousands ("Preface," B4–B4v).

Arranged in groups with one elected ruler for every ten households, these elected officials would form a council of five, governing fifty families, a council of ten for every one hundred families—all the way up to the highest council of rulers headed by Christ. Eliot's government would thus be administered by councilors convening in progressively higher courts while receiving guidance from the Holy Scriptures. Thus, the Word of God would become the supreme measure for all the world. Eliot instituted this form of government in his communities of praying Indians with some success. If his Mosaic administration was thus closer to biblical precedent than any colonial government in Boston, then Eliot, ironically, set some sort of beacon for the capital of the Bay. He was wise enough not to press the issue.

The layperson's point of view on matters apocalyptic is represented in Edward Johnson's *Wonder-Working Providence of Sions Saviour in New-England* (London, 1654). Like Judge Samuel Sewall's much later *Phaenomena quaedam Apocalyptica* (Boston, 1697), Johnson's text demonstrates that millennialism was not solely in the domain of the clergy. As a military leader of Woburn, Johnson (1508–1672) knew much about service in the militia. It is therefore not surprising that his millennialism is surcharged with images of the church militant—the church in battle against Antichrist—led by Christ and "freeing his people from their long servitude under usurping Prelacy" (*Johnson's Wonder-Working Providence*, ed. J. F. Jameson [New York: Charles Scribners's Sons, 1910], 23). Assuming the prophetic voice of some latter-day military leader in the army of Christ, Johnson intoned his millenarian rallying cry: "You are called to be faithful Souldiers of Christ, not onely to assist in building up his Churches, but also in pulling downe the Kingdome of Anti-Christ, then sure you are not set up for tollerating times" (p. 30). It is significant that throughout his *Wonder-Working Providence,* Johnson speaks of the battle against Antichrist as having begun—a clear indication that his fervency was informed by an imminent millennium. No wonder Johnson does not shrink from encouraging his Christian soldiers to die gleefully, for the promised resurrection would almost be instantaneous: "Babylon is fallen. . . . Nay I can tell you a farther word of encouragement, every true-hearted Souldier that falls by the sword in this fight, shall not lye dead long, but stand upon his feet again, and be made partaker of the triumph of his Victory: and none can be overcome, but by turning his back in fight" (p. 271). It is unclear whether Johnson believed that those who died fighting against Antichrist were saints of the first resurrection, who would then (as Alsted and Davenport believed) share in the corporeal first resurrection and in Christ's government on earth.

As can be gathered from the evidence so far, millennialism was certainly a significant facet in the works of the leading ministers of the period. But we must be cautious not to project such fervency back into the settler's motivation for emigrating to New England in the first place—certainly not during the first wave of migration (1620–1640s). The earliest Puritan documents with sustained millennial fervor in New England can be dated from 1639. There was no divine "Errand into the Wilderness" at the outset. Rather, with the political crisis in England, the coming Civil War and Interregnum, just as much as with the proliferation of eschatological theories in the early decades of the seventeenth century, millennialism became a defining feature in the sermon literature of the time. As can be seen in Johnson's providence history, New England millennialists (clergy and laypeople alike) invented a religious errand as a means to stem the tide of reverse migration to Old England—when the crown of England was likely to be offered to the king of kings. We also need to be reminded that neither Johnson nor any of his confreres believed that perfection was possible on either side of the millennium. In fact, there is sufficient evidence that at least until the time when, in his "Triparadisus" manuscript, Cotton Mather

(1663–1728) began to advocate a supernatural millennium of immortal saints both in heaven and on earth, the inchoate millennium of progressive sanctification tempered by sin, disease, and death (even among the saved nations) was the standard form of millennialism—certainly in the authors discussed here.

☞ PREMILLENNIALISM, THE CONFLAGRATION, AND THE CONVERSION OF ISRAEL

The debate about whether the millennium of peace was past or future spilled over into the next generation of American eschatologists. Perhaps the best example of how some of its leading representatives struggled with this issue can be seen in Increase Mather's "New Jerusalem" (ca. 1689–95) and in *A Dissertation on the Future Conversion of the Jewish Nation* (London, 1709) as well as in Cotton Mather's eschatological tract "Problema Theologicum" (1703). It is safe to say that both father and son were of one mind on these issues until roughly 1720, when son Cotton began to put forth his new theories in "Triparadisus," recently published in *The Threefold Paradise of Cotton Mather* (1995). His earlier "Problema Theologicum" (ca. 1695–1703) (ed. Jeffrey S. Mares, *Proceedings of the American Antiquarian Society* 104/2 [1994]) is an attempt to persuade his Salem colleague Nicholas Noyes (1647–1717) to relinquish his preterist millennium in favor of Alsted's futurist system. At the opening of his argument, Mather identifies as his principal opponents those who placed the millennium of the church either (1) at *Christ's birth,* or (2) at *Christ's death,* or (3) at the *fall of Jerusalem* by the Romans in 70, or (4) at the *baptism of Constantine I,* who became the first Christian emperor of Rome in 306, or (5) at *Luther's Reformation* in 1517. And in one fell swoop, as only Cotton Mather knew how, the pastor of the Second Church of Boston attempted to set the record straight: Christ will appear at the beginning *and* end of the millennium; the first and second resurrection are both literal and corporeal; the raised saints of the first resurrection would rule visibly in a *literal* New Jerusalem in the heavens, hovering over the restored Jerusalem in the new earth ("Problema," 423; *Threefold Paradise,* 245); the millennium begins with a literal yet partial conflagration confined mostly to Italy and ends with a global fire dissolving the elements; and last but not least, an inchoate millennium of raised saints ruling over the saved nations of mortals who had escaped the partial conflagration.

For our purposes, Cotton Mather's views on the first resurrection are again crucial for the development of his later eschatological system in his *Threefold Paradise.* He berated his allegorizing colleagues who saw the first resurrection merely in terms of a person's conversion and of the church's reformation. But, as if remembering that his illustrious grandfather John Cotton had espoused the exact same allegorical position in *The Resurrection of the Churches* more than sixty years earlier, Mather became more conciliatory: "It will not Do! It implyes that the Martyred Saints, *Lived again,* only in their *Successors,* not in their *own Persons;* whereas, the *Resurrection,* as the word itself imports, is of *the Same.*" In fact, it would be disheartening to these saints and martyrs if they came alive only in their successors, who carry out their bidding in the millennial earth (p. 407). To settle the issue once and for all, Mather enlisted Justin Martyr (ca. 100–ca. 165), Irenaeus (ca. 130–ca. 200), Papias (ca. 60–130), and Polycarp (ca. 69–ca. 155) in his battle against the allegorizers of the first resurrection, among whom Mather identified

Jerome (ca. 342–420), Eusebius (ca. 260–ca. 340), Cornelius à Lapide (1567–1637), and Caesar Baronius (1538–1607).

If Mather seemed more than certain on the issue of the corporeal nature of the raised saints in heaven, he was more cautious on the issue of their mortal counterparts on earth. Like his predecessors, he believed in an inchoate millennium of saved, albeit mortal, nations. In this early work, he did not quite know what to make of those nations who had not yet come to accept Christianity. These "Nations in the Remoter Skirts of the World," Mather speculated, "will not be under so high a Dispensation of Christianity, as those that ly nearer to ye *City of God,* & under its more Direct and Shining Influences" (p. 422). These intractable nations required "a Rod of Iron" to make them see the light, their remaining sinfulness constantly leading them astray. Thus wondering, Mather raised the issue point blank: "How far *Sin* shall be extinguished and Extirpated among the *Righteous,* by whom the *New Earth* is now inhabited?" (p. 423). Thus wondering, Mather listed it as a theological query alongside the issue of the rapture (2 Thess. 4:15) and invited his fellow millennialists to present their written answers in print or at their next meeting.

Mather was not happy with such an imperfect millennium, in which saints and sinners would still be plagued by sin, disease, and death. Neither did he like the idea of two separate conflagrations, a partial one destroying the papal dominions of Italy at the beginning, and a global one at the end of the millennium—offered as a hermeneutical compromise in Drue Cressener's *Judgements of God upon the Roman-Catholick Church* (London [1689], 284–99). But how else would the saints alive at Christ's second coming escape the burning fire, unless the conflagration were limited in space and time to a particular region of the Old World? Joseph Mede had not solved this issue to his satisfaction either, for he too had opted for a double conflagration when he limited the initial conflagration to "exactly M.DC furlongs, or 200 Italian miles" of the papal territories in Italy—however, leaving the ancient terrain "occupied by the *Babylonians, Persian,* and *Graecian* Kingdomes . . . untouched" (*Works,* 4th ed. [1677], 593). Neither was Mather happy with Mede's vacillation between an inchoate millennium of gradual improvement within history and a supernatural millennium in which the saints alive on earth would attain their immortality suddenly and rapturously in the clouds of heaven (2 Thess. 4:17), before being returned to fill the earth with their immortalized offspring (*Works,* 775).

These issues rankled him a great deal and were subject to countless debates with his father Increase at least until 1720, yet Cotton tried to make amends in his final treatise on the issue. Instrumental in Mather's break with his predecessors and decisive for the development of premillennialism in America was a little-known tract by Praisegod Barbon (fl. 1670s), whose *Good Things to Come* (London, 1675) addressed the issue of an inchoate millennium as well and argued for a supernatural solution. The immortality of the saints would be attained either by a corporeal resurrection of the dead or by a corporeal transformation of the living: "the one, is by dying; and after lying a time in the grave: rising again, or being raised out of the prison grave at the sounding of the trumpet of God. . . . The other way is, by not dying, but being changed, in a moment, at the very same time, the dead are raised [2 Thess. 4:17]. This change: is a mistery; a secret: not much taken notice of" (p. 53). In short, the raised saints, just as much as the changed saints (saved nations), would attain their immortality miraculously, the one by corporeal resurrection, the other by corporeal transformation without first incurring death. Both classes of saints would be endowed with immortal bodies, yet their function in the millennial earth would differ greatly. No doubt the position of the raised saints would be more illustrious, their principal function to serve as kings, priests, and governors over their fellow inhabitants; the changed saints, though not far behind, would be mainly concerned with the more menial tasks of rebuilding and repopulating the burned earth with immortal offspring—duties from which their superiors were exempted (*Good Things,* 59–65). Suddenly, all the pieces of his eschatological puzzle seemed to fit together, and Mather could now iron out the remaining kinks as he penned down his new system less than a year before his death.

The Petrine conflagration of the globe (2 Peter 3) was one of those problems that could now be addressed with some consistency, for the earth's predicted dissolution was now no longer impeded by the saved nations, whose remaining mortality had necessitated a limited conflagration to allow for their escape. Indeed, this inelegant solution had been less than satisfying, but with Mather's new system of the changed saints in place, he could turn his back on Mede, Cressener, even his father, Increase, and assert a single, yet global conflagration at the opening of the millennium (*Threefold Paradise,* 314–16). With this puzzle solved, Mather could now address a much more threatening problem of a different sort raised by the Dutch jurist and theologian Hugo Grotius (1583–1645) and by his English colleague Henry Hammond (1605–1660). In its literal sense, Grotius and Hammond argued, the Petrine conflagration was applicable only to the historical destruction of Jerusalem; any futurist application of the fire dissolving the heavens and the earth would violate the historical context of the prophecy and had to be understood in an allegorical sense. Preterists like Grotius and Hammond thus subverted the very foundation on which much of the literalist's expectation of the future conflagration depended.

That the Atlantic proved no barrier to the hermeneutical tempests gathering strength in Europe can be seen in Mather's *Threefold Paradise.* His incessant calculations of prophetic chronometry repeatedly provoked a retrenchment of his avowed literalism. Yet while Mather willingly compromised on his literalist stance on the restoration of the Jewish nation, he drew his line of battle in front of the camp of the metaphorists, who ridiculed the hyperbolical language of the Hebrew prophets. Grotius's allegorist disciples missed the whole point by ignoring the prophetic intent of scripture, Mather countered. Nor did they understand the typological design of the "Prophetic Spirit," for which "the lesser *Particular Judgments*" were "an *Earnest* as well as a *Figure,* of the *General One,* wherein the *Frame* of Nature shall be dissolved" (p. 184). Preterist exegesis, Mather retorted, attenuated the prophetic spirit, which, true to God's design, intended a double fulfillment. The smaller event generally accomplished in the historical past of the prophet's own time really signified a second, much larger, and most of all, literal fulfillment in the latter days. This was certainly the case with the Petrine prophecy, Mather judged, which in predicting the immediate fall of Jerusalem actually intended the passing away of heaven and earth at Christ's second coming. In redressing the contradictions of his millenarian thought, Mather—like his English colleagues—was forced to adjust his taxonomy to maintain the interior logic of his system. At the same time, he safeguarded his literalism by merging Cartesian notions of the earth's fiery magma with the modifications introduced by John Ray (1628–1705), Thomas Burnet (ca. 1635–1715), and ultimately by William Whiston (1667–1752), whom Mather admired greatly. Mather was not far behind his English colleagues in explaining the supernatural conflagration in terms of its feasibility. And gathering evidence about volcanoes existing in every hemisphere, he was convinced that the Lord of Hosts would muster at his coming the unextinguishable fire of the deep to do his bidding: "What Commotions, what Convulsions has this Planet, in many Parts of it suffered from Subterraneous *Com-*

bustions, and such Amassments of *Igneous Particles,* which are an *Eternal Fire,* breaking forth at those formidable *Spiracles,* which if they had not been afforded, the Globe would, no doubt, have been torn to Peeces!" (*Threefold Paradise,* 209). In short, the holocaust of nature did not require supernatural intervention—all that God had to do was to withdraw his restraint from the fiery magma locked up in the earth, and the whole globe would turn into a lake of fire.

Praisegod Barbon's *Good Things to Come* (1675) also helped Cotton Mather to solve yet another puzzling issue that had long resisted clarification. Most millennialists of the seventeenth and eighteenth centuries insisted that the Jewish nation would play a central part in the second coming of the Messiah and in the theocracy of the new heavens and the new earth. St. Paul had foretold the restoration of the Jews in Romans 11, predicting that their unbelief would be removed, and natural Israel would then embrace Christianity in everlasting communion with the Ancient of Days. Most millenarians agreed, therefore, that the Jews' return to the Holy Land and their national conversion were the most reliable signs of Christ's second coming and of the end of the times of the Gentiles. More important, these events were prerequisite to the golden age, which would be postponed until their accomplishment. Few millenarians differed from this mainstay of Christian exegesis popularized by Joseph Mede. He theorized that nothing short of a miracle could effect this conversion, whose smaller type was evidenced in St. Paul's mystical conversion on the road to Damascus: "That of the *Jews* may be like it; *viz.* That though many were present with S. *Paul* at that time, yet none saw the apparition of Christ, nor heard him speak, but *Paul* alone" (*Works,* 767). This exegetical issue did not enter the limelight of eschatological speculations until the renowned Dutch Rabbi Menasseh ben Israel (1604–1657) published his tractate *Spes Israelis* (1648), in which he validated earlier eyewitness accounts by Antonio de Montezinos that the Lost Tribes of Israel had been discovered in the Peruvian Andes. This alleged discovery in America raised tremendous hopes among millennialists all across Europe, and when Sabbatai Sevi (1626–1676), a Turkish Jew from Smyrna, proclaimed himself the Messiah and called on European and Ottoman Jews to return to the Holy Land, the excitement of the 1660s reached a feverish pitch.

Increase Mather spoke for all of his Puritan colleagues in New England when he pleaded for the literal restoration of Israel in his book-length *Mystery of Israel's Conversion* (London, 1669) and in his updated interpretation *Diatriba de Signo Filii Hominis* (Amsterdam, 1682) in response to several European colleagues who were prone to read Romans 11 as an allegory of the Christian church. Championed by Hugo Grotius, Henry Hammond, Jacob Batalerio (1593–1672), James Calvert (d. 1698), John Lightfoot (1602–1675), later joined by Richard Baxter and others, these notable scholars adopted a preterist interpretation of Romans 11 and asserted with Grotius that St. Paul's prophecy had literally been fulfilled in the first two centuries of the Christian church when the churches of Palestine, Asia Minor, and Rome mostly consisted of Christian Jews. St. Paul's prediction, so they argued, must therefore be understood literally only of the Christian Jews and their offspring, who through intermarriage with their Gentile brethren lost their distinction. Any latter-day conversion of the Jews as a nation was therefore illogical and had to be understood of the surrogate Israel, the Christian church. This radical subversion of millenarian hope triggered a widespread debate in which the literalist and allegorist camps positioned their arms at each other's hermeneutical foundation.

In his old age, the renowned English clergyman Richard Baxter (1615–1691) defected and went over to the allegorists—much to the dismay of all those who appreciated his conservative Presbyterianism. In justifying his new position in *The Glorious Kingdom of Christ* (London,

1691), he dedicated his treatise to Increase Mather, then residing in London and negotiating New England's second charter at the court of William and Mary, calling on his American friend to debate the issue. Mather complied in his *Dissertation Concerning the Future Conversion of the Jewish Nation* (London, 1709), but did not publish his rejoinder until almost two decades after Baxter's death. Back in New England, Cotton Mather joined the debate by issuing his *Faith of the Fathers* (Boston, 1699), a catechism that aimed at converting Jewish readers in America. The anticipated conversion of the Jewish nation just before the millennium never quite squared with Cotton Mather's own conjecture that Christ's sudden coming, like a thief in the night, would find the whole Christian world in a dead slumber. How could the sleepy world be caught off guard by his coming, if such telling signs as Israel's national conversion were to precede the second coming? Something did not jibe here. And to join the postmillennialist camp of Daniel Whitby, whose *Treatise of the True Millennium* (1703) asserted the rise of a Jewish monarchy during the millennium, was altogether out of the question to Mather. Perhaps Hugo Grotius's preterist reading deserved another chance. If St. Paul's prediction was really fulfilled in the times of the early church and in the surrogation of the Gentiles as the elect, then the Jews' literal conversion was already past and thus the surprise of Christ's coming in the clouds of fire could still be maintained. So ruminating in the last decade of his life, Cotton Mather defined his ultimate thoughts in his *Threefold Paradise* (pp. 295–318), in which he turned allegorist on the issue of Israel's conversion by insisting on their surrogation by Gentile Christians, yet lambasting all those who dared to join Grotius and allegorize the envisioned conflagration. The fine lines between literal and allegorical exegesis had to be drawn somewhere to keep the house in order.

Mather's friends in Boston were shocked to find a defector amidst their own conservative ranks. Judge Samuel Sewall (1652–1730) tried to ward off such deist inroads by dusting off his earlier *Phaenomena* (1697), reminding Cotton of his father's orthodox position in *Mystery* (1669) and *Future Conversion* (1709), and appending Samuel Willard's literalist defense, *The Fountain Opened* (1700), to the second edition of his *Phaenomena* (Boston, 1727). In the next generation, Jonathan Edwards (1703–1758) held fast to orthodoxy and pointed to Judea as the land where God's promise would be fulfilled: "Without doubt, they will return to their own land" yet "remain a distinct nation" even after their conversion, to be "a visible monument of God's wonderful grace and power in their calling and conversion." In the Holy Land, "Religion and learning will there be at the highest; more excellent books will be there written," and "all nations will be as free to come to Judea, or to dwell in Jerusalem, as into any other city or country, and have the same privilege there as they themselves" ("Notes on the Apocalypse," ed. Stephen J. Stein, in *The Works of Jonathan Edwards* [New Haven: Yale University Press, 1977], 5:135). Postmillennialists like Joseph Bellamy and Samuel Hopkins were not far behind their master in asserting the literal accomplishment of Romans 11. The destruction of Antichrist and his pagan and Moslem allies prior to the millennium "will open the way for their return to the land given to their ancestors," Hopkins determined. But whether God's ancient people would "continue a distinct people" during the millennium or "intermix with others" can only be settled after the fact (*A Treatise of the Millennium* [Boston, 1793], 119, 120). At the fall of the Roman Antichrist and of his Turkish ally, the "powerful obstacles to the coming in of the Jews" would be removed, Connecticut's own Thomas Wells Bray (1738–1808), pastor of Guilford, Connecticut, intoned in his *Dissertation on the Sixth Vial* ([Hartford, 1780], 39), during the American Revolution.

It is safe to say that with a few exceptions, the return of God's ancient people remained an exegetical touchstone in the millenarian treatises throughout the seventeenth and eighteenth centuries. Yet such niceties of interpretation were not always taken too literally as the pressures of political upheavals in America called for a prompt response from the pulpit. Perhaps the zeal of the moment prevailed as the revolution loomed on the horizon; for as America's patriotic clergy called on God's newly chosen people to defend his American Israel against the tyranny of the English Antichrist, the civil millenarians of the period had long forgotten Nicholas Noyes's neat (perhaps too neat) distinction between the literal application of God's prophetic promises to his ancient people and the *"Analogical sence"* and *"Analogical Accomodation"* to God's surrogate Israel, the Protestant church in America (*New-Englands Duty and Interest* [Boston, 1698], 10, 42).

☞ THE GREAT AWAKENING
AND JONATHAN EDWARDS

Much, perhaps too much, has been made of Jonathan Edwards's heady assertion that the revivals in his day might be "the beginning or forerunner of something vastly great" in America (*Thoughts on the Revival of Religion in New England* [1742], *The Works of President Edwards*, 4 vols. [New York, 1864], 3:316). If his conniving colleagues ridiculed him for reading the spiritual awakening in New England as signs of the millennium lately begun in Northampton, modern critics are no less liable to fall into the same trap—albeit for different reasons. Roughly until the early 1980s, historians of the period were wont to see the events of the First Great Awakening (1734–35; 1739–43) as some sort of latter-day manifestation of the Puritan errand into an American wilderness. The surprising conversions up and down the Connecticut Valley began in the winter of 1734–35, sporadically swept across New England, and climaxed in mass revivals in the years between 1739 and 1743. Such unprecedented outpourings of the spirit certainly required official interpretation especially in the wake of charges by Old-Light theologians that Jonathan Edwards and his compeers had fallen prey to dangerous enthusiasms and delusions. But there were others who looked on these occurrences in New England with much more expecting eyes. Inquiries from home and abroad kept fueling the debate. Thomas Prince (1687–1758), for instance, was eager to publish eyewitness accounts of the surprising conversions in his *Christian History* (2 vols.; Boston, 1744–45) for his inquiring readers on both sides of the Atlantic. Likewise, John Gillies (fl. 1740–1760s) edited his *Historical Collections* (2 vols.; Glasgow, 1754) and involuntarily supplied grist for the mills of later historians in search of their own usable past. If Edwards's contemporaries constructed their interpretations as signs of providential history unfolding in front of their very eyes, early-nineteenth-century participants in the "Second Great Awakening" (1790–1840) just as much as late-nineteenth-century historians reinvented Jonathan Edwards as an ideal if not convenient figure to reify their own views of a First Great Awakening as a formative event in American religious history. This "interpretive fiction" says as much about our present need of reconstructing cultural history in our own image as it does about past historians who inscribed their own agendas into the subtexts of their histories. Whether "great" or small, the Great Awakening and its principal participants are presently being reinvented not the least in the republication of Jonathan Edwards's works in the mighty Yale edition (1957–).

Be that as it may, we may do well in examining the development of Edwards's eschatological thought in terms of the continuity or discontinuity of his interpretive environment. If Edwards really did focus myopically on America as the center of latter-day activities (as historians searching for the roots of America's national identity are wont to discover), then we should be able to substantiate these interpretations in the deep structure of his millenarian theories. Among his most valuable works on the issue are his "Notes on the Apocalypse," a running commentary on Revelation, begun in 1723 and continuously revised until his death in 1758; *An Humble Attempt* (Boston, 1747), a transatlantic endeavor to encourage concerted prayers to hasten the millennium (both in *Apocalyptic Writings*); *A History of the Work of Redemption* (1774), a historical and prophetic interpretation of soteriology from the creation to the end of the millennium, in thirty sermons preached in 1739 (ed. John F. Wilson, *Works* [1989] vol. 9); and his recently published *The "Miscellanies"* (ed. Thomas A. Schafer, *Works* [1994], vol. 13), Edwards's encyclopedic commonplace book on all issues relevant to his theology. If Edwards did expect to hear the silver trumpets in his own day, his public and private calculations of the millennium should provide us with helpful insight into the matter. The earliest published example of Edwards's calculations is his *Humble Attempt*. Here Edwards voices his dissatisfaction with Moses Lowman (1680–1752), whose *Paraphrase and Notes on the Revelation of St. John* (London, 1737) is central to an understanding of Edwards's theology. Lowman conjectured that Antichrist's 1,260-year reign would terminate in 2016 "more than two hundred and fifty years hence" (*Humble Attempt*, 394). Edwards did not like this late date at all and objected that Lowman placed Antichrist's rise "300 years later" than Joseph Mede did in his chronology (p. 403). Mede's old mainstay of commencing the rise of Antichrist at Genseric's destruction of Rome in 456 or with the deposing of Romulus Augustulus, Rome's last emperor, in 476, yielded much earlier dates, according to which the fall of Antichrist could be expected either in 1716 or 1736. But while the latter date may have played some part in Edwards's response to the first outpouring of the spirit in the winter of 1734–35, by the time he was writing his *Humble Attempt* (1747), Mede had long been proven wrong (*History*, 412). But neither Lowman nor his French Huguenot colleague Charles Daubuz (1673–1717) seemed to furnish satisfactory calculations. Perhaps a much more revealing comment can be found in his private "Notes on the Apocalypse," esp. nos. 11–16, which have been dated to the "late spring or early summer of 1723" (p. 77). Commenting on Revelation 13 and 20, Edwards conjectured that Antichrist's reign began in 606 and would therefore "end about 1866," even though he did not completely dismiss Lowman's conjecture about the year 2,000 ("Notes," 129). These two references provide a framework for Edwards's own expectation of Antichrist's fall. Yet Edwards is quick to remind us that this crucial event would *not* occur all at once, but during a period of gradual decline ("the drying up of the Euphrates") at which time Antichrist's revenues exacted from his regal supporters would totally dry up (*Humble Attempt*, 410).

In explaining these events, Edwards kept supernatural explanations to a minimum, stressing Antichrist's gradual decline over a long period of time, rather than resorting to a miraculous intervention of God. Antichrist's waning power was already apparent since Luther's reformation in 1517. The loss of French Canada to the British, terminating the French-Indian War (1754–63) further contributed to the pontiff's loss of revenue, the rebellion of Spain and Portugal, and "the late peeling and impoverishing the Pope's temporal dominions in Italy, by the armies of the Austrians, Neapolitans and Spaniards"; the "almost miraculous taking of Cape Breton, in the year 1745, whereby was dried up one of the main sources of the wealth of the kingdom of France"; the great earthquake of Lima (1746), which disrupted the flow of silver and gold to the Spanish crown; the loss of the French fleet under Duke D'Anville in 1747 (King George's War, 1744–48)—these and more were all signs of the sixth vial poured out on Antichrist, whose gradual, yet inevitable demise was already in progress (*Humble Attempt*, 421, 422, 423). Whatever the year of this final dissolution and whatever shape, form, or opinion Antichrist might assume, Edwards called for concerted prayers on both sides of the Atlantic to cast him out—even if Antichrist lately changed his spots, appearing in the guise of Anabaptism, Quakerism, Socinianism, Arminianism, Arianism, and Deism (*History*, 430–32).

That Antichrist would not relinquish his reign without battle unto death was all too clear to anyone who understood the prophetic "slaying of the witnesses" (Rev. 11:7–10). In fact, Jonathan Edwards worried in his *Humble Attempt* that if Moses Lowman were right in placing this dreadful calamity in the future, such an expectation of carnage just prior to the millennium of peace would be "a great damp to their hope, courage, and activity, in praying for, and reaching after the speedy introduction of those gloriously promised times" (p. 378). The anticipation of such doom would positively "deaden and keep down, life, hope and joyful expectation in prayer," for in quickening the coming of Christ's kingdom, the saints were in effect hastening their own doom: never in this life would they see the glory of Christ's coming (p. 379). Edwards could not reconcile himself to this futurist application. And like Mather before him, he was certain it was an event of the past as described in the martyrology of John Foxe, where the slaughter of the Waldenses, Albigensians, Bohemians, Huguenots, and Calvinists in Poland, Palatine, Lithuania, Holland, even in England under Queen Mary and King Charles I, fully answered the description of this prophetic event (*History*, 419–29). It is interesting to note here that Edwards's American colleagues distanced themselves from Edwards's preterization, even as they joined his concerted effort to pray for the coming of Christ (*Humble Attempt*, "Preface," 310).

Besides, Edwards objected, the gradual decline of Antichrist's power since the Reformation would render this slaughter impossible—even if Satan's visible empire on earth would join forces against true religion: the Antichristian kingdom (the beast), the Mahometan kingdom (the false prophet), and the heathen kingdom (the dragon). They would join forces in all parts of the world as the heathens would battle "against Christianity in America, and in the East Indies, and Africa," just like "the Mahometans and papists do in the other parts of the world" ("Notes," 174). Of all these looming events, the bloody defeat of the Ottoman Turks in 1697 and during the Russo-Turkish War (1735–39) was a harbinger of things to come ("Notes," 190–91). As is clearly evident from the many pages of commentary that Edwards invested in this issue, the horrors of Antichrist's global warfare in Edwards's postmillennialist system were not all that different from the awesome description of Christ's supernatural destruction of Antichrist as championed by premillennialists of Cotton Mather's persuasion. In either system, the events leading up to the millennium pictured fearsome desolation that only the strong in faith could broach with some measure of confidence. Whatever the precise nature of this imminent catastrophe, God would see to it that his people would not come to harm.

The main features of Edwards's millennialism were certainly not new in his day, and neither Daniel Whitby, nor Moses Lowman, nor Charles Daubuz can be credited for being his principal source of inspiration on these issues. Again crucial here is that Edwards followed the Augustinianism of his predecessors Brightman, Alsted, and Cotton and allegorized the first resurrection (Rev. 20:5) as a spiritual conversion of individuals (Edwards, "Notes" 144–45; see also 151). Significant too is that Edwards's millennium remains inchoate, a mixture of the

saints in heaven ruling through their spiritual successors over their mortal and sinful counterparts on earth. The corporeal resurrection of body and soul would be "absolutely necessary" for
both classes of saints (Rev. 20:6, 14), for the soul in separation from the body cannot achieve
"complete happiness" ("*Miscellanies,*" 179). This union, however, would not occur until judgment day, when God would establish his literal new heavens and new earth, of which its
inchoate counterpart was merely a spiritual type. St. John's Revelation is not hyperbolical,
Edwards insisted, but employs "mixed prophecies" that have "an eye to several events"
("Notes," 150) adumbrated in double manifestations: the first during the golden age of Christ's
spiritual reign and the second after the literal resurrection at the end, when the New Jerusalem
descending from heaven (Rev. 21:2) would be established on a literal new earth located in an
altogether different part of the universe ("Notes," 151–52).

Edwards's double application of the new heavens and new earth has frequently been mistaken for the same eschatological event in time. It is evidently inspired by his British colleagues
Thomas Burnet, William Whiston, and Isaac Newton (1642–1727), who had much to say about
the predicted conflagration of the earth (2 Peter 3), its condition, and location following its dissolution. Edwards was certainly familiar with their daring theories. Adopting some of their
interpretations, Edwards insisted that the Petrine conflagration was not a metaphor for human
warfare, as Sir Isaac Newton opined in his famous *Observations upon the Prophecies* (London,
1733), nor an allegory of the Roman destruction of Jerusalem, as Grotius and Hammond
argued in their *Annotations* (1642) and *Paraphrase* (1653), but a literal melting and total dissolution of the earth's elements (Thomas Burnet, *Sacred Theory of the Earth* [1684–91]). This
hyperliteralism becomes significant in light of William Whiston's conjecture that after its conflagration by a passing comet "the Earth will desert its present Seat and Station in the World,
and be no longer found among the Planetary *Chorus*" (*A New Theory of the Earth* [1696], 5th
ed. [London, 1737], pt. 2, pp. 289, 291). Edwards was not far behind his English colleagues. As
the eternal abode of the corporeal saints following the universal resurrection, the new earth
must surpass in glory even its millennial predecessor. A purging by fire, Edwards felt, could no
more than facilitate the "primitive state" of this new earth, but not a "new creation." It was
therefore more likely that "this globe with all its appurtenances is clear gone, out of the way;
and this is a new one, materially as well as in form." Its location, though the Bible did not say so,
would likely be in "some glorious place in the universe prepared for this end by God, removed
at an immense distance from the solar system" ("Notes," 140–41), while the old earth consumed in the flames of fire "shall be the place of the damned" (*"Miscellanies,"* 376, no. 275).
Edwards knew enough about the state of contemporary science to assert with Burnet and Whiston that God's prophecies did not represent these cosmic phenomena "according to philosophic verity, but as they appeared to our eyes." Yet Edwards was convinced "that this place
shall be remote from the solar system" ("Notes," 141–42). A totally new creation of the globe
was all the more logical, Edwards observed, because nothing in nature could last forever. The
habitation where the blessed would reign forever and ever (Rev. 22:5) must needs be an eternal
abode not subject to mutability: "'Tis manifest God did not make these fleeting systems for an
eternal duration as might be more fully shown, if the place were proper for such a philosophical
discourse" ("Notes," 141–42). From these passages we can gather that for Edwards the restitution of all things after the day of judgment, when the corporeal saints would enjoy immortality
in primitive purity, did not imply stasis or cessation of all deterioration, but an everlasting rise

and fall of all matter. Not even God's restitution of all things could offset the inevitable laws of nature.

What then did Edwards's millennial earth look like, when Satan was bound, the gospel preached universally (albeit the saints on earth retaining their mortality and sinful disposition)? For Edwards, the whole earth would be filled with universal peace and love. Naturally, there would be righteous governors who love their people, ministers who cherish their parishioners in sweet harmony, people who joyfully submit to their rulers, churches without division or strife, discipline without dissent, and all inscrutable points of biblical exegesis clarified for good. "It may be hoped that then many of the Negroes and Indians will be divines, and that excellent books will be published in Africa, in Ethiopia, in Turkey—and not only very learned men, but others that are more ordinary men, shall then be very knowing in religion" (*History*, 480). In short, all nations in all parts of the habitable globe would be united in "sweet harmony." Geographic isolation would cease through improved communication and "the art of navigation" fully dedicated to holy uses, as the saints the world over would gather around Christ's throne in Judea, "at the center of the kingdom of Christ, communicating influences to all other parts" ("Notes," 134). With all things in beautiful proportion, there would be "a time of great temporal prosperity," improvement of health, ease, material wealth, and "great increase in children," as each and every one "shall build houses, and inhabit them" (*History*, 480–85) and benefit from all useful knowledge and improvements in "the arts and sciences" (*Humble Attempt*, 338–39, 342–43, 359).

Edwards's inviting description of these Edenic prospects reverberates in the works of his principal disciples, the Congregationalist minister Joseph Bellamy, of Hartford, Connecticut, and Samuel Hopkins, fervent abolitionist pastor of the First Congregational Church in Newport, Rhode Island. Both clergymen were faithful to the Edwardsian tradition of the millennium and differed only in minor points from his New Light exegesis. For instance, in his homily *The Millennium* (Boston, 1758), Bellamy largely dissociated his millennialism from direct references to contemporary events. Yet everyone of his parishioners knew what he meant when he offered comfort in visions of hope and peace so befitting this "terrible darkness" of the French-Indian War (1754–63). In the glorious days of the millennium, universal peace would prevail, all war would cease, and the nations beat their swords into plowshares and their spears into pruning hooks (Isa. 2:4). No doubt, such soothing words (no matter how apolitical in outlook) were welcome balm in the face of wartime ravages, when death and desolation depleted the resources of the colonies. But come the millennium in 2016, as Moses Lowman seemed to suggest, Bellamy was certain everyone would diligently work in his calling, live in his own house, and eat the fruits of his own labor, while all the losses and suffering of the great war would be forgotten in the billions of new offspring populating the new earth: "And if *all* these shall *know the Lord* . . . it will naturally come to pass, that there will be more saved in these thousand years, than ever before dwelt upon the face of the earth from the foundation of the world" (in *The Great Awakening*, ed. A. Heimert and P. Miller [1967], 628–29). And if Bellamy were not mistaken in modifying the conjectures of Thomas Burnet and William Whiston, then the ratio between the eternally lost and saved would be 1 in 17,476 during a millennial period of peace and plenty that might last as long as 360,000 years (*Millennium*, 617–20, 628–30).

That Bellamy's popular *Millennium* greatly impressed parishioners far and wide is well known, notwithstanding the fact that Hopkins at century's end did not see why God would need 360,000 years to accomplish the task of saving his elect. A literal period of a thousand years would be totally sufficient. In chapter 2 of his *Treatise of the Millennium* (Boston, 1793), Hopkins agreed with Lowman and Bellamy that the hoped-for millennium was little more than two hundred years off. Yet that did not deter Hopkins from dedicating his tract to all those who would live during those halcyon days. In fact, Hopkins's glowing description rose to a veritable crescendo of symphony and anticipated bliss as he sketched his picturesque vision on the canvas of his readers' imaginations. Though far from being immortal, human beings would continue to incur death, yet without "painful sickness or distress of body and mind" and without grief to their "surviving relatives and friends" who would "expect soon to arrive" in the invisible world as well (p. 75). While here on earth, they would enjoy eminent degrees of holiness short of perfection. Holy teachers would enlighten the nations in all useful branches of the arts and science that promote spiritual and bodily comforts in this life. Unanimous belief in God and unanimity in his worship would banish all sectarian strife and disagreeable doctrines while promoting political harmony through separation of church and state (p. 79). Though hardly a republican government of, by, or for the people, Christ's monarchy would uphold material prosperity through improvements in the "art of husbandry" and the cultivation of the soil, increasing its productivity "20, 30, and perhaps an 100 fold more" (p. 71). Great discoveries and inventions in the mechanical arts would ensure that "all utensils, clothing, buildings, &c. will be formed and made, in a better manner, and with much less labour . . . beyond our present conception" (p. 71). No "more than 2 or 3 hours in a day" would be necessary to acquire one's wherewithal, leaving ample time for "reading and conversation" and the improvement of one's mind (p. 72). No doubt, the global population would increase in an unprecedented fashion without leading to strife, famine, or war.

International communication would be fostered by one universal language taught throughout the world. And "this useless and imprudent waste of time and money" to which millions of young scholars were subjected in learning dead languages, Hopkins's Yankee ingenuity surmised, would finally cease (p. 75). That Samuel Hopkins not even once alluded to the American Revolution or the independence of the United States so painfully acquired during his lifetime certainly speaks loudly. The internecine rhetoric of Federalists and Anti-Federalists, the contrasting visions of Alexander Hamilton and Thomas Jefferson, clearly indicated to Hopkins that the political Messiah had not come to the young republic, the millennium not begun. It was far safer to concentrate on the timeless promises of God than to be swept up by the patriotic rhetoric of his misguided colleagues.

If Hopkins's vision of abundant happiness struck a responsive chord in his parishioners, then Elhanan Winchester's *Universal Restoration exhibited in a Series of Dialogues* (London, 1793) would equally appeal to those who had no patience with a wrathful God condemning all sinners to eternal perdition. An English Baptist turned Universalist, Elhanan Winchester (1751–97) came to the United States late in his life and preached his new doctrine to whoever was willing to listen. His tract is modeled after Justin Martyr's famous *Dialogue with Trypho* (ca. 156), in which a sympathetic interlocutor raises questions to facilitate the teacher's programmatic answers. In his *Universal Resurrection,* Winchester took issue with the Calvinist doctrine of arbitrary election and eternal reprobation, asserting instead that all humans, no matter how sinful, would ultimately attain redemption through a cycle of retribution, conviction, and conversion. The doctrine of eternal punishment (no matter how small the crime) seemed unreasonable to this former Baptist, for a God of fairness could not be presumed to punish humanity eternally: "The current doctrine of *endless misery,* destroys this rule of equity and proportion: for though it contends for degrees of future punishment, yet it makes the duration the same, whether men sin more or less" (p. 5). Besides, such indiscriminate punishment would merely harden reprobates in their belief that God's punitive measures were akin to vindictiveness.

More to the point, Winchester argued, the apostles rarely ever used the term *everlasting* (*aiōnian*) in the context of "damnation" (p. 17). And mustering more than fifty passages in which the terms *everlasting* and *forever* signified a limited period of time (e.g., Hab. 3:6), Winchester brushed aside all those who relished the eternal fires of hell where the worm dieth not, and the fire is not quenched (pp. 18–19). Even the "second death" (Rev. 20:14) could not be everlasting, but was limited to a specific duration of time, while the earth's elements were turned into liquid fire. Besides, since the melting earth would be the seat of hell, it could only last as long as there were "combustible matter" available. It followed that those who partook in the second death would also be restored to eternal life on the new earth, their period of punishment in the lake of fire terminated, when sinners had sufficiently atoned for their iniquity. Subsequent to their restoration, they would willingly undergo conversion and gladly join the saints of the New Jerusalem in the worship of Christ their Redeemer. In this manner, the "universal deliverance of all men from the bondage of sin" would be accomplished (p. 181), and eternal happiness be the lot of all humanity. Such promises of universal redemption certainly appealed to Winchester's spiritual descendants in early-nineteenth-century America, as the Transcendentalists formulated their credo of humanity's divinity in union with an all-loving Over-Soul.

☞ MOUNTAIN GLOOM AND MOUNTAIN GLORY: THE AMERICAN REVOLUTION AND THE ARMS OF THE BLACK REGIMENT

If Winchester represents the first stirrings of Universalism in the young republic, then David Austin (1760–1831), Yale graduate and Presbyterian colleague in Elizabethtown, New Jersey, is a milestone of rabid millenarian fervor, wedding his patriotic rhetoric of freedom and independence to liberty of (Protestant) conscience. Austin's *Downfall of Mystical Babylon* (Elizabeth Town, 1794) eagerly asserts his Edwardsian roots by reprinting Bellamy's *Millennium* and Edwards's *Humble Attempt.* Yet Austin's mixing of the sacred with the profane goes beyond anything that either of his predecessors would have deemed appropriate or safe. The United States of America represented to David Austin the apocalyptic "stone cut out of the mountain" soon to cover the whole earth (Dan. 2:31–45). Young America, to Austin, is that prophetic "kingdom of the stone," born on 4 July 1776, steeled in the War of Independence, and soon to become the kingdom of the mountain in its conquest of the political pagans the world over: "Behold the *regnum montis,* the kingdom of the mountain, begun on the Fourth of July, 1776, when the *birth* of the MAN-CHILD—the hero of the civil and religious liberty took place in these United States. Let them read the predictions of heaven respecting the increase of his dominion—that he was *to rule all nations with a rod of iron.* . . . Behold, then, this hero of America wielding the standard of civil and religious liberty over these United States" (pp. 392–93). The American man-child must spill the blood of civil and ecclesiastical tyranny by smashing the feet of Nebuchadnezzar's Antichrist, Austin intoned, as he called on his fellow ministers to wield their spiritual weapons in pulling down the anti-Christian strongholds across the Atlantic.

Thus, for the United States to become the kingdom of the mountain and cover the whole earth, a second, albeit spiritual, revolution would have to take place (sometime in 1813) in which the ideas of liberty, democracy, and Protestantism would mop up the rubble of the anti-Christian Babylon. "Is not the *Stone* now rolling against the feet and toes of the mighty image?" Austin enthusiastically appraised the French Revolution and its break from the tyranny of church and state (p. 390). But while the European world was doing its share of fighting the beast, the church, escaped on the wings of an eagle, was safely ensconced in the American wilderness: "she hath her station upon the broad seal of the United States; and from thence has perched upon the pediment of the first government-house, dedicated to the dominion of civil and religious liberty, where she is still to be seen, an emblem of the protection of Providence towards our present government, and towards this our happy land" (p. 415). And while thus celebrating the victory of good over evil, David Austin built landing piers in the Long Island Sound to facilitate the return of American Jews to the Holy Land: the second coming was at hand. The notion of a civil millennium in which miter and scepter were supplanted by liberty of conscience and political independence can be traced to the emergence of a republican eschatology in the decade before the French and Indian War. While some historians see this civic millennium as a direct outgrowth of the Great Awakening with its New Light emphasis on prayer, piety, and conversion, other historians point to eighteenth-century political philosophy and millenarian apocalyptic shared by both New and Old Light theologians. To suggest, however, that disillusioned postmillennialists turned to statecraft for signs of the second coming when the religious awakenings in the mid-1740s dwindled to a mere trickle seems to ignore the secular application of the prophecies implicit in Daniel and Revelation. New Light millennialists did not have to replace their pious dictums with political metaphors to reawaken their parishioners, because all prophecies were to be interpreted by their post-facto accomplishment in the course of empire. Jonathan Edwards's *History of Redemption,* first preached between March and August 1739, is certainly no exception. Be that as it may, it is fair to suggest that this hybrid eschatology of politics and religion breathed new life into an ancient script when in the wake of the Stamp Act of 1765 and the Quebec Act of 1774 millenarian tracts featured King George as Antichrist, the American colonists as the New World Israelites shackled in Egyptian bondage, and Jehovah of armies as an American minuteman ready to cast his plagues upon any English (or French) pharaoh unwilling to let his people go. On this basic level, all denominations could make common cause and enlist behind the banner of virtue, liberty, and providence in God's American Israel. Opportunities for such a cause came early on.

Early in King George's War, New England's regiments captured the French bastion of Louisbourg, in Nova Scotia, in July 1745 and founded Halifax as an English stronghold against the Catholic Acadians and their Indian allies. Newspapers and sermons up and down the east coast celebrated Protestant victory over their antichristian enemy to the north. This blow against the "Man of Sin" furnished new themes for the political sermons in the decades before the Revolutionary War. As if Thomas Prince and Joseph Sewall of Boston had dusted off Cotton Mather's inveterate *Shaking Dispensations* (1715) and his only sermon in French *Une Grande Voix Du Ciel A La France* (1725), the fall of that "French Leviathan, the oldest son of Antichrist" was nothing less than "the Doings of God" (Prince, *Extraordinary Events the Doings of God* [Boston, 1745]). And as King George's War wore on into the French and Indian War

(1754–63), the "Gallic threat" in French Canada virtually engrossed the spotlight in the sermon literature of the period. Painting images of bloodshed and rape, enslavement in Catholic dungeons and forced conversions by Jesuits no less, the black regiments of Ebenezer Pemberton (1705–1777), Gad Hitchcock (1719–1803), Solomon Williams (1700–1776), Isaac Stiles (1697–1760), and a whole host of others thundered from their pulpits doom and destruction—if God's people in Protestant New England did not unite behind the banner of their British majesty: "It is possible, our land may be given to the beast, the inhabitants to the sword, the righteous to the fire of martyrdom, our wives to ravishment, and our sons and daughters to death and torture" (John Mellen, *The Duty of All to be Ready for Future Impending Events* [Boston, 1756], 19–20).

This Gallic threat to Protestantism was little short of rivaling the heinous Gunpowder Plot of 1605, when Guy Fawkes (1570–1606) tried to blow up king and parliament for the glory of the Church of Rome. By invoking the ominous language of warfare between Satan and Christ in the battle of Armageddon, ministers lent cosmic significance to the minutiae of infantry combat, mixing pious maxims with the ideals of civic liberty. Sermons were surcharged with ominous forebodings as parishioners flocked to the churches to hear the latest news from Quebec improved with apocalyptic significance. In the unfolding events of the period, Old- and New-Light millenarians made common cause in focusing more on Antichrist's fall than on saving souls. This shift in focus set the stage for the Peace of Paris (1763), in which France relinquished her Canadian colonies to the British crown. Babylon has fallen, Harvard's euphoric Samuel Langdon (1723–1797) proclaimed; "the final ruin of that spiritual tyranny and *mystery of iniquity*" was at hand (*Joy and Gratitude to God* [Portsmouth, New Hampshire, 1760], 42–43).

The genre and language of the apocalypse proved so adaptable to the civic needs of clergy and statesmen that the myth of the Puritan Errand was put to new use: our ancestors came to America for freedom of religion and to preserve their political liberties. And just like Jonathan Mayhew (1720–1766), Andrew Eliot (1718–1778), Nathaniel Appleton (1693–1784), Eli Forbes (1726–1804), Mather Byles (1707–1788), and Abraham Keteltas (1732–1798), James Cogswell (1720–1807) yoked the sacred with the profane: "Liberty is one of the most sacred and inviolable Privileges Mankind enjoy; without it Life itself is insipid and many Times burdensome.... Endeavor to stand as Guardians of the Religion and Liberties of *America;* to oppose Antichrist ... [as] the art of War becomes a Part of our Religion" (*God, the Pious Soldier's Strength and Instructor* [Boston, 1757], 26, 11). In the excitement of the moment, the fine line between God's will and colonial politics was largely obliterated. As usual, Jehovah of armies was on the side of the victor. In celebrating the victory of the British crown over Antichrist's eldest son, the American colonists were proud to be English subjects.

All of that would change with one stroke. Scarcely had the colonial troops returned home when the Stamp Act of 1765 incensed the pulpit with the tyranny of arbitrary taxation without representation. The corruption of the Hanoverian court was all too obvious when King George III threatened his American subjects with loss of liberty if they did not pay for the expense of the recent war. If that were not enough, the Quebec Act of 1774 added insult to injury as royal George restored Canadian civil law and confirmed freedom of worship for all Acadians, Roman Catholic or no. Such a betrayal of the Protestant cause betokened King George's complicity in this Catholic plot. Samuel Sherwood's famous *Church's Flight into the Wilderness* (Boston, 1776) is a representative example of the sermon literature of the period: French atrocities against Christ's "humble followers" are ominous, and the "corrupt system of tyranny and oppression, that has of late been fabricated and adopted by the ministry and parliament of Great-Britain, which appears so favourable to popery and the Roman catholic interest . . . awfully threatens the civil and religious liberties of all sound protestants" (in *Political Sermons of the American Founding Era: 1730–1805*, ed. Ellis Sandoz [1991], 502). In short, the blending of apocalyptic fervency with civil liberty forged expectations for a civil millennium that climaxed in the American Revolution. In this eruption, political rationalists and millenarians of all shades made common cause in unleashing the full force of their pulpit rhetoric that had previously battered the walls of the fortress of Louisbourg. Satan's plot to enslave God's people in America was most of all evident in the tyranny of British power: standing armies, corrupt politicians, taxation without representation. The fervor of the moment heightened the divine mandate against all types of oppression, as the pulpit issued the call to arms: "We must beat our plowshares into swords, and our pruning-hooks into spears." Remember "that terrible denunciation of divine wrath against the worshippers of the [British] beast and his image." For all those who received his mark in their forehead would be tormented forever and ever in the fire and brimstone of Christ's coming (Samuel West, *A Sermon Preached before the Honorable Council, May 29th, 1776*, in *The Pulpit of the American Revolution*, ed. John Wingate Thornton [Boston, 1860], 318).

The conflation of sacred and secular metaphors mobilized intellectuals just as much as it did backwoods farmers who were tilling their stony glebe. It also inspired a group of visionary poets among the Connecticut Wits, who celebrated America's rising glory in their epic poems about the young republic. In hindsight, it is not surprising that the revolutionary pulpit did not develop any fully matured eschatological system until long after those heady days were over and theologians had sufficiently distanced themselves from the events to give them meaning. By that time, the Second Great Awakening was taking shape, and American patriots, employing sacred and secular metaphors with ease, reinvented the Puritan Errand, the Edwardsian Awakening, and the Revolution to give mythic dimension to the new nation. Of all the many writers who incorporated these new myths into their works, Herman Melville said it best in his antebellum novel *White-Jacket: or The World in a Man-of-War* (1850):

> We Americans are the peculiar chosen people—the Israel of our time; we bear the ark of the liberties of the world. God has given to us, for a future inheritance, the broad domains of the political pagans, that shall yet come and lie down under the shade of our ark. The rest of the nations must soon be in our rear. We are the pioneers of the world, the advance guard, sent on through the wilderness of untried things, to break a new path in the New World that is ours. (*The Writings of Herman Melville*, ed. Harrison Hayford et al. [Evanston: Northwestern University Press, 1970], 151)

☞ BIBLIOGRAPHY _____

Bercovitch, Sacvan. 1975. *The Puritan Origins of the American Self.* New Haven: Yale University Press. *Puritan Origins* traces the rhetorical origin of America's myth as a chosen nation from its formulation in the seventeenth century to its culmination in the Transcendentalism of the nineteenth century.
———. 1978. *The American Jeremiad.* Madison: University of Wisconsin Press. *American Jeremiad* describes a homiletic genre of moral and political exhortation that has played a vital role in American life and thought through the Civil War.

Bloch, Ruth H. 1985. *Visionary Republic: Millennial Themes in American Thought, 1756–1800.* Cambridge: Cambridge University Press. This revisionist study asserts a middle ground between postmillennialism (Heimert, Tuveson) and republican ideas of civic liberty (Hatch) as playing a defining role in the American Revolution.

Bozeman, Theodore Dwight. 1988. *To Live Ancient Lives: The Primitivist Dimension in Puritanism.* Chapel Hill/London: University of North Carolina Press. The Puritan exodus was not informed by expectations of the millennium until at least a full decade after their arrival and was more concerned with soteriology and primitive church purity than with establishing an American New Jerusalem.

Butler, Jon. 1990. *Awash in a Sea of Faith: Christianizing the American People.* Cambridge, Mass.: Harvard University Press. Popular piety, magic, divining rods, and occultism were frequent phenomena in colonial America, demonstrating that the Revolution was a profoundly secular and interdenominational event that sacralized religious freedom and political independence.

Conforti, Joseph A. 1995. *Jonathan Edwards, Religious Tradition & American Culture.* Chapel Hill: University of North Carolina Press. The publishing history and appropriation of Edwards's work by succeeding generations evinces their manipulation of his legacy to reify their own agendas.

Davidson, James West. 1977. *The Logic of Millennial Thought: Eighteenth-Century New England.* New Haven: Yale University Press. A remarkable continuity of millenarian logic shaped Puritan responses to the political events of the eighteenth century.

De Jong, J. A. 1970. *As the Waters Cover the Sea: Millennial Expectations in the Rise of Anglo-American Missions, 1640–1810.* Kampen: J. H. Kok N.V., 1970. This helpful study examines eschatological speculations in action: their impact on ecumenical missionary activities through the early nineteenth century.

Delbanco, Andrew. 1989. *The Puritan Ordeal.* Cambridge, Mass.: Harvard University Press. The ordeal of Americanization of the Puritan immigrants is examined here as they tried to "escape" from the religious and political chaos of Jacobean and Carolingean England.

Elliott, Emory. 1975. *Power and the Pulpit in Puritan New England.* Princeton: Princeton University Press. Elliott employs the methodologies of structuralism and psychohistory to examine the language of Puritan sermons as a literary art form.

Froom, Leroy Edwin. 1946–54. *The Prophetic Faith of Our Fathers: The Historical Development of Prophetic Interpretation.* 4 vols. Washington, D.C.: Review and Herald Publishing Association. Though denominational in orientation, this old mainstay provides a monumental survey of the eschatological ideology and literature from the early church to the twentieth century.

Gilsdorf, Joy Bourne. 1964. "The Puritan Apocalypse: New England Eschatology in the Seventeenth Century." Ph.D. diss., Yale University. This influential study examines how seventeenth-century eschatological beliefs shaped Puritan responses to conversion and church membership codified in a Federal Covenant.

Hatch, Nathan O. 1977. *The Sacred Cause of Liberty: Republican Thought and the Millennium in Revolutionary New England.* New Haven: Yale University Press. Hatch investigates the rhetorical changes in the millennial ideology of colonial New England from the late seventeenth century to its transformation in a civil millennium during the last two decades before the American Revolution.

Heimert, Alan. 1966. *Religion and the American Mind: From the Great Awakening to the Revolution.* Cambridge, Mass.: Harvard University Press. Heimert's controversial thesis that eighteenth-century Calvinism (more so than liberal philosophy) inspired America with a nationalist ideology has sparked an ongoing debate.

Holstun, James. 1987. *A Rational Millennium: Puritan Utopias of Seventeenth-Century England & America.* New York: Oxford University Press. Displaced populations were subjected to a program of rational domination in both Englands.

Knight, Janice. 1994. *Orthodoxies in Massachusetts: Rereading American Puritanism.* Cambridge, Mass.: Harvard University Press. The split between rationalist and mystical strains of piety in New England informed the struggle between such preparationists as Hooker and Bulkeley on the one hand and anti-preparationists such as Cotton, Davenport, and Norton on the other.

Lowance, Mason I., Jr. 1980. *The Language of Canaan: Metaphor and Symbol in New England from the Puritans to the Transcendentalists.* Cambridge, Mass.: Harvard University Press. The author studies the figurative language and the prophetic symbolism of New England's homiletic literature from its rise to the Transcendentalism of Thoreau.

Miller, Perry. 1956. *Errand into the Wilderness.* Cambridge, Mass.: Harvard University Press. This seminal work, along with his two-volume compendium *The New England Mind* (1939 and 1953), establishes the myth of the Puritan errand and America as God's elect as one of the most abiding legacies of Puritan culture in America.

Niebuhr, H. Richard. 1988. *The Kingdom of God in America.* 1937; Middletown, Conn.: Wesleyan University Press. A classic interpretation of American religion and its impact on American self-perception.

Patrides, C. A., and Joseph Wittreich, eds. 1984. *The Apocalypse in English Renaissance Thought and Literature.* Ithaca, N.Y.: Cornell University Press. This collection provides background information on English and American millennialism from the Renaissance to the late eighteenth century.

Smolinski, Reiner. 1995. *The Threefold Paradise of Cotton Mather: An Edition of 'Triparadisus.'* Athens/London: University of Georgia Press. Mather's millenarian tract is a hermeneutical defense of revealed religion that negotiates between the literalist positions of orthodoxy and the new philological challenges to the scriptures by European theologians and scientists.

Toon, Peter, ed. 1970. *Puritans, the Millennium and the Future of Israel: Puritan Eschatology 1600–1660.* Cambridge: James Clarke & Co. This is a useful collection of essays on the eschatological role of the Jewish nation in Puritan millennialism on both sides of the Atlantic.

Tuveson, Ernest Lee. 1968. *Redeemer Nation: The Idea of America's Millennial Role.* Chicago/London: University of Chicago Press. This early examination of millennialism in American national ideology remains a helpful introduction to the subject.

Zakai, Avihu. 1992. *Exile and Kingdom: History and Apocalypse in the Puritan Migration to America.* Cambridge: Cambridge University Press. Anglican settlers extended a "Genesis-type" concept of England as a chosen nation into America while Puritan settlers employed an "Exodus-type" ideology borne out in apocalyptic crisis and constructed in terms of the church's flight into the wilderness.

18

Apocalypticism in Mainstream Protestantism, 1800 to the Present

James H. Moorhead
Princeton Theological Seminary

A N ACCOUNT OF APOCALYPTICISM in mainstream American Protestantism from the late eighteenth to the early twentieth century resembles a famous episode in Arthur Conan Doyle's portrayal of Sherlock Holmes. In one story the great detective calls attention to the "curious incident of the dog in the nighttime," the incident being the fact that the dog did *not* bark. In mainstream Protestantism, apocalypticism was the dog that did not bark. Or to render the analogy more precise, it was the dog whose barking, muted from the outset, became ever fainter until it was little more than a whimper.

Before that assertion is defended, however, a word on terminology is in order. The phrase "mainstream Protestantism" is here used to denote those churches that historically provided much of the leadership for various interdenominational ventures, sought to be culturally engaged with the central issues of American life, and understood themselves to be in some sense custodians of a common Protestant tradition that they believed was closely related to the American national identity itself. At the close of the eighteenth century, mainstream Protestantism included the Congregationalists, Presbyterians, and Episcopalians. By the mid-1800s, Methodists and Baptists had attained mainstream status; and by the early twentieth century, most observers would include the Disciples of Christ and the major Lutheran bodies.

The assertion that apocalypticism gradually became a mere whimper within mainstream Protestantism begins with the assumption, succinctly stated by a recent scholar, that "the essential claim of apocalyptic argument can be reduced to the statement: 'The world is coming to an end'" (O'Leary 1994, 77). At the outset of the nineteenth century, mainstream Protestants still believed that the world would have an end; but they would not admit that it should arrive with unseemly haste and terminate history prematurely. Asserting that history did move toward an end, these leaders also sought to affirm the nearly boundless possibilities of temporal existence. By the late nineteenth and early twentieth centuries, this tenuous equipoise was lost in many quarters; and the sense of open-ended temporal progress gradually displaced belief in a definitive end. As a result, mainstream Protestantism, at least significant sectors of it, ceased to participate in apocalyptic discourse.

This story is intimately connected with the rise and eventual declension of postmillennialism as the regnant eschatology among leading Protestants. Postmillennialism is the belief that the second coming will occur *after* the millennium or golden age foretold in Revelation 20. It is usually distinguished from premillennialism, which holds that the second coming will transpire *before* the millennium. Daniel Whitby (1638–1726), a latitudinarian English theologian, often receives credit for initiating postmillennialism in *A Paraphrase and Commentary on the New Testament* (1703); and the historian C. C. Goen has ascribed to Jonathan Edwards (1703–1758) and his theological disciples such as Samuel Hopkins (1721–1803) and Joseph Bellamy (1719–1790) the introduction of postmillennialism in America and has styled it "a new departure in eschatology."

Such attributions are misleading, for both Whitby and Edwards merely stated more systematically what had been implicit in certain earlier theories. Moreover, one must not attach greater significance to the early manifestations of postmillennialism than contemporaries did. The position of the second coming relative to the millennium was only one of many disputed eschatological questions and not necessarily the one on which exegetes placed the greatest weight. The fact that the term "postmillennialism" was not used before the nineteenth century—even among those who held the view—underscores the point. Even more significantly, postmillennialists prior to that period did not make the chronology of Jesus' return the key to a consistent view of the meaning of time. But after 1800 this situation began to change. Postmillennialism started to become more than a matter of dating the second advent. It came to denote an understanding of history as gradual improvement according to rational laws that human beings could learn and use. It was becoming a faith in an orderly ascent of history into the golden age—a hope, as Perry Miller once said aphoristically, that America might find the "the way, without any Fifth-Monarchy nonsense, into the millennium" (1965, 79).

In part this new view of history derived from the apparent success of revivals. Beginning with the so-called Great Awakening of the 1740s, periods of religious excitement and numerous conversions intermittently rumbled across the American landscape and continued well into the nineteenth century. It was logical for Protestants to associate these awakenings with the millennial hope, for various passages in the New Testament link the Spirit to the last things: for example, the prophecy that in the latter days God's Spirit will be poured out on all flesh (Acts 2:17) and the assertion that the "firstfruits of the Spirit" in the hearts of believers point to the redemption of the entire creation (Rom. 8:18–25). Thus Jonathan Edwards in the midst of the excitement generated by the Great Awakening wrote in 1743: "'Tis not unlikely that this work of God's Spirit, that is so extraordinary and wonderful, is the dawning, or at least a prelude, of the glorious work of God, so often foretold in Scripture, which in the progress and issue of it, shall renew the world of mankind" (Stein 1977, 26). Although in response to criticism Edwards later hedged his bets more cautiously, his initial enthusiasm represented a common pattern among evangelicals: revivals prompted expressions of hope that the millennial era was on the horizon.

These scattered effusions of hope, however, still fell short of a new view of history until many Protestants rethought the nature and origin of revivals. Initially deemed a surprising work of God, these outpourings of the spirit recurred with such frequency as to appear, especially after the Second Great Awakening, the normal state of the church. "They have become," said Robert Baird in his influential study of American religion in 1844, "a constituent part of the religious system of our country" (Bowden 1970, 202). At first, many Protestants still in the grip of predestinarian theology regarded the revivals as something to be awaited from the hand of God. At least this posture was the official one despite the fact that George Whitefield (1714–1770), the folk hero of the Great Awakening, had achieved his triumphs in large part through careful advance publicity and self-promotion. But as Calvinistic doctrine was attenuated, the theory of revivals began to resemble the practice. Awakenings were overtly touted as objects of promotion and calculation. By studying the laws underlying revivals, persons could use appropriate tactics to produce revivals virtually at will. Thus, evangelist Charles G. Finney (1792–1875) declared in his *Lectures on Revivals of Religion* (1835) that a revival "is not a miracle or dependent on a miracle, in any sense." It is "the result of the right use of the constituted means" (McLoughlin 1960, 13). And this promotionalism had an impact on the millennial hope as well. As they cooperated with the Spirit, believers could themselves be the agents for introducing the millennial age. "If the whole church as a body," declared Finney, "had gone to work ten years ago, . . . [t]he millennium would have fully come in the United States before this day" (ibid., 305).

The organization of numerous benevolent or voluntary societies in the first quarter of the nineteenth century also manifested the same spirit. Groups such as the American Board of Commissioners for Foreign Missions (1810), the American Bible Society (1816), the American Education Society (1816), the American Colonization Society (1817), the American Sunday School Union (1824), and the American Tract Society (1825) attempted through their respective causes to make the nation and the world Christian. In drumming up support for their programs, these institutions frequently offered a postmillennial rationale. Thus William Cogswell of the American Education Society in *The Harbinger of the Millennium* (1833) painted a picture of a glorious millennial future: "Soon," he promised, "the whole earth will chant the praises of the Redeemer, and the song of salvation will echo from shore to shore." Lest anyone believe, however, that such progress would be automatic, Cogswell quickly added that human cooperation with God's purposes was necessary; commitment had to be redoubled and purse strings needed to be loosed. In order for the millennium to come, "there must be more fervent prayer, more abundant labors, more enlarged charities. In this conquest of the world to Christ, the church must become a well-disciplined army, and every member of it must know her place and duty." "All this," Cogswell insisted, "is to be accomplished . . . not by miracles, but by the blessing of God accompanying the use of suitable means" (1833, 299–300). In the hands of people like Cogswell, postmillennialism served as an instrument of religious mobilization for the renovation of the world.

Postmillennialism also provided a means whereby Protestants accommodated the apocalyptic hope to Enlightenment ideals of rational order and benevolence. Although many Protestants attacked what they perceived as the "infidelity" of the more radical forms of the Enlightenment, they nevertheless absorbed many of the movement's central emphases, especially as mediated by the so-called Scottish Common Sense philosophy. Theologians wrote their works in a new key, stressing the reasonableness of Christian orthodoxy. In particular, they felt constrained to demonstrate that God ruled benevolently so as to promote the greatest happiness of the universe and to show that God exercised sway over humanity through persuasion rather than fiat. Postmillennialism, as commonly interpreted in the nineteenth century, served as a prime example of these commitments. By denying the premillennial notion that time might end at any moment thus foreclosing the possibility of future conversions, postmillennialism guaranteed that history would culminate in a lengthy era when all (or nearly all) men and women would be regenerate Christians. Then at the last judgment the final tally of all who had ever lived would disclose that the redeemed far outnumbered the damned. (As early as 1758, Jonathan Edwards's disciple Joseph Bellamy had calculated that the final ratio of the saved to the lost might well be more than 17,000 to 1!) For many Protestants, such computations were far more than idle speculations. They were a way of demonstrating that God indeed governed the universe with a view toward promoting its greatest happiness. In 1843, Charles Finney drew out the implications explicitly. If the world, he asked, "should now be swept out of the universe [by a premillennial second coming], could we suppose that it was created with a benevolent design?" Since "a great majority of those who have inhabited the earth, have gone to hell," a premature end to the world would call into question the rationality and benevolence of its Creator *(Oberlin Evangelist* [December 6, 1843]: 195). Moreover, if the millennium were to be introduced by a naked display of supernatural power (once again the premillennial foil appeared), this fact would suggest that God ruled *not* by moral means but rather by force. It would imply that God had to launch a celestial army of invasion to coerce a world he could not win by persuasion.

This rational, progressivist vision also made room for "secular" improvements to serve as instruments of the kingdom. As early as 1793, Samuel Hopkins in his *Treatise on the Millennium* was arguing that the golden era would be marked by improved material and technological conditions. He envisioned labor-saving devices reducing work to two or three hours a day, printing innovations rendering books cheaper, and a communications revolution enabling "correspondence . . . with much less expense of time and labour, perhaps a hundred times less, than that with which men now correspond" (Hopkins 1793, 77). Although Hopkins did not make these improvements instruments for the advance of the kingdom, later postmillennialists amid the nineteenth century's scientific advances and market revolution took that step. Increasingly, millennialists enumerated more sophisticated technology, greater prosperity, and the flourishing of the arts and sciences as signs of the millennium. For example, a writer in a Methodist women's magazine in 1859 declared of the invention of the telegraph: "This noble invention is to be the means of extending civilization, republicanism and Christianity over the earth. . . . Then shall come to pass the millennium" *(Ladies' Repository* [February 1850]: 61–62). Five years later when Presbyterian minister Nathan L. Rice commented on *The Signs of the Times*, he saw evidence of the impending millennium in the "rapidity of travel, the consequent increase of intercourse between the different nations, and the amazing facility of communicating intelligence." In this "providential arrangement" lay the means of history's consummation. "From the more enlightened, free and prosperous [nations], light will be diffused through the darker masses, and liberal principles will triumph, in spite of the efforts of tyranny[,] and every important change will become universal in its consequences" (1855, 17, 18–19).

Protestant experience by mid-century lent considerable plausibility to that heady dream. Improvements in printing had permitted the inundation of the nation with religious tracts and newspapers; the steamboat and the merchant opened the doors of foreign lands to the missionary; and affluence made possible the host of Christian colleges from which evangelical influences emanated. Rightly understood, secular improvements had, in Presbyterian Albert Barnes's (1798–1870) words published the year after his death, "an essential connection with Christianity. They become incorporated with it. They carry Christianity with themselves wherever they go" (1871, 130–31).

Progressivist millennialism also glided easily into assertions of American exceptionalism and special mission. It is not surprising that the sacred and the profane thus overlapped, for millennialism in whatever form, envisioning a time when "the kingdoms of this world are become the kingdoms of our Lord" (Rev. 11:15), tends to blur these distinctions. Moreover, so many of the symbols of the Apocalypse describe political and social upheavals that even relatively apolitical millennialists have usually been compelled to relate the rise and fall of nations to the history of redemption. But nineteenth-century postmillennialists had even stronger reasons to associate their country with the coming millennial glory. Having converted technological and material progress into handmaids of evangelical advance and having conflated the liberty of the Gospel with political liberty and republicanism, they readily identified their nation as the purest exemplar of these trends, and thus styled America, in Ernest Tuveson's phrase, a "Redeemer Nation." Occasionally some postmillennialists argued that the Bible explicitly foretold the United States' millennial role. For example, the Reverend Joseph Berg (1812–1871), a German and later Dutch Reformed pastor, contended that the United States fulfilled the prophecy in Daniel 2 of a fifth and final (or millennial) kingdom. More often, however, postmillennialists eschewed an exegesis of scriptural proof texts in favor of an exegesis of contemporary events: the contours of history suggested that America had been providentially positioned to fulfill a great millennial destiny.

This use of apocalyptic themes was credible in large measure because of the peculiar historical position of Protestantism in the late eighteenth and early nineteenth centuries when the American republic was born and reached its brassy adolescence. The great modernizing forces—the Enlightenment, independence from the British Crown, democratization, and the market revolution—did not arrive in America as strident opponents of traditional religion. By contrast to their impact in much (though not all) of Europe, these changes possessed no sharp anti-ecclesiastical or heterodox edge, forcing persons to choose between the new order and faith. In fact much of the initial thrust toward a modern America came from the Protestant churches, which prospered and enjoyed considerable cultural eminence. Under these circumstances, it was plausible to invest secular changes with positive religious meaning and to use traditional eschatological symbols to depict a future in which sacred and profane forces would advance in harmony, a future over which the saints would enjoy mastery. Certainly that was the vision inspiring a Presbyterian minister who spoke to a foreign missions society in New York City in 1860. "For eighteen centuries," said the Reverend Walter Clarke in *The National Preacher* in February 1861,

> the saints have been gradually getting possession of the world, of its intelligence, of its arts, of its property, of its positions of power and influence. . . . Project this Church into the future now! Let the saints of God go on for the centuries to come, acquiring and accumulating as they have done in times gone by; and is not here an argument to attest what the prophet [Daniel] foresaw? That the kingdom and dominion, and the greatness of the kingdom under the whole heaven, shall be given at length to the people of the saints of the Most High God? (pp. 56–57)

Yet there was another side to the postmillennial vision other than serene, unabated progress. To be sure, its adherents often spoke, in the words of Methodist bishop Leonidas Hamline (1797–1865), of the coming kingdom as "a gradual, not an instantaneous work. It will be, not like the springing up of worlds from chaos, but like the stealing dawn or the cautious tread of Spring, its march will be clandestine, and its gentle, noiseless conquests will be almost unobserved among the nations." (1869, 337.) Although postmillennialists often spoke in that fashion, they also adopted another vocabulary, one characterized in Mark Hanley's words by the "withering fire of salvation messages [and] . . . final judgment scenarios" (1994, 126). Even for postmillennialists the future was latent with a sense of the final end, of transcendent judgment and calamity.

How was it that a sense of an impending end and of cataclysmic upheaval remained lively among those who had postponed the last day for at least a thousand years and who often spoke of the advance of the millennium by "gentle, noiseless conquests . . . almost unobserved among the nations"? The answer involves the complex interaction of Protestant beliefs about the nature of biblical predictions, the notion of multiple fulfillments of apocalyptic prophecy throughout history, and the sense of the religious life of each person as a recapitulation in miniature of the Apocalypse.

Like other Christian visions of the last things, postmillennialism claimed its authority from the Bible. To be sure, not everyone invoking eschatological images or themes offered a thorough exegesis of scripture. Throughout the nineteenth century, hundreds, if not thousands, of Protestants often limned pictures of millennial glory or of apocalyptic judgment without stopping to provide systematic scriptural warrant. Yet even when its texts were not carefully plumbed, the Bible loomed in the background. Allusions to biblical prophecy carried weight because men and women assumed that biblical predictions would in fact come to pass. Lines from the *Biblical Repertory and Princeton Review* in January 1861 summarized the prevailing view: "The predictions uttered by the prophets were real disclosures of future events, and must therefore of necessity always be accomplished" (p. 84). There were, to be sure, divergent interpretations about how many vials had been poured out, whether the Man of Sin was papal Rome or a sinister figure yet to be revealed, and when the travail of the witnesses would end. Likewise, some voices urged caution, reminding others how enigmatic biblical predictions were and how frequently persons had made fools of themselves trying to extrapolate a time-specific chronology from Revelation. That exegetical wrangling, however, testified to a consensus taken for granted by the disputants: The Bible did contain a unified and accurate set of predictions. Among these were prophecies of a terrible day of wrath, a literal second coming, and a dramatic overturning of the present age. Since these were motifs deeply embedded in the Scriptures and since postmillennialists believed the Bible to be God's authoritative word, they could not dismiss such themes. Although postmillennialism delayed the supernatural destruction of this age until after the millennium—that is, until after the gospel and secular progress had run their appointed courses without unseemly intrusion—they believed that the end, though postponed, had to come, for the Bible had foretold it. Like marine navigators, postmillennialists could tack across apocalypticism, but they could not sail directly against it.

Moreover, the terrors of the Apocalypse were by no means held in complete abeyance until the end of time. Because the majority of postmillennialists viewed Revelation as an encoded history of the church from the incarnation (or sometimes earlier) to the end of the world, the sharply dualistic struggle of good against evil, the pouring of the vials of wrath, the earthquakes, wars, and famines were not merely reserved to the end. They constituted the fabric of all history. Christ might not return in person for many centuries, but in the interim the rise and collapse of kingdoms would portend that final event. And even if one denied that the Apocalypse contained a detailed chronology, the present relevance of apocalyptic categories was not thereby contradicted. The Revelation, said biblical scholar Moses Stuart (1780–1852), "is a τύπος [type] of all that is to happen in respect to the church. I regard the whole book as particular illustrations of a general principle"—the principle that God will overthrow his foes and establish his perfect kingdom (*Commentary on the Apocalypse*, 1:478). These prophecies, then, had perennial relevance, for they not only embraced specific occurrences but also provided models of the way in which God would always act and posited a view of history as a succession of fulfillments, each prefiguring some aspect of the last things. In that sense, every era was contemporaneous with the end; and in the words of a Civil War editor, prophecy is "fulfilled anew from age to age . . . in all these great events that baffle human foresight" (*Independent* [December 19, 1861]: 4).

Apocalypticism also remained powerful because it resonated with themes at the heart of evangelical piety. Evangelical Protestantism summoned each person to move from sin to holiness, a passage requiring the acknowledgment of one's lost condition before one could enter a state of blessedness. The central dynamic was that abasement preceded exaltation in the spiritual life. These struggles surrounding conversion, along with the accompanying dreams of the heaven or hell into which death would shortly usher each person, constituted a miniature apocalypse paralleling the historical scenario of the book of Revelation. Just as the kingdom of God arrived only through overturning and judgment, so, too, believers achieved assurance of salvation only after a season of terror, during which they knew themselves to deserve hell. Indeed, the two processes were one, for the history of redemption was the sum of all the individual stories of men and women fleeing the wrath to come. Or as one advocate of postmillennialism declared in 1837, the approach of the golden age would cause increasing numbers of people to engage in introspection until "every one will feel himself to be lost, and as standing on the brink of destruction, and as not having a moment to lose without fleeing to the Saviour" (Adam 1837, 161).

The quest for salvation provided an imaginative participation in the last things. The agonies of the unregenerate carried them forward to the hour of death, when they would be hurled into the flames of hell; and that terrifying moment in turn prefigured the day when all people would stand before God's judgment seat. In a word, the struggle surrounding each believer's conversion was for the believer a premonition of the final battle between Christ and Antichrist. Through conversion and the subsequent struggle for holiness it was as if time were collapsed and the saint projected forward to the judgment. As one Baptist minister argued in 1840, "in three years, *eighty millions* of the inhabitants of this earth will have been summoned to give up their account; and they will know their eternal destiny as surely as if the Judge were to come in the clouds, seated on his great white throne. Beloved reader, whose eye now rests upon this page, THOU MAYST BE ONE OF THEM! Art thou prepared?" From that perspective, it mattered not "whether the Judgment shall set tomorrow, or thousands of years to come" (John Dowling, *An Exposition of the Prophecies, Supposed by William Miller to Predict the Second Coming of Christ*, 162–63, 165). For each person the struggle determining the judgment was today.

Postmillennialism, then, struck a balance between a progressive view of history and the apocalyptic outlook of the book of Revelation. By delaying the second coming and last judgment to the far side of the millennium, the eschatology assured that God would not ring down the curtain of history prematurely or coerce an earthly kingdom into existence via displays of supernatural might. By moral government or persuasion, God would establish the millennial age, the saints themselves would cooperate, and all of the accouterments of progress—for example, technological improvements and republicanism—would likewise work toward that goal. Yet the apocalyptic outlook remained. Postmillennialists generally endorsed the popular evangelical piety whose stress upon conversion and unpredictable death as the moment of the fearful divide between heaven and hell lent vivid existential immediacy to the notion of an imminent apocalyptic judgment. Moreover, believing that the cataclysms of the book of Revelation described upheavals that the church would face throughout history, not merely at the end of time, postmillennialists expected tumults as well as gradual progress as the kingdom advanced. Writing years later of his antebellum boyhood, the liberal theologian William Newton Clarke (1841–1912) gave pointed expression to the double-sided eschatology he had been taught. "The theory [postmillennialism]," he said, "put the end indefinitely far away, and yet I listened trembling for the trump of God in every thunder-storm" (1909b, 102).

Given Clarke's boyhood confusions, one must ask about the extent of postmillennialism within American Protestantism. Among leading clerical figures, it clearly became the dominant view in the antebellum period—"the commonly received opinion," as a theological quarterly called it in 1859 (*American Theological Review* [November 1859]: 655). There were, of course, significant exceptions. The Baptist preacher William Miller (1782–1849) from Low Hampton, New York, gathered a substantial following in the early 1840s and piqued the curiosity of perhaps millions when he predicted that Jesus would return around 1843. After 22 October 1844, a date in which Millerites invested considerable hope, came and went without the visible appearance of Christ, outsiders ridiculed the movement; and Millerism became a kind of negative reference point, discrediting premillennialism in the eyes of many. The challenge of that eschatology did not end, however, once the Millerite excitement abated. Within the major denominations, vocal advocates kept premillennialism before the public. While eschewing the setting of specific dates, these people expected an early end to the present world order and an imminent second coming. Yet they won relatively few prominent Protestants to their cause prior to the Civil War.

When one asks how widespread pre- or postmillennialism was among the rank and file in the pews, a definitive answer is impossible to give; but there are tantalizing hints. Surveying numerous diaries and letters of obscure Americans in the antebellum period, historian Lewis Saum has found little evidence of an explicit postmillennialism. "When millennial intimations surfaced in the writings of the common folk," Saum writes, "they often did so as little more than predictions of cataclysmic retribution"—in other words there was little of the genial hope of gradual progress usually associated with postmillennialism (1980, 74). Similarly, the historian William J. Gilmore, after an extensive canvass of personal libraries recorded in the estates of persons in Vermont during the early nineteenth century, has noted that premillennial works tended to outnumber postmillennial ones (1989, 316, 323, 338). Moreover, postmillennialism lacked the unambiguous clarity and cosmic drama of the premillennial hope. It is difficult to imagine a postmillennialist movement—at least one fully embodying that eschatology's ambivalent stance between progress and apocalypse—exciting the fervor or even curiosity that the Millerites aroused when they predicted that Christ would return around 1843. Perhaps historian Ruth Bloch is correct when she writes: "On the level of popular culture, the image of

Christ appearing in the flesh had probably always dominated over the idea of a purely spiritual coming, both because of its greater dramatic power and because of its greater faithfulness to the literal biblical word" (1985, 33).

To make these observations is not to suggest that the so-called average person was either a confirmed post- or premillennialist. Most persons probably had not sorted out their views clearly but lived with a mental hodgepodge of images of the last things which they had not ordered into a distinct or coherent theory. They might alternately hope for the gradual conquest of the world to Christ and the sudden return of the Lord. Many were no doubt like Clarke, who awaited an "end indefinitely far away and yet . . . listened trembling for the trump of God in every thunder-storm." The genius of postmillennialism, however inconsistent we might judge it to have been, was that it permitted appeals in both the progressive and apocalyptic modes. In fact, much of the cultural power of postmillennialism came from its evocation of cataclysmic images of the End whose energy was then harnessed in service to the incremental construction of an evangelical empire.

Although postmillennialists did not promote a single blueprint for that empire, they did in general advance an agenda of reform. The various societies of the evangelical united front, which so often appealed to a postmillennial rationale to drum up support, sought to create a more thoroughly Christian America and world. Initially the reformism of these groups hewed to moderate, gradualist, and noncontroversial programs. The Colonization Society, founded in 1817, is a case in point. The organization, whose goal was to colonize freed slaves in Africa, placed its faith in voluntary emancipation of slaves and compensation for slaveholders. Avoiding all attacks on the owners of slaves and asking only for gradual manumission, the colonization movement tapped into the optimistic view that slavery was a dying institution, but remained pessimistic that blacks could be integrated into American society. Its solution to the problem of slavery—seeking the migration of African Americans out of the country—was thoroughly compatible with a racist desire to make America lily-white. Yet the movement also drew upon an idealistic postmillennial hope, for black emigrants from bondage would spread to Africa the Christianity, republicanism, and material progress that they had learned in America and thereby hasten the latter day.

By the 1830s, a more militant reformism appeared in some Protestant quarters. As various forms of perfectionist doctrine merged with the idea of God's coming kingdom, the postmillennial hope became the charter for more immediate, thoroughgoing, and uncompromising efforts to alter the character of American society. Again the issue of slavery is illustrative. The American Anti-Slavery society, formed in 1833, called for the immediate abolition of slavery, denounced slaveholding as a sin that all people should renounce at once, and demanded the granting of full civil liberties to the freed slaves. Although one group of abolitionists, led by William Lloyd Garrison (1805–1879), moved increasingly away from orthodox Christianity, much of the impetus among rank and file abolitionists came from people like Theodore Dwight Weld (1803–1895), a Finneyite who merged millennial hope with perfectionism to demand an all-out attack on the slave system. The millennial perfectionism of abolitionism also found parallels in other reform movements. Temperance advocates, for example, began moving in the 1830s from a platform permitting the moderate use of alcohol to one demanding total abstinence. Similarly, the millennial and perfectionist impulse that caused some to question the legitimacy of slavery prompted a broader re-examination of other social arrangements in which illicit human coercion preempted the moral government of God. Thus, some abolitionists moved toward advocacy of equal rights for women and toward a rejection of participation in government and in war.

One must not, however, overemphasize the extent to which perfectionist millennialism triumphed in the 1830s. Aside from a growing tendency to equate the temperance reform with total abstinence from alcohol, the more radical forms of reform remained anathema to most mainstream Protestants. The vast majority scoffed at pacifism, nonresistance, and women's rights. Abolitionists, assailed by angry mobs in many communities, remained a hated minority down to the Civil War, even among many who styled themselves antislavery. Leonard Bacon (1802–1881), a prominent Congregationalist minister in New Haven and well-known proponent of colonization, continued to argue the gradualist case throughout the 1830s and 1840s. Condemning abolitionists for impeding true reform by making slaveholders more intransigent, he insisted that the true path to reform was "to make *men* better—individual men—by inspiring them with new ideas and new principles of action." Christianity, he explained, "leaves these new ideals to work out their own effects upon the structures of society." Bacon was content to allow a "benignant providence" to override slavery, and soon it would be apparent that the cause of reform and the advance of the millennium have "been imperceptibly approaching the hour of final triumph" (*Slavery Discussed in Occasional Essays*, 35, 36, 98, 177, 178). With such logic, the great majority of mainstream Protestants continued to the Civil War to think of themselves as simultaneously antislavery and anti-abolitionist.

In a few instances, postmillennial reformism was not even mildly antislavery. Some southern Protestants advocated what Jack P. Maddex has called "proslavery millennialism." Presbyterian ministers such as James H. Thornwell (1812–1862), Robert Dabney (1820–1898), John Girardeau (1825–1898), and John Adger (1810–1899) shared the hope of northern postmillennialists that Christian principles would gradually triumph, yielding a golden age; but unlike their counterparts, they did not anticipate that progress would gradually bring emancipation. As part of God's providential plan for solving the problem of labor management and of ordering the relations between superior and inferior races, slavery might well endure into the millennial age. These apologists acknowledged that features of the system—for example, laws forbidding the education of slaves or recognition of their marriages—would have to be abolished in due course. Then, purged of its abuses, slavery could stand to the end of time as a boon to masters and bondpeople alike.

Although they invoked postmillennialism on behalf of progressive social change, Protestants after the 1830s were increasingly divided over the content and strategy of reform. Their goal of establishing the millennium via persuasion had become increasingly problematic. Once secession occurred and Confederate forces fired on Fort Sumter in April 1861, the hope appeared to have been refuted altogether. After decades of evangelical enterprise, Americans had not been persuaded to move toward an orderly millennium. They marched instead into the four bloodiest years of American history. Yet postmillennial dreams, filled with images of apocalyptic judgment as well as pictures of peaceful progress, adapted remarkably well to the new context.

In the North, many Protestant leaders argued that the struggle to preserve the Union was a holy war fraught with millennial significance. A handful of expositors tried to demonstrate that the crisis of the Union and the North's ultimate victory were specifically foretold in biblical prophecy. Although most mainstream Protestants rejected such exegesis, they affirmed the basic interpretation of the war contained in these idiosyncratic pieces. They asserted that the war was purging the nation of its sin, providing a moral rebirth through a baptism of blood, and preparing the way for America to resume a grand millennial mission. William B. Sprague (1795–1876), the usually cautious Old School Presbyterian editor of *Annals of the American Pulpit*, predicted that the war would bring "a flood of millenial [*sic*] glory" and introduce "the Great Thanksgiving Day of the World" (1861, 58). In the last year of the war, *Christ in the Army*, a collection of addresses and sermons produced for distribution to northern troops was equally expansive: "The Lord is mustering the nations to the last great struggle between freedom and slavery, truth and error. . . . We are entering, fellow-citizens, upon a period foretold by prophets of old—looked for and longed for by lovers of their country in past generations—which kings and prophets waited to see, and have not seen—a period of the overthrow of despotism, and the downfall of Anti-Christ" (pp. 137–40.)

No less than their northern counterparts, southern clergy viewed the Confederate cause as sacred. Several noted ministers, such as Presbyterians James H. Thornwell and Benjamin Morgan Palmer (1818–1902), played a prominent role in the drive for secession. When the conflict began, the clergy justified it as a classic instance of a just war—and more. Upon the citizens of the new nation rested a special mission. Theirs was the task of setting before the world ideals of ordered liberty, states' rights, and biblical values that Yankees had corrupted by radical democracy, centralized federal tyranny, and "infidel" (that is, abolitionist) readings of the Bible. The South's mission was to save the world from the false ideas of democracy; and some preachers popular with the troops asserted that God might use the Confederacy to inaugurate the kingdom of God on earth. Although the ideal of millennial mission so prevalent in the North appears to have been generally more muted below the Mason-Dixon line, it was by no means absent.

For the North at least, the successful outcome of the conflict appeared to vindicate dreams of eschatological triumph. Three years after the close of the Civil War, Methodist Jesse Peck (1811–1883) assembled this argument within the pages of *The History of the Great Republic*. Cribbing his facts largely from George Bancroft (1800–1891) and other nineteenth-century historians, Peck constructed (or so he fancied) an epic postmillennial drama with the United States as the central actor in the history of the world. Much of the plot was drawn from standard antebellum Fourth of July orations and sermons: God had hidden the New World from European settlement until the Protestant Reformation prepared a pure Christianity for transplanting in America. There, aided by abundant natural resources, a civilization dedicated to the gospel and political liberty was to usher in a new epoch for humanity. Heretofore, the taint of slavery and despotism impeded that mission; but now, with the defeat of the Confederacy, the nation was fully ready to assume its destiny. "How potentially," he said in a vision of national millennial glory, "will it command wars to cease, and all the forces of Christian civilization to march on for the conquest of the world!" (1871, 707, 708, 709). The postmillennial hope was alive and well as mainstream Protestants faced the Gilded Age.

Yet that hope was soon altered in subtle but profound ways. In the decades after Appomattox, postmillennialism's tenuous balance between progress and apocalypse came undone. The progressive elements of the older postmillennial vision displaced its apocalyptic features. What remained was the notion of an immanent, this-worldly kingdom of God from which the sense of a definitive end had been removed. The change had roots partly in the new higher criticism, which undermined belief that the Apocalypse provided accurate predictions of the future. The transformation also reflected the significant reconfiguration of piety in which mainstream Protestants were engaged. They ceased depicting hell in lurid detail, participated in the growing denial of death, displaced conversion from the center of the spiritual life in favor of nurture and development, stressed the natural over the supernatural, and generally emphasized this life rather than the life to come. All of these changes weakened patterns of thought and practice that had kept nineteenth-century postmillennialists at least partially grounded in the world of the Apocalypse.

As a system of biblical interpretation, postmillennialism was already vulnerable, for it had always been something of a Janus—one face looking toward the literal accomplishment of apocalyptic hopes, the other turned away, slightly embarrassed by such crudities. It wanted to treat the hope of the Apocalypse partly as figurative truth and partly as literal. As Methodist Bishop Stephen M. Merrill (1825–1905) summarized in an 1879 book, a proper interpretation of the Apocalypse had simultaneously to avoid two extremes: the premillenarian notion that Jesus might return at any moment "to wield an earthly scepter over the nations" and a "liberal-ist" view that denied altogether a literal second advent and last judgment (1879, 13, 282). Thus against the premillenarians, for example, postmillennialists fought verse by verse, insisting that prophecy had spiritual, not carnal, fulfillment. Prophecies of a political kingdom for the Jews were types of Christianity's religious influence; the promise of a special resurrection of the mar-tyrs was a metaphor for the resurgence of their values; and the picture of Christ reigning in the millennium was only an emblem of his presence in the hearts of all men and women. Yet when postmillennialists came to the passages speaking of a second coming in which Christ would raise the dead and subject them to judgment, figurative and spiritual interpretation ceased. These prophecies were deemed literal descriptions of future events, albeit events that would occur after the thousand years. Given the basic principle of interpretation postmillen-nialists had enunciated, it was not clear why such predictions should be exempt from a spiritual reading. If descriptions of an earthly millennium required a spiritual interpretation, why should not the same hermeneutic dissolve the literal facticity of a postmillennial second coming and end of the world?

After 1880, the acceptance of modern biblical criticism in major seminaries, universities, and pulpits made many Protestants even more uncomfortable with the notion that the Bible contained *any* literal predictions. This new scholarship was not so much a set of agreed conclu-sions—critics debated the "assured results" of their craft—as it was a new and sometimes dis-turbing angle from which to view the scriptures. Basic to that perspective was a commitment to analyze the Bible in the same fashion as other documents. In purporting to discover the mean-ing of scripture by placing it in temporal context through the tools of philology, comparative religion, literary analysis, or historical research, the new learning generally diminished the role of the supernatural as an explanatory device. It also tacitly confessed that all things were histori-cally conditioned. Thus, the Bible often ceased to resemble a record of the unchanging faith once delivered to the saints and became instead a record of an ancient Near Eastern people's developing views of religion.

The apocalyptic scriptures in particular were subjected to a rigorous scrutiny. During the nineteenth and into the twentieth century, European scholars such as Friedrich Lücke (1791–1855), Adolf Hilgenfeld (1823–1907), Wilhelm Bousset (1865–1920), Johannes Weiss (1863–1914), and preeminently R. H. Charles (1855–1931) shattered older understandings of apocalypticism. As a result of this research, the books of Daniel and Revelation, long the main-stays of millennial speculation, lost their uniqueness as critics analyzed them as mere instances of a larger genre of literature, much of it noncanonical. Moreover, scholars contrasted the apocalyptic mentality with that of Hebrew prophecy. They portrayed the latter as hopeful of redemption within history and characterized the former as despairing of the current age, apocalypticists entertaining the faulty expectation that the present order would shortly end in a supernatural upheaval. This contrast undercut traditional millennial speculation by suggesting that the Bible contained multiple views that could not be assembled into a single eschatology. In addition, critics usually set prophecy against apocalypticism in order to derogate the latter. While prophecy allegedly represented the mainstream of biblical thought, the apocalyptic dream was an aberration, born perhaps of non-Jewish sources and representing the slightly unbalanced hopes of desperate men and women. The chief novelty of this critique was its overtness. Christians from Augustine to nineteenth-century postmillennialists had often found themselves uneasy with apocalypticism and had used various interpretive devices to mute it; but the canonical status of Daniel and Revelation had prevented direct onslaughts against that eschatology. Now, in light of newer scholarship and looser views of biblical inspiration, the attack was more direct and self-conscious.

Apocalypticism was, in short, becoming an embarrassment to many Protestants. That view, said British exegete Arthur Peake (1865–1929) in a widely read commentary in 1919, seems "remote and bizarre, its imagery pretentious or grotesque" (1919, 368). According to one author, Revelation was a "queer bird" hatched from "visions of the impossible"—visions that the Christian community had fortunately dropped for "saner and more spiritual conceptions" (*Bibliotheca Sacra* [January 1907]: 54, 55, 59). The *Biblical World* asserted that modern scholarship had brought about the "passing of apocalypticism." The editor wrote: "A study of its origins inevitably brings its validity under suspicion for us." A product of a "highly imaginative Jewish thought," apocalypticism seduced the early Christian community for a time but was never consistent with the basic thrust of the church's message (*Biblical World* [September 1910]: 147–51).

In place of the apocalyptic vision was a new understanding of the kingdom of God as a present ethical reality advancing according to organic laws of growth and requiring no dramatic intrusions. Little of apocalypticism remained. At best, books such as Daniel and Revelation provided exotic images of a morally satisfying outcome to history, but no intelligent person could any longer expect to draw from them an actual picture of the future. In fact, one could know very little about ultimate destiny, said William Newton Clarke, in the 1909 edition of his influential *Outline of Christian Theology*.

> But his [Christ's] coming is not an event, it is a process that includes innumerable events, a perpetual advance of Christ in the activity of his kingdom. It has continued until now, and is still moving on. . . . No visible return of Christ to the earth is to be expected, but rather the long and steady advance of his spiritual kingdom. . . . We find ourselves on the stream, but see neither the fount nor the ocean, nor can we tell how far away either is, except that both seem far remote. After all, what need have we of seeing either? (1909, 444, 446)

With clear prophetic landmarks knocked down, there was no longer a definite eschatological goal toward which history moved. Humanity now floated on a stream in ignorance of both its origins and destination. What remained of postmillennialism was the genial hope that the tide was benign.

Changed views of individual eschatological destiny likewise diminished ideas associated with an apocalyptic outlook. An important part of evangelical piety had been the fearsome shadow cast by hell, but that specter gradually receded during the nineteenth century. Postmillennialism, with its assertion that vast numbers of conversions in the millennial era would reduce the final number of the damned to a tiny percentage of the human race, had already taken an important first step toward making hell appear to be far less significant in the ultimate scheme of things. As William G. T. Shedd (1820–1894), professor of theology at Union Seminary in New York and a defender of the doctrine of hell, argued in 1887, "Compared with heaven, hell is narrow and limited. Sin is a speck upon the infinite azure of eternity; a spot on the sun. Hell is only the corner of the universe" (1887, 159). By the time Shedd penned these lines, some mainstream Protestants began openly expressing their discomfort with traditional notions of damnation. In the 1880s, the faculty at Andover Theological Seminary advanced a theory of future probation—the notion that those who had never had a fair hearing of the gospel in this life would receive another chance in the next. Some prominent figures—most notably Lyman Abbott (1835–1922), Henry Ward Beecher's successor in the pulpit of Plymouth Congregational Church in Brooklyn—argued that the finally impenitent, rather than suffering for countless ages, would simply pass out of existence at death. Moreover, many in the rising liberal movement argued as did influential Boston Congregationalist George A. Gordon (1853–1929) in 1897 that it was utterly nonsensical to suppose that God loves sinners now but will, immediately after their decease, become an implacable foe. Since God's gracious love is the fundamental law of the universe, that love operates in all places and times. To claim that it ceases operation at death "is the same thing logically as to say that one can cut out a circle in space, within which the law of gravitation operates, and where the order and beauty that always follow may be beheld; but beyond which there is no gravitation, no law of space, and where nothing exists except chaos and utter contradiction" (1897, 78). But more significant than overt questioning of traditional notions of hell was frequent silence about the subject. Writing of the state of theology at the dawn of the twentieth century, one Episcopal minister asked: "What has become of hell?" "There has been," he noted, "a remarkable change of late years in religious teaching with reference to future punishment. Whereas formerly in theological papers, in sermons and books of instruction, much was said about hell, now it is but rarely mentioned. . . . You do not hear of it in the pulpit, or see reference to it in the religious press, or in the modern theological book, nor is it often brought up in religious conversation. It is tabooed by the pulpit generally" (Morgan et al. 1901, 159–60).

At the same time time hell assumed a less terrifying appearance, the image of heaven also changed. For many, heaven was becoming continuous with the present life; it was a place where the best of this world would be writ large and where the fulfillment of earthly dreams would be at least as important as the glory of God. What historian Geoffrey Rowell has written of Victorian Britain describes late-nineteenth-century America equally well: Many Protestants came to look forward to "an immortality of self-realization, rather than an immortality of salvation" (1974, 15). This eschatological revision, born among earlier visionaries and literary figures such as John Milton (1608–1674), Emanuel Swedenborg (1688–1722), William Blake (1757–1827), and Jean-Jacques Rousseau (1712–1778), had begun to work its way into the thought of mainstream Protestant leaders.

Consolatory literature carried this trend to its logical extreme. William Branks's *Heaven Our Home* (1864), published on both sides of the Atlantic in several editions, and Adeline Bayard's *Views of Heaven*, written for the American Sunday School Union in 1877, were notable examples of a genre that depicted heaven as a scene of family reunions and domestic bliss. In her wildly popular novels *The Gates Ajar* (1867) and *Beyond the Gates* (1885), Elizabeth Stuart Phelps (1844–1911), a daughter and granddaughter of Andover Seminary faculty, portrayed heaven as a place so natural, so like this world, that death was as uneventful as walking from one room to another. In the next life, people lived in pleasant middle-class homes. They continued the occupations begun on earth and also busied themselves with a round of museums, universities, and concerts. Never did God, in Phelps's portrayal, intrude in such a way as to mar the earthlike quality of heaven; and Jesus moved about unobtrusively, sometimes unrecognized by the inhabitants. Perhaps the character of her heaven is best explained by one of her characters who observed: "Here we unfold like a leaf, a flower. He [God] expects nothing of us but to be natural" (1885, 47).

Leading clergy echoed these themes, albeit with less speculation about the precise contours of the heavenly state. Death was but an incident in each person's eternal progression, and heaven was the place of that everlasting growth. Presbyterian theologian William Adams Brown (1865–1943) best summarized the new thought about heaven.

> Too often in the past the contrast between the present and the future has been unduly exaggerated. The life after death has been isolated from all relation to the present, and defined purely by contrast. The result is a certain hollowness and unreality which all the glowing imagery of the Apocalypse . . . has been powerless to warm into the semblance of a true life. How empty and shallow the heaven to which we have often been asked to look forward, a heaven of untroubled bliss, with nothing to achieve and nothing to anticipate, a heaven freed from suffering indeed, but free also from the struggle of which suffering is born, a heaven in which there is nothing to do but to enjoy, year after year, and aeon after aeon, through a monotonous eternity.

But heaven would not be monotonous. It was an eternal progressive purposeful activity already begun here. "Our hope for the life to come is not different from our hope for the life here. There is but one life here and hereafter, and the change we call death is but opening the door from one room to another in the Father's house" (1917, 18). As contemporary scholars Colleen McDannell and Bernhard Lang have argued in *Heaven: A History*, such changes constituted a "kinetic revolution in heaven"; that is, they recast heaven as a state of becoming rather than being, of doing rather than resting (1988, 277).

Funeral customs symbolized the transformed perception of death and what followed it. Beginning in the 1830s, the rural cemetery movement sought to make the necropolis a beautiful park to which the living would repair for edification and recreation. In its environs vanished the negative associations of the old graveyard—the place where, in Jonathan Edwards's vivid language, the "ghastly" corpse lay "putrifying and rotting and becoming exceeding loathsome" (1948, 43). Funerary art often depicted the dead in lifelike settings, and the topography of the rural cemetery evoked the sense of the sublime not of the morbid. After the Civil War, the lawn cemetery, characterized by inconspicuous markers and open spaces, continued the revolution in burial practice. While the rural cemetery had sentimentalized the home of the dead, the lawn cemetery went a step further and removed the most blatant reminders that the dead were present; but both institutions agreed in making the cemetery a pleasant site, devoid of negative associations. The increasing use of undertakers and funeral parlors served the same end. The distasteful business of preparing the deceased for burial—formerly a task of the family—could be remanded to the professionals; and the now more common practice of embalming guaranteed that the corpse would appear lifelike rather than "ghastly" when presented for burial. Cremation, though remaining the choice of only a tiny minority of the bereaved, did win greater popularity after the Civil War; and it, too, served to eliminate the reminders of mortality. By a swift sanitary stroke, the body was gone, spared the gruesomeness of decomposition. Yet whether sentimentalized or hidden from view, death was transformed by such rituals into little more than an incident along the path of unfolding life.

These changes converged in a new understanding of the religious life itself. With hell diminished to insignificance and heaven transformed into a mere enlargement of this life, with eternal life depicted as an arena for the ever-deepening realization of the self's longings and death reduced to a minor incident in this progression, it no longer made sense to portray the Christian life according to the old conversion-centered model as a stark choice between sin or salvation, life or death, eternal terror or joy. An earlier generation of Protestants had believed that the essence of Christian piety consisted in living, said a writer in the *American National Preacher* in 1850, "as if we were acting our own death-scene, which in reality we are doing." True religion had entailed acting "as if the flaming eye of our divine Judge were now turned full upon us, . . . as if the thunders of eternal retribution were already rolling over our heads" (p. 99). In large sectors of Protestantism such descriptions of Christian experience sounded increasingly quaint or anachronistic, for in the new vision of human destiny there were neither flaming eyes nor the thunders of eternal retribution. Humanity instead engaged in a life-affirming quest for never-ending self-improvement. Adopting and refining notions of Christian nurture first advanced by Horace Bushnell (1802–1876) in the 1840s, many Protestants argued that gradual and natural growth were the normal mode of engendering Christian piety and practice. The dramatic conversions favored by the older piety were explained in terms of natural processes in the life cycle. Research in the psychology of religion by G. Stanley Hall (1844–1924), Edwin D. Starbuck (1866–1947), James H. Leuba (1868–1946), and George A. Coe (1862–1951)—all indebted indirectly to Bushnell—related conversion to natural processes of human growth such as the onset of puberty. Many hoped that, as the laws of human development were better understood and applied by clergy and educators, the traumas of religion would recede in importance and in fact had already begun to do so. In their place was a more natural Christian growth, stressing sunnier themes and practical service rather than morbid introspection.

The preoccupation with natural growth, the denial of limits (especially death), the desire for open-ended movement, and the fear of stasis were rooted in major cultural and intellectual transformations. The triumph of a consumerist ethos offered interesting parallels with the new eschatology. In the late nineteenth century, America was becoming what contemporary scholar William Leach has called, in a book by the same name, the *Land of Desire*. The emerging corporate economy required that men and women consume more goods, and with that purpose sellers stimulated desire. Through magnificent displays of color, light, and glass showcasing their wares, merchants created a vision of an alluring fantasy world. (It was not inappropriate that L. Frank Baum [1856–1919], author of *The Wonderful Wizard of Oz* [1900] and that tale's glittering Emerald City, was an authority on department store displays.) Merchants and advertisers sold dreams of perfect contentment—visions of an Emerald City. Because they vended fantasies, their actual products could never fully satisfy the longings they had aroused. In fact, the logic of the market demanded that want remain partly unslaked, for if this year's goods indeed delivered paradise, no one would purchase next year's supply. The Emerald City gleaming in the distance always receded with the horizon, and the pleasures of consumption aroused the desire for more. Unquenchable desire, as Leach observes, "fostered anxiety and restlessness. . . . And because of its associations with the new and its attachment to fantasy, it tended to reinforce the American refusal to face death as a fact of life" (1993, 7). In many respects, new eschatological views stressing kinesis and eternal progression offered a theological analogue to the consumer culture.

Similarly, the triumph of the theory of biological evolution lent credibility to the new eschatology. Although Darwin's *On the Origin of Species* had been debated sporadically in America since shortly after its publication in 1859, it was not until the late 1870s that prominent clergy began espousing evolution in significant numbers. The liberal Protestant recension of the theory, emphasizing God's immanence within biological change and the progressive and teleological character of the entire process, gave a distinctly non-Darwinian cast to the transmutation hypothesis. The departure from Darwin, however, made biological evolution more serviceable to the liberal theological agenda. Evolution became, in one scholar's words, "paradigmatic of all divine activity" and "was equated with gradual, continuous, and progressive development" (Roberts 1988, 145, 156). "God has but one way of doing things," Lyman Abbott declared in 1897. That way "may be described in one word as the way of growth, or development, or evolution." From this fact, Abbott concluded "that there are not occasional interventions in the order of life which bear witness to the presence of God, but that life itself is a perpetual witness to His presence" (1897, 9–10). Change, in short, was the basic fact of the universe; it occurred according to natural, uniform principles of growth, and God was resident in the process.

Amid these intellectual and cultural transformations, many mainstream Protestants looked for a kingdom of God which, while in important respects continuous with the old postmillennial hope, diverged from it in important respects. The kingdom was decisively oriented to this world. As Congregationalist theologian Lewis French Stearns (1847–1892) argued in *Present Day Theology* (1893), the kingdom "consists in the doing of God's will on earth as it is done in heaven." Since it was to be achieved within history and was not limited to the church, Stearns cautioned against "too narrow a view of the kingdom." Advancement of the kingdom entailed more than adding converts to the church; it included finding a solution to the problems between labor and capital, ending war, creating better sanitation in cities, conserving the products of nature, and elevating the tone of politics. No less than the church, all other human institutions—the family, the state, "labor, commerce, the trades and professions, science, art, and literature"—were to fall under the sway of the kingdom, for that reign was to be "as wide as the earth itself" (1893, 110, 123, 124, 125). The secular fruits of the millennium, previously regarded as by-products of the kingdom, were increasingly sought as objects worthy of direct pursuit in their own right.

The new theology of the kingdom also exulted in the prospect of never-ending improvement. As Walter Rauschenbusch (1861–1918) argued in his *A Theology for the Social Gospel* (1917),

> An eschatology which is expressed in terms of historic development has no final consummation. Its consummations are always the basis for further development. The Kingdom of God is always coming. . . . If he [God] called humanity to a halt in a "kingdom of glory," he would have on his hands some millions of eager spirits whom he has himself trained to ceaseless aspi-

ration and achievement, and they would be dying of ennui. . . . [But] we are on the march toward the Kingdom of God, and getting our reward by every fractional realization of it which makes us hungry for more. A stationary humanity would be a dead humanity. The life of the race is in its growth. (1917, 227)

The images are significant: a kingdom always coming, "ceaseless aspiration and achievement," unlimited growth as the goal of humanity. Eternal motion had replaced the sense of a definitive apocalyptic end of time, and the kingdom of God had become virtually identical to one scholar's description in 1991 of "the modern conception of progress." What is distinct about that concept, Christopher Lasch avers, is "not the promise of a secular utopia that would bring history to a happy ending but the promise of steady improvement with no foreseeable ending at all" (1991, 47).

This eschatology found numerous embodiments in mainstream Protestantism. Advocates of the Social Gospel such as Washington Gladden (1836–1918), Walter Rauschenbusch, and Graham Taylor (1851–1938) sought to apply the moral imperatives of Christianity to the reconstruction of American society along more equitable lines. They grounded their endeavor in the conviction, as lay theologian and economist Richard T. Ely (1854–1943) put it in 1889, that "Christianity is primarily concerned with this world, and it is the mission of Christianity to bring to pass here a kingdom of righteousness and to rescue from the evil one and redeem all our social relations" (1889, 53). The ecumenical spirit that brought thirty-three denominations to form the Federal Council of Churches in 1908 drew upon a similar vision. Faced with a vast influx of non-Protestant immigrants and in light of major dislocations wrought by urbanization and industrialization, many Protestants feared that in their divided state they were not up to the challenges of the hour. Protestantism, Congregationalist Newman Smyth (1843–1925) charged, "has frayed out into so many separate strands. No single thread of it is strong enough to move the whole social mechanism; it is like so many ravellings; at most one strand may move a few wheels" (1908, 28–29). Yet "the whole social mechanism" *had* to be moved if the kingdom were to be built—hence the necessity of unity in order to reknit the ravelings and move more than "a few wheels." Federation, it was hoped, would supply that unity and yield greater Protestant influence in American society. Thus, the founders of the Federal Council envisioned their movement as a consolidated thrust that would enable the churches to fulfill the mandate that Frank Mason North (1850–1935) set before the Council at its first meeting. "Primarily we are engaged," he avowed, "in establishing his [God's] kingdom in these United States." Before adjourning, the Council pledged itself to "wiser and larger service for America and for the Kingdom of God"; and one of its leaders declared that the Council was the living embodiment of the churches' duty "to hasten the coming of the day when the true King of Men shall everywhere be crowned as Lord of all. This Council stands for the hope of organized work for speedy Christian advance toward world conquest" (Sanford 1908, 229, 323, 508). The foreign missions movement, reaching its high tide between 1880 and the 1920s, also gathered strength from this motivation. Despite the presence of alternate eschatological rationales, much of the zeal for missions in these decades drew upon the hope of shaping not only the United States but also the entire world into the kingdom of God.

In conducting crusades to subdue the world to Christ, mainstream Protestants adopted worldly instruments. In an age of mushrooming corporations and proliferating forms of scientific and professional specialization, these instruments included creation of new religious orga-

nizations—as well as the revamping of old ones—in accord with the principles of rational planning, businesslike management, and professional expertise. Like business, government, and
research universities, the churches increasingly bureaucratized and professionalized their internal life. Although this transformation was by no means the result of Protestant eschatology, the
idea of a coming kingdom in this world was used to legitimate it. Organizations were created and
reshuffled in the name of building the kingdom. For many, advancing God's reign became as
much a matter of structure, technical knowledge, and competence as it was of piety or devotion.

Many Social Gospelers, for example, wished to employ as handmaids to the kingdom the
social sciences then emerging as distinct disciplines within American universities. That affinity
was eminently logical because the professors who set the parameters of these sciences frequently came from strongly Protestant homes and brought to their subjects a moralistic vision.
With considerable justice, contemporary scholar Jean Quandt has argued that the work of such
thinkers represented "the secularization of postmillennialism," for social scientists frequently
assumed that their empirical studies could be used to build an ideal social order. Sharing that
assumption, Richard T. Ely asserted that building a better social order required more than good
intentions. "What is wanted," he declared, "is not dilettanteism [sic] with respect to those
duties which we owe our fellows, but hard study, pursued with devotion for years." Since not all
were capable of such study, the churches needed to frame their policies in light of what these
experts had to say (1889, 17). Similarly, Warren H. Wilson (1867–1937), a Presbyterian
denominational official who sought to craft a Social Gospel for rural churches, argued in 1915
that Christian activism could indeed hasten the time "when the world shall have all been
redeemed, . . . when the Kingdom of God shall have indeed come." But that kingdom would
advance only as Christians allied themselves with academic expertise. Churches had to serve as
the "channels by which the knowledge that the universities have in store can come to the use of
the people" (1915, 29).

With specialized knowledge also came the deepening professionalization and bureaucrati-
zation of ecclesiastical life. Those who wished, for example, to promote the Social Gospel
secured the creation of new agencies for social witness in the various denominations. The Presbyterian Church in the U.S.A. formed such a department in 1903, the Congregationalists and
Methodists in 1907, the American Baptists in 1908. As the foreign missionary movement
increased dramatically in size, it too contributed to the proliferation of agencies, their subdivision into departments, and to the self-conscious desire to pattern the work after successful
business corporations. A new kind of leader flourished in this environment. An earlier generation had thrilled to the adventures of missionaries like Adoniram Judson (1788–1850) and his
wife Ann Haseltine (1789–1826) as they braved the dangers of Burma. Although the romance of
missions did not die out entirely, the missionaries themselves were generally less prominent by
1900. The commanding presence was the missionary executive. Often a layman and more a
man of affairs than a theoretician, the administrator was a hero because he set himself to great
organizational tasks and accomplished them. Missionary leaders were themselves aware of the
change and spoke in new accents. "The Lord's work as well as man's," said one missionary executive, "calls for business methods." He boasted that missions boards often included "bank presidents, successful merchants, railroad directors, great lawyers, managers of large corporations,"
who applied their commonsense skills to "the extension of the kingdom of God" (A. J. Brown
1908, 35, 39). Kingdom building now required a great deal of organization tending.

The mania for technique, businesslike management, and professional expertise converged in an efficiency movement in the early twentieth century. A widespread cultural phenomenon, the mania for efficiency was perhaps best epitomized by Frederick W. Taylor (1856–1915), whose *Principles of Scientific Management* (1911) made him something of a guru to many in the movement. Taylor's system involved the analysis of every task scientifically, the breaking of it into component parts, and the determination by the stopwatch of the time each segment (when optimally performed) should take. Although supposedly secular in nature, Taylorism had powerful religious and moral overtones. It promised a moral housecleaning, checking the greed of employers and the laziness of workers. It also held out the hope of establishing perfect harmony between capital and labor; in other words, it heralded a golden age. It was appropriate then that at Taylor's funeral in 1915 he was eulogized as one who not only longed for "an industrial social millennium," but "told in detail exactly how this long-hoped for condition might be actually accomplished at once" (1920, 4). Although many disputed the precise formulations of Taylor's system, it symbolized a much more widespread cultural fascination with efficient technique as the key to a better future. It fit well with the ethos of political progressivism, then at its zenith, for progressives often championed an expanded role for the expert and administrator—witness their desire for professional city managers, their fondness for expert fact-finding commissions to draft legislation, and the various governmental regulatory agencies they created.

Because of its moral and even millennial overtones, the gospel of efficiency was readily adopted by numerous Protestants. A torrent of religious books extolled efficiency as a panacea for the churches' effort to realize the kingdom of God. These included *Scientific Management in the Churches* (1912) by Shailer Mathews (1863–1941), dean of the University of Chicago Divinity School; *The Reconstruction of the Church* (1915) by Rochester Presbyterian Paul Moore Strayer (1871–1929); *The Social Engineer* (1911) by Drew Seminary's professor of Christian Sociology Edwin Earp (1867–1950); *The Community Survey in Relation to Church Efficiency* (1915) by Charles E. Carroll (1877–1946); and the multiple works on church management, finance, and program by Albert F. McGarrah (1878–1962) of McCormick Theological Seminary. These pieces invariably urged churches to adopt a hierarchical system of committees reporting to the pastor/executive of the church. The books also portrayed church efficiency as the key to more fully realizing the immanent kingdom of God on earth. The ideal minister of the early twentieth century was one who, in Earp's description, "can help . . . establish a desired working force in any field of need, and keep it in sympathetic cooperation with all other forces working for the establishment of the Kingdom of God on earth" (1911, xviii). Or, as Charles Carroll contended, the efficient clergy and church were the very people who knew how "to bring religion from the stars to the streets" and to achieve "the Kingdom of God in this world" (1915, 3).

The grandest experiment in church efficiency on behalf of the kingdom took place at the close of World War I. Inspired by the example of Americans' willingness to cooperate for a great cause during the just-ended war to buy Liberty Bonds, to subscribe to Red Cross drives, and to observe "meatless Tuesdays," many Protestant denominations united in a new cooperative venture, the Interchurch World Movement, "to make the kingdoms of this world the kingdoms of our Lord" ([Interchurch World Movement], *Speakers' Manual*, 17). Through the IWM, they expected to raise a huge sum of money, to help direct the disparate Protestant forces in the United States, and to establish a joint headquarters for various religious agencies in New York City. John D. Rockefeller, Jr. (1874–1960), the devout Baptist multimillionaire and a major bankroller of the enterprise, claimed that the IWM "gives the best hope that has appeared yet that the wasteful era of ecclesiastical competition is over and that one of ecclesias-tical efficiency and co-operation has begun" (*New Era Magazine* [June 1920]: 418–19). For Rockefeller, the restructuring of American Protestantism along more efficient lines meant nothing less than the redemption of the world. "I see the church," he declared in a *Saturday Evening Post* article anticipating the formation of the new organization, "molding the thought of the world as it has never done before, leading in all great movements as it should, I see it liter-ally establishing the Kingdom of God on earth" (Fosdick 1956, 206).

These efforts at kingdom building soon waned dramatically. The Interchurch World Movement swiftly collapsed because its fundraising drive fell woefully short. By the 1930s, both the foreign missionary drive and the Social Gospel had also lost energy. Divisions within the Protestant house contributed to this result.

For more than a generation, a conservative backlash against liberal trends in American theology had been brewing. It erupted into the so-called Fundamentalist Controversy of the 1920s. Although that struggle chiefly revolved around the nature of the Bible, the nature of doc-trine, and the relationship of science and religion, it also turned on the nature and meaning of God's activity in history. The issue was this: Was time bounded by the purpose of a God who gave it a definitive End beyond itself and beyond human control? Or was time a virtually limit-less process which humans could master and whose only goal lay in its own indefinite improve-ment? The kingdom builders who spun out a plethora of new organizations, professional specializations, and bureaucratic procedures opted decisively for the latter opinion. By con-trast, the rising premillennial party, growing in power in conservative sectors of Protestantism since the mid-1870s, assessed the possibilities of time very differently. That group regarded the current age as hopelessly corrupt and incapable of redemption until the supernatural advent of Christ inaugurated a new heaven and new earth; and this conviction became even more pro-nounced within the dispensational premillennialism that had largely arrogated the millenarian mantle to itself by the beginning of the twentieth century. Accordingly, premillennialists often spoke contemptuously of the efforts to build a kingdom of God. Isaac M. Haldeman (1845–1933), a premillennialist pastor in New York City, ridiculed the Interchurch World Movement as an effort to construct "a colossal machine," "to multiply wheels within wheels, to extend the system of internal and humanly created organizations" until the church succumbed to "ecclesiastical sovietism" and a "concentrated dictatorship." The Interchurch campaign ignored the true mandate of the church—to preach Christ to perishing sinners. At the root of this apostate endeavor lay a false eschatology. The IWM, he charged, was "the combined, aggressive effort" of would-be kingdom builders "to render meaningless the last promise of an ascended Lord: 'Surely I come quickly'" (1920, 4, 17, 18, 46).

Although premillennialists constituted only one portion of the fundamentalist coalition that emerged after World War I, they were among the most visible and numerous segments of the movement; and it was chiefly against them that the advocates of kingdom building turned their fire. In a series of articles, books, and pamphlets beginning during World War I and stretching well into the 1920s, moderate and liberal Protestants savagely attacked the premil-lennial view. Shailer Mathews fired one of the first salvos. In a pamphlet entitled *Will Christ Come Again?* (1917), he accused premillennialists of espousing a "miraculous militarism," a divine reign of terror in which Christ would impose his kingdom by supernatural brute force. The true conception of Christ's reign was the progressive "discovery of God and his laws in social evolution"—a process of development fully congruent with "the growing knowledge of the universe and society given by science" (1917, 4, 6, 13–14, 16, 20, 21). The association of Christian hope with methodical progress in accord with uniform laws amenable to human control was a consistent theme of the critiques of millenarianism.

This liberalized eschatology was almost as uncongenial to traditional postmillennialism as it was to premillennialism. Those who believed that the Bible contained discrepant and frequently mistaken eschatologies had no basis for drawing any *specific* predictions from it. Thus Professor George Cross (1862–1929) of Rochester Theological Seminary argued that premillennialism was a deluded but "consistent attempt to resuscitate ancient millenarianism with its primitive world view," and postmillennialism represented "an inconsistent attempt to unite modern spirituality with the primitive view" (*Biblical World* [July 1919]: 3–4). Neither offered a viable option to the contemporary church, which needed to move beyond millennialism of any sort. Writing in *The Christian Century*, Herbert Willett (1864–1944) reached a similar conclusion. While he allowed that traditional postmillennialism was far better than its premillennial counterpart, he contended that biblical scholarship and natural science "have made less and less convincing any theory of millennialism whatever" (September 5, 1918: 6). In its place was the belief, as Methodist George Mains (1844–1930) put it, that humanity "carries in itself the prophecy of infinite possibilities of development. No goal is in sight beyond which the race may not make unmeasured increase in knowledge and wisdom" (1920, 92).

Those who held this view rallied a coalition of liberals, moderates, and some irenic conservatives to win a victory over the millenarians and their other conservative allies. The triumph, however, was a highly qualified one. Despite the fact that fundamentalists lost the struggle to control the denominations for which they had contested, they were far from beaten. Some remained as (for the moment) relatively quiescent enclaves in major denominations; others withdrew to form independent denominations. Even more significant was the expansion in the 1920s and 1930s of a vast fundamentalist subculture sustained by a network of publishing houses, Bible institutes, and dynamic leaders. More impressive still was the astonishingly rapid growth of various Pentecostal bodies during the 1920s and 1930s. A relatively new family of churches, most of which traced themselves directly or indirectly to the so-called Azusa St. revival of 1906 in Los Angeles, had grown out of the nineteenth-century holiness tradition and made their distinctive doctrinal contribution through the claim that God had restored the primitive gifts or charismata (healing and speaking in tongues) enjoyed by the earliest Christian church. Such trends were symptomatic of the very limited victory won by liberals. Though unquestionably secure within their denominations, they now discovered that these very organizations exercised influence over a more limited domain. The fundamentalist-modernist battles had, as Martin Marty notes, "split up what was left of a Protestant establishment, leaving it ever less prepared to hold its place of dominance in the decades to come" (1991, 214).

Moreover, the kingdom-building theology would soon be in disrepute even within the highest precincts of mainstream Protestantism, as liberalism found itself embattled on a wide front against a new theological enemy. That foe, usually called Neo-Orthodoxy (but sometimes termed dialectical theology, the theology of crisis, neo-Reformation theology, or Christian realism), exerted a powerful influence on American seminaries in the 1930s. More a mood and a common perception of crisis than a single intellectual system, Neo-Orthodoxy turned with renewed appreciation to Christian themes neglected by nineteenth-century liberalism: the centrality of biblical revelation, the transcendence of God, and the sinfulness of humanity. What this new theological perspective meant for eschatology was succinctly expressed by Drew Seminary's Edwin Lewis (1881–1959) in *A New Heaven and a New Earth* (1941): Notions "about 'bringing in the Kingdom' . . . [are] exceedingly remote from the complete Gospel." "There is," said Lewis, "a growing conviction that the New Testament idea of the Kingdom of God cannot be fitted into any naturalistic evolutionary scheme; or into any philosophy of history which operates exclusively with the category of divine immanence" (1941, 106, 115–16).

Seldom, of course, does any idea or movement die completely. One might argue, in fact, that, once the Neo-Orthodox moment had passed by the mid-1960s, notions of "building the kingdom" enjoyed an Indian summer among various advocates of so-called secular or religionless Christianity. For example, although he eschewed its rhetoric, Harvey Cox in his best-selling *Secular City* (1965) exhibited many affinities with the old liberal vision of kingdom building. Calling upon Christians to forsake the metaphysical for the practical, he gloried in the achievements of a technocratic age and urged Protestants to pour their energies into the search for pragmatic solutions to the problems of urban civilization. Yet in the retrospect of more than a quarter century, the enthusiasms of the 1960s do not appear to have reversed the theological judgment rendered by mainstream Protestantism in the 1930s: talk about "building the kingdom" became increasingly passé.

With the waning of postmillennialism into an open-ended theology of the kingdom of God and then with the gradual disappearance of the latter, large segments of mainstream Protestantism had effectively cut themselves off from a biblically based apocalyptic discourse. It had not always been so. Despite very real differences and often heated exchanges between premillenarians and their critics, there had been no irrevocable parting of the ways in the nineteenth century. Certain common assumptions about the Bible, conversion, heaven, hell, and the afterlife made possible a genuine discourse. Today in libraries, gathering dust, are countless old volumes testifying to this fact: Millerite and anti-Millerite tracts, pre- and postmillennial polemics, all attempting to grapple with each other's arguments within at least a partially shared frame of reference. That frame of reference had been lost by the early twentieth century. When in the 1970s, premillenarianism once attained greater visibility as Hal Lindsey's *Late Great Planet Earth* appeared on the bookracks of almost every drug store in the country, mainstream Protestants could at best lapse into the silence of total incomprehension, utterly bewildered by what sounded like a foreign tongue, or simply dismiss it as utter nonsense.

Secularized intellectuals are likely to be well aware of the dangers of believing too literally in the notion of an end. Assurance that the end is nigh often brings with it profoundly dangerous baggage. The conviction tends toward the demonizing of opponents and toward the glorification of the divine violence that will supposedly usher in the new order. Adherents of such views all too easily assume the position of detached spectators, placidly awaiting the inevitable destruction; or, more ominously, they may be tempted to shed the pose of bystander, to enter the arena, and to nudge history toward its appointed cataclysm. "The panoramas of destruction," contemporary writer A. G. Mojtabai has reminded us, "depicted in loving detail, with no human solution offered but flight from the world, are helping to create the conditions through which they become scenes from a self-fulfilling prophecy" (1986, 163). In the aftermath of the apocalyptic violence at the Branch Davidian Compound in Waco, Texas, and with growing numbers of armed militias preaching their own Doomsday scenarios, Mojtabai's warning cannot be ignored.

Yet if the dangers of taking the end too literally are self-evident, the story of mainline Protestant eschatology in the nineteenth and twentieth centuries warns of a less obvious peril.

In espousing a theology that exalted eternal becoming over the sense of an end, that eliminated the more somber elements of eschatology, and that valued this world over the next, mainstream Protestants succeeded in promoting a crusading activism, many of whose goals and results were laudable. But in the process, they may also have lost the capacity to address humanity's more primal fears and longings and to provide symbols of a transcendent resolution and closure of these issues. Those who have wished to find such an eschatology had to turn to one of the many permutations of premillennialism, to pentecostalism, or to the various surrogates for an eschatological vision provided by science fiction and stories of alien abduction. For weal or woe, it would appear, a religious movement must provide its adherents with a satisfying vision of the end; when it fails to do so, many people will be drawn elsewhere. Indeed in the long run, the attempt to live without a sense of the end may exact from the human spirit something as costly as any vision of the *Dies Irae*.

⌘ BIBLIOGRAPHY

Abbott, Lyman. 1897. *The Theology of an Evolutionist.*
Adam, M. T. 1837. *The Millennium.*
Bacon, Leonard. 1846. *Slavery Discussed in Occasional Essays.*
Barnes, Albert. 1871. *Life at Threescore and Ten.*
Bloch, Ruth. 1985. *Visionary Republic: Millennial Themes in American Thought, 1756–1800.* Cambridge: Cambridge University Press. The most comprehensive examination of millennial themes in the Revolutionary epoch.
Bowden, Henry Warner, ed. 1970. *Religion in America: A Critical Abridgement.* New York: Harper & Row.
Brown, Arthur Judson. 1908. *The Why and How of Foreign Missions.* 3rd ed.
Brown, William Adams. 1917. *The Christian Hope.*
Butler, Jonathan M. 1991. *Softly and Tenderly Jesus is Calling: Heaven and Hell in American Revivalism, 1870–1920.* Chicago Studies in the History of American Religion 3. Brooklyn, N.Y.: Carlson Publishing. An analysis of the ways in which heaven and hell functioned in the preaching of revivalist Dwight L. Moody and his successors.
Carroll, Charles. 1915. *The Community Survey in Relation to Church Efficiency.*
Clarke, William Newton. 1909a. *Outline of Christian Theology.*
———. 1909b. *Sixty Years with the Bible: A Record of Experience.*
Cogswell, William. 1833. *The Harbinger of the Millennium.*
Davidson, James West. 1977. *The Logic of Millennial Thought: Eighteenth-Century New England.* New Haven: Yale University Press. Examines the way in which an apocalyptic paradigm—what the author calls "the afflictive model of progress"—shaped ideas toward religion, politics, and culture.
Doan, Ruth Alden. 1987. *The Miller Heresy, Millennialism, and American Culture.* Philadelphia: Temple University Press. An analysis of the way in which opposition to William Miller's prediction of the end of the world around 1843 helped to define the boundaries of mainstream Protestantism and culture.
Earp, Edwin. 1911. *The Social Engineer.*
Edwards, Jonathan. 1948. *Images or Shadows of Divine Things.* New Haven: Yale University Press.
Ely, Richard T. 1889. *Social Aspects of Christianity and Other Essays.*
Fosdick, Raymond B. 1956. *John D. Rockefeller, Jr.: A Portrait.* New York: Harper & Brothers.
Frederick Winslow Taylor: A Memorial. 1920.
Gaustad, Edwin S., ed. 1974. *The Rise of Adventism: Religion and Society in Mid-Nineteenth Century America.* New York: Harper & Row. Essays examining not only William Miller's movement but the larger social, intellectual, and cultural context of Adventism.

Gilmore, William J. 1989. *Reading Becomes a Necessity of Life.*

Goen, C. C. 1959. "Jonathan Edwards: A New Departure in Eschatology." *Church History* 28:25–40. The classic statement of the argument that American postmillennialism originated with Edwards.

Gordon, George A. 1897. *Immortality and the New Theodicy.*

Haldeman, Isaac M. 1920. *Why I Am Opposed to the Interchurch World Movement.*

Hamline, Leonidas. 1869. *Works of Rev. Leonidas L. Hamline, D. D.: Sermons.*

Hanley, Mark Y. 1994. *Beyond a Christian Commonwealth: The Protestant Quarrel with the American Republic, 1830–1860.* Chapel Hill/London: University of North Carolina Press. An argument that early-nineteenth-century Protestants were far more critical of American culture than historians have often supposed.

Hatch, Nathan O. 1977. *The Sacred Cause of Liberty: Republican Thought and the Millennium in Revolutionary New England.* New Haven: Yale University Press. An analysis of the manner in which New England clergy invested the struggle for liberty and independence with eschatological significance.

Hopkins, Samuel. 1793. *A Treatise on the Millennium.*

Laderman, Gary. 1996. *The Sacred Remains: American Attitudes toward Death, 1799–1883.* New Haven: Yale University Press. An examination of changing American attitudes toward death with special emphasis on the role of the Civil War.

Lasch, Christopher. 1991. *The True and Only Heaven.*

Leach, William. 1993. *Land of Desire: Merchants, Power, and the Rise of a New American Culture.* New York: Pantheon Books.

Lewis, Edwin. 1941. *A New Heaven and a New Earth.*

Maddex, Jack P., Jr. 1979. "Proslavery Millennialism: Social Eschatology in Antebellum Southern Calvinism." *American Quarterly* 31:46–62. Demonstrates that postmillennialism was not invariably associated with political reform but might in fact co-exist with conservative politics.

Mains, George. 1920. *Premillennialism.*

Marsden, George M. 1980. *Fundamentalism and American Culture: The Shaping of Twentieth-Century Evangelicalism, 1870–1925.* New York: Oxford University Press. The standard history of Fundamentalism.

Marty, Martin. 1991. *The Noise of Conflict, 1919–1941.* Volume 2 of *Modern American Religion.* Chicago: University of Chicago Press.

Mathews, Shailer. 1917. *Will Christ Come Again?*

McDannell, Colleen, and Bernhard Lang. 1988. *Heaven: A History.* New Haven/ London: Yale University Press. A survey of changing attitudes toward heaven from antiquity to the present.

McLoughlin, William G., ed. 1960. *Lectures on Revivals of Religion by Charles G. Finney.* Cambridge, Mass.: Harvard University Press.

Merrill, Stephen M. 1879. *The Second Coming of Christ Considered in Its Relation to the Millennium.*

Miller, Perry. 1965. *Life of the Mind in America: From the Revolution to the Civil War.* New York: Harcourt, Brace & World.

Mojtabai, A. G. 1986. *Blessèd Assurance: At Home with the Bomb in Amarillo, Texas.* Boston: Houghton Mifflin.

Moorhead, James H. 1978. *American Apocalypse: Yankee Protestants and the Civil War, 1860–1869.* New Haven: Yale University Press. Argues that Northern Protestants heavily employed apocalyptic rhetoric to portray the struggle for the Union as a sacred cause.

———. 1984a. "Between Progress and Apocalypse: A Reassessment of Millennialism in American Religious Thought, 1800–1880." *Journal of American History* 71:524–42. Contends that postmillennialism was a complex compromise between an apocalyptic and progressive view of history.

———. 1984b. "The Erosion of Postmillennialism in American Religious Thought, 1865–1925." *Church History* 53:61–77. Treats the religious, intellectual, and cultural sources of the gradual disappearance of postmillennialism.

———. "The Millennium and the Media." In *Communication and Change in American Religious History*, edited by Leonard I. Sweet, 216–38. Grand Rapids: Eerdmans, 1993. Assesses the impact of the advent of cheap mass printing upon American millennialism.

Morgan, J. Vyrnwy, et al. 1901. *Theology at the Dawn of the Twentieth Century.*

O'Leary, Stephen D. 1994. *Arguing the Apocalypse: A Theory of Millennial Rhetoric.* New York/Oxford: Oxford University Press. A sophisticated rhetorical analysis demonstrating how apocalyptic discourse can shape a variety of responses to religious, political, and cultural events.

Peake, Arthur. 1919. *The Revelation of St. John.*

Peck, Jesse. 1871. *The History of the Great Republic.*

Phelps, Elizabeth Stuart. 1885. *Beyond the Gates.*

———. 1867. *The Gates Ajar.*

Quandt, Jean. 1973. "Religion and Social Thought: The Secularization of Postmillennialism." *American Quarterly* 25:390–409. Shows that the thought of many late-nineteenth- and early-twentieth-century social theorists was heavily influenced by postmillennialism.

Rice, Nathan L. 1855. *The Signs of the Times.*

Roberts, Jon H. 1988. *Darwinism and the Divine in America: Protestant Intellectuals and Organic Evolution, 1859–1900.* Madison: University of Wisconsin Press.

Rowell, Geoffrey. 1974. *Hell and the Victorians: A Study of the Nineteenth-Century Theological Controversies Concerning Eternal Punishment and the Future Life.* Oxford: Clarendon Press.

Sandeen, Ernest. 1994. *The Roots of Fundamentalism: British and American Millenarianism, 1800–1930.* Chicago/London: University of Chicago Press. Contends that an ongoing premillennial tradition was the primary shaper of what became Fundamentalism.

Sanford, Elias B. 1908. *Federal Council of the Churches of Christ.*

Saum, Lewis. 1980. *The Popular Mood of Pre-Civil War America.* Westport, Conn.: Greenwood Press.

Shedd, William G. T. 1887. *The Doctrine of Endless Punishment.* 2nd ed.

Smith, Timothy L. 1979. "Righteousness and Hope: Christian Holiness and the Millennial Vision in America, 1800–1900." *American Quarterly* 31:21–45. Argues that nineteenth-century postmillennialism coupled with a perfectionist theology promoted a progressive and reformist approach to American society.

Smyth, Newman. 1908. *Passing Protestantism and Coming Catholicism.*

Sprague, William B. 1861. *Glorifying God in the Fires.*

Stearns, Lewis French. 1893. *Present Day Theology.*

Stein, Stephen J., ed. 1977. *Apocalyptic Writings.* Vol. 5, *The Work of Jonathan Edwards.* New Haven: Yale University Press.

Tuveson, Ernest Lee. 1968. *Redeemer Nation: The Idea of America's Millennial Role.* Chicago: University of Chicago Press. The now classic statement of the way in which millennial imagery came to shape notions of American national identity and mission.

Whalen, Robert K. 1972. "Millenarianism and Millennialism in America, 1790–1880." Ph.D. diss., State University of New York, Stony Brook. Though now dated in approach, a valuable overview of the primary literature of American millennialism in the nineteenth century.

Wilson, Warren H. 1915. *The Second Missionary Adventure.*

19

Apocalypticism Outside the Mainstream in the United States

Stephen J. Stein
Indiana University

T HE WIDESPREAD INTEREST in apocalyptic in the United States has often reached its fullest and most radical expressions in religious communities situated on the margins of American life. These communities, sometimes referred to as sects and "cults," or alternative and outsider religions, or new religious movements, invite special attention because for many of them apocalypticism is central to their beliefs and practices. But any effort to catalogue or classify the varieties of apocalypticism outside the mainstream in America confronts the challenge of bewildering diversity.

The United States has been a fertile seedbed for alternative religions. This nation has been an especially hospitable environment for such groups as a consequence of the constitutional guarantee of religious liberty, the abundance of open space and cheap land, the spirit of independence, the high value placed on individual judgment, and the prevalence of the "Protestant principle." In every period of national history new groups featuring an apocalyptic message have arisen or arrived. The formal names of a few bear witness to the centrality of apocalypticism among religious outsiders: the United Society of Believers in Christ's Second Appearing, better known as the Shakers; the Church of Jesus Christ of Latter-day Saints, or the Mormons; the Seventh-day Adventists; and Zion's Watch Tower Tract Society, later renamed the Jehovah's Witnesses. These and other outsider groups are the focus of this essay.

Several preliminary concerns require comment at the outset. First, "apocalypticism" is defined as belief in an imminent end to the present order, either through catastrophic destruction and conflagration or through establishment of an ideal society—millennial or utopian. This broad definition is necessary because the apocalyptic views associated with America's alternative religions are extremely diverse. A narrow definition does not do justice to the range of ideas found in these communities.

Second, contemporary scholars who criticize the use of "mainstream" and "margin" as categories have not yet offered alternatives with greater explanatory value. The critics of this terminology fail to take into account the self-perception of the members of outsider groups. "Mainstream" and "margin" depict real differences in power, influence, and position. Persecution and hostility provide proof that some groups are inside and some outside. R. Laurence Moore demonstrates persuasively that outsider religious groups occasionally choose "outsiderhood" because of its advantages. Some seek the edges of American society as a refuge; others use the margins to establish a distinctive identity. The essence of outsiderhood is dissent in its various forms—dissent against more powerful religious denominations, against social or economic establishments, against prevailing cultural values, or against some combination thereof. Problems may develop from the use of these terms, but it is impossible to deny that the mainstream and the margin exist.

Third, a comment about the usefulness of the contrast often drawn between varieties of millennialism is in order. The common distinction between postmillennialism and premillennialism has limited usefulness when discussing the apocalypticism of outsider religious groups. In many of these communities apocalyptic optimism and pessimism exist side by side; the forces of construction and destruction operate in tandem; and the fulfillment of prophecy involves both human actions and divine activity. As an added complication, alternative religious communities often modify their outlook on apocalyptic matters. As a result, it is more instructive to identify the principal apocalyptic themes employed by these groups than to force the data into pre- or postmillennial constructs.

Finally, in this essay I divide the history of apocalypticism outside the mainstream into four periods even though the story involves continuities as well as discontinuities. Typical concerns of those for whom apocalyptic has been a matter of life and death include a sense of urgency, appeal to scripture, confidence in prophecy, preoccupation with the passage of time, concern with the contrast between good and evil, and a desire to create a community of like-minded individuals. These themes figure prominently in the story that follows.

☞ APOCALYPTIC OUTSIDERS IN THE YOUNG NATION

The first period in this history of apocalypticism among outsider religious groups in the United States witnessed the displacement and hardship attendant on the War for Independence as well as subsequent struggles to establish a new government. Geographic and demographic expansion followed as the young nation moved across the Alleghenies into the heartland of the continent. Religious groups faced new challenges, too, in coping with these changes. Historians underscore the role of the evangelical churches in creating a coalition that exercised religious and cultural dominance over the young society. In the first third of the nineteenth century, that alliance manifested its religious energy in the Second Great Awakening and its social influence through a network of reform and benevolent organizations. But on the edges of that mainstream alliance and crossing back and forth across its boundaries were dissenting groups that did not participate in it and sought to establish their own identity apart from it. Several such groups made use of apocalypticism in their efforts to negotiate a place in the new nation.

Two individuals who left the evangelical mainstream as a consequence of their radical apocalyptic views illustrate the movement across boundaries. Simon Hough, a member of the Congregational church in Stockbridge, Massachusetts, published his views concerning the imminent return of Christ in *An Alarm to the World* (1792). Using biblical citations to confirm his eschatological timetable, he combined a zealous apocalyptic outlook with strident support for the young American republic. Hough also attacked the learned ministry and the established churches of his day, actions that eventually resulted in his excommunication. David Austin (1759–1831), minister at the First Presbyterian Church in Elizabethtown, New Jersey, spoke of the millennial significance of the American Revolution. Based on visions he received, he identified the fourth Sunday in May 1796 as the date when Christ would return to the earth, a prophecy he thought confirmed by the American and French revolutions. The failure of his prediction did not deter Austin, who traveled widely, preaching his message. When he persisted with his millennial views, his congregation dismissed him. Austin, too, harshly criticized members of the clergy, whom he identified with the figure of the Beast in the book of Revelation. Hough, Austin, and others like them were initially religious insiders whose unconventional apocalyptic views moved them into the camp of outsiders.

Two religious outsiders deeply influenced by the Enlightenment speculated in different ways on apocalyptic matters. Benjamin Rush (1745–1813), a Philadelphia physician and supporter of the American Revolution, interpreted progress in the eighteenth century in religious categories, seeing God's design in such disparate developments as scientific discoveries and the establishment of the new republic. Educated at Princeton College, he celebrated the triumphs of Christianity and of liberty, assured that America was leading toward a moment when "the kingdoms of this world are probably to become the kingdoms of the Prince of Righteousness and Peace" (1951, 1:466–67). His confidence in the outcome of the Christian republic was almost boundless, as was his belief in the progressive nature of history. Joseph Priestley (1733–1804), noted English scientist, philosopher, and Unitarian minister who came to America in 1794, wrote extensively on apocalyptic topics including the fall of Antichrist, the timing of the millennium, and the restoration of the Jews to Palestine. But it was the French Revolution that most absorbed his interest and intensified his views on prophecy. He was influenced by the American Universalist Elhanan Winchester (1751–1797) whose publication *The Three Woe Trumpets* (1793) linked the fall of the French monarchy with Revelation 11. Priestley believed that prophecy was being fulfilled at that very moment. He spent his last ten years in Northumberland, Pennsylvania, where he was unsuccessful in attracting support for his controversial religious views on the atonement, the Trinity, and the soul. He and Rush became friends and shared apocalyptic interests, though they disagreed on other issues.

Several small religious communities during the revolutionary period reflect continuities with the apocalypticism of the colonial era. One sect formed around Jemima Wilkinson (1752–1819), who was nurtured within a Quaker family in Cumberland, Rhode Island. Illness and radical revivalism fanned her early religious interests. Spiritual experiences persuaded her that she had died and that her body had been possessed by "the Spirit of Life from God" (Wisbey 1964, 12). Wilkinson adopted the name "the Public Universal Friend" and traveled throughout southern New England, preaching a message of salvation and exhorting hearers to holiness in the face of an impending day of judgment. She wore clerical robes and a white Quaker hat, and she spoke with great boldness. By the 1780s Wilkinson and her converts had established several congregations. In preparation for the end-times she regulated the work, food, dress, and other details of their lives. She also counseled celibacy, but did not require it. In 1788 her followers, called Universal Friends, purchased land near Seneca Lake in New York and founded a communal settlement named Jerusalem. The precise claims she made for herself lie under a cloud of conflicting testimony. One "neighbor," defending Wilkinson after her death, denied the persistent report "that she professed to be the *Messiah*" (Wisbey 1964, 21).

Shadrach Ireland (d. 1778), an artisan in Charlestown, Massachusetts, who became a Separate minister, later a Baptist, and by the 1770s a self-proclaimed prophet, had no such reluctance. His prophetic claims, including the notion that he was the second Messiah, led him to abandon his wife and family and to preach a doctrine of "spiritual wifery." Ireland and his followers constructed "the Square House" in Harvard, Massachusetts, where they lived communally. He hoped to create a perfect society, believing that celibacy was a necessary step toward that goal, a step ultimately to be superseded by other social arrangements. Ireland claimed immortality for himself. When illness threatened his life, he struck an apocalyptic note, announcing, "I am going but don't bury me; for the time is short; God is coming to take the church" (Marini 1982, 51). Following his death, the Irelandites obeyed his command, but only for a time. They interpreted his death as a sign of the impending second coming. Three years later many of them joined the infant Shaker movement.

Ann Lee (1736–1784), an English laborer who came to the New World, was the principal founder of the Shakers in America. In England she had joined a small sect known as the Shaking Quakers that proclaimed impending judgment and engaged in ecstatic worship and prophetic activity. In 1774 Lee, who emerged as a leader because of her charismatic gifts, led a small group of followers to America. The Shakers eventually located at Watervliet, near Albany, New York. They were first noticed during the Revolutionary War when they refused to support the patriot cause. Lee and several followers were jailed as British sympathizers. Later, in 1780, the small group began to attract attention from evangelicals in the region who heard curious tales about this "strange new religion." Lee and her colleagues preached that sin involved sexuality and that confession was required as prerequisite for membership. The famed "Dark Day" of May 19, 1780, when an eerie daytime darkness fell over New England, fueled apocalyptic fears in the populace, and the Shakers capitalized on those anxieties. The next year Lee and several companions began a twenty-six-month missionary journey throughout eastern New York and New England. They attracted hundreds of converts but also experienced hostility and physical abuse. Within a year of her return to Watervliet, she died. Local newspapers reported Lee's death and the fact that her followers called her the Elect Lady and the Mother of Zion.

In the years following, Lee's successors gathered the scattered converts and built villages. They adapted her teachings to the changing circumstances in the young nation and established institutions that lasted more than two hundred years. They structured a communal life that required of its members celibacy, confession of sins, common property, and obedience to the ministry. Men and women shared leadership responsibilities. The society codified its rules and regulations in a collection entitled "Millennial Laws." They defended their religious ideas in a series of major publications, including *The Testimony of Christ's Second Appearing* (1808) and *Summary View of the Millennial Church* (1823). The Shakers developed distinctive worship patterns, including dances and marches. In 1813 they published a collection of hymn texts entitled *Millennial Praises*. In this period the Shakers also fashioned peculiar ideas concerning the dual nature of God, as both Father and Mother, and about the role of Ann Lee as parallel to that of Jesus of Nazareth—a kind of second Christ. It is difficult to know for certain what Lee claimed for herself. Her enemies spoke of the fact that the Shakers called her "mother" and associated her with "the woman clothed with the sun" (Revelation 12). Others spoke of her as "Christ's wife." By the 1820s the United Society of Believers had established villages from Maine to Indiana. The "Millennial Church" succeeded in a manner without parallel among early outsider groups.

The followers of George Rapp (1757–1847) comprised another imported alternative group for whom apocalypticism was central. Born in Württemberg, Germany, Rapp—a weaver—rejected the formalism of the Lutheran Church and adopted a mystical, pietistic approach to religion. By 1791 he felt called as a prophet and set out to organize a community of religious dissenters. In 1803 he traveled to America looking for a refuge for his followers. The next year three hundred came to Pennsylvania, where they built the town of Harmony and formed the Harmony Society. In 1814 the Rappites, as they were also known, moved from Pennsylvania to a site in western Indiana, also named Harmony, and a decade later back to a new location in Pennsylvania named Economy. The Harmonists accepted Rapp as their undisputed religious authority. They practiced communal living and celibacy, although their physical arrangements differed from the strict separation of the sexes carried out by the Shakers. Rapp believed that the second coming was approaching rapidly and that it was his responsibility literally to deliver his community to Christ. At one point Rapp declared 1829 to be the date when Christ would return. When that date came and went, the Harmonists lived through their disappointment by continuing to build their community here on earth. At each of the sites they prospered economically.

The 1820s and 1830s were formative years for a new American religion that eventually overshadowed the Shakers and the Harmonists in size and importance. Mormonism's inauspicious beginnings involved a young lad in western New York, Joseph Smith (1805–1844), who hailed from a family preoccupied with religion and the occult. Visions and revelations guided Smith at every turn. In 1830 publication of the *Book of Mormon,* Smith's "Golden Bible," described as a translation of ancient records, signaled the start of his effort to restore the church of Christ. This scripture told of the early inhabitants of the Americas, of Christ's postresurrection appearances in the New World and of future dispensations. In it a prophet named Nephi spoke of "evil and unbelief" in the last days. Smith and a growing band of followers regarded the book itself as a sign that the end was nigh.

Smith moved rapidly from being a translator of ancient records to being a living prophet. He proclaimed a new gospel to those who would listen, declaring that Mormonism represented the true restoration of New Testament Christianity. In Mormon eyes, the world divided sharply between Latter-day Saints—what they called themselves—and Gentiles, those who rejected the gospel. The hardship and persecution suffered by the Saints in New York, Ohio, Missouri, and Illinois confirmed their belief that apocalyptic destruction was close at hand. In 1833 *The Evening and the Morning Star,* a Mormon periodical, listed wars, calamities, pestilence, selfishness, and rampant evil as signs of the time, evidences of "that great day fast approaching when this scene of wickedness shall close . . . and the Son of God be seen coming in the clouds of heaven, with all his holy angels, with power and great glory" (vol. 2, no. 15, p. 1).

The first generation of Mormons anticipated Christ's return inaugurating an earthly millennium during which the inhabitants of Zion—the Latter-day Saints—will "reign with Christ a thousand years on the earth." Smith was cautious about setting a specific date for that return, though he and others watched closely for time-honored signs such as the conversion of the

Jews, which the *Book of Mormon* had connected with the arrival of the fullness of the gospel (III Nephi 20:30–31). Smith developed a distinctive notion of "two places of gathering" in the latter days: Jerusalem in Palestine for the Jews, and Zion in western Missouri for the Gentiles. The early Mormons were confident that they would be vindicated in their beliefs and that their enemies would be destroyed.

One group contesting the Mormon claim to be the restored church of the New Testament was the movement associated with Alexander Campbell (1788–1866), a Presbyterian and native of Ireland who came to America in 1808. Both he and his father, Thomas, withdrew from the Presbyterians and sought to recover the essence of apostolic Christianity, free from denominational and creedal developments. Campbell formed societies called simply "Disciples of Christ," known also as "Campbellites." His program represented a sharp rebuke of the denominational pattern. He used the power of the press to attack the churches of his day and to call for the unity of Christendom. In 1830 he launched the *Millennial Harbinger,* a journal devoted to "the destruction of Sectarianism" and to the "introduction of that political and religious order of society called THE MILLENNIUM" (January 1830: 1–2). For Campbell, the unity of Christians was a necessary precondition for the arrival of the millennium. He expected a millennial age that mirrored the apostolic era. He gained a substantial following, but ironically was responsible for the formation of yet another Protestant denomination.

One outsider whose apocalyptic views led to open armed revolt was Nat Turner (1800–1831), an African-American slave and lay Baptist preacher in Virginia. Turner, a mystic and visionary, believed that he had been chosen by God for a special messianic vocation, a task similar to that of the Hebrew prophets who called down God's wrath on sinful people. He waited for a sign that would signal the time for open rebellion against white slaveholders. A solar eclipse in February 1831 alerted him to the impending moment when the slaves should rise up and slay their enemies. Five months later other signs in the sky—strange atmospheric phenomena—convinced Turner that the time had come for him to act. On August 22 and 23 Turner and a band of some fifty slaves, armed initially with axes and hatchets, murdered fifty-seven whites in the name of justice and freedom. This slave insurrection, the bloodiest in American history, resulted in as many as one hundred slave deaths. Turner, who remained confident in his prophetic role, eluded captors for more than two months; following capture, he was tried, convicted, and executed, after which his body was skinned and grease was made of his flesh. The Nat Turner rebellion sent shock waves throughout southern slaveholding society.

The public attention paid to all of these apocalyptic movements pales in comparison with that given to the adventist movement associated with William Miller (1782–1849). Miller, another Baptist lay preacher, formerly a deist and soldier in the War of 1812, following his conversion in 1816 became preoccupied with the study of the Bible, particularly with the books of Daniel and Revelation. He concluded that biblical prophecies had a literal fulfillment and that the Bible contained its own rules for interpretation. His apocalyptic calculations drew on the widespread theory that a "day" in prophecy equals a year. Using Dan. 8:14, he concluded that the world was to end in 1843. But lack of confidence and nagging uncertainty kept him from announcing his judgment for more than a decade. Finally in 1831 he began to speak publicly, traveling throughout New England and New York. In 1836 Miller published *Evidence from Scripture and History of the Second Coming of Christ about the Year 1843.*

Millerism became a widespread popular movement after Joshua V. Himes (1805–1895), an evangelical leader in Boston, accepted the adventist message. Himes, skilled and experienced in reform activity, transformed adventism into a nationwide crusade. He organized conferences and camp meetings, published periodicals—*Signs of the Times* and *Midnight Cry*—and newspapers, preached the cause, established adventist libraries, developed chronological charts, and sent lecturers throughout the land. The message of the movement, in Miller's own words, was quite simple: "I believe that the Scriptures do reveal unto us in plain language that Jesus Christ will appear again on this earth, that he will come in the glory of God, in the clouds of heaven, with all his Saints and angels" (1841, 33). Following this "first resurrection," the saints will reign with Christ for a thousand years on a new earth cleansed by fire. Bowing eventually to pressure, Miller calculated that Christ's coming would occur more precisely between March 21, 1843, and March 21, 1844.

With the approach of these dates, the Millerites became more aggressive, their opponents more resistant, and the level of excitement higher. Local churches were often the scene of conflict because adventists for the most part remained in their congregations. In 1843 activity reached new heights; the Millerites used every possible means to spread their message. When March 1844 passed without Christ's return, the movement suffered widespread disappointment and public ridicule. Miller confessed his error, but affirmed, "I still believe that the day of the Lord is near, even at the door." He counseled his followers to remain watchful (Numbers and Butler 1987, 50).

Not all adventists conceded defeat. Himes continued to proclaim the necessity of living in constant expectation of the impending end. He was joined by the editors of a new journal, *The Advent Message to the Daughters of Zion*. In the May 1844 inaugural issue, Clorinda Minor and Emily Clemons warned their counterparts throughout the nation that the "glorious hour" of Christ's coming was close at hand. Despite disappointment, they affirmed "a sure word of prophecy" (vol. 1, no. 1, p. 1). By August, Samuel S. Snow, a Millerite preacher, was arguing that miscalculations had occurred and the proper date was 22 October 1844. Skeptical at first, Himes and eventually Miller bowed to pressure and reluctantly accepted the revised date. A new tide of enthusiasm crested as the date approached, and then passed.

The second disappointment—the "Great Disappointment"—delivered a body blow to the adventist movement: Millerism lay in shambles. Himes wrote, "We admit that it is proved that we do not yet know the definite time" (Numbers and Butler 1987, 52). Critics heaped ridicule on adventism and accused the Millerites of destroying families, creating financial instability, and causing insanity as well as suicide. Miller rationalized the movement as God's way of turning people to Bible study. Despite the miscalculation, he affirmed, each day was one day closer to Christ's return.

The year of the Great Disappointment was also a moment of special significance for the Shakers and the Mormons. In the United Society 1844 was a time of widespread spiritualistic activity. Scores of spirits visited the Shakers, including Ann Lee and Jesus as well as the Almighty Father and Holy Mother Wisdom, the two "persons" in the Godhead. This Shaker version of a second coming was not date specific but rather repeated and repeatable. In several villages the Shakers were also caught up in the Millerite excitement and attended adventist camp meetings. After the Great Disappointment, several hundred Millerites turned to the Shakers for a brief time. In 1844 the main body of Latter-day Saints resided in Nauvoo, Illinois, where Joseph Smith presided as both prophet and civic leader. He received numerous revelations spelling out new theological ideas and religious practices. His vision of the impending millennium involved responsibility for building Zion but also led to conflict among the Mormons and to growing hostility from those outside the community. Rumors of the practice of polygamy led to the jailing and murder of Smith on 27 July 1844—a severe blow to the young community.

EXPANDING APOCALYPTIC SECTS IN THE NINETEENTH CENTURY

The second period in this history of apocalypticism saw the lines in the sectional struggle harden as antislavery and proslavery forces, buttressed by religious arguments, squared off against each other. The idea of secession was in the air as the United States moved steadily across the continent, its citizens attracted by land, resources, and the sheer thrill of expansion. The annexation of Texas in 1845 brought war with Mexico. Simultaneously, immigrants from western Europe, especially Germany and Ireland, flooded into the country, changing the ethnic and religious makeup of the nation. When the war between the states came, it devastated the nation, killing more than six hundred thousand. The union was preserved, but not without immense costs; and the sectional rivalry did not end. After the war, African Americans experimented with freedom in the South at the same time that waves of new immigrants from southern and eastern Europe arrived in the North. Cities full of factories grew on the landscape, and laborers filled those factories. The nation grew more powerful even though both wealth and poverty were products of this "progress." New conflicts erupted over science, industry, politics, and religion.

These difficult times contributed to continuing interest in apocalyptic among former Millerites. In the aftermath of Christ's failure to return, many abandoned the adventist cause; others pulled back from public view; and only a handful persisted in setting dates. All lived in the shadow of the Great Disappointment. The impulse to set specific dates suffered a crushing blow, but belief in an imminent second coming did not die. On the contrary, reaffirmation of adventist tenets often accompanied the reinterpretation of recent events. For example, Hiram Edson, a former Millerite, argued that the 1843–1844 dates were intended not to identify the destruction of the earth but rather to signal a new phase of Christ's ministry in heaven. He and others found renewed strength by reinterpreting the miscalculation.

Another ex-Millerite whose faith in adventism did not flag was Ellen Harmon (1827–1915), who in 1844 at the age of seventeen experienced the first of many visions. She met and married the adventist preacher James White, and subsequently they traveled together, itinerating as a team. They also became converts to Sabbatarianism. Among their beliefs, in addition to the seventh-day Sabbath, were a primary affirmation concerning Christ's imminent personal return and acceptance of the principle of prophecy. For example, they reinterpreted the prophecies used to support 1844 as references to Christ's cleansing of the sanctuary in heaven (Rev. 11:19) and blotting out sins in advance of his second coming. They regarded their recovery of the Sabbath as fulfilling Revelation 14 and thus preparing the world for Christ's coming. Ellen White the visionary and James White the organizer, working in tandem, moved adventism from its early unstructured stage to a formal organization by 1860, named the Seventh-day Adventists. James White was especially effective in the use of publications, including the *Review and Herald,* launched in 1850.

Ellen White's adventism included a vigorous reformist dimension. Her own illnesses led to an abiding interest in health reform. She advocated a simple vegetarian diet and urged a drugless variety of health care, including use of the water cure, or hydropathy. In 1866 the church opened a sanitarium dedicated to health reform, an act that began a long and profitable association between Seventh-day Adventists and health care institutions. White also supported establishment of Seventh-day Adventist colleges in order to keep young Adventists from worldly associations. The first such school opened in 1874 at Battle Creek, Michigan, setting a pattern for subsequent colleges. Another continuing emphasis in the community was missionary activity, first in the settled portions of the United States, then in new states and adjacent territories, and finally also in Europe. Initially the missionaries proclaimed the need to prepare for Christ's coming. By the mid-1870s, however, the emphasis changed as Adventists urged concern for the salvation of others through Christlike activity.

The 1890s were a time of institutional crisis for Seventh-day Adventism and growing concern on the part of some that the church had expanded too quickly. Internal tensions flared, and reliance on the prophetic guidance of Ellen White increased with some resulting tension over her leadership. When a coalition of religious and political organizations moved to enforce Sunday legislation, Seventh-day Adventists suffered arrest, fines, and imprisonment. They interpreted this opposition as a sign of the approaching end-times. These developments also moved Adventists for the first time to use the political process on their own behalf.

The uncertainties of antebellum America stoked the fires of apocalyptic interpretation. For example, John Humphrey Noyes (1811–1886), converted in an evangelical revival at Putney, Vermont, during the 1830s, attended Andover and Yale seminaries, where he developed several distinctive theological ideas, including the notion that the second coming of Christ had taken place in A.D. 70 with the destruction of the Jewish Temple in Jerusalem. He maintained that the first resurrection in the spiritual world had inaugurated the kingdom of God. The second resurrection was now fast approaching. Noyes seized on the concept of Christian perfection as the instrument by which the millennium might be established on earth. Claiming personal holiness for himself, he struggled to establish a society committed to social perfection. He founded a community at Putney that was organized communally. The group also experimented with an alternative to conventional marriage, a practice known as "complex marriage." Noyes condemned exclusive sexual relations and celebrated the spiritual possibilities of intercourse between men and women as an aid for attaining perfection. Male continence, or coitus reservatus, accompanied the practice of complex marriage, thereby controlling the propagation of children. In 1847, when charged with adultery, Noyes fled from Vermont, and the next year he established a new community at Oneida, New York. By the mid-1870s more than three hundred Perfectionists resided there in the dwelling known as the Mansion House, where they practiced complex marriage accompanied by a unique discipline known as "mutual criticism" and also, for a time, a form of eugenics directed by Noyes known as "stirpiculture." Noyes, a prolific writer whose interests ranged widely over social and religious issues, dominated life at Oneida. The community prospered economically until 1879, when new legal action forced Noyes to flee to Canada. The following year the community abandoned complex marriage and converted its assets into a joint-stock community, Oneida Community, Ltd.

William Keil (1812–1877), an Austrian who came to America in 1831, founded another communal society grounded in apocalyptic ideas. He believed that he was one of the witnesses mentioned in Rev. 11:3, and on that basis he formed a sect in Pennsylvania. Some of his early followers were former disciples of Bernard Muller (1787–1834)—Count Leon—a German mystic and prophet who had led an exodus of Harmonists from Economy, Pennsylvania, and subsequently founded short-lived colonies at Phillipsburg, Pennsylvania (New Philadelphia Society), and Grand Ecore, Louisiana (New Jerusalem). Muller claimed that he was "of the Stem of David and the Root of Jesse." In 1844 Keil and his followers relocated to Bethel in Shelby County, Missouri. Within less than a decade the community numbered a thousand members. In 1854 Keil changed locations one more time, on this occasion leading his followers across the continent to Oregon, where they founded the Aurora colony in the Willamette Valley. The community prospered as a cooperative society until 1881, four years after Keil's death.

Most of the outsider groups in nineteenth-century America in which apocalypticism figured prominently were Protestant in background. They often used prophetic language to condemn Roman Catholicism as anti-Christian. One notable exception is the St. Nazianz colony in Manitowoc County, Wisconsin, a community founded in 1854 under the leadership of Ambrose Oschwald (1801–1873), a German Catholic priest condemned by the church for his mystical ideas and apocalyptic predictions. In his writings, for example, he predicted that the New Jerusalem would come before 1900, and he warned his followers to prepare for the coming of Jesus. At St. Nazianz, property was held in common, some members lived in nuclear family units and others in celibate orders, and all observed a structured religious life. The community also experimented with occult medical practices, a special interest of Oschwald. This Catholic utopian community declined shortly after his death.

The Civil War itself gave rise to apocalyptic speculation similar to that discredited by the Great Disappointment even among those nominally associated with mainstream denominations. Events such as the raid in 1859 on the federal arsenal at Harpers Ferry in Virginia by John Brown, the radical abolitionist, were "signs of the times." Hollis Read, an agent for the American Tract Society, viewed the outbreak of the Civil War as evidence that God's plan for history was moving toward its conclusion. In an 1861 publication, *The Coming Crisis of the World, or the Great Battle and the Golden Age,* he predicted that the millennium was close at hand. A Methodist minister in Brooklyn, L. S. Weed, took stock of contemporary events throughout the world, including "the rage of civil conflict and the boom of cannon on our shores," and concluded on the basis of Revelation 12 that the Confederacy would be defeated and eventually the gospel prevail in all nations, followed by the millennium. Both Read and Weed were optimists, but in their schemes the millennium was to arrive only after immense suffering and bloodshed (Moorhead 1978, 57–59).

Perhaps the most unusual expression of apocalyptic in the period was the revivalistic movement among Native Americans known as the Ghost Dance. Beginning first among the Northern Paiute Indians in Nevada in the 1870s, this movement grew out of the distress experienced by Native Americans. It promised renewal of the earth, return of the dead, and restoration of tribal life. In 1890 Wovoka—Jack Wilson—received a vision promising reunion with the dead if the Indians followed his counsels and performed the dance. The movement spread rapidly among Plains Indians, who came to regard Wovoka as a Messiah. The United States army interpreted this religious movement as a call to insurrection and moved against the Indians with military force, resulting in the massacre at Wounded Knee in December 1890. This catastrophe brought an end to enthusiasm for this messianic revival. The apocalyptic themes in the Ghost Dance movement reflect the impact of Christian missionaries on the natives.

The list of self-proclaimed prophets and charismatic leaders who engaged in apocalyptic speculation and founded communities in this period is almost endless. Thomas Lake Harris (1823–1906), the Spiritualist founder of Mountain Cove in Virginia and later of the Brotherhood of the New Life in New York and Fountain Grove in California; Peter Armstrong (1800–1892), an ex-Millerite who established Celesta in Pennsylvania; William W. Davies (1833–1906), a convert to the Morrisite sect of Mormonism who eventually founded the Kingdom of Heaven in Washington state; and Cyrus Read Teed (1839–1908), founder of the Koreshan Unity, located first in Chicago and later in Florida—these examples document the geographical distribution of such communities. Almost all such groups had difficulty surviving after the death of the founder.

One denomination with a distinctive interpretation of the Apocalypse that did survive following the death of its founder, Mary Baker Eddy (1821–1910), was Christian Science. Eddy's overcoming of early persistent ill health and personal misfortunes gave rise to metaphysical views that became the basis for a system of religious thought and an approach to healing. Her struggles led to the publication of *Science and Health* (1875), the textbook and foundation for a new church, the Church of Christ, Scientist. Eddy's interpretation of the Bible included a spiritual exposition of the book of Revelation in which she identified the "serpent" of Rev. 12:9 with the belief that the material world is real—a notion she declared "pure delusion" destroyed by Christ, or Truth. Her approach to spiritual healing based on a monistic understanding of reality placed Christian Scientists outside the circles of conventional science and medicine.

One group, the Shakers, whose greatest numerical expansion was in the 1840s, began a steady decline in membership and a geographical retreat following the Civil War. Economic success brought accommodation to the world. Many Shakers adopted a liberal religious outlook and joined other reformers supporting women's rights, vegetarianism, temperance, and the peace movement. The most prominent spokesperson for the community in this period was Frederick W. Evans (1808–1893), English by birth, who served as an elder for fifty-seven years. Despite his liberal social program, the closing words of his *Autobiography of a Shaker, and Revelation of the Apocalypse* (1869) sounded a traditional note concerning Ann Lee: "Yet, glory be to our Eternal Father and Mother,—the *Most* High God,—the *female Messiah has come,* in the 'still small voice' of *Shakerism . . .* " (pp. 147–48).

By contrast with the Shakers, the Latter-day Saints expanded rapidly during this period. The schisms they experienced in the 1840s following the murder of Joseph Smith produced several short-term communities, including the Kingdom of St. James on Beaver Island in Lake Michigan comprised of the followers of James Strang (1813–1856), and one continuing denomination, the Reorganized Church of Jesus Christ of Latter Day Saints, headed by the lineal descendants of Joseph Smith and headquartered eventually in Independence, Missouri. The bulk of the Latter-day Saints, however, joined Brigham Young (1801–1877) and fled the scene of persecution in Nauvoo to the western wilderness near the Great Salt Lake. There they reestablished Zion and laid the foundation for institutional expansion into a worldwide religious community. The Mormons dominated the economic, political, and religious life of the intermountain region; they prospered despite the opposition provoked by the practice of plural marriage and federal efforts to suppress it. Eventually those pressures forced capitulation by the Mormons: in 1890 the president of the church, Wilford Woodruff, issued a manifesto directing Latter-day Saints to give up the practice of plural marriage. That accommodation made statehood possible for Utah and represented a step toward the mainstream.

The most successful new apocalyptic group to arise during this second period came from the efforts of Charles Taze Russell (1852–1916), a Congregationalist layman in Allegheny, Pennsylvania, who established study groups, which he organized as the International Bible Students' Association in 1872. His study of the Bible focused on the prophetic sections. Russell adopted a radical adventist position, maintaining that the millennial dawn already had occurred in 1874 and that the end would be in 1914. But, according to his interpretation, Christ had not returned to earth at the former date; rather his return had been spiritual. Russell drew sharp lines between the forces allied with Christ and those allied with Satan. Among the latter he lumped the churches, governments of the world, and commercial institutions. Russell's most celebrated statement, "Millions now living will never die," underscored his view of the nearness of the end. He developed distinctive ideas concerning the godhead, distinguishing sharply between Jehovah and Jesus Christ. He rejected the traditional notion of hell, substituting a doctrine of annihilation followed by a re-creation and then a period of probation, after which extermination for those refusing the gospel. By the close of the century Russell had attracted thirty thousand members to this apocalyptic community.

In September 1893 representatives of the mainstream Protestant denominations in America, as well as Roman Catholic and Jewish spokespersons, and several delegates from abroad representing Asian religions, assembled in Chicago for the World's Parliament of Religions. Held in conjunction with the Columbian Exposition, this gathering was hailed as a pioneering event, providing an occasion for religious exchange. The tone of the meeting was undeniably liberal and Protestant. Part of its agenda was justification for Christian missionary efforts. This parliament, celebrated as "the morning star of the 20th century," embodied an alternative vision of the millennium to that held by most of the outsider groups (Barrows 1893, 1:74). The representatives were optimistic about a future ideal society in which religious conversation among diverse groups would be civil and enlightening. The World's Parliament of Religions is significant in another way, however, because most of the groups discussed above were absent from the assembly, uninvited and unwelcome. Therein lies further evidence of their continuing outsiderhood near the turn of the century.

☞ APOCALYPTIC PROPHETS AND ALTERNATIVE
COMMUNITIES IN THE FIRST HALF
OF THE TWENTIETH CENTURY _____

The beginning of the third period was marked by the United States' entry into the Spanish American War in 1898 and by the turn of the century itself. Conflict and change continued with ethnic and economic turmoil at home and the First World War abroad. The same decades witnessed the migration of millions of African Americans from the South to northern cities. In the aftermath of the World War old hatreds reared their heads again: the Ku Klux Klan revived, and nativists secured the passage of anti-immigration legislation in 1924. Prohibition and speakeasies, radios and automobiles, flappers and Fundamentalists followed; and then the Depression. Roman Catholics and Jews appeared on the religious landscape in greater numbers than ever before, creating with Protestants what later observers described as the triple melting pot. The period ended in warfare, too, as the Nazi menace in Europe and the Japanese attack on Pearl Harbor brought Americans together.

This period produced still more prophets and apocalyptic communities. Frank Weston Sandford (1862–1948), a Baptist minister from Maine interested in biblical prophecy, began receiving visions dealing with apocalyptic topics. He resigned his pulpit and in 1895 opened the Holy Ghost and Us Bible School in Durham, Maine. The next year he began building the Shiloh community. Sandford believed that he had been chosen as an Elijah to prepare the world for Christ's second coming, and Shiloh was to be the center of his activities. He made extreme demands on his followers as they gave of their time and resources to build the community. Often they had little to eat, and sickness took its toll. Sandford forbade conventional medical assistance because he believed in faith healing. These circumstances led to charges of manslaughter and child abuse. In 1905, directed by a vision, he sailed for Palestine, leaving behind followers at Shiloh, and hoping to convert others on the trip around the world. For a time he established a small community in Jerusalem, where he expected the center of end-time events to occur. On his return in 1909, he was arrested and charged with responsibility for the death of one of his followers on shipboard, for which he was convicted and sentenced to federal prison. Several years later, shortly after his parole, the colony at Shiloh disbanded.

Another prophetic figure who emerged during this period was Benjamin Purnell (1861–1927), a native of Kentucky who itinerated as a preacher in the Midwest before joining a sect known as the New House of Israel in 1892. When that group broke up, he announced his own messianic mission. In 1903 Purnell relocated in Benton Harbor, Michigan, and founded a celibate community called the House of David, which, he declared, was to be the location of the "gathering in." He took the name King Benjamin and called his wife Queen Mary. Purnell predicted that the millennium would begin in 1905. The sect attracted followers from as far away as Australia and managed to develop a successful economic base, including a baseball team that attracted attention because all the men wore long beards. The colony, and Purnell in particular, evoked negative criticism when rumors of unusual sexual activities surfaced in conflict with a public commitment to celibacy. Lawsuits were brought against Purnell for seduction and fraud, but he died in hiding before the conclusion of the proceedings. His wife subsequently defected and founded the rival City of David Community.

Far more significant was the emergence after the turn of the century of Pentecostalism, a new family of outsider religious groups. Derived in great part from Holiness churches, this movement reflected apocalyptic ideas widely disseminated in those assemblies. For example, the Niagara Bible and Prophecy Conferences in the closing decades of the nineteenth century had spread notions of dispensational millennialism through Holiness ranks, accompanied by doctrines defining a Rapture of the saints and a time of great tribulation preceding Christ's return and the millennium. Much of this millennial tradition continued in Pentecostalism, but the definitive feature of modern Pentecostalism was the notion that the spiritual experiences of the early Christians are repeatable in every age. Therefore the gifts of the Spirit described in the New Testament (e.g., speaking in tongues, healing, miracles, prophecy, etc.) are the evidences of true Christianity. Pentecostals regarded the restoration of these charismatic gifts as a necessary precondition of Christ's return. This movement spawned scores of new denominations, several very large, many very small; it splintered repeatedly, reflecting theological, racial, class, and regional differences.

Among the Pentecostal denominations formed after the beginning of the century were the Church of God (Cleveland), the Assemblies of God, the Pentecostal Assemblies of the World, the United Pentecostal Church, and the International Church of the Foursquare Gospel. The last of these developed from the ministry of Aimee Semple McPherson (1890–1944), wife of a missionary to China who, after his death, herself became a highly successful itinerant evangelist. She preached with great flare and an entertaining style. McPherson eventually established a ministry in Los Angeles and built a large church—the Angelus Temple—in 1923, which became the center of her operations. Her ministry featured the "foursquare gospel" of Christ as Savior, Healer, Baptizer, and Coming King. With regard to the last of these, she called on her hearers to prepare for the coming of Christ. The words of Rev. 22:17 were on the masthead of her publication, *The Bridal Call*. In it she expressed a sense of urgency at the shortness of the time remaining before Christ's return. McPherson gained notoriety in 1926 when she was allegedly kidnapped. Subsequent disclosures suggest that she may have hidden out with a lover. Perhaps the most colorful figure ever in this tradition, she died of an overdose of pills.

The migration of African Americans to the northern cities set the stage for the development of several outsider groups comprised largely or exclusively of blacks. One of these formed around George Baker (ca. 1877–1965), a native of Maryland and former itinerant preacher. By 1919 he was located on Long Island, where he attracted attention by serving banquets to his followers and assisting them with finding employment. He took the name Major Jealous Divine and was known widely as Reverend Divine and also as Father Divine. During the next decade the number of persons—both black and white—taking part in his banquets, worship services, and other functions increased dramatically, and then the Depression came. In 1932 Divine was arrested and convicted for maintaining a public nuisance, jailed for a short period, and then released. The judge who sentenced him died shortly after the sentencing, and Divine's reputation expanded. Father Divine claimed that he was God come to the earth to bring righteousness, justice, and peace to all. He declared that he was the fulfillment of the prophecies in the book of Revelation, and that the new day had dawned. Divine provided for the needs of his followers; in turn, they gave him their love and possessions. He demanded that they be celibate, honest, and hard-working. The Peace Mission Movement called its houses of prayer "heavens," and Divine's followers were "angels." He forbade distinctions on the basis of race or color of skin. His message was one of optimism and hope. This movement spread across the nation during the Depression with centers located in most major cities. Changing times in the 1940s resulted in a loss of membership and precipitate decline.

A far different apocalyptic message emanated from Wallace D. Fard (d. 1934?), a mysterious peddler of silk, who appeared in the black ghettos of Detroit in the 1930s, announcing that he had been sent from Mecca to wake up the Lost Nation of Islam. Fard's message echoed themes that Noble Drew Ali (1886–1929), founder of the Moorish Science Temple in Newark, New Jersey, had sounded earlier, namely, that salvation for African Americans lay in self-knowledge, and that Islam—not Christianity—was the true religion of blacks. Fard organized a Temple of Islam and a number of auxiliary groups before he disappeared in 1934. His successor, a black from Georgia named Elijah Poole (1897–1975), whom Fard renamed Elijah Muhammad, took control of the young movement. Elijah Muhammad declared Fard the incarnation of Allah and himself the last messenger of Allah. This community, the Nation of Islam, known widely as the Black Muslims, rested on a peculiar view of the races and their respective histories. Blacks were the original superior race, and whites were created by a mad scientist named Yakub, who bred all good out of them, creating a devil race. For six thousand years Allah permitted whites to dominate the world, but that period was about to end with the massive destruction of white society. Then blacks could assert their superiority and rule again. In the meantime, "so-called Negroes" were to separate from white society and follow Islam instead of Christianity, which has always been a religion of oppression. Elijah Muhammad's social program called for economic independence and non-participation in government and politics. Black Muslims were to avoid drugs and alcohol, develop strong family units based on fidelity between spouses, and pursue education, health, and financial stability. The Nation of Islam's apocalyptic views included both the impending destruction of white society and ultimate vindication for blacks.

Some communities founded in earlier periods continued their steady growth. The Seventh-day Adventists' leader, Ellen White, spent her last years, after returning from travels throughout Europe and Australia, lecturing, writing, and participating in the governance of the community. She emphasized evangelism and the fulfillment of Christ's commission to go into all the world with the gospel. The Seventh-day Adventists used every means at their disposal to accomplish that goal, including the press and the new medium of radio. The *Voice of Prophecy,* for instance, carried the church's message throughout the United States. The First World War produced a spate of apocalyptic declarations in Adventist publications—*Signs of the Times, Signs of the Times Magazine,* and *Watchman Magazine*—in which special attention was given to Turkey's role in the conflict, a country linked with the "king of the north" in Daniel 11. Some Adventists speculated that the war might be a step toward Armageddon, but other voices cautioned against specific prophetic claims. The war posed another problem for members of the church, which in the nineteenth century had associated the "beast with two horns like a lamb" (Revelation 13) with the United States government and a coalition of Roman Catholics and politicians intent on destroying churches through Sabbatarian legislation. The Adventists were unwilling to enter the war as combatants even though large numbers did serve as cooperating noncombatants. On the doctrinal level, the Seventh-day Adventists continued to espouse certain apocalyptic views. For instance, in 1941 when the General Conference adopted a revised and expanded statement of beliefs it included propositions dealing with the Bible as the inspired word of God, the imminent second coming of Christ as king, and Christ's ministry in the heavenly sanctuary. Yet the church was slowly accommodating to the American scene.

Similar growth, expansion, and accommodation occurred among the Latter-day Saints during this period. After the Woodruff Manifesto, the Mormons set out to improve their public image. Despite the fact that America occupied a special place in Mormon theology, the Latter-day Saints were forced to spend time defending themselves against charges that they were un-American. (For example, the Mormons could not be true patriots because they were waiting for the kingdom of God in which they were to play a special role.) To counter this attack, leaders stated forthrightly that expectation of the millennium did not compromise Mormon allegiance to the United States. Furthermore, they declared, they had no way of knowing when the millennium would begin. Other changes affecting the doctrine of the millennium were evident, too, including a general deemphasis of the issue, avoidance of questions regarding its imminence, and great caution in suggesting any connection with politics. During this period the idea that the Latter-day Saints ought to gather in Zion, that is, in Utah, also changed; Zion became wherever the Saints gathered. Another way the community moved into the mainstream was through its participation in the First World War—LDS soldiers in the trenches, chaplains serving their needs, and strong support on the home front. At least one development moved in the opposite direction: the Word of Wisdom, a revelation given to Joseph Smith prohibiting the drinking of alcohol, coffee, tea, etc., became an increasingly important marker separating Mormons and Gentiles (*Doctrine and Covenants,* sect. 89).

By contrast with the expansion of the Seventh-day Adventists and Mormons, at the start of the twentieth century the Shakers were a shadow of their former self, having declined to eight hundred members most of whom were aging. Their villages were closing rapidly, and the distinctive testimony of the community was muted. The Shakers were on their way to becoming American artifacts. When the headquarters at Mount Lebanon, New York, closed in 1947, only three small villages remained. The notion of the "millennial church" that once informed their existence now seemed remote.

The tradition begun by Charles Taze Russell continued to expand during this period. The community changed its name to Zion's Watch Tower Tract Society and in 1909 moved the headquarters of the organization to Brooklyn, New York. Russell was a tireless worker on behalf on his apocalyptic message—a message that predicted Jehovah's defeat of Satan's forces at the battle of Armageddon. He identified 1914 as the critical date. One means of spreading his views was the publication series entitled *Studies in the Scriptures* (1886–1917), which was distributed in millions of copies. The onset of the First World War seemed to confirm his apocalyptic scenario. Russell, whose followers regarded him as "the faithful servant" of Matt. 24:45, died during the conflict. Following his death many of his followers joined Joseph Franklin Rutherford (1869–1942), a disciple of Russell who had entered the organization in 1906. For the next twenty-five years Rutherford worked to bring organizational coherency and discipline to the movement. During the war he and others refused to participate, and as a result Rutherford spent time in federal prison. Under his leadership the organization expanded and solidified; in 1931 it officially became the Jehovah's Witnesses. Rutherford, who regarded 1914 as the start of the millennium, never lost sight of the movement's apocalyptic expectations. He built a special mansion in San Diego, where Abraham and the prophets might dwell during the millennium.

The Depression produced economic and social chaos, fueling fears of impending disaster. The threat of Hitler and the Nazis in Europe as well as Japanese expansion throughout the Pacific Ocean made apocalyptic scenarios seem even closer. Then the United States dropped atomic bombs on Hiroshima and Nagasaki. Doomsday became a potential reality giving pause to all, whether apocalyptically minded or not; now everyone was forced to ponder the threat of nuclear destruction.

☞ APOCALYPTICISM ON THE EDGE
IN THE RECENT PAST _____

The second half of the twentieth century began under the shadow of the mushroom cloud with the world divided between East and West. Armed confrontations beginning with the Korean War followed as the nuclear powers faced off against each other. Anxiety never seemed far away, yet the postwar boom produced prosperity, suburbs, cultural change, and religious revival. The nation added "under God" to the Pledge of Allegiance in 1954 and adopted "In God We Trust" as the "official" motto in 1956—hedges perhaps against a nuclear disaster—but life went on in increasingly secular ways. A series of blows to the body politic followed—the

Vietnam War, the civil rights movement, Watergate. Alternatives embodied in the youth culture, the drug culture, and Eastern cultures seemed to undermine traditional values, and an inevitable conservative swing occurred in politics, culture, and religion. As the century wore on fears once attached to communism and nuclear war transferred to AIDS, environmental disasters, and terrorism. But side by side with these were new prospects symbolized by computers, the Mars probe, and laser surgery. Much had changed in two hundred and twenty-five years, and yet little had changed.

The same was true in the history of apocalypticism. Familiar patterns continued even though by the end of the twentieth century the religious situation in America was more complex than ever before, both because of the influx of the world's religious traditions and because of changing value systems. Some outsider groups continued to accommodate to the world around them, and others retained their distinctive apocalyptic markers.

The Mormons have been the most successful group, reaching nine million members worldwide by the end of the century, half of whom are in the United States. No longer content to manifest the presence of Zion only in the intermountain area, they have expanded visibly throughout the United States and the world, marking their presence with new temples, including one in Washington, D.C. Their close identification with American culture is evident in their ardent support of capitalism, the defense industry, and family values. At least one residual, however, remains from the earlier apocalyptic mind-set. Mormons are responsible for maintaining a year's supply of food and clothing in the event of catastrophic disaster. Yet fear is no longer the characteristic emotion of the Latter-day Saints; nor is "the latter day" the most prominent theme of the community. Zion has been built successfully, and the Mormon Tabernacle Choir is "America's choir." The fate of Mormonism and the future of America are now inescapably linked.

The Seventh-day Adventists still conduct seminars on the imminence of the second coming, and they continue to support missionary work, hospitals, and educational institutions. But the rationale for much of this activity has lost its sectarian edge. In the United States there are more than eight hundred thousand Adventists today; church membership abroad has grown at an even faster rate. In an effort to retain a notion of being God's remnant selected for a special role at the close of history, the Adventists needed an explanation for the delay of the end. In 1966 the General Conference president called for reformation and for the church to fulfill its responsibility in spreading the word throughout the world—then Christ will come again. In 1980 the Adventists affirmed, "The second coming of Christ is the blessed hope of the church, the grand climax of the gospel. The Saviour's coming will be literal, personal, visible, and worldwide. . . . The time of that event has not been revealed, and we are therefore exhorted to be ready at all times" (Land 1986, 249).

The Jehovah's Witnesses have maintained an apocalyptic mentality throughout the twentieth century. They stand ready to fight with Jehovah against the forces of Satan, but they have not been willing to participate in America's wars. The Witnesses set themselves apart from other Americans by several other practices, too, including their unwillingness to salute the flag, to observe religious holidays such as Christmas and Easter, or to accept blood transfusions. They invest large amounts of time in witnessing and distributing literature, such as *Awake* and *The Watchtower,* and in Bible study, all focusing on apocalyptic themes. Their activities bring public disrepute as well as harassment and persecution, which they accept as necessary marks of true witnesses. More than any other major group, they have retained the impulse to set dates.

For instance, they "marked" several years for special attention, including 1975. The Witnesses, numbering more than half a million in that year in the United States and some two million worldwide, still live expecting the end.

Pentecostals in their denominational diversity have retained an affinity for the apocalyptic mind-set. That outlook finds expression in their critique of American society and their determination to draw sharp boundaries by prescribing clothing and hairstyles and proscribing personal ornamentation and popular entertainment, and by relying on practices such as faith healing. Yet the forces of accommodation also have been felt in the Pentecostal churches. The sense of outsiderhood has been reduced by economic upward mobility and by the fact that a "pentecostal" outlook has been carried into the mainstream churches by the charismatic movement in the 1960s. The career of Oral Roberts (b. 1918) is striking evidence of this mainstreaming. He has gone from tent revivalist and faith healer to television preacher and entrepreneur, to founder of a university and hospital complex, to ordained minister in the United Methodist Church. His apocalyptic comments have a very different ring today than when he launched his independent ministry in 1947.

The independent ministries arising from the Holiness/Pentecostal lineage reflect the distinctive apocalyptic visions of their founders. Such was the case with William Branham (1909–1965), an independent healer and evangelist whose center of operations was Jeffersonville, Indiana. Following the Second World War, he launched a healing ministry based on his claim of an angelic commission. He achieved remarkable success, rivaling Oral Roberts in reputation. He did not, however, follow Roberts's path of accommodation, and as a result his ministry declined. He claimed to be an end-time prophet of God. Following his death, his followers elevated him and declared his sermons to be the message of God to the last generation.

Many independent ministries have made effective use of newly emerging media—first radio, and then television. Their congregations are often "virtual congregations" comprised of audiences who tune in across the airwaves or on television. The expansion of the electronic church has increased the capacity to create such communities of contributors. One example that focuses almost exclusively on apocalyptic themes is the ministry of Jack Van Impe (b. 1931), who for several decades has used the media to warn of the approaching end. His programs and publications, including *Perhaps Today,* feature contemporary "signs of the times." He writes, "I have always preached imminence, that Jesus could come at any moment, and I believe we are in the windup now" (May/June 1993: 16). Van Impe's success and the presence of scores of others testify to the continuing resonance of an apocalyptic gospel in the late twentieth century.

One group that reversed its direction twice in the recent past is the Nation of Islam, which rose to prominence in the early 1960s when Malcolm X (1925–1965) was a public spokesperson for the movement. In that period membership reached nearly one hundred thousand African Americans. Following Elijah Muhammad's death in 1975, his son Wallace D. Muhammad (b. 1933) assumed leadership. Almost immediately he set in motion a process of Islamization, transforming the community religiously and politically. One effect of these changes was the spiritualization of the apocalypse. Rather than predicting massive destruction, Wallace Muhammad described future spiritual possibilities. He also ended the demonization of the white race as he moved the Nation of Islam toward orthodox Islam. Organizational changes followed as the movement blended into the American religious scene. One powerful minister in the movement, Louis Farrakhan (b. 1933), a native of the West Indies, who had replaced Malcolm X at the Harlem Temple, resisted these changes. By 1977 he and other leaders set out to reestablish the Nation of Islam in accord with Elijah Muhammad's views. In 1985 he received a vision confirming his role in this resurrection process. He was told to return to Elijah's original teachings and to expect a final great battle against evil. His newspaper, *Final Call,* reasserted the original apocalyptic message of the Nation of Islam. Farrakhan has received harsh criticism for his public pronouncements against Jews and for his entrance into the world of national politics with the Million Man March in 1995.

One group that came from the East but embodies Western apocalyptic ideas is the Unification Church founded in Korea by Sun Myung Moon (b. 1920). Moon, born in North Korea, experienced a vision in 1936 in which Jesus told him to restore the kingdom of God on earth. Subsequent visions became the basis for his distinctive theological ideas, later published as *Divine Principle* (1966). (During the Korean War, he spent time in a communist labor camp in North Korea.) According to Moon, the original plan of salvation called for creation of a God-centered family. Jesus was unable to complete the task of restoring the world to its pre-Fall situation because he was murdered before marrying. Using the Bible, Moon concluded that a second Messiah would be born in Korea between 1917 and 1930. Unificationists regard Reverend Moon as that Messiah, and they are confident that through his marriage in 1960 he has established the foundation for the kingdom on earth. The second Messiah is to accomplish salvation and also unite all religions. The final struggle between good and evil is now under way; it is a struggle between "godism" and "atheistic communism." At one point Moon identified 1967 as significant, and then later 1977. As each of these dates passed, adjustments were made in apocalyptic expectations. Moon, who came to the United States in the 1970s, supports conservative political causes, engages in numerous successful business ventures, and conducts mass weddings for his followers. The Unification Church has experienced sustained opposition over the past twenty-five years. In 1982 Moon was convicted of tax evasion and served time in prison.

The 1960s and 1970s witnessed the rise of a host of outsider groups that mixed Western and Eastern religious beliefs and practices with apocalypticism. The Holy Order of MANS, founded by Earl Blighton (d. 1974) in California, is one example of a syncretistic new religious movement. Some groups combined such disparate notions as devotion to Krishna with an end to the present age (International Society for Krishna Consciousness), or ancient meditation techniques with a new age of material well-being on earth (Transcendental Meditation). Others focused attention on the world of outer space and spoke of extraterrestrial beings and Unidentified Flying Objects as agents of either catastrophic destruction or redemption from such a disaster. Those beliefs lay behind the collective suicide in 1997 of thirty-nine members of Heaven's Gate in San Diego, California, the followers of Marshall Applewhite. Still others keep their attention on the earth first, warning of ecological disasters if more responsible stewardship of the environment is not made a top priority.

One outsider group that rose from the heartland of America, migrated to the west coast, and eventually left the United States was the Peoples Temple, founded by James Warren Jones (1931–1978), a native of Indiana. Jones served as pastor of a church he established in Indianapolis while attending college. In 1963 he named his congregation the People's Temple Full Gospel Church. Jones, an ordained Disciples of Christ minister, was active in interracial religious activities and social causes. In 1965 he warned his congregation of impending nuclear war and the next year relocated with a portion of his followers to California. He recruited new members in both San Francisco and Los Angeles. He also gained a reputation for political activism increasingly informed by Marxist ideology, for bold preaching, and for faith healing. When rumors surfaced linking Jones with sexual improprieties, he made plans to move again, this time to Guyana, South America, where he held a lease on some land. In 1977 he led the bulk of his followers to Guyana, described by him as the promised land, where they established an agricultural colony in the jungle—Jonestown. There Jones exercised dictatorial control over his followers' lives, activities, and financial resources. Jonestown adopted socialist principles and Jones's brand of apocalyptic religion. He warned of threats from the United States government and from concerned relatives, who wanted to remove family members from the commune. Jones became ill and increasingly demonic in his leadership. The experiment in the jungle was moving toward failure as his paranoia mounted. A visit by Congressman Leo J. Ryan brought Jonestown to a screaming end. After Ryan and members of his entourage were murdered, on the night of November 18, 1978, more than nine hundred members of the Peoples Temple, including Jones, committed mass suicide/murder—literal fulfillment of Jones's apocalyptic predictions.

One final apocalyptic example is the community initially led by a Bulgarian immigrant, Victor Houteff (d. 1955), who split from the Seventh-day Adventists. After being disfellow-shipped, Houteff formed his own church patterned after the Adventists, but also with distinctive beliefs including the notion that he was a divine messenger chosen to interpret the seven seals in the book of Revelation and to gather the 144,000 in advance of the second coming. In 1935 he established an agricultural community in Waco, Texas, called Mt. Carmel. In 1942 the group took the name of Davidian Seventh-day Adventists based on their expectation that a faithful remnant would found a kingdom of David in Palestine. Following Houteff's death, his wife Florence led the community and predicted that in 1959 the kingdom would begin on earth. The failure of that prophecy produced a major defection. Among the remnant, Benjamin Roden (d. 1978) emerged as a new leader, proclaiming that the kingdom would begin when the faithful fulfilled God's law. The Davidians established a small commune in Israel in 1958. After Roden's death, his wife Lois took over leadership in 1978, but her son contested that succession.

This was the scene in Waco when Vernon Howell (1959–1993) arrived and became a competitor to Roden's son. Howell assumed the role of teacher, married the daughter of a respected member, and consolidated his position in the community. The conflict developed into an armed standoff, followed by legal maneuvering and a shootout. By 1987 Howell was in control of the community. Residents at Mt. Carmel lived in expectation of Christ's imminent return. Prohibitions governed food, drink, clothing, entertainment, and other aspects of life. Howell changed his named to David Koresh in 1990, by which he laid claim to messianic aspirations and biblical ancestry. He set out to interpret the seven seals prior to the close of the age. He also claimed a special responsibility to raise up children by taking women in the community as wives. Daily Bible study was a principal activity at the compound. In 1993 the Branch Davidians, as they were called, came into conflict with federal authorities over possession of firearms. A raid on 28 February by the Bureau of Alcohol, Tobacco, and Firearms resulted in the death of four agents and six members of the community. A fifty-one day armed confrontation followed, which ended when government agents launched a gas attack on the compound. Fire broke out, and more than eighty members, including Koresh, died in the resulting inferno.

☞ CONCLUDING OBSERVATIONS

Several closing observations are in order concerning apocalypticism among outsider religious groups in the United States. Outsiderhood is a relative status and, for many religious groups in America, a passing state. There is no apparent correlation between particular apocalyptic beliefs and the longevity of the communities holding those views. Most alternative communities, regardless of their millennial outlook, pass from the scene rather quickly, often after the founding charismatic leader is no longer present. Others, again regardless of their millennial outlook, responding to pressures to relinquish religious ideas or practices that set them apart, modify their dissenting stance and move from the margin into the mainstream.

One usual development among groups outside the mainstream is gradual reduction in the sense of apocalyptic urgency and an increasingly comfortable sense of belonging in the world. Some describe this as a shift from an otherworldly to a this-worldly orientation. Others explain the change as evolution from a pre- to a postmillennial outlook. But more to the point is the fact that millennial rhetoric remains a favorite form of discourse despite the change in perspective. Apocalyptic language is exceedingly plastic; it can be employed both literally and metaphorically. Doctrinal formulas often continue in use long after they have ceased reflecting real convictions.

The failure of apocalyptic predictions rarely results in the complete disintegration of outsider groups or the discrediting of their beliefs. On the contrary, when prophecies fail there seems to be renewed determination to discover a way to salvage those beliefs. Apocalyptic speculation knows no creative limits. Visions and revelations provide possibilities for reinterpretation of prophetic claims. The historical record demonstrates that the most likely way for an outsider community to fulfill its apocalyptic vision is for them to take things into their own hands—witness the fate of Nat Turner's band, Jim Jones's followers, the Branch Davidians, and the members of Heaven's Gate.

Apocalyptic speculation among groups outside the religious mainstream is not an abstract activity. Convictions regarding such matters have motivated prophets and visionaries to establish societies in order that their principles can be embodied in practice. Behavior follows belief, and community provides the best forum for achieving apocalyptic objectives. Social experimentation has been a prominent mark of outsider apocalyptic groups in America. Radical economic proposals, unconventional sexual practices, innovative family arrangements, alternative approaches to healing, resistance or non-cooperation with governmental agencies—these and other practices have distinguished outsiders.

Outsider groups are by definition critical of mainstream values. Apocalypticism has been a powerful weapon in their hands. It will most likely remain so in the future with the result that such groups will continue to experience hardship and persecution. Those who use this armament cannot expect to be welcomed, for prophets still are not accepted in their own lands.

There is no reason to suggest that America will cease producing or attracting new prophets and new apocalyptic movements. The years surrounding the turn of the new millennium will, no doubt, produce a flurry of such activity. Witness the outsider groups already presenting themselves on the Internet. It is likely that the dynamics observed in this essay will continue in the years ahead. Biblical texts will attract attention; visions will guide prophetic figures; the apocalyptic calendar will evoke speculation; the forces of good and evil will divide; communities will rise and fall; and the apocalypse probably still will not come.

☞ BIBLIOGRAPHY

Anderson, Robert Mapes. 1979. *Vision of the Disinherited: The Making of American Pentecostalism.* New York: Oxford University Press. A valuable historical account of the origins of Pentecostalism in the early decades of the twentieth century.

Arrington, Leonard J., and Davis Bitton. 1979. *The Mormon Experience: A History of the Latter-day Saints.* New York: Alfred A. Knopf. The most useful general history of the Mormons.

Barkun, Michael. 1986. *Crucible of the Millennium: The Burned-Over District of New York in the 1840s.* Syracuse: Syracuse University Press. An insightful examination of the leading millennial movements in this hotbed of religious ferment.

Barrows, John Henry. 1893. *The World's Parliament of Religions.*

Bloch, Ruth H. 1985. *Visionary Republic: Millennial Themes in American Thought, 1756–1800.* Cambridge: Cambridge University Press. A historical account of the role of millennial thinking in the age of the American Revolution.

Boyer, Paul. 1992. *When Time Shall Be No More: Prophecy Belief in Modern American Culture.* Cambridge, Mass.: Harvard University Press. A path-breaking study of the role of apocalyptic belief in the United States with special attention to popular culture and the period after World War II.

Chidester, David. 1988. *Salvation and Suicide: An Interpretation of Jim Jones, the Peoples Temple, and Jonestown.* Bloomington, Ind.: Indiana University Press. A probing analysis of the religious and cultural dimensions of the tragedy at Jonestown.

Davidson, James West. 1977. *The Logic of Millennial Thought: Eighteenth-Century New England.* New Haven: Yale University Press. A penetrating study of the impact of eschatology in eighteenth-century New England.

Fogarty, Robert S. 1980. *Dictionary of American Communal and Utopian History.* Westport, Conn.: Greenwood Press. An essential reference work for anyone wishing basic information on such communities in American history.

———. 1990. *All Things New: American Communes and Utopian Movements 1860–1914.* Chicago: University of Chicago Press. A careful examination of utopian experiments in the United States in a period which has received only modest attention from scholars.

Fuller, Robert C. 1995. *Naming the Antichrist: The History of an American Obsession.* New York: Oxford University Press. A popular history of the changing interpretations of the figure of the Antichrist in America.

Gardell, Mattias. 1996. *In the Name of Elijah Muhammad: Louis Farrakhan and the Nation of Islam.* Durham, N.C.: Duke University Press. A history of the Nation of Islam from its origins during the American Depression to the present, featuring the contemporary role of Louis Farrakhan.

Harrell, David Edwin, Jr. 1975. *All Things Are Possible: The Healing and Charismatic Revivals in Modern America.* Bloomington, Ind.: Indiana University Press. A historical study of independent Pentecostal revivalists after World War II.

Klaw, Spencer. 1993. *Without Sin: The Life and Death of the Oneida Community.* New York: Allen Lane. An examination of the rise and fall of John Humphrey Noyes's perfectionist experiment at Oneida.

Land, Gary, ed. 1986. *Adventism in America: A History.* Grand Rapids, Mich.: Eerdmans. A collection of useful historical essays focusing on the development of the Seventh-day Adventist movement.

Lucas, Phillip Charles. 1995. *The Odyssey of a New Religion: The Holy Order of MANS from New Age to*

Orthodoxy. Bloomington, Ind.: Indiana University Press. A study focusing on a contemporary example of a new religious movement.

Marini, Stephen A. 1982. *Radical Sects of Revolutionary New England.* Cambridge, Mass.: Harvard University Press. A probing historical study of the Shakers, Universalists, and Freewill Baptists in late-eighteenth- and early-nineteenth-century New England.

Miller, Timothy, ed. 1995. *America's Alternative Religions.* Albany, N.Y.: State University of New York Press. A valuable collection of essays spanning a wide range of diverse sects and cults present in America.

Miller, William. 1841. *Views of the Prophecies and Prophetic Chronology.* Boston: Joshua V. Himes.

Moore, R. Laurence. 1986. *Religious Outsiders and the Making of Americans.* New York: Oxford University Press. A thoughtful revisionist look at the role of religious outsiderhood in American history.

Moorhead, James H. 1978. *American Apocalypse: Yankee Protestants and the Civil War.* New Haven: Yale University Press.

Numbers, Ronald L., and Jonathan M. Butler, eds. 1987. *The Disappointed: Millerism and Millenarianism in the Nineteenth Century.* Bloomington, Ind.: Indiana University Press. An instructive collection of essays situating William Miller's movement in the larger framework of American religious history.

O'Leary, Stephen D. 1994. *Arguing the Apocalypse: A Theory of Millennial Rhetoric.* New York: Oxford University Press. A rhetorical explanation for the appeal of millennialism featuring the Millerite movement as a case study.

Penton, M. James. 1985. *Apocalypse Delayed: The Story of Jehovah's Witnesses.* Toronto: University of Toronto Press. A systematic overview of the history, doctrines, and organization of the Jehovah's Witnesses.

Rush, Benjamin. 1951. *Rush Letters: Letters of Benjamin Rush.* Edited by Lyman H. Butterfield. Philadelphia: American Philosophical Society.

Spann, Edward K. 1989. *Brotherly Tomorrows: Movements for a Cooperative Society in America 1820–1920.* New York: Columbia University Press. A study of the social idealism that drove efforts to create a cooperative society in America.

Stein, Stephen J. 1992. *The Shaker Experience in America: A History of the United Society of Believers.* New Haven, Conn.: Yale University Press. The most useful general history of the Shakers.

Tabor, James D., and Eugene V. Gallagher. 1995. *Why Waco? Cults and the Battle for Religious Freedom in America.* Berkeley, Calif.: University of California Press. A historical account and analysis of the tragedy at Mt. Carmel.

Underwood, Grant. 1993. *The Millenarian World of Early Mormonism.* Urbana, Ill.: University of Illinois Press. A helpful analysis of the implications of millennialism in the early period of Mormon history.

Watts, Jill. 1992. *God, Harlem U.S.A.: The Father Divine Story.* Berkeley, Calif.: University of California Press. An account of the life and career of Father Divine, featuring the formative religious influences on him.

Wisbey, Harold. 1964. *Frontier Prophetess: Jemima Wilkinson, the Publick Universal Friend.* Ithaca: Cornell University Press.

20

The Growth of Fundamentalist Apocalyptic in the United States

Paul Boyer
University of Wisconsin

"HE'S COMING SOON!" "the end is near!" close attention to the apocalyptic beliefs summed up in exhortations such as these can illuminate vast tracks of American religious history, and indeed of American politics and culture. From the beginnings of European settlement in North America through the end of the twentieth century, a supernaturalist worldview that finds the terminal events of human history foretold in the prophetic and apocalyptic portions of the Hebrew and Christian scriptures has profoundly shaped the national experience. But the apocalyptic worldview has never been contained within a single homogeneous belief system. Rather, throughout American history, apocalyptic belief has taken many different forms, attracted widely divergent groups of adherents, and undergirded a broad spectrum of social and political views.

Within this diversity, the strand that one might call "fundamentalist apocalyptic" has played a major role. This approach to the Bible's prophetic and apocalyptic passages has been characterized by a literalistic interpretative hermeneutic in which the key texts are viewed not as allegorical representations of spiritual realities, or as a record of apocalyptic expectations at the time the works were composed, but as a guide to God's plan for human history, verbally dictated and inerrant in every detail.

This approach has invited minute textual analysis, from which specific details of human history past and future can be extracted. Drawing on a wide range of seemingly disparate prophetic and apocalyptic passages written over a span of several centuries under vastly different historical conditions, a succession of ingenious interpreters and popularizers have pieced together detailed and more-or-less cohesive end-time scenarios as one would patiently assemble the pieces of a jigsaw puzzle until the full picture emerges.

Though many variants and disagreements about detail exist, as we shall see, the broad contours of one major strand of fundamentalist apocalypticism includes the following elements, each of which is documented by specific scriptural citations. According to this scenario, human history is rapidly nearing its climax, as contemporary events correspond ever more precisely to a series of "signs" of the last days foretold in the Bible. The increase of apostasy, wickedness, warfare, famine, and natural disasters in the present age will culminate in the seven-year Great Tribulation, when a demonic figure, the Antichrist, will rule the earth.

At the end of the Great Tribulation, Jesus Christ will return to earth with his saints as an avenging warrior-king to defeat the Antichrist in a final cosmic conflict, the Battle of Armageddon. Ruling from the restored Jewish Temple in Jerusalem, Christ will establish his thousand-year millennial kingdom on earth, imposing righteousness and justice on the whole world. Next will come a last judgment, at which every person who has ever lived will be forever consigned to heaven or hell. After one final abortive uprising, the Antichrist will be defeated forever and cast into the Lake of Fire. As the "new heaven and new earth" pictured at the close of the book of Revelation (the Apocalypse of John) replace the present cosmos, history gives way to eternity. Christ and the saints reign forever; the long human drama ends at last with righteousness triumphant.

One major strand of fundamentalist apocalyptic, premillennial dispensationalism, as we shall see, also encompasses the doctrine of the Rapture. This is the belief that just before the onset of the Great Tribulation, the church—Christ's true followers—will be spirited away from the earth to join Jesus Christ in the skies and then return with him to share in the triumph over the Antichrist at Armageddon and participate in the millennial kingdom.

Elements of this particular end-time scenario may be traced far back in the history of Christian apocalyptic interpretation. But in its fully articulated modern form, it arose in Great Britain in the early nineteenth century and emerged as a powerful force within American Protestantism in the late nineteenth and early twentieth centuries. Apocalyptic belief played a central role in the histories of several major Protestant denominations and sectarian movements. In the form called dispensational premillennialism, it figured prominently in the emergence of Fundamentalism as a distinct form of evangelical Protestantism.

Though the movement grew less visible and became more culturally marginalized after World War I, losing much of the intellectual standing it had once enjoyed, it remained vital at the popular level. In the Cold War and post–Cold War eras, fundamentalist apocalyptic belief influenced the worldview of millions of Americans and helped shape the climate of opinion on important public issues. As the century ends, all indications suggest that fundamentalist apocalyptic, though without much intellectual support in mainstream theological circles or cultural institutions, will remain influential among ordinary American believers of the evangelical or fundamentalist persuasions.

To approach a fuller understanding of this important and neglected facet of American religious history, this essay will first place fundamentalist apocalyptic in historical context, explore its emergence and development from the mid-nineteenth century through the era of two world wars, and finally examine its evolution and influence in the later decades of the twentieth century.

☞ BACKGROUND: THE VARIETIES
OF APOCALYPTICISM_____

Throughout Christian history, some religious leaders and textual interpreters adopted a literal-istic approach to the prophetic and apocalyptic texts of the Hebrew and Christian scriptures (the Old Testament and the New Testament, in the Christian Bible). The cryptic language, mys-terious imagery, and sometimes terrifying visions woven through the books of Daniel and Rev-elation (the principal complete apocalypses in the biblical canon) as well as apocalyptic sections found in Isaiah, Ezekiel, Mark, 1 and 2 Thessalonians, 1 Corinthians, 2 Peter, and other books of the Bible tested the ingenuity of pious expositors over the centuries.

Several broad interpretative strategies emerged. One approach, which became dominant within the Roman Catholic Church, views these texts as essentially spiritual in their meaning: they evoke the ongoing struggle between righteousness and evil in human history and within each individual heart, and they offer hope that righteousness will ultimately triumph. But the details of this consummation lie in God's hands, beyond human knowledge. This strand has been designated *amillennial* (nonmillennial), since it envisions a transcendent spiritual fulfill-ment of the apocalyptic texts, beyond history. Amillennialists foresee Christ's ultimate triumph outside the temporal realm, not in an actual earthly reign of one thousand years. After an inter-val of sometimes feverish end-time speculation among early Christians, this spiritualized hermeneutical approach to the apocalyptic texts was espoused by Origen (185?–254), Augus-tine (354–430), and other church fathers, and became the doctrine of the Roman Catholic Church. Within Protestantism, the Lutheran and Reformed churches remained generally amil-lennial in outlook.

But despite official disapproval, the literalistic approach to the apocalyptic texts never lost its appeal for religious mystics and ordinary Christians. Prophetic interpreters such as the Calabrian monk Joachim of Fiore (ca. 1135–1202) found in these texts not only an allegorical expression of spiritual truth but a key to actual events within history.

This literalistic interpretative approach, in turn, took various forms. Some expositors adopted a *historicist* hermeneutic, viewing the successive scenes and events described in the apocalypses of Daniel, Revelation, and other scriptural passages as a kind of mosaic of the entire span of human history viewed from a Christian perspective. Others, by contrast, embraced a *futurist* interpretative model, viewing the fulfillment of the apocalyptic texts as still lying ahead. For prophecy expositors of this persuasion, the apocalypses unfolded not the whole of human history but its final chapter.

As time went by, the futurist position, in turn, branched into two broad interpretative streams, sometimes designated *premillennial* and *postmillennial.* Premillennialists, who in recent times have espoused the end-time scenario summarized at the outset of this essay, despaired of the human role in achieving the blessed state of justice and righteousness foreseen in the Bible as the final stage of history. Indeed, premillennialists, citing the wickedness of Noah's day that led God to destroy most of humanity in a great flood, predicted not gradual betterment but increasing evil, conflict, and unbelief leading to a cataclysm of horrendous destruction. Only at the end of this downward spiral, they concluded, and entirely by supernat-ural means, would the divine new order be established on earth. The postmillennialist position, by contrast, which emerged in its modern form in the early eighteenth century, held that the establishment of Christ's earthly kingdom will come as the culmination of a long cycle of human progress and moral advance achieved through the prayerful efforts of Christian believers in the present age.

The interaction of these quite distinct and partially contradictory strands of futurist apocalyptic interpretation illuminates important aspects of Christian history and biblical hermeneutic. And, as historian Norman Cohn has made clear, apocalyptic exposition in the Middle Ages—as in our own day—was not the sole domain of monks, priests, and scholars. Wandering prophets and mystics preached their own version of apocalyptic truth across Europe, winning followers and sometimes suffering execution for their pains.

The swelling ranks of Europeans from many different religious traditions who colonized North America from the late sixteenth century through the era of the American Revolution were heirs of this long and multifaceted tradition of apocalyptic interpretation. In British North America, the apocalyptic scriptures were nowhere searched more assiduously than in Puritan New England. Among the early New England Puritan divines, one may find elements of both "postmillennial" and "premillennial" thought (occasionally even in the same individual). Some foresaw the establishment of Christ's kingdom as a direct outgrowth of the spiritual efforts of Christians in these New World outposts of the purified Protestant faith. Other ministers, however, particularly as the piety that had inspired the first settlers gave way to secular and "worldly" pursuits, adopted a more pessimistic "premillennial" view. Sadly contemplating the rising tide of wickedness, they foresaw a day when God would wreak terrible judgment upon a sinful, backsliding people.

The Great Awakening, the wave of religious enthusiasm that arose in New England in the 1730s and swept the colonies in the 1740s, revived and strengthened the more hopeful "postmillennial" variant of the apocalyptic vision. The revivalist and theologian Jonathan Edwards (1703–1758) foresaw the coming of Christ's kingdom—perhaps by the year 2000—through the intercessory prayer and unfailing religious exertions of the saints. As Edwards wrote in 1739, "the preaching of the gospel and the use of the ordinary means of grace" could be sufficient to usher in the millennium. Others caught up in the religious fervor of the time shared Edwards's hopeful view.

In somewhat secularized garb, this hopeful, activist reading of the apocalyptic scriptures carried over into the Revolutionary era and the early decades of the nineteenth century as the United States, having achieved political independence from Great Britain, set out to define itself as a nation. In the years between 1815 and the Civil War, a high-octane blend of millennial fervor and patriotic enthusiasm fueled a wave of reform effort in the new nation. Across the North, especially, middle-class Americans imbued with the spirit of evangelical Christianity plunged into a whirl of benevolent activity to reanimate the vision of the early New England Puritans and of Jonathan Edwards: to build on the American soil a society worthy of the exalted vision of the New Jerusalem found in the book of Revelation. Sunday schools, moral-uplift crusades, tract and Bible societies, temperance campaigns, Sabbatarian efforts, penitentiaries to turn malefactors into productive citizens, asylums for society's outcasts, struggles against slavery, and a host of other reform efforts gained energy from the impulse to construct a Christian nation—an impulse rooted in the apocalyptic vision of a redeemed social order arising within history, through human effort.

But even in these years of soaring reformist aspiration, the darker variant of apocalyptic interpretation made its presence felt. Those drawn to this tradition shared the longing for a righteous social order, but combined it with deep pessimism about the possibilities of achieving the Christian utopia by the instrumentalities of government, legislation, and reform effort. In these antebellum decades, a succession of millennial groups, from Shakers and Mormons to the followers of John Humphrey Noyes and other perfectionists, rejected the larger society as irredeemably wicked and depraved and withdrew into separatist communities where they believed the kingdom of God could most likely be achieved.

This separatist, otherworldly strand of apocalyptic thinking also underlay the Christian (Disciples of Christ) movement that emerged from the frontier revivals of the early nineteenth century. The movement's leader, Alexander Campbell (1788–1866), preached the imminent return of Jesus Christ in his sermons and in the pages of his aptly named journal, the *Millennial Harbinger*. The last days before the blessed event, Campbell wrote in 1831, would see "the most tremendous calamities and sudden disasters" coupled with the destruction of all earthly governments as well as the Roman Catholic Church "as preliminary to the commencement of the reign of a thousand years." Turn from wicked society and its vain endeavors, Campbell urged his followers when he was in this otherworldly frame of mind, and concentrate on things eternal.

This apocalyptic strand of end-time belief also underlay the upsurge of feverish end-time anticipation in the 1830s and early 1840s known as the Millerite movement. The Millerite phenomenon is particularly germane to the themes of this essay, since the fierce popular reaction against the Millerites' propensity for pinning the second coming to a specific date created a favorable climate for an alternative system of prophetic interpretation: dispensational premillennialism.

The Millerite movement began in the early 1830s with the preaching of William Miller (1782–1849), an earnest, self-taught Baptist biblical scholar and itinerant evangelist from the "burned over" district of western New York (so called because of the successive waves of religious enthusiasm that swept the region). Adopting a historicist approach to prophetic interpretation, Miller focused his attention especially on the book of Daniel, particularly Dan. 8:14, which states: "Unto two thousand and three hundred days; then shall the sanctuary be cleansed." Converting these 2,300 "days" to years (a common convention among Bible interpreters of prophecy), and starting from 458 B.C.E., when Artaxerxes I of Persia authorized the exiled Jewish priest Ezra to rebuild the Temple in Jerusalem, Miller concluded that Jesus Christ would return "about the year 1843."

Miller's preaching attracted growing numbers of followers. He did not rant or rave, but simply explained his interpretative system in a low-keyed schoolmasterish fashion. In a democratic and generally well-schooled society proud of its skills of literacy and numerology, Miller's complex and ingenious reading of the biblical texts, the product of his own unaided study, exerted a powerful appeal. Soon other Millerite exegetes elaborated the master's calculations to fix upon a precise date for the end: October 22, 1844. As the appointed day drew nearer, many thousands of converts flocked to the movement. The cause was advanced by great outdoor services conducted in big tents that could readily be moved from place to place; by mass-produced tracts and periodicals such as the *Midnight Cry* and *Signs of the Times;* and by colorful charts—replete with lions, bears, and dragons drawn from the rich apocalyptic imagery of the book of Daniel—illustrating Miller's interpretive system.

Though the Millerite movement collapsed overnight when the eagerly awaited day came and went, it remains crucially important in the history of fundamentalist apocalyptic belief in

America for a number of reasons. First of all, out of the ruins of the movement eventually emerged a new Protestant evangelical denomination, the Seventh-day Adventist Church. As we shall see, this group in the late nineteenth and through the twentieth century loomed large among the religious organizations most active in promulgating premillennial beliefs in America and throughout the world.

Beyond this direct organizational link with later prophecy-based religious movements, the Millerites helped set the tone of future premillennial thought through their profoundly negative view of human government and human institutions. In an age when some reformers were turning to government as an instrument for achieving a purified social order rooted in the biblical millennial vision, the Millerites focused not on human effort for betterment in the present age but on a supernatural apocalyptic event that would remove the saints from the earthly social order altogether. (In fact, Millerite behavior was not always consistent with the logic of their beliefs: some espoused antislavery and other reforms while they awaited the end.)

The Millerites also pioneered organizational and publicity techniques that would provide a model for later popularizers of apocalyptic belief. Operating largely outside the framework of Protestant denominationalism, they set up an alternative organization held together by the charisma of the movement's leaders, by the peripatetic open-air tent services that rallied the faithful and attracted new recruits, and by use of the latest techniques of mass communication—the new high-speed printing presses of the day—to produce their tracts, posters, charts, periodicals, and hymnals.

Finally, while the Millerite movement successfully employed a perennially appealing mode of literalistic, historically rooted apocalyptic interpretation, it also became the definitive cautionary example of the dangers of setting a date for the second coming. After 1844, other leaders and prophetic interpreters would emulate the Millerites' exploitation of popular fascination with the "end-times" while avoiding the kind of specificity that brought the Millerites to grief. While continuing to preach that "the end is near," they added stern caveats against setting a specific date for the glorious event. Premillennialist expositors now quoted the words of Jesus that the Millerites had rashly ignored: "But of that day and hour knoweth no man, no, not the angels of heaven, but my Father only" (Matt. 24:36). After 1844, most proponents of fundamentalist apocalyptic would master the art of keeping end-time yearnings at a peak of expectation, while avoiding the hazard of linking their interpretive system to a specific date.

⌒ 1820–1920: THE RISE OF DISPENSATIONAL PREMILLENNIALISM

While Americans had launched their new nation on a wave of millennial fervor and the Millerite movement had arisen and collapsed, Great Britain had also seen strong stirrings of prophetic interest, particularly of the premillennial variety. Why did the early nineteenth century produce this upsurge of interest in Bible prophecy, and especially in interpretations that despaired of human institutions and looked to a cataclysmic end-time crisis as the only means of transforming the social order? While historians offer no fully persuasive answer to this question, some relate it to the mood of disillusionment that the French Revolution left in its wake. As the exalted revolutionary hopes of 1789 gave way to the Terror, the guillotine, and the

Napoleonic wars, these historians suggest, the entire Enlightenment worldview, with its faith in progress through human reason, was seriously undermined. In this climate, conditions became ripe for a biblically grounded scheme of history less rosy in its view of the human condition, less confident of progress through human endeavor, more reliant on supernatural intervention at the end of time.

Whatever the intellectual and social sources, the early and middle decades of the nineteenth century in Great Britain—and eventually in the United States as well—witnessed a dramatic growth of interest in apocalyptic prophecies of the last days. One early leader of this movement was Edward Irving (1792–1834), a handsome, charismatic young Scotsman who in 1822 became pastor of a London chapel where his sermons on Bible prophecy soon attracted large audiences. Irving also translated into English *The Coming of Messiah in Glory and Majesty*, a millennialist tract written in the 1790s by a Chilean Jesuit, Manuel Lacunza.

Irving's moment in the sun proved short-lived. He alienated many sympathizers in 1831 when his wife and other members of his congregation began practicing glossolalia (speaking in unknown tongues) in imitation of the apostles on the Day of Pentecost. By the time of his early death in 1834, Irving's reputation had faded.

But "Irvingism"—an interest in and fervent anticipation of the imminent return of Jesus Christ to earth—lived on in Great Britain. The millennial hope was furthered by a number of prophecy journals that sprang up in the 1820s and 1830s. The movement was also spread by a series of annual prophecy conferences at the Albury Park estate of Henry Drummond (1786–1860), a wealthy banker and statesman with a consuming interest in prophecy. Beginning in 1826, Drummond's Albury gatherings attracted a diverse array of ministers, Bible scholars, and lay prophecy enthusiasts, who explored fine points of interpretation and delivered lectures that were then reprinted as tracts or as articles in the prophecy magazines.

The thrust of the developing movement was premillennial and apocalyptic. Participants in Drummond's conferences, and the writers in the prophecy journals of the day, elaborated and refined the last-days scenario sketched at the outset of this essay: humankind is now living in the "last days," as a sobering concentration of signs and portents makes clear; the present age will grow ever more sinful, culminating in a crescendo of wickedness and apostasy; just as conditions reach their nadir, and the forces of Satan seem triumphant, Jesus Christ will return to defeat the enemies of righteousness at Armageddon and establish his millennial kingdom.

Like the Millerites in America, these early-nineteenth-century British apocalypticists, while mainly futurists, also incorporated a historicist strand in their interpretive approach. In the events of the French Revolution and its aftermath, they saw the completion of various historical time spans mentioned in the book of Daniel and the pouring out of the seven vials referred to in the sixteenth chapter of the book of Revelation.

These British prophetic expositors also displayed keen interest in the history of the Jews. The conversion of the Jews and their restoration to the promised land, they taught, would figure prominently in the succession of prophetic fulfillments that would mark the last days. Accordingly, many prophecy teachers immersed themselves in missionary projects to persuade the Jews to accept Jesus as the Messiah. As we shall see, this link between prophetic belief and attentive interest in the Jews and their destiny would remain a central component in fundamentalist apocalyptic belief in the twentieth century.

No one played a more central role in shaping this early-nineteenth-century upsurge of interest in the apocalyptic scriptures, and particularly in premillennial interpretive systems, than the British religious leader John Nelson Darby (1800–1882). Ordained a priest of the Church of Ireland when he was twenty-five, Darby gradually became disillusioned with the formulaic ritual and hierarchical structure of organized religion and in the early 1830s threw in his lot with the Brethren, a group of dissenters centered in Plymouth and other English cities that would eventually evolve into a sect known as the Plymouth Brethren.

Energetic, strong-willed, and absorbed in Bible prophecy, Darby traveled and lectured widely, painstakingly shaping his complex (indeed, nearly impenetrable) prophetic interpretations into a full-fledged system that he buttressed with extensive biblical references. The first complete articulation of his framework of interpretation apparently came in a series of prophecy lectures delivered in Lausanne, Switzerland, in 1840, just as the Millerite movement in America was moving toward its climax.

Darby's system came to be called "dispensational premillennialism," but neither term really distinguishes it from the teachings of many other prophecy expositors of his day. He was indeed a premillennialist, but so were most other evangelical prophecy preachers and teachers of the time. As for the term "dispensational," this simply meant that Darby viewed history as divided into a series of distinct stages, or dispensations, in each of which God dealt with humankind in different ways, and in which the means of grace differed. This periodization of history was not unique to Darby, although he did elaborate it more fully and draw sharper distinctions between the successive "dispensations" than did most other prophecy interpreters. For example, he saw an absolute distinction between God's plan for the Jews and God's plan for the Gentiles. The Bible presents a distinct scheme of salvation and a distinct prophetic destiny for Jews and non-Jews, Darby taught, assigning some prophetic passages to one group, some to the other.

But if Darby's system had much in common with other prophetic schemes of the 1830s and 1840s, it incorporated certain distinctive features that did set it apart from the larger world of premillennial thinking in his day, and that enhanced its viability and grassroots appeal. He rejected all vestiges of the historicist interpretation. The last events of prophetic significance, he taught, had occurred nearly two thousand years ago when the Jews rejected Jesus as the Messiah and God turned his attention to non-Jewish believers, "the church." The present dispensation, the Church Age, was a "great parenthesis" devoid of prophetic significance except as a prelude to the next dispensation, the Kingdom Age, which would be rich in apocalyptic import as the separate end-time destinies of the Jews and the church unfolded.

In denying that one could fit events such as the French Revolution into a biblically grounded prophetic scheme, Darby circumvented a troubling problem in the historicist approach. Even if one refrained from setting a precise date for the second coming, the very act of placing recent historical occurrences in a sequence of prophetic fulfillments implicitly suggested that other prophesied events, including Christ's return itself, would soon follow according to a discernible chronological timetable. The historicist approach, in short, led all too easily down the dangerous path of setting a date for the end. Darby's system, firmly rejecting the view that contemporary historical events can be matched up with specific prophecies (except as general "signs" that the end is approaching), avoided this pitfall.

Darby also professed almost contemptuous hostility not only toward secular governments and the human social order but also toward all organized religious bodies. He even kept a wary distance from his own group, the Plymouth Brethren, and engaged in contentious disputes with other Brethren leaders. The true church was a mystical and spiritual body, he taught, and

all institutional forms of religion were deeply suspect. While this anti-government, anti-institu-
tional position was not unique to Darby, he elevated it to a position of centrality and insisted on
it with a vehemence that set his system apart from that of other premillennialists. In an age
when the ideology of *laissez-faire* individualism, suspicion of the state, and hostility to social
constraints was being espoused by social theorists such as John Stuart Mill (1806–1873) and
Herbert Spencer (1820–1903), and soon by William Graham Sumner (1840–1910) in America,
this feature of Darby's system fit the spirit of the times perfectly and doubtless enhanced its
appeal for many.

The most distinctive feature of Darby's system was the doctrine of the Rapture. He derived
this doctrine from a passage in Paul's first letter to the Thessalonians:

> For the Lord himself shall descend from heaven with a shout, with the voice of the archangel,
> and with the trump of God: and the dead in Christ shall rise first: then we which are alive and
> remain shall be caught up together with them in the clouds, to meet the Lord in the air: and so
> shall we ever be with the Lord. Wherefore comfort one another with these words. (1 Thess.
> 4:16–18)

Though the passage seems to suggest that Paul anticipated this event during his own lifetime, Darby placed it in the future. The Church Age would end, he taught, and the prophetic
clock would again start to tick, when all the saints suddenly vanished from the earth to join
Christ in the clouds. Only after this event would the full horrors of the Great Tribulation and
the reign of the Antichrist unfold.

With the doctrine of the Rapture, Darby sidestepped the most harrowing and frightening
aspect of premillennial teaching: the belief that everyone alive on the earth at the end-times,
including faithful Christians, would endure the terrors of the Tribulation and Antichrist's persecution. Darby's system assured believers that while the wicked (and those converted to Christ
after the Rapture—the "Tribulation saints") underwent the agonies of the Tribulation, the rap-
tured saints would be safely removed from the awful scenes unfolding below, preparing to
return in triumph to rule with Christ.

Darby's system steadily gained ground in prophetic circles in Great Britain. He preached
widely, wrote voluminously, and, from 1831 on, expounded his apocalyptic interpretation at an
annual prophecy conference held in Ireland on the County Wicklow estate of Lady Theodosia
Powerscourt, a wealthy and pious young widow who much admired him.

This upsurge of premillennialist teaching and writing in Great Britain had powerful ramifications in the United States. In the period of disorientation that followed the Millerite fiasco
of 1844, Bible prophecy, and particularly premillennialism, seemed discredited, and popular
interest waned. But it gradually revived, encouraged, perhaps, by a series of events that served
to undermine the reformist optimism of earlier decades. The revival fires that had burned so
brightly on the frontier and in eastern cities earlier in the century had largely sputtered out. The
arrival of many thousands of poverty-stricken Irish-Catholic immigrants in the 1840s and
1850s, escaping the dreadful potato-blight famine in their homeland, exacerbated the social
problems of urban America and heightened Protestant-Catholic religious tensions in New
York, Philadelphia, Boston, Baltimore, and other urban centers. Conflicts over the expansion
of slavery increasingly roiled the body politic, culminating in 1861 in civil war. Amid these
unsettling developments, prophetic interpretations that placed less emphasis on the ability of

Christians to transform the world and more stress on end-time conflict, human wickedness, and apocalyptic interventions in human history exerted more appeal.

In this context, British prophecy teachers of the premillennial persuasion provided an ideological framework around which fundamentalist apocalyptic in the United States could reorient itself. John Darby, in particular, played a major transatlantic role. Darby visited North America seven times between 1859 and 1877, expounding his views in lectures, Bible readings, and meetings with key evangelical leaders. Darby was not a charismatic evangelist on the order of Charles Grandison Finney (1792–1875) or Dwight L. Moody (1837–1899). Indeed, after an interview with Moody in Chicago, the British visitor expressed considerable skepticism toward the American revivalist's extemporaneous preaching style and ignorance of the nuances of scriptural interpretation. But while Darby never gained a mass following, he excelled as a biblical expositor, and on each American visit he won significant recruits among leading evangelical clergymen, particularly Presbyterians and Baptists in such major cities as New York, Boston, Chicago, and St. Louis.

Though Darby's American recruits did not generally join his sect, the Plymouth Brethren, or even separate themselves from their denominational affiliation, as Darby believed they should, they did embrace the essential elements of his interpretation of the apocalyptic scriptures. These ministers in turn gradually diffused his version of premillennialism among the laity. While premillennial dispensationalism remained a minority position within the spectrum of American Protestantism in these years, it was taken seriously and its advocates given a respectful hearing. "The doctrine is spreading wonderfully," observed Darby as he completed his seventh (and last) U.S. visit in 1877.

As in Great Britain, premillennial prophecy belief was also promulgated in late-nineteenth-century America by a network of periodicals such as the monthly *Prophetic Times* (founded in 1863). Again drawing on British precedent, American premillennialists also spread the word through a series of interdenominational prophecy conferences. The American Bible and Prophetic Conference, the first of seven gatherings of that name held over a forty-year span, convened in 1878 at Holy Trinity Episcopal Church in New York City. Attendance was large and journalistic coverage extensive. And (despite Darby's reservations about him) Dwight L. Moody, the best-known American evangelist of the late nineteenth century, preached at least a generalized version of premillennial doctrine and provided a forum for British and American premillennialists at the annual Bible conferences he hosted at his retreat in Northfield, Massachusetts.

The most important of these interdenominational prophetic gatherings, the Niagara Bible Conference, met each year from 1875 to 1897, usually at Niagara-on-the-Lake, New York. At these and other conferences, the leading premillennialists assembled, shared interpretations, and strengthened one another in the faith, which they then carried back to believers in their home areas—primarily in the Northeast and Midwest.

The 1878 Niagara conference adopted a creedal statement that summed up what the leaders saw as the basic doctrinal principles of evangelical Christianity. This creed was firmly premillennial in foreseeing "a fearful apostasy" in the last days, followed by "the personal and premillennial advent" of Christ to "introduce the millennial age." The Niagara conference would soon embrace the doctrine of the Rapture as well.

These were years of rapid growth for premillennial doctrine. When the second American

Bible and Prophetic Conference convened in Chicago in 1886, a leading Baptist publication (not itself premillennialist) acknowledged the impact of the prophecy-conference movement:

> A new impulse was thereby given to subjects of prophetic study, the religious press of the country gave larger and larger space to the treatment of the . . . book of Revelation and kindred Scriptures. . . . Pre-Millennial views, whatever may be said of them, have become so widespread in the various denominations, not excluding the Baptists, that it is folly to ignore this mode of Christian thinking, or to attempt to silence the discussion which is in progress. (Sandeen 1970, 154–55)

The impressive cadre of premillennialist leaders included such well-known figures on the evangelical scene as James H. Brookes (1830–1897) of the Walnut Street Presbyterian Church in St. Louis; Adoniram Judson Gordon (1836–1895) of Boston's Clarendon Street Baptist Church; Nathaniel West (1826–1906), a Presbyterian churchman from Cincinnati; Arthur Tappan Pierson (1837–1911), a prominent evangelist and convert to premillennialism; Reuben A. Torrey (1856–1928) of Moody Bible Institute, who succeeded Dwight Moody on the evangelistic circuit; and William G. Moorehead (1834–1914), a professor at United Presbyterian Seminary in Xenia, Ohio. Along with scores of others, leaders like these exerted a powerful influence in turning evangelical Protestants toward premillennial dispensationalism.

As historian Ernest Sandeen has argued, this scheme of fundamentalist prophetic interpretation played a leading role in the emergence of a larger evangelical reaction against the late-nineteenth-century inroads of Darwinian evolutionary theory and the new historical-critical biblical scholarship, which eroded the Bible's status as a sacred and inerrant text. Like the staunchly evangelical Charles Hodge (1797–1878) of Princeton Theological Seminary, author of the influential 1874 text *Systematic Theology*, premillennialists rejected liberal and rationalistic theological trends and affirmed the divine inspiration and inerrancy of the Bible as the literal Word of God.

Premillennialists also battled turn-of-the century liberal ministers and theologians such as Washington Gladden (1836–1918) and Walter Rauschenbusch (1861–1918), who were appropriating the apocalyptic scriptures for their own purposes. In the *post*millennialist tradition, these theological advocates of what came to be called the Social Gospel proclaimed that the kingdom of God would come as Christians joined others of goodwill in supporting labor unions, battling child labor, campaigning for laws to protect factory workers and immigrant slum dwellers, and otherwise joining the struggle for social justice in urban-industrial America.

Premillennialists rejected this allegorizing and liberalizing hermeneutic approach as a dangerous heresy. With ever-greater vehemence they insisted on their very different interpretive position: progress is an illusion; the world is growing more wicked; and no human effort can reverse the process. Only with Christ's return and the defeat of the Antichrist in an apocalyptic final conflict will the millennium be achieved.

But while premillennialists disparaged social reform, they avidly embraced missionary activity. If the end could come at any moment, sinners must be warned. Premillennialists may have given up on Christianizing the world, but they fervently believed in snatching individual souls from Satan's grasp before the Rapture. As Dwight Moody put it:

> I look on this world as a wrecked vessel. God has given me a lifeboat, and said to me, "Moody, save all you can." . . . This world is getting darker and darker; its ruin is coming nearer and

nearer. If you have any friends on this wreck unsaved, you had better lose no time in getting them off. (Weber 1987, 53)

As the twentieth century dawned, this fundamentalist apocalyptic perspective continued to figure importantly in religious and cultural discourse. Though the postmillennial Social Gospel theologians were obviously central voices in shaping progressive reform ideology, a significant minority of Protestant evangelicals stood aside. Reiterating the apocalyptic end-time scenario articulated by John N. Darby and other nineteenth-century premillennialist leaders, their early twentieth-century successors looked with skepticism at all schemes of reform. Continuing to view human nature and human institutions with deep pessimism, they dismissed all talk of social betterment through human effort.

Despite the inroads of liberalism, the premillennialist infrastructure remained strong. Nearly every major evangelist of these years preached this doctrine. While the Niagara conferences had ended, other annual prophecy conferences, particularly those at Asbury Park, New Jersey, and Sea Cliff on Long Island, continued to gird up the faithful. A network of some fifty evangelical Bible schools and institutes trained Christian workers in the core doctrines set forth at the 1878 Niagara conference, including the premillennial return of Jesus Christ. Such schools as Moody Bible Institute in Chicago (1889), the Bible Institute of Los Angeles (1907), and William Bell Riley's Northwestern Bible Training School in Minneapolis (1902) trained thousands of ministers, foreign missionaries, and Christian laypersons, who carried the fundamentalist apocalyptic vision throughout the nation and the world. These Bible schools hosted prophecy conventions and published books and magazines (and soon would operate radio stations), providing a sense of community and organizational structure to the vast but diffuse body of premillennial believers in many different evangelical denominations.

A major boost to the cause came in 1910, when the brothers Lyman and Milton Stewart, the millionaire owners of California's Union Oil Company, financed the publication and distribution of *The Fundamentals,* a series of essays by leading conservative theologians and churchmen setting forth the key doctrines that Fundamentalists (as they were beginning to be called) considered vital to true Christianity. Published in eleven volumes between 1910 and 1915 under the general editorship of the Rev. Amzi C. Dixon (1854–1925), pastor of Chicago's Moody Memorial Church, *The Fundamentals* was distributed free to hundreds of thousands of U.S. Protestant ministers. One of the "fundamentals," and the subject of two essays in the series, was Christ's premillennial return. The Stewart brothers also financed in 1908 the reissue of *Jesus is Coming,* a premillennialist treatise of the 1880s by the Chicago real-estate developer and prophecy writer William E. Blackstone (1841–1935). Thanks to the Stewarts' largesse, nearly seven hundred thousand copies of this work went out to ministers across America.

Another landmark event in the early-twentieth-century promulgation of dispensational premillennialism was the publication in 1909 of the *Scofield Reference Bible.* Cyrus R. Scofield (1843–1921) was a colorful, strong-willed individual with a rather shadowed past. After fighting on the Confederate side in the Civil War, Scofield had become involved in Kansas politics. He fled the state in 1877, abandoning a wife and two children, to escape prosecution for embezzling campaign contributions made to a Republican senator. (His wife later secured a divorce on grounds of desertion.) While in a St. Louis jail on forgery charges, Scofield experienced a religious conversion under the influence of the Darbyite leader James H. Brookes, who introduced him to the study of prophecy. Appointed pastor of a Congregational church in Dallas, Texas, Scofield soon became a fixture on the prophecy-conference circuit and wrote books, tracts, and articles defending and promoting dispensational premillennialism.

The *Scofield Reference Bible,* the work that has transmitted Scofield's name to posterity, remains in print, with total sales estimated by the publisher (Oxford University Press) as high as ten million. Scofield had labored on this project for several years with the assistance of an editorial board of leading premillennialists. The work consists of the full text of the King James Bible with Scofield's commentary printed at the bottom of each page. Well-thumbed Scofield Bibles occupied an honored place in the homes of vast numbers of evangelical Christians, many of whom had difficulty remembering precisely where they had acquired a particular idea: from the sacred text itself, or from Scofield's notes, with their dispensational premillennialist message woven throughout.

Scofield's scant education and lack of theological training did not hamper his success. Indeed, it may have helped it. In egalitarian America, do-it-yourself prophetic interpretation seemed the quintessentially democratic hermeneutic mode. Anyone could join in. As one author wrote in 1919, the only requirements were "a bit of spare time daily, some simple, comprehensive plan of reading, a reverent spirit and daily practice with the [Bible's] spirit and teaching."

The outbreak of war in Europe in 1914, and America's entry into the conflict in 1917, provided a major stimulus to the premillennialist position. The wholesale slaughter of 1914–1918, after decades when many people had confidently assumed that the world was moving toward universal peace, seemingly confirmed the premillennialists' insistence on the innate wickedness of all human institutions. Further, the war precipitated a series of events that premillennialists invested with prophetic significance. The 1917 Bolshevik Revolution in Russia added fresh cogency to a long-established tradition in prophetic interpretation that identified Russia as Gog, the mysterious northern kingdom whose end-time destruction is foretold in the thirty-eighth chapter of Ezekiel.

Of even greater significance was the capture of Jerusalem from the Turks by the British general Edmund Allenby in September 1918, which struck premillennialists as a crucially important prophetic sign. Despite John Darby's insistence that the course of history since biblical days was irrelevant to the prophetic timetable, many premillennialists had continued to pay close attention to current events. In particular, they had watched for evidence of the Jews' interest in returning to Palestine as a portent of the last days. Indeed, as early as 1891, several years before Theodore Herzl formally launched the Zionist movement, William E. Blackstone had presented to President Benjamin Harrison a petition urging U.S. support for a Jewish return to the promised land.

Allenby's victory, following upon the 1917 Balfour Declaration by which the British government endorsed the Zionist goal of a Jewish homeland in Palestine, seemed a miraculous prelude to precisely that outcome. A prophecy conference that convened in Philadelphia shortly after Allenby's capture of Jerusalem focused heavily on the prophetic significance of events in Palestine. The Reverend A. B. Simpson (1844–1919), a leading premillennialist and founder of the Christian and Missionary Alliance Church, wept as he read the Balfour Declaration to his congregation. Among believers, interest in Bible prophecy reached almost a fever pitch as the war drew to a close.

☞ ADVENTISTS, PENTECOSTALISTS, AND JEHOVAH'S WITNESSES: VARIANT VERSIONS OF FUNDAMENTALIST APOCALYPTIC _____

While dispensational premillennialism was gaining ground among evangelical Protestants in the late nineteenth and early twentieth centuries, new religious movements had arisen that espoused variant forms of literalistic interpretations of the apocalyptic scriptures. The Seventh-day Adventist Church, for example, made steady advances in these years. As we have seen, the "Great Disappointment" of October 22, 1844, had seemingly dealt a death blow to the Millerite movement and fatally discredited its prophetic teachings. Many chastened converts did, indeed, abandon millennialism and return to their churches in the Protestant mainstream.

But some Millerites sought to reanimate the fragmented movement. An eschatological event had, indeed, occurred on October 22, 1844, they now concluded, but in heaven, beyond human perception. Christ's second coming to earth still lay in the future. While the precise date could never be known (to this extent William Miller's teachings were rejected), one could determine through careful study of the prophetic and apocalyptic texts the "signs of the times" that showed the end was near.

These ex-Millerites gradually formed new associational ties, from which emerged the Seventh-day Adventist Church in 1863. A leader of the new organization was the visionary, prolific writer and itinerant speaker Ellen G. White (1827–1915), who with her husband, the Rev. James S. White, is honored by Adventists as the founder of their church. Through some fifty books, scores of pamphlets, and thousands of articles, Ellen White formulated the central tenets of the post-Millerite Adventist movement, including not only prophetic interpretation but also vegetarianism, sexual purity, health reform, avoidance of alcohol and tobacco, the observance of Saturday as the Sabbath, and a firm commitment to worldwide missionary activity.

Following Ellen White's teachings, the Seventh-day Adventists' understanding of the end-times exhibited certain distinctive features. They held, for example, that the dead exist in a kind of dreamless sleep until the second coming, when they will be resurrected and judged. And they taught that Christ's millennial reign will be in heaven, while Satan continues to rule the earth; only after Satan's final defeat at the end of the millennium would Christ and the saints return to earth for all eternity. Adventists also rejected the doctrine of eternal punishment, teaching that the wicked will simply be annihilated after the last judgment. But in their adherence to the core premillennialist belief—that human history will soon end in a series of apocalyptic events foretold in the Bible—the Adventists were fully a part of the larger movement. By the time of Ellen White's death in 1915, the Seventh-day Adventist Church had become a major force in promulgating worldwide the urgent message of Christ's second coming.

The emergence of the modern Pentecostal movement in the early twentieth century added another strong voice to the chorus of religious groups and individuals proclaiming fundamentalist apocalyptic belief. Modern Pentecostalism, usually dated from a 1906–1907 revival among an interracial group of believers in Los Angeles, focused on the spiritual gifts associated with the "baptism of the Holy Spirit" granted to the apostles at the first Pentecost after Christ's ascension to heaven. These spiritual gifts included miracles, faith healing, and speaking in unknown tongues.

Pentecostalism emerged from a fusion of several American religious traditions of the late nineteenth century, including dispensational premillennialism. Like the followers of Edward Irving in early-nineteenth-century England, who combined millennial expectations with glossolalia, Pentecostalists demonstrated intense interest in prophetic themes and in the signs of Christ's second coming. Indeed, the gifts of the spirit that rained down in Pentecostalist worship services were seen as clear evidence of the nearness of the second coming. As one leader wrote in 1908: "'Jesus is coming soon' is the message that the Holy Ghost is speaking today through nearly everyone that receives the baptism with the Holy Ghost" (Anderson 1979, 79). Or, in the words of a formula proclaimed by many early Pentecostal churches, Jesus Christ was "Savior, Baptizer, Healer, and Soon Coming King."

Pentecostal churches such as the Assemblies of God (which emerged in 1914 from the amalgamation of several smaller groups) and the Church of God in Christ (a predominantly African American denomination whose roots date to 1897), became major channels for disseminating the fundamentalist apocalyptic message. Eventually the highly diffuse American Pentecostal movement would spawn more than three hundred separate denominational bodies, all committed to belief in Christ's premillennial return.

Pentecostalism proved especially important in promulgating fundamentalist apocalypticism in the South and West, where premillennial dispensationalism had enjoyed less success than in the Northeast and Midwest. Pentecostalism also helped instill a fervent anticipation of Christ's second coming in the African American community, where the new movement took deep root.

A quite different but highly influential literalistic interpretation of the apocalyptic scriptures was offered by Charles Taze Russell (1852–1916), a Pennsylvania haberdasher and Bible student who in 1884 founded the Watchtower Bible and Tract Society (incorporated in 1931 as the Jehovah's Witnesses). Adapting a historicist interpretive approach, Russell promulgated his distinctive reading of the apocalyptic texts in *The Plan of the Ages* (1881) and other books published in six volumes under the general title *Millennial Dawn* (1886–1904). Russell proclaimed that the first stage of the millennium as a spiritual event had already dawned in 1874 and that Christ's reign in heaven would begin forty years later, in 1914. (The outbreak of war in 1914 heightened interest in Russell's teachings.)

Christ's thousand-year earthly reign, Russell taught, could begin at any time and would be launched by the annihilation of all existing governments, churches (especially the Roman Catholic Church, toward which he had a special antipathy), and human institutions of every description. Other distinctive features of Russell's highly complicated system included a sharp distinction between Jehovah and Jesus Christ as separate beings, and elimination of the Holy Spirit, the third person of the Trinity in orthodox Christianity. Russell also abandoned the concepts of hell and eternal punishment. All sinners are annihilated at death, he taught, to be "re-created" during the millennium and given a second opportunity for salvation. If they once more reject the truth, they will again be annihilated, this time forever. Focusing attention on the 144,000 servants of God mentioned in Rev. 7:3–4, Russell taught that 144,000 believers would soon be gathered out of the world to become saints in the coming kingdom.

Through the voluminous writings of Russell and the organizational skills of his successor, Joseph F. Rutherford, the Watchtower movement grew rapidly. The publications that poured from the movement's headquarters in Brooklyn, New York; the spread of Jehovah's Witnesses meetinghouses (called "Kingdom Halls" rather than churches); and an endless round of door-to-door evangelism brought a continued flow of new converts and an ever-widening spread of the Witnesses' particular understanding of the apocalyptic events that will herald Christ's return and the end of history.

Apocalyptic expectations involving a literalistic reading of the prophecies and a despairing view of all human institutions obviously ran counter to what is conventionally thought of as the main currents of intellectual and cultural development in the late nineteenth and early twentieth centuries. This was the era, after all, when postmillennial Social Gospel theologians added their blessing to Progressivism, and when the historical-critical mode of biblical study became dominant among theological modernists in mainstream seminaries. But although the fundamentalist apocalyptic expectations of Protestant conservatives and various sectarian movements may appear a reactionary backwater from one point of view, it represented a major strand of American religious life and posed a standing challenge to the prevailing assumptions of the age. From their different perspectives, dispensational premillennialists, Seventh-day Adventists, Jehovah's Witnesses, the many varieties of Pentecostalism, and vast numbers of premillennialists in the pews of mainstream churches, bore witness to the continuing appeal of an apocalyptic worldview that powerfully blended the terrifying and the inspiring in its vision of history's approaching end.

☞ THE INTERWAR YEARS: CONTINUED VITALITY DESPITE MARGINALIZATION

As we have seen, the World War I era represented a high-water mark for fundamentalist apocalypticism as a respected and dynamic movement within the spectrum of American Protestantism. The 1918 Philadelphia prophecy conference brought together the leading lights of the premillennialist camp. The World's Christian Fundamentals Association, founded in Philadelphia in 1919, further consolidated the movement. If the long-term prospect for humanity looked grim, the immediate outlook for premillennialism seemed bright as the 1920s dawned.

But the 1920s was in fact a key transitional decade that would decisively alter the status of conservative evangelical Protestantism—and of premillennial apocalyptic belief—in American society. By 1920, many of the older intellectual leaders of the movement had died or were in retirement. Nathaniel West died in 1906, William G. Moorehead in 1914, A. T. Pierson in 1911, and Cyrus Scofield in 1921. Few younger figures of the same caliber emerged to take their places. And in this decade, what had been a serious and generally well-regarded component of the larger spectrum of Protestant thought was increasingly marginalized and stigmatized as "Fundamentalism." In mainstream seminaries, the "modernists" grew more confident and assertive. The prominent liberal New York City minister Harry Emerson Fosdick (1878–1969) threw down the gauntlet in 1922 with a provocative and widely discussed sermon "Shall the Fundamentalists Win?" Shailer Mathews (1863–1941) of the University of Chicago Divinity School, offering a liberal credo in 1924, firmly rejected the Fundamentalists' insistence on a literal second coming and last judgment. The "ultimate triumph of love and justice" would come through the spread of knowledge of God through Christ, he suggested, not in an apocalyptic final crisis. The commentator on the book of Ezekiel in the 1929 *Abingdon Bible Commentary,* a liberal enterprise, flippantly observed of the work's apocalyptic section: "These very difficult and obscure chapters raise many problems too intricate for discussion here, a loss the less serious in that few of them have been solved" (Eiselen et al. 1929, 741).

And in this decade, too, many Fundamentalists turned their attention from the close of the biblical drama to its beginning, as they channeled their energies, and staked their cause, on a defense of a literalistic reading of the Genesis account of creation against the advocates of Darwinian evolutionary theory. In terms of the larger secular culture, the result was a public-relations disaster. At the famous 1925 Scopes "Monkey Trial" in Dayton, Tennessee, involving a state law banning the teaching of evolution in the public schools of Tennessee, the biblical literalist position, championed by the aging statesman William Jennings Bryan, was held up to ridicule by the freethinking Chicago attorney Clarence Darrow and a corps of big-city reporters led by Henry L. Mencken.

Literalist interpreters of the biblical apocalyptic texts had for decades been closely identified with the larger conservative movement in American Protestantism, and as that movement—now stigmatized as Fundamentalism—came under attack, this approach to prophecy interpretation was pushed to the cultural fringes as well. By the end of the decade and beyond, literalistic prophecy interpretation no longer enjoyed much status or respectability in American intellectual life, either in the forums of secular discourse or in the mainstream seminaries, pulpits, and religious publications. During the early 1930s, as the Depression and the New Deal dominated public attention, interest in fundamentalist apocalypticism seemed decidedly muted in contrast to the late-nineteenth- and early-twentieth-century years.

But this interwar era resists simple generalizations. While Fundamentalism seemed to be in retreat, the movement was in fact undergoing a complex process of reorientation that the historian George Marsden has characterized as "withdrawal and regrouping." Beyond the purview of the mass media, the intellectual elite, and most cultural observers, a thriving fundamentalist network of Bible schools, magazines, and local congregations survived and even flourished. While modernism and the historical-critical approach to biblical scholarship were indeed strong in mainstream denominations, Fundamentalism remained alive and well in many evangelical denominations, sectarian groups, and independent churches.

This little-noted process provided an institutional framework within which premillennialism and a literalistic reading of the apocalyptic scriptures survived. The older Bible schools such as Moody Bible Institute remained bastions of premillennialism, and new ones were launched, notably Dallas Theological Seminary (1924) and Westminster Theological Seminary of Philadelphia (1929), founded by J. Gresham Machen (1881–1937) and other dissident faculty members from Princeton Theological Seminary, where a more latitudinarian outlook had won the upper hand. Though marginalized by the higher-education establishment and its accrediting agencies, these institutions continued to indoctrinate thousands of young ministers and laypersons in the principles of the faith long embraced by evangelicals, including the premillennial return of Jesus Christ.

While the ranks of the older premillennialist leaders were thinning, a few survived, such as James M. Gray (1851–1935) of Moody Bible Institute; Arno C. Gaebelein (1861–1945), editor of the prophecy magazine *Our Hope;* and William Bell Riley (1861–1947), the "fundamentalist pope" who led a large ultraconservative Baptist church in Minneapolis. Riley's Northwestern Bible Training School graduated hundreds of ministers, who held pulpits across the Upper Midwest, creating a kind of fundamentalist empire. John Roach Straton (1875–1929), an unbending premillennialist, held forth from New York's Calvary Baptist Church throughout the 1920s. Across the border in Toronto, Oswald Smith (1889–1986), a spellbinding preacher and prophecy expositor, attracted large audiences and published a number of books explicating biblical prophecies in the 1920s.

The two best-known religious celebrities of the 1920s—Billy Sunday (1863–1935), whose fire-and-brimstone revivals attracted large audiences across the nation, and Aimee Semple McPherson (1890–1944), the flamboyant leader of Angelus Temple in Los Angeles—preached the imminent end of the present age and Christ's imminent return. Other revivalists, while lacking the celebrity status of Sunday and McPherson, spread the word of Christ's second coming from pulpits and evangelistic tents throughout the land.

The rise of the fascist dictators Benito Mussolini in Italy and Adolph Hitler in Germany stimulated popular interest in apocalyptic speculation, as some prophecy expositors identified these feared tyrants as forerunners of the Antichrist. It was widely noted, for example, that if the letter *A* is given the value 100, *B* 101, *C* 102, and so on, the name HITLER adds up to 666—the number of the Beast as recorded in Rev. 13:18.

Mussolini, however, was more frequently pinpointed as the Evil One. A long-standing interpretative tradition which held that in the last days the Antichrist would arise in Rome and initially rule over a revived Roman Empire lent weight to this identification. Toronto's Oswald Smith declared as early as 1926 that Mussolini appeared to be "a foreshadowing at least of the coming super-man" (Smith 1926, 65). The concordat signed between Mussolini and the Vatican in 1929 offered further evidence of his end-time role, since many Fundamentalists viewed the Roman Catholic Church as the abominable "Whore of Babylon" portrayed in Revelation 17. *The Sunday School Times,* a premillennialist weekly widely read in evangelical circles, argued for Mussolini as the probable Antichrist up to the moment of his death in 1945.

And despite the more marginal status of literalistic readings of the Bible prophecies, a new generation of expositors continued in the tradition of Darby and Scofield, expounding the apocalyptic scriptures for believers. Some of the prophecy teachers and preachers who emerged in the 1930s would enjoy long careers well beyond that decade, including Wilbur M. Smith (1894–1977) of Moody Bible Institute; Harry Ironside (1876–1951), a member of the Plymouth Brethren who pastored Chicago's Moody Memorial Church; and Donald Grey Barnhouse (1895–1960) of Philadelphia who edited the prophecy journal *Revelation* and conducted a popular weekly religious program on CBS Radio.

Fundamentalist prophecy expositors avidly embraced the new medium of radio just as they would utilize television in future years. By 1930, evangelical programs offering a fundamentalist perspective on the apocalyptic scriptures filled the airwaves, including those on Moody Bible Institute's powerful station WMBI and Charles E. Fuller's *Old-Fashioned Revival Hour*, which originated in Long Beach, California, and was carried on more than 450 stations by the 1940s. Fuller's program, according to one admirer, was "saturated with the truth of Christ's near return."

Despite marginalization and declining intellectual status, fundamentalist apocalyptic belief continued to thrive at the grassroots level in the interwar years. The movement was well positioned for a resurgence as World War II came to a close, ushering America and the world into an anxiety-filled new age.

⌒ FUNDAMENTALIST APOCALYPTIC
SINCE WORLD WAR II_____

Statistics on the extent of literalistic prophetic belief are notoriously imprecise, but the ranks of believers clearly included many millions of Americans in the last half of the twentieth century. According to a 1983 Gallup Poll, 62 percent of Americans had "no doubt" that Jesus will come to earth again. A 1980 poll by the same organization revealed that 85 percent of Americans regarded the Bible as divinely inspired, with 40 percent holding that the Bible is inerrant and to be taken literally, word for word. Such beliefs in inerrancy, of course, encompass the apocalyptic texts along with the rest.

From the 1970s on, evangelical, fundamentalist, holiness, and pentecostal churches, in which Bible-prophecy belief runs high, were the fastest-growing sector of American religion. By the 1990s, membership in the Assemblies of God Church stood at more than two million. The Church of the Nazarene, a holiness group, reported 562,000 adherents.

Premillennial belief in these years pervaded the nation's largest Protestant denomination, the fifteen-million-member Southern Baptist Convention. Although Southern Baptists place great emphasis on the autonomy of the individual congregation, and thus do not have an official creed binding on all members, a 1987 survey of nearly seven hundred Southern Baptist ministers found that about 63 percent, when asked to classify their beliefs about Bible prophecy, chose the "premillennialist" category. (Only five respondents, 0.7 percent of the total, checked the "postmillennial" option.) In response to another question, more than 30 percent of the ministers defined themselves as "Dispensationalists." Presumably at least as high a percentage of the Southern Baptist laity embrace the prophetic beliefs preached and taught by their ministers.

Sectarian groups that espoused particular variants of prophecy belief grew by leaps and bounds as well. In 1996 the Seventh-day Adventist Church boasted 6 million members worldwide, while the Jehovah's Witnesses claimed 4.5 million adherents throughout the globe.

The most popular evangelist of the postwar years, Billy Graham, whose revival crusades attracted many thousands throughout the world, proclaimed the imminent apocalyptic end of history in no uncertain terms. In the early years of his ministry, Graham even ventured into the risky realm of date setting. "I sincerely believe that the Lord draweth nigh," Graham preached to a crusade audience in 1950. "We may have another year, maybe two years to work for Jesus Christ, and [then] ladies and gentlemen, I believe it is all going to be over. . . . Two years, and it's all going to be over." In 1952, as the end of the designated two years approached, he was still insisting: "Unless this nation turns to Christ within the next few months, I despair of its future." In *World Aflame* (1965), while avoiding date setting, Graham remained firmly committed to the classic premillennialist message with its despairing view of the world's short-term future. Christ's kingdom would arise from the ruins of earthly institutions, he proclaimed. "Secular history . . . is doomed. . . . The whole world is hurtling toward a war greater than anything known before." Nuclear holocaust, he speculated, might be God's chosen means of achieving the earth's "purification"[1] (1967, 165, 191).

Belief in premillennialism spread to other parts of the world, notably Central and South America and Africa, as fundamentalist and pentecostalist missionaries taught these doctrines to their converts. The introduction of global telecommunications satellites provided another medium by which prophecy-preaching evangelists beamed their message worldwide.

A few fundamentalist prophetic interpreters such as Rousas J. Rushdoony (b. 1916) embraced a postmillennialist hermeneutic, looking to the Christianization and moral purification of the world in the present age. And some premillennialists espoused a "post-Trib, pre-Mill" position, arguing that Christ will return before the millennium, but *after* the Great Tribulation. George Ladd (1911–1982) of Fuller Theological Seminary in California, for example, embraced this position in several works published before his death in 1982. But among prophecy popularizers who reached a mass audience, premillennial dispensationalism as formulated by John Darby and Cyrus Scofield remained by far the preferred interpretive system.

Even more than in earlier decades, the literalistic interpretations of Bible prophecy were purveyed in these years not by established theologians or church leaders, but by itinerant evangelists, radio and television preachers, and the writers of popular paperbacks. Frequently, these popularizers had only loose denominational affiliations, or none at all. Collectively, these promoters reached many millions of Americans, spreading more widely than ever the fundamentalist version of apocalyptic belief.

Among the better-known electronic evangelists who incorporated a strong emphasis on Bible prophecy in their message were pentecostalists Oral Roberts (b. 1918) and Jimmy Swaggart (b. 1935). (The latter's television ministry faltered in the early 1990s when he was twice arrested with a prostitute.) Also prominent were M. R. DeHaan (1891–1964) of Grand Rapids, Michigan, whose *Radio Bible Class* aired on five hundred stations in the 1950s and 1960s, and his son Richard DeHaan (b. 1923), who made the transition to television. Jack Van Impe (b. 1931), Jerry Falwell (b. 1933), and Pat Robertson (b. 1930) all hosted highly popular religious television programs that heavily emphasized apocalyptic themes. Robertson, while conducting his own program, *The 700 Club,* also elaborated his apocalyptic worldview in a series of best-selling paperbacks and directed the Christian Broadcasting Network, which provided a forum for other "televangelists" who shared his end-time interests.

The postwar paperback explosion served prophecy popularizers well. Throughout these decades, and particularly after 1970, the market was literally flooded with inexpensive paperbacks offering end-time scenarios based on each author's interpretation of the apocalyptic and prophetic scriptures. Cumulatively, these works sold many millions of copies. Boasts of "over 100,000 sold" or "250,000 copies in print" adorned the covers of many prophecy books. But this phenomenon went largely unnoticed because these works were issued mainly by religious publishing houses far from New York City and were marketed through a vast but little-known network of Christian bookstores.

The publishing phenomenon that best illustrated this broad diffusion of mass-market prophecy books was Hal Lindsey's *Late Great Planet Earth* (1970). Indeed, Lindsey's career epitomizes many central aspects of the role of fundamentalist apocalypticism in modern America. Born in Houston in 1930, he served a stint in the U.S. Coast Guard and was working as a Mississippi River tugboat captain in the 1950s when he experienced a religious conversion. His interest in Bible prophecy was aroused during four years (1958–1962) at Dallas Theological Seminary, a premillennialist bastion whose faculty included several prominent prophecy writers, among them the president, John Walvoord (b. 1910).

Joining the evangelical Campus Crusade for Christ, Lindsey was engaged in open-air preaching at the University of California-Los Angeles in the late 1960s when he announced a series of lectures on Bible prophecy. To his surprise, the week-long series attracted larger and larger audiences, until by the last night the auditorium was packed. From these lectures, and with the aid of a ghostwriter, Lindsey wrote *The Late Great Planet Earth,* published initially by Zondervan, a religious house in Grand Rapids, Michigan.

The book essentially presents the dispensational premillennialist scheme of prophetic interpretation worked out some 130 years earlier by John Darby and promulgated in America by Cyrus Scofield and others. Citing an array of biblical texts, Lindsey offered the familiar sequence of end-time events: increasing evil and wickedness, the Rapture, the Tribulation, the Antichrist's rise, Armageddon, the millennium, the last judgment.

What distinguishes Lindsey from his nineteenth- and early-twentieth-century predecessors is that he unabashedly targeted a mass audience, writing in a slang-filled, colloquial style and freely drawing on current events and mass-culture allusions. The Antichrist, for example, becomes "The Future Fuehrer," while Armageddon is "World War III." When Lindsey discusses the history of Jewish persecution, he refers to the Jews as being taken to "God's Woodshed." A chapter on a cryptic biblical reference to "the kings of the east" (Rev. 16:12) is entitled "The Yellow Peril." The "great whore" of Revelation 17 becomes "Scarlet O'Harlot." Of the Rapture, Lindsey (or perhaps his ghostwriter) commented in the drug-influenced argot of the 1960s: "It will be the living end. The ultimate trip" (1973, 126). While the apocalyptic scenario of *The Late Great Planet Earth* mirrored that of Darby, Scofield, and their peers, the breezy tone differed radically from the sober vocabulary and careful biblical exegesis of those earlier writers and teachers.

Lindsey's work differed from earlier premillennialists' writings in another key respect as well. Darby, aware of the pitfalls of date setting, had cautioned against linking current events to the prophetic timetable, and his followers had generally heeded the warning. To be sure, events such as World War I, the Balfour Declaration, the Bolshevik Revolution, and the rise of Mussolini and Hitler had been viewed by some popularizers as "signs" that the last days were approaching, but the more sober premillennialists had generally avoided the temptation to measure biblical apocalyptic texts against the morning headlines. Lindsey represented a very different approach. His work is full of allusions to contemporary political and social issues and world events. And he readily relates the sequence of post-Rapture events—the rise of the Antichrist, the Battle of Armageddon, the invasion of Judea by a northern kingdom, the arrival at Armageddon of a 200-million-man army from the East, and so forth—to contemporary international tensions and Cold War power alignments.

The Late Great Planet Earth represented a departure from classic premillennial dispensationalism in still another way: Lindsey came perilously close to date setting as he predicted that the Rapture might come in the year 1981—eleven years from the publication date of his book. He reached this date by an ingenious if somewhat tortuous series of interpretative moves based on the parable of the fig tree (Mark 13), in which Jesus lists various signs that will signal the approaching end, compares them to the blooming of a fig that heralds the coming of summer, and goes on to prophesy: "Verily I say unto you. This generation shall not pass, till all these things be fulfilled." The blooming of the fig tree, Lindsey contended, represented the end-time restoration of the Jews to the promised land, a process consummated with the establishment of the State of Israel in 1948. That year became the starting point of the "generation" that would see the fulfillment of all the prophesied end-time events. Defining a biblical "generation" as forty years, Lindsey concluded that the Battle of Armageddon might well occur by 1988. Deducting seven years for the Great Tribulation, he arrived at 1981 as a plausible date for the Rapture.

Though Lindsey surrounded this prediction with enough cautionary escape hatches to avoid a repeat of the Millerite fiasco, the readers who made his book a best-seller through the 1970s had every reason to conclude that they were living in the very final moments of human history.[2]

Lindsey's breezy, breathless approach paid off. *The Late Great Planet Earth* sold more copies than any other nonfiction book published in the entire decade of the 1970s, going through thirty-six printings by 1981. By the mid-1990s, the estimated total sales in successive editions and many translations stood in excess of twenty million copies. A 1977 feature film based on the book, narrated by Orson Welles, reached a large moviegoing public. While a succession of sequels such as *The 1980s: Countdown to Armageddon* (1980) and *Planet Earth 2000 A.D.* (1994) did not achieve the runaway bestsellerdom of *The Late Great Planet Earth,* they all followed Lindsey's successful formula, matching current events—particularly events that were a source of public anxiety—with the biblical passages that supposedly foretold them.

Although Lindsey was the most successful of the contemporary popularizers of fundamentalist apocalypticism, he was by no means alone. Scores of other writers produced their own works aimed at a mass readership. John Walvoord's *Armageddon, Oil, and the Middle East Crisis* (1974), published as Mideast tensions and spiraling gasoline prices agitated the public mind, sold 750,000 copies. (A revised edition, capitalizing on the surge of prophecy interest stirred by the Persian Gulf War, appeared in 1991.) Few of the authors were trained theologians or Bible scholars, but they had mastered the sensationalized, present-minded approach perfected by Lindsey, and their books collectively reached a vast reading public.

The pervasiveness of apocalyptic belief in America, generally overlooked by the secular media, tended to enter the realm of media awareness when such beliefs were linked to a high-visibility public figure. Such a moment occurred in 1984, for example, when media scrutiny for a time centered on President Ronald Reagan's long-standing and well-documented belief in Bible prophecy. Journalistic attention focused particularly (and understandably) on whether Reagan's view of the Battle of Armageddon might make him more likely to launch a nuclear war against the Soviet Union. Queried on this point on national television during one of the presidential debates of the 1984 campaign, Reagan delivered a rather bland answer clearly designed to sooth public fears, and the issue faded.

The political mobilization of religious conservatives in the 1980s and 1990s focused attention on the so-called New Christian Right, including their apocalyptic beliefs. Interest centered especially on the voluble televangelist Pat Robertson, who briefly sought the Republican presidential nomination in 1992 and then emerged as a power in Republican politics as founder of the Christian Coalition, a conservative political lobby. Robertson's books of apocalyptic interpretation, including *The New World Order* (1991) and *The End of the Age,* a 1995 prophecy novel, were scrutinized by analysts seeking clues to his political thinking.

Public awareness of fundamentalist prophecy belief in American culture sharpened, too, in the 1990s when a number of tightly knit right-wing groups, inspired at least in part by their apocalyptic beliefs, denounced the federal government as evil, denied its legitimacy, and withdrew into separatist, heavily armed enclaves. One such group, the Branch Davidians of Waco, Texas, a heretical offshoot of the Seventh-day Adventist Church dating from the 1930s, fell under the leadership of David Koresh (originally named Vernon Howell). Koresh used his mastery of biblical prophecy to coerce his followers into absolute obedience and to exploit sexually the women and girls of the sect.

In February 1993, a battle erupted when agents of the federal Bureau of Alcohol, Tobacco, and Firearms (ATF) sought to enter the Branch Davidians' compound to arrest Koresh on firearms charges. Four ATF agents and six Davidians died of gunshot wounds. During the fifty-one-day siege that followed, Koresh released several long letters and a tape for radio broadcast filled with his rambling commentary on the biblical prophecies and warnings of an apocalyptic denouement ahead. On April 19, 1993, the Davidian compound erupted in flames as government armored vehicles rumbled in to end the standoff. Some eighty Davidians, including Koresh himself, perished in the fiery holocaust.

But while the apocalyptic beliefs of presidents, public figures, and armed separatist groups fleetingly captured media attention, the more general phenomenon of endemic prophecy belief in late-twentieth-century America, and its political implications, attracted less notice. The fact remained, however, that throughout the Cold War era and beyond, the popularizers of fundamentalist apocalypticism offered commentary on public issues that helped shape the worldview and political ideology of believers who took these teachings seriously. Prophetic pronouncements on nuclear war, the Soviet Union, Israel and the Jews, the environment, and the rise of a multinational global economy illustrate the point.

The atomic bombs that destroyed Hiroshima and Nagasaki in August 1945, and the forty-five-year nuclear arms race that followed figured prominently in the writings of Hal Lindsey and many other prophecy popularizers. Countless works of premillennial exposition published in these years included a chapter interpreting the Battle of Armageddon as a thermonuclear holocaust. Many writers quoted 2 Peter 3:10 as a foretelling of nuclear war:

> But the day of the Lord will come as a thief in the night; in the which the heavens shall pass away with a great noise, and the elements shall melt with fervent heat, the earth also and the works that are therein shall be burned up.

Atomic-age prophecy popularizers did not explicitly *advocate* nuclear war, and the more scrupulous acknowledged that Revelation portrays Armageddon as an eschatological event, not as a war between human armies using human weaponry. But many popularizers blurred the distinction, so that biblical depictions of a cosmos-destroying end-time apocalypse became indistinguishable from a thermonuclear World War III. It is thus not surprising that throughout the years of maximum nuclear threat, premillennialist writers generally dismissed anti-nuclear activism as pointless, since the scriptures so plainly foretold an apocalyptic cataclysm at the end of time.

A similar perspective shaped the premillennialists' view of the larger Cold War confrontation between the United States and the Soviet Union. As we have seen, from the early nineteenth century on, some prophecy interpreters had speculatively identified Russia as Gog, the doomed northern power mentioned in Ezekiel 38. Cyrus Scofield in his *Reference Bible* lent the weight of his prestige to this interpretation. Following the Bolshevik Revolution of 1917 and during the Red Scare of the 1920s, this theme had been much discussed. Premillennialists were thus well prepared for the Cold War. From the late 1940s into the 1990s, scores of popularizers hammered heavily on the theme of Russia's coming destruction. Televangelist Jack Van Impe produced many TV programs, videotaped sermons, and paperbacks elaborating this theme.

As with thermonuclear war, these popularizers did not advocate an actual attack on the

Soviet Union. The prophesied destruction of Russia and godless communism, they conceded, would ultimately be by divine intervention, not by human means. But, again, this view of Russia's divinely ordained fate contributed a theological and apocalyptic dimension to the Cold War, and undercut efforts to ease United States–Soviet tensions. If Russia's destruction was foretold in scripture, what was the point of attempts to forestall that preordained outcome?

The theme of Israel and the Jews also figured prominently in the work of post–1945 fundamentalist apocalypticists. Again, as we have seen, this was hardly a new theme for prophecy interpreters. Throughout the interwar years, prophecy writers had continued to cite the Balfour Declaration and Jewish settlements in Palestine as momentous prophetic events. But the developments of the postwar years, especially the establishment of the State of Israel on May 14, 1948, and the Israelis' recapture of the Old City of Jerusalem in 1967, were hailed by Hal Lindsey and scores of other prophecy expositors as events of the first magnitude in the unfolding of the end-time sequence.

Indeed, fundamentalist interpreters of the apocalyptic scriptures ranked among Israel's strongest supporters, particularly favoring the Jewish state's more hard-line and expansionist parties. Not only did they proclaim that the Jews' right to their ancient homeland had been sealed by God himself, but many taught that in the millennial future Israel would expand to the boundaries promised by God in his covenant with Abraham recorded in Gen. 15:18, from the Euphrates to the "river of Egypt." As John Walvoord proclaimed at a 1971 prophecy conference in Jerusalem: "Of the many aspects of prophecy relating to Israel, none is more pointed than the promise of the land" (Boyer 1992, 193).

In common with some ultra-orthodox Jewish sects, many fundamentalist prophecy writers also taught that the scriptures foretold the reconstruction of the Jewish Temple on its ancient foundations in Jerusalem—currently the site of the Dome of the Rock, the second most sacred Islamic shrine, after Mecca itself, the spot from which the Prophet Muhammad ascended to heaven. Premillennialists who embraced this interpretation typically dismissed the protests of Palestinians or Arab leaders against the claims of Israeli hard-liners to full sovereignty in Jerusalem or to expansion into the West Bank or other disputed territories. What did mere human claims or grievances weigh against God's own prophetic plan for the Jews?

But the prophetic destiny of the Jews sketched by many postwar premillennialist writers had another, and far grimmer, dimension. The same writers and publicists who wrote eagerly of Israel's vast future expansion offered a harrowing prophetic interpretation of the fate of the Jewish people. The long history of anti-Semitic persecution, including the Nazi Holocaust, they explained (as always, with a flourish of biblical texts), was part of God's prophesied "chastisement" of his chosen people for their rejection of Jesus as the promised Messiah.

Further, these writers continued, the apocalyptic future will be even worse. During the Great Tribulation, they predicted, the Antichrist will launch a horrendous persecution of the Jews. With chilling specificity, they quoted Zech. 13:7–8 as a prophecy that Antichrist will slaughter two-thirds of all Jews in a Holocaust worse than anything unleashed by Hitler:

> [S]mite the shepherd, and the sheep shall be scattered: and I will turn mine hand upon the little ones. And it shall come to pass, that in all the land, saith the Lord, two parts therein shall be cut off and die; but the third part shall be left therein.

As with their commentaries on nuclear war and the coming destruction of Russia, these premillennialist popularizers took no joy in their blood-drenched accounts of Jewish slaughters past and future. They expressed sorrow over the fate of the Jews, but they saw it as inevitable and foreordained so long as the Jews persisted in their rejection of Christ.

Post–1945 fundamentalist apocalyptic, in short, especially as offered up in cartoonlike versions for mass consumption, had significant implications for the way Bible-believing Americans viewed a broad range of important public issues. This is not to suggest that popular attitudes on any one of these issues were absolutely determined by a particular reading of Bible prophecy. The presidency of Ronald Reagan would alone cast doubt on such a simplistic cause-and-effect explanatory model. Over the years, Reagan had frequently expressed the view (common in the premillennialist world of his boyhood and youth) that Russia's annihilation is foretold in the prophecies. His 1983 labeling of the Soviet Union as an "evil empire" was not a casual bit of political hyperbole but a quite literal expression of a theological position deeply embedded in his worldview. Nevertheless, when the political winds shifted toward the end of his second term, he was quite ready to fly to Moscow for amiable meetings with Mikhail Gorbachev, head of the nation whose divinely ordained destruction he had long believed inevitable.

For presidents and ordinary citizens, obviously, worldviews and ideologies are complex and often contradictory—and rarely a direct reflection of any one source, even so potent a source as biblical prophecy. Nevertheless, if apocalyptic scripture was not the only influence shaping the outlook of millions of American believers during the Cold War, it was unquestionably one important factor that merits close attention in any effort to understand American culture and politics in these decades.

In 1989–1990, a series of seismic upheavals transformed the basic contours of global power alignments. As liberalization swept aside the Communist Party that had ruled Russia for more than seventy years, the Soviet Union itself collapsed, unleashing unpredictable energies in Eastern Europe and in breakaway republics of the former Soviet Union itself. Almost overnight, it seemed, the Cold War, the global conflict that many Americans had known all their lives, was over. Its evil twin, the nuclear arms race, quickly faded as well.

These dramatic events initially threatened an epistemological crisis in the world of prophecy belief. An end-time scenario that for half a century had mirrored in lurid apocalyptic terms the central realities of a world divided between two nuclear-armed superpowers suddenly seemed out of date. Some elements of the system remained in place, of course, notably those relating to Israel and the Jews, but the alarming predictions of global thermonuclear war and the destruction of the Soviet Union that had enlivened countless prophecy popularizations for decades now seemed embarrassingly passé.

But the prophecy popularizers barely missed a beat. One of the great strengths of literalistic apocalypticism over the centuries had been its resourcefulness in adapting to new realities. The Emperor Saladin gave way to Napoleon, and Napoleon to Mussolini, as the prime candidate for the Antichrist. The Ottoman Empire gave way to Russia as the doomed kingdom of the north. The Millerite movement, with its unfortunate propensity for date setting, gave way to Darby's dispensational premillennialism, which neatly avoided this pitfall.

Prophecy popularizers demonstrated the same resourcefulness as they adjusted their scenario to the new realities. Some themes were quietly downgraded, others shifted to center stage. The popularizers cited environmental hazards such as pollution, global warming, genetic mutation, shifting tectonic plates, and the gap in the ozone layer as preludes to the end-time disasters foretold in the Apocalypse of John: the sun and the moon darken, earthquakes wreak global devastation, the seas turn to blood, hideous monsters emerge from the earth, and terrible sores afflict the human race.

In *Planet Earth—2000 A.D.*, the ever-resourceful Hal Lindsey highlighted the prophetic significance of these environmental fears while also devoting several chapters to Islamic Fundamentalism. Where Russia had once occupied his attention, he now suggested that such nations as Libya, Iran, and Iraq might comprise the end-time power alignment that would confront Christ's wrath at Armageddon.

And post–Cold War prophecy interpreters dwelled with renewed emphasis on a theme that had been somewhat muted during the years when America had led the crusade against godless communism: the terrible and ever-worsening wickedness of the United States itself. With new fervor they reiterated the theme insisted on by Scofield and other premillennialists of an earlier day: the United States, having long since lapsed from divine favor, is sinking ever deeper into sin and evil. They cited a variety of evidence, from radical feminism and New Age mysticism to AIDS, abortion, drugs, and illegitimacy, as proof that America's prophesied descent into end-time apostasy is far advanced. The *Roe* v. *Wade* decision legalizing abortion, the outlawing of school prayer, and governmental support for homosexual rights, they mourned, proved that the federal government, once viewed by postmillennialists and Social Gospellers as a potential ally in Christianizing the world, was in fact becoming a demonic power leading humankind's march to the age of the Antichrist.

With equal resourcefulness, the Bible prophecy popularizers of the 1990s pointed to recent global developments that they claimed heralded the rise of the Evil One. They cited international trade agreements, multinational corporations and investment banks, and political institutions such as the United Nations as part of an emerging world system that will be in place when the Antichrist finally bursts upon the scene. Elaborating the point, they discussed the rise of a computerized economy, plastic credit cards, and a worldwide satellite communication system as means the Antichrist will use to impose his control over world politics and the world economy during the Great Tribulation.

The Beast's ability to appear to everyone in the world simultaneously and to control every individual economic transaction, described in Revelation, had puzzled prophecy interpreters of earlier generations. In the era of computerized data, MasterCard and Visa, and endlessly orbiting communications satellites, the technical means by which the Antichrist will maintain his rule had become clear, and the prophecy popularizers elaborated the possibilities with vivid imaginative flair.

In earlier times, speculation about the Antichrist and his mysterious number, 666—mentioned in Rev. 13:18, the best known of all the apocalyptic scriptures—had generally focused on a specific individual. In the prophecy popularizations of the late twentieth century, attention shifted to the technical means by which the demonic world system will function during the Great Tribulation. Some writers, for example, sought to show that the computerized bar codes found on consumer products in supermarkets and department stores are based on a 6-6-6 numerical system.

In short, in the years after the Cold War, fundamentalist apocalyptic underwent a refashioning analogous to the rise of premillennial dispensationalism after the Millerite episode. As they had since time immemorial, late-twentieth-century prophetic interpreters identified an interconnected set of concerns that troubled many Americans—environmental worries, the globalization of the economy, the dominance of the mass media, the complexity of the computer age, the reduction of politics to TV images and sound bites, the alienating anonymity and social disconnectedness of modern life—and wove them into a compelling end-time scenario.

Pat Robertson's *New World Order* (1991) summed up some of the central themes of the post–Cold War apocalyptic message. "[A] giant plan is unfolding," Robertson warned; "everything perfectly on cue" for the Antichrist (1991, 176). Among the conspirators, Robertson singled out the Masons, the eighteenth-century Bavarian Illuminati, the first U.S. Congress (which had adopted the Great Seal of the United States with its sinister motto *Novus Ordo Seclorum*), the Rothschilds and other "international bankers," President Woodrow Wilson's shadowy advisor Colonel Edward M. House, the Trilateral Commission, the Council on Foreign Relations, Visa, MasterCard—and John Lennon, whose song "Imagine" had injected internationalism like a poison in the consciousness of "millions of misty eyed teenagers and young adults." Even President George Bush, with his pronouncement that the end of the Cold War would give rise to a "new world order," roused Robertson's suspicions. Robertson even suggested that the entire Cold War was arranged by the international bankers to divert attention from their emerging global system. As the conspiracy entered its final phase, Robertson predicted, the full demonic nature of the Antichrist's "counterfeit world order" would soon be unveiled.

But Robertson, like countless of his predecessors, pointed beyond the frightening days immediately ahead to the ancient millennial hope: Antichrist's dictatorship will fail; Christ's true kingdom will come at last. "*God's* new world order," he concluded triumphantly, "is much nearer than we believe" (1991, 247).

Whatever their subtext of conspiracy, paranoia, and social alienation, the late-twentieth-century expositors of fundamentalist apocalypticism offered a message that resonated powerfully for millions of Americans. For those who eagerly embraced this message, its intellectual or theological standing was largely irrelevant. The prophecy popularizers' gripping narratives of the end-times addressed an array of disturbing contemporary trends and placed them within a meaningful framework. And with the doctrines of the Rapture and the millennium, they offered the consoling hope that the redeemed would escape the horrors ahead and finally reign in triumph over a radically transformed world.

Fundamentalist apocalyptic invested history with drama and meaning. Whereas the "secular" history of the public schools and the textbooks offered no clue to history's overarching pattern or ultimate goal, the prophecy popularizers insisted with confident assurance that history is following a clear trajectory determined by God and that it is headed toward an ultimate, glorious consummation.

Further, fundamentalist apocalyptic continued to provide an anchor to those for whom biblical inerrancy remained a foundational element of faith. In the face of skeptical critical challenge, the amazing "prophetic fulfillments" demonstrated by ingenious interpreters offered reassurance in a world of uncertainty and doubt.

As the twentieth century ends and the portentous year 2000 looms, all evidence suggests that fundamentalist apocalyptic interpretations, endlessly refashioned, infinitely adaptable, and seemingly impervious to intellectual challenge, will retain their grip on the popular imagination, as they have for centuries.

⌒ NOTES

1. In later years, as he prayed with presidents at the White House and was idolized as the elder statesman of American evangelicalism, Graham tempered his fundamentalist apocalyptic message. In sermons and books of the 1980s such as *Approaching Hoofbeats* (1983), on the Four Horsemen of the Apocalypse (Rev. 6:1–7), he tended to interpret the prophecies allegorically rather than literally, and to speak more favorably of human effort against such scourges as nuclear war, epidemics, and famine.

2. In his later books, and in subsequent editions of *The Late Great Planet Earth,* Lindsey, like Billy Graham, retreated from specific date setting and adopted the cautious position more typical of dispensationalists: the end is "near," but the precise date is known only to God.

⌒ BIBLIOGRAPHY

Anderson, Robert Mapes. 1979. *Visions of the Disinherited: The Making of American Pentecostalism.* New York: Oxford University Press. Scholarly history of the origins of a twentieth-century popular religious movement immersed in end-time belief.

Bass, Clarence B. 1977. *Background to Dispensationalism: Its Historical Genesis and Ecclesiastical Implications.* Grand Rapids, Mich.: Baker Book House. Useful study of the roots of premillennial dispensationalism.

Boettner, Loraine. 1957. *The Millennium.* Grand Rapids, Mich.: Baker Book House. A useful study that includes a brief but factual biographical sketch of Cyrus Scofield, for whom no full-scale modern biography exists.

Boyer, Paul. 1992. *When Time Shall Be No More: Prophecy Belief in Modern American Culture.* Cambridge, Mass.: Harvard University Press. Traces origins of biblical apocalyptic genre and its interpreters, emergence of premillennial dispensationalism, and political ramifications of prophecy belief in post–World War II America.

Butler, Jonathan, and Ronald Numbers. 1986. "The Seventh-day Adventists." In *The Encyclopedia of Religion,* edited by Mircea Eliade. New York: Macmillan. Valuable overview essay by two leading scholars.

Eiselen, Frederick C., Edwin Lewis, and David G. Downey, eds. 1929. *The Abingdon Bible Commentary.* New York: Abingdon Press.

Gallup, George, Jr., and Jim Castelli. 1989. *The People's Religion: American Faith in the Nineties.* New York: Macmillan. A revealing collective profile based on public-opinion data.

Graham, Billy. 1967. *World Aflame.* New York: Penguin Books. Original publication, 1965.

Hadden, Jeffrey K., and Anson Shupe, eds. 1986. *Prophetic Religion and Politics: Religion and the Political Order.* New York: Paragon House. Interesting essays placing American fundamentalist apocalypticism in a larger context of prophetic movements worldwide.

Halsell, Grace. 1986. *Prophecy and Politics: Militant Evangelists on the Road to Nuclear War.* Westport, Conn.: Lawrence Hill. Polemical and highly critical journalistic exposé of the relationship between American fundamentalists and right-wing expansionists in Israel.

Harrell, David E., Jr. 1987. *Pat Robertson: A Personal, Religious, and Political Portrait.* San Francisco: Harper & Row. Valuable study of the early stages of Robertson's career.

Hatch, Nathan O. 1989. *The Democratization of American Christianity.* New Haven: Yale University Press. Path-breaking study of the revivalist culture from which the Disciples of Christ and other antebellum millennialist movements arose.

Hunter, James Davison. 1983. *American Evangelicals: Conservative Religion and the Quandary of Modernity*. New Brunswick, N.J.: Rutgers University Press. Thoughtful sociological monograph offering a wealth of data on American evangelicals in the early 1980s.

Lindsey, Hal. 1973. *The Late Great Planet Earth*. New York: Bantam Books.

Marsden, George. 1980. *Fundamentalism and American Culture: The Shaping of Twentieth-Century Evangelicalism, 1870–1925*. New York: Oxford University Press. Well-researched history situating Fundamentalism and dispensational premillennialism within a broader cultural and intellectual context.

Mojtabai, A. G. 1986. *Blessed Assurance: At Home with the Bomb in Amarillo, Texas*. Boston: Houghton Mifflin. Witty, perceptive, and sympathetic account of premillennial belief in the city where hydrogen bombs were assembled.

Moore, R. Laurence. 1986. *Religious Outsiders and the Making of Americans*. New York: Oxford University Press. Valuable explorations of the byways of American popular religion, including premillennial dispensationalism.

Moorhead, James H. 1984. "Between Progress and Apocalypse: A Reassessment of Millennialism in American Religious Thought, 1800–1880." *Journal of American History* 71:524–42. Thoughtful analysis of American postmillennialism in the era between Jonathan Edwards and the Social Gospel.

Noll, Mark A. 1994. *The Scandal of the Evangelical Mind*. Grand Rapids, Mich.: Eerdmans. Harsh but fair-minded and scholarly critique of the "intellectual sterility" of Darbyite dispensationalism, by a leading evangelical scholar.

Numbers, Ronald, and Jonathan M. Butler, eds. 1987. *The Disappointed: Millerism and Millenarianism in the Nineteenth Century*. Bloomington, Ind.: Indiana University Press. Essays exploring the Millerite movement from a variety of perspectives.

Penton, M. James. 1985. *Apocalypse Delayed: The Story of Jehovah's Witnesses*. Toronto: University of Toronto Press. Definitive history of a religious movement shaped by the founder's distinctive interpretation of the biblical apocalyptic texts.

Rausch, David A. 1979. *Zionism Within Early Fundamentalism, 1878–1918: A Convergence of Two Traditions*. New York: Edwin Mellen Press. Sympathetic study of evangelical Protestants' view of Jews and Zionism, as influenced by prophetic belief.

————. "Arno C. Gaebelein (1861–1945): Fundamentalist Protestant Zionist." *American Jewish History* (September 1978). Biographical treatment of a prominent premillennialist who was particularly interested in the prophetic destiny of the Jews.

Robertson, Pat. 1991. *The New World Order*. Dallas: Word Publishing Co.

Sandeen, Ernest. 1970. *The Roots of Fundamentalism: British and American Millenarianism, 1800–1930*. Chicago: University of Chicago Press. Important monograph documenting the centrality of dispensational premillennialism in the emergence of American Fundamentalism.

Smith, Oswald. 1926. *Is the Antichrist at Hand?* Toronto: Tabernacle Publishers.

Trollinger, William Vance, Jr. 1990. *God's Empire: William Bell Riley and Midwestern Fundamentalism*. Madison, Wis.: University of Wisconsin Press. Well-researched biography offering valuable insights on a leading exponent of Fundamentalism and premillennialism in the interwar years.

Trumbull, Charles G. 1920. *The Life of C.I. Scofield*. New York: Oxford University Press. The only full-scale biography, but dated and incomplete in coverage of Scofield's early life.

Weber, Timothy P. 1987. *Living in the Shadow of the Second Coming: American Premillennialism, 1875–1982, With a New Preface*. New York: Oxford University Press. Update of a valuable functionalist study that includes a wealth of valuable information and thoughtful critical reflections.

Wilson, Dwight. 1977. *Armageddon Now! The Premillenarian Response to Russia and Israel Since 1917*. Grand Rapids, Mich.: Baker Book House. Path-breaking critical examination of the role of premillennialist doctrine in shaping believers' attitudes toward Russia, Zionism, and Israel, from World War I through the 1970s.

21

Apocalyptic Movements in Latin America in the Nineteenth and Twentieth Centuries

Robert M. Levine
University of Miami

L ATIN AMERICAN SOCIETY in the nineteenth and twentieth centuries witnessed an array of religious expressions and movements. Among them were many, mostly small, communal-based millenarian experiments with negative apocalyptic underpinnings. That is, rather than believing that the millennium would heal and reform society, they emphasized the imminence of severe divine judgment and the final destruction of the world. This essay examines the most prominent of such movements that occurred throughout the region. It devotes considerable attention to the region's major millenarian event, the destruction by government forces in rural Brazil in 1897 of Canudos, a religious settlement of more than twenty-five thousand believers peacefully living in anticipation of the approaching day of judgment. For the most part, Latin American millenarian movements were religious, not political, in nature. Only a few utilized apocalypticism as a weapon against colonial rule or its survival; rather, most pitted the beliefs and perceptions of the under class against the modernizing thrust of elites, who feared them as primitive and atavistic.

The centralized structure of Iberian state religion constantly reinforced orthodoxy when it could, but in sparsely populated hinterland regions this proved nearly impossible. The diversity of religious expression in post-independence Latin America more often than not played out through syncretism—among groups nominally Roman Catholic but borrowing heavily from African or Amerindian spiritual expression and ritual. Latin American religious practice, then, has encompassed a broader array of forms than, in contrast, North America. And while institutional Roman Catholicism (which in most of Latin America remained tightly in the control of a conservative hierarchy) remained strong enough to combat most break-away impulses in large population centers, in the hinterland's small towns and rural villages, unorthodoxy proliferated.

545

Although isolated from one another, the post-independence Latin American movements shared common beliefs linking salvation to penitence and separation from the secular world. Given the region's history, this should not be surprising. The original Spanish and Portuguese colonial polemic for justifying empire involved Judeo-Christian ideas about the teleological nature of time and history, that the world would end when all people had converted to Christianity. Political theorists began to promote the idea of a universal Christian monarchy (one king, one nation, one religion), and for many Spaniards (and some Portuguese), Charles V in the sixteenth century seemed the perfect leader for it. Dissent from this doctrine was rare not only during the colonial period but after independence as well. Comtean positivism gained important adherents during the middle and late nineteenth century, especially in Mexico, Brazil, and Argentina, but positivist influence remained an upper-class phenomenon, while the lower classes retained their Roman Catholic identity.

During the great age of European popular insurgency from the fourteenth to the seventeenth century, lower-class groups reacted actively to deterioration in their living standards, and, when they fought for alternative social structures, it was usually at the behest of religious visionaries or charismatics. Traditional millenarian protest movements drew their inspiration from Christian eschatology, envisioning the replacement of existing society by paradise on earth. In the case of most of the Latin American movements, we simply do not know what significance leaders gave to the imminence of the apocalypse. Followers tended to accept the premise that society was basically unchangeable, and that when the climate changed to the detriment of the poor or when disease ravaged the land, this was an expression of God's will. As Friedrich Engels noted, however, even during the Middle Ages there was a kind of revolutionary underground tradition appealing to apocalyptic scripture and making a conscious social as well as religious appeal to the poor.[1] Whether Latin America inherited this tradition remains to be seen. Millenarianism is one thing; utopianism another.

The arrival of thousands of evangelical Protestants in Latin America in the nineteenth century sowed the seeds for receptivity of millenarian movements out of that tradition as well. Settlers from northern Europe often migrated to communities where they could speak their own language and practice their faith: Welsh to mining colonies in Patagonia; Swiss to the low mountains outside of Rio de Janeiro; Presbyterian and Evangelical Lutheran Germans to Minas Gerais (Lavras), São Paulo (Santa Barbara), and the states of Santa Catarina, Paraná, and Rio Grande do Sul. New Methodists and Church of God sects were established in many places; Baptists, some of whom came from the United States Confederacy after Lee's surrender, established churches and schools in many Latin American cities. Workers imported from Jamaica and Barbados brought Protestantism with them to Venezuela, Colombia, and the Brazilian Amazon.

A dual pattern emerged of Protestant settlements in farming and mining communities in rural areas and in large cities, where arrivals of foreigners from Europe and the United States came to do business. Protestant congregations in the cities received a constant influx (and outflow) of members, leaving little room for doctrinal mutations. In the countryside, many of the original settlers intermarried and dropped their Protestantism, although small isolated communities, especially among German-speaking immigrants, retained their national identities and Protestant observance. In the 1960s, a third locus of Protestant activity emerged, rooted in urban evangelical Protestant congregations founded by missionaries. Located in impoverished areas of Latin American cities, these grew at an enormous pace, winning tens of thousands of adherents. In some cases, the local Roman Catholic Church was forced to modify its use of

Latin in favor of new forms of worship that included incorporation of African music, vernacular language, and, in the 1980s and later, a new focus on personal salvation and disengagement from communal-based movements for social reform. Evangelical Protestant groups, many linked to sects in the United States, rode such a heady wave of growth that zealots within their ranks publicly mocked Roman Catholicism: in 1995, for example, a Brazilian bishop of the Universal Church of God's Reign, Sérgio Von Helder, kicked to pieces a plaster statue of a Catholic saint during a televised revival meeting, a taunt against what he called "idol worship."

In circumstances where the Roman Catholic Church was strong, then, with its emphasis on group ritual and worship rather than on individual salvation, and its deemphasis—especially in contrast to Protestantism—on interpretations of biblical prophecy, millenarianism arose rarely. But in small towns and in shabby blue-collar districts of large cities, charismatic and millenarian impulses have been strongest, especially when abetted by evangelical missionary Protestantism. Here, as well as among the remnants of native populations, apocalyptic movements have thrived, rooted in the belief that God has revealed the imminent conclusion to the struggle between good and evil through history. The religious climate in these remote places nurtured related behavior, especially the tradition of penitential pleas for direct intervention by saints to relieve drought, cure disease, or alleviate poverty.

It must be recognized that Latin America's social struggles have often had little to do with one religion or another, although they have tended to blend spontaneous class-based resistance with mystical interpretation and the quest for salvation. It is telling that the uprising of Mayan peasants in southern Mexico in 1848 against Mexican landowners started as an economic protest. Four years later it took on millenarian overtones when a wooden "Speaking Cross" appeared, redirecting the Mayan forces to fight a race war in favor of Indian unity. Leaders proclaimed that the Indians were God's children fighting God's war, and that victory would bring spiritual redemption. These violent social upheavals resulted from specific historical pressures. Race-based uprisings of Indians in Mexico in the early nineteenth century led by the *mestizo* priests Hidalgo and Morelos occurred as peninsular elites tried to establish their hegemony after Napoleon's defeat of Spain. As the decades passed, popular religious expression in Latin America remained colored by the preservation of a vast gap between haves and have nots: in a Gramscian manner, the poor's internalization of an elite ideology diffused over generations by the church, the government, and by social institutions (see Parker 1996).

The dominant form of rigid social order in the region yielded another effect as well. Ordinary people, conditioned to obey authority, became easily captivated by charismatic leaders, not only political but religious. Latin American millenarianism, then, invariably followed individuals. When such men (the paternalistic heritage kept women from playing these roles) linked demands for social justice to moral regeneration, millenarian movements emerged, perceiving the world as dominated by sinfulness and redeemable only by a holy war in the name of God. Such movements thirsted for salvation, not only from political and economic oppression but from manifestations of evil in the everyday world.

In Argentina, immigrants who settled in rural areas became involved in millenarianism during the last third of the nineteenth century. These were short-lived and had little lasting impact. The major Argentine event took place on the first day of 1872 in the pampa town of Tandil. The area had attracted immigrant wheat farmers, from Denmark, the Basque region of Spain, and from Italy. In 1871 a healer, Geronimo G. de Solané, familiarly known as "Tata Dios," established a clinic and began to attract clients. He had a long, flowing beard, and an imposing presence, although he was barely literate. Like other lay missionaries, he preached what historian Richard Slatta terms "a skillful blend of miraculous cures, herbal remedies, and conventional Catholicism" (1986, 171–72). Trouble came when dozens of his gaucho followers, led by two of his close disciples, met at a balancing rock in the fills above Tandil to await the appearance of God and the coming of a terrible earthquake. This would destroy the old society and usher in a new society cleansed of immigrants.

On dawn on New Year's Day, the armed gauchos attacked the town square shouting epithets against foreigners and Masons. Slatta described what happened:

> They freed the only prisoner in the city jail, an Indian named Nicolas Oliveira, who joined the group. Gathering more arms, they began a murderous rampage. Near the plaza they struck down their first victim, a forty-five-year-old Italian organ player who died of a fractured skull. Turning north, they fell upon a group of sleeping Basque carters . . . and slit the throats of several. A Basque merchant met the same fate. The killers spared his Argentine wife but dispatched a young Italian peon. Several English settlers died at a store owned by a Mr. Thompson. The band slit the throats of the clerk and his wife, both in their mid-twenties. . . . The raiders destroyed the account books of the pulperia (dry goods store), filled with those mysterious little marks that held the gaucho in debt to the foreign merchant. A native, Honorio de la Canal, rode up to the store during the attack. The killers spared his life when a black member of the band assured them that he was Argentine, not foreign. (1986, 171–72)

A posse led by a military officer tracked down the band and killed or captured most of its members. Although Tata Dios was not present at the rampage and disavowed any involvement or knowledge of the massacre, he was arrested and held for trial. During his incarceration, however, he was shot to death through the window of his cell. It is not known who killed him, although some of the town's foreigners may have taken revenge. The episode generated heated debate throughout the country and even in Europe. Voices decried gaucho primitivism, but others blamed the government for oppressing gauchos and for favoring foreigners. The millenarian aspect of the rampage especially shocked Argentines, who had long considered the gauchos superstitious and prone to violence. The British consul complained that the Argentine government had been too lax in pursuing the rioters, and for a while the news in the foreign press may have dampened interest among would-be immigrants to Argentina from the continent.[2]

This was only one of many similar movements in the hemisphere during the nineteenth and twentieth centuries. Conspirators in the Peruvian city of Cuzco participated in a thwarted millenarian insurrection seeking to drive out the Spaniards and install a descendant of the Inca as king. Settlers inspired by Fourier established utopian communities for peasants in northern Mexico roughly at the same time. These were not very similar to the peasant movements springing up throughout Latin America seeking to restore Inca or Aztec or Mayan rule, although they shared utopian and millenarian elements. Bolivia witnessed its Tahuantisuyu-Kollasuyu restorationist uprising, linked to the "prepolitical" efforts of rebels in Peru. In Mexico, Atanasio Tzui mobilized fifty-five thousand Indians against the central government; in the Yucatán, the Caste War raged for decades. Between 1868 and 1870 a corresponding movement in southern Chiapas erupted, a millenarian rebellion that caught up Mayan peasants from Tabasco to Guatemala. Quintín Lame, in Colombia, led a millenarian rebellion between 1910 and 1918 seeking to restore Indian self-rule. On the whole, though, these movements were likely motivated more by the personal aims of their leaders, who took advantage of local economic deprivation and pent-up resentment against European domination to rally indigenous men and women behind restorationist slogans made more dramatic by millenarian appeals to divine retribution.

Millenarian movements were relatively more numerous in Portuguese-speaking Brazil. Hierarchical Roman Catholicism was always weaker in Brazil than in the former Spanish colonies. Over time, Brazilian elites—perhaps they because they were outnumbered to a much greater extent by the illiterate under class formed by African slaves, their descendants, and native populations—took fewer and fewer steps to combat syncretic and other varieties of popular religious expression. The result was that the Brazilian Roman Catholic Church concentrated its relatively meager institutional resources in its wealthy city dioceses, leaving the poor (and the vast hinterland) to their own devices. These places proved unusually fertile soil for a penitential and Manichean religious idiom apocalyptic in nature.

The movements that erupted under these conditions followed in the footsteps of similar phenomena occurring in virtually every part of Latin America and stretching from the colonial period to the mid-twentieth century. Their historical antecedents extended back at least four centuries, to the 1500s. In Brazil, among indigenous populations dozens of insurrections broke out, some of them magico-religious or messianic in nature, such as the *Confederação de Tamoios* (1563), the *Santidade de Jaguaripe* (1584, reappearing at least five additional times down through 1892), as well as Tupí-Guaraní resistance which took the form of migratory flight. The first of Brazil's millennial impulses rooted in Christianity took the form of sporadic dramatizations of Portuguese Sebastianism, a mystical movement whose followers awaited the resurrection of the fallen King Sebastião, who had been killed in 1578 while fighting the Moors, and which held popular currency in Portugal for centuries. Sebastianism also erupted periodically in diverse parts of the Luso-Brazilian world. Sebastianism was deeply rooted in rural folk religion and exercised a much stronger influence in the backlands than on the coast. Sebastianism's persistence in Luso-Brazilian history is remarkable, as the literary historian Frederic Amory has observed (1996, 677), and it strongly influenced individuals in the lower classes who dreamed that kingly divine intervention would bring relief from their marginalized lives.

The first of the nineteenth-century movements occurred in the Rodeador mountains in southern Pernambuco. There, beginning in 1817, backlanders became caught up in a religious crusade which declared that, without bloodshed, they would be able to march to Jerusalem, free it from its worldly capture, and witness the coming of the kingdom of God on earth. Their leader was Silvestre José dos Santos, an ex-soldier hailed as a prophet, who, with four hundred disciples, founded a "City of Earthly Paradise." Skeptics would be dazzled by the peaceful return of King Sebastião and his armies. The movement was suppressed by authorities, who believed it to be connected to the political separatist movement of that same year in Pernambuco, but there was apparently no link.

There was some evidence of dissatisfaction with the repressive governor at the time, and with the military draft system, but the main cause of the movement, as far as can be determined, was the millenarian hope of salvation. What is fascinating in the light of later (and unproven) claims about Canudos is that prisoners captured at Rodeador believed unshakably that once the faithful initiated their march there would be no need to fight: enemies would be converted to their faith, a latter-day version of the medieval Children's Crusade (see Ribeiro 1970, 66). Most of the faithful were massacred when the governor ordered Rodeador attacked on October 25, 1820.

In central Pernambuco, Pedra Bonita was the site of a terrible incident in the 1830s, the Enchanted Kingdom of Vila-Bela. There, between two monoliths reaching a height of one hundred feet, rural folk, presuming that they had to demonstrate their unequivocal faith, offered blood sacrifices to bring about the return to earth of King Sebastião. The first to be killed in this way was the prophet's own father. Three days later, on May 14, 1838, dozens more were sacrificed, including thirty children, twelve men, eleven women, and fourteen dogs. The religious leader João Ferreira, aided by subordinates, slit the children's throats or dashed their heads against the rocks. It is believed locally that the fanatics were convinced that in addition to salvation, the worldly order would become inverted: mulattos and blacks would be transformed into whites, and the poor would be granted riches and eternal life. The movement ended abruptly when the police invading the sacrificial site encountered no resistance, because, as Sebastianists, the believers had been taught that an attack on them would signal the beginning of the restoration of the kingdom. Most of the faithful died singing religious songs, and the leaders of the movement were imprisoned. The originator of the cult, a *mestizo* named João Santos, was arrested and killed by the soldiers who detained him.

The Cabanada was a grassroots millenarian crusade in Pernambuco's *agreste* between 1832 and 1836. More than most of the other Brazilian movements with millenarian underpinnings, what was called by contemporaries the Cabanada, or the War of the Cabanos, in fact started for expressly political reasons. It was triggered in April 1832 by restorationist rebellions in Recife and Rio de Janeiro, but, although the instigators, mostly Portuguese militia men, were crushed, the movement spread into the hinterland. It soon became transformed into a three-year guerrilla war. Outside support came from Portuguese merchants in Recife and restorationist politicians in Rio de Janeiro. The movement took on millenarian proportions when the guerrilla commander, an ex-sergeant who had deserted from the army, Vicente Ferreira de Paula, used the news of the death of Emperor Pedro I in September 1834 to warn his followers that they were living in sin. He convinced them that they had to fight to save both the new emperor and their religion from the anti-Portuguese upstarts who were governing independent Brazil, whom they labeled Jacobins. Ferreira de Paula, who was the son of a priest, escaped after the main body of rebels capitulated in 1835 and managed to survive with a small band of the faithful in a kind of wretched colony in which the residents subsisted by eating snakes, insects, wild fruits, and lizards. The survivors had held out because they feared that if they were captured they would be skinned alive and that their own leaders would kill them if they did not obey.

In the south there were the "Muckers." *Mucker,* a German term for a religious hypocrite, was the derisive label applied to members of a messianic sect living in Ferrabrás in São Leopoldo, Rio Grande do Sul, beginning in 1868. The movement was also referred to as "*os Santarrões,*" the term mocking the devout nature of the followers' beliefs. The sect resided in the midst of a German colony of impoverished agricultural settlers. The leaders of the movement were Anabaptist healers Jacobina Maurer and her husband, João Jorge Maurer. As monarchists, the Maurers claimed that they had been elected by God to lead the faithful to establish a holy kingdom on earth. The intrusion of the outside world, most visibly in the form of steamship links between Pôrto Alegre and São Leopoldo and the arrival of a railroad line in 1871, seems to have had unsettling effects on the region's former isolation; the Muckers even tried to prevent the railroad from operating. Their followers were almost exclusively illiterate (German and German-Brazilian) farmers suffering declining social status and economic hardship.

The religious movement's exclusivity angered its neighbors and led to acts of arson, armed conflict, and eventually the sect's refusal to obey local authorities. On June 28, 1873, the Muckers defeated a force of one hundred police, killing its commander. The army subdued the rebels only after a series of engagements using artillery. The survivors were not executed but were sentenced to prison terms of up to thirty years; all were pardoned in 1883. They then returned to Ferrabrás, and the old conflict with their neighbors started up again. Skirmishes continued through the 1890s, and in 1896 it was rumored that the sect was regrouping at Nova Petrópolis. By 1898, one year after the fall of Canudos, the remaining Muckers had all been killed. Traces of the movement survived until at least the mid-1950s, when adepts held a "reunion" of families in Taquaraçu in anticipation of the return of their leader.

Brazil's rejection of monarchy in late 1889 and its adoption of republican government rooted in positivist ideology and hostile to the Roman Catholic Church set in motion events that, during the next decade, would erupt in a millenarian, apocalyptic movement whose members would ultimately be wiped out in a massacre championed by the national elite as a cleansing defense of civilization against fanaticism. The event, incorrectly dubbed the Canudos Rebellion, shocked the Brazilian upper classes, who had embraced the heady atmosphere of the replacement of the monarchy, an event that the London *Statesman*'s editors, in an uncharacteristic fit of hyperbole, had euphorically called "the most important world event" in 1889. Still, Canudos so traumatized Brazilian life that for decades after it was destroyed it colored the way Brazilians saw themselves and the lower classes. For this reason, this essay analyzes Canudos in depth as a case study of an apocalyptic occurrence with deep national reverberations.

CANUDOS

Canudos, or Belo Monte, was a religious settlement founded by a pious lay Catholic mystic, Antônio Vicente Mendes Maciel (1830–1897), known to his followers as Antônio Conselheiro (the Counsellor). Belo Monte took form on the grounds of an abandoned cattle ranch owned by the Jeremoabo clan in the parched backlands interior of the state of Bahia. The region was afflicted by a severe climate and generally barren terrain that intimidated visitors. The backlands conjured up images of backwardness and inhospitability of place and people, although on the whole its dry climate was neither intolerable nor oppressive. Backlands residents were not peasants like the sedentary rural peoples of the Andean highlands or Middle America, where the term "peasant" is used mostly to describe poor rural families with little freedom or independence, living and working on land once communally shared but now either divided into minifundia (units too small to yield profit) or larger properties owned by others. Most rural backlanders lived as renters or sharecroppers under miserable conditions, but they retained a limited freedom of movement and a grudging spirit of self-reliance. Before 1893, few outsiders passed through the Bahian *sertão* except en route to the São Francisco River one hundred and thirty kilometers to the north.

Conselheiro's followers willingly accepted prescriptions for life that provided comforting structure and direction. At Canudos, residents were assigned work and lived according to a set routine, which must have brought a sense of security to men and women whose lives had been traumatized by deprivation and by the vicissitudes of drought, disputes between clans, and economic uncertainty. Many ordinary citizens of the backlands questioned the secularized republican order. It is untrue that the backlands residents of Canudos were driven by crazed religious fanaticism. Economic depression, residual effects of crippling drought, increased use of the state police to enforce political demands, and the disappearance of the monarchy and its traditional prescriptive authority combined to make the structured life promised by Conselheiro seem powerfully desirable.

Not only was the world changing, but the closing years of the nineteenth century actually witnessed a broadening gulf between the emerging national elite culture, on the one hand, and the world of the countryside, on the other. Coastal Brazilians gentrified religion (or, in the influential Masonic lodges and parlors of the secular humanists, ignored it), while backlands religionists, through means remarkably similar to what historian Robert Darnton calls the remote mental universe of the eighteenth-century French village, "presented man as a slave of passion," and fill(ed) their heads "with visions of threatening, occult forces . . . miracles, and hagiography" (see 1990, 239–40).

In the backlands of the state of Bahia, the dislocations created by the changes on the coast disoriented the lower classes. They were angered by the reports that Emperor Pedro II (1826–1891), their beloved father figure, had been sent into exile. The backlander followers of Conselheiro questioned the secularized republican order. Married couples feared that the new separation of church and state would fail to recognize their religious marital vows, making their children illegitimate and depriving them of religious burial when they died. Some viewed the new requirement for civil registration and census questions about racial origins as a threat to restore slavery, which had been abolished by the monarchy a year before it fell. Conselheiro had pulled down and burned notices of new municipal taxes in 1893. Even the election of a president rather than the lifetime investiture of a fatherly monarch raised fears; many backlanders preferred to seek refuge in Canudos, a communal settlement led by a protective patriarch.

Conselheiro's charismatic appeal was rooted in diverse factors. Given the scarcity of priests in the remote backlands of northeastern Brazil in the last quarter of the nineteenth century, it should be no surprise that itinerant lay preachers were heavily influential. Imperfect as all human beings, they inevitably stamped their own mark on the theology they transmitted to the faithful. They adopted and added to the assumptions present among their flocks, and they contributed new emphases to the stream of popular religious culture. It is understandable that the Canudos conflict has lent itself to symbolism of dramatic proportions, for Conselheiro did at some point promise his followers salvation—even under the duress of invasion—the second coming in the millennial year 1900. But most of his preachments were not apocalyptic or thaumaturgic: they simply demanded personal morality and hard work and invoked spiritual protection from the corrupted secular world. That world, in the *sertão*, was also locked in economic crisis, as it had been to a greater or lesser degree for generations. Belo Monte was thus a place in which the faithful would lead disciplined lives according to Catholic precepts, removed not only from modern infamies but from hunger and want; yet it also seemed an environment of primitivism and audacity.

The survival of Conselheiro's settlement from 1893 through 1897 indicates clear evidence of growing symbolic withdrawal from the dominant regional culture by the thousands of backlanders who opted to take up residence there. Whether this withdrawal was based on foolish gullibility or "mystic evasion," Conselheiro's cult offered "a critique of the existing order and a [potentially explosive] alternative symbolic universe." Canudos nurtured new social links and cultural dissent in the form of a variant—exaggerated but not necessarily heretical—of the dominant Roman Catholic religion.

Nationally, influential citizens had dreaded that the stubborn independence shown by the *Canudenses* would spread beyond its own locale and ultimately incite regionalist insurrection. This never happened. What coastal elites refused to comprehend was that Conselheiro's words were rhetorical, not a summons to aggression. His followers withdrew to Canudos to await the day of judgment. They tended to themselves and did not proselytize. Conselheiro's hatred of the Republic was real enough, but at least in the early days of his settlement he and his lieutenants managed to ally themselves with local landowners and other members of the backlands elite on a purely pragmatic basis.

The nature of Conselheiro's ministry in Canudos, and the physical exodus of northeasterners to join him in his holy city, doomed his movement to inevitable intervention by the state. Prophecy coupled with diatribes against sin played a regular part of lay Catholicism as communicated to backlanders not only by Conselheiro during the wandering phase of his ministry but by many others in the region. The Canudos episode occurred at the height of the Vatican's ultramontanist campaign to restore orthodox religious practice to its followers throughout the world. Lacking Brazilian-born priests, the coastal church hierarchy sent for European-born replacements. These men, conservatively trained and speaking French, German, or Italian—not Portuguese—were assigned exactly to the remote places where penitential folk Catholicism had taken its greatest hold. The foreign priests were horrified at what they found: men and women praying to saints' figures and icons, the popularity of flagellation cults, and widespread lack of the use of Latin. Conselheiro, in turn, an educated man familiar with the work of church missionaries in India and Asia, treated his flock with austere compassion. One of the main elements of his teachings was the apocalyptic Portuguese-language *Missão Abreviada*, written by the Portuguese priest Miguel Couto for use among the heathen. The clash with lay missionaries like Conselheiro was inevitable, and the harshness of their response—labeling him a dangerous heretic—in some cases had the opposite effect, encouraging men and women to seek refuge in his settlement.

Conselheiro's "New Jerusalem" grew rapidly until it contained more than five thousand mud-and-wattle huts scattered in close proximity below a ring of hills and low mountains. Its population of twenty-five thousand (at its height in 1895 probably closer to thirty-five thousand) made it the largest urban site in Bahia after Salvador, the capital, seven hundred kilometers distant to the southeast. Canudos drained labor across several states, especially from the Rio Real in southern Sergipe and Inhambupe in Bahia. Between 1893 and 1897 it became the expression of a popular movement atavistic to outsiders but vigorous and pragmatically adapted to the region's limitations. Conselheiro was a product of his unique backlands religious environment. Since colonial days, the São Francisco Valley had been known for the powerful influence of flagellant penitential brotherhoods. The backlands population, largely self-instructed in its Catholicism, tended to blend everyday stoicism and resignation with messianic hopes. It sanctioned an apocalyptic view of life, indulgences, and the cult of personal saints. The *beatos* (lay persons living as if they were members of a religious order, consecrated by a curate in this status) and other late-nineteenth-century wanderers were laymen in religious garb. They offered quasi-sacramental functions and combined moral and practical advice with fire-and-brimstone millenarian allegories, becoming an institutionalized form of popular religion. Herein lay the heart of the clash between the "modern" and "backwards" cultures embodied in the Canudos conflict: the characteristics of which coastal observers disapproved and which they scorned were the very ones that brought vitality to Conselheiro's followers.

The depletion of surplus labor from surrounding regions as well as exaggerated tales of religious fanaticism told by visitors to Conselheiro's self-proclaimed "holy city" led local elites to demand intervention. When Conselheiro stubbornly held firm, the decision was made first to disarm the "rebels" and ultimately to destroy their city. After three military expeditions failed, a fourth expedition of more than eight thousand men commanded by three generals and the minister of war shelled Canudos into submission in October 1897. Only a handful of women and children survived. Canudos went down in Brazilian history as a glorious victory for the forces of civilization against the dark forces of primitivism and insurrection. The remarkable tenacity of those faithful who did not flee Belo Monte but who resisted to the end may possibly be explained by theories about the "density" of popular culture. Social psychologists have also suggested that when belonging to or joining a group demands great sacrifice from a member, that person tends to give greater prestige to his association with that group. This seems to fit with what we know about behavior within Canudos under Conselheiro's leadership. The same determination that was seen by outsiders as a primitive effort to block change may be seen as a form of coping or even assertiveness in which group cohesiveness under Belo Monte's utopian framework was reinforced by Conselheiro's imprecations that the faithful, not the outside world, would be redeemed.

The attitudes and erroneous suppositions held by educated coastal Brazilians about the nature of life in the rural hinterland made even greater the shock from news about the army's inability to subdue Conselheiro's defenders, whose ranks combined backlands ruffians with pious residents lacking any kind of fighting experience. Although their stereotypes of the rural poor conjured up images of resistance to authority and latent violence, at the same time educated Brazilians subscribed to the long-standing myth that even in the northeast the period after 1850 represented a kind of golden nonviolent age. In reality, the region was swept by both urban and rural conflict between 1850 and 1900, including food riots in Salvador and slave revolts in the interior. No fewer than fifty-nine violent conflicts were enumerated by the provincial Ministry of Justice through 1889, and many others undoubtedly went unreported. Major outlaw gangs roamed the backlands. Nor did the government's victory over Canudos mean any cessation of politically linked violence. The 1899 municipal elections pitted anti-incumbent interests against the governor's allies, just as before, with the usual attendant beatings, attacks on commercial establishments, and murder.

Until the settlement was attacked by soldiers and earmarked for destruction, Canudos coexisted peacefully with its neighbors. Up to twenty-five thousand men and women flocked to it, but hundreds of thousands more in the region did not and showed no inclination to do so. Canudos also became a victim of circumstance: its birth and explosive growth fatally coincided with the opportunity to mount a propaganda campaign depicting Canudos as a monarchist plot. In the aftermath of the carnage that ensued, jingoism shored up the shaky civilian government. Under the weight of carefully orchestrated patriotism, the "politics of the governors" emerged—a brokered arrangement through which the strongest states in the federation gained unprecedented power—and alliances between state machines and rural bosses, or *coronéis*, through which the agro-commercial oligarchy secured unopposed control of rural Brazil.

What outsiders wanted to see as a rebellion was a collective statement by an integrated and unified community demanding the right to relocate to a place they considered a haven from an unfriendly world. Belo Monte had to be crushed because it upset the stability of the status quo in the *sertão*. It affected two major elements of rural oligarchical power: the pliant labor system and the "herd vote," the arrangement by which rural bosses captured all the votes under their control and delivered them in exchange for local autonomy. Migration from all parts of the backlands to Canudos posed an immediate, real threat to the labor system.

Conselheiro never claimed to be the Messiah. His supernatural charisma was always attributed to him by others. He did, of course, exercise a powerful spell over his flock, and his acerbic (and antisocial) personality frightened many. What have never been questioned are his unshakable personal faith and determination to shield his followers from the sins and temptations of modern life. To those who encountered him he projected a "sense of foreboding . . . pervasive and unappeasable."[3] Conselheiro broke the hold of the traditional system of social control and offered new lives for the faithful, especially in the heady period before the settlement was attacked by enemies.

Conselheiro neither spoke frequently about miracles nor claimed miraculous powers. Backlands folklorists have uncovered three miraculous acts attributed to Conselheiro during Canudos's lifetime, but no evidence links them to him. As miracles, they are very small in scale. At best, they likely were journalistic adaptations of backlands stories, fitted to the Canudos events. All of them date from the period of heaviest combat, during a period in which journalists, as all war correspondents do, were scratching for copy to send to their newspapers. The first story claimed that when he sat under a tree, the leaves fell when he departed. The second told of a chronically ill woman who requested a piece of Conselheiro's robe. When she received it, she burned it, made a potion of the ashes, drank it, and was cured. The third account told of a nursing woman whose breasts were dry. She asked Conselheiro to touch them, and they were said to fill with milk.

Canudos's residents behaved rationally. They willfully and courageously abandoned their former lives to enter Conselheiro's holy city. It is insufficient to dismiss Canudos and like movements as responses to *anomie*, or breakdowns of the traditional extended family owing to the rise of urbanization, the decline of paternalism, and other factors. Nor was Belo Monte simply a kind of "dumb theater," as outsiders tended to regard it—a pathetic, year-round version of the carnivalesque practice whereby the poor become rich and enact waking dreams of social inversion. Those that elected to live in Conselheiro's austere commune were likely motivated by the dislocations caused by the accelerating pace of change bringing instability to the backlands, and to the always-present condition of hardship in individual lives.

The end came in October 1897, when Canudos was encircled and pounded into submission by a furious assault by the Brazilian armed forces. Male captives had their throats slit, often with family members forced to watch. News of the military campaign was reported daily over a period of months by newspaper correspondents; the campaign itself was personally conducted by the Brazilian Minister of War, situated at a safe distance from the front. When Canudos finally capitulated, after months of resistance, the community's 5,200 homes were burned to the ground. The few surviving women were evacuated to the coast, where they were made servants (and in some cases, prostitutes); some of the surviving children were "adopted" by some of the onlookers or otherwise taken as trophies of war. Spiritual revolt at Canudos yielded messianic hope and the determination to take leave of the secular world by finding refuge in a disciplined, protected community. The willingness of rural men and women to accept authority and to shrink from confrontation itself predisposed many of them—perhaps the most depressed members of the population—to heed Conselheiro's message, to have the courage to follow him, and to accept the strictures of Belo Monte's austerity.

Here we see a contrast between Canudos and apocalyptic movements elsewhere in Latin America. More often than not these were antinomian, breaking significantly with Christian orthodoxy on practice, theology, and social behavior. At Canudos, however, precisely the opposite occurred. Conselheiro preached to his followers that they were the authentic Christians, that Brazilian society had become immoral, anti-Catholic, and dissolute; that his was the true faith.

Yale University's James C. Scott has reminded us that "(if) it requires no great leap of the imagination to reverse the existing social order, then it should come as no surprise that it can as easily be negated" (see Scott 1985, 232). On the other hand, the radicalism underlying Conselheiro's millenarian and utopian vision may be seen as a negation of the existing pattern of misery and exploitation. What the faithful thought they were going to experience was essentially a reflexive symbolism implying a post-earthly society *not* in which there be no rich or poor— which is the typical goal of a millenarian movement—but, in keeping with Conselheiro's dark, unforgiving Catholicism, an inverted future in which the rich will become poor and the poor rich.

☞ PADRE CÍCERO

The last schismatic movement of notable size after Canudos was named for its patron, Padre (Father) Cícero (1844–1934). It arose in the 1850s in southern Ceará's backlands Carirí Valley. A newly ordained priest, Cícero Romão Baptista, came to the area in the early 1870s, immediately before the calamitous droughts of 1877–1879. Padre Cícero encouraged his followers to dig wells, build shelter, and plant crops of manioc. In 1889 Cícero became involved in a religious dispute over the veracity of a supposed miracle which had occurred under his jurisdiction. During a mass the host had been divinely transformed into the blood of Christ. The more his backlands settlement in the Ceará hamlet of Juazeiro attracted followers, the more church officials found fault with his religious practices, and in 1892 he was partially suspended from orders by Ceará's bishop. Now firmly entrenched in the backlands hamlet of Juazeiro, he became involved in a lifelong conflict with the church, which looked askance at his command of thousands of devout backlanders, many of whom came to settle permanently.

Historian Ralph della Cava notes that by attracting pilgrims to labor-shy regions of Bahia and Ceará, both Conselheiro and Padre Cícero accumulated the equivalent of political power. Work-hands, under the domination of local bosses, represented potential wealth and votes. Unlike Conselheiro, Padre Cícero initially displayed a greater willingness to work with the local archdiocese. Later he sent appeals directly to Rome, when Ceará's bishop refused to acknowledge the claimed miracle, and he sought support from local *coronéis* and lay leaders for his request to be reinstated as a priest. When threatened with excommunication, Cícero's followers raised funds through lay Catholic associations to send emissaries to argue their case. They used both the religious and secular press in addition to gathering dozens of petitions to plead their case. Padre Cícero himself traveled to Rome in 1898, although without success. During Padre Cícero's lifetime, his messianic movement became institutionalized. Miracles and extreme forms of religiosity were discouraged, and social relationships and the political machinery at Juazeiro were almost "indistinguishable from those prevailing in general in Brazilian peasant society" (Ribeiro 1970, 67).

Both Juazeiro and Canudos illustrate the fact that rural violence accompanied manifestations of popular religion. We know that *beatos* and other religious figures found it necessary to surround themselves with bodyguards, often rough-and-tumble men carrying arms. Sometimes violence was directed the other way. At Alagoa de Baixo, in Pernambuco, after a sermon by the local priests disparaging the well-known "miracles" of Padre Cícero at Juazeiro, followers and penitents loyal to Cícero invaded the town and assaulted the church, attempting to beat and expel the prelate on the grounds that he had become an agent of the devil. For years and even up to the present, backlands families well integrated into the regular Catholic Church, in most of Ceará as well as throughout the Northeast, have hung images and effigies of the "saint" Padre Cícero in the front room of their houses to ward off evil spirits and to invoke his protection.

☞ CONTESTADO

On the remote contested border between the southern states of Paraná and Santa Catarina, a monarchist uprising known as the *Contestado* broke out in 1912 when a *curandeiro* (herbal medicinal faith healer) and seer, José Maria, gathered three hundred homeless followers and appealed to them to reject the Republic. Parallels with Canudos were striking. José Maria had been an itinerant holy man wandering through the backlands. José Maria, born Miguel Lucena Boaventura, was a literate man of about forty, probably a deserter from the police force of the state of Paraná. Erudite to an unusual degree for even a man of his background, José Maria read aloud passages from *The History of Charlemagne* to his followers to encourage monarchist feelings, and to remind them of the holy war against the Moors. He dressed twenty-four of his soldiers for battle in white robes draped with green crosses, naming them the *Pares de França*, the Peers of France, for Charlemagne's imperial guard.

José Maria preached that the Republic was evil and that the monarchy should be restored. He frequently invoked the name of Saint Sebastian. Conselheiro and José Maria both asked the faithful to withdraw from civil society to a holy city, to wait for evil to consume the rest of the world. Women played a major role in the Contestado movement, joining José Maria's settlement on the whole with greater enthusiasm than their husbands. Like Canudos, the holy city was open to all: *patrões* as well as the landless.

Local landowners instigated an attack by police forces and José Maria was killed; but under a successor, José Eusébio Ferreira dos Santos, a "holy" settlement was established on lands which he owned. A lay religious organizer, José Eusébio had invited José Maria to participate in the annual Bom Jesus festival at Perdizes Grandes, a tiny hilltop village. The regional political boss, Francisco de Albuquerque, expelled them, driving the band, by now known as *os fanáticos* (the fanatics), into Paraná. Citizens on the coast began to receive reports of the nascent conflict, with memories of Canudos fresh in their minds. Some officials interpreted the movement of José Maria's band as a disguised effort by Santa Catarina to occupy disputed Paraná land. The migrants settled near Irani on hilly land populated by *posseiros* (squatters). Many of these men were armed, the nucleus of José Maria's volunteer fighting force. The new holy city was named Taquaraçu. In March 1914, men, women, and children defended themselves against machine-gun fire by draping themselves in a large white and green cross flag, convinced of their immunity to the army's weapons. A massacre ensued. At its height the Contestado rebellion went further than Canudos. After the Taquaraçu massacre the rebels took the offensive, attacking and burning nearby properties. Twenty thousand insurgents took control of 3 percent of the national territory, or twenty-eight thousand square kilometers. The population of the holy city numbered ten thousand. In 1915, the Brazilian army used a scorched-earth policy to starve the colony into submission. The rebellion was eradicated in 1916.

☞ THE POSTWAR PERIOD

Post–World War II movements, like most of their predecessors, likely represented only a small fraction of the dozens of millenarian cults that never developed to the point of threatening the status quo and therefore went unrecorded. The millenarian, and particularly the Sebastianist, tradition was very much a part of Luso-Brazilian life during the colonial period. Although the influence of organized religion diminished in the nineteenth century (marked by the formal separation of church and state in Brazil in 1891), millenarian sects not only continued to be born but underwent a flowering during the late twentieth century. Some of the most prominent movements included the Fraternal Universal Eclectic Spiritist church in Rio de Janeiro in 1945 (a branch moved to Brasília in 1960 when that new capital was inaugurated). The Fraternal Universal Church was headed by Master Yokaanam, who instructed his disciples in a melange of spiritist doctrine taken from Alain Kardec and evangelical, apocalyptic Protestantism. The "Blue Butterfly" cult was formally known as the Charitable House of Jesus in the Garden and was located in the inland city of Campina Grande, Paraíba, from 1961 to 1979. Cult leaders demanded that followers fast, pray, and perform penance, and taught that disease did not exist except as a state of mind induced by physicians. Sickness was a punishment; the way to health lay in gaining God's protection. The continued popularity of such movements may have pointed to the reservoir of alienation in Brazilian life, and to the shock of a growing clash between the Brazilian Catholic Church and evangelical Protestants.

These movements stressed religious, not political, goals, although some groups in the region, notably Peru's Shining Path guerrillas, borrowed from native myths of millennial renewal to justify their insurgency. There is a regional tradition for this. Following the Chilean government's campaign against the Araucanian Indians (1860-1883), the surviving Indians revived millennial legends to assert their confidence that divine intervention would punish the Europeans and restore their lands. Indian priests warned that earthquakes would destroy the urban settlements of the occupiers, and that larger earthquakes would topple the very Andean *cordillera*.

What is striking about the Latin American experience with millenarian movements is that since the Second World War the pace of their formation has accelerated. As in the past, they have been almost exclusively lower-class in composition. A more aggressive example of lower-class millenarian beliefs was identified by John H. Bodley in the 1960s in his study of the Asháninkas in Amazonian Peru. This tribe, living among thirty-eight mostly Protestant mission communities in their territory, seemed to still be influenced by the missionary preaching of a Seventh-day Adventist mission along the Río Perené in the early and mid-1920s. Pastor Stahl, who preached the imminent return of a destructive Christ, led the Asháninkas to believe that such intervention was to be expected any day. Bodley wrote:

> This coming was to be an extremely cataclysmic event. One informant said the dead would arise, all evil would be destroyed, and the believers and risen dead would be taken to the house of God in the sky where there would be no more sickness, death, or growing old. Some confused Stahl with the promised messiah, and there were reports that God had already descended to earth at Metraro [Stahl's mission station]. (Brown and Fernández 1991, 75)

In a manner strikingly similar to what had happened at Canudos in the Brazilian backlands eighty years earlier, hundreds of Asháninkas gathered to await the predicted millenarian event. As a result, local landowners faced significant labor shortages and organized reprisals against the balky workers, including at least one murder. When the Messiah failed to appear, most of the Asháninkas dispersed, although small groups remained in two settlements organized by natives at La Cascada and Tambo. In still another outbreak of apocalyptic excitement, in the late 1950s or early 1960s the arrival of a Protestant missionary named Bulner attracted many Asháninkas to his settlement at Puerto Rico, to await the day of judgment. Brown and Fernández relate the comments of Marta, a Nomatsiguenga woman, about what happened:

> At that time we were living there in my village, and I heard people speaking this way: "Upcountry there is a gringo, a little gringo who is a brother, who is a god. he is white." He was white. The people said: "You ought to believe it! He's [the] Sun, our god!" Since he was a gringo, everyone believed him, every last person believed him. People from everywhere came to see this gringo. The People believed that he was Itomi Pavá (Son of the Sun).

But Bulner and many of his followers contracted malaria and died. Then people said that he was not divine; he was not Itomi Pavá. He was an impostor, and he "finished off all our people" (Brown and Fernández 1991, 76–77).

Another Peruvian Amazon community, in Chiriguania, experienced in 1969 and 1970 a series of events that were not only similar to the phenomenon created by Bulner but which were remarkably like Canudos itself. To this distant region came José Francisco da Cruz, a fifty-five-year-old preacher and lay missionary who entered Peru at Pucallpa in 1969 and who remained for four years among Indian tribes. Later, after returning to Brazil, he founded a settlement named the Union of Peace and Love. His Peruvian disciples, most Cocama Indians of Tupí-Guaraní origin from the most marginalized region of the Peruvian Amazon near Iquitos, in turn formed an evangelical church, the Brotherhood of the Cross, which taught that Cruz was the Messiah, destined to achieve a world without evil and an earthly paradise.

Like Conselheiro, the bearded Cruz walked from place to place wearing a long caftan tied by a cord and with sandals on his feet. He wore a large wooden cross on his chest and carried a walking stick. When he arrived in a town he would erect a large cross hewn from tree trunks, sometimes meters high. He preached and offered advice and, in many places, people attributed miracles to him. His disciples dressed in white, even in mourning, and wore wooden crosses with the initials STA ("Salva Tu Alma," or "Save Your Soul"). Men were instructed to let their beards grow, like their leader. They withdrew from the secular world, awaiting the impending end of the world and God's wrath against human misbehavior. Their religion mixed Catholic and evangelical Protestant practices with Tupí notions about nature. They believed that God spoke to men in three phases, the first heralded by Christ, the second by Calvin, and the third (and final phase) by José Francisco da Cruz.

Cruz put his flock to work in communal agriculture, feeding his settlement and selling what was not needed to pay costs. Those owning their own properties were asked to tithe a tenth of their income to the movement and to give more if they could. Cruz also asked for donations from his followers in case of special need—if a "brother" or "sister" fell ill, for example. To administer this fund Cruz established AEBMCC, the Emergency Assistance Charitable and Cooperative Bank. Cruz oversaw the construction of chapels, where he preached, and which offered Bible study. All aspects of behavior were controlled. All icons and images were prohibited.

On the last day of every month Cruz would lead a procession accompanied by flutists and drummers. New followers were baptized in the river. In more remote areas, followers would light candles to celebrate their leader's work. Liquor, dancing, playing cards, and practicing black magic were banned. By 1980, the organization had four thousand members in Peru and six thousand in Brazil, and had developed a hierarchy headed by a Bishop-Patriarch who directed priest-missionaries. Their goal was to find paradise on earth, a communal society that would survive the coming deluge. This followed Tupí belief as well as Christian millenarianism, for the Tupís believed that the world would be destroyed and then recreated. Groups of followers were sent to explore the hinterland to find the site of this paradise. In 1977 one of the groups founded a holy settlement on the Blanco River, which was sanctified by the Bishop-Patriarch as the holy land site. Hundreds flocked to reside at the site, but there were food shortages and many of the settlers fell ill. The colony, which was called New Jerusalem or Palestine, was abandoned. Instead, the movement inspired smaller settlements in different locations, all designated *tierra santa,* where followers could live beyond the influence of secular society and its evils.

As a frontier region populated by immigrants who often built settlements together, and as a destination of utopian dreams, the western hemisphere from north to south hosted many religious communities. Scholars have probed not only Latin American Christianity for apocalyptic elements but native religions themselves, especially Aztec worship. Inasmuch as the Aztecs believed that time unfolded in five cyclical stages, it is difficult to see how they could be said to await an "end-time," but other facets of Aztec beliefs sustain the notion that they expected an end-of-the-world judgment day. Since we know little about the specific nature of pre-Columbian worship, these arguments remain speculative. Other indigenous groups, however, had beliefs that were definitely millenarian and apocalyptic. Perhaps the most pronounced were the Tupí-Guaranís, who lived in present-day Brazil and the Peruvian Amazon. They believed that a demiurge, a subordinate god, would return to earth and demolish it, and would save only the faithful. Some Tupí clans wandered the rainforest searching for a place to await this event, a place that would shelter them from impending destruction.

These beliefs survived among the dwindling remnants of indigenous Tupí clans. Anthropologists have studied them through narratives passed on from generation to generation. Most of the Surui people, for example, know the traditional myths and folk tales. They begin with the story of the Dirty Palop, a demiurge, the Creator of the World. The story of the moon is about incest; the Surui story of the tapir is a Don Juan parable warning against stealing women's hearts. The story of the eagle is a fairy tale; the story about the locust (*cicada*) comments on the need to protect children. The stories are playful, filled with tricks and moral lessons and the propensity of the Surui to laugh. They deal with a wealth of human behaviors and emotions: madness, pregnancy, initiation rites, health, homesickness, magic, scatological wisdom, fire, agriculture hunting, and dreams. In the case of the Surui and many other indigenous peoples, belief in the coming destruction of the world remained part of the oral tradition but had lost its imminence. Missionaries rekindled fears about impending divine retribution to the point that native peoples and peasants allowed themselves to be mobilized to join millenarian communities.

Is there a connection between group insecurities and the rise of millenarian movements? After all, history is filled with examples of nonmillennial social protests and revolts. The answer must lie in the religious mentality of the participants in the movements seeking a fantasy of a perfect age: beyond growing social tension and fear of change, there must be an underlying religious element provoking desperate measures to find salvation.

Studies of the social character of millennialist sects underscore accumulated tensions from social causes as well as from religious anxiety or fear, but the spiritual element, harder to pin down, is usually slighted. After all, illiterates groping for meaning in the harsh landscape of poverty do not leave historical testimony. Lacking the ability to read people's minds, we must rely on what we can figure out about the pressures on them. Millenarian and apocalyptic movements took shape not only when near-psychopathic individuals stirred up the collective fears of followers but also in cases when individuals trapped in the under class and alienated from the dominant elites in their society who disparaged and feared them clung to their own forms of religious expression as a shield against encroachment from modernizers who rejected them as recalcitrant obstacles to progress.

☞ NOTES

1. See Mullett 1987, citing Karl Marx and Friedrich Engels, *On Religion* (Moscow: Progress Publications, 1972), 33, 74.

2. Francisco Fernández's important novel *Martín Fierro* was published in the same year as the Tandil massacre; it portrayed the gaucho as inarticulate and violent. See Slatta 1986, 174.

3. Ironically, the description was written about John Calvin, but it fits Conselheiro perfectly. See John Gross, review of William J. Bouwsma's *John Calvin: A Sixteenth Century Portrait* (Oxford: Oxford University Press, 1987), in *New York Times* (December 8, 1987), 29.

☞ BIBLIOGRAPHY

Amory, Frederic. 1996. "Historical Source and Biographical Context in the Interpretation of Euclydes da Cunha's *Os Sertões.*" *Journal of Latin American Studies* 26:667–86. Contends that recent studies of Brazilian millenarian movements have unwisely been willing to circumvent or disqualify da Cunha, the leading nineteenth-century chronicler of Canudos.

Brown, Michael F., and Eduardo Fernández. 1991. *War of Shadows.* Berkeley: University of California Press. Analyzes what the authors term the Evangelical Protestant "struggle for Utopia" in the Peruvian Amazon.

Burdick, John. 1993. *Looking for God in Brazil.* Berkeley: University of California Press. Analyzes in detail the growing tension between Roman Catholics and Protestants in Brazil during recent decades.

Chilcote, Ronald H., ed. 1972. *Protest and Resistance in Angola and Brazil.* Berkeley: University of California Press. Some of the essays deal with millennial movements and their followers.

Cohn, Norman, 1961. *The Pursuit of the Millennium.* 2nd ed. New York: Harper Torchbooks. A basic study of millenarianism in history.

Da Matta, Roberto. 1981. *Carnavais, Malandros e Heróis.* Rio de Janeiro: Zahar Editores. An anthropologist's controversial interpretation of Brazilian popular culture and religious expression, emphasizing the psychological traits of civic and religious celebration and ritual.

Darnton, Robert. 1990. *The Kiss of Lamourette: Reflections in Cultural History.* New York: W. W. Norton. Offers useful comparative insights with Europe.

della Cava, Ralph. 1970. *Miracle at Juaseiro.* New York: Columbia University Press. A careful account of Padre Cícero's millenarian movement, which arose in the Brazilian backlands about the same time as Canudos but which ended peacefully several decades later.

Diacon, Todd A. 1991. *Millenarian Vision, Capitalist Reality.* Durham, N.C.: Duke University Press. A study of Brazil's Contestado movement with some comparison to other movements of similar nature.

Levine, Robert M. 1990. *Vale of Tears.* Berkeley: University of California Press. Analyzes Brazil's traumatic Canudos movement and its destruction.

Mindlin, Betty, and Susui Narrators. 1995. *Unwritten Stories of the Susui Indians of Rondonia.* Austin: Institute of Latin American Studies, University of Texas. Narrates and analyzes the millenarian legends of one of the few remaining indigenous tribes in Amazonia.

Mullett, Michael A. 1987. *Popular Culture and Popular Protest.* London: Croom Helm. An insightful overview of this history of popular mobilization and resistance to it by dominant societies.

Nina Rodrigues, Raimundo. 1935. *A Animismo Fetichista dos Negros Bahianas.* Rio de Janeiro: Companhia Editora Nacional. An examination by a forensic law expert of the psychology of charismatic religious practice among Afro-Brazilians.

Parker, David S. 1996. H-NET review of Susan C. Stokes, *Cultures in Conflict: Social Movements and the State of Peru* (Berkeley: University of California Press, 1995), 3 June 1996, books@h-net.msu.edu.

Ribeiro, René. 1970. "Brazilian Messianic Movements." In *Millennial Dreams in Action: Studies in Revolutionary Religious Movements,* edited by Sylvia L. Thrupp, 55–69. New York: Schocken Books. A Brazilian psychiatrist from the Northeast analyzes the cultural and behavioral basis of membership in millenarian movements.

Scott, James C. 1985. *Weapons of the Weak.* New Haven: Yale University Press. Offers useful comparative information about peasant experiences in Southeast Asia.

Seigel, Bernard J. 1977. "The Contestado Rebellion, 1912–1916." *Journal of Anthropological Research* 33:199–215. Links the Contestado Rebellion to larger national events and considers the reasons for the movement's growth.

Slatta, Richard W. 1986. *Gauchos and the Vanishing Frontier.* Lincoln: University of Nebraska Press. Offers useful information about the Argentine Tata Dios and his movement.

Spindler, Frank MacDonald. 1980. "Francisco Bilbao, Chilean Disciple of Lamennais." *Journal of the History of Ideas* 41:487, 496. Discusses Chile's religious setting and the conflict between church and state in the 1850s.

Stern, Steve, ed. 1987. *Resistance, Rebellion, and Consciousness in the Andean Peasant World: 18th to 20th Centuries.* Madison: University of Wisconsin Press. Contains several essays on insurgent political movements in the Andean region that may be considered to have had religious coloration.

22

The Messianism of Success
in Contemporary Judaism

Aviezer Ravitzky
Hebrew University of Jerusalem

The world is already sufficiently defiled, Master of the Universe. Given that this muck will doubtless continue, there's no reason for You to wait for things to get worse; You can go ahead and send us the Messiah. (Agnon 1976, 428)

It is obvious, that after the Holocaust, calamity will not rise up a second time. . . . On the contrary: there will be only goodness and mercy, apparent and revealed, for all the children of Israel, wherever they may be; I stress—goodness that is sensed and manifest!!! (M. M. Schneersohn [the Lubbavitcher Rebbe] 1992)

CONTEMPORARY JEWISH REALITY has spawned two movements of messianic redemption, two comprehensive and intensive religious awakenings, without precedent in Jewish history over the past three hundred years. The prevailing opinion is that the failure of the messianic Sabbatean movement of the seventeenth century and its traumatic aftermath stifled or neutralized any acute Jewish expectation for collective historical redemption. It led to an internalization and spiritualization of the messianic idea. Even if messianic tensions occasionally rose to the surface and charismatic figures emerged out of them, they did not generate mass movements or leave a significant historical imprint. During the mid-twentieth century, however, a notable shift took place. Since then we have witnessed two prominent instances of messianic revival—messianic religious Zionism, on the one hand, and Lubbavitcher (Habad) Hasidism, on the other.

In my recent book, *Messianism, Zionism, and Jewish Religious Radicalism*, I devoted two chapters to these movements and their ideological development. The present article will go a step further and examine these modern phenomena from a comparative historical perspective.

The appearance of the two new movements poses two central questions. First, is messianic ferment inherently rooted in a sensation of collective distress? Does redemptive turmoil necessarily stem from a consciousness of calamity and crisis, from a catastrophic or apocalyptic expectation of the uprooting of existing historical reality? Does not Jewish history—from the days of the Bar Kokhba revolt in ancient times until the present day—also manifest a different pattern of messianic tension, one that arises out of a sense of success, fulfillment, and historical triumph? And have we not witnessed comparable phenomena in the history of Christian Europe, when millenarian expectations based themselves on military victory, cultural renewal, or even a belief in the historical progress of the human race?

Second, what correlation is there between the burgeoning of messianic agitation and the basic religious stance of the believer? Can one anticipate such awakenings also among individuals and schools that tilt toward pantheism, positing an immanent divine presence, all-penetrating and all-encompassing? On the face of it, such a religious standpoint would have been expected to remove human concern from actual history, from the present moment, directing it to the continuing cosmic drama instead. It would be assumed to redirect our attention to the universe as a whole—already saturated with divinity, or to the individual soul—already filled with God's presence, rather than to a future redemptive, transcendent eruption from the "outside," which will penetrate the inner core of history. Can messianic turmoil then emerge from a pantheistic religious consciousness as well?

The two redemptive Jewish movements of our day—despite the deep distinctions between them—supply similar and "surprising" answers to these questions. First, in both the case of Lubbavitcher Hasidism and that of redemptive religious Zionism (the disciples of Rav Kook), messianic tension gathered force from a consciousness of progress, conquest, and divine favor, rather than from distress and debacle. Both based themselves on the potent belief that the present is an era of historical fulfillment (at least until recently), or even of cosmic completion. In both of them, the awakening reached its climax in view of and by virtue of reality, rather than in opposition to it.

Second, these movements sprang up in the heart of religious traditions characterized by a clear pantheistic emphasis. Both the Lubbavitcher Rebbes over the generations and Rabbi Avraham Yitzhak Kook and his students laid great stress on the immanent aspect of the divine. (The latter also explicitly supported the pantheistic line of thought in the teachings of Habad [Kook 1965, 399].) And lo and behold, precisely these two religious movements have generated open displays of messianic tension in our times, without precedent among the Jewish people for generations.

Is this really surprising? Is it a unique, anomalous development, or perhaps an organic religious development, the expression of a potential that is inherent within the messianic idea? I will explore this question by examining the historical precedents and theological reasoning underlying the contemporary phenomena. In addition, I will attempt to reach a general conclusion regarding the nature of messianic turmoil and its relation to the appearance of the historical drama.

☞ PATTERNS OF MESSIANIC TENSION _____

Messianic awareness creates a strained relationship between present and future, history and utopia. It exalts the future, at times even endowing it with a transcendent dimension. Yet the tense transition between present and future assumes different and even opposing guises in the believer's eyes. In times of crisis and affliction, it may take the form of a sharp, severe shift, a sort of paradoxical leap from one extreme to its polar opposite; for example, the light of redemption will arise out of the darkness and pierce it through. The transition is meant to contradict a given reality, rather than to grow out of it organically. In other words, the very distress and disaster experienced today are the express portents of the savior's imminent arrival. In the language of the Babylonian Talmud: "If you see a generation afflicted by many tribulations, await him" (*Sanhedrin* 98a). This is, to be sure, a characteristic expression of messianic expectation,[1] one that has been greatly stressed in the scholarly literature as well.

It is worth presenting this messianic pattern in its more extreme version. That is, the deeper the abyss, and the more sharply the straits hem us in on either side, the greater the demand for the transcendent deliverance that is the only logical solution. Hence, since salvation is a necessity, it will inevitably come: "Reason dictates, that the arrival of our righteous Messiah will be no further prolonged, for we find ourselves on such a level that it is not possible for us to be worse and sink lower." Such was the clarion call of Rabbi Israel of Radin (the "Hafetz Haim") at the beginning of the twentieth century, in view of the severe deterioration, spiritual and physical, he found around him. "The King-Messiah must come speedily, for in a little while there will not be anyone for whom to come!" (Prager 1958, 6, 12; Levinstein 1978, 27).

Indeed, messianic demands of this kind have appeared frequently in Jewish history, in the face of different traumas.[2] As Rabbi Avraham Saba, a Spanish and Portuguese exile of the late fifteenth century, wrote: God must not further delay the time of redemption, because "if God waits to redeem Israel until that [distant] day hinted at by the prophets . . . given that more troubles are piling up against them every day, when that time comes there won't be anything left of them" (Saba 1985, 11). Saba admittedly put these words into the mouth of the prophet Jeremiah, as a reaction to the destruction of the First Temple. He also alluded to other disasters that had visited the Jewish people in the past. Yet he deliberately added on to these the pressing distress of his own time and place.

In other words, according to this pattern, precisely because historical reality is experienced to be beyond fixing, and because one cannot find any rational opening for extricating the community, so reality must be grasped mythically. It should be turned upside down and be afforded a redemptive significance. Otherwise, the only alternative to paradox would be despair.

Over and against this, however, the importance of a different pattern of messianic tension needs to be stressed. There exist historical situations, or states of consciousness, in which a sense not of defeat but rather of success is the factor spawning expectations of redemption. There are times when precisely the seeds sprouting before us today betoken a full flowering tomorrow. In such a state of affairs, redemption is no longer poised over and against reality as its veritable antithesis; rather, it is assumed to be embodied in the historical process itself, leaving its imprint in concrete developments. It is likened to the morning star, which shines higher and higher: "Thus will be the redemption of Israel. . . . First it will glimmer, then sparkle, then shine forth ever more brightly" (*Shir haShirim Rabah* 6, 16; cf. Jerusalem Talmud *Berakhot* 1.1; *Yoma* 3,2). In this messianic mode, the connection between the historical present and the redemptive future is expressed no longer by paradoxical transformation but through the swelling tide of a historical drama. Signs presaging the Messiah are henceforth to be found in very present events, in any concrete and auspicious turn of history.

Naturally, here as well the messianic hope fundamentally derives from a basic human distress, an uneasiness with existing reality. It is also conceivable that the current messianic tension first arose under conditions of debasement and persecution. Yet at a certain stage a watershed is reached (in terms of external reality, or of consciousness), and believers find themselves in a new, promising historical phase. From now on, the religious ferment will be fed precisely by this feeling of progress and triumph. Thus, for instance, while the Jewish revolt against the Roman Empire admittedly broke out in response to pressure and oppression, the initial military successes then tipped the scales in the direction of a messianism of success (see examples below). Similarly, the Jewish anticipation of the demise of Christian rule arose, admittedly, under conditions of degradation and persecution, yet it was the encouraging developments on the international plane that suddenly galvanized expectations of redemption (see below). Again, despite all the historical distinctions, the horror of the Holocaust sparked in some hearts a catastrophic messianic expectation, yet the ensuing national revival in the land of Israel (in the case of religious Zionists) and the Jewish flourishing in the modern world (in the case of Habad Hasidim) shifted this horror to a mode of triumphant messianism.

Finally, we can identify a third, mixed pattern of messianic ferment. According to this approach, neither defeat nor resurrection alone is an intrinsic harbinger of redemption. Rather, it is their joint, dialectic appearance within the very same development, the internal tensions and contradictions experienced within the same historical process. Redemption grows and ascends from the deep opposition between shadows and light, blessing and curse, destruction and construction, all of which are mixed up together within the very same reality. Admittedly, such a complex conception is no mere ingenuous expression of religious fervor, but the product of a historiosophical outlook. It represents a scrutiny of and reflection on reality, rather than a spontaneous reaction to it. Accordingly, the contradictions and oppositions of which it speaks are reflected not primarily in the concrete, physical plane but on the ideological and spiritual one, in the moral stature of the generation to be redeemed: "It is composed of polar opposites. . . . It is humble and degraded, also high and exalted; utterly guilty, and utterly innocent" (A. Y. Kook 1967, 108).

In all three of the above patterns, messianic tension can arise even in the absence of a personal Messiah. The redemptive ferment at issue centers not necessarily on a living charismatic figure but on a historical development and what it portends. To be sure, the personal Messiah will indeed come (even if he tarries), yet conceivably it is the current redemptive turning point that will generate him organically from within.

☞ MESSIANISM OF SUCCESS:
HISTORICAL CONTEXT

The numerous studies devoted to the phenomena of Jewish messianism and Christian millenarianism have usually focused only on the first, the catastrophic mode of these phenomena. Quite often one may even get the impression that this is the only possible expression of redemptive agitation, as if messianic zeal always originates in disaster and distress, directing itself entirely against current reality.

Some scholars have grounded this proposition in a sociological claim (Hobsbawn 1965; Worsley 1957; Wallace 1956). To their mind, the messianic outpouring is in its very essence an awakening of deprived groups, of individuals and communities who suffer from want and oppression, and consequently long for radical change. These men and women are the ones who seek to emerge from the straits; they are the ones who require redemption. The same cannot be said for their successful neighbors, who rule the former complacently. The latter are primarily interested in social stability and seek to preserve the existing historical state of affairs.

In contrast, other scholars have ascribed the phenomenon of messianic ferment to a feeling of comprehensive historical calamity.[3] In their opinion, even if the ferment does not necessarily express the specific aspirations of a particular disadvantaged sector of society, it does reflect a deep consciousness of collective decline and debacle. It arises out of a pessimistic attitude of disappointment and rejection of the present reality, or even alarm in the face of it. Accordingly, the believer anticipates the incipient collapse of history and a redemption to rise upon its ruins. How much the more so when united with the above attitude is a general apocalyptic line of thought, whereby only total destruction can cleanse the existing universe and purify it of all its contamination.

Yet neither of these two explanations appears to exhaust the phenomena of messianic upheavals. The first argument, the sociological one, has already been refuted empirically by several studies. These showed that members of the dominant elite were also likely to be swept up in messianic outbursts (Scholem 1973, 1:3–5; Cohen 1967, 143–46) and that religious ardor frequently transcends all social and economic barriers. The redemptive movements that have sprung up in contemporary Judaism as well clearly demonstrate this fact. Neither religious-messianic Zionism nor contemporary Habad Hasidism has been successful among the disadvantaged sectors of society in particular. Both of them confound all attempts at sociological and economic (Marxist?) reductionism; in fact, the former movement, that of religious Zionism, was constituted chiefly by members of the more privileged strata of Israeli society.[4]

The same reasoning applies to the second argument. In my earlier works on the ideology and theology of these movements, I had already stressed the centrality ascribed by them to the pattern of triumphant messianism, based on a consciousness of progress and ascendancy (1984, 146–67; 1990, 18–30; 1996, 28–29, 79–144, 196–200). Recently Moshe Idel (1990, 8–10; 1992, 14; 1995, 142) and Albert Baumgarten (1998) have pointed out other manifestations of messianic tension, which are also connected to victories and achievements. Evidently, then, the time has come to sharpen the historical picture by proposing a new outlook on these phenomena as a whole. My contention is that neither distress and calamity per se nor victory and prosperity are the galvanizing factors for acute redemptive tensions. Rather, it is the historical turning point in itself, the sense that we are witnesses to an unprecedented drama, whether for good or for bad, that invites a mythical interpretation of events. Not the intrinsic quality of the event but its overwhelming force is decisive here; not the content, but the intensity. This is what endows events with a transhistorical, even cosmic, dimension.

In order to base this argument on solid ground, I will first expand the historical picture to show that messianic ferment arises in tandem with conflicting historical phenomena and is not limited to the catastrophic pattern alone. I will rely primarily on Jewish sources, although some parallels from the chronicles of Christian Europe are also worth noting.

At the outset, it bears mentioning that Jewish scholars in the Middle Ages were not oblivious to the stated distinction between two types of messianic tension. Several of them even explicitly preferred one messianic mode over the other. The most prominent of these was Maimonides, who forcefully rejected, in his legal Code, all of the traditional motifs of catastrophic redemption, and fixed on historical success alone as the conspicuous centerpiece of the messianic consciousness (*Mishneh Torah,* The Laws of Kings, 11–12; Ravitzky 1996, 73–112). To be more precise, Maimonides was keenly aware of the alternative, crisis-centered concept of the redemptive process. In his populist *Epistle to Yemen,* in which he exerts himself to the utmost to rescue a Jewish community from the dangers of a false Messiah, he himself resorts to such menacing motifs (1960, 112). Yet when it came to legislating for future generations and to shaping a model of Jewish messianism in a systematic and commanding fashion (in his Code, *Mishneh Torah*) Maimonides swept aside all the classic descriptions of premessianic tribulations. He also deliberately ignored the figure of the "Messiah son of Joseph," the mythic personality to whom previous Jewish traditions had linked the catastrophe projected for Israel on the eve of deliverance. In Maimonides' eyes, the sole legitimate criterion for evaluating any messianic phenomenon was historical success, that is, the religious, political, and even military accomplishments of the prospective Messiah.

Accordingly, Maimonides adopted a positive stance toward the traditions regarding the Bar Kokhba Revolt against the Romans (132–137 C.E.) and toward the messianic hopes that fastened on the leader of that revolt. So long as Bar Kokhba's star was in the ascension, argued Maimonides, a general consensus prevailed regarding his messianic status. Not only did Rabbi Akiva champion his cause, but "all Israel, together with the greatest Torah scholars, presumed him to be the King-Messiah" (The Laws of Fasting 5:3). Of course, once the man fell into the hands of the Romans and "was killed for sins" (The Laws of Kings 11:3), they realized that he was not the true Messiah. Yet even then, after the debacle, the story's conclusion does not necessarily dictate the significance of its beginning. Apparently Maimonides held that, were it not for the sins, the successful onset of the revolt would ultimately have been likely to produce the desired fruit (Ravitzky 1996, 98–99). In any event, historical achievements alone are the essential criterion at every stage of the messianic process: "It will only be demonstrated by success, as R. Moses [ben Maimon] wrote, and this is the truth" (Shem Tov Ibn Gaon [fourteenth century], *Migdal Oz,* Hilkhot Melachim 11:3). The importance of this normative messianic model, originating with Maimonides, cannot be overemphasized when one comes to address contemporary Jewish redemptive movements.

In contrast, the opposing model was formulated in flowing style in the writings of R. Yitzhak Abrabanel, first and foremost among the Spanish exiles. Abrabanel championed the catastrophic and apocalyptic concept of redemption unreservedly. To his mind, not the historical successes, but rather the failures, presage the arrival of the redeeming transformer. "When the time of redemption is drawing near, terrible troubles will proliferate against Israel," predicted Abrabanel, "so that their condition should shift from the extremity of evil and loss and utter annihilation, to exaltation and the pinnacle of success" (Abrabanel 1961, 33a). And when did "terrible troubles" proliferate against Israel, if not in his own generation, that of the expulsion and mass conversions? "The King-Messiah will be born or revealed when all of Israel are expelled from the Roman and Christian lands. . . . [He] will be like one of the children of these edicts and annihilations, in one of the periods in which Israel suffers severe distress and numerous afflictions" (ibid., 23b).

Besides the contemporary context of his words, Abrabanel expresses through their agency a preference in principle for the messianic pattern of crisis and extremity, while explicitly rejecting its alternative—the false mode of historical victory. And who better embodies this false pattern than the personality and enterprise of Bar Kokhba? Here the inverted symmetry prevailing between Abrabanel's concept and that of Maimonides is clearly distinguishable. Abrabanel, in contrast to Maimonides, sharply criticized the support Rabbi Akiva and his colleagues extended to the revolt, and to the messianic presumption it exemplified.[5] He took this line of thought to even greater lengths, attributing the sages' bitter mistake to their seduction at the hands of (ephemeral) historical success, and their willingness to make the redemption of Israel contingent upon the latter. In the words of Abrabanel:

> This is a most astonishing fact . . . how the sages of Israel believed Ben Koziva to be the Messiah King; how Rabbi Akiva could so err in this respect as to become his adjutant. . . . It seems to me, therefore, that upon seeing Ben Koziva's successes in battle, R. Akiva thought the Holy One, Blessed be He, had accelerated the inevitable conclusion of the exile, and changed His mind concerning the affliction. . . . Consequently, Rabbi Akiva thought that Ben Koziva was the Messiah. . . . What happened to him happens often to every wise person—to think and believe that which one yearns for, and what his soul is expiring for. Similarly, Rabbi Akiva, in his longing for Divine redemption, upon seeing Ben Koziva's valor and his military successes, which were not in the way of nature, considered them to be a visitation from God, who had repealed His decree, having mercy on His people. (1961, 31b)

Abrabanel brooks no compromise in the matter. With regard to Rabbi Akiva: "And who knows, whether it was not for this sin that Rabbi Akiva was called to task in his death, for the manner of his death was more severe than that of the other martyrs of the regime" (ibid., 31a).

And as for Bar Kokhba, it was the sages of Israel who first condemned him to death, although he ultimately fell in battle with the Romans. (This is an interesting combination of two conflicting versions that appear in the Talmuds—Babylonian, *Sanhedrin* 93b; and Jerusalem, *Ta'anit* 4:5). Furthermore, elsewhere Abrabanel lumps together the names of three false messiahs who succeeded in publicly disseminating their false message: Jesus, Muhammad, and Ben Koziva! (ibid., 20a).[6] Given these difficult precedents, then, "In what way will we recognize the generation of the [true] Messiah?" Abrabanel answers, predictably, according to the trenchant logic of catastrophic messianism: "That in other generations, once an evil has afflicted Israel for a time, a respite is provided and they are able to rest at ease and dwell securely for some period of time. But at the time of the Messiah, the troubles will be so incessant, that even while one trouble still persists, a new one comes along" (ibid., 23b).

The Bar Kokhba Revolt, then, has been preserved in the Jewish historical memory as the symbol of a messianic ferment that brewed from within success and victory: a positive symbol in the eyes of one, negative in the eyes of another. In both cases, however, the symbol does not conform to the accepted scholarly theories regarding the tight connection between messianism and calamity. Both of the sages mentioned above, Maimonides and Abrabanel, at odds though they were on the question of which was the legitimate, normative messianic pattern, would have dismissed the approach that confines the phenomenon to the catastrophic mode alone.

Does our historical information confirm their opinion? As recently argued by Baumgarten, the victories of the Maccabeans or the Hasmoneans may have raised certain messianic hopes at the time (Baumgarten 1996, 58–60).[7] In any event, this was the case with regard to the Great Revolt against the Romans, when temporary successes ignited people's hearts and were taken by many as signs of redemption. Take, for instance, the excitement generated pursuant to the conquest of Massada by Menahem haGalili, and his return to Jerusalem with the trappings of royalty (Stern 1991, 302); that following the great victory over Castius Gallus on the slope of

Beit Horon (Kasher 1983, 88); and that following the severe crisis which shook the Roman Empire in the year 68, upon the death of Nero and the killing of two subsequent emperors ("I will overturn the thrones of kingdoms" [Haggai 2:22]).[8] The messianic climate admittedly preceded the Great Revolt, yet in no few cases the signs of blessing that arose during its course were what fostered and amplified it. And ultimately, with regard to the Bar Kokhba Revolt, few would dispute the fact that it was only at the time of the wave of conquests that the man's messianic status ascended[9] and was widely acclaimed.[10]

Once the revolts had been quashed with a heavy hand, and following the hardships and ruination that succeeded them, the Jewish people lost their political/military option and also were sworn in the Talmud and Midrash not to revolt again against the nations of the world. Yet even now, in the era of exile, the messianic longings that continued to manifest themselves from time to time were not necessarily connected to suffering and disaster. They were often associated with encouraging omens of promise and success, that is, with social and international developments that seemed likely to overthrow the kingdom of evil, to transform the world order, and to smooth the way for the King-Messiah.

Encouraging omens of this sort appeared, for example, when the Christian empire seemed liable to fall at the hands of foreign armies or, alternatively, when the reigning Christian faith gave signs of imploding from within. The first hope evidently arose already at the time of the Persian and Arabic wars against the Byzantine Empire (Eshkoli 1988, 117–30; Lewis 1950, 323). It returned with heightened intensity in the thirteenth century, in the face of the Mongol raids against Europe. This mysterious host, which issued abruptly out of the unknown and struck terror into the hearts of the ruling peoples, evoked messianic expectations among many Jews (Eshkoli 1988, 165, 213). Various communities even identified the Mongol legions with the ten lost tribes of the ancient kingdom of Israel, who were said to be returning from afar to deliver their persecuted brethren. In those days, "Stories abounded in the mouths of many," in the words of the poem by Meshulam of Epaireh of Spain:

> A kingdom will be renewed in our times, for a lost people and dispersed [Jewish] communities, and a gift will be brought to the son of David and Yishai . . . who will build and establish my sanctuary. . . . Tribes which were exiled before, and now have left the land of their habitation. . . . My time is a time of great rejoicing. . . . This host is accustomed to miracles, since its hands are assisted by the merit of my king. . . . On the border of Ashkenaz, cities are in panic, and confronting a sword of terror. (Shirman 1972)

As pointed out by Moshe Idel, a similar messianic ferment arose simultaneously in North Africa and Italy as well. Avraham Abulafia even made personal efforts to befriend the Mongol heralds of redemption (1990, 8–9). Here an illuminating fact is disclosed. The rise of the Mongolian empire fueled great hopes, at the outset, particularly among the Christians: the victory of Genghis Khan over the Muslim kingdom in central Asia (1221) was perceived by the Christians as abetting the success of the Crusades, and some of them even deemed the Mongols the key to the fulfillment of Christian apocalyptic hopes (McGinn 1979a, 150). Only later, when the tables were turned and the Mongols began raiding Christian Europe, did the event fuel new messianic longings among the Jews.

A similar excitement infected Jewish hearts pursuant to the fall of Constantinople to the Turks in 1461 (Scholem 1978, 26; ben Sasson 1981, 225; Tishbi 1985, 53; Idel 1992a, 84–85).

Similarly, some Jews found portents of deliverance during the same period in the ascendancy of the Falashas in Ethiopia (Eshkoli 1928, 412–16; 1988, 355). In every instance, it was precisely occurrences that seemed to favor the Jews which supplied the foothold for messianic fervor. Since the Jews were unable to achieve the political and military turnaround through their own efforts, they pinned their hopes on the valor of others. And it was precisely the more promising victories that were now accorded a new construction and new significance, and were awarded cosmic redemptive significance.

Even the Reformation was grasped in this context as a war of deliverance that Martin Luther had declared not only against the pope but against the Christian faith as a whole.[11] The kabbalist Avraham ben Eliezer haLevi, a Spanish exile, even ventured a daring historiosophic judgment about it. He equated, obliquely, the dialectical role played by Jesus Christ and the Christian religion in the dissemination of monotheistic ideas among the pagan peoples (as interpreted by Maimonides, The Laws of Kings 11:4 [the uncensored version]), with the role attributed by him to Hebrew studies and the Reformation in bringing the Christians closer to Judaism. Both the former and the latter came only to "pave the way for the King-Messiah" (the language of Maimonides regarding Jesus Christ [ibid.]). It is my sense that Eliezer haLevi attempted to sketch a kind of dialectic, messianic history of the universal conquest of humanity by the true faith: from the pagans to Jesus Christ, and from him to Martin Luther, and onward to the true (Jewish) Messiah, who is on the verge of making his presence known.

These phenomena of messianic expectations, which seized upon historical successes, should not be viewed as a unique Jewish development. Parallel developments can be identified in the chronicles of Christian Europe as well. (I already noted above the Christian expectations connected with the initial successes of the Mongols.) For instance, the millenarian movement in Florence at the end of the fifteenth century centered entirely on an optimistic sense of realization regarding the special role accorded the city in the renaissance of Christianity ("the myth of Florence") (Weinstein 1970a, 1970b; McGinn 1979b; Baumgarten 1998). It is unsurprising, then, that this example of Florence features as a central problem in Michael Barkun's important book *Disaster and the Millennium* (1974, 17–174), whose title attests to its basic thesis.

Other examples can be presented: After the English Civil War during the mid-seventeenth century, there sprang up broadly based millenarian sects, precisely out of the providential sensation that an unprecedented era in national history had arrived (St. Clair 1992, 192–217). The French Revolution as well, although it failed to generate large religious movements, was grasped in eschatological terms by various persons. It featured in their eyes as a new and promising era, in which human history was reborn under the influence of the Holy Spirit (ibid., 230–54). How much the more so with regard to the successes of the colonization of America and the victors of the American Revolution, which were viewed by many as the realization of biblical prophecies, spawning messianic outbreaks during the course of the eighteenth and nineteenth centuries (ibid., 270–74).

Beyond all of the above, the sanguine belief in historical progress that was part and parcel of the European Enlightenment, was already identified in the seventeenth century with the millenarian tradition! Henry More even argued later that God delivers humanity through a gradual historical process, which from time to time manifests pivotal messianic turning points. The period of the Enlightenment represents such an important watershed, and it paves the final route to the age of redemption.[12] This tight connection between messianic expectations and the sanguine theory of progress clearly testifies to the fact that the catastrophic, apocalyptic emphasis is not critical to the messianic idea, and certainly does not exhaust the rich potential embodied in the messianic phenomenon.

☞ HISTORICAL DRAMA

We have illustrated that messianic expectations and agitations emerge in relation to conflicting experiences. Collective disaster may represent the horrors of premessianic tribulations, while collective renewal may attest to the "growth of redemption" and its flowering. What then do all of these phenomena have in common? It is my contention that they all arise and seethe out of a sense that one is at the height of an unprecedented historical drama; a conviction that taking place in front of one's eyes is a transformation so far-reaching that it invites a messianic interpretation. As stated above, neither distress in itself nor success is the agent of ferment; it is not the content of events that endows them with a transcendent dimension but their power and intensity. The messianic myth is likely to tell its story in varying circumstances, at both low points and upturns, so long as the historical reality appears in the eyes of the believer no longer as normal and neutral but as aberrant and unique. The present moment must no longer show itself in grey and undistinguished tones. It must be painted in brilliant hues, sufficiently bold to herald the coming of the other age.

Furthermore, the fact that messianic ferment is neither linked to a particular (disadvantaged) social stratum nor dictated by a particular historical mode (catastrophic) further accentuates the decisive role played by internal, immanent religious motives in generating the ferment. The dramatic power of events is not measured by the scholarly criterion of the sociologist or historian alone. Religious longings and anxieties take an important part in shaping the drama. They also dictate the manner in which reality is evaluated.

Hence, some distinguished Hasidic leaders were so shocked by the Napoleonic wars and their casualties,[13] or by the First World War and its losses, that they were convinced that they were witnessing the apocalyptic afflictions that usher in the messianic age ("Let them walk up to their kneecaps in blood, so long as the end comes!" [Shapira 1962, A, 231][14]). For other religious authorities, even the Second World War and the Holocaust of European Jewry fitted smoothly into the traditional experience of exile and served as a repeated confirmation of the religious order existing since time immemorial (reward and punishment, guilt and atonement) (Teitelbaum 1978, 5–7; Ravitzky 1996, 64–66). The same rule that applies to the fears also applies to the hopes: there were those who saw in the emancipation of the Jews at the time an unequivocal sign of imminent redemption and a call from on high to settle the Land of Israel (Rabbi Zvi Hirsh Kallisher) (Katz 1983, 290). Yet there were those who leveled sharp criticism against this messianic approach (which "was grounded on a deceptive light seen in the western countries") and sought to detach the settlement activity in the Land of Israel from any messianic rhetoric (Rabbi N. T. Y. Berlin) (Gaerlitz 1974, 2:15). In sum, messianic awakenings construe and supplant historical reality, no less than historical reality evokes and supplants the awakenings.

The messianic ferment that has permeated Habad Hasidim in our times provides a living example of the above arguments. It began in the face of a clear and distinct historical reality—

the Holocaust and its horrors. At its inception, then, this was a conspicuous example of cata-strophic messianism, a cry of hope that was sounded (in America) despite the abyss that had opened in Europe, perhaps even because of that abyss. "The troubles of Israel have now reached the most terrible degree," the Rebbe of Lubbavitch (Yosef Zvi Schneerson) declared to his disci-ples. "Therefore, the days of the redemption are imminent. This is the sole genuine answer to the destruction of the world and the anguish of Israel. . . . Be ready for redemption soon, shortly, in our day!" The suffering had evidently reached such dimensions that the cosmic scales were in danger of subversion. Damage of this magnitude is irreparable, unless it can be understood as the final throes of the premessianic birth pangs. Accordingly, the Rebbe promised, "The righteous redeemer is just around the corner" (Y. Z. Schneerson 1943; 1941, issues 9–11; 1942, issue 25; see also Ravitzky 1996, 194–203; Schweid 1994, 39–64; Greenberg 1992, 61–84).

Yet such was not the case at the time of the ferment that intensified afterwards, in the pres-ent generation, under the leadership of the last Rebbe (Menaham Mendel Schneerson). This turmoil was informed entirely by a feeling of welfare, the optimism of success and fulfillment. The Rebbe pointed to an unprecedented Jewish flowering in both the Holy Land and the Dias-pora, to the fall of the atheist communist empire, and to the process of ethical and religious refinement that humanity is experiencing. On the contrary, cried the Rebbe, the messianic birth pangs have passed for good. After the calamity of the Holocaust, he promised, "Distress will not rise up a second time. On the contrary: there will be only goodness and mercy, apparent and revealed, for all the children of Israel, wherever they may be" (M. M. Schneerson 1992). The redemption is burgeoning now for all to see, but no longer in opposition to reality, no longer despite history, but within and by virtue of contemporary history, accompanied by a sense of progress and prosperity. As Rabbi Menahem Brod, the spokesman for Habad in the Holy Land, summed up:

> All the great events that have been happening in recent times, prepare the climate for the idea of Messiah. For example, the ingathering of exiles. Suddenly, we see a tremendous revolution, that the country [the former Soviet Union] which forcibly held in all of the Jews is beginning to release them at a tremendous pace. . . . The messianic period is manifested also by "beating their swords into plowshares," and what do we see before our very eyes if not the cessation of the arms race, with tanks being turned into tractors. One more point: in messianic times, the whole world will unite in faith in the Creator of the World. And behold, you see that commu-nism, which was a big stumbling-block to faith, has collapsed, and there is a renewed flocking towards religion. (Sheleg 1992, 40)

Evidently, then, the religious tension has preserved its continuity, and the Lubbavitcher mes-sianic consciousness has found itself a secure foothold, both in times of curses and in times of blessing. Even if at present this tempest is slated gradually to spend itself, this is due not to external reality but rather to the internal crisis following the incapacitation and death of the charismatic Rebbe, the inspiring leader, upon whose redemptive personality all messianic hopes were fastened. Furthermore, from the point of view of the scholar, a fascinating phenom-enon has come to light: only a few months sufficed from the time the Rebbe fell ill for the Hasidim to perform an open about-face in the messianic rhetoric that had been serving them for years, that is, in order to make the shift from an explicit messianic pattern of success, to one based chiefly on crisis and paradox. Suddenly, the ancient midrashim about the sufferings of the Messiah, his personal fall, and the collective premessianic tribulations, were on their tongues. Suddenly the familiar voice of the catastrophic and apocalyptic concept of redemption was being heard in public:

> The exile cries out on account of everything that is happening around us. Jewish history has never experienced such a self-destructive period as the present one. . . . And precisely at the height of the crisis, [the Rebbe] has left us. . . . [However,] from within the grief and mourning, the hope grows and the expectation intensifies. . . . From within the peak of the darkness, the light will shine. (Sichat haShavuah 393 [1994], Parashat Devarim [15.7.94])

> Just before the redemption, the general degeneration peaks, the low point reaches its climax . . . [and this] informs us that the redemption is near indeed. (Sichat haShavuah 291 [1992], Parashat Matot [24.7.92])

> When something falls, there is no need for any reconstruction or assembly, but only to raise it up. . . . This is also the essence of the Messiah, for when the time comes this power will be revealed in him, and he will arise from his "fall" and be revealed in all his glory. (Sichat haShavuah 228 [1992], Parashat Hukat [3.7.92])

"The unbearable lightness" with which all of these transitions are taking place drives home the ability of the immanent religious motive to express itself and to tell its messianic saga, by means of varied images and in conflicting historical circumstances. So long as the historical drama persists, so will it. Given the current condition of Habad Hasidism, however, it is highly doubtful whether it will be possible to maintain this drama among the Lubbavitcher community.

What about the competing redemptive movement, that of contemporary messianic Zionism? Here the messianic tension always flourished from an optimistic awareness of national renaissance and historical actualization. The movement's guides always championed a gradual, evolutionary process of redemption, which takes place entirely by means of natural law and is not conditioned upon a miraculous messianic revelation. They fixed the Zionist enterprise and the revival of the State of Israel at the heart of this development and exalted them to sublime heights ("Zionism is a Divine matter." "The State of Israel is a Divine entity") (Z. Y. Kook 1987, 244, 246; cf. 1967, B, 157–58). It is difficult to find a better example, either in Jewish history or in the histories of other nations, of a redemptive awakening that is so exclusively based on sensations of success and divine favor. Furthermore, in contrast to Habad Hasidism, the tension has been preserved and intensified over time, despite the absence of a live messianic leader.

Admittedly, the trauma of the Holocaust left its indelible imprint here as well. Yet again, the remedy for that trauma is to be found in full in the redeemed State of Israel. As I have written elsewhere, only a definitive messianic construction of the Zionist revival could, from their point of view, impute a religious "sense" to the Holocaust (1996, 126–27). That is to say, the calamity was immeasurable, unfathomable, yet also the regeneration that succeeded it was total and unprecedented; the debacle would have been demonic, if a transcendent redemption had not grown out of it. In other words, only one (messianic) myth could neutralize the other (satanic) myth, and thus prevent the moral abyss and religious chaos from dominating our lives.

Hence, one encounters here a movement of redemption that rejected to the extent possible the catastrophic messianic expectation and strove for many years to expose the welcome signs of the "redeemed End" in the Land of Israel. The question that now occupies the scholar is, What religious reactions will take shape in the future, if the withdrawal from substantial sections of the Land (in accordance with the Oslo agreements) continues to proceed? From the point of view of the believers, this withdrawal is not territorial alone, but first and foremost an organic dismemberment, a critical blow to the process of redemption. Will the messianic tension be neutralized? Will the familiar passage from one messianic pattern to another transpire here as well? Which of the messianists will compose a new midrash (reinterpretation) exposing the redemptive tidings concealed in present events as well? Which will develop a general alienation, ideological and theological, from the entire enterprise of Zionist revival (in ultra-orthodox style)? In my estimation, all of the above responses will be expressed in different circles. Yet it is worth emphasizing that, at the time of the writing of these words (in early 1997), it is precisely a theological silence that most conspicuously characterizes the religious leadership of the movement. This is a thundering silence indeed, given that at issue is an activist leadership, which for several decades has not refrained from reacting and interpreting, from displaying historical sensitivity, and seeking to find the hand of God manifested in events.

The most enlightening reaction I have heard to date was given on Independence Day 1995 by one of the rabbinic discussants on the settlers' radio station ("Channel 7").[15] In his words, the Oslo agreements and their "evil" will pass and vanish from the world, yet one benefit will result from them, which will persist in perpetuity. As known, the people of Israel were sworn, according to the Talmud and Midrash, not to rise up against the nations of the world. Consequently, the Jews are in (theological) need of recognition by the Gentiles regarding their right to political regeneration in their land. Until the present time, only distant peoples have recognized this right, and therefore the oath has yet to be entirely dissolved. Yet now that the Palestinian inhabitants of the land have consented to this through their signature, the apprehension regarding the oaths has been quelled once and for all. This is, therefore, the hidden inner meaning of the Oslo agreements.

These words demonstrate beautifully how triumphant messianism charts its course among obstacles and succeeds in drafting the idea of the cunning of history into its service.

☞ MESSIANISM AND PANTHEISM

Finally, how are we to construe the fact that the two contemporary Jewish redemptive movements have sprung up precisely in the heart of the theological conceptions leaning toward pantheism? Why did this messianic agitation flourish precisely among religious streams that believe in an immanent divine presence, of which no place is free? On the face of it, one would have anticipated the opposite development: if the whole world is full of divine glory, why should all the religious hopes focus on a future transcendent redemptive eruption, one that will penetrate "from the outside" inward? If the divine presence already dwells in every person and is constantly actualized in every time, is this not sufficient to neutralize the taut expectation for messianic fulfillment in present history?

This is admittedly the accepted logical conclusion. Yet the stated developments that have transpired among Jewish movements in the twentieth century demand our renewed attention to this question. They attest to the existence of another option, that of a messianic potential concealed within the heart of the religious concept of divine immanence. It is my understanding that such potential revealed itself in modern European thought as well in the transition from the static idea of pantheism (Spinoza) to the historical concept of pantheism (Hegel), and from them to the messianic application of pantheism (Moses Hess). At present, however, with regard to the movements in question, it has revealed its power in actual religious life as well. At this juncture I will present some preliminary thoughts on the subject, in the hope that they will prompt additional research and systematic inquiry.

I will start by honing the theological positions at issue: no Jewish religious stream in recent generations has emphasized the immanent aspect of the divine more than Habad Hasidism and the school of Rav Kook. The teachings of Habad have always stressed the axiom that God is the exclusive real being. Rabbi Schneer Zalman of Ladi, the founder of Habad, states: "For everything is truly like nothing compared to His substance and His essence" (1982, 219). "His substance and essence is to be found below just as truly as it is found above, without any differentiation or change at all" (1978, Vaʾerah, 110).[16] Rabbi Avraham Yitzhak Kook as well explicitly adhered (to a large extent, under the influence of Habad) to "the monotheistic concept which tends to the pantheistic, Spinozist interpretation, once the latter has been purified of its dross." (This is the original text in his handwriting. In the published version, the editor omitted the word "Spinozist") (Kook 1964, B, 399). These theories do not identify the divinity with the cosmos: the divinity is not exhausted by the world but rather extends beyond it. Yet the world has no separate existence of its own, distinct from the divinity (but see ben Shlomo 1984, 289–309). These religious conceptions afterwards reached the Hasidim and students, and they prevail among them to this day. Yet among these very same movements, more than among any others in contemporary Judaism, a redemptive agitation has broken out. Moreover, it has appeared primarily in the guise of a turmoil of success and triumph. In what way do these movements differ from the others?

It seems that the very concept of the immanent divinity opens before the believer two different options. The first, more common one, is that religious attention focuses entirely on being, on the cosmic fullness. Similarly, it also focuses on the human soul and the divine presence dwelling within it. In this case, the arena of the religious drama is the cosmic and psychological realms, not the historical one. On the contrary, the believer is likely to divert attention entirely from the historical dimension, for goodness, holiness, and divinity are a given at all times, and beyond time.

There is, however, another possibility as well. Let us assume that for various reasons a new sensitivity toward history has arisen in the heart of the believer, a new attentiveness to transformation in time. Will the latter not henceforth expand the arena of the religious drama to them as well? Won't immanence and sanctity and fulfillment henceforth be expected to manifest themselves in history as well? In other words, will the believer not expect to encounter a redeemed and harmonious world? After all, this belief in a universe saturated with divinity, to which modern historical sensibilities have now been united, invites, according to its internal logic, a consciousness of present deliverance and messianic fulfillment. For in such a state of mind, redemption is the natural state! If the divine bounty encompasses and suffuses not only cosmic reality but also the historical sphere, how can there be any place left for an unredeemed person and for unredeemed time?

In fact, it is difficult to find streams in Jewish orthodoxy over the last generations that have developed an attentiveness to history similar to that developed by the two movements in question. Even if this attentiveness did not arise from internal religious motives; even if it is not a logical outgrowth of pantheism per se but was projected onto it from the outside by virtue of a series of dramatic events and ideological confrontations (see Ravitzky 1996, chaps. 3, 5); nevertheless, this new sensibility has had a fertilizing effect on theology.[17] It has activated the messianic potential that was incorporated from the outset in the concept of immanent divinity.[18]

Evidently, then, according to this redemptive logic, there is a place first and foremost for the messianic pattern of success and triumph rather than of debacle and calamity. If afflictions occur in objective reality, they present a difficulty, a problem, no longer a paradoxical promise. They evoke the question of why it is that historical reality hobbles along behind ontological reality like a poor cousin, when the latter is all holiness and actualization. After all, evil was supposed to be only an illusion, a defect in understanding! For in truth, from the divine perspective, redemption is already a given, and only actual history seems to refuse to admit this fact and to embody redemption in itself.

In other words, if one adheres to the transcendent concept of God, one is likely to speak of a catastrophic fall from divine favor, of a God who has distanced himself for a time from the people, from humanity, and from history. Yet this possibility has been closed to pantheists. Their God is supposed to be present here and now, within the cosmic and historical order, and not outside it. It is no accident, then, that precisely the Rebbe of Lubbavitch, M. M. Schneerson, on the one hand, and Rabbi Z. Y. Kook, on the other, were the two contemporary Torah sages who explained the Holocaust as a healing process, as divine "surgery" and "treatment" performed on the body of the nation in preparation for its salvation. "With all the horrifying pain of this tragedy, it is clear that 'no evil comes from Heaven,' and that within the very evil and suffering of the afflictions, a sublime spiritual good is embodied. . . . The Holy One, Blessed be He, as that professor-surgeon, did everything He did for good" (M. M. Schneerson 1980, 116–17); the Holocaust is a "deep and hidden internal Divine treatment, of the cleansing of impurity" (Kook in Aviner 1967, 21). These are their words. The first admittedly spoke of the spiritual "salvation" of the dead of Auschwitz, and the second of the national redemption of the Jews living in the Land of Israel. Yet for both of them, God's glory fills the world, and Auschwitz is also included in this world.[19]

Indeed, from the point of view of the two contemporary Jewish redemptive movements, the God of Israel returns and appears now before his children, as befits him—the saving God, who chooses Israel and brings the people out of Egypt, not the God of the apocalypse. God returns and reveals himself to believers by the light of his face, not within the demonic darkness. This perhaps is the penetrating significance of the ascendance of the messianic mode of success and conquest in the generation after the Holocaust.

Translated from the Hebrew by Rachal Yarden

⌒ NOTES _____

1. The theoretical model for this is naturally to be found in the apocalyptic and rabbinic literatures. Yet here we are addressing the current translation of this model into the urgent language of messianism in times of calamity.

2. Such a messianic demand is also capable of leading to destructive practical conclusions, as in the case of some of the rebels in the Great Revolt against the Roman Empire on the eve of the destruction of

the Second Temple. Yet it has been formulated over the generations chiefly as a sort of prayer or cry of protest.

3. Barkun 1974; Adas 1979; Thrupp 1970; Wilder 1971; Scholem 1971, chap. 1.

4. Members of this group admittedly felt alienated in the ideological-political realm in the past: a dissonance was generated between the central position designated for them (according to their own religious outlook) in leading the historical redemptive process, and the actual position they were pushed into in Israeli society. This sort of feeling galvanized them during the 1970s and 1980s to move from the margins to the political center. See Ravitzky 1996, 122.

5. This criticism admittedly issued from the question of the appointed time for the redemption, yet it also incorporated the direct confrontation between catastrophic messianism and the messianism of success and conquest.

6. It is worth comparing the writings of Abrabanel on this subject to a Christian concept that presented Bar Kokhba as the "Messiah," that is, as a kind of Antichrist. See Aharon Oppenheimer, "Meshichiuto shel Bar Kochbah," in *Meshichiut ve-Eschatologiah,* ed. Zvi Baras (Jerusalem, 1984), 165; S. Applebaum, *Prolegomena to the Study of the Second Jewish Revolt* (Oxford: British Archaeological Reports, 1976), 60.

7. Cf. J. A. Goldstein, "How the Authors of 1 and 2 Maccabees Treated the 'Messianic' Promises," in *Judaisms and their Messiahs,* ed. Jacob Neusner, W. S. Green, and Ernest Frerichs (Cambridge: Cambridge University Press, 1987), 69–96; J. J. Collins, "Messianism in the Maccabean Period," in *Judaisms and their Messiahs,* 97–110.

8. My thanks to Prof. Daniel Schwartz for his advice.

9. Aharon Oppenheimer ("Meshichiuto shel Bar Kochba," 162) limited the "messianic" status of Bar Kokhba to political and military activism, in contrast to supernatural utopianism. According to his emphasis, the apocalypse began pursuant to the failure of the revolt.

10. Messianic optimism was linked to the personality of R. Yehudah "the Prince" as well. E. E. Urbach pointed out, in this context, the messianic longings which accompanied the renewal of the "Holy Community in Jerusalem." See *Chazal: Emunot ve-Deot* (Jerusalem, 1969), 609.

11. The letter of R. Avraham haLevi on this matter was edited by Gershom Scholem, *Kiryat Sefer* 7 (1920–21): 442–48. See also H. H. ben Sasson, "HaYehudim Mul haReformatziah," *Proceedings of the Israeli Academy of Arts and Sciences* 4, 5 (Jerusalem 1970): 75–81; Scholem 1978, 40.

12. Ernest Tuveson, *Millenium and Utopia* (Gloucester, Mass.: Peter Smith, 1972), ix–x. Cf. Reinhold Niebuhr, *Faith and History* (New York: Macmillan, 1949); J. B. Bury, *The Idea of Progress* (New York: Dover Publications, 1932). Some scholars have argued that such a theory of progress naturally neutralizes messianic tension. According to them, an expectation of gradual evolution is not compatible with a messianic movement. However, precisely the Jewish contemporary example would seem to refute this claim. Messianic-religious Zionism is based solely on such a concept of gradualism, maintaining simultaneously both the theory of progress and redemptive activism. See, nevertheless, Barkun 1974, 8–27.

13. This, reportedly, was the reaction of R. Menachem Mendel of Rimanov. See A. H. S. Michaelson, *Ateret Menachem* (New York, 1944), 124.

14. Compare with the response of Rabbi Kook, written during the same period (*Orot* [Jerusalem, 1963], 13–17).

15. My thanks to Reuven Campanino, who directed my attention to this.

16. See Moshe Halamish, *Mishnato haIyyunit shel R. Shneur Zalman miLadi,* (doctoral diss., Jerusalem, 1976); Rachel Elior, *Torat Achdut haHafachim* (Jerusalem, 1993) and the detailed bibliography therein; Amos Funkenstein, "Gevulot haHakarah beTorat haRav miLadi," in *Sefer haKen* (Jerusalem, 1969), 117–22; Naftali Loewenthal, *Communicating the Infinite* (Chicago: University of Chicago Press, 1990).

17. The direct encounter with secularism, Zionism, and world war impelled Rabbi A. Y. Kook to develop not only a theology but a historiosophy as well. Later on, the horror of the Holocaust and the victories of the state drove his son, Z. Y. Kook, to become a political as well as a spiritual leader. Habad Hasidism does not fall short of this either. As I have shown (1996, 194), the confrontation with Zionism at

the beginning of the century forced the Rebbe Sh. B. Schneerson to respond historiosophically: he could no longer keep quiet in view of an activist movement he regarded as false messianism. Later on, persecution and the Holocaust, on the one hand, and the contemporary Jewish flowering on the other, led his successors (Y. Z. and M. M. Schneerson) to construe the events of the time in their own original fashion.

18. The dynamic interpretation of pantheism did not originate in our times. It was inherent in the Kabbalah, particularly the Lurianic one. The myth of the breaking of the vessels and the repair introduced a kind of "historical" motive into the divinity itself. It itself is now exposed to the dynamics of improvement and perfection: the divine immanence is portrayed as a process, not a static entity. However, this dynamic element was still centered exclusively in the spiritual realm, in the gradual process of the mystical repair of the upper worlds. Along came the school of Rabbi A. Y. Kook and transferred this to the concrete physical realm. This school henceforth focused on historical, national, and political construction, which was awarded senior status in the process of cosmic improvement and emendation. Habad Hasidim, on the contrary, saw no redemptive significance in the earthly political activity of Jews. They ascribed such value only to their spiritual, *halakic,* and mystical endeavors. Nevertheless, at least after the Holocaust, they also found in external historical events signs and testimony to the immanent divine Presence. Among them as well, the pantheistic conviction bestowed an unshakable faith in God's dwelling in history, including his redemptive activity.

19. I am grateful to the late Amos Funkenstein, to Rachel Elior and to Yosef ben Shlomo, for their illuminating comments on the question of pantheism and messianism.

⟅ BIBLIOGRAPHY

Works in English

Adas, Michael. 1979. *Prophets of Rebellion.* Chapel Hill: University of North Carolina Press.

Almog, Shmuel. 1987. *Zionism and History.* New York: St. Martin's Press. A study of the relationships between history and national identity in the early Zionist ideology.

Aran, Gideon. 1991. "Jewish Zionist Fundamentalism: The Bloc of Faithful in Israel." In *Fundamentalisms Observed,* edited by M. E. Marty and J. R. S. Appleby. Chicago: University of Chicago Press. An analysis of the ideology and theology of messianic religious-Zionism.

Barkun, Michael. 1974. *Disaster and the Millennium.* New Haven/London: Yale University Press.

Baumgarten, A. I. 1998. "The Pursuit of the Millennium in Judaism." In *Tolerance and Its Limits in Early Judaism and Early Christianity,* edited by G. Stanton and G. Stroumsa. Cambridge: Cambridge University Press.

Cohen, G. D. 1967. "Messianic Postures of Ashkenazim and Sephardim." In *Studies of the Leo Baeck Institute.* Leo Baeck Institute.

Davies, W. D. 1952. *Torah in the Messianic Age and/or the Age to Come.* Philadelphia: Society of Biblical Literature. An examination of the antinomian elements in the doctrines of redemption of the rabbis.

Elior, Rachel. *The Paradoxical Ascent to God: The Kabbalistic Theosophy of Habad.* Albany: State University of New York Press. A study of early theology of Habad Hasidism, including its pantheistic emphasis.

Greenberg, Gershon. 1992. "Redemption after Holocaust according to Mahane Israel—Lubavitch 1940–45." *Modern Judaism* 12:61–84.

Hobsbawn, Eric. 1965. *Primitive Rebels.* New York: W. W. Norton.

Ish-shalom, Benjamin. 1993. *Rav Avraham Itzhak Ha-Cohen Kook: Between Rationalism and Mysticism.* Albany: State University of New York Press. A systematic description of the philosophy of Rabbi Kook.

Lewis, Bernard. 1950. "An Apocalyptic Vision of Islamic History." *Bulletin of the British School of Oriental and African Studies* 13: 315–30.

Liebman, C. S., and Eliezer Don-Yehia. 1983. *Civil Religion in Israel.* Berkeley: University of California Press. An analysis of the relationships between traditional Judaism and political culture in Israel.

Loewenthal, Naftali. 1990. *Communicating the Infinite.* Chicago: University of Chicago Press. A study of Habad theology and philosophy.

Luz, Ehud. 1988. *Parallels Meet.* Philadelphia: Jewish Publication Society. A historical description of the encounter of religion and nationalism in the early days of the Zionist movement.

Maimonides. 1960. "Epistle to Yemen." *Igrot haRambam.* Jerusalem.

McGinn, Bernard. 1979a. *Visions of the End.* New York: Columbia University Press.

———, ed. 1979b. *Apocalyptic Spirituality.* New York: Paulist Press.

Ohana, David, and Robert S. Wistrich. 1995. *The Shaping of Israel's Identity: Myth Memory and Trauma.* London: F. Cass. A collection of essays by different authors on myth and memory in contemporary Israel.

Ravitzky, Aviezer. 1990. "Religious Radicalism and Political Messianism in Israel. In *Religious Radicalism & Politics in the Middle East,* edited by Emmanual Sivan and Menachem Friedman, 18–30. Albany: State University of New York Press.

———. 1996a. *Messianism, Zionism, and Jewish Religious Radicalism.* Chicago: University of Chicago Press. An examination of Orthodox and ultra-Orthodox responses toward Zionism and the State of Israel.

———. 1996b. *History and Faith.* Amsterdam: J. C. Gieben.

Rotenstreich, Nathan. 1968. *Jewish Philosophy in Modern Times: From Mendelssohn to Rozenzweig.* New York: Holt, Rinehart, Winston. An analysis of the philosophical doctrines of the great modern Jewish thinkers (including Rabbi Kook).

Schatz, Rivka. 1993. *Hasidism as Mysticism.* Princeton, N.J.: Princeton University Press. A study of the quietistic elements in Hasidism.

Scholem, Gershom. 1971. *The Messianic Idea in Judaism and Other Essays.* New York: Schocken Books. An analysis of the messianic concepts of the rabbis and the kabbalists.

———. 1973. *Sabbatai Sevi.* Princeton, N.J.: Princeton University Press. A historical account of the greatest messianic agitation in Jewish history.

Sivan, Emmanual, and Menachem Friedman, eds. 1990. *Religious Radicalism & Politics in the Middle East.* Albany: State University of New York Press. A collection of essays by different scholars on religion, messianism, and politics in contemporary Judaism and Islam.

St. Clair, M. J. 1992. *Millenarian Movements in Historical Context.* New York: Garland Publishing.

Thrupp, L., ed. 1970. *Millennial Dreams in Action.* New York: Schocken Books.

Urbach, E. E. 1979. *The Sages: Their Concepts and Beliefs.* Jerusalem: Magnes Press. A comprehensive study of the theology of the rabbis, including their messianic beliefs.

Wallace, A. F. C. 1956. "Revitalization Movements." *American Anthropologist* 58:264–81.

Weinstein, Donald. 1970a. *Savonarola and Florence.* Princeton, N.J.: Princeton University Press.

———. 1970b. "Millenarianism in a Civic Setting: The Savonarola Movement in Florence." In Thrupp 1970, 187–203.

Wilder, A. N. 1971. "The Rhetoric of Ancient and Modern Apocalyptic." *Interpretation* 25:436–53.

Worsley, Peter. 1957. *The Trumpet Shall Sound.* London: MacGibbon & Kee.

Works in Hebrew

Abrabanel, Yitzhak. 1961. *Yeshuot Meshicho.* Königsberg.

Agnon, S. Y. 1976. *Me Atzmi el-Atzmi.* Tel Aviv.

Aviner, Schlomo, ed. 1967. *Sichot haR. Z. Y. Kook.* Holocaust Memorial Day.

Baumgarten, Albert. 1996. "Lihiyot Am Hofshi beArtzenu." In *Eretz Yisrael biTkufat haHashmonaʾim,* edited by Uriel Rappaport, 58–60. Tel Aviv.

ben Sasson, H. H. 1981. "Galut u-Geulah beEinav shel Dor Golei Sefarad. In *Sefer Yovel leYitzhak Baer.* Jerusalem.

ben Shlomo, Yosef. 1984. "Shelemut ve-Hishtalmut beTorat haElohut shel haRav Kook. In *Bein Iyyun leMaʿaseh,* edited by Yirmihhahu Yovel and Paul Mendes Flor. Jerusalem.

Eshkoli, A. Z. 1928. "Yehudei Habash beSifrut haIvrit." *Zion,* A.

———. 1988. *HaTenuʾot haMeshichiot beIsrael.* Jerusalem.

Gaerlitz, M. M. 1974. *Mara d'Arah Yisrael.* Jerusalem.

Idel, Moshe. 1990. "Reshit haKabbalah biTzefon Afrikah." *Peamim* 43:8–10.

———. 1992a. "Hibburim Zenuchim shel Baʿal Sefer Kaf haKetoret." *Paʾamim* 53.

———. 1992b. *Meshihiyut u-Mystikah* (University On Air). Tel Aviv.

———. 1995. "Historiah shel haKabbalah ve-Historiah shel haYehudim." *Teoriah u-Vikoret* 6.

Kasher, Aryeh. 1983. "HaReka haSibati ve-haNesibati shel Milhemet haYehudim baRomaʾim." In *HaMered HaGadol,* edited by Aryeh Kasher. Jerusalem.

Katz, Jacob. 1983. *Leumiut Yehudit.* Jerusalem.

Kook, A. Y. 1965. *Orot haKodesh.* Jerusalem. The most systematic text of Rabbi Kook, the mentor of redemptive Zionism.

———. 1967. *Eder haYekar ve-Ikvei haTson.* Jerusalem.

Kook, Z. Y. 1967. *LiNtivot Yisrael.* Jerusalem.

———. 1987. *LeHilkhot Tsibur.* Jerusalem.

Levinstein, Yehezkel. 1978. "Hovat haHitchazkut beIkveta diMeshihah." Published with the booklet of the "Hafetz Haim," *Tzipita Lyshua.* Jerusalem.

Prager, Moshe, ed. 1958. *LeʾOr haEmunah.* New York.

Ravitzky, Aviezer. 1984. "HaTsafui v-haReshut haNetunah." In *Israel Likrat haMeah ha-21,* edited by Aluf har-Even. Jerusalem.

Saba, Avraham. 1985. *Tseror Hamor.* Jerusalem.

Schneerson, M. M. 1980. *Emunah u-Mada.* Kefar Habad.

———. 1992. *Devar Malchut.* Parashat Vayera. Lacks page numbers.

Schneerson, Y. Z. 1941. *HaKeriah haKedoshah.*

———. 1943. *Arbaʾah Kol haKoreh mehaAdmor Shlitah meLubbavitch.* Jerusalem.

Scholem, Gershom. 1978. *Mavo le ʾMaʾamarʾ leRabbi Avraham ben Rabbi Eliezer haLevi.* Jerusalem.

Schweid, Eliezer. 1994. *Bein Hurban lishuah.* Tel Aviv.

Shapira, Rabbi Elazar, of Munkacz. 1962. *Shaʾar Yissachar.* Jerusalem.

Sheleg, Yair. "Ve-Af Al Pi She-Yitmahmehah." *Kol HaʾIr* (14.2.92).

Shirman, Hayim. 1972. *HaShira haIvrit biSefarad u-viProvence.* Jerusalem and Tel Aviv.

Stern, Menachem. 1991. *Mechkarim beToldot Israel bimei haBait haSheni.* Jerusalem.

Teitelbaum, R. Yoel, of Satmar. 1978. *VaʾYoel Moshe.* Jerusalem.

Tishbi, Yeshayahu. 1985. *Meshichiut beDor Gerushei Sefarad u-Portugal.* Jerusalem.

Zalman, Schneer, of Ladi. 1982. *Taniah—Likuttei Amarim.* Brooklyn.

23

The Resurgence of Apocalyptic in Modern Islam

Abbas Amanat
Yale University

A POCALYPSE IN THE ISLAMIC CONTEXT primarily corresponds to the fundamental doctrine of resurrection (*qiyama*) and applies to eschatological speculations concerning the return of the dead, the day of judgment, the process of salvation and damnation, and their complex realizations at the end of time (*akhira al-zaman*). In a broader sense it also encompasses preparatory events preceding the resurrection including the advent of the Mahdi (the [divinely] guided, the Islamic Messiah), symbolic reenactment of the sacred past, and the ultimate triumph of the forces of Islam over disbelief. Though the evidence in the *Qurʾān* and the *hadith* (the words and deeds attributed to the Prophet Muhammad) are employed as apocalyptic prophecies, apocalypse in the biblical sense—namely, the revelatory dreams and visions—rarely occurs in the Islamic tradition (see chapter 15). In historical reality, apocalyptic applied to all speculative or redemptive experiences and movements aspiring to transform the normative Islam, the existing political order, and the ethics of the Muslim community, by claiming a new divine mandate and by declaring commencement of an era of rejuvenated faith. Such experiences, often triggered by messianic, utopian, and apocalyptic potentials embedded in the Islamic tradition and led by charismatic figures, punctuate Islamic history throughout its course. While the Sunni world witnessed numerous examples of Shariʿa-oriented Mahdism with a distinct desire to restore pristine Islam of Muhammad's time, the Shiʿi world regenerated messianic impulses with distinct apocalyptic features aiming at a break with the Shariʿa and creation of a postmillennial order.[1]

Modern Islamic times have often been dated from the latter decades of the eighteenth century and the beginning of the nineteenth, when Muslim thinkers, statesmen, and reformers began to air a sense of anxiety for what they believed to be their communities' moral and material decline. In part the outcome of political disarray, or total disintegration, of the Muslim

I would like to thank Said Arjomand, Magnus Bernhardsson, and Juan Cole for their assistance.

582

empires of earlier centuries, this sense of decline often equated with decay of Islam as a religion. In the same period, Muslim societies, from Indonesia and India to Central Asia, the Middle East, and North Africa, began to experience the presence of the West through commerce and diplomacy. By the beginning of the nineteenth century the impact of Europe's colonial domination and its military, industrial, and later cultural and ideological manifestations became apparent not only to the Muslim states but to the Muslim peoples. These coinciding processes in turn contributed to the Muslim notion of modernity as an indigenous effort to revitalize religious, political, and social institutions (see Cleaveland 1994; Hourani 1991, 265–458; Hodgson 1974; Lewis 1994). Concepts of renewal (*tajdid*) and reform (*islah*), though not foreign to Islamic thought from earlier times, were widely used by reformers, visionaries, prophets, and revolutionaries to transform Muslim culture and material life and to resist political subordination to the West.[2]

◯ SUNNI FRONTIER MESSIANISM AND THE PROPHETIC WAY

The earliest of what may be called proto-messianic trends appeared in North Africa as part of a greater religious revival in the peripheries of the Islamic world. Inspired by such figures as Shaykh Ahmad Sirhindi (1564–1624), the founder of the Mujaddidiya Sufi order in India, and Muhammad ibn ʿAbd al-Wahhab (1703–1792), the founder of the Wahhabi puritanical movement in the Arabian peninsula, the most significant among North African trends were the Tijaniyya and Idrisiyya neo-Sufi orders at the turn of the nineteenth century, followed by the Sanusiyya order a few decades later. Differences aside, all these orders were founded by charismatic figures with puritanical proclivities and with intuitive and visionary aspirations calling for austere observance of a monolithic Shariʿa and repudiation of any monistic notion of the divinity. Warning against alien infiltration into the domains of Islam and denouncing as heretical any form of "innovation" (*bidʿa*) in religion, these mystic guides looked upon the pristine Islam of the Prophet's time as the only sacred model for emulation, a tendency that often was complemented by a claim to receive guidance from the Prophet himself. "The Muhammadan Way" (*Tariqa Muhammadiyya*) thus entailed a call against normative and popular Islam and toward restoration of a utopian community on the model of the Prophet's time. Endogenous to North African Islam, this pattern of Mahdism went back in time to the Almohad movement of Ibn Tumart (ca. 1078–1130) and before.[3]

Although restoring the glory of the Islamic past could trigger an apocalyptic scenario, in reality restoration remained distant from it and closer to the Salafiyya, a trend that called for restoring the way of the forefathers (*salaf*). It is important to note that, since Islam regarded Muhammad's revelation as complete and final and ruled out the possibility for future prophetic revelation of any kind, adherents to the Muhammadan Way could only employ intuitive experiences in order to call for restoring the "pure Islam" of the early Islamic community and strive to regain Islam's predominance through political power and, if necessary, through *jihad*. Developing in the stateless periphery of urban Islam and at a time when North Africa was experiencing the dwindling power of the Muslim states and intrusion of the Western colonial powers, these movements were bound to acquire a political character. Although Tijaniyya and

Sanusiyya began as purely Sufi revivalist trends with little overt political ambitions, they soon gave birth to political expressions that eventually, in defiance of European colonialism, led to the emergence of new states.[4]

The first among these visionary mystics with what may be called proto-messianic propensities was Ahmad al-Tijani (1737–1815), the Algerian founder of the Tijaniyya order. Experiencing visionary encounters with the Prophet in the state of wakefulness, al-Tijani arrogated to himself the status of the "master of masters" (qutb al-aqtab), a position that implied supreme spiritual supervision over all Sufi orders of his times. In his works al-Tijani even hinted at a status of infallibility, a quality exclusively reserved in Sunni Islam for the prophets. He believed that his infallibility, a gift endowed on him by the Prophet Muhammad, would enable him on the Day of Resurrection to intercede (shifaʿa) with God on behalf of his followers in the spirit of the Prophet. On the day of judgment he and his followers will be saved whereas his enemies will be banished into hell (Abun-Nasr 1965, 14–50; Trimingham 1971, 107–10).

Ahmad Ibn Idris (1760–1837), a Moroccan peripatetic Sufi scholar and the founder of the Idrisiyya order (whose influence on the early development of neo-Sufism was felt throughout North Africa, Egypt, the Sudan, and as far as Yemen) also experienced prophetic visions. A co-citizen of al-Tijani, Ibn Idris claimed that the Prophet Muhammad appeared to him in the company of al-Khidr (otherwise known as Ilyās, the Hebrew prophet Elijah), who acted as an intermediary instructing him with new Sufi litanies and prayers. Yet these mystical experiences barely took a messianic direction beyond allusions to the apocalyptic "signs of the hour," one of which he identified as the ignorance of the ʿulama of his time. No doubt the antagonism of the clerical establishments in Fez, then an active center for Moroccan scholarship, and in Mecca, where he spent some years during the Wahhabi presence, was influential in his rejection of the four traditional schools of Sunni law in favor of the exercise of ijtihad (deduction of legal opinions on the basis of the Qurʾān, the hadith, logical rudiments, and the consensus of the experts) (O'Fahey 1990, 46–49, 73, 105–10).

The same desire for establishing direct spiritual communication with the Prophet can also be observed in the teachings of Muhammad ibn ʿAli al-Sanusi (1787–1859, also known to the Europeans as the Grand Sanusi), the founder of the influential Sanusiyya order of Cyrenaica in eastern Libya. A student of Ibn Idris and al-Tijani, influenced by the Meccan revivalist circle at the turn of the nineteenth century, al-Sanusi sensed an even greater urgency than his teachers in seeking a spiritual remedy to Islam's political and moral infirmity, a worldview no doubt touched by al-Sanusi's residence in Egypt, where he was denounced by the ʿulama of al-Azhar for his emphasis on ijtihad and for his strict adherence to the Muhammadan Way.[5]

Even more than the intellectual environment of al-Azhar and Fez, it was the threat of European domination that motivated al-Sanusi and his successors to undertake a largely peaceful missionary expansion of the Sanusi order among the mixed nomadic population and the peasantry of present-day Libya, Algeria, and Chad, as far south as equatorial Africa, and along the southern Mediterranean coast. In this endeavor al-Sanusi and his son and successor, al-Sayyid al-Mahdi (1844–1902), initially prescribed a course of moral reconstruction of the community on the Muhammadan model as an alternative to an outward jihad. Although Sayyid al-Mahdi was viewed by his followers as the Mahdi (and mujaddid of the turn of 1300 AH [1882–1883]), he preferred to publicly play down the messianic attribute. He nevertheless drew upon the North African cult of saints and the dormant expectation for the advent of the Mahdi, especially among the Berbers, to preserve an aura of Mahdihood. In due course the changing political climate in North Africa transformed the Sanusiyya's political quiescence into an out-ward revolt. By the turn of the twentieth century the movement took a definite anticolonial bent as the Sanusiyya spearheaded a formidable force of indigenous resistance against French, and later Italian, occupation of Libya. The bonds of loyalty to the Sanusi leadership were upheld with a messianic zeal and throughout the First World War and after. In the post–Second World War era the residue of the movement's charismatic past contributed to the legitimacy of the Sanusi monarchy of Libya.

Yet it was with the rise of the Mahdi of the Sudan, perhaps the most well known of the Sunni claimants to Mahdihood, that African neo-Sufism found its most intense expression of puritanic messianism. Muhammad Ahmad ibn ʿAbdullah (1844–1885), a *faki* (*faqir*, as Sufi adapts were known in Sudanese Islam) from a family of boat builders in Donghola, on the southern edge of the Nubian desert, received formal madrasa education and rigorous Sufi training before settling in 1870 in the strategically located island of Aba, which served as a gate-way for the slave trade of equatorial Sudan and for the Baqqara tribal confederacy in the adja-cent Kordofan and the Darfur ranges. This was at a time when the Egyptian conquest of the Sudan from around 1810–1820 had created a political vacuum in the region which the Egyptian Khedival administration had difficulty filling. In the frontiers of the Nilotic Sudan with a com-plex and volatile tribal structure, the Egyptian attempt to enforce administrative control through a harsh taxation policy disturbed not only the agricultural and urban patterns of tradi-tional life but the delicate tribal balance, which had already been upset by massive movements of population. Equally disruptive was the British-backed Egyptian attempt in the 1860s to enforce a ban on the lucrative slave trade of the south. Intrusive centralization measures, com-bined with the excesses of the alien and haughty officials and a rapidly transforming economy aided by the introduction of modern communication aroused popular discontent at all levels, to which al-Mahdi's movement became an indigenous response (Holt 1970, 2:329–38).

As one of the leaders of a Sammaniyya Sufi order, Muhammad Ahmad gained a reputa-tion for being a deeply pious and observant man, a predictable precondition for claim to Mahdihood. Infusion of neo-Sufi orders may be seen as a Sudanese response to the penetration of the madrasa-oriented Islam of al-Azhar sponsored by the Egyptian administration. Muham-mad Ahmad first aired in secret his messianic claims around 1880 shortly after coming into contact with his most influential follower and later his successor, ʿAbdullah ibn Muhammad of Darfur, a Sufi devotee suffused with Mahdistic longings. More explicit manifestation (*zuhur*) as the expected Mahdi (*al-Mahdi al-muntazar*) of the Islamic world, came in June 1881, following his adoption of the title Muhammad al-Mahdi, which he claimed was conferred on him by Muhammad the Prophet. In numerous proclamations (*manshurat*) dispatched in the course of the next four years, al-Mahdi defined his mission as one inspired through intuitive communi-cation with Muhammad in which he was given the task of erasing the corruption and decay that plagued the Muslim community and restoring the unspoiled Islam of the Prophet's time. He drew upon Islamic apocalyptic prophecies as well as Sufi prognostications (such as Ibn ʿArabi's) to justify his own prophetic "signs," both physical and behavioral, which he compared with those of the Prophet of Islam. He further viewed his manifestation at the impending end of the thirteenth Islamic century (which was to arrive in 1300 AH/1883), not only as a divine will to "renovate" Islam but a manifestation from the world of "concealment," a notion closely associ-ated with the Shiʿi notion of Occultation (*ghayba*). Al-Mahdi's emphasis on his sacred lineage from the "prophetic house" and the fashion in which he claimed to have received inspirations also pointed in a Shi'i apocalyptic direction. Yet in rendering his mission, al-Mahdi seldom, if ever, trespassed the bounds of a Shari'a-restoring Mahdism. He believed himself to be the locus for the "prophetic lights," from the "niche of [Muhammadan] prophecy" and recipient of "divine voices" who was called upon to "revive" the essence of the prophecy and "return matters to their beginning," by "filling the earth with justice," as the famous messianic *hadith* prescribed, "when it is filled with oppression and tyranny." To rebuild the Prophet's Shari'a, which has been "obliterated" by the enemies of Islam, and to restore the "true religion," like Muhammad he had to resort to the sword in order to remove not only the spurious four schools of the Sunni law and to replace them with the "pure Islamic rules" and "God's punishing limits," but also to declare jihad against the most virulent enemies of Islam.

Symbolic reenactment of early Islamic history held sway over much of al-Mahdi's action. The infidels of his manifestation were the Turks, a generic term applied in his parlance to the Egyptian Khedival authority (after the assumed Turkish origin of the dynasty) and to all Egyptian and European officials, officers and troops in its service. It was even stretched to include the Ottoman state, the nominal suzerain of the Egyptian rulers, and the European powers supporting the Khedivate. Al-Mahdi's profound enmity toward the Turks was probably rooted in the harsh treatment the northern Sudanese tribes, among them the Danghula, received at the hands of Muhammad 'Ali's conquering armies earlier in the century but more so because he viewed the Turko-Egyptian domination and their modernizing measures as deviations from Islamic norms and thus tantamount to idolatry. In his messianic worldview the distinction between the forces of good and evil was sharp. Any deviations, whether advancing the madrasa-based Islam of the heartland, neglecting the Islamic "prohibition of the evil," relaxing restrictions on veiling of the women, or enforcing unlawful taxes, were all justifiable ground for declaring a holy war. As an evidence of Islam's subjugation, he labeled state taxes alien to the Sudanese society as a form of *jizya* (Islamic poll tax imposed on religious minorities) which, he believed, was antithetic to Islam's sovereignty especially as they were imposed upon Muslims by Christian agents (Holt 1958, 37,116; Shaked 1978, 50–200; Voll 1979, 145–66).

Reconstructing his mission on the model of early Islam in late 1881, al-Mahdi embarked on the symbolic act of "immigration" (*hijra*) from Aba to Qadir to the safety of the Baqqara tribes in the Kordofan. He consciously portrayed his *hijra* as a replication of Muhammad's departure to Medina in 622, a symbolic act of breaking with unbelievers and striking a new covenant with his "helpers" (*ansar*). The capture of the provincial capital, al-'Ubayd, in 1883, at the turn of the fourteenth Islamic century, was the first of the victories affirming al-Mahdi's belief that he was repeating Muhammad's victories in the battlefield. Coinciding with the 'Urabi Pasha's revolt in Egypt, which led to the British occupation of that country in September 1882, al-Mahdi succeeded further in the battle of Shaykhan to annihilate another expeditionary force led by Colonel William Hicks. It was the fall of Khartoum to al-Mahdi's forces in January 1885, however, and the slaying of General Charles Gordon that were seen by his followers as the pinnacle of the new prophet's success and a prelude to victories beyond the Sudan. To the Western public, anxiously following the events through extensive press reports, the rise and the success of al-Mahdi were viewed as nothing but the resurgence of fanaticism, tribal savagery, and senseless resistance to the benevolent forces of white civilization (Daniel 1966, 416–58). To Muslims, who read about his successes with a reserved interest, he remained a pseudo-Mahdi (*al-Mutamahdi*), even though he was sometimes praised for his defiance to the British. By June 1885 when al-Mahdi died, possibly because of an epidemic, he controlled most of the Sudan through conquest and tribal alliances and laid the foundation for a theocratic state under his successor, Khalifa ʿAbdullahi, and his lieutenants.

Thirteen years later, in 1898, a British expedition under General Kitchener routed the Khalifa's forces in the decisive battle of Omdurman, a brutal operation that led to the destruction of al-Mahdi's state. Winston Churchill, then a young war correspondent, was thrilled with the military action and welcomed the British imperial reassertion but could not hide his disgust with the British command's vengeful retaliation for Gordon's death (Gilbert 1991, 90–100). The British strategic concerns were primarily with the French advances in central Africa, which in the same year as the battle of Omduran led to the famous Fashoda incident in the south Sudan. Al-Mahdi's messianic drive no doubt was regressive in its orientation and oppressive in its application, but it was, to the extent that it was realized, a formidable force consolidating desperate and divided tribal loyalties into a centralized political-religious entity (Holt 1958, 202–4).

☞ SHIʿI MAHDISM AND THE END OF TIME

Even in modern times expectations for the Mahdi were more prevalent in Shiʿi Islam, particularly in Iranian Shiʿism, than in the Sunni world. Deeply ingrained in its belief system and, in turn, into the Shiʿi psyche, the doctrine of Imamate ensured continuity of divine inspiration. As designated descendants of the Prophet who inherited in a direct line the leadership of the community, the Imams' continued existence was considered "proof" (*hujja*) of the continuity of divine grace toward the "guided" Shiʿi community. In Twelver Shiʿism the Mahdi is the Twelfth (and the last) Imam in the line, who is believed to have entered in the year 260 AH/873–874 into a state of Occultation and hence is invisible to believers through normal means. Essential to the Shiʿi apocalyptic beliefs is that the advent of the Hidden Imam (*al-Imam al-Ghaʾib*) will set in motion a course of events ultimately leading to the destruction of the world and the end of time. Though no specific time was ever set for his advent, it was generally believed that his revolt (*khuruj*) would occur at the turn of a millennium after his Occultation. As the Lord of Time (*al-Sahib al-Zaman*) and the Riser (*Qāʾim*) of the House of the Prophet, he will restore justice and equity to the world when it is filled with evil and oppression. This sense of restoring justice was tied in Shiʿi prophecies with reinstalling the right to political leadership of the House of the Prophet, vengeance against the usurpers of that authority, and consequently expansion through jihad and the Imam's world domination. This millennial scenario, elaborated and embellished over centuries in a vast body of apocalyptic literature, presented the advent of the Imam and his accomplishments against the forces of the Dajjal, the false Messiah, as the prelude to the resurrection and the final judgment. Contrary to the Sunni Mahdi, whose advent was aimed to enhance the foundations of Islam on a periodic (centennial) basis, the Shiʿi Islam essentially strived to invoke the Imamate paradigm so as to bring about the resurrection and an end to the prevailing dispensation. The Imam's advent will differentiate the forces of good from evil in two confronting armies and establish the sovereignty of the House of the Prophet, but his kingdom was predicted to be ephemeral and only a preparatory stage before the cataclysmic end of the material world, the commencement of the day of judgment, and thereafter the final departure of the saved to paradise and the damned to hell.[6]

Despite this rich and dynamic apocalyptic tradition, however, during the period of expectation (*intizar*) for the Lord of Time to bring relief from oppression, no course of action was
prescribed for the believers except vigilance and, if need be, dissimulation of true beliefs in the
face of danger. Although Shi'ism began to develop, almost immediately after the Occultation,
an elaborate body of formal religious sciences crowned by the study of jurisprudence, the question of political leadership of the community during the interregnum of the Imam's absence
remained essentially unaddressed. A long tradition of madrasa education, reenforced under the
patronage of the Safavid dynasty (1501–1732), led to the emergence of a community of jurists
(*mujtahids*) who claimed a collective vicegerency (*niyaba*) on behalf of the Hidden Imam while
condoning the shahs' vague notion of political vicegerency. Partially independent from the
state, these 'ulama, who assumed for themselves the task of preserving the "essence of Islam" as
experts in the holy law and its sole implementors, became increasingly self-conscious of their
status after the fall of the Safavid state in the early eighteenth century. By the time the Qajar
dynasty (1785–1925) consolidated, the 'ulama of the predominant Usuli legal school presented
a socioreligious force to be reckoned with in the domain of the judiciary and of education. They
seldom, however, in theory or practice, laid any claim to political authority in the state beyond
occasional challenges to its conduct. The clergy–state equilibrium, a legacy of the Safavid
period, had the natural tendency to relegate the advent of the Hidden Imam to a distant future
and in turn dismiss as unorthodox, if not heretical, all such speculations. The actual messianic
aspirations were tolerated even less, having routinely been labeled as fraudulent and heretical.[7]

Yet Shi'ism never fully dissociated itself from messianic aspirations, even though preoccupation with jurisprudence and supplementary sciences steered mainstream learning in a nonmessianic direction. No less important a scholar than Mulla Muhammad Baqir Majlisi
(1628–1699), the celebrated theologian most responsible for popularizing Shi'ism, dedicated a
substantial portion of his famous *Al-Bihar al-Anwar* and a number of his Persian works to the
subject of the Hidden Imam, the circumstances of his manifestation, the struggle against the
Dajjal, and the consequent eschatological occurrences leading to the return (*raj'a*) of the past
prophets and Imams, the raising of the dead on the Plane of the Gathering, the Final Judgment,
the Heaven's bliss, and the torments of Hell. The apocalyptic literature produced by Majlisi,
and later writers up to the twentieth century, was influential not only in keeping alive debates
about the advent of the Imam in the madrasa circles, but more significantly, in the popular
imagination. Beyond the calm and stern surface of formal Shi'ism there continued to surge a
mass of millennial yearning often with revolutionary potentials against the prevailing religion
of the 'ulama and the institutions of the state (Amanat 1989, 1–47, 70–105).

Speculative Shi'ism also elaborated on Shi'i eschatology and, more specifically, on the circumstances of resurrection. The immortality of the soul, modes of existence in the hereafter,
and, most troubling of all, the doctrine of the corporal resurrection (*al-ma'ad al-jismani*) came
to occupy such philosophers as the Sadr al-Din Shirazi, better known as Mulla Sadra (d. 1640),
perhaps the greatest of Muslim philosophers of recent centuries. In contrast to Sunni Islam's
relinquishing serious philosophical discourse, learned Shi'ism preserved a thriving and highly
diverse philosophical tradition and articulated within the framework of mystical philosophy
notions of time and modalities of being essential for innovative conceptualization of the end.
Unlike the historically static worldview of the Shari'a-minded 'ulama, Mulla Sadra and his students, known as Muta'allihin (theosophists), envisioned a dynamic view of time that in final
analysis was at odds with the conventional notion of the eschaton as the permanent point of

termination. Sadra'ians essentially remained loyal to a blend of Peripatetic and Neoplatonic philosophy expounded by classical Muslim philosophers, but their notion of beings' everlasting motion in time was a breakthrough. In what Mulla Sadra defined as the "essential motion" (*al-haraka al-jawhariyya*) of all things, the universe "is ceaselessly being renewed and passing away, originating and ending." Unlike the theory of the fixed cycles or the ahistorical approach of mainstream theology, the Sadra'ian concept of "essential motion" (or transubstantiation) pointed to an unending spiral, if not linear, course of humankind's spiritual and material progression. Even in its dormant philosophical rendition, this concept challenged conventional interpretation of the End and cast doubt on its occurrence as a providential cataclysm destined to bring the world to a permanent end. Yet Shi'i philosophical speculations remained essentially loyal to the doctrine of Islam's perfection and finality (Morris 1981, 119–29).

With the emergence of the Shaykhi school and the visionary theology of its founder, Shaykh Ahmad Ahsa'i (1756–1826), Shi'ism generated a new mystical-philosophical synthesis that was highly influential in shaping later millennial trends. A peripatetic and widely read scholar from al-Ahsa' (north of Arabian peninsula), Ahsa'i was familiar not only with the theosophist school of Isfahan (though he violently denounced Mulla Sadra) but also with the speculative Sufism of Ibn 'Arabi and the illuminist philosophy of Shihab al-Din Suhrawardi, both known for their apocalyptic propensity. Ahsa'i's contribution to the Shi'i eschatological thinking was in three areas, which corresponded to the problematic that was long troubling Shi'i theology. Dealing with the Hidden Imam's physical endurance in the state of Occultation, Ahsa'i proposed a celestial visionary space, which he called *Hurqalya*, where the Hidden Imam resides until his return to the physical world. Speculating on the metaphysical means of communicating with the Imam, Ahsa'i emphasized personal and intuitive experiences. Furthermore, he redefined corporal resurrection through a complex process that aimed at humankind's spiritual recreation once the Imam returns to the physical world.

The luminous *Hurqalya*, a purgatory through which all beings must pass before being finally judged on the day of resurrection, was perceived as a world whose "state was neither the absolutely subtle state of separate substances nor the opaque density of the material things of our world." In this liminal space the Imam, who endured in a refined frame, could be encountered by the believers through intuitive visions, holy dreams, and occult sciences. The placement of the Imam in this visionary space in effect rescued him from the timeless, confused, and inaccessible tangle to which he was relegated by the Shi'i prophecies and instead subjected his existence to the dictates of time and space. Ahsa'i further maintained that so long as the Imam was in Occultation and while the world was still undergoing pre-resurrectional preparation, only one person could acquire perfect awareness of the Imam at any moment of time. The belief in the Perfect Shi'a (*al-Shi'a al-Kamil*), the one who can visualize the Imam in an all-embracing state of intuitive experience, became the Fourth Principle (*al-Rukn al-Rabi'*) of the Shaykhi school and the central point for its messianic speculations. Ahsa'i's chief disciple and successor, Sayyid Kazim Rashti (d. 1844), who further elaborated on his teacher's philosophy and created an organizational rudiment for Shaykhism, was viewed by his followers as the Perfect Shi'a and the gate (*bab*) through which the Imam's presence could be grasped though such identification was never made explicit beyond the circle of the adepts. Employing the same idea of celestial conservatory, Ahsa'i conceived of a fourfold human existence which goes through a complex process of quintessential overhaul before being refashioned in its original form at the final judgment (Amanat 1989, 48–58; Corbin 1960, 281–338; 1977, 180–221).

Under Rashti, a small but active group of Shaykhi seminarians, trained in the madrasas of the Shi'i holy city of Karbala in Iraq, preached Shaykhism in mostly Iranian urban and rural communities. As Shaykhism gradually evolved from a theological school into a proto-messianic movement with followers among the lower- and middle-rank clergy, members of the urban guilds, merchant families, local government officials, and some peasant communities, it was increasingly received as a threat by the higher ranks of the clerical establishment. By the end of Rashti's time, the Shaykhis fully nurtured a sense of expectation for some form of messianic advent, which they hoped could save them from the harassment and denunciation of their opponents. With this sense of expectation there also emerged among the Shaykhis a more humanlike picture of the Lord of the Age and of his mission. He no longer was perceived as a superhuman with fantastic powers which allowed him, according to Shi'i prophecies, to survive a thousand years; he was seen as a human being born to mortal parents. Nor was his divine mission for universal conquest to be accomplished through a set of bizarre and confused apocalyptic events that would ultimately lead to the destruction of the world. His main task, to restore justice and equity, was seen no longer as mere vengeance for the long-standing feud with the historical enemies of his holy family but as a gradual process whose success against his enemies depended on the support and sacrifice of his followers (Amanat 1989, 58–69).

☞ THE BABI MOVEMENT
AND THE BAHA'I FAITH

The rise of what came to be known as the Babi movement in Iran in the 1840s and 1850s was an outgrowth of a wide range of messianic speculations of which Shaykhism was the most prevalent. In May 1844 the founder of the new movement, Sayyid 'Ali Muhammad Shirazi (1819–1850), a self-educated young merchant with Shaykhi leanings from Shiraz (the capital of the Fars province), declared that he is the *bab* (gate) to the Hidden Imam and the sole source of legitimate authority. Though the Bab, as he came to be known to the general public, employed the early Shi'i notion of "gateship" now revived by the Shaykhis, even in his earliest declarations he was equivocal about his exact status. To Mulla Husain Bushru'i, an ardent student of Rashti who became the Bab's first convert, as well as to a group of mostly Shaykhi clerics who constituted his circle of early believers, the Bab gradually confided that he was not merely a gate to the Hidden Imam but the manifestation of the expected Imam, the Qa'im himself, whose appearance the Shi'is expected for a thousand years. Preoccupied with numerology and occult sciences, the Bab drew on the fact that his "manifestation of the [divine] cause" occurred in the year 1260 AH, a thousand years after the presumed Greater Occultation of the Twelfth Imam, Muhammad ibn Hasan al-'Askari, in the year 260 AH/873–874. He also drew on the fact that he was a *sayyid*, a descendant of the house of the Prophet, from which the Mahdi will appear, while stressing his own intuitive experiences and visions, his purity of character, and his ability to utter holy verses similar to the *Qur'an*. Implicitly denying the doctrine of Occultation, he further stated that his manifestation was a symbolic return of the Lord of the Age and not the flesh-and-blood reappearance of Muhammad ibn Hasan al-'Askari, who had died a millennium earlier (Amanat 1989, 109–211).

What was also remarkable about the Bab's claim, as it evolved in the course of the next five years, was that he considered his call not as a reassertion of Islamic Shariʿa, as was the case with the Sunni Mahdis, but as the beginning of an apocalyptic process that was destined to bring the Islamic dispensation to its cyclical end and to inaugurate instead a new dispensation, which he called the era of *Bayan*. Relying on a hermeneutical interpretation of the Shiʿi prophecies, for the first time in the history of modern Islam, he claimed that with his advent the age of resurrection has started and the End of Time is to be understood as the end of the past prophetic cycle. Employing the ancient Iranian tree metaphor and its seasonal renewal, he explained in his major work, the Persian *Bayan* (literally, explication [of the past scriptures]) that religious dispensations come in cycles so as to renew for humankind the "pure religion," a concept with a long history in "esoteric" Islam. In his theory of progressive revelation he compared the successive dispensations to the life cycle of a tree with a spring of inception and early growth, a summer of strength and maturation, an autumn of gradual decline and decrepitude, and a winter of barrenness and death. This key notion of continuity in revelation not only legitimized the Bayan religion but recognized and anticipated future prophetic occurrences after the Bab. Contrary to the prevailing Islamic notion of a cataclysmic end, the Bab believed that the "time cycle is in progress."[8]

Beyond the theme of progressive revelation, Babi theology, deeply rooted in Perso-Islamic antinomian thought, brought to the surface new anthropocentric potentials. His manifestation, the Bab asserted in the *Bayan*, was not only the fulfillment of the Shiʿi expectations for the Qaʾim and the beginning of a new prophetic dispensation but also a new stage in humankind's continuous spiritual elevation in the process of reunification with the Creator. Though wrapped in a complex and convoluted language with much neology, the Bab's emphasis on humanity as a corporal mirror reflecting the essence of the sun of divine truth offered a new outlook, in which believers collectively, rather than the sheer will of Providence, were responsible for the success or failure of the new dispensation. This sense of collective enterprise was apparent from the start in the nascent organization of the movement and in the beliefs and conduct of early Babis. The Letters of the Living, as the Bab named the inceptive Babi Unit of nineteen consisting of himself and eighteen early believers, was at the heart of the renewed dispensation. In his conception of the new religion, the Bab was influenced also by the story of Jesus and his disciples as narrated in newly accessible printed translations of the New Testament. In his religious scheme, the Bab constituted the Primal Point (*Nuqta-yi Ula*) of a scriptural universe in which each convert was considered a building block, a symbolic point, in the *Bayan*'s book, which was uttered not only in letters and words but in their human equivalents of the sacred text of the physical world. At the same time the Bab's assumed epithet to be the Sublime Lord (*Rabb-i Aʿla*) was close to the Christian characterization of Jesus, Son of God and the Savior, whose account of life and sufferings was appreciated by the Bab.

In the Bab's scripture-oriented worldview, the Europeans, whose increasing presence was felt in Iran around the middle of the nineteenth century, were recognized as the "letters of the Gospel." They were praised for their material advances and their savvy but were frowned upon for their unsavory intrusion into the land of the believers—a reflection, one may surmise, of the growing European commercial and diplomatic dominance. Indeed, the Bab, himself from the ancient province of Fars, expressed in his writings a nascent national awareness exemplified not only by his ban on Christian intrusion into the land of Bayan but also by the use of Persian (along with Arabic) as a scriptural language. His fierce criticism of conventional Islamic madrasa scholarship of his time, which was exclusively in Arabic, brought him to the point of banning the study of jurisprudence and scholastic philosophy and calling for burning all books that were contrary to the essence of the *Bayan*. He also adopted a new solar calendar (in part based on ancient Iranian time reckoning) in place of the Islamic lunar calendar and marked the date of his own manifestation as a beginning of a novel (*badiᶜ*) era.[9]

Yet the new Babi identity still carried a powerful Shiᶜi component that was best discernible in the reenactment of the Shiᶜite apocalyptic paradigm. Based on the sufferings of the Shiᶜite saints of the early Islamic period and aimed at redressing them, the apocalyptic myth was invoked as the Babis faced harassment and persecution. Following the arrest and incarceration of the founder of the movement and experiencing a number of humiliating episodes, the initial Jesus-like program for peaceful propagation was surpassed by the ever-present Husain paradigm of martyrdom in the battlefield. In this shift of paradigms the Bab saw his own fate as identical with the fate of the Lord of the Age as foretold by prophecies. He was to be killed at the hand of the Dajjal of his time in the same way that the Third Imam, Husain ibn ᶜAli, was martyred at the hand of his Umayyad adversaries in the battle of Karbala.

The Babis, too, reflected this convergence of the Persian and the Shiᶜi identities. The sociogeographic composition of the Babi movement revealed national characteristics consonant with the Babi beliefs but in contrast to the compartmentalized structure of the society in which it appeared. Babism was the first movement in the modern Middle East that brought together a wider spectrum of converts from different walks of life and throughout a vast geographical span. Confrontations with the forces of opposition, first the Shiᶜi clerical establishment and later the Qajar state, further reenforced this national fusion. In the siege of Tabarsi in Mazandaran province in northern Iran, when in 1848–1849 the Babis put up a stiff and bloody resistance against the government forces and their clerical allies, there came together converts from all over Iran, as well as Afghanistan and Iraq, of different social classes with diverse occupational background, education, and religious leanings. The Tabarsi resistance, like a number of other Babi armed struggles around the same time in Zanjan and Nayriz, embodied the anticlerical and antistate sentiments that were combined at times with indigenous communistic proclivities, giving expression to urban and rural grievances and ethnic strife (Amanat 1989, 260–94, 332–71).

In addition to lower ranks of the clergy and members of the bazaar guilds, a number of women also joined the movement. Most notable among them was Zarrin Taj Baraghani (1814–1852), better known by her titles Qurrat al-ᶜAyn (the Solace of the Eye) and later, Tahira (the Pure). An ardent Shaykhi scholar and orator from a well-known clerical family, she probably was the first Muslim woman in modern times to remove her facial veil in public, reportedly while preaching to a male audience. A mystic and a poet, she highlighted the independent nature of the Babi dispensation in the gathering of Badasht in 1848. She held that the ongoing age of resurrection has put an end to the Islamic Shariᶜa and that during the interregnum between the old religion and the birth of the new one, such obligations as prayers and fasting and even institutions of marriage and divorce are abolished. Her very act of removing her facial veil was as much an expression of protest against women's inferior position as it was a symbolic declaration of the age of apocalypse and the occurrence of the sedition (*fitna*). She declared that the age of "delivering the word" has only brought abuse and persecution and that the only option open to the Babis was resort to the sword (Amanat 1989, 295–331, and sources cited there).

By 1848, as the Babi armed resistance culminated, the government's attitude hardened toward the Babis. The new premier, Mirza Taqi Khan Amir Kabir, who viewed the movement as a revolutionary threat to the very survival of the state, with much trouble managed to suppress the revolts, and subsequently, in 1850, he executed the Bab in Tabriz. The leadership of the movement suffered badly, and large numbers of the Babis were killed in action and massacred and their families enslaved. Two years later the remnant of the movement's elite was executed or lynched in the aftermath of a Babi assassination plot against the new shah, Nasir al-Din Qajar (1848–1896). Only a few of the leaders, most significantly Mirza Husain ʿAli Nuri, better know as Bahaʾullah (1817–1892), were sent to exile to the Ottoman Iraq. Suppression of the Babi millennialism at the hands of a reform-minded premier, with the full blessing of the ʿulama, was symptomatic of the triumph of one vision of change over another, namely, that of the state-sponsored secular modernism over an indigenous messianic revolution. The Babi movement, perhaps the most intensive example of apocalyptic aspirations in the modern Middle East, was thus militarily defeated and driven underground.

Disillusioned and persecuted, Babism nevertheless survived and even thrived in the following decades as a force of religious and political dissent. Despite horrifying mistreatment at the hand of government officials, the fierce animosity of the ʿulama, and frequent mob attacks and scenes of gruesome lynching, known as *Babi-kushi*, and despite internecine conflicts and ideological divisions within the exiled leadership, the Babis continued to attract converts from discontented elements of all ranks. Bahaʾullah, who led the Babi-Bahaʾi majority faction from exile in Baghdad, then Ederna, and later Akka in Palestine, was supported by converts from among the petty merchants and other sectors of the middle classes. A member of the bureaucratic elite, Bahaʾullah renounced the Babi militant stance against the state in favor of a pacifist approach based on a moral reassessment of the Babi principles. The minority Babi-Azali faction, on the other hand, remained theoretically loyal to the Babi revolt against the state and the ʿulama and refused redefinition of the Babi scripture (Amanat 1989, 372–416).

The emerging Babi-Bahaʾi faith represented a religious outlook based on Bayani religion but in many respects, particularly its socio-moral message, distinct from it. Bahaʾullah, who first claimed in 1864 to be "He whom God shall manifest," the awaited savior of the Bayani dispensation, combined in his teachings aspects of mysticism with utopian discourse of possible European origin while preserving the Babi messianic outlook and communal vigor. In the spirit of the Babi theophany, he claimed to be the manifestation of the divine word uttered in the day of encounter with God. His ecumenical call drew upon Islam as well as Judaism and Christianity as he claimed to be the messianic fulfillment of all monotheistic religions, a manifestation aimed at elevating humankind to the status of cognition while Bahaʾullah himself was to be the ultimate pinnacle of this divine manifestation. Bahaʾullah viewed the arrival of this apocalyptic moment, God's Day, as a sign of maturation of human moral and civil potentials. The call for the "unity of humankind," the ultimate goal of the anticipated "universal peace," reflected the Bahaʾi wish to break with the ethnic, racial, and gender norms and loyalties prevalent at the time. Bahaʾullah's later writing emphasized racial and gender equality, economic harmony, constitutional monarchy, and religious toleration. His independent investigation of truth as the guiding principle for personal enlightenment and for the community's intellectual life also dismissed religious conviction on the bases of ancestral, communal, or scriptural identities and instead underscored a shade of modern individuality. "Universal maturation" was thus viewed as the prelude to a new age of cognition, rather than abiding dogma, and individual responsibility, rather than collective ritualism. The Babi teachings were further modified so as to remove the relics of the Islamic past in the areas of devotional acts, legalistic provenance of the ʿulama, women's segregation, strictures in dealing with nonbelievers, and dietary rules. More importantly, as a post-apocalyptic faith, Baha'ism sought to disengage from Islam's preoccupation with the hereafter, at least in its heaven–hell dichotomy, and to highlight instead the gradual elevation of human soul in the afterlife.[10]

The unfolding of millenarian potentials of Iranian Shi'ism in the Babi movement, and its later Baha'i and Azali manifestations, occurred at a critical juncture when Islamic societies had begun to encounter the threatening and yet luring West. The Babi movement thus represented a novel answer to the question of religious modernization by breaking with Islam while preserving the continuity of the Middle East's prophetic tradition.

In contrast to the Babi trend to break from Islam, the Ahmadiyya movement of the Indo-Muslim prophet Mirza Ghulam Ahmad Qadiyani (1839–1908), demonstrates the foreboding obstacles in the way of movements of messianic renewal that strived to remain within the pale of Islam. Mirza Ghulam Ahmad, a Sufi-oriented advocate of continuity in prophethood, viewed divine revelation as the only remedy to Islam's evident doctrinal ailment and intellectual decrepitude. Being part of the Muslim (and Hindu) eclectic modernism of colonial India and having been exposed to the messianic Christian missionary propaganda (mostly by American Presbyterians), from around 1880 Ghulam Ahmad claimed to be the locus of divine revelation and the advent of both the Islamic Mahdi and the second coming of Jesus Christ (*Masih*).

Rejecting the doctrine of crucifixion (as does the *Qur'ān*), Ghulam Ahmad made the extraordinary claim that in reality Jesus recovered from his wounds and left Palestine for Kashmir, where he died a natural death and was buried. He believed that as Jesus' ministry transpired 1400 years after Moses, Ghulam Ahmad's divine mission, too, occurred 1400 years after Muhammad's divine mission, a juncture that corresponded also to the beginning of the twentieth century of the Christian era. Yet his claim to be in the "likeness" of Jesus who confesses Islam did not entail the approach of the apocalypse, nor was his claim to Mahdihood to be understood as waging an apocalyptic jihad. As he eventually asserted after facing bitter opposition from the Sunni 'ulama, Hindu reformers, and Christian missionaries, he was a *nabi* (prophet) whose peaceful advent was to revitalize true Islam and reveal the secrets of its scripture. This claim was not in essence different from that of the Mahdi of the Sudan, whom Ghulam Ahmad had attacked for his militancy, nor was it essentially distinct from North African intuitive Mahdis, insisting on remaining within the pale of Islam while striving to revitalize it through prophetic inspiration (Lavan 1974, 22–63).

Under Ghulam Ahmad's son and successor, Bashir al-Din Mahmud Ahmad Masih II, the majority of the Ahmadiyya, known as Jama'at Ahmadiyya, came even closer to an Islamic revisionist creed. Despite its exclusive sense of community and its missionary drive, Jama'at Ahmadiyya still fully complied with the doctrine of Islam's finality and its superiority. The troubling Qur'anic assertion respecting *khatam al-nabi'in* (33:41) thus was rendered by Ahmadiyya, based on semantic variations, as affirmation of Muhammad's superior virtue, hence being the "seal of the prophets," and not the "last of the prophets." Ghulam Ahmad viewed himself as a prophetic manifestation under the aegis of Muhammadan Shari'a and not an end to it. For the Ahmadiyya hereafter was meant to be a continuous journey of the soul toward spiritual perfection, an interpretation distinct from literal Qur'anic rendition of heaven and hell but close to the Sufi, and the later Baha'i view. The rival Anjuman Ahmadiyya, led by Mawlana Muhammad 'Ali, reverted to the Islamic fold even more than the majority Jama'at

Ahmadiyya by recognizing Ghulam Ahmad not as a prophet but as an Islamic centennial renovator (*mujaddid*) (Lavan 1974, 92–121).

⌒ ECLIPSE OF THE HEREAFTER AND THE
RISE OF ISLAMIC UTOPIANISM

With the dawn of Western-style modernism, in the late nineteenth and early twentieth centuries, messianic aspirations and the creative interpretation of eschatology largely disappeared
from mainstream Sunni discourse. Facing the formidable threat of colonial domination and
Western ideological and cultural preeminence, Muslim reformist trends became increasingly
preoccupied with preserving Islam's identity and redefining its political community. Debates
about the end and the hereafter were viewed as essentially irrelevant to such endeavors except as
obligatory tenets necessary for the believers' steadfast devotion to their faith. Modernist trends
often strived to justify, revise, and redefine Islam as a religion concerned with the affairs of this
world and adaptable to the norms of modernity while, understandably, excluding critical
reassessment of Islam's fundamental doctrines. In their vision of rejuvenated Islam, reformists
saw might and glory in cherished virtues of religious enlightenment, political unity, material
progress, modern sciences and technology, and mass education—themes they began to redis-
cover in an idealized picture of Islam's past—while blaming the obscurantist ʿulama for their
short-sighted clinging to arcane intricacies of the holy law. Thinkers and political activists of
the late nineteenth and early twentieth centuries such as Jamal al-Din Asadabadi (al-Afghani),
Muhammad ʿAbdu and Rashid Rida in the Arab world and Sayyid Ahmad Khan and Muhammad Iqbal in India seldom paid attention to serious reassessment of doctrines of prophethood
and resurrection not only out of fear of denunciation and charges of heresy but because they
genuinely traced the roots of Islam's "decay" in the believers' preoccupation with the hereafter
and failure to appreciate the this-worldly dimensions of Islam (Smith and Haddad 1981,
127–46).

Muhammad Iqbal's reflection on the question of corporal versus spiritual resurrection is
typical of modernists' resort to a mystical interpretation with a this-worldly bent. He believed
that "Heaven and Hell are states, not localities" and that *Qurʾān*'s descriptions of the hereafter
are "visual representations of an inner fact." Hell, in the words of the *Qurʾān*, he stated, is
"God's kindled fire which mounts above the hearts" and a "painful realization of one's failure
as a man." Heaven, on the other hand, "is the joy of triumph over the forces of disintegration"
(Iqbal 1962, 123; see Smith and Haddad 1981, 138). Iqbal's interpretation, however, was not
always shared by Muslim intellectuals with secular proclivities. If not dismissed as intellectually
inexplicable, or sneered at with silent skepticism, the hereafter was abided only as articles of
faith. Whenever formulaic rationalizations were employed by the scientifically-minded Muslims to reconcile such troubling questions as corporal resurrection, heavenly recompense, and
torments of hell, with the precepts of modern sciences, the result was conveniently comforting
to their authors.

The literalists' view of the hereafter, on the other hand, remained blissfully mundane if not
entirely obsolete even when modern secular values began to corrode the time-honored convictions regarding the eschaton. Fascination with the intricacies of the hereafter and with the nar-

ratives of the resurrection is well attested in the vast publication of classical accounts and more often in contemporary popular renderings on postmortem interrogation and torments of the grave, signs of the Hour, mischiefs of the Dajjal, sedition and calamities, raising of the dead, horrors of the final day, reckoning and judgment, and vivid depiction of heavenly bliss and torments of hell. Nearly always following traditional literature and reiterating the Qurʾanic and the *hadith* evidence, these accounts in Arabic, Persian, and Urdu were written by traditional scholars, lay fundamentalists, and popular preachers. Yet beyond attempts to streamline the mass of confused and contradictory prophecies, they seldom place the eschatological narrative in any spatial or chronological frame or identify preconditions for the eschaton with historical time. Such timeless approaches to prophecies no doubt conformed with prohibitions in Islam (as in Judaism) for setting a time for the resurrection.

Absence of critical inquiry about the hereafter, however, did not diminish aspirations for Islamic utopia in this world, nor did it curtail endeavors for realizing it. In the works of Islamic writers and activists of the twentieth century one can detect a shift from yearnings for the otherworldly kingdom to a desire for establishing a perfect Islamic society in this world with recognizable eschatological paradigms. Ideas of Hasan al-Banna (1906–1949), the Egyptian founder of the Society of the Muslim Brothers, and later, those of Sayyid Qutb (1906–1966), the chief articulator of the Muslim Brothers' ideology, were prototypical of trends in the Sunni world often known as fundamentalist. A charismatic figure with the zeal of a messianic claimant and with a following as devout and motivated as any millenarian community, Banna's program for establishing a "true" Islamic order was pursued as a divinely ordained plan to reconstruct a community on the Muhammadan model, the same Salafiyya idea that fascinated his puritan and messianic predecessors. In his hierarchical organization, Banna himself was the "general guide" whose mission was to "teach" (*taʿlim*) his disciples. These concepts were borrowed from Islam's esoteric past and wedded with a sophisticated administrative and ideological scheme with modern trappings. More importantly, Banna's return to the *Qurʾān* and the *hadith* as bases for a new political and ethical Islam and his attack on the traditional ʿulama for their legalistic obscurantism and submissiveness to corrupt secular powers had a clear messianic ring. The decay and humiliation of the Islamic faith and the corruption of its political and religious leaders, he believed, required a regeneration of an international "Islamic order" which was to be achieved in Egypt following a revolution and the establishment of an Islamic state. Banna's Islamic "renewal" (*tajdid*) was firmly based on reassertion of the Islamic Shariʿa as the only way to confront, and ultimately prevail over, the diabolic Western imperialism. His Shariʿa-based order was in effect as much a rejection of the Western secularism as it was a substitute for otherworldly promises of the judgment, bliss, and torment of traditional religion. His conscious and systematic effort to realize a this-worldly ideal society was to be accomplished by an implicit disengagement from the hereafter while paying it a theological lip service. His mission for "reawakening and deliverance," as he addressed his brethren, was like the light glowing amidst darkness, not to hoard up wealth, or achieve fame, or to dominate over the earth but to "liberate the Islamic fatherland from foreign domination" and to establish "a state according to the precepts of Islam, applying its social regulations, proclaiming its sound principles, and broadcasting its sage mission to all mankind" (Banna 1978, 32–33). Banna's tacit dismissal of Mahdism as an untenable, even unfounded, popular belief was complemented by his disavowal of its historical manifestations as misguided if not false. Yet he himself achieved in the eye of his followers, particularly after his assassination, the status of a martyred messiah reminiscent of Christ's crucifixion (Mitchell 1993, 299).[11]

Even Sayyid Qutb's book-long study of resurrection in the *Qur'ān* barely exceeds the age-old Islamic debate about the nature of resurrection (1975). Though he does not reject outright the *Qur'ān*'s assertion of corporal resurrection and the afterlife's sensual recompense and sufferings, he offers a new "metaphorical" rendition different from earlier commentators for emphasizing the "psychological" dimension of reward and punishment both in this world and after death. For him the exact nature of the afterlife is unknown, but he acknowledges that "one does not die so he can have rest, nor does he live so he can have enjoyment"; there is a continuity in human moral evolution (Smith and Haddad 1981, 138–39). Metaphorical interpretation, however, does not persuade Qutb to overtly associate the "signs of the Hour" with circumstances of his own time. Instead he articulates the Muslim Brothers' unambiguous differentiation between the community of true believers and the infidels, a familiar pre-apocalyptic distinction presented in a new guise. For Qutb the contemporary Muslim community is reverted to a new state of "ignorance" or "barbarism" (*jahiliyya*), a state identified with pre-Islamic "dark ages," when the pristine religion of Muhammad was denied and opposed by the infidels. To combat the forces of contemporary ignorance, Qutb prescribes a symbolic withdrawal, an "immigration" (*hijra*) from the doomed sources of power, wealth, and corrupt culture, denouncing (*takfir*) barbaric society's material mischiefs, and taking refuge in the diaspora of a community of authentic Islam. Contrary to the voluntary withdrawal of the mystics and esoterics of earlier times, Qutb's objective for withdrawal is to prepare actively for a showdown with the forces of disbelief. The intensity of Qutb's dormant apocalyptic program, primarily directed toward Nasser's regime and his determined efforts to suppress all forms of political dissent, appealed to a later generation of Muslim Brothers and especially to extremist splinter groups such as al-Takfir wa al-Hijra (Denunciation and Withdrawal), who were responsible for Anwar Sadat's assassination in 1981. Like the earlier radical trends, the prime target for Muslim Brothers' ideological offensive was the Arab regimes whose legitimacy was blemished in their eyes not only because of their deviation from Islamic Shari'a but because of their ineptitude in repulsing military, political, and cultural aggression directed against Islam and the Muslim peoples (Sivan 1985, 23–26, 66–69, 86–90).

The Arab–Israeli conflict and the creation of the state of Israel in particular occupied a central position in the worldview of Muslim radicals. Zionist victories in the battlefield and loss of territory in three rounds of Arab–Israeli conflict were viewed by them as the ultimate humiliation of the Muslims, especially the Arabs, at the hands of the Jews. The *Qur'ān*'s condemnation of the Jews of Medina for opposing Muhammad's message provided a historical context for many fundamentalist writers to view the Arab–Israeli conflict in an apocalyptic context. Defeat was the outcome of the absence of divine blessing for Muslims and the punishment for their grave moral and material weaknesses. In this regard the ultimate triumph against the Jewish state could be achieved only if Muslims, like the Jews, recapture their true religious identity and draw strength from their faith. Occasional references in the works and statements of radical fundamentalists to Jewish conspiracy and citing such anti-Semitic publications as the *Protocols of the Learned Elders of Zion* also gave a certain sense of doom to the Arab–Israeli conflict and thus an apocalyptic urgency to the Muslim task of defending Islam and Muslim lands against the Jewish plans for world domination, or its destruction. Such conspiratorial perspective was primarily applied to the "Zionist entity's" occupation of the Muslim Holy Lands and its usurpations of the Palestinian territory with the support of Britain and, later, the United States. Occasionally this literature also portrayed Communism as the other side of Jewish conspiracy aiming at destruction of Islam through atheism, tyranny, and immorality.[12]

MODERN SHIʿISM
AND THE ISLAMIC REVOLUTION

The desire to create a "true" Islamic community found in modern Shiʿism a resonance no less intense than in the Sunni world, albeit with an undercurrent of messianic deliverance. Though Shiʿi Islam was generally less exposed than Sunnism to religious modernization, in the decade leading to the Islamic Revolution of 1979 there were some attempts to reassess such themes as the nature of the hereafter, the coming of the Mahdi, and the utopian order he will establish. Likewise, topics such as the duties of believers during the Occultation were more assertively linked to the questions of political legitimacy and clerical leadership on behalf of the Imam. Evident in these pre-messianic reflections was a gradual distancing from the traditional narrative of the apocalyptic end in favor of portraying the Imam's return as an all-embracing revolution with this-worldly causes and consequences. This new tendency may be detected first in polemical responses to Marxists, secularists, and Bahaʾi critics who raised questions about doctrines of Occultation, corporal resurrection, and the last judgment.

One such advocate of seeking rational and scientific explanation for eschatological questions was Mehdi Bazargan (1907–1995), a university professor of thermodynamics who later became the premier of the Islamic Revolution's provisional government. In several of his works Bazargan, a prolific writer on religious themes, questioned the very existence of the human soul (rawh) and its scientific provability, though he did not deny the existence of the hereafter, which he argued could be explained by means of modern sciences. Though his science, which he avidly applied to all aspects of Islamic beliefs and practices, was not entirely novel to the contemporary Islamic discourse, it did stir in the mid-1970s some controversy in religious circles and in turn encouraged further questioning about the circumstances of the Imam's appearance. His "scientific" explanations for the Hidden Imam's millennial longevity, in particular, rested on farfetched biological theories and outlandish applications of modern theories of physics. He speculated, for instance, that, unlike matter and energy, a "third element" endures after death which will be reanimated at the time of the resurrection (Bazargan 1966).

Reflections of ʿAli Shariʿati (1933–1977) on the subject of expectation clearly illustrate how modern Shiʿi activists, influenced by Western ideological trends of their time, grappled with central themes of messianic advent and the eschaton. In a pamphlet entitled "expectation, a school of protest," Shariʿati, a major ideologue of revolutionary Shiʿism and one of the forebears of the Islamic Revolution, regarded the End of the Time as nothing but an "ultimate revolution" for humanity. The "Mahdi's revolution" (inqilab-i Mahdi), as he called it, however, could not come about without Muslims arriving at a new understanding of expectation as a way of acquiring social responsibility, working toward a just and equitable order and rejecting political oppression and cultural degradation. Complying with the Shiʿi prophecies, he repeated that the Lord of the Age will come when "the entire life of humanity reaches the lowest ebb of corruption," but until that time, he recommended, the community of believers should settle on the leadership of a democratically elected jurist (*faqih*) to serve as the "general deputy" (*naʾib-i ʿamm*) of the Hidden Imam. The true understanding of the end, he stated, will advance only when Muslims abandon troubling theological entanglements concerning circumstances of the resurrection (and in effect the Occultation) and instead develop a perspective conforming to modern "social and human sciences" and based on a sociological analysis of class conflict. Infused with Third World socialism of the 1960s, Shariʿati's "ideological" dimensions of expectation go only so far as endorsing a Marxist-inspired Islamic revolution. His Islam is an "imperishable and lively religion" that has been misunderstood and misapplied by the obscurantists who exploited the doctrine of Occultation to compromise with corrupt worldly powers. This "negative expectation" for the Imam, as he labeled it, stood in contrast to "positive expectation," during which the "disinherited of the earth" will hasten the coming of the Mahdi through vigorous resistance to the "corruptor of the earth" and triumph over "satanic forces." Led by their "Imam-type" (*imam-gunih*) leader, the elected vicegerent of the Imam, the "disinherited of the earth" actively bring about a "revolution of universal scale," destroy the satanic superpowers and realize the "dictate of history." True expectation, Shariʿati concluded, is "believing that in the life of humankind on this very earth and before death, not in the Resurrection after death, history will bring about the triumph of the oppressed and destruction of the oppressors" (1396 Q./1976, 4–24).

Conscious effort to transform the Shiʿi expectations into a worldly revolution reduced the Hidden Imam's function to a merely nominal one. Interestingly enough, Shariʿati's rendition was not entirely oblivious to a modern understanding of messianism from a sociological perspective. He acknowledges that the "yearning instinct" for a savior is a universal phenomenon in all human cultures and that Islamic yearning for the Mahdi is identical to the expectation in Christianity of Christ's second coming and to a universal hope for establishing a "golden age." *Messianisme* and *futurisme* (both terms cited in original French) in his view were the outcomes of a "synthesis between the ideals and the realities" of Islam, an ambition to restore the ideals of ʿAli's just rule and to redress his defeat in reality at the hands of his enemies. To reconstruct such an idealized past, Shariʿati believed, the "disinherited (*mustazʿafin*) of the earth" should strive for a "classless society" in which justice and equality will triumph over exploitation, imperialism, and tyranny. Though there is no explicit reference to contemporary political regimes, Shariʿati's *Intizar*, like his other works, was suffused with implicit hints to the Pahlavi monarchy as a contemporary embodiment of the corrupt and oppressive rule of the Umayyad dynasty, the historical (and apocalyptic) enemies of Shiʿism and the killers of the most celebrated Shiʿi martyr, Husain ibn ʿAli, whose martyrdom is to be avenged by the Mahdi. In the true spirit of the prevalent radicalism of the time, Shariʿati also portrayed Muhammad Riza Shah's most ardent supporter, the United States, along with its ideological rival, the Soviet Union, as the "world-devouring" superpowers who exhibit the diabolical powers of the Dajjal (1396 Q./1976, 25–53).

Shariʿati's revolutionary messianism had a resonance in the rapidly politicizing environment of Iran of the 1970s and no doubt influenced ongoing debates on the question of communal leadership in the absence of the Hidden Imam. One can observe gradual articulation of these themes among radical clergy such as Murtaza Mutahhari, a prominent student of Khomeini and a teacher of philosophy. In his essay on the uprising and the revolution of the Mahdi, he treated the advent of the Lord of the Age no longer as a sudden and cataclysmic event outside the pale of history, but as the final stage in an ideologically driven revolution to establish Islam's "ideal society." Mutahhari conceived the coming of the Mahdi, this "eminent and holy personality," as the climax of a revolutionary struggle that in its primary stages requires the believers' active involvement (Mutahhari 1354 Sh./1975, 5–10). Unlike Marxist theory of revolution, Mutahhari believed, Mahdi's revolution is divinely inspired yet is still contingent on the alertness and action of the community. For Mutahhari the "great expectation" for the coming of the Mahdi by itself was to sketch out the forthcoming Islamic utopia; optimism for humanity's salvation; triumph of morality, justice, and freedom over unscrupulous capitalism and political arrogance; establishment of world peace and global government; material development and utilization of earth's natural resources; humanity's maturity and liberation from bestial and barbaric bonds; equality of wealth for all; elimination of all moral depravities; and harmony with the natural environment (ibid., 57–60). Though wrapped in an Islamic guise, such utopian Mahdism was a far cry from the customary Shiʿi view of Mahdi's return and in some respect close to the Babi-Bahaʾi ideals a century earlier as well as to the very Marxist utopianism against which he proposed his "Islamic ideology." Establishing a "just state" thus became for Mutahhari and like-minded activists a legitimate first step toward the final revolution of the Mahdi.[13]

The publication in 1971 of Ayatullah Khomeini's well-known work *Wilayat-i Faqih* ([authority of the jurist], otherwise known as *Hukumat-i Islami* [Islamic government] [1981, 27–149]) was clearly meant to render an answer to the most urgent of these concerns. In this work, which almost coincides with Shariʿati's *intizar*, Khomeini unequivocally, and in sharp contrast to the traditional Shiʿi view, advocated the necessity for instituting an Islamic government in the absence of the Hidden Imam. Other theological considerations aside, his argument with regard to the Occultation revolved around a bold (and in many respects contradictory) interpretation of the doctrine of *wilayat* (guardianship, vicegerency, authority) whereby the jurists were called upon to preserve the "essence of Islam" from chaos and to defend its sacred values at a time when it had fallen into a state of alienation. It stands to reason, Khomeini argued, that while the Imam is in the state of Occultation, these tasks are to be accomplished by an Islamic government under the aegis of a "guardian jurist" who, though not infallible, by the virtue of his position is to be upheld as the "vicegerent" (*naʾib*) of the Hidden Imam and hence superior to all other temporal powers. Identifying a set of pre-apocalyptic "signs" generally associated with the advent of the Imam and offering them as evidence for the necessity of forming an Islamic government, he in effect appropriated the function of the Imam to himself though staying short of claiming divine inspiration and infallibility. In support of this doctrine, Khomeini cites, among other evidence, one of the Hidden Imam's decrees in which the ʿulama were upheld as "proofs" (*hujaj*) of the Lord of the Age—who himself is "the proof of God"—and assigns to them the right to interpret the "events of the time." Both terms, *hujjat* and the "events of the time," implied a clear apocalyptic undertone. He paralleled these upheavals with the perceived malaise of his own time including "dissemination of vices," such as prostitution and drug addiction, by the "corruptor of the earth" and the mischievous idol-worshiping (*taghuti*) rulers who allied themselves with the satanic superpowers to destroy Islam, to isolate and humiliate its ʿulama, and to corrupt and violate its women. These vices were part of a conspiratorial scheme in which the threat of "Jewish domination" over the Muslims, exemplified by Israel's occupation of the Muslim holy lands, was complemented by distortion of Islam's sacred text by agents of colonialism, anti-Islamic propaganda by the Baha'is and the Christian missionaries, and the evil designs of the British and other colonial powers to exploit Muslim natural resources and to ensure Muslims' material and cultural backwardness. The United States, in particular, occupied a prominent place in this house of Western demons not only for conducting an unjust and brutal war in Vietnam and for supporting the heinous policies of the Zionist state but also for reimposing the colonialist capitulatory rights over the Iranian people, backing the Pahlavi dictatorial regime, conspiring to deprive Muslims through its spying agencies, and above all for tempting the believers to imitate the vilest immoralities of the West. Such anti-American rhetoric was further embellished during the course of the Islamic Revolution and confrontation with the United States. He labeled the United States the Great Satan (*shaytan-i buzurg*), an epithet probably adopted from the Marxist-Leninist propaganda of earlier decades in an Islamic guise and with an apocalyptic undertone (Khomeini 1357 Sh./1978, 6–24; 1981, 27–54).

The vehemence with which Khomeini called for destruction of the monarchical shambles and for erecting in its place an Islamic government under the guidance of the guardian-jurist displayed an unmistakable messianic resolve. Complemented by his single-minded sense of mission to rescue Islam from the ebb of disgrace and humility, his shrewd yet ruthless maneuvering against all other reformist and revolutionary forces, and his uncompromising stance in dealing with domestic and international opposition, he loomed large as a prophetic figure in late-twentieth-century Islam—in the eyes of his supporters, perhaps larger than any in Islamic history. He was not merely a "vicegerent" of the Imam, as he theoretically claimed to be, but an *imam*, as he was universally addressed in the Islamic Republic, an unprecedented honorific exclusively reserved for the Shiʿi Imams and not assumed by any Shiʿi figure since the Occultation of the Twelfth Imam in the ninth century. The fact that the victory of the Islamic movement and Khomeini's rise to power in November 1979 coincided with the beginning of the fifteenth Islamic century only added to his prophetic aura, which in the popular mind was further embellished with tales of supernatural feats.[14]

With the establishment of the Islamic Republic, the debate about the Mahdi's revolution was partially cast aside. The intensity with which the Pahlavi monarchy was overthrown created a certain momentum and a confidence in the totality of the revolution among its religiously motivated supporters. Dramatic events such as the hostage crisis and confrontation with the United States, massive human casualties and material destruction in the war with Iraq, and the struggle to acquire a monopoly of power in the face of domestic opposition further prompted Khomeini's followers to view the revolution as an end in itself. The Islamic Republic was no longer viewed as the fulfillment of the "positive expectation" for a Mahdi-like revolt but came to supplant the authority of the Mahdi with the "authority of the jurist," as Khomeini outlined it.

Pivotal though the doctrine of the "authority of the jurist" was for the Islamic Republic, it was not accepted by all parties even within the revolutionary spectrum. In the years following the revolution, the secular opposition and the Islamic modernists questioned its validity because of its antidemocratic presumptions, while some of the high-ranking ʿulama implicitly took issue with its juristic soundness. A more vociferous objection to its unrestricted authority, however, came from the members of the Hujjatiyya Society, a splinter religious organization dedicated, as it claimed, to the Twelfth Imam, after whom it was named. Led by Shaykh Mahmud Halabi, an old preacher and an extreme anti-Baha'i activist with an expressed messianic bent, the Hujjatiyya acknowledged, at least in public, the collective "authority of jurists" within its legal bounds but only as an interim to the impending advent of the Hidden Imam. Hujatiyya's position, in contrast to those who defended the jurists' total authority, is best illustrated in the competing slogans. While the Hujjatiyya party exclaimed: "Until the Mahdi's Revolution the movement continues," its opponents replied: "Khomeini! Khomeini! You are the Imam's manifestation." Partly isolated for its antiwar position during the Iraq–Iran war, the Hujjatiyya Society was banned in 1983 by Khomeini's order (see Baqi 1363 Sh./1984).

There were ample "apocalyptic" manifestations in the unfolding of the revolution itself, both in theory and in practice, to ward off the endemic resistance to the doctrine of the "authority of the jurist." Protracted war with Iraq with its horrendous scenes of bloodshed and destruction set the stage for the characterization of the war in the official media as a cataclysmic "struggle of truth against falsehood," which could be won only by martyrdom, as Khomeini reassured armies of ill-equipped and untrained teenage volunteers who were dispatched to the fronts only to serve as fodder for the Iraqi guns. The cult of martyrdom perpetrated throughout the war reminded all Iranians by means of dramatic war murals that "all days are ʿAshura, all lands are Karbala." This was a deliberate and highly effective use of an old Shiʿi mourning chant invoking Husain's tragic fall in the battle of Karbala on 10th Muharram (ʿAshura) 61 AH/ 10 October 680. The messianic undertone of the story of Karbala, the ultimate paradigm for martyrdom, is evident, for it is this event that serves as the chief motive for Mahdi's vengeance in his final showdown with the forces of Dajjal, now reincarnated in the Iraqi leader, the "infidel" Saddam Husain. The messianic myth was further reinvoked by frequent citations on the war front of the Mahdi himself exhorting the "warriors of Islam" to sacrifice in the way of true religion; by the prosaic yet moving "testimonies of the martyrs," invariably aspiring to "adjoin the face of God," an ostensibly apocalyptic yearning; and by the equally innocent wearing of a plastic "key to paradise" around the neck. In the battlefields of southern Iraq, the scene of Shiʿi apocalyptic prophecies, the warriers of the revolution were assured on makeshift signsposts that "the road to Quds [Jerusalem] was through Karbala." Celebration of martyrdom as a shortcut to eternal salvation was reenforced by public displays of ornate *hijla*, replicating the wedding chambers of martyrs who were about to taste the sensual recompenses of paradise, and by the tinted water gushing from the fountains of Tehran cemetery reminding visitors of the martyrs' ever-flowing blood, which nurtures the Islamic revolution.

Revolutionary rage and righteous martyrdom could not thrive without their antagonist, no longer an apocalyptic beast or a hated tyrant from early Islamic history but a contemporary superpower or its perceived subordinate. As the Hidden Imam now was effectively replaced by his modern revolutionary vicegerent, so the old enemies were to be replaced with new ones. Khomeini and his propaganda machine labeled the United States the Great Satan, lurking in the shadow of the revolution, conspiring, seducing, and devouring. Insatiable in its appetite for the flesh and blood of the martyrs, Khomeini assured his crowd, the Great Satan was to be revoked by hysterical calls of "Death to America!" almost as if it were a demon-repelling chant.

Most Islamic militants shared the Islamic Republic's anti-Western sentiments. In the post–Cold War era hard-line fundamentalists, from Algeria, Egypt, and the Sudan to Saudi Arabia, Lebanon, Palestine, and Afghanistan chastised the United States not only for supporting anti-Islamic dictatorial regimes or for backing Israel's aggression against its neighbors but for disseminating what they believed to be a culture of immorality and materialism. Anti-Westernism proved to be a potent weapon in the hands of all preachers of radical Islam who grudgingly admired the West for its scientific and industrial achievements but were anxious to resist its cultural and political influences. An idealized image of the Islamic revolution in Iran thus became for many throughout the Islamic world a prototype of steadfastness against temptations and mischiefs of the West, and Khomeini, regardless of his Shiʿi identity, a renovator of modern Islam if not its prophet.

With the end of the eight-year Iraq–Iran war in 1988 and, soon after, in 1989, the death of Khomeini, the tides of revolutionary zeal began to subside as though an exhausted nation was ready to bury with the militant prophet the decade-long memoirs of a Mahdi-like revolution. The post-Khomeini Iran quietly cast aside the myth of martyrdom along with the urge to restore power and privilege to the disinherited of the earth. Even calls to confront the Great Satan no longer moved the masses as they once did, though such tiresome rhetoric still comes to the aid of the clerical elite anxious to regain their waning popularity. The Party of God, once a dreadful force of Islamic reprisal, turned for the most part into a political tendency occasionally flexing its muscles in mob action and within the Army of Defenders of the Islamic Revolution (the Revolutionary Guards) and retreated to the barracks, acting as a shadow of the regular armed forces. A set of new Islamic institutions emerged to define and preserve—and if need be to modify—the constitution of the Islamic Republic, but as yet a crucial question concerning the theological justification for the central doctrine of the "authority of the jurists" hangs in the balance. Khomeini's successor, often referred to as the leader (*rahbar*) of the revolution, strives to adhere to his predecessor's charismatic image by stressing the divinely ordained nature of his office, yet Khomeini's messianic charisma as the supreme master of the revolution defies routinization.

In the late twentieth century, as the Islamic world moves further in the direction of a new monolithic outlook and ideology, and as differences between Shiʿi and Sunni creeds, historical and theological, gradually dim into insignificance, messianic characteristics of both creeds also seem to embrace a common pattern. Belief in the hereafter and in the events of the last day remain strong and continue to generate messianic impulses for salvation, though such impulses often find expression in "fundamentalist" trends with predominantly regressive paradigms of glorious early Islam and revival of Muhammadan Shariʿa. Yet at the same time most of these trends are not devoid of utopian paradigms for material and cultural renovation. The revolution in Iran no doubt was permeated by such motifs, though the Shiʿi legacy that motivated Khomeini and his followers maintained its urge to break with the past—which, one may argue, is unique in the contemporary Islamic experience. The mixing of these paradigms is symptomatic of Islam's dilemma in an enlarging world system and is likely to bring a new synthesis with latent or manifest apocalyptic characteristics.

☞ NOTES

1. For Islamic messianism, see J. Blichfeldt, *Early Mahdism: Politics and Religion in the Formative Period of Islam* (Leiden: E. J. Brill, 1985); J. Darmesteter, *Le Mahdi depuis les origines de l'islam jusqu'à nos jours* (Paris: Gautnier-Villars, 1885); A. A. Sachedina, *Islamic Messianism: The Idea of the Mahdi in Twelver Shiʿism* (Albany: State University of New York Press, 1981). See also W. Madelung, "al-Mahdi," in *The Encyclopedia of Islam*, 2nd ed. (Leiden: E. J. Brill, 1960–). For a selection of primary sources on Mahdism, see J. A. Williams, ed., *Themes of Islamic Civilization* (Berkeley: University of California Press, 1971), 189–251. See also J. Macdonald's series of seven articles in *Islamic Studies* on aspects of Islamic eschatol-

ogy: "The creation of man and angels in eschatological literature," 3(1964): 285–308; "The angel of death in late Islamic tradition," 3 (1964): 485–519; "The twilight of the dead," 4 (1965): 55–102; "The preliminaries to the Resurrection and Judgment," 4 (1965): 137–79; "The Day of Resurrection," 5 (1966): 129–97; and "Paradise," 5 (1966): 331–83.

2. For reform and renewal in Islam, see A. Merad, H. Algar, N. Berkes, and A. Ahmad, "Islah," in *Encyclopedia of Islam,* vol. 2. J. O. Voll, *Islam: Continuity and Change in the Modern World* (Boulder: Westview Press, 1982).

3. For North African Islam, see A. Faure, "Islam in North-West Africa (*Maghrib*)," in *Religion in the Middle East,* ed. A. J. Arberry (London: Cambridge University Press, 1969), 171–86. For the Muhammadan Way, see O'Fahey 1990, 1–24. For a comparative study of North African trends, see A. Dallal, "The Origins and Objectives of Islamic Revivalist Thought, 1750–1850," *Journal of the American Oriental Society* 113 (1993): 341–59.

4. For North Africa in the eighteenth and the early nineteenth centuries, see A. Raymond, "North Africa in the Pre-Colonial Period," in *The Cambridge History of Islam,* ed. P. M. Holt, A. K. S. Lambton, and B. Lewis, 2 vols. (Cambridge: Cambridge University Press, 1970), 2:266–98; *Eighteenth-Century Renewal and Reform in Islam,* ed. N. Levtzion and J. Voll (Syracuse: Syracuse University Press, 1987), 3–38.

5. Dallal, "Origins," 355–58; K. S. Vikor, *Sufi and Scholar on the Desert Edge* (Evanston, Ill.: Northwestern University Press, 1995), 218–40; N. Ziadeh, *Sanusiyah* (Leiden: E. J. Brill, 1958), 35–51, 73–98.

6. On Shi'i Mahdism and the Occultation, see M. A. Amir-Moezzi, *Divine Guide in Early Shi'ism* (Albany: State University of New York Press, 1994); S. A. Arjomand, "The Crisis of Imamate and the Institution of Occultation in Twelver Shi'ism: A Sociohistorical Perspective," *International Journal of Middle East Studies* 28 (1996): 491–515; H. Modarresi, *Crisis and Consolidation in the Formative Period of Shi'ite Islam* (Princeton: Darwin Press, 1993), 53–105; Sachedina, *Islamic Messianism,* 78–183.

7. For Shi'i messianism in the early modern period, see S. A. Arjomand, *The Shadow of God and the Hidden Imam: Religion, Political Order and Societal Change in Shi'ite Iran from the Beginning to 1890* (Chicago: University of Chicago Press, 1984), 66–104; H. Halm, *Shiism* (Edinburgh: Edinburgh University Press, 1991), 71–91. See also A. Amanat, "The Nuqtawi Movement of Mahmud Pisikhani and His Persian Cycle of Mystical-Materialism," *Mediaeval Isma'ili History and Thought,* ed. F. Daftary (New York: Cambridge University Press, 1996), 281–98.

8. *Bayan* (Tehran, n.d.), 2:7 (pp. 30–33) and 3:13 (93–97); cf. *Le Beyan Persan,* trans. A. L. M. Nicolas (Paris: Librairie Paul Geuthner, 1911), 68–73, 50–58. For other pertinent references, see E. G. Browne's "Index of chief contents of the Persian Bayan," in his edition of Hajji Mirza Jani of Kashan, *Kitab-i Nuqtatul'-Kaf* (Leyden: E. J. Brill/London: Luzac & Co., 1910) under "Resurrection" (p. lxxxvii), "Revelation" (p. lxxxvii), and "*Zuhur*" (p. xciv).

9. For a summary of the Babi doctrine, see E. G. Browne, "The Babis of Persia: II, Their Literature and Doctrines," *Journal of the Royal Asiatic Society* 21 (1889): 881–933 reprinted in *Selections from the Writings of E.G. Browne on the Babi and the Baha'i Religions,* ed. M. Momen (Oxford: George Ronald, 1987), 187–239.

10. For Babi-Baha'i fulfillment of past prophecies, see Baha'ullah, *Kitab-i Iqan* (Cairo, n.d.), trans. Shoghi Effendi as *Kitab-i Iqan, the Book of Certitude* (Wilmette, Ill.: Baha'i Publications Committee, 1931). On the Baha'i faith, see J. R. I. Cole, *Modernity and the Millennium: The Genesis of the Baha'i Faith in the Nineteenth Century Middle East* (New York: Columbia University Press, 1998); P. Smith, *The Babi-Baha'i Religions: From Messianic Shi'Ism to a World Religion* (Cambridge: Cambridge University Press, 1987).

11. For the Muslim Brothers' view of the West and return to Islam, see Mitchell 1993, 224–45.

12. For a specimen, see I. R. al-Faruqi, "Islam and Zionism," in *Voices of Resurgent Islam,* ed. J. L. Esposito (New York: Oxford University Press, 1983), 261–67. See also G. Kepel, *Muslim Extremism in Egypt: The Prophet and Pharaoh* (Berkeley: University of California Press, 1985), 110–24.

13. See also M. Mutahhari's discussion on resurrection (*ma'ad*) and his debates with Mahdi Bazargan during late 1960s in his *Majmu'a-i asar* (Tehran: Intisharat-i Sadra, 1374 Sh./ 1995), 4:621–840.

14. For Khomeini and the idealogy of the Islamic Revolution, see S. A. Arjomand, *The Turban for the Crown: Islamic Revolution in Iran* (New York: Oxford University Press, 1988), 91–102, 147–88; S.

Bakhash, *The Reign of the Ayatollahs* (New York: Basic Books, 1984); H. Munson, *Islamic Revolution in the Middle East* (New Haven: Yale University Press, 1988).

⌁ BIBLIOGRAPHY

Abun-Nasr, J. 1965. *The Tijaniyya: A Sufi Order in the Modern World.* London: Oxford University Press. A study of history, organization, and doctrine based on primary research and some analysis of the doctrine and the proto-messianic intuitive trait.

Amanat, A. 1989. *Resurrection and Renewal: The Making of the Babi Movement in Iran, 1844–1850.* Ithaca: Cornell University Press, 1989. Part 1 surveys learned and popular Shiʿi millennialism; Parts 2 and 3 examine the life of the Bab and the Babi movement's intellectual and socioreligious origins and development.

Arjomand, S. A. 1984. *The Shadow of God and the Hidden Imam: Religion, Political Order and Societal Change in Shiʿi Iran from the Beginning to 1890.* Chicago: University of Chicago Press. A masterful sociohistorical analysis of interactions between Shiʿi messianic trends and the religious and political establishments. Part 3 covers the modern period.

Bab, The. (Sayyid ʿAli Muhammad Shirazi). *Bayan-i Farsi* (in Persian). 1911. Translated by A. L. M. Nicolas as *Le Beyan Persan* (Paris: P. Geuthner). Theological and doctrinal exposition of the Bayani religion by its founder providing the most consistent defense of the Bab's millennial claims.

Bahaʾullah, Husain-ʿAli Nuri. 1931. *Kitab-i Iqan.* Cairo. Translated by Shoghi Effendi as *Kitab-i Iqan, the Book of Certitude.* Wilmette, Ill.: Bahaʾi Publications Committee. An early apologia based on Islamic and other prophecies in support of progressive revelation and Baha'ullah's own implicit claim.

al-Banna, Hasan. 1978. "Between Yesterday and Today." In *Five Tracts of Hasan al-Banna (1906–1949),* translated by C. Wendell. Berkeley: University of California Press.

Baqi, ʿA. 1363 Sh./1984. *Dar shinakht-i hizb-i qaʿidin-i zaman.* Tehran: Nashr-i Danish-i Islami.

Bashi-ud-Din Mahmud Ahmad. 1980. *Invitation to Ahmadiyyat.* London: Routledge & Kegan Paul. A systematic exposition of the movement's doctrine by its third leader.

Bazargan, M. 1959. *Rah-i tayy shudah.* Tehran: Shirkat-i Sahami-i Intishar.

———. 1966. *Zarrih-i bi intiha.* Tehran: Shirkat-i Sahami-i Intishar.

Browne, E. G., ed. 1910. *Kitab-i Nuqtatuʾl-kaf being the Earliest History of the Babis compiled by Hajji Mirza Jani of Kashan Between the Years A.D. 1850 and 1852.* Leyden: E. J. Brill/London: Luzac & Co. Persian original of an early history of the movement and apologia with introduction and index of the Bab's Persian *Bayan.*

Cleaveland, W. L. 1994. *A History of the Modern Middle East.* Boulder: Westview Press.

Cole, J. R. I. 1998. *Modernity and the Millennium: The Genesis of the Bahaʾi Faith in the Nineteenth Century Middle East.* New York: Columbia University Press. Fresh treatment of Bahʾullah and evolution of his writings with emphasis on sociopolitical teachings and based on extensive research.

Corbin, H. 1960. *Terre celeste et corps de résurrection de l'iran mazdeen à l'iran shiʿite.* Paris. Eng. trans.: *Spiritual Body and Celestial Earth from Mazdean Iran to Shiʿite Iran* (Princeton: Princeton University Press, 1977). A broad selection of philosophical writings on eschatology and apocalypse with two introductory chapters demonstrating continuity in the Iranian millennial tradition.

Daniel, N. 1966. *Islam, Europe, and Empire.* Edinburgh: Edinburgh University Press.

Gilbert, M. 1991. *Churchill: A Life.* New York: Holt.

Hodgson, M. G. S. 1974. *The Venture of Islam.* 3 vols. Chicago: University of Chicago Press.

Holt, P. M. 1958. *The Mahdist State in the Sudan, 1881–1898.* Oxford: Clarendon Press. A thorough examination of the history and organization of the al-Mahdi's messianic state based on primary sources but sparsely covering the doctrinal aspects.

———. 1970. "Nilotic Sudan." In *The Cambridge History of Islam,* edited by P. M. Holt, A. K. S. Lambton, and B. Lewis, 2:329–38. Cambridge: Cambridge University Press.

Hourani, A. H. 1991. *A History of the Arab Peoples.* Cambridge, Mass.: Harvard University Press.

Iqbal, Muhammad. 1962. *The Reconstruction of Religious Thought in Islam.* Lahore: Javid Iqbal.

Khomeini, Ayatullah. 1971. *Wilayat-i Faqih* (Authority of the jurist). Tehran. New ed., 1357 Sh./1978. Translated and annotated by H. Algar as *Islam and Revolution: Writings and Declarations of Imam Khomeini* (Berkeley: Mizan Press, 1981). First delivered as a series of lectures in Arabic in the early 1970s, this work was then translated into Persian for publication. The English is an accurate though laudatory translation of Khomeini's writings and speeches on the Islamic revolution and the Islamic government.

Lavan, S. 1974. *The Ahmadiyah Movement: A History and Perspective.* Dehli: Manohar Book Service. An adequate history and selective treatment of the doctrine.

Lewis, B. 1994. *The Shaping of the Modern Middle East.* New York: Oxford University Press.

Mitchell, R. P. 1969. *The Society of Muslim Brothers.* 1st ed. Oxford: Oxford University Press. 2nd ed., New York: Oxford University Press, 1993. Thorough study of early history and doctrine. Part 3 provides a summary of the ideology.

Momen, M. 1985. *An Introduction to Shiʿi Islam: A History and Doctrine of Twelver Shiʿism.* New Haven: Yale University Press. Useful survey with ample biographical, bibliographical, and chronological references covering aspects of learned and popular Shiʿism. Chapter 6 is on modern times and chapter 14 on the contemporary period.

Morris, J. W. 1981. *The Wisdom of the Throne: An Introduction to the Philosophy of Mulla Sadra.* Princeton: Princeton University Press. Annotated translation of an important work of the seventeenth-century philosopher with a long introduction and notes. Chapters 5 and 6 of the introduction highlight eschatological dimensions.

Mutahhari, M. 1354 Sh./1975. *Qiyam va inqilab-i mahdi az didgah-i falsafah-yi tarikh* (The uprising and the revolution of the Mahdi from the perspective of philosophy of history). Tehran: Intisharat-i Wahyy.

O'Fahey, R. S. 1990. *Enigmatic Saint: Ahmad Ibn Idris and the Idrisi Tradition.* Evanston, Ill.: Northwestern University Press. A study of North African Islam based on new primary sources and focusing on the founder of the influential neo-Sufi order. Fresh observations on the Muhammadan Way.

Qutb, Sayyid. 1975. *Mashahid al-qiyama fi al-Qurʾan.* Beirut: Dar al-Shuruq.

Shaked, H. 1978. *The Life of the Sudanese Mahdi: A Historical Study of Kitab saʿadat al-mustadhi bi-sirat al-Imam al-Mahdi.* New Brunswick, N.J.: Transaction Books. Annotated translation of an apologia and chronicle of the Mahdi of the Sudan by Ismaʿil b. ʿAbd al-Qadir with a useful introduction and notes.

Shariʿati ʿAli. 1392 Q./1972. *Intizar mazhab-i iʿyiraz.* N.p. 3rd ed., 1396 Q./1976.

Sivan, E. 1985. *Radical Islam: Medieval Theology and Modern Politics.* New Haven: Yale University Press.

Smith, J. I., and Y. Y. Haddad. 1981. *The Islamic Understanding of Death and Resurrection.* Albany: State University of New York Press. Pioneering study of an important but neglected area based on ample classical and contemporary Arabic sources covering eschatological interpretations in modern times (chapters 4 and 5).

Smith, P. 1987. *The Babi and Bahaʾi Religions from Messianic Shiʿism to a World Religion.* Cambridge: Cambridge University Press. A concise survey of history and doctrine based on studies and primary sources tracing doctrinal and institutional development to the present with attention to the evolving millennial theme.

Trimingham, J. S. 1971. *The Sufi Orders in Islam.* Oxford: Clarendon Press.

Vikor, K. S. 1995. *Sufi and Scholar on the Desert Age: Muhammad b. ʿAli Sanusi and His Brotherhood.* Evanston, Ill.: Northwestern University Press. A new study of the history of the founder of the order and his writings.

Voll, J. O. 1979. "The Sudanese Mahdi: Frontier Fundamentalism." *International Journal of Middle East Studies.* 10:145–66.

———. 1982. *Islam: Continuity and Change in the Modern World.* Boulder: Westview Press. Concentrates on Islam since 1800. A useful overview of modernist and fundamentalist trends.

Ziadeh, N. 1958. *Sanusiyah: A Study of a Revivalist Movement in Islam.* Leiden: E. J. Brill. Still a useful study of the Sanusi order but sparse on messianic dimension.

24

Apocalypticism in Modern Western Europe

Sandra L. Zimdars-Swartz
Paul F. Zimdars-Swartz
University of Kansas

T HE APOCALYPTIC WORLDVIEWS of nineteenth- and twentieth-century Europeans have been grounded in many of the same kinds of hopes, fears, and concerns as those of their ancestors. In the wake of the violent French Revolution and with the rise of secular governments that repressed or severely regulated religious institutions, many Europeans sought reassurance that these developments were not without meaning and, indeed, that they were part of a divine plan that would assure them of God's mercy and bring judgment upon their enemies. To gain this reassurance they turned to what they assumed were scenarios of the end-time events in the Hebrew Scriptures and the New Testament and to the recorded visions and oracles of many post–New Testament prophets. But they also turned to some of their contemporaries, whose religious experiences appeared to reinforce, clarify, or bring these prophecies up to date. Drawing on these materials, on compilations or anthologies of these materials, and on the commentaries and interpretations of various authorities, they sought and found scenarios of the final events that allowed them to see where they stood in relation to the end and what role they should play in the divine plan that they understood to be unfolding before them.

Christian apocalypticism in modern Western Europe, which will be the focus of the first two parts of this essay, tended in the nineteenth century to revolve around concerns relating to the Enlightenment, the French Revolution, the fall of the papal states, and growing interest in national identities and destinies. In the twentieth century the locus of concern shifted to events associated with the two world wars and the rise of important secular movements such as National Socialism and Communism. The various apocalyptic worldviews of Christians in these two centuries have provided many thousands of people with vivid pictures of the meaning of these and of other important contemporary events, and they have given these people a sense of control over these events by participating in activities that have reinforced this meaning.

⤳ PROTESTANT APOCALYPTICISM

Many forms of Christian apocalyptic thought and many of the Christian apocalyptic movements that have appeared in Western Europe in the past two centuries have been distinctly Protestant. In nineteenth-century Germany, for example, there were some important manifestations of end-time awareness associated with Württemberg pietism that drew on some apocalyptic sources of the late eighteenth century, notably the calculations of the biblical critic J. A. Bengel (1687–1752) and the writings of the occult philosopher F. C. Oetinger (1702–1782). Bengel, a major figure in modern German Protestant biblical interpretation, presented a system of calculations suggesting that the second coming would occur in the 1840s, and many early-nineteenth-century intellectuals were fascinated by his calculations, including the physician and author J. H. Jung-Stilling (1740–1817). In the wake of the French Revolution, Jung-Stilling, in his popular series of tracts *Der Graue Mann* and his novel *Das Heimweh,* issued a call to Christians to repent of their unbelief and love of luxury and indicated that the church of the last days would be saved by turning toward "the East" (that is, toward Russia and Eastern Orthodoxy).

Oetinger, whose thought was influenced by Jakob Boehme and Emanuel Swedenborg, devised a comprehensive *philosophia sacra* with apocalyptic overtones, which seems to have been of some importance for both Friedrich Schelling (1775–1854) and Georg Hegel (1770–1831), and it influenced Protestant Christianity through the well-known preacher and pastor Johann Michael Hahn (1758–1819). One of the ancestors of later Swabian pietism and the author of numerous biblical commentaries, Hahn proclaimed a form of Christian theosophy imbued with millennialist ideas that has been perpetuated within the evangelical churches of south Germany by the so-called *Hahnische Gemeinschaft.*

While there are some studies that have focused on the importance of Oetinger for early-nineteenth-century German philosophy, and a few suggesting that apocalyptic thought may lie in the background of early-twentieth-century Christian socialism in Germany and Switzerland, little scholarly study as such has yet been done of the Protestant apocalyptic thought and movements indigenous to Germany, or indeed, to continental Europe.

Great Britain and Ireland, on the other hand, have been the home of several modern Protestant apocalyptic movements and forms of apocalyptic thought that have spread beyond the borders of these lands and have attracted considerable scholarly attention. Because of this, and because such a focus will allow us to sketch the development and changing fortunes, within a rather diverse Protestant context, of some prophetic-apocalyptic traditions, it seems appropriate to restrict the bulk of this essay to a consideration of Protestant apocalypticism in these countries. Particular attention will be given to apocalyptic prophecies and movements of the nineteenth and early twentieth centuries since the significance of these is clearer and more firmly established.

The first years of the nineteenth century in Western Europe were marked by a plethora of hopes and fears unleashed by the French Revolution, and it is not surprising that this event figured prominently in the apocalyptic thought that appeared in these years in England. Indeed, the first major British apocalyptic prophet of that century, Richard Brothers (1757–1824), saw such significance in this event that he was arrested on charges of treasonable activities and was imprisoned for about twelve years.

Brothers, who had been a lieutenant in the British navy, proclaimed that the death of Louis XVI in 1793 had been foretold in the book of Daniel, that all European monarchies would soon collapse, that the French revolutionaries had been agents of God's will in their actions against the Roman Catholic Church, and that it would be senseless for England to go to war against a people "who had the judgment of God in their favor." He saw himself, moreover, as "a nephew of the Almighty" and as the herald of a great change that would soon convulse the world, an important part of which would be the restoration of the Jews to the promised land, which he himself would direct.

As a result of the publication of his book *Revealed Knowledge* (1792) and other shorter works, Brothers attracted a considerable following. Moreover, his arrest in 1795 on charges of being a Jacobin and subsequent imprisonment as a lunatic seem only to have given wider circulation to his ideas. Apparently, however, some of the more important persons who had been attracted to his prophecies were disillusioned by his long imprisonment, and during these years their attention turned toward another apocalyptic prophet, Joanna Southcott (1750–1814).

The celebrated "prophetess of Exeter" was a young domestic servant who, in 1792, claimed to be the recipient of a vision in which she was told that she was the woman of the twelfth chapter of Revelation, that the second coming of the Lord in which he would bring deliverance to the poor was imminent, and that upon the Lord's return, she would become his bride. At this time she also began to receive communications from the Spirit, which she began to transcribe in a script that a contemporary observer said was illegible to anyone except her.

Southcott proclaimed that the bad harvests and other catastrophes occurring at that time in England and, a few years later, the dismal progress of the war against France were judgments of God. However, she did not share all of Brothers's views with respect to France. While she did see the French Revolution as the beginning of God's last judgments, she and her followers believed that France had then surrendered to the beast (Napoleon). The war against France was thus a holy war in which England was destined to triumph. The many current tribulations of England, according to Southcott, were the result of the English people not heeding her revelations and acknowledging her special status. Southcott acknowledged Brothers's divine mission and advocated his release from prison, but she held that because of his spiritual pride, he had fallen from the Lord and that she was his legitimate successor.

Southcott arranged for most of her communications to be printed and widely distributed, many pamphlets being handed out without charge. She attracted a large following, among both the poor and the educated elite. Her communications received in the course of thirteen years, many of which are contained in the volumes *The Strange Effects of Faith* (1801 and 1802), filled some sixty-five books and pamphlets containing over 4,500 printed pages. Some of her followers argued that the prolixity of these writings in itself testified to their divine origin. Others, however, became convinced of her vocation through various signs or confirmatory visions or through some of her prophecies, for example, of the death of a bishop and of bad harvests, which seemed to have been fulfilled.

Southcott's followers argued that since the first coming of Christ was told to a few simple shepherds, it was reasonable that he would make known his second coming to the meek and lowly of spirit. While their leader offered no detailed blueprint of the coming millennial kingdom, she did speak of the coming golden days when "Christ would renovate the land," and she also noted, probably much to the relief of some of her followers, that in this kingdom "all kinds of trade will go on" much as before.

Southcott's followers believed, and Southcott encouraged the belief, that through her they could be "sealed" and thus enrolled among the 144,000 of the book of Revelation. It was acknowledged that the sealed would be subject to everyday trials and misfortunes, but it was thought that they would be protected from threatening apocalyptic dangers such as a French invasion. While opponents claimed that among Southcott's followers there was "traffic in seals" (buying and selling of the documents testifying to this special status), her followers themselves denied that this ever took place.

The Southcottian movement, which began in 1802 when Joanna was brought to London to meet with a group of prominent men attracted to her ideas, came to a critical focus in 1815, when she announced that through her divine spouse she was pregnant and that "Shiloh" would soon be born. Apparently many people, including some doctors, believed that this was a real pregnancy, but when Southcott became increasingly weak and finally expired without delivering a child, and when an autopsy found no sign of a fetus, the course of the movement was profoundly altered. Some followers maintained their faith in Southcott's prophecies and mission by concluding that she had meant all along that this would be a "spiritual birth," but others drifted away, and without any visible leader or any consensus about how to maintain their beliefs, the movement soon came to an end.

Many nineteenth-century British devotees of prophecy had little use for high-profile prophets such as Brothers and Southcott, and many of these persons turned to simple correlations of biblical prophecies with contemporary events. For example, in his *Dissertation on the Prophecies* (1804), the controversial British preacher and author George Faber (1773–1854) proclaimed that the French Revolution was one of the woes predicted in the book of Revelation, and that at the time of his writing, the fourth vial noted in chapter 16 of that book was beginning to be poured out on the world. Faber calculated that the period of the seventh vial would begin in 1866, and that seventy-five years later, in 1941, all the prophecies would be fulfilled and the millennium would begin. While Faber held that Christ would not come again literally until after the millennium, he did speak of a figurative coming of Christ beforehand, and thus his work had some influence on both later premillennial and postmillennial thinking.

The categories pre- and postmillennial, however, hardly seem applicable to most of the early-nineteenth-century British works on biblical prophecies. For example, James Frere (1779–1866), in *A Combined View of the Prophecies of Daniel, Esdras, and St. John* (1815), argued that while the millennium would be ushered in by Christ's second advent and while there would be no gradual improvement of the world leading up to these events, there would be a premillennial period of progress of the kingdom of Christ in which the pagan nations would be converted. This, according to Frere, would begin in 1822 and end in 1867, when Christ would return and the millennium would begin. Frere, like Faber, saw the French Revolution as the beginning of the period of woes associated with the opening of the seventh seal, and, more or less in accord with Faber's timetable, he saw the woes of the sixth vial as about to be poured out in 1815.

A more clearly premillennial position was set forth about a decade later by the Scottish minister Edward Irving (1792–1834). In his work *Babylon and Infidelity Foredoomed by God* (1826), Irving repeated and affirmed the premillennial timetables of Faber. The 1260 years suggested by the 1260 days of Rev. 11:3 had ended in 1793 with the French Revolution, he said, and this was immediately followed by the commencement of the judgment on Babylon. The pouring out of the first vial had spanned the years from 1793 to 1823; this was followed immediately by the emptying of the second through the sixth vials; and the emptying of the seventh, he believed, was now imminent. Armageddon, according to Irving, would occur in 1868, and this would be quickly followed by Christ's advent and the beginning of the millennium.

Irving's views were influenced by the work of a controversial Chilean Jesuit, Manuel de Lacunza (1731–1801), *The Coming of the Messiah in Glory and Majesty,* which Irving himself translated and published in 1827. Lacunza had researched and sketched what he saw as the qualified acceptance of apocalyptic thinking by the Roman Church, and Irving praised his work as "the finest demonstration of the Orthodoxy of the ancient system of the millenarians."

Irving was influenced also by Henry Drummond (1786–1860), an Anglican member of Parliament with an intense interest in prophecy, and by the so-called Albury Conferences held at Drummond's estate from 1826 to 1830, which had been called for the purpose of examining contemporary political and social events in the light of scriptural prophecies. Irving himself was a minister of the [Reformed] Church of Scotland who had been preaching at a small church in London. As Irving's reputation as a prophetic preacher grew, however, and as he began to proclaim an "Apostolic Restoration" characterized by manifestations such as glossolalia, which he said were signs of the imminence of the second coming, a public scandal arose. Irving was removed from his pulpit in 1832, and he, Drummond, and several other participants in the Albury Conferences then began to hold meetings that became the seedbed of the Catholic Apostolic Church.

Within a few decades, this new church, led by twelve apostles chosen through charismatic visions and prophecies, grew to encompass many congregations in England, Scotland, and Germany. The apocalyptic ideas that had led to its formation, however, seem gradually to have moved into the background, while more emphasis was put on its unique polity and on a distinctive set of doctrines and practices, including, for example, a well-defined liturgy, sacraments, and speaking in tongues. While the Catholic Apostolic Church no longer formally exists—its sacraments were officially suspended early in the twentieth century with the death of the last of the twelve apostles—it has been of some importance for the ecumenical movement, and scholars have been interested in it both as a precursor of later Pentecostalism and as a structure inviting comparison with the Church of Jesus Christ of Latter-day Saints.

A number of later premillennial authors and preachers followed Faber, Brothers, and Irving in attempting to correlate the events of their times with biblical prophecies and in setting at least approximate dates for the second coming. For example, the Scotsman John Cumming (1807–1881) who, like Irving, was a minister of the Scottish National Church serving the Crown Court congregation in London, published in 1855 two best-selling books, *Signs of the Times; or Past, Present and Future,* and *The End; or the Proximate Signs of the Close of This Dispensation.* Cumming was convinced that a number of important biblical prophecies would be fulfilled in the year 1864. He was especially interested in the Middle East, and, noting the recent return of some Jews to Jerusalem and reviving a theme of Faber and Brothers, he predicted that the Jews would soon be restored to their own land. Cumming saw Russia as crucial in this scenario, equating it, like Faber, with that great northern power that was "doomed to perish ultimately in Palestine." When subsequent events suggested to him that these things might not transpire as quickly as he originally predicted, he extended his timetable a few years, and in *The Great Preparation* (1861) he announced that the repossession of Jerusalem would take place in 1867, at which time the affliction of the Jews and their oppression by the Gentiles would cease.

A type of premillennial apocalypticism less susceptible to disconfirmation emerged around the mid-nineteenth century in the thought of the Irish Protestant John Nelson Darby (1800–1882). A clergyman of the National Church of Ireland, Darby began meeting in the late 1820s with some other members of the Irish upper class who sought a simple New Testament Christianity unencumbered by traditional church structures. The movement begun by these men, who called themselves "Brethren" and who were zealous missionaries, spread to England in the 1830s, where its adherents, whose meetings at Plymouth were especially well publicized, began to be called "Plymouth Brethren." In the course of several more decades it had spread to Switzerland, Germany, Canada, and the United States. While Darby's leadership of the Brethren was not uncontested, he became their best-known spokesperson as a result of his extensive worldwide travels, and it was his "dispensationalism," which took shape during a long sojourn in Switzerland in the 1840s, that gave new life to late-nineteenth-century premillennialism.

Dispensationalism, or the idea that history was divided into distinct periods, or dispensations, characterized by distinct modes of divine operation, was not a teaching peculiar to Darby or the Brethren. Darby, however, gave it a new importance by arguing that in the present dispensation all attempts to correlate biblical prophecy with contemporary events were futile. Darby held that this dispensation (the dispensation of the church) was a "great parenthesis" or gap about which scriptural prophecies had nothing to say, and that since the true church was purely spiritual and heavenly, "forming no part of the course of events of the earth," the sole object of its hope must be the secret rapture in which the true followers of Christ would be taken up into the air to meet their Lord. This, according to Darby, could come at any time, and while it would be followed by Christ's public appearing, this initial phase of the second advent would be secret in the sense that it would be experienced only by those persons who would be subject to it (Sandeen 1970, 63).

Benjamin Wills Newton (1807–1894), who led a rival faction of the Brethren, attempted to refute Darby's idea of the "anytime rapture" by pointing out that there were a number of prophecies in the New Testament, some of which had been fulfilled, that did pertain to the dispensation of the church. Darby responded by noting that such prophecies were not for Christians at all but "for the Jews."

Darby's futurist approach to biblical prophecy (the notion that any outstanding prophecy must pertain to a future time) stood in contrast to the historicist approach of the majority of premillennial thinkers, who were obliged to seek out those prophecies that were being fulfilled in their own times, and it appealed to many who had no taste either for the detailed predictions of the historicists or for the postmillennial optimism of the liberals. Large numbers of conservative Protestants, especially in America, were attracted to Darby's ideas, but to his dismay few of them thought it necessary to leave the "corrupt church structures" that he and other members of the Brethren so detested.

Meanwhile, as the historian Ernest Sandeen has noted, the many failed prophecies of popular prophets such as Cumming were contributing to a growing skepticism about setting dates for the events of the end-times. But, of course, this practice did not cease, and persons who claimed to know when Christ would return continued to attract considerable attention. One of the best known of these date-setters was Michael Paget Baxter (1834–1910). A British publicist and preacher who toured the United States for many years beginning in 1861, Baxter predicted various times for the second coming, for example, between 2:30 and 3:00 in the afternoon of 12 March 1903.

Somewhat more successful than either Cumming or Baxter was the British author H. Grattan Guinness (1835–1910). In his 1878 book *The Approaching End of the Age,* Guinness pointed to 1923 as the time of the last possible culmination of the prophecies of Daniel, emphasizing that before then, the Jews would surely be restored to Palestine. The subsequent rise and progress of the Zionist movement, followed in 1917 by the occupation of Jerusalem by British and French troops and the Balfour Declaration, suggested to many that Guinness's predictions had been correct, and his popular book was reprinted in 1918.

The heyday of premillennial prophecy in Britain, however, seems to have come to an end about this time. It is interesting, for example, that the 1923 book of the British champion of women's suffrage, Christabel Pankhurst (1880–1958), entitled *The Lord Cometh,* and two later prophetic books by Pankhurst, were published not in London but in the United States, where her lectures had been attracting a great deal of attention. Pankhurst stressed that the Zionist plan for the return of the Jews and the removal of the Turks from Palestine were signs of the end of the age and a practical guarantee that the Son of God was soon to appear. While she said that 1925 would be the year in which a number of nations would confederate and be ruled by a dictator who would be the Anti-Christ, she continued her lecturing for some time thereafter, and in 1940 a major London publisher did publish her work *The Uncurtained Future.*

In more recent years in Great Britain and Ireland, some forms of Protestant premillennial thinking have continued to attract attention and to influence how some have understood some difficult situations and events. One might, for example, think of "Bloody Sunday" in Londonderry in 1972, when fourteen Roman Catholic demonstrators were shot and killed by British troops, and recall that the long-standing disputes there between Catholics and Protestants have been fueled by denunciations of the papal Antichrist by followers of the fervent Irish nationalist, the Rev. Ian Paisley.

ROMAN CATHOLIC APOCALYPTICISM

The most important Roman Catholic apocalyptic thought of modern Western Europe arose in nineteenth-century France, as French Catholics, bereft of the security of their beloved monarchy, struggled to maintain their faith and identity in a very new and uncertain world. More than their counterparts in other European lands, French Catholics struggled to find an explanation for the social and political turmoil that had been unleashed on their soil; and the many prophetic books and tracts published in France in these years provided them with at least the rudiments of such an explanation. The apocalyptic scenarios sketched in these materials shifted in response to the rapidly changing politics of these years, but there were some common themes in these prophetic writings grounded in a deep sense of the unity and common destiny of the French nation.

The most important of these themes was that of collective sin and chastisement. For example, Soeur Nativité (Jeanne Leroyer, 1730–1798), whose revelations recorded in the 1790s were published in 1818 (*Vie et révélations de la Soeur de la Nativité*), upbraided her people for their prideful trust in human reason and surrender to the spirit of the Enlightenment. The philosophers who led that intellectual movement, she said, were agents of the devil, and their aim was to promote the earthly reign of Antichrist. The French Revolution was a divine punishment for these collective sins and a call to the French people to make reparation so that France could move on to assume its appointed role in the divine plan of the last days.

The special place reserved for France in the scenario of the end-times was the second major theme of early-nineteenth-century French prophecy. This theme was especially pronounced in the prophecies that circulated in the years following the restoration of the Bourbon monarchy (1815–1830). Many popular prophecies of these years spoke of the French monarch gaining sovereignty over and bringing peace to the whole world, of the conversion of the infidels and the restoration of Jerusalem, and of the appearance, just before the end, of a pope of exceptional holiness.

While the revolution of 1830 once again removed the Bourbons from the throne, it seems to have had little effect on popular belief in the crucial role of France and especially of a Bourbon monarch in the last days. The prophecies pointing to such a scenario, however, were now linked to the subversive cause of the Legitimists, who sought to restore to the throne one of several competing claimants. The best known of the apocalyptic legitimist movements during the so-called July Monarchy was the "Oeuvre de Misericordie," which expected the dawn of a third age of the Holy Spirit, inaugurated by the restoration of one of these Bourbon claimants known as Naundorff. This movement was quickly denounced as heretical by French Roman Catholic officials, and its leader, Eugene Vintras (d. 1875), whose divine mission and support of Naundorff had been confirmed in the eyes of his followers by his reputed healing powers, was arrested and prosecuted for fraud.

While it was in early-nineteenth-century France that nationalistic apocalyptic scenarios were most evident, a type of politicized apocalypticism less specifically tied to France developed at the same time in connection with a Catholic revival that had erupted in aristocratic circles both in France and in several other Western European lands. At the forefront of this revival was Joseph de Maistre (1754–1821), a Catholic aristocrat from Savoy, who denounced the French Revolution as the scourge of God, who expected a coming Catholic monarchical restoration that would bring peace and universal well-being, and who sought support for his vision from the czar in St. Petersburg. Also important in this Catholic revival was the Livonian aristocrat Juliane Kruedener (1764–1824), who was more specific with her prophecies and who is alleged to have had considerable influence on the czar and on the "Holy Alliance" of 1815. Drawing on the spirit of this revival, on the ideas of the French Masonic prophet Claude Saint-Martin (1743–1803), and on the apocalyptic thought of the German Protestants J. A. Bengel and F. C. Oetinger, some prominent Bavarian Catholics, who had close ties to the romantic movement and whom the modern historian Paul Gottfried has called "conservative millenarians," developed a variety of futurist views and optimistic politically oriented end-time prophecies. The most important of these was Munich philosopher Franz von Baader (1775–1841).

What proved to be most important for European Roman Catholic apocalypticism, however, was neither that form of early-nineteenth-century French prophecy which revolved around the destiny of the French nation nor the somewhat softer forms of political prophecy of the conservative millenarians. It was rather the development, within the nineteenth-century French Catholic context, of an emphasis on visible apocalyptic signs that could become a focal point for traditional devotional practices and at the same time function as concrete indicators of an unfolding apocalyptic scenario.

One of the best early examples of such a sign occurred in 1827 at Migné, near Poitier, where, at the conclusion of a sermon, a cross was seen in the sky, after which hundreds of people reportedly fell to their knees in a dramatic gesture of contrition and repentance. The interpretative framework in which this event was reported was precisely that of the apocalyptic prophecies described earlier—that is, that France had sinned in the Enlightenment and had been chastised in the Revolution, but that now, through such repentance, it was on its way to assuming its crucial role in the Christian millennium.

Three years later, Catherine Labouré (1806–1876), a young nun in a convent on the Rue du Bac in Paris, reported a series of visions of the Virgin Mary, in the course of which she was directed to have the image that had appeared to her imprinted on a medal. Mary had appeared to her, she said, standing on a globe of the earth, with rays radiating from her hands, and Catherine then heard a voice saying, "These rays are the symbol of the graces Mary obtains for all men, and the point toward which they flow most abundantly is France." During the next decade, millions of so-called "Miraculous Medals" were minted and distributed throughout France, as were thousands of pamphlets describing the history and miracles associated with the medal. As the historian Thomas Kselman notes, it was the popularity of the Miraculous Medal that kept alive the idea of France's special role in world history during the July Monarchy.

The appearance and the immense success here of a specifically Marian apocalyptic sign were portents of what was to come. In politically uncertain times, free-floating prophecies of a coming Great Monarch and an Angelic Pope proved to have less appeal for French and other European Catholics than prophecies associated with the Mother of God and with actual places that could be visited and objects that could be touched.

This pattern became clear a few years later in 1846 in connection with the Marian apparition at La Salette. While its site was remote and its message much more sober than that associated with the Rue du Bac visions, news of the appearance of the Virgin to two shepherd children on this hillside high in the French Alps soon spread throughout France, as did a number of threatening apocalyptic prophecies associated with it. These were years of famine, and the image of Mary connected with this apparition was that of a distraught mother warning her children to return to the mandates of the church, lest the hand of her Divine Son be loosed in some more terrible judgment. Catholics throughout France found here both a way to confront the divine judgment that they believed had been unleashed on their nation and a way to mitigate this judgment by recommitting themselves to traditional religious observances.

While it is unlikely that many of the early devotees of the Rue du Bac and the La Salette visions needed any help fitting these events into an apocalyptic framework, it may not have been clear at first why these last days of the world should be marked by appearances, specifically, of the Virgin Mary. In 1842, however, a manuscript was discovered of a lost work of the French monk, Grignion de Montfort (1673–1716), *Traite de la vraie devotion à la saint vierge,* which explained this. In the midst of pious meditations on Mary's life and power in heaven, Montfort posited that the second coming of Christ would be preceded by an "Age of Mary." Basing his ideas on a recapitulation of Mary's role in the incarnation, he argued that just as Mary first gave Christ to the world, so she will cause him to "burst forth" in his second appearance. Or, more precisely, as the Virgin Mary with the help of the Holy Spirit produced what was heretofore the greatest thing, that is, the God-Man, so only "this excellent and miraculous Virgin" with the Holy Spirit could bring the greatest things in the end-times.

Montfort held that the task of the Virgin just preceding the second coming would be "the formation and education of the great saints who will come at the end of time," and Montfort referred to these persons as "apostles of the latter times" (1985, 21).

Montfort's treatise, which became one of the most popular Catholic devotional works of the nineteenth century, gave clarity and theological sanction to ideas that were implicit in much French Catholic Marian piety even before its discovery. And as more reports of Marian apparitions began to surface, in the wake of the church's official approval of the La Salette devotion in 1851, many French Catholics became convinced that Montfort's "Age of Mary" had begun and that they themselves might be the apostles of the last times of whom Montfort had spoken.

The apparition reported by Bernadette Soubirous (1844–1879) at Lourdes in 1858, which was declared worthy of the assent of the faithful in 1862 and which in the next few decades brought millions of pilgrims to this town in the foothills of the Pyrenees, was the next major event to become a sign and a point of anchorage for this Marian apocalyptic framework. While the messages reported here were basically brief admonitions to devotion, for example, "Penance, penance, penance!" and were lacking in apocalyptic content, this does not mean that this event was without apocalyptic significance.

Mary's reported message at Lourdes on March 25, 1858, "I am the Immaculate Conception," was quickly understood as a confirmation of the Dogma of the Immaculate Conception, declared by Pope Pius IX in 1854, which was itself understood by many as a sort of apocalyptic sign. Many French Catholics, who by now were presumably growing skeptical of the prophecies that a French monarch would soon appear who would play a decisive role in the events of the end-times, were now beginning to believe that the Virgin Mary herself, having visited France at least three times in recent decades, was fulfilling that role, and that by attending to Mary's messages and instructions they themselves were now playing a crucial role in God's plan for the last days.

For many, this redemptive role was associated with the image of suffering that was prominent at La Salette and that would emerge in many later Marian apparitions. Mélanie Calvat (1831–1904) and Maximin Girard (1835–1875), the two young seers of La Salette, had reported that they had encountered a bright light that slowly faded, revealing a seated woman who was weeping. She rose and began to speak to them in words that emphasized her vicarious pain.

> For a long time I have suffered for you; if I do not want my son to abandon you, I am forced to pray to him myself without ceasing. You pay no heed. However much you would do, you could never recompense the pain I have taken on for you. (Zimdars-Swartz 1991, 30)

Devotees of La Salette and of some later French apparitions found here a model for the redemptive work to which they believed they had been called. Indeed, some of them found in the later, troubled life of Mélanie a living model of such vicarious, redemptive suffering. In a century in which secularism continued to gain ground and in which they seemed to be surrounded more and more by unbelievers, faithful French Catholics could take heart from and join in devotions associated with these models, believing that their own sacrifices and sufferings were atoning for the sins of others, and that thereby they were carrying out their nation's unique end-time mission.

France, however, had no exclusive claim on the Virgin Mary. Not long after Lourdes, appearances of the Virgin began to be reported in other Catholic regions of Western Europe, and while the messages of some of these apparitions were quite militant, the devotions and devotional contexts they inspired were not unlike those inspired by the earlier French apparitions. The concrete grounding, the devotionalizing, and finally the universalizing of apocalyptic thought that took place in these French Marian apparitions and in their aftermath have been perhaps the most important development in Roman Catholic apocalypticism in recent centuries.

While a Marian apparition is potentially of universal appeal, the forms of thought or knowledge that come to be associated with it are very particular. The particular forms of knowledge that grow up around a Marian apparition are perhaps best studied by looking at the "secrets" that the Virgin typically entrusts to her visionaries. It is these secrets, typically, that become the bearers of quite specific apocalyptic hopes and fears.

The special information that the seers of modern Marian apparitions, beginning with La Salette, have said they were instructed not to share with anyone was originally thought to be relevant only to these persons themselves. However, some of the first devotees of La Salette, anxious to make sense of the social and political chaos of their time, became convinced that Mélanie and Maximin had been given insights into the nature and future course of the events unfolding around them. The seers' "secrets" were thus inserted into a framework of prophecy, and while presumably only the seers themselves knew what these secrets were, this prophetic framework allowed for and encouraged a great deal of speculation about what they might be.

The public message of La Salette had specified simply that a chastisement from God was imminent if people did not amend their religious lives. There was much speculation at the time, however, about France's religious and political destiny, understood as part of a scenario of end-time events, and rumors were soon circulating that such things were the subject of the La Salette secrets. There was a rumor, for example, connecting La Salette with the already well-known apparition on the Rue du Bac. The nun who had seen Mary in the Rue du Bac convent, it was said, had traveled on foot to La Salette, where she allegedly had had a revelation linking contemporary events to the imminence of the second coming. Concern with the La Salette secrets, of course, was chiefly focused on the two young seers, and they were pressed by many persons, both devotees and skeptics, to reveal their secrets, if not to those who besieged them, then to some appropriate authorities. The proper recipients of the secrets, most agreed, would be their confessors or the pope, and in fact both Mélanie and Maximin were finally persuaded to write down their secrets and send them to Pius IX, who never made any public statements about their content.

The transmission of the secrets of the La Salette seers to the pope did little to discourage public interest in these secrets. Texts alleged to be the secret of Maximin were in circulation as early as 1854, and these were often included in late-nineteenth-century prophetic anthologies, where they were represented as authentic. More interesting, however, is a text of Mélanie's secret that she herself published in 1870, which is an unrelenting account of the evils that will beset the world in the last times.

This text begins with a strong denunciation of evil priests who through their dissolute lives had become cesspools of iniquity, and it then speaks of a coming vindication of the righteous, when Christ will command his angels to put to death the persecutors of his church and all persons addicted to sin. Various evils will follow this, but in the midst of these a call will be issued to the true imitators of Christ, the apostles of the last times, to come forth and strengthen the world. Then, finally, the beast will be defeated by the archangel Michael, the earth will be purified and the works of human pride consumed, all things will be renewed, and God will be served and glorified.

Especially notable in this text is Mélanie's claim that the Virgin had given her a rule of life for the "Order of the Mother of God." It was the male branch of this order, she said, who would be the apostles of the last times and who would preach the gospel of Jesus Christ throughout the world in the last days. While she was reluctant to put this rule into writing, Mélanie apparently did devote a great deal of time and effort in her later years to trying to establish this religious order.

This published text of Mélanie's secret attracted a great deal of attention among Catholics in France, England, and Italy, who feared that their church, or at least many of its leaders, had been conscripted by the powers of evil and had sold out to powerful secular governments. This text was officially repudiated by the Roman Catholic Church in 1923.

While the secrets of La Salette became the focal point of the apocalyptic fears of many later-nineteenth-century European Catholics, the secrets of another Marian apparition would assume a place of even greater importance in the consciousness of many Catholics of the twentieth-century. In the spring of 1917, at Fatima, Portugal, three peasant children reported that the Virgin Mary had appeared to them. Subsequently, on the thirteenth day of each month, from May to October, with the exception of August, Lucia dos Santos (1907–) and her cousins Jacinta Marto (1910–1920) and Francisco Marto (1908–1919) reported similar appearances, and large crowds began to assemble around them during these experiences.

It was the appearance reported on July 13, 1917, that gave rise to the famous secret of Fatima. Between two and three thousand people were present on this occasion, and in the course of the apparition, Lucia, who seemed to be in conversation with someone, suddenly took a deep breath, turned pale, and cried out in terror. Later, when asked what it was that had been so unpleasant, she replied that it was a secret, and upon further questioning, she suggested that it was good for some people and bad for others. The children also began to say at this time that the lady of their vision had told them not to tell this secret to anyone.

These were difficult times for Portugal and especially for Portuguese Catholics. These were the years of the Great War; there were serious food shortages; and the new government, moreover, seemed to be determined to wipe out religious institutions. While the claims of the three Fatima children were met initially with skepticism and resistance, an immense groundswell of interest in and support for the Fatima visions developed very quickly. It was not until some years later, however, that the story of Fatima became well known outside of Portugal.

Modern devotional accounts of the Fatima apparition almost all relate the two parts of the secret that Lucia eventually revealed as if these were simply parts of Lucia's vision of July 13. But in fact this secret has a rather complicated history. Lucia's secret—or, rather, what she said were the first two of its three parts—was not published until August 1941, when it appeared in her so-called *Third Memoir*. In this document, written twenty-four years after the apparition itself, Lucia said that on July 13, 1917, Mary had first showed them a vision of hell, "where poor sinners go." Then, she said, the Virgin gave her the second part of the secret, which consisted of instructions for devotion to her Immaculate Heart, and Lucia, writing in 1941, put these instructions into a distinctly apocalyptic framework.

The Virgin told her, Lucia said, that if this devotion were established, many souls would be saved and there would be peace. The current war, World War I, would end, but Mary warned that if people did not cease offending God there would be, during the pontificate of Pius IX, an even greater war. Mary said, according to Lucia, that this would be preceded by a sign: "When you see a night illumined by an unknown light, know that this is the great sign given you by God, that he is about to punish the world for its crimes, through war, famine, and persecutions of the Church and of the Holy Father" (Santos 1976, 162). To prevent this, Mary had asked for the establishment of two devotions: the consecration of Russia to her Immaculate Heart, and the Communion of Reparation on the First Saturdays.

If her requests were heeded, Mary said, "Russia will be converted and there will be peace; if not, she will spread her errors throughout the world, causing wars and persecutions of the Church." Then good people would be martyred, the pope would suffer much, and various nations would be annihilated. In the end, however, Mary's Immaculate Heart would triumph. "The Holy Father will consecrate Russia to me, and she will be converted, and a period of peace will be granted to the world" (Santos 1976, 162).

This "secret," in fact, pulls together into a single narrative the content of a number of religious experiences that Lucia had reported earlier to her confessors or superiors in the convent. Between 1925 and 1927 she had reported a series of experiences relating to the establishment of a First Saturdays devotion. The Virgin had appeared to her, she said, and had asked that on the first Saturdays of five consecutive months, Catholics should confess, receive absolution, recite five decades of the Rosary, and then, while making reparation to the Virgin, meditate on the fifteen mysteries. Then, on June 13, 1929, Lucia reported a vision in which the Virgin had requested the Consecration of Russia, saying, "The moment has come in which God asks the Holy Father in union with all the bishops of the world to make the consecration of Russia to my Immaculate Heart, promising to save it by this means." And Lucia herself later noted that, in 1939, she had understood and had told her confessor that a spectacular aurora borealis of that year was a sign from God that the prophesied second war was about to take place.

In her *Third Memoir* Lucia noted that there was a third part of the secret which the Virgin had not given her permission to reveal, and this has subsequently come to be known simply as "the third secret of Fatima." Late in 1943, after a serious illness, during which some concern had been expressed that this third secret might be forever lost, Lucia was persuaded to write it down, seal it in an envelope, and put this in one of her notebooks. In 1944 she sent this envelope to Jose Correia da Silva, the Bishop of Leiria, who kept it in a chancery safe until 1957. At that time, the Sacred Congregation for the Doctrine of the Faith requested photocopies of all of Lucia's writings, and this became the occasion for the transmission of this text to Rome.

The Secret of Fatima has figured prominently in both the hopes and fears of Roman Catholics in the second part of the twentieth century. What appeared to be the correct prediction, in the second part of the secret, of the end of the First World War and the beginning of the Second (although this may in fact be an *ex post facto* prophecy) drew much attention to this secret in the wake of its publication. In the later 1940s and 1950s European as well as American Catholics were deluged with popular accounts of the Fatima apparition and its secrets. The European clergy in particular found the Fatima devotions and statements about the threat of Russia useful in their campaigns against the growing socialist and communist movements, and millions of Catholics worldwide in the 1950s and 1960s understood the so-called Cold War in the apocalyptic framework set forth in Lucia's *Third Memoir*.

As had happened earlier with the secret of La Salette, many Catholics assumed that the Third Secret of Fatima was prophetic, sketching a scenario of end-time events. And since the content of the secret was unknown, speculation fed by the fears and anxieties of the times was rampant. As early as 1956, reports were circulating that the Third Secret contained prophecies of various impending tragedies, for example, involving the pope, and soon texts were circulating on mimeographed sheets and in popular magazines purporting to reveal some of this information. According to one of these texts, the pope would be taken prisoner by the Nazis and made into a Nazi puppet; according to another, he would be captured, tortured, and finally killed by Italian communists; and according to a third, the pope would abandon Rome and transfer the See of Peter to a new location. Many of these texts predicted widespread apostasy and impending judgments, and, typically, it was the Virgin Mary who was identified as the last anchor of salvation.

The most famous of the texts purporting to be the Third Secret of Fatima was printed in the German weekly *Neues Europa* on October 15, 1963. Many people at that time were concerned about the proliferation of nuclear arms, and there was much talk about the recent test-ban treaty. In the commentary published along with this text, it was reported that Paul VI had arranged for this secret to be read and studied by the leaders of the United States, Great Britain, and the Soviet Union, and that it was because they had been so impressed by this document that they had drawn up and promoted the treaty, signed by ninety nations on August 6 of that year, which banned atomic experiments on land, in the air, and under water. The article said that journalist Louis Emrich had obtained extracts of the secret that had been presented to these leaders in Washington, London, and Moscow, and that it was these extracts that were now being published.

According to these alleged extracts of the Third Secret, a great punishment would come upon all humankind in the second half of the century. People had been sacrilegious, order was lacking, and Satan ruled in the highest levels of many institutions. This would be a time of severe trials for the church, and there would be a great war. But after Satan's henchmen had ruled the earth for a time, there would come a time when God and his glory would again be invoked and served. The text concludes with this call to all true Christians and latter-day apostles: "The time of times is coming and the end of all ends, if people are not converted and if this conversion does not come from the directors of the world and the church" (Zimdars-Swartz 1991, 214).

The apparitional focus of modern Roman Catholic apocalypticism has continued into the late twentieth century in the wake of the reported appearances of the Virgin to six young people beginning in 1981 in Medjugorje in the former Yugoslavia. Again, the messages of the Virgin have included admonitions to return to traditional devotional practices and criticism of modern materialism and atheism, and they have become the bearer of apocalyptic expectations, especially through the ten secrets reportedly given to each of the visionaries.

Pilgrimages to Medjugorje were very popular among European Catholics until the outbreak of the ethnic conflicts that led to and have followed the breakup of Yugoslavia. In the wake of these pilgrimages, there have been reports of several other Marian apparitions in Western Europe such as that at Melleray in the Republic of Ireland in the summer of 1985. There the Virgin issued warnings concerning Ireland's future and spoke of the need to return to traditional devotions and of the role of the Irish people in these last days in conveying God's messages to the world. Similar phenomena were soon being reported in the United States, as large numbers of people returned from pilgrimages to Medjugorje. The best known of these was in Conyers, Georgia, where the visions of housewife Nancy Fowler on the thirteenth of each month became the basis for large public gatherings beginning in 1991.

☞ SECULARIZED APOCALYPTICISM _____

In contrast to those who saw in the French Revolution and its aftermath the opening of the seventh seal and the pouring out of the vials of wrath of the Apocalypse, many nineteenth-century Europeans saw in these years the beginning of the fulfillment of the radical hopes and promises of the Enlightenment. While most of these persons granted no supernatural authority to the biblical writings that were the traditional basis of Jewish and Christian apocalyptic thought, they found symbolic truth in the texts that pointed to the coming of a peaceful millennial kingdom; and, to the extent that they expected an imminent, radical transformation which would be the beginning of such a kingdom, it is reasonable to think of them as representatives of a secularized apocalypticism.

Indeed, it is becoming increasingly clear that vast numbers of Enlightenment and post-Enlightenment thinkers were influenced by apocalyptic religious traditions, and that through some of these persons, elements of these traditions have been mediated to and reconstituted in important modern political movements such as National Socialism and Communism. The apocalyptic character of some modern political and social movements is now rather widely acknowledged, and some work has been done to identify crucial antecedents of their apocalyptic ideas. But it is not at all clear the channels through which these apocalyptic ideas have been (or are now being) mediated, and thus, which of the many modern representatives of secularized apocalyptic thinking are really worth our attention. In the meantime, the best strategy may be to focus on a few of the best and most intriguing candidates.

One of the first and most interesting of these persons was Robert Owen (1771–1858). Owen was a self-taught Welsh entrepreneur and industrialist whose radical ideas and projects attracted the attention of large numbers of England's elite. Like some earlier representatives of the Enlightenment, Owen held traditional religion in contempt, and from some of his statements one might judge him simply to be a deist, for example, in his speaking of "that hitherto undefined, incomprehensible Power which directs the atom and controls the aggregate of nature." But he goes on to say that this power "has in this era of creation made the world to wonder at itself" and to forecast the imminent demise of many of the world's formerly most-esteemed institutions. Indeed, these statements are part of a discourse in which Owen cites many passages from both the Hebrew and the New Testament scriptures to illustrate his conviction that the world is on the verge of a "new era of charity" and a "new religion of truth" (1991, 222). Although it is not always clear in Owen's writings what is literal conviction and what is impassioned rhetoric, one can scarcely miss the apocalyptic character of the climax of this discourse, where he repeats and adds a few words of commentary to a well-known passage of the New Testament, Luke 21:25-28.

> And there shall be signs in the sun and in the moon and in the stars; and upon earth, distress of nations, with perplexity; the sea and the waves roaring; men's hearts failing them for fear and for looking after those things which are coming on earth; for the powers of heaven shall be shaken. And they shall see the Son of Man (or TRUTH) coming in a cloud with power and glory. And when these things begin to come to pass, then look up and lift your heads, for your redemption (FROM CRIME AND MISERY) draweth nigh. (1991, 221)

Owen was a proponent of "pure and undefiled religion" or "natural religion," in contrast to the "artificial religion" of the churches, and his most radical idea was that proper education, especially of the working classes, in a properly ordered external environment, would trigger a change in human nature and quickly usher in a utopian future. The fact that some of his earlier attempts to create such environments at New Lanark seemed to be successful lent much credibility to his ideas in the 1820s and 1830s, and this, along with his unbounded optimism, gave an immense boost to the socialism (Owen apparently coined this word) that he sought to establish.

While the element of imminence is not so pronounced in the thought of Owen's contemporary, the Frenchman Charles Fourier (1772–1837), he put such emphasis on an impending and inexorable cosmic transformation that he too can certainly be seen as an apocalyptic thinker. Fourier, who in his early writings spoke of himself as the "Messiah of Reason" and who is known today as the prophet of a universal harmony that would replace our "vicious and perverse" civilization, believed, like Owen, that he was translating into practice the message of the New Testament Gospels. According to Fourier, his (or the Enlightenment's) second revelation, that is, the revelation of the destiny of societies, paralleled and fulfilled the first revelation made by Jesus, of the salvation of souls. Imbued with a sense of a supremely high mission and embittered by the rejection that he encountered during his lifetime, Fourier claimed that "[he] alone . . . followed the instruction of Jesus" and that he was the "prophet post-cursor announced by him . . . completing his work of the rehabilitation of men" (Riasanovsky 1969, 103).

Fourier held that in a matter of a few years not just human society but the earth itself, and indeed the whole universe, would be transformed by a host of new human inventions and technologies. In contrast to the passivity advocated by the traditional apocalypticist, he saw human beings as very much involved in and as bringing about this transformation, presumably by employing the obtuse theories he had set forth in his writings. Like his apocalyptic ancestors, Fourier really believed that he had "found the code" that would unlock the future, and while he was not the most rational of his contemporaries to hold such a view, the boldness and exuberance of his convictions attracted many admirers after his death in both Europe and America.

The most important of these admirers was the German Karl Marx (1818–1883). Marx appropriated the basic apocalyptic structure of Fourier's thought, that is, the thorough condemnation of existing civilization and the expectation of an imminent world transformation, triggered by informed human activity. With the help of Hegel's dialectic, he shaped this into a philosophy of history and a theory of class warfare culminating in the collapse of capitalism and a worldwide workers' revolt. Marx thought of himself as a scientist, but the ponderous economic science of *Das Kapital* (1867) for which he is often remembered and which, indeed, he himself regarded as his greatest achievement, was only a lengthy preface to the theory of proletarian revolution that he crafted with the help of his collaborator Friedrich Engels (1820–1895), which was an adaptation of the apocalyptic structure already noted.

One of the most remarkable things about this theory of proletarian revolution is the extent to which it became, through the personal efforts of Marx and Engels, the focal point and rallying cry of the radical workers' movements of the late nineteenth century. Almost as remarkable, however, was the extent to which Marx's and Engels's own contributions to this theory, that is, their understanding of through whom and under what circumstances this revolution would occur, were significantly modified, both in these movements and in the radical thought and politics that grew out of them in the next century. Modern "Marxist" political leaders from Leon Trotsky and Vladimir Lenin to Mao-Tse-Tung, Che Guevarra, and Fidel Castro have adapted this theory to suit and to sanction ideas of revolution and ways of facilitating it that

Marx and Engels surely would have considered heretical. Modern theorists of various persuasions have used elements of this theory and of its apocalyptic structure to construct a wide variety of philosophies and critical theories.

The Russian propagandist and provocateur Michael Bakunin (1814–1878) distinguished himself clearly from the Marxists and has not usually been seen as an apocalyptic thinker. Nevertheless, he had such an impact on the radical thought and politics of modern Western Europe that he can scarcely be omitted from this discussion. Retreating from Fourier's and Marx's expectation of an imminent, one-time world transformation and portraying the future more as an unfinished human project, Bakunin expected a series of national revolutions that would finally coalesce in a universal social revolution. He emphasized that this revolution would be the work not of an organized proletariat, as Marx and Engels thought, but a free and spontaneous uprising of the masses. After being expelled by Marx and his supporters from the International Working Men's Association, Bakunin worked for some time in Western Europe as a labor organizer and propagandist, and in Switzerland, Italy, and Spain his ideas proved more popular among the workers than those of his more authoritarian protagonist.

The justification for regarding Bakunin as an apocalyptic thinker lies in his radical concept of the revolutionary act, rooted in the apocalyptic idea of total and immediate world transformation. Characterized by the modern social critic Edward Hyams as "a romantic in whom violence was for ever imminent" (1974, 88–89) and known for his vehement atheism, Bakunin, like Marx and some other left-wing Hegelians, was attracted to the secular crystallization of this idea in that mysterious moment of Hegel's dialectic in which the negative is suddenly transformed into the positive. To an extent unmatched by other followers of Hegel, however, Bakunin translated this moment into a life-orienting principle which he called the "principle of Revolution," and which he understood to involve "the radical overthrow of all presently existing religious, political, economic and social organizations and institutions . . . and the reconstitution . . . of world society on the basic of liberty, reason, justice, and work" (1973, 64).

Bakunin called his theory "anarchism," but this politically oriented term tends to obscure its apocalyptic roots, as well as the influence exercised by Bakunin and some like-minded mystical atheists not just on the politics but on the mind-set of the intellectual and cultural elite of Europe in the late nineteenth and early twentieth century. One important proponent of Bakunin's principle of revolution was the French syndicalist Georges Sorel (1847–1922), who observed in his work *The Decomposition of Marxism* that the general strike represents the advent of the new world and corresponds to the biblical Apocalypse.

A somewhat similar but more philosophically sophisticated theory of apocalypse emerged early in the twentieth century in the writings of the German essayist and philosopher Ernst Bloch (1885–1977), and a sketch of this theory will be a fitting conclusion for this essay. Bloch was a lifelong devotee and collector of romantic stories and images, but he was also devoted to classical German philosophy, and he brought these two interests together in a rather striking manner in his first major work, *Spirit of Utopia* (1917).

This work was a collection of essays on topics as diverse as an old jug and "Karl Marx, Death, and the Apocalypse." Bloch noted, however, that on another level, it was an attempt to rescue and rehabilitate the word "utopia," which in the aftermath of the Great War had fallen into disfavor, in a semi-dialectical structure similar to that of Hegel's phenomenology. Bloch, who always thought of himself as a socialist and who in the period between the two wars was drawn more and more to Marxist and materialist modes of thought, held that at the heart of the cosmos was a utopian tendency that could only develop as it was mediated by informed human activity from its "source" in existing material forms to its "mature formation" in what he called not-yet-being.

Bloch, however, was not a metaphysician of some cosmic utopian process. Following Marx and perhaps also Hegel, Bloch avoided the terminology of process and emphasized rather the dialectical "leap" triggered by a sudden flash of insight and realized in subsequent human praxis. It is only here, he insisted, that the old is negated, that the utopian tendency in material forms is released, and that the new, in the guise of a new and better form or image, makes its appearance in the world. In his several writings dealing with biblical religion, the atheist Bloch consistently identified this leap, this sudden flash of insight, and this mediation of the new through informed human praxis with "apocalypse."

Creation and apocalypse, he explains in his work *Atheism in Christianity* (1968), are contrary principles, the former being summed up in the phrase, "And behold, it was very good!" and the latter in the phrase, "Behold, I make everything new!" (1972, 29). Bloch makes it clear here that it is the latter, that is, the principle that leads out of the world as it is into the better world foreseen by the biblical prophets, that is at the heart of his own worldview. The apocalypse, he had said some years earlier, is "the apriori of all politics and culture" and represents an "awakening into totality" (1971, 341).

Perhaps the most striking thing about Bloch's theory of apocalypse is its emphasis on knowledge. Bloch has replaced Bakunin's idea of the revolutionary act, where the destruction of the old mysteriously gives birth to the new, with the idea of an apocalyptic insight or vision which guides and directs the transformation of specific material forms. This, Bloch himself observed, marks a return to the original biblical meaning of apocalypse, that is, unveiling, and it is significant that it was in the context of the Marxist-Christian dialogue of the 1970s that Bloch's rather obtuse writings began to attract serious attention.

CONCLUDING REMARKS

The materials sketched in this essay demonstrate that, in the midst of perceived social and political disorder, many modern Europeans have turned to ancient prophecies promising a new or transformed world, updated by messages associated with visions and other kinds of experiences reported by their contemporaries, or simply by prophetic insights offered by some trusted authorities. Prophecies ancient and modern, free-floating and grounded in concrete places, religious and secular, have been the points of orientation that have enabled many thousands of people of modern times to continue with their lives in meaningful ways even in the most unsettling of circumstances. Sometimes these prophecies have inspired changes in the social or political order, and sometimes they have functioned to maintain or justify some existing orders or practices. But at all times they have given reassurance that contemporary events were moving toward an appropriate and desirable goal and that they could be affected by a program of appropriate behavior.

The future of these patterns may be suggested by the visions and prophecies of the late-twentieth-century American seer Annie Kirkwood, whose best-selling 1991 book *Mary's Message to the World* combines Marian apparitions with the new-age concerns of ecology and personal growth. The non-Roman Catholic Kirkwood claims that because humans have completely "disregarded the earth as a planet," Mary has come to warn the residents of planet earth of impending natural disasters. Not God, she says, but the planet herself will punish them in order to renew the land and the "minds of mankind." Included among Mary's predictions, according to Kirkwood, are nearly daily UFO sightings, an increasing number of appearances of civilizations from other planets, a decline in the power of the Catholic Church, and a call by religious leaders for the unity of all religions. Here, the apocalyptic dimension of Marian apparitions has become the basis for an eclectic scenario of last things incorporating late-twentieth-century obsessions with the environment, human potential, and extraterrestrial life and contact. Kirkwood's book demonstrates the resilience and adaptability of apocalyptic prophecy in the contemporary Western world, and it suggests that such prophecy is likely to continue to be popular in the next century, both in Western Europe and in America.

⤳ BIBLIOGRAPHY

Bakunin, Michael. 1973. *Selected Writings of Michael Bakunin.* Edited by Arthur Lehning. London: Cape.
Bloch, Ernst. 1971. *Gesamtausgabe,* Bd. 16. Frankfurt am Main: Suhrkamp Verlag.
———. 1972. *Atheism in Christianity: The Religion of the Exodus and of the Kingdom.* Translated by T. J. Swann. New York: Herder & Herder. This relatively short work of this twentieth-century Marxist-atheist philosopher illustrates more clearly than his massive three-volume *Principle of Hope* his unusual reading of the Hebrew and New Testament scriptures and his distinctive understanding of apocalypse.
Buber, Martin. 1949. *Paths in Utopia.* Translated by R. F. C. Hull. London: Routledge & Kegan Paul. A survey and critique of some important theorists and experiments in utopian socialism of the nineteenth and twentieth centuries, this work by a well-known Jewish theologian offers an interesting perspective on the achievements and failures of Marx and Lenin, and presents a vision, born of a sense of crisis, of new forms of communal life which the author saw emanating from Jerusalem.
Christian, William A., Jr. 1996. *Visionaries: The Spanish Republic and the Reign of Christ.* Berkeley/Los Angeles: University of California Press. A detailed reconstruction of apparitions of the Virgin Mary reported by persons at Ezkioga in the Basque region of Spain beginning in 1931, this book shows how an apocalyptic perspective gradually works itself into the worldview of apparition devotees, both emerging from and shaping their sociopolitical situation. Christian notes that the visionaries began to report apocalyptic messages only as their audience expanded to include outsiders, who encouraged them to fit their visions into a more universal and timeless framework, defined to a considerable extent by earlier prophecies.
Flegg, Columba. 1992. *Gathered under Apostles: A Study of the Catholic Apostolic Church.* Oxford: Clarendon Press. This study by a scholar with close ties to what remains of the Catholic Apostolic movement sketches the historical contexts in which this movement arose and includes a careful discussion of its eschatology. The author minimizes the significance of Irving and stresses the catholic and Christian ecumenical character of this church.
Gerlich, Fritz. 1920. *Der Kommunismus als Lehre vom tausandjaehrigen Reich.* Munich: Bruckmann Verlag. While Gerlich collects considerable evidence here to show that communism is a secularized version of the millennial kingdom, the scope of this work is much broader. Taking his cue from a remark of Kant that Lessing was a philosophical chiliast, Gerlich shows that chiliastic motifs permeated not just the thought of Lessing but also that of Kant, Fichte, and Hegel, and that their probable origin was the chiliastic pietism of J. A. Bengel.
Gottfried, Paul. 1979. *Conservative Millenarians: The Romantic Experience in Bavaria.* New York: Fordham University Press. This is an exemplary study exploring, in the author's own words, "the seculariza-

tion, and modernization, of a mode of looking at historical change which may be called apocalyptic." While formally limited to some Catholic circles in early-nineteenth-century Bavaria, Gottfried's work also sheds light on some German Protestant apocalyptic traditions, on apocalyptic elements in German philosophy, and on the interface between apocalyptic thought and early German romanticism. There is also a valuable annotated bibliography.

Harrison, J. F. C. 1979. *The Second Coming: Popular Millenarianism, 1780–1850.* London: Routledge & Kegan Paul, 1979. This is the classic study of the major British and American millenarian prophets and prophetic movements of the early nineteenth century. Harrison calls his work "an experiment in the writing of popular history," and he succeeds admirably in situating these persons and movements in the popular culture of their times.

Hobsbawm, E. J. 1965. *Primitive Rebels: Studies in Archaic Forms of Social Movement in the Nineteenth and Twentieth Centuries.* New York: Norton. In this study of selected "revolutionary" movements of nineteenth- and twentieth-century Europe, Hobsbawm argues that millenarianism, the hope for a complete and radical change in the world, is present in all such movements and may be a necessary device for effecting profound social change. He sees these movements occurring primarily in regions influenced by Judeo-Christian propaganda, expressed in the language of apocalyptic religion.

Hopkins, James K. 1982. *A Woman to Deliver Her People: Joanna Southcott and English Millenarianism in an Era of Revolution.* Austin: University of Texas Press. This is an impressive study, based on a University of Texas dissertation, of Southcott and the Southcottians and of the early-nineteenth-century historical and prophetic contexts in which this movement appeared.

Hyams, Edward. 1974. *The Millennium Postponed.* London: Secker & Warburg. A wide-ranging and very readable survey of the history of socialism from the French Revolution to the New Left of the 1970s, this work is a good introduction to the most important strands of radical thought and politics of nineteenth-century Europe by a sympathetic critic who is aware of the importance of utopian visions.

Irving, Edward. 1823. *For the Oracles of God: Four Orations: For judgment to come: an argument in nine parts.* London: Printed for T. Hamilton. While quite lengthy, this is one of the more accessible of Irving's prophetic works.

Kirkwood, Annie. 1991. *Mary's Message to the World.* London: Piatkus.

Kselman, Thomas A. 1983. *Miracles and Prophecies in Nineteenth Century France.* New Brunswick, N.J.: Rutgers University Press. This is the definitive study of the social and historical contexts of the Marian apparitions and other popular religious phenomena in nineteenth-century France and of how Roman Catholic officials dealt with these phenomena.

Martins, A. M., ed. 1984. *Novos Documentos de Fatima.* Sao Paolo: Edicoes Loyola. This is an edited collection of documents important for establishing the chronology of events at Fatima and the subsequent experiences and recollections of Lucia.

Marx, Karl, and Friedrich Engels. 1992. *The Communist Manifesto.* Edited with an introduction by David McLellan. Oxford/New York: Oxford University Press. This is a modern edition of one of the most important and most apocalyptic of Marx's and Engels's works.

Montfort, St Louis-Marie Grignion de. 1985. *True Devotion to the Virgin Mary.* Translated by Frederich William Faber. Rockford, Ill.: TAN Books.

Owen, Robert. 1991. *A New View of Society and Other Writings.* Edited with an introduction by Gregory Claeys. London/New York: Penguin Books. In the first and title essay of this collection Owen sketches clearly and succinctly his radical idea of the impending, imminent transformation of human nature and the educational and social reforms that he is convinced will bring this transformation.

Perry, Nicholas, and Loreto Echeverria. 1988. *Under the Heel of Mary.* London/New York: Routledge. A biased but nonetheless important survey of connections between modern right-wing politics and devotion to the Virgin Mary in predominantly Roman Catholic nations throughout the world, this work will at least suggest some contexts in which one might do more careful study of the relationship between Catholic apocalyptic thinking and modern fascism.

Riasanovsky, Nicholas. 1969. *The Teaching of Charles Fourier*. Berkeley: University of California Press.

Sandeen, Ernest. 1970. *The Roots of Fundamentalism: British and American Millenarianism, 1800–1930.* Chicago: University of Chicago Press. Sandeen's work, in contrast to Harrison's, focuses on millenarian thought in the context of Protestant institutional structures such as churches, Bible conferences, missionary societies, and various schools and institutes, and it traces this more-institutionalized millenarianism up to and through the Fundamentalist movement of the 1920s. It includes a lengthy discussion of John Nelson Darby and the Plymouth Brethren.

Santos, Lucia dos. 1976. *Fatima in Lucia's Own Words*. Edited by L. Kondor. Translated by the Dominican Nuns of Perpetual Rosary. Fatima: Postulation Centre. This is a translation of Lucia's four memoirs, in the third and fourth of which she relates the first two parts of the secret that she said she had received in 1917.

Stern, Jean, ed. 1980, 1984. *La Salette: Documents authentique.* 2 vols. Paris: Desclee de Brouwer and Cerf. This is a collection of documents important for reconstructing the sequence of events associated with La Salette, including the prophecies and apocalyptic messages.

Zimdars-Swartz, Sandra. 1991. *Encountering Mary: From La Salette to Medjugorje.* Princeton: Princeton University Press. This work surveys the original reports of the major nineteenth- and twentieth-century European Marian apparitions, the many accretions to these reports and subsequent developments at the apparition sites, and finally the apocalyptic interpretations that have grown up around these phenomena in modern popular Roman Catholicism.

25

Apocalypticism in Eastern Europe

J. Eugene Clay
Arizona State University

APOCALYPTICISM HAS PLAYED a dramatic role in eastern Europe in all three of the Abrahamic traditions. From the tenth century on, the Eastern European Orthodox states have legitimized their rule by drawing from Byzantine realized eschatology. In the seventeenth century, the Jewish messiah Sabbatai Sevi (1626–1676) announced the end of time, and in the nineteenth century, Muslim guerrilla fighters in the Caucasus appealed to the tradition of the *mahdi*, the rightly guided leader who would appear at the eschaton. But the history of apocalypticism is filled with paradoxes and contradictions. In some cases, apocalyptic theology helped legitimize the status quo; in other cases, it justified social revolt. Some apocalypticists optimistically prophesied an earthly millennium when God would rule with his saints; others saw only a future judgment. Although apocalypticism originally sprang from a religious vision, by the early twentieth century, secular Marxists had embraced an ideology that greatly resembled Christian eschatology. Through human labor, the atheistic Bolshevik leaders hoped to usher in a communist millennium; yet their very efforts provoked an apocalyptic religious backlash, as persecuted Christians and Muslims prophesied God's final judgment on the new regime. In the wake of the dissolution of the Soviet Union, eschatology continues to provide believers with a supernatural narrative that helps to render comprehensible the dizzying events of the past decade.

Because the history of apocalypticism in Eastern Europe is so vast, this article deals exclusively with the Christian apocalyptic tradition and concentrates primarily on Russia, whose rich eschatological tradition has been more thoroughly explored.

THE BEGINNINGS OF THE APOCALYPTIC TRADITION

From the ninth century on, Byzantine and Western efforts to spread Christianity to Eastern Europe began to bear fruit as one by one the rulers of the major states converted, were baptized, and invited and supported teachers and priests of the new religion into their lands. In 863, Rostislav (r. 846–870), the ruler of Moravia (in the area of today's Czech Republic), accepted the Byzantine missionaries Cyril (827–869) and Methodius (825–884); within two years, the Bulgars adopted Christianity. A century later, in 966, Grand Duke Mieszko (930–992) of Poland (r. 963–992) was baptized; and in 988, Vladimir (956–1015), the Viking ruler of the Kievan state (r. 980–1015), followed suit. The Christian priests and scholars who entered these countries brought with them the elaborate apocalyptic mythologies of the Bible and the church fathers.

As in Western Europe, this Christian apocalyptic mythology provided an interpretative framework for both rulers and historians as they sought to make and understand their place in history. When the nomadic Cumans attacked Kiev in 1096, one chronicler identified them as one of the eight unclean races that, according to Pseudo-Methodius, had to issue forth before the end of the world. As the Byzantine empire weakened, the independent rulers of new states incorporated apocalyptic elements into state ideology and ritual to legitimize their rule. Alluding to the stories of the Last Emperor, the great Serbian king Stefan Dushan (1308–1355, r. 1331–1355) styled himself *tsar* (the Slavic form of Caesar) and Emperor of the Romans. The chroniclers of Bulgaria referred to their capital, Trnovo, as the New Rome that had replaced the first and second Romes of Italy and Constantinople.

The Ottoman conquest of southeastern Europe in the fourteenth century ended these dreams but also contributed to the elaboration of an apocalyptic mythology among the South Slavs. Serbian nationalists of the nineteenth and twentieth centuries have seen the Serbian defeat at the Battle of Kosovo in 1389 as their sacrifice to save Christian civilization from the Muslim onslaught. But by subjugating the states of southeastern Europe, the Ottomans also prepared the way for the rise of an apocalyptic interpretation of Moscow, whose ruler, though a vassal to the Muslim Mongols of the Golden Horde, nevertheless ruled his own territory. In 1390, Cyprian (1336–1406), a bishop from Trnovo, Bulgaria, became the Metropolitan of Moscow and carried with him the ideologies that had been developing in the South.

☞ MOSCOW, THE THIRD ROME

The Ottoman conquest of Constantinople in 1453 played an important role in the imagination of Muscovite rulers. Moscow considered the Byzantine capitulation to Latin demands at the Council of Florence in 1439 to be the cause of their destruction. The fall of Constantinople left Moscow as the only Orthodox state that had been continually ruled by an Orthodox ruler since its conversion. (Even though Moscow was a vassal to the infidel Mongols from 1240 to at least 1450, the Mongols had chosen to exercise their authority through the Grand Prince.) In 1448, Moscow became autocephalous by overthrowing the Greek Metropolitan Isidore (1385–1463), who had signed the Council of Florence, and choosing a new, Russian metropolitan. The rulers of Moscow, like Bulgars and the Serbs before them, began to see themselves as the successors to the Byzantine empire. To bolster such claims, Grand Prince Ivan III (1440–1505) of Moscow (r. 1462–1505) married Sophia, the niece of the last Byzantine emperor, in 1472.

The Byzantine calendar, which dated the first day of creation to Sunday, September 1, 5508 B.C.E., contributed to apocalyptic speculation, since the seventh millennium of the universe ended on August 31, 1492, and several Christian writers had held that Christ would return in the seventh millennium. In 1487, Archbishop Gennadii (Gonzov, d. 1505) of Novgorod (r. 1484–1504), anxious to dispel rumors of the approaching end, wrote an epistle to confirm his faith in Christ's ultimate return but also to reject any speculation as to its exact date. Even so, when the world did not end in 1492, a group of proto-Protestants attacked the authority of tradition in favor of the Bible.

"The Tale of the White Cowl," composed in Novgorod about the same time, also actively promoted the idea that true Christianity survived in Russia alone. A symbol of the true faith, the white cowl of the tale was initially given to the pope by Constantine. As long as the Roman Church maintained the true faith handed down from the apostles, they also revered the cowl; but once they broke with the Eastern Church and added new doctrines (including the *filioque* [the Roman doctrine that the Holy Spirit proceeds from both the Father and the Son instead of from the Father alone, as the Orthodox Church teaches] and papal supremacy), they also profaned the cowl and decided to destroy it. An angel miraculously preserved the cowl and forced the pope to send it to Patriarch Philotheos (Kokkinos, 1300–1379) of Constantinople (r. 1353–1355, 1364–1376). Warned in a vision by Pope Sylvester (r. 1314–1335) that Constantinople would fall to the Muslims, Philotheos sent the cowl to Archbishop Vasilii (Kaleka, r. 1331–1352) of Novgorod. Russia thus symbolically became the heir of Rome and the leading Christian nation.

In 1511, in a letter to the Grand Duke Vasilii III (1479–1533, r. 1505–1533), the monk Filofei of the Eleazar Monastery in Pskov' further developed this apocalyptic scheme:

> The church of ancient Rome fell because of the Apollinarian heresy, as to the second Rome— the Church of Constantinople—it has been hewn by the axes of the Hagarenes [i.e., the Muslims]. But this third, new Rome, the Universal Apostolic Church under thy mighty rule radiates forth the Orthodox Christian faith to the ends of the earth more brightly than the sun. . . . Hear me, pious tsar, all Christian kingdoms have converged in thine alone. Two Romes have fallen, a third stands, a fourth there shall not be. . . . (Malinin 1901, 50, 54–55.)

Influenced by this realized eschatology, Ivan IV (r. 1533–1584), the son and successor to Vasilii, consciously sought to make Moscow the leader of the Orthodox world. He began an ambitious program of church construction, a massive translation of relics to Moscow, a major revision of church law, and crusades against the Muslims to the east and the Livonian Catholics to the west. In 1547, Ivan formally took the title Tsar, or caesar, to indicate that he was in fact the successor of the Byzantines.

☞ THE APOCALYPTIC STRUGGLE BETWEEN CATHOLICISM AND ORTHODOXY, 1550–1650 ⎯⎯⎯⎯⎯⎯⎯⎯⎯⎯

Apocalyptic ideas seemed especially relevant in the context of the struggle with Catholic Europe, which intensified in the late sixteenth century. The Orthodox Christians of Ukraine and Poland came under increasing pressure to join the Catholic Church. In 1596, at the Union of Brest, a group of Orthodox bishops agreed to recognize the authority of the pope and the validity of the *filioque* on the condition that they be able to maintain their own liturgical language, rites, canons, and customs. The Union created the Greek Catholic (or Uniate) Church, which continues to play a significant role in western Ukraine.

For the Jesuits, who had gained influence over the Polish throne, the Union of Brest marked the culmination of an apocalyptic hope—the rejoining of the Orthodox and Catholic branches of Christianity and the healing of the Great Schism of 1054. The Poles used eschatological symbols to vindicate their efforts to conquer Muscovy in 1605–1612. In 1610, the Polish poet Stanislaw Grochowski (1540–1612) called Cracow the "New Rome," and two years later King Sigismund III (1566–1632, r. 1587–1632) justified his foreign adventures by claiming that he wished to establish a universal Christian commonwealth. But by 1613, these dreams had only provoked a vigorous Orthodox reaction that united Muscovy to drive out the Catholic invaders and establish a new Orthodox dynasty, that of the Romanovs.

At the same time, Belarusian and Ukrainian Orthodox Christians regarded the Union of Brest as a dangerous apostasy heralding the end of the world. Lavrentii Zizanii (fl. 1596–1627), author of the first Slavonic grammar, also compiled the *Book of Cyril,* an important collection of anti-Catholic apocalyptic writings. One of Zizanii's anonymous colleagues put together a similar anthology called *The Book of the One True and Orthodox Faith* (1648). Both of these anti-Uniate works became popular in seventeenth-century Muscovy, whose most dangerous enemy was arguably Catholic Poland. Published in large editions in Moscow in 1644 and 1648 respectively, the two books attacked the Roman Catholic Church for breaking with Orthodoxy in the eleventh century, and regarded the Council of Brest as an apostasy from the true faith. More ominously, the *Book of Faith* predicted a third and final global apostasy: according to the author's timetable, the first apostasy had taken place about 1000 C.E. when the Roman Church ended a millennium of Christian unity by falling away from the Greek Church. The second apostasy had occurred at the Council of Brest, about six hundred years later, and the third and universal apostasy would begin sixty years after that. In the context of the enserfment of the peasantry (accomplished by the 1649 Law Code), the long and protracted struggle with Catholic Poland, and the expansion of an increasingly effective centralized Moscow bureaucracy, such ideas gained wide currency; by the 1650s church officials were reporting a variety of apocalyptic preachers.

The most important mass movement of Christian apocalypticism in Eastern Europe arose in reaction to the liturgical reforms that Patriarch Nikon (Nikita Minin) of Moscow (r. 1652–1658) introduced to make Russian practice conform to that of the Greek Orthodox. In an apparently trivial—but far-reaching—change, Nikon ordered Christians to make the cross with three fingers (the thumb touching the index and middle fingers) to represent the Trinity instead of with two (the index and middle fingers) which had represented the two natures of Christ. Since Orthodox believers crossed themselves several times a day, this change was particularly significant. The sign of the cross was simply the first of many similar reforms: the Orthodox were to proceed around the church counterclockwise rather than clockwise; to place five loaves of altar bread before the altar instead of seven; to spell the name of Jesus *Iisus* instead of *Isus* in order to conform more closely to the Greek *Iesous;* to pronounce a triple, rather than a double, alleluia in worship; and so on. Nikon also forbade new styles of icon painting and certain types of church architecture.

Although to Western eyes these changes seem innocuous, they provoked the first mass movement of religious dissent in Russia. Officially condemned at the Council of Moscow of 1666–1667, those who opposed the changes came to be known as Old Believers (*starovertsy*), or Old Ritualists (*staroobriadtsy*). Some of the Old Believers, such as Archpriest Avvakum Petrov (1620–1682), objected to Nikon's attack on the cherished idea of Muscovite religious superiority contained in the third Rome doctrine. Others, such as the monks of the Solovetskii monastery, who suffered a seven-year siege by government troops rather than introduce the new service books, rejected the centralization of power implicit in the newly imposed reforms. Both groups made the two-fingered sign of the cross a rallying symbol.

The Old Believers took four different approaches to eschatology: (1) a literal reading of apocalyptic texts which viewed the Antichrist as a single, human opponent of Christ; (2) a figurative interpretation that held the Antichrist to be a spiritual force; (3) an eschatology of despairing acquiescence to the state church; and (4) a realized eschatology that considered the *parousia* as already accomplished.

First, the most moderate Old Believers condemned the Nikonian reforms, but did not modify traditional Orthodox eschatology. Like the official church, these dissenters believed that, although the church had faced and would face many Antichrists, the last and greatest Antichrist would appear as a human being, a Jew of the tribe of Dan, who would be born in Babylon, reign in Capernaum, imitate Christ's miracles (including a pseudo-resurrection and ascension), proclaim himself to be God at the rebuilt Temple in Jerusalem, persecute the church, murder the prophets Enoch and Elijah (who had returned from heaven to unmask him), and ultimately be defeated by Christ.

In the wake of Nikon's reforms, many of the Old Believers tried to identify the Antichrist responsible for the mass apostasy of the church. Patriarch Nikon (r. 1652–1658), Tsar Aleksei (r. 1645–1676), and the Greek Arsenii Sukhanov (fl. 1610–1666), who helped to publish the new service books, were all candidates for the dubious honor, but none of them fit the literal requirements of the Orthodox tradition. Nor were Enoch and Elijah, the prophets who had been bodily assumed into heaven and who would return to denounce the Antichrist, anywhere to be found. Those Old Believers who continued to hold to the literal truth of the patristic tradition also took the most moderate position toward the official Russian Church, which they regarded as schismatic, but still in some sense Christian. They continued to believe that the sacraments and the priesthood existed even after the Nikonian apostasy. When these dissenters found themselves without a bishop of their own to consecrate priests for their communities, they accepted converted Orthodox priests in their orders. Most of these priestly Old Believers, as they came to be known, required converts from the official church to renounce their heresy and undergo chrismation.[1] Today—perhaps because they eschewed eschatological excesses— these priestly Old Believers are the largest and best organized of those who resisted the Nikonian reforms. They are represented by two rival hierarchies: (1) the Russian Orthodox Old Believer Church with its center in Rogozhskoe Cemetery in Moscow; and (2) the Ancient Orthodox Church led by the Archbishop of Novozybkov.

More radical Old Believers developed a very different eschatology, which completely reinterpreted traditional apocalypses. In the 1670s, in an important work entitled "On the Antichrist and His Secret Kingdom," a Siberian Old Believer argued that the Antichrist was not a physical person but a spiritual force. Writing sometime before 1676, the author built a powerful and appealing case that the Antichrist was alive in the sacraments of the Nikonian Church. The traditional Orthodox legends spoke of the "abomination of desolation," which would appear in the Temple in the last days and demand to be worshiped as God; the anonymous author interpreted this "abomination" to be the new loaves of altar bread, now marked with the Latin four-cornered cross instead of the traditional eight-cornered cross. During the liturgy, the loaf consumed as the sacrament was supposed to be transformed into the body of Christ and thus made the blasphemous claim to deity prophesied in church tradition.

Orthodox literature also predicted that the Antichrist would (through some false trickery) raise the dead and ascend into heaven. The Old Believer pointed out that those who partook of communion in the Orthodox Church falsely believed that they had eaten of the body of Christ and thus had been raised from spiritual death. Moreover, in the Nikonian service, the priest at one point lifted up the Eucharist and said, "Ascend into heaven, O God," thus fulfilling the ancient prophecies concerning the Antichrist's pseudo-ascension into heaven.

The Old Believers who embraced this reinterpreted eschatology adopted a much more pessimistic view of the official church and of the world that they lived in, a world in which the Antichrist reigned. They believed that it was necessary to rebaptize converts from the official church, and hence came to be known as Rebaptizers (*perekreshchentsy*).

Along the Volga River, far from the northern regions where the Rebaptizers dominated, a third group of Old Believers developed an entirely different way of understanding the world. Although like their spiritual cousins in the north they believed that they lived in the time of the Antichrist, they held that none of the sacraments had survived the evil one's advent. Salvation in this evil age could come only through the miraculous grace of the Savior, who might, in his mercy, make invalid rites effective. Thus, rather than try to administer their own sacraments, most of the Saviorites turned to the official church for baptism, and simply prayed that God might accept the sacrament performed by the priest, who, "though a heretic, was still a priest in a cassock, not a peasant."

Other groups of Old Believers carried this process of demythologization even further. They spiritualized not only the advent of the Antichrist but also the second advent of Christ, which, according to the Bible and Orthodox tradition, was destined to follow the Antichrist's appearance. The scriptural descriptions of Christ's second coming indicate that the entire world will be aware of it; the messianic preachers of the mid-seventeenth century spoke of a Christ who had arrived so quietly that his arrival had to be announced.

As early as 1656, Patriarch Nikon wrote against "false Christs" and "false prophets" who declared, "Lo, here is Christ." Other documentary evidence indicates that messianism was especially prevalent in the Volga-Oka basin. These observers may have been referring to the Kostroma peasant Danilo Filippov (fl. 1660–1700), who apparently declared himself to be a second incarnation of Christ in the latter half of the seventeenth century; he and his followers claimed to have restored original Christianity in their prayer meetings, and they appropriately called their faith, the Faith of Christ (*khristovshchina, khristovoverie*). Danilo's grave in Kriushino hamlet, near the city of Kostroma, drew pilgrims for at least a century and a half after his death around 1700. Danilo's disciple, Ivan Suslov (fl. 1690–1710), who became a trader in Moscow, continued to lead the movement after its founder's death; he, too, was regarded as an incarnation of Christ.

The members of the Faith of Christ promised to live by a strict moral and ascetic code that demanded abstinence from sex and alcohol. Gathering together regularly for long prayer meetings, they recited the Jesus prayer ("Lord Jesus Christ, Son of God, have mercy on me a sinner") until the Holy Spirit possessed their prophets, who then danced and predicted the future. They understood this encounter with the divine as the promised *parousia*, and believed that their leaders were so filled with the Holy Spirit that they were themselves new incarnations of Christ.

Just as the Old Believers vigorously debated the nature of the Antichrist and other eschato-logical theories, they also differed over the correct response to the Nikonian apostasy. By the end of the seventeenth century, the dissenters had demonstrated six different options by which the true Christian might contend against the evil that had befallen the Russian Church: (1) social revolt, (2) mass suicide, (3) martyrdom, (4) flight, (5) psychological withdrawal, and (6) accommodation.

In 1668, the powerful monastic elite of the Solovetskii monastery rejected the new service books, not because they objected to the liturgical changes but because they resented the central-ization implicit in the Nikonian reforms. Behind the fortresslike walls of their cloister, the monks battled state troops for eight years until they were finally defeated in 1676. Later, Old Believers took part in the Cossack revolts of Kondratii Bulavin (1705) and Emelian Pugachev (1773–1775). Overall, however, social revolt was not a successful or rational strategy for an iso-lated religious minority to pursue, and Old Believers tended to favor other means of struggling against evil.

Collective suicide, usually by self-immolation, was the most disturbing of the Old Believ-ers' options; for some, suicide seemed to be the only way to escape the Antichrist, whose seal would destroy both body and soul. Generally, such suicides corresponded to periods of inten-sive persecution. The worst such period occurred in the last two decades of the seventeenth cen-tury, when the state actively sought out schismatics and tried to force them to convert; according to the incomplete data currently available, over eight thousand Old Believers died by their own hands from 1687 to 1700. In later years, as persecution abated, the numbers of sui-cides also fell; never again did they reach the dizzying heights of the seventies and eighties. Still, in times of crisis—when the church or government tried to register or convert a group of "schismatics"—Old Believers could and did turn to mass suicide as a means of resistance.

On the other hand, many Old Believers explicitly rejected suicide. It did, after all, violate canon law. Horrified by what he regarded as the fanatical acts of his co-religionists, the moderate priestly Old Believer Evfrosin wrote a tract in the 1680s strongly condemning the practice. Still, in the face of overwhelming state power, collective suicide or the threat of collective suicide gave the Old Believers important leverage in their negotiations with bishops and army commanders.

A few brave Old Believers such as Avvakum Petrov (1620–1682), who was burned at the stake in 1682, provided their communities with admired examples of uncompromising devo-tion to truth. Eighteenth-century Old Believers lionized these individual heroes of faith in such manuscript collections as the *Russian Vineyard*. But as important as such figures were, most believers had to avoid martyrdom if their community was to survive.

The severe persecution of the 1680s pushed Old Believers into the periphery, where they began to construct their own communities. The first great centers of Old Belief—Vetka in Poland, Starodub on the Polish frontier, the Vyg River monastery in northern Olonets province, the hermitages of the Kerzhenets forests on the Volga—were located on the frontier, far from the Muscovite chancelleries. This withdrawal from the larger society allowed the Old Believers the possibility of developing their own institutions for the long struggle with the heretical Nikonian church.

In addition to physical withdrawal from the broader society, religious dissenters also with-drew psychologically by setting ritual boundaries with the outside world and by reinterpreting their interaction with that world. Both the Saviorites and the Faith of Christ employed this strategy; their adherents attended the local Orthodox church and participated in its rituals, but reinterpreted them. For the Saviorites, Orthodox baptism was not valid in itself, but became valid only through the miraculous grace of God in response to prayers from true believers. Similarly, the members of the Faith of Christ regarded the Orthodox church rituals as secondary to their own private prayer meetings in which the Holy Spirit descended to speak to his people face to face.

Finally, some Old Believers sought to accommodate themselves to the Orthodox Church. This was possible only for those Old Believers with moderate eschatological views. From the early eighteenth century, some priestly Old Believers even tried to obtain an Old Believer bishop through and with the consent of the official church. In 1800, in an effort to heal the schism, the Russian Orthodox Church created a uniate movement (*edinoverie*) that allowed Old Believers who recognized the official church to use the pre-Nikonian liturgical books. But until 1918, the church refused to consecrate a uniate bishop. And because the church lifted the anathemas of the Council of 1666–1667 against the old rite only in 1971, few religious dissenters accepted this uniate compromise without state coercion.

☞ PETER THE GREAT AS THE ANTICHRIST

Many Russians, both Old Believers and Orthodox, believed that the powerful, reforming tsar Peter the Great (r. 1682–1725) was the long-awaited Antichrist. Seeking to Europeanize Russia, Peter consorted with foreigners, openly mocked the church in his drunken revelries, and forced his urban subjects to wear Western clothing. To finance his wars, he secularized monasteries and melted down church bells to make cannons. When Patriarch Adrian died in 1700, Peter did not permit a successor to be chosen; finally, in 1721, he abolished the patriarchate and replaced it with a council of bishops, the Holy Synod. He ordered men to shave their beards, an irreligious act from the point of the Old Believers. By creating a standing army and a draft, he placed new, heavy burdens on the peasants and townsmen, the vast majority of the Russian people. He also invented the oppressive head tax and instituted the first tax census to ensure that it was collected. For civil purposes, he adopted the Gregorian calendar, changed the New Year from September 1, to January 1, and began to date years from the birth of Christ instead of from the creation of the world. Finally, he took the Western title Emperor. Peter's legendary cruelty also lent credence to claims that he was the Antichrist: in 1698, Peter violently crucified hundreds of musketeers who had risen against him. His own son, Aleksei, whom he suspected of plotting against him, was tortured to death in 1718.

Orthodox as well as religious dissenters thought that he might be the Antichrist. In 1700, Peter's ecclesiastical policies led Grigorii Talitskii, an educated member of the official Orthodox Church, to proclaim that Peter was the Antichrist. Old Believers made similar accusations, basing their case most often on three of Peter's reforms: his introduction of the soul tax and tax census, his calendar reform, and his adoption of the title Emperor.

Outbreaks of apocalyptic despair in the eighteenth century were generally linked to the state's efforts to force Old Believers to recognize its legitimacy through three symbolic forms of submission: (1) loyalty oaths; (2) the tax and recruit census; and (3) prayers for the tsar.

After he had ordered his son Aleksei tortured to death in 1718 for plotting against him, Peter the Great modified the rule of succession to allow the ruler to choose his or her own heir. Without making his choice public, he decided to have his subjects swear their fealty to his as yet unnamed successor. The most radical Old Believers regarded this as a clever ruse to make them swear loyalty to the Antichrist, who of course could not be named. In 1722, this demand provoked a major uprising in the town of Tara in Siberia; when government agents tried to force the townspeople to take the oath, they incited a mass suicide.

Later, Empress Elizabeth (r. 1741–1762), who had come to power thanks to a palace coup, faced similar opposition when her bureaucrats tried to force her subjects to swear their fealty to her. In 1742 and 1743, such efforts again set off collective suicides, as Old Believers refused to pledge their allegiance to the ruler.

The tax and recruit census also provoked resistance among the Old Believers. In 1716, Peter legalized the existence of the Old Belief by requiring its adherents to register, wear special clothing, and pay a double tax. But registration presented several practical and ethical difficulties for the Old Believers. Legally, even registered Old Believers had no right to raise their children in their faith. Marriages performed by Old Believer priests or preceptors were not valid in the eyes of the law. Registered Old Believers could expect additional pressure from the state, which sometimes extracted promises from the registered dissenters that they not harbor fugitives or keep heretical works. Finally, registered Old Believers declared themselves to be schismatics, when in their own eyes they were Orthodox.

Before abolishing the double tax in 1782, the Russian state undertook four tax and recruit censuses: in 1719, 1744, 1762, and 1782. Each of these censuses provoked mass protests, including collective suicides, as Old Believers sought to escape the agents of the Antichrist who wished to enroll them.

Prayers for the tsar represented another serious problem for the Old Believers, whose pre-Nikonian service books included litanies asking divine help for the "pious" (*blagochestivyi*) and "right-believing" (*blagovernyi*) tsar. For all the Old Believers, the tsar was at best a schismatic and at worst the Antichrist himself; in the latter case, following the traditional formulas would have resulted in true Christians praying for Satan's victory. The Rebaptizers, headed by the Vyg monastery, initially refused to pray for the tsar. Unfortunately for them, the government was by no means indifferent to this question, which struck at its legitimacy; in 1739, under the guns of a state investigative commission, the Vyg community began to pray for the tsar.

The decision to pray for the tsar, however, caused a schism in the community. One of its most important leaders, the monk Filipp (Fotii, d. 1743), left the monastery and established his own denomination of Rebaptizers, the Filippites. When government troops tried to force Filipp's followers to pray for the tsar, they burned themselves. Filipp himself died in such a conflagration in 1743; his successor Terentii killed himself and ninety-eight followers four years later; and the monk Matfei, who took up the leadership, committed himself and his followers to the flame in 1750. Despite these incidents, the firm convictions of the Filippites attracted a strong following, especially in the Russian north, and they became serious rivals for the Vyg community.

☞ APOCALYPTICISM UNDER ENLIGHTENED DESPOTISM, 1762–1800

In the latter half of the seventeenth century, three new apocalyptic movements arose: the Wanderers (*stranniki*) of the northern regions of Olonets, Iaroslavl', and Tver'; the Dukhobors (or

Spirit-Wrestlers) in the southern black-earth provinces of Tambov and Voronezh; and the Castrates (*skoptsy*) in Orel province. Surprisingly, they appeared in the period when Peter III and Catherine II drastically reduced the persecution of religious dissenters. But at the same time that Catherine lifted legal restrictions on Old Believers, she placed new, heavy burdens on the peasantry, who had to supply the men and the funds for her to conduct her wars.

The Wanderers broke away from the radical priestless Filippite Old Believers, whose position on the census proved to be too moderate. A Filippite council in 1765 condemned certain forms of registration, in which the Old Believer called himself a schismatic or promised not to provide refuge to runaways. But at the same time, the council refused to impose a penance on believers who paid the double tax without formally declaring themselves to be schismatic. This implicit recognition of the census drove some Filippites to form a new movement, that of the Wanderers or Pilgrims in the 1760s. But the Wanderers would have remained a small and relatively uninfluential schismatic group had not their ideas attracted the radical Filippite monk Evfimii (1743/44–1792) in 1784.

Evfimii made significant modifications to the theology of the earlier Wanderers. When he decided to leave the Filippites, Evfimii took an unprecedented step—he rebaptized himself and then rebaptized seven of his followers. Disappointed by the moral failings and disputes he had witnessed in the Filippite community, Evfimii concluded that constant contact with the world of the Antichrist prevented the Old Believers from living truly Christian lives. True believers had to flee from the Antichrist before they could receive baptism and be counted Christians.

Like the other Rebaptizers, Evfimii believed in a demythologized "spiritual" Antichrist, who nevertheless worked through his "vessels," the most powerful of which was the reigning emperor. Drawing on earlier arguments that Peter had been the Antichrist, Evfimii especially emphasized the injustice of the Petrine social hierarchy and tax system. The internal passport system and the police measures Peter had introduced prevented Christians from seeking salvation in the wilderness, as had the monastic ascetics of old.

Evfimii's uncompromising demand that baptism—and thus salvation itself—be reserved for those who had fled the world of the Antichrist created many practical problems for the Wanderers. Those who had accepted baptism had to depend on their unbaptized disciples, the "friends of Christ" (*khristoliubtsy, strannopriimtsy*), who remained in the world to provide support and shelter for the true Christians. The problem of how Christians should relate to these special friends continues to plague the present-day Siberian Wanderers, whose council of elders as recently as 1986 reaffirmed the principle that those who remain in the world cannot receive baptism.

The Wanderers, especially the most radical branches, remained keenly aware of the imminent end of time. In 1828, during a bitter dispute among *strannik* leaders about whether a true Christian could handle money, the radical elder Mikhail Andreev Kuvshinov predicted the end of the world on 25 March, one of the rare times when Easter and the Feast of the Annunciation coincided. When his prediction failed, he rejoined the Wanderers' more moderate branch.

Despite frequent schisms, the Wanderers developed a very effective underground organization that has survived the efforts of both the tsarist and the Soviet government to destroy it. The "friends of Christ" remained in the world, and often became very prosperous, like Vasilii Rukavitsyn (fl. 1890–1908), the owner of a soap factory in Perm' at the turn of the century. They supported, fed, and clothed the Christians who spent their lives in prayer, teaching, and the copying of holy books. When close to death, the "friend of Christ" would also accept baptism.

The movement known as Spiritual Christianity arose from the intense apocalyptic expectations of Orthodox peasants in the black-earth region of Tambov and Voronezh provinces in the 1760s. In 1762, Kirill Petrov (fl. 1762–1769), the sacristan of the church in Goreloe village, and Ilarion Pobirokhin (fl. 1762–1785), a state peasant who had become wealthy by trading in wool, began to teach their friends and neighbors that the day of the Lord was at hand and that this present age was coming to an end. God had placed his word directly in the hearts and on the lips of his true followers; for this reason, Christians had to cease the idolatrous worship of icons, crosses, and images. Saying that they worshiped God in spirit and in truth, Pobirokhin and Petrov rejected the Orthodox sacraments and priesthood. To replace the corrupt and drunken priests of the state church, they chose their own spiritual leaders; instead of venerating icons, Christians were to venerate men created in the image and likeness of God. To this end, at the conclusion of their assemblies, Pobirokhin had his followers bow to him and kiss him as they would an icon. Meeting together regularly, they prayed, sang psalms, and listened to their teachers interpret the Bible.

The early hymns of the Dukhobors demonstrate that they believed that the struggle against the Antichrist was intensifying as the *parousia* approached. Pobirokhin preached on the apocalyptic text of Zechariah 14 and compared the worship of icons to the worship of the Beast of Revelation: "for he who worships the icon of the Beast and accepts its mark on his forehead will be burned with fire and brimstone" (Vysotskii 1914, 42). Yet the hymns also express confidence that Christ would return to rescue his true church from its persecutors. By 1767, this conviction led the Dukhobors to confront the state church. At the midnight liturgy on Easter Sunday in Lysye gory village, three Dukhobors interrupted the service by shouting "indecent words" when the priest held up his cross. In the same year, a delegation of four Dukhobors traveled to St. Petersburg to demand legal recognition of their movement and the right to worship as they pleased. A third group in Zhidilovka village, Tambov province, made their convictions known to the new bishop, who promptly denounced them.

Not surprisingly, these actions provoked a strong campaign of state persecution to eradicate the new heresy. The Tambov governor publicly tortured the three Dukhobors who had dared interrupt the Easter service. As for the rest, those who refused to abandon their convictions were sentenced to military service on the Crimean front, where Russia was conducting a war against the Ottoman Empire. The state also seized their children and placed them in foster homes or military boarding schools, where some of them died. Despite these harsh measures, few Dukhobors returned to Orthodoxy, and hundreds chose to suffer exile to the southern military frontier rather than renounce their faith.

Despite this repression, these early spiritual Christians gave rise to two movements that have survived to the present: the Dukhobors and the Molokans. Believing that God had placed his word directly in their hearts, the Dukhobors neglected written scriptures. The Molokans, led by the Tambov peasant Semen Matveev Uklein (1733–1809), held the Bible in higher regard and broke with the Dukhobors over this issue. Uklein and his followers energetically proselytized on the southeastern frontier and made many converts in Orenburg, Saratov, Tambov, and Astrakhan provinces.

Both the Molokans and the Dukhobors claimed the title of Spiritual Christians; both groups also retained elements of their apocalyptic beginnings. Several Molokan prophets predicted the end of the world in the 1830s; and in the late 1880s, the Dukhobor leader Petr

Vasil'evich Verigin (d. 1924) prophesied the imminent return of Christ and urged his followers to burn their weapons, take up vegetarianism, and abstain from sexual relations.

At the same time, in the 1760s, some of the celibate adherents of the Faith of Christ decided to castrate themselves. By 1800, these Castrates had broken away from the Faith of Christ to form their own movement under the leadership of Kondratii Selivanov (d. 1832), an Orel peasant who claimed to be an incarnation both of Christ and of Emperor Peter III (1728–1762, r. 1762), the unfortunate husband of Catherine II (1729–1796, r. 1762–1796). According to the Castrates, Selivanov had been miraculously born of the virgin Empress Elizabeth (1709–1762, r. 1741–1762) in Orel province, where she had disguised herself as the peasant Akulina Ivanovna. The miraculous child was the future Emperor Peter III, who was raised in Holstein and castrated in his youth. When he married the future Catherine II (the Great), his lustful wife, disappointed by her husband's impotence, took the devil as a lover and gave birth to an Antichrist, Napoleon Bonaparte. She then unsuccessfully tried to assassinate her husband, who barely escaped her plot; one of his faithful followers obligingly took his place and was killed in his stead. He traveled back to his home province of Orel, where he was ultimately arrested and exiled to Irkutsk in Siberia. After thirty-three years of redemptive suffering, Selivanov was recalled to the capital by his son, the emperor Paul (1754–1801, r. 1796–1801).

From this point, the legend can be verified. Paul's son and successor, Alexander I (1777–1825, r. 1801–1825) allowed Selivanov to live and teach freely in St. Petersburg from 1802 until 1820. At that time, the Castrate Christ was arrested and placed in monastic imprisonment in the Suzdal' Monastery of the Savior, where he died—or ascended into heaven—in 1832.

Selivanov called for his followers to undergo the "fiery baptism" of castration. Although many adepts never underwent castration, the operation remained an important ideal for both sexes: females excised their vaginal lips, clitorises, and nipples. According to one reconstruction of their mythology, the Castrates believed that when the number of those who had been emasculated reached 144,000 (Rev 14:1), then Selivanov would descend from heaven to claim his rightful place as emperor, ring the bell in the Dormition cathedral in the Moscow Kremlin, and judge the world.

MILLENNIALISM, 1800–1861

In the nineteenth century, for the first time, millennialism became an influential idea and the subject of several fascinating manuscripts by religious virtuosi. Old Believers traditionally were not chiliastic; following the *Book of Faith*, they understood Christ's millennial kingdom as identical with the first thousand years of church history, before Rome's fall into heresy. Under the reign of Alexander I, however, native Russian thinkers embraced the Protestant pietist idea of a millennial kingdom. Correspondingly, the apocalyptic thinkers of the nineteenth century placed more emphasis on the positive possibilities of human action than did the amillennial Old Believers.

Alexander I and his court initially encouraged a pietistic, mystical form of Christianity. Russian aristocrats such as Ivan Lopukhin (1756–1816) and Aleksandr Labzin (1766–1825) embraced the visions of the German pietistic philosophers Johann Heinrich Jung-Stilling

(1740–1817) and Karl Eckartshausen (1752–1803), who believed that a new universal church, free of dogma, would emerge to unite all people of faith. This pure Christianity also promised to put an end to the revolutions that had troubled Europe—an attractive prospect for the Russian emperor, who had to contend with Napoleon Bonaparte, the carrier of the French Revolution.

Influenced by these ideas, Alexander in 1812 helped to found the Russian Bible Society, which carried out a program of widespread distribution of scripture. He also encouraged the translation and dissemination of Jung-Stilling's and Eckarthausen's works; as he marched toward Paris, Alexander even found time to meet with the aging Jung-Stilling. And with the defeat of Napoleon, whom Jung-Stilling believed might be the Antichrist, Alexander sought to incarnate the pietist ecumenical vision by creating the Holy Alliance that united the Catholic emperor of Austria, the Protestant emperor of Prussia, and the Orthodox emperor of Russia.

Alexander's ecumenical pietism resulted in a policy of religious toleration. In a series of decrees issued from 1802 to 1805, he allowed the Molokans and Dukhobors to settle on land near the Molochnaia river of Mariupol' district in Ukraine, where they could freely practice their faith. For almost two decades, he made no effort to arrest the Castrate Christ, Kondratii Selivanov, who lived at liberty in St. Petersburg from 1802 to 1820. And he permitted fugitive Orthodox priests to convert to and serve priestly Old Believer congregations.

The dissemination of the scriptures and of pietist writings also created a religious climate that encouraged apocalyptic thinking. Jung-Stilling in particular was convinced that the end of the world was near, and he calculated that it would occur in 1836. Labzin's translation of Jung-Stilling's *Victorious History of the Christian Church* in 1815 helped to spread his eschatological views, especially among the Molokans, who were active in the regional chapters of the Bible Society.

The apocalyptic vision that helped bring forth the first Molokans remained a powerful force long afterwards. At the beginning of the nineteenth century, Sidor Andreev (fl. 1810), a runaway soldier, began to preach among the Molokans of Saratov province that Christ would soon return to take his people to the land of milk and honey located somewhere near Mount Ararat. Before he could lead his followers there, however, Andreev was arrested and exiled to Siberia. But this failed to stem the apocalyptic movement; the retired soldier Nikolai Bogdanov (b. 1770) took up the preacher's mantle until he was exiled to a monastery in 1833.

In the early 1830s, at the time of a severe crop failure, several prophets from various Russian provinces warned of Christ's second coming. While migrating from his native Orenburg province to the Transcaucasia, the peasant preacher David Ivanov (fl. 1830s) claimed that the Holy Spirit had possessed him and that the world would end on Trinity Sunday. Even though this date passed by without event, three years later in 1836, another Molokan prophet, Evstignei Iakovlev Filimonov (b. 1808), testified to the reality of the Spirit's presence in Ivanov's life. About the same time, Luk'ian Petrov Sokolov (d. 1858), a fugitive from Moldova, proclaimed that Christ would return on Mount Ararat in 1836. He traveled through Melitopol' in Ukraine to Saratov and Samara provinces, where he helped organize a mass migration to Transcaucasia. Two of Sokolov's companions, who represented themselves as the prophets Elijah and Enoch, performed miracles to support his claims. Another peasant preacher, Fedor Osipovich Bulgakov (fl. 1830s), who called himself by the messianic title of David, the son of Jesse, championed Sokolov's millennial vision in his "Book of Zion," composed between 1833 and 1838. Unlike the apocalypses of most of the Old Believers, Bulgakov emphasized Christ's millennial kingdom rather than the reign of Antichrist that would precede it.

Encouraged by these visions, hundreds of Molokans left for Ararat. When 1836 came and went without incident, most Molokans abandoned chiliasm and became known as "constant" Molokans. But the millennialist movements of the 1830s did leave a lasting legacy in two new sects. The Spiritual-Christian Jumpers (*pryguny*), led by Maksim Rudometkin (d. 1877), carefully preserved and revered Sokolov's and Bulgakov's prophecies, for they marked the beginning of an outpouring of God's spirit that continued in the dances and the ecstasies of their worship. On the other hand, the utopian and (initially communistic) community Common Hope (*Obshchee upovanie*), led by the Saratov peasant Mikhail Akinfievich Popov (1790–1873), sought to recover the radical egalitarianism and communalism of the early 1830s.

Nikolai Sazontovich Il'in (1809–1890), a retired captain of the artillery, founded the Righteous Brotherhood (*desnoe bratstvo*), one of the most remarkable apocalyptic movements in Russia. In 1846, he broke with the Orthodox Church and began to preach a highly imaginative new gospel. Il'in regarded God as an extraterrestrial named Jehovah who had a physical body and a human soul. He soon would return to earth to defeat his enemies at Armageddon and to establish his millennial kingdom, where he would reign for a thousand years with his immortal followers, the Righteous Brotherhood. After the millennium, God would begin the process of creating and recreating a new heaven and a new earth that he would eternally improve. The New Jerusalem, built by extraterrestrials, would descend complete from heaven to become the center of this new creation; the fruits of its trees would provide immortality for its citizens within and healing for those outside.

To a far greater extent than the Old Believers, who for the most part did not believe in a future millennium, Il'in emphasized the positive possibilities of human action. Significantly, his utopia, the New Jerusalem, was to be built by extraterrestrials, not by a transcendent God; it was also to undergo eternal improvement. He rejected the idea of salvation by faith, but at the same time, contemporary pietist groups that had successfully colonized the Russian frontier (such as the Mennonites and Herrnhutterites) attracted him. The Righteous Brotherhood imposed the Mosaic ethical and dietary restrictions on its members. In preparation for the apocalypse, they energetically hectographed and distributed their teacher's poetry and tracts.

Although in monastic confinement from 1859 to 1879, Il'in continued to write to and direct his followers, who had their headquarters in Nizhnii Tagil of remote Perm' province. The Brotherhood survived the 1917 revolution; the Soviet secret police destroyed the Nizhnii Tagil center in 1931 and then again in 1939. Despite these depredations, the Brotherhood endured well into the 1970s. Moving to the Northern Caucasus and Kyrgyzstan, members of the Brotherhood continued to hectograph their master's works, which they mailed and left in buses and other public places.

WESTERN PROTESTANTS AND SECULAR UTOPIANS, 1861–1917

In the years following the emancipation of the serfs in 1861, thousands of Russians for the first time began to turn to Western free-church Protestantism—the Baptists, Adventism, and Pentecostalism—and the premillennialist eschatology that these movements espoused. At the same time, the intelligentsia became enamored of immanentizing social utopias by education, reform, or revolution. The main ideologies of the period—Slavophilism, Populism, and Marxism—each aimed toward a utopian end.

By the end of the nineteenth century, as they saw their world change ever more rapidly, artists and writers also began to explore apocalyptic themes in their work. As part of his personal religious quest, Dmitrii Merezhkovskii (1866–1941) wrote a trilogy of novels entitled *Christ and Antichrist*. In his *Three Conversations with a Short Story of the Antichrist* (1900), the great philosopher Vladimir Solov'ev (1853–1900) imagined the Antichrist as the ruler of an oriental empire, whose wicked designs are ultimately foiled by an alliance of righteous Jews and Christians. In his dark novels *The Silver Dove* (1910) and *Petersburg* (1916), Andrei Belyi (1880–1934) took up this theme as well, portraying cabals of secret sectarians and revolutionaries bringing the final judgment nearer. In his *Apocalypse of Our Time* (1919), Vasilii Rozanov (1856–1919) attributed the Russian Revolution to the failures of the Christian Church.

☞ THE RUSSIAN REVOLUTION _____

The Russian Revolution marked a turning point in apocalypticism. On the one hand, the new Bolshevism was itself an apocalyptic ideology containing dire predictions of a final struggle between the bourgeoisie and the proletariat before the rise of Communist paradise. In the *ABC of Communism*, the Bolsheviks Evgenii Preobrazhenskii (1886–1937) and Nikolai Bukharin (1888–1938) predicted that under Communism the average person would be the equal of Aristotle and Plato; simply by eliminating economic exploitation, the early Bolsheviks imagined that they would usher in a new utopia.

On the other hand, most religious believers looked at the regime suspiciously. Soviet Russia (and from 1924 the Soviet Union) was the first officially atheist state in history. Several delegates to the Russian Orthodox Church Council, which was meeting when the Bolsheviks took power, condemned the revolutionaries as "satans" and "antichrists." And although religious toleration was in principle protected by law, the young Communist state, which regarded religion as the ideological tool of its enemies, engaged in a serious effort to destroy religion altogether.

For the first ten years of Soviet power, it was the Orthodox Church, the former state church, that bore the brunt of the state's anti-religious campaigns. The constitution of the Russian Soviet Federated Socialist Republic, adopted in 1918, separated the church from the state and the school from the church. By disestablishing the church, the Soviets deprived it of most of its wealth. In 1922, the Bolsheviks used a nationwide famine as an excuse to seize more property from the church, and to arrest, try, and execute some of the most important churchmen, including the popularly elected Metropolitan Veniamin (Vasilii Pavlovich Kazanskii, 1874–1922) of Petrograd (r. 1918–1922). They encouraged a left-wing schism, known as the Living Church, which broke with the newly elected Patriarch Tikhon (Vasilii Ivanovich Belavin, 1865–1925) in 1922 and followed a policy of collaboration with the Bolshevik regime. The Soviet government placed Patriarch Tikhon under house arrest, and when he died in 1925, they refused to allow the church to hold a council to replace him.

In 1927, in a desperate effort to create a *modus vivendi* with the Communist state, the *locum tenens* of the patriarch, Metropolitan Sergii (Ioann Nikolaevich Stragorodskii,

1867–1944), issued a strong statement of loyalty to the Soviet regime. This accommodationist policy drew a strong reaction from Metropolitan Iosif (Petrovykh, 1872–1938) of Leningrad (r. 1926–1928), who formally separated from Sergii. Many ordinary believers followed the Metropolitan; they regarded themselves as the true followers of Patriarch Tikhon. Called the "Josephite schism" by those sympathetic to Sergii, the followers of Iosif came to call themselves the "True Orthodox Christians."

All religions, including the True Orthodox Christians, faced a fierce new challenge in 1929 when the Communist Party instituted a major antireligious campaign as part of the First Five-Year Plan. A new law passed in April restricted religious organizations and resulted in the closure of thousands of churches. At the same time, peasants were being forced to join collective farms, and the secret police was placing wealthier peasants, called *kulaks,* into corrective labor camps. The drive to eliminate religion intensified during the second Five-Year Plan (1933–1937), which called for the complete eradication of all faith.

Many believers resisted these new measures. During the forced collectivization campaign of 1929 in the village of Novaia Kalitva, Voronezh Province, the followers of Fedor Prokofievich Rybalkin (fl. 1920s) declared that the archangel Michael would soon appear to punish the Communists and those who joined the collectives. In their struggle against the atheists, the "Fedorite crusaders" used arson as well as prayer. The Soviet government lost no time in trying and executing fourteen of the apocalypticists and sending over two thousand others to prison camps.

Christians also actively distributed apocalyptic literature. "Heavenly letters" supposedly written by the Mother of God or Christ urged believers to quit the collective farms. "The Visions of John of Kronstadt," a work attributed to the charismatic parish priest Ioann Sergiev (1829–1908, canonized 1990), but probably written in the 1920s, was especially popular and described the Soviet state and the Bolshevik revolution as the last desperate acts of the Antichrist before his doom. Similar apocryphal works attributed to the wonder-working saints Serafim of Sarov (1754–1833, canonized 1903) and Tikhon (Sokolov, 1724–1783, canonized 1861) also identified the Soviets as agents of Antichrist.

In 1941, the German invasion of the U.S.S.R. pushed the Soviet leader Joseph Stalin (1879–1953) to grant new freedoms to religious believers. In 1943, he allowed the Orthodox Church to elect a new patriarch to replace Tikhon, who had died eighteen years earlier; in the same year, he let Muslims choose an official mufti; and a year later, he permitted the Baptists to hold their own council and create an officially recognized national body, the All-Union Council of Evangelical Christians and Baptists. This policy of relative toleration lasted until 1959, when the First Secretary of the Communist Party, Nikita Sergeevich Khrushchev, attempted once again to eradicate religion.

This temporary relaxation of persecution simply permitted new eschatological forms to appear. Toward the end of the war, True Orthodox Christians in the Tambov region mailed chain letters warning believers and unbelievers alike that the Antichrist had already appeared, and that the end of the world was approaching. Writing about 1957 in Alma-Ata, Kazakhstan, the True Orthodox Christians P. G. Sorokin and G. K. Tsimbal reinterpreted the passage in Revelation that limited the Antichrist's reign to forty-two months. Identifying the Bolsheviks as the Antichrist, they argued that each of the scriptural months actually represented a year and predicted that the Soviet Union would fall—and the world would come to an end—in 1960.

Nikita Khrushchev's (1894–1971, r. 1953–1964) renewed persecution of religious believers strengthened these apocalyptic tendencies. Beginning in 1959, Khrushchev initiated a campaign to eradicate religion by introducing new, more restrictive legislation governing religious organizations; closing churches, mosques, theological schools, and synagogues; and arresting and convicting religious activists. The campaign ultimately failed to eliminate religion, but did succeed in driving activists of various denominations underground. These activists often appealed to their fellow believers by evoking vivid eschatological images that encouraged and justified an almost hopeless struggle against overwhelming odds. For example, the anonymous author of "The Cross and the Star," a manuscript written around 1960, predicted that the "abomination of desolation" would appear in June 1962 when the Soviets replaced church crosses with red stars—a clear reference to Khrushchev's mass closures of churches. For Christians, the proper response to such blasphemy was to destroy one's internal passport and flee, for only forty-two months later, Christ would return to establish the true Communist utopia in place of Khrushchev's false hopes.

Among the underground Baptists, the visions of Ivan Moiseev (1952–1972), a Soviet draftee who was persecuted to death for his religious convictions, were widely circulated in the 1970s and 1980s. While serving in the army, Moiseev had seen signs in the sky of Christ's second coming. Even legally recognized Baptist preachers emphasized eschatological themes, though they had to choose their words with care; spreading rumors about the end of the world was punishable under Soviet law.

THE POST-SOVIET PERIOD

In 1990, the Supreme Soviet passed a new law granting unprecedented freedom for religious organizations. Many apocalyptic groups, including the Jehovah's Witnesses, the Church of Jesus Christ of Latter-day Saints, and the Seventh-day Adventists, used their new freedom to organize and proselytize openly without fear of repression.

Emerging from the underground, the True Orthodox Christians have splintered into several different movements even as they have attracted new converts from the broader society. One branch of the True Orthodox Christians has allied itself with the monarchist Russian Orthodox Church Abroad; a second group, led by Bishop Gurii (Simon Pavlovich Pavlov, 1906–1995) of Kazan' (r. 1991–1995), who spent more than sixty years in the catacombs, has recognized the jurisdiction of Archbishop Auxentios (Constantine Pastras, 1912–1994) of Athens (r. 1963–1994), the leader of one faction of the Old Calendar Orthodox Church of Greece. The independent followers of the catacomb Metropolitan Gennadii (Grigorii Iakovlevich Sekach, 1898–1987) have divided into two groups. One is led by Metropolitan Feodosii of the Kuban'; the other, by Archbishop Ioann (Bereslavskii), the founder of the Church of the Transfiguring Theotokos (the Center of the Mother of God).

Bereslavskii's group is the most active and apocalyptic of True Orthodox Christians. In November 1984, Bereslavskii began to witness apparitions of the Mother of God, who has continued to provide him with special revelations. She has predicted a future third world war between good and evil, but at the same time she has inaugurated a new spiritual movement, the church of the Holy Spirit, to counter the world's current corruption. Her new revelation represents a third testament, the testament of the Holy Spirit. However, not all Christians will accept this new revelation; even priests will accept "the seal of the enemy on their foreheads," and the church will be divided. Bereslavskii is currently isolated; his movement has been condemned by every other branch of the Russian Orthodox Church.

The new religious and press freedoms have also permitted the emergence of what the American scholar Michael Barkun has called "eclectic apocalypticism." Throughout Eastern Europe, there is great popular interest in unidentified flying objects, magic, astrology, and Oriental religions. The apocalyptic Japanese sect Aum Shinrikyo (the religious movement thought to be responsible for the sarin gas attack in a Tokyo subway in 1995) had more followers in Russia than in any other country outside Japan. And the White Brotherhood, a syncretic religious faith that combines elements from Hinduism, Theosophy, the Kabbalah, and Orthodox Christianity, created a major scandal when on November 1, 1993, five hundred of its members gathered in Kiev to witness the end of the world and the crucifixion and ascension of their leader Marina Tsvigun (b. 1960), who had taken the name Maria Devi Khrystos. The news media also falsely reported that they were planning a collective suicide. In 1996, Khrystos and her vatic husband, Iurii Krivonogov (b. 1941), were sentenced to four- and seven-year prison terms, respectively, for disrupting public order.

Perhaps the most influential source of apocalyptic warnings in Eastern Europe comes from six visionaries in Medjugorje, Bosnia. In 1981, the Virgin Mary began to make regular appearances to six children, members of a Catholic, Franciscan parish that is struggling to remain independent of the diocesan bishop. The peculiar power struggle between the Franciscan order and the bishop prevented the diocese from co-opting and concealing the visionaries, who have gained international fame, especially in Catholic charismatic circles; as a result, the apparitions continue to this day. Warning of a future terrible and imminent judgment, the Mary of Medjugorje calls for repentance, prayer, and fasting. She is also in the process of giving ten secrets to the visionaries, only the first of which has been revealed to the world: soon a sign visible to believers and unbelievers alike will appear on the hill where Mary first spoke to the children. The Medjugorje phenomenon has sparked imitators across the globe as pilgrims travel to the site and return to form their own Marian devotional groups.

☞ CONCLUSION

Apocalypticism is a complex phenomenon that defies facile interpretations. In Eastern Europe, the apocalyptic narrative has served to legitimize states (as the Third Rome doctrine legitimized Moscow) and to support social protests (as Old Believer ideology supported the monks of the Solovetskii monastery). Not every social crisis precipitated an apocalyptic response; none of the many nomadic invasions, for example, sparked apocalyptic movements in Russia. And although social oppression did play a role in the rise of the Dukhobors, Wanderers, and the Old Belief, these movements also attracted relatively prosperous peasants and townsmen and even members of the elite.

Christian eschatological narratives provided a way for Russians and other Eastern Europeans to make their own historical situations meaningful. The theodicy implicit in that narrative also implied a sociodicy, and thus eschatology helped historical actors to critique their own societies and sometimes to try to build better ones. From the beginning of the nineteenth

century, millenarianism—and a positive view of human action—became increasingly significant in Russia, so that by 1917, the new Bolshevik rulers tried to create their own millennium.
The failure of Communism has not, however, discredited millennialism, which continues to
exert a powerful influence on religion and politics in Eastern Europe.

NOTES

1. Chrismation is the Orthodox sacrament corresponding to Catholic confirmation. It represents
the believer's reception of the Holy Spirit and is usually administered at the same time as baptism. In this
sacrament, a priest anoints the believer with holy myrrh that has been consecrated by a bishop. Schismatics who wish to rejoin the church usually must confess their error and be chrismated.

BIBLIOGRAPHY

Sources

Avvakum. 1979. *The Life Written by Himself.* Michigan Slavic Publications 4. Ann Arbor: University of
    Michigan. This is the colorful autobiography of one of the most important leaders of the seven-
    teenth-century schism, Archpriest Avvakum.
*Bozhestvennye izrecheniia nastavnikov i stradal'tsev za Slovo Bozhie, veru Iisusa i dukh sviatoi religii
    Dukhovnykh khristian Molokan-Prygunov* (The divine utterances of the preceptors and sufferers for
    the word of God, the faith of Jesus, and the spirit of the holy religion of the spiritual Christian
    Molokan Jumpers). 1928. Los Angeles. A valuable source for the eschatological movements of the
    1830s, this is a collection of the inspired prophecies of the Molokan leaders Maksim Rudometkin,
    Fedor Bulgakov, and Luk'ian Petrov Sokolov. The Molokan Jumpers continue to revere these
    prophets and have preserved their writings.
Bukharin, Nikolai Ivanovich. 1922. *The ABC of Communism: A Popular Explanation of the Program of the
    Communist Party of Russia.* London. Bukharin and Preobrazhenskii's famous book describes their
    vision of the Communist millennium.
Evfrosin. 1895. *Otrazitel'noe pisanie o novoizobretennom puti samoubiistvennykh smertei* (A letter objecting
    to the newly invented means of suicide). Edited by Khrusanf Loparev. Pamiatniki drevnikh pis'men-
    nostei 108. N.p.: Tipografiia I. N. Skorokhodova. Evfrosin condemned the practice of collective sui-
    cide in the 1680s.
Otkrovenie Bozhiei Materi v Rossii (1984–1991) proroku episkopu Ioannu Odigitriia-Putevoditel'nitsa (The
    revelation of the Mother of God in Russia [1984–1991] to the Prophet Bishop Ioann). Moscow:
    Bogorodichnyi tsentr. This is one of many pamphlets published by the Center for the Mother of God
    containing the prophecies that the Virgin Mary has revealed to their bishop.
Vysotskii, Nikolai Gavriilovich, comp. 1914. *Materialy iz istorii dukhoborcheskoi sekty* (Materials from the
    history of the Dukhobor sect). Sergievskii pesad: I. I. Ivanov. Nikolai Vysotskii, an official in the
    Department of Ecclesiastical Affairs in the Ministry of Internal Affairs, published several collections
    of archival documents dealing with the apocalyptic movements of the Castrates, the Dukhobors, and
    the Faith of Christ. This book contains his analysis of heresy trials of the Dukhobors from the 1760s
    and 1770s.

Studies

Bax, Mart. 1995. *Medjugorje: Religion, Politics, and Violence in Rural Bosnia.* Amsterdam: VU Uitgeverij.
    An anthropological study of the apparitions at Medjugorje, Bosnia.

Bethea, David. 1989. *The Shape of Apocalypse in Modern Russian Fiction*. Princeton, N.J.: Princeton University Press. Bethea analyzes the influence of apocalyptic ideas on Russian literature.

Billington, James. 1966. *The Icon and the Axe: An Interpretive History of Russian Culture*. New York: Knopf. In this work of breathtaking scope, Billington surveys the cultural landscape of Russia and demonstrates the importance of apocalyptic thought.

Brandenburg, Hans. 1977. *The Meek and the Mighty: The Emergence of the Evangelical Movement in Russia*. New York: Oxford University Press. This work explores the growth of pre-millennial Protestant Christianity in Russia.

Butkevich, Timofei I. 1910. *Obzor russkikh sekt i ikh tolkov*. Khar'kov: Tipografiia Gubernskogo Pravleniia. Although extremely biased against religious minorities, Butkevich's work is a useful introduction to the various apocalyptic movements of the late imperial period.

Clay, J. Eugene. 1985. "God's People in the Early Eighteenth Century: The Uglich Affair of 1717." *Cahiers du monde russe et soviétique* 26/1:69–124. This article analyzes the first heresy trial of the Faith of Christ.

Conybeare, Frederick C. 1962. *Russian Dissenters*. New York: Russell & Russell. Although outdated and at times inaccurate, this book is the best survey available in English.

Crummey, Robert Owen. 1970. *The Old Believers and the World of Antichrist: The Vyg Community and the Russian State, 1694–1855*. Madison, Wis.: University of Wisconsin Press. Crummey examines the history of the Vyg monastic community, which led the Pomorian branch of the Rebaptizing priestless Old Believers until the monastery was destroyed in 1850s. This work remains the best in English on the early Old Belief.

Engelstein, Laura. 1996. "Rebels of the Soul: Peasant Self-Fashioning in a Religious Key." *Russian History* 23/1–4:197–213. A historian who has written brilliantly about sexuality in prerevolutionary Russia, Laura Engelstein examines the Castrates in this article and in her forthcoming book.

Fletcher, William. 1971. *The Russian Orthodox Church Underground, 1917–1970*. New York: Oxford University Press. A sociologist at the University of Kansas, Fletcher has provided a useful analysis and survey of underground Orthodox movements, many of which were apocalyptic.

Gur'ianova, Natal'ia Sergeevna. 1988. *Krest'ianskii antimonarkhicheskii protest v staroobriadcheskoi eskhatologicheskoi literature perioda pozdnego feodalizma*. (Peasant Anti-Monarchical Protest in the Old Believer Eschatological Literature of the Late Feudal Period). Edited by Nikolai Nikolaevich Pokrovskii. Novosibirsk: Izd-vo "Nauka," Sibirskoe otd-nie. A former student of Nikolai Pokrovskii, Gur'ianova has carefully analyzed hundreds of apocalyptic texts written by the various schools of Rebaptizing priestless Old Believers. She understands these movements within a Marxist framework as a form of social protest.

Kazakova, N. A., and Iakov Solomonovich Lur'e. 1955. *Antifeodal'nye ereticheskie dvizheniia na Rusi XIV—nachala XVI veka*. Edited by Vladimir Dmitrievich Bonch-Bruevich. Moscow-Leningrad: Izdatel'stvo Akademii Nauk SSSR. In this work on proto-Protestant movements in the Russian northwest, Kazakova and Lur'e explore the theological controversies surrounding the end of the seventh millennium in 1492.

Klibanov, Aleksandr Il'ich. 1977–78. *Narodnaia sotsial'naia utopia v Rossii* (Popular social utopia in Russia). Edited by L. V. Cherepnin. Moscow: Nauka. This two-volume work, which won the Academy of Sciences' Grekov Prize, is a sympathetic analysis of archival and printed sources about utopian movements among the Russian peasantry. Although Klibanov made many errors of fact and interpretation, his books are pioneering works achieved at great personal cost that helped pave the way for other scholars.

———. 1982. *History of Religious Sectarianism in Russia (1860s–1917)*. Edited by Stephen P. Dunn. Translated by Ethel Dunn. New York: Oxford University Press. Until his death in 1994, Aleksandr Klibanov was the dean of Russian scholars studying religious dissent. This is an English translation of Klibanov's flawed *Istoriia religioznogo sektantstva v Rossii* (Moscow: Nauka, 1965). Written at the end of the Khrushchev persecution, this book nevertheless managed to present an interesting interpretation of sectarianism, including many apocalyptic movements.

Malinin, V. 1901. *Starets Eleazarova monastyria Filofeia i ego poslaniia* (The elder Filofei of the Eleazarov Monastery and his epistles). Kiev: Tipografiia Kievo-Pecherskoi Uspenskoi Lavry. Malinin wrote the unsurpassed study of Filofei, the creator of the Third Rome doctrine.

Mal'tsev, Aleksandr Ivanovich. 1996. *Starovery-stranniki v XVIII—pervoi polovine XIX v.* (Old Believer Wanderers in the Eighteenth and the First Half of the Nineteenth Century). Novosibirsk: Sibirskii khronograf. Mal'tsev was a member of the Novosibirsk school; this work, based on previously unknown archival sources, has transformed our understanding of the most apocalyptic of the Old Believer movements, the *stranniki*.

Margaritov, Sergii. 1914. *Istoriia russkikh misticheskikh i ratsionalisticheskikh sekt* (The history of Russian mystical and rationalistic sects). 4th ed., rev. and corr. Simferopol': Tavricheskaia Guber. tip. Margaritov's textbook provides a useful, though biased, survey of Christian minority movements in Russia before the revolution.

Michels, Georg Bernard. Forthcoming. *Myths and Realities of the Russian Schism : The Church and Its Dissenters in Seventeenth-Century Muscovy.* Stanford: Stanford University Press. The first Western scholar to work extensively in seventeenth-century archives on the Old Belief, Michels argues that the schism became a mass movement only in the eighteenth century.

Moskalenko, Aleksei Trofimovich. 1978. *Ideologiia i deiatel'nost' khristianskikh sekt* (The ideology and activity of Christian sects). Novosibirsk: Nauka. Moskalenko has written one of the better antireligious works from the Brezhnev period. He provides many interesting documents and facts on apocalyptic movements under Stalin and Khrushchev.

Pascal, Pierre. 1969. *Avvakum et les débuts du raskol.* Etudes sur l'histoire l'économie et la sociologie des pays slaves 8. Paris: Mouton. The eminent French scholar Pierre Pascal has given us in his biography of the Archpriest Avvakum the best book in any Western language on the schism.

Pokrovskii, Nikolai Nikolaevich. 1974. *Antifeodal'nyi protest uralo-sibirskikh krest'ian-staroobriadtsev v vosemnadtsatom (XVIII) v.* (The anti-feudal protest of the Uralo-Siberian peasant Old Believers in the eighteenth century). Novosibirsk: Nauka. Nikolai Nikolaevich Pokrovskii is without question the foremost authority on the history of the Old Belief in Siberia. This extraordinary work, his doctoral dissertation, is based on previously unexplored archives.

Robson, Roy. 1995. *Old Believers in Modern Russia.* DeKalb, Ill.: Northern Illinois University Press. This recent work by an American Old Believer explores these religious communities at the end of the nineteenth and the beginning of the twentieth centuries.

Sapozhnikov, Dmitrii Ivanovich. 1891. *Samosozhzhenie v russkom raskolie so vtoroi poloviny XVII veka do kontsa XVIII : istoricheskii ocherk po arkhivnym dokumentam* (Self-immolation in the Russian schism from the second half of the seventeenth century to the end of the eighteenth: A historical essay based on archival documents). Moscow: Univ. Tip. Sapozhnikov's examination of collective suicides provides valuable data on the most disturbing phenomenon of the Russian schism.

Smirnov, Petr Semenovich. 1895. *Istoriia russkogo raskola staroobriadstva* (The history of the Russian schism of Old Ritualism). St. Petersburg: Tipografiia Glavnogo upravleniia udelov. This survey was the main textbook for the study of the history and unmasking of the schism in Russian seminaries and academies before the Revolution of 1917.

———. 1909. *Spory i razdieleniia v russkom raskolie v pervoi chetverti XVIII veka* (Arguments and divisions in the Russian schism in the first quarter of the eighteenth century). St. Petersburg: M. Merkushev. A careful analysis of manuscripts written by Old Believers, this work was Smirnov's crowning achievement.

Viola, Lynne. 1996. *Peasant Rebels under Stalin: Collectivization and the Culture of Peasant Resistance.* New York: Oxford University Press. Viola demonstrates the importance of apocalyptic ideology for peasant resistance to Stalin.

Index of Ancient Sources

Index of Names